D0002451

MODERN ARCHITECTURAL THEORY

Modern Architectural Theory is the first book to provide a comprehensive survey of architectural theory, primarily in Europe and the United States, during three centuries of development. In this synthetic overview, Harry Mallgrave examines architectural discourse within its social and political context. He explores the philosophical and conceptual evolution of its ideas, discusses the relation of theory to the practice of building, and, most importantly, considers the words of the architects themselves as they contentiously shaped Western architecture. He also examines the compelling currents of French rationalist and British empiricist thought, the radical reformation of theory during the Enlightenment, the intellectual ambitions and historicist debates of the nineteenth century, and the distinctive varieties of modern theory in the twentieth century up to the profound social upheaval of the 1960s. *Modern Architectural Theory* challenges many assumptions about architectural modernism and uncovers many new dimensions of the debates about modernism.

As a distinguished historian, Harry Francis Mallgrave has long dedicated himself to mining the architectural ideas of the past three centuries. For nearly two decades he served as the Editor of Architecture and Aesthetics for the highly acclaimed "Texts and Documents Series" of the Getty Research Institute, in which capacity he was engaged in the publication of more than twenty volumes devoted to theoretical matters. He has authored, edited, and translated numerous books, including his intellectual biography, *Gottfried Semper: Architect of the Nineteenth Century*, which won the prestigious Alice Davis Hitchcock Award from the Society of Architectural Historians. He currently teaches history and theory at Illinois Institute of Technology.

MODERN ARCHITECTURAL THEORY

A Historical Survey, 1673–1968

HARRY FRANCIS MALLGRAVE

CAMBRIDGE
UNIVERSITY PRESS

CAMBRIDGE
UNIVERSITY PRESS

University Printing House, Cambridge CB2 8BS, United Kingdom

One Liberty Plaza, 20th Floor, New York, NY 10006, USA

477 Williamstown Road, Port Melbourne, VIC 3207, Australia

4843/24, 2nd Floor, Ansari Road, Daryaganj, Delhi - 110002, India

79 Anson Road, #06-04/06, Singapore 079906

Cambridge University Press is part of the University of Cambridge.

It furthers the University's mission by disseminating knowledge in the pursuit of education, learning and research at the highest international levels of excellence.

www.cambridge.org
Information on this title: www.cambridge.org/9780521130486

© Harry Francis Mallgrave 2005

This publication is in copyright. Subject to statutory exception and to the provisions of relevant collective licensing agreements, no reproduction of any part may take place without the written permission of Cambridge University Press.

First published 2005
Reprinted 2007 (twice), 2009
First paperback edition 2009

A catalogue record for this publication is available from the British Library

Library of Congress Cataloging in Publication data
Mallgrave, Harry Francis.
Modern architectural theory : a historical survey, 1673–1968 /
Harry Francis Mallgrave.
p.   cm.
Includes bibliographical references and index.
ISBN 0-521-79306-8 (hb)
1. Architecture – Philosophy – History.
2. Architecture, Modern. I. Title.
NA2500.M28   2005
720'.1 – dc22   2004045916

ISBN 978-0-521-79306-3 Hardback
ISBN 978-0-521-13048-6 Paperback

Cambridge University Press has no responsibility for the persistence or accuracy of URLs for external or third-party internet websites referred to in this publication, and does not guarantee that any content on such websites is, or will remain, accurate or appropriate. Information regarding prices, travel timetables, and other factual information given in this work is correct at the time of first printing but Cambridge University Press does not guarantee the accuracy of such information thereafter.

To Susan

CONTENTS

D0025487

LIST OF ILLUSTRATIONS

PREFACE

An encounter with the architectural ideas of the past few centuries is a little like rushing upon a sleeping Proteus – the mythical sea god and herdsman of seals who (to Odysseus) had the power to take all manner of shapes. One has to hold on fast as theory evolves through its many guises until at last it is forced to reveal its true identity. In the seventeenth century, it was codified and was more or less restricted to one or two academies; its main ideas were expounded through lectures and treatises. During the Enlightenment, it steps out into the public forum for the first time, and nonacademic viewpoints begin to challenge accepted academic dogmas. The rise of national identities and the availability of architectural journals in the nineteenth century vastly expanded and facilitated theoretical discourse. And of course the manifestos of the twentieth century were usually short, minimalist polemical statements, sometimes cogently reduced to axiomatic diagrams or simple sketches. We shall take architectural theory in its broadest sense and define it simply as the history of architectural ideas, literary or otherwise. Further, as every generation possesses the need to define itself in relation to what exists, architectural theory has almost always been a reaction to the past.

The present work seeks to narrate the main lines of modern architectural thought from 1673 to the troubling year of 1968. These dates may appear arbitrary, but they have a foundation. To start with, the words *theory* and *modern* both first came into prominence in the late seventeenth century. The Greek and Latin word *theoria* – related to the Greek words *theoros* (spectator), *theos* (divine being), and *theatron* (theater) – had several meanings in early antiquity. It could refer to a person consulting an oracle, someone participating or assisting in a religious festival, or (perhaps most

anciently) the experience of looking at a god. Reflecting on this fact, David Leatherbarrow, in a discussion of the poetic meaning of *theory*, highlighted someone experiencing a religious epiphany or turning one's life around.[1] In later antiquity, the term came to mean "looking at, viewing, or contemplation." Aristotle, for instance, employed *theoria* to signify "to contemplate, to consider," as well as to refer to an "object of contemplation."[2] Cicero, in a letter to Atticus, used the Greek word loosely in this sense, but this interpretation remained relatively rare in Latin until the word was applied to philosophical matters during the Middle Ages.[3] The Roman architect Vitruvius, in making his famous distinction between theory and practice, for instance, employed *ratiocinatio* for the former, a word meaning "the process of reasoning, calculation, ratiocination, or theorizing."[4]

The Italian word *teoria* appears occasionally in artistic literature in the late Renaissance.[5] In the 1558 edition of *Le vite* (Lives), Georgio Vasari used *teorica* at the beginning of his sketch of Alberti to refer to a set of theoretical beliefs that an artist should successfully marry with *pratica* (practice).[6] One year earlier, Daniel Barbaro, in his Italian translation of Vitruvius' *De Architectura*, translated *ratiocinatio* as *discorso*.[7] Because the Italian words *calculatione* and *ratiocinatione* were the preferred terms for translating *ratiocinatio* earlier in the century, Barbaro was probably following the lead of Jean Martin, who in 1547 had translated this term into French as *discours*.[8] In any case, it was not until the next century that *théorie* became widely adopted into French, *theory* into English, first in the sciences. In 1656, Blaise Pascal, in his seventh *Provincial Letter*, used *théorie* entirely in the modern sense, that is, to refer to the opposite of practice.[9] More importantly, Claude Perrault, in his 1673 translation of Vitruvius, chose *théorie* for the Latin *ratiocinatio*. This term and its variants almost immediately became standard in architectural discussions throughout Europe. An English translation of an abridged version of Perrault's text, published in 1692, first established its architectural usage in this language.[10] *Theory* seems to have fit the body of architectural thought so well that, in a reprint of this book eleven years later, the title was changed to *The Theory and Practice of Architecture; or Vitruvius and Vignola Abridg'd*.[11]

Conveniently, *modern* also came into usage around this time. Its Latin root *modernus* first appeared in the late fifth century A.D., although other words in early antiquity were used to express the same concept.[12] Its use finally became prevalent by the eight or ninth century, in such forms as *modernitas* (of the present day) and *moderni* (modern people). It was the "quarrel of the ancients and moderns" in the late seventeenth century, however, that popularized *modern* as an art term. The "quarrel," an artistic and literary controversy of the 1670s and 1680s, was crucial to the formation of modern theory. It pitted those who defended the artistic superiority of the classical Greek and Roman periods against those who espoused the superiority of modern artists, with their more "reasoned" rules and refined tastes.[13] The "ancients," to put it generally, preferred the "ornaments" devised in classical times to newer and more modern inventions. The "moderns," while acknowledging the profit to be gained by studying the past, dared to criticize antiquity for its "imperfections" and sought to improve on them. And whereas this quarrel in most studies is generally consigned to the late 1680s, it really began in architectural circles as the result of a single footnote – again found in Perrault's 1673 translation of Vitruvius.

The choice of the year 1968 to conclude this study also deserves a few words. To begin with, this year was chosen not because it signifies an end to modernity or the death of architecture, nor because it signifies some greater paradigm shift within the conceptual development of global thought. This book will not debate the relevancy of the culture industry, the notion of an avant-garde predicated on the "scars of damage and disruption," or even the montage of artistic life suspended in a Benjaminian postauratic world.[14] Francesco Dal Co recently pointed out the odd coincidence of the current success of theory in academe with "a depletion of theoretical production on the part of practicing architects and with an increasingly accentuated autonomy claimed by historical research."[15] This suggestion – that theory prospers where theory in practice falters, and vice versa – is indeed an intriguing one because it highlights the resistance of a theory to overly conceptualized modeling. Architectural theory is perhaps better seen as a relatively closed body or culture of ideas formed over centuries, ideas that remain remarkably stable in the face of constantly changing contexts. And in this sense it can certainly be argued that architectural discourse moves quite seamlessly through the late 1960s and early 1970s with no discernible sign of a rupture or breakdown of thought.

Nevertheless, the year 1968 is more than a convenient resting point. It was a year of dramatic social confrontation and upheaval characterized by a dislocation of strategies and sensitivities comparable to what would result from a war or a severe economic downturn. The year and its events challenged the relevancy of the current body of architectural theory and, in the process, injected a measure of intellectual fatigue, politics, and cynicism into the discourse – even if these features resonated with very different political overtones in Europe and Asia than in North America. We also should not overlook feelings of anger and futility and the widespread loss of confidence on the part of architects in their timeless desire to change the world. If theoretical deliberation in the 1970s moves, on the one hand, to resemanticize forms and, on the other hand, to desemanticize their former content, both efforts can be seen as born of the very same impulse. Theory did not change in 1968, but its context radically shifted.

I also want to stress that a history of theory is different from a history of architecture. The emphasis in the former is on ideas, and some major architects have had only a small effect on the course of theory whereas some minor architects have had a large impact. Thus, the pattern of theory is different from that of history. Similarly, if I have privileged certain movements or institutions – such as the De Stijl movement and the Bauhaus in the 1920s – it is not because I necessarily give historiographic preeminence to them within the context of this decade (as, admittedly, many historians have done in the past) but rather because they had a larger and more immediate influence on the theoretical terrain than other contempory events. Further, although this study can by no means be comprehensive, I have striven to provide a balanced account of the development of Western theory in both its European and (somewhat later) North American manifestations.

Every book takes on a life of its own. The efforts that led to this book began with an invitation to the Clark Art Institute study center, and for this I owe a considerable debt to

Michael Conforti and Michael Holly and to the library staff at this idyllic facility in scenic Williamstown. The final chapters of the book were completed at the Canadian Centre for Architecture in Montreal, and I wish to thank Phyllis Lambert for her invitation and generosity and to express my gratitude to Louis Martin, Martin Bressani, Mario Carpo, Dirk De Meyer, and Spyros Papapetros for many discussions. The book owes much to the bibliographic resources of this great institution, supervised by Gerald Beasley, Pierre Boisvert, Renata Gutman, Suzie Quintal, Paul Chenier, and Françoise Roux. I owe a special debt of gratitude to Christina Contandriopoulos for her work on the illustrations. Also providing invaluable assistance at the Canadian Centre for Architecture were Nathalie Senecal and Aliki Economedes. I express my appreciation to Peg Wilson at my local library for her interlibrary-loan assistance. A very important grant from the Graham Foundation for Advanced Study in the Fine Arts allowed me at one point to work full time on the project. I also owe a debt of gratitude to many other people for discussions over the years relating to this study, among them J. Duncan Berry, Marco Frascari, Barry Bergdoll, Henrik Karge, and Joan Ockman. Perhaps the strongest supporter of this enterprise was Beatrice Rehl, the distinguished editor at Cambridge University Press.

One final editorial note: I have in my citations employed the original spellings and accentuation even when they differ from modern usage. Also, a book of this historical scope can only be built on the historical investigations of many others. I have striven in all cases to recognize the sources I used, but the large scope of this enterprise makes it impossible to recognize in every case the efforts of those who shaped aspects of my own work over the years and to construct a comprehensive bibliography. I therefore apologize to all historians whose work I have not cited.

1

PRELUDE

The taste of our century, or at least of our nation, is different from that of the Ancients.

Claude Perrault

1. François Blondel and the French Academic Tradition

Architectural thought in France at the start of the seventeenth century, like that in Italy and Spain, was predicated on the notion that the art of architecture participated in a divinely sanctioned cosmology or natural order: a stable grammar of eternally valid forms, numbers, and proportional relations transmitted to the present from ancient times. Jean Bautista Villalpanda, in his 1604 commentary on the prophet Ezekiel and Solomon's Temple, attempted to prove that these numbers and proportions not only were compatible with the Vitruvian tradition but were given to Solomon directly by God himself.[1] Within a few years, this tenet, more broadly considered, would meet philosophical resistance in the person of René Descartes (1596–1650). In his *Rules for the Direction of the Mind,* written sometime before 1628, Descartes noted: "Concerning objects proposed for study, we ought to investigate what we can clearly and evidently intuit or deduce with certainty, and not what other people have thought or what we ourselves conjecture."[2] In this clash of two different systems of values – inherited tradition and the confident power of human reason – resounds the first stirrings of modern theory.

Descartes's third "rule," as he termed it, is even richer in its implications. Inherent within it is the principle that came to be known as "Cartesian doubt," that is, the provisional and methodic suspension of belief in any knowledge gained simply through books or idle speculation. Such critical skepticism was necessary, the philosopher insisted, both to separate modern science from the prejudices of late scholastic and ancient thought and to ground it anew on

"clear and distinct" ideas. The teachings and terminology of Aristotle, to cite an example used by Descartes himself, were no longer to be taken as sacrosanct; the modern critical mind should approach each problem anew on the basis of empirical results and the methods of deductive reasoning.

Cartesianism would become very much in vogue in French scientific circles by midcentury, and around this time we also begin to find similar attitudes expressed in the arts. Writing in 1650, the architect Roland Fréart de Chambray (1606–76) opened his *Parallèle de l'architecture antique avec la moderne* (Parallel of ancient architecture with the modern) with the suggestion that contemporary architects should eschew the "blind respect and reverence" that antiquity and long custom had imposed on architectural thinking, because "the mind is free, not bound" and "we have as good right to invent, and follow our *Genius,* as the *Antients,* without rendering our selves their Slaves."[3] Fréart's distancing of modern architecture from that of the ancients, however, was not unqualified. In the philosophical tenor of the day, he bases his book "on the *Principles of Geometry,*" because essential beauty in architecture resides in the "*Symmetry* and *Oeconomy* of the *whole,*" or rather in the "visible harmony and consent, which those eyes that are clear'd and enlightened by the real Intelligence of *Art,* contemplate and behold with excess of delectation."[4]

Delectation aside – Fréart's skepticism toward the past incited little enthusiasm among his colleagues, and his admonition to moderate one's "blind respect and reverence" for antiquity found few adherents. France in the second half of the century, in fact, pursued the classical ideal with increasing attention and aplomb. The cultural backdrop to this classical revival was the reign of Louis XIV, who assumed the throne in 1661 with a compelling ambition to elevate the standing of France in every field. Initially, at least, he was enormously successful, in part because France had emerged from the Thirty Years' War (1618–48) as the strongest and most prosperous nation of a much transformed Europe. Given that the population of France was four times that of England and eighteen times that of the Dutch Republic, Louis possessed both the manpower and resources to plan great ventures. He was also fortunate in having at his side, as his chief minister and superintendent of building, the very capable Jean-Baptiste Colbert (1619–83).[5] Writing almost a century later – and addressing himself specifically to readers possessing both intelligence and the "still more rare" attribute of good taste – Voltaire equated the era of Louis XIV with those of Alexander, Augustus, and the Medicis, the era "in which the arts were carried to perfection, and which, by serving as the era of greatness of the human mind, are examples for posterity."[6]

It was an era of wonder to be sure. French missionaries of the Jesuit order were probing the reaches of the world in such distant places as China and North America. Colbert was sending emissaries to other exotic or little known spots, both to forge relations and to seek out selected treasures for the French crown. Typical of these ventures were the efforts of Charles François Olier, the Marquis de Nointel, who in 1670 was sent to Constantinople to negotiate a trade treaty with the Ottomans. Nointel returned by way of Egypt and Greece, where his two artists (foremost Jacques Carrey) famously recorded the (still intact) sculptures decorating the Athenian Parthenon. At home, Colbert focused his attention on founding or reorganizing various academies as well as on directing building enterprises on behalf of the young king. His efforts in both these endeavors conspired to change the course of architectural theory.

The term *academy* of course goes back to the park within Athens in which Plato conversed with his students; the word was revived in fifteenth-century Italy, when it became widely applied to any philosophical discussion, formal or informal. The circle of intellectuals gathered around Giangiorgio Trissino in Vincenza, where Palladio began his higher education in the 1530s, was called an academy because of its emphasis on propagating classical learning. In 1555, Palladio helped to organize the Accademia Olimpica, which deliberated not only on classical works but also on questions of mathematics. One of the first academies devoted entirely to the arts was the Accademia del Designo, founded in Florence in 1563. It held regular weekly meetings and planned an ed-

ucational program, although this program remained largely confined to paper. By contrast, the Accademia de San Luca in Rome, inaugurated in 1593, quickly became celebrated as the premier school for instruction in the theory and practice of the arts.[7]

In France, the early academies were also private, but in 1635 Cardinal Richelieu founded the French Academy. The concern of this institution initially was limited to producing a dictionary of the French language and providing rules for literary composition. More important was the founding of the Royal Academy of Painting and Sculpture in 1648, which was conceived – after the Roman model of San Luca – as a school for practical instruction. In the 1660s, after Louis XIV ascended to the throne, the state embarked on an ambitious program of academic expansion and reorganization. The Academy of Dance was founded in 1661; two years later the so-called Little Academy, an offshoot of the French Academy and the forerunner to the Academy of Inscriptions and Belles Lettres, came into existence. In 1664, Colbert completely reformed the Academy of Painting and Sculpture and provided it with a constitution mandating instruction; in conjunction with its reformation, he opened the French Academy in Rome in 1666, to which the best students in the arts were invited to complete their training. In the same year was founded the Academy of Sciences, and in 1669 the Academy of Music. Perhaps the crown jewel of this elaborate academic bureaucracy was the Royal Academy of Architecture, which opened its doors in 1671.[8] With the founding of these institutions, Colbert and the king had accomplished several things. First, they created a prestigious class of "academicians" with special privileges and responsibilities for instruction; second, they brought all artistic instruction under a centralized authority. The rules of each discipline were now to be strictly mandated; further, they were to be based on ancient and Renaissance precedents.

The first director of the Royal Academy of Architecture was a fifty-three-year-old mathematician and engineer, François Blondel (1618–86).[9] Although he had come late to architecture, Blondel was an interesting polymath with considerable intelligence and solid accomplishments. Over the course of a lengthy career, he had distinguished himself in military and naval battles; undertook a diplomatic mission to Turkey; visited Italy, Greece, and Egypt; gave lectures on mathematics at the Collège de France; and served as an ambassador to Denmark. In France he had attended to fortifying arsenals and to improving the defense of seaports. Immediately preceding his appointment, he had served as the mentor to Colbert's second son on his Italian tour.

The purpose of the Royal Academy of Architecture was not only to codify the principles of classical design but also to espouse these principles, which it did by holding two public lectures a week. The first hour of each session was devoted to the theoretical side of architecture; this was followed by a talk on a technical aspect of the field, such as the rudiments of Euclidean geometry. With much fanfare, the inaugural address by Blondel took place on 31 December 1671. The new director, after reciting the litany of advantages to be acquired from mastering the nuances of architecture, urged his students to pursue their profession by taking advantage of the financial generosity of the king – "the grandeur of his virtues and actions" – under the management of Colbert.[10]

That Blondel's mandate had been defined by the curricula of earlier academies goes without saying, but architecture too had its unique set of problems. Perhaps foremost was the reform of the classical tradition in light of the perceived abuses of the baroque period. And herein also lay France's declaration of architectural independence – its desire to define itself apart from the Italian classical legacy and to surpass the works of Italian architects with its own achievements. Thus in many ways antiquity and not the Renaissance became the new starting point for French theoretical development. If modern French architecture, in line with the other arts, was to emulate the masterworks of Roman antiquity, great care had to be taken to select approved models. In the realm of theory, the teachings of Vitruvius naturally took precedence, and only when this author left matters in doubt were the Renaissance interpretations of Palladio, Scamozzi, Vignola, Serlio, and Alberti to be consulted for edification.[11]

Blondel was also charged with publishing his own lectures on theory, which he did between 1675 and 1683 in two large volumes, *Cours d'architecture* (Course of architecture). His teachings rested on the very traditional notion that architectural beauty derives primarily from proportions.[12] Further, he believed that architectural proportions (perceived by the eye), like musical tonalities (perceived by the ear), emanate from a higher cosmic order, and the perception of these consonances is made possible by an idea divinely implanted in the mind. Indeed, Blondel accepted the arguments of his friend, the musicologist René Ouvrard, who in his *Architecture harmonique* (Harmonic architecture) would insist "that a building cannot be perfect if it does not follow the same rules as composition or the harmonizing of musical chords."[13] Proportional relations were still considered to compose the essence of architectural practice; beauty as an ideal was presumed to be absolute in the mind's discernment of these proportional ratios. The skepticism that Fréart de Chambray had voiced toward antiquity a quarter of a century earlier is occasionally echoed in Blondel's analyses, but not in a way that would offend the votaries of the past. Architecture at the start of the reign of Louis XIV was repositioned squarely within the classical tradition.

2. Claude Perrault and the Louvre

The second front of Colbert's influence on the arts derived from his position as superintendent of buildings, royal manufacturers, commerce, and fine arts – a post he assumed on 1 January 1664. This position gave him nearly full control of the many new artistic and architectural initiatives of the monarch. One of Colbert's first acts, for instance, was to nationalize the Gobelin tapestry factory in Paris and bring it under the authority of Charles Le Brun, the first painter to the king. Hundreds of workers with skills in painting, sculpture, engraving, goldsmithing, cabinet making, weaving, dyeing, and mosaics were enticed from abroad (mainly from Italy) – all, of course, for the greater glory of France.

The principal architectural project under consideration at this time was the eastern extension of the Louvre, the building that was to serve as the urban residence of the new king. The history of its construction is a complicated one.[14] The original turreted castle on the site dated back to early medieval times, but it had been gradually dismantled during two building campaigns undertaken in the sixteenth and early seventeenth centuries. In 1546, Pierre Lescot (d. 1578) produced his masterful design for the southwest corner of the now existing square court, which formed the anchor for the new expansion. Beginning in 1624, Jacques Lemercier (1582–1654) devised a more ambitious master plan and doubled this building, adding as well a new central pavilion. The plan was to construct northern and southern wings at each end and join them at the eastern end with a new building, forming a square with an interior court. Some work was completed on the basement of the north wing, but construction was halted in 1643 when Louis XIII died.

In 1659, as Louis XIV approached his ascension to the throne, work resumed. In that year, the king's first architect, Louis Le Vau (1612–70), prepared a new design for the complex, and construction resumed. Soon the south wing was largely finished, and the foundations and a portion of wall along the eastern ceremonial front were erected. Then Colbert assumed office, and the situation just as quickly changed. Unhappy with Le Vau's design, Colbert, as early as 1662, had been privately seeking alternatives. Upon assuming his new post in 1664, Colbert solicited proposals from other French architects, including Jean Marot, Pierre Cottart, and François Mansart. Two schemes in particular had an important influence on the final outcome. One was for an open colonnade of Corinthian columns along the eastern front, a feature not present in Le Vau's design. This design, exhibited anonymously in Paris in 1664, turned out to be the work of Claude Perrault (1613–88), the older brother of Colbert's private secretary, Charles Perrault (1628–1703). The second design also had a freestanding colonnade along the eastern facade, but its columns were arranged in pairs. This alternative was proposed by François Le Vau (1613–76), the younger brother of Louis Le Vau.[15]

François Le Vau's proposal, however, was not sent to Colbert until December 1664. Earlier, in March of that year, Colbert had requested a proposal from the Italian baroque architect Gianlorenzo Bernini (1598–1680), which arrived in Paris in June. By December 1664, Colbert had evidently decided in favor of the Italian architect, and on behalf of the king, he asked Bernini to prepare a revised proposal and undertake the journey from Rome to Paris. The story of Bernini's triumphant (and costly) carriage ride into the French capital on 2 June 1665 has often been recounted.[16] In the end, however, the trip would prove futile, because his revised design would be greeted with harsh criticism by French architects as well as by Colbert's secretary, Charles Perrault, and eventually it would be ignored by the king himself.[17] Construction of the east wing was halted in October, shortly after Bernini's departure, and the project languished until the spring of 1667. Then Colbert appointed a new committee (a *petit conseil*) to reconsider the design and come up with a new proposal.[18] This design committee was composed of three individuals: Charles Le Brun (the king's first painter), Louis Le Vau (still the king's first architect), and the author of the unsolicited design proposal of 1664, Claude Perrault.

From an historical distance of more than three hundred years, it is of course impossible to understand fully the reasons for the selection of the architecturally inexperienced Perrault, although the political support of his younger brother, together with Colbert's desire to have a voice on the committee, almost certainly played a role. But it can be said that he was a man of considerable stature (Fig. 1). Up to the time of his first proposal for the Louvre, the fifty-one-year-old Perrault had shown no interest in architecture, except possibly for some changes he made to his country house at Viry.[19] He had taken his medical degree

1. Claude Perrault, from *Artist Portraits: Scrapbook, 1600–1800.* Courtesy Collection Centre Canadien d'Architecture/Canadian Centre for Architecture, Montréal.

from the Ecole de Médecine in 1642 and over the next two decades occasionally gave lectures on anatomy and pathology there. He maintained a small medical practice, although his professional interests eventually gravitated toward scientific research. He was, in fact, a consummate Cartesian in his scientific outlook. In addition to conducting numerous anatomical dissections on animals from the royal menagerie, he had studied problems of botany, geology, and mechanics. On one occasion he even conducted experiments on the speed of sound with the famed Dutch physicist Christiaan Huygens. In 1666, one year before his appointment, both Perrault and Huygens were elected to the first class of the Academy of Sciences, a prestigious appointment that had to be approved by Colbert. Thus his scientific accomplishments were certainly known to the latter.

Claude Perrault also possessed another skill that was relatively rare in Paris, a command of both Latin and Greek. This must have stood him in good stead when – probably late in 1666 – Colbert sought a translator for his state-sponsored

2. The Louvre, 1674, engraving of Sébastien Le Clerc, *Lifting of the Louvre Pediment Stones, 1674*. Courtesy Collection Centre Canadien d'Architecture/Canadian Centre for Architecture, Montréal.

translation of Vitruvius, a project no doubt conceived together with his plans for the future Academy of Architecture. Perrault's selection for the translation also seems to have accelerated his architectural interests or perhaps dovetailed with them. Late in 1666 he made a proposal for an obelisk to be dedicated to Louis XIV.[20] Perrault was also commissioned in the spring of 1667 to be the architect of the new Royal Observatory, the building that was to house the meetings of the Academy of Sciences.[21] This commission preceded by only a few weeks the first meeting of the building committee for the Louvre.

To what extent Perrault contributed to the final design of the Louvre (for which he would later take sole credit) has always been a point of historical contention, but it seems likely that the design was genuinely a committee project. (Figs. 2 and 3).[22] The atelier of Louis Le Vau produced the

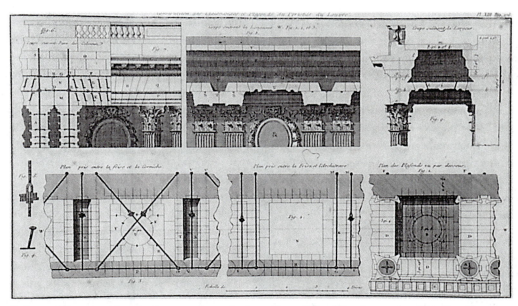

3. Iron reinforcement bars in Louvre colonnade, from Pierre Patte, *Mémoires sur les objets les plus importans de l'architecture* (Paris, 1769). Courtesy Collection Centre Canadien d'Architecture/Canadian Centre for Architecture, Montréal.

first drawings in April and May 1667. These contained the motif of coupled or paired columns along the main story of the eastern front, and it is likely that the seed for this design had been planted by the earlier scheme of François Le Vau. But Perrault also contributed much to the new design during its stages of development, and his responsibilities seem to have expanded as the project underwent refinements, down to the final design of 1668.[23] With his background in science and his broad knowledge of mechanics, he no doubt assisted in devising the ingenious structural solution for the colonnade, with its hidden but elaborate network of iron bars holding the masonry parts together.[24] He also probably devised some of the constructional machinery for the work. In any case, the straight entablature of the Louvre, spanning nineteen feet between its paired columns, would eventually be hailed as one of the great masterpieces of French classicism. Perrault's authorship, real or merely claimed, was sufficiently known for him to include the building – together with his other architectural designs – in the frontispiece of his similarly masterful translation of Vitruvius, which appeared in 1673.

3. The Quarrel of the Ancients and the Moderns

The Louvre design and the translation of Vitruvius together represent one of those rare moments in architecture when revolutions in practice and theory perfectly coincide. Perrault employed his annotations to the translation, in fact, to explain the Louvre design. The crucial note appears in the third chapter of Book 3, in which the Roman author lauds the innovations of the Hellenistic architect Hermogenes, specifically his modification to the dipteral temple through the removal of the inner row of a double range of columns.[25] This design simplification, Vitruvius argues, had both the functional advantage of creating a passage for people behind the outer colonnade and the aesthetic advantage of visually lightening the appearance of the temple and thus endowing it with a certain majesty. Perrault shrewdly seizes this passage as a justification for the use of coupled columns along the east facade of the Louvre:

The taste of our century, or at least of our nation, is different from that of the ancients and perhaps it has a little of the Gothic in it, because we love the air, the daylight, and openness [dégagemens]. Thus we have invented a sixth manner of disposing of columns, which is to group them in pairs and separate each pair with two intercolumniations.... This has been done in imitation of Hermogenes.... What he did by removing

a range of columns in each aisle, we do within a colonnade by removing a column from the middle of two columns and pushing it toward the adjacent column. This manner could be called the Pseudosystyle.[26]

Perrault's reference to "a little of the Gothic" alludes not to the formal or decorative aspects of Gothic architecture but rather to the efficiency of its structural system, that is, to the lightness of its vertical supports when contrasted with the squatter proportions of classical columns. In 1669 Perrault had undertaken a trip to the south of France, where he sketched and took notes on both medieval and classical buildings, among them the vaults of the church of Saint-Hilaire-le-Grand in Poitiers ("la structure est assez particulière") and the cathedral of Saint-André in Bordeaux.[27] In the latter city, he also studied the ruins of the amphitheater and the columnar remnants of a Gallo-Roman temple (now destroyed), the Piliers de Tutelle.[28] These two works were important to Perrault for what they displayed of the constructional techniques of Roman architecture. More important, however, was his exposure to and appreciation of the comparative structural efficiencies of medieval or Gothic works ("l'ordre gothique"). He returned to Paris not only with a sense of their structural ingenuity but also with an aesthetic taste for their visual lightness.

Also noteworthy in the quoted passage is the term rendered as "openness" – dégagmens or dégagement, which literally means "disengagement." Perrault is referring to the separation of the colonnade from the wall of the palace behind and to the overall lighter spatial sensation that results from this separation. It was a criticism of Italian Renaissance architecture, the fact that it relied on heavy exterior walls with reinforcing pilasters. Perrault argues that the openness of the colonnade and the reduction in the load to be borne by the wall behind allow larger windows in the wall and thus the enhancement of natural light and ventilation (air). This point was made by Perrault despite the fact that the original windows planned for the Louvre wall were (in 1668) transformed into solid niches.[29]

A third important term that appears in Vitruvius's original text, the Latin word asperitas (translated into French as aspreté, now âpreté, also the English asperity), which Vitruvius used to describe the visual effect of the new design of Hermogenes. This was the effect of the lighter colonnade throwing the temple walls into deep relief. The word signifies a roughness or unevenness of surface, but Perrault employs the term in French to refer to the "lively aspect" or "picturesque vista" induced by the colonnade, in other words the visual tension in relief when perceived in perspective.[30] *Dégagement* and *âpreté* will later become key terms in French theory and discussions in which they occur inevitably point back to this particular passage.

Perrault's very unclassical allusion to Gothic taste, as well as his defense of a coupled column for the Louvre (with few ancient or Renaissance precedents), interestingly, did not evoke an immediate reaction within academic circles. In fact, when this particular passage was read to the Academy of Architecture in December 1674 (as part of weekly readings of the entire book), it passed without comment, even though the assembly did find a "difficulty" with another footnote, on columnar diminution, that appeared a few lines later.[31] The sense of professional decorum apparent in these proceedings may have hindered overt confrontation, but Perrault's various concerns regarding accepted features of classical theory at the same time called into question the teachings of Blondel. A response was therefore inevitable, and it came in 1683, when Blondel published the second volume of his *Cours d'architecture*. The academy director, in fact, devoted three chapters of his book to contesting this particular footnote and also mounted a harsh attack on the Louvre design. His response essentially defined the opening round of a broader cultural debate in France, later known as the "quarrel between the ancients and the moderns," in which Blondel, through his defense of antiquity, took the side of the ancients.

With regard to the Louvre design, Blondel was above all suspicious of the amount of reinforcing iron used in the colonnade. Solidity in architecture, he insisted, requires architects not to take shortcuts that reduce "confidence" in the stability of the design, and in any case the ancients, with their heavier buildings, did not have to rely on this recourse.[32] He also questioned the structural advantages of the coupled-column solution, which Perrault had argued was structurally superior because the composite beam spanning the larger intercolumniation of paired columns rested wholly on the inner column at each end. Blondel replied that these structural advantages were not real – essentially by incorrectly speculating that the negative bending movement of a cantilevered beam causes its ends to raise up, thus inducing greater stress at the inside corners of the supporting columns.[33] As there was no way at the time to consider these issues mathematically, it should be noted that Perrault originally demonstrated the coupled-column, quasi-cantilevered solution to his peers by building a model in iron and stone in the laboratory, to the scale of one inch per foot.[34]

In his book, Blondel devotes much time to searching for ancient and Renaissance precedents for Perrault's scheme and its rationalization. On the first front, he finds too few precedents of coupled columns or pilasters in antiquity or the Renaissance (for the latter, he cites the Belvedere, the House of Raphael by Bramante, as well as Michelangelo's use of them in St. Peter's). He also expresses surprise that this motif – through Perrault's example – has become so widely accepted in the intervening decade: "I am astonished, I say, that they [the architects employing it] have not seen the difference between those ruins that have received universal approbation, and those buildings, half Gothic, on which the ancients coupled columns or pilasters."[35]

This taint of Gothicism in the bundling of structural supports now emerges as the main issue: "I have nothing to say of that love that he attributes to our nation for daylight and openness, because we can admit at the same time that it still partakes of the Gothic, and in this it is therefore very different from that of the ancients."[36] And if Perrault uses Hermogenes to justify his new invention, Blondel insists that the sword has a double edge: "It is also very true that this same reasoning has opened the door at all times to the disorder that is found in architecture and in the other arts." Now he approaches the heart of the matter: "Gothic architects only filled their edifices with such impertinences because they believed that it was permitted to add to the inventions of the Greeks and Romans."[37]

Blondel's sentiments here seem remarkably doctrinaire and opposed to all innovation, but we should keep in mind that the issue for him carried very high stakes, of which his reputation as an engineer and teacher was not the least. Perrault was nevertheless forced to rejoin, and his initial response – resonating with the Cartesian doubt that imbued his scientific training – took the form of a greatly expanded footnote in the second edition of his translation of Vitruvius, issued in 1684. His reasoning is now quite clever. On the one hand, he argues that a blind adherence to ancient practices would effectively stifle all progress or modern innovation; on the other hand, he proudly admits to the taint of Gothicism:

The principal objection on which he [Blondel] leans the most is founded on prejudice and on the false assumption that it is not permitted to depart from the practices of the ancients; that everything which does not imitate their manners must be either bizarre and capricious, and that if this rule is not inviolably protected, the door is opened to license, which leads the arts into disorder. But just as this reasoning proves too much it cannot prove anything at all, because it is much more disadvantageous to close the door to all beautiful inventions than to open it to those that are so ridiculous that they will destroy themselves....

But the greatest reproach he believes to make against our Pseudosystyle is to say that it resembles the Gothic. I might hesitate to agree with this fact in my note, but assuming that the Gothic in general (and taking into account everything that composes it) is not the most beautiful style of architecture, I do not think everything in the Gothic must be rejected. The daylight in their buildings, and the openness that results are things in which the Gothic people differed from the ancients, but they are not things for which the Gothic is to be disdained.[38]

Thus, the issues first defining the architectural debate between the ancients and the moderns were neatly laid out on the table by 1684, but Perrault, with his deeply felt skepticism toward the authority of the classical past, did not stop here. One year before the second edition of Vitruvius appeared, Perrault published his own architectural treatise, *Ordonnance des cinq espèces de colonnes selon la méthode des anciens* (Ordonnance for the five kinds of columns after the method of the ancients), which issued an even more threatening challenge to Blondel's academic teachings.[39] It did so ostensibly by raising a problem that Renaissance theory (both in Italy and in France) had been unable to resolve – that of devising a uniform system for the proportioning of columns.

The problem was in fact a long-standing one, as Renaissance architects had recognized. The system proposed by Vitruvius was unacceptable, first because the Roman architect had not provided sufficient details, second because he himself had admitted that the basic proportions for the orders had changed over time, and third because the columns in surviving Roman buildings (mostly from imperial times) did not have the proportions that he prescribed. In searching for a unified system in keeping with the belief in absolute beauty, Renaissance architects from Leon Battista Alberti (1404–72) to Vincenzo Scamozzi (1552–1616) had proposed systems for quantifying dimensions. More recently, in 1650, Fréart de Chambray had taken another approach; he simply compiled the dimensions given by ten authors so that the architect could decide upon the best solution.[40] Thus, an urgent problem of the newly established Academy of Architecture was to define with precision the system used by Roman architects and so make it available as a guide for modern use.

To this end Colbert sent the student Antoine Desgodetz (1653–1728) to Rome in 1674 with the mission of measuring the principal Roman monuments.[41] The trip proved eventful from the start, as both Desgodetz and his traveling companion, Augustin-Charles d'Aviler, were kidnapped by pirates on their way south and had to be ransomed by the crown before they could start work. When Desgodetz eventually returned to Paris in 1677, he brought with him measurements of almost fifty buildings. Twenty-five monuments were chosen to be engraved in a volume published by the crown in 1682, under the title *Les Edifices antiques de Rome dessinés et mesurés très exactement* (The ancient buildings of Rome drawn and measured very exactly).[42] Yet far from revealing the system used in antiquity, Desgodetz's research rather demonstrated that no common dimensional system prevailed and that the measurements of such renowned Renaissance authors as Serlio and Palladio were filled with inaccuracies when compared with his "very exact" measurements.

Blondel seems not to have cared much for the conclusions of Desgodetz's study (not least because they were inconsistent with his belief in absolute beauty), and it was most certainly Blondel's decision to suppress the results, or at least to keep them from serious examination.[43] Perrault, who was also following the events closely, was by contrast intrigued by Desgodetz's findings, and they must have served as a challenge to his scientific mind. Indeed, the first goal of Perrault's *Ordonnance* was to propose a new system of proportional ratios for the columnar orders, which he devised by working in an empirical fashion. He gathered measurements from buildings and treatises of ancient and modern authors and derived from them the arithmetical mean for each unit of the columns and entablatures – invoking the premise that "good sense" on the part of the architect prescribed the choice of the mean between two extremes.[44] His system of "probable mean proportions" was also based on an innovation of his, the *petit module* (a third of the diameter of a column), which allowed the architect to employ simple numbers (instead of fractions) for smaller parts.

Still, it was the theoretical introduction to the *Ordonnance* that had the most important implications for the debate, for there Perrault seized the opportunity to wrap his earlier objections to Blondel's teachings under a broader theory. In several footnotes to the 1673 edition of Vitruvius, for instance, he had voiced his belief that proportions, far from possessing a "positive, necessary, and convincing beauty," were rather a product of the human mind (*fantasie*), arrived at by "a consensus of architects" based on what they deemed to be the best works to be imitated.[45] This belief now led him to propose two different types of beauty for architecture: positive and arbitrary. In the first category belong those beauties based on "convincing reasons" easily apprehended by everyone, such as "the richness of the materials, the size and magnificence of the building, the precision and cleanness of the execution, and symmetry."[46] Positive beauty is thus reminiscent of absolute beauty, but only in the sense that its appreciation is universal. Arbitrary beauty, on the other hand, is "determined by our wish to give a definite proportion, shape, or form to things that might well have a different form without being misshapen and that appear agreeable not by reasons within everyone's grasp but merely by custom and the association the mind makes between two things of a different nature."[47] Here, under the rubric of "affectivity" or "association," is where architectural proportions reside. Thus Perrault's argument presages a relativistic rather than an absolutist aesthetics.[48]

Perrault's distinction between positive and arbitrary beauty also becomes the basis for calling into question other tenets of academic theory. Drawing upon his continuing medical research, for instance, he denounces the notion of shared harmonic values for music and architecture on the grounds that the ear and the eye process perceptual data in different ways. The former works without the mediation of the intellect, while the eye perceives entirely through the intervention of knowledge.[49] Musicians never differ on the correctness of the notes of a chord, he points out, whereas architects (as the many books with rules for column orders show) almost always hold distinct opinions on proportions. Perrault challenges as well the idea that architectural beauty should be predicated on imitation, either of nature or of reason, and prefers to ground it entirely on habit or custom.[50] His harshest words – words that also articulate his "modern" position most clearly – are directed against those architects who express an undue reverence for antiquity: "The extent to which architects make a religion of venerating the works they call ancient is inconceivable. They admire everything about them but especially the mystery of proportions."[51] Perrault compares this "exaggerated respect" for the past in his day to the "cruel war waged on the sciences" by the barbarism of the Middle Ages, forcing many branches of culture to take refuge in monasteries. Thus his long scientific training obviously stood behind his desire to demystify the foundations of architecture and place its basic tenets on a rigorous rationalist footing.

But this desire was expressed near the time that the architectural debate was drawing to a conclusion. And in the short term at least, Perrault's views would not win many followers. Blondel died in 1686 and his successor, Philippe de la Hire (1640–1718), would leave in place his teachings regarding absolute beauty and proportions. Perrault himself

would die in 1688 – conscientious scientist that he was, of an infection incurred while dissecting a camel.

4. The First Project for the Church of Ste.-Geneviève

Even before Claude Perrault passed away, the quarrel between the ancients and the moderns had entered a new phase. The stimulus to the new debate was a poem by Charles Perrault read to the French Academy on 27 January 1687. It was entitled "The Century of Louis the Great," and in it Charles glorified the accomplishments of the age of Louis XIV and the great strides that had been made in the arts over the last quarter-century.[52] He even went so far as to liken these accomplishments (architectural and otherwise) with the achievements of "the beautiful age of Augustus."

Reactions to such comparisons within the literary world were swift and for a while unrelenting. The classicist Nicolas Boileau-Despréaux got up and walked out of the hall during the reading, by some accounts slamming the door on his way out. He later proceeded to attack the Perrault brothers unmercifully for their cultural conceit, as did other "ancients" within his literary circle, including La Fontaine and Racine.[53] Charles, however, was well equipped to respond. After retiring as Colbert's secretary in 1682, he had returned to his literary pursuits (he was well known as the author of fairytales, many of which were collected and published between 1812 and 1815 by the Grimm brothers).[54] To Boileau he responded with a four-part Socratic dialogue, *Parallel of the Ancients and the Moderns*, which appeared between 1688 and 1697. Here he greatly expanded his earlier arguments in favor of progress in the arts and sciences and again defended the right of his age to define its own artistic spirit even if this meant going outside of the stylistic confines of the past. In commenting on Charles's rationalist fervor (no doubt also evident in his brother), one nineteenth-century chronicler of the quarrel between the ancients and moderns even referred to him as "the son of Descartes."[55]

This quarrel, however, was largely a literary affair. Far more important for architectural theory was a brief *mémoire* Charles published in 1697 under the title "Dessin d'un Portail pour l'Église de Sainte-Geneviève a Paris."[56] This was a proposal that both he and Claude had made in the mid-1670s to enlarge the ancient church of Ste.-Geneviève, the patron saint of the city of Paris. The proposed addition had been designed a few years after the appearance of Claude's translation of Vitruvius, and a surviving interior perspective and elevation recall, in fact, several plates contained in Claude's translation.[57]

Two features of the design made it of great interest to the eighteenth century. One was the entrance porch to the church, a freestanding colonnade supporting an uninterrupted flat entablature above. The second was the flat entablature of the interior nave, which is supported on each side by a row of columns, while the ceiling above is vaulted (actually supported by trusses above). The use of freestanding columns in the nave of a basilica, as Perrault would have known from his research, is reminiscent of a few surviving works from late Roman antiquity as well as the early Renaissance, but the practice of using columns in the naves of larger churches had ceased during the Renaissance. Structurally, the weight and lateral thrust of a vaulted ceiling (desired for reasons of fireproofing) demanded the heavier support of more massive piers.

The scheme of the Perrault brothers, like the Louvre colonnade, was structurally daring in its slender proportions, and it no doubt derived from the same argument made in Claude's footnote defending his scheme for the Louvre. The interior daylight allowed by the more slender columns, the Gothic lightness of their appearance, and the openness (dégagement) of the floor plan – these were the elements of Gothic architecture that Claude had approved, whatever paradoxes they might pose for classical theory. There is even an internal formal consistency here, as Michel Petzet has suggested: "The more classical church, the church with columns and architraves, is at the same time more Gothic in its structure."[58]

In 1698 work also began on the chapel at Versailles, following the design made almost a decade earlier by Jules Hardouin-Mansart (1646–1708).[59] The chapel presented a unique architectural problem in that the royal pew was to be on the second level whereas the lower level was reserved for less important members of the king's retinue. Matching the height of the narrow chapel with the existing elevations of Versailles also mandated a vertical solution.[60] Hardouin-Mansart's design was ingenious: He created a two-part scheme that featured a low range of piers at ground level and a taller colonnade of freestanding Corinthian columns above, supporting a straight entablature and vaulted ceiling (of wood and stucco). The daylight pouring through the upper-story windows behind the columns, contrasting with the darkened spaces below, accentuate this royal division. Various historians have commented on the Gothic feeling of this classical chapel, with its slender columns reinforced with iron bars and chains buried in the architraves –

not to mention the flying buttresses outside. Wherever Hardouin-Mansart found the inspiration for his light and elegant design, it perfectly reflects the innovative mind of Claude Perrault.

Hardouin-Mansart's design also falls in with another historical development then taking place. When Perrault traveled to Bordeaux in 1669, he made mention of the *l'ordre gothique*, which he contrasted in the same sentence with the *l'ordre antique*. He was therefore making a stylistic distinction between Gothic and classical architecture that was in one respect new to seventeenth-century France. It is not that Gothic architecture was unknown or unstudied at this time; rather, the converse is closer to the truth. As Robin Middleton has noted, the Gothic building tradition and its guilds remained strong in French secular and ecclesiastical circles throughout the sixteenth and seventeenth centuries.[61] The first major proponent of Italian Renaissance taste, Philibert de L'Orme (1515?–70), in fact devoted several chapters of *Le premier tome de l'architecture* (The first book of architecture; 1567) to Gothic vaulting techniques.[62] Various guidebooks and building studies in the last part of the sixteenth century discussed in some detail the medieval monuments of France. And by the early seventeenth century, various authors, among them André Duschesne and François Derand, not only had a sophisticated appreciation of Gothic formal and structural characteristics but stressed the "elegance," "delicacy," and "lightness" of Gothic structural solutions.[63] What Perrault's stylistic distinction suggested – aside from granting Gothic architecture a certain credibility as a style – was that classical architecture might indeed be enriched by a better understanding of the formal and structural techniques of Gothic buildings.

This point was not entirely lost on the Academy of Architecture. Blondel himself, though fiercely opposed to the forms and ornaments of Gothic architecture, had (with his engineering background) some appreciation for the constructional aspects of Gothic works. Still, when the Academy of Architecture began to read de L'Orme's treatise in 1676, it skipped over his analyses of Gothic structures and began with book 5, dealing with the classical orders.[64] Two years later, at the request of Colbert, members of the Academy of Architecture made several field trips in and around Paris to study the properties and deteriorating stonework of medieval churches.[65] Aside from visiting such Parisian works as Notre-Dame, architects and students ventured to Saint Denis, Rouen, and Chartres.

The Gothic style was given another measure of legitimacy a decade later, in 1687, when Jean-François Félibien

(c. 1656–1733) – the son of the academy's first secretary, André Félibien (1619–95) – published his *Recueil historique de la vie et des ouvrages des plus célebres architectes* (Historical compilation of the life and works of the most celebrated architects).[66] The younger Félibien, who later would inherit his father's position, assigned the start of Gothic practice in the South to the reign of Honorius (384–423) but in France to the reign of the sons of Hugh Capet, around the start of the eleventh century.[67] Félibien also distinguished between *gothique ancien* and *gothique moderne*; the former, roughly equivalent to the Romanesque, is characterized by its "solidity and grandeur."[68] *Gothique moderne*, which commenced in 1140 with the Church of St. Denis, possesses, by contrast, a "rather grand excess of delicacy."[69] Félibien discusses at some length all of the major French cathedrals and does not hesitate to place Chartres "within the rank of the most sumptuous that can be seen today in Europe."[70]

Félibien's historical survey, combined with Perrault's earlier reference to Gothic style in his defense of the Louvre and in the proposal for the Church of Ste.-Geneviève, set the stage for a more radical consideration of this style with respect to classical theory. We can see a growing fascination with this "Graeco-Gothic Ideal," to use Middleton's expression, at the beginning of the eighteenth century, indicated by the publication of two books.[71]

Michel de Frémin's *Mémoires critiques d'architecture* (Critical memoirs on architecture, 1702) was the first of these studies. It is a salty text, lacking the decorous composure a respected academician would give it but rather is embued with the critical enthusiasm of someone removed from the academy's august deliberations concerning the orders. Frémin, who was a financial administrator, engineer, and inspector of roads and bridges, in fact belittled the importance of the column orders altogether (which he deemed to be the "least part of architecture") and focused instead on architecture's more practical pursuits.[72] He chose the format of forty-eight letters, he noted at the start, so that the book might be read even by "people a little short on intelligence."[73] The letters do tend to ramble, as they deal with such topics as exposing the malpractice of workers, the design of smokeless chimneys, machines of Frémin's own invention, and the worthwhile properties of plaster. One curious letter disputes "the ridiculous opinion that the moon eats stonework."[74]

What makes this book important is that Frémin draws specifically upon the implications of Perrault's footnote regarding *dégagement* and gives it a functionalist turn. In the

sixth letter, he compares the two Gothic churches of Notre-Dame and Ste.-Chapelle with the two classical churches of St. Eustache and St. Sulpice. The design of the Church of St. Eustache (begun in 1532) is an interesting hybrid, basically a Gothic plan outfitted in Renaissance forms; the interior piers are classical instead of Gothic but have proportions more closely approaching the latter. St. Sulpice (begun in 1645) also combines classical and Gothic elements but has piers and proportions more classical than Gothic. Frémin is quite critical of both efforts, chiefly for their inefficient use of interior space. He criticizes St. Eustache for the "crudeness" of its mass of pillars, especially in the case of the organ supports, where "more than half of the ground area is taken up by stonework!"[75] The Church of St. Sulpice fares even worse, with its squared "monstrous pillars" nine feet in width. Not only do these pillars take up too much space, they represent the timidity of architects, who "pile up entire quarries to support a small pedestal, then tremble lest the work will collapse when they remove their hands."[76]

The two Gothic works, by contrast, are entirely fitted to ecclesiastical services and provide ample spaciousness and daylight. Ste.-Chapelle is a "model of true architecture" because of its lack of side aisles and its colorful oversized windows, the advantage of which is strengthened by the slender Gothic piers.[77] Notre-Dame is lauded for the spaciousness of its plan; for its accommodation of the needs of acoustics, daylight, and ventilation; and for its ingenious and economical vaulting system.[78] Frémin, like Perrault before him, was advocating not a return to Gothic style but rather the incorporation of this style's functional and structural efficiencies into church design.

Frémin's book received a cool reception from the Academy of Architecture, which found its observations "quite remote" from the subject of architecture.[79] Nonetheless, it helped shape the arguments of another book that appeared four years later, the *Nouveau traité de toute l'architecture* (New treatise of all architecture, 1706), written by Jean-Louis de Cordemoy. Though a layman, Cordemoy constructed his book along the lines of a traditional treatise and explicitly acknowledged the connection between his ideas and Perrault's. He was the fifth son of Gerauld de Cordemoy (1626–84), a Cartesian philosopher and historian. Jean-Louis, a canon at the Church of S. Jean des Vignes in Soissons, seems to have had no architectural training; and, like Frémin's, his views stand in sharp contrast to academic teachings.[80] His study is in part a book on the orders, and he admits at the start that he wants to follow the system proposed in the *Ordonnance* of Perrault – "ca sçavant *homme*" – but to simplify the more diffuse and obscure parts of Perrault's ideas.

Cordemoy is above all a rationalist, and his sense of architecture can almost be seen as an attenuation of Perrault's notions of *âpreté* (visual tension) and *dégagement* (spaciousness). In general, Cordemoy prefers less ornament, plain surfaces, and rectilinear architectural forms; he opposes a host of baroque and rococo devices, such as multiple pilasters, giant pilasters or columns, twisted columns, columns on pedestals, statues on roofs or in niches, niches themselves, and gabled roofs. There is, however, one modern invention that he very much favors: the freestanding colonnade with coupled columns and flat entablature. This post-and-lintel solution is preferred not only for its "true proportions" and "true beauty" but also "because it alone has that beauty that results from the visual tension (*âpreté*) or squeezing together (*serrement*) [of columns] that pleased the ancients so much, and the spaciousness (*dégagement*) for which the moderns so carefully search."[81]

The same is true with regard to church interiors. Many people, Cordemoy notes, claim that St. Peter's in Rome is the most beautiful church in the world because of its vast expanse, prodigious height, and correctness of ornament. But he disputes this judgment because the pilaster-and-arcade system supporting its interior vaults and dome at the same time established these features as a bad precedent for church interiors. Cordemoy regards the Church of Val-De-Grâce in Paris as a better example of a church interior, but even it could have been improved:

Would it not be infinitely more beautiful if, instead of all those useless and ponderous arcades, those pilasters and large piers that occupy so much space and necessarily create gloom, we had placed there columns in order to carry the rest of the edifice . . . ? Would not its dome have been more beautiful if it were supported by a colonnade, instead of by the square arcades on which it is falsely supported?[82]

Instead of this church, with its lack of boldness and excess of sterility, Cordemoy regards "a church in the taste of the portico of the entrance to the Louvre, or that which is

the invention of the illustrious P. de Creil at the Abbey of Ste.-Geneviève in Paris, as the most beautiful thing in the world."[83]

Cordemoy's views, like Perrault's before him, would soon come under fire, in this instance by Amédée François Frézier (1682–1773), a young infantry officer and engineer. Frézier's hostility centered on Cordemoy's lack of knowledge and constructional experience, in particular his rather naive belief that domes as large and heavy as that of St. Peter's or Val-de-Grâce could be supported simply with columns. Frézier also defended most of the other things that Cordemoy wanted to eliminate from practice, including the arcuated system for masonry presently in use, and he insisted that flat lintels or entablatures were not possible with the small stones available in France.[84] His review prompted several exchanges between the two men from 1709 to 1712.[85] In 1714 Cordemoy published a second edition of his book, in which he responds directly to Frézier's charges.[86] The abbé now defends, among other things, the right of laymen to critique architecture, the notion that columnar churches are more beautiful ("a faith I have in common with the Ancients"), and the structural ingenuity of the Louvre colonnade. He also reiterates his earlier argument that Bramante and Michelangelo took a wrong turn with their use of pilasters and arcades for church interiors. Cordemoy thus emerges as a strict Perraultian in his thinking, and he finds ample precedents for his ideal church in the basilicas of early Christianity.

Cordemoy's spirited defense of his position perhaps could have made some headway in the early years of the eighteenth century – were it not for a strong contrary current driving French architectural practice. The increasingly sumptuous interiors introduced at Versailles by Hardouin-Mansart found many emulators in France, among them Gilles-Marie Oppenord, Robert de Cotte, Jean Aubert, and Jules-Aurèle Meissonnier. By the middle of the 1730s, the ornate rococo style had established itself – now across Europe – as a fully mature "*nouvelle manière*." Thus, the debate initiated by Perrault was, temporarily at least, pushed into the background.

2

THE ENLIGHTENMENT AND
NEOCLASSICAL THEORY

Suddenly a bright light appeared before my eyes. I saw objects distinctly where
before I had only caught a glimpse of haze and clouds.

Marc-Antoine Laugier (1753)

1. The Enlightenment in France

The relative lull in architectural debate in the first decades
of eighteenth-century France mirrors a more pervasive
lethargy that both shifted and sapped intellectual performance at large. Rococo theory, on the one hand, turned
the focus of architectural attention from monumental practice toward residential planning – a trend discernible in the
three editions (the second and third each greatly expanded)
of Augustin-Charles d'Aviler's *Cours d'architecture* (Course
of architecture; 1691, 1710, 1738) and Jacques-François
Blondel's *De la distribution des maisons de plaisance, et
de la décoration des edifices en general* (On the layout of
country seats, and the decoration of edifices in general;
1737–8).[1] French rococo theory, on the other hand, was a
body of thought planted on soft political and economic underpinnings. The great promise of the early reign of Louis
XIV soon dissipated. The fate of his cultural renaissance in
France was largely sealed by the revocation of the Edict of
Nantes in 1685, which sent tens of thousands of productive Huguenots into permanent religious exile. The whimsical overbuilding at Versailles and the disastrous War of
Spanish Succession (1701–13) further depleted state cof-
fers and undermined French morale, so much so that when
the corpse of the monarch was wheeled to its burial place
at Saint Denis in 1715, it was jeered along the way by angry mobs. The regency government of the Duke of Orleans
(1715–23) promised reforms but did not deliver, and the
early nominal rule of Louis XV (1723–74) did little to improve the situation. Wars, disease, famine, poverty, religious
persecution, and political suppression were more the rule
than the exception during the first half of the eighteenth

century – across Europe. Architectural theory in France was
more or less relegated to the confines of the academy, and
the lack of a viable tax base meant that no large architectural
projects could be contemplated.

But these facts do little to explain the phenomenon of
the European Enlightenment around midcentury. It was
a discourse that took place almost simultaneously across
Europe and would soon be felt as far away as the United
States. Within the short span of eight years – between the
War of the Austrian Succession (1740–8) and the Seven
Years' War (1756–63) – various proponents of the new
"reason" gathered in Paris, among them Etienne-Bonnet
de Condillac, Anne-Robert Turgot, Denis Diderot, Jean Le
Rond D'Alembert, and Jean-Jacques Rousseau. In the realm
of French architecture, the decision was made to tear down
and build a new Church of Ste.-Geneviève. In architectural theory, the Abbé Marc-Antoine Laugier published his
controversial *Essai sur l'architecture* (1753). Although the
"ancient regime" survived for a few more decades before
its violent collapse, the intellectual forces that set in motion the idea of modernism were already in evidence at
midcentury.

The great *Encyclopédie* edited by Denis Diderot defiantly
led the way. This critic and philosopher originally came to
Paris in 1728 to pursue an ecclesiastical career, but the writings of Voltaire (in particular, the banned *Letters Concerning
the English Nation*, 1733) dissuaded him from this course. By
the end of the 1730s, he had settled into a bohemian life in
which he split his time between learning languages and attending university lectures. His first published work, *Pensées
philosophiques* (Philosophical thoughts, 1746) – a defense
of the passions and an indiscrete attack on religion – was

sufficiently risqué for the city of Paris to order the book burned. Another early book, *Lettre sur les aveugles à l'usage de ceux qui voient* (Letter on the blind for the use of those who see), landed him in a prison cell in the summer of 1749. In this work, he reconsiders an epistemological problem raised by John Locke and Condillac and insists that a person is born without any innate moral sense.[2]

Diderot's imprisonment delayed, but did not prevent work on the encyclopedia from moving forward. The project was initiated by the Paris publisher André François Le Breton in 1743 as a French translation of the Ephraim Chambers's *Cyclopaedia* (1728). Diderot joined the editorial staff in 1745; two years later he was named editor-in-chief, from which position he convinced the publisher to abandon the English model and start the project anew. The prospectus, published in 1750, describes the new work as largely complete and consisting of at least ten volumes, including 600 illustrative plates.[3] It divides human knowledge into the three realms of memory, reason, and imagination, under which fall the disciplines of history, philosophy, and the arts, respectively.

D'Alembert's "Preliminary Discourse" in the first volume (1751) further defines the project's philosophical direction.[4] The impact of English philosophers (Francis Bacon, Isaac Newton, and John Locke) is fully acknowledged, as is the influence of Descartes (especially Cartesian doubt), Montesquieu, and Voltaire. The encyclopedia espouses the spirit of rigorous analysis and the method of reason; no self-evident or a priori principles are to be conceded, even in such sensitive matters as politics and religion. D'Alembert, himself a royal academician, mathematician, and physicist, wrote most of the scientific entries. Diderot wrote many more, but he was also joined by other authors, including his close friend Rousseau. Jacques-François Blondel wrote the article "Architecture" but with little insight into the dramatic changes that were about to overtake the art.[5]

The high level of most of the entries was, however, unable to stave off the disapproval of state censors and church officials.[6] The first two volumes appeared in June 1751 and January 1752, and by February all further volumes had been prohibited. Voltaire encouraged Diderot to shift his base of operations to Berlin, but Diderot sought allies within royal circles, and through the intervention of Madame de Pompadour (mistress of Louis XV), the ban was lifted in the spring. Volumes 3 to 6 appeared between 1753 and 1756, but under stricter censorship. The seventh volume, with Voltaire's article on fornication and d'Alembert's essay on Calvinism, resulted in a royal condemnation in 1759. Most participants, fearing arrest, now deserted the project, but

Diderot persisted and secretly published the remaining volumes. Over the next six years, he guided another ten volumes through production and then supervised eleven volumes of plates. That the project was completed at all is a testimony to his intellectual integrity.

The two discourses of Rousseau, of 1750 and 1755, further defined the ideas of the Enlightenment. Rousseau, who was a native of Geneva, migrated to Paris in the early 1740s, where he unsuccessfully sought to introduce a new system of musical notation. Under the influence of Diderot, he turned to a life of letters, commencing in the summer of 1749, when he heard that the Academy of Dijon was offering a prize for an essay in response to the question "Has the Restoration of the Sciences and Arts Tended to Purify Morals?" After discussing the matter with Diderot in the latter's prison cell, Rousseau decided to enter the contest and won first prize.

Rousseau's leading thesis − contrary to the jury's expectations − was that the sciences and arts had not purified morals but had rather corrupted them. The essay first distinguishes between simple men in their natural condition and "respectable men" of social seasoning. The first are like Greek athletes who competed in the nude; they exalted in their strength and disdained the vile ornaments invented by others to hide some deformity. Customs were rustic but natural. With the advent of arts and sciences, however, simplicity began to give way to the affectation of manners: "One no longer dares to appear as he is; and in this perpetual constraint, the men who form this herd called society, placed in the same circumstances, will all do the same things unless stronger motives deter them."[7] Rousseau then draws the famous distinction between Athens and Sparta. The latter banned the arts and sciences from the city walls and remained moral and pious in temper; the former (the abode of civility and good taste, the city of art, rhetoric, and philosophy) by contrast fell into corruption. Early Rome was militant and courageous; imperial Rome, enervated by literature and the arts, collapsed under the weight of its immorality.

Rousseau's second discourse pursues a similar theme, only in a more rigorous way. The question now proposed by the Academy of Dijon was "What Is the Origin of Inequality among Men; and Is It Authorized by Natural Law?" Rousseau responds by portraying "natural man" sleeping under an oak, taking his meals from sources immediately available, his drink from a nearby stream. He lives at the level of his sensations; he is free, healthy, and robust, and he has no feelings of unhappiness, no sense of deprivation, no understanding of vice and virtue. "Social man," accustomed to soft and effeminate ways of living, by contrast experiences all of the ills of civil society. The introduction of property is the first turning point in the natural order; the arts of metallurgy and agriculture later introduce the concepts of labor, social servitude, and inequality. "Crimes, wars, murders," not to mention simple tyranny, ensue from these civilizing conceits.[8]

It does not take much effort to read the revolutionary fervor underlying Rousseau's analyses. The first part of the second discourse is, in fact, an encomium to the "Republic of Geneva" and the idealized democracy of this small city-state, which stands in vivid contrast to the unmentioned monarchy of France, guided by a few men "gutted with superfluities while the starving multitude lacks necessities."[9] Such ideas were dangerous to the existing order, and it would only take a few years before Rousseau himself was forced to flee Paris out of fear of arrest. What is important to note, however, is that this generation of idealists who scrutinized the premises of the political and social worlds were not working alone; similar efforts were also underway in architectural theory and practice.

2. Soufflot and the Church of Ste.-Geneviève

When Madame de Pompadour intervened in 1752 to save Diderot's encyclopedia project, it was not the first time that she exercised a major influence on France's cultural life. Since her formal "presentation" at Versailles as the king's mistress in 1745, her power on various fronts had steadily mounted. She was born Jeanne Antoinette Poisson, the daughter of a steward to powerful bankers. She married well and – being beautiful, intelligent, and sincerely interested in the arts – aspired to have a salon that would rival the more exclusive social gatherings in Paris. She succeeded in her plan, enticing the likes of Voltaire, Montesquieu, Fontenelle, and Helvétius into her home. Then in 1745 she caught the eye of Louis XV at a masked ball. When the king went off that summer to overview the military victory at Fontenoy, the new mistress was conveyed to the château at Etioles to be trained in the social graces of the court. By the end of the year, Madame de Pompadour had profoundly changed the artistic climate at Versailles. Not only did she prove to be a friend and an ally of the *philosophes*, but she also became a benefactor of the arts. One of her first political maneuvers at court was to have her younger brother Abel-François Poisson, later the Marquis de Marigny, designated as the future director of royal buildings for Paris. This lofty promotion required him to take an extended tour of Italy so as to

gain an architectural education. She chose as one of his three mentors on his travels a young but "very gifted architect" from Lyons, Jacques-Germain Soufflot (1713–80).[10]

Soufflot shared the desire for reform of so many of his generation. Born near Auxerre, he first came to Paris to study law, but in 1731 he set off for Rome to pursue his interest in architecture. By the end of 1734 he had taken up residence at the French Academy and had begun his studies of Roman churches. Only in 1738 did he return north to Lyons to practice architecture, but he soon achieved some notable results. His most significant work in Lyons was the extension along the Rhône of the city's hospital, the Hôtel-Dieu (1739–48). He also designed various houses, the Loge des Changes (1748–50), and the city's theater (1753–6). He seems to have nurtured important social connections as well. One was Cardinal de Tencin, a former ambassador to Rome; his sister was Madame de Tencin, who until her death in 1750 ran another renowned salon for intellectuals in Paris.

Important for Soufflot's development were several papers he presented to the Société Royale des Beaux-Arts de Lyon, to which he had been elected in 1738. In the first of these, "Mémoire sur les proportions de l'architecture" (Memoir on architectural proportions, 1739), he raises the issue of the quarrel between Blondel and Perrault and somewhat interestingly (in light of his later work) proclaims that he, on the question of proportions and absolute beauty, had "always deferred more to the sentiments of M. Blondel than to those of M. Perrault."[11] From his measurements of three Roman churches, Soufflot modestly concludes that, while there are a wide range of proportions in nature that are pleasing, a few, at least as far as the design of churches go, "necessarily cause pleasure."[12]

In another paper, "Mémoire sur l'architecture gothique" (Memoir on Gothic architecture, 1741), Soufflot returns to another issue posed by Perrault.[13] Soufflot is well aware that the majority of French writers have labeled the Gothic style "bizarre and contemptible," but he laments the lack of serious studies of Gothic structural innovations. He finds, in fact, much that could be of use to present-day church design: the larger windows and more abundant light, the openness of the plan induced by the more slender supports and the diagonal placement of the piers, and the absence of disruptive horizontal projections in the entablature. The lightness and delicateness of Gothic construction is especially praiseworthy; it is "more ingenious, more daring, and even more difficult than ours."[14] Disregarding Gothic's "bizarre ornaments" and "extreme proportions," Soufflot encourages architects to find "a right mean between their style and our own," claiming that he who achieves this – presaging Soufflot's own later accomplishment – will win everyone's acclaim.[15]

At this time, interest in the constructional aspects of Gothic architecture was once again on the upswing in France. In 1736 the architect Ferdinand Delamonce presented a spirited defense of "delicate" Gothic architecture to the Academy of Dijon.[16] Two years later, Frézier – the same engineer who had earlier condemned Cordemoy's book – lauded the ingenuity of the Gothic structural system.[17] Also, sometime before 1741 André Clapasson, who, like Soufflot, was admitted to the Academy of Dijon in 1738, presented a paper on Gothic churches in which he insisted that a more serious study of this style could greatly contribute to the progress of architecture.[18]

In 1744, in a third paper presented before the Academy of Lyons, Soufflot made known his opposition to the rococo style. The paper actually addresses the question of whether taste in architecture is preferable to the science of rules or whether rules are preferable to taste. His answer, based on his own experiments with proportions, is simple: "The rules are taste; taste defines the rules."[19] In the final part of the lecture, he criticizes the "extravagant productions" and "bizarre assemblage of ornaments" connected with the rococo style. While Soufflot concedes that he prefers the creations of unstudied genius to those of the uninspired pedagogue, he nevertheless insists that true beauty in ar-

chitecture resides "in a true disposition of more universal parts; these parts are all known and their proportions are rather well established."[20]

Soufflot's second trip to Italy, in 1750–51, provided further material for his intellectual consumption. The future Marquis de Marigny, Soufflot, Abbé Le Blanc, and the engraver Nicholas Cochin left Paris in December 1749. Throughout their travels, they were entertained in the highest circles, and in Rome they stayed at the Palazzo Mancini, the home of the French Academy. In returning to that city, Soufflot was made a member of the Accademia de San Luca, complementing his admission earlier in the year to the second class of the Royal Academy of Architecture in France.[21] The trip proved a great success in that Marigny acquired his classical education and Soufflot made an important friend. When Marigny returned to France in 1751, Soufflot and Cochin continued south to Naples to observe the first excavations of the newly discovered Roman town of Herculaneum. The highlight of the trip, however, was their subsequent visit to the Greek colonial site of Paestum, where Soufflot, together with his old friend Gabriel-Pierre-Martin Dumont, made extensive measurements and sketches of Greek temple ruins.[22] The two men thus became the first French architects to study Greek works.

Upon Cochin and Soufflot's return to France, their careers were more or less assured. Marigny assumed his new post as director of royal buildings in November 1751, and

4. Jacques-Germain Soufflot, exterior view of Church of Ste.-Geneviève, Paris. Photograph by author.

5. Jacques-Germain Soufflot, interior view of crossing in the Church of Ste.-Geneviève, Paris. Photograph by author.

although he was modest, even insecure in his personality, he possessed both an appreciation of antiquity and the necessary administrative skill to rely heavily on the advice of mentors and friends. As an early token of his generosity, he provided Cochin and Soufflot with an apartment in the Louvre. Later he would appoint Cochin to the post of secretary of the Royal Academy of Painting and Sculpture. In 1755 he rewarded Soufflot with the most important architectural commission of the century – the new Church of Ste.-Geneviève (Figs. 4–5). 9

This building (converted into a pantheon to great Frenchmen in 1793) was the same monastic church for which the Perrault brothers had made their renovation proposals in the mid-1670s. The site possessed great antiquity and sanctity. The illustrious St. Geneviève, the patron saint of the city, was buried on the spot in the year 500, and seven years later the ruler Clovis decided to build a basilica in her honor. This work was burned by the Normans in the ninth century but rebuilt in the eleventh century. Subsequently modified with Gothic vaults, it became the headquarters for the Augustian order in France. The proposal of the 1670s indicates that the building was in need of repairs at this time; when these were not made, the fabric continued to deteriorate. It took a half-century and supposedly divine intervention to rectify the situation. In 1744 Louis XV fell ill on the battlefield at Metz and attributed his recovery to St. Geneviève. Ten years later, in November 1754, he made a pilgrimage of gratitude to her site in Paris and saw firsthand the sad condition of the church. A few days later he ordered a new church to be built, and he put up a substantial sum of his own money. The idea was to build a church of symbolic grandeur equal to St. Peter's in Rome or St. Paul's in London.

This task normally would have fallen to the king's first architect, Ange-Jacques Gabriel, but the latter was already fully engaged in numerous building activities at Versailles and Paris. On 6 January 1755, Marigny suggested Soufflot's name to the king, and by February Soufflot was in Paris surveying the site.[23] His new position was that of Controller of Royal Buildings for Paris, and thus his duties became broader than the design of Ste.-Geneviève. By the fall of 1755, the first plans were drawn up, but the initial design was superceded by revisions in 1757, 1758–9, 1764, and 1770. Construction initially proceeded slowly, in part because of the extensive foundations needed, in part because of the intervention of the Seven Years' War (1757–63). The building was brought up to ground level only in 1764, when the cornerstone was officially laid. The dome was not started until 1785, or five years after Soufflot's death. Work was not complete until 1791, at which time the Revolutionary Council decided to withdraw its religious sanction and transform the building into the Panthéon. At that point Antoine-Chrysostôme Quatremère de Quincy, the later *Secrétaire Perpétuel* of the Academy of the Beaux-Arts, supervised various changes to the work, the most damaging of which was blocking up the windows to darken the interior of what was now a funerary monument. Also in the summer of 1791, the remains of Voltaire were ceremoniously brought to the site in a carriage topped with his full wax image, drawn by twelve white horses arrayed three by three. The body of Rousseau followed three years later.

What makes this building so important to architectural theory, however, is the break that it signals with the past, in particular, Soufflot's objective – as later recorded by Maximilien de Brébion – "to join under one of the most beautiful forms the lightness of the construction of Gothic edifices with the purity and magnificence of Greek architecture."[24] In fact, nearly all of the issues raised by

Perrault a century earlier are here revisited, and Soufflot was not alone in addressing them. Pierre Contant d'Ivry (1698–1777) began exploring the possibility of a Graeco-Gothic structural synthesis earlier in the decade with his designs for St.-Vasnon at Condé-sur-l'Escaut (begun 1751) and St.-Vaast at Arras (begun 1753). Soufflot, however, would make the idea of a synthesis the main issue. Built in the form of a Greek cross, Ste.-Geneviève is entered through an "antique" portico consisting of twenty-four colossal Corinthian columns supporting a flat lintel wired together with iron bars similar to those used in the Louvre. Inside, the nave and five domes are supported with slender columns modeled on the decorative Corinthian order at Baalbek, whose proportions closely follow the ratios proposed by Perrault. The lightness of the structure is made possible by a system of iron and concealed flying buttresses above, inspired by medieval churches.

The building was carefully engineered in every respect. One of Soufflot's first tasks in Paris was to repair and finish the east wing of the Louvre. The cornices and parapets had never been completed, and some of the metal ties in the entablature had rusted, causing voussoirs to fracture.[25] The Louvre thus became Soufflot's structural laboratory, even though his use of reinforced masonry at Ste.-Geneviève far exceeded his instructional model. Together with Jean-Rodolphe Perronet (1708–94), the chief engineer and director of the Ecole des Ponts et Chaussées, Soufflot carried out a series of experiments to measure the expansion of iron. Perronet's assistant, Émiliand-Marie Gauthey (1732–1808), also devised a machine to measure the compressive strength of stone. When Pierre Patte in 1770 criticized the dimensions of the slender interior supports, Perronet and Gauthey defended the design with actual structural calculations. As one historian has noted, Patte in his report employed such terms as *weight* and *load*, while Perronet defended the structure as an organic system of forces and resistances.[26] Modern structural theory was being born.

The "Greek" aspects of Soufflot's design are no less interesting. The initial crypt for the church was a small chamber outfitted with Greek decorations and baseless Doric columns. Although the crypt was later much enlarged and altered by the addition of rustic Tuscan columns, the exquisite stereotomy still enhances its appearance. The dome as originally designed was quite modest, but it was greatly enlarged in the design of 1764, and this change also intensified the lighting effects. On the exterior of this design, the silhouette of the cupola forms a stepped cone, creating a pedestal for the colossal statue of St. Geneviève at the top.

Allan Braham suggests that the inspiration for the design goes back to experiments of French students in Rome in the 1740s and in particular to a project by Soufflot's friend Dumont.[27] Joseph Rykwert traces its source to an engraving published by Caylus of a late Hellenic Numidian tomb.[28] In any case, the dome of 1764, later modified, is altogether new in its formal vocabulary, as was the design for the church as a whole. By the time that this masterpiece was finished, however, the "goût grec" that it helped to usher in had long since spent itself.

3. Marc-Antoine Laugier

The challenges that Soufflot's design for the Church of Ste.-Geneviève posed for academic practice was matched in theory by the *Essai sur l'architecture* (Essay on architecture, 1753) of Marc-Antoine Laugier (1713–69).[29] And even though there are important differences in the backgrounds of these two men, there are also interesting points of commonality. Laugier's idealism again marches in accord with the broader intellectual climate of the Enlightenment. For instance, the opening lines of his *Essai*, in which he describes early man as guided simply by instinct, may have drawn inspiration from Rousseau's allusion to natural man in 1750. And Rousseau's description of this individual in his second discourse, written in 1755 – someone sleeping under a tree and simply satisfying his needs of hunger and thirst – may well have been suggested by Laugier's portrayal of him in 1753.

Born in Provence in the same year as Soufflot, Laugier entered the noviciate of the Jesuits in 1727 and embarked on the lengthy and highly disciplined requirements for higher education. After finishing the initial phase of his training at Avignon, he took further schooling at the Jesuit colleges at Lyons, Besançon, and Marseilles before returning to the college at Avignon around 1740. His residence at Lyons, in fact, may have coincided with Soufflot's first return from Italy.[30] Yet in 1744 Laugier moved to Paris and took his final vows. There he became known for his oratorical skills, which he first put on display at the Church of St. Suplice. Late in 1749 he was commanded to Fontainebleu to sermonize before the king, which he did on several occasions, culminating with a sermon on Christmas day.

Laugier published the *Essai* anonymously in 1753, at a time when the threat of revolution was in the air. Political unease had been stirred by the king's dispute with clerics over new taxes. Against political opposition, Louis XV shut down both chambers of parliament and sent their leaders away from Paris. This action set off a constitutional confrontation that lasted well into 1754 and threatened to bring down the government. Laugier's tract, of course, did not address the political crisis, but its immediate reception in government circles is interesting. In October 1752, the censor Tanevot sent a letter to the chief censor Malesherbes in Paris, informing him that he had read the manuscript of the essay and found it to be a work "very dignified" and "full of taste and genius." He noted, further, that he wanted to sit down personally with "so esteemed" an author – not because of the content of the work but because of the author's occasional display of "a little too much spirit."[31] In this regard, it is not surprising that one of the first reviews of the *Essai* came from the anticlerical circle of the *philosophes*. Diderot's close friend, the editor Friedrich Melchior Grimm, made mention of the book toward the end of 1753. He was favorably reviewing a brochure that Laugier had penned on the Salon of 1753, and he took the occasion to laud the *Essai* and its author: "This work, for which a much expanded second edition is being prepared, has been a great success in Paris, at a time at which its author judiciously lies in hiding in Lyons."[32] Grimm also connects Laugier's enthusiasm with the architectural efforts of Soufflot – "the only architect today celebrated in France" – and concludes with this telling comment: "Father Laugier is young; it seems that his talent and his taste for the arts will not stay buried in a cloister, and that he will soon be counted among the number of ex-Jesuits who have brought honor to literature."[33]

This passage suggests that Grimm had not only met Laugier during the summer of 1753 but was privy to information that Laugier himself would have preferred not to have been made public, at least not yet. In any case, Laugier made his break with the Jesuits in a very public way in the following spring, when the political situation had grown particularly tense. In his Easter sermon at Versailles, he deplored not only the king's moral lapses and indiscretions but also his indecision with respect to the parliament. He further urged him to dissolve the impious body that had perpetrated the crisis and not to fear shedding blood in a just cause. Louis XV was appalled and reaction within the order was swift. Laugier was quickly recalled to Lyons, where he commenced the necessary paperwork to gain his release from the Jesuits. In the spring of 1756, he completed his transfer to the Benedictine order and was soon back in Paris, now with an editorial position at the *Gazette de France*. From this base he fashioned a second career in letters. The expanded second edition of the *Essai* had meanwhile appeared in 1755.

Between 1759 and 1768 Laugier wrote a twelve-volume history of Venice. In 1765 he also published his *Observations sur l'architecture* (Observations on architecture), largely devoted to the issue of proportions.[34] This book never came close to matching the appeal of his shorter *Essai*, which by this later date was well known throughout Europe.

The principal theme of the *Essai* is deceptively simple yet philosophically complex in its nuances (Fig. 6). Grimm, in his review of the book in 1753, pointed out that Laugier had succeeded in producing a work that was not only "instructive" in its argument but at the same time "very agreeable" in its presentation.[35] The first chapter opens with a description of a man in a primitive state of nature relying only on his instincts. He is resting on a stretch of grass at peace with himself and the world until the sun forces him to seek shelter. He first tries the forest, but rain disturbs him; he next seeks shelter in a cave, but the darkness and stagnant air force him outside. He eyes some fallen branches and sets upright four straight ones in a square plan; across their tops he lays four horizontal branches. Finally, he inclines some other branches to from a gable and covers the roof with leaves. These three elements – columns, entablature, and gabled roof – thus constitute what is essential to architecture. All else – arches, pedestals, attics, even doors and windows – are by definition extraneous. Some elements, such as walls and doors, have a certain functional necessity and therefore are allowed back into the scheme, but those elements lacking this necessity fall under the rubric of "caprice" and are to be stricken from architectural use. Architecture has been rationally purified.

The list of those elements to be removed is lengthy, as Laugier devotes several chapters to enumerating the multitude of faults of contemporary practice. These include the use of engaged columns, pilasters, the swelling of columns, columns on pedestals, arches, broken pediments, niches, immoderate use of sculpture, extravagant arabesques, and excessive bulk in the building fabric – in short, almost everything related to the traditions of Renaissance, baroque, and rococo practice. The two models foremost in Laugier's ideal architecture are Perrault's colonnade at the Louvre and Hardouin-Mansart's chapel at Versailles – works to which he repeatedly refers the reader. Neither is altogether without faults, however. The former has the unfortunate pediment in the center of the long east facade (a motif that should appear only along the narrow side of a building), and below it the arch of the main portal cuts into the upper socle for the columns.[36] The chapel at Versailles is marred by its ground-level arcades.[37] From antiquity, the building Laugier most

admires is the Maison Carrée at Nîmes, which he knew firsthand. As far as theory is concerned, the writings of Perrault and Cordemoy are repeatedly cited.

Laugier's reliance on Perrault is further seen in his use of the terms *âpreté* and *dégagement*. The abbé uses the former term, which was defined earlier as the visual tension induced by a row of columns when viewed in perspective, exactly as it was used by Cordemoy and Perrault. Laugier invokes it to describe the beauty of the columns in the chapel at Versailles – the "picturesque vista through its intercolumniations."[38] The word *dégagement* is used so often by Laugier that it essentially becomes the leading tenet on which he builds his theory. The "disengagement" of the column from the wall (the prohibition of the pier and pilaster) becomes the principal means of obtaining that air of lightness, unobstructed view, spaciousness, simplicity, and elegance by which all beautiful architecture is measured.[39]

But given Laugier's appreciation of Perrault's rationalist rigor and his similar views on design, it is interesting that on the matter of proportions and absolute beauty he takes a different stance. Indeed, the issues of the earlier dispute – the quarrel between the ancients and the moderns – come back into fashion in the early 1750s, and Laugier is not the first to raise them. In 1752, the nonagenarian architect Charles-Étienne Briseux (1660–1754) published his *Traité du beau essentiel dans les arts* (Treatise on essential beauty in the arts). Briseux, who witnessed parts of the earlier debate firsthand, devotes his entire preface to praising the efforts of Blondel and attacking those of Perrault, whose theories, based on "cunning paradoxes," he blames for the subsequent decline in academic theory and for creating an "epoch of decadence in French architecture."[40]

Briseaux's approach to the matter, in fact, does not differ greatly from the earlier argument of Blondel. He revives the theories of Alberti, Palladio, and Vignola and insists on an absolute or "essential beauty" found in nature, that is, the constant of harmonic ratios naturally in accord with human constitutions. Only with regard to the psychology of beauty (the issue of taste) does he take account of more recent tendencies. Sensations of beauty and correct proportion arise mechanically from the stimulation of nerves, and they vary in human perception for two reasons. First, there are differences in the mental capacities and sentiments of the perceiving subjects, particularly when the mind is not fortified by principles. Second, there are differences in the impressions of objects, which are disfigured, as it were, "by the vice of the senses on which they are impressed."[41] In short, the mind is content with the pleasure of simple sensation when it is not

6. Marc-Antoine Laugier, frontispiece to *Essay on Architecture* (1753). Collection Centre Canadien d'Architecture/Canadian Centre for Architecture, Montréal Courtesy.

educated by the higher precepts of reason. These precepts, it seems to follow, are innate ideas. Briseux in his study also provides abundant examples of "harmonic ratios," but it interesting that he also concedes, in the face of Perrault's argument, that as yet no fixed proportions for columns have been established. Nevertheless, architects should agree on the necessity of observing harmonic ratios.[42]

Briseux's views on the issue of proportions and beauty may be contrasted with those of Diderot, who also addressed the problem in an essay published in 1751.[43] Diderot's position, to start with, is far more subjective, although the strategy he utilizes and many of his assumptions resemble those of Briseux. He first reviews theories of beauty historically but then grounds the idea of beauty not in a capacity for innate ideas but rather in Lockean sensations or, more specifically, in the perception of relations or proportions. For instance, in viewing the east facade of the Louvre (the example he uses), the conjunction of parts may call to mind the presence of certain pleasing proportions even if they are only vaguely felt or indeterminate. But this does not mean that the idea of beauty is merely reduced to sentiments or feelings or that there is no absolute beauty. The symmetry and proportional relations of parts of a building, particularly of a novel or complicated arrangement of parts, demand also the higher concepts of reason or understanding to mediate the effect of the whole.[44] The judgment of beauty thus operates on two levels: first, in the experience of certain relations of lines, colors, or sounds, and, second, in the mental associations that these relationships or proportions stimulate. In line with this, Diderot distinguishes between "real beauty," based on the consideration of the object in relation to itself, and "relative beauty," based on the consideration of the object in relation to other objects.[45] And to further confuse the matter, he later falls back on the Earl of Shaftesbury's concordance of beauty with ethics – the correlation of the beautiful with the good.[46]

Laugier's notion of beauty mirrors elements from each of these schemes. His position in fact only came into focus in the expanded second edition of the *Essai* of 1755, where he responds to negative reviews of the book by Briseux and Frézier.[47] In 1753 Laugier had spoken vaguely of how the artist needs firm principles to guide artistic creation; the process of architectural creation was not simply controlled by instinct but needed logical reasoning and experience in the ways of beauty.[48] He insists, like Briseux, that there is an essential beauty in architecture independent of mental habit and human prejudice, although he grounds it not only in proportions but also in the elegance of forms and the choice and distribution of ornaments.[49] He also argues that, in architechure, the proportional ratios are precise, that is, there are never two ways of creating the same correct effect.[50] The problem is simply that these ratios are still unknown and the matter needs more research; his hope is that some day a great architect will come along and disclose architecture's fixed and unchangeable laws.[51]

By 1755 Laugier's position, although firm on the issue of absolute beauty, had shifted in other respects. Frézier had attacked Laugier's insistence on precise proportional ratios

essentially by falling back on Perrault's earlier position that beauty is a matter of convention or education and therefore changes with fashion. That this is so is shown by the great differences in national taste and style – the differences, say, between Greek and Chinese architecture. Laugier counters in the "Response" attached to the second edition, in which he insists that "there is an essential beauty in the arts" independent of fashion and that Perrault only rejected its presence out of a "spirit of contradiction" or "sheer obstinacy."[52] But Laugier is also adverse to siding with Briseux, who, following Blondel, wanted to ground essential beauty solely in harmonic proportions.[53] Proportions may be an important part of the foundation of beauty for Laugier, but they are not its only determinants. Laugier thus momentarily draws close to the formulation of Diderot by arguing that we can unconsciously feel essential beauty but cannot explain it because perception first operates on the level of sensation. Moreover, precedents and fashions accustom the eyes to certain forms or styles, thus further influencing or distracting the operation of sentiment. In the end, essential beauty emerges only through the higher mediation of reason, which effectively weans sensations from these distractions. The domain of beauty is thus "enhanced by reflection."[54] And Laugier even speaks of "primitive beauty that results from the conjunction of a multitude of individual qualities," an essential beauty that underlies differing national tastes and to some extent parallels his paradigm of the primitive hut.[55]

Laugier's position on the matter of beauty and proportions is significant because it discloses that the earlier position of Perrault was still a minority position in the 1750s, even as other issues of architectural theory and practice were beginning to be called into question. In the first three months of 1755, the year that the second edition of the *Essai* appeared, the Academy of Architecture once again began to read Perrault's translation of Vitruvius. The footnotes on more than one occasion sparked a lively debate, although the transcriptions of the proceedings allude only to "several reflections" that were made in response to them.[56] In 1765, the same year in which Laugier published his *Observations sur l'architecture*, the Academy of Architecture returned to the issue, this time by reading the relevant passages of François Blondel's *Cours d'architecture*. There is no mention of intervening "reflections," and it seems that Blondel's views regarding proportions, including those on harmonic proportions, were accepted without debate.[57] At no point between 1753 and 1765 is the name of Laugier raised. The academic establishment in France was still marching to the drumbeat of its original program.

But Laugier's *Essai* indeed had an effect on French theory by 1765, especially its exaltation of "reason" as the lodestar for all deliberations. If rationalism in architecture could trace its lineage back to the Cartesianism of Perrault, it now takes on a new cast within neoclassical theory as a result of being paired with the Enlightenment notions of progress and institutional reform. Laugier's message of reform – his plea for a return to a simplified classicism – at the same time would not have had the resonance it did were it not for the timing of the *Essai*'s publication and the confluence of ideas that it came to share with Soufflot's work on Ste.-Geneviève. Both the *Essai* and Sufflot's design reflect a critical attitude toward contemporary (rococo) practice and an appreciation of the constructional advantages of the Gothic style.

Although French rococo had its start in the last decade of the seventeenth century, it came to maturity in France only around 1730, where it was known as the *Style Louis XV*, later the *Style Pompadour*. Fiske Kimball, in fact, placed its culmination in France in the period between 1740 and 1755.[58] Nevertheless, opposition to its decorative excesses also appeared quite early. In 1737 Jacques-François Blondel, who was schooled in the style, at the same time opposed "everything that the caprices of novelty have for some years been ushering in."[59] Soufflot, as we saw earlier, opposed the trend in the 1740s, as did everyone involved with the classical circle of the Comte de Caylus.[60] Laugier's undying opposition to the "les folles imaginations de l'arabesque" was thus impeccably timed to join with the efforts of other opponents, and he even presciently indicated that "this dangerous epidemic is nearing its end."[61]

Laugier's championing of the superiority of Gothic constructional technique also parallels Soufflot's endeavors. Many of the innovations incorporated into the design of Ste.-Geneviève – freestanding interior columns on low socles, flat entablatures, ample lighting, tall vaults, and an air of lightness – were cited by Laugier with approval before the design was started because he was drawing on the same sources (Perrault and Cordemoy) as Soufflot. But Laugier seems to have known little of the work similarly inspired and undertaken in the first part of the century. The chapel at Versailles, for instance, gave rise to many imitations, such as Germain Boffrand's chapel at the Chateau de Lunéville (1703–19, rebuilt 1740), which carried similar proportions but substituted columns for the arcades at ground level. Also in this category was Guillaume Hénault's design for the Church of Notre-Dame-de-Bonne-Nouvelle of 1718, which copied the interior of the chapel at Versailles but clad it with a Gothic exterior. Of greater interest would have been

the recent churches designed by Contant d'Ivry, in which stone vaults were supported on tall columns and a straight entablature.[62] And as regards the structural lightness, Contant d'Ivry's design for the Church of the Madeleine in Paris, begun in 1763, would have rivaled Soufflot's efforts at Ste.-Geneviève – had it been completed.[63]

Nevertheless, it was Laugier's passion for architecture, combined with the logic and clarity of his ideas, that brought his tract to the forefront of contemporary discussions, and his circle of readers was as large outside of France as within. In France, as already noted, the book received a positive mention by Grimm and negative assessments by Briseux and Frézier. Jacques-François Blondel concluded his *Discours sur le nécessité de l'étude de architecture* (Discourse on the necessity of studying architecture, in 1754) by listing Langier's *Essai* among his recommended books, describing it as "a work full of new ideas and sagaciously written."[64] Soufflot himself held a high opinion of Laugier, as did David Le Roy.[65]

In England the *Essai* was translated in 1755, and many of its tenets were soon incorporated (some literally) into the text of Isaac Ware's *Complete Body of Architecture* (1756).[66] William Chambers was familiar with it but was more critical of its content.[67] Laugier had an even greater influence on the next generation of English architects, among them George Dance and John Soane. The latter is said to have owned at least eleven copies of the *Essai* and made translations of various parts.[68]

Laugier's influence was equally long-lived in Germany, where the *Essai* was translated in three editions between 1756 and 1768. Laugier's most famous reader in Germany was Johann Wolfgang von Goethe, who was ambivalent toward it. While sympathetic with the plea for simplicity and its anti-rococo sentiments, Goethe at the same time ridiculed the notion of a primitive hut and more generally the rationalist basis of Laugier's theory.[69] Nevertheless, Laugier's reputation survived until classicism took root in Germany in the 1780s and 1790s, and his ideas later resonated within the circles of David and Friedrich Gilly.[70]

In Italy, too, Laugier's views would have a significant impact. In 1756, for instance, the architect Andrea Memmo asserted that Laugier had been in Venice prior to writing the book and plagiarized the architectural ideas of Carlo Lodoli.[71] Although this charge had no basis, it nevertheless indicates the emotion that the work inspired. The *Essai* was also avidly read at the French Academy in Rome, where a new generation of French students, building upon the earlier efforts in the 1740s of Jean-Laurent Legeay (c. 1710 to c. 1788), Gabriel Dumont, and Nicolas-Henri Jardin (1720–99), were developing a columnar style that would become the hallmark of French neoclassicism.[72] Also reading Laugier's words in Rome was a young architect and engraver just stepping into international prominence with the publication of his *Antichità romane* (Roman antiquities, 1756). The incomparable Giovanni Battista Piranesi would, however, have a very different take on the correctness of Laugier's tenets.

4. The "Rediscovery" of Greece

Coincident with the efforts of Soufflot and Laugier in the 1750s was the so-called rediscovery of Greece. Though difficult to evaluate in all of its aspects, this event would have an equally dramatic effect on European architectural consciousness.

The richness of classical Greek culture was of course very well known. Greek philosophers, playwrights, poets, rhetoricians, and historians were widely read, and many architectural treatises over the centuries had made at least a passing reference to the beauty of Greek architecture. But surprisingly little was known of actual Greek buildings or their differences from Roman examples. Nearly every Renaissance account, beginning with that of Alberti, had described architecture as arising in Asia (sometimes Egypt), flowering in Greece, but attaining its glorious maturity in Rome. François Blondel echoed this view in 1675 when he noted that if the rules for architecture had been first devised by the Greeks, they had been greatly enhanced by imperial Rome, the majesty of whose edifices stood as a testament to their "grandeur and spirit."[73] A few theorists along the way had differing views on the matter. In 1650, for instance, Fréart de Chambray alluded to the "glory and immortality" of the Greeks, the "inventors" of the arts, "which perhaps only in this country were seen in their perfection."[74] And in 1747, Jacques-François Blondel opened his book on country residences by remarking that the Greeks, though they had not succeeded in extending the grandeur of their monuments, had been the first to have endowed architecture with "grace" and that it has since been impossible to add anything to their proportions, "rules that our most capable architects are again observing today."[75] Laugier also expressed himself on this matter: "Architecture owes all that is perfect to the Greeks, a nation privileged to have known everything regarding science and to have invented everything connected with the arts."[76] The problem, of course, was that without a clear image of Greek architecture all of these opinions had little basis.

The lack of visual documentation began to be rectified around 1750. The visit that Soufflot and Dumont paid to Paestum toward the end of 1751 had not been initially planned. Only upon meeting Count Felice Gazzola in Naples did they learn of the ruins of the Greek colonial temples at that site (originally the Greek colony of Poseidonia); these dated back to the sixth and fifth centuries B.C. At this time there was considerable uncertainty about whether the ruins were Greek, Roman, or Etruscan.[77] Gazzola, who was a prominent engineer and the commander of the royal artillery for the Kingdom of Naples and Sicily, had known of the ruins since 1746 and had even prepared drawings for publication. They may indeed have been the basis of some of the engravings published by Dumont in 1764.[78] By this date, Paestum had been visited by several travelers. The German historian Johann Joachim Winckelmann went to the site in 1758, and between 1764 and 1784 no fewer than eight fully illustrated books on the temple ruins were published.[79]

The Greek colonial cities on Sicily were also but recently visited. The first traveler to study them, Jacques-Philippe d'Orville, had done so in 1727, although his drawings were only published posthumously in 1764.[80] Giuseppe Maria Pancrazi recorded several Greek monuments in the two volumes of his *Antichità Siciliane spiegate* (1751–2). This work, together with measurements conveyed to him by the Scottish architect Robert Mylne, inspired Winckelmann to publish his *Anmerkungen über die Baukunst der alten Tempel zu Girgenti in Sicilien* (Reflections on the architecture of ancient temples at Girgenti in Sicily) in 1759. Winckelmann lingered over the squat dimensions of the Temple of Concord, compared it with temples presented by Vitruvius and Diodorus and with reports of the temples at Paestum, and solemnly concluded that the Sicilian temple was "undoubtedly one of the oldest Greek buildings in the world."[81]

Travelers to Greece and the Middle East were more numerous but often no less helpful in conveying their impressions and findings. The region had been under Ottoman control since the fifteenth century, although Venice governed Attica and Morea from 1685 to 1687, in which year Venetian cannons blew up the Parthenon. Greek marbles began to pass to the West in the first part of the seventeenth century, often through the agency of diplomats and entrepreneurs.[82] Travelers, however, become more common in the last quarter of the century. We have already noted the visit of the Marquis de Nointel in 1674, during which the artist Jacques Carrey made his famous sketches of the sculptures; no attention was paid to the monument itself. A private expedition in 1675 by Jacob Spon and George Wheler also focused on the Parthenon. Spon stood in awe of what he saw, but in his *Voyage d'Italie, de Dalmatie, de Grèce, et du Levant* (1678) he could produce nothing better than a childlike sketch of the Parthenon, greatly distorting its main features and proportions.[83] This inaccurate drawing nevertheless became the basis for Bernard de Montfaucon's reconstruction of the building in his *L'antiquité expliquée*, which appeared in fifteen volumes between 1719 and 1724. Montfaucon's reconstruction in turn became the basis for Fischer von Erlach's reconstruction of the temples at Palmyra and Olympia in 1721.[84]

Relaxation in the political tensions between the Ottoman East and European West in the 1740s allowed a new stream of European travelers to visit Greece and the Middle East, although the conditions of travel were still quite difficult. Richard Pococke (1704–65) and Richard Dalton (*c.* 1715–91) visited the eastern Mediterranean separately in the late 1730s and the 1740s, respectively, and both men recorded their impressions.[85] The decade of the 1750s, however, belonged to two expeditions of far greater significance, that of the Englishmen James Stuart (1713–88) and Nicholas Revett (1720–1804) and of the Frenchman Julien-David Le Roy (1724–1803).

The drama of these ventures can be gleaned from the contemporary account of Robert Wood (1716–71) of his expeditions to Palmyra (Syria) and Baalbek (Lebanon).[86] Inspired by Desgodetz's earlier study of Roman monuments, Wood had set out in 1750 with James Dawkins and two others to visit Greece, Asia Minor, Syria, Phoenicia, Palestine, and Egypt and to make a similar survey. In Athens, they even ran into the "two English painters" delineating Attic works, but Wood and Dawkins had already decided to concentrate on Asia Minor. Wood recounts some of the dangers and pleasures they encountered: unexpected desert horsemen, avarice, "shameless venality," and the hospitality of local emirs. The "armed servants" employed by Wood and Dawkins were along both to serve as a show of force against local threats and to protect the booty that they were amassing. The chronology of Palmyra and Baalbek, both late Hellenistic cities – "perhaps the two most surprising remains of antient magnificence which are now left" – was much in doubt.[87] Although Wood was dubious that either was pre-Solomonic in origin (Palmyra by one account was founded on the spot where David slew Goliath), he nevertheless accepted the local belief that both cities were started by Solomon, subsequently destroyed by Nebuchadnezzar, and

rebuilt in Roman times. Both cities, with their columnar streets, were still relatively well preserved, although their buildings lay in ruins. Still, the layout of Baalbek, in Wood's view, constituted "the remains of the boldest plan we ever saw attempted in architecture."[88]

James Stuart arrived in Italy in 1742 with slightly different expectations. The son of a Scottish mariner, he made his way to Rome (on foot) relatively late in life and at his own expense. For "6 or 7 years" he studied painting in the studio of Marco Benefial and did classical studies at the Collegio di Propaganda Fide. While on a tour of Naples in 1748, he discussed with Nicholas Revett, Gavin Hamilton, and Matthew Brettingham the possibility of making a trip to Greece. At some point Hamilton and Brettingham withdrew, but Stuart and Revett continued planning, and later that year Stuart wrote the first prospectus of their venture. In the version of the prospectus published in the first volume of his later book, he describes Athens as the "fountainhead" of Greek art, "the Mother of elegance and politeness, whose magnificence scarce yielded to that of Rome, and who for the beauties of a correct style must be allowed to surpass her."[89] This book, funded by subscriptions and facilitated by the Society of Dilettanti, was intended to appeal to "those Gentlemen who are lovers of the Arts" as well as to artists.[90] The two men left Rome in March 1750, but not until the following January did they depart Venice for Zanthe, from which they traveled, after several stops, to Athens on March 18. Here they were met by the "Grand Signor's firman," whose services as a bodyguard had been arranged by the British ambassador at Constantinople.[91] Stuart and Revett spent almost two years in Attica and scrupulously took measurements; they returned to Britain separately in 1754.

At this point their saga becomes defined by what they did not do. Interest in Greece had grown enormously since the start of their well-publicized trip, as had the international expectations of their findings, but Stuart and Revett appeared all but oblivious to this interest and in no hurry to publish their results. Moreover, in their original prospectus of 1748, they had proposed to survey the antiquities of Greece in three volumes, of which the first was to delineate the works on and around the Athenian acropolis. Instead they chose to defer presenting their research on these buildings until the second volume and to focus instead on a few secondary works of lesser artistic importance in the first volume (1762). The second volume, containing impeccable images of the Parthenon, in fact did not appear until after Stuart's death in 1788 (Fig. 7). The fourth and last volume

7. James Stuart and Nicholas Revett, view of the Parthenon, from *The Antiquities of Athens*, vol. 2 (1788).

was not published until 1816, making its appearance timely only to a much later controversy regarding Greek art.

Because Stuart and Revett failed to seize the day, precedence in publication fell by default to the Frenchman Julien-David Le Roy. The son of the royal clockmaker, Le Roy had been a student of Jacques-François Blondel, among others, and in 1750 he won the *Prix de Rome* for his design of a "vaulted orangery," winning out over designs by Pierre-Louis Moreau-Desproux (1727–94) and Charles de Wailly (1730–98). Once in Rome he befriended Charles-Louis Clérisseau (1721–1820) and soon alienated the director of the French Academy, Charles Natoire, for his "arrogance" in refusing to sign the certificate of Easter Communion.[92] Le Roy nevertheless applied himself to his artistic development and – after learning of Stuart and Revett's proposal – obtained permission from Natoire as well as from envoys of the French government in Rome and Venice to visit Athens and sketch its major monuments. His efforts, financed in part by the government, thus constituted a race to publication, in French eyes pitting the national honor of France against that of Britain. Le Roy sailed from Venice on the ambassador's ship of eighty guns in the spring of 1754. He only stopped briefly in Attica, because he had to go first to Constantinople to obtain the necessary permits from Ottoman officials. He arrived in Athens in February of the following year and was able to stay in that city less than three months.

By July he was already back in Rome, and he returned to Paris in the fall of 1755 to start work on his publication.

Le Roy had been in contact with Comte de Caylus during his trip, and it is likely that the latter took charge of the project back in Paris, for which the "proposal" was issued in March 1756.[93] The delay may have had something to do with the quality of Le Roy's drawings. Cochin, a friend of Soufflot, later related that when he and Caylus saw them shortly after Le Roy's return, they realized that they were "so crude" that they had to be redone. This was a task for the engravers Jacques-Phillippe Le Bas and Jean-Joseph Le Lorrain – the latter, according to Cochin, a "mediocre painter" but able to draw "agréablement et avec goust."[94]

The finished volume of *Les Ruines des plus beaux monuments de la Grece* (The ruins of the most beautiful monuments of Greece) appeared in 1758 to high acclaim within French artistic circles. The *Correspondance littéraire* boasted that it was a "magnificent work ... very superior to anything that the English have published in this genre."[95] At the Academy of Architecture, Blondel praised it lavishly in mid-November 1758, and the next week he nominated Le Roy to the vacant seat within the academy. Thus the honor of France had been upheld, and a bright future was virtually assured for this once "arrogant" student.

Much has been made of the many "inaccuracies" of Le Roy's publication (first pointed out by Stuart and Revett

8. David Le Roy, view of the Temple of Minerva (Parthenon), from *Les Ruines des plus beaux monuments de la Grece* (1758). Photo courtesy of the Getty Research Institute for the History of Art and the Humanities.

in 1762), but the criticisms often miss the point. Le Roy had intended to produce not a strict archaeological study, but rather select impressions of "ruins" supported in a secondary way by drawings of details. One of his inspirations, in fact, had been Wood and Dawkins's publication on Palmyra, which combined a series of picturesque views of ruins with a historical sketch and travel anecdotes.[96] The finished drawings were exceedingly accomplished and emotionally powerful (Fig. 8). Le Lorrain, in particular – notwithstanding Cochin's assessment – was a highly talented artist who, during his apprenticeship in Rome, had been influenced by Giovanni Paolo Panini and Giovanni Battista Piranesi.[97] In addition, student drawings at the French Academy in the 1740s and 1750s generally were moving away from strictly measured presentations and toward more imaginative and pictorially stimulating compositions. Although Le Lorrain's engravings of Le Roy's drawings fail to achieve the intense psychological intensity of Piranesi's mature style, they are not far behind. Not only do they bring the forms and character of Greek architecture to European consciousness for the first time, they do so in a highly seductive manner. Their ap-

peal was directed not to the "lovers of Polite Literature" or to the British aristocracy, but rather to artists and architects.[98]

Another reason Le Roy's book resonated so strongly within architectural circles was the fact that Le Roy himself was an architect, and the work was informed by his architectural sensibilities. He divided the study into two parts; the first devoted to an account of his endeavors and the history of Greek architecture; the second to measured drawings and matters of theory. In his "Discourse on the History of Civil Architecture," he waxed sufficiently poetic on Greece's progress (beyond Egyptian architecture) along the path of perfection. He portrayed Greece as ultimately "ascending to the most sublime ideas and descending to the most subtle refinements" and discovering "everything in architecture that is beautiful and ingenious."[99] On this path the Romans were a distant second. They may have learned some of their better building habits from the Egyptians, he speculates, but their temples and orders derived entirely from Greece. For their most important building projects, the Romans (in Rome, Athens, Cyzicus, Palmyra, and Baalbek) employed the most celebrated Greek architects. "In the end," he concludes, "it seems that the Romans lacked the creative genius that led the Greeks to so many discoveries."[100]

Similar sentiments echo in Le Roy's "Discourse on the Nature of the Principles of Civil Architecture," in part 2 of his lengthy study. Greek architecture is to be praised for evoking "notions of grandeur, nobility, majesty, and beauty" – aesthetic accomplishments recognized by everyone from Horace to Montesquieu.[101] As for specific aesthetic principles, however, Le Roy is only able to speak in a vague way of the proportions, harmony, and solidity of Greek architecture and to propose three evolutionary stages for the development of the Doric order. It seems that Greek architecture, for Le Roy, was almost entirely a visual and emotional experience – an intense moment in architectural drama to be recaptured by his generation. Such a view also becomes evident near the end of the discourse, where he ponders the question of whether contemporary architecture should imitate Greek proportions. His solution is to pursue a "path of conciliation," which would involve studying the ruins of all nations and all times in the hope that some consensus could be reached. Le Roy therefore follows Perrault in his belief that proportions are not "essential" in their beauty but are rather the result of a judicious agreement among talented architects. In his belief in the relativity of proportions, he stood virtually alone among French architects in 1758 – but not for long.

5. The Historiography of Winckelmann

Le Roy followed his publication on Greece with a book that further plots his development as a historian and theorist. His *Histoire de la disposition et des formes différentes que les chrétiens ont données à leurs temples depuis le règne de Constantin le Grand jusqu'à nous* (History of the disposition and different forms that the Christians have given their temples since the reign of Constantine the Great to our time) appeared in 1764 and was written in part to coincide with the laying of the cornerstone of Ste.-Geneviève.[102] Three of its four chapters constitute a comparative study of church design in which he draws a line of progressive development commencing with the Vitruvian basilica and culminating with the spectacular interior colonnades of Contant d'Ivry's Madeleine (never finished) and Soufflot's Ste.-Geneviève. In the third chapter, which draws heavily on the new aesthetics emanating from both Britain and Diderot's *Encyclopédie*, Le Roy discusses the psychological or perceptual experience of a colonnade and building interiors. For instance, he takes

Perrault's argument to the next level and applauds the use of columns less for their logical value and more for their visual attractiveness or psychological sense of grandeur. He also refers to the recent popularity of colonnades in neo-classical practice and dwells on the experience of walking past Perrault's Louvre colonnade, which is now "the finest piece of architecture in Europe."[103] In discussing interiors, he considers the disparity between the apparent and actual size of buildings, again drawing out the perceptual factors affecting architectural design. His treatments of these topics, many of which will find their way into the second edition of *Les Ruines des plus monuments de la Grece* (1770), also draw upon other historiographic innovations of Enlightenment thought, such as the concordance of a nation's art with its climate, social structure, and political system.

Le Roy's important comparative study, however, was eclipsed internationally by a second book that appeared in 1764. The *Geschichte der Kunst der Alterthums* (History of the art of antiquity) of Johann Joachim Winckelmann (1717–68), in fact, was the preeminent work of neoclassical theory and represented the consolidation of historical sentiments taking place in Rome in the decade of the 1750s. Not only did Winckelmann bring a coherent historical and aesthetic framework to the new movement, but the full implications of his "system" for art history were realized only in the nineteenth century, when his reputation was even greater than during his lifetime.

Born the son of a cobbler in provincial Prussia, he briefly studied theology and medicine at the Universities of Halle and Jena before becoming interested in the classics.[104] In 1748, at the age of thirty, he obtained a position as a librarian to Count Heinrich von Bünau in Saxony and for six years assisted him in writing a history of the Holy Roman Empire. In 1754 he moved to Dresden to take the same position with Cardinal Passionei in order to be closer to that city's famed collections of art and antiquities. His work there led him to Rome in 1755 as the librarian to Cardinal Archinto. Three years later, through the offices of the collector Baron von Stosch, he obtained the post of librarian to Cardinal Albani, the nephew to Pope Clement XI and the greatest collector of antiquities in Europe. In 1763, in recognition of his erudition, Winckelmann gained the additional post of prefect of antiquities at the Vatican. His grand *Geschichte* appeared in the following year, announcing Winckelmann as Europe's foremost authority on classical art (Fig. 9).

Winckelmann's contribution to architectural theory was twofold. First, his antiquarian and philological inquiry into the past, drawing heavily on the methodology of

9. Opening page of preface to Johann Joachim Winckelmann, *Geschichte der Kunst der Alterthums* (1764).

Montesquieu, succeeded in depicting Greek art as the embodiment of sensibilities and values pervasive in Greek culture as a whole. His vision of Greek art may have been more late Hellenistic or Graeco-Roman than high Greek, but it nevertheless was a vision highly charged with spiritual and plastic values that could be readily applied to architectural practice. Second, he conceptualized a system for the rise and fall of Greek art, indeed for the art of antiquity as a whole: a system that was quite specific in its formal, creative, and temporal stages and that offered insights in the very nature of art as well. That the highpoint of ancient art for Winckelmann fell in the years between Pericles and Alexander also implied that Roman art, of necessity, was artistically inferior –

the "art of the imitators." This system thus fractured the very foundation of earlier academic models. If there was a third way in which this historian influenced the direction of architectural thinking, it was through the power of his images and the persuasiveness of his language. Winckelmann composed his vision not only with authority but also with passion, a vision of a time and a place remote yet vividly and fantastically reconstructed.

These qualities are first seen in his brochure of 1755, *Gedanken über die Nachahmung der griechischen Werke in der Mahlerey und Bildhauer-Kunst* (Reflections on the imitation of Greek works in painting and sculpture).[105] He composed it in Dresden working only from a knowledge of

Greek classical casts, engravings, and verbal descriptions. Greek art was superior to Roman art, he argued, first by virtue of the physical beauty of the Greek people, whose bodies were nurtured by a perfect climate, whose diets included a minimum of corrupting substances, and who were reared on incessant physical exercise. The soul of Greek culture for Winckelmann was on display at the Olympic games at Elis, where the strongest and bravest youths of the land assembled to compete for the honor of a statue and godlike immortality. The training centers for artists were the gymnasia, where artists came to study nude bodies in rigorous physical training and displayed without a sense of shame or false modesty. But the representation of Greek deities in marble nevertheless required more than a single model. Greek artists not only worked from nature in its near perfect manifestations but also assembled the best parts of all bodies to compose an idealized and especially refined beauty. To this physical perfection were added the gesture and expression of a "noble simplicity and quiet grandeur." This was best personified for Winckelmann by the statuary group Laocoön, where the hero endures the most violent suffering and pain but faces his agonizing moment of death with divine restraint and dignity, thereby ennobling the human condition. The phase "noble simplicity and quiet grandeur" may have appeared here and there in previous discourse, but with Winckelmann it expresses the distilled essence of the new artistic movement.[106]

Winckelmann's two writings on architecture do not add significantly to the contemporary debate (as neither was widely read or known at the time), but they offer an interesting counterpoint to Laugier's theory. Both his trip to Paestum in 1758 and the (already noted) essay of the following year on the temple at Agrigento stand behind his *Anmerkungen über die Baukunst der Alten* (Reflections on the architecture of antiquity), published in 1761. In the preface, Winckelmann recounts the state of archaeological discoveries at this time. He is familiar with the measured drawings of Paestum of Count Gazzola (which the count showed him in Rome) and with Pancrizi's two volumes on Sicily.[107] He is familiar as well with the ruins of a few other sites around Italy, many of which were actually Etruscan. He further applauds the studies of Le Roy and of Wood and Dawkins and notes the "great anticipation" with which the forthcoming work of Stuart and Revett was awaited – an anticipation that would soon turn into disappointment.[108]

The main body of Winckelmann's work is divided into two parts, the first dealing with the "essential" (*Wesentliche*) and the second with the "decorative" (*Zierlichkeit*). Under the first heading he treats constructional materials and methods, the overall form of a building and its necessary parts, and a building's proportions. Winckelmann's lone innovation here is his suggestion to add a fourth phase to Le Roy's tripartite scheme for the development of the Doric order.[109] In part 2 of the work, however, his deliberations break fresh ground. After defining the decorative in a conventional sense – "A building without decoration is like health in poverty, which nobody regards as a happy condition"[110] – he points out, based on his observations at Paestum, that the oldest buildings have the least decoration; conversely, the works of late Roman antiquity, starting with the reign of Nero, have the most. His conclusion is to elevate "simplicity" as an aesthetic norm lest architecture suffer the fate of the ancient languages, "which became richer as they were losing their beauty."[111]

Winckelmann, following Vasari, adheres to an evolutionary scheme according to which architecture moves from the barest forms at its stylistic origin to a tasteful simplicity and then to baroque excess. And it does not take him too many pages to connect this scheme with current baroque excesses – decorative extravagance spawned in the "fertile imagination" of Michelangelo but later exaggerated even more by Borromini.[112]

Winckelmann uses a similar scheme in his *Geschichte*, only now the model is refined by his introduction of the word *style* into art historical parlance.[113] He divides all ancient art, in fact, into four stylistic periods: the most ancient style, the grand or high style, the beautiful style, and the style of the imitators. The first style lasted in Greece until the time of Phidias, or the mid-fifth century. The high style ran from Phidias until the period of Praxiteles, or around the mid-fourth century. The beautiful style flourished from the period of Praxiteles to that of Lysippus and Apelles, at the end of the fourth century. The style of the imitators extended to the close of antiquity and therefore encompassed all Roman art.

These stylistic distinctions, founded mainly, though not entirely, on sculptural works, were formally and spiritually defined. The high style possessed an austere kind of beauty distinct from the stiff hardness of the most ancient style, yet the high style subsequently was transformed into the more refined beautiful style, with its graceful and sensuous forms, before this tendency was carried too far and led to the overly worked style of imitation. The cultural forces guiding these stylistic transformations also informed art, thus suggesting that for architecture the high style was best represented by the Parthenon and the temple of Zeus at Olympia. This was, of course, a radically new view of the past, one that stripped the art and architecture of Rome entirely of its artistic preeminence and validity. If Laugier's *Essai* had established the primitive hut as the conceptual paradigm against which good architecture should measure itself, Winckelmann's *Geschichte* points to the golden age of Greece as the more appropriate model for neoclassicism to emulate. The two perspectives, combined with Le Roy's visual documentation, were in fact mutually supportive.

6. The Graeco-Roman Debate

Although Winckelmann completed the manuscript for his great history at the end of 1761, the book lay in the publisher's hands in Dresden for over two years and did not appear until early 1764, or just as the debate over classical antiquity was about to heat up. For in November of that year, the antiquarian Pierre-Jean Mariette, who was part of the circle of Caylus and Le Roy in Paris, published a letter in which he challenged some views expressed in 1761 by Giovanni Battista Piranesi on the superiority of Roman art, which Mariette now compared unfavorably with the "beautiful and noble simplicity" of the Greeks.[114] The derisive, even hectoring tone of the letter, published in a newspaper, demanded a forceful response from the Italian artist.

From Rome, Piranesi (1720–78) indeed had been watching the growing Graecophilic sentiments during the 1750s with increasing agitation (Fig. 10). Born in Venice, he had first studied architecture in that city, a fact that very much shaped his outlook. He initially trained in the office of his mother's brother Matteo Lucchesi, later in the studio of Giovanni Scalfarotto, who was both a highly regarded engineer and a historian of Venetian architecture. Piranesi studied perspective under Carlo Zucchi and became familiar with the stage designs of the Bibiena family, but he was also familiar with the architectural teachings of Carlo Lodoli (1690–1761), a Franciscan friar and peripatetic philosopher with strong architectural interests. The latter's views, in fact, deserve attention in their own right, as we have already noted the charge of plagiarism made against Laugier by a member of the Lodoli circle.

Lodoli's brand of rationalism, although truly a search for first principles, was grounded in a very different approach from that of the Frenchman.[115] Lodoli had studied mathematics and philosophy in Dalmatia, at that time a Venetian territory. After further studies in Rome, during which time he pursued his artistic interests, he moved to Verona in

10. Giovanni Battista Piranesi, from *Artist Portraits: Scrapbook, 1600–1800*. Courtesy of the Collection Centre Canadien d'Architecture/ Canadian Centre for Architecture, Montréal.

1715. Here he advanced his classical understanding in the antiquarian salon of Marchese Francesco Scipione Maffei, a historian of ancient statuary whose work was later known and repeatedly criticized by Winckelmann.[116] In 1730 Lodoli moved back to Venice, where he supervised a hostel for pilgrims to the Holy Land and served as a state censor. Through Maffei's intercession, the now highly regarded polymath also ran (until 1748) an architectural seminar for the sons of nobility, in which he espoused the new ideas of the Enlightenment that was spreading across Europe. He was an admirer of Voltaire and Montesquieu, later of Rousseau, and he strongly supported the efforts of the historian and sociologist Giambattista Vico, the intellectual leader of the early Italian Enlightenment.

Lodoli's "rigorist" architectural theory, which formed an important part of his seminar, is known from two drafts for a proposed treatise on architecture, subsequently published by Andrea Memmo.[117] His argument begins with a call for a critical review of all existing theoretical systems, especially that of Vitruvius and his latter-day baroque interpreters. Lodoli counters with the demand for "new forms and new terms" responsive to present needs – forms and terms logically dictated by reason and inductive demonstration. In short, architecture should now take the "guise of science" and be construed as such. The first of its integral parts is solidity of structure, which is conjoined with the other primary integral parts of proportion, regularity, and symmetry; its secondary integral parts are convenience and ornament. The last "should always be derived from the complex of human and structural requirements adjusted to the chosen materials in every respect."[118]

The second draft sheds further light on his thinking. "Proper function and form are the only two final, scientific aims" of architecture, and they should become one.[119] Function relates principally to the structural efficiency of the building and its members. Form is the expression that results when the materials are directed to their desired end according to geometric, mathematical, and optical laws. Again, structural solidity, proportion, and convenience are essential properties of correct form; ornament is inessential but now also takes on both a mathematical and rational character – that is, it must be true and "legible" in terms of how it is made and works. Thus parts of the traditional vocabulary can be used but only after they have been critically tested against these criteria. On one point, Laugier and Lodoli differed sharply. Laugier believed that Greece provided the ideological grounding for "truth" in architecture, whereas for Lodoli actual stone construction was invented by the Egyptians and passed to the Romans through the Etruscans. The timber forms supposedly imitated in stone by classical Greek architects were thus by definition lacking in logic and truth.

It is unclear how much of Lodoli's theory was absorbed by Piranesi, but it suffices to say that this artist arrived in Rome in 1740 with a solid architectural education, one that was well attuned to theoretical concerns.[120] In Rome, Piranesi

studied etching with Giuseppe Vasi and became familiar with the architectural fantasies of Panini.[121] Early in his stay, he also drew close to a circle of students at the French Academy, among them Jean-Laurent Legeay, Michel-Ange Challe, and Le Lorrain. Piranesi published the first twelve plates of his first book of engravings, *Prima parte di architetture e prospettive* (Part one of architecture and prospectives), in 1743. He visited the site of Herculaneum and contemplated a work depicting these ruins, but his financial situation forced him back to Venice in the spring of 1744. Now falling under the influence of Giambattista Tiepolo, Piranesi took a new and more expressive approach to drawing, signaled by the engravings in *Invenzioni Capric de Carceri* (Fanciful images of prisons), first issued in 1745.

By the end of 1745, Piranesi had returned to Rome. Once again he worked closely with students at the French Academy and over the next two decades composed an ever more expansive portfolio of engravings, writings, and designs, which brought him international fame. Among the French students coming to Rome in the 1750s were Le Roy, Marie-Joseph Peyre, Charles de Wailly, and Victor Louis, all of whom would become major neoclassical architects. Among the British students paying homage to Piranesi were William Chambers, Robert Mylne, Robert Adam, and George Dance. In the second half of the 1740s, Piranesi produced numerous *vedute* (views) of Rome, many of which included ruins, but in the 1750s his attention turned increasingly toward archaeological themes. These plates often depict fantastic reconstructions of Roman works at an imagined scale resounding with greatness. The culmination of this trend were the four volumes (250 plates) of *Le antichità romane* (Roman antiquities, 1756), which boasted of the colossal feats of Roman architecture and engineering through a creative array of images, inscriptions, and implements.[122]

Piranesi's development took another turn in the next decade with the publication of his *Della magnificenza ed architettura de' romani* (Of the magnificence and architecture of Rome, 1761), which combined a slim group of thirty-eight plates with over 200 pages of text. The book was conceived as early as 1758 in response to Allan Ramsay's "Dialogue on Taste" (1755) and Le Roy's publication on Greece. The former, the work of the Scottish portrait painter and friend of Piranesi, takes the form of a dialogue between two protagonists on art, one of whom not only proclaims the superiority of Greek architecture but also chides the Romans for merely imitating Greek buildings.[123] An angry Piranesi now steps forward to defend Roman culture. Drawing upon the scholarly hypotheses of recent Etruscan investigations as well as Vico's belief in the autonomy of Roman civilization, Piranesi argues that the Romans were well advanced in the arts prior to their contact with the Greeks and that (as claimed by Lodoli) their mentors were the Etruscans rather than the Greeks.[124] And if the Etruscans (for Piranesi, an older race than the Greeks) provided the architectural foundation for later Roman civilization, Etruscan stone architecture, in turn, can trace its roots back to the Egyptians. Thus it was the Etruscans and not the Greeks who brought "every art to its ultimate perfection," and the unfortunate Greeks, for their part, were only able to affect an "empty elegance."[125] The examples that Piranesi cites are mainly Roman engineering achievements: roadways, drainage systems, and aqueducts such as the Cloaca Maxima. Like Lodoli before him, he therefore exalts truth, technical skill, practical function, and decorum.

The plates of *Della Magnificenza* reveal another side of this polemical story. Several plates, for instance, were directed Laugier's way and the idea of transposing the timber forms of a hut into stone. Many others respond explicitly to images of Le Roy.[126] The latter's drawing of the Greek Ionic order, for example, lies "unraveled" on a plate depicting more richly ornamented Roman capitals.[127] The suggestion here is that the Romans were more creative precisely because of their decorative exuberance.

Themes of Roman grandeur continued to occupy Piranesi's imagination for much of the first half of the 1760s, and he followed *Della Magnificenza* with graphic works depicting – at an exaggerated scale – the Roman water system (1761); the Emissarium, or water works, for Lake Albano (1762); and other engineering feats at Albano, Castel Gandolfo, and Cori (1764). Certainly the grandest of these speculative, if not feverish, reconstructions was *Campo Marzio dell' Antica Roma* (Campus Martius of ancient Rome, 1762), which sought to reconstruct the architectural grandeur of Rome's Campus Martius (the plain northwest of the Capitoline Hill) in several stages of development and at a fantastic scale. The work is built around a six-plate plan, the *Ichnographia*, which brings together in an accretive and collisional manner a network of buildings and urban complexes reminiscent of concomitant student projects at the French Academy but far more elaborate and sophisticated in geometry. The work was dedicated to Robert Adam and in fact was partly based on material assembled during Adam's studies with Piranesi in the mid-1750s. Archaeological correctness was no longer an issue for Piranesi; artistic license and bravado were the call of the day.

Given the fervor of Piranesi's defense of the Romans, it is surprising that a response was so long in the making. Yet when the Frenchman Mariette did train his sights on Piranesi late in 1764 (in response to a review of *Della Magnificenza*), he did so in a way that both overstated the case and managed to be nationally offensive. He begins his letter by chiding the Italian for insisting that Roman architecture owes nothing to the Greeks; for believing that Roman monuments were greatly superior in solidity, size, and magnificence; and for insisting that Roman models and building methods were learned from the Etruscans before the Romans had contact with Greece. In fact, the last issue, for Mariette, is meaningless, because the Frenchman wrongly believed that the Etruscans were Greek in origin. Mariette next sharpens his attack by adopting the view of both Le Roy and Winckelmann – that when the Romans first came into contact with the Greeks Hellenic art had already attained its highest point of perfection, that is, it "was still governed by the rules that ordained a beautiful and noble simplicity."[128] Hence the Romans, possessing no natural aptitude for art and being merely skilled at plundering Greek cities, could do nothing but lead art down the path of decline. Moreover, Greek slaves were responsible for whatever beauty the Romans, in their own modest way, did attain.

Piranesi's response was prompt. In 1765, he produced two texts that developed his earlier views in significant ways, and in 1769 he added a final statement of his position. In the first of these three works, "Osservazione di Giovanni Battista Piranesi sopra la Lettre de M. Mariette" (Observations of Giovanni Battista Piranesi on the letter of Monsieur Mariette), he presents a point-by-point rebuttal of Mariette's letter, with Mariette's text placed on one column of the page and Piranesi's response lying opposite. The illustration of the Tuscan order on the title page effectively sets out the polemical guidelines for the discussion, as Piranesi implies that the Tuscan order was an Etruscan–Italic invention predating the Greek Doric order (Fig. 11). On the left side of this same page, a "sinister" (left) hand writes a letter to the *Gazette*, and below it the circular modules within the outline of a Tuscan order contain the tools of the noble artist-architect.[129] The two inscriptions above each image – "aut cum hoc" and "aut in hoc" (either with this or in this) – reveal Piranesi's disdain for *littérateurs* who only dabble in issues of art, as opposed to those who daily labor in its practice.

The text is unrelenting in its pitch, as Piranesi (recounting his views in the third person) savages the arguments of Mariette. He corrects Mariette's overstatements, reproves

11. Title page of *Osservazioni sopra la Lettre de M. Mariette* (1765). Courtesy of the Getty Research Institute for the History of Art and the Humanities.

12. Plate IX from *Osservazioni sopra la Lettre de M. Mariette* (1765). Courtesy of the Getty Research Institute for the History of Art and the Humanities.

him for his insinuations, but above all ridicules the dilettantish arrogance with which his views are presented: "As for yourself, Signor Mariette, what are you, who in your letter bestow and refuse credit for the possession of taste and talent in the fine arts. Neither a painter nor a sculptor nor an architect."[130] Piranesi insists that he had never denied that the Romans owed something to Greek taste but rather had merely claimed that they had nothing to learn with regard to the science of construction and building practice. He challenges the false assertion that the Etruscans were Greek in origin. He rails, at times incessantly, against the comment that only Greek slaves practiced the arts in Rome. And he is especially offended with the suggestion that the Romans were vulgarians or men lacking in taste:

In his book, Piranesi has asserted (and this I repeat for the last time) that the Romans . . . built things that it had never crossed the minds of the Greeks could be built by a living soul. That very many of the Romans (that is, of the citizens) were from time to time able architects. That they corrected many of the innumerable defects that they found in the architecture of the Greeks. That they achieved a magnificence equal to that of the Egyptians and the Greeks, and therefore greater than that of any other nation. What more could the Romans have done to honor the fine arts?[131]

In the end, the issue turns on national pride, and Mariette becomes, in Piranesi's eyes, "one of those Frenchmen *who, as Signor [Francesco] Algarotti says, now regard the journey to Italy as utterly useless for young artists.*"[132]

The second part of Piranesi's text of 1765, the *Parere su l'architetture* (Opinions on architecture), expands earlier arguments through both graphic and theoretical innovations. The former consist of a series of intensely ornate and barque architectural designs by the hand of Piranesi (Fig. 12); the latter take the form of a dialogue between two architects discussing Piranesi's designs. The "rigorist" defender of recent trends, Protopiro, accuses Piranesi of inconsistency by extolling truth and simplicity in *Della Magnificenza* while employing a highly decorative style in practice. Protopiro next alludes to Laugier and praises the recent tendencies toward simple round columns, straight lines, and clean surfaces. His antagonist, Didascalo, criticizes his position on two counts. First, he extends Protopiro's rigorist logic to the extreme − by eliminating bases, capitals, moldings, friezes, cornices, and vaults, thereby reducing architecture to primitive huts and to monotonous "laws that have never really existed."[133] Second, he condemns Protopiro for criticizing "the very spirit that invented the architecture that you praise."[134] This is the creative competitive spirit that elevates the rank of the architect above that of the simple tradesman, and one of the principal architectural outlets for this spirit is indeed the ornamental vocabulary, for

take away every man's freedom to decorate as he sees fit, and you will very soon see the architectural sanctum open to all and sundry. When everyone knows how to practice architecture, everyone will despise it. As time goes by, buildings will grow worse, and the architectural manners that you gentlemen consider so rational will be destroyed by the means whereby you seek to preserve them. You will lose the will to compete, and to stand out from all other architects − since there will be no architects.[135]

By 1765 Piranesi had in fact already entered the architectural arena itself. In 1763 he was given a commission by Pope Clement XIII to design a new altar and choir for the Church of San Giovanni in Laterno. Although his highly elaborate design was never used, Piranesi received a second commission in the following year to renovate Santa Maria Aventina, the headquarters of the Knights of Malta. His intensely personal and eclectic design for this church won for him the papal title of *Cavaliere die Sperone d'oro* and election to the Accademia di San Luca.

Piranesi's final theoretical statement, *Divers Manners of Ornamenting Chimneys*, appeared in 1769. The heart of this trilingual publication (in Italian, English, and French) is his "Apological Essay in Defence of the Egyptian and Tuscan Architecture." It is just this − an extended homage to the originality and refinement of the architectural styles of these two nations, which he incorporates into his fireplace designs. The essay is not anti-Greek in the manner of his earlier writings, yet Piranesi remains adamant that the Greeks were not the inventors of all that is beautiful in architecture. The scrolls of the Ionic order, for instance, he traces to the volutes of seashells, and he prefers to credit the Phoenicians with introducing "into Greece the three above mentioned orders of architecture."[136] Piranesi also defends the ornamental exuberance of his own designs with the argument that "it is not the multiplicity of ornaments which offends the Spectator but the bad disposition of them," the want of a "high and low."[137] But the clincher to his apology, and a

fitting evolution of his ideas, is his remarkable conclusion, namely, that architects should consult not only the Greeks for ornamental ideas but also the Etruscans and Egyptians: "And by prudently combining the Grecian, the Tuscan, and the Egyptian together, he ought to open himself a road to the finding out of new ornaments and new manners."[138] In saying this, Piranesi becomes the first architect to arrive at a position of historical relativism or architectural eclecticism.

7. Neoclassicism and Character

The baroque eclecticism that Piranesi advocated in 1769 in several respects defined the path that neoclassicism would traverse over the remainder of the century. The foreign students who had lived in Rome in the 1750s and 1760s had returned north by this date and as practicing architects were now experimenting with architectural forms quite different from those of the past. This burst of creativity in the second half of the eighteenth century drew upon a multitude of sources, but what resulted formally could scarcely have been predicted from the individual spurs giving rise to it. The innovative and playful nature of neoclassical architecture underlines the very inappropriateness of the term itself. If Greek and Roman motifs were important sources for design, they were by no means the only ones, or even the predominant ones. For neoclassicism, especially as it came to maturation in the late 1760s, principally defined itself through the erosion of classical values. In France, the period from Soufflot's first design for Ste.-Geneviève (1755) to the French Revolution became one of intense experimentation, and at its close the last vestiges of academic classicism had all been swept away − at least temporally.

Various projects depict the evolution of this process. The Petit Trianon at Versailles (1761−68) of Ange-Jacques Gabriel (1667−1742) represents a compromise between the academic style of French rococo and the new impulses taking shape.[139] The client was the king's mistress, Madame de Pompadour, who died before its completion. It was intended to be her personal pavilion, situated within the newly created botanical garden at Versailles. Yet the cool elegance of the Petit Trianon is somewhat misleading. In Gabriel's original design, the building was square and the four pilasters in the front (columns in the rear) were compressed in the center, suggesting a triumphal arch or even a Palladian church motif. The central portal was framed with a segmental pediment, and festoons were applied to the sides. When the building was redesigned to include five bays along the

13. Ange-Jacques Gabriel, Petit Trianon, Versailles, 1761–8. View of front façade.

front, the spacing of the columns was made regular, the exterior decoration was removed, and the neutral rustication of the original basement story was replaced with the strong horizontal blocking of the final design (Fig. 13). Thus the building, with its symmetry and slight compositional inflection, evokes the essence of classicism, yet its blocklike form and simple roof balustrade (without pediment or statues) led many contemporary observers to perceive it as "Greek."[140] Inside, Gabriel departed from the classical tradition even more forcefully. All of the principal rooms are rectangular and without cove cornices (except the salon). The walls are paneled with rectilinear forms, and the ornaments and profiling are sharp and strictly classical. Only a few traces of rocaille shellwork survive here, and even the pale, neutral tones of the rooms (without gilding) suggest a new austerity. The pavilion is restrained yet deceptively so.

The Petit Trianon was finished in 1768, shortly before two other buildings with more revolutionary designs, one by Jacques Gondoin (1737–1818) and the other by Claude-Nicolas Ledoux (1735–1806). Both architects were students of Jacques-François Blondel, yet neither won the Prix de Rome (Gondoin did study four years at the French Academy in Rome). Both, however, were among the first to assimilate the new tendencies and translate them into convincing architectural forms.

Gondoin's Ecole de Chirurgie (School of Surgery, 1769–74) in Paris is one of the few buildings designed by him.[141] In 1764, he had returned to the city from Rome, where he had been influenced by Piranesi's archaeological fervor and eclectic imagination. The commission for the school

seems to have been due to his friendship with Germain Pichault de la Martinière, the first surgeon to the king, and Gondoin responded to the cramped site by devising a traditional U-shaped plan, with the courtyard open to the street. But the architect also partially enclosed the courtyard with a screen of Ionic columns (a double row of paired columns in depth), which support a library at the second level (Fig. 14). The impression from the street is of a forest of columns, a form of homage paid to the spirit of Perrault if not to the psychological observations of Le Roy. Within the intercolumniation on each side of the center portal Gondoin slipped in sculptural panels, which, together with the monumental bas-relief above, evoke the vestige of an honorific triumphal arch. The principal room of the complex, the surgical arena, lies opposite the main portal and is defined by a giant Corinthian porch, alluding to Soufflot's nearby porch at Ste.-Geneviève. Goindoin's rendering of the semicircular Greek amphitheater behind, crowned with a coffered ceiling and demioculus, is fully Piranesian in its lighting effects and spatial drama. Even the detailing is revolutionary. The Ionic colonnade of the screen wall and courtyard omits the epistyle or architrave, leaving the plain frieze to rest directly on unadorned Ionic capitals. The two-story Corinthian porch of the courtyard, stepping out from smaller Ionic columns running behind, appears to be snatched from another building, for it seems vastly overscaled and rudely attached to the front of the amphitheater. Its shallowness prohibits any human use other than as a symbolic gesture. To emphasize the collision of scales, the Ionic columns behind are coupled at each end of the porch.

14. Jacques Gondoin, School of Surgery, Paris, 1769–74. View from the street. Photograph by author.

Everything about the composition is slightly awkward and very unclassical in feeling.

Ledoux's pavilion and private theater for Mlle. Guimard (1769–72) was designed later in the same year (Fig. 15).[142] The client was a celebrated dancer with the Comédie-Française and Paris Opera, and the construction of the building seems to have been funded by several of her lovers. The leading motif of the "Temple of Terpsichore," as it was known in its day, is the semicircular entrance niche, entered through a screen of four Ionic columns carrying a full entablature open above. The coffered ceiling of the niche recalls a Piranesi engraving of the Temple of Venus and Rome in the Roman Forum, but Ledoux's source is more likely Robert Adam, who in the 1760s employed similar domed niches in the interiors of his houses at Syon, Kenwood, and Newby. As a colossal exterior motif, it is stunningly successful here, and Ledoux highlights the austere cubic form with bas-reliefs and horizontal rustication, the latter bending down over the windows in an allusion to keystones. The circular wall of the entry also allows him – in a very unclassical manner – to swing the main entrance off at a forty-five–degree angle (a *cabinet de bains* lies directly behind the center of the niche); the entrance leads into an oval antechamber, from which another axial line is established with a similar rotation.

Another feature in this early work of Ledoux is his use of rhetorical or allegorical motifs. At the Hôtel d'Uzès, completed in 1769, Ledoux honored his military client with a triumphal-arch gateway, in front of which he placed free-standing Doric columns bearing torsos, shields, helmets, arms, and trophies. At the townhouse for Mlle. Guimard, the entablature above the entrance features a statuary group in which Terpsichore is festively crowned as the Muse of dance. In the bas-reliefs of the niche, she is drawn in a chariot by cupids and bacchantes and followed by a procession of Graces and dancing fauns. The result, fittingly so, is theatrical, and the townhouse, even without the notorious social festivities of its owner, created a sensation.

The revolutionary designs of Gondoin and Ledoux are best considered under the notion of "character," a notion then gaining wide currency in French theory but also with a lengthy academic pedigree. The starting point is certainly Charles Le Brun's 1668 lecture to the Royal Academy of Painting and Sculpture, entitled "The Expression of the Passions."[143] The principal concern of Le Brun (who was at the time working with Claude Perrault on the design of the Louvre) was with individual expressions in historical paintings, and in fashioning his theory he drew upon a variety of sources both classical and modern. The rhetorical concept of decorum, for instance, demanded that a speech must display a particular character appropriate to an occasion, and for the arts this idea translated into a theory of literary styles or musical modes such as the Phrygian, Dorian, Aeolian, and Lydian or architectural styles such as the Doric, Ionic, and Corinthian. Le Brun joined these nuances with the physiology of Descartes to postulate artistic formulae for the expression of each passion, for which the eyes and eyebrows (because of their proximity to the pineal gland in the center of the brain) were the most revealing. Terror, for instance, causes the eyebrows to rise up high in the middle and the eyes to open wide, whereas horror causes the lids to frown downward and the pupil to draw up under

15. Claude-Nicholas Ledoux, Pavilion for Mlle. Guimard, Paris, 1769–72. From *Architecture de C. N. Ledoux* (1847).

the lid. The manifestation of expression was also dependent on the individual's facial type, age, and social rank.

The architect Germain Boffrand (1667–1754) was the first to translate this theory of expression into the architectural notion of character in his *Livre d'architecture* (Book of architecture, 1745).[144] Boffrand had originally studied architecture in the office of Hardouin-Mansart, the architect of the Versailles chapel, and in 1700 he embarked on what would become a successful private practice as a designer of aristocratic residences. Over the next half-century he became one of the leading practitioners of the French rococo as well as a highly respected academician. His *Livre d'architecture* consists of four essays directed to different themes, "enriched" with an abundance of engravings of his own designs. Most important among the essays is the one entitled "Principles Derived from Horace's *Art of Poetry*," which he originally presented as a lecture to the Royal Academy of Architecture in 1734.

The text is in large part a transposition of Horace's literary principles into architecture. Because the arts share a common heritage and purpose in playing upon human emotions, Boffrand argues, it is possible to graft the rules for poetry, which "has its different genres; and the style of one does not suit another," onto architectural theory.[145] Buildings not only have the general capacity to speak, but the architect should learn to exploit architecture's ornamental vocabulary in such a way that a rapport is established with the spectator. Thus beauty is but a prelude to a building's elocutionary purpose: "It is not enough for a building to be handsome; it must be pleasing, and the beholder must feel the character that it is meant to convey."[146] The orders provide the initial framework for this discourse, yet the typology of character, following the breadth of human emotions, is more effusive and elicits distinct impressions through the smallest nuances of detail. Some of Boffrand's axioms for character are quite general, such as the need to impress a building with a consistent character, "so that it must appear cheerful where it is intended to communicate joy, and serious and melancholy when it is meant to instil respect or sadness."[147] Others, however, are more

39

specific, such as his reflections on the difficulty of pro-filing moldings ("what words are in a discourse")[148] so that "there is a grace and elegance that only the masters of the art can truly appreciate, and this is very difficult to obtain."[149]

Boffrand's theory of character was to undergo elabora-tion in the teachings of Jacques-François Blondel, who, to-gether with Laugier and Soufflot, should be deemed one of the most influential architects of the second half of the eighteenth century.[150] Blondel was foremost a teacher and he wrote extensively. In 1739–40, on the rue de la Harpe in Paris, he opened his own private school of architecture, against initial opposition from the Royal Academy of Archi-tecture. The purpose of the new school, as he later explained in a prospectus, was to bring students together in a single studio and move them through a structure of courses (which the academy did not), from elementary principles of design to higher theory and the technical principles of practice. The program soon proved successful, and Blondel attracted a number of the next generation's best students, includ-ing Gondoin, Ledoux, Étienne-Louis Boullée, and William Chambers. In 1755 Blondel gained entry into the second class of the Academy of Architecture, and in 1762 his school, along with its program of instruction, was formally incorpo-rated into that institution.

Blondel was also active within the intellectual circles of the *Encyclopédie* and contributed numerous articles to Diderot's venture. His four-volume *Architecture Françoise* (1752–6) composed what was, in effect, an encyclopedia of the major works of French practice. In his outlook, how-ever, Blondel was hardly a revolutionary. His tastes grav-itated toward the traditional forms of French classicism (and in particular the classical period of François Mansart, Perrault, and François Blondel). He first praised but later condemned the teachings of Laugier, and he opposed as-pects of the rococo as well as the growing interest in Greece. He valued the importance of reason or rational analysis, yet his theory favored precepts and rules and paid allegiance to the academic notion of *convenance* (fitness with propri-ety). Ornament is not so much devalued as the touchstone of architectural beauty as "distribution" or planning – in Blondel's view, the French contribution to the ever more perfect line of architectural development – is elevated in stature and placed alongside decoration. In short, Blondel stayed an academic course against the currents of his time, yet he nevertheless educated a generation of students who fell in with contemporary tendencies. He also employed the term *style* for the first time in architectural theory, using it

to refer to the multitude of characters that a building may represent.

As with Boffrand, the orders for Blondel supply the first measure of magnificence to the art by defining such domi-nant themes as rusticity, delicacy, and sublimity. But subtler expressions of character are called for: "Do not doubt that it is by the assistance of those imperceptible nuances that we are able to make a real distinction in the design of two buildings of the same genre but that nevertheless announce themselves differently: preferring in one a style sublime, no-ble, and elevated, in the other a character naive, simple, and true."[151] Blondel's list of "imperceptible nuances," based on the three principal orders, runs over thirty pages and distin-guishes among the styles manly, firm, virile, light, elegant, delicate, rustic, naive, feminine (Petit Trianon), mysterious, and grand, among many others. Although Blondel was wary of the perceived excesses of his day, he did allow the ar-chitect greater latitude or more personal discretion than earlier. In the end the lodestar for him was "taste," that "which establishes, which determines the proper style to each genre of building, and which – guided by the rea-soning of the architect – allows him to vary his facades to infinity."[152] Blondel's theory of character was neverthe-less conceived entirely within the confines of the academic tradition, and if we follow the concept over the remain-der of the century, we find it taking on a very different life of its own – now exploiting theatrical effects or what would become known as *architecture parlante* (speaking architecture).[153]

A new psychological reading of character was advanced in 1780 by Nicolas Le Camus de Mézières (1721–89) in *Le Génie de l'architecture; ou l'analogie de cet art avec nos sen-sations* (The genius of architecture; or the analogy of that art with our sensations). Although the bulk of this book is concerned with rules for planning the French residence, Le Camus in his short introduction writes of the inexhaustible moods and characters evoked by natural and architectural forms: "The more closely I have looked, the more I have found that every object possesses a character, proper to it alone, and that often a single line, a plain contour, will suf-fice to express it."[154] Aspects of Le Camus's discussion may at first seem decidedly backward looking – such as his ref-erences to the expressionist theory of Le Brun and to the mathematical work of Ouvrard on harmonic proportions as well as his criticism of Perrault for his skepticism toward absolute ratios – but Le Camus actually places the mat-ter of character almost entirely on a sensationalist footing by interpreting character solely through human sensations or responses: "What emotions do we not feel in the contrast between deep shadow and limpid light, or between the delights of calm weather and the confusion of winds and Tempests: Every nuance, every gradation, affects us."[155] In the end there is a close affinity between forms and our sensations, but architecture also becomes an impressionist art: "The whole, the masses, the proportions, the shadows, and the lights are the bases of our compositions."[156]

Le Camus's text is often read as a prelude to the better known theory of character of Boullée, but we might first consider another book, *Lettres sur l'architecture des anciens et celle des modernes* (Letters on ancient and modern architecture) of Jean-Louis Viel de Saint-Maux – the letters that make up its contents appeared between 1779 and 1787. Little is known of Viel other than that he was the younger brother of the architect Charles-François Viel (1745–1819) but his Masonic book stands far outside of the academic tradition. In fact he disdainfully accuses the treatise of Vitruvius, along with "the centuries that have adopted it," of arresting the progress of this art, and claims that it is a textual memorial to the "perpetual stupidity of mankind."[157] The author turns instead to the growing body of antiquarian and travel literature on Indian, Japanese, Chinese, Babylonian, and Persian architecture, from which he reconstructs an ancient architecture that is intensely symbolic, a "poême parlant" to the early emblematic themes of agriculture, cosmogony, cosmology, and fertility. All of ancient architecture is symbolic for Viel, from the first menhirs raised as sacred calendars to column capitals "expressing natural causes and the genius of each people"[158] to representational friezes "like the Zodiac encompassing the heavens."[159] A pediment features a triangular form not in imitation of a rustic hut but because in ancient times the triangle, like the circle, was the universal symbol of the supreme being.

On how this "symbolic style" could inform and rejuvenate contemporary practice and culture, Viel was much less clear. He is not shy, however, about calling Jean-François Blondel "the Charlatan of architecture" or accusing Ledoux of pillaging the forms of his entry columns for the Hôtel d'Uzès from a design of Jean-Laurent Legeay.[160] In another attack on the symbolic confusion of Ledoux's partially completed Hôtel des Fermes in Paris, Viel sarcastically wonders if its stepped pyramidal entries and "torso of Mercury" would denote – when construction was completed – a church, hospital, theater, college, or tobacco shop.[161] Viel more generally faults modern practice for lacking fixed thematic content or "distinctive character," and thus he favors expanding the use of symbolic forms.[162]

A fascination with characteristic effects and a recognition of the capacity of architecture to become symbolic converge in the theory and drawings of Étienne-Louis Boullée (1728–99).[163] In his work, and in that of his colleague and contemporary Ledoux, we in fact see a culmination of revolutionary tendencies festering since the 1750s. After early training in painting, Boullée studied architecture under Blondel and Boffrand and more importantly in the Paris office of Jean-Laurent Legeay, the *grand-prix* winner of 1732, who was renowned for his delineatory skill. Boullée never ventured south but established a career in Paris, both as a teacher and, like Ledoux, as a designer of fashionable townhouses. His most highly regarded commission, the Hôtel de Brunoy (1774–9), featured on its garden front a three-sided arcade of windows wrapping around a taller temple porch of six Ionic columns. Atop the stepped pyramidal pediment above the porch he placed a statue of the goddess Flora, the symbolic leitmotif of the garden. Thus he too viewed character in allegorical terms. In 1778 Boullée was named to a government post, but his various efforts to win official commissions mostly ended in failure. In 1782 he retired from practice in order to concentrate on his visionary drawings and projected book. His incomplete textual manuscript, "Architecture, Essai sur l'art," was not published until 1953, but both it and the bold visual documentation of his ideas (in his will bequeathed to the French nation) were well known to his students and other architects during his lifetime.

Boullée's theory transcends the academic notion of character by emphasizing the emotional impressions received from simple prismatic forms – spheres, cubes, pyramids – and by forging these elements into a sparse aesthetics. The *Essai* opens, interestingly enough, with a lengthy discussion of the Perrault–Blondel debate in which Boullée concedes that most architects now side with Perrault and believe architectural proportions are inherently "fantastic," that is, the product of human imagination. But Boullée disagrees. Architecture is the poetic creation of mental images or visual tableaux, but it creates these through a play of volumes, of which regularity, symmetry, and variety are the basic principles. Proportion, then, is the "combination of these properties," the effect produced by a volume's regular order. "It is easy for the reader to surmise," he notes, "that the basic rule and the one that governs the principles of architecture, originates in regularity and also that any deviation from symmetry in architecture is as inconceivable as failing to observe the rules of harmony in music."[164]

Character is conjoined with these principles, although in a highly symbolic manner. It is the "effect of the object which makes some kind of impression on us," or more specifically, "the judicial use of every means of producing no other sensations than those related to the subject."[165] Character is also fostered by good taste and by that "delicate, aesthetic discernment" that allows us to be delighted in the depths of our being. The impression of architectural grandeur, for instance, "lies in the disposition of the volumes that form the whole in such a way that there is a great deal of play among them, that their masses have a noble, majestic movement and that they have the fullest possible development."[166] All can be further enhanced by a play of light and shadow, a subtle use of color, and a discriminate disposition of the secondary parts. In this way the revolutionary shift from viewing character as something ordained by academic convention to viewing it as something gained by immediate sensation – a shift presaged by the theory of Le Camus – is complete. Buildings through their geometry acquire their individual nature and distinctive character.

If Boullée's theory is purposely archaic in its pristine Platonic splendor, his well-known sepia drawings are even more strikingly an exercise in architectural reduction. He presents only regular forms here, often composed with rows of columns stripped to their classical essence. His design for a metropolitan church is based on Soufflot's Ste.-Geneviève but idealized at a fantastic scale, one defying human imagination. The Perraultian splendor of its interior columns, multiplied to metaphorical excess, appropriately serve as a backdrop to a Masonic ceremony of initiation. In his text, Boullée draws heavily on the article of his "friend" Le Roy in recounting the perceptual nuances of scale and the experience of perceiving columnar screens. In a similar way, the vast basilica for a national library, with its amphitheater of books, "is crowned with an order of architecture so conceived that far from distracting attention from the spectacle of the books, it would offer only that decoration necessary to give yet more brilliance and nobility to this beautiful place."[167] Again, the proposed "Tomb for the Spartans" supports no colonnade, but its roof is borne by a frieze of soldiers arrayed for battle. The much admired "Cenotaph for Newton" is a gigantic sphere whose interior play of light is calculated to produce the characteristic effect of sublimity.

Boullée's architectural drawings, in their conscious distillation of classical forms, are allegories of the human spirit, esoteric essays in the pursuit of geometric ideals. In this sense, they differ little from the later designs of Ledoux, who, after many Palladian detours, also crossed the classical boundary in his search for forms sustained primarily by their pictorial content. The turning point in Ledoux's career took place in 1771, when, through his association with Madame du Barry, he was given a sinecure as the inspector of saltworks for the province of Franche-Comté. He thus began to supplement his earlier work, mostly for private patrons, with a bevy of proposals for large public commissions. Though many of his projects were never built, a few were erected and all have survived through engravings. A seemingly capricious line of formal exploration runs through them. In the buildings for the saltworks at Arc-et-Senans, constructed between 1775 and 1780, he explores in a serious way a generic, geometric classicism stripped for the most part of emblematic decoration. The double-cube of the director's house, with the giant proportions of its rusticated columns, occupies the focus of the half-circular plan as a carefully measured gesture of power over a confined community of workers. The theater in Besançon, built during the same years, originally employed the same antique theater plan as the site plan at Chaux, but for its interior Ledoux forsook the traditional loges. He delineated the physiognomy of his proposed prison for Aix-en-Provence (1787) simply with squat, baseless columns in the porch, the "funeral" roof motifs of the corner towers, and the horizontal slits of its infrequent windows. In his controversial *barrières* (tollhouses) for the perimeter of Paris (the scheme for which he also envisioned eight large taverns and a "house of pleasure" for Montmartre), Ledoux allowed his eclectic fantasies to run wild, trampling in the process every rule of classical order and decorum. And finally in his imaginary designs for the ideal city of Chaux, conceived in fits of activity over the last twenty-five years of his life, Ledoux was in the end successful in ridding architecture entirely of its classical legacy, transforming it, in the words of Anthony Vidler, into "hieroglyphic signs" and "pictographic writing."[168]

For all of this, Ledoux has of course been hailed as a "revolutionary architect," no doubt with justification.[169] But there is also a very interesting (architecturally less subversive) side of Ledoux that emerges in the first and only volume of a monograph published in 1804, *L'Architecture considérée sous la rapport de l'art, des moeurs et de la législation* (Architecture considered under the relation of art, mores, and legislation) (Fig. 16). The project began around 1780 as a collection of engravings depicting his built and imagined projects for the saltworks near Chaux. The number of plates greatly expanded over the course of the decade and then was halted by the Revolution and by Ledoux's imprisonment in 1793–4 for his royalist sympathies. When the project resumed, Ledoux felt the need not only to defend his architectural honor but also to vindicate his symbolic vision

16. Title page of Claude-Nicholas Ledoux, *L'Architecture considérée sous la rapport de l'art, de moeurs et de la législation* (1804).

of architecture as something that should stand in service to and legitimize the aspirations of the state, in his words, "the propagation and purification of morals."[170] Thus in his ideal city every house announces its purpose: The Oikéma, or house of pleasure, has a phallic floor plan; the workshop for the river guards has the river flowing through it; and the house of the coopers takes the form of barrel hoops.

In such a conception, architecture must assume its "proper physiognomy."[171] The lure of beauty becomes a questionable "despotism," and decoration is a flirtatious and "artful coquette, supported by the sweet arts of civilization."[172] Architecture speaks like a mythical oration: "Architecture is to masonry what poetry is to literature: it is the dramatic enthusiam of the craft; one can only speak of it with exaltation. If design gives the form, it is that which bestows the charm that animates all productions. Just as there is no uniformity in thought, there can be no uniformity in expression."[173]

His Masonic underpinnings aside, Ledoux's hieroglyphic characters far overstepped the classical boundaries of decorum, as many of his contemporaries observed. Quatremère de Quincy used the designs of Ledoux in his encyclopedia of 1788 to clarify the meaning of such terms as "Abuse" and "Bizarre."[174] The architect Charles-François Viel referred to Ledoux in 1800 as someone "celebrated for the extent of his ruinous enterprises."[175] But Ledoux's reputation effectively survived his detractors, and the sheer inventive power of his creations in many ways served as a fitting tribute to the libertarian underbelly of the Enlightenment. His is an architectural conception both utopian and utilitarian at the same time: an endgame born of guillotines and anarchy. After him came the deluge; postrevolutionary French architecture would need a retrenchment.

3

BRITISH THEORY IN THE EIGHTEENTH CENTURY

But it appears very clearly to me, that the human figure never supplied the architect with any of his ideas.

Edmund Burke (1759)

1. The Legacy of Jones and Wren

There are many reasons for Great Britain's relatively independent course of intellectual development in the eighteenth century. Politically, the two most significant events were the revolution of 1688 and the Treaty of Utrecht of 1713. The former resulted in constitutional reforms that enhanced liberty of expression and stabilized the governing process, while the latter concluded a dozen years of war with France and instilled in the British both pride and an ambition for international political standing. The ascension of the House of Hanover in 1715 further consolidated these gains and led to a period of unmatched colonial expansion and economic prosperity that lasted until midcentury. Attention to such luxuries as art and architecture was of course congenial with these developments.

Thus Britain over the course of the century increasingly competed with France and Italy on the European cultural stage, yet with some unique traits in its national makeup. Until late in the century, it possessed no academic structure in the arts and hence had no organizational means of defining a unified set of artistic beliefs. British architects learned their trade either as apprentices in offices or through self-education by reading the principal texts of the Italian Renaissance or French classicism. Where advanced schooling was desired, one embarked on a tour of the south to imbibe the classical tradition firsthand. As a consequence, British architectural theory remained captive, at least initially, to the Vitruvian traditions of Italy and France.

But Britain was also a country with a competitive spirit and well-defined national mannerisms, and in the eighteenth century these tendencies increasingly came to the fore. Already by the start of the century, certain aesthetic sensibilities can be recognized as distinctly British. Whether one chooses to ground these aesthetic proclivities in the utilitarian aesthetics of Francis Bacon (1561–1626) or in the empiricism of John Locke (1632–1704) is immaterial.[1] What is important is the manifest change in eighteenth-century sensibilities – a change, as Rudolf Wittkower once aptly characterized it, toward "that which is dictated by the senses as opposed to the reasoning faculties."[2] At the start of the century, absolutist and relativist tendencies stand side by side in theory, with no perceived incongruities or contradictions. But by the time David Hume published the first two books of his *Treatise of Human Nature* (1739–40) – in which reason is now inextricably wedded to sense impressions as yet another perception of the mind – such a commingling of vantage points is no longer possible.[3] The classical belief in absolute beauty and proportion that assumed such a prominent place within the British Palladian movement of the first quarter of the century (the legacy of the French and Italian Renaissance) is scarcely to be found on the theoretical map of Britain in the second half of the century. Picturesque theory, grounded in the new associational and sensational psychology, had emerged victorious.

Within architectural theory, the clash between classical and relativistic values begins to appear in the respective views of Inigo Jones (1573–1652) and Christopher Wren (1632–1723). Jones – a younger contemporary of Francis Bacon and William Shakespeare – illustrates Britain's early fascination with Italian theory and its classical appeal. Originally a costume designer and court artist, Jones learned architecture entirely from his study of treatises and his travels to the South (Fig. 17). His first trip to Italy took place

17. Inigo Jones, from *Artist Portraits: Scrapbook, 1600–1800.* Courtesy of the Collection Centre Canadien d'Architecture/Canadien Centre for Architecture, Montréal.

around the turn of the seventeenth century, when his principal interest was still the theater. He returned to Italy in 1613 for another nineteen months, during which time he met Scamozzi and immersed himself in Palladian lore, utilizing a 1601 edition of Palladio's treatise to study the works of this master and to chronicle monuments of Roman antiquity.[4] Thus, when Jones began his architectural career in 1616 as surveyor of the king's works, he did so within the context of a living Renaissance tradition and with the belief in a metric and universal harmony governing the world of high art. His celebrated designs for London's Banqueting House (1619–22) and the Queen's House at Greenwich (1616–35) visually articulate the depth of his thought; their crisp and clean classical lines, together with details gleaned from his careful study of Renaissance sources, later served as the milestones for the English Palladian movement that took shape in the first quarter of the eighteenth century.[5]

Jones's architectural perspective also shares affinities with Henry Wotton's *The Elements of Architecture* (1624).[6] Some have speculated that Wotton, who was an ambassador to

Venice and an enthusiast of the arts, not only knew Jones but also assisted him in purchasing Palladio's drawings.[7] Wotton's short treatise, famously exalting "Commoditie, Firmness, and Delight" as the linchpin of theory, of course derives from Vitruvius, although it is Vitruvius harmonically recast in the absolute aesthetics of Alberti, Dürer, and Palladio. In addition, the treatise places an emphasis on practicality or attention to use, as it was intended to be a guidebook for English gentlemen builders.

At the start of his career, Wren similarly embraced the classical spirit, although in a few cases – such as the design for Tom Tower at Oxford – the context necessitated that the design "ought to be Gothick to agree with the Founder's Worke."[8] Wren, like Jones, was a self-educated architect (Fig. 18). But he was a mathematician and an astronomer of the first rank: a founding member of the Royal Society and a professor of astronomy at Gresham College in London, later the Savillian Professor at Oxford. He came

18. Christopher Wren, from *Artist Portraits: Scrapbook, 1600–1800.* Courtesy of the Collection Centre Canadien d'Architecture/Canadian Centre for Architecture, Montréal.

to architectural practice almost accidentally upon being asked to give structural advice on the remodeling of the old Cathedral of St. Paul's (in 1663 and 1666). Through local contacts with college officials, he prepared designs for the chapel at Pembroke College, Cambridge (1663–5), and the Sheldonian Theater at Oxford (1664–9). On a trip to France in 1665, he pursued his fledgling architectural interests by surveying that country's major monuments. There he also met Bernini, who was at work on the Louvre, and he is said to have met François Mansart and Louis Le Vau as well, whose buildings effected a change in his earlier Renaissance style. The Great London Fire of 1666 was the immediate cause of his near full time devotion to architecture. He was first appointed to the six-member committee charged with rebuilding the city; by 1669 he was appointed surveyor general for all new construction in London.

Wren's trip to France deserves to be considered in greater detail, because at this point he also became interested in architectural theory. His "Letter to a Friend from Paris," written in the fall of 1665, reflects his penchant for noticing the details of daily Parisian life, reminiscent of Thomas Jefferson's later fascination with the city. He surveyed the "most esteem'd Fabricks" of the city and the surrounding countryside, including the Palais Mazarin, the Château de Maisons, the royal estate at Fontainbleau, the Château-Neuf at St. Germain, and the early work at Versailles.[9] He admired the work of Bernini and Mansart, but he could also be critical of such buildings as Le Vau's Collège de Quatre-Nations. On his two visits to Versailles, where women have "sway," he reacted strongly to the excessive luxury: "Not an Inch within but is crouded with little Curiosities of Ornaments." These fashionable "little Knacks" he contrasts with a vision of architecture whose art "certainly ought to have the Attribute of eternal, and therefore the only Thing uncapable of new Fashions."[10]

The trip seems to have inspired him to put his ideas on architecture down on paper. His writings, later organized into "tracts" by his son, open with the affirmation that architecture aims "at Eternity, and therefore the only Thing uncapable of Modes and Fashions in its Principals, the *Orders*."[11] Its three basic (Vitruvian) principles are beauty, firmness, and convenience; the first two depend on the "geometrical Reasons of Opticks and Staticks," the last on variety. Beauty, which is defined as "a Harmony of Objects, begetting Pleasure by the Eye," has two causes. Natural beauty derives "from Geometry, consisting in Uniformity (that is Equality) and Proportion." Customary beauty results from the "Use of our Senses to those Objects which are usually pleasing

to us for other Causes, as Familiarity or particular Inclination breeds a Love to Things not in themselves lovely." Customary beauty (custom) is also the source of errors in architectural judgment, for "always the true Test is natural or geometrical Beauty."[12]

These few comments are rich in theoretical implications, and they have been interpreted in different ways. One may first be tempted to correlate these two causes of beauty with Perrault's near contemporary distinction between positive and arbitrary beauty – except that Perrault placed proportion within the category of arbitrary beauty. And then again, Wren did not postulate two different kinds of beauty but rather two causes of beauty. As one historian has pointed out, Wren's emphasis on the proof of geometric beauty is closer in words and spirit to Fréart de Chambray's geometric formulation of the same as the "Harmony and Consent" of enlightened judgment.[13]

Still, Wren's more rational or scientific approach to the issue of beauty differs from Renaissance theory. The "Harmony of Objects, begetting Pleasure by the Eye" at least allows an underlying empiricism – that is, importance is placed on the visual discernment of the spectator. And even though "Uniformity" and "Proportion" remain at the center of architectural design, Wren is equally critical of those who "have reduced them into Rules, too strict and pedantick, and so as not to be transgressed, without the Crime of Barbarity"; for him, rather, "they are but Modes and Fashions of those ages wherein they were used."[14] This cultural and aesthetic relativism, at heart opposed to his apparent classicism, raises again the interesting question of where Wren would have stood in the contemporary debate between the ancients and the moderns. His scientific interests and experimentation clearly place him on the side of progress, but his emphasis on the "Eternal" and his warning that "an Architect ought to be jealous of Novelties" suggest otherwise.[15]

It is only through his subsequent practice that this question finds a resolution, although here again his achievements are disputed. In 1936 John Summerson decreed that Wren was a "Royal Society type of mind," a "man of science" and a "classical scholar," but at the same time an architect of little imagination who engaged in "empirical, arbitrary methods of composition."[16] Recent interpretations of his work have tended to see him in a more positive light yet still struggle to mediate the classical foundations of his theory with the increasingly baroque sensibilities of his practice.[17] The evolution of Wren's designs for St. Paul's, the inventive and varied designs for the London churches, his willingness to accommodate an existing Gothic tradition, and the baroque features of his later work – all point to a scientifically reasoned flexibility that enabled him to change with the times.

Wren's tracts on "history" shed some light on his position regarding antiquity. To begin with, his interests were by no means confined to the Roman or Hellenic past. The postulation of a "Tyrian order" preceding the refinement of the Doric falls in line with his cultural relativism. His fascination with Hebraic and biblical buildings – the Temple of Dagon (pulled down by Sampson), the Temple of Solomon, the tombs of Porsenna and Absalom, the pyramids and walls of Babylon, as well as the Temple of Diana at Ephesus and the Mausoleum of Halicarnassus – suggests a store of forms richer in possibilities than any true interpretation of classicism would allow.[18] In short, one must allow Wren both his experiments expanding the formal repertoire of architectural motifs and his perceptual preference for abstracting "geometrical Beauty."

Wren's near eclecticism undoubtedly had an effect on the early eighteenth century designs of Nicholas Hawksmoor (1661–1736) and John Vanbrugh (1664–1726).[19] Collectively and apart, they define the first great line of British architectural development in the eighteenth century, an approach clearly eclectic in its methods. Hawksmoor's ties to Wren are the most explicit, as he began his career as a teen in Wren's office and worked his way up to become a collaborator on many projects. Between 1691 and 1710 he served as the chief draftsman for the Cathedral of St. Paul's; in 1698 he assisted Wren in the design of Greenwich Hospital. One year later he began his association with Vanbrugh, initially by detailing and executing the latter's designs for Castle Howard (1699–1712) and Blenheim Palace (1705–25).

Hawksmoor's historical understanding and inventiveness has only come to be appreciated recently. He was more curious than Vanbrugh in searching out historical themes, and he was more prone to use them in practice. The annotated drawings that he prepared for Worcester College shortly before 1720, for instance, drew upon a variety of sources. One design for the library refers to the "Arc sur le Pont du Xaintes," the triumphal arch at Saintes. Another sheet refers to the "Antiquity at Bordeaux," the Piliers de Tutelle as sketched by Perrault. Still other sheets cite Vignola, the Tower of the Winds at Athens, the Pantheon, the Arch of Constantine, and "The Rusticks according to Mr Jones, at St James Chapell."[20] The "Gothic" lantern of the Church of Saint Anne, Limehouse (1714–19), was based on the Tower of the Winds. The Mausoleum of Harlicarnassus, which fascinated both Wren and Hawksmoor, finds its way atop

St. George's, Bloomsbury (1716–35), where its twenty-four pyramidal steps support a statue of George I.

Hawksmoor's views on Gothic architecture were also unusual and much in advance of their time. In a letter written to the dean of Westminster in the mid-1730s, Hawksmoor defends the word "Gothick" against those who disabuse it by applying it to "every thing that displeases," similar to how the Greeks and Romans used the word "Barbarous."[21] For Hawksmoor it signified an admirable and logical style of building that derived from changed building types and from the necessity of using small stonework. With regard to the Gothic forms that he brought to the north quadrangle of All Souls College, Oxford (1718–24), it is clear that what pleased him was less the quadrangle's structural or material logic and more the storybook character of its pinnacled roofline (punctured regularly with Gothic finials), the bold romantic towers, and the dappled play of light and shadow. That the interiors were classical in style underscores the scenographic nature of his designs.

Vanbrugh gave in to pleasure of poetic license only to a slightly lesser extent. When he succeeded Wren as the surveyor to Greenwich Hospital in 1716, he celebrated his promotion by erecting his medieval-inspired "Vanbrugh Castle" nearby, replete with a crenellated gateway, the "white towers," and a nunnery. This fantastical work of architecture was constructed during the same years that Vanbrugh and Hawksmoor populated the grounds of Castle Howard with an obelisk, pyramid, pyramid gate, temple, and mausoleum. If Hawksmoor's eclecticism, as manifest in his idiosyncratic choice of sources, presages tendencies that generally become evident in the "revolutionary" architecture of the late eighteenth century, Vanbrugh's theater of effects provides an outlet for nascent picturesque sensibilities.[22] Both men in their outlook stand far apart from developments on the continent.

2. The Palladian Movement

The baroque tendencies of Hawksmoor and Vanbrugh also supplied fodder to the opposing Palladian movement, which likewise begins to take shape in England in the first years of the eighteenth century. The godfather to the movement was naturally Inigo Jones, with his earlier Palladianism. Upon his death in 1652, his library of books and designs was passed on to his capable assistant, John Webb (1611–72), who continued the Palladian tradition in the third quarter of the century. The architecture of Palladio also continued to interest Wren, among others. Palladio, for instance, had a strong following in Oxford in the last decade of the century, centered in the circle of Henry Aldrich (1648–1710), dean of Christ Church, and George Clarke (1661–1736). Aldrich compiled unpublished treatises on geometry and architecture, and in 1706 he prepared an impressive Palladian design for Peckwater quadrangle at Christ Church. Clarke, who was a close friend of Hawksmoor, may even have stimulated the latter's interest in Palladio; he prepared several Palladian designs, among them one for the North Lodging at All Souls College (c. 1710). Others enamored with Palladio in the first decade of the century include Alexander Fletcher, William Talman, and William Benson.[23]

Thus the stirrings of a Palladian revival were well advanced by 1712, when Anthony Ashley Cooper, the third earl of Shaftesbury, composed his influential "Letter Concerning Design." Shaftesbury's letter is often said to signify the dethronement of Wren within intellectual circles, as this Neoplatonic philosopher laments the fact that so many important buildings "have miscarried amongst us," by "retaining much of what artists call the Gothic kind."[24] Wren is censured directly for his work at Hampton Court and St. Paul's, and Vanbrugh's design at Blenheim is called "a new palace spoilt." Nevertheless, Shaftesbury is optimistic about the British nation's improving public taste, which in the future, he feels, should manifest itself in a new royal palace and parliament. Shaftesbury also pleads for an "academy for the training of her youth in exercises."[25]

Although Shaftesbury does not mention Palladio by name, the earl's personality and character were entirely classical in bearing.[26] He was educated by no less a mind than John Locke (who was the personal secretary and physician to the first earl of Shaftesbury), and he cultivated his artistic sensibilities during his tour of Italy in the late 1680s. His idealist moral philosophy was predicated on the classical notions of harmony, proportion, and the much admired "good taste," and his *Characteristics of Men, Manners, Opinions, Times* (1711) gives instruction on how to acquire the necessary virtues and moral sense to become a man of proper breeding. He deems beauty – in contrast to Locke – to be an innate idea, perceived through the "inward eye."[27]

English Palladianism consolidates itself as a movement around 1715, first through the efforts of Giacomo Leoni (1686–1746) and Colen Campbell (1676–1729). The Venetian Leoni had arrived in England two years earlier, and the first installment of his two-volume *The Architecture of A. Palladio; in Four Books* (1715–20) put the master's words and buildings before the English public for the first time

(Fig. 19). In the translator's preface Nicholas Du Bois describes Palladio as the "most eminent" of the "great masters of Civil Architecture." Du Bois also optimistically observes that the present is tending toward "the noble and majestick Simplicity of the Ancients," which opposes the "ridiculous mixture of *Gothick* and *Roman*, without Judgement, Taste, or Symmetry."[28] Leoni reports in the second edition of the book that it took him five years and the greatest effort to correct and visually enhance Palladio's original woodcuts. Leoni did more than simply enhance the original drawings, however; in some cases he altered their design and imparted to them a distinctly baroque character.[29]

Shortly before Leoni's edition of Palladio, Campbell, in 1715, published the first part of his equally ambitious *Vitruvius Britannicus or the British Architect*. The book was originally conceived as a survey of national architecture, and in fact various buildings of Wren and Jones are proudly displayed. Campbell intended the work to counter "so mean an Opinion of what is performed in our own country" and to enter the name of Inigo Jones to the "Lists" beside the "Renowned Palladio."[30] But Campbell reserves a special place for "the great *Palladio*, who has exceeded all that were gone before him" and has become the "*Ne plus ultra* of his Art."[31] The works of Bernini and Fontana and the "odd and chimerical Beauties" of Borromini are roundly condemned. Campbell, however, includes in his liberal survey baroque designs of Thomas Archer, Nicholas Hawksmoor, and John Vanbrugh.

The efforts of Leoni and Campbell, nevertheless, soon came up short. For by the early 1720s leadership of the Palladian movement (now more strictly defined) had passed to Richard Boyle, the third earl of Burlington and fourth earl of Cork (1694–1753).[32] Born into wealth and cultural circumstance, Burlington assumed his titles upon reaching his majority in 1715. In the previous year he had undertaken his first tour of Italy, where he indulged his taste for music, theater, and purchasing paintings. He was at this time pursuing Shaftesbury's ideal of a "virtuoso," that is, someone who dispassionately appreciates aesthetic form. During his tour, no less an architect than James Gibbs was hired to make changes to the Burlington House on Piccadilly. When Burlington returned home in 1715, the books by Leoni and Campbell seemed to have piqued his architectural interest. He decided to replace Gibbs with Campbell in renovating the Burlington House, and there are indications that the latter mentored Burlington over the next few years. This period ended in 1719, when Burlington, now critical of Campbell's impure classical style, decided to undertake a second trip to

19. Frontispiece, portrait of Andrea Palladio, in Giocomo Leoni, ed., *The Architecture of A. Palladio in Four Books* (London, 1715).

ANDREAS PALLADIVS VICENTINVS.

Italy specifically to study Palladio at the source. He not only surveyed many of Palladio's works but purchased all of the surviving drawings that could be found. Upon his return to London, he bought a large part of Inigo Jones's collection, which also contained drawings by Palladio.

Thus all of the elements for his architectural success were in place by the start of the 1720s, when Burlington set about refurbishing the manor at his second estate in Chiswick. A fire in that building in 1725 led to his decision to build a new Palladian rotunda between 1725 and 1730, and the accomplished design for this building became the paradigm for the Palladian movement. But Burlington would not stop there. In 1724 Burlington commissioned William Kent, whom he had met in Italy, to prepare *The Designs of Inigo Jones*, which appeared in two volumes in 1727.[33] He also seems to have been of assistance to Robert Castell, who in the following year published *The Villas of the Ancients Illustrated*, resurrecting Pliny's descriptions of the villas of Laurentinum and Tuscum. The little-known Castell dedicated

the book to Burlington, after reflecting "that many Works of Inigo Jones's and Palladio's had perish'd but for Your Love to Architecture."[34] In 1730 Burlington followed with his *Fabbriche antiche*, which presented (from his own collection) previously unpublished reconstructions of ancient buildings by Palladio.[35]

The professional relationship of Burlington and Kent, which defines the heart of this circle, is a complex and interesting one. Burlington first met Kent in Rome in the winter of 1714–15, where Kent was acting as an agent for his purchases. He invited Kent back to England in 1719 to work as a decorative painter. Kent, living within the Burlington household, was employed in outfitting the Burlington House on Piccadilly and later the villa at Chiswick. In the late 1720s Kent also contributed to redesigning the gardens at Chiswick. These efforts eased Kent's transition into architecture in the early 1730s, which began in a serious way with the sumptuous plans for Holkham Hall, Norfolk (1734), probably in collaboration with Burlington.[36] In the same decade Kent also prepared classical schemes for a new treasury, a royal palace, and houses of parliament – schemes reviving the earlier advice of Shaftesbury.

Also contributing much to the Palladian cause was Isaac Ware (d. 1766), who had worked for Burlington and remained within his circle. His *Designs of Inigo Jones and Others* seems to have first appeared in 1735.[37] Three years later, Ware began publishing a new translation of *The Four Books of Andrea Palladio's Architecture*.[38] Burlington, who had long rejected Leoni's alterations to the master's text, was so concerned with accuracy in this new edition that he revised the translation himself and provided the financial support for its publication.

Perhaps the most active writer on classical architecture during these years was Robert Morris (1701–54), who stood at least at the fringe of the Burlington circle. Little is known of him aside from his extensive literary activities. He was a native of Twickenham and a "kinsman" of the architect Roger Morris, but he apparently built little. The dedication of his first book, *An Essay in Defence of Ancient Architecture; or a Parallel of the Ancient Buildings with the Modern* (1728), is addressed to all "Encouragers and Practitioners of Ancient Architecture," and he singles out Burlington, the earl of Pembroke, and Andrew Fountaine for special praise.[39] The title of his book, of course, alludes to Fréart de Chambray's earlier work as well as to the quarrel of the ancients and the moderns. Morris, with near religious fervor, is decidedly on the side of the former, although in a way quite different from the French position. The destruction wrought by the "Goths and Vandals" on those "unerring Rules, those perfect Standards of the Law of Reason and Nature" of classicism, was repaired by the architects of the Renaissance, of whom "Palladio bears away the Palm."[40] More recently, the "English Palladio" Jones and after him Wren rectified the situation in England. Central to Morris's theory is the notion of harmony, by which he means the "agreeable Symmetry and Concordance of every particular separate Member, centered and united in the Oeconomy of the Whole."[41] He champions an architecture ruled by absolute mathematical precision, not the "effeminate" search for "Novelty and Singleness."[42]

A similar respect for correct "Harmonik Proportions" occupies several of Morris's *Lectures on Architecture*, issued in 1734–6, even though now he is slightly less enamored with Palladio. His analysis is also less classical in its overall character. Though he still views proportions as essential, he lends equal importance to the "situation" of architecture as well as to the "convenience" of the thing to be designed.[43] Situation in his thinking is a broad concept, embracing not only the characteristics of a building's site or landscape but also the associational qualities that these evoke – the landscape's capacity to raise "such elevated *Ideas*."[44] Indeed, in his follow-up publication, *An Essay upon Harmony as it relates chiefly to Situation and Building* (1739), he describes situation as having "some influencial Force over the Faculties of the Soul." This harmony of nature is possible because "our Bodies are organized, to tally with those Graces that Nature produceth."[45] In effect, then, the Palladian ideals in Morris's theory undergo a subtle transmutation as the absolute and objective standards of classical beauty mingle with the associational and subjective ideals of emerging picturesque thought.

Another sign of the weakening of Palladianism in Britain around midcentury is the neoclassical influence emanating from France. This influence is discernible, at least, in Isaac Ware's *A Complete Body of Architecture* (1756), where Palladio remains the "best and greatest" fountainhead of practice even if he is not altogether beyond reproach.[46] Yet just as important in Ware's new compendium of classical theory – really the first of its kind in British literature – are the ideas of Laugier's *Essai sur l'architecture* (1753). Ware not only takes over many of Laugier's dicta but sometimes presents direct translations as his own without acknowledging his debt.[47] Columns, for instance, should be round, not twisted, detached from walls, without swelling, and without pedestals.[48] Ware also disdains arches but admits the use of pilasters, yet only in those rare instances where columns, the correct alternative, cannot be employed.[49]

He allows the diminution of columns but is opposed to optical adjustments; even the fluting of columns has "no foundation in reason" and is therefore a "false ornament." British architects may not know this, but they should observe the situation in France, where "there is not a fluted column of any order to be found in their latest and most correct works."[50] Ware further pleads for a "nobleness in simplicity," where "no ornament should be admitted but what is reasonable; and nothing is reasonable in architecture which is not founded on some principle of use."[51] The most surprising aspect of Ware's new interpretation of classicism is his warm acceptance of Perrault's coupled column, for here is an instance where "the moderns have made an absolute and great addition to these [ancient] rules, and an improvement upon them."[52]

A similar French influence is also clearly evident in the *Treatise on Civil Architecture* of William Chambers (1759).[53] This work of the French-trained Chambers (1723–96), a book written relatively early in his career, in fact defines the end of Palladianism in Britain. The treatise is succinct (originally intended as a small volume of designs) and is exquisitely illustrated with drawings; comments of a theoretical nature appear only in places where one would not normally expect them. His general tenor and position with respect to his contemporaries, however, is very evident. He makes abundant references to French and Italian authors, relies on precedents, but is liberal in his questioning of the same. Perrault is often cited as a model but is held in no higher esteem than his contemporary Blondel. Palladio is frequently invoked as a valuable source, but only in the third edition (1791) is he singled out for his "correct and elegant" style.[54] Chambers is decidedly cool toward the many strictures of Laugier, who "very cavalierly banishes at once all Pedestals, Pilasters, Niches, Arcades, Attics, Domes, etc. and it is only by special favour, that he tolerates Doors or Windows, or even Walls."[55]

In the two most revealing chapters of the *Treatise*, he comments on the issue of proportions. In the chapter on the Doric order, Chambers argues that "a strict attachment to harmonic relations seems to me unreasonable" because "different figures and situations" of viewing contribute to the overall effect and the sensations that arise from it.[56] Here, in fact, he invokes the proportional relativism of Edmund Burke (despite Burke's intrinsic antipathy to classicism), which also posits that "simple forms will operate more speedily than those that are complicated, and such a project will be sooner perceived than those that are more retired."[57] In a later chapter, he returns to this theme, again in an anticlassical vein, and argues that "pleasure or dislike" excited by proportions must "be ascribed either to prejudice, or to our habit of connecting ideas with the figures, rather than to any particular charm inherent in this, as some people are apt to imagine."[58] In a Perraultian fashion, he now takes the position: "Perfect proportion consists in a Medium between these Extremes: which Medium the rules of Architecture tend to fix."[59]

Interestingly, this is a position that he later emends. In the extensively revised third edition of 1791, he invokes the Perrault–Blondel dispute but is now unwilling to decide in favor one side or the other. Both the "maintainers of harmonick proportions" and the supporters of relative proportion, he insists, base their ideas of perfection on the same buildings of antiquity and their "infallible way of pleasing . . . which is so universally approved."[60] In the end, the proportional relativism that in 1759 he shares with Le Roy in France and Piranesi in Italy (both of whom he personally knew) now tends toward absolutism – at a time that support for absolute proportions elsewhere virtually disappears. To this oddity might be added the fact that in 1791 Chambers is more Palladian in spirit than he was in 1759.

3. The Origins of the Picturesque and the Sublime

The related notions of the "picturesque" and the "sublime" cut a broad swath across eighteenth-century British aesthetic theory, and their increasingly frequent invocations (either by word or idea) often mutually support one another. Together, they define an aesthetic that steers issues and interests away from more the traditional theme of beauty, and they therefore have far-reaching architectural implications. The notions of the picturesque and the sublime are intrinsically anticlassical in that they posit a concern with attributes altogether alien to such classical interests as geometry, symmetry, and proportion.

The word *pittoresk* (a bold and striking picture) appears in English as early as 1685, but the consistent development of the picturesque as a concept begins in earnest in the eighteenth century.[61] The word is frequently – and rightly – aligned with landscape theory, but it also suggests a more general aesthetic outlook that is almost innately British. As an early example of this outlook, consider John Vanbrugh's often-cited plea to the duchess of Marlborough in 1709 to preserve the old manor and chapel on the grounds of Blenheim Palace, "as they move more lively and pleasing Reflections (than History without their Aid can do) On

the Persons who have Inhabited them; On the Remarkable things which have been transacted in them, Or the extraordinary Occasions of Erecting them."[62] Vanbrugh goes on to point out the scenic effects of enhancing these ruins with natural features, such as "(principally Fine Yews and Hollys) Promiscuously Set to grow up in a Wild Thicket," such that "it wou'd make One of the Most Agreable Objects that the best of Landskip Painters can invent."[63]

The idea of the picturesque also appears early in the century in the writings of the earl of Shaftesbury and Joseph Addison. In a frequently cited passage of Shaftesbury's *Characteristics*, he expresses his preference "for things of a natural kind, where neither art nor the conceit or caprice of man has spoiled their genuine order by breaking in upon that primitive state." He continues, "Even the rude rocks, the mossy caverns, the irregular unwrought grottos and broken falls of waters, with all the horrid graces of the wilderness itself, as representing nature more, will be the more engaging and appear with a magnificence beyond the formal mockery of princely gardens."[64]

Allusions to the notions of the picturesque and the sublime abound in the writings of Shaftesbury's friend Joseph Addison, in particular, in his essays written for the *Spectator* in the summer of 1714. Subtitled "Pleasures of Imagination," they speak to the feelings "such as arise from visible Objects, either when we have them actually in our View, or when we call up their Ideas in our Minds by Paintings, Statues, Descriptions, or any the like Occasion."[65] Among these pleasures, Addison distinguishes between "Great, Uncommon, or Beautiful" ideas. Whereas he aligns the concept of beauty with such traditional aesthetic notions as symmetry, proportion, and an orderly disposition of bodies, he attributes the appearance of the great (the idea of the sublime) to "Largeness of a whole View, considered as one entire Piece."[66] Greatness in nature, "that rude kind of Magnificence," is evoked by broad expanses, such as of "a vast uncultivated Desart, of huge Heaps of Mountains, high Rocks and Precipices, or a wide Expanse of Waters."[67] In architecture he associates greatness with "the Bulk and Body of the Structure, or to the Manner in which it is built," and he gives the examples of the pyramids, the Tower of Babel, the Wall of China, and the Pantheon, where on first entering one's "Imagination is filled with something Great and Amazing."[68] The concept of the sublime as sketched by Addison, though rife with aesthetic possibilities, nevertheless had to wait until midcentury to find significant elaboration.

The idea of the picturesque develops somewhat earlier and is given life in Addison's many expressed preferences for

20. Grotto in Alexander Pope's Garden. From John Serle, *A Plan of Mr. Pope's Garden, as it was left at his death: with a Plan and Perspective View of the Grotto* (London, 1745).

"rough careless Strokes of Nature," "wide Fields of Nature," and "wild Scenes" in general:

Hence it is that we take Delight in a Prospect which is well laid out, and diversified with Fields and Meadows, Woods, and Rivers; in those accidental Landskips of Trees, Clouds and Cities, that are sometimes found in the Veins of Marble; in the curious Fret-work of Rocks and Grottos; and, in a Word, in any thing this hath such a Variety or Regularity as may seem the Effect of Design, in which we call the Works of Chance.[69]

The gardener Stephen Switzer, who earlier in his career had worked for John Vanbrugh at Castle Howard, conveys a similar idea of the picturesque in the three volumes of his *Ichnographia Rustica* (1718) simply by contrasting the "regular gardener" with the "natural gardener."[70]

Alexander Pope advanced the notion of the picturesque in several important ways. To start with, he helped to popularize the word itself, both in the notes to his translation of *The Iliad* (1715–25) and in his correspondence.[71] Just as important were his efforts to incorporate picturesque effects in the design of his own garden. Pope's family had moved to Chiswick in 1716, which introduced the poet into the circle of Burlington. In 1718 Pope leased his own villa along the banks of the Thames in nearby Twickenham, and after alterations on the house were complete, the poet turned his attention to altering the five acres of vegetation behind it, based on the premise that "all gardening is landscape

painting."[72] The garden's most notable feature was the underground grotto, which visitors entered from under the road from Hampton Court to London (Fig. 20). It seems to have been initially conceived as a classical nympheum but was later modified by Pope to take on the appearance of a cave in the tin mines of Cornwall.[73] The garden further contained a "mount" (or vantage point), a vineyard, an orangery, winding paths, an obelisk, and a shell temple.

Pope's efforts may have influenced Burlington, who began to relax the symmetry of his gardens at Chiswick in the late 1720s through a combination of serpentine paths, water, bridges, and cascades. Two of Burlington's models were Pliny's villas at Laurentinum and Tuscum, which Robert Castell had reconstructed in his *Villas of the Ancients Illustrated* (1728). In his remarks on the site of Tuscum, Castell reported that Roman landscape architects had passed through three stages of design. The first was the "rough Manner" of "little or no Alteration," and the second involved laying out gardens "by the Rule and Line."[74] In the third and most advanced stage, the architects departed from this formality and devised another style, "whose Beauty consisted in a close Imitation of Nature; where, tho' the Parts are disposed with the greatest Art, the Irregularity is still preserved."[75] This last style also employed the use of "Rocks, Cascades, and Trees, bearing their natural Forms."[76]

Similar ideas were also espoused in a contemporary study, *New Principles of Gardening* (1728) by Batty Langley

(1696–1751). This native of Twickenham opens his book by assailing the "stiff, regular Garden" and suggests instead "to copy, or imitate Nature" and "trace her Steps with the greatest Accuracy that can be."[77] Parts of his study draw upon traditional elements, but parts are genuinely novel. His section "Of the Situation and Disposition of Gardens in General" presages later developments with his emphasis on naturalness, variety, and "new Pleasures at every Turn."[78] On walks whose views cannot be extended, he recommends such terminations as "Woods, Forests, mishapen Rocks, strange Precipices, Mountains, old Ruins, and grand Buildings."[79] Groves should be planted with a "regular Irregularity."[80]

Still, picturesque theory originated within the Burlington circle and finds its first clear elaboration after 1730 in the work of William Kent (Fig. 21). The painter, as we have seen, was beginning at this time to turn his attention to architecture, and it seems that by the late 1720s he had participated in several of the landscape changes made on Burlington's estate in Chiswick. Kent is credited with the design of the theater (or orangery), which was completed in 1728. He made plans for a garden exedra (which was not built), and he is said to have designed the "wilderness" to the west of the villa, together with the rustic cascade. It was at Carleton House, Stowe, and Rousham, however, that he put his "new taste" in landscape design – much influenced by Pope at Twickenham – fully into practice. Writing to Lord Carlisle in 1734, Sir Thomas Robinson famously described Kent's innovation as working

without level or line. By this means I really think the 12 acres the Prince's garden consists of, is more diversified and of greater variety than anything of that compass I ever saw; and this method of gardening is the more agreeable, as when finished it has the appearance of beautiful nature, and without being told one would imagine art had no part in the finishing, and is, according to what one hears of the Chinese, entirely after their model for works of this nature, where they never plant straight lines or make regular design.[81]

At Stowe between 1731 and 1735 Kent relaxed an earlier garden scheme of Vanbrugh with "Elysian Fields." In a wooded valley with meandering paths and a stream he placed his "Temple of Ancient Virtue" (based on the Temple of Vesta at Tivoli), "Temple of Modern Virtue" (a picturesque ruin), and "Temple of British Worthies" (based on an exedra that he had earlier designed for Chiswick). At Rousham, beginning in 1737, Kent transformed another radial scheme into a wooded "Venus's Vale," complete with two rustic cascades and connected to the upper park and

21. William Kent, from *Artist Portraits: Scrapbook, 1600–1800*. Courtesy of the Collection Centre Canadien d'Architecture/Canadian Centre for Architecture, Montréal.

house by a seven-arch terrace, or "Praeneste." These two early masterpieces of picturesque garden design, however, would be eclipsed a little over a decade later by the younger Henry Hoare's idyllic transformation of his Palladian estate at Stourhead, Wiltshire, where a massive artificial lake was created to connect visually a series of Virgilian garden follies. Most were designed by the Burlington disciple Henry Flitcroft, including the miniature Pantheon and one folly based on the temple of Venus at Baalbek, recently published by Dawkins and Wood.

In an influential essay written later in the century, "History of the Modern Taste in Gardening" (1771), Horace Walpole (1717–97) credited Kent for being the first to give poetic form to the new landscape style: "He leaped the fence, and saw that all nature was a garden."[82] Kent's innovations included a mastery of perspective, painterly contrasts of light and shape, the natural grouping of trees, and select architectural terminations at points of interest. Above all, there was Kent's unaffected use of water, where "the gentle stream was taught to serpentize seemingly at its pleasure."[83]

Appreciation for the beauty of nature as well as the picturesque sensibilities to which it gave rise were augmented by two other fashions impressing themselves on British thought. One was a new interest in Gothic architecture, which ultimately would be viewed as quintessentially British; the other was a fascination with all things Chinese, emanating from British colonial interests. Both trends in fact would merge seamlessly with the picturesque movement.

Gothic design, as we have seen, never entirely disappeared from British architectural practice, even during the height of the Palladian movement. All Souls College, Oxford, designed by Hawksmoor in the Gothic style, was constructed between 1715 and 1734, and his two Gothic towers at Westminster were built even later, between 1735 and 1745. Pope was known to be curious about the Gothic style, and Kent too had a fascination with medievalism. In the 1730s, Kent designed additions to a medieval seat, Esher Place, with turrets, battlements, and Gothic windows. In 1732, the same architect rebuilt part of the Clock Court and the vaulted gatehouse at Hampton Court in the Gothic style. He later added Gothic screens to Westminster Hall (1738–39) and Gloucester Cathedral. Among his many follies was a mill converted into a Gothic oddity at Rousham.

Others were pursuing the same effects. On the grounds at Stowe, in 1741, James Gibbs designed a remarkable two-story Gothic temple in red ironstone. Efforts such as these may have prompted Batty Langley in the following year to publish his *Ancient Architecture, Restored and Improved by a Great Variety of Grand and Usefull Designs, entirely new, in the Gothick Mode, for the Ornamenting of Building and Gardens*.[84] In addition to supplying designs for Gothic temples, pavilions, and umbrellas for the intersection of walks in gardens, Langley delineated five classicized Gothic orders, suggesting a parity of this style with the classical style.

A new phase of the Gothic revival begins with Walpole's efforts at Strawberry Hill. This noted parliamentarian, son of the first earl of Orford, purchased a small house in Twickenham in 1748 and turned his attention to cultivating the grounds in a natural manner. The next year he decided on a series of expansions to the house in the Gothic style. Over the next quarter of a century he made significant additions to his "castle," completing the library and refectory in 1753; the gallery, round tower, and great cloister in 1761; the great north bedchamber in 1770; and the Beauclerc tower in 1776. The result was an amalgam of Gothic wings and turrets informally laid out but with increasingly correct Gothic detailing and designed by many of the best architects of the second half of the century. The medievalism of Strawberry Hill, whatever its other failings, defined the start of a Gothic revival movement in Britain that carried down through the nineteenth century.

Walpole in his essay on the modern taste in gardening also alluded to the contemporary fascination with China. Throughout Europe, in fact, interest in China had been expanding since the reports of Jesuit missionaries in the midseventeenth century. Chinese tea began to be imported to England around 1650. Chinese porcelain pottery became highly desirable, especially after the secret of porcelain manufacturing was rediscovered in the West in the first decades of the eighteenth century.

The Englishman William Temple (1628–99) was the first to discuss Chinese gardens in a remarkable essay entitled "Upon the Gardens of Epicurus; or, Of Gardening, in the Year 1685." In contrasting Chinese and European gardens, Temple noted the scorn that the Chinese held for the symmetries and regularities of the European style of gardening and described their contrary approach: "But their greatest reach of imagination is employed in contriving figures, where the beauty shall be great, and strike the eye, but without any order or disposition of parts that shall be commonly or easily observed."[85] Temple even gave the Chinese word for this artful contrivance, *Sharawadgi*. Interestingly, Temple counseled Europeans against adopting this approach to gardening – not because of its lack of beauty but because of the difficulty of achieving success.

Temple's remarks were undoubtedly the source for Addison's comments on Chinese gardening in 1714, when he noted that "they chuse rather to shew a Genius in Works of this Nature, and therefore always conceal the Art by which they direct themselves."[86] Another contribution to this growing interest in China was made by no less a Palladian figure than Burlington himself, when he, in 1724, purchased the engravings of the Jesuit missionary Matteo Ripa depicting Emperor Chien Hsi's palace and gardens at Jehol, outside of Peking. Some even speculated that it was these engravings that had led him to reconsider his own gardens at Chiswick.[87] In any case, Burlington's interest reflected a growing fascination with Chinese building forms, and in the 1740s and 1750s Chinese structures begin to find their way into various English gardens. At his Grove House, Old Windsor, Dickie Bateman in the 1740s added a Chinese bridge and a Chinese house to his other English and Gothic ornaments.[88] The chinoiserie fashion was sufficiently advanced by midcentury for William Halfpenny to publish *New Designs for Chinese Temples* (1750) and *Chinese and Gothic Architecture properly ornamented* (1752).

22. Plate from William Chambers, *Designs of Chinese Buildings, Furniture, Dresses, Machines and Utensils* (London, 1757).

The interest in China culminated in the design efforts and publications of William Chambers. This Swedish-born, French-trained architect, as we have seen, preceded his architectural training with a career in the Swedish East India Company, for which he made three trips to China and the Far East in the 1740s. Chambers's first book, *Designs of Chinese Buildings, Furniture, Dresses, Machines, and Utensils*, appeared in 1757 and played upon the current fascination with China (Fig. 22). It contains a chapter on the "Art of Laying Out Gardens Among the Chinese," in which Chambers lauds their efforts and affinities with English examples: "Nature is their pattern, and their aim is to imitate her in all her beautiful irregularities."[89] By this date Chambers had already built the "House of Confucius" in the gardens at Kew. He did so at the urging of Frederick, Prince of Wales, whom he had met in Paris in 1749, that is, as Chambers was beginning his architectural studies. Chambers later transformed the gardens at Kew between 1757 and 1763 – 1763 also being the year in which he published his *Plans, Elevations, Sections, and Perspective Views of the Gardens and Buildings at Kew in Surry*.[90] These picturesque gardens are still visited today for their exotic structures, perhaps the best known of which is Chambers's ten-story Great Pagoda,

erected in 1761. Chambers followed these efforts with *A Dissertation on Oriental Gardening* (1772), which appeared at a time when interest in China was beginning to wane.[91]

4. The Scottish and Irish Enlightenment

The intellectual transformation only vaguely reflected in British architectural theory in the 1750s is more apparent elsewhere during this decade – an aesthetic shift as subtle and as profound as that which was taking place in France. One early indication of this change is Allan Ramsay's "Dialogue on Taste," which appeared under the title *The Investigator* in 1755.[92] Ramsay, whom we encountered in the previous chapter as a protagonist in the Graeco-Roman debate, was a Scottish painter then living in Rome, and his essay vividly isolates the troubling aesthetic issues of the day. Ramsay wrote it on a nine-month visit to Edinburgh in 1754. It was conceived in connection with the founding of the Select Society, an Edinburgh debating society that he, together with David Hume (1711–76) and Adam Smith (1723–90), established in 1754 to address new artistic and scientific issues. The young architects Robert and

James Adam were also founding members. Ramsay was a close friend of Hume, and it is likely that he discussed the ideas expressed in the dialogue with the philosopher. It has even been suggested that the dialogue's principal skeptic, Colonel Freeman, was modeled on Hume.[93]

The theme of the dialogue is whether taste can have any absolute standard or whether it is simply a matter of individual preference. Freeman argues the latter position, essentially by insisting that the classical ideal of human beauty (the ideal soon to be reinstated by Winckelmann) was in fact not an enhancement or selection of beautiful features but a physiognomic typing of features predicated on eliminating everything outside of the norm. This averaging, as it were, was done to overcome the problem of the relativity of taste, or in other words to establish a neutral convention sufficiently abstract in its features to conform with everyone's particular mental impressions.

Architecturally, aesthetic relativism leads Ramsay to some interesting places. First there is his great respect for Gothic architecture – an appreciation he shares with Robert and James Adam.[94] Then there is his insistence on the impossibility of any universal standard. Comparing taste in architecture to cooking, he notes,

An Artist may, by a Palladian receipt alone, without any taste, form a very elegant Corinthian pillar; as a cook, without any palate, and by the help of the housewife's *vade mecum* only, make an unexceptional dish of *beef a la daube*. These rules are plainly no more than the analysis of certain things which custom has rendered agreeable; but do not point out to us any natural standard of beauty or flavour, by which such things, whether pillars or dishes, could have been originally contrived to answer the purpose of pleasing. I should be exceedingly glad to hear a reason why a Corinthian capital clapt upon its shaft upside-down should not become, by custom, as pleasing a spectacle as in the manner it commonly stands.[95]

Hume soon responded to the relativism of Ramsay's dialogue. In earlier writings he had defined beauty as a power "felt," arising from a pleasurable sentiment.[96] And in the early essay "On the Delicacy of Taste and Passion," he had noted the desirability of cultivating this delicacy of sentiment through exercises intended to strengthen judgment.[97] In his important essay of 1757, "Of the Standard of Taste," he followed this logic to its conclusion. "Beauty is not a quality in things themselves," he argued, "it exists merely in the mind which contemplates them; and each mind perceives a different beauty."[98] This subjectivist formulation would seem to preclude the possibility of universal standards or rules for beauty, but this is actually not the case for Hume.

Those "finer emotions of the mind" require rather "the concurrence of many favorable circumstances" coming together or being conjoined, for which one needs an inherent "delicacy of imagination," "practice in a particular art," "a mind free from all prejudice," as well as "good sense."[99] What effectively distinguishes the judgments of people possessing such attributes from pretenders are two things. The first is the distance of time, by which the appreciation of Homer in Athens and Rome later becomes mirrored in Paris and London; the second is the fact that "the general principles of taste are uniform in human nature."[100] The philosophical problem of mediating both the subjectivity and universality of taste will later become the focus of Immanuel Kant's second moment of beauty.[101]

Following closely on the heels of Ramsay's "Dialogue on Taste" and Hume's "Of the Standard of Taste" was Edmund Burke's *A Philosophical Inquiry into the Origin of our Ideas of the Sublime and Beautiful*. This book, monumental in its influence, appeared in 1757, only a few months after Hume's essay, and the Irishman Burke (1729–97) in fact seems to have held back his introductory essay, "On Taste," until the second edition (published in 1759) to respond more fully to Hume's position. Burke also noted in the preface to the first edition that the work had lain substantially complete since 1753.

The position articulated in Burke's *Philosophical Inquiry* is groundbreaking for several reasons. First, he appends to the sensationalist strain apparent in British thought since Locke – sensationalism defined as the dependence of mental ideas on the senses – the argument that ideas of beauty are caused by the body's neurological response to objects rather than to mental operations alone. Second, whereas Hume had maintained skepticism with respect to judgments of taste by arguing that they are in fact displayed only by people possessing a superior delicacy of imagination, Burke takes a much clearer position. He seeks to isolate "some invariable and certain laws" underlying judgments of taste, which he defines as "that faculty or those faculties of the mind, which are affected with, or which form a judgement of, the works of imagination and the elegant arts."[102] Burke now strips the notions of the sublime and the beautiful of all their classical trappings and considers them as parallel and complementary aesthetic categories.

The notion of the sublime, as we have seen, had first been developed by Addison through the companion idea of greatness but then had received little conceptual elaboration. The word *sublimity* itself had been prevalent in European thought for almost a century, finding broad discussion, for instance, in Nicolas Boileau-Despréaux's 1674 translation of and commentary on the treatise *On the Sublime* by Longinus.[103] The term was first employed in a literary sense, to mean a "majesty of words," but later it came to mean any feeling of emotional intensity. Addison alluded to the new concept in 1714 by distinguishing the "Great" from the "Beautiful," and Hume also related the idea of the sublime to "distance" and its effect on exciting passions.[104]

Another important step in the development of its meaning is found in Alexander Gerard's *An Essay on Taste*, published in 1759. Gerard's lengthy consideration of taste, however, was actually written in 1756 for the Select Society of Edinburgh, for which he won the first of its annual prizes. Gerard defines "grandeur or sublimity" as "a still higher and nobler pleasure [than novelty], by means of a sense appropriated to the perception of it; while meanness renders any object to which it adheres, disagreeable and distasteful. Objects are sublime, which possess *quantity*, or amplitude, and *simplicity*, in conjunction."[105] Examples of natural phenomena that excite sublime emotions are the Alps, the Nile, the oceans, the heavens, "or the immensity of space uniformly extended without limit or termination."[106]

Burke in his *Philosophical Inquiry* conceives of sublimity as an aesthetic category itself, different from beauty. If the "beautiful" can be defined as "that quality or those qualities in bodies, by which they cause love, or some passion similar to it," the sublime is "whatever is fitted in any sort to excite the ideas of pain and danger, that is to say, whatever is in any sort terrible, or is conversant about terrible objects, or operates in a manner analogous to terror."[107] His definition is not as startling as it may first appear. Such pain is only a surrogate pain or terror, in that the body is not actually placed in terrifying circumstances but responds with exhilaration to the idea of danger when standing, for instance, at the edge of a cliff. Beauty, by contrast, is caused by things with attributes of smallness, smoothness, gradual variation, delicacy, clear and bright colors.

What makes Burke's distinction so important for architectural theory are the nuances of his system. Fitness to purpose, for instance, can bear no relation to beauty because fitness implies the intervention of reason beyond sense impressions. Under the experience of sublimity he also discusses magnitude, difficulty, and light in architectural terms. Magnitude concerns the effect of a building dimension, whereas Stonehedge serves as the example for difficulty; the last is a sublime work that required immense force and labor. Under the heading of "Light in BUILDING," Burke speaks of dark and gloomy spaces producing the idea of the sublime and also of the need for striking transitions of light, "when therefore you enter a building, you cannot pass into a greater light than you had in the open air; to go into one some few degrees less luminous, can make only a trifling change; but to make the transition thoroughly striking, you ought to pass from the greatest light, to as much darkness as is consistent with the uses of architecture."[108] Not only did William Chambers and John Soane study this passage, but such ideas would shortly find their way to France.[109]

Finally, Burke takes on the issue of proportion squarely and entirely apart from the classical tradition. Proportion too cannot be a cause of beauty, he argues, because it relates to convenience and, more importantly, because pleasing proportions could not have been derived from observations of nature or from proportional ratios of the human figure. Referring to Leonardo da Vinci's drawing of a man with outstretched arms within a circle and square, Burke noted,

But it appears very clearly to me, that the human figure never supplied the architect with any of his ideas. For in the first place, men are very rarely seen in this strained posture; it is not natural to them; neither is it at all becoming. Secondly, the view of the human figure so disposed, does not naturally suggest the idea of a square, but rather of a cross; as that large space between the arms and the ground must be filled with something before it can make anybody think of a square. Thirdly, several buildings are by no means of the form of that particular square, which are notwithstanding planned by the best architects, and produce an effect altogether as good, and perhaps a better. And certainly nothing could be more unaccountably whimsical, than for an architect to model his performance by the human figure, since no two things can have less resemblance or analogy, than a man and a house or temple; do we need to observe, that their purposes are entirely different?[110]

The radicality of Burke's position is even better appreciated by comparing the *Philosophical Inquiry* with the nearly contemporary *Elements of Criticism* (1762) of Lord Kames (1696–1782). Taste, for Kames, occupies a middle place in human experience, between organic and intellectual pleasures. Regarding proportion, Kames is critical, on the one hand, of strict mathematical relations, but he is opposed, on the other hand, to proportional relativism, which in his view neglects the human delight in perceiving proportions, regularity, order, and propriety. His position is that there is a range of agreeable proportions for any given situation, for "if these proportions had not originally been agreeable, they could not have been established by custom."[111]

By the time Kames published his work, the issues with which he had been concerned were already beginning to be decided in practice. They are found to a certain extent in the architectural theory of Chambers, who initially shared Burke's views on the relative nature of proportions. They are even more apparent in the work of Robert Adam (1728–92) and his brother James (1732–94). Both were close friends of Ramsay and Hume, and both knew Kames as well. Robert's friendship with Hume dates from around 1752, which is significant, as Hume at this time was something of a social outcast, having twice been rejected for university positions because of his antireligious and skeptical views. Also in that year Hume obtained the post of keeper of the Advocates's Library in Edinburgh, which is why the meetings of the Select Society were held in that venue.

Robert Adam's friendship with Ramsay is better documented. It begins in earnest in Rome. Ramsay left Edinburgh in the summer of 1754 for his second stay in the south, and Adam embarked on his grand tour in October of the same year. Ramsay invited Adam to his weekly "conversations" in Rome, which attracted a number of artists – a type of social event that Adam, emulating Ramsay, soon began to put on himself.[112] They sketched and traveled together in Italy, and in 1757 they even returned part of the way home together. Robert was also close to Clérisseau, a friend of Le Roy's who had been expelled from the French Academy in Rome. Clérisseau had been briefly employed by Chambers to teach him drawing, and Adam hired him full time in the same capacity. Clérisseau, in turn, introduced Adam to Piranesi, who seems to have taken a genuine liking to the Scotsman. Piranesi frequently joined Adam and Clérisseau on their sketching expeditions around Rome, and he attended Adam's weekly soirees. In the frontispiece to Piranesi's *Antichità romane*, Adam and Ramsay were both given honorary tombs along the Via Appia. Afterwards, Piranesi, after his bitter break with Lord Charlemont, dedicated his *Ichnographia* – his stupendous six-plate map of Rome – to Adam. The dedication did not come without a price, however, for Adam in turn agreed to purchase "eighty or a hundred copies of it."[113]

One of the highlights of Adam's stay in the south was his excursion to Spalatro (Split, now in Croatia) to record the ruins of Diocletian's palace, a trip hastily arranged near the end of his stay. In the company of Clérisseau and two other draftsmen, Adam hired a felucca and sailed from Venice in July 1757. After delays in obtaining permission and some hesitation by the local military governor, Adam directed the team in surveying the imperial Roman palace

in a stay that lasted five weeks. The resulting text, *Ruins of the Palace of the Emperor Diocletian at Spalatro in Dalmatia*, did not appear until 1764, in part because Adam wanted to wait for Stuart and Revett's proposed work on Greece to appear.

Another reason for the delay in publication was the rapid success Adam would find back in London, to which he returned in 1757 with bundles of drawings and two carefully selected Italian draftsmen. The "Adam style" was already beginning to take concrete form before James left for his three-year tour of the South in 1760, and its elements have been extensively discussed.[114] It is a highly refined compositional and decorative style of a kind not seen in Britain before, featuring varied geometric spaces, detached interior columns and columnar screens, abundant grotesques, and a vivid polychromy of detailed stucco work, paint, variegated marbles, and ormolu (Fig. 23). Like Chambers, Robert Adam gave preference to the Roman past, but the Adam brothers also expanded the historical palette to include motifs from Etruria, Pompeii, Herculaneum, the Renaissance, Burlington Palladianism, and even Vanbrugh. To this must be added their personal design proclivities, which can only be described as *rocaille*.

Some of the ideas underlying their conception of architecture can be gleaned from the preface to *The Works in Architecture of Robert and James Adam*, published in three volumes between 1773 and 1822. This preface, however, has an earlier origin. In 1762 James Adam, in correspondence with Kames, began an essay in which he spoke of the possibility of a "sentimental" architecture, that is, one appealing primarily to the senses, and it has been suggested that his comments sprang from discussions with Robert as far back as 1758.[115] This seems likely, because some of James's unpublished passages find their way into their joint preface to *The Works*. Most important is their desire to create "greater movement and variety" in their designs, concepts they define in a footnote:

Movement is meant to express, the rise and fall, the advance and recess, with other diversity of form, in the different parts of a building, so as to add greatly to the picturesque of the composition. For the rising and falling, advancing and receding, with the convexity and concavity, and other forms of the great parts, have the same effect in architecture, that hill and dale, fore-ground and distance, swelling and sinking have in landscape: That is, they serve to produce an agreeable and diversified contour, that groups and contrasts like a picture, and creates a variety of light and shade, which gives great spirit, beauty and effect to the composition.[116]

23. Robert and James Adam, ceiling of music room of Sir Watkin Williams Wynn, Saint James Square, London. From *The Works in Architecture of the Late Robert and James Adam* (London, 1822).

The note further singles out the dome of St. Peter's, the college and church of the Four Nations in Paris, and the "genius" of Vanbrugh, whose Blenheim Palace and Castle Howard serve "as great examples of these perfections."[117]

A Humean aesthetic is also evident in these pages. Architecture, which has no direct standards in nature, must be improved by "correct taste, and by diligent studies of the beauties exhibited by great masters," for it is only through such effort and meditation that "one becomes capable of distinguishing between what is graceful and what is inelegant; between that which possesses, and that which is destitute of harmony."[118] Hence taste is entirely subjective but at its highest level is acquired only through training and experience.

In the preface to the second volume, published in 1779, we find the two Adams spiritedly affirming Piranesi's view that the Romans acquired their architectural knowledge from the Etruscans long before their contact with the Greeks.[119] Their adherence to this position reinforces the fact that Robert Adam, among all of his contemporaries, was the most

baroque, the most eclectic, and the most profoundly affected by the artistic beliefs of the great Italian artist.

5. Picturesque Theory

The aesthetics of neoclassicism, which flowered in France in the last third of the eighteenth century, remained in Britain something imported from abroad. In the end it would fail to meld with evolving British sensibilities, as the remarks of the Adam brothers – overt classicists – make clear. The long-term direction of British architecture rather lay with an evolving picturesque tradition, which came together as a theory in the last decades of the century.

The great picturesque gardens of the first half of the century achieved an early synthesis in the work of another Scotsman, Lancelot "Capability" Brown (1716–83). Brown shifted his operations to England in 1739 and two years later was hired by Lord Cobham as the head gardener at Stowe. Thus he can be seen as a protégé of Kent, who was charged with transforming these gardens during this period, but Brown also developed his own style. Upon the death of Cobham in 1749, Brown began to take on other jobs, and by the middle of the next decade he was the most sought after gardener in Britain, ultimately planning hundreds of gardens in every corner of the island. His style has been called purist, in the sense that he preferred to work solely with the elements of nature – water, trees, gentle open spaces, and natural vistas. He avoided architectural and sculptural elements, and his pathways were always serpentine and followed the contours of the landscape. Rolling surfaces of grassland were meticulously manicured by combinations of concave and convex surfaces. An artificial lake, formed by damning a creek, was also a typical feature of his work.

Brown's work was admired by Walpole but also by the parliamentarian Thomas Whately, whose *Observations on Modern Gardening* (1770) was very much influenced by it. Whately seeks to elevate gardening to a place among the liberal arts, treating it as not unrelated to landscape painting, and he analyzes the modern garden under its five "materials": ground, wood, water, rocks, and buildings. He placed great importance on the sentimental or associational ideas evoked by landscapes and in particular the ideal and moral attributes of character. The term *character*, in fact, epitomizes the gist of his theory, and when his treatise was translated into French in 1771, it not only brought the achievements of the "l'art des jardins anglois" to the Continent but also influenced the theory of character of Le Camus de Mézières.

Whately used the word *picturesque* only sparingly and still in the sense of pictorial composition. William Gilpin (1724–1804) defined it similarly in 1768 as "a term expressive of that peculiar kind of beauty, which is agreeable in a picture."[120] But when his *Observations on the River Wye* appeared in 1782 – the first of his many guidebooks to the countryside of Britain – Gilpin could subtitle his essay "Relative chiefly to Picturesque Beauty." Gilpin had made various excursions around the island in the 1760s and 1770s, specifically to engage in and ultimately to publicize a new aesthetic pursuit, "that of not barely examining the face of a country; but of examining it by the rules of picturesque beauty: that of not merely describing; but of adapting the description of natural scenery to the principles of artificial landscape; and of opening the sources of these pleasures, which are derived from the comparison."[121] For Gilpin, nature takes on a quasi-religious complexion, as shown, for instance, in his description of Goodrich Castle: "A reach of the river, forming a noble bay, is spread before the eye. The

bank, on the right, is steep, and covered with wood; beyond which a bold promontory shoots out, crowned with a castle, rising among the trees."[122] Gilpin terms this scene "*correctly picturesque*, which is seldom the character of a purely natural scene."[123] The artist, however, "lays down his little rules therefore, which he calls the *principles of picturesque beauty*, merely to adapt such diminutive parts of nature's surfaces to his own eye, as come within its scope."[124] Gilpin also illustrated his verbal descriptions with a series of soft aquatints, drawings conveying an almost startling impressionist quality.

The various guidebooks of Gilpin form the transition to the fuller development of picturesque theory that takes place toward the end of the century in the work of Humphry Repton (1752–1818), Uvedale Price (1747–1829), and Richard Payne Knight (1750–1824).

Repton became the century's most important practitioner of picturesque gardening. He came to the profession somewhat late in life, but he was immediately successful and by the mid-1790s had built a practice that in the number of commissions rivaled that of Brown, whose general principles he sought to emulate. Part of the reason for his success was his great skill as a watercolorist and his ability to sketch out proposed views, part was the professionalism of his approach and the practicality of his designs and working relationships. At the same time, he was not an articulate thinker or theorist, and his presumed want of "attentive study of what the higher artists have done" led to a spirited dispute with Price and Knight over the artistic success of his endeavors.[125]

Repton's *Sketches and Hints on Landscape Gardening* (1795) is a practical guide to his work. One of the more interesting parts of the book is the appendix, where he responds to the attacks of Price and Knight by presenting twenty-one "Sources of Pleasure in Landscape Gardening." These include such general attributes as congruity, utility, order, symmetry, variety, simplicity, and contrast. He defines "association" as "one of the most impressive sources of delight; whether excited by local accident . . . the remains of antiquity . . . but more particularly by that personal attachment to long known objects."[126] The "Picturesque effect" is another of these sources, as it "furnishes the gardener with breadth of light and shade, forms of groups, outline, colouring, balance of composition, and occasional advantage from roughness and decay, the effect of time and age."[127] It has been noted that the word *picturesque* for Repton still means the pictorial, the wild, and the rugged in nature – the meaning suggested by Gilpin.[128] Thus he did not view the picturesque as necessarily a good thing in landscape design, and he was still somewhat traditional in his handling of nature. Picturesque effects in architecture, by contrast, mean a certain irregularity in plan or compositional outline that does enhance the character of the design.

More ambitious as an undertaking was Repton's *Observations on the Theory and Practice of Landscape Gardening* (1803), although the ideas expressed there were not much advanced. "*Relative fitness* or UTILITY, and *comparative proportion* or SCALE" now become the cornerstone of his theory. He defines relative fitness as "the comfort, the convenience, the character, and every circumstance of a place that renders it the desirable habitation of man, and adapts it to the uses of each individual proprietor."[129] Such ideas stand in stark contrast to the pictorial or poetic character of Repton's designs, which include the naturalist attributes of Brown's model. As far as architecture is concerned, Repton preferred the Gothic style over what he deemed to be the Greek alternative.

It thus remained for Price and Knight to pull together the elements of picturesque thinking into a coherent theory. Price's *Essays on the Picturesque*, which first appeared in 1794, actually preceded Repton's book. Price, a parliamentarian and classical scholar (translator of Pausanias), also implemented his landscape ideas at his own country estate in Herefordshire. What knowledge he lacked in the specifics of horticulture, he more than made up for by his command of landscape painting, especially the works of Claude Lorraine, Nicolas Poussin, and Jean-Antoine Watteau. Price, in fact, was following the lead of Whately and Joshua Reynolds, who in his thirteenth discourse before the Royal Academy in 1786 had sought to elevate gardening into an art form.[130] This painterly perspective was the basis of Price's feud with Repton, who conversely emphasized the differences between the two arts. Price was, in general, unrelenting in his assault on the tradition of Kent and Brown, whose formulae Price regarded as both monotonous and unnatural because they had substituted a new formality of regular curves for the geometrical formality of older gardens. Price was contemptuous of the serpentine driveways, walks, and canals of Brown. And he opposed as well the "clump" or the massing of trees of similar age and size at near equal distances and without their natural undergrowth.[131] Price insisted instead on the importance of time and accident in nature, and he championed what his opponents referred to as gardening by neglect, that is, an approach wholly natural in the diversity, intricacy, and haphazardness of its details.

Price's most important contribution, however, lay in his effort to add the "picturesque" to the system of Burke as a third aesthetic category alongside the "beautiful" and the "sublime." The picturesque, in his view, not only differs from beauty but arises from qualities almost diametrically opposed to those of beauty. Burke had said that the two most important attributes of beauty were smoothness and gradual variation. Price defines the picturesque as caused by "roughness, and of sudden variation, joined to that of irregularity," and in addition he cites the attributes of age or decay, lack of symmetry, and autumnal hues.[132] The architectural ruin epitomizes the notion of the picturesque for Price; he exalts broken or fragmented forms, weather stains, partial incrustations such as vines and moss, and an overall irregularity of effects. If sublimity has to do with greatness of dimension, awful and terrifying objects that evoke the idea of astonishment, the picturesque can be found in the smallest or largest of objects, in the light and playful, in the shaping and disposition of boundaries. Invoking Burke's physiology, Price describes the picturesque as a neurological reaction occupying a midway position between the beautiful and the sublime. A beautiful scene, for Burke, relaxes the nervous fibers of the body below their normal tone; a sublime image conversely stretches the same fibers beyond their normal tone. Price argues that the picturesque creates a natural tone between languor and tension and "that the effect of the picturesque is curiosity."[133] This physiological explanation, however, is presented very succinctly, and the psychological or associational basis of his descriptions remains the more prominent.[134]

In 1798 Price supplemented his *Essays on the Picturesque* with three new texts, the last of which, "An Essay on Architecture and Buildings," applies the concept to architectural design. Perhaps its most interesting aspect is Price's effort to resurrect the reputation of John Vanbrugh as the most eminent of Britain's "*architetti-pittori*," that is, as an architect who studies landscapes and buildings and applies to both the principles of painting. Vanbrugh's masterpiece in this regard is Blenheim Palace, a "bold and difficult design" that unites the "magnificence of Grecian architecture" with the "picturesqueness of the Gothic," whose "various bold projections of various heights," "variety of outline," "violation of rules," "neglect of purity," and "new and striking effects" set a worthy standard for picturesque design.[135] Price's remarks, as the author himself notes, again derive from the thirteenth discourse of Joshua Reynolds, who lauds Vanbrugh as "an Architect who composed like a Painter."[136] Price also ventures some fascinating conclusions regarding design itself. Not only should a building be consciously designed to harmonize with the landscape, but picturesque architecture should also promote irregular and asymmetrical additions and a new flexibility of plan, allowing one to draw "an idea of comfort from it."[137] Of buildings in the various styles, Price finds Gothic structures and old castles to be the most picturesque, because of their "breaks and divisions, and the parts highly and profusely enriched."[138] Hence the implications of Walpole's Strawberry Hill have been canonized, and Price's book forges an invaluable passage to nineteenth-century theory.

Richard Payne Knight, a neighbor of Price in Herefordshire, shared a similar enthusiasm for the picturesque, and his *Analytical Inquiry into the Principles of Taste* (1805) is one of the crowning achievements of eighteenth-century British thought.[139] The grandson of a Shropshire mine owner, Knight inherited 10,000 acres in Herefordshire upon coming of age in 1771 and immediately began building his own turreted and crenellated castle, Downton, high above the river Teme. By this date he had made his first tour of Italy, but in 1776 he embarked on another – this time to visit Paestum and Sicily. In his diary of 1777, he describes the tints of Paestum's ruins as "at once harmonious, pleasing, and picturesque."[140] The second trip earned him a membership in the Society of Dilettanti, and when Knight returned to Downton, he pursued a life of antiquities collecting and philological scholarship. Like Winckelmann, he was fascinated with the ancient cult of Priapus, or phallic worship.[141] Later, around 1805, he became a somewhat discredited protagonist in the dispute surrounding the Elgin Marbles, when he argued that they were Roman restorations and scarcely worth the £35,000 that the Earl of Elgin was asking from the British Museum.

In any case, his main importance lies with his authorship of the *Analytic Inquiry*. Ten years before its publication, in the second edition of his poem *The Landscape*, he had questioned Price's sharp distinction between the beautiful and the picturesque as well as the separate category of the sublime.[142] Knight's approach to the problem in fact was less Burkean and more Humean in its underlying reasoning, in that he chose to carry out his analyses under the headings of sensation, association of ideas, and passions. A key (Burkean) assumption in the first part, on sensation, is the premise that sight is nothing other than "impressions or irritations upon the optic nerves,"[143] from which Knight deduces that "the beauties of light, shade, and colour are all that affect the eye, or make any impression upon organic sense and perception."[144] Nevertheless, the experience of the picturesque is psychological: It is a quality arising not from the objects themselves but rather from the habituated ideas that are prompted by optical stimulation. The picturesque is thus an acquired taste – what he terms an "improved perception" – such as when a musician learns to tune an instrument or a vintner develops the ability to distinguish between the chemical components of a wine. The picturesque is apparent only to people who have become conversant with the art of painting, although it scarcely transfers to an appreciation of nature. Further, the picturesque cannot be analyzed because it lacks rules. Claude's landscapes with ruins are picturesque, but so are his painterly scenes of quays and palaces. Symmetry plays no role in its appearance, and neither does proportion, because both are arbitrary conventions formed by association. And the picturesque exists alongside other characters such as the "sculpturesque" and "grottoesque" and has finer modalities such as the classical, romantic, and pastoral.[145] In responding to criticisms made by his friend Price, Knight insists that the ideas of the beautiful and the picturesque are not synonymous, and it is clear that he thinks the latter is little more than a category of the former.

Still, Knight's definition of the picturesque is not entirely open-ended, for when he turns his attention to architecture, he enters entirely original terrain. His discussion centers on his criticism that modern architecture is "too rigid" in its adherence to Greek and Gothic models, shown by the Italianized villas of Jones and Palladio planted across Britain and the recent trend toward building "pure Gothic" castles and cathedrals. But what are the rules, proportions, and definitions of Gothic works? Historically, Knight argues, Gothic is a late style that emerged only after the fall of Rome, although such elements as battlements and pointed arches are much older than either Greece or Rome. Hence Gothic architecture is but a corruption of the sacred architecture of the Greeks and Romans, with a mixture of Moorish or Saracenesque elements harking back to Egypt, Persia, and India.[146] This is not necessarily a bad thing, because, according to Knight, the pristine Greek temple should be banned as a model for modern times owing to its feigned regularity. Essentially, the mixing of Greek and Gothic forms that he first offers by way of intimation (already melded in vernacular Italian practice and further sanctioned by the paintings of Claude and Poussin) suggests a suitable direction for contemporary practice.

Fifty pages later, Knight's picturesque and eclectic model becomes more explicit when he speaks of his own castle at Downton: "It is now more than thirty years since the author of this inquiry ventured to build a house, ornamented with what are called Gothic towers and battlements without, and with Grecian ceilings, columns, and entablatures within; and though his example has not been much followed, he has every reason to congratulate himself upon the success of the experiment."[147] In a thinly veiled swipe at the theories of Repton and Walpole's Gothic manor at Strawberry Hill, Knight lauds the recent tendency to adapt the forms of country houses to the character of the surrounding landscape. Yet he states one caveat. Ideas of irregularity in plan have been drawn from "the barbarous structures of the middle ages," and worse, ornaments and proportions are servilely copied from "the rude and unskilful monuments of those times," with the result that these houses are "heavy, clumsy, and gloomy within."[148] Knight, by contrast, seeks to join the advantages of the picturesque object with elegant and convenient interiors, and to do so while still avoiding "the appearance of trick and affectation." Therefore, he arrives at a position very close to that of Piranesi:

The best style of architecture for irregular and picturesque houses, which can now be adopted, is that mixed style, which characterizes the buildings of Claude and the Poussins: for as it is taken from models, which were built piece-meal, during many successive ages; and by several different nations, it is distinguished by no particular manner of execution, or class of ornaments; but admits of all promiscuously, from a plain wall or buttress, of the roughest masonry, to the most highly wrought Corinthian capital: and, in a style professedly miscellaneous, such contrasts may be employed to heighten the relish of beauty, without disturbing the enjoyment of it by any appearance of deceit or imposture.[149]

Thus in Knight's interpretation of the picturesque, one can employ battlements, pinnacles, and flying buttresses and still safeguard the character of the landscape and meet modern needs. The lone British architect, in his view, who was successful in pursuing such a goal was Vanbrugh – a view soon to be shared by one prominent architect.

6. John Soane

Until recently, it was difficult to consider John Soane (1753–1837) a picturesque architect in any sense. He was trained as a classical architect at the newly founded Royal Academy in London, made a conventional tour of the South, was decidedly Francophilic in most of his tastes, and became a Royal Academician. But now, owing in large part to the efforts of David Watkin, we know much more of his mind and personality than before.[150] If his practice was ruled by his single-minded desire to craft a modern architecture from the

eclectic tendencies of his time, his theoretical efforts show him as an Enlightenment thinker *par excellence*: the erudite and eccentric synthesizer of various and sundry currents of eighteenth-century British and Continental thought. Soane, within his historical context, is altogether unique in his intellectual bearing.

Soane differs from his British predecessors, in fact, in almost every way. The son of a Berkshire builder, he came to his profession without social standing or other privilege of rank and wealth. At the age of fifteen he joined the office of George Dance as an errand boy. Three years later he had shown sufficient progress in drafting to be accepted into the newly founded British Royal Academy, which maintained a small architectural program. With the gold medal in hand for his design of a triumphal bridge in 1776, Soane began his much anticipated tour of the South. Passing through Paris he was excited by the contemporary works of Ledoux, Boullée, Gondoin, and Jean-Rodolphe Perronet. In Rome he met Piranesi only a few months before the artist's death. He visited, like so many others, the ancient sites around Naples, Paestum, and Sicily. In the tradition of Chambers and the Adam brothers, he focused his efforts in Italy on meeting English noblemen in the hope of future commissions, but he met with little success. When he returned to England prematurely in 1780, it was because of what proved to be the empty promise of a commission by Frederick Hervey, the Bishop of Derry.

Soane's career started very slowly in the 1780s. He was able to cobble together a number of jobs doing additions and renovations of estates during this decade, among them Letton Hall, Shotesham Hall, and Langley Park in Norfolk; Malbery Hall in Warwickshire; Chillington in Staffordshire; and Mulgrave Castle on the Yorkshire coast. Slowly but surely he built a private practice, aided by the encouragement of such well-placed friends as Thomas Pitt, his reputation for producing economic designs, his attention to construction details, and a good marriage (from which he would eventually inherit financial independence). By the time he had secured an appointment as surveyor for the Bank of England in 1788, his professional success was assured.

More interesting, however, are other aspects of his development. To begin with, his *Designs in Architecture*, an illustrated book of fanciful copperplates for "decorating Pleasure-Grounds, Parks, Forests, etc.," was published in 1778. It was prepared, in fact, before he left for Italy.[151] Its various tearooms, temples, casinos, and garden structures are the work of a young architect with a penchant for experimentation, eroticism, and imaginative flights. Designs such as those for a herm-supported "Garden Seat" and "Gothic Summer House" are entirely whimsical, while the "Elevation of a Diary House in the Moresque Stile" features a pair of obelisks, a full-size statue of a cow mounted over the entrance, and a series of bulls' heads placed atop urns at ground level.

A similar playfulness is seen in his *Sketches in Architecture* (1793), in which Soane presents watercolored renderings of rustic and rural designs, often with an odd marrying of features, such as thatch roofs with classical symmetry (Fig. 24).[152] Occasionally he would even persuade a client to build one of his follies, such as the brick barn with coupled brick columns "à la Paestum" that he constructed for Henry Greswold Lewis in 1798.

Equally unrevealing of his mindset is his *Plans, Elevations, and Sections of Buildings* (1788), which documents his designs for country houses. Soane prefaces this monograph with a somewhat pompous introduction in which he waxes decorously on the duties and responsibilities of the architect by citing passages (in Latin and Italian) from Vitruvius, Martial, Horace, Pliny, and Alberti. After informing us that architecture is a "coy mistress that can only be won by unwearied assiduities, and constant attention," Soane ventures a few gems of theoretical speculation.[153] "Ornaments," he insists, "are to be cautiously introduced; those ought only to be used that are simple, applicable and characteristic of their situations: they must be designed with regularity and be perfectly distinct in their outlines."[154] Proper caution precludes the "puerile and disgusting" practice of decorating English houses with such antique emblems as "skulls of victims, ram heads and other ornaments peculiar to their religious ceremonies."[155] Despite his own advice, he nevertheless allows himself to place a cow in the pedimental field of his Doric-inspired "Dairy at Hammels."[156]

Soane also speaks here of Gothic architecture. By "Gothic" he means not "those barbarous jumbles of undefined forms in modern imitations of Gothic architecture: but the light and elegant examples in many of our cathedrals, churches, and other public buildings, which are so well calculated to excite solemn, serious and contemplative ideas, that it is almost impossible to enter such edifices without feeling the deepest awe and reverence."[157] King's College chapel in Cambridge, with its "boldness and mathematical knowledge," presents "a glorious example." Soane concludes this passage with a stirring plea for the recording and preservation of these works.

One can only begin to discern the breadth of Soane's theoretical outlook, however, by turning to the formal lectures he gave at the Royal Academy; these start in 1810 and run – with a few interruptions – until 1836. The fascinating details surrounding their origin are now known, and copious annotations penned inside the books of his extensive architectural library testify to his extraordinary efforts in preparing them.

Soane's connections with the Royal Academy were longstanding. He regularly exhibited (with few exceptions) at the annual exhibitions from 1772 onward, and in 1795 he gained associate membership to the institution through the successful lobbying of his friend and former mentor George Dance. The death of William Chambers in the following year left a vacancy within the first class of the Academy, and on the very day of Chambers' demise, Soane, somewhat incautiously, sought to secure political support for his appointment. It nevertheless took him six years to defeat Joseph Bonomi (1739–1808) and become a full member. Soane's conflicts with other academicians soon surfaced, including one in which he acted ungraciously toward Dance. The latter held the professorship of architecture and had been charged since 1798 with delivering the annual cycle of lectures on architecture to students and the public. But Dance had failed to deliver them, chiefly because of his heavy workload as a municipal architect. In 1805 Soane began to lobby privately for Dance's resignation from the post. Dance found out and resigned toward the end of the year, embittered by the awkward circumstances in which he found himself placed through the private efforts of his friend. Soane was nevertheless unperturbed, and in the following year he was successful in gaining the vacant post. In all fairness to him, Soane had devoted much energy during this time to making lengthy translations of French and Italian authors in anticipation of achieving his goal. He also soon embarked on the tedious task of preparing more than a thousand large-scale drawings of buildings that he exhibited as an accompaniment to his lectures.

Soane in his talks eclectically draws upon a bevy of competing and sometimes conflicting sources to fashion what sometimes appears to be an apology for his own architectural inclinations.[158] He discusses the ideas of Rousseau, Diderot, and d'Alembert as well as Perrault, Laugier, Jacques-François Blondel, Piranesi, Francesco Milizia, Le Camus de Mézières, Soufflot, and Ledoux. Among British thinkers he refers to Addison, Shaftesbury, Burke, Kames, and Reynolds, the picturesque thought of Price and Knight, Burlington, Robert Morris, Robert Adam, Chambers, and Thomas Sanby, among many others. At the head of the luminaries of English architecture he places

24. Design from John Soane, *Sketches in Architecture* (London, 1793).

John Vanbrugh – whom he knights with "the high distinctive appellation of the Shakespeare of architects."[159] The resurrection of this formerly disdained baroque architect is now complete.

Vanbrugh's apotheosis is symbolic of Soane's eclectic viewpoint. As a true believer in the superiority of the ancients over the moderns as regards architectural magnificence, construction, and decorum, for example, Soane surprisingly sides with Perrault over Blondel in that earlier debate, but in an odd sort of way. Soane defines beauty, for instance, as "either intrinsic, relative, or compounded of both."[160] By intrinsic beauty he means "certain forms and proportions," such as circles, squares, and polygons; by relative beauty he means the "dimensions" demanded by use and character. He claims, "Intrinsic beauty combined with relative beauty produces that symmetry and proportions which distinguish the works of real artists from those of humble copyists. In a word, an edifice can only be considered beautiful when all its parts are in exact proportion, well balanced and combined together with proper quantities of light and shadow, richness and repose."[161]

These last few qualifications, as we shall see, entail a group of more elaborate concerns, which in the end strike down any notion of absoluteness in mathematical proportion. In commenting on Ouvrard's theory of harmonic proportions, for instance, Soane finds the correlation of architecture with music "neither applicable nor useful," and he again invokes the name of Perrault to insist that architecture cannot be reduced to any mechanical system: "It has no fixed proportions: taste, good sense, and sound judgement, must direct the mind of the architect to apply harmony and justness of relative proportions, that correlation of parts with the whole, and of the whole with each part."[162]

As to what constitutes "taste, good sense, and sound judgement," Soane directs us down avenues of both classical and picturesque thought. On the classical side, we have his warnings that ornament should be governed by strict rules of propriety, which would lead to the rejection of such decorative features as unnecessary pediments, interior columns, and ritualistic or political emblems of antique times, such as ox heads, garlands, griffins, sphinxes, lions, and serpents. On the picturesque side, there is Soane's appreciation of the "light and fanciful style of decoration" introduced by the Adam brothers, which, in residential design, broke "the talismanic charm" of both English Palladianism and the monumental school of neoclassicism.[163] Nevertheless, the Adams' failure to learn from the best examples of antiquity led Soane to pursue his own decorative abstractions using classical language, including such devices as incised geometric lines, sunken moldings, and domed canopies. Hence his underlying conservatism becomes the basis for some of his more interesting design innovations.

Central to Soane's architectural conception is the notion of character, a theme that owes much to French theory even if Soane provides his own shading:

Every building, whether great or small, simple or elegant, must, like the picture, speak intelligibly to the beholder. Each must have a positive character peculiar to itself, sufficient to point out the purposes and uses for which it was erected. This cannot be attained if the work is deficient in character. The Athenian orator being asked what were the great requisites in his art, replied, action, action, action. So if it were asked what constituted the distinctive beauties in architectural compositions, the answer would be, character, character, character.[164]

Propriety is one determinant of architectural character. Suitability for use and accommodation to the landscape also condition it. But character for Soane mostly resides in the expressive manipulation or nuancing of natural light and the details, for "even a moulding, however diminutive, contributes to increase or lessen the character of the assemblage of which it forms a part."[165] One of the recurring keynotes of his own practice was his exploitation of natural light – also its coloring and reflection – for its emotive qualities, as his home at Lincoln's Inn Fields has long demonstrated. Light forms an essential aspect of his architectural conception: "The 'lumiere mysterieuse,' so successfully practiced by the French artists, is a most powerful agent in the hands of a man of genius, and its power cannot be too fully understood, nor too highly appreciated."[166] Lighting effects must therefore be orchestrated "with all the fine feelings and nice discrimination of the artist," for only in this way will the architect be able "to move the soul, or speak to the feelings of mankind."[167]

Character too epitomizes Vanbrugh's design at Blenheim and the attraction of Gothic architecture. As for Blenheim, "the great extent of this noble structure, the picturesque effect of its various parts, the infinite and pleasing variety, the breaks and contrasts in the different heights and masses, produce the most exquisite sensations in the scientific beholder, whether the view be distant, intermediate, or near."[168] Judging such a composition "by the strict rules of Palladian tameness," Soane further argues, would be equivalent to judging the powerful language of Shakespeare by the "frigid rules of Aristotle."[169] In a similar way, Gothic works are attractive because of "all the astonishing variety, harmony, and grandeur of the different masses, as well as the intricacy and movement of the whole assemblage, the play and contrast of light and shadow, together with the exclusion of all glaring lights."[170]

In the end, the classicist Soane appears – through his abstraction of the classical language, his fondness for exaggerated proportions, and his use of abrupt spatial transitions and staged lighting effects – as a picturesque architect, but here again his private feelings are ambivalent and difficult to define with much precision. On the one hand, he greatly appreciated the aesthetics of picturesque theory and the liberal rein it allows the artist's powers of expression. On the other hand, after reading and annotating with approbation Knight's lengthy study for its architectural implications, Soane could not go so far as to permit his "dangerous tendency, calculated to destroy all relish," of marrying those Gothic battlements and flying buttress of Downton Castle with its "Grecian ceilings, columns, and entablatures," or even of applying such forms to modern buildings.[171] Classical propriety simply would not permit it. Soane, in such (nonstylized or ahistorical) designs as that for Dulwich Gallery, was often interpreted in the twentieth century as a forerunner of abstract modernism. In view of the color and richness of his ideas, it is perhaps more correct to nominate him as the last major architect of the eighteenth century. Such an appellation does not make him any less modern.

4

NEOCLASSICISM AND HISTORICISM

Why should not architecture also have its little revolution?
Léon Vaudoyer (1830)

1. Durand and Quatremère de Quincy

If the storming of the Bastille on 14 July 1789 has long served as the dividing line between premodern and modern European history, it was in many ways a symbolic one. The event (which liberated but five prisoners and two madmen from a prison already scheduled for demolition) represents, on the one hand, the collapse of the "old regime" in France and the aristocratic and clerical privileges it protected, on the other hand, the dawning of a new era of individual rights and democratic government. The social and political implications of the French Revolution were certainly not felt in France alone. The period 1789–1815 was an exceedingly convulsive one for a still largely feudal Europe, now forced to undergo a radical reconsideration of the existing body politic. Wars and related incidents of social unrest were nearly continuous. And to these cataclysms must be added, in the more advanced states, the economic pressures of the Industrial Revolution. In the end, modern values for the first time become clearly discernible, manifesting themselves no less in architectural thought than in other cultural fields.

The political and military events neatly encapsulate the stages of progressive turmoil. The unrest in France in the summer of 1789 led to a "Declaration of the Rights of Man" (emulating the American model) and a limited or constitutional monarchy. Intellectuals across Europe and America – save the perspicacious Edmund Burke – were enthralled with the possibilities for social change.[1] A French war with Austria (soon followed by wars with Prussia and Britain) and continued social unrest resulted in a second revolution in the summer of 1792 and the seizure of the government by Jacobin radicals. The insidious Reign of Terror ensued, led by Maximilien Robespierre, and from the summer of 1793 to the summer of 1794 (when Robespierre himself was put to death), over 20,000 victims lost their heads on the guillotine, among them the monarch Louis XVI. The so-called Directory (a regime of five directors) assumed leadership of France in 1795, but it in turn was ousted by the coup-d'etat of Napoleon Bonaparte in 1799. Napoleon was, of course, obsessed with military expansion, and he succeeded all too well, creating strong nationalist reactions to his conquests that would survive a century and more. By 1810 he had conquered or gained control of nearly all of Europe (except for Britain and Russia), yet his disastrous march on Moscow in 1812 decimated his once "Grand Army." At the start of 1814, a coalition of Austrian, Russian, Prussian, Bavarian, and British forces crossed the Rhine and bore down on Paris. In March they occupied the capital, and Napoleon fled to Fontainebleau. He was forced to abdicate but was given the sovereignty of Elba. His escape from Elba and return to Paris the next year led to another round of military fighting, culminating at Waterloo. The principal military powers at the Congress of Vienna (1814–15), seeking to put an end to twenty-six years of almost continuous warfare, debated their interests, traded lands, and redrew the national boundaries of Europe.

Of course, not all of the effects of the French Revolution were destructive. In sweeping away aristocratic and church privileges, the Revolution implemented a series of administrative, financial, educational, and legal reforms, both in France and in the conquered lands. Napoleon, himself an ardent Jacobin in earlier years, in fact saw his reform efforts as the realization of the ideal of human equality under law. In the various German states, many intellectuals – among them Friedrich Klopstock, Friedrich Schlegel, Immanuel Kant, Georg Wilhelm Friedrich Hegel, and Friedrich Hölderlin – initially hailed the events of 1789 as a prelude to a larger moral and spiritual renewal of Europe.[2] Even the subsequent Reign of Terror and Napoleon's campaign of conquest did little to temper the enthusiasm of some of these onlookers. When Napoleon entered Jena in October 1807, on the eve of his rout of the Prussian army, Hegel was enthralled by having seen this "world-soul" from his window.[3] A few months later, in Berlin, Johann Gottlieb Fichte (1762–1814) began his spirited *Reden an die deutsche Nation* (Addresses to the German nation, 1807–8), which initiated a strong nationalist backlash to the humiliation of the French occupation.[4]

The political and social changes set in motion by the French Revolution dovetailed nicely with the equally momentous changes created by the Industrial Revolution, which also became increasingly evident during these unsettled years. The impulse to industrialize – to replace the techniques of manual labor by mechanized modes of production – came largely from Britain, which over the course of the eighteenth century had transformed the processes of textile manufacturing, coal mining, and metal manufacturing. The first steam-powered factories appeared in Britain in the 1770s, contemporary with the capitalist monetary policies advocated by Adam Smith in *The Wealth of Nations* (1776). Thus when Soane began working on his revolutionary designs for the Bank of England in 1788, he was operating on the central nervous system of Britain's economic prosperity and colonial expansion. In 1797, the Bank of England issued the first pound notes, thereby simplifying monetary exchange.

Britain's early lead would be increasingly challenged in the nineteenth century by France, Germany, and the United States. The impact of industrialization, however, was everywhere the same. Changes in production required mass migrations of workers out of rural areas, the expansion of old cities and the creation of new ones, new and speedier modes of transportation (canals, later railways), the creation of a middle class of entrepreneurs, and the emergence of an urban working class. To these changes must be added the explosion of Europe's population in the late eighteenth century. During the years 1789–1815, Prussia doubled its population, from 3 to 6 million people, France grew from 20 to 29 million, and Britain from 9 to 16 million.

Architectural changes could certainly be expected. Not only did industrialization bring forth new types of buildings, such as exchanges, banks, and factories, but it also had effects of a subtler nature. When France adopted the metric system in 1793, for instance, this system made it more difficult to use traditional proportional formulae. In France the aristocratic associations of classicism were now (at least temporarily) to be disdained, as were some of the country's leading architects. Claude-Nicholas Ledoux, for instance, never revived his career after his imprisonment in 1793–4. Yet others of his generation thrived on the political changes, as when the revolutionary government of the early 1790s initiated scores of architectural competitions to symbolize the new "democratic" taste.[5] Few of the proposed designs, however, were actually used because of the continued political turmoil. One exception was the conversion of Soufflot's Church of Ste.-Geneviève into a national Panthéon to honor France's "great men."

Two important architectural events did occur during the tumultuous years 1789–1815: the founding of the Ecole Polytechnique in 1794 and the creation of the Ecole des Beaux-Arts. These institutions have always been tied to the teachings of two individuals who initially gave them their direction: Jean-Nicolas-Louis Durand (1760–1834) and Antoine-Chrysostome Quatremère de Quincy (1755–1849).

Durand, more than any other architect, speaks to revolutionary ideals and their importation into architectural theory.[6] Born in Paris, he briefly attended the Collège de Mantaigue before focusing on architecture in the mid-1770s. He worked in the office of Pierre Panseion and then for Boullée while attending the Royal Academy of Architecture and the lectures of Le Roy. He placed second in the *grand-prix* competitions of 1779 and 1780, visited Italy, and returned to France for what was initially an uneventful career. The revolution energized his thinking, however, and around 1790, inspired by Boullée and Piranesi, he began to prepare an architectural publication consisting of 168 pencil sketches of urban scenes. Together with Jean-Thomas Thibault, he threw himself into fifteen architectural competitions in 1793–4 and placed first in one with the scheme for a "Temple of Equality" (Fig. 25) – a simple temple with square columns whose capitals consisted of idealized classical heads representing republican virtues.

In 1794 Durand was hired to teach drafting at the newly founded Ecole Polytechnique; three years later he was promoted to assistant professor and charged with providing an architectural course for French military engineers and scientists. Between 1799 and 1801 he published his *Recueil*

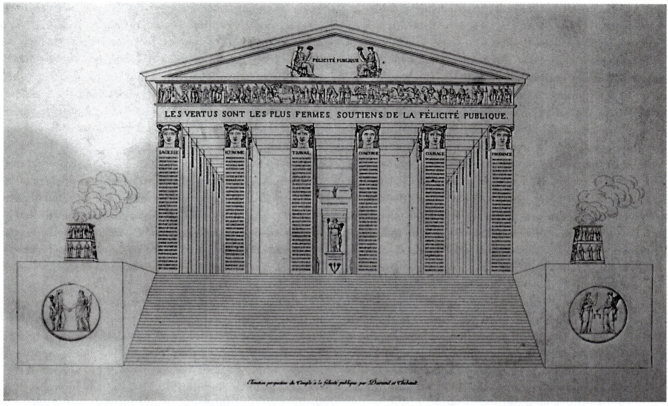

25. Jean-Nicolas-Louis Durand and Jean-Thomas Thibault, Temple of Equality, 1794, from *Projets d'architecture, et autres productions de cet art qui ont mérité les grands prix accordés par l'Academie* (Paris, 1834).

et parallèlle des édifices en tout genre, anciens et modernes (Collection and parallel of buildings of every type, ancient and modern), which, owing much to Le Roy's earlier study of churches, presented a lavish visual comparison of global architecture.[7] Durand followed this endeavor with the publication of his architectural lectures at the Ecole Polytechnique, *Précis des leçons d'architecture* (Précis of the lectures on architecture, 1802–5).[8]

Durand's theory was informed by contemporary events and by the circumstances of his teaching position. The revolutionary government founded the Ecole Polytechnique in 1794 as an advanced engineering school, a polytechnical college for military engineers focusing on mathematics, mechanics, physics, and chemistry. In line with these scientific and technological pursuits, Durand was charged with providing the rudiments of architectural training, more practical than theoretical in nature. This task allowed Durand to rethink the classical underpinnings of architecture, or rather to reassess classical architecture's social relevance to modern industrial society. Underlying his deliberations were three powerful impulses. One was the

simple exhaustion or faltering relevance of the Vitruvian tradition. Another was the "sentimental" assault that his former teacher Boullée had launched on the same tradition – "sentimental" in the sense of relating to emotion or character. Durand's premises were in this regard more politically motivated, and it was not the classical language that he would reconsider but rather the design process itself. A third force coming into play was the growth of structural theory and the new standards of professionalism in architectural practice. Once again the design method became of paramount importance to Durand; efficiency and utility were its dual objectives. It is scarcely coincidental that the first volume of Durand's *Précis* appears in the same year as the first volume of the *Traité théorique et pratique de l'art de bâtir* (Theoretical and practical treatise on the art of building, 1802–17) of Jean-Baptiste Rondelet (1743–1829).[9] The latter, a pupil of both Jacques-François Blondel and Boullée, was responsible for completing the Church of Ste.-Geneviève, and he viewed architecture largely in structural terms, foremost as a scientific discipline in search of progress.

Durand's revolutionary fire is immediately evident in the opening pages of the *Précis*. His tactic is to discredit the idea that architecture imitates nature (the analogy of the orders with human forms) or that it emulates some hypothetical model like the primitive hut of Laugier. He pursues this tactic by questioning the value and meaning of the three principles of the Vitruvian tradition – distribution (convenience), construction (solidity), and decoration. If the first two principles are to be elevated, decoration is now to be scorned in the new age, and his conclusion is in keeping with the postrevolutionary disdain of royalist excesses: "It is evident that pleasure can never have been the aim of architecture; nor can architectural decoration have been its object. Public and private utility, the happiness and the protection of individuals and of society: such is the aim of architecture."[10] Thus design becomes transformed into "fitness and economy," which are "the only principles that can guide us in the study and exercise of the art."[11]

Convenance, the French word for fitness, harks back to the theory of Jacques-François Blondel and implies a classical sense of propriety or decorum. But Durand now more strictly defines it as referring to construction that is "solid, salubrious, and commodious" to its purpose.[12] Further, economy, which he clarifies through the notions of regularity, symmetry, and simplicity, is not just a matter of fiscal restraint. The notion of simplicity in particular suggests less a minimum of material means and more a visual slenderness or ingenious elegance in the design concept. Durand's famous example for demonstrating his idea of economy is Soufflot's Church of Ste.-Geneviève. He criticizes the ratio of exterior wall to usable floor area in the recently completed church and proposes instead a circular solution with a low dome, which, while employing with the same materials, would enlarge the floor area by 600 square meters![13]

The abstract nature of the principles of fitness and economy, of course, can guide the architect only in a very general way, and Durand next proposes an analytical method for design, a simple procedure of combining possible topological elements (Fig. 26). The starting point is the axial grid (an architectural innovation that itself appears around 1770), which serves as a base for design components that can be plugged into its coordinates, as it were. Accompanying the idea of a grid is a series of charts or plates depicting formal possibilities: generic floor plans, porches, vestibules, staircases, fountains, vegetation, building elevations, and roof shapes. The purpose of the taxonomy of parts is to provide the designer with a variety of plans and massing variations upon which to exercise his compositional skill. The styles of the elevations, interestingly enough, are only vaguely classical and more often resemble French or Italian vernacular forms. A building's style in fact means nothing to Durand; the rational method of design is here what takes center stage. In another group of drawings, Durand provides generic plans for such buildings as libraries, palaces of justice, museums, colleges, and hospitals. In effect, he provides the student (of engineering) with a package appropriate for a home-study course.

Assessing the influence of Durand's new method of design is difficult. Although the book would be widely read in Germany (where it was quickly translated), its initial impact in France is more tenuous, no doubt owing to the fact that it was a course of lectures intended for military engineers. Its utilitarian emphasis would also run counter to the reconstitution of academic theory under the aegis of the Ecole des Beaux-Arts in 1803.

This last event grew out of the suppression of academic institutions during the tumultuous revolutionary years. The Royal Academy of Architecture was already beset by growing turmoil throughout the 1780s, and its students appeared before the Paris Commune early in 1790 to denounce the school as antirevolutionary. In 1791 the school proposed a series of reforms, but the measures could not still the hostility of revolutionaries, especially that of the painter Jacques-Louis David (1748–1825). He demanded the abolition of all royal academies, and the activists succeeded in achieving this goal on the night of 16 August 1793, when the doors of the various institutions were sealed. The architecture school existed in a state of limbo for the next two years, even though, under a plan of reform, Le Roy and Antoine-Laurent-Thomas Vaudoyer (1756–1846) continued to lecture privately. In 1795 the school received a new name, the Ecole Spéciale de l'Architecture, but the process of reform was not complete until 1803, when Napoleon created the Classe des Beaux-Arts, bringing together painters, sculptors, architects, engravers, and musicians under one administrative umbrella. War interests nevertheless took precedence, and it was only with the restoration of the Bourbon monarchy in 1816 that the term *Académie des Beaux-Arts* – to refer to the institution that encompassed the Ecole de Beaux-Arts – came back into use.

The education of architects was therefore severely interrupted during the revolutionary and Napoleonic years. Le Roy had managed to save the academy's library in 1793, but students were few. There were no *grand-prix* competitions during the next four years, and the situation became more complicated in 1798 when Neapolitan armies burned down

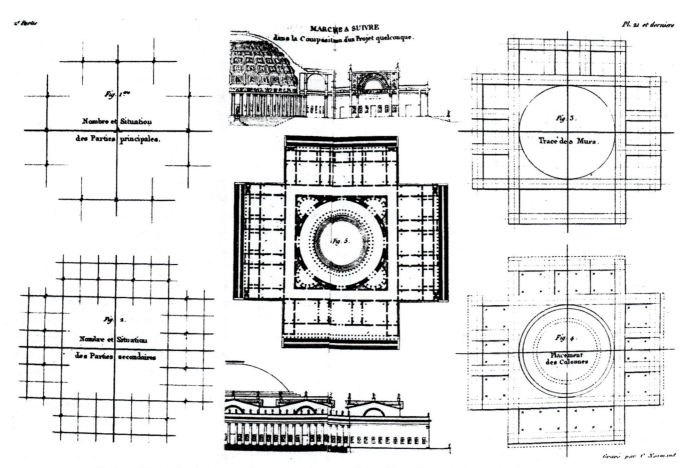

26. Jean-Nicolas-Louis Durand, plate on the "Course to Follow" from *Précis des leçons d'architecture données à l'École Royale Polytechnique* (Paris, 1802–5).

the home of the French Academy in Rome, the Palazzo Mancini. It was not until 1802 that France took over the Palazzo Medici and not until 1806 that the *Prix-de-Rome* was formally reinstated on an annual basis. Le Roy directed the education of architects until his death in 1803. Léon Dufourny (1754–1818) succeeded him and adhered to the existing program of classical teachings. Upon Dufourny's death in 1818, Louis-Pierre Baltard (1764–1846) assumed control of the architecture department within the Ecole des Beaux-Arts. The most powerful force directing the school, however, was Quatremère de Quincy, who in 1816 assumed the post of Secrétaire perpétuel de l'Académie des Beaux-Arts, a directorship he would hold until 1839.

Although architecture would become one of his principal concerns, Quatremère de Quincy was not an architect.[14] He was foremost an intellectual, and his lengthy personal life was filled with dramatic turns and changes of fortune. The son of a cloth merchant, he studied sculpture in the studio of Guillaume Coustou before traveling to the south

at his own expense in 1776, where he visited Rome, Naples, Pompeii, Paestum, and Sicily. Except for one brief interlude, he remained in Italy until 1785, traveling mostly with the *grand-prix* painter David and meeting such luminaries as Piranesi and Canova. Upon his return to France, he won an academic prize for his historical essay on the origins of Egyptian and Greek architecture. Soon thereafter he was commissioned to write the architectural component of the *Encyclopédie méthodique*, a new encyclopedia for the arts. The large first volume of alphabetized articles (*Abajour* to *Colonne*) appeared in 1788, volume 2 (in two parts) in 1801 and 1820, and volume 3 in 1825. Hence Quatremère de Quincy had established his scholarly reputation prior to the Revolution.

Still, the Revolution changed everything, and it was a cause that Quatremère de Quincy first supported with vigor. He was elected to the Commune de Paris and appointed to the influential Committee of Public Instruction. He worked there with his friend David and developed an important relationship with Charles-Maurice de Talleyrand. In 1791 he was also appointed to overview the transformation of the Church of Ste.-Geneviève into the Panthéon, which he did while writing two pamphlets on reforming design education. As the radicals gained greater political control, however, Quatremère de Quincy's support for the Revolution waned. He defended Lafayette, one of the leaders of the Revolution, after Lafayette had been declared a traitor for opposing the Jacobin party. This led to one attempt on Quatremère de Quincy's life in 1793; in the same year Jean-Paul Marat named Quatremère de Quincy a royalist sympathizer, and the sculptor was arrested in March 1794 on a warrant signed by his friend David. With the fall of Robespierre in July, Quatremère de Quincy gained his release but now openly opposed the government of the Convention, and in 1795 he demonstrated his antipathy by inciting a crowd to riot. He narrowly escaped pursuing solders, but he was subsequently condemned to death in abstentia and had his property confiscated. Remarkably, when captured, he successfully argued for his acquittal. His attendance at a royalist meeting at Clichy in 1796, however, led to a new warrant of arrest. With Tallyrand's help, Quatremère de Quincy escaped to northern Germany, where between 1797 and 1800 he devoted himself to studying German philosophy, aesthetics, and archaeology. With Napoleon's general amnesty of 1800, the activist and scholar returned to France and began his academic career. In 1804 he was elected to the Académie des Inscriptions et Belles-Lettres, and in the following year he began delivering lectures. He continued to write as well, and his publications contributed to his prestigious appointment in 1816.

Although the theoretical core of his classical position was formed prior to the Revolution, Quatremère de Quincy did more than simply reinstitute the earlier body of academic doctrines; it is not an exaggeration to say that he fundamentally rethought the conceptual premises of architecture. In this regard, his two essays on Egyptian architecture foreshadow his innovations and set out the guidelines for subsequent development.

The first of these, written for a literary competition of 1785, responds to the question "What was the condition of Egyptian architecture and what did the Greeks seem to have borrowed from it?" Drawing upon Le Roy's earlier musings on the origins of Egyptian and Greek architecture, Quatremère de Quincy responds with a relativist explanation of Egyptian and Greek architecture that presents a series of social (primordial and cultural) and geographic conditions as determinants of the stylistic forms of each nation's architecture. The explanation is based on the anthropological (biblical) premise that early societies evolved from three modes of life, those of hunters, shepherds, and farmers. Hunting and fishing societies needed no fixed homes, and thus they inhabited the shores of seas and rivers and found natural lodgings in nearby caves. Shepherds, by contrast, had migratory living habits and thus required light mobile dwellings such as tents. Agricultural societies tended to be stable, and therefore solid timber huts were their prototypical dwellings. Moreover, for reasons of race and geography, some regions tended to favor specific types of dwelling. Tents were commonplace among the shepherds in the arid deserts of western Asia and in China. Agriculture was an art first practiced by Indo-European tribes, especially by the early peoples of Greece. The cave was the natural architectural prototype for hunting and fishing tribes of Egypt. Quatremère de Quincy's argument is that the subsequent architectural forms in these regions retained certain formal characteristics of the dwellings associated with the original modes of living. Hence the troglodyte Egyptians, for example, favored simple plans and large masses as well as uniform and solid construction.

But Quatremère de Quincy's theory was more complex than first might appear. In the essay of 1785, he noted that there was a double origin to Egyptian architecture: the cave and the hut both influenced Egyptian forms. In an expanded version of the essay published in 1803, he views Greek and Egyptian architecture as entirely separate in their underlying motives, each derived entirely from the types of huts and caves characteristic of the particular region. Invoking linguistic theory, he notes the difference between the general principles of universal grammar, which apply to all languages, and the syntax of a particular language, which is unique. He wants to discourage those who try (as he himself did in 1785) to derive Greek forms (such as the Doric order) from Egyptian prototypes. Columns, in effect, belong to the universal grammar and thus appear everywhere, whereas the particular syntax of the three Greek orders is what elevates Greek architecture above all others.

This qualitative distinction is also supported by considering the two countries' original types of dwelling. As the tent and the cave offer few architectural possibilities for development, nothing of interest can be derived from them; the tent has only extreme lightness as a formal attribute, while the cave has monotony and extreme heaviness. The wooden forms of the hut, however, are easily modified and capable of rich and logical formal development – indeed, with so many possible nuances that "one is able to affirm that only the school of carpentry is able to make architecture a rational art."[15] From this premise, Quatremère de Quincy takes another important step (one that rebuts the teachings of Lodoli) in affirming that it is the hut's specific material transposition from wood into stone (realized for him in the Greek temple) that elevates Greek architecture above that of any other nation. Monumental architecture, in short, is based on this illusion of forms and material: "In effect, it will take little to recognize that the essence of architecture, and in large part the means by which it pleases us, is in raising this agreeable fiction, this ingenious mask, which, in association with the other arts, permits them to appear on its stage and furnishes architecture with an occasion to rival them as well."[16] Hence, classical architecture's "happy metaphor" – its imitation of prototypical timber forms – is what endows it with a superior aesthetic basis.

Quatremère de Quincy developed his idea in the articles he wrote for the *Encyclopédie méthodique* beginning in 1788. Architecture is first defined in a traditional manner, as "the art of building following determined proportions and rules."[17] Equating the art with the "charm of music, the song of poets, and the illusions of the theater," Quatremère de Quincy draws attention to the feigned "trickery" of architecture's material transposition of the timber cabin, "at the same time illusionary and real."[18] But classical architecture is in fact doubly imitative: It is a theatrical imitation of the conceptualized hut and a figurative imitation of nature, that is, nature's general principles and laws. Thus there arises a surprising flexibility in Quatremère de Quincy's definition of architecture, for proportional laws serve only as a general guide in which variations are permitted, just as nature creates exceptions to its formative rules: "The general imitation of nature in its principles of order, of harmony relative to the affections of our senses, and to perceptions of judgment has given it a soul, and has made it an art no longer copyist, no longer imitative, but a rival to nature herself."[19] Architecture becomes, in essence, ideal. And based on this Platonic sense of harmony and order, Quatremère de Quincy, in the late 1780s, harshly condemns modern architecture (surely alluding to the work of Ledoux) for its lack of a "clear and precise idea," for its linguistic distortions and allegorical confusion, and for its becoming "a puerile plaything for artists and an enigma for the community of men."[20]

Quatremère de Quincy's encyclopedia article on "Character," by far the longest article in the first volume, may well have been considered in Chapter 2 – except that here too he endows the concept with an entirely new life. Arguably he mediates the academic notion of character with the new historical and aesthetic systems of the Enlightenment (Montesquieu and Winckelmann in particular), while at the same time stripping away the idea of any emotional or sentimental content. He begins by defining character as "the sign by which nature inscribes on each object its essence, its distinctive qualities, its relative proprieties," for which reason he distinguishes between essential, distinctive, and relative character.[21] Each kind of character is further delineated in physical and moral terms, leading to such general attributes as species/inclinations, physiognomy/momentary modifications, talents/proprieties of use. Such a model, in all its biological abstraction, is then applied to architecture, with varying results.

Architectural character resides "in a manner of being, in a necessary conformation between physical needs and moral habits, and in that developed by the climate, ideas, customs, taste, pleasures, and the character of each people."[22] Nuances follow. Essential character is the most original but also the most expressive of force or grandeur. It is found in the expression of architectural types, such as carpentry, and in such general modes as the three orders. Interestingly, among the latter, the Doric has the most character because its force or expressiveness has not yet been decoratively treated in a society of refinement. Distinctive character is the physiognomy or originality of the architectural work, the sign of its particular style. Relative character is the most fecund for architectural development, because it arises through the expressive use of materials, through the invocation of ideal and artistic qualities ("what poetry is to language"), and through observing the rules of decorum: "See how nature, simple in her types, economical in her means, is however inexhaustible and varied in all the combinations that modify her works."[23]

Quatremère de Quincy's classicism is thus a classicism not of hard and fast rules but of decorous nuance: the propriety of selecting appropriate types, of applying decorative attributes, of invoking that subtle linguistic expression, or "occular eloquence" that has been compiled over centuries and is now, in his view, threatened with extinction. When he later completes his model in the third volume of the encyclopedia (1825) using such concepts as "Type," "Style," and "Theory," its philosophical subtlety becomes all the more refined. An architectural type is not an image of a thing to copy or imitate but rather "the idea of an element that must itself serve as a rule or model."[24] Style is no particular formal language but rather something "synonymous with *character*, or with the proper manner and the distinctive physiognomy that pertains to each work, to each author, to each genre, to each school, to each country, to each century, etc."[25] And theory possesses its practical and didactic aspects but more importantly its higher "metaphysical" dimension, that "degree of superior instruction" that

presents not rules but points to the sources from which the rules emanate; it is not that which drafts the laws but that which investigates and penetrates the spirit behind them; it is not that which takes its principles in works but that which gives its principles to works, the same laws of nature, the causes for the impressions that we experience, the means by which art touches us, moves us, pleases us.[26]

Thus the reconstituted Ecole des Beaux-Arts was provided with a classical foundation of great subtlety and intellectual refinement. This theoretical base would, however, prove to be of very short duration. For no sooner was the final volume of the encyclopedia completed in 1825 than the system of Quatremère de Quincy came under fire. The threat of still another revolution – both political and architectural – was in the air.

2. The Polychrome Debate

Within architecture, the European-wide polychrome debate represented the first stage of this revolution. It started innocently enough with the polite "discovery" of Hellenic polychromy early in the century. The discovery had in fact been made three-quarters of a century earlier, when Stuart and Revett recorded outlines of painted decorations on a few Athenian temples, among the temple on Theseus (Fig. 27). They saw the remnants of paint but did not see the far-reaching implications of its presence on these monuments, which otherwise exhibited bare white marble. Neither could others at the time. Working principally from marble copies of Hellenic sculptures, Winckelmann had defined the neoclassical view that the essence of sculptural beauty was contour or form, which in turn was enhanced by the material nobility of white marble. Winckelmann even argued that the degree of a marble's whiteness affected the beauty of the sculpture, because the color white best reflected light and thus best defined the contour or outline.[27] Such a view was easily transposed to architecture. Writing in 1801, the German historian Christian Ludwig Stieglitz summarized the neoclassical position by noting, "Works of architecture receive their beauty through beautiful form, which in this

art, as in the other fine arts to which it is related, is evoked through order and symmetry, through propriety and good proportions."[28]

Overlooked or lightly considered at this time were several classical references to the existence of architectural polychromy. Vitruvius himself had referred to a blue wax applied to the triglyphs of wooden temples, and Pausanias in his account of his second-century travels had mentioned seeing red and green Athenian tribunals.[29] The assumption, however, was that color was applied to buildings only as an accent and that the main parts were white. The issue of wall painting, however, complicated the matter. The first-century Roman historian Pliny the Elder had noted that the Greeks in the best period did not practice true wall painting (a Roman degradation) but rather painted on panels that were inserted into walls.[30] Winckelmann had refuted this contention (to the comfort of his later opponents), but the passage nevertheless allowed a "white view" of Greek antiquity to remain undisputed until the end of the eighteenth century.[31] Greek architecture was deemed to be principally white (its best monuments executed in Parian and Pentelic marble), and where color was shown by accumulating evidence to have been used extensively – such as on Egyptian tombs and bas-reliefs, the colorful decorations of the Treasury of Atreus at Mycenae, and in the wall murals of Pompeii and Herculaneum – these places and periods were identified as being of artistic infancy or provincial decadence. The high style of the Age of Pericles stood above these times in all its pristine artistic glory.

This view began to be challenged shortly after 1800, as a spate of travelers, mostly British, visited Greece and carried out further investigations. Between 1799 and 1802, the Scotsman Thomas Bruce, seventh earl of Elgin (1766–1841), was the envoy extraordinary at Constantinople, where he conceived his plan to remove the decorative sculptures from the Parthenon and ship them back to England. Also in Greece at this time were the travelers William Wilkins, an architect; William Leake, a topographer; and Edward Dodwell, an antiquarian – all of whom found evidence of polychromy. Wilkins detected traces of paint on the entablatures of the propylaeum and Temple of Theseus (Hephaisteion).[32] Leake noted "various colors" applied to the Parthenon's wall surfaces and sculptures.[33] And Dodwell found extensive remnants of blue, red, and yellow paint on the Parthenon. He stated,

It is difficult to reconcile to our minds the idea of polychrome temples and statues; but it is certain that the practice was

27. Detail of the painted entablature of the Temple of Theseus, from Stuart and Revett's *The Antiquities of Athens* (1788).

familiar to the Greeks in the earliest times, and even in the age of Pericles. No doubt all the Grecian Temples were ornamented in the same manner . . . with the highest finish and the greatest elegance, corresponding with the sculptural parts.[34]

Another wave of travelers to Greece arrived around 1810 – among them C. R. Cockerell, the German Carl Haller von Hallerstein, the Russian Otto Magnus von Stackelberg, and the Dane Peter Oluf Brøndsted – and their findings were even more dramatic. In 1811, on the island of Aegina,

Cockerell, Hallerstein, and Brøndsted unearthed the pedimental sculptures of a partially standing temple; they detected color not only on the statuary but also on the moldings of the cornice. One problem, however, was that the paint evaporated shortly after its exposure to air and sunlight. Later that year, the same group discovered the Arcadian temple ruins at Bassae and again found extensive traces of paint.[35] This finding was most significant because the architect of the temple was Ictinus, also the architect of the Parthenon.

This is where the matter stood in 1815 when Quatremère de Quincy published his philological study *Le Jupiter olympien, ou l'art de la sculpture antique considéré sous un nouveau point de vue* (The Olympian Jupiter, or the art of antique sculpture considered under a new point of view). This book, which he had begun in 1803, did not specifically take into account the recent discoveries, although the author was certainly aware of the (mostly unpublished) findings. The goal of his study, which he describes as a "supplement" to Winckelmann's great history, was to reconstruct the famed chryselephantine (gold-and-ivory) statues of Phidias – the colossal statues of Zeus and Athena that had been placed inside their respective temples at Olympia and Athens. Classical writers, such as Pausanias, had hailed these works as masterpieces of antiquity, yet neoclassical authorities, such as Caylus, were considerably less enamored of the use of these two materials to depict cloth and skin. Their censures, as Quatremère de Quincy summarizes them, were four: (1) the colorful use of gold and ivory represented a taste foreign to the usual practices of the Greeks; (2) the mixing of two materials was "bizarre" and less pure than using one noble material, such as marble; (3) their material richness falsely swayed the ancients as to the works' artistic merit; and (4) the use of color produced "a kind of illusion" that was contrary to the most "elementary principle" of sculpture, which is form.[36]

Quatremère de Quincy counters these criticisms with an argument that unfolds over 400 pages, supported by myriad classical sources. The historical models for these works, he argues, were not foreign but rather the primitive wooden idols of early Greek times – *les statues-mannequins* – painted and dressed with actual materials. The painting and dressing of these mannequins evolved into the technical process of toreutics (embossing or engraving metal). Color continued to be applied to other materials to protect them against the effects of weather and time, to correct material deficiencies, and to relieve the coldness and monotony of larger surfaces. Thus by the time of Pericles, the use of color had enjoyed a long tradition in Greek statuary, one both symbolic in content and sanctified by religious practices. In his beautifully rendered drawings of these two gold-and-ivory works, Quatremère de Quincy depicted them as sheathed in a transparent colored sheen, "a sort of painting without being colored, that is to say, of being colored without being painted, it offers finally the appearance and not the reality of the illusion."[37]

As Quatremère de Quincy had crafted this argument in response to a specific archaeological and philological

problem, he was surely unconcerned with the architectural implications of his reasoning. Other architects and archaeologists did, however, take note of the argument. Thus when Cockerell published his findings regarding the marbles from Aegina in 1819, he described them as "a very remarkable, and very ancient example of the practice which prevailed among the Greeks, of painting their sculpture."[38] He saw this practice as a means "of distinguishing the several parts, and heightening the effect by a delicate variety of tones, so as to relieve what might otherwise be inanimate or monotonous."[39] Two years later the German architect Leo von Klenze – who had been commissioned to design the Munich Glyptothek, the museum intended to house these same marbles – opened a lecture on ancient architecture by chastising Winckelmann and Caylus for their "dry, cold, and rigid" view of antiquity and then went on to praise Quatremère de Quincy and Cockerell, among others, for correctly reassessing the past.[40] In his restoration of a temple that was to serve as backdrop to the marbles, he painted the columns and metopes yellow, the cella walls red, and the triglyphs blue.

Other explanations for antique polychromy followed in short order. In 1826 Baron von Stackelberg published a book on the discovery of the temple at Bassae in which he reiterated Quatremère de Quincy's arguments but also enhanced them with observations on the colorful landscape of the South and the ruddy Greek spirit:

Color, even today indispensable to all Southern peoples to enliven the architectural masses, was used by the Greeks on the greatest architectural masterworks of the Periclean Age, both Doric and Ionic, as seen on Theseum, the Parthenon, the Temple of Minerva Polias, and the Propyläen, where colors were even applied to the exterior building decorations. In addition, several examples of memorials, Greek vase paintings, and frescoes from Pompeii demonstrate the universality of painted decorations on architectural works themselves. The mild climate favored this use, and the Doric temple appeared much more richly decorated than we might imagine.[41]

The second edition of Stuart and Revett's *Antiquities of Athens*, issued in 1825–30, advanced the argument further. William Kinnard, in his newly written annotations on the Parthenon, acknowledged that paint was still "distinctly perceptible" and now insisted that it was applied to other than decorative elements: "The polished columns of white marble with their architrave, triglyphs, and the chief part of the cornice, may therefore have thus been relieved in a manner agreeable to the eye, in so sunny an atmosphere, by the enrichment and combination with colours and gilding judiciously applied."[42] The reasons cited for the use of color now included the need for the architectural surfaces to conform to the brilliantly decorated sculptures within, as well as to the Athenians' purer sense of design.

A similar view was voiced by Brøndsted in the folio presentation of his polychrome findings, *Reisen und Untersuchungen in Griechenland* (Travels and investigation in Greece, 1825–30). He transposed Quatremère de Quincy's four-stage scenario for Greek statuary to architecture (the temple evolving from its wooden prototype and therefore initially in need of paint) and treated color as more fully exploited at each succeeding stage. By the Age of Pericles, "the first kind of color application, namely, that used for actual architectural purposes, was so general in the most beautiful period of Greek architecture that one can, as already noted, confidently assert that all Greek temples were more or less painted."[43] For Brøndsted this meant the painting of columns, walls, and all other surfaces.

Thus by 1825 the "white view" of Greek antiquity was largely a thing of the past. In theory, the problem that color posed for classicism was simply one of emphasis: By giving increasing importance to color in classical compositions, one at the same time lessened the emphasis placed on symmetry, decorum, and, most of all proportions. Nevertheless, the issue of polychromy became more divisive than this suggests; it became, as it were, a pretext seized by many French students in the second half of the 1820s to attack the aesthetic heart of academic theory. Indeed, Quatremère de Quincy's defense of proportional values in the face of mounting evidence of polychromy weakened his authority.

The most damaging event in this regard – and one that clearly crossed the archaeological line – was the restoration of a small Sicilian monument by Quatremère de Quincy's one-time friend Jacques-Ignace Hittorff (1792–1867). This architect had been born in German Cologne, but Napoleon's annexation of the west bank of the Rhine in 1810 had allowed him to declare French citizenship and enroll at the Ecole des Beaux-Arts. Hittorff quickly moved up within the French professional hierarchy, and in 1821, stimulated by his visit to England to see the Elgin Marbles and by Quatremère de Quincy's book, he began to plan a trip to the South specifically to make a new polychrome discovery.[44] He departed Paris in September 1822 and first went to Rome, where he met and was encouraged by Bertel Thorwaldsen, the sculptor who had restored the Aeginetan marbles before their transportation to Munich. Upon hearing that the Englishmen William Harris and Samuel Angell had made a discovery of painted metopes at Selinus, Hittorff sped to the Sicilian site (as it turned out, in a race with the German architect Klenze) to undertake his own diggings there. He met up with Angell in Palermo (Harris had just died of malaria) and viewed firsthand the reddish metopes.[45] Hittorff commissioned diggings at Agrigento with some success, but then he moved his team to Selinus, where he uncovered the remains of a small temple (Temple B), parts of which were partially covered with stucco and paint. He returned to Rome to prepare a colored restoration, but after showing his results to various architects there, he decided against publishing them immediately.[46] In fact, not until 30 April 1830 did he display his restoration drawings and formally present his "system" of polychromy to the full Académie des Beaux-Arts.[47]

Hittorff's system, as its turns out, was nothing more than speculation, although he never pretended otherwise. Like Brøndsted he transposed the main lines of Quatremère de Quincy's color theory to architecture, and like Stackelberg he emphasized the need for architecture to accommodate itself to the "brilliant vegetation" and "the inexhaustible richness of nature" of the sunny South. What he brings new to the debate – aside from his vividly rendered, fully polychrome drawings – was his insistence that a single system of polychromy existed in antiquity, in fact as a subsystem of the larger modality of the orders. Color, in his view, provided architecture an additional and powerful means to express the character of the building: "It was the degree of ornamental richness for which painting was most especially suited that served more or less to define the visible magnificence of sacred buildings, depending on the glitter with which they wished to surround the gods."[48]

What Hittorff also presented by way of visual documentation was an "artistic" restoration. With little excavated evidence to draw upon, Hittorff, as he freely admitted, reassembled his Sicilian heroum (and by extension "the Hellenic monuments of every epoch") using a patchwork of colors and decorative motifs from such far-flung places and times as Tarquinia, Pompeii, Aegina, and Jerusalem. The result was not altogether unexpected. Quatremère de Quincy's eventual successor at the Académie des Beaux-Arts, the historian Désiré Raoul-Rochette, quickly changed his assessment of Hittorff's restoration from "a satisfactory restoration" to "an arbitrary and hypothetical idea" – leading to full-scale warfare on the academic front.[49] In a flurry of articles over the next six years, Hittorff and Raoul-Rochette (and their defenders) exchanged fistfuls of increasingly insulting barbs in a public debate on polychromy that soon spread to Germany, England, and Spain.[50]

3. Socialism, Romanticism, and the "Petite Révolution"

Hittorff's address to the Académie des Beaux-Arts was also auspicious, for it was presented in April 1830, three months before another revolution engulfed France. The problems went back to the Vienna Conference of 1814–15, when the victorious European powers, having defeated Napoleon, restored the Bourbon line of monarchs. France thus inherited the unpopular and ineffective Louis XVIII, a sharply divided parliament, much contracted borders, and heavy war indemnities. The government at the very beginning was therefore in a tenuous position, and anarchy – a term that first came into use during these revolutionary years – festered not far beneath the surface. The situation did not improve much in 1824, when Louis died and was succeeded by his brother Charles X, who proved even more unpopular. By the late 1820s France was abuzz with talk of revolution.

The situation came to a head in March 1830, when the politician and historian François Guizot, from the floor of the Chamber of Deputies, made his historic plea for political freedom. Charles X responded by calling new elections, which only had the unintended effect of strengthening the opposition to the crown. Finally, on 24 July 1830 Charles X signed secret orders suspending the freedom of the press and curtailing the power of the parliament. When the orders became known a few days later, 600 barricades were erected across Paris. On 7 August a delegation of deputy members reconvened the assembly, stripped the monarch of his office, and presented the crown to Louis-Philippe, the duke of Orleans. Ten days later the disposed monarch, hunted by mobs across France, crossed the English Channel into permanent exile.

The political events in themselves only mirrored a more deeply rooted social crisis growing out of industrialization. The bloody years of terror and almost continuous warfare in the decades surrounding the turn of the century had resulted in a general European malaise and various efforts to rethink society as a whole. In Britain, reformers such as Jeremy Bentham (1748–1832) and Robert Owen (1771–1858) pushed strategies for social change. Bentham, the principal theorist of utilitarianism, is perhaps today best known for his Panopticon, or model prison, but he made various proposals as well for the humane treatment of the poor and for transforming factories into efficient, safe, and sanitary workplaces. Owen, who was one of the first theorists of socialism, created in the 1790s a model factory commune in New Lanark, Scotland, in which children were educated and cared for during the day while adults were "improved" by following the strict work rules of the community. Much later, in 1825, Owen purchased 30,000 acres in Indiana, but his experimental town New Harmony ended three years later in failure.

In France the two leading utopians were Charles Fourier (1772–1837) and Claude-Henri Saint-Simon (1760–1825). Fourier believed he had made a momentous sociological discovery – the discovery of an "analytic and synthetic calculus of passionate attractions and repulsions" – in 1799, but his plan for creating phalanxes, or planned communities, with seven industrial functions (domestic, agricultural, manufacturing, commercial, educational, scientific, and artistic) evolved more slowly.[51] He was at heart an anarchist and a deist who sought to solve social problems by means of scientific and rational cooperatives encompassing production and consumption. The arts were to play an important educational role in these new communities, but so were such reforms as the legalization of polygamy. The Fourierist movement did not fully materialize until after 1830, and its few attempted phalanxes soon collapsed. They did, however, attract the attention of such later thinkers as Karl Marx.

The socialist theories of Saint-Simon were far more popular in the 1820s and strongly influenced architectural theory. A spiritual heir to Rousseau, the aristocrat Saint-Simon had fought briefly in the American War of Independence and had, like Fourier, been imprisoned during the Reign of Terror. His philosophical beliefs also evolved slowly. Beginning in 1816 he called for the creation of a new "organic" epoch: a radically changed social order based on the tools of industrial production.[52] The order would be a meritocracy and thus would have a social hierarchy; women would have full political equality, and the goal was to eliminate poverty. At the top of the structure would be a ruling scientific elite, an administrative cadre of artists, scientists, and industrialist-artisans guiding production and progress – reminiscent of the later visions of Le Corbusier.

Saint-Simon's theories gained several followers in the second half of the 1820s. One of his early disciples, Auguste Comte, developed aspects of his thought into the sociology of Positivism. According to Positivism, in the current historical stage, which has succeeded the theological and metaphysical stages, the world is to be explained strictly in terms of scientific truth, and facts are to be based exclusively on the methods of the physical or "positive" sciences. Another new concept to emerge from Saint-Simonism during this decade was the notion of an artistic "avant-garde" who would lead the march toward a more humane world. In invoking this idea in 1825, Olinde Rodrigues vests the concept with militant and political connotations:

It is we – artists – who will serve as the avant-garde; the power of the arts is indeed the most immediate and the most rapid. We have arms of every kind. When we want to spread new ideas among people we inscribe them on marble or canvas; we popularize them by poetry and song; in turn, we employ the lyre or flute, the ode or song, history or the novel. The dramatic scene is open to us and it is through it that we have an electric and victorious influence.[53]

An artistic and architectural reiteration of this message was published in 1830 by Emile Barrault (1799–1869), in his polemical tract *Aux artistes* (To artists). Barrault begins his pamphlet with the claim that "the decadence of the arts is evident" and that architecture, though superficially agreeable and elegant in its formal compositions, lacks both an underlying animation and poetry.[54] He then goes on to discuss where the present falls within the Saint-Simonian framework of "organic" and "critical" epochs. Organic epochs are relatively short historical periods in which religious, social, and artistic ideals reside in harmony and mutually reinforce one another; in the succeeding critical epochs, the same forces compete with and co-opt one another. Western civilization has seen but two organic epochs: The first began with the rise of Greek civilization, the second with the consolidation of Christianity in the Middle Ages. The last epoch exhausted itself by the fifteenth century, however. Barrault concludes his book by suggesting that the French Revolution and the teachings of Saint-Simon have signaled the dawning of a new organic epoch of reconciliation, for "the arts are only able to flourish during an organic epoch, and inspiration is only powerful and salutary when it is social and religious."[55] In this scenario, architecture becomes a collective discipline serving the needs and aspirations of a new socialist society. Underlying this view of the world is the historical notion that chosen societies advance not only cyclically but also progressively toward their desired ends. Cultural or anthropological factors, relative to each situation, are therefore paramount.

Such ideas were, again, easily transposed to architectural thinking. Quatremère de Quincy himself had already provided French theory with the seeds of a relativist foundation in 1788 by propounding his notion of character and stressing the uniqueness of each culture. Also informed with such ideas were the architectural lectures of Jean-Nicolas Huyot (1780–1840), presented to students at the Ecole des Beaux-Arts beginning in 1823.[56] Huyot had won the *grand-prix* in

1807, and his spectacular *envoi* reconstruction of the Temple of Fortune at Palestrina (1811; later displayed on the walls of the Villa Medici) enchanted an entire generation of international students in Rome.[57] In 1819 Quatremère de Quincy appointed Huyot as professor of architectural history. His earlier historical outlook cannot be stated with certainty (as the earliest notes for his lectures date from 1830), but it is clear that his ideas, although classically based, differed in important respects from those of the director. He focused on ancient architecture, but rather than viewing each culture's architecture in terms of some primordial type, he attempted to situate it within the geographic, social, and historical context of the Mediterranean basin.

Huyot's lectures in any case resonated with a talented group of *grand-prix* winners – self-styled "romantics" – who lived at the French Academy in Rome in the 1820s, among them Félix Duban (1797–1874), Henri Labrouste (1801–75), Louis Duc (1802–79), and Léon Vaudoyer (1803–72).[58] Students winning the *grand-prix* were awarded five years of study in Rome and lived in the Palazzo Medici. The first three years were to be devoted to "analytic" archaeological studies of details, starting with the orders. In the fourth year students were expected to prepare a restoration of a major work of antiquity, supplemented with a historical explanation. In the fifth year they were expected to design a contemporary French monument, drawing upon their classical knowledge and archaeological experience, as a prelude to a high government post. Each year the drawings were exhibited in Rome and then sent back to Paris for a formal exhibition and a review by the larger academy. The professors there provided written critiques of each student's progress and artistic accomplishments. The presumed model for architectural design, as in the eighteenth century, remained the classicism of imperial Rome.

In the mid-1820s these guidelines were beginning to be ignored, although the reasons may have been as much political as aesthetic. A hint of student dissatisfaction can be seen in 1826, when students in Paris interrupted a eulogy for a deceased given by Quatremère de Quincy with hoots and catcalls, leading to the hall being cleared by police. It is unclear, however, if their anger was directed more toward Quatremère de Quincy's royalist allusion to the "happy restoration" of the Bourbons or toward his references to the architect's classical ideals.[59]

By 1828, the ideas of Saint-Simon had made their way to Rome, and the students drew closer to open revolt. The *grand-prix* winners now became less interested in studying the approved models of imperial times and more interested in examining republican Roman works, Sicilian works, Etruscan sites, and even Renaissance architecture. Part of the reason for this may have been archaeological, for Hittorff had made his Sicilian discovery a few years earlier, and important Etruscan grave sites were found at Corneto (now Tarquinia) in 1827. Yet the desire to subvert the system surely played a role, as three students in 1827 submitted unorthodox projects. Vaudoyer, for his third-year project, submitted a comparative study of three early Roman temples, one of which, the Doric Temple of Hercules at Cori, he claimed to be Etruscan in its proportional style.[60] For his fifth-year project, Duban presented not a major classical monument but a "Protestant temple" or meeting house, which of course had no Roman Catholic or classical precedents.[61] But the project that aroused the most controversy was the fourth-year restoration project of Henri Labrouste. He reconstructed not a Roman work but three Greek temples at Paestum, the very buildings that had attracted Soufflot and others almost eighty years earlier.[62]

Labrouste's project was conceived in every way as a challenge to academic expectations. The temples by this date were rather well known and had been measured and correctly dated, but Labrouste, with his twenty-three restoration drawings, took a different interpretation. To start with, in his written essay he reversed their accepted chronology and argued that the Temple of Hera II (presumed to be the most recent because its proportions best approached those of Greek temples) was actually the earliest of the three. His reasoning was that its proportions were truly Greek and thus reflected the recent arrival of the colonists from the mainland, but as the colony at Paestum came to experience its own material, historical, and cultural transformations, its architecture mirrored the changing conditions. Hence, design moved not from squatter proportions to lighter ones better approaching the classical ideal, but rather, in a relative way, followed the evolution of social institutions. In keeping with this reasoning, Labrouste identified Hera I, with its coarser and presumably older forms, not as a temple at all but rather as a late civic basilica erected to honor secular rituals. In his drawings he endowed it with a coat of stucco and paint, with decorative lances and shields, and with painted inscriptions (graffiti) on its walls. Thus the building – as Neil Levine has interpreted it – served as a kind of "album" chronicling civic events and the spoils of successful military campaigns; such an affront to academic teachings was simply "blasphemy deserving of excommunication."[63]

Even before Labrouste's drawings arrived back in Paris, the opposing parties had arrayed their forces. In a letter,

Quatremère de Quincy scolded the director of the French Academy in Rome, Horace Vernet, for allowing younger students to travel outside of the city. Vernet, in turn, garnered the support of highly placed friends and defended Labrouste. When the drawings were exhibited in Paris in August 1829, a furor erupted. Quatremère de Quincy saw the controversy as a plot to destroy the teachings of the Ecole des Beaux-Arts, which it certainly was; some students seized the event as a chance to destroy the director for his royalist support. Still others saw the controversy as an instance of the "romantic" embrace of freedom, in keeping with the romanticism of the age. In a letter from Rome to his father in Paris, the younger Vaudoyer denounced Quatremère de Quincy as someone who was "eternally boring" and "would like it if we were still living in 1780."[64]

The controversy did not simmer down. In 1829, Labrouste defied the academy once again with his fifth-year *envoi* project, whose topic was not a classical monument but a small provincial bridge, meagerly decorated and hypothetically serving as a crossing point between France and Italy. But even before this project could prompt its expected uproar, Labrouste, early in 1830, returned to Paris and was petitioned by a group of students (defecting from other prestigious ateliers) to open his own atelier. During the tumultuous days of the July uprising, he was reportedly hoisted on the shoulders of fellow students and carried around Paris as a sign of victory. The fallout was not long in coming. Vernet offered to resign his post on 7 September 1830, but his published letter of resignation was rejected by the new minister, François Guizot. Quatremère de Quincy clung to his position another nine years, but his authority had been broken.

But the story does not end here. Sometime in 1830 Labrouste was approached by the novelist Victor Hugo and asked to consult on a chapter on architecture that Hugo had planned to include in his new novel, *Notre-Dame de Paris* (translated into English as *The Hunchback of Notre-Dame*). Hugo possessed a keen interest in architecture; as early as 1824 he had expressed the hope that the nascent romantic (or Gothic) movement in France would reinvigorate the arts and architecture by liberating them from the clutches of classicism.[65] Hugo's architectural chapter in *Notre-Dame* – later embraced by Frank Lloyd Wright as his personal artistic credo – is more pessimistic, however. Entitled "Ceci tuera cela" (This will kill that), it follows as an excursus to a conversation between Archdeacon Claude Frollo and King Louis XI in disguise, in which the archdeacon, in turning from a book on his desk to the Cathedral of Notre-Dame outside his window, sadly utters the comment that "this will

28. Henri Labrouste, La Bibliothèque Ste.-Geneviève, Paris, 1838–50, from César Daly, *La Revue Générale d'Architecture et des Travaux Publics*, vol. 10 (1852).

kill that."[66] Hugo offers two explanations for the statement, in the second of which he makes known his views on architecture. The "this" refers to the invention of the printing press or the published word, the "that" refers to the erstwhile "great book" of architecture that is about to be super-seded as a tool for expression. Hugo's reasoning is what is most interesting, as he launches into a history of the art in which the upright stone becomes the first letter, the laying of one stone on another becomes the first word, and the monuments (with their statuary and stained glass) become the first books recording the great ideas of the human race. It is a process that spanned 6,000 years, from the pagodas of Hindustan to the art's great culmination in the medieval cathedral. Gutenberg's invention changed everything, however. The printed book is easier to access, less costly, and more effective as a form of social expression; as a consequence, architecture has withered since its invention. The classicism of the Renaissance was cold, dry, and naked, and between the reigns of Francis II and Louis XV the disease of classicism spread at a geometric rate until architecture became "nothing but skin clothing bones."[67] Hugo concludes that "architecture will never be the social, collective, dominant art it was. The great poem, the great structure, the great masterwork of humanity will never again be built; it will be printed."[68]

Hugo's chapter, first added to his novel in the second edition (1832), described French architecture as in a state of crisis. We can view it as at a crossroads from which three paths are discernible.

One is a renewed interest in Gothic architecture – pleaded for by Hugo – which will encourage a strong Gothic restoration and revival movement in France in the 1830s and 1840s. This path will lead to the rationalist theories of Eugène-Emmanuel Viollet-le-Duc.

A second path will be defined by Labrouste himself, most especially in the Renaissance-inspired design for the Ste.-Geneviève Library (1838–50) on the Place du Panthéon, facing Soufflot's masterpiece. This path too will be interpreted as a form of rationalism, but it is a technically innovative rationalism tempered by expressive allegory: a building dressed metaphorically with the sepulchral facade of Alberti's S. Francesco at Rimini (Fig. 28). The spirit of Boullée now dons not classical but Renaissance cladding; the pessimism of Hugo is contested.

Still a third path will be charted by the lesser known architect Léonce Reynaud (1803–80), who long had connections with Saint-Simonism and student dissident groups. He had originally enrolled at the Ecole Polytechnique in 1821 but was expelled on the suspicion that he belonged to an anarchist organization. A few years later he enrolled at the Ecole des Beaux-Arts, but he never competed for the *grand-prix*. Instead, in 1828 he traveled at his own expense to the French Academy in Rome, where – Robin Middleton has surmised – he made known the ideas of Saint-Simon to Labrouste and Vaudoyer.[69] By 1832 Reynaud had joined a circle of intellectuals led by Pierre Leroux, who in 1831 had taken over the *Revue encyclopédie* and (together with Léonce's brother Jean) planned to turn it into a new ency-

clopedia project predicated on Saint-Simonism. Toward the end of 1834, Léonce Reynaud wrote the entry "Architecture," intended in fact to replace the now outdated article by Quatremère de Quincy.

In openly opposing the doctrines of the Ecole des Beaux-Arts, Reynaud proudly announces that "none of the systems of the past can be considered as having an absolute value" and that none "is able to serve as a definite model or formally impose its laws on us."[70] In advancing the earlier historical premises of Saint-Simon, he sees architecture not so much as an art engaged in the dialectic of organic versus critical development but as an art marching arm and arm with science and technology in progressive evolution.[71] The trabeated (post-and-lintel) system found its early perfection in Greek architecture; the arch, an invention of the Etruscans, only found its full realization in Gothic times. The recent decline of Christianity signals the social exhaustion of these forms, and it is up to the present to conceive a new and original architecture expressing a new "grand moral idea." Another innovative feature of Reynaud's article is its version of rationalism. Styles may represent larger social ideas, but in a real way their forms are determined by materials and the ingenuity of their structural solutions: factors contributing to a trend toward less massive proportions. This pathway, of course, leads to the end of historicism itself.

4. Classicism and the Gothic Revival in Britain

The popularity of picturesque theory notwithstanding, British architecture in the first half of the nineteenth century experienced a strong classical revival. The reason for this new interest in classicism had much to do with the conservative nature of many British institutions. The much delayed publication of Stuart and Revett's books on Athens – volumes two through four appearing between 1788 and 1816 – did much to keep classical interest alive, as did the landed gentry's continuing penchant for touring the South and the activities of such classically inspired organizations as the Society of Dilettanti and later the Institute of British Architects (founded in 1836). Archaeological investigations in Greece likewise continued unabated, especially in the first three decades of the nineteenth century. Of all of these causes, the arrival of the Elgin Marbles in London certainly had the greatest impact. Their arrival had been anticipated from the time they left Greece, though it was delayed when one of the vessels foundered off Cape Malea in 1803, and the marbles in that vessel had to be recovered by divers. They were not fully reassembled in London until 1807–12. The preparations for their display prompted still another expedition to Greece, by a team of architects and classicists led by William Kinnard. The goal of this team was to supplement and prepare a less expensive, annotated second edition of Stuart and Revett's *The Antiquities of Athens*; this edition appeared between 1825 and 1830.

A convenient starting point for the translation of this interest into architectural practice is 1804, the year of the controversy over the recently endowed Downing College at Cambridge University. The neoclassicist James Wyatt had shortly before submitted plans for the new college based on classical Roman forms. The master of Downing, Francis Annesley, sought comments from the noted collector and dilettante Thomas Hope (1769–1831). The choice of Hope as a referee is an interesting one, for he was born in Amsterdam, the son of a wealthy English merchant, and between 1787 and 1795 had made a particularly ambitious grand tour, which included Sicily, Egypt, Turkey, Syria, and Greece. At the time of Annesley's request, Hope was in the midst of redesigning the interiors of a house designed by Robert Adam on Portland Square – indeed, outfitting it as his new residence.

Hope responded to Annesley with a thirty-five-page pamphlet, *Observations on the Plans and Elevations designed by James Wyatt, Architect, for Downing College, Cambridge.*[72] After detailing at length his extensive travels and sensitivity toward architecture, Hope expressed his keen disappointment with the proposed design: "In a building which, from the immensity of the sum allotted to its construction, is enabled, as well as intended, to become one of the first ornaments to a country, I could still wish that instead of the degraded architecture of the Romans, the purest style of the Greeks had been exclusively exhibited."[73] Hope went on to argue that a monument "in the true Grecian style would thus be really unique" and that as a model "Mr. Wilkins has lately brought home, and soon intends to publish, designs of a Greek temple."[74] Hope reinforced this last point by arguing that the black-and-white engravings of Greek forms published so far did little justice to the style's true character – a claim with which John Soane (though later critical of Hope's interior designs) would voice his full agreement.[75]

Hope's pamphlet dissuaded Annesley from hiring Wyatt, and Annesley sought an alternative design from George Byfield. Also making proposals were William Wilkins (who had just returned from Greece), Francis Sandys, and Lewis Wyatt (the nephew of James). Wilkins's winning scheme of 1806

(partially built) combined a building with Ionic porches (whose capitals were modeled on those of the Erechtheum) with a Doric propylaeum, intended to serve as the entrance to the college. The archaeological character of his effort was supported the following year by the publication of his *Antiquities of Magna Graecia*, which focused in large part on the Greek colonial works of Sicily and Paestum.[76] Wilkins's commission for Downing College launched him on a successful career in which he designed several other classical works, among them University College, London (1826–30), and the National Gallery and Royal Academy, London (1832–8).

His scheme for Downing College also initiated a phase of neoclassicism in Britain that was noted for its archaeological character and cubic austerity. Another practitioner of this style was Robert Smirke (1780–1867), who first made his mark with his design for the Convent Garden Theater (1808–9). Smirke had briefly studied with Soane in the mid-1790s, and in 1799 he won the gold medal at the Royal Academy, allowing him to tour France, Italy, Sicily, and Greece. The theater was notable for its unadorned simplicity, Doric porch, and continuous bas-relief across the front. The design was first applauded but became an object of contention when, in January 1810, Soane displayed and ridiculed it in a lecture to the Royal Academy. With Smirke present in the audience, Soane condemned the "glaring impropriety" of the building's parsimonious lack of symbolic context – leading some in the audience to hiss and the academy to censure Soane for his remarks.[77] Soane, in turn, suspended his lectures for two years, effectively closing down architectural instruction at the academy. The controversy, however, did not injure the reputation of Smirke, who in 1815 advanced to a top government post at the Office of Works alongside Soane and John Nash.

This phase of British classicism, which was noted for its Hellenic simplicity and archaeological correctness, was superceded by another that began to take shape around 1830, one more creative and more eclectic in its underpinnings. Perhaps its most gifted practitioner was Charles Robert Cockerell (1788–1863).[78] After training by his father (Samuel Pepys Cockerell) and by Smirke, Cockerell spent no less than seven years in the South. Between 1810 and 1815 he made his archaeological discoveries on the island of Aegina and at Bassae; over the next two years he resided in northern Italy and Rome, where, inspired by the ever more ambitious restorations of the French students, he similarly impressed the new wave of British students with his visual panoramas of Athens, Pompeii, and the Roman Forum.[79]

29. Charles Robert Cockerell, Ashmolean Museum, Oxford, 1841–5. Photograph by author.

Cockerell's architectural career, however, evolved slowly. His early buildings, done in the 1820s, especially his prize-winning attempt to place a "Parthenon" on Carlton Hill, Edinburgh, as the Scottish "National Monument" (1824–9), betray his training under Smirke. But eventually Cockerell's own design sensitivities – a somewhat Piranesian taste for assembling and combining Greek, Roman, Palladian, and baroque motifs – came to the fore, and by 1830 they culminated in a highly original style that included layering the outside of buildings with plastic details. The Westminster Life and British Fire Office, London (1831–2), the University Library, Cambridge (1837–40), and Ashmolean Museum, Oxford (1841–5) are three superb examples of his convincing and dignified exterior style (Fig. 29). His finishing touches to the Fitzwilliam Museum, Cambridge (1846–7), and St. George's Hall, Liverpool (1851–4), display as well a mastery of interior effects.

The exteriors of the last two buildings are also testimonials to a still vibrant classical tradition lingering in Britain up to and past midcentury.[80] The grandiose portico of the Fitzwilliam Museum, inspired by the Capitolium at Brescia, was designed by George Basevi (1794–1845), a student of Soane. He had embarked on a trip to Italy, Greece, and Asia Minor in 1816, but his promising career as a classicist was cut short by a fatal fall from a scaffold at Ely Cathedral in 1845. The columnar design for Saint George's Hall, Liverpool (1839–54), was fashioned by Harvey Lonsdale Elmes (1814–

47) after the competitions of 1839 and 1840 – initially separate competitions for a concert hall and the assize courts. Elmes had won the gold medal at the Royal Academy in 1837 and was much inspired by the work of Cockerell, but illness claimed his life prematurely. Cockerell stepped in and designed the caryatids and other details of the elliptical music hall, and he applied the finishes to the concert hall, a room inspired by the *tepidarium* at the Baths of Caracalla.

Other competitions and commissions from this era reveal a range of classical solutions. William Tite (1798–1873) won the competition for the Royal Exchange in 1839. James Pennethorne (1801–71), another traveler to the South, is best known for the top-lit gallery of his Museum of Economic Geology, London (1844–8), which illuminates a Doric hall below. And there were the many Scottish classical monuments designed by Thomas Hamilton (1784–1858), William Playfair (1790–1857), and Alexander Thomson (1817–75). All were celebrations of classicism and attest to its late appeal.

Nevertheless, the choice of the classical style for the majority of public monuments in Britain in the first half of the century soon came under attack by proponents of the Gothic revival. The roots of this movement, as we have seen, can be traced back through the eighteenth century, and its aesthetic justification in part lies with the emergence of picturesque theory. Horace Walpole's estate at Strawberry Hill (begun in 1748), Richard Payne Knight's Downton

30. Plate from John Britton *The Architectural Antiquities of Great Britain* (1807–26).

Castle (1772–8), and James Wyatt's design at Fonthill Abbey (1796–1807) are monuments to this picturesque fascination. But the style was also furthered by archaeological journals and antiquarian interests, such as the founding of the Society of Antiquaries in 1717, which over the century developed the mandate to chronicle early British monuments.[81] Britain was certainly not alone in developing a national interest in its architectural history. Johann Wolfgang Goethe's famous paean to Erwin von Steinbach and the Strasbourg Cathedral – "Von deutscher Baukunst" (On German architecture) – was written in 1772 and helped to spawn the German romantic movement.[82] François-René Chateaubriand's equally celebrated chapter "Gothic Churches" appeared in *Le Génie du christianisme* (The genius of Christianity) in 1802.[83]

Around the turn of the nineteenth century in Britain, however, the Gothic movement began to track a course independent of and more scholarly than that on the Continent. Interest in Gothic architecture became more archaeological and historical, as it was bound up with curiosity about the medieval roots of the nation. Two early studies were James Benthan's *History of Gothic and Saxon Architecture in England* (1798) and John Milner's *The History, Civil and Ecclesiastical, and a Survey of the Antiquities of Winchester* (two volumes, 1798–1801). Another was John Carter's *Ancient Architecture of England*, which appeared between 1795 and 1814.[84]

Other early studies were published by James Dallaway and George Downing Whittington. Dallaway's *Observations on English Architecture, Military, Ecclesiastical and Civil* (1806) presented a survey of classical and medieval architecture. It is notable both for the structural value he places on the Gothic style (citing Soufflot) and for his suggestion that the style may have first appeared in France.[85] This suggestion contradicted not only the predominant English view of the style's national origin but also the opinions of most Germans, for whom Gothic was called the *altdeutsch* (old German) style. Precisely the same suggestion was defended by Whittington in *An Historical Survey of the Ecclesiastical Antiquities of France* (1809).[86] He had traveled to France in 1802–3 with the intention of writing a survey of French medieval architecture, and he is one of the first modern historians to regard the Cathedral of St. Denis as the seminal work of the new style. His effort, in turn, provided the framework for the highly influential investigations of John Britton (1771–1857), Thomas Rickman (1776–1841), and Augustus Charles Pugin (1768–1832).

Britton was foremost a topographer, and his chief contribution was to compile illustrations of measured plans, sections, and elevations of medieval British works. His initial studies – *Beauties of Wiltshire* (three volumes, 1801–25) and *Beauties of England and Wales* (ten volumes, 1801–16) – prepared the way for *The Architectural Antiquities of Great Britain* (five volumes, 1807–26), which through its abundant and stunning engravings surveyed not only Romanesque and Gothic buildings in Britain but many Elizabethan and Renaissance buildings (Fig. 30).[87]

Britton failed to organize Gothic architecture into a compelling system of stylistic phases, and instead this was the contribution of Thomas Rickman's *An Attempt to Discriminate the Styles of English Architecture, from the Conquest to the Reformation* (1817).[88] Rickman's book was the first popular study of English Gothic intended also to serve as a guide for restorationists and builders working in this style. Rickman had engaged in various professions (including medicine) before turning to architecture in 1812, and the book evolved from a paper he first published in 1815.[89] He argued that just as classical architecture was Greek and Roman by heritage, so Gothic architecture was essentially "English" in character. He defined four principal phases: the Norman style (until 1189), the early English style (until 1307), the decorated English style (until 1377), and the perpendicular English style (until 1630 or 1640). As the book appeared in six editions between 1817 and 1881, these terms were soon etched into English historical consciousness.

Another study that focused on accurately depicting Gothic details was *Specimens of Gothic Architecture* by Augustus Charles Pugin.[90] Its two volumes were published in 1821 and 1823. Pugin had emigrated from France in 1792 and had studied painting at the Royal Academy. He then began a long association (seventeen years) with John Nash in the capacity of an architectural draftsman and expert on Gothic architecture. He pursued at the same time his interest in colored aquatints for publishers and topographers, such as Britton and E. W. Brayley. *Specimens of Gothic Architecture* differs from other antiquarian studies of this period in that it provided the architect with precisely drawn plates of "geometrical proportions, plans, and construction of genuine Gothic architecture."[91] Pugin stressed first authenticity of detail, second need for scale, and third harmony or consistency of style. His commitment to truthfulness was intended to counter the "sneers and contempt" with which earlier attempts at "modern Gothic" had been greeted because of the abuses of ignorant builders and architects. The appended "Remarks on Gothic Architecture; and on Modern Imitations," written by the architect E. J. Willson, echo these sentiments. In his historical review, Willson condemns the Gothic works of Wren, Hawksmoor, Langley, and Walpole ("a heap of inconsistencies, and altogether a mere toy") but lauds James Wyatt for his early efforts on behalf of Thomas Barrett at Lee (1782).[92] Obviously, Willson sees the present as the start of a new and archaeologically more correct phase of Gothic design.

Pugin's manual for designers prepared the ground for the confrontation between the Gothic style and the classi-cal style as they openly vied for supremacy in Britain in the 1830s. One force instigating this showdown was the prodigious talent of Pugin's son, Augustus Welby Northmore Pugin (1812–52). Another was the competition for the new Palace of Westminster and Houses of Parliament.

The competition of 1836, in fact, was the largest and most important British architectural competition of the nineteenth century, although interestingly the significance of its influence on architecture can be debated. The competition came about because a fire in the autumn of 1834 had gutted much of the old Palace of Westminster. Robert Smirke, employed in the Office of Works, prepared a "Tudor" design for a rebuilt complex, but the design found little sympathy with politicians or with King William IV. In 1835 a select committee reconsidered the issue and insisted on an open competition for the new building; it further mandated that the style be either "Gothic or Elizabethan." The choice of these two styles grew out of the desire to have the new work conform in style with nearby Westminster Cathedral and Abbey and to display symbolically the medieval roots of the English government. But this choice emerged only after considerable controversy, as the classical tradition too had its many supporters. The competition, as written, received ninety-seven entries, and four were passed to William IV for the final decision. In February 1836 Charles Barry (1795–1860) was announced the winner.[93]

In the career of this architect, in fact, is where the classical and Gothic lines cross over, for Barry was another student traveler to the classical lands. He set out for the South in 1817 and visited France, Italy, Greece, Turkey, and – after a chance encounter and offer of employment – Syria and Egypt. In the mid-1820s Barry designed several Gothic churches, but he made his reputation with his Greek design for the Manchester Royal Institution of Fine Arts (City Art Gallery, 1824–35) and for his two Renaissance-inspired clubs on Pall Mall. The earlier of these clubs, the Travellers' Club (1829–32), was the first Palladian building constructed in London since the end of the eighteenth century, while the Reform Club (1837–41) emulated the Renaissance Palazzo Farnese. Barry's design for the Westminster complex also was classical in plan; the long river facade is actually symmetrical, save for the placement of Victoria Tower and Big Ben. The division of functions around the central hall and axes is a marvel of simplicity and logic. To attend to the Gothic detailing, however, the classicist Barry was forced to seek a partner well versed in the nuances of this style, and for this type of help he turned to the younger Pugin.[94]

Barry was a gifted designer and a superb delineator, but Pugin was a better detailer. Pugin, of course, had all of the advantages of his familial upbringing, including a bilingual education, travel to the Continent, a fine private library, and a passion for historical understanding. But he also possessed something that no one of his architectural generation possessed in greater measure: a fire in his belly and the zeal to pursue his cause with every last breath of energy. His artistic and literary output was astounding, but it cost him dearly. By 1852 he had depleted all of his physical and mental forces and died at the age of forty.

Pugin was not trained as an architect in the conventional way. In his early years he cultivated his drawing skills, assisted his father on his publications, and developed an interest in designing furniture. By the age of fifteen he was producing furniture designs for Windsor Castle through the auspices of Morel & Seddon. Pugin next turned his attention to scenery painting for the stage while at the same time freelancing his delineatory talent to the architect James Gillespie Graham. He also tried his hand at producing furniture and interior designs, but with less success. In 1832 (still only twenty years of age) he began producing small manuscript books of Gothic and ecclesiastical designs.[95] The death of his father in 1832 led Pugin to take over the production of the second volume of *Examples of Gothic Architecture*, which appeared in 1836.[96] In 1835 Pugin also began a series of small pattern books for Gothic furniture, iron and brass work, and gold- and silversmithing.[97] In the same year he met Barry and was engaged to make some Gothic designs for a grammar school in Birmingham.

On 6 November 1834, Pugin had watched the conflagration at Westminster and lamented the possible involvement of Smirke in the rebuilding. In a letter to E. J. Willson, he vowed to counter Smirke's "diabolical plans and detestable details" by charging "boldly to the attack," for "his career has gone on too long, and this will be a capital opportunity to show up some of his infamous performances."[98] Pugin employed his graphic talents to assist two teams, those of Barry and Graham, during the competition, and when Barry's victory was announced at the end of January 1836, Pugin threw himself into the design development stage. Construction commenced in 1840, and Pugin's contribution to the interiors, in particular, was immense.

By this date Pugin had made his reputation on another front – with the publication of *Contrasts: or, A Parallel between the Noble Edifices of the Middle Ages, and Corresponding Buildings of the Present Day; Shewing the Present Decay of Taste* (1836).[99] The idea for the book had been

hatching in his mind since the early 1830s, when he first developed an interest in Catholicism and its rituals (he converted to the religion in 1835). He was impressed by the disparity he saw between elaborate medieval designs and the more austere and inexpensive productions of the Industrial Age. The fire at Westminster and Smirke's possible involvement in the rebuilding increased his contempt for the present, and his intention now was not only to exalt the superiority of medieval forms (and their superior theological underpinnings) but to demonize classicism as aesthetically and morally inept – even worse, as "pagan." The opening sentence of the first chapter of *Contrasts* proudly announces this theme: "On comparing the Architectural Works of the last three Centuries with those of the Middle Ages, the wonderful superiority of the latter must strike every attentive observer; and the mind is naturally led to reflect on the causes which have wrought this mighty change, and to endeavour to trace the fall of Architectural taste, from the period of its first decline to the present day; and this will form the subject of the following pages."[100]

Adopting the argument that each nation defines an architectural style suited to its climate, customs, and religious practices, Pugin, like Rickman, insists upon the special "national" character of pointed (i.e., Gothic) architecture. And if the forms and details of classical architecture accurately represented the different deities and "heathen rites" to which the original monuments were dedicated, pointed architecture stakes much higher claims to our admiration, because "in it alone we find *the faith of Christianity embodied, and its practices illustrated.*"[101] Following that claim, Pugin begins a historical sketch of Gothic architecture that focuses not so much on the details of its formal development as on the ethical decline that commences with the Reformation and (dovetailing with classical tendencies) continues down to the "present degraded state of ecclesiastical buildings."[102]

The well-known plates depict this degraded state by showing images of present-day buildings contrasted with idealized and pious images of medieval buildings. Opposite a saintly medieval title page is a mock Soanian version of the same, ridiculing at the same time the "new square style" and the works of Wilkins, Smirke, and Nash, among others (Figs. 31 and 32). Another frontispiece announces a church competition in a "Gothic or Elisabethan" style (satirizing the Palace of Westminster and Houses of Parliament competition) and goes on to condemn the practice of nineteenth-century architecture "on new improved and

31. Medieval title page from Pugin's *Contrasts* (London, 1836).

cheap principles." The large contrasting plates at the end of the book somewhat viciously attack the work of other modern designers by reducing their buildings to rude images (often enlivened with scenes of moral turpitude) and contrasting them with the always devout scenes of more sympathetically rendered medieval examples. "The Professor's own House" (Soane's house at Lincoln's Inn Fields), for instance, is contrasted with a particularly ornate medieval house from Royen. In plates added to the second edition (1841), Pugin contrasts a medieval town of 1440, silhouetted by an abundance of church steeples, with that of a modern town of 1840, dotted with ugly factories, chimney stacks, and a panopticon prison in the foreground. Rarely had the work of living architects been so pointedly attacked, seldom before had modern architectural theory been made entirely subservient to such an external force as a religious crusade, and never before had the plea for a single national style been more passionately made.

32. Mock Soanian title page from Pugin's *Contrasts* (London, 1836).

The popularity of *Contrasts* and the controversy it raised catapulted Pugin into the public eye. Given his fame as Barry's Gothic designer and his historical grasp of Gothic principles, it was only natural that he would next turn to the practice of architecture. In the 1840s he began a prolific career in which he specialized in ecclesiastical projects, eventually designing and renovating more than a hundred (mostly parish) churches across the British Isles. To these must be added thousands of designs for wallpaper, furniture, ceramics, books, jewelry, metalwork, stained glass, and textiles.[103] Indeed, the Pugin medieval guild of the 1840s became one of the most productive ever organized.

Pugin's polemical edge fit with the continuing and ever more detailed historical investigations taking place in Britain and elsewhere during the 1830s. In this decade alone appeared the last part of Sulpiz Boisserée's *Geschichte und Beschreibung des Domes zu Köln* (History and description of the Cologne Cathedral, 1823–31), William Whewell's *Architectural Notes on German Churches* (1830), Arcisse de Caumont's *Cours d'antiquités monumentales* (Course on monumental antiquities, 1830–41), Robert Willis's *Remarks on the Architecture of the Middle Ages, especially of Italy* (1835), a second English translation of Georg Moller's *Denkmähler der deutschen Baukunst* (Monuments of German architecture, 1836), and Henry Gally Knight's *An Architectural Tour of Normandy* (1836). In 1840 Alfred Bartholomew published his *Specifications for Practical Architects preceded by an Essay on the Decline of Excellence in the Structure and in the Science of Modern English Buildings.*

Aroused by Pugin, in 1839 John Mason Neale (1818–66) and Benjamin Webb (1819–85) founded the Cambridge Camden Society, whose purpose was to reintroduce medieval ritual into the Anglican Church, provide approved guidelines for the restoration of older churches, and serve as a stylistic watchdog for new church construction. The society, as Pugin had insisted, strove for authenticity in all things, which, in the realm of architecture, meant a faithful return to the English Gothic style of the mid-twelfth century to the mid-thirteenth century. The society became successful, and its members soon numbered in the hundreds. In 1841 Neale and Webb founded the journal *The Ecclesiologist*, which became a prominent voice in what would later become a fierce stylistic debate.[104]

Pugin, however, remained the most articulate and impassioned voice for the Gothic style in Britain. In 1841 he published *The True Principles of Pointed Architecture*, which carried forward the themes introduced by *Contrasts* in light of further historical research. Its two opening rules – *"1st, that there should be no features about a building which are not necessary for convenience, construction, or propriety; 2nd, that all ornament should consist of enrichment of the essential construction of the building"* – have often been hailed as the precursors of functionalist theory, but such a judgment both belies the growing complexity of the debate and oversimplifies Pugin's position.[105] For Pugin, these two principles can be realized only by designing in Gothic style; and then again, Pugin was the most talented ornamentalist of his day, in whose work, as he himself later admitted, construction and ornament can scarcely be distinguished.[106] But this does not mean that these rules were without influence, for they were soon to be enshrined as tenets of reform by Henry Cole and members of his circle. The remainder of Pugin's text is given over to demonstrating on every level the superiority of the Gothic style over classical design and to condemn the abominations produced in the factories of Birmingham and Sheffield – some dutifully illustrated.

Other writings of Pugin during the 1840s tend to be more moralizing in their tone and sometimes more inflexible in their demands, yet the books are beautifully produced and filled with wit, scholarship, and logic. His last book devoted to architecture, *An Apology for the Revival of Christian Architecture in England* (1843), illustrates several of his own church designs, but more importantly it is a trenchant attack on academic eclecticism and the "carnival of architecture" of his day. By this last phrase Pugin means styles "*adopted*" rather than "*generated*," the "confused jumble of styles and symbols borrowed from all nations and periods."[107] Pugin's personal attacks on those within the architectural establishment are no more veiled than earlier, and Cockerell, now a professor at the Royal Academy, in particular receives harsh words. Not only is he poisoning the minds of students with his "erroneous opinions of Christian architecture," but with his design of the Ashmolean Museum in Oxford, "the same architect is erecting another unsightly pile of pagan details, stuck together to make up a show, for the university galleries immediately facing the venerable front of St. John's, and utterly destroying this beautiful entrance to the most Catholic-looking city in England."[108] Soane and his "eccentricities" are treated with no more kindness; his New Dividend Office at the Bank of England is a room "overloaded with all sorts of unmeaning plaster ornament, stuck up without the slightest propriety, or reference to the purpose of the building."[109] Tite's new Royal Exchange "is another stale dish of ill-adapted classicisms, – heavy, dull, and uninteresting, – nothing to awaken national or civic associations in the minds of its citizens."[110] Pugin, by this time, was even reconsidering the implications of his earlier Gothicism: "Any modern invention which conduces to comfort, cleanliness, or durability, should be adopted by the consistent architect; *to copy a thing merely because it is old, is just as absurd as the imitations of the modern pagans.*"[111] By 1843 the "Battle of the Styles" in Britain had begun.

5

THE RISE OF GERMAN THEORY

Every principal age has left behind its architectural style. Why should we not also
seek to discover a style for our own age?

Karl Friedrich Schinkel

1. The German Enlightenment

The turmoil that engulfed the Ecole des Beaux-Arts in the early 1830s marked the beginning of the decline of that institution's control over much of European architectural theory. The institution itself would of course survive the nineteenth century and continue well into the twentieth, but French dominance in architectural theory would now gradually diminish. The new but still unrecognized challenger on the horizon in 1830 was Germany. Few would suspect that by century's end this once rural and divided country would dominate European theory at large.

This development is all the more remarkable if we consider how late an independent Germanic line of thought formed. Germany's artistic "provincialism" in the seventeenth and early eighteenth centuries had everything to do with its political and economic fragmentation. Germany existed during this period not as a country but as a medieval affiliation of over 300 states and cities, nominally confederated under the aegis of the ancient *Reich*, or Holy Roman Empire. These entities were largely feudal in constitution, not always German speaking, both Catholic and Protestant in religion, and variously ruled by an assortment of emperors, kings, counts, dukes, margraves, bishops, and electors. Fifty-one of these entities functioned as free cities, led by the Hanseatic trading centers of the north.

By the middle of the eighteenth century, political and military power came to be concentrated in the hands of the Habsburgs in the south and Prussia-Brandenburg in the north. The Habsburg dynasty, which acquired the crown of the Holy Roman Empire in 1438, was centered in baroque Vienna, and at different times this empire governed large parts of Europe, including Spain, the Netherlands, Bohemia, Hungary, and parts of northern Italy. Eventually it was challenged by the Prussian monarch Frederick the Great (1712–86), who ascended to the throne in 1740 and soon engaged in campaigns of expansion against Habsburg interests. By 1763 he had largely succeeded in his aims and turned his attention (over the next twenty-three years) to instituting economic, agricultural, and legal reforms, all of which greatly enhanced the economic standing of Prussia. Frederick was in many ways a child of the Enlightenment, despite the internal harshness of his rule. He allowed religious freedom, and his tolerance swelled the population of Prussia with skilled immigrants. He was a friend and protector of Voltaire, supported the *Encyclopédie*, and wrote extensively on various issues.

The intellectual excitement spawned by the Enlightenment found a particularly strong resonance in the German lands because it awakened sentiments that had long lain dormant. The second half of the eighteenth century produced a litany of important German writers and thinkers who responded positively to the new ideas, among them Immanuel Kant (1724–1804), Gottfried Ephraim Lessing (1729–81), Johann Gottfried Herder (1744–1803), Johann Wolfgang von Goethe (1749–1832), and Friedrich von Schiller (1759–1805). The psychological dramas of Lessing, Goethe, and Schiller were in the vanguard of a Germanic literary renaissance that for the first time competed successfully with trends from abroad. The polymath Herder is famed for fostering the notion of a uniquely gifted Germanic people (*Volk*) guided by common cultural ideals. Kant essentially laid the intellectual groundwork for modern German philosophy and aesthetics. His *Critique of Pure Reason*

(1781), *Critique of Practical Reason* (1788), and *Critique of Judgment* (1790) established, respectively, the epistemological, ethical, and aesthetic foundations of nineteenth-century German idealism. It is also important to note that these efforts, although supportive of a nascent Germanic consciousness, were broadly European rather than nationalist in their ideological underpinnings. Kant, living in remote Königsberg, credited David Hume with awakening him from his "dogmatic slumber."[1] Kant's ethical notions were largely derived from Rousseau, and his aesthetics were informed by such disparate sources as Plotinus, Shaftesbury, and Burke.[2] Conversely, Herder's relativist critique of European historiography has been called "one of the greatest intellectual triumphs of the philosophy of the Enlightenment."[3]

Perhaps no one better personifies the depth of artistic passion of this generation than the so-called sage of Weimar – Goethe. As a law student in Leipzig, he took private drawing lessons with Winckelmann's former art instructor, Adam Friedrich Oeser, and thereby gained a familiarity with the art history of Winckelmann.[4] In 1770 he moved to Strasbourg and met Herder, from whom he drew the nationalist inspiration for his romantic panegyric to Erwin von Steinbeck and the Strasbourg Cathedral – the first glorification of the emotional power of Gothic architecture in Germany.[5] His conversion to classicism came in 1787 after his epiphany before the Greek temples of Sicily and Paestum, which he visited in the company of the architectural historian Alois Hirt (1759–1834).[6] Goethe's intellectual partnership with Friedrich Schiller (1759–1804) was formed in 1794, that is, shortly before Schiller began to compose his Winckelmannian essay *On the Aesthetic Education of Man* (1795). Goethe's friendship with Schiller resulted a few years later in his founding the journal *Propyläen*, through whose classical portal he hoped to enter the "inner sanctuary" of art.[7] These very same years (1794–1798) were the golden years of German romanticism, led by August Schlegel (1767–1845), Johann Christian Hölderlin (1770–1843), Novalis (1772–1801), Friedrich Schlegel (1772–1829), Johann Ludwig Tieck (1773–1853), Wilhelm Wackenroder (1773–1798), and Friedrich Schelling (1775–1854).

Eighteenth-century German architecture generally followed trends imported from elsewhere. In the first half of the century, the Germanic lands were largely dominated by the Italian-inspired late-baroque in the south and French classicism in the north. Vienna, with its aristocracy and imperial wealth, was home to the baroque and rococo, which found a new synthesis in the designs of Fischer von Erlach

(1656–1723) and Johann Lucas von Hildebrandt (1668–1745). Bohemia was the center of activity for the celebrated Dientzenhofer family of architects. The late-baroque also found favor in Bavaria, in the work of Balthasar Neumann (1687–1753) and Johann Michael Fischer (1692–1766), and in Saxony where Georg Bähr (1766–1738) and Matthäus Daniel Pöppelmann (1662–1736) mastered the style.

Austria, Bohemia, Bavaria, and parts of Saxony remained Catholic in religion and culture, and if we turn to the Protestant lands of northern Germany and Scandinavia, we find a very different approach to practice. The influence of France and Britain was strong, especially the former. The talented French architect Nicolas de Pigage (1723–96) worked on the Elector's Palace at Mannheim (1755–65), and the Neues Schloss at Stuttgart was finished by the French-trained architect Philippe de la Guêpière (1715–73). The gifted Nicolas-Henri Jardin, who first made his mark as a *grand-prix* winner in Rome in the 1740s, was called by Frederick V to Denmark in 1754, where he worked for seventeen years. His fellow *pensionnaire* in Rome, Jean-Joseph Le Lorrain, prepared interior designs for the castle of Count Tessin in Sweden. Palladian influence is also evident in the North at an early date, as seen in the publications of the Swede Erik Jönsson, Graf von Dahlberg (1625–1703), and the Dane Lauritz Lauridsen de Thurah (1706–59).[8]

Nowhere, however, is the combination of diverse geographic and stylistic influences more apparent than at the court of Frederick the Great. His leading architect was the classicist Georg Wenzeslaus von Knobelsdorff (1699–1753) and his artistic advisor was no less than the Venetian Francesco Algarotti (1712–64), a student of Lodoli. Knobelsdorff built a new wing to the palace at Charlottenburg (1740–3) in a classical style, and he designed the Berlin Opera in 1741. The latter project is interesting for its Palladian character, apparently advocated by Algarotti, who was familiar with the work of Lord Burlington. When Frederick moved the court to Potsdam, Knobelsdorff renovated the old palace and later designed the park and the small pink-and-white Schloss Sanssouci (1745–7), a building noted for its French-inspired rococo elegance. One of his last designs, the church of Saint Hedwig in Berlin (1747–73), was modeled on the Roman Pantheon.

Also active in Potsdam was the French architect Jean-Laurent Legeay (1710–86), a friend of Jacques-Gabriel Soufflot and a one-time collaborator of Piranesi. Frederick brought Legeay to Potsdam in 1756 to become his royal architect, but the Frenchman soon quarreled with the headstrong king and left Prussia in 1763. The imposing colonnade of his service wings for the New Palace, concluding with open temple forms at each end, is extraordinary for its date and represents one of the first neoclassical works in Europe. After Legeay's departure, construction of the complex was entrusted to Karl von Gontard (1731–91), who in 1777–80 built the King's Colonnade on the Royal Bridge in Berlin. Thus in a curious way Berlin-Potsdam between 1750 and 1780, with its architectural dependence on France, was in the forefront of European architectural fashion.

If Frederick looked principally to France, other rulers in the North looked elsewhere. In 1766 Prince Leopold Friedrich Franz instructed his friend and architect Friedrich Wilhelm von Erdmannsdorff (1736–1800) to build the schloss and "picturesque" park at Wörlitz, near Dessau. Both men were avid students of European developments, having toured England, Scotland, France, and Italy together on two trips in the 1760s. While they were in Rome, Winckelmann had served as their daily companion (for no less than six months!), and there they had also met Clérisseau and Piranesi. In England they visited picturesque gardens and studied the early work of the Adam brothers. The estate at Wörlitz displays all of these influences, and more. The main building is Palladian, yet its interiors follow the Pompeian lead of the Adam brothers. The park, featuring a copy of Rousseau's burial island at Ermenonville, is entirely picturesque, and, like Stourhead, has several temples scattered around the grounds.

Interest in the English garden was well advanced in the North by this date. In 1779 the Holsteinian Christian Cay Laurenz Hirschfeld (1742–92) issued the first of the five-volumes of his *Théorie de l'art des jardins*, which among other things argued that the informality and asymmetry of English picturesque gardens were better suited to modern democratic times than the severity of formal gardens.[9] Hirschfeld, a professor at the University of Kiel, contrasted the "new taste" of the British with the "old taste" of the French and lauded in particular the writings of William Chambers, Thomas Whately, and Horace Walpole. The qualities he sought to promote, aside from a certain "rural" character, were vivid contrast, variation, color, movement, charm, novelty, and unexpectedness – all of which the designer was suppose to exploit in a sophisticated yet sensitive way.

Another seat of the German Enlightenment was the Hessen town of Kassel. The "upper new town" was built for a community of French Huguenots, following their ouster from France in 1685. The architect for the urban extension was Paul du Ry (1640–1714), who had been trained in Paris by François Blondel. Paul's grandson, Simon Louis du Ry (1726–99), continued the French-inspired tradition. After training in Sweden, he studied at Jacques-François Blondel's school in Paris, and his most important contribution to neoclassicism was the Museum Fredericianum (1769–79), whose horizontal skyline and austere Ionic portico are said to be based on a design of Jean-François de Neufforge, but mediated by Simon's interest in the British Palladians.[10] The Landgrave of Hesse also invited Claude-Nicolas Ledoux to Kassel in the mid-1870s, and the Frenchman offered several design proposals. Friedrich again solicited a design for the renovation of Schloss Wilhelmshöhe, high above the town of Kassel, from the Paris architect Charles de Wailly. Simon du Ry and his student Heinrich Christoph Jussow (1754–1825) eventually carried out the project.

Finally, we should note the work of the Dresden architect Friedrich August Krubsacius (1718–89). His architectural treatise *Betrachtungen über den Geschmack der Alten in der Baukunst* (Reflections on the taste of the ancients in architecture, 1745) served as a textbook for Winckelmann when he moved to Dresden in 1754.[11] Krubsacius quite possibly was also the German translator of Laugier's *Observations sur l'architecture* in 1771.[12] The Tuscan portico and crisp rectilinearity of Krubsacius's design for the Dresden Landhaus (1770–6), now City Museum, is said to have been inspired by Soufflot, although the cast-iron railings of his staircase still owes much to baroque sensibilities. His books on architecture, however, place him alongside Soufflot as an early champion of neoclassicism.[13]

2. Friedrich Gilly and Karl Friedrich Schinkel

The German classical architects of the 1760s and 1770s, although still taking heed of the fashions of France and Britain, laid the essential groundwork for the consolidation of Germanic theory toward the end of the century. Travel to the South, as elsewhere, played an important role in fostering this classically oriented independence. Beginning in the 1770s German visitors to Rome began increasing dramatically in numbers, and by the end of the century they formed one of the largest contingents of foreigners in Rome. Intellectuals and artists traveling to this city in the 1780s included Goethe, Alois Hirt, Karl Philipp Moritz, Heinrich Meyer, Hans Christian Genelli, and Johann Gottfried Schadow; they were joined by the architects Heinrich Christoph Jussow, Peter Joseph Krahe, Christian Frederick Hansen, and Johann August Arens. In the early 1790s the architects Heinrich Gentz (1766–1811) and Friedrich Weinbrenner (1766–1826) resided in the city, along with the painter Asmus Jacob Carstens. Many of these artists would assume leadership in artistic matters once they returned home. Moritz, Hirt, Genelli, and Schadow, for instance, would all later teach at the Berlin Academy of Fine Arts, while Weinbrenner raised the banner of classicism in Karlsruhe. And as the "Storm and Stress" era of the 1770s and 1780s gave way to a softer yet broader cultural flowering under the dual impulses of classicism and romanticism, the first signs of a German national identity became manifest.

For architectural theory, the key event was the founding of the Berlin Architecture Academy in 1799 – the Bauakademie. Classicism, which had already had an influence on the architecture of the city, was promoted in the 1780s by Friedrich Wilhelm II, who was interested in cultivating a "German" taste with a Greek cast. In 1787 he commissioned Erdmannsdorff to renovate the Berlin Schloss in a severe classical style, and between 1789 and 1791 Carl Gotthard Langhans built the Brandenburg Gate. The Silesian Langhans had distinguished himself first in Breslau, and he based his gateway design on the Athenian propylaea of Stuart and Revett. Its flat entablature supported a bas-relief by Christian Bernhard Rode and a colossal quadriga with a winged Victory by Schadow. Another architect to be summoned to Berlin by Friedrich Wilhelm in the late 1780s was the Pomeranian David Gilly (1748–1808). Gilly's practice had been mainly rural, but in 1783, in the town of Settin, he had operated a small architectural school that drew in part upon French teaching methods (Gilly was of Huguenot extraction). After settling in Berlin, Gilly reopened his school in 1793 as a *Lehranstalt* (institute), and the school was officially sanctioned by the crown in 1799 as the Bauakademie. By this date, however, Gilly had been upstaged by his talented son Friedrich Gilly (1772–1800), around whom a cadre of romantic architects had formed.

To his friends and colleagues, Friedrich Gilly, who tragically died of consumption in 1800, epitomized the romantic ideal of genius.[14] After training with his father and moving to Berlin, he enrolled in the Berlin Academy of Fine Arts and then entered state service as a building inspector, working briefly for Erdmannsdorff and Langhans. On an inspection tour of Pomerania in 1794, he prepared a series of drawings of the thirteenth-century schloss at Marienburg that earned him a four-year travel stipend from the crown. He delayed his departure because of political unrest in France and Italy,

and in the summer of 1796 he entered the competition for a monument to Frederick the Great.

The competition was another sign of Germany's growing national consciousness. Langhans won the competition with a design of a small circular temple with both Doric and Ionic variants. Hirt, in an allusion to an earlier proposal that Genelli and Schadow had made in Rome in 1787, proposed a simple Greek temple. Gentz presented a very accomplished design of a circular temple set on a high podium, drawing elements from his earlier proposal for a royal *Lusthaus* and from the architecture of Ledoux. Nevertheless, it was Gilly's design and drawings that captured the day. Similar to the project of Gentz, he located his Greek temple high atop a substructure containing the sarcophagus of the king. Because of its scale, he placed it not on the site stipulated by the program but rather within a temple precinct on Leipziger Platz, just south of the Brandenburg Gate. A massive triumphal arch with quadriga (serving as a gateway into the city), Doric colonnades, and a series of obelisks and lions further defined the sanctuary of the new urban square. Other sketches of the cryptlike spaces of the substructure revealed a highly romantic interpretation of a mausoleum, made especially dramatic by the contrasting play of light and dark.

By the late 1790s Gilly had moved to the forefront of the German romantic movement. The writer Wackenroder, in a letter to Tieck written in 1793, had already judged Gilly to be a prodigy: "This is an artist! Such a consuming enthusiasm for ancient Grecian simplicity! I have spent several very happy hours in aesthetic conservation with him. A godlike man!"[15] Part of Gilly's charisma had to do with his contemplative and artistic personality, but part had to do with his expansive circle of friends, which included the architects Hirt, Martin Friedrich Rabe, and Carl Haller von Hallerstein (who would later join up with Cockerell in Greece); the sculptor Schadow; and the linguist Wilhelm von Humboldt. Gentz not only was a member of the circle but was Gilly's brother-in-law, and in 1798 he began work on Berlin's new mint, which was noted for its crisp cubic form and continuous classical frieze (designed by Gilly, executed by Schadow) running above the rusticated ground story. The top story of the building became the first home of the Bauakademie.

In 1799 Gilly and Gentz founded the Private Society of Young Architects, a fraternity of seven communicants dedicated to group readings, discussions, and the fostering of mutual criticism regarding their designs.[16] Gilly read several papers to the gatherings, foremost among them "Some

Thoughts on the Necessity of Endeavoring to Unify the Various Departments of Architecture in Theory and Practice." It constitutes a convenient starting point for modern German theory.

Gilly's paper actually grew out of his criticism of the curriculum of the newly created Bauakademie, where he served as a professor. The academy had initially been modeled on the Ecole Polytechnique in Paris and therefore emphasized engineering in its training of architects for state service. Gilly begins his critique by discussing one of the principal theoretical concerns of the nineteenth century: the mediation of architecture's increasing technical demands with its historical and artistic underpinnings. On the one hand, he argues, there is modern construction with its ever escalating technologies and the resulting push toward utilitarian design and specialization; on the other hand, there is the tendency of academies to reduce art to abstract rules and antiquarianism – "a pernicious *one-sidedness*" leading to pure "scholarly pursuit" or degenerating into "the futile feuds and controversies between the academic architects and their various adversaries in France and England, with all their dire consequences."[17] What is needed to overcome this false division, Gilly continues, is what Goethe has called "a universal and active love of art, *with a predisposition toward greatness.*"[18] Only in this way can a German monumental art be summoned to enhance the productions of science.

In April 1797, Gilly set out on his long-delayed study tour. However, instead of going to Italy, where Napoleon's armies had insinuated themselves, he traveled to Paris, London, Vienna, Prague, and Hamburg. The few known pages of his sketchbooks confirm that he was a discerning but unsettled artist. In France he sketched the work of Ledoux yet said nothing about it. He admired the work of the engineer Jean-Rodolphe Perronet and visited various county estates, including Louis Le Vau's chateau at Raincy, but he seems to have been most moved by the small pavilion in Paris, the Bagatelle, built in 1777 by the architect François-Joseph Bélanger (1744–1818). For Gilly, Bélanger is "one of the few architects to have given an entirely new direction to French architecture."[19] Gilly's one important architectural design of 1799 – his competition design for the new Berlin Playhouse – betrays the influence of France, but Gilly lost the competition to Langhans in a much disputed decision.

Gilly's name in architectural history books will, however, always be tied to that of Karl Friedrich Schinkel (1781–1841), arguably, the most significant architect of the nineteenth century. Schinkel was a sixteen-year-old student when he presented himself – or so the story goes – to David Gilly in 1797, upon seeing the younger Gilly's competition drawings for the monument to Frederick the Great. The youth was not only accepted into the school but also into the Gilly household and, just as importantly, was taken under the Friedrich's wing. When Friedrich died in 1800, Schinkel inherited his portfolio of drawings. In 1805, in a letter to David, still grieving over his son's early death, Schinkel went so far as to describe Friedrich as "the creator of what I am."[20]

Schinkel was born in Neuruppin, a village thirty miles northwest of Berlin. In 1787 a fire destroyed the village and took his father's life. His widowed mother moved the family to Berlin in 1795, where Schinkel attended a classical gymnasium (another student was Peter Christian Beuth, later his friend). After graduating from the Bauakademie in 1803, Schinkel embarked on an eighteenth-month tour of Italy and Sicily. The timing of his return to Germany was unfortunate, as in October 1806 Napoleon crushed the two prongs of the Prussian army at Auerstedt and Jena and subsequently occupied Berlin. The entire next decade was exceedingly grim for Prussian architects, because the French occupation carried with it ruinous economic consequences and the end of building activity.

Schinkel handled these distractions with determination. Always philosophically inclined, Schinkel met the young philosopher Wilhelm Ferdinand Solger in 1801 and threw himself into the idealism of the time. The lone book he took with him on his tour of the South was Johann Gottlieb Fichte's *The Vocation of Man* (1800), which argued for subsuming one's ethical behavior or sense of duty under the progressive course of humanity. When in the South, Schinkel visited the usual sites but also many unusual ones. He scoured the Croatian coastline for its scenery and vernacular building traditions. The highlight of his tour was his ascent of Mount Aetna, where he camped near the peak at night to arrive on its acme at dawn. In considering a book of his travels, he downplayed the relevance of classicism and promised instead to focus on "those works carrying the true character of their land and purpose."[21] These buildings were neither classical nor Rennaissance but from the period of development that lay between these two – what he termed "Saracenic," a style he defined as "arising from the blending of Eastern and antique architecture in the time of the mass migrations."[22] His interest in the late Roman and Romanesque styles developed more than three decades before any other European architect would devote similar attention to this period.

The period 1805–15 was equally crucial for his intellectual development. Robbed for the most part of an architectural outlet (in 1810 he was appointed an aesthetic "advisor" to the state on architecture), Schinkel focused his enormous imagination on landscape painting, panoramas, dioramas, and stage designs. While in Rome, Schinkel had admired the heroic classical landscapes of Joseph Anton Koch, whose style had in turn been influenced by Carstens and Nicolas Poussin. Schinkel derived from Koch his landscape style: atmospheric scenes profuse with hints of human events, often with abrupt spatial breaks from foreground to backdrop. Architecture was generally the focus of these paintings, and with his growing interest in Gothic architecture around 1810, he often featured medieval or Gothic themes. The paintings lack the inward spirituality and lonely melancholy of the works of his contemporary Caspar David Friedrich, but they share a romantic intensity of feeling and a similar depth of philosophical and historical reflection. They are, as Kurt W. Forster has characterized them, *Stimmungsbilder* – images of poetic feeling – composed in space and light with discerning intelligence.[23] In 1844 Gustav Friedrich Waagen noted that if Schinkel had given all of his attention to painting, he would have been "the greatest landscape-painter of all time," because "he combined the Nordic temperament's intensely vital feeling for simple, unpretentious delights – made so appealing to us by the pictures of Ruysdael – with Claude Lorrain's sense of magical effects of light, for which the landscape of southern Europe offers abundant inspiration."[24]

Then there was Schinkel's fascination with panoramas and dioramas.[25] The panorama, which Schinkel first experienced in Paris in 1804, was in many ways a forerunner of the modern cinema. Patented by the Scotsman Robert Barker in 1788, it was a process in which spectators, standing on a raised platform inside a circular room (originally sixty feet in diameter), viewed continuous (urban or natural) images surrounding them. The space between the images and the platform was darkened, and the images themselves were lit from above and behind with concealed lighting. Special lighting effects also changed over time or even created visual illusions. Schinkel's famous panorama of Palermo was exhibited in 1808 to large crowds in Berlin, but one year earlier he invented (in collaboration with the theater owner Wilhelm Gropius) a new genre of "perspective optical views," a type of diorama in which large flat transparent images (originally thirteen feet by twenty feet) were viewed thirty feet away through darkened rows of columns. In 1807

Schinkel's one-man show consisted of four such images: interior views of St. Peter's and Milan Cathedral, and landscapes of Mount Vesuvius and Mont Blanc. Images in other years depicted distant cities (such as Constantinople and Jerusalem) or historical landscapes (such as the ruins of a theater at Taormina against the backdrop of Mount Etna). In 1812 the burning of Moscow was depicted, and in the following year Schinkel painted a scene from the battle near Leipzig in which the remnants of the French army were routed by Prussian forces. These shows were wildly popular, and Schinkel was heralded as a "genius" for his panoramas. In 1810 the king and queen returned to Berlin from Königsberg and even asked for a private showing from the artist. Friedrich Wilhelm III was so moved by the display that he offered Schinkel a position as an architectural advisor and soon engaged him to renovate rooms for his palaces in Berlin and Charlottenhof.

Finally, one should also take note of Schinkel's stage designs for the Berlin Playhouse. His dioramas were in essence stage scenery, but in 1813 he made a proposal to the Berlin Playhouse director, August Wilhelm Iffland, to renovate the building that Langhans had designed in 1799. Following proposals of Goethe and Tieck, Schinkel suggested eliminating the cumbersome stage sets and coulisses and replacing them with flat transparent images lit from behind. To separate further the unreal world of the actors from the spectators, he also proposed deepening the proscenium and placing four Corinthian columns on each side, thereby creating a false-perspective effect. The intention was to condense and enhance the theatrical experience by making the stage scenery less literal and more atmospheric in character. Schinkel failed to convince Iffland, yet Iffland's successor, Graf Brühl, was quite open to his talents. Between 1815 and 1828, Schinkel created over one hundred sets for forty-five plays. His sensational sets for the 1816 production of Mozart's *Magic Flute* colorfully transported the dazzled viewer to a dozen exotic landscapes in primeval time and served as a fitting culmination to the coronation ceremonies of that year.[26]

Schinkel turned his attention back to architecture in a serious way in 1815, when he was promoted to the post of *Geheimer Oberbaurat*, which gave him control of much of the state building activity in Prussia. As a hedge against French aggression, the Congress of Vienna had enhanced the status of Prussia by giving it mineral holdings in the Ruhr and Sahr valleys (vital for its industrial development) as well as areas of the Rhineland, Westphalia, and Saxony. Thus the capital of Berlin was poised to become a major

33. Karl Friedrich Schinkel, Berlin Playhouse, 1819–21. Photograph by author.

European center just as Schinkel was approaching his prime as an artist.

His architectural sensitivities were also evolving during this time. Influenced by the romantic currents of the war years, during which the "old German" (Gothic) style was championed as a way of opposing the French occupation, Schinkel became enamored with this language, and in his designs for rebuilding the Berlin Petrikirche (1810) and for his proposed Cathedral to the Wars of Liberation (1814), he even combined the Gothic style with classical elements. In his commission for the Neue Wache, or royal guardhouse (1816–18), however, Schinkel chose a spartan Doric style for the porch – perhaps in homage to the classicism of Gilly.

In the summer of 1817 a fire destroyed the Berlin Playhouse, for which Schinkel had made renovation proposals four years earlier. Through his relationship with Brühl, the theater director, Schinkel was well placed to vie for the commission, and eventually he produced a building entirely novel in its architectural treatment. Brühl took the opportunity offered by the fire to reconsider the function of the playhouse. He argued that it should no longer host operas and comedies but should be a classical theater that focused mainly on Greek drama, although still presenting the works of Goethe, Schiller, and other modern dramatists. Schinkel responded with a design that was classical, but only vaguely so (Fig. 33). The auditorium and

stage house consist of a double square within a tripartite composition; the seating, reminiscent of Gilly's earlier proposal for this theater, has a near semicircular form for better sightlines. The exterior overtly assumes a classical mantle with its sculpted pediments and groups of statuary defining the building on all four sides. Apollo leads a quadriga atop the monument; below him the three Muses crown the lower pediment. In describing the published plates of the work, Schinkel says that he "tried to come as close as possible to Greek forms and constructions."[27]

But the building is scarcely classical in its proportions, massing, and details. Forced to use the earlier theater's foundations, Schinkel fulfilled his ambition to create a work that would "rise above ordinary urban buildings" by placing it on a grand rusticated podium with a steep flight of stairs (whose extension was limited by adjacent French and German churches), spilling down to an enhanced civic square.[28] Carriages with theatergoers enter the building from below the staircase; lower-story entrances on the side wings allow access into the concert hall and practice areas. Aside from the innovative pyramidal massing of the building (whose parts were made compositionally distinct for fire concerns), the most interesting feature of its exterior is the fenestration. Schinkel forsook isolated windows in favor of horizontal banks of openings seemingly divided by squared "pilasters" – without capitals but slightly articulated.

Although he rationalized this abstract device on classical grounds (citing Stuart and Revett), it is an entirely novel creation. The theater opened to a performance of Goethe's *Iphigenia in Taurus* on 26 May 1821, inaugurated by a prologue written by the playwright himself. Schinkel with this design had created his first architectural masterpiece, and his quest thereafter was to devise a new style suited to the cultural aspirations of bourgeois German society.

The 1820s and early 1830s were Schinkel's brilliant years, a period of prodigious architectural production. They were also expansive years for the city of Berlin, as it became a center for commerce, manufacturing, and the arts. Schinkel's particular contribution to architectural theory – his quest for a new style – situates itself along two interrelated fronts: the technical and the aesthetic. Both are alluded to in a passage he probably penned in the mid-1830s, in which he reflected on his efforts of the previous twenty years:

After I began my architectural studies and had made some progress in the different branches, I soon felt a stirring in my soul, which became all the more important the more I sought to clarify it.

I noticed that all architectural forms were based on three basic ideas: 1) on forms of construction; 2) on forms possessing traditional or historical importance; 3) on forms meaningful in themselves and taking their model from nature. I noticed further that an enormous treasury of forms had already been invented or deposited in the world over many centuries of development and through the executed works of very different peoples. But I saw at the same time that our use of this accumulated treasury of often very heterogeneous objects was arbitrary, because each individual form carries its own particular charm through a dark presentiment of a necessary motif – be it historical or constructive – that intensifies and continues to seduce us as we employ it. We believe that by invoking such a motif we invest our work with a special charm, even though the most pleasing effect produced by its primitive appearance in old works is often completely contradicted by its use in our present works. It became especially clear to me that this willfulness of use is the reason for the lack of character and style that seems to plague so many of our new buildings.

It became my life's goal to clarify this matter. But the more I considered the problem, the more I saw the difficulties opposing my efforts. Very soon I fell into the error of pure radical abstraction, by which I conceived a specific architectural work entirely from utilitarian purpose and construction. In these cases there emerged something dry and rigid, something that lacked freedom and altogether excluded two essential elements: the historic and the poetic.[29]

Schinkel's "error of pure radical abstraction" (really the first precursor of twentieth-century German modernism) evolved from his long-standing fascination with constructional techniques and innovations. This began with his early training under David Gilly at the technically oriented Bauakademie, his attendance at the lectures of Hirt (which included a history of construction), and his Italian comments on materials and techniques. It was later encouraged by the various technical tasks associated with his government post.[30] The matter of technical innovation had to do with the fiscal near-ruin of Prussia during the war years and the state's efforts after 1815 to confront directly the issues of industrialization and modernization. It also had something to do with Schinkel's friendship with Peter Christian Beuth.

Schinkel and Beuth were childhood friends, and both entered state service in 1810. By 1818 Beuth had risen within the Interior Ministry to become the director of the Department of Trade and Industry. The goal of this agency was to advance industrialization and further Prussian trade, which Beuth and his agency did through a variety of activities ranging from industrial espionage abroad (in England, France, and the United States) to educational reform at home. One of the fruits of his reforms was the creation in 1821 of the Institute for Industrial Arts and Trade, a technical college and forerunner of today's Technical University in Berlin; under its leadership were created a series of local craft schools specializing in fostering design skills for industry. In 1821 Beuth also founded the Union for the Promotion of Industrial Efficiency, a professional association dedicated to accelerating the pace of industrial change. Schinkel served on many of Beuth's commissions, and in 1822 the two succeeded in their plans to dislodge the Bauakademie from the jurisdictional control of the Academy of Fine Arts and to relocate it under Beuth's Department of Trade and Industry. The purpose for this shift was to allow greater flexibility and specialization in architectural training.

It was also Beuth who accompanied Schinkel on his important trip to France, England, and Scotland in 1826.[31] Schinkel was at the time engaged in the design of the Altes Museum, and the ostensible reason for the trip was to study the museums of Paris and London. In Paris, Schinkel and Beuth were accompanied on their tours by Alexander von Humboldt, the geographic explorer and brother of Wilhelm.[32] Schinkel also met many of the leading French architects, yet his attention was almost as highly focused on technical matters. He studied the iron-and-glass galleries of the Palais Royal, the dome of the Panthéon, the Pont Neuf, the iron dome of the Halle au Blé, and the iron roof of the Bourse. In England and Scotland, the two travelers visited a number of factories, workshops, bridges, machinery, and iron works. Although Schinkel saw the Bank of England and Soane's house in London, the highlight of his stay was his introduction to Marc Brunel (1769–1849), who was just starting to drill his tunnel under the Thames. The two Germans also went to Manchester, York, Edinburgh, and Glasglow and sought out the bridges of Thomas Telford (1757–1834). Schinkel was particularly impressed with the recently completed Menai suspension bridge, which had been open only nine days.

In addition, Beuth played a role in getting Schinkel to work on creating an architectural textbook (*Lehrbuch*). With the founding of the Institute for Industrial Arts and Trade in 1821, Beuth and Schinkel wanted to provide new textbooks for students, which for architectural instruction meant replacing the earlier textbook of Heinrich Gentz.[33] Schinkel assisted Beuth in producing four volumes of the *Vorbilder für Fabrikanten und Handwerker* (Models for manufacturers and craftsmen), essentially a pattern book of designs to train industrial designers in the principles of form and ornamentation.

The issue of Schinkel's architectural *Lehrbuch*, or theoretical textbook, is complex, due to many historical infelicities. When Schinkel died in 1841, his drawings and literary manuscripts were gathered together and catalogued in a way that separated the drawings from the text, and they were also arranged by content rather than chronology. These different writings were subsequently cut and spliced together on different pages by later archivists, thus making a chronological understanding of the textbook's development exceedingly difficult if not impossible. The most gallant effort to achieve such an understanding is Goerd Peschken's arrangement of the material according to five different conceptions of the *Lehrbuch* spanning the years 1803 to 1840.[34] While this arrangement has been open to dispute, it is clear at least that Schinkel's theoretical development unfolds in a way that reflects his interest in romantic philosophy, tectonics, and the artistic integrity of architectural creation.

Schinkel's romanticism emanates from his youthful interest in the idealist theories of Solger, Fichte, Schelling, August Schlegel, and Carl Gustav Carus.[35] In his early notebooks, he would sometimes create aphorisms by giving an architectural turn to a philosophical or political statement. Scott Wolff notes, for example, that in one instance Schinkel changed a passage by the political activist Joseph Görres: by substituting the word "art" for "constitution," thereby changing a political polemic into an artistic manifesto.[36]

Schinkel's early aphorisms on architecture frequently mention the idea of "purposiveness" (*Zweckmässigkeit*), which takes its start in German theory in Kant's *Critique of Judgment* (1790). In Kant's "third moment" for beauty, he defines beauty as "the form of purposiveness of an object, insofar as it is perceived without the idea of purpose."[37] In modern usage, *Zweckmässigkeit* can signify "suitability," "appropriateness," even "functionality," but in Kant the term takes on a more subtle meaning as a playful locution between teleological purpose and the nature of aesthetic judgments, which for Kant should not take the object's purpose or utility into account. Ernst Cassirer defines Kant's idea of *Zweckmässigkeit* as "the general expression for every harmonious unification of the parts of a manifold," closely related to Gottfried Leibniz's idea of "harmony."[38] Stephen Körner defines the concept through the notion of "purposive wholes," that is, as an inner form or formal accord of parts that we expect to see displayed in beautiful objects.[39] Just as we impose on works of nature a functional and formal unity in line with human understanding, so works of art or architecture should be coherently structured and exhibit this harmonious melding of parts.

The notion of *Zweckmässigkeit* underwent further elaboration after 1800 in the aesthetic theory of Schelling and August Schlegel. As Schelling's (then unpublished) lectures on art were given in Jena in 1802–3 (and repeated in Wurzburg in 1804), it is unlikely Schinkel knew of them, and thus they need not be considered here.[40] Schlegel's lectures, however, were given in Berlin in 1801–2, and Schinkel was almost certainly present. Schlegel begins by defying Kant and allowing the notion of purpose back into architecture. He defines architecture in a twofold way as "the art of designing and giving beautiful forms to objects without a definite model in nature, freely after an original idea of the human mind," but also as an art that "must be directed to a purpose."[41] Now his problem becomes that of rescuing architecture's "beautiful forms" from the grasp of mundane purpose, which he does by embarking on an instructive survey of theories of imitation. Mirroring what Durand was simultaneously doing in France, Schlegel dismisses both the contention that stone architecture imitates or allegorizes the timber hut and the Vitruvian belief that architecture imitates the proportions of the human body. Schlegel is left with the thesis that architecture does not imitate nature but rather her idealized "methods," that is to say, such higher concepts as regularity, symmetry, and proportion and the physical and psychological laws of form (against gravity).[42] When these principles are filtered through the creative mind of the architect, architecture escapes mundane "purpose" effectively by advancing to a higher "appearance of purposiveness." Schlegel concludes the argument by citing Cicero's famous passage in which the orator mentions the gabled roof-form of a temple, whose original purpose was to discard rain water.[43] Over time, Cicero insists, the pedimental form acquired a higher religious value, so much so that if a citadel were built in heaven, where no rain could fall, it would be entirely lacking in dignity without this gable. The original purpose of the form is thus transcended by the higher purposiveness of form, now symbolically displayed.

Schinkel seems to invoke the notion of purposiveness precisely in this sense, for instance, in his early aphorism: "Just as purposiveness is the basic principle of all building, so the greatest possible presentation of the ideal of purposiveness, that is to say the character or physiognomy of a building, defines its artistic value."[44]

Such a conception calls into question Schinkel's relationship with his former teacher Alois Hirt, whose academy lectures, with their constructional emphasis, were published in 1809 under the title *Die Baukunst nach den Grundsätzen der Alten* (Architecture according to the principles of the ancients).[45] Schinkel responded in his notebook by copying passages of Hirt specifically to refute them. He reacted sharply, for instance, to Hirt's belief in the primordial nature of the Greek temple (transposed from wood) and the eternal validity of this sacrosanct ideal. Whoever believes in the former, Schinkel writes, necessarily becomes a "slave to imitation," and as to the matter of classicism's perfection, "this question displays the greatest narrow-mindedness, the perfection of architecture as a whole may well evolve to infinity."[46] Against Hirt's suggestion that the classical ideal had been suppressed during the "dark" Middle Ages, Schinkel with equal firmness insists that future research will show that medieval times were in fact not so dark but "the beginning of a completely new development."[47] Once again, such a historical attitude was extremely rare for this date, and in holding it he was far ahead of his architectural contemporaries.

Nevertheless, Hirt's conception of architectural beauty – as defined almost solely in terms of convenience and construction[48] – portends the second phase of Schinkel's theoretical concerns: his focus on tectonics. This is the concern that takes center stage in the 1820s when he, encouraged by Beuth, begins a book dealing with construction. Schinkel's notebooks during these years are filled with the most ingenious sketches, and collectively they represent one of the most original attempts to posit a theory of architecture entirely based on structural issues. Schinkel

in effect sets out to define a morphological taxonomy of constructional forms related to the epoch in which they arise. He begins with the remarkable assumption that architecture is a constructional play of visible forces – a psychology of architectural form, if you will. One source for such a conception may have been Arthur Schopenhauer's *The World as Will and Representation* (1819), in which the philosopher interprets architecture as a dynamic play of gravitational forces held in check by the architect's ingenious system of static equilibrium.[49] Schinkel assumes a similar animistic tone, yet with the crucial distinction that he reads these dynamic forces not strictly as gravitational ones but rather as evidence of historical sentiments or cultural expressions. In his words, "Architectural proportions rest on very general dynamic laws yet they become truly meaningful only through their relation and analogy to personal human existence or to that of a similarly articulated and organized being of nature."[50] Construction forms the starting point of design, and thus "everything essential must remain visible," and it is "through the characteristic of visible constructional parts the building receives something living," a pleasurable sensation of rest, strength, and security.[51] Still, according to this conception, construction not only must be "enhanced with an aesthetic feeling" but overlaid with an ethical mantle: "Very different from sensible pleasures, forms thereby awaken moral-spiritual pleasures, which arise partly from the pleasure of ideas evoked, partly from the delight that unmistakably arises through the mere activity of clear understanding."[52]

Hundreds of sketches support this thesis, as Schinkel moves from a demonstration of abstract tectonic forms (first with respect to stone) to complex post-and-lintel and vaulted structural systems. After his 1826 travels to France and England, his formal topology expands to include a visual consideration of brick, timber, iron, and other modern building materials. No other theoretical text of this period even vaguely approximates the tectonic writings of Schinkel – all of which remained unpublished. Interesting also were his experiments in the 1820s with "pure radical abstraction." His buildings for the customs administration – the Packhof – were started in 1825. Two are simple masonry blocks (one with rectangular, one with arched windows) without historical detailing. In 1827, upon returning from France and England, Schinkel devised an (unsolicited) proposal for a new brick market in downtown Berlin. Marrying an interior structure of vaults and columns with an exterior wall of glass, he created an interior gallery of shops not unlike the Palais Royal in character. Perhaps the most

34. Karl Friedrich Schinkel, The Altes Museum, Berlin, 1823–30.

remarkable design of this period was for a new wing of the Institute of Industrial Arts and Trade (1828). The building consists of three stories of large glazed openings divided by a simple post-and-lintel grid of supports. Again, because historical forms are discarded, to our eyes it looks as if it had been designed a century later.

Around 1830, however, Schinkel began to see his "error of pure radical abstraction," and he now moved into the third phase of his theoretical development: when he again outfits buildings using an ornamental vocabulary. This phase was not a reversion to classical or Gothic forms but rather an evolution of his tectonic conception, for he now seeks to re-clad a tectonically pure architecture with those elusive attributes of "the historic and poetic." Two built works, in particular, articulate this grand vision.

The first is the Altes Museum (1823–41), Berlin's first art museum and, like the Berlin Playhouse, a monument to the high cultural aspirations of the young bourgeois state. (Figs. 34 and 35).[53] With its colonnaded front and central pantheon, it is overtly a classical work, yet overlaid with a sophisticated gown of modern metaphor. Its principal artistic motif is not the screen of eighteen Ionic columns (which Schinkel viewed as a formal device to anchor its place on the Lustgarten, opposite the Royal Palace and the Berlin Cathedral); it is rather the colossal urban

stoa behind, for which Schinkel, between 1828 and 1832, designed two giant frescoes, placed across the upper half of the wall. Their purpose was to articulate the building's essential cultural function – that is, to narrate the mythological and metaphysical history of the heavens and the early deities and present selected moments of nature and the human race.[54] The narrative was continued in the open vestibule behind the monumental staircase, truly defining the work as urban theater or setting for cultural rituals: educating and refining public taste. Hence architecture is made a station for civic instruction and deliberate historical self-reflection.

Schinkel continued these ideals in his design for the new Bauakademie (1831–6). Only here his tectonic ideas have come to full maturity in a work remarkable for its segmental fireproof construction. Built like a highrise, the building consists of an independent structure wrapped in exposed, nonbearing brick walls. The shallow interior vaults are highlighted on the exterior by segmental arches, but the additional "historic and poetic" values are again woven into the fabric, with terra-cotta panels employed in the spandrels, mullions, sills, and door surrounds, where Schinkel once again wrote a mythological and cultural history of architecture (Fig. 36).[55] Because the ground floor was given over to shops, even casual visitors were able to

35. Karl Friedrich Schinkel, The Altes Museum, Berlin, 1823–30.

view this urban processional sculptural frieze. Schinkel's Bauakademie (demolished only in 1961) has to be regarded as his greatest triumph and a vivid expression of his architectural theory. His contemporaries were no less aware of his efforts and his genius. When he died in 1841 (after a physical collapse reportedly brought on by exhaustion), he was given a hero's farewell – "a funeral procession such as the great court had seldom seen."[56]

3. Weinbrenner, Moller, Klenze, and Gärtner

Although Schinkel's outpouring of ideas and built works would scarcely be matched by any other German architect in the first third of the nineteenth century, the pace of architectural activity picked up across Germany. Most importantly, the educational groundwork was laid for Germany's famed engineering and architectural schools, which excelled later in the century and into the next. One city with high aspirations was Karlsruhe, the capital of Baden. Karlsruhe was founded along the Rhine in 1715 by Margrave Karl Wilhelm of Baden-Durlach, and it followed a baroque plan in which the palace formed a segment of a circle and thirty-two streets radiated from a central ring. In 1806 Baden allied itself with Napoleon, an act that enlarged its borders

and allowed the province to escape the misery of the war years. In the same year, the architect Friedrich Weinbrenner (1766–1826) began implementing his plans for a new town square.

Weinbrenner was a native of Karlsruhe, but he visited Vienna, Dresden, and Berlin before embarking on a six-year Italian tour in 1791. He met Langhans and Friedrich Gilly in Berlin, and he befriended Hirt in Italy. Weinbrenner participated in the Berlin competition for the monument to Frederick the Great, but even before this, in 1791, he presented the Baden margrave with a proposal for the extension of the area south of the palace: the creation of a major town square.[57] This became the basis of the plan of 1797 that he prepared and implemented after his return to the city and his appointment as city architect.

In 1800 Weinbrenner also founded a private architecture school, which in the 1820s would be incorporated into the city's new polytechnical school. His interest in teaching led him to write a textbook, *Architecktonisches Lehrbuch*, which he published in three volumes between 1810 and 1819. The first two volumes deal with issues of geometry and perspective, and in the third he sets out his views on architecture. He places emphasis on local customs, climate, materials, solidity, and convenience in planning, but he holds that all of these factors must remain subservient to the essential idea that is to be represented. One of his more interesting formulations is the notion of beauty, which he defines (evoking Kant) as "the perfect harmony of form [*Form*] with purpose, and the form is perfect when the object appears complete in itself, such that for a given design [*Gestalt*] nothing additionally can be thought for it or about it."[58] He calls this harmony a "purposive perfection," and claims that "beauty in art rests on an idea, and the true and genuine artist must possess – together with a talent for technical execution – that inspired power that freely prevails in the realm of forms and knows how to give birth to and animate them."[59]

One of Weinbrenner's first students, Georg Moller (1784–1852), carried his vision of classicism to Darmstadt, where he became the architect to Grand Duke Ludwig I in 1810. Early works of Moller, such as his Kasino (1812), emulate Weinbrenner's unassuming and sometimes severe academic style, but later works, such as the Church of St. Ludwig (1820–7) and the Renaissance-inspired royal theater (1829–33), the latter influenced by designs of Gilly and Durand, display both imagination and great artistic talent.[60]

Moller's most important contribution to theory, however, came in 1814, with his discovery in a Darmstadt barn (where apparently it had been discarded by rummaging French au-

thories) of half of the original drawing for the west elevation of Cologne Cathedral. When Sulpiz Boisserée shortly thereafter found the other half of the drawing in a Paris art shop, the completion of the long-unfinished cathedral (started in 1248 but suspended in 1560) became a national political cause.[61] Moller further contributed to the Gothic revival in Germany with his three-volume history, *Denkmäler der deutschen Baukunst* (Monuments of German architecture, 1815–21).[62] This well-respected survey of German medieval architecture, beginning with the period of Charlemagne, was read by many in the Gothic revival movements in Britain and France. Moller, however, argued against a return to Gothic forms and insisted that styles must arise out the climate, building materials, and sentiments and manners of the nation; he therefore rejected "everything foreign and unsuitable."[63]

Munich was home to two talented architects, Leo von Klenze (1784–1864) and Friedrich von Gärtner (1791–1847), both of whom left a significant imprint on theory.[64] Klenze was an architect of lofty ambition. Born near Braunschweig, he enrolled at the Berlin Bauakademie in 1800 and was a fellow student of Schinkel. After completing his studies there, he moved to Paris, where, for a few months, he attended Durand's classes at the Ecole Polytechnique and

36. Karl Friedrich Schinkel, Berlin Bauakademie, 1831–6. From *Sammlung architektonischer Entwürfe* (1819–40).

worked for Percier and Fontaine. On his subsequent tour of Italy, he met a nobleman in Genoa who provided him with a letter of introduction to Napoleon's brother Jerome, soon to be installed on the Hessen throne at Wilhelmshöhe. Klenze was only able to build a small Palladian theater at Wilhelmshöhe before the ill fortunes of war intervened and Jerome was forced to flee to Italy. Klenze spent the year 1815 traveling between the peace talks in Paris and Vienna – in search of a new patron. He discovered his Maecenas when he met Crown Prince Ludwig of Bavaria; the young prince invited Klenze to his father's court in Munich.[65]

Klenze's relationship with Ludwig (who ascended to the throne in 1825) would prove contentious over the years, but Klenze enriched the aspiring metropolis with over twenty buildings. His two finest works are undoubtedly his two museums, the Glyptothek (1815–34) and Pinakothek (1822–36). The competition for the Glyptothek was arranged by Ludwig specifically to house the sculptures from Aegina that had been unearthed in 1812. (Fig. 37).[66] In the intervening years they had remained in Rome undergoing restoration at the hands of Berthel Thorwaldsen, whom Ludwig knew personally from his days in Rome. Klenze's Ionic entrance to the museum is exquisite in its proportions, but even better are the interior spaces, based on a floor plan of Durand and entirely comfortable in their scale, ornamentation, and lighting. The Pinakothek, or painting gallery, besides being an early example of a Renaissance movement in Germany, has an innovative floor plan of top-lit galleries.

Klenze's interest in theory has been largely ignored because so many of his writings still lie unpublished.[67] His theorizing began as early as 1809, when he started preparing "Notes and Excerpts as Ideas on the Origin, History, and Rules of Architecture."[68] He failed to complete this project, but in 1821 he published two works devoted to archaeology: *Der Temple des olympischen Jupiter von Agrigent* (Temple of Olympian Jupiter at Agrigento), and his lecture "Versuch einer Wiederherstellung des toskanischen Tempels nach seinen historischen und technischen Analogien" (Attempt at a restoration of the Etruscan temple from its historical and technical parallels).[69] The following year he published a pattern book of church design, *Anweisung zur Architektur des christlichen Cultus* (Instructions on the architecture of the Christian faith) – in part in response to objections from the Nazarene painter Peter Cornelius over the use of the classical style in church design.[70] It appeared in the same year as the first volume of Johann Gutensohn and Johann Michael Knapp's *Denkmale der christlichern Religion* (Monuments of the Christian religion, 1822–7).

Klenze's archaeological concerns grew out of several trips to the South, two in the company of Crown Prince Ludwig. Klenze, as we have seen, actively participated in the polychrome controversy in the 1820s, first through his painted backdrop to the Aeginetan marbles displayed inside the Glyptothek, second by giving various lectures arguing that polychromy was used in antiquity. Although he lost his personal competition with Hittorff in 1824 over diggings at Selinus, Klenze nevertheless produced an abundance of sketches and measured drawings during his travels. In 1834 Klenze fulfilled his lifetime dream of visiting Athens. The trip was an official one, as Otto, the second son of Ludwig, had been installed by the European powers (following the Greek war of independence) as the new king of Greece. Klenze was able both to study Greek works in detail and to make proposals for their preservation and restoration – really the starting point for the celebrated German archaeological school of the nineteenth century. That this trip took place at the same time that Schinkel was making his grand polychrome plans for the new palace for Otto on the Acropolis underscores once again the parallel paths of these two former students of the Bauakademie.

An archaeological and classical sense also pervades his treatise on church architecture. Although architecture, for Klenze, "in an ethical sense is the art that arises out of forming and joining natural materials for the purposes of human society and its needs" and with "the greatest possible stability and duration," this pragmatism and propriety do not preclude the adoption of Greek classicism for church design.[71] Klenze is opposed to the early stirrings of a Gothic revival, and because he is later forced to admit that the liturgical demands of Christianity have evolved over the centuries, he is thus led to a prototype of a classicized basilica for church design not unlike in character such French models as Soufflot's Church of Ste.-Geneviève or Giovanni Servandoni's façade on the Church of St.-Sulpice. This said, Klenze's lone church design – the court Church of All Saints (1826–37) in Munich – was inspired by the richly polychrome Romanesque style of the Palatine Chapel at Palermo, where Klenze and Ludwig twice spent Christmas together.[72] It is sometimes referred to as the first *Rundbogen* (rounded-arch) building in Munich, but its initiation of this style seems almost accidental.[73]

In general, Klenze's architectural views always paid lip service to his great esteem for Greek classicism, even if he was quite flexible in his own design tendencies. If Greek architecture provided modern-day Bavaria with its "inner living principle" and proper "spiritual bearing," the Greeks

37. Leo von Klenze, Glyptothek, Munich, 1815–34. Photograph by author.

themselves unconsciously nurtured the principles of their architecture, seemingly out of natural necessity. The period of the early nineteenth century, by contrast, is one of "thinking, of investigating, and of self-conscious reflection" and is therefore intrinsically remote from that earlier state of cultural naiveté.[74] Adding a distinct note of Durandian utility to these sentiments, Klenze also argues that "a clearly articulated architectural demand of the present is the combination of practical purposiveness with the greatest possible economy."[75]

A very similar French influence can be detected in the work of Klenze's great rival in Munich, Friedrich von Gärtner. The latter's main contribution to practice and theory resides with his two masterpieces, the state library (1827–43) and the Ludwigskirche (1828–1844), both of which defined the early *Rundbogen* movement. Gärtner, the son of a prominent Munich architect, studied at the Munich Academy with Karl von Fischer and briefly with Weinbrenner in Karlsruhe, before making his way to Paris in 1812. There he attended the lectures of Rondelet, was exposed to the work of Percier and Fontaine, and learned the design system of Durand, although probably through the efforts of Charles-Pierre-Joseph Normand (1765–1840).[76] Gärtner next lived in Italy and Sicily, and in 1819 he visited England and met C. R. Cockerell. Thus, when he received his appointment as professor of architecture at the Munich Academy of Fine Arts in 1820, he was exceedingly well qualified, and

in fact he succeeded in making the school one of the most prestigious in all of Germany.

Yet Gärtner's career was for many years thwarted – by Klenze, it now seems. It was not until 1827 that Ludwig offered him the commissions for the state library and the new church. The most prominent feature of the state library is the grand staircase, which Gärtner spatially modeled on Jean-François-Thérèse Chalgrin's staircase at the Palais du Luxembourg in Paris (1803–7). Gärtner's decoration of the vaults and column capitals, however, is highly original. On the exterior Gärtner was limited to a planar solution without projections, in keeping with the precedent of Klenze's nearby neo-Renaissance War Ministry. Gärtner responded with an inspired solution: the exposed brickwork of the upper two stories (set on a rusticated ground story) is exquisitely detailed, the upper stories have simple rounded windows, and the building is capped with a corbel table and medieval cresting.

In the case of the Ludwigskirche, Gärtner's intentions are even clearer (Fig. 38). Here he made known his aversion to Klenze's classicism and ideas on ecclesiastical architecture by designing a church "that lies somewhere between these severely Greek – or more generally – these strict and methodical architectural rules and the purely heartfelt fantasies of the Middle Ages, which, if they could be combined, would surely be the best for Christian, and particularly for Catholic churches."[77] Gärtner himself referred to his creation in 1829 as reflective of a "purified Byzantine style," by which he meant a scaled-down Italian Romanesque style modified to suit present needs.[78] The superbly scaled twin towers and central portico give way in the interior to a polychrome drama of great spatial and ornamental integrity, highlighted by a large fresco by Peter Cornelius. Indeed, the stylistic synthesis achieved in this work – the prototypical *Rundbogen* (rounded-arch) church design – would be widely emulated in Europe and North America. It certainly influenced as well the theoretical arguments of *Die Basiliken des christlichen Roms* (The basilicas of Christian Rome 1842–4) by Christian Carl Josias Bunsen (1791–1860), which advocated using early Christian basilicas as models for Protestant churches in Germany.

4. In What Style Should We Build?

Within the context of the rising historicist tendencies of the nineteenth century, Gärtner's designs for both the state library and the Ludwigskirche can be interpreted as early essays in the nascent neo-Romanesque movement that came to be more defined in large measure by a polemical pamphlet that appeared in 1828. Its author was the then little known Karlsruhe architect Heinrich Hübsch (1795–1863).[79] With the pamphlet's title, *In welchem Style sollen wir bauen?* (In what style should we build?), Hübsch did more than simply pose a question. He ignited a German debate and in the process impelled German architectural theory in a new direction.

That Hübsch accomplished this feat with a text of only fifty-two pages underscores the magnitude of his philosophical effort. He had, in fact, begun his higher studies at the University of Heidelberg in 1813 as a student of philosophy and mathematics. There he came under the sway of the noted philologist Georg Friedrich Creuzer, who over the course of the previous decade had supplied a new scientific foundation for understanding Greek historiography and mythology. Hübsch, however, turned his attention to architecture and moved to Karlsruhe to study with Weinbrenner. There he got a solid technical education and was given the encouragement to travel to the South.

Hübsch's tour of Italy and Greece in the years 1817–21 had the opposite effect of what his teacher may have expected. From the beginning he seems to have been attracted less by the spirit of classicism and more by Italy's medieval architecture. In Rome he came under two formative influences. One was the German Nazarenes, an artistic

brotherhood of painters who had rejected classical academic training and searched for a new religious style inspired by the frescoes of the Middle Ages and early Renaissance. The other was the art historian Friedrich von Rumohr (1785–1843), who since 1805 had been a semiregular member of the German community in Rome.[80] Rumohr's major historical innovations have yet to be fully appreciated. In 1827–31 he published his *Italienische Forschungen* (Italian investigations), where he attempted to lay "a documentary foundation for the new art history."[81] Volume 3 contains his lengthy essay "On the Common Origin of the Architectural Schools of the Middle Ages," really the first historical study of Italian medieval architecture. Rumohr (well before French historians would do the same in the 1840s) emphasized the continuity of the Graeco-Roman tradition back through the Byzantine schools of the Eastern Roman Empire and argued that the change from the Greek trabeated system to the Roman arcuated systems was due not to artistic or technical decline but rather to such factors as climate, different materials, new building types, and new needs. In his long critical preface to the work, Rumohr promised to cut a middle course between the idealism of Winckelmann and the romanticism of Schelling, one in which "style" becomes defined qualitatively "as the successful accommodation of the artist to the inner demands of the material, by which the sculptor actually creates his forms, the painter makes visible his images."[82] Hegel, in his lectures on aesthetics at the University of Berlin, would soon take umbrage at such a materialist explanation for art.[83]

Hübsch certainly knew something of Rumohr's views before he departed Rome in 1818 for an extended stay in Greece with Josef Thürmer and Franz Heger. And even though he greatly appreciated what he saw there, at the same time he came away convinced that classical forms should no longer be used in contemporary practice. He returned to Germany in 1821, convinced "that in order to establish a new style, alive to the demands made by the present, I had to proceed more radically than I had done so far."[84] His radicalism was promulgated the next year in his study *Über griechische Architectur* (On Greek architecture, 1822), the first installment of his attempt to liberate architecture "from the chains of antiquity."[85]

In this book Hübsch did not present Greek architecture in a negative light; rather, like Moller, he viewed its tectonic logic as deriving from local materials and methods of construction, mediated by the specific exigencies of climate and social conditions. The indirect target of his remarks consisted of the teachings of his former mentor,

38. Friedrich Gärtner, Ludwigskirche, Munich, 1828–44. From Friedrich von Gärtner, *Sammlung der Entwürfe ausgeführter Gebäude* (Munich, 1844–5).

Weinbrenner; the direct target consisted of the theories of Hirt, specifically the classical primer he put forth in *Baukunst nach den Grundsätzen der Alten* (Architecture according to the principles of the ancients). If Schinkel, a decade earlier, had rejected the historical implications of Hirt's "system," Hübsch challenges its premises at their very foundation. He not only dispenses with Hirt's belief in the universal "mechanistic" laws deriving from the transposition of the wooden temple into stone but even rejects the contention that the stone temple had a timber prototype. Instead, Hübsch counters with the argument that the Greek

temple arose only from the material, structural, and social conditions peculiar to Greece itself. It is thus absurd, he concludes, to try to transpose such forms into different climates, different materials, and different social conditions.

Hübsch's book drew an angry response from Hirt, and by 1825 even Weinbrenner had voiced his objections to the arguments of his former student.[86] Weinbrenner, however, died the following year, and Hübsch, as fate would have it replaced him as the municipal architect of Karlsruhe. At this time Hübsch was already preparing a more ambitious response to the recent controversy he had caused, and in April 1828, coinciding with a Nazarene celebration of Albrecht Dürer in Nuremberg, he published his pamphlet *In What Style Should We Build?*[87]

The title is almost misleading, as Hübsch has already found his answer, but the method of his analysis is what is especially innovative. Against the "sophistry" of those who "believe that the beauty of architectural form is something absolute, which can remain unchanged for all times and under all circumstances, and that the antique style alone presents these forms in ideal perfection," Hübsch proposes a simple alternative.[88] He wants to identify the "objective" principles for the creation of a new style based on need, which he defines through the double purposiveness (*Zweckmässigkeit*) of commodity and solidity. A style, he feels, is best defined by the primary structural elements of roof and supports, and the two basic types are the trabeated (post-and-lintel) and arcuated (arched) systems, best illustrated in classical and medieval times. Other factors affecting the creation of a style are the local and traditional building materials, climate, cultural needs, and technostatic progress. "Technostatic progress" refers not only to the level of structural progress or knowledge but to the collective or cultural perception of structural proportions. Hübsch also seems to be using "purposiveness" here in a purely utilitarian or functional sense.

On such a basis, Hübsch sets out on a historical study of structural systems and their forms, seeking a direction for the present. His survey is ruthless in its logic. The columnar system is quickly eliminated from consideration because of its structural inefficiency with regard to mass and material expenditure, and because of its unsuitability to a northern climate. This leaves Hübsch with the option of arcuated systems, whose arches can be either pointed (Gothic) or rounded (Byzantine). Pointed arches have great structural efficiencies, yet their "exceedingly steep proportions" make them "incompatible with our needs," primarily the need for interior daylight.[89] The *Rundbogen* system, which he finds perfected into the Romanesque Abbey of Maria Laach near Koblenz, is preferable for a host of reasons. But Hübsch, in his quest for a new style, was not advocating the German imitation of earlier Romanesque examples, but rather the abstract principle of the rounded arch, "as it would have evolved had it developed freely and spontaneously, unimpeded by all harmful reminiscences of the ancient style."[90] His pragmatism is everywhere apparent: "The theory of art developed here is not, therefore, like those scholarly theories that relate to reality in only a few issues and in which rules abstracted from such theories are unhesitatingly made into

general laws. This theory is thoroughly practical."[91] Again, he is opposed to viewing the *Rundbogen* as a style: "The buildings of the new style will no longer have a historical and conventional character, so that emotional response is impossible without prior instruction in archaeology: they will have a truly natural character, and the layman will feel what the educated artist feels."[92]

The materialist nature of Hübsch's formulation in 1828 – and indeed its relevance to the contemporary dialogue – may be seen by comparing it with the idealist formulations of Hegel in lectures he was then giving at the University of Berlin. For Hegel, art is fully the world of Spirit (although inferior to philosophy and religion in the presentation of the Idea), and architecture, because of its sensuous materiality striving against gravitational limitations, is the least spiritual or idealistic of the arts. Architecture, in its earlier stages at least, is also predominantly a symbolic art, which again places it at the lowest end of Hegel's dialectical staging of cultural development. Architecture nevertheless did advance, in part. From its symbolic stage, best represented by the Egyptian pyramid, it entered the classical stage in Greece, where the Idea gained equality with the subject matter. Finally it arrived in Gothic times at the romantic stage of development, where (in the cathedral) the "infinite significance" of the Idea became "exalted above all mere intentional serviceableness" and the infinite became expressed "through the spatial relations of the architectural forms."[93] The problem with such an idealized scheme is that the highpoint of architectural production for Hegel necessarily resides in the thirteenth century, and the architecture of the nineteenth century (built upon the dialectic of classical and medieval foundations) is thus left without much of an artistic future, that is, without the possibility of additional formal or structural development. Hübsch's formulation, by contrast, is free of all metaphysical restraints: "We have now reached the goal that we tried to attain and have established a strictly objective skeleton for the new style, sufficiently articulated, I believe, for the artist to enliven with his own individuality."[94]

5. Karl Bötticher and the Style Debate

Hübsch's pamphlet appeared in 1828, around the time that Gärtner was beginning work on the state library and the Ludwigskirche and three years before Schinkel began to design the Bauakademie. Hübsch himself had already attempted to implement the *Rundbogen* style in 1825 with an arcaded design for a theater, whose structure featured a remarkable arched roof composed of an open iron trusswork.[95] The flat, undecorated, exposed brick facades of his Karlsruhe Finance Ministry (1829–33) and Karlsruhe Polytechnic School (1833–6) again mirror the progressive lines of his theory, as do his designs for St. Cyriacus, Bulnach (1834–7), and the *Trinkhalle* in Baden-Baden (1837–40). Hübsch's twin-tower Romanesque design for a Protestant church in Pforzheim, exhibited in Munich in November 1829, may even have influenced Gärtner's design for the Ludwigskirche.[96] Conversely, Hübsch's *Rundbogen* design for his polytechnical school seems to owe something to Gärtner's state library.

But it is the fallout over Hübsch's book more than its architectural manifestation that makes it so important. One reviewer, the young architect Rudolf Wiegmann, acknowledged classical architecture's present decline and the resulting state of eclecticism – "on crutches and in the rags of every nation and period" – but Wiegmann is at the same time skeptical about "exchanging one set of fetters for another," especially for something as un-Germanic as the "Byzantine arch-style," which had its origin elsewhere.[97] What Wiegmann also objects to is Hübsch's emphasis on material and constructional factors, whereby "matter dominates mind."[98] For Wiegmann, style is something "spiritual" that defines either broader national and temporal tendencies or the emotive responses provoked by artistic genius. Materialist precepts "of this kind only nip artistic creation in the bud, clip the wings of genius," and do little to bring the artist's spirit in line with the tenor of his age.[99]

The young Berlin historian Franz Kugler also alludes to Hübsch's study in 1834 and takes a very similar tack. He rightfully juxtaposes Hübsch's argument with the classicism of Klenze and concedes the latter's obstruction of progress. But Hübsch in his study has also failed because of his belief that "a work of art could ever evolve out of the material and extraneous conditions."[100] Kugler insists, rather, that a new style could only arise out of a nation's religious traditions.

Slowly but surely, Hübsch's consideration of the problem of historicism came to be taken more seriously. By 1840 there was nearly universal consensus among German architects – as elsewhere in Europe – that not only was contemporary architecture in a state of crisis over the issue of a style but no plausible solution was in sight. Everyone agreed that a new direction had to be taken, but no one could agree on what approach would lead to the desired end. The debate was also fueled by a burst of new architectural journals and newspapers that appeared during this decade. In Vienna, Ludwig Förster founded the *Allgemeine Bauzeitung* in 1836, and five years later, in Leipzig, Johann Andreas Romberg began his influential *Zeitschrift für praktische Baukunst*. Both dealt extensively with the question of style, as did the first congress of the Association of German Architects and Engineers, which formed in Leipzig in 1842. As a result, various camps coalesced around different stylistic directions.

By this date the medieval camp had already split into *Rundbogen* and Gothic factions. An early proponent of the Gothic style was the architect Eduard Metzger, a student of Klenze and Gärtner, who in 1833 was appointed a professor at the Munich Polytechnikum. In 1837 Metzger published a lengthy stylistic analysis in which he – in reviewing Greek, Egyptian, and medieval architecture – argues that styles arise from the three factors of national character (culture and religion), nature (landscape and climate), and building materials (their natural and structural laws). The last factor actually takes precedence in his analysis. In his consideration of German medieval styles, he reviews the structural evolution of the Gothic style from the Romanesque style and sees Gothic as a form of "higher poetry" whose vaulted ribs form a network or "system of well ordered tension, closely bound together and mutually supportive, producing for the individual vaulted field a latticework that could exist as a whole or for itself."[101]

Other supporters of the Gothic cause focused less on its structural ingenuity. In a letter addressed to all members of the Association of German Architects and Engineers in 1844, Carl Albert Rosenthal, a graduate of the Bauakademie, reviewed all styles for their contemporary relevance and again decided on the superiority of the Gothic style. He interpreted the Romanesque, with its heavy forms, as the last vestige of Roman decline and viewed it as less appropriate for the present than the "Arabic style," whose principal fault (outside of its lack of the Christian element) is "an almost total disregard for the symbolic expression of structural forces."[102] The Germanic or Gothic style, by contrast, is superior because of its Hegelian "upward striving and the dominance of form over mass, which symbolizes the dominance of spirit over matter and of spirituality over sensuousness."[103] Such a style, Rosenthal held, is at its core Germanic.

An even more vehement partisan of the Gothic cause was the politician and polemicist August Reichensperger (1808–95), who in 1844–5 published *Die christlich-germanische Baukunst und ihr Verhältnis zur Gegenwart* (Christian-Germanic architecture and its relation to the present).

Reichensperger, a native of Koblenz, is a fascinating individual.[104] In his youth he studied law at Bonn, Heidelberg, and Berlin Universities and even attended the lectures of Hegel. He mended his liberal ways by 1838, however, when he confronted the teachings of the Catholic apologist Joseph Görres (who now was opposing Protestant Prussia's control of the Catholic Rhineland). Reichensperger converted to the Catholic faith and two years later became active in the campaign to complete the Cologne Cathedral, which since 1815 had served as a symbol of German nationhood; he was on the platform of luminaries in 1842 when construction ceremoniously resumed. In the same year he also first read Pugin's *The True Principles of Pointed or Christian Architecture* and became a convert to its position. Reichensperger's book of 1844–5 effectively transposes Pugin's principles to the Germanic discussion, thereby turning his campaign into a moral crusade for "truth."[105]

The *Rundbogen* movement by this date also had many followers. Aside from Hübsch, who remained a very active proponent, the *Rundbogen* cause was espoused by Hübsch's one-time critic Wiegmann, now a professor at the Dusseldorf Academy. In 1841 Wiegmann wrote an important article for the *Allgemeine Bauzeitung*, "Thoughts on the Development of a Contemporary National Style of Architecture," which underscores the level of sophistication that the discussion had now achieved. Wiegmann's task is to seek an "organic relation" of architecture with "the spirit of our time," and while he is appreciative of the great strides being made by industrial technology, he does not want to limit architecture's "spiritual expression."[106] Every people should have their own architecture, and thus he is opposed to the rampant use of Greek, Roman, Byzantine, Gothic, and Italian forms. "This eclecticism has only brought confusion into this art, with scarcely an end in sight," he notes, and modern buildings are considered "more from the perspective of fashion, than as genuine art."[107] To counter this "Babylonian confusion," Wiegmann considers what can be gleaned from the past, and he sets up a duality between the inner subjectivity and spirituality of the Gothic style and the rational objectivity of antique forms. In between – and serving as the middle course – is the *Rundbogen* style, whose forms are simple, rational, and suited to the Germans' materials, climate, and needs. But the *Rundbogen* style cannot be simply taken directly from its historic sources; it must undergo further refinement because its development had been interrupted by the rise of the Gothic style in the thirteenth century. Only through this (*Rundbogen*) synthesis of Gothic inner spirit and Greek cultural worldliness (*Bildung*) – this

"mediation of the spiritual with the sensuous" – can the present age achieve the desired "perfect harmony between the outward and the inward."[108]

Wiegmann's attempted synthesis was opposed on several occasions in the 1840s by the classicism of the Kassel professor Johann Heinrich Wolff (1792–1869), who in 1843 rose to the defense of the "universal truth" of classicism.[109] Two years later, in responding to a speech given by Friedrich Stier to German architects assembled in Bamberg in 1843, Wolff reiterated his position by stressing that the principal architectural forms have already been invented, leaving the present with the task of simply "modifying and rearranging the architectural elements that naturally evolved from antiquity."[110] Instead of seeking particularity or any national style, he encouraged architects to focus on what is universally valid: "If every artist strives after what is true and right, then his work will in itself carry the imprint of his mind."[111]

Wolf, incidentally, was no simple pedagogue. He had trained under Klenze (in Kassel) and Charles Percier (in Paris) and in 1816–18 had lived in Rome, where he found his religion in classicism. His *Beiträge zur Aesthetik der Baukunst oder die Grundgesetze der plastischen Form* (Contribution to the aesthetics of architecture or the basic principles of plastic form, 1834) provided the new German architectural schools with a solid primer on classical theory.[112] He further engaged Wiegmann (through a series of published articles) in a running and sometimes testy debate that lasted most of the decade.

The culmination of this intense stylistic controversy came sooner rather than later – in fact in a somewhat dramatic fashion in 1846. In that year a newly appointed professor at the Berlin Bauakademie, Karl Bötticher (1806–99), was charged with delivering the annual commemorative address in celebration of Schinkel, who had died in 1841. The title of the address was "The Principles of the Hellenic and German Ways of Building with Regard to their Application to our Present Way of Building."

The theorist Bötticher epitomizes the rapid strides that German architecture had made since 1815. He had been one of the students attracted to Beuth's reorganized industrial art schools in the 1820s and was trained in ornamentation relating to textiles. He subsequently taught at several of the new craft schools, and in 1839, at Schinkel's invitation, he joined the faculty at the Bauakademie. He now focused on architecture and in 1844 passed the state examination for practice. By this time he had completed the first volume of his celebrated book on Greek tectonics, to which we will turn momentarily.

The theme of Bötticher's address of 1846, the synthesis of Greek and Gothic principles, derives in part from the teachings of Schinkel. The latter had sought a stylistic synthesis in several church designs as early as 1810 and even more explicitly in his design for the Hamburg theater in 1825.[113] The Hamburg design contains double-story arches intersected at their imposts with flat lintels supported on a middle pier. Schinkel discussed his idea of a stylistic synthesis in several passages of his notebooks, and in an 1833 letter to Crown Prince Maximilian II of Bavaria responding to a specific series of questions, Schinkel explicitly rejects the notion of an eternal ideal while insisting that a historical synthesis might still be possible, but only "if one could hold fast to the spiritual principle of ancient Greek architecture, while broadening it with the conditions of our new world era and with the harmonic blending of the best features of all intervening periods."[114] The dream did not end with his passing in 1841. In the following year, Friedrich Wilhelm IV sent two of Schinkel's pupils, Friedrich August Stüler (1800–65) and Johann Heinrich Strack (1805–86), to Britain to study recent churches for the purpose of generating ideas for prototypical Protestant churches. Stüler's and Strack's drawings were displayed at the Bamberg congress of architects of 1843. The next year saw the appearance of the first volume of *Entwürfe zu Kirchen, Pfarr- und Schulhäusen* (Designs for churches, parish houses and schools), with officially sponsored church designs by Stüler and two other Schinkel students, August Soller (1805–53) and Ludwig Persius (1803–45). In crossing such classical themes as columns and domes with medieval plans, the formal solutions in an odd way take on a *Rundbogen* character.[115]

A second impulse motivating Bötticher's 1846 address was a study published in 1845 by Metzger, "Contribution to the Contemporary Question: In What Style Should We Build!" Metzger's analysis is remarkably perspicacious by any measure. He begins by considering the dramatic social and material changes of his day – the multitude of new needs, the wealth of practical and theoretical experience, the large engineering projects involved in the development of railways, canals, and other arteries of trade – and the apparent conflict in which they have placed science and art. In search of a solution, he proceeds, as before, with a historical survey, but this time through the Hegelian stages of the pyramid, column, and vault. Each constructional concept is seen to build upon the other preceding one, and the ever more dramatic vaulting techniques of Romanesque and Gothic times again represent the acme in the development of the vaulting principle. And if the last significant structural system was

thus perfected in the fourteenth century, it is also true historically, he insists, that something new always evolves out of the most efficient aspects of the previous system. And the one new variable to enter the present stylistic equation, he now concludes, is the structural possibilities of iron – that "scary word," as he characterizes it, to the ears of sculptors and architects![116]

At this point Metzger draws a most instructive parallel between the "thin, finely-felt linear configuration" of iron and "the network of the pointed-arch system in its collective bracing."[117] His aim – vaguely presaging such works as the Eiffel Tower – is to show that the triangulated ribs of the Gothic vault, which he earlier deemed to be structural, possess ready applicability to iron systems such as trusses, especially when the horizontal is suppressed and the trusses assume arched or pointed forms. Although industrial examples of this formal principle are already evident in England, France, Belgium, and Russia, Metzger is at the same time cautious in applying the principle to German architecture. In his view, this formal transformation of architecture, brought on by the enrichment of an old principle through new technical processes, should only come about gradually. In fact, the media he suggests to enhance and shape the coming debate with respect to iron's new forms are competitions restricted to paper.

Metzger's analysis is nevertheless persuasive, and it had a great influence on Bötticher, whose 1846 address more succinctly brings into focus the issues raised over the previous two decades. First he defines a style (in the manner of Hübsch) as a space-covering system, and he agrees with Hübsch in noting that the two existing spatial styles, the classical and the Gothic (which he calls "Germanic"), have perfected the systems of trabeation (relative strength) and arcuation (reactive strength), respectively and thus are incapable of further development. For a new style to emerge – now a "historical inevitability" – a new spatial system must be devised, one that uses a new material (the possibilities of stone have been exhausted) and is able to satisfy every spatial and functional need. This new material will be lighter and will thus reduce the amount of material required for the supporting walls. This new material does in fact exist and is being tested – it is iron. Its principle is absolute strength in tension, and with its adoption a style will soon emerge that "will in times to come be as superior to the Hellenic and medieval systems as the arcuated medieval system was to the monolithic trabeated system of antiquity."[118]

Bötticher's Hegelian synthesis – now stripped of its limitation – is remarkable, if only because industrialization in the smaller German states still lagged far behind that in England and France. His solution was therefore more conceptual than empirical in its postulation. Another notable aspect of the address is that the bulk of Bötticher's argument is not structural, as the account just given would suggest, but rather historical. Its focus on history in fact heralds the architectural issue that was most compelling during the second half of the century, much more so in Germany than elsewhere.

Bötticher, like many others of his day, saw the contemporary debate as dominated by the classicists and Gothicists. The former adhered to the Greek ideal as the apogee of human constructional activity and eschewed the Gothic style as barbaric in conception and notable only for its structural and spatial possibilities. The latter held Greek aesthetic principles to be foreign to the German national spirit and therefore ill suited to present-day functional and cultural values. Both factions denied architecture its rightful history, Bötticher argued, because the principles of one system cannot be penetrated without knowledge of the other. The result must necessarily be the "colossal emptiness" of a culture that has lost its historical footing and is left with "the future as the only basis on which further development is possible."[119] Intellectual progress must therefore embrace the past, and Bötticher posed three alternatives for the present. The first is to adhere to traditional forms and deviate from them as little as possible. The second is to attempt a mediation of the two systems by "clothing" the structural system of the Gothic with the forms of the Greek style – the early fascination of Schinkel. The third, preferred by Bötticher, is to investigate historically the spiritual and material qualities of the existing traditions in order to gain a better understanding of their essential nature and resulting forms. In short, Bötticher sought a mediation between the principles of the two existing styles: The new style is to borrow the spatial possibilities and structural principles from the Gothic and develop them artistically in the way that the Greeks invested their forms with symbolic meaning. In his words, "While penetrating in this way the essence of tradition, we simultaneously recapture an awareness of the principle, the law, and the idea inherent in traditional forms; destroy lifeless eclecticism; and once again tap the source of artistic invention."[120]

Bötticher's synthesis derives in part from his earlier and concurrent investigations into the nature of Greek tectonics, the theme to which Schinkel directed his attention in the late 1830s. The first volume of his enormously influential *Der Tektonik der Hellenen* (Greek tectonics, 1844) in fact introduced into German architectural theory the term *tectonics*, which he defined broadly as "the building and furnishing activity."[121]

The outline and leading premises of this difficult conceptual study were first presented in an article in the *Allgemeine Bauzeitung* of 1840 entitled "Development of the Forms of Hellenic Tectonics." Following the philosophical fashion of the day, it reads like a series of geometrical propositions or theorems, and each proposition, building upon the previous, is followed with remarks and explications. His contention is that the decorative forms developed for the Greek temple (a column capital or a molding, for example) symbolize the mechanically functioning idea of each part and its location. The conceptual duality underlying this scheme is the distinction he draws between the "core-form" (*Kernform*) and its "decorative dressing" (*dekorative Bekleidung*) or "art-form" (*Kunstform*). The core-form consists of the functional demands that a building component has to satisfy, such as support or load, arching, walling, or terminating. Each part, however, is never simply represented as a core-form but always through some kind of symbolic modulation or art-form (the rounding and tapering of a column, for instance), which formally explicates and is identical with the structural function represented. The expressive means for these ideal modulations or art-forms are existing either through allusions to similarly functioning members existing elsewhere (in nature, for instance), or from "inner sensations" emanating from the nature of the function itself.[122] As a third concept to his scheme, Bötticher defines the "juncture" (*Junktur*) as the organic connection of all parts.

In *Die Tektonic der Hellenen*, the leading thesis now also becomes a biological one. The "principle of Hellenic tectonics" is identical with "the principle of creative nature," and the Greeks alone developed an ornamental language symbolic of the purpose represented.[123] Bötticher now simplifies his two leading concepts – the core-form (the "mechanically necessary, statically functioning scheme") and the art-form (the "functionally clarifying characteristic")[124] – but vastly expands his material with a learned and near religious exegesis of every component of the Greek temple. For instance, the Greek cyma (ogee molding) was applied at transitional points in a temple, in such places as the cornice and the echinus of a Doric capital. In the latter case it became a symbol of "load and support in conflict," whereas in the first case it functioned merely as a "seam" and symbolized the concept of "uprightness, free-finishing."[125] The curvature of the molding thus varied, but in all cases it depicted the intensity of the load to be

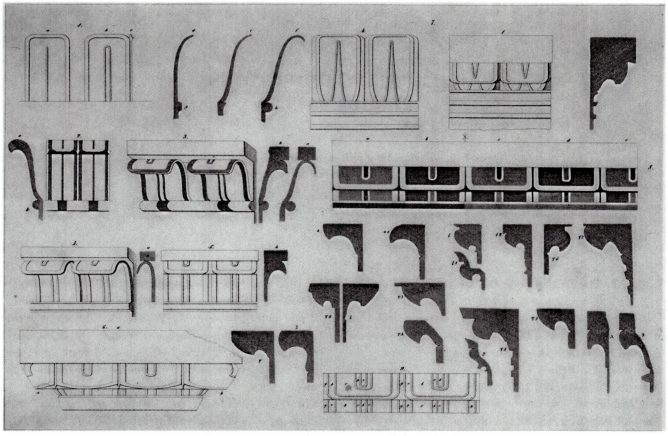

39. Karl Bötticher, plate from *Die Tektonic der Hellenen* (Potsdam, 1844–5).

symbolically supported by the form. On another level, art-forms were also applied to the cyma in the form of painted patterns. In the burdened situation of an echinus, the profile tends toward a horizontal angle of inclination; when placed in the unburdened situation of a cymatium, the cyma now assumes a more vertical profile and becomes a transitional molding to whatever roof emblems may terminate the roofline. Similarly, the ornaments painted on the cyma say something within this discourse. In the echinus, its analogous leaves (painted or plastic) are so loaded down with weight that they effectively bend over upon themselves and create the decorative motif of the egg-and-dart ornament (Fig. 39). The point of Bötticher's exalted analysis is that every part of the Greek temple from the stylobate to the angle of the roof displays consciously artistic or symbolic expression. No one before had looked at Greek architecture

in such a rigorous or scientific way or with such abstracted idealism. Bötticher dedicated his book both to Schinkel and to the archaeologist Carl Otfried Müller.

Bötticher's study of the Greek temple was also influential in another regard. When King Maximilian of Bavaria, for instance, encouraged the Munich Academy in 1850 to hold an architectural competition specifically "to invent a new style" for the present age, the attempt failed miserably.[126] But when the new material "iron" was plugged into Bötticher's formula – effectively as the "core-form" for a new style – the task of the architect was to endow its spatial possibilities with a suitably purposeful and exquisitely expressive "art-form." Many German architects now took up the task. If the Greeks could scale such subtle and sublime heights of artistic expression, why could not the Germans of the nineteenth century?

6

===

COMPETING DIRECTIONS
AT MIDCENTURY

People reproach us architects for a lack of inventiveness – too harshly, as nowhere
has a new idea of universal historical importance, pursued with force and consciousness, become evident.

Gottfried Semper (1869)

1. The British Style Debate 1840–1860

The lively debate about style among German architects
in the 1820s, 1830s, and 1840s parallels a growing sense
of disquiet evident among British architects during the
same years. The debate in England, however, formed along
somewhat different and generally less philosophical lines.
Here institutions such as the Royal Academy and the Institute of British Architects (founded in 1834) represented
the status quo and therefore became objects of attack,
both from new institutions (London's Architectural Association and Henry Cole's Department of Practical Art) and
from powerful individuals (Augustus Welby Pugin and John
Ruskin). And the backdrop to the debate was of course
Britain's advanced industrialization, which in 1851 resulted
in the first international exhibition devoted to art and
technology.

The Cambridge Camden Society, along with its polemical
organ, *The Ecclesiologist*, was another of these institutional
voices. The society had been founded in 1839 with thirty-
eight members, but by 1843 it counted over seven hundred enthusiasts, including many leaders of the Anglican
Church. *The Ecclesiologist* became a strident voice championing liturgical and architectural "truth."[1] It unequivocally opposed all competing styles for churches, once noting
that the introduction "of a new style, whether Romanesque,
Byzantine, or Eclectic, is to be earnestly deprecated," as
"Gothic architecture is, in the highest sense, the only Christian Architecture."[2]

Occasionally rival groups challenged the society's dogmatism and acceptance of Pugin's goal of advancing liturgical
reforms. John Weale (1791–1862), for instance, launched

his *Quarterly Papers on Architecture* in 1843 as an organ
for defending Protestantism and opposing the Camdenians.[3]
By midcentury, however, the Ecclesiological Society (as the
Cambridge Camden Society was renamed in 1846) dominated the Gothic revival in England to such an extent
that Pugin's passing in 1852 did not noticeably diminish its
voice.

In Pugin's place, in fact, stepped another important
Gothic partisan in the person of George Gilbert Scott (1811–
78), whose architectural office would soon be one of the
largest in London. Scott came from a religious background,
and in 1838 he designed his first church. Upon first reading
Pugin in 1841, he joined the Cambridge Camden Society
and dedicated himself to its aims in his church designs.[4]
His relationship with the society was severely tested in 1845
when Scott won the competition for a Lutheran church in
Hamburg, the Church of St. Nicholas. *The Ecclesiologist*
haughtily condemned the design as a prostitution of the
Christian Church to a "heretical sect," for which "we are
sure that the temporal gains of such a contract are a miserable substitute for its unrealness, and, – we must say it, –
its sin."[5] Scott's standing was repaired two years later when
he received the commission to restore Ely Cathedral, and
in 1849 he became the surveyor to Westminster Abbey. His
views on Gothic architecture were made known in his book
A Plea for the Faithful Restoration of Our Ancient Churches,
published in 1850.[6]

The book has dual themes. The first, as the title suggests, is the need to halt what Scott describes as "the torrent
of destructiveness, which, under the title and in the garb
of 'Restoration,' threatens to destroy the truthfulness and
genuine character of half of our ancient Churches."[7] This

sounds progressive within the context of nineteenth-century restoration practices, but Scott's view of what is "faithful" is somewhat sketchy, and he was not always true to the past in his own restorations.[8] The second theme concerns the more general use of Gothic forms "everywhere" in contemporary architecture practice. Scott saw the past 300 years of architecture as a series of "mistaken paths," for which reason he urged a return to the northern Europe Gothic style that predates this period, specifically the "Middle Pointed" style of the thirteenth century. The reason for this revival is in part disciplinary, for only by an apprenticeship in this Gothic style can architects develop the skill and discipline to adapt its forms to present needs. The same view is reiterated in Scott's *Remarks on Secular and Domestic Architecture, Present and Future* (1857) and his *Lectures on the Rise and Development of Medieval Architecture* (1879), although in the last book Scott prefers to "revivify" rather than simply "revive" the style for modern purposes.[9] Scott's highly picturesque design for Saint Pancras Station (1868–74) colorfully displays his vision for adopting Gothic forms to modern needs.

Other visions were also put forth. One early contribution to the debate was Thomas Hope's *Historical Essay on Architecture* (1835).[10] Hope, as we have seen, had earlier championed Greek classicism and furthered the career of William Wilkins, but over the course of remodeling his own houses in London and in Surrey, his tastes expanded to encompass the French Empire, the picturesque, and the Renaissance. *An Historical Essay* reflects the same eclectic tastes. Hope admired the *Rundbogen* style, and he had a high regard for the Italian Renaissance – the *Cinque-cento* style – although he had some reservations as well. The most often cited passage of his book is the very last paragraph, in which he, following Piranesi, articulates a position of eclecticism:

No one seems yet to have conceived the smallest wish or idea of only borrowing of every former style of architecture, whatever it might present of useful or ornamental, of scientific or tasteful; of adding thereto whatever other new dispositions or forms might afford conveniences or elegancies not yet possessed; of making the new discoveries, the new conquests, of natural productions unknown to former ages, the models of new imitations more beautiful and more varied; and thus of composing an architecture which, born in our country, grown on our soil, and in harmony with our climate, institutions, and habits, at once elegant, appropriate, and original, should truly deserve the appellation of "*Our Own.*"[11]

The historian Peter Collins pointed out several years ago that the term "eclecticism" throughout the nineteenth century,

particularly in England and France, was not the pejorative term that it later became. In its strict philosophical sense, it signifies a reasoned and judicious blending of the best doctrines (models) from the past with the intention of creating something new and entirely fitted to modern times.[12]

In his appreciation of the Renaissance, Hope found a companion in Charles Barry, as shown by Barry's designs for the Travellers' Club (1829–32), the Athenaeum in Manchester (1836–9), and the Reform Club (1837–41). The Renaissance style was also defended by William Henry Leeds in 1839 in "An Essay on Modern English Architecture."[13] And this style was utilized on occasion in the work of Cockerell, who in 1839 succeeded Wilkins and Soane as the professor of architecture at the Royal Academy. Cockerell's lectures, delivered from 1841 to 1856, reflect Soane's catholic tastes over those of Wilkins and were appreciative of the artistic unity achieved during the Renaissance and of its interpretation by such later architects as Inigo Jones, Christopher Wren, and John Vanbrugh. They are also notable for the emphasis that Cockerell placed on history as the grounding for architectural education.[14]

The Renaissance style was also practiced, among other styles, by several of the founders of the Institute of British Architects, including Thomas Leverton Donaldson (1795–1885). Donaldson was entirely cosmopolitan in his outlook, having traveled extensively in France, Italy, and Greece. As a former gold-medal winner at the Royal Academy (1816), he had a high regard for and scholarly interest in the potential drama of architecture. Donaldson sought to align the Institute of British Architects (the designation "Royal" was added later) with traditional European academies, and in his founding address of 1835 he announced the objective of facilitating member and student travel abroad, especially to Rome.[15] To this end he also nominated honorary foreign members to the institute, among them Charles Percier, Pierre Fontaine, Karl Friedrich Schinkel, Leo von Klenze, and Jacques Ignace Hittorff. In 1841 Donaldson was appointed the first professor of architecture at University College, London, and here he spoke very directly to the issue of eclecticism:

Styles in Architecture may be compared to languages in literature. There is no style, as there is no language, which has not its peculiar beauties, its individual fitness and power – there is not one that can be safely rejected. A principle reins in each, which the Architect may hap[pi]ly apply with peculiar propriety on some emergency. And as the traveller, who is master of several languages, finds himself at home and at ease among the people with whose language he is familiar, so the Architect is more fitted for the emergencies of his difficult career, who can command the majesty of the classic styles, the sublimity of the Gothic, the grace of the revival or the brilliant fancies of the Arabic.[16]

The issue of imitation, also known as "copyism," soon became a contested one in the pages of Britain's leading architectural journal, *The Builder*, which was founded in 1842 by George Godwin (1815–88). Godwin seems to have enjoyed fanning controversies, as he opened his journal to worthy protagonists of every persuasion. One of the more memorable running disputes was started in 1850 by James Fergusson (1808–86), who sharply took Pugin to task for attempting to bring back medieval building practices and design.[17] Pugin responded in the next issue with a defense of his approach, "How Shall We Build Our Churches?" which also condemned Fergusson's "common-sense" approach.[18] The latter seems to have won this debate, as in follow-up articles Edward Lacy Garbett and Robert Kerr supported Fergusson in calling for an end to copyism, and Kerr went so far as to label the Gothic revival "mere fashion."[19]

Fergusson, a former indigo manufacturer in India, would go on to succeed Hope as Britain's leading historian of architecture. In the preface to his *Enquiry into the True Principles of Beauty in Art* (1849) – a serious yet failed attempt to define architecture as a "universal science" – he first promoted his common-sense style against the "monkey styles of modern Europe, from the time when men first began to copy, instead of thinking, till the present time, when they have ceased to think, and can only copy."[20] He further refined his position in his popular *History of the Modern Styles in Architecture* (1762), in which he countered both the Gothic and classical revivals with a position almost unique within the debate: "He [the philosophical student of art] knows that both are wrong, and that neither can consequently advance the cause of true art. His one hope lies in the knowledge that there is a '*tertium quid*,' a style which, for want of a better name, is sometimes called the Italian but should be called the common-sense style."[21] For Fergusson, this was the one style capable of forming a middle path between the futile search for new forms and the spiritually crushing practice of imitation: "It does not require a man or set of men, as some have supposed, to invent a new style; the great want now is self-control and self-negation. What we require is that architects shall have the moral courage to refrain from borrowing, and be content to think, to work, and to improve

bit by bit what they have got."[22] And what they have got, in Fergusson's view, is the Renaissance tradition.

Another regular contributor to *The Builder* was Robert Kerr (1824–1904). A native of Aberdeen, he began his practice in New York City in 1843, then resettled in London in the following year. Three years later he became one of the founders (and first president) of a new school of architecture, the Architectural Association.[23] It was envisioned to be as much a debating club as a school, and it arose in opposition to the teachings of the Royal Academy and the Institute of British Architects, which Kerr attacked with a fury. He was equally unsympathetic to the Gothic revivalists. In Kerr's *Newleafe Discourses on the Fine Art Architecture* (1846), he proceeds to ridicule as well those who view architecture as a business, or as mere construction, or as the application of the orders, or as antiquarianism, but most especially those who view it as a "style." What he is left with is freedom, reason, fitness, convenient planning, and "principles of pictorial Effect," that is, the architect's capacity to evoke emotions in the beholder.[24] Kerr moderated his inflated tone in the 1850s, and in his own work he tended toward the common-sense style of Fergusson. He nonetheless remained a shrewd critic of the contemporary scene throughout his life.

Another thoughtful book to appear around this time was the *Rudimentary Treatise on the Principles of Design in Architecture* (1850) by Edward Lacy Garbett (d. 1898). The first part of the text deals with architecture largely from a Victorian moral perspective, beginning with the opening chapter on politeness, beauty, expression, and poetry in design, in which the ideas of Ruskin and Joshua Reynolds are seconded. As Garbett moves away from his preliminary definitions, the tenor of his historical analysis changes. Under the notions of "constructive truth" and "constructive unity," he musters the premise that not only should a building "never appear to be constructed on different statical principles from those really employed" but any attempt to imitate the forms of past styles without also imitating the same structural principles and intention is a lie.[25] Hence, employing Gothic forms without employing Gothic building methods is deceitful, as is employing classical forms without a strict post-and-lintel system. In sum, both styles are dead styles that cannot be revived. Joining this "false use of precedent" is the equal sin of "novelty hunting" – "the "Scylla and Charybdis between which, the many, and the architects of the many, are for ever destined to be wrecked" – leaving the architect seemingly with no way out.[26]

40. The Crystal Palace, Great Exhibition of 1851. From Peter Berlyn, *The Crystal Palace: Its Architectural History and Constructive Marvels* (London, 1851).

Garbett's sympathies really lay with the Renaissance, but his ultimate solution to the issue of architectural style is in fact far more radical. Taking up a line of argument perhaps owed to Karl Bötticher, he notes that the Greek and the Gothic styles, the two past styles that attained stylistic unity, employed two different structural principles. The Greek temple was built on the principle of "cross-strain," or what he also termed the "Depressile" structural principle, in which the loads of the post-and-lintel system are transmitted vertically to the ground. The Gothic system, on the other hand, was a "Compressile" system of vaults and arches.[27] But there is a third structural possibility (the discovery of which he attributes to Alfred Bartholomew), a "Tensile" system, in which loads are transmitted in tension: "The third constructive principle has yet to be elaborated into a system. The two systems are past and dead; we may admire the fading vestiges of their loveliness, but can *never* revive them. The third is the destined architecture of the future."[28] This system for Garbett is represented in the possibilities of the truss.

Garbett's rather remarkable feat of structural reasoning seems to have been little noticed in Britain, and perhaps with good reason. For London in the fall of 1850 was already buzzing in anticipation of what many cultural historians regard as the single most important event that occurred in nineteenth-century Britain – the Great Exhibition of the Industry of All Nations of 1851. Architecturally, it may also have been the moment when, in the words of Robert Kerr, the "Fine Art of Architecture" stepped down from its privileged pedestal to join the other applied arts and became the "Industrial Art of Architecture."[29]

In discussing the Great Exhibition, historians of architecture have focused mainly on its iron-and-glass building, and thus the exhibition's effect on theory has in some ways been misunderstood (Figs. 40 and 41). It was not so much Joseph Paxton's design (generally favorably reviewed by the contemporary press) that heralded a new direction for architecture as the speed and economy of its erection. It was designed, fabricated, and erected in eleven months, a feat that might be compared with the construction of the recently completed British Museum, which had taken twenty-three years. And it was not the industrial implications of the fabric (which most architects at the time understood) that generated the greatest excitement but rather the sensation of its spaces, combined with the technology and art on display. Half a million people crowded into Hyde Park on 1 May to greet the arrival of the queen and the prince consort. Thirty thousand more were gathered inside to hear the opening speeches, trumpets, and benedictions – some nervously fearing the glass roof would shatter when the royal salute was fired from a model frigate on nearby Serpentine Pond. Within its 93,000 square meters of floor space 14,000 exhibitors displayed 100,000 articles from the around the world, including raw materials, industrial machinery, agricultural implements, wagons, locomotives, textiles, jewelry, and fine art. *The Times* reported that "the edifice, the treasures of art collected therein, the assemblage and the solemnity of the occasion, all conspired to suggest something even more than sense could scan, or imagination attain."[30] Another critic referred to the Crystal Palace as a "magical glass" cabinet that brought together goods from different nations in different stages of artistic progress and that thus revealed that "man is, by nature and universally, an artificer, an artisan, an artist."[31]

The man who put it all together was Henry Cole (1808–82).[32] He was in many respects a quintessential Victorian: industrious, religious, ambitious, politically ruthless. Charles Dickens parodied him in the second chapter of *Hard Times* as a "professed pugilist; always in training, always with a system to force down the general throat like a bolus."[33] Prime Minister Lord Derby once called him "the most generally unpopular man I know."[34] Cole seems not to have minded. He began his career as a record keeper for the Exchequer of Pleas and climbed the bureaucratic ladder, pursuing art merely as a hobby at first. He started a popular series of children's books called the "Summerly Home Treasury," for which he employed a number of talented artists as illustrators. In 1845 he created the Summerly Art Manufactures, an alliance of artists willing to sell designs to manufacturing firms. In the same year he was appointed to the Society of the Arts, a government council under the aegis of Prince Albert that was studying the problem of Britain's lagging competitive position with respect to exports. The council, between 1846 and 1849, induced Cole to orchestrate a series of exhibitions intended to put the fruits of English industry on display. For the planned national exhibition of 1851, Cole

came up with the daring idea of making the event international. He next chaired the royal commission that planned the event and saw to it that none of the 245 competition entries for the exhibition building, even the joint design of the building committee, was accepted. It was therefore Cole who handed the commission off to Joseph Paxton (1801–65), whose one qualification was that he had experimented with large hothouses. Cole, it must be said, despised architects and their stylistic pretensions.

For Cole the Great Exhibition of 1851 was not just an end in itself but a means to another end. In 1848 he had been invited to give a series of lectures at the London School of Design, one of several industrial art schools set up by Parliament in 1837 to further British exports by upgrading industrial design. But the schools in their first decade had been unsuccessful; as one historian has noted, "they were distracted by feuds, encumbered by debts and convulsed by mutinies."[35] The feuds, in particular, chewed up three directors over the first eight years, and by the end of 1847 a triumvirate of three artists – Richard Redgrave, H. J. Townsend, and J. R. Herbert – nominally ran the schools. It was at this point that Cole was invited to lecture, and he declined on the grounds that the program was in disarray. Instead he wrote three reports to the Board of Trade (the regulatory agency) and insisted on thorough educational and administrative reforms. And lest it was not clear to everyone who was the man most capable of effecting the necessary changes, Cole embarked on yet another venture, *The Journal of Design and Manufactures* (1849–53). One purpose of this organ was "to present to the designer treatises developing sound principles of ornamental art"; another was to serve as a mouthpiece for Cole's criticisms of the schools of design.[36] Cole next formed an alliance with three individuals equally enamored with reform: Richard Redgrave (1804–88), Owen Jones (1807–88), and Matthew Digby Wyatt (1820–77).

The alliance is surprising only in that two of the three individuals who wedded their professional fortunes with those of Cole were architects. The exception was Redgrave, a royal academician and painter who had first made his name producing landscapes and compositions with historical themes but later favored sentimental and sermonizing depictions of female subjects.[37] In 1843 he became a commissioner of fine art and soon thereafter began teaching at the London School of Design. In 1850 he joined Cole on the exhibition committee and was charged with writing the official *Reports by the Juries* on the goods displayed, to which he appended his highly critical "Supplementary Report on

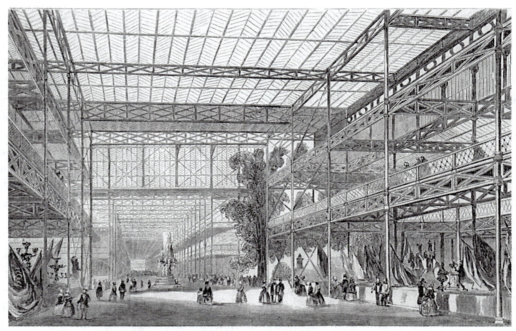

41. The Crystal Palace, Great Exhibition of 1851. From Peter Berlyn, *The Crystal Palace: Its Architectural History and Constructive Marvels* (London, 1851).

Design." Redgrave was an astute critic, and, following Pugin, he lambasted the machine-made products displayed at the exhibition for constructing ornament rather than ornamenting construction. He was also critical of the contemporary architectural situation:

In other ages of the world, nations have been fortunate in so adapting design to prevailing wants, and in sympathy with existing feelings, as to produce a national style. But in the present day men no longer attend to such considerations; they are wholly without such guiding principles, and consequently are totally without a characteristic style. They are satisfied with the indiscriminate reproduction of the architecture of Egypt, Greece and Rome, or of Christendom in any, or all, of its marked periods. Originality they have none.[38]

A few years later Wyatt would refer to Redgrave's exhibition report as an amplification of the principles that Owen Jones had laid down in his "Gleanings from the Great Exhibition of 1851," a series of articles published in the *Journal of Design and Manufacturers*. The Welshman Jones had trained under Lewis Vulliamy and first gained accolades for his *Plans, Elevations, Sections and Details of the Alhambra* (1836–45), an astonishing chromolithographic depiction of the Moorish palace prepared after his tour of Turkey, Egypt, and Spain. His two London buildings in the 1840s emulated this "Saracenic" style, and in 1850 he was hired to paint the interior iron members of the Crystal Palace, which he did – following the color theories of Michel Chevreul – in shades of red, blue, and yellow. In his exhibition articles, he too criticized the goods of the Western nations, but he lauded those of India, Tunis, Egypt, and Turkey, especially the textiles, with their harmonious color tones and abstract surface decorations – which he reduced to six stylistic principles.[39] In his formal exhibition lecture of 1852, he expanded these principles into twenty-two propositions, and in his highly influential *Grammar of Ornament* (1856), this list had grown to thirty-seven propositions. Atop was this thesis: "The Decorative Arts arise from, and should properly be attendant upon, Architecture."[40]

Wyatt shared Jones's penchant for pedantic proposition making. As an architect, he is best remembered for his odd collaboration with George Gilbert Scott in the Renaissance design of the Foreign Office Building (1856–73), after the prime minister, Lord Palmerston, personally intervened to halt Scott's medieval design. Wyatt was also a discerning critic. He was born into the Wyatt dynasty of architects and artists, the best known of which had been the neoclassicist James Wyatt (1746–1813).[41] Matthew devoted his European tour to medieval themes, which led to his first book, *Specimens of Geometric Mosaics of the Middle Ages* (1848), a work admired by John Ruskin. He accompanied Cole on a trip to France in 1849, when they together hatched the idea of an international exhibition. He also was active in producing the exhibition, first as the secretary to the Royal Commission, later as the architect overseeing the construction of the Crystal Palace.

Wyatt's various lectures and essays on the Great Exhibition bring a somewhat different perspective to the events. In one article prepared for the *Journal of Design*, he refers to the pace of industrial change as "double speed" and argues that the exhibition would ultimately benefit British industry and soften nationalist prejudice everywhere.[42] In his introduction to his exhibition catalogue, *The Industrial Arts of the Nineteenth Century*, he describes the Great Exhibition as a beacon of the industrial age, similar to what the Olympic games were to Greece. It was the culmination of a thirty-six – year industrial process, beginning in 1815, that reflected "the universality of development attained by combining the division of labour in manufacturing with the aggregation of its results in commerce."[43] On the exhibition building itself, he was equally perspicacious, noting on the eve of its opening, "Whatever the result may be, it is impossible to disregard the fact, that the building of the Exhibition of 1851 is likely to accelerate the 'Consummation so devoutly to be wished,' and that the novelty of its forms and details will be likely to exercise a powerful influence upon national taste."[44]

Cole certainly shared these sentiments, and in his capacity as journal editor and as exhibition director he cast his lot with industrialization. He took the exhibition, which was a major cultural and fiscal success, to have proved his point, and at the end of 1851 he was awarded the administrative directorship of the schools of design. By the mid-1860s, from his new offices in South Kensington, Cole was managing over ninety art schools, a museum (now the Victoria and Albert Museum), and 16,000 students – a model of education and display that would be widely emulated across Europe. Appraisals of his accomplishments differed widely. Kerr stated in 1891 that "the triumph of Cole was that he had laid a foundation for the popularity of the whole world of decorative arts."[45] Another contemporary voice dissented, noting that "the Professorship of Sir Henry Cole at Kensington has corrupted the system of art-teaching all over England into a state of abortion and falsehood from which it will take twenty years to recover."[46] This critic, one of Cole's many sworn enemies, was none other than John Ruskin (1819–1900).[47] Capitalism versus socialism, ugliness versus beauty, industrialism versus piety – the British debate here enters a new and distinct phase.

Ruskin's influence on the main issues in the debate would become incomparable. This precocious son of a wealthy businessman only seemingly burst upon the architectural scene with the publication of *The Seven Lamps of Architecture* in 1849. While studying at Oxford in the late 1830s, he wrote several articles for John Claudius Loudon's *Architectural Magazine* using the pseudonym "Kata Phusin." These articles, collectively titled "The Poetry of Architecture," exalted the picturesque charm of peasant cottages and their unaffected adaptation to the landscape, their innate good taste, and their reflection of national characteristics. Ruskin at this time aspired to be a geologist, but when he met the painter Joseph Turner in the summer of 1840, he changed his mind. The first volume of Ruskin's *Modern Painters* – largely a celebration of Turner – appeared in 1843, and Ruskin was suddenly famous for his artistic criticism and effusive prose. The second volume appeared in 1846. Before and after its publication, he traveled regularly to the continent and sketched tirelessly. The medieval structures of Rouen, the natural beauty of the Alps, and Venetian polychromy became especially dear to him. Sometime late in 1847 he decided to write another book on architecture, but he seemingly had little knowledge of the London debates and even less of traditional architectural literature. He knew architecture almost entirely from his visual meditations on medieval works.

What must have made *The Seven Lamps* so perplexing in 1849 was just this remoteness or aloofness from the professional scene, as the book makes almost no reference to contemporary discussions. The seven lamps – Sacrifice, Truth, Power, Beauty, Life, Memory, and Obedience – are ethical beacons or "large principles of right which are applicable to every stage and style."[48] They are moral precepts clad in the mantle of eternal truth. Architecture has nothing to do with academic strictures; it is "the art which so disposes and adorns the edifices raised by man for whatsoever uses, that the sight of them contributes to his mental health, power, and pleasure."[49] Ornament is central to this conception. In Ruskin's famous illustration, a simple masonry wall is mere building or construction, but if a supplementary feature is affixed to it, such as a cable molding, it becomes architecture. Thus architecture "impresses on its form certain characters venerable or beautiful, but otherwise unnecessary."[50]

The lamps, each in their own way, impress these characters on form. Sacrifice prompts the architect to offer up precious things, be they fine materials or labor. Truth, which "forgives no insult, and endures no stain," demands the absence of falsehoods, be they structural, the painting of one material to represent another, or the use of machine-made ornaments.[51] Power is the expression of human imagination exercised on a breadth of surface or quantity of shadow. Beauty derives from nature and follows from the use of natural decorative motifs in keeping with the system that nature itself employs. Life insists on the human impression with which we endow materials, and memory pays homage to the historical. Obedience prescribes not the invention of a new style but the use of "*some* style," that is, a generally accepted stylistic framework within which the architect can exercise imagination.[52] As regards style, Ruskin somewhat naively reduces the present stylistic options to the four with which he was most familiar: Pisan Romanesque, early Italian Gothic, Venetian Gothic, and English earliest decorated. His preference for the last – "the safest choice" – is scarcely convincing, even if he would mingle with it "decorative elements from the exquisite decorated Gothic of France."[53]

But the importance of Ruskin's book does not reside in such facile judgments. His prose sparkles with biblical authority; his discussion of the laws of proportion ("which will never be either numbered or known") and color appeal intuitively to the architectural mind; his excursus on the picturesque (defined as "Parasitical Sublimity") is a classic summary of Ruskinian aesthetics predicated on the frank admission of human frailty or imperfection.[54] His views on iron are also instructive. "Abstractly," he writes, "there appears no reason why iron should not be used as well as wood," and he even concedes that "the time is probably near when a new system of architectural laws will be developed, adapted entirely to metallic construction."[55] But history cautions us otherwise, and "even in periods of more advanced science" the "chief dignities" of architecture will continue to be "the materials and principles of earlier ages."[56]

Ruskin proposes a theory of ornament but not superficially so. The cable molding, for instance, should never be applied to the walls of a railway terminal, because "the whole system of railroad travelling is addressed to people who, being in a hurry, are therefore, for the time being, miserable."[57] Similarly, millions have been spent in recent years on building roads, tunnels, train lines, and locomotives, but suppose, he asks, "that we had employed the same sums in building beautiful houses and churches."[58] The answer is obvious, "instead of the very doubtful advantage of the power of going fast from place to place, we should have had the certain advantage of increased pleasure in stopping at home."[59] Again, the principal question to ask with regard to ornament is, "Was it done with enjoyment – was the carver happy while he was about it?"[60] If he was, the most

abundant ornament can never be too excessive; if not, the smallest ornament is always bad and overcharged.

The unnamed reviewer of Ruskin's book in the October issue of the *Journal of Design* understood the "excellent spirit" of "this thoughtful, eloquent book," but also its limitations. Instead of considering the means to improve present tendencies, he noted, Ruskin "either puts his back against their further development, or would attempt to bring back the world of art to what its course of action was four centuries ago!"[61] And with regard to the four prospective styles: "Does he not see that the creation or establishment of a style lies in causes much deeper than men's options?"[62]

Surely Ruskin saw this, but he imagined with even greater clarity the world of his own making. Then again, he probably did not see this particular review, because in September 1849 he was traveling (by slow carriage, of course) to Venice, a city that after its declaration of independence from Habsburg rule in 1848 had suffered a six-month siege and daily bombardment by Austrian forces. It had surrendered in August 1849 and was still under martial law; cholera and starvation abounded. Ruskin was perhaps the lone Englishman to venture into the city at this time, but art, for Ruskin, suspended reality: his mission now was to record every detail of every Byzantine and Gothic building in the threatened city. He compiled, according to one biographer, no fewer than ten notebooks totaling over 1,100 pages, in addition to 168 large worksheets of architectural details.[63] The result was one of the great literary masterpieces of the nineteenth century, *The Stones of Venice* (three volumes, 1851–3). Its opening sentences reveal its apocalyptic intentions: "Since the first dominion of men was asserted over the ocean, three thrones, of mark beyond all others, have been set upon its sands: the thrones of Tyre, Venice, and England. Of the First of these great powers only the memory remains; of the Second, the ruin; the Third, which inherits their greatness, if it forget their example, may be led through prouder eminence to less pitied destruction."[64]

Ruskin commences his chronicle of the city and its architecture against "the warning which seems to me to be uttered by every one of the fast-gaining waves, that beat, like passing bells, against the Stones of Venice."[65] If in his earlier book he at times gave the appearance of an amateur venturing into a new field, in this work he speaks with the authority of an expert who has examined every pitted crevice of Venice's architectural past – in his words "stone by stone, but every fragment throughout the city which afforded any clue to the formation of its styles."[66] The book is, above all, a celebration of the city. The first volume, entitled "Foundations," talks generally about architecture and its formal progression. Volume 2 and 3 trace Venetian architecture through its Byzantine, Gothic, and Renaissance phases (emanating, respectively, from Japeth, Shem, and Ham), with the architectural Fall of Adam for the city coming in the year 1418. Architecture generally follows the three human virtues of acting well (good construction), speaking well (with polish and decorum), and looking well (good decoration), but these are really aspects of architecture's larger moral law, ornamentally "the expression of man's delight in God's work."[67] Ruskin follows with abundant drawings depicting the elements of Venetian architecture, building upon the earlier illustrative studies of Gothic architecture (Fig. 42). By the time he reaches the mezzotint comparing a rusticated Renaissance wall and impost and a highly polychrome wall segment from the cathedral at Pistoia, every reader is convinced of the latter's superiority and of Ruskin's critical infallibility.[68]

The second volume contains his most important essay, "The Nature of Gothic," which would later serve as the manifesto of the Arts and Crafts Movement. The essay opens with the premise that Gothic architecture possesses not only a formal vocabulary but also a living soul, that is, an animate character exploiting the picturesque attributes of savageness, changefulness, naturalism, grotesqueness, rigidity, and reduction. Pages follow elucidating each of these. Under "Savageness" Ruskin draws his famous contrast between the "Servile" nature of Greek and Renaissance ornament and the ethical supremacy of medieval decorations.[69] The straight lines and geometrical perfection of Greek ornament enslaved the spirit of the sculptor by making him servile to a simplified pattern: "If you will have that precision out of them, and make their fingers measure degrees like cog-wheels, and their arms strike curves like compasses, you must unhumanize them."[70] The Renaissance, which for Ruskin fell under the sway of the cardinal sins of pride and infidelity, fared no better and produced only "a wearisome exhibition of well-educated imbecility."[71] Gothic ornamentation was superior in every respect. It allowed invention, accepted human imperfection, despised symmetry, and in fact reveled in the individuality of every soul. Ugly goblins and formless monsters peering out of shadowed imposts were free inventions, signs of life, and evidence of the workers' happiness. The Greeks were able to invent only five orders, yet "there is not a side chapel in any Gothic cathedral but it has fifty orders, the worst of them better than the best of the Greek ones, and all new."[72] Once again, Ruskin's perspective on these matters is entirely new.

Everything is ethical for Ruskin. The Gothic window should be introduced into domestic architecture because "it is the best and strongest building, as it is the most beautiful."[73] The rectangular window is inherently base and insecure. At the end of a vivid description of St. Mark's, he concludes that "the school of incrusted architecture is *the only one in which perfect and permanent chromatic decoration is possible.*"[74] An equally impassioned portrait of the Ducal Palace leads him into a discussion of Dante, and then we learn that the "exactly equal proportions" of Roman, Lombard, and Arab influences merging in this civic landmark make it "the central building of the world."[75] His opinion in this case was tactilely formed; he traced the palace's every line with arthritic fingers in the unusually cold winter of 1849–50.

The Stones of Venice is also rife with comments on topical issues. Against Garbett's "grave charge" that Ruskin used the words "beauty" and "ornament" interchangeably, Ruskin responds proudly, "I do so, and ever shall."[76] He then corrects Garbett on a finer point: "What right has he to assume that ornament, rightly so called, ever was, or can be, superfluous? I have said before, and repeatedly in other places, that the most beautiful things are the most useless; I never said superfluous."[77] He concludes these remarks by venturing an opinion on the Crystal Palace based on the axiom that "the value of every work of art is exactly in the ratio of the quantity of humanity which has been put into it." In this case, this rule turns out to be a harsh yardstick:

The quality of thought it expresses is, I suppose, a single and very admirable thought of Mr. Paxton's, probably not a bit brighter than thousands of thoughts which pass through his active and intelligent brain every hour, – that it might be possible to build a greenhouse larger than ever greenhouse was built before. This thought, and some very ordinary algebra, are as much as all that glass can represent of human intellect.[78]

Ruskin, as many of his contemporaries now realized, was at war with the architectural profession.

And it was a war that he would win rather easily by the end of the decade. First there came the Ruskinian architects – William Butterfield (1814–1900), George Edmund Street (1824–81), Benjamin Woodward (1816–61), and Thomas Deane (1792–1871) – who were inspired by his love of hand-hewn materials and medieval polychromy. Next came Ruskin's growing fame as a speaker and his increasing tendency to focus his critical powers on what he saw as the evils of laissez-faire capitalism. His *Lectures on Architecture and Painting*, delivered in Edinburgh in 1853, wrapped his

42. Plate from John Ruskin, *The Stones of Venice* (London, 1851–3).

architectural principles in popular form while not extending them.[79] But in his Kensington lecture of 1858, he momentarily allowed access to the depth of his mystical world when he commented on the unnatural thinness of the portal statues of Chartres:

These statues have been long, and justly, considered as representative of the highest skill of the twelfth or earliest part of the thirteenth century in France; and they indeed possess a dignity and delicate charm, which are for the most part wanting in later works. It is owing partly to real nobleness of feature, but chiefly to the grace, mingled with severity, of the falling lines of excessively *thin* drapery; as well as to a most studied finish in composition, every part of the ornamentation tenderly harmonizing with the rest. So far as their power over certain tones of religious mind is owing to a palpable degree of non-naturalism in them, I do not praise it – the exaggerated thinness of body and stiffness of attitude are faults; but they are noble faults, and give the statues a strange look of forming part of the very building itself, and sustaining it – not like the Greek caryatid, without effort – nor like the renaissance caryatid, by painful or impossible effort – but as if all that was silent, and stern, and withdrawn apart, and stiffened in chill of heart against the terror of earth, had passed into a shape of eternal marble; and thus the Ghost had given, to bear up the pillars of the church on earth, all the patient and expectant nature that it needed no more in heaven. This is the transcendental view of the meaning of those sculptures.[80]

On a rhetorical level, Henry Cole could not compete with Ruskin, but their personal feud marked the larger clash of intellectual, political, and moral forces coming together in the 1850s. Cole, the realist, embraced the machine and the capitalist forces giving rise to a new economic and social order; he was at heart a reformist. Ruskin, the spiritualist, too saw the pending upheaval, but glimpsing as well the inhumanity displayed by these same industrial forces, he simply retreated, as his critic of 1849 had correctly suggested. History, however, is sometimes written in riddles. If Cole's embrace of modernity presages the welcome it received around 1900, it was Ruskin's consciously backward looking views that for the next half-century carried the day in much of the Anglo-Saxon world. Such is the power of simple passion.

2. Viollet-le-Duc and the Debate in France

Ruskin's importance to British theory in the mid-nineteenth century was matched in France by the influence of Eugène-Emmanuel Viollet-le-Duc (1814–79).[81] The French architect came upon the architectural scene in France a few years earlier than Ruskin did in England, and although he wrote as profusely, he failed to achieve a following until near the end of his career. And if Viollet-le-Duc was driven by a similar passion for Gothic architecture, it was for different reasons.

The situation in France with respect to Gothic architecture in fact had always been different than elsewhere.

Gothic works had been admired throughout the eighteenth century by various architects, among them Soufflot, but almost exclusively for their structural efficiencies. The Royal Academy of Architecture disapproved of Gothic ornaments and proportions, historical research was virtually nonexistent, and the harsh reality of the Revolution cut short any outpouring of romantic sensibilities, such as appeared in Germany and England. Indeed, the revolutionary council of the 1790s nationalized all church properties and vandalized many by removing their treasures to Paris. In 1795 the painter Alexandre Lenoir, who had been charged with safeguarding medieval artifacts at the former Paris convent of the Petits-Augustins, took advantage of the situation to open a Musée des Monuments Français, which he filled largely with medieval treasures arranged chronologically.[82]

Sympathies for the Gothic style quietly developed along other fronts. François-René Chateaubriand included a chapter on "Gothic Churches" in Le Génie du Christianisme (The genius of Christianity, 1802), in which he discussed the aesthetic impression – "a kind of awe and a vague sentiment of the Divinity" – that one experiences upon entering these churches.[83] One of the first English studies translated into French was George Downing Whittington's Gothic investigations in Normandy, An Historical Survey of the Ecclesiastical Architecture of France. This book spurred French investigations of Gothic churches, led by those of Arcisse de Caumont (1801–73), whose first book, Sur l'architecture du moyen-âge particulièrement en Normandie (On medieval architecture, particularly in Normandy) appeared in 1824.[84]

In the 1830s the Gothic movement increased its momentum largely through the efforts of three individuals: Victor Hugo, François Guizot, and Prosper Mérimée. Hugo had been involved with the Gothic movement since 1823, and his hosanna to the cause, Notre-Dame de Paris (1831), became a clarion call for many students, among them Adolphe-Napoléon Didron and the Comte de Montalembert. Lending government support to these efforts was the historian Guizot, who in 1830 was named interior minister of the new government. He created the post of Inspecteur Général des Monuments Historiques, to which he named Ludovic Vitet. In 1834 Vitet was succeeded by Mérimée, who had an interest in both literature and preservation. In 1837 another government commission was formed by Jean Vatout, the Commission des Monuments Historiques.[85]

Yet it was Mérimée, with long-standing connections to the family of Viollet-le-Duc, who aided the youthful Eugène and later became one of his closest friends. Viollet-le-Duc was born into a family of modest circumstance; his father had a government job supervising royal residences and was an avid book collector. In the attic of the Viollet-le-Duc household lived his mother's brother, the painter Etienne Jean Délecluze, who had been a student of David and who wrote for the Journal des Débats. Délecluze helped Eugène to develop drawing and painting skills, underappreciated elements of an architect's talent.[86] The father and uncle held regular salons that attracted a number of artists and writers, among them Stendhal, Sainte-Beuve, Vitet, and Mérimée. Eugène was also influenced by the Saint-Simonian movement, and in 1830 he manned the barricades during the July Revolution. Spurred on by Hugo, Eugène decided to pursue architecture, but he refused to enter the Ecole des Beaux-Arts. Instead he apprenticed with the architects Marie Huvé and Achille Leclère and traveled extensively in France, Italy, and Sicily. Upon returning to France in 1837, he rejoined the office of Leclère, but three years later (through the intercession of Mérimée) the twenty-six-year-old architect was offered the commission to restore the Church of the Madeleine at Vézelay.

Within a couple of years, the gifted Viollet-le-Duc had vaulted to the head of the French preservation movement. He cut his teeth on the Church of the Madeleine, which was one of the largest surviving Romanesque churches in France and in need of extensive structural repair. It thus became a lab in which he developed and tested his ideas regarding medieval architecture. In 1840 Viollet-le-Duc also became the "second inspector" for the restoration of Ste.-Chapelle in Paris, working under Félix Duban. The "first inspector" at Ste.-Chapelle was Jean-Baptiste Lassus (1807–57), with whom Viollet-le-Duc would now work closely. In 1844, in fact, Lassus and Viollet-le-Duc would win the prestigious commission to restore the Cathedral of Note-Dame in Paris, which had been extensively damaged by the Revolution. By 1845 the two men had no fewer than twelve French monuments under restoration.

It was in the mid-1840s that Viollet-le-Duc first turned his attention to theory. His outlet was the Annales archéologiques, a new journal founded in 1844 by Adolphe-Napoléon Didron. Beginning in volume 1, Viollet-le-Duc was given a featured place for his nine-part history of Gothic architecture, "On the Construction of Religious Buildings in France, from the Beginning of Christianity until the 16th century."[87] The essays are scarcely historical in the traditional sense; rather, they present the history of an idea by focusing on the two buildings Viollet-le-Duc knew extremely well, the Church of the Madeleine and Notre-Dame de Paris.

The saga takes the form of a momentous rediscovery of "a science and an art unknown until then and lost today," an intellectual moment of enlightenment first attained at Vézelay, when the master mason constructed two bays of groin vaults on top of ribbed ogival arches left in place rather than on the usual timber centering.[88] Here the new "elastic" conception of architecture manifested itself – elasticity (a term frequently used by Viollet-le-Duc) suggesting as well a certain vitalism of form.[89] The next step was the thirteenth-century invention of the pointed arch, the moment of "greatest perfection," when art "submitted to fixed rules, to an order."[90] Hence, "this charming construction, so simple, so clear, not needing an explanation in order to be understood," and "full of sense and reason" appeared as a highpoint in human history.[91] Gothic architecture for Viollet-le-Duc was a structural system almost divinely derived from an increasingly precise understanding of vaulted forces held in equilibrium, supported by an ever more efficient use of materials. Every molding, every ornamental detail, was similarly endowed with a rational or functional value, and the rationlist ideals of Perrault, Cordemoy, and Soufflot now achieved a kind of apotheosis.

Behind such a summary, of course, lay the issue of the relevance or continuing validity of this style for contemporary design. For Viollet-le-Duc, the Gothic style was preeminently Christian and French and hence still valid. The opposition to his position, interestingly, came not from the Ecole des Beaux-Arts but rather from a still evolving circle of Saint-Simonian disciples. The issue, in fact, was quite complex, because much historical investigation had been done over the previous decade, and the debate had by now grown refined in its nuances.[92]

Perhaps the seminal event took place in 1831 when the Saint-Simonian movement itself split in two. Prosper Enfantin, with his messianic aspirations, took one group to the suburb of Ménilmontant to build a temple to his new religion, but another contingent of social activists remained behind in Paris. These dissidents were led by Pierre Leroux, Hippolyte Fortoul, Jean and Léonce Reynaud, and Albert Lenoir (the son of the medieval museum curator). Leroux was a socialist who had rejected the Saint-Simonian historical thesis of organic and critical stages in favor of the notion of continuous progress. In assuming the editorship of the *Encyclopédie nouvelle* in 1833, he set out to promulgate his new universal system of knowledge.

As we have seen, in 1834 Léonce Reynaud wrote the entry on "Architecture," attempting to put architectural developments on a more "scientific" footing. Two points are central to his thesis. First, as mentioned earlier, he notes that if each style of architecture corresponds to a developmental stage of human science, no system of the past can possess absolute value.[93] Second, he asserts that "there will be [architectural] progress every time that the supports and loads will be disposed in a manner that the ratio of solid to void is diminished, or that one has been able to use less material."[94] Architectural progress thus follows constructional and technological progress, and architecture always moves toward greater structural efficiency.

Also associated with this theory of continuous progress was Edouard Charton, who in 1833 had launched the journal *Le Magasin pittoresque*. Beginning in 1839 he commissioned Léon Vaudoyer and Albert Lenoir to write a history of French architecture, a task that would consume the next fourteen years. The timing was impeccable, as both men had traveled extensively in the 1830s in search of the origins of medieval architecture. Vaudoyer, together with Fortoul, had studied monuments in France and Germany. Lenoir had ventured as far the Middle East in 1836 to test his thesis that medieval architecture had formed from two relatively autonomous Roman offshoots: the *Style Byzantin* and *Style Latin*. In addition, both men held the same position regarding progress as Reynaud: Architecture involves a process of continuous formal development and stylistic synthesis within which the Gothic style enjoys no special standing.[95]

In fact, the Gothic style, in Vaudoyer and Lenoir's opinion, had too quickly overreached itself structurally and therefore had never fully constituted itself formally. Such a view left the present time with but two stylistic options. One was to return to an early stage in the *affranchissement de l'arcade* (emancipation of the arch) – to the Romanesque – and employ it as a starting point for a new desired synthesis. The second was to go back to a later stage of synthetic development, either the early Renaissance or its later counterpart, the French Renaissance. Labrouste's Bibliothèque Ste.-Geneviève, on which construction began in 1842, followed the model of the early Renaissance. Vaudoyer and Lenoir, however, favored the French Renaissance, and thus we can understand Lenoir's incredulous response to Viollet-le-Duc's assertions on behalf of Gothic imitation in 1844: "What, Gothic can be claimed as our national art? Should we thus renounce all the advances that have been made since!"[96]

Actually, another front to the debate was opening around this time, one emanating from the *Revue générale de l'architecture et des Travaux Publics*, which was founded in 1840 (Fig. 43).[97] Its editor was César Daly (1811–94), a follower of the utopian thinker Charles Fourier and therefore someone favorably disposed toward advances in engineering and science. Thus in the first years of publication as much emphasis was placed on engineering developments as on historical and artistic themes – even though Lenoir was the journal's principal historian. Daly's architectural position, however, evolved over the years. Initially he saw the possibility of a new style as something that would emerge from a scientific understanding of the past and present, and he could applaud such architects as Labrouste (a friend) while not opposing the medievalism of Didron and Viollet-le-Duc. In the second half of the 1840s, though, Daly began to turn against the Gothic revivalists. In a spirited essay of 1847, "On Liberty in Art," he criticized in very pointed terms the restoration policies of Vitet and opposed those who in their historical passion "want to impose the exclusive cult of the Gothic," which he characterized as a tyranny born out of "fetishism."[98] The nineteenth century, by contrast, needs to define its own era: "It believes in progress, it respects the past, it wants liberty."[99]

Also attacking the Gothicism of Viollet-le-Duc was Léonce Reynaud, whose *Traité d'architecture* (Treatise on architecture, 1850–8) encapsulated his teachings at the Ecole Polytechnique in the 1840s. His position had not fundamentally changed since his earlier encyclopedia article, although it had now been strengthened by historical research. He again places great emphasis on the influence of science and industry in providing this "eminently rational" art with its means of realization and its elementary forms.[100] He also devotes an entire section to iron and its role in renewing architecture with new forms and proportions, which he sees evident in Labrouste's recently completed Bibliothèque Ste.-Geneviève, a modern work of a "most distinguished taste."[101] In volume two of his treatise, Reynaud underscores the idea of continuous progress in architectural development by tracing Gothic architecture back through its Romanesque and Lombard stages to its Byzantine roots. In 1852 Viollet-le-Duc would dispute this lineage and argue that the Lombardian elements found in French medieval architecture were "exotic" and contrary to the normal path of development.[102]

Reynaud's criticisms nevertheless led Viollet-le-Duc in the 1850s to refine his position. It was an especially fertile decade for this writer – his professional career continuing to rise with the ascendancy of Napoleon III – as he embarked on his two sizable encyclopedia ventures and began his famous *Entretiens sur l'architecture* (Lectures on architecture,

1858–72).[103] His ten-volume encyclopedia of medieval architecture, *Dictionnaire raisonné de l'architecture française du XIᵉ au XVIᵉ siècle* (1854–68), stands as one of the great historical works of the nineteenth century. Viollet-le-Duc chose a dictionary format because he believed the wealth of information and examples would become "confusing and almost intelligible" if presented in a historical narrative.[104] The objective of his analyses is neither to focus the artist's attention on the past nor to furnish the nineteenth century with examples to copy but rather to study the art of these centuries as one would study an inexhaustible mine teeming with original ideas, a period with a unity of conception and accord of details lacking in almost all other times. The *Dictionnaire* is also a nationalist pursuit specific to modern-day France, intended "to render to architects that suppleness, that habitude of applying a true principle to each thing, that native originality and that independence that derives from our national genius."[105]

With such an aim, Viollet-le-Duc proceeds over nine volumes (the tenth contains an analytical table of contents) to dissect medieval architecture with a surgeon's scalpel: to expose its "imperious laws of logic" and the dialectical system of historical evolution that culminated in the creation of the Gothic style. Further, in contrast to Reynaud, Viollet-le-Duc treats this style as privileged historically. The 336 pages of Viollet-le-Duc's entry on "Architecture" reveals both his fascination with monastic buildings and his extensive knowledge of military architecture.[106] The entry on "Construction" is 279 pages in length and relies heavily on his investigations at Vézelay.[107] It also follows closely his earlier essays in the *Annales Archéologiques* in that aesthetics plays no discernible role in design; each form arises as a logical solution to a structural problem. The entry is superbly argued and illustrated with a plethora of anatomically inspired drawings.[108]

Other articles reveal his nationalist feelings, such as his article on "Sculpture." If Ruskin read into the unnaturally thin statuary of Chartres the spiritual transcendence to which his theory was directed, Viollet-le-Duc's analyses are more methodical yet equally impassioned. French sculpture displays a certain canon of beauty, a certain harmony, and a certain French physiognomy that differ from those of classical sculpture but are in no way inferior. A virgin on the north portal of Notre-Dame is modeled on a "a woman from a good family, a noble lady," someone whose qualities of intelligence and energy are delicately portrayed.[109] Another virgin, from Strasbourg Cathedral, has a "grand nature" chiseled with "excellent execution" and is "modeled very beautifully."[110]

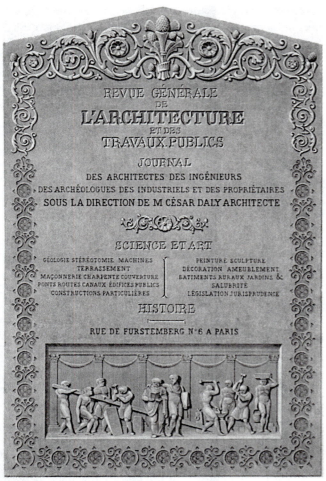

43. Title page from César Daly's *Revue générale de l'architecture et des Travaux* Publics (Paris, 1840).

So is the harp player at Reims. The sworded and blindfolded female nude riding a horse placed over the central portal of the Paris cathedral alludes – Viollet-le-Duc tells us – to the revelation of Jesus Christ to Saint John.[111] By contrast, those terrible birds and beasts feeding on men and animals which together compose a column at the abbey church of Sainte-Marie at Souillac betray not French but Hindu sensitivities.[112] Certainly few architects before Viollet-le-Duc would have ventured into such historical reaches.

Given that Viollet-le-Duc took fourteen years to complete the *Dictionnaire*, it is not surprising that his views evolved. For example, the early entries tend to focus on local history, the later ones encompass a broader historical span, including those that reflect Viollet-le-Duc's developing interest in Orientalism. Nonetheless, the later articles maintain a "scientific" bearing. In the article on "Restoration," which appears in volume 8 (1866), Viollet-le-Duc likens the his-

torical efforts of the present to the anatomical and geologic investigations of Georges Cuvier as well as to the supporting efforts of contemporary philologists, ethnographers, and archaeologists.[113] In the article on "Style," in the same volume, he carries the analogy one step further by means of another allusion to Cuvier: "Thus, just as in viewing a single leaf it is possible to reconstruct the entire plant, and in viewing an animal bone, the animal itself, it is also possible to deduce the members of an architecture from the view of an architectural profile."[114] The idea of "style," which he immediately distinguishes from the "styles" of historical schools, is a key concept. It is an inner yet visible sign of unity and harmony – "what blood is for the human body" – a phenomenon that both develops with and vitally nourishes artistic form.[115] Better known is his second definition of style as "the *manifestation of an ideal based on a principle.*"[116] Style is furthermore a "consequence of a principle pursued methodically"; it is an "adherence to a law that is unimpeded by exceptions," yet it is not an attribute that can be consciously sought.[117] Style develops – as with a plant – naturally or in accordance with the laws of nature; that is, it derives from the materials employed, how they are used, the goal to be achieved, and the logical deduction of details from the greater unity of the whole. Viollet-le-Duc can thus claim that he is encouraging not the resurrection of the Middle Ages but rather the understanding and assimilation of its principles into contemporary artistic efforts. Hence his theory now comes to define an idealized but scientific functionalism:

That each stone of a building fills a useful and necessary function; that each profile has a precise purpose and that that purpose be clearly indicated in its line; that a building's proportions be derived from principles of geometric harmony; that ornamentation be based on natural flora, as observed truly and with imagination; that nothing be left to chance; that materials be employed in accordance with their qualities and that these qualities be indicated by the form they are given – does it follow from all of this that art is absent and science alone operative?[118]

The answer is not cut and dry, for these words, written in 1866, need to be interpreted within the context of his *Entretiens sur l'architecture*, (Lectures on architecture) which he began writing almost a decade earlier, in 1858. They were conceived in 1856, when Labrouste decided to close his popular studio. Fifteen of his students, lead by Anatole de Baudot (1834–1915), approached Viollet-le-Duc and asked him to open a studio. Viollet-le-Duc, daring to enter the pedagogical arena of the Ecole des Beaux-Arts, responded with an architectural program and a course of lectures. He did not succeed, however. He failed to arouse enthusiasm from his students, and his professional responsibilities as a preservationist kept him away from Paris for prolonged periods of time. One by one the students left the studio. Upon returning from one trip and finding himself the object of caricature, Viollet-le-Duc quit the atelier and never returned. The first four lectures were written for these students, but after the studio's demise Viollet-le-Duc continued writing until 1863, when the first volume of ten lectures was complete.

By this date another event had intervened. The long and intensifying debate over reforming the Ecole des Beaux-Arts – an institution of which Viollet-le-Duc had for years been a harsh critic – came to a head in 1863, and one outcome was that the school was detached from the purview of the Académie des Beaux-Arts. Mérimée was placed on the governing council of the school, and he named his close friend (and fellow participant in the intrigue) as the new professor of art and aesthetics. The appointment was greeted with anger by both the faculty and students, and it proved to be a disastrous experience for Viollet-le-Duc as well. The new professor became the object of the widespread opposition, and at his first public lecture, given in January 1864, and attended by some high government officials, he was greeted with shouts and catcalls. Interruptions occurred on subsequent occasions, and after his seventh lecture, given on 18 March, he submitted his resignation – throwing the plans for reforming the Ecole des Beaux-Arts once again into abeyance.

A trip to Italy and northern Africa eventually salved Viollet-le-Duc's bitterness, and he returned to Paris and once again threw himself into the fray by supporting a new school of architecture, the Ecole Centrale, conceived in opposition to the Ecole des Beaux-Arts. During these same years he continued writing his lectures, completing the twentieth and last lecture in 1872. For Paris, these had been the giddy years of the prefecture of Baron Georges-Eugène Haussmann (1809–91), when so much of the city was under construction. Still, the period would end badly. In 1870 France declared war on Germany, and its armies were quickly routed by Prussian forces. The new German Empire (in essence, Germany after unification as a nation-state) was declared at Versailles. For the French yet another civil war ensued, followed in the winter of 1871 by the destructive trauma of the Paris Commune. The fifty-six-year-old Viollet-le-Duc volunteered for military service in August 1870, in fact on the day on which, with French armies in retreat, Napoleon III resigned as commander-in-chief.

Viollet-le-Duc's lectures, which were to exert an important influence on architects of the next generation, deal with a variety of themes, but their lodestar remains the faculty of reason. They also follow the turns of Viollet-le-Duc's own fortunes in their composition. The first five lectures are largely didactic and historical in their formal development. The Greeks were "lovers of form" and instinctively a "colony of artists"; their aim was to derive form logically from construction, with strict attention to clarity or distinct expression. The Romans were organizers and rulers, and in their development of the vault, the idea of economy played an important role. Also, for them ornament constituted an additional "clothing" or covering for the structure.[119] More generally, in each of the ancient nations there was close connection between manners, habits, laws, religion, and art.

In the sixth lecture, written in 1859, Viollet-le-Duc takes up the theme of style and begins his history of the early Middle Ages. In the first of his many attacks on current practice, he condemns contemporary architects for their lack of inventiveness and for adhering to a system that in the scientific world would be Galilean in its underlying concepts: "We architects, shut up in our art – an art which is half science, half sentiment, – present only hieroglyphics to the public, which does not understand us, and which leaves us to dispute in our isolation."[120] One reason for the lack of progress (echoing Rousseau) is the enfeeblement bred of overcivility and cultural refinement, and, like Saint-Simon, Viollet-le-Duc holds that "the periods most fruitful in intellectual productions have been periods of the greatest agitation".[121] Another reason is the want of style, which he now defines as "inspiration subjected to the laws of reason."[122] It too is inversely proportional to the advance of civilization and demands human imagination.[123] For instance, he considers the example of a simple copper vessel, which has style first because it is functional, second because it is fashioned in a way suited to the material, and third because its form also corresponds with the material and function (Fig. 44). A second coppersmith comes along and tries to improve it by softening its angular lines, but he only robs the logic of the style. A third coppersmith ruins it altogether by artfully stripping it of its functional and material reasoning. This leads Viollet-le-Duc to speak of style in relation to the industrial age:

The locomotive, for example, has a special physiognomy which all can appreciate and which renders it a distinct creation. Nothing can better express force under control than these ponderous

44. Eugène-Emmanuel Viollet-le-Duc, plate from the sixth lecture, *Entretiens sur l'architecture* (1858–72).

rolling machines: their motions are gentle or terrible; they advance with terrific impetuosity, or seem to pant impatiently under the restraining hand of the diminutive creature who starts or stops them at will. The locomotive is almost a living being, and its external form is the simple expression of its strength. A locomotive therefore has style.[124]

This pivotal turn in his theory becomes even more apparent in the first lectures of the second volume, which are devoted to the use of iron. These were written in 1866–8, predictably amid yet another polemical dispute. César Daly, in his "introduction" to the year 1866 in his journal, attacked the new Ecole Centrale and its "rationalist" curriculum, "which tends at this moment to transform the *architectural art* into an *industrial architecture*" and proclaims reason as the "only judge."[125] Daly in his article goes on to defend "art" against the excesses of the classical, Gothic, and rationalist schools, while advocating an intelligent and tasteful "eclecticism" as a transitional solution to the current style dilemma. Three years earlier he defined this "isthmus" of eclecticism as "destined to facilitate in our weakness the passage from the collapsing old world to this new world that emerges slowly from the depths of the unknown."[126]

Another volley was shortly thereafter fired across Viollet-le-Duc's bow – in this instance an attack on his student Anatole de Baudot by the critic Bourgeois de Lagny, who condemns what he terms "architectural realism (or construction with the absence of art)."[127] Alluding specifically to Champfleury and the "realist" movement evident in literature and painting, de Lagny argues that architectural realism (suited only to "those periods of civilization rather rude and barbaric") overlooks the fact that monumental art is in essence idealistic and that beauty therefore resides in both "choosing" and "concealing."[128] Monumental art should display graceful contours, harmonious proportions, elegant forms, and originality in disposition and effects; it should conceal everything that suggests the struggle with materials and resistance to force and weight. Obviously iron

falls into the latter category, and its visible use should be delimited.

Viollet-le-Duc responds in his twelfth lecture with his remarkable series of drawings suggesting how iron might be visibly introduced in contemporary practice (Fig. 45). His argument is multifaceted. The escalating costs of materials and labor, together with the growing authority of the engineer, are making architects both expensive and professionally obsolete. Viollet-le-Duc suggests that architects respond forcefully by embracing the new technologies and constructional efficiencies. One issue is the extent to which iron should be employed, and the foil for Viollet-le-Duc is the design of the Halles Centrales of Victor Baltard (1805–74). This group of urban markets had been started in 1845 in masonry, but at the command of Haussmann they were demolished and reerected in iron and glass in 1853–7. They personified "realism" to Zola, who in his later novel *Le ventre de Paris* (The market of Paris, 1873) would see them as the much desired destroyer of the old art and its archaic social order as well as "a timid revelation of the twentieth century."[129] Viollet-le-Duc too is respectful of Baltard's efforts, but he – and here is where he differs from the realists – nevertheless rejects the design because metal has completely superseded the use of masonry. What he proposes is a mediation of these two materials, and with regard to large halls this means: "to obtain a shell entirely of masonry, walls, and vaulting, while diminishing the quantity of material and voiding obstructive supports by the use of iron: to improve on the system of equilibrium adopted by the mediaeval architects, by means of iron, but with due regard to the qualities of that material."[130] Viollet-le-Duc goes on to propose several composite designs, employing masonry for the wall shell and iron for the supports and roof structure. It is in some respects a stunning response to a theoretical issue, but then again it is an architectural solution lacking reality and was therefore unable to convince many readers. Within the context of the engineering displayed at the Paris Exhibition of 1867 (on which Gustave Eiffel first worked), it is even a timid response.

Viollet-le-Duc wrote much more in his lifetime, but his theoretical efforts would largely cease after 1872, when, because of the military defeat of France, he retired to the mountains of Switzerland. In the aftermath of the war his concern was to resurrect the honor of French culture and the French race. Perhaps his most interesting later work is *L'Art russe, ses origines, ses éléments constitutifs, son apogée, son avenir* (Russian art, its origin, its constructive elements, its apogee, its future, 1877), which dissects the elements of Russian architecture and speculates on how traditional forms might be renewed within a culture. It was translated into Russian in 1879, the year of his death in Lausanne.

Viollet-le-Duc's legacy is presently undergoing a reevaluation, for his reputation as a functionalist is far too one-dimensional. He also articulated a distinct French line of rationalist theory that is difficult for an outsider to appreciate fully. His great successor was Auguste Choisy (1841–1904), the engineer and teacher, whose *Histoire de l'architecture* (1899) is a fitting testimony to Viollet-le-Duc's belief that logical construction is the essence of good architecture. For Choisy even more than for Viollet-le-Duc, architectural history is the march of technological development; good form is always the succinct expression of function. Speaking of Labrouste's celebrated reading room at the Bibliothèque Nationale, Choisy asserts in the final paragraph of his book that "a new system of proportions is being created today, where the harmonic laws will be not other than the laws of stability."[131] Viollet-le-Duc could not have said it better himself.

3. Gottfried Semper and the Idea of Style

The more metaphysical writings of Gottfried Semper (1803–79) underscore the vast differences separating German theory of midcentury from its counterparts in France and Britain, but Semper differs from theorists such as Viollet-le-Duc and Ruskin in another important respect.[132] This architect of high standing (possessing a large portfolio of monumental buildings) dominated German theory to a much greater extent than these two other individuals did within their cultural context. Not only did Semper almost single-handedly chart the course of Germanic theory for the next three decades, but it is impossible to understand the impulse of German modernism at the turn-of-the-century without recourse to his ideas.

Semper was born into a family of modest wealth in Hamburg and endured a childhood colored by the Napoleonic occupation and the consequent desolation of the region. He attended Göttingen University for little more than a year, where he first specialized in mathematics. In 1825 he enrolled in the Academy of Fine Arts in Munich, as a pupil of Friedrich Gärtner, but seems to have attended few classes. A duel in Regensburg is the presumed reason for his setting out – in December 1826 – for Paris, where he attended a private school run by Friedrich Christian Gau, a friend of Hittorff. This places Semper in this tumultuous city during the revolt by students at the Ecole des Beaux-Arts in the late 1820s. Semper also watched the July Revolution with the keenest interest and enthusiasm, before setting out for the South in the fall of 1830.

In terms of his artistic development, Semper's trip would be momentous. After a few months in Rome, he joined a group of French students who rented a boat to sail to Sicily, with a stopover at Paestum; together they planned a collective portfolio of Greek monuments in response to the polychrome efforts of Harris, Angell, and Hittorff. Next Semper ventured with Jules Goury to Greece. A little over a decade before, this trip would not have been startling, but with the onset of the Greek war of independence in 1821, travel to the region had become exceedingly dangerous. Greece, with European support, was seeking independence from Ottoman control, but warring factions within the country complicated the situation. Semper, in fact, found himself trapped in Greece for seven months, although he was able to conduct archaeological investigations on the Athenian Acropolis and on Aegina. He was even briefly pressed into the German diplomatic service by Friedrich Theodor Thiersch, who was mediating a cease-fire on behalf of the Bavarian government. Finally, at the end of May 1832, Semper caught a ship out of Greece and – after an encounter with pirates on the high seas – made it back to Italy.

Semper's trip to Greece handed him the polychrome issue when the debate was reaching full stride. He made numerous colored drawings of his findings, particularly of the Parthenon. With the help of the Archaeological Institute in Rome, he did further studies on Etruscan gravesites and scaled Trajan's Column in search of traces of paint. When Semper left Rome for Altona late in 1833, he passed through Berlin and showed his drawings to a very interested Schinkel. And even though his projected folio on ancient polychromy never materialized, Semper published a

18

45. Eugène-Emmanuel Viollet-le-Duc, plate from the twelfth lecture, *Entretiens sur l'architecture* (1858–72).

polemical tract under the title *Vorläufige Bermerkungen uber bemalte Architectur und Plastik bei den Alten* (Preliminary remarks on polychrome architecture and sculpture in antiquity, 1834).[133] He thus entered the international fray over polychromy.

Semper argued that Greek temples were entirely dressed with paint, a radical position that Hittorff had only championed with regard to colonial works in Sicily. He buffered his case with three arguments. First, he presented the historical argument (earlier used by Quatremère de Quincy) that polychromy had been a practice sanctified by tradition: a practice resplendent in Homeric times but becoming more lawful and disciplined in later times. Second, he reiterated the environmental argument of Baron von Stackelberg and

Hittorff: the sunny climate and variegated landscape of the South had made color a necessity, both to mitigate the glaring effects of the sunlight and to harmonize the building with its surroundings. Third, he offered the aesthetic argument that Greek polychrome temples were, in effect, staged platforms in service to communal rituals, consciously choreographed by the first architects to higher artistic ideals. The first temples were rough scaffolds upon which were attached decorative flowers, festoons, sacrificial animals, implements, shields, and other emblems; later these elements became conventionalized as fillets, egg-and-dart motifs, arabesques, rosettes, meanders, and labyrinths. Color was the means by which architects articulated these effects, in essence highlighting the work as a *Gesamtkunstwerk* (artistic synthesis) of dramatic effects. In his words,

In addition to painting, we should not forget the metal ornaments, gilding, tapestry-like draperies, baldachins, curtains, and moveable implements. From the beginning the monuments were designed with all of these things in mind, even for the surroundings – the crowds of people, priests, and the processions. The monuments were the scaffolding intended to bring together these elements on a common stage. The brilliance that fills the imagination when trying to visualize those times makes the imitations that people have since fancied and imposed on us seem pale and stiff.[134]

Semper at the same time weakened his argument by failing to provide hard archaeological documentation, even though he had brought back from Greece several paint samples that he had removed from temple surfaces.

Semper prefaces his pamphlet with various architectural remarks that demonstrate he had absorbed the Saint-Simonian fervor. He strongly denounces the eclectic tendencies of the day (especially the work of Klenze), Durand's use of the grid (which produces mechanical designs), and the invention of tracing paper (which leads architects to copy). He pleads instead for a new "organic" era in which art can flourish "on the soil of need and under the sun of freedom."[135] Organic architecture will emerge, he feels, by scaling back on monumental tendencies, by directing all efforts to meeting human needs, and by insisting on material honesty in architectural expression. Yet these were the words of a thirty-one-year-old architect who had yet to receive a significant commission.

Both his views and his career would soon advance. Semper's "extreme" polychrome position was greeted rudely on the European stage, criticized in particular by the Berlin historian Franz Kugler. But his pamphlet of 1834 also led to his appointment as a professor at the Dresden Academy of the Fine Arts and the chance to begin a practice. In 1838 (with the blessing of Schinkel) he was given the prestigious commission to design the new royal theater for the Saxon court. As the building was originally to be attached to Matthäus Daniel Pöpplemann's rococo complex – the Zwinger – Semper chose an arcuated Renaissance vocabulary to continue the rhythm and scale of the arches. In the interior Semper introduced some of the reforms suggested by Goethe, Tieck, and Schinkel. When it opened on 12 April 1841, to a performance of Goethe's *Torquato Tasso*, it was regarded by many as the finest theater in Germany.[136]

Semper followed this work over the next decade with several major commissions, the largest of which was the Dresden Art Museum (1839–55). His lone architectural setback came in his native Hamburg. In 1845, his Florentine-inspired design for the Church of St. Nicholas won first place in the competition, but the decision was overturned by an alliance of partisans of the Gothic style who favored the design of G. G. Scott. Semper nevertheless reigned as Germany's most brilliant architect, and in the cultural world of Dresden he befriended the sculptors Ernst Rietschel and Ernst Hähnel, the musicians Franz Listz and Richard Wagner, and the Devrient family of actors. Semper's friendship with the then little known Wagner, whose first operas were performed in the theater designed by Semper, sheds light on the subsequent theoretical development of both men. Wagner first met Semper (ten years his senior) in a Dresden music shop while the architect was purchasing the libretto of *Tannhäuser*. Semper, Wagner later noted, "made it clear to me immediately that he despised me for my choice of such [medieval] material."[137] Their cafe discussions on several occasions nearly resulted in fisticuffs, but there can be no doubt that their individual notions of a *Gesamtkunstwerk* were each nurtured during these spirited exchanges.

These happy years for Semper came to an end with the political events of 1849. The revolution in Paris of the previous year had incited long-delayed political efforts to unify Germany through the creation of a national parliament and the writing of a constitution. A draft of the constitution was finished in March 1849, and in April the titular national crown was offered to the Prussian monarch Friedrich Wilhelm IV. When Wilhelm rejected it and the limitations it imposed on his power, sporadic uprisings occurred in various German states. In Saxony the situation grew particularly tense as barricades were erected. The Saxon ruler Friedrich Augustus II dissolved the Saxon Diet and called for military assistance from Prussia. Semper, who commanded the city militia's "academic legion," and Wagner both fought on the side of the insurgents. Semper achieved battlefield notoriety for his construction of a particularly large and well-engineered barricade, which, as Wagner later recalled, was built "with all the conscientiousness of a Michel Angelo or Leonardo da Vinci."[138] As Prussian and Saxon troops entered the city, both men (now facing warrants of arrest for treason) fled. Wagner went to Zurich, and Semper made a harrowing escape to Paris.

Semper's life now lay in ruins. He had left behind his wife and six children with no means of support. He had lost his practice and academic position. He arrived in France penniless and with no prospects for work. After nine months of struggling in vain, he decided to emigrate to the United States, but he was lured off a steamer at Le Havre at the last minute by a letter offering what turned out to be a bogus commission in London. He struggled in London for the next two years, before Henry Cole offered him a position in the newly formed Department of Practical Art. He remained in London until 1855, when he accepted the architectural directorship at the new federal polytechnikum in Zurich.

What had been disastrous for his career, however, gave support to his inclination for theory, which now took center stage in his life. The first fruit of his endeavors was a small study entitled *Die Vier Elemente der Baukunst* (The four elements of architecture, 1851).[139] It was on many levels a pathbreaking study. Over the years Semper had grown increasingly attracted to ethnological, archaeological, and linguistic research, whose advances were sweeping away previous anthropological models. For instance, Quatremère de Quincy's thesis of three primitive types for architecture – the cave, the tent, the hut – had been predicated on a biblical chronology of six thousand years of human antiquity, which allowed him to argue that these types had developed historically within the early cultures of Egypt, China, and Greece. This chronology gave way in the face of scientific advances of the 1830s. Charles Lyell's *Principles of Geology* (1830–3) suggested that the earth was millions, not thousands, of years old. Franz Bopp's *Comparative Grammer of the Sanskrit, Zend, Greek, Latin, Lithuanian, Gothic, German, and Slavonic Languages* (1833–52) further indicated that the linguistic evolution of the Indo-European language had been longer and more complex than a few thousand years would admit. The issues of race and biological evolution were also becoming lively topics. It was in the 1840s that Charles Darwin formulated his theory of natural selection, although he refrained from publishing it until 1858.

Two events of the 1840s sparked Semper's thinking. One was the discovery of the Assyrian civilization by the com-

46. Assyrian winged figure. From Austen Henry Layard, *The Monuments of Nineveh* (London, 1849).

peting archaeological expeditions of Paul Émile Botta and Henry Layard. The existence of Assyria (c. 1350–612 B.C.) had been known from Greek historians and from descriptions in the Old Testament, but the exquisitely chiseled alabaster wall panels excavated from its buried cities began to reveal the nature of this civilization (Fig. 46). In Botta's explanation, the Assyrians (at this time not culturally distinguished from the older Sumerian and Chaldean civilizations to the south) represented an artistic mean between the cultures of Egypt and Greece. In terms of naturalism, Assyrian figures surpassed the figures (portrayed only in profile) of the Egyptians, who were still tightly bound to the fetters of theocracy, while they fell short of the sculptures of the

Greeks, who pursued the ideal of beauty with freedom. For Semper, Assyria displayed architectural forms quite different from those of any other nation known before, yet there were some interesting parallels with the forms of Greece.

The second event of the 1840s to affect Semper's theory was the publication of Gustav Klemm's *Allgemeine Cultur-Geschichte der Menschheit* (General cultural history of mankind, 1843–52). Klemm, who was also living in Dresden, set about writing a history of human culture from its rudest beginnings in time to its fusion "into organic, social bodies."[140] His book delineates three stages of development, those of savagery, tameness, and freedom. The phenomenon of culture appears only in the second of these stages, in Malaysia, Mexico, Egypt, the Middle East, and China. The third stage of freedom is largely a Western achievement, initiated once the yoke of autocratic rulers was broken. The Persians and Arabs were able to reach the beginning of this stage of development, but the Greek, Roman, and German nations followed through to its near conclusion. Myriad factors contributing to cultural achievement support each of these stages. Klemm's study reads in fact as a catalogue of human activities and artifacts repeated for each nation or ethnic group. Initially he considers humanity under such headings as physical and mental characteristics, family and social life, eating and burial habits, dwellings, dress, decoration, tools, weapons, utensils, religion, and language. As culture advances, these categories expand and multiply. The use of fire and language mark the beginning of cultural development, but cultural stages better coincide with the adoption of family life and the appearance of ownership. His perusals of so-called primitive societies, of their early implements and technical prowess, of body decorations, song, and dance – all bring a fundamentally new perspective to the course of human development.

Semper in *Die vier Elemente* draws upon this ethnological and archaeological evidence to propose four motives (motifs) as the essential conceptual building blocks of all architectural creation – hearth, mounding, roofing, and enclosure.[141] Each of these affects formal development in a particular way, and each is associated with early technical crafts. The social hearth, or fire, is the element around which the first tribes gathered after the hunt. It therefore became the symbolic embryo of all social institutions, including the family (the hearth) and society (altar). It also gave rise to the ceramic arts. Mounding, roofing, and walling were involved in safeguarding the sacred flame. The mound – the origin of all later substructures – raised the flame off the damp earth. It eventually developed into such types of construction as dams, canals, terracing, and masonry construction. Roofing shielded the flame overhead and spawned the notion of carpentry or of a fixed structural framework. Walling, first seen in textile fabrics and simple mats, shielded the flame from the winds; at the same time it defined a spatial interior or a private world distinct from the exterior. Semper goes on to speculate on the relation between certain architectural forms and social institutions. He associates the gabled form, for instance, with the start of patriarchal life in the northern Mediterranean highlands, while the courtyard style of building was better suited to the warmer climate and rigidly hierarchical life of Egypt. The Assyrian wall panels, with their textile-like patterns, represent for Semper the direct transformation of the textile motive from fabric into a hard material. It is an example of the way architectural motives can jump along entirely different lines of formal development and undergo both material and cultural change.

Die vier Elemente appeared in the winter of 1851, just as Semper was trying to establish himself in London. The Crystal Palace was under construction, and through an intermediary Semper was introduced to Henry Cole, who helped him find work as a designer of exhibits for the exhibition. Semper prepared the layouts for Turkey, Canada, Sweden, and Denmark and thus had special access to the exhibition building. He was much impressed with the artifacts of the North American Indians, as he was with Maori decorative designs and African grass skirts. At the exhibition he found that the model of a "Carib" hut from Trinidad perfectly illustrated his four-motive thesis in seemingly primordial form (Fig. 47). The hearth was raised on a log substructure, a roof of reeds was supported on a bamboo framework, and wall mats were hung vertically between the roof supports: "Every element of the construction is speaking for itself alone and has no connection with the others."[142] He was no less impressed with the latest industrial implements and machinery – steam hammers, Bessemer pumps, boilers – which were in advance of what he was familiar with in Germany.

The outgrowth of his fascination with the exhibition was the book *Wissenschaft, Industrie und Kunst* (Science, industry, and art), which he wrote in the fall of 1851.[143] Here his theory broadens in unexpected ways, as Semper comes to see the current crisis in architectural production as the result not of ideas but of "certain anomalies" in the workplace fostered by the industrial process. Industrialization, with its commensurate "excess of means," was indeed destroying or devaluing the traditional practice of art, which had been based on the labor of the human hand. But for Semper – in

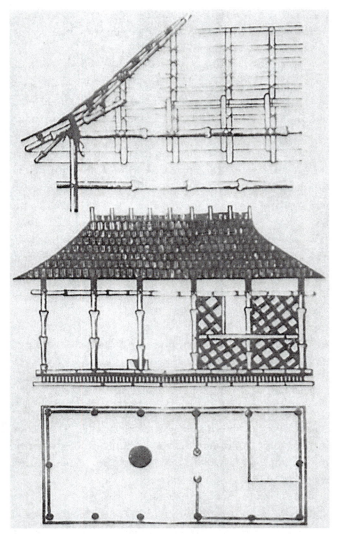

47. Gottfried Semper, "Carib" hut from Trinidad, displayed at the Great Exhibition. From Gottfried Semper, *Der Stil in den technischen und tektonischen Künsten oder praktische Ästhetik*, vol. 2 (1863).

tional, and personal factors affecting the work. The hope here is that once we properly analyze the current variables and their artistic implications, we can once again produce works with style. Art has effectively moved into the industrial age, and its production must respond to these new parameters.

The chapters of *Wissenschaft, Industrie und Kunst* devoted to reviewing the goods displayed at the Great Exhibition were written very much with Henry Cole in mind. Semper was aware that Cole was taking control of the schools of design, and he applied for a position. Cole was not unsympathetic to Semper's plight. On a trip to Germany at the end of 1851, Cole had sought out Semper's Hoftheater in Dresden and was amused by the story that the Saxon king had threatened to hang Semper in his own theater if he could ever get his hands on him.[146] But bureaucratic delays set in, and it was not until the fall of 1852 that Cole appointed Semper as an instructor "in the principles and practice of Ornamental Art applied to Metal Manufactures." The appointment meant that Semper, after years of isolation and poverty, was finally able to have his wife and children join him in London.

The one other tract that Semper wrote in England was a mathematical study of Greek slingshot projectiles.[147] It grew out of a debate that the Royal Institute of British Architects was having on whether the Greeks possessed universally valid laws of proportion. Semper responded by studying the dynamic properties of Greek and Arabian slingshot projectiles at the British Museum. He produced a hundred pages of complex trigonometric and derivative functions, replete with diagrams, through which he attempted to prove that the aerodynamic forms of Greek projectiles (as well as the directional axes of birds and fish) resembled the profiles used in architecture – not because the Greeks designed their temples using mathematical formulas but because "the law of nature followed by the Greeks in the limits of their form-making, everywhere letting the tension dominate, was not vaguely intimated but clearly recognized."[148] These laws were not absolute, because each form can only be judged within its specific medium or context.

In 1855 Semper became head of the architecture school at the Polytechnikum in Zurich (now ETH), and over the next five years he wrote the first volume of his great theoretical work, *Der Stil in den technischen und tektonischen Künsten oder praktische Ästhetik* (Style in the technical and tectonic arts or practical aesthetics, 1860–3).[149] The second volume was published three years later, while a third volume, intended to deal exclusively with architecture and the

vivid contrast to Ruskin – this "disintegration" of the existing art types was not to be mourned. In fact, it revealed a way out of the current situation – of replicating "borrowed or stolen" motives – by allowing "something good and new" to emerge.[144] Semper thus argued that the current architectural crisis was not economic or social but stylistic. "Style," he wrote, "means giving emphasis and artistic significance to the basic idea and to all intrinsic and extrinsic coefficients that modify the embodiment of the theme in a work of art."[145] The basic idea or theme is central to this definition; the "intrinsic and extrinsic coefficients" are those variables that affect the theme's presentation. Intrinsic variables are the materials and technical means employed in a work's production; extrinsic variables are the local, temporal, na-

problem of style, was planned but never written. Nevertheless, the study is vast in its ambition.

With his "comparative method" or "practical aesthetics," Semper in *Der Stil* makes a break with earlier Germanic theory by specifically seeking to overturn the abstract aesthetic theorizing of Georg Wilhelm Friedrich Hegel and other romantic philosophers. In a lecture given in Zurich shortly after his arrival, "On the Formal Lawfulness of Ornament and its Meaning as an Artistic Symbol," he signals his new approach.[150] He builds the lecture around the dual meanings of the Greek word *kosmos* (cosmos, also cosmetic), which signifies both an order found in the movement of the heavens and the notion of adornment. Thus to decorate for the Greeks implied the imposition "of a natural order on the object that is adorned," which is the formal lawfulness by which art imitates or mirrors the cosmic laws of nature.[151] After taking us through some of the earliest ethnological examples of this decorative instinct – ranging from the bison heads worn by North American Indians to the masks, amulets, and tattoos of the South Sea islanders – Semper argues that the Greeks were the first to exploit this decorative lawfulness consciously in their jewelry and dress. Greek ornaments in fact fall into three classes: (1) hanging ornaments such as earrings, tassels, and hair styles; (2) ring ornaments such as necklaces, bracelets, and belts; and (3) directional ornaments, such as diadems, miters, and warrior helmets. The value of such a categorization becomes evident when Semper analyzes the decorations of the Greek temple in precisely the same way: Guttae and mutules are hanging elements; tori, taenias, and astragals are ring elements; and roof sculpture and ridge tiles are directional elements. The directional frieze panels, for instance, form a eurythmic necklace tied together with sculptural gems, while acroteria assume forms similar to the plume ornaments of warrior helmets.

The same comparative framework is brought to *Der Stil*. It opens with general remarks on art and the crisis in which architecture finds itself in the mid-nineteenth century. Semper's aim is "to explore within individual cases the regularity and order that becomes apparent in artistic phenomena during the creative process of becoming, and to deduce from that the general principles, the fundamentals of an empirical theory of art."[152] The idea of an "empirical theory" is slightly misleading, in that he uses the term simply to oppose the speculative tendencies of German idealist philosophers and their lack of practical values or guidance for the artist. His theory seeks to be practical by providing concrete guideposts for invention: "It looks for the constituent parts of form *that are not form itself* but rather the idea, the force, the material, and the means – in other words, the basic preconditions of form."[153]

Contemporary architecture he sees dominated by three false schools of thought. The "materialists" are swept away by the possibilities of new materials and constructional feats, and they therefore place material factors above the idea in the creation of form. The "historicists," by contrast, adhere to past models and therefore fail to let the present evolve as freely as it should. Alluding to the writings of August Reichhensperger, he even criticizes the Gothic school for treating "northwestern and northern Europe as a pagan country to be conquered anew for Christianity."[154] The third false school – the "purists, schematists, and futurists" – also fail the present. They treat architecture as either a philosophical exercise or a form of "aesthetic Puritanism," thereby placing too much emphasis on interpretative meaning and ultimately depriving architecture of any means of expression.[155] Architecture, for Semper, is born out of the same lawful and playful instincts we celebrate everywhere around us: the interlacings of a wreath, the curl of a scroll, a circular dance, the beat of an oar. "These are the beginnings out of which *music* and *architecture* grew," he notes, "the two highest purely cosmic (nonimitative) arts, whose legislative support no other art can do without."[156] The same instincts thus conform to the spatial moments of symmetry, proportion, and direction, though not bound to any strict rules for interpretation or creation.

With this structure Semper begins his analysis of style's four basic motives as they unfold in the artistic industries of textiles, ceramics, tectonics (carpentry), and stereotomy (masonry). At times the writing takes on an encyclopedic character and Semper seems to lose himself in detail, but just as often with a simple remark he provides the reader with a fundamentally novel insight. His section on ceramics, for instance, with its lexicon of forms, becomes important because, in Semper's view, the profiles of forms devised in the ceramic quarter of Periclean Athens were also the profiles applied to architectural moldings. In one instance, he goes so far as to interpret the shapes of the Greek hydria and Eyptian situla as collective or "national emblems." In the low center of gravity of the situla he reads the "basic features of all Egyptian architecture," while in the higher center of gravity of the hydria he finds "certain types found in Doric architecture."[157] This transposition of motives or typical forms from one medium to another comes about also through a process of *Stoffwechsel*, or "material transformation," whereby artistic forms that undergo changes of material always carry forward vestiges or residues of the earlier styles, sometimes symbolically. A basket weave developed in textiles, for instance, might be transposed into a conventional ornamental design or even become applied to a column capital as a motif for tensile strength.

In the sections on tectonics and stereotomy, other novel points are made. In considering the "spatial" motive inherent in the development of the Roman vault, for instance, Semper raises the issue of space in itself as a valid realm for architectural consideration. In his discussion of iron, he again sets the theoretical parameters for the Germanic discussion of this material for the remainder of the century. Because iron as a material becomes more perfect or efficient the thinner it is, it is by nature an "infertile ground for art!"[158] If it could be given greater dimension through the use of tubular forms in large trusses, however, "it might be possible to pin our hopes for the future of art on it."[159]

The largest section is devoted to textiles, and here Semper's analyses are exceptionally creative, even far-flung, as he winds through the complex history of these pliable and tough materials highly resistant to tearing. In his lengthy excursus on the crucial notion of the "dressing" (*Bekleidung*) – he finds an analogy between human clothing and architectural dressing – he develops at length the leitmotif of his architectural theory. Historically, the theme of textiles derives from primitive mat walls hung vertically as spatial dividers. Next came the transition from the plaiting of branches to the plaiting of basts and grasses, then the transition to the use of threads spun from vegetable matter, until finally came weaving. At this stage of development, polychrome tapestries were still hung vertically against solid walls to symbolize the spatial motive, but eventually this theme was transplanted to the wall itself as a dressing – the most obvious case being the textile-like wall panels of Assyria. In Greece, however, another decisive step was taken when these textile wall dressings were painted, for they became "spiritualized," that is, no longer simply decorating surfaces but now "masking" them in a highly symbolic and expressive fashion. For Semper this pivotal movement in Western art – "the [thematic] masking of reality in the arts" – coincided with the development of the Greek drama and arose from the same theatrical instincts:

I think that the *dressing* and the *mask* are as old as human civilization and the joy in both is identical to the joy in those things that drove men to be sculptors, painters, architects, poets, musicians, dramatists – in short, artists. Every artistic creation, every artistic pleasure presupposes a certain carnival spirit, or

48. Gottfried Semper, portrait by W. Ungers, 1871. From *Zeitschrift für bildende Kunst*, 1879.

to express myself in a modern way, the haze of carnival candles is the true atmosphere of art.[160]

This "denial of reality," this masking of thematic content, in Semper's view is the same impulse that inspired the dramas of Shakespeare and Mozart's *Don Juan*, the same "carnival spirit" that resides in the stone dramas of Phidias. It is for Semper, in a curious way, the reason for monumental architecture's very existence.

Semper completed the second volume of *Der Stil* in 1863 and almost immediately became diverted by what would have been one of the grandest architectural projects of the century. Richard Wagner, who had been on the move since 1849, had at last found his long-sought patron in young King Ludwig II of Bavaria, who ascended to the throne in 1864. The new king desired to have Wagner (who was writing the Ring Cycle) as his resident composer, and to that end

49. Gottfried Semper, second Dresden Hoftheater, 1870–8. Photo by author.

he offered to build him the largest theater in the world to stage his operas. Semper was commissioned to design it, and during the next three years he worked on the design in its many details. Wagner, meanwhile had quickly grown accustomed to palatial luxury and made repeated monetary demands on the state treasury, which scarcely endeared him to the taxpayers of Bavaria. When his adulterous affair with Cosima von Bülow became public in the fall of 1865, the result was a near riot against his presence in the city. Richard was quietly put on a train to Switzerland, and

the grand theater project was doomed from that moment forward.

Semper's work on the design in any case interrupted his work on the third volume of *Der Stil*, and it was only toward the end of the 1860s that Semper returned to the book, but with little success. His last public lecture, "On Architectural Styles" (1869), is notable on two counts. One is his recognition that in the "mighty art of spatial creation" lies the "future of architecture in general."[161] The second is the apologetic resignation of this sixty-six-year-old architect and his thesis that the time is just not right for a new architectural style to emerge. In arguing this thesis, Semper passed the burden of innovation to the next generation, to "one or the other of our younger colleagues."[162]

There is, however, an interesting postscript to Semper's despondency. Beginning in 1869, Semper revived his monumental practice with several major commissions in Vienna and Dresden. In the latter city, a fire in 1869 burned down Semper's first theater, and after some hesitation the Saxon king invited the now celebrated architect back to the city to build a new one (Figs. 48 and 49). These events took place when another German intellectual – Friedrich Nietzsche – had become fascinated with Semper's theory. In reading *Der Stil*, Nietzsche was especially drawn to those passages dealing with Greek drama and the "masking of reality."[163] Nietzsche was at the time developing his ideas on Greek drama in two lectures composed in the fall of 1869, and they became the starting point for his first book, *The Birth of Tragedy from the Spirit of Music* (1872). The book has two main themes. The first is that Greek tragedy was born out of a union of Apollonian and Dionysian forces, a union in which Dionysian tendencies dominated. This union effectively ended at the time of Euripides and Socrates, when the irrational component was purged, as it were, by the ascending rational forces of what would become Western civilization. The second theme is that for the Greeks the "narcotic draught" of Dionysus offered a means to escape from the primal condition of angst and effectively – through the mediation of the chorus – find spiritual redemption in the symbolic sacrifice of the tragic hero. Through drama, the Greeks were able to rid themselves of their civilizing conceits

and release their pent-up irrational urges: "For this chorus the Greek built up the scaffolding of a fictitious *natural state* and on it placed fictitious natural beings. On this foundation tragedy developed and so, of course, it could dispense from the beginning with a painstaking portrayal of reality."[164]

In his design for the second Dresden theater, Semper was pursuing similar ideas. In the iconographic program for the new theater – prepared just as Prussian armies were marching into France – Semper reversed the long-accepted priority given to Apollo in the decorative appointments of theaters and crowned his great work with a bronze quadriga in which Dionysus leads his bride Ariadne to Mount Olympus. The "Return of Dionysus" is also the leading theme articulated throughout the theater's interior. In a brochure of 1874 consisting of two memoranda, Semper defended his iconography by insisting that – in contrast to such brutal natural laws as survival of the fittest – he was appealing in his design to the higher laws of humanity, best understood in mythical terms when art is directed to the national consciousness of a people.[165] The increasing ascendancy of rationalized industry with its ever greater potential for human destruction, he argued, was essentially depriving art of its primordial redemptive role of appeasing or taming the baser human instincts. A more frank celebration of the irrational was therefore needed if art was to continue to fulfill its social task of ridding humanity of its civilized demons. In the end, then, Semper's stylistic resignation appears to have been principally metaphysical; in his vision of the artist, he was almost certainly the last architect of the nineteenth century to view himself in terms similar to those he applied to his favorite artist – Michelangelo.

7

HISTORICISM IN THE UNITED STATES

The Genius of architecture seems to have shed its maledictions over this land.

Thomas Jefferson (1781)

There is a time in every man's education when he arrives at the conviction that envy is ignorance; that imitation is suicide; that he must take himself for better, for worse, as his portion.

Ralph Waldo Emerson (1841)

1. The Tradition of American Classicism

Architectural theory in the United States, as we might expect, was a relatively late developing phenomenon – a philosophical luxury rarely engaged in before the 1840s. But this does not mean that national characteristics in thinking were not evident before this date. If American architecture in the beginning was heavily influenced by the cultural values and historical perspectives of European settlers, it soon exhibited important differences from European architecture, variations forced on it by the new geographic and cultural milieu. For one thing, American architects lacked ready access to the monuments of the past – the architecture of Greece, Rome, the Middle Ages, and the Renaissance – or those models that provided the immediate context for European historical conceptions. Then there were the economic and physical hardships of pioneering life, which quickly tempered the pretensions of European culture with a necessary respect for frugality and practicality. We should also take into account the unspoiled and mostly unpopulated landscape of North America with its large distances and scale, which helped to foster a generally rural or antiurban outlook. Again, of great importance were the egalitarian ideals of the American political system and the antiroyalist sentiments of the populace, who initially shunned personal excess and civic pomp. Finally, there was a well-defined ideological split (political and cultural) growing out of northern and southern social views and patterns of immigration. Many of the early New Englanders came from the lower classes of British society, and they brought with them strict religious principles and communal beliefs, including a puritanical eschatology that viewed the future of the nation in terms of a divine plan. The early settlers drawn to the South were, by contrast, attracted by the profit motive; by the more temperate climate of the abundant tidewater areas; and by the fertility of the land, on which they soon cultivated crops such as tobacco, rice, and cotton. These landowners were proud "self-made" individuals who literally carved a civilization from the wilderness. Thus from the early days of the Republic, a principled (and eventually near ruinous) political division was in place.

The difference between the regions can also be seen in the architectural orientations of the first two significant American architects, Charles Bulfinch (1763–1844) and Thomas Jefferson (1743–1826).[1] The Bostonian Bulfinch, a graduate of Harvard University, embarked on a two-year European tour in 1785. There he met Ambassador Jefferson and followed his suggestion to visit the south of France and Italy. It was England, however, that shaped Bulfinch's architectural outlook and provided him with his library. Two early designs, for the Federal Street Theater (1793–4) and the Tontine Crescent (1794), were modeled on British sources, and Bulfinch's major work, the Massachusetts State House (1795–8), owes much to the river facade of William Chambers's Somerset House. Yet Bulfinch's architectural detailing is lighter and more austere than his British models, and his overall proportions are scaled to the timber traditions of the Northeast. The development of his American sensitivity is best seen in the puritanical simplicity of the Lancaster Meetinghouse (1816–18), truly one of the early masterpieces of American practice.

Jefferson's architectural outlook is no less derivative but somewhat more cosmopolitan in its sources. We also know far more of his ideas. His schooling began in the early 1760s

140

at the College of William and Mary, where he also came upon his first architectural books (perhaps in the library of William Byrd at nearby Westover). Jefferson began the construction of his beloved Monticello in 1767, the original design for which was based on a plan from a book by Robert Morris. The three-room plan was modest and classical, English Palladian in character, and its construction, redesign, expansion over the next several decades provided Jefferson with a means to test his continually evolving ideas on architecture. In the early 1770s he also made various designs for buildings at Williamsburg: an octagonal chapel, an addition to the so-called Wren Building at the College of William and Mary (which he described as "rude, misshapen"), and a remodeling of the Governor's Palace.[2] All seem to have been based on Palladian precedents. In 1780, as the head of the committee in charge of planning the new capitol at Richmond, Jefferson made his first design for the Virginia State Capitol, with a classical portico at each end.[3]

Jefferson's five years as ambassador to France, between 1784 and 1789, were architecturally very rewarding. Well known is his infatuation ("like a lover at his mistress") with the Maison Carrée at Nîmes – the building that had served Laugier as the model of architectural perfection. It was this temple form, of course, that he had earlier transposed to the Virginia State Capitol.[4] For the American Embassy, he rented the somewhat luxurious Hôtel de Langeac, a neoclassical work designed by Jean-François-Thérèse Chalgrin (1739–1811). It was situated on the Champs Elysées, across the street from one of Ledoux's toll buildings. Jefferson was also "violently smitten" with the construction of Pierre Rousseau's Hôtel de Salm.[5] He sketched Jacques Soufflot's Panthéon and much admired the laminated timber dome of the Halle au Blé (grain market). He was also a frequent visitor to the home of the Countess de Tessé at Chaville, designed by Etiénne-Louis Boullée. His classicism thus took on a distinct French coloration.

In the spring of 1786 Jefferson traveled to England with John Adams and toured various English estates and gardens, among them Lord Burlington's Chiswick (whose dome has "an ill effect" and whose garden shows "still too much of art"), Alexander Pope's Twickenham, William Kent's Stowe, and Kew.[6] The English approach to gardening, in his view, "surpasses all on earth" and "went far beyond my ideas."[7] By contrast, English architecture "is in the most wretched stile I ever saw, not meaning to except America where it is bad, nor even Virginia where it is worse than in any other part of America, which I have seen."[8] In 1788

he also toured in Holland and Germany, rounding out his rather sound architectural education.

All of these experiences transformed his architectural thinking. He began a new wave of construction at Monticello in 1793 and incorporated ideas from many of the French examples. Of greater importance, perhaps, was the imprint that he, as secretary of state and president, left on the new city of Washington. When George Washington commissioned the French painter and architect Pierre-Charles L'Enfant (1754–1825) to prepare the plan for the new capital city in 1791, the president instructed him to contact Jefferson – from whom L'Enfant promptly received plans of several European cities. In Jefferson's letter of response, he also suggested for the Capitol "the adoption of some one of the models of antiquity, which have had the approbation of thousands of years"[9] (Fig. 50). After L'Enfant had been dismissed from his post in 1792, Jefferson organized a competition for the president's house and one for the Capitol. In the first of these, won by the Irishman James Hoban (c. 1762–1831), Jefferson entered the fray anonymously with his own design based on Palladio's Villa Rotunda. He later fought for changes to Hoban's design and was responsible for Benjamin Latrobe adding the front porch to the White House in 1807 (Fig. 51).

The early designs for the Capitol had generated greater controversy. No scheme was judged victorious in 1792, although one of the competitors, Etienne-Sulpice Hallet (c. 1760–1825), was retained by the building commission to "improve" his entry. At this point William Thornton (1759–1828) came forward with a new design that drew upon a design of Colen Campbell. Over the next year or so, Thornton and Hallet exchanged alternative designs, with Thornton gradually taking control. A sketch made by Jefferson of one of Hallet's revised plans, passed on to George Washington, yet reveals that Jefferson was also critical of Thornton's plan.[10] Thornton, for the near term, succeeded with his scheme, that is, until Jefferson, then president, replaced him with Benjamin Latrobe in 1803. Jefferson in this way continued to influence the project. Against the architect's severe objections, Jefferson prevailed in his pitched two-year battle with Latrobe over the roofing design for the House of Representatives. The glare and condensation caused by Jefferson's skylights (based on the roof design of the Halle au Blé) would soon prove an embarrassment to the president, but only until British torches neatly eliminated the problem. All things considered, it is not unfair to say that Jefferson was the person most responsible for endowing the new capital with its classical character.

50. View of the Capitol and Washington, D.C., in 1810. From J. W. Moore, *Picturesque Washington: Pen and Pencil Sketches* (Chicago, 1886).

Jefferson's most important design, of course, was that for the University of Virginia (1817–26; Fig. 52). It is also the work in which his classical idealism found its fullest realization. The preeminently civil idea that "an University should not be a house but a village" – possibly emanating

from the encyclopedia article on "Collége" by Quatremère de Quincy – was articulated at the start of 1805 and altogether refined by 1810.[11] Latrobe suggested to Jefferson the idea of a focal building at the head of the complex, "which ought to exhibit in Mass and details as perfect a specimen

51. The White House from Pennsylvania Avenue. From J. W. Moore, *Picturesque Washington: Pen and Pencil Sketches* (Chicago, 1886).

52. Thomas Jefferson, campus of the University of Virginia, 1817–26. From William Alexander Lambeth, *Thomas Jefferson as an Architect and a Designer of Landscapes* (Boston, 1913).

of good Architectural taste as can be devised."[12] Jefferson's use of the Roman Pantheon (at one-half scale) for this focal point endows the overall design with elegance and credibility. The pavilions of the ten professors, linked by a colonnade, form a kind of architectural encyclopedia with their varied elevations, plans, and details – as Latrobe too suggested. The use of the entry exedra of Ledoux's Hôtel de Guimard for Pavilion IX is a Jeffersonian stoke of genius. The terracing of the lawn and the gradually increasing spacing of the pavilions also demonstrate a sense of visual subtlety. The campus is one of the finest architectural creations of the nineteenth century: quintessentially American in its antiurban, individualist yearnings.

The wide acceptance of classicism in the first half of the nineteenth century also owes much to Benjamin Henry Latrobe (1764–1820).[13] Latrobe emigrated to the United States in 1796, already an experienced engineer and architect, and he brought with him a library of 1,500 books. He was born in England and attended religious Moravian schools in Saxony and Silesia (Poland). Later in London he worked in the offices of John Smeaton and Samuel Pepys Cockerell. He then set up his own practice and designed two houses in a distinct Soanian style before the war with France and the death of his young wife led to his departure for Virginia. His success in the new country came slowly. His design and engineering skills were first displayed in the Virginia State Penitentiary (1797) but were given greater expression in Philadelphian projects, the Bank of Pennsylvania (1799–1801) and the waterworks (1799). The bank, with its Roman temple design, contained the first vaulted, circular hall in the United States, while the bold and muscular forms of his pump house on Centre Square betray the influence of Ledoux as well as Soane.

Latrobe still struggled until Jefferson came to his rescue. Shortly after landing in Virginia, Latrobe had attempted to cultivate political connections, first by visiting George Washington at Mount Vernon in 1796 and then by meeting Vice President Jefferson two years later.[14] It was not until 1802 that President Jefferson, after an exchange of letters regarding a canal between the Delaware River and Chesapeake Bay, invited Latrobe to Washington to design a naval dry dock, with a roof "in the manner of the Halle au Blé at Paris."[15] The project did not go forward, and up to this point the two men had apparently never discussed architecture. But at two presidential dinner parties in November of that year, Jefferson discovered the kindred classical spirit that he was seeking.[16] Early in 1803 he chose Latrobe for the revived post of surveyor of public buildings in Washington and charged him with advancing work on the Capitol, which had been languishing.

Latrobe's structural corrections and plan modifications to the hitherto disastrous building campaign were not accepted without a fight. As a friend of Jefferson, he was fiercely opposed by the Federalist Thornton, who was still a building commissioner, and the latter did his best to destroy Latrobe's reputation.[17] Despite Thorton's objections, between 1803 and 1811 Latrobe created a series of classical spaces that, with their plastic proportions, domed canopies, and lighting effects, owed much to Soane's halls at the Bank of England. Latrobe's debt to these halls is even more pronounced in his revised designs for the Capitol in 1815, after the British had burned the first building to the ground.

Latrobe was in every way a versatile designer. For the Baltimore Cathedral in 1805, he initially proposed both "Gothic" and "Roman" designs, stating that he "should prefer the former."[18] He nevertheless provided this lone Catholic diocese in America with a superb classical church and dome. Books that Latrobe mentions in letters are the usual classical texts – ranging from Vignola to such modern authors as Stuart and Revett (whose *Antiquities of Athens* was a principal source for the Capitol), William Chambers, and David Gilly.[19] In his often cited letter to Jefferson of 1807, Latrobe referred to himself as a "bigotted Greek, to the condemnation of the roman architecture of Balba, Palmyra, Spalatro, and of all the buildings erected subsequent to Hadrian's reign."[20] This remark has a revealing context. In an earlier letter, Jefferson had touched a sore point by insisting that the dome and cupola with which Latrobe hoped to roof the House of Representatives was simply "an Italian invention" with no ancient or classical precedent.[21] Latrobe responded – in what was surely a rebuke to Jefferson's bookishness – by condemning the slavish copying of antique buildings:

Our religion requires churches wholly different from their temples; our government, our legislative assemblies, and our courts of Justice buildings of entirely different principles from their basilica's; and our amusements could not possibly be performed in their Theatres or amphitheatres. But that which principally demands a variation in our buildings from those of the ancients is the difference of our climate.[22]

Latrobe concludes, "I cannot admit that because the Greeks and Romans did not place elevated cupolas upon their temples, they may not, where necessary, be rendered also beautiful."[23]

Latrobe's strengths included his geometric planning, engineering competence, and inventiveness as a designer, which collectively had no equal among American architects in his day. His noble second design for the House of Representatives exalted modern precedents. It drew upon the domed legislative amphitheater (Chambre des Députés) of the Palais Bourbon of 1795–7, which in turn invoked the amphitheater of Goindoin's school of surgery.[24] In its overall polychrome and spatial drama, the Capitol – vilified unceasingly by contemporary politicians – was exquisitely conceived to serve as the symbol for the young and struggling democracy.

Latrobe was not the only immigrant with architectural talent. Joseph-François Mangin appeared in New York in 1794, became a city surveyor, and won the competition for the New York City Hall in 1802 (executed by John McComb in 1803–12). He built several other works in this decade but then apparently returned to France around 1817. The French-trained architect Maximilian Godefroy (1765–1840?) arrived in 1805 and worked primarily in Baltimore. He befriended Latrobe and even collaborated with him on the Baltimore Exchange, although this partnership resulted in a dispute between the two men, and Godefroy returned to England in 1819.[25] Still another talented French émigré was Joseph Ramée (1764–1842), a pupil of François-Joseph Belanger. Ramée came to the United States in 1812 via Belgium, Germany, and Denmark.[26] In 1813 he received the commission to design Union College in Schenectady, New York, and his U-shaped plan for the college buildings, featuring a central rotunda with a classical pediment, certainly caught the eye of Jefferson a few years later when the latter began to finalize his scheme for the University of Virginia. Also in 1813 Ramée entered the competition for the Washington Monument in Baltimore with an exquisitely rendered design of a triumphal arch. The two-column screen and entablature recessed within the central opening – the "Guimard motif" – add an unmistakable French flavor to the ensemble. Ramée's design placed second to that of Robert

Mills, and his failure to sustain a practice led to his return to Europe in 1816.

Finally, there were the Englishmen George Hadfield (1763–1826) and William Jay (c. 1793–1837).[27] The latter lived in Savannah only from 1817 to 1824 but left the city with an indelible imprint of exceptional neoclassical works. Hadfield too possessed considerable talent. He trained at the Royal Academy, worked for James Wyatt, traveled to Italy on a scholarship, and then immigrated to the United States in 1795 to oversee the construction of the Capitol. Conflicts with the irascible Thornton led to his resignation two years later, but he remained in the city and designed a number of federal buildings. His most notable work is just across the Potomac River in Arlington – the Curtis-Lee Mansion (1817). Situated on a lush hillside and with a massive portico of six unfluted Doric columns modeled on the forms at Paestum, it remains a prominent local landmark.

Like their foreign-born counterparts, American-born architects struggled to maintain their practices in the first decades of the new century. In Boston the classical style of Bulfinch found three notable adherents in Alexander Parris (1780–1852), Solomon Willard (1783–1861), and Isaiah Rogers (1800–69).[28] A guide to their styles can be found in the six editions of Asher Benjamin's *American Builder's Companion*, which appeared between 1806 and 1827.[29] Benjamin (1773–1845), also a practicing architect, can lay claim to publishing the first American text on architecture, *The Country Builder's Assistant: Containing a Collection of New Designs of Carpentry and Architecture* (1797), the first of seven handbooks published by him.[30] The first edition of *The American Builder's Companion* drew its examples from James Gibbs's *Book of Architecture* as well as the work of Bulfinch and Benjamin. By the third edition (1816), Benjamin had turned to William Chambers as his principal source. In the sixth edition of 1827, Benjamin adds a section on "Grecian Architecture," which illustrates, among other things, the orders of the Parthenon and the Ionic temple on the River Ilissus. Benjamin's discussion of theory is slim and seems to derive entirely from Laugier. Architecture, he argues, imitates nature, specifically the primitive hut as described by this French neoclassicist. The structural parts of a building are necessary or essential, while ornaments are "only accessories" and must therefore be both tasteful and moderate. Benjamin presents a Vitruvian explanation for the origin of the orders but warns that its veracity "has been much questioned, and is, probably, not much to be depended on."[31]

An earlier declaration in favor of Greek classicism – and one that better prepares the ground for the Greek revival – is an essay that appeared in 1814.[32] Its author was the Philadelphian George Tucker, who was an admirer and early biographer of Jefferson.[33] Tucker opens with the question whether Greek architecture, which for two thousand years has held sway over the architectural world (save for the "short period" of Gothic architecture around the thirteenth century), was indeed the unchanging standard of excellence in this field. Citing the aesthetics of Shaftesbury and Burke, Tucker considers the many reasons for its near universal adoption by civilized man, among them its utility and convenience, its intrinsic beauty, its modest but effective ornament, habit or tradition, and classical authority. This last reason in fact leads him into something of a dilemma. On the one hand, Tucker acknowledges the need for variety and contrast as well as the human instinct for invention; on the other hand, he is critical of both Latrobe's innovative column capital designs for the Capitol and Jefferson's use of side entrances on the Virginia State Capitol. Tucker concludes that

the moderns, though they may have as pure a taste for the beautiful and the grand, as their Grecian preceptors, as happy an invention, and as fair a field for its exertion in the erection of as magnificent fabrics as ever existed before, must be content to rank with the *servum pecus*, and however original they may aspire to be in other arts, to remain slavish imitators in architecture.[34]

Another early champion of Greek architecture was Benjamin's student Ithiel Town (1784–1844), although he mediated his training in classicism with knowledge of contemporary European trends. Town had worked under Benjamin in 1805–6 and by 1810 had opened a practice in Boston. In 1813 he moved to New Haven to build Trinity Church (1813–16), one of the earliest Gothic revival churches in the United States. His interest next turned to bridges, and in 1820 he patented a clever lattice truss that behaved almost like a monolithic structure.[35] He returned to architecture in 1825 and erected a number of important classical buildings, among them the New York Theater (1826) and the Connecticut State House, New Haven (1827–31). In 1829, on the eve of his partnership with Alexander Jackson Davis, Town sailed to Europe to visit England, France, and Italy.[36] In London he was impressed by the buildings of John Soane, John Nash, Robert Smirke, and C. R. Cockerell, and in Italy he visited Herculaneum and Pompeii. He returned to the United States and with Davis built one of the largest offices in the country (1829–36).[37] His own "fireproof" home (1834–6) in New Haven, which was conceived to accommodate what was then the largest architectural library in the country, exhibits distinct Soanean overtones, while the firm's designs for the state capitols of Indiana (1831–5) and North Carolina (1833–40) are heavily classical. Town also put much time into upgrading the status of the profession in America. As an honorary and corresponding member of the Institute of British Architects, he worked tirelessly for the founding of an "Institution of Architects" on American soil. His educational expectations are voiced in his pamphlet *Outlines of a Plan for Establishing in New York an Academy and Institution of the Fine Arts* (1835).

Town's embrace of Greek classicism in the 1820s fell in line with the classical designs of Robert Mills (1781–1855), William Strickland (1788–1854), and John Haviland (1792–1852). The works of all three men testify to Latrobe's widespread influence.

Mills – a South Carolinian who viewed himself as "the first native American who directed his studies in architecture as a profession" – trained first with Hoban and later with Jefferson before being directed by the latter to Latrobe's office in 1803.[38] He remained with Latrobe for nearly five years, handling his commissions in Philadelphia, then struck out on his own in 1808. His use of a colonnaded exedra or Guimard motif in Washington Hall, Philadelphia (1814–16), indicates his early infatuation with the stylish neoclassicism that also attracted Jefferson, yet his more original designs for the Sansom Street Baptist Church, Philadelphia (1811–12), the Octagon Unitarian Church, Philadelphia (1812–13), and the Monumental Church, Richmond (1812–17) display his architectural strengths as well as his limitations. Each of the three churches possesses an interior rotunda and is severe in its geometry and Spartan in its ornamentation.

The same limitation can be seen in the winning schemes for his two monuments to George Washington. The first, the Baltimore monument built between 1814 and 1842, is a Doric pillar modeled on Trajan's Column yet admirably fitted to its urban square. The monument in the nation's capital (1833–84) was originally designed in the form of a low-capped obelisk with a circular "pantheon" at its base. In Washington, Mills followed the lead of Latrobe with his classical solutions for the Patent Office (1836–40), the Treasury Building (1836–42), and the Post Office (1839–42). All are well-constructed, technically innovative, and fireproof

buildings, admirable for their simplicity. Mills also built several important buildings in Virginia and South Carolina, and it is in such smaller works as his County Record Building in Charleston (1821–7) that his skills as a designer become most evident.

Mills left behind several writings and a partially completed monograph on his own works. In the notes for his planned essay "The Progress of Architecture in Virginia," Mills "deprecated the servile copying of the buildings of antiquity," as well as those of Europe, Asia, and Egypt.[39] Instead, he encouraged architects to study the "original models of their country" and "go not to the old world for your examples. We have entered a new era in the history of the world; it is our destiny to lead, and not to be led. Our vast country is before us and our motto Excelsior."[40] In the introduction to his projected monograph "The Architectural Works of Robert Mills," he distinguishes between Jefferson's "Roman style" and Latrobe's improved "purely Greek" style and commends the latter – also applauding Stuart and Revett for illustrating the "chaste style of the Grecian buildings."[41] In commenting on his own innovations, however, he takes a more practical slant and urges "utility and economy" with "as much harmony and beauty of arrangement as practical."[42]

Strickland's Greek classicism, by contrast, seems to spring from more expressive impulses.[43] He trained under Latrobe during the designing of the Bank of Pennsylvania, but his first commission was the quaint Gothic Masonic Hall in Philadelphia (1808–11). After the War of 1812, he returned to practice with great fanfare by winning the 1818 competition for the Second Bank of the United States in Philadelphia, whose program mandated "a chaste imitation of Grecian architecture, in its simplest form" (Fig. 53). Strickland responded with an imitation of the Parthenon, minus the lateral colonnades. Shortly after its completion, the bank was lauded by one foreign visitor as "the most beautiful building I have yet seen in the United States," while for James Fenimore Cooper it was the second most beautiful nineteenth-century building in the world – second to the Paris Bourse, designed by Alexandre Théodor Brongniart.[44] With the exception of experiments with an Egyptian style, Strickland remained true to his Greek vocabulary throughout his highly successful career.

Strickland is notable too for the start he gave to architectural education in Philadelphia. The question of architectural training, in fact, had long been an issue in the nation's largest city. In 1790 it formed part of the charter of the

53. William Strickland, Second Bank of the United States, Philadelphia, 1818–24. Photograph by author.

Philadelphia Carpenters' Company, and in 1804 the idea of a school was again given serious consideration by this guild before being rejected for reasons unknown. The matter of formal training took another turn in 1824 with the creation of "The Franklin Institute of the State of Pennsylvania, for the Promotion of the Mechanic Arts." The term "mechanic arts" referred to the sciences and construction, and the five hundred members who joined the Franklin Institute in its first year testify to the support behind the institute's mandate "to improve the condition and elevate the character of the operative class of society, by affording them the only effectual means for this purpose, *education*."[45] Strickland was one of the two architects to join the Franklin Institute, and he was then given the professorship in architecture. He responded with at least eight lectures in 1824–5, the first presentation on American soil of the history of architecture.

The lectures exalt the classical spirit, now approaching its height of popularity. Six deal with Greek architecture and the orders, while one discusses the Tuscan order. The first, the introductory lecture, paints a vivid portrait of the architectural aspirations in 1824. After commenting on Hindu, Persian, and Egyptian architecture, Strickland arrives at the Greeks, whose "skill and taste in the art far surpassed all other nations before and since their time."[46] Strickland describes the transposition of wooden forms into stone; he cites

the Elgin Marbles and the principal Athenian works made known by the "laudable exertions" of Stuart and Revett; he lauds the Roman invention of the arch and dome and even more the Gothic works, with their expansive scale and use of stained glass, "which produces the most brilliant and transparent effect."[47] "Decided character" seems to lie at the heart of his message: "Buildings of a public nature ought to express in their design the uses and purposes for which they are erected; so that when we behold a *Church, Bank, Courthouse, Prison* etc. we may understand them to be such from some external characters in the design without the aid of a painted sign or inscribed tablet" – though not excluding the use of allegorical decoration.[48] Strickland concludes his talk with general remarks on the architecture of the day, noting that the United States Capitol "is perhaps the greatest effort of our Republic in point of extent and workmanship," although in beauty is less than Philadelphia's own Bank of Pennsylvania and Bank of the United States. It is because of these buildings that Philadelphia should claim "the proud title of the Classical City."[49]

The other Philadelphia architect to join the Franklin Institute in 1824 was John Haviland (1792–1853).[50] He had been trained in England and considered emigration to Russia before settling in Philadelphia in 1816. With few commissions, he first supported himself by running an architectural drawing school with his friend the artist Hugh

Bridport. The first fruit of their endeavors was the three-volume *Builder's Assistant* (1818–21), a definitive, strikingly illustrated, and highly detailed textbook for architects and carpenters.[51] All of the first volume is devoted to the orders and to "the best specimens of Grecian and Roman Antiquities" as well as to a selection of "the best modern works extant in Europe."[52] These contents are reflected in the program the two men inaugurated at the Franklin Institute late in 1824. Haviland was also a designer of considerable talent. He designed the new building for the Franklin Institute in 1825, the same year in which he began the speculative Philadelphia Arcade (1825–8). It was the first American enclosed shopping gallery, based on the successful Burlington Arcade (1818–19) in London.

America's last important classical architect, Thomas U. Walter (1804–87), was also raised in Philadelphia.[53] He began his career as a mason under his father, who was in charge of the construction of Strickland's Second Bank. He spent some time in Strickland's office and in 1824 enrolled in the Franklin Institute. His first great professional success was his competition-winning design for Girard College in 1833. Behind this project was Nicolas Biddle (1786–1844), one of the more interesting residents of the city. This prodigy graduated from the University of Pennsylvania at the age of thirteen, finished a degree in the classics from Princeton at the age of eighteen, and traveled to Paestum and Greece at the age of twenty. He was the editor of the first American literary journal, *Port Folio*, which published George Tucker's article in 1814. After serving as a diplomat, Biddle was appointed by President James Monroe to the board of the Second Bank of the United States in Philadelphia and thus wrote the classical competition program for the bank. Biddle was also president of the board of trustees of Girard College in 1833 and worked closely with Walter in altering the latter's original design for the central building – Founder's Hall – and transforming it into a large Corinthian temple that housed three (vaulted) floors of classrooms. A few years later Walter added the Paestum-inspired portico to the main house of Biddle's estate, Andalusia. To what extent Walter was "straightjacketed" by Biddle remains a point of contention, but Walter certainly used the temple form with grace elsewhere, most notably in the elegant Ionic portico of Charleston's Hibernian Hall (1835). The greatest achievement of Walter's career was the iron dome he placed atop the Capitol (1855–65).

In 1840 Walter accepted the architectural professorship of the Franklin Institute and in the fall of that year began a series of lectures. Most instructive is the fifth lecture – given December 1841 and entitled "On Modern Architecture" – in which Walter traces the course of architecture since the Renaissance. He speaks of Philibert de L'Orme and Claude Perrault in France, Inigo Jones and Christopher Wren in England, as well as William Chambers and James Stuart, the last of whom "has established a taste for Grecian chasteness and elegance in Architecture throughout the civilized world."[54] The best American examples of this classical taste are New York's City Hall, the Senate Chamber of the Capitol, and Latrobe's Bank of Pennsylvania, which affords "a high degree of intellectual pleasure" and is "a memento worthy of his lofty genius."[55]

But Walter at the same time speaks of the classical style as a movement already in decline. On the one hand, he admits that its laudable chasteness has presently evolved into an excessively "poor and meagre" style, "a sort of blank style to which we are mainly indebted for the brick-pile appearance of many of our best streets."[56] On the other hand, modern inventions and improvements, the proliferation of engravings, and the steam engine and its effects on quickening transportation and disseminating knowledge have conspired to render the notion of a single or national style obsolete. Any style or set of styles, from the "massy style of Egypt" to the "pointed styles of England," can be used to express more succinctly the purpose of a particular building. Moreover, a uniquely American architecture is making itself evident, by virtue of America's continuing democratic principles and growing wealth: "Instead of the magnificence, grandeur, and showy gorgeousness always affected under hereditary monarchies, we shall gradually settle down into a simpler, chaster, and more decided taste – a taste like that which marked the triumphant career of Republican Greece."[57] For now, says Walter, "the people are the nobility."[58]

2. Stylistic Pluralism around Midcentury

Walter's remarks about the decline of the Greek revival in the United States came more than a decade before his involvement in building the Capitol dome, yet they accurately reflect changing sensibilities. By the start of the 1840s, challenges to the so-called Greek revival were well underway, as both the forces of immigration and the growing knowledge of alternative styles brought American practice more into line with the stylistic pluralism of Europe. From

Britain came the Gothic revival, which was championed by an American ecclesiology movement. From Germany came the *Rundbogen* style, whose reach in the United States was extensive. And from France – in the late 1850s – came the Second Empire style.

Coincident with these pluralistic tendencies were the twin phenomena of industrialization and the social discord that culminated in the Civil War. If the quick acceleration of industrialization fueled the growth of capital and rapid economic expansion, the Civil War, besides resulting in the emancipation of a vast number of slaves, devastated a whole section of the country economically and consigned it to decades of deprivation. Economic and political power would now shift entirely to the North – that is, until the overflow of money and resources found outlets in westward expansion.

The Gothic revival was not a phenomenon new to the 1840s; in fact, it is more accurate to say that from the time the Second Trinity Church in New York City was constructed (1788–90), Gothic was the preferred style for ecclesiastical buildings. Almost all classical architects at some point in their careers practiced the style, though with varying degrees of accuracy and assurance. Latrobe had proposed a Gothic design for the Baltimore Cathedral in 1805, and he succeeded in building a Gothic church for the nation's capital three years later. Godefroy built the classicized Gothic Chapel of Saint Mary's in Baltimore in 1806. Charles Bulfinch endowed his Federal Street Church in Boston (1809) with vaguely Gothic forms. Dozens of other examples can be cited, but most were "bookish" in their inspiration, drawing upon such eighteenth-century published sources as James Gibbs and Batty Langley.

This situation began to change rapidly in the 1830s, as the historical studies of Thomas Rickman and John Britton found their way across the Atlantic. In 1830 the Yale professor Benjamin Silliman published a series of articles in the *American Journal of Science and Arts* that discussed Gothic architecture at length, including its origins and structural principles.[59] In 1836 the historian Henry Russell Cleveland also discussed the style but found its American possibilities limited because of the high cost of construction.[60] And in the same year the Vermont Episcopal bishop, John Henry Hopkins, published his *Essay on Gothic Architecture*, which was intended to serve as an introduction to this style for churchmen.[61]

A clearer direction was given to the Gothic movement at the start of the 1840s by Richard Upjohn (1802–78), an Englishman who had immigrated to America in 1829.[62]

Upjohn had been trained as a cabinetmaker in his native Dorset, and after a few years living in New Bedford, Massachusetts, he moved to Boston to join the office of Alexander Parris. Upjohn assisted him on several projects in Maine, including the Church of Saint John's in Bangor (1835–6). With his growing knowledge of Gothic forms, he was asked in 1839 by Dr. Jonathan Wainright, the rector of Trinity Church in New York, to oversee repairs on the now aging church, completed in 1790. Shortly thereafter, it became clear that the existing building had structural problems, and the decision was made to build a new one (Fig. 54).

What happened next is a remarkable chapter in American architecture.[63] Upjohn prepared a series of designs, the earliest of which resembled his design for Saint John's in Bangor. He studied the recent developments in England, the efforts of the Cambridge Camden Society, and the writings of Pugin. His final design of 1841, with its front tower and spire, resembled closely the ideal church proposed by Pugin in *The True Principles of Pointed Architecture*, which had just appeared. Upjohn was aware of Pugin's design, but how much of his own design was based on it is unclear. Nevertheless, the built church, still a landmark at the base of Wall Street, brought the American Gothic revival in line with the English movement. The church's spire (for many years the tallest structure in New York City), the chancel's perpendicular window, and the rib-vault ceiling (constructed of plaster and lath) defined a formally correct Gothic style that had not been seen before in North America – although soon other churches, such as St. George's in Montreal, started by William Footner in 1842, showed the influence of Pugin as well.[64]

Following Upjohn in his understanding of the Gothic style was the architect James Renwick (1818–95).[65] He launched his prolific career at the age of twenty-four with the commission for New York's Grace Church (1843–6). Grace Church shares features with Upjohn's Trinity (for example, the frontal tower and spire), but they also have important differences (Grace Church has a cruciform plan and curvilinear tracery). Renwick is best known as the architect of New York's Saint Patrick's Cathedral, commissioned in 1853. Here the Gothic sources are more French than British, but the cathedral's complex design history is essentially a reflection of Renwick's urbane and eclectic tastes rather than the result of a clear stylistic bias.

The case for using Gothic forms as an alternative to Greek forms was strongly argued in the 1840s by the Boston architect Arthur Delavan Gilman (1821–82). In a book review written in 1844 for the *North American Review*, Gilman seized the occasion to compose forty-four pages on American practice. The result was in fact a Puginesque diatribe against the "weak puerilities of Latrobe and his rivals," Stuart and Revett's *The Antiquities of Athens* ("that inexhaustible quarry of bad taste"), and the nearly completed Customs House in Boston ("so incongruous and absurd a pile").[66] Gilman's list of architectural infamies do not stop here: he goes on to denounce the work of Alexander Jackson Davis, Thomas Walter, and nearly everyone else practicing the classical style. In contrast, he praises the axioms of Pugin's recently published *True Principles of Pointed or Christian Architecture*, but only for religious buildings. He is particularly appreciative of Upjohn's Trinity Church, "rising, in almost mediaeval grandeur, upon our western shores. It is truly gratifying to perceive such substantial evidences of the wealth, the taste, and the piety of a people."[67] Gilman allows the possibility of other styles for other building types, and he is accepting, for instance, of the English Renaissance styles of Jones, Wren, Vanbrugh, Lord Burlington, and Charles Barry. At this stage in his career, Gilman is simply an Anglophile, although he would later be smitten by the Second Empire style of France.

Upjohn and Renwick possessed the same eclectic instinct, and neither worked exclusively in the Gothic style. During the mid-1840s both men experimented with the German *Rundbogen* style – effectively initiating a Romanesque revival in this country. The impulse to use the *Rundbogen* style seems to have been at least twofold. First, the works of such German architects as August Soller and Friedrich Gärtner were becoming known through publications; second, a wave of German-trained architects emigrated to the country, particularly after the political turmoil of 1849.[68] Upjohn again anticipated Renwick in this regard with his *Rundbogen* designs for the Church of the Pilgrims, Brooklyn (1844–6), the Bowdoin College Chapel (1845–55), and the Harvard College Chapel (1846, unbuilt). The choice of the *Rundbogen* style for the Brooklyn church resulted from efforts of the American Congregational Church to define a style for its churches different from the English Gothic favored by the Episcopalians. The sect's primer in this regard, *A Book of Plans for Churches and Parsonages* (1854), was officially noncommittal on the question of style, although it did suggest that such stylistic modifications (to the Gothic and classical) as the Rural English, Norman, or Romanesque "are adapted to a great diversity of situations, and they are, al-most any of them, a great improvement upon the miniature temples and cathedrals which have been so much in vogue in our country for years past."[69] Of the eighteen church designs presented, four were in the *Rundbogen* style, including two of the largest designs prepared by Upjohn and Renwick.[70]

Other architects working in the *Rundbogen* manner in the 1840s were Charles Blesch (1817–53), Leopold Eidlitz (1823–1908), Alexander Saeltzer, and Thomas Alexander Tefft (1826–59). Blesch, who studied with Gärtner in Munich, teamed up with Eidlitz (who studied in Vienna) to design St. George's Episcopal Church (1846–48), for some years the largest church in New York City. It was based on Gärtner's Ludwigskirche in Munich.[71] Saeltzer, who studied at the Berlin Bauakademie, won the prestigious competition for the Astor Library, New York (1849–53), with a Romanesque design loosely based on Gärtner's state library in Munich. The Rhode Islander Tefft seems to have embraced the *Rundbogen* style as a matter of principal and personal preference. Henry-Russell Hitchcock once lauded his remarkable round-arch design for the Union Depot, Providence (1847–8), as "the finest early station in the New World."[72] In an instructive lecture given in Portsmouth in 1851, Tefft reflected on the architecture of his day. He praised the exterior of the Capitol building but not its "miserably arranged" interiors. He admired several churches of Upjohn but not such constructional artifices as his plaster-and-lath ceilings and sham clerestories. Tefft spoke most highly of the "round arch school of Germany," which "is employing much invention and originality in their designs and we hasard but little in predicting a favorable result."[73] What this means to Tefft only becomes apparent a few pages later when he underscores the need for architecture to "possess an unmistakable expression of its purpose" as well as to exalt in its materiality. In his words, "It is in far better taste, besides being much less expensive to build buildings of the simplest durable materials – if they are legitimately ornamented – than to adorn less permanent construction with profuse decorations."[74] He illustrates this point with his own railroad station.

The *Rundbogen* style gained in popularity in the 1850s, as German immigrants flooded into New York, Philadelphia, and a host of Midwestern cities. The competition for the Philadelphia Academy of Music (1854), for instance, produced a slew of Romanesque designs and was won by Napoleon LeBrun and Gustav Runge, the latter a recent German émigré. For some architects the *Rundbogen* style

54. Richard Upjohn, Trinity Church, New York City, 1839–46. From *Trinity Church: Bicentennial Celebration, May 5th, 1897* (New York, 1897).

represented a "modern" alternative to the historically exhausted classical and Gothic styles; for others it offered for secular works an economical and functional solution, material expression, and spatial possibilities in planning.[75] The *Rundbogen* style's rather sudden popularity, however, was followed by an equally precipitous decline, beginning with the economic crash of 1857. The resulting depression halted most construction and forced many recent European immigrants back to their native countries.

The American Civil War, which began in 1861, had an equally disastrous effect on building activity, but by this date the *Rundbogen* style was already being overtaken by the Second Empire style for larger commissions. Synonymous with this style is the name of Richard Morris Hunt (1827–

95), although this association is somewhat misleading. Hunt, however, did come to epitomize the upper echelon of the newly forming architectural profession.[76] The son of a congressman, he had every privilege the new plutocratic society could offer: a respected family, a good education, extensive travel, and marriage into a family of greater wealth, not to mention professional recognition as one of the founding members of the American Institute of Architects in 1857. He also had the distinction of being the first American to be educated at the Ecole des Beaux-Arts, having gained acceptance into the second class in 1846. He was a pupil of Hector-Martin Lefuel, the *grand-prix* winner of 1839, who in early 1854 was appointed the architect of the Louvre. Hunt had just returned to Paris from his tour of Italy, Sicily, Egypt, Palestine, Syria, and Greece, and he worked for Lefeul for two years. And it was a reluctant Hunt – at this stage in his life more European than American – who returned to the United States in 1855, where "greater numbers of luxurious houses were now being built in New York City than in Paris."[77] Perhaps equally important was the fact that "all things French" had recently become the rage – that is, within the parvenu circles of the Astors, Vanderbilts, and other pretenders to European aristocratic tastes.

Hunt built little during his first decade in practice. Instead, he joined the right social clubs, established several offices, trained several students (to high competence) in the French atelier system, sketched in his spare time, and, perhaps most importantly, established his summer residence in Newport. It was not until his return from his third extended European tour of 1867 that he began to practice what he rightfully termed "the French school of academic architecture, the school of a style which takes splendor, dignity and a certain monumental feeling as the most necessary merits of its construction."[78] Although this allegiance sometimes translated into the luxurious but hapless "early-French châteaux" style, Hunt was an architect of discipline and considerable talent.

Nevertheless, the Second Empire style of Napoleon III, especially the popular mansard roof, did indeed prosper in the decade of the 1850s and 1860s, as shown by such buildings as Renwick's Cocoran Gallery, Washington, D.C. (1859–71), Gridley Bryant's Boston City Hall (1861–5, designed by Arthur Gilman), and Fuller and Laver's New York State Capitol (started in 1867).

What should not be overlooked in this importation of European "culture" during these years was the industrial progress being made. The country's physical and geographical makeup was also rapidly changing. The first horse-drawn railway line appeared in Pennsylvania in 1829, but by 1850 a steam-powered railway line had crossed the Mississippi, and by 1869 a unified-gage transcontinental line was in place. The first telegraph line between Washington, D.C., and Baltimore was completed in 1844; twenty-two years later a successful transatlantic line was in service. The first documented balloon-frame structure appeared in Chicago in 1833, and balloon-frame construction soon proliferated there and in the new cities of the West, especially San Francisco. Elisha Graves Otis proudly displayed his elevator at the New York World's Fair in 1853. In 1846 the German-American engineer John Augustus Roebling built his first suspension bridge over the Monongahela River at Pittsburgh, then larger ones over Niagara Falls (1855) and the Ohio River at Cincinnati (1867). The following year he began work on the Brooklyn Bridge.

And no less significant to architectural practice were the efforts of James Bogardus (1800–74).[79] This one-time watchmaker (later successful inventor) from upstate New York lived in Britain in 1836–40 and observed the architectural use of cast iron there. On a trip to Italy in 1840 he hit upon the idea of a modular cast-iron structural system for buildings. In 1847, while living in New York City, he settled down to solving the problem in earnest, and within two years he found the financial backing to erect a four-story cast-iron frame manufactory and warehouse – the Duane Street Factory – illustrating his ideas. Tubular, fluted cast-iron Doric columns ran up the outside of the building; window glass and spandrel panels filled the space in between; the entire interior structure was iron. His taller Sun Iron Building, Baltimore (1851), carried the concept of all-iron construction further, and for the New York World's Fair of 1853 he proposed a gigantic coliseum with a central round iron tower 300 feet tall. Though he was unsuccessful in getting this proposal accepted, he still spawned a new industry of cast-iron construction, which, aided by the California Gold Rush of 1850, rapidly spread to the West.

The efforts of Bogardus and others challenged the American architectural profession. In one of the first papers given to the newly formed American Institute of Architects, "Cast Iron in Decorative Architecture" (1858), Henry Van Brunt (1832–1903) rallied to the support of this new material and criticized its rejection by an arrogant profession, "sitting haughtily on her acropolis."[80] Van Brunt, who had just been accepted into Hunt's studio, also called into question Ruskin's belief that good architecture lies in the costliness of materials and time expended on execution; he insisted rather that "the cheapness of iron, its rapidity and ease of workmanship, the readiness with which it may be made" are indeed valuable attributes in a democratic society.[81] Eidlitz responded by presenting a paper two weeks later in which he rejected iron for anything other than a secondary and utilitarian purpose. At the lecture's conclusion, Hunt was prompted to rise to the defense of his student, and he did in fact later experiment with this material in two shop fronts along Broadway – although it would take him twelve years to do so.[82] Van Brunt would go on to become the first American translator of Viollet-le-Duc's *Discourses on Architecture*, and later in the century he became one of America's most astute architectural critics.

3. Emerson and Greenough

Despite the expanding cultural dependency of American architects on European fashions and trends in the middle years of the century, uniquely American sensitivities were being quietly cultivated. One front of this theoretical development is represented by the ideas of Ralph Waldo Emerson (1803–82) and Horatio Greenough (1805–52).[83] Both were graduates of Harvard, though they did not meet until later. Emerson completed his studies in 1821, and in 1825 he entered Harvard Divinity School in order to follow in the footsteps of his father, a Unitarian minister. In 1829 he obtained the post of junior pastor at Boston's Second Church, but the death of his wife in 1831, at the age of nineteen, led Emerson to reconsider the course of his life. In 1832 he resigned his position and undertook a trip to Italy, France, England, and Scotland to further his intellectual education. When Emerson returned to Massachusetts, he moved to Concord and turned his attention to writing. Around him gathered the so-called Concord circle of transcendentalists, which ultimately comprised Theodor Parker, Margaret Fuller, Bronson Alcott, Henry David Thoreau, and Walt Whitman. Gradually it expanded into a potent intellectual force.[84]

Emerson first met Greenough in his Florence studio in 1833. The latter had completed his studies at Harvard in 1825 and had immediately left for Rome to study sculpture, armed with a letter of introduction to Bertel Thorwaldsen.[85] He joined the international student community there, and after having apprenticed with the classicist Lorenzo Bartolini in Florence, he received in 1832 the congressional commission to execute a statue of George Washington for the rotunda of the Capitol. His partially nude, seated figure of Washington, however, found little approbation in the nation's capital, as did several of his later classical pieces. Emerson once noted to Thomas Carlyle that Greenough's "tongue was far cunninger in talk, than his chisel to carve," but Emerson also absorbed many of his aesthetic ideas from Greenough.[86] In *English Traits* (1856), Emerson was more honest in reporting that the now deceased sculptor was "a superior man, ardent and eloquent, and all his opinions had elevation and magnanimity. . . . his paper on Architecture, published in 1843, announced in advance the leading thoughts of Mr. Ruskin on the *morality* in architecture, notwithstanding the antagonism of their views of the history of art."[87]

The transcendental vision of Emerson is key for understanding the spiritual accord between the two men, although Greenough was never a part of Emerson's circle. The gist of Emerson's theory is found in his 1836 essay "Nature," in which he first articulates his quasi-pantheistic notion of an "Over-Soul" (divine spirit) of which humanity is but an extension or projection: "Standing on the bare ground, – my head bathed by the blithe air, and uplifted into infinite space, – all mean egotism vanishes. I become a transparent eye-ball; I am nothing; I see all; the currents of the Universal Being circulate through me; I am part or particle of God."[88] He borrowed the notion of the transcendental from Kant, who used it to characterize a class of ideas – space, time, causality – that were not learned from experience but were intuitions by which the mind organized the material of the senses. Emerson defines the transcendental more simply as the philosophical counterpart to materialism, as an "excess of faith" that, while not denying reality, nevertheless grounds the world in a deeper spiritual consciousness: "The Transcendentalist adopts the whole connection of spiritual doctrine. He believes in miracle, in the perpetual openness of the human mind to new influx of light and power; he believes in inspiration, and in ecstasy."[89]

Another pole of Emerson's thought is found in his famous essay "Self-Reliance," published in 1841. The title, soon to become a motto for American intrepidity, refers to self-reliance not in any material or economic sense but rather to the intellectual self-reliance of a person or an entire nation. Here is where his eschatological or revelatory vision for the New World becomes manifest – America's fated role in the redemptive story of humanity. "It is for want of self-culture," he notes, "that the superstition of Travelling, whose idols are Italy, England, Egypt, retains its fascination for all educated Americans."[90] He continues, "We imitate; and what is imitation but the travelling of the mind? Our houses are built with foreign taste; our shelves are garnished with foreign ornaments; our opinions, our tastes, our faculties, lean, and follow the Past and the Distant. . . . And why need we copy the Doric or the Gothic model?"[91] Emerson thus demands an independent American culture while at the same time disdaining any form of antinomian eccentricity or liberal elitism:

Beauty, convenience, grandeur of thought, and quaint expression are as near to us as to any, and if the American artist will study with hope and love the precise thing to be done by him, considering the climate, the soil, the length of the day, the wants of the people, the habit and form of the government, he will create a house in which all these will find themselves fitted, and taste and sentiment will be satisfied also.[92]

The architectural translation of these ideas become even more evident in another essay of 1841. Art, for Emerson, must contain a universal and creative element; its forms must be subordinate to nature but at the same time serve as a continuation or extension of nature's formative powers, the "reappearance of one mind" working toward a definite end. Fitness is thus an indispensable component of beauty, even in the fine arts: "We feel, in seeing a noble building, which rhymes well, as we do in hearing a perfect song, that it is spiritually organic, that is, had a necessity in nature, for being, was one of the possible forms in the Divine mind, and is now only discovered and executed by the artist, not arbitrarily composed by him."[93] This notion of the organic for Emerson will eventually translate into a "perfect economy" of material and means, strict veracity in their use, and a Puritanical scorn for all ornamental trappings: "Hence our taste in building rejects paint, and all shifts, and shows the original grain of the wood: refuses pilasters and columns that support nothing, and allows the real supporters of the house honestly to show themselves. Every necessary or organic action pleases the beholder."[94]

The notion of the organic is given richer development by Greenough. For all of his classical training, Greenough was highly critical of the American Greek revival. In 1836, during a visit to the United States, he remarked to a friend, "The Architecture flounders on in obstinate Greekism and at enormous expense.... Rail Roads alone seem to be *understood*."[95] Even more remarkable is a letter of five years earlier, written from Paris to Washington Allston, in which Greenough devotes several pages to the subject of architecture. Again he begins by demeaning the "universal and indiscriminate admiration" for the Greek school – in particular, Strickland's recently completed "parthenon in Philadelphia, shoved in between the common buildings of a street – shorn of its lateral colonnades and pierced every where for light reminds us of a noble captive stripped alike of arms and ornaments and set at work with the other drudges of his conqueror."[96] He is no more enamored with the Gothic, "at once grand and pathetic," and in its place he argues for a return to nature, "the only true school of art."[97] What this translates to in 1831 is a moderate use of historical forms, yet these – like a ship – should be entirely subservient to practical or functional considerations: "we would that the shell of each fabric be as it were, moulded on the wants and conveniences desired – Such has been the case with naval architecture – and he who has seen a ship at sea will confess that in that work man has approached nearest his maker."[98]

Greenough uses this nautical analogy – here presented almost a century before Le Corbusier was to employ it – again in an essay of 1843, "American Architecture," yet now within a larger theory. The leitmotif is whether "these United States are destined to form a new style of architecture" or whether America will remain "content to receive our notions of architecture as we have received the fashion of our garments and the form of our entertainments, from Europe."[99] Again the Greek revival and the "small Gothic" are decried: "It is make believe," he notes, "it is not the real thing. We see the marble capitals; we trace the acanthus leaves of a celebrated model – incredulous; it is not a temple."[100] Greenough counters with the metaphor of nature: the skeletons of animals (lacking any arbitrary proportions), the functional forms of swans, eagles, and horses, all of which satisfy what he, in speaking of evolution, terms the "law of adaptation." Here he again employs the naval metaphor: "Could we carry into our civil architecture the responsibilities that weigh upon our shipbuilding, we should ere long have edifices as superior to the Parthenon, for the purposes that we require, as the *Constitution* or the *Pennsylvania* is to the galley of the Argonauts."[101] As regards architecture, he makes this plea: "Instead of forcing the functions of every sort of building into one general form, adopting an outward shape for the sake of the eye or of association, without reference to the inner distribution, let us begin from the heart as the nucleus, and work outward."[102] This "organic" approach, it should be noted, does not apply to monumental buildings "addressed to the sympathies, the faith, or the taste of a people," but strictly to useful buildings: "They may be called machines each individual of which must be formed with reference to the abstract type of its species."[103] Such is Greenough's remarkable functionalist credo.

The credo is further elaborated in letters and the essays published in 1852 under the title *The Travels, Observations, and Experience of a Yankee Stonecutter*. In a letter to Emerson dated 28 December 1851, Greenough recaps his "theory of structure" in this way:

A scientific arrangement of spaces and forms to functions and to site – An emphasis on features proportioned to their *gradated* importance in function – Colour and ornament to be decided and arranged and varied by strictly organic laws – having a distinct reason for each decision – The entire and immediate banishment of all make-shift and make believe –.[104]

In his essay "Relative and Independent Beauty," he is decidedly Emersonian in refusing to "purloin" the glory of Schiller, Winckelmann, Goethe, and Hegel for his own "crudities." Beauty is now simply "the promise of Function," and the first downward step in architectural production was "*the introduction of the first inorganic, nonfunctional element, whether of shape or color*. If I be told that such a system as mine would produce nakedness, I accept the omen. In nakedness I behold the majesty of the essential instead of the trappings of pretension."[105] In his essay "Structure and Organization," he again defends himself against the idea that his system would produce an economic and cheap style: "No! It is the dearest of all styles! It costs the thought of men, much, very much thought, untiring investigation, ceaseless experiment."[106]

Such words would reverberate within Emerson's circle. When Emerson showed Greenough's letter to Henry David Thoreau in 1851, the latter recorded in his journal that Emerson liked it "very much," although he himself was not so approving and he accused Greenough of dilettantism.[107] Nevertheless, when Thoreau a few pages later outlines his views on architecture, he betrays the influence of Greenough: "What of architectural beauty I now see, I know has gradually grown from within outward, out of the character and necessities of the indweller and builder, without even a thought for mere ornament."[108] What Thoreau opposes is ornamented architecture in any form; in his pursuit of simplicity he prefers the "logger's hut" and the "suburban box," that is, "when the life of the indweller shall be as simple and as agreeable to the imagination."[109] A few years later he even speculates – like Diogenes – that a three-by-six-foot box with a few auger holes bored in it to "admit the air" might provide someone with adequate shelter.[110] He also scoffs at the notion of a professional designer: "An enterprise to improve the style of cottage architecture! Grow your own house, I say."[111]

Greenough, in architectural matters, was surely not the dilettante that Thoreau supposed; he was well traveled, astute, and versed in European architecture. Sometime after his arrival in Italy in the 1820s, he is said to have become familiar with the French rationalist tradition and to have met Henri Labrouste at the Villa Medici.[112] He knew of the work of Schinkel, as seen in his inquiry to a friend who had recently visited Germany: "If you should have leisure pray tell me your impression of the works of Shinkel [*sic*] the architect, as regards distribution & adaptation, *organization* in short. That's the *germ* of future architectures."[113] And it is highly probable that Greenough – with his emphasis on function – was indeed familiar with Memmo's edition of Lodoli's theory, which appeared in 1834.[114] In short, Greenough appears to have been a learned and discerning critic

of European theory, which makes his later impact on American theory more understandable.

4. Davis and Downing

Thoreau's sarcastic reference to improving "the style of cottage architecture" points to his awareness of a second front coincidentally developing within American theory, represented by Alexander Jackson Davis (1803–92) and Andrew Jackson Downing (1815–52). With their respect for nature and emphasis on adapting architectural forms to the nuances of the landscape, Davis and Downing were receptive to the ideas of Emerson, and in later years both men even drew personal endorsements from the sage of Concord. The starting point for this parallel movement, however, was not transcendentalism but the aesthetics of picturesque theory, about to evolve into something uniquely American.

Davis, in fact, can be considered, with Latrobe, Richardson, and Sullivan, as one of the most significant American architects of the nineteenth century.[115] He was born in New York City, raised in Newark and midstate New York, and trained as a typesetter in his half-brother's newspaper office in Alexandria, Virginia. By 1823 Davis had moved back to New York and begun to study art. He apparently trained at the American Academy of Fine Arts (whose director was John Trumbull), at the New York Drawing Association, and at the National Academy of Design. At these institutions he met Samuel B. Morse, Rembrandt Peale, and probably Thomas Cole, whose paintings of Catskill Falls formed the centerpiece of the American Academy's exhibition of 1825. Davis's own production gradually turned toward architectural rendering (pen and wash) and illustration, and after a year in the architectural office of Josiah Brady, he had become one of the most talented draftsmen in the country. He met Town in 1827, and the latter encouraged his architectural ambitions and gave him access to his library. Davis poured over Town's vast holdings, and on extended trips to Boston in 1827 and 1828, he further pursued his architectural education at the library of the Boston Athenaeum. When he officially joined Town as a partner in January 1829, he was a young but already mature artist, supremely gifted with the pencil and extraordinarily well read. But he brought to architecture not a bookish outlook but a pure painterly perspective; his tools of design were scale and proportion, light and tone, texture and color.

In the first half of the 1830s, Town and Davis advanced to the forefront of American practice. In 1831 the firm won the competition for the Indiana State Capitol (1831–5), and two years later it won the commission for the North Carolina State Capitol (1833–40). In 1833 Davis designed the most important neoclassical work in New York City, the United States Custom House (1833–42). Between 1832 and 1834 Davis also prepared several classical designs for the United States Patent Office in Washington, D.C., the last of which paid homage to Perrault's design for the east wing of the Louvre. Despite their success, Town and Davis decided to part ways in 1835, a split that seems to have been caused by Davis's frustration with the vocabulary of Greek classicism. During these years his deep appreciation for the American landscape attracted him to the writers and artists of the Hudson River school. He befriended Asher B. Durand, Thomas Cole, and William Cullen Bryant and became a regular on their "nature" excursions to the Catskills and Berkshires. His architectural interests now shifted to residential design and the home's setting within a landscape.

The key work documenting his changing interests was a house and gatehouse he designed for Robert Donaldson in 1836. Two years earlier, the firm of Town and Davis had designed a flamboyant "Residence in the English Collegiate Style" for Donaldson, but the latter decided to sell the partially wooded site prior to building. In 1836 Donaldson purchased another tract along the Hudson River, near Barryton, with an existing house – renamed Blithewood by the new owner – and invited Davis to make alterations (Fig. 55). The simple change that Davis proposed was to wrap a veranda around three sides of the house, supported on trellises. Davis's famous rendering of the veranda displays not the house but a view through the porch, underscoring the scenic beauty of the Hudson River. Also for the grounds of Blithewood, Davis designed a simple "Gate-House in the Rustic Cottage Style." It was a seven-room, two-story cottage with ornamental verge boards within three of its visible gables. With its hooded windows and tree-trunk porch supports (for a second-floor central balcony), it seems indeed "rustic," yet it contained a significant design innovation. Its plain wooden siding ran vertically in a board-and-batten pattern.

The significance of Blithewood's veranda and gatehouse first became evident when the architect illustrated both – together with Donaldson's first Gothic villa – in his book *Rural Residences*, which appeared in 1837. Davis intended to produce designs for rural building types in six parts, although only two appeared. These two consisted of hand-colored lithographs of cottages, farmhouses, villas, and village churches, with brief descriptions, plans, cost estimates,

and materials. In essence, the book was a portfolio and pattern book for residential and other designs. Davis's sources were the "picturesque Cottages and Villas of England," he noted in the preface, simply for their lessons of variety in both plan and outline.[116] English villas were too large in scale and costly for American needs, while English cottages, he argued, were "too inconsiderable and humble for the proper pride of republicans."[117] Davis further hoped to counter the present "bald and uninteresting aspect" of American dwellings with regional designs that exalted their connection with their natural settings. This was the lesson of Blithewood's veranda: a sheltered place to enjoy the scenic landscape. Even the use of the word "villa" was a novelty in American literature. As William H. Pierson has noted, it now came to signify "not just a house, but a country house built for a man of means and discriminating judgment, and sympathetically designed in relation to a particular natural setting."[118] Blithewood's "rustic cottage," with its spatially suggestive biaxial plan, also had important design implications; it carried a seed conscientiously nurtured by Davis over the next several decades – the seed of a specifically American residential type for suburban development.

Blithewood piqued the interest of Downing.[119] In 1838 this young horticulturalist from the Hudson Valley town of Newburgh was traveling the river to study its finer estates for their situations. Upon arriving at Blithewood, he was encouraged by Donaldson to write to Davis and express his desire to come to his office and view examples of his work. Downing was at this time completing his own treatise on landscape gardening, and he was in search of architectural ideas to complement his thoughts. The meeting between the two men could not have been more fortuitous. Davis agreed to supply Downing with architectural designs and drawings for his book, and Downing, in turn, provided Davis with a literary exposition of their mutually evolving ideas regarding the landscape and dwellings. Their collaboration was to last the next twelve years.

Downing, in fact, had arrived at Davis's office with a well-defined mission. The son of a successful nurseryman, he had married the great niece of John Quincy Adams in 1838 and had begun to build a somewhat luxurious "Elizabethan" house adjacent to the nursery, which he designed after studying examples from Loudon's *Encyclopedia* and from Francis Goodwin's *Rural Architecture* (1835). Not surprising, Downing's *Treatise on the Theory and Practice of Landscape Gardening* (1841) owes a debt to these and to other British sources. The title, many of the aesthetic principles, and even the physical layout of the book are derived from Humphry

55. Alexander Jackson Davis, view of the veranda and grounds at Blithewood, residence of Robert Donaldson. From Andrew Jackson Downing, *A Treatise of Theory and Practice of Landscape Gardening Adapted to New America* (New York, 1841).

Repton's *Observations on the Theory and Practice of Landscape Gardening* (1803). But Downing's book, like Davis's, is not simply a matter of transposition. Downing brings to it a decidedly Yankee character, beginning with its dedication to John Quincy Adams, "the Lover of Rural Pursuits, as well as the Distinguished Patriot, Statesman, and Sage."[120] Downing's goal is to "adapt" the motherland's (England's) cultural root and its principles of gardening to a specifically American soil and climate and American political aspirations:

Whatever, therefore, leads man to assemble the comforts and elegancies of life around his habitation, tends to increase local attachments, and render domestic life more delightful; thus not only augmenting his own enjoyment, but strengthening his patriotism, and making him a better citizen. And there is no employment or recreation which affords the mind greater or more permanent satisfaction, that that of cultivating the earth and adorning our own property.[121]

The text of Downing's *Treatise*, as one might expect, is almost entirely devoted to landscape issues and the various species of American trees and plants. But near the end he includes a chapter on "Landscape or Rural Architecture," in which he makes known his views on architecture. He begins by distinguishing between town and country residences, and though with the first class he has "little complaint,"

his assessment of the second – "without the least attempts at adaptation to situation" – could not be worse.[122] What character, then, should a rural residence possess? A residence worthy of approbation "not only gives ample space for all the comforts and conveniences of a country life, but by its varied and picturesque form and outline, its porches, verandas, etc., also appears to have some reasonable connection, or be in perfect keeping, with surrounding nature. *Architectural beauty* must be considered conjointly with the *beauty of the landscape* or situation."[123] Its leading principles should be (1) fitness for the end in view, (2) expression of purpose, and (3) expression of some particular architectural style.

These principles are given greater elaboration in his next book, *Cottage Residences*, which appeared in 1842 and was dedicated to Robert Donaldson. It is also a book in which Downing makes excellent use of Davis's talents. Its subject is rural architecture, and the original edition contained nine prototypical designs: two based on commissions of Davis, one based on a design by John Notman, and seven based on sketches by Downing. In this last group of designs, Davis took Downing's sketches and refined their proportions and details in elaborately finished drawings executed on woodblocks. In the preface, Downing expresses his desire to "to contribute something to the improvement of domestic architecture" and "to inspire all persons with a love of beautiful forms," which he hopes to achieve through his presentation of "compact, convenient, and comfortable houses."[124] Above all, he hopes that "at no distant day our country residences may rival the 'cottage homes of England,' so universally and so justly admired."[125]

The book opens with the chapter "Architectural Suggestions," in which Downing expands upon the three principles discussed in the *Treatise*. The leading principle, fitness, concerns not only comfort and the convenience of the plan (how to employ such features as closets) but also the fitness of materials, with wood (the least durable), brick, and stone forming an ascending hierarchy. Expression of purpose speaks to truthful expression but also to such other issues as color. Here the designer is to steer away from bright and glaring tones and seek overall – citing Uvedale Price – "that mellow golden hue so beautiful in itself."[126] Expression of style more or less equates with "the sentiment associated with certain modes of building" and has certain other aesthetic features such as unity, formal regularity, and what Downing calls a "symmetrical irregularity" (an asymmetrical balance) of parts. Styles possess no intrinsic beauty but acquire their meaning by their sentiments. He uses a linguistic analogy to state his position that domestic architecture needs not the exalted formal language of epic poems but is most suited to such "every-day" languages as "Rural Gothic cottage" or "Italian villa." Again, style should not be some overreaching convention but rather an overall picturesque sensation emanating from seemingly minor but functional details: "For domestic architecture, we would strongly recommend those simple modifications of architectural styles, where the beauty grows out of the enrichment of some useful or elegant features of the house, as the windows or verandas, rather than those where some strongly marked features, of little domestic beauty, overpower the rest of the building."[127]

The designs and drawings of Davis harmonize perfectly with the text. Despite Downing's aversion to timber construction, wood is featured in many designs, and there is an illustration of Davis's board-and-batten technique to show this new and unfamiliar type of construction. Other features of the architectural designs, such as the omnipresent veranda, the grouping of interior chimneys, and the ornamental treatment of verge boards and cornices with decorative pendants (visually softening the linearity of the forms), are also owed to Davis. Downing is especially excited with his own design for "A Cottage Villa in the Bracketed Mode," through whose careful study "a very ingenious architect might produce an *American cottage style*"[128] (Fig. 56).

In an 1843 review of Downing's first two books, Arthur Gilman expressed appreciation for the looseness of the author's approach to style and praised in particular the cottage villa in the bracketed mode. In a country where "every one is weary of the eternal Grecian" and "the Gothic too, so far as cottages are concerned, has nearly had its day," Downing has shown that "there may be appropriate forms, not slavishly borrowed from any other, nor yet fastidiously rejecting any of their advantages."[129] One example is this "American cottage style, which shall be so well adapted to our wants, so harmonious with our landscape, and so grateful to the eye, as gradually to supplant all others, and to become the prevailing domestic architecture in this country."[130] He further applauds the bay windows, the decorative gables, the roof's graceful brackets, and the toned-down colors – in short, everything except the ever-present verandas, which he feels might take too much light away from the interiors. This was but a small reservation, for these designs "are beautiful always, and everywhere, not simply as ornaments, but as signs and expressions of the refinement and grace of life."[131]

By midcentury both Davis and Downing had advanced their careers. Davis had by now emerged as the most prominent residential architect in the country, and he built up a national practice – like Frank Lloyd Wright after him – by selling house designs to clients across the country by mail. Downing intensified his pace of writing and in 1846 sold his nursery to take over the editorship of the journal *The Horticulturist*. The next year he published *Hints to Persons about Building in the Country* (1847), which was copublished with George Wightwick's *Hints to Young Architects*.[132] It largely reiterated his earlier views while more strongly "abjuring all styles or modifications of styles not warranted by our social and domestic habits."[133] Focusing his interest ever more on architecture, Downing proposed a formal partnership to Davis in 1848, which the latter seems to have declined. In July 1850 Downing left on a trip to England specifically to seek out an architectural partner, whom he found in Calvert Vaux (1825–95). Two months earlier, in April, Downing and Davis completed work on their last collaborative venture, *The Architecture of Country Houses* (1850).

This is generally considered to be their supreme achievement as book collaborators, and it certainly is when judged by the number and breadth of the designs presented. Downing now feels it imperative to take on the issue of smaller, less expensive dwellings and thus divides the book into sections on cottages ("of a family, either wholly managing the household cares itself, or, at the most, with the

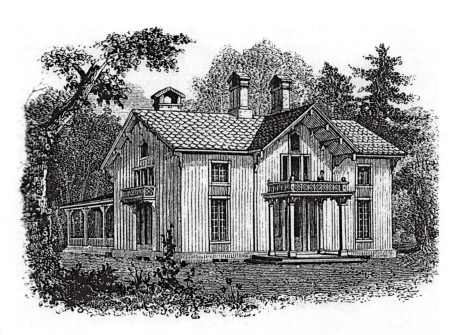

56. "A Cottage Villa in the Bracketed Mode."
From Andrew Jackson Downing, *Cottage Residences* (New York, 1842).

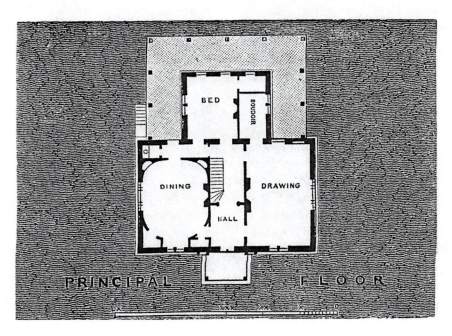

assistance of one or two servants"), farmhouses, and villas ("of a person of competence or wealth sufficient to build and maintain it with some taste and elegance").[134] A number of the cottages are actually smaller than his definition may suggest and are intended for simple laborers; in these cases Downing becomes a champion of less expensive timber construction and Davis's board-and-batten technique. By contrast, many of the villas (such as Newport's King house, de-

signed by Richard Upjohn) approach the size of a mansion, indicative of the growing prosperity of many Americans.

In its theory, the book is less successful. Downing wrote the ambitious introductory essay, "On the Real Meaning of Architecture," shortly after reading Ruskin's *Seven Lamps of Architecture* (1849), and he was obviously much impressed by the book. A Ruskinian ethic, for instance, pervades the three reasons Downing gives to explain that his countrymen should now have good housing with a particular American resonance: (1) Good housing serves as a powerful means of civilization, (2) it has great social value, and (3) it exerts a moral influence. "The mere sentiment of home, with its thousand associations," he writes, "has, like a strong anchor, saved many a man from shipwreck in the storms of life," and thus a house "shall symbolize the best character and pursuits, and the dearest affects and enjoyments of social life."[135] This optimism, with its ecological grounding, is certainly one of Downing's greatest achievements. Of course, Vincent J. Scully also famously credited him with having "decisively established the principles of asymmetrical, picturesque design in America and thereby laid the foundation for a whole new sequence of experiments in planning and spatial organization."[136]

Downing's life was tragically cut short. When he returned from England in 1850 with Vaux, he commenced on what promised to be a successful practice, first by winning the national competition for the design of the Capitol Mall, for which he and his partner proposed a meandering, quasi-picturesque plan. When the design began to be implemented in the following year, however, it met much political resistance in Washington. On 28 July 1852 Downing was aboard the steamboat *Henry Clay* when it caught fire on the Hudson River and was one of the seventy people who drowned. He was thirty-six years old. Work on the mall was soon suspended.

Downing's domestic and picturesque legacy was nevertheless immense. In 1852 the Philadelphia architect Samuel Sloan (1815–84) published the two volumes of *The Model Architect: A Series of Original Designs for Cottages, Villas, Suburban Residences*, which in its designs and presentations follows in the tradition of Downing.[137] Even more solidly in this tradition is Calvert Vaux's *Villas and Cottages* (1857), which both documents Downing and Vaux's collaborative work and carries it forward in some significant ways. Vaux places much emphasis on the economy of good design and the importance of a skillful arrangement of forms, harmonious proportions, fitness, and variety. Now basking in the spirit of Emerson, Vaux lauds republican distaste for the "pomps and vanities so closely connected with superstition, popery, or aristocracy" and for European art "as it then existed, a tender hothouse plant ministering to the delights of a select few."[138] In addressing the issue of "style," this immigrant strongly advocates the cultivation of a genuinely native American architecture arising from the nation's distinct climate, habits (individuality), and democratic political

system. Architecture for Vaux thus becomes the "rock" of his populist and freedom-loving vision for the new but evolving society: "In American this rock commands a boundless prospect, and no fitting or enduring edifice can be erected on it that does not include the most liberal manners, the most generous aspirations, the most noble institutions, and the most pure and beautiful arts that unfettered humanity is capable of conceiving."[139]

Also influenced by Downing are the ideas of Frederick Law Olmsted (1822–1903), who in 1857 formed a partnership with Vaux. A native of Connecticut, Olmstead absorbed both the picturesque thought of Britain as well as the American transcendental tradition of Emerson and Thoreau before embarking on various travels, the first to China at the age of twenty-three. In 1847 Olmstead began an experimental farm on Staten Island, and his success there encouraged Vaux to ask him to participate jointly in the competition for New York's Central Park in 1857. Their winning proposal, which was inspired in part by Downing and Vaux's earlier scheme for the Capitol Mall, launched the two men (working separately and together) on brilliant careers and led to commissions for parks in Brooklyn, Philadelphia, Montreal, Washington, D.C., San Francisco, and elsewhere.

5. Richardson and Sullivan

Architecture in the United States just before the Civil War was characterized by a number of conflicting theoretical positions. The Jeffersonian tradition that had evolved into a popular "Grecian" style in the first half of the century had by the end of the 1860s lost favor – save for the monuments still under construction in the nation's capital. The transcendental tradition of Emerson and Thoreau, together with the aesthetics of Greenough, had established a rather firm foothold in theory by this date, but as yet it had had little effect on practice. In addition, the somewhat related naturalist ideas of Downing and Davis had initiated a line of development that would eventually align itself with the rapid development of the single-family house. Nevertheless, architects in the newly developed metropolitan centers, particularly in the Northeast, were walking ever more tightly in lockstep with the stylistic fashions of Europe. The few architects who took exception, such as Alexander Jackson Davis, often found themselves professionally isolated, even embittered – in his case he resigned from the newly formed American Institute of Architects to express his displeasure with the institute's focus on the high Gothic and French styles. Pressure, however, continued to mount to place an American stamp on design and several talented American architects did in fact emerge in the immediate post-bellum years.

The fresh and vigorous style of Frank Furness (1839–1912) is indicative of the higher aspirations of this generation.[140] He was the son of William Henry Furness, a prominent Unitarian minister from Massachusetts, an abolitionist, and a classmate and lifelong friend of Emerson. After William Furness had moved his ministry and home to Philadelphia, Emerson still took a keen interest in Frank's early development and on one occasion even presented him with the gift of a stereo viewer to spark his appreciation of nature and architecture.[141] On the basis of his father's reputation, Frank was accepted into the private atelier of Hunt in 1858, where he was challenged artistically. He planned to study in Paris, but the Civil War intervened. Between 1861 and 1865 he served courageously as a cavalry officer in Colonel Rush's famed lancer regiment. Decorated, he returned to Hunt's office in 1865 but left within a year to move to Philadelphia and open a practice.

Furness's first important commissions came in 1871, when he, in partnership with George Hewitt, won the competition for the Pennsylvania Academy of Fine Arts. The building is an original and hybrid work, designed collaboratively by the two men. In his early years, Furness had practiced what he had learned in Hunt's office: a French manner of design that combined an emphasis on composition and axiality with a modest richness of ornamental detailing. Hewitt, by contrast, had been trained in a Ruskinian Victorian manner that emphasized Gothic forms and a lavish polychrome display of materials. The Pennsylvania Academy of Fine Arts brings these disparate elements together in one of the most sparkling creations of the century. The variegated entrance facade, with its Second Empire central pavilion, weaves together an ensemble of vermiculated bluestone, smooth sandstone, polished granite, patterned panels of red and black brick, ogival openings, and classical bas-reliefs – an orchestrated drama of textural effects loosely fitted into classical proportions. Even more seductive is the main stair hall, whose satrapic splendor of colors derives from its skylights and starry deep-blue canopy, set atop gilded, Nile-red spandrels. Here carved, cast, punched, and incised floral motifs gleaned from French and English sources join a panoply of squat columns of polished marble, ebullient floral capitals, and painted cast-iron columns and

girders. The building is neither Victorian nor French nor Islamic in character but a conscious caricature of competing themes and muscular forms freely drawn from a bevy of sources.

This feeling for textural inflation became, in essence, the firm's style, although the polychromy is toned down after illness caused Hewitt to leave the firm in 1876. In Furness's numerous banks, railway stations, houses, and apartment and office buildings, he reached ever outward for formal and decorative motifs that could be playfully abstracted. His library at the University of Pennsylvania (1888–90) – with its reddish tones of brick, sandstone, and terra-cotta – was his final masterpiece. The virtues of his forms, Lewis Mumford once noted, "sprang out of their defiance of correctness," and the four-story reading room and the gargantuan iron girders of this building now constitute a soldier's act of defiance in the face of yet another wave of refined beaux-arts "culture."[142] Furness's legacy resides in the way his buildings always surrender their pretense to high art.

A similar exaggeration – not to say individuality – is found in the work of Furness's near contemporary, Henry Hobson Richardson (1838–86).[143] The two men in fact met in New York shortly after the war, as both were being inducted into the American Institute of Architects. Furness had just returned from the battlefield, but Richardson – a Southerner from Louisiana – had returned to New York after his architectural studies in Paris. There was another odd connection between the two men. Richardson was a great-grandson of the noted chemist and Unitarian minister Joseph Priestly, who, upon immigrating to the United States in 1794, had settled in Philadelphia and established the Unitarian ministry that William Henry Furness would later inherit.

Richardson's architecture is frequently described with the epithets "massive," "presence," and "weight," but these are insufficient to prepare the beholder for the true bigness of scale of his buildings when seen up close. There is nothing puling or mean in Richardson's architecture; he himself was a big man, 300 pounds and with a large girth, caused by his insatiable appetite for champagne and cheese. He is often cited for being the first architect to define a distinctly American style as well as for the first American designer to win European approbation. "Richardsonian Romanesque" is a term that has slipped into the general architectural vocabulary, although this appellation becomes problematic the more one studies his work in its entirety. His sources were more modern than historical, and anything but simple.

The son of a Louisiana plantation owner, Richardson graduated from Harvard in 1859, one of six Southerners in a class of ninety-nine. Harvard provided him with contacts and future clients, and he left immediately upon graduation for France to seek entry to the Ecole des Beaux-Arts. He enrolled in the atelier of Louis-Jules André in November 1860 and after one failed effort gained acceptance into the school the following year. His time at the Ecole was for the most part undistinguished, in part due to the onset of the Civil War in 1861, which cut off his financial support. He returned to Boston briefly that year, contemplated practice there or returning to the South, but in the end he decided that schooling in Paris was a better alternative. To support himself once back in France, he took a job in the office of Théodore Labrouste, the younger brother of Henri. The only other incident we know of during his years at the Ecole was his arrest in 1864 for rioting, following one of the controversial and short-lived lectures of Viollet-le-Duc. For one night, the rowdy student thus got to share a jail cell with the writer Théophile Gautier.

In 1865 Richardson returned neither to Louisiana nor to Boston but instead moved to New York. After building a (mansard-roofed) house on Staten Island for his new wife and family, he began a life-long friendship with Olmstead (who lived nearby) and formed an architectural practice, initially in partnership with Charles Gambrill. His first two churches in Massachusetts – the Church of the Unity, Springfield (1866–9), and Grace Church, Medford (1867–9) – were English Gothic in inspiration, though Grace Church's expressive boulder walls provided an intimation of what was to come. He broke with the Gothic in his *Rundbogen* design for the Brattle Square Church (1869–73), in which the rose window, round-arched portal, and random pattern of ashlar walls are altogether dominated by the highly original corner tower, seemingly defending the street intersection. Beneath its corbeled attic story, Richardson placed his colossal frieze of saints representing the sacraments (carved in place by Auguste Bartholdi) and buttressed at the corners with angels blowing gilded trumpets – a metaphoric expression of the tower's function almost coinciding with Whitman's composition of *The Mystic Trumpeter* (1872).

If Brattle Square Church summoned Richardson's name before his colleagues, his competition design for nearby Trinity Church in 1872 – winning out over designs by Hunt, Ware and Van Brunt, Peabody and Sterns, William A Potter, and John Sturgis – catapulted him into the forefront of American practice. Though often judged to be his most "archaeological" work, this early polychrome masterpiece (composed in Dedham granite ashlar with bands and arches of East Longmeadow sandstone) is scarcely bookish. From the French region of Auvergne he may have borrowed the idea of a "color church," and from Salamancha the seed of his tower, yet Trinity Church defines a novel architectural conception simply through its imposing silhouette and massive presence. It is above all a tower church, with a colorful 100-foot tall central room dominating the modified Greek-cross plan. True, the tower itself is a collaborative structural masterpiece (as it was supported on 4,400 piles driven into the fill of Boston's back bay), and the vivid polychrome interior is in part due to the genius of John La Farge, but the design's imaginative audacity and rugged plasticism are entirely the gifts of Richardson. The confident architect would never look back to the work of his colleagues, nor would his work again be so stylistically accurate.

The architectural accomplishments of Richardson's career (cut short by his death at age forty-seven from a renal disorder) are both numerous and well known. What he brought to American practice and theory was an independence and self-confidence that drew upon contemporary intellectual traditions, though often joined to aspects of European (French and English) modernity, and the resulting designs were consistently novel. His residential work, in particular, the Watts-Sherman house in Newport (1874–6), illustrates this point. It is sometimes cited as an example of the Queen Anne or Shavian Manorial style making its way to America's shores, but its sources of inspiration are far broader, with features emanating directly from the American colonial and picturesque traditions – from the saltbox silhouette of its overhanging front gable to its shingle fields and the living-hall focus of the plan.[144] It in fact draws a crucial line from the innovations of Davis to the perfection of the so-called shingle style, not coincidentally also found in Richardson's Stoughton House, Cambridge (1882–3), which has long been regarded as one of the triumphs of American domestic design.

Equally intriguing, however, is the Ames Gate Lodge (1880–1) in North Easton, which Richardson built in collaboration with Olmstead on a purposefully surreal boulder-strewn landscape. It stands as a memorial to the close relationship of the two men, now enriched by years of working together. In 1870 Olmstead brought Richardson onto his Staten Island planning commission, which was charged with developing for this community an ideal suburban plan. The two men and their wives took an extended "Cook's Tour" of Niagara Falls in 1875. The architect and landscape architect had also worked together on the New York State Capitol in 1876; on two "natural" bridges in Fenway Park, Boston, in 1880; and on the vegetation surrounding the North Easton train depot the following year. In 1880 Richardson designed the Ames Gate Lodge, consisting of a gardener's house, guest rooms, and "Bachelor's Hall" on one side, a winter storage room for plants on the other, joined by a "Syrian" arch over the roadway. Lacking any stylistic pretense, the lodge was built almost entirely of massive boulders found on the site; the occasional use of red Longmeadow sandstone gives only the vaguest indication of nature being tamed by the architect's hand. For the landscaping, Olmstead laid out a series of rocky outcroppings, but he also supplied the architect with his leitmotif – as we know from Olmstead's later remark that Richardson was attracted to the boulder style "after he had examined two works of rough-hewn stones and boulders built in Central Park twenty years before."[145] The two bridges to which he alludes were those built by Vaux and Olmstead in the early 1860s, and they sprang from the intention to create a primeval lithic landscape softened by natural vines and greenery for areas of Central Park.

Richardson is of course best known for his larger works, but even here the rounded arch is only a formal and spatial principle developed by him in his own imaginative way. In his masterful and fantastic design for the Allegheny County Courthouse and Jail, Pittsburgh (1883–8), the rounded arch is simply a repetitive foil played off against the cyclopean blocks of granite ashlar – the 300-foot entrance campanile, the "Bridge of Sighs," the impenetrable jailhouse walls (Fig. 57). This Piranesian drama achieves its crescendo in the main interior stairway, where full and segmental arches crisscross and intersect with a virtuosity previously dared only in engravings. "If they honor me for the pygmy things I have already done," the architect is said to have noted shortly before his death, "what will they say when they see Pittsburgh finished?"[146] Writing an obituary for Richardson a few months later, Henry Van Brunt saw the deeper significance of the architect's overall achievement:

At the present moment we are under the dominion of an impulse so vigorous, healthy, and stimulating, so different from any which has preceded it, so elastic to practical uses, that, in the hands of a profession far more accomplished and far better trained than ever before, it gives us the right to hope for results of the first importance in the development of style.[147]

Concurrent with the construction of the Allegheny County Courthouse was the building of the Marshall Field Wholesale Store in Chicago (1885–7), the other building that Richardson hoped to see completed before his death. Here the purpose of utilitarian "plainness" takes a distinctly Florentine cast, but this was a commercial monument to a booming American spirit that transcended its organizational impulse. Louis H. Sullivan perhaps described this "oasis in our desert" best when he referred to it as a living being: "No; I mean, here is *man* for you to look at. A man that walks on two legs instead of four, has active muscles, heart, lungs and other viscera; a man that lives and breathes, that has red blood; a real man, a manly man; a virile force – broad, vigorous and with the whelm of energy – an entire male."[148]

It is no secret, of course, that Sullivan (1856–1924) coveted the architectural mantle of Richardson, though he also inherited the transcendental legacy of Emerson and Thoreau.[149] In addition, it is well known that he especially admired the words of Walt Whitman (1819–92), the buoyantly optimistic and rhapsodic oracle of democracy, who saw "in vistas, a copious, sane gigantic offspring" of the New World to be realized.[150] In 1887 Sullivan sent the American bard a copy of his lyrical essay "Inspiration" with the confession that "I, too, 'have pried through the strata, analyzed to a hair,' reaching for the basis of a virile and indigenous art."[151] The previous year Sullivan had read this opaque essay on wondrous organic growth to the convention of the Western Association of Architects and stunned the audience into silence.[152] The subject of architecture was never even broached in its pages.

Sullivan was certainly not lacking in gumption. A native of Boston, he was one of the first students to enroll in the new architectural program at the Massachusetts Institute of Technology in 1872, then dropped out the following spring. The program had started a few years earlier under the direction of William Robert Ware, and the Frenchman Eugène Letang taught design following the compositional methods of the Ecole des Beaux-Arts. After his short stay, Sullivan moved to Philadelphia, where he brazenly offered himself for employment to Furness (after seeing one of his buildings) and actually obtained the job. The panic of 1873, however, ended his brief tenure there, and his next stop was Chicago, where he worked in the office of William Le Baron Jenney and befriended his first intellectual mentor, John Edelmann. The next year Sullivan set sail for Paris, where he joined the atelier of Émile Vaudremer and attended the Ecole des Beaux-Arts. Once again he remained only six months. Vaudremer seems to have had little influence on his pupil, but the American seems to have attended the drawing course of Victor-Marie Ruprich-Robert at the Ecole des Arts Décoratifs – with whose decorative designs he may already have become familiar in Furness's office.[153] If the last experience defined a principal focus of his practice, Sullivan was still anxious. After undertaking a trip to Italy specifically to view Michelangelo's Sistine Chapel, the nineteen-year-old architect returned to Chicago in the summer of 1875. Success came slowly, as Sullivan moved from office to office as a freelance designer and draftsman. In 1880 he joined the office of the German-born Dankmar Adler (1844–1900), but it was not until his elevation to full partner three years later that the "myth" of Sullivan began to take hold.

When the young Sullivan returned to Chicago in 1875, he was most accomplished in the area of ornamentation. If Emerson had been wary of architectural ornament, and Richardson often left the ornamental details to such gifted office hands as Stanford White, Sullivan exalted in decoration. He also advanced his thought in other ways. He befriended the engineer Frederick Baumann (1826–1921), another of Chicago's many German immigrants and a very serious Semperian. Sullivan read vociferously as well. In working for Adler in 1880, he immediately applied his ornamental pencil to the cornices and spandrels of the Borden Block (1880), the first of a string of such designs. After the partnership of Adlar & Sullivan was formed in 1883, Sullivan began to experiment more broadly, although still tentatively. In a talk he gave to the Western Association of Architects in Saint Louis in 1885, he raised the idea of a national style and of moving beyond the stylistic legacy of Europe, but he never quite got to the heart of the matter. He spoke of "a more rational and organic mode of expression" and "innate poetic feeling," but simply concluded that a new national style could not emerge "Minerva-like" and must be "a slow and gradual assimilation of nutriment."[154]

Late in 1886 Adler & Sullivan received the commission for the Auditorium Building, the partnership's largest and most complex commission thus far and a building that was to serve as an icon for the cultural arrival of the city.[155] The timing was also propitious for the designer. Sullivan had just happened upon – "quite by accident" – the poetry of Whitman, and construction was starting on Richardson's Marshall Field Warehouse. Sullivan, following Richardson's lead, avoided the exterior use of decoration and instead chose massive lithic walls with rhythmic openings. He still employed an abundance of ornamentation inside, especially in the auditorium itself. As the auditorium was nearing completion, however, Sullivan abruptly ended this phase by producing highly ornate designs for the Getty Tomb (1890) and the Wainwright Building, Saint Louis (1890–1). It is here that the elements of Sullivan's innovative style first come to maturity – harkened by debates in Chicago.

These were the formative years of the so-called Chicago School, and Sullivan was especially active in discussions about style. He was one of the founding members of the Western Association of Architects in 1884 and remained an active member until its merger with the American Institute of Architects in 1889. In 1885 Sullivan began to support the Chicago Architectural Sketch Club, which was dedicated to "the development of an unaffected school of modern architecture in America."[156] Sullivan, Jenney, and Root often served as judges at the club's annual drawing exhibits, and in 1888 and 1889 Sullivan read two papers to the club: highly philosophical musings on style in nature and the artistic use of the imagination.[157]

More revealing were Sullivan's contributions to symposia sponsored by the Illinois State Association of Architects, the local chapter of the Western Association of Architects. The Illinois chapter held monthly meetings in Chicago, several of which were devoted to theoretical issues. One symposium, held in March 1887, concerned the question "What Are the Present Tendencies in Architectural Design in America?" and Sullivan, Root, Adler, Baumann, Clarence Stiles, and W. W. Boyington debated the issue. Root underscored the need for historical study and identified the elements of a future American architecture as catholicity (adaptation of various styles), gravity, practicality, and splendor. Stiles disagreed with Root's contention that American architects should simply modify existing styles, and he predicted the blossoming of a genuinely American architecture in the near future. Baumann stressed the need for utility in style, but also cited Semper's definition of the concept. Sullivan countered that style was not something external but rather something within ourselves, residing in "the character and quality of our thoughts and our observations."[158] Against Root's acceptance of Romanesque motifs, Sullivan claimed "that the use of the historical motive, which once had a special significance, now seems rather thin and hollow when used in our designs."[159] The Richardsonian Romanesque walls of the Auditorium, of course, were then under construction.

In another discussion that featured Sullivan, held in May 1887 and dealing with the theme "What Is the Just

57. Henry Hobson Richardson, Allegheny County Courthouse and Jail, Pittsburgh, 1883–8.

Subordination of Details to Mass?" the architect is suddenly Emersonian. For now he addresses the question only in a highly rhetorical way and in fact denounces all efforts at theorizing:

I say present theories of art are vanity. I say all past and future theories of art were and will be vanity. That the only substantial facts which remain after all the rubbish, dust and scientific-analytic-aesthetic cobwebs are brushed away are the facts, which each man may take to himself, namely: that I am; that I am immersed in nature here with my fellow men; that we

are all striving after something which we do not now possess; that there is an inscrutable power permeating all, and the cause of all.[160]

Baumann's reference to Semper's definition of style at the March 1887 meeting, incidentally, is important. It was in fact the first of several efforts by this architect to expound Semper's ideas, including two papers he read before the American Institute of Architects in 1889 and 1892, both published in the Chicago journal *The Inland Architect and News Record*.[161] This interest in Semper even encouraged

John Root to translate Semper's last lecture, "On Architectural Styles," for the same journal in 1889.[162] Hence Semper's thought, particularly the conceptual model of four architectural motives, was clearly "in the air" in Chicago in the late 1880s.[163] Also driving interest in Semper is the fact that in the 1880s Adler & Sullivan was largely staffed with German-trained draftsmen and engineers. Edgar Kaufmann Jr. notes that the recent German immigrant Paul Mueller introduced Frank Lloyd Wright to Sullivan in 1889 – perhaps leading to Wright's affectionate Germanic appellation for Sullivan, "Lieber Meister."[164] Others have noted the conceptual relationship between Semper's "dressing" thesis and the "curtain wall."[165]

All of this, however, only underscores Sullivan's personal aversion to theorizing, or at least his discomfort with putting his architectural inspiration into words. In his famous essay "Ornament" (1892), for instance, he notes that it "would be greatly for our aesthetic good" if architects temporarily refrained from the use of ornament, in order "that our thought might concentrate acutely upon the production of buildings well formed and comely in the nude."[166] This seems like a transparent statement, yet it in no way accords with his personal view, expressed a few pages later, that a building "is in its nature, essence and physical being an emotional expression" and that a decorated structure, harmoniously conceived, well considered, cannot be stripped of its system of ornament without destroying its individuality."[167] In 1892, the year of this essay, Sullivan designed the ornate "Golden Doorway" for the Transportation Building at the World's Columbian Exposition.

In another important essay, "Emotional Architecture as Compared with Intellectual: A Study in Subjective and Objective" (1894), Sullivan elaborated upon his notions of "Intuition," "Imagination," and "Inspiration." While he acknowledges the value of rational thought, Sullivan's admonition to architects to animate their works with the "Great Spirit" clearly takes on pantheistic overtones: "There can be no doubt that the most profound desire that fills the human soul, the most heartfelt hope, is the wish to be at peace with Nature and the Inscrutable Spirit; nor can there be a doubt that the greatest Art Work is that which most nearly typifies a realization of this ardent patient longing."[168] The classical and Gothic styles, he concludes, deftly served their purpose and represented, as it were, the objective and subjective side of the human mind. Yet both are now inadequate and should be replaced by a truly poetic architecture, "which shall speak with clearness, with eloquence, and with warmth, of the fullness, the completeness of man's intercourse with Nature and

with his fellow man."[169] It is Emerson pure and simple, and these thoughts were voiced on the eve of his commission for the Guaranty Building, Buffalo (1894–5), his artistic masterpiece.

Sullivan's celebrated adage – "Form ever follows function" – was first voiced in the 1896 essay, "The Tall Office Building Artistically Considered." Although the term "function" is used with regard to the commercial and mechanical functions of an office building, Sullivan's meaning is already more pregnant, for he introduces the term by way of Greenough's biological analogy, indeed with many of the sculptor's examples of form-function relationships in nature – those exemplified, for instance, in the eagle, horse, and swan.[170]

Not to be overlooked in this crucial reformulation of Greenough is the importance of Leopold Eidlitz's *The Nature and Function of Art: More Especially of Architecture* (1881), a much underappreciated book of nineteenth-century American theory.[171] Born in Prague and trained in Vienna, Eidlitz had immigrated to the United States in the early 1840s. As we have seen, he was an early proponent of the *Rundbogen* style and also built various Gothic works. If his polychrome designs are difficult to evaluate today (much of his work has been destroyed), his book reveals an individual of intellectual depth. Further, he is philosophically inclined and draws upon not only British theory but also the German romantic and American transcendental traditions. G. W. F. Hegel is discussed, as are the ideas of J. J. Winckelmann, Friedrich Schiller, Franz Kugler, Plato, Socrates, Aristotle, and Lord Shaftesbury, to mention but a few. Eidlitz's idealism, however, is both original and inspired by Germanic psychological aesthetics as well, which he translates into an "organic" analogy: "The Architect, in imitation of this national condition of matter, so models his forms that they also tell the story of their functions."[172] And just as a human being has both physical and emotional aspects, so architecture has a skeletal side of bones and sinews and also an ideal side of emotional expression. "When constructive expression is heightened by decoration," he claims, "it tells more plainly and promptly the nature of the functions performed by the organism."[173] Therefore, chief among architecture's expressive devices are carved ornament and color decoration, which effectively animate the functional masses: "Carved ornament and color decoration have no other purpose than to heighten the expression of mechanical resistance to load and pressure in architectural organisms. They do this (as hereafter more minutely shown) by their density, magnitude, projection, form, and the direction in which they are placed, which direction must coincide with the direction of resistance to load and pressure."[174]

The analogy between architectural form and function is also treated broadly by Sullivan in *Kindergarten Chats*, a series of weekly articles he wrote in 1901–2. The articles take the form of a meandering dialogue between a sagacious but exacting master (Sullivan) and an architecture school graduate who now seeks to obtain a true education. On a mundane level, a building's form must express certain typological functions of its contents, but this is far from Sullivan's point. We live in a universe, he insists, "where all is function, all is form," that is, "behind every form we see there is a vital something or other which we do not see, yet which makes itself visible to us in that very form."[175] That this "vital something" is nothing less than the "Infinite Creative Spirit" takes us to the core of his philosophy.[176]

Therefore for Sullivan function bears no resemblance to mundane purpose. It is always a "living force," an immaterial or vitalist force, while form is simply "organic" structural expression. The architect's task may be to animate materials "naturally, logically and poetically," but he should also instill in them greater values, such the American "spirit of democracy" that seeks expression in organized social form."[177] The "real function of the architect" is metaphysical, moral, and altruistic: "to vitalize building materials, to animate them collectively with a thought, a state of feeling, to charge them with a subjective significance and value, to make them a visible part of the genuine social fabric, to infuse into them the true life of the people, to impart to them the best that is in the people, as the eye of the poet, looking below the surface of life, sees the best that is in the people."[178] Ultimately, then, the functional expression of form for Sullivan is an ethical totality wrapped in his messianic vision for the promise of democracy; ornament is the medium for poetic expression. The Emersonian Over-Soul is present, "for Nature is ever the background across which man moves as in a drama: that dream within which man, the dreamer, moves is his dream; that reality which is man's reality. For all life, collectively is but one vast drama, one vast dream, and the soul of man its chief spectator."[179]

Sullivan's metaphysics never later budged from this point, but his "scientific" ethics swelled with an abundance of philosophical sources, from the psychologies of Charles Darwin and William James to the sociologies of Thorstein Veblen, John Dewey, and Oscar Lovell Triggs.[180] The passion of Nietzsche and Whitman also never stray far from his inspirational field. The latter's allegorical distinction between

"feudalism" and "democracy" in fact becomes the historical dialectic of Sullivan's 162-page philosophical manuscript "Democracy: A Man-Search" (last edited in 1908; published in 1961).[181] Feudalism signifies not a political system but all that is past, all that is represented by the failed and confining systems of dualistic thought. Democracy, likewise, is no abstract political order but the future – a kind of collective psychological liberation that comes when humans think naturally and recognize the limitlessness of their mental powers. The promise of American democracy therefore goes beyond national boundaries and exists as a grand promise of human psychological liberation that all of humanity will eventually benefit from and partake of.

The same ideas find a more specific architectural interpretation in Sullivan's remarkable essay "What is Architecture?: A Study in the American People of Today" (1906). It deals with architecture only in the most general manner and with some measure of pessimism. It argues that buildings are always the expression of human thought and that each building of the past and present serves "as a product and index of the civilization of the time, also, as the product and index of the thought of the people of the time and place."[182] Because human thought is always a process in motion, any effort to imitate the architecture of the past is unworthy of a free people: "It says, in a word: The American people are not fit for democracy."[183]

The assumption underlying this falsehood is that architecture is a closed system of forms, which can therefore only be selected, imitated, and adapted. Of greater importance for Sullivan, however, is the breakdown of "organic reasoning," that is, the artificial division between theory and practice and the absence of modest, truthful, and sincere feelings for expression. "Your buildings show no philosophy. So you have no philosophy," he intones.[184] What passes for common sense is "light as folly: a patent-medicine folly, an adulterated-food folly, a dyspeptic folly, a folly of filth and smoke in your cities."[185] The tonic for these feudal and arrogant ways is nothing less than to seize nature's creative energy and equipoise, which in turn will lead to a radical change in human thinking:

THEN, TOO, AS YOUR BASIC THOUGHT CHANGES WILL EMERGE A PHILOSOPHY, A POETRY, AND AN ART OF EXPRESSION IN ALL THINGS; FOR YOU WILL HAVE LEARNED THAT A CHARACTERISTIC PHILOSOPHY, POETRY AND ART OF EXPRESSION ARE VITAL TO THE HEALTHFUL GROWTH AND DEVELOPMENT OF A DEMOCRATIC PEOPLE.[186]

Emerson, in effect, now meets Dewey.

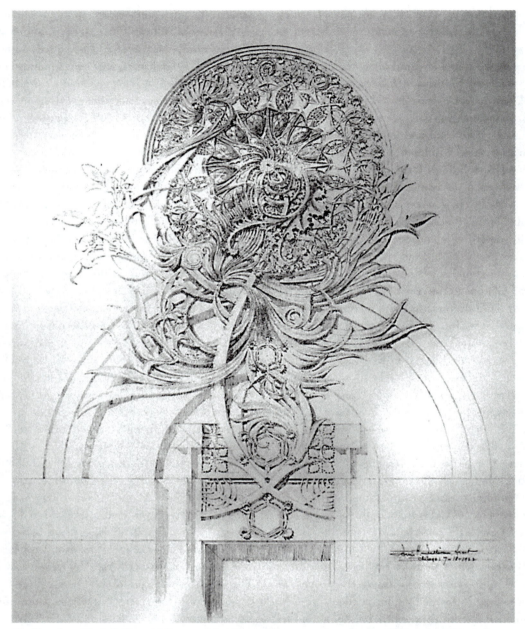

58. Plate from Louis Sullivan, *A System of Architectural Ornament According to a Philosophy of Man's Powers* (Chicago, 1924).

Sullivan's final literary endeavor, *A System of Architectural Ornament According to a Philosophy of Man's Powers* (1924), summarizes his fifty years of intellectual development, verbally and also visually, in twenty stupendous plates (Fig. 58). In the brief introductory essay, "The Inorganic and the Organic," he rhapsodizes once again on human creative powers – the power to will, the power to sympathize, but above all the power to bring forth "that which hitherto was non-existent."[187] There may well be, as

has been suggested, the theosophy of Emanuel Swedenborg behind these lines, but there is also much of the personality of Sullivan as well: "The dreamer-man becomes the seer, the mystic, the poet, the prophet, the pioneer, the affirmer, the proud adventurer."[188] The plates start with simple inorganic forms, such as a square or pentagon, and organically progress "through man's manipulation of a central idea, into plastic, mobile, and fluescent phases of expression tending towards culmination in foliate and efflorescent forms."[189] Ultimately the rigid geometry vanishes in a "mobile medium"; restraint surrenders to freedom.

When Sullivan died of alcoholism in 1924, shortly after viewing his published drawings, he did it as a "proud adventurer" having genuinely accomplished much of his self-proposed task. He was a draftsman and form maker of extraordinary expression and depth, but he also brought to a conclusion a line of American philosophical thought that had been fermenting for three-quarters of a century. Even the intellectual powers of his immediate successor, Frank Lloyd Wright, could extend it no further.

8

THE ARTS AND CRAFTS MOVEMENTS

Art is not healthy, it even scarcely lives; it is on the wrong road, and if it follow that road will speedily meet its death on it.

William Morris (1881)

1. The British Arts and Crafts Movement

The generally negative view of the artistic creations of the Victorian Age presented in many studies of modern architecture has not always been shared by critics, especially those writing closer to the time. For instance, writing at the end of the nineteenth century, the architect Robert Kerr saw the Victorian Age as the start of the great "popularising of art," whereby artistic design for the first time became a middle-class pursuit. Beginning with the Great Exhibition of 1851, Kerr argued, the formerly pedantic "Fine Art of Architecture" stepped down from its pedestal in order to merge with the "Minor Arts" and become the new "Industrial Art of Architecture." The arts and crafts, once deemed ornamental and inferior, were thus embraced by architecture as "no longer of unequal dignity with herself, but of altogether equal and similar comeliness of grace."[1]

Kerr's assessment makes a very salient historical point. The Great Exhibition of 1851 did indeed represent a turning point in European theory, in the sense that critics of the event were nearly universal in their realization that the artistic principles recognized over centuries had become estranged in their adaptation to the industrial practices of fabrication. This was the central theme of Richard Redgrave's "Supplementary Report on Design," which he appended to his official *Reports by the Juries* (1852). He repeatedly lamented the excessive ornamentation on the vast number of objects displayed at the exhibition and came "to admire those objects of absolute utility (the machines and utensils of various kinds), where use is so paramount that ornament is repudiated and, fitness of purpose being the end sought, a noble simplicity is the result."[2]

Redgrave was in a position to act on his beliefs. When Henry Cole was named the administrative director of the schools of design in 1852, Redgrave was named the artistic director, and thus it became his task to write a new curriculum and repair the deficiencies. His appointment also coincided with increased government spending in the arts. The Great Exhibition had generated an unexpected windfall in profits, and Prince Albert (the German-born husband of Queen Victoria) decided to plow the money back into industrial arts education. To this end, the commission purchased land in South Kensington with the intention of creating a college of art and manufactures. The first iron-and-glass structures erected on the site in 1856 – the somewhat infamous "Brompton Boilers" – proved an embarrassment to everyone because of their problems with leakage and condensation. Beginning in 1862, the engineer Francis Fowke (Cole still shunned architects) erected the first buildings of what became the Victoria and Albert Museum – the first combination of an industrial arts school, library, and museum. The nucleus of the industrial arts collection consisted of purchases made at the conclusion of the Great Exhibition by a committee composed of Cole, Redgrave, Augustus Welby Pugin, Owen Jones, and J. R. Herbert.

To provide the newly named Department of Practical Art (formerly the London School of Design) with interim lodgings, Prince Albert offered the Marlborough House to the school in 1852. The new faculty chosen by Cole and Redgrave included Octavius Hudson, Henry Townsend, Ralph Wornum, Gottfried Semper, and J. C. Robinson, among others. Altogether seven classes were established, in metalworks, textiles, wood engraving, lithography, anatomy, painting on porcelain, and practical construction. Cole's stated aim for the institution was "*to elevate the Art-Education of the whole people*, and not merely to teach artisans, who are the servants of manufacturers, who themselves are the servants of the public."[3] Drawing remained the foundation of the school, and students generally copied from prescribed examples.

The pedagogy of the new school – lampooned by Charles Dickens in *Hard Times* (1854) – sought to instruct by means of design principles. In a memo from Redgrave to Cole in the fall of 1852, the former noted, "I think Mr. Hudson & Professor Semper should prepare a set of Dogmas, Canons or Axioms – The Principles of Design applied to their various sections – to be publicly exhibited in their class room – something in the shape of Owen Jones' propositions – These should be considered and approved."[4] Jones had established the first of these axioms in the school's inaugural lectures, given in June 1852: "The Decorative Arts arise from, and Should be Attendant Upon, Architecture."[5] In the first lecture, he also criticized the state of architecture in his day, foremost its stylistic disorder: "We have no principles, no unity; the architect, the upholsterer, the paper-stainer, the weaver, the calico-printer, and the potter, run each their independent course; each struggles fruitlessly, each produces in art novelty without beauty, or beauty without intelligence."[6] Then there is architecture's "universal practice of copying and reproducing extinct styles," which "increases daily most unblushingly" with increasing knowledge of the past.

Many of Jones's propositions were incorporated into the department's catechism of principles published in 1853, a manual probably written by Redgrave.[7] Also stressed is the need for decoration to be subservient to utility and construction and for it to be adapted to each material. Perhaps the most general proposition is that ornament should always be conventionalized rather than be naturalistic: "True Ornament does not consist in the mere imitation of natural objects; but rather in the adaptation to their peculiar beauties of form or colour to decorative purposes, controlled by the nature of the material to be decorated, the laws of art, and the necessities of manufacture."[8] In stating this position, Redgrave was specifically opposing Ruskin's naturalism.

Other books also spoke to conventionalization in design, which became inextricably linked with the eclecticism of the day. Ralph Wornum's *Analysis of Ornament* (1856) analyzed nine principal ornamental styles as "analogous to *hand* in writing," that is, as ready-made systems or vocabularies placed at the artist's disposal.[9] Far more ambitious was Owen Jones's *Grammar of Ornament* (1856). The book

had grown out of his interest in the Moorish architecture of the Alhambra as well as the works of the nonindustrialized nations at the Great Exhibition. The colored lithographs, in fact, compose a visual extravaganza: a systematic panorama of ornamental motifs beginning with designs from what he calls "Savage Tribes" (from Tahiti, the Sandwich Islands, New Zealand, and other South Seas locations), followed by exotic Persian, Turkish, Hindoo, Chinese, and Celtic designs, and concluding with familiar Western styles. Of the prefatory thirty-seven design propositions, only thirteen actually deal with design, and then mostly with constructing conventionalized representations of natural objects. The other twenty-six propositions concern the issue of color – principles Jones adopts from the chromatic theories of Michel Chevreul and George Field.[10]

Jones's emphasis on the perceptual dimension of color (obtaining visual repose) is new. Also novel is his ornamental hierarchy of styles. The acme of ornamental pattern making for Jones remains the Alhambra, in which "every ornament contains a grammar in itself" and all thirty-seven propositions are followed: "We find in the Alhambra the speaking art of the Egyptians, the natural grace and refinement of the Greeks, the geometrical combinations of the Romans, the Byzantines, and the Arabs."[11] Jones also likes Egyptian ornament, which he believes exceeded Greek decoration in terms of its symbolic values and range of ornamental development. It also differs from other styles in that "the more ancient the monument the more perfect is the art." Hence it composes a kind of ur-language for decorative designers: "In the Egyptian we have no traces of infancy or of any foreign influence; and we must, therefore, believe that they went for inspiration direct from nature."[12]

Undoubtedly the most important chapter for the author is the final one, "Leaves and Flowers from Nature," for here he turns to the matter of a new decorative and architectural style (Fig. 59). In the second proposition he had defined architecture as "the material expression of the wants, the faculties, and the sentiments, of the age in which it is created. Style in Architecture is the peculiar form that expression takes under the influence of climate and materials at command."[13] In the final chapter, however, he ventures the observation that decoration indeed can take the lead, in fact "would be one of the readiest means of arriving at a new style." Then, as a caveat, he states that "if we could only arrive at the invention of a new termination to a means of support, one of the most difficult points would be accomplished."[14] What he means by this is unclear, but what he suggests from the decorative side is not a copying of past styles but rather a return to nature and an "idealizing" of her organic principles of creation.

Jones achieved little in his own design practice, unlike Christopher Dresser (1834–1904), the Department of Practical Art's most distinguished student.[15] Dresser entered the School of Design in 1847, but in the 1850s was attracted to the work of Owen Jones, for whom he prepared a drawing for *The Grammar of Ornament*. In 1856 Dresser became a lecturer on botany at the South Kensington school, and on the basis of his lectures and writings he was awarded a Doctor of Philosophy by the University of Jena in 1859. He soon became one of England's leading industrial designers, producing numerous "modern" and timeless designs noted for their clean, functional lines.

Dresser's theories of design were first enunciated in his 1862 book *The Art of Decorative Design* (Fig. 60).[16] It builds upon Jones's effort and was intended as a primer on ornamental design. Based on a novel psychological premise – "Refined forms are an expression of refined minds, and delicate subtleties in shapes indicate a keen power of perception" – the book is filled with astute observations.[17] Central to Dresser's efforts is his contention, perhaps influenced by his interest in Japanese art, that the beauty of ornamental forms unfolds as a hierarchy of ideal content or knowledge. Naturalistic ornament is ranked the lowest (a swipe at Ruskin), conventionalized ornament is next, and the highest level is reserved for the most sublime ideas: "Purely ideal ornament is that which is most exalted, it being wholly a creation of the soul; it is utterly an embodiment of mind in form, or an offspring of the inner man, and its origin and nature give to it its elevated character."[18] Dresser goes on to consider the affinity of ornamental design with musical composition and with such variables as order, repetition, curves, proportion, alternation, and adaptation. The most innovative feature of his study is his downplay of the importance of symbolism, and he even suggests that the need for a symbolic ornamental system has passed and will never again return. He seems to have been familiar as well with the expanding body of Germanic aesthetic and psychological theory, which partially explains why he became the first Englishman to present an animate reading of form from a psychological perspective. For this reason alone he is a major theorist. His follow-up study, *The Principles of Decorative Design* (1873), is a less philosophic and more pedagogic explication of his ideas.[19]

Dresser in his functional idealism differed sharply from the social teachings of William Morris (1834–96), and here in fact we have the second phase of the divide seen earlier between the theories of Cole and Ruskin.[20] The rebellious Morris had every financial and intellectual advantage in his nontraditional quests. His father died at a young age but with a fortune sufficient to insulate the family against material wants. In 1853, while at Oxford, Morris befriended the future painter Edward Burne-Jones (1833–98), and out of their reading of Ruskin was hatched the idea of a feudal brotherhood devoted to the arts. It was not to be a secluded monastic life but a naively militant one, in Burne-Jones's words, a "Crusade and Holy Warfare against the age."[21] Although the plan faltered, the passion behind it did not. Upon completing his studies in 1855, Morris articled himself to the architect George Street, in whose Oxford office he would soon meet Philip Webb (1831–1915). The following year, Morris gave up his interest in architecture and followed Burne-Jones to London to study painting under the Pre-Raphaelite Dante Gabriel Rossetti (1828–82). These were bohemian years for these two young men, highlighted by their participation in the Rossetti circle and their first contacts with Ruskin himself.[22] The end came in 1859, when Morris married Jane Burden – a model of Rossetti and a woman of striking beauty, to whose charms the older painter never relinquished his claims. It would not be an entirely successful marriage.

The marriage, however, prompted Morris to collaborate with Webb on the design of the "Red House" in Bexleyheath. This house has long been deemed one of the shrines of the early modern movement, but its architectural significance has been overstated. Sometimes considered medieval because of its Gothic overtones, the house, with its simple brick exterior and asymmetrical layout, rather emulates rural vernacular architecture; its interiors are more sophisticated, owing to their heavy, handmade furniture, decorative patterns, and glasswork. In any case, its importance lies mostly in the fact that it served in 1861 as the site of and first studio for the firm of "Morris, Marshall, Faulkner & Company, Fine Workmen in Painting, Carving, Furniture and the Metals."

Hence the idea of a monastic brotherhood evolved into a commercial venture. In the firm's prospectus, Morris attributed the recent growth of the decorative arts "to the effort of English Architects," by which he was probably alluding to the highly ornate interiors of Street, William Butterfield, and George Bodley. The execution of these designs "hitherto have been crude and fragmentary" because of the lack of artistic coordination and supervision.[23] This problem is to be solved through the unified approach of a single decorative firm, whose partners included the talents

59. Plate from Owen Jones, *The Grammar of Ornament* (London, 1856).

formed the Marxist Socialist League. Through his preaching and his propaganda of the late 1880s, he became one of the best known socialists in England.

The idea of artists dedicating their lives to the arts and crafts (instead of high art) proved to be an especially alluring one in the last quarter of the century.[24] Many smaller firms or workshops came out of Morris's studio or were created at his urging, such as those of William De Morgan (1839–1917) and William A. S. Benson (1854–1924). Guilds of a medieval type were also popular. The first was Ruskin's socialist Guild of Saint George, a short-lived agrarian, non-industrial community set up in 1871 and in part funded by the writer's royalties. More successful was the Century Guild, founded in 1882 by Arthur Mackmurdo (1851–1942) and Selwyn Image (1849–1930).[25] Mackmurdo had trained as an architect, but in 1871 he began reading Ruskin and shifted his focus. He traveled with Ruskin to Italy in 1874, and three years later he met Morris. The Century Guild too

of Burne-Jones, Charles Faulkner, Ford Madox Brown, Rossetti, and P. P. Marshall.

The idea of a guild of artists dedicated to rejuvenating and unifying the various arts through handicraft methods of fabrication was not entirely new (Pugin had prepared the way), but the profitable operation of such a firm was. Many of the firm's orders – especially for its stained glass work, tapestries, and murals – came from architects with church commissions. The firm also made furniture, some pieces on consignment and some for the firm's later showroom on Oxford Street in London. Morris specialized in weavings, dyes, printed fabrics, wallpapers, chintzes, and book printing. All in all, the firm was a commercial success, and in later decades it would employ hundreds of workers. And behind the venture lay Morris's political activism. In 1883 he joined the Democratic Federation, the nascent socialist party of Great Britain. Two years later, with the blessing of Frederick Engels, he led a split from this organization and

60. Christopher Dresser, cover of *The Art of Decorative Design* (London, 1862).

sought "to render all branches of art the sphere no longer of the tradesman, but of the artist."

Another of the early guilds, the Art-Workers' Guild, had close ties with the politics of Ruskin and Morris. It was founded in 1884 by a number of young designers, led by the architect and historian William Richard Lethaby (1857–1931).[26] Among this informal group of artists was Lewis F. Day (1845–1910) and Walter Crane (1845–1915).[27] The intention was to counter the influence of the Royal Academy and the Royal Institute of British Architects by creating an activist organization devoted to artistic reform from below. An important offshoot of this guild was the Arts and Crafts Exhibition Society, which held its first event in 1888. In *Arts and Crafts Essays*, published by the society in 1893, Crane described its efforts "as a protest against the conviction that, with all our modern mechanical achievements, comforts, and luxuries, life is growing 'uglier every day,' as Mr. Morris puts it."[28] Crane was adamant in his belief that "the true root and basis of all Art lies in the handicrafts," and he followed Morris as well in joining the Socialist League.[29]

Crane's most influential book, *The Claims of Decorative Art* (1892), was a collection of papers he had written over the previous decade. In it, he tirelessly attacks the "hideous luxury and squalor," the "huge, ever-spreading, unwieldly, unlovely cities" of modern life, which he attributes to "unscrupulous commercialism," private ownership of land, runaway industrialism, and the inability of artists to earn a living wage.[30] All were also being driven by society's "fluctuating harlequin of fashion and trade."[31] Crane pleads for "a new view of life upon an economic basis," which for him is the "religion" and "moral code" of socialism.[32] Crane's book was translated into German in 1894, and it affected the reforms already underway there. One year earlier, the English journal *The Studio* ran its first edition, also making better known to Europeans the full dimensions of the English arts and crafts movement.

The other important theorist of the arts and crafts movement in Britain is Charles Robert Ashbee (1863–1942).[33] Educated at Cambridge, he also began his career as an architect in the London office of George Bodley. While working there, he took up residence in Toynbee Hall, an experimental university settlement of living and learning, upon which Hull House in Chicago was later based. At Toynbee Hall he taught art and formed the School of Handicraft, which in 1888 he joined with a new Guild of Handicraft – the first successful combination of a design school and a commercial workshop. Ashbee's designs became a regular feature of the Arts and Crafts Exhibition Society's displays, and by the late

1890s they were regularly shown and admired abroad. All of this encouraged him in 1902 to move the Guild of Handicraft (and its 150 craftsmen and family members) to the Gloucestershire village of Chipping Campden, where, following Ruskin, he hoped to create a feudal socialist society as an alternative to modern cities and industrial methods of production. Like the earlier ventures, this one too failed, and Ashbee returned to London and eventually to architectural practice.

Among all of the leaders of the arts and crafts movement, Ashbee was the most active as an architect, and we can expect – given the large number of architects involved with the movement – a sympathetic sharing of ideals, particularly in residential design. Philip Webb, of course, was the architect closest to Morris at the start of the movement, and he remained true to their mutual ideals over the years, even if his later formal "classicism" also revealed his artistic independence.[34] The Red House's informality of plan, brick exterior (itself a novelty), tiled roofs, and large chimneys and fireplaces place it at the threshold of the Queen Anne style – only Webb's use of Gothic openings stood in opposition to what was to come. The attribution of this style to the baroque reign of Queen Anne (1702–14) is somewhat misleading, as the intention of the proponents of this style, many of whom had by now grown weary of the Gothic revival, was to emulate the commonplace and vernacular British architecture of the seventeenth and eighteenth centuries. Aside from the features noted above, the style espoused functional and practical planning, bay and strip windows with leaded and wooden frames, and simple unpretentious effects achieved through the manipulation of materials, color, and massing.

Much of Webb's work of the 1860s and 1870s fell in with these tendencies, but the name most associated with the Queen Anne was the Scotsman Richard Norman Shaw (1831–1912), who came up through the Gothic revival movement.[35] He was originally trained in the office of William Burn but was soon drawn to the teachings of Pugin (whose funeral he attended in 1852). After working for Anthony Salvin, he joined the office of George Street in 1859 as chief draftsman, actually succeeding Webb, who was starting the design of the Red House. In 1862 Shaw ventured out on his own but shared an office with his close friend William Eden Nesfield (1835–88), and this loose association proved invaluable to both. Nesfield had spent almost five years on the Continent, gathering material for his *Specimens of Mediaeval Architecture* (1862).[36] It was Nesfield who seems to have been first attracted to the "Old English" vernacular, and with his farmhouse at Shipley Hall (1860–1)

61. Richard Norman Shaw, Leyeswood, Sussex, 1868–9. From supplement to *The Building News*, March 31, 1871.

and two lodges in Regents Park (1864–5), which exhibit a medley of rural English forms, he pointed the way for others to follow.

Nesfield considerably refined the aesthetics and scale of the style in the next decade, but by then Shaw had seized the lead with his two manorial estates, Glen Andred, Sussex (1866–8), and Leyswood, Sussex (1868–9) (Fig. 61). It was the publication of the perspectives for these two estates in the pages of *Building News* that attracted the attention of Richard Morris Hunt and H. H. Richardson and inspired a parallel path of development in the United States. The early Shavian style is characterized by meandering but functional floor plans, brick exteriors, tile surfaces with textural effects, half timbering, enormous chimney stacks, a free use of gables and dormers, and large banks of windows. The overall feeling is sophisticated, rural, and picturesque – but the style is also very costly. Shaw's early townhouses are more restrained but no less original and indicative of his talented hand. Perhaps his most admired buildings were those done at Bedford Park in 1877–80. The developer Jonathan Carr conceived this new garden suburb west of London, but Shaw gave it a highly attractive form with designs for community buildings and houses, all conveniently and artistically laid out. The suburb, with its natural vegetation intact, quickly became a center for artists and writers, and Shaw, at least among British architects, probably deserves

the epithet awarded him by Hermann Muthesius as "the first in the history of nineteenth-century architecture to show this freedom from the trammels of style."[37]

Shaw's talent and success appealed to many within the movement. Lethaby was his chief draftsman between 1879 and 1889, while also devoting his time to founding the Art-Workers' Guild. He did not open his own office until the 1890s, and then his teaching, organizing, and craft design still overshadowed his architectural practice. Still, his first large commission, the almost idiosyncratic composition of forms for the manor Avon Tyrell, Hampshire (1891–2), was much lauded by Muthesius, who felt it brought "a delicate, distinctive atmosphere to the sombre grandeur of the English house."[38]

Also influenced by Shaw was Edward William Goodwin (1833–86), who began his career as a Gothic revivalist but gave up his practice for a while after moving to London in 1865 and becoming involved with furniture and stage designs. His famous Chelsea "White House" (1878), designed for the painter James Whistler, betrays the sudden influence of Shaw. The same influence is also seen in the work of Mackmurdo, whose architectural practice was severely limited by his teaching and his craft designing. His Shavian first house, at 6 Private Road, Enfield (1872–6), defines the start of a career that does not resume until his second house on Private Road, at no. 8 (1886–7).

The most talented domestic architect to be engaged with the arts and crafts movement was Charles F. A. Voysey (1857–1941), a close friend of Mackmurdo.[39] He began his practice in 1881, but it was not until later in the decade that he received his first commission for a dwelling, and in the interim he designed textiles, wallpapers, and furniture for the Art Workers' Guild. In his architectural practice, which began in earnest around 1890, he drew upon the elements of vernacular architecture but now abstracted and mediated them with European avant-garde influences. Other architects working in a similar vein in the 1890s were M. H. Ballie Scott (1865–1945) and Edwin Lutyens (1869–1945) – the latter of whom, of course, would eventually shift his base of operations to India.

What is lacking in this transformation of British domestic architecture in the last quarter of the nineteenth century, however, is a definitive statement of theory. One of the more intriguing books of the early 1890s is Lethaby's esoteric *Architecture, Mysticism and Myth* (1892). The subject is ancient architecture's essential cosmological and symbolic nature, which he traces through the occult cultures of the Chaldeans, Jews, Egyptians, Arabs, Minoans, Hindus, and Chinese, among others. Lethaby admits that such religious symbolism is a thing of the past, but at the same time he insists that modern architecture cannot be "a mere envelope without contents."[40] Citing Cèsar Daly, he argues that "we must have a symbolism immediately comprehensible by the great majority of spectators" but without the message of "terror, mystery, splendor."[41] The proper message, nevertheless, is only vaguely defined by him: "The message will still be of nature and man, of order and beauty, but all will be sweetness, simplicity, freedom, confidence, and light; the other is past, and well is it, for its aim was to crush life: the new, the future, is to aid life and train it, 'so that beauty may flow into the soul like a breeze.'"[42]

Lethaby was influenced by Mackmurdo, by the Orientalism that was also fascinating the circle of the so-called Decadents, among them Aubrey Beardsley, Arthur Symons, and Oscar Wilde. One architect who was much enamored with Lethaby's book was Charles Rennie Mackintosh (1868–1928).[43] He returned to Scotland from a tour of Italy in 1891. Over the next two years he gave two lectures in Glasgow, the first of which discussed at length the principles of Ruskin's *Seven Lamps*. In his lecture of 1893, simply entitled "Architecture," he drew extensively on Lethaby's ideas; indeed, nearly half of his talk is drawn directly from Lethaby's introduction, a fact that he may or may not have acknowledged to his audience.[44] What is interesting, however, is the direction in which he directs his thoughts near the end of the talk. After expressing his belief that "all great & living architecture" has been an expression of the "the needs & beliefs of man at the time of its creation," he goes on to denounce eclecticism in every form: "We must clothe modern ideas, with modern dress – adorn our designs with living fancy. We shall have designs by living men for living men – something that expresses fresh realization of sacred fact – of personal broodings of skill – and joy in nature in grace of form & gladness of colour."[45]

Yet these words too were borrowed – not from Lethaby but from John D. Sedding (1838–91), another influential arts-and-crafts designer who had just passed away.[46] Such usurpation on the part of Mackintosh should not be unexpected, for during these years he too was borrowing architectural motifs from Sedding and others in such designs as the Gothic Railway Terminus competition (1892) and the Glasgow Herald Building (1893). What is striking, however, is how Mackintosh seems to use the ideas of Lethaby and Sedding to advance his own thinking. His famous competition design for the Glasgow School of Art was made in 1896.

Finally, we have the writings of Morris.[47] His references to architecture throughout his voluminous essays, lectures, and letters are scattered and generally of little substance. Few speak to architecture directly, and these for the most part are political in nature and pessimistic in tone – not at all dissimilar to the essays of Crane. In his London lecture "The Prospects of Architecture in Civilization" (1881), Morris decries at length the marring of the earth by the "haste or carelessness of civilization," the "sordidness of city life of to-day," and the "universal ugliness" everywhere present.[48] His alternative, the laborer's cottage of "cotswold limestone" built when "beauty still lingered among peasants' houses," nevertheless seems extreme.[49] And the means that he offers to effect such a change, preservation societies and ridding ourselves "of all the useless luxuries (by some called comforts) that make our stuffy art-stifling houses more truly savage than a Zulu's kraal or an East Greenlander's snow hut," are both inadequate and affectedly naive.[50]

In another essay, "The Revival of Architecture" (1888), he discusses the Gothic revival of the past generation – emanating for Morris entirely from Ruskin's insight "that the art of any epoch must of necessity be the expression of its social life." For Morris, however, it has largely resulted in failure.[51] He is also at best lukewarm about the Queen Anne style, which "is surely not too sublime for general use" and has conquered modern taste, but only because in it "there was yet left some feeling of the Gothic" and it was generally practiced by architects of good taste.[52] Ultimately it, like its Gothic predecessors, is "too limited in its scope," for a fundamental revival in architecture must be utterly dependent on the revival of society as a whole.[53] Saying this another way, architecture's true improvement must await a socialist revolution: "Meantime we are waiting for that new development of society, some of us in cowardly inaction, some of us amidst hopeful work towards the change; but at least we are all waiting for what must be the work, not the leisure of taste of a few scholars, authors, and artists, but of the necessities and aspirations of the workmen throughout the civilized world."[54]

It is noteworthy that in Morris's futuristic novel of 1890, *News from Nowhere* (set in twenty-second–century England), the theme of architecture is scarcely raised. We learn of the time traveler's joy at finding the Hammersmith suspension bride (1887) replaced by "a wonder of a bridge" evoking the Ponte Vecchio at Florence, and then there is his mannered taciturnity at finding the "ugly old building" of the British Museum still intact.[55] The closest thing to an architectural description of this new utopia occurs when the time traveler, in approaching London, first encounters "a splendid and exuberant style of architecture" that seems to embrace "the best qualities of the Gothic of northern Europe with those of the Saracenic and Byzantine, though there was no copying of any one of these styles."[56] Once again medieval Florence is evoked – this time the Bapistry, yet an improved model "most delicately ornamented."

There is something very quaint in Morris's medieval vision for the twenty-second century. In another part of the novel the time traveler converses with two protagonists (Clara and Dick) about their art and the fact that most of the artistic themes (works produced by common people rather than by "artists") are drawn from fanciful fairy tales, such as Jacob Grimm might assemble. The time traveler finds this "childishness" curious, as Clara and Dick are both aware of "realist" art of the past and its concern with the themes of modern life. Dick reasons that his century's art is owing to the fact that the "child-like part of us" is that which produces works of imagination; hence his society of innocents responds to the joy of having recovered its childhood. Clara, however, is not so sure. "Well, for my part," she says, "I wish we were interesting enough to be written or painted about."[57]

In Morris's view, on architecture too must await the socialist coming of the "second childhood," but, however sincere politically, his is a vision based on privilege and characterised by egotistical Oxford genteelness bordering on vanity. Morris lived in and immeasurably contributed to a period of dramatic social and artistic change, but he remained until the end seemingly oblivious to its most significant accomplishments. Even more so than the novel's protagonist, he never strayed far from his earlier concerns with the unreal world of folklore.

2. Domestic Reforms on the Continent of Europe

Since the appearance of Hermann Muthesius's *The English House* (1901–2), it has been almost axiomatic to treat the arts and crafts movement as largely a British phenomenon that subsequently spread to the Continent and North America. But such a view simplifies the complexity of related national movements of reform with diverse aims and ideological origins. Indeed, Muthesius was sent to London as an attaché to the German Embassy to assess English domestic architecture and design partly as a means of comparing the arts and crafts movement in England with similar efforts at reform in Germany.

The rise of the industrial arts museum on the Continent is an instructive case in point. The London Museum of Ornamental Art, established by Cole at the Marlborough House in 1852, is the first museum of this kind in Europe, although specialty industrial arts museums, generally associated with regional and imperial crowns, had long been in existence. Dresden for more than a century had been noted for its porcelain collections and the treasures of the "Green Vault." Vienna was renowned for its Schatzkammer at the Hofburg Palace. France had long had its famed tapestry and porcelain collections on display, respectively, in the manufactories of the Gobelins and at Sèvres. In 1832 Alexandre du Sommerard began displaying his collection of furniture, carvings, ceramics, textiles, and metal works at the Hôtel de Cluny; eleven years later the collection was purchased by the French government and given permanent sanction.[58]

Contemporary with Henry Cole's efforts in London was the founding of the Germanic National Museum in Nuremberg (1852) and the Bavarian National Museum in Munich (1853). Both were historical museums that focused on Germany's medieval past. This limited conception would change in the 1860s, beginning with the creation of the Museum for Art and Industry in Vienna (1863) and the Museum of Applied Arts in Berlin (1867). These two museums were influenced by developments in South Kensington, but both were directed toward contemporary reform by their first curators and directors: Rudolf von Eitelberger (1817–85) and Jakob von Falke (1825–97) in Vienna, Julius Lessing in Berlin.

Eitelberger, in fact, contacted Semper in Zurich in 1867 and asked for a copy of the catalogue on metals that he had prepared for Henry Cole in 1852.[59] The art historian was interested in the manuscript because of Semper's introductory remarks on the arrangement of industrial arts collections – really a historical review of this "sort of index to the History of Culture" and its educational possibilities for both the public and designers. Semper also stressed the need for "re-uniting what has been artificially separated and divided in modern times" – high art and the so-called minor arts – and he concluded with a sketch for an ideal museum in which ornamental artifacts are grouped according to four motives: textiles, carpentry, ceramics, and masonry.[60]

Semper's ideas influenced both Eitelberger and Lessing and also Julius Brinckmann, who in 1874 became the founding director of the Museum for Art and Applied-Arts in Hamburg. In the 1870s, other museums focusing on the industrial arts opened their doors in various cities, including in cities such as Dresden, Frankfurt, Kassel, Kiel, Leipzig, Brunn, and Budapest. These new institutions – which, following the lead of South Kensington, also featured lectures, libraries, and traveling exhibitions and thereby established the essential foundation for the reform of arts and crafts in Germany and elsewhere in central Europe.

Other influences were also coming to bear. The efforts of early proponents of the Gothic revival in Germany – August Reichensperger, Sulpiz Boisserée, and Ernst Zwirner – came to fruition in 1842 when contruction of the Cologne Cathedral recommenced. The resumption of work intensified interest not only in the Gothic style but also in how its lessons might be applied to modern architecture.

In the new generation of medieval enthusiasts was Georg Gottlob Ungewitter (1820–64).[61] Even before his first contact with Reichensperger around 1850, this Hessian had begun producing pattern books showing how to adapt *Rundbogen* and Gothic forms to modern constructional techniques. The designs often have asymmetrical plans and emphasize natural materials. Perhaps the most important of these books was his two-volume *Entwürfe zu Stadt- und Landhäusern* (Designs for urban and country houses, 1856–8), in which he produced original designs for informally planned houses compositionally influenced by late medieval sources (Fig. 62).[62] Here was a direct parallel with the Queen Anne fashion in England, although it was based upon earlier mod-

els and placed a greater emphasis on Gothic verticality. Similar to the style of Ungewitter was that of Conrad Wilhelm Hase (1818–1902). His own house in Hanover (1859–61) is contemporary with Webb's Red House and comparable to it in that it is built of exposed brick, is asymmetrical in plan, and has Gothic detailing for some of the windows and portals.

The Gothic revival and the medieval *Rundbogen* school were not alone in preparing the ground for reform in Germany. In Berlin the so-called Schinkel school extended well into the nineteenth century. This school included Friedrich Hitzig (1811–81), Johann Heinrich Strack (1805–80), and Ludwig Persius (1803–45), all of whom cultivated a free villa style that drew upon rural Italian models. Similar tendencies are found in the work of the Hamburg architect Alexis de Chateauneuf (1799–1853), who also brought to his work a knowledge of English domestic architecture.[63] And then there was the free Renaissance manner of Gottfried Semper, who influenced numerous designer's, among them Constantine Lipsius (1832–94), Alfred Friedrich Bluntschli (1842–1930), Hans Auer (1847–1906), and Heinrich von Ferstel (1828–83).[64] The last architect, in fact, was chosen by Eitelberger to design the Austrian Museum for Art and Industry in 1868. By this date, the scattered reform efforts of the previous two decades had advanced into a full-blown movement, particularly in housing design.

An early indication of this is found in the concluding pages of Hermann Lotze's *Geschichte der Aesthetik in Deutschland* (History of German aesthetics, 1868), which exempts domestic design from the rules of monumental practice. If the purpose of the monument is "to hold up to consciousness an ideal purpose of life" (generally represented by the formality of a unified style), domestic life cannot really be governed by any single idea, Lotze argues. The design of a residence should rather proceed from a way of thinking that is more "painterly and scenic," that is, free of the constraints of symmetry or unity of plan and therefore capable of "serving modern life."[65]

The Berlin architect Richard Lucae (1829–77) seems to have come to the same conclusion at the same time. In a 1867 lecture entitled "Der Mensch und sein Haus – my home is my castle," this later director of the Bauakademie deplored contemporary housing for its lack of functionality, natural light, and ventilation and underscored the domestic associations of the family, the hearth, and comfort.[66] Lucae had traveled to England and was a shrewd critic of the ramifications of industrialization.

62. Georg Gottlob Ungewitter, house design from *Gotische Stadt- und Landhäuser* (Berlin, 1889?).

German critics of the arts and crafts as practiced in Germany formed another front to this movement. Friedrich Pecht devoted a full-length study to the Paris Exposition of 1867, and in page after page he lamented that the Germans in their handicraft production lagged far behind the French in terms of standards of execution and expression of a contemporary style.[67] This view was echoed a few years later by Julius Lessing, the first director of the Museum of Applied Arts in Berlin. In reviewing the Vienna World Exhibition of 1873, he pointed to the superiority of the French in these areas and to the confusion of the Germans in trying to relate to international developments.[68] Lessing would go on to become an advocate of industrialization and a foe of all historical tendencies.

It was in Vienna and Munich that the German reform movement was most pronounced. Two people associated with the Museum for Art and Industry in Vienna – Eitelberger and Ferstel – led the charge on housing reform. In a joint pamphlet written in 1860 in response to housing

along the newly constructed Ringstrasse, they condemned the urban speculative apartment building, which often shields a "nomadic life" behind the facade of pomp and false elegance. They also had praise for the moral idea of home ownership as displayed in the native Austrian dwelling.[69] The museum's first curator, Jakob von Falke (1825–97), joined the cause when he introduced stylized rooms into the museum as a way to educate the public about tasteful and practical appointments. In his *Geschichte des modernen Geschmacks* (History of modern taste, 1866), Falke argued for using the Renaissance as a rational and moderate haven to guard against the *Stillosigkeit* (absence of style) that he saw evident in his day. This position was given support by Wilhelm Lübke's *Geschichte der deutsche Renaissance* (History of the German Renaissance, 1873). Lübke looked back to the time of Albrecht Dürer not only as a period of simple honesty and reform in the arts but as an age in which the southern sense of form merged with northern spirituality to good effect.

179

In 1871 Falke published a compendium of rules for domestic design, *Die Kunst im Hause* (Art in the house), which would go through several editions and appear in an English translation in 1879.[70] Style is defined variously, but a piece of furniture has style "when it is exactly what it ought to be, when it is suited to the purpose for which it was intended, and it has that purpose unmistakably inscribed upon it."[71] Falke also emphasizes that a common, unstylized piece of furniture can and should have style, though given the rapid change of "modern life" he now questions whether it is advisable to strive for a stylistic unity in the manner of his earlier "period" rooms. He reduces artistic harmony in interior design to color and form and in fact places the greatest emphasis on the latter.[72] Falke's importance also lies in the fact that in 1878 he published a study entitled the "English House," in which he exalted the lessons of recent English domestic architecture.[73]

Rivaling Falke's efforts were those of Georg Hirth (1814–1916) in Munich. Hirth gravitated to Munich in the early 1870s to serve as a political editor for the *Allgemeine Zeitung*. In 1875, aided by the publishing interests of his father, he cofounded the publishing house of Knorr und Hirth, which specialized in high-quality art books. He was an avid collector of art and in the 1890s was instrumental in founding the art nouveau journal *Jugend*. His interest in domestic reforms is first seen in the items that he contributed to the Munich Applied Arts Exhibition of 1876. In 1880 he published *Das deutsche Zimmer der Renaissance* (The German Renaissance room), one of the most copiously and beautifully illustrated books of the second half of the century. Carrying the subtitle "Suggestions for a Domestic Cultivation of the Arts," the book is an intelligent plea for reform according to the tasteful principles exhibited in the German Renaissance: clean logical lines, neutral tones, unity of ornament and structure, and harmony of parts. The book's longest chapter is devoted to "the innate love of the Germans for the colorful," but the basic principle of the new style should be *Stoffgerechtigkeit*, or the correct use of materials (Fig. 63).[74] Hirth's color preference for lighter browns led him to favor the warmth of unstained wood for floors, walls, and ceilings – against which a few select decorative tones and objects could be allowed to stand out. Behind these recommendations was his long-held conviction "that among the conditions that must work together for the enhancement of our economic life, the cultivation of a good national taste occupies a prominent, perhaps the leading place."[75]

Working alongside Hirth was the architect Gabriel von Siedl (1848–1913), whose Renaissance-inspired reconstruction of a "Room with an inserted corner Alcove" was shown at the exhibition of 1875 and illustrated by Hirth. Beginning with his designs for the Kunstgewerbehaus (Museum of Applied Arts, 1877) and Gasthof Deutsches Haus (1879), Seidl was popularizing a local style that would later be described as "realism," that is, an architecture emphasizing the "truth" of a nonacademic regional style consisting of smooth wall surfaces and thinly profiled sill and head moldings.

The 1880s, as in Britain, saw a great consolidation of the German reform movement as the participants of various reform efforts of the previous decade joined with adherents and propagators of the Queen Anne style. One example is Robert Dohme's enchanting study *Das englische Haus* (The English house, 1888), which neatly summarized what had transpired in England. Dohme (1845–93) in the previous year had published his *Geschichte der deutschen Baukunst* (History of German architecture), but a journey to England led him to write a semiofficial report of new developments there. He begins his study with nothing less than a historical survey of England that starts with the Roman and Norman invasions and leads the reader down through Gothic, Renaissance, and baroque times. The contributions of picturesque theory are not overlooked, nor are the efforts of Pugin, George Godwin at *The Builder*, Henry Cole, and the "Esthetics" of Rossetti and Burne-Jones. Foremost, however, is the innovative work of Shaw, who is perhaps most responsible for instituting "a new evolutionary period of culture."[76]

With this point made, Dohme begins to dissect the individual elements of the English house. The superiority of the English approach resides "neither in spaciousness and monumentality nor in wealth and luxury . . . but in the harmony of the individual rooms, their skillful grouping – in short, in fulfilling that sum of demands that his practical sense and refined need of life have shown to be prerequisites for a comfortable existence."[77] These demands or attributes are seven: site selection, aspects/prospects, light and ventilation, cheerfulness, comfort, convenience, privacy, and fastidiousness. Such attributes, Dohme admits, are not yet evident on the Continent, but they are found "in our modern wagons and ships, whose beauty, in fulfilling the task, we have sought by limiting any and all decorative ornaments merely to the graceful lines accompanying the object's most possible attention to function, to the greatest simplicity of form, and to divesting it of all superfluities."[78] Thus Dohme becomes the second theorist (following Greenough) to invoke the analogy between architecture and modern vehicles and ships.

63. Georg Hirth, room design from *Das deutsche Zimmer der Renaissance* (Munich, 1880).

But Dohme's book of 1888 is misleading in that he seems little informed of parallel German efforts at reform. This is not the case with the second important study to appear in this year, *Im Bürgerhause* (Inside the middle-class house) by Cornelius Gurlitt (1850–1938). The author of ninety-seven books, Gurlitt was arguably the most brilliant German critic on the scene. A Saxon native, he had trained as an architect in Berlin and Stuttgart before turning to history and criticism in the 1870s. In 1879 he became a curator at the Dresden Museum for the Applied Arts and was later appointed a professor at that city's technical college. *Im Bürgerhause*, which carries the subtitle "Pleadings on Art, Applied Art, and Domestic Furnishings," is aimed not at designers but at the new class of urban dwellers. The German term *Bürger*, related to the English word "burgher," connotes not only the "middle-class" but also the attributes of plainness, honesty, simplicity, and unpretentiousness. Thus the book is something of a primer on how to choose and economically outfit a modern dwelling.

The first eighty or so pages deal not with issues of design but with "culture," specifically the growing sense of a German culture and what it meant at that time to be a German – only seventeen years after national unification. Gurlitt dwells at length on the philosophies of neoclassicism and romanticism and the aesthetic outlooks of these periods. He credits Semper in particular for laying the basis of the reforms of the previous two decades. Against those (such as Dohme) who want the Germans to look to England for models of modern life, Gurlitt's response is succinct and

surprising – "delusion." In his words, "The nature of the English style consists in the fact that it imitates no one, that its motives, although perhaps drawn from all the styles of the world, are completely national. So long as we do not become Englishmen, we cannot make an English style."[79]

Gurlitt espouses the now familiar refrain of simplicity, color, material and productive honesty, and satisfaction of purpose. But in his concluding remarks he also emphasizes that styles and fashions are ephemeral things that continually change: "They change not only the form of things, but also our eyes. This table that appears so charming to us today can in five years appear ponderous. Are there laws for such change? Are there rules of beauty, such as how thick a table leg should be? Surely not."[80] Therefore, all efforts to create aesthetic laws are in vain, and if a work of art is to have virtue, it should both be "congenial" and express its time. "The march of our nation goes ever forward," he concludes. "We no longer live in the realm of dreams and history; our actions and thoughts direct themselves first to what is going on around us, in which we have to take an active part, in which we have to maintain our position. And when we turn our heads forward to see the greatness of our people perpetually active, then will our art also be modern and *only* modern."[81] The depth of a people's character thus supercedes principled aesthetic reasoning.

It is difficult to underestimate the importance of these appeals of the 1880s. If Dohme's book sparked an interest in English design that lasted through the 1890s, Gurlitt's book more directly drew upon native Germanic developments and

64. Stave church from Johan Christian Dahl, *Denkmale einer sehr ausgebildeten Holzbaukunst aus den frühsten Jahrhunderten in den inneren Landschaften Norwegens* (Dresden, 1837).

was certainly no less influential in setting the stage for the events of a decade later – when "realism" and *Sachlichkeit* (simplicity) became the cornerstones of modern German theory.

The issue of relating design to the emergence of a national identity was also evident in Czarist Russia and the Nordic countries.[82] In Scandinavia, the search for cultural and national identities parallels the resurgence of interest in "old Norse" mythology and vernacular decorative traditions, which in architecture largely meant the techniques and ornamental devices of timber construction. The first great historian of Norse architecture, Johan Christian Dahl (1788–1857), was born in Norway, was trained in Denmark, and lived most of his professional life in Dresden, where he taught landscape painting. His *Denkmale einer sehr ausgebildeten Holzbaukunst aus den frühsten Jahrhunderten in den inneren Landschaften Norwegens* (Monuments of a highly developed timber architecture from the earliest centuries in the interior parts of Norway, 1837) is known especially for its depiction of exotic stave churches (Fig. 64). The images in this book not only cultivated concern for the preservation of these buildings but also eventually led Norway and Sweden to construct medieval farmhouses at the Paris Exposition of 1867.[83] These farmhouses in turn inspired such Swedish and

Norwegian intellectuals as Axel Key, Lorentz Dietrichson, and Carl Curman to build "old Norse" houses in the 1870s and early 1880s as models for how the past might be given a modern look.[84]

Also experimenting in the timber vernacular style in the 1880s were the Danish architects Hans Jørgen Holm (1835–1916) and Martin Nyrop (1849–1921). Like Gurlitt, Holm believed that neoclassicism had displaced native cultural traditions, and his built essays in timber and brick architecture attempted to recapture the simple yet expressive techniques of the past for contemporary use. Nyrop was simply one of the most talented architects practicing anywhere in Europe in the last decades of the century. His vividly polychrome gymnasium for the Folk High School at Vallekilde (1884) is extraordinary for this date – not only for its color but also for its clean and "modern" use of timber planking without stylistic pretense. His buildings for Cophenhagen's Nordic Exposition of 1888 are fantastic exercises in traditional timber sheathing and structural techniques, with trusses actually modeled on those of stave churches. Four years later Nyrop began his much acclaimed Copenhagen City Hall (1892–1905), the work that was one of the models for H. P. Berlage's Amsterdam Exchange.

Besides architects who drew inspiration from vernacular and traditional forms, Scandinavia was home to communities of artists who not only were attracted to rustic and cottage forms, natural settings, and simple materials but filled their houses with innovative textiles and furnishings inspired by folk art. In Norway a circle of artists formed around Erik Werenskiold (1855–1938) and Gerhard Munthe (1849–1929). In Sweden the artists Anders Zorn, Emma Lamm, and Carl Larsson settled in the Mora district of Dalarna and outfitted their houses with Swedish-inspired modern artworks, textiles, and furnishings. Perhaps the most interesting of these early artistic communities, however, were those in the Karelia region of Finland, a country whose language, unlike those in the rest of Scandinavia, is not Germanic. Yet the country had been ruled by Sweden from medieval times until 1809. In 1815 the European powers ceded Finland to Russia, which, with increasing severity, imposed "Russification" on the country, that is, until the Russian Revolution, when Finland at last gained its independence. One reaction to this external cultural imposition

in the latter part of the nineteenth century was the rediscovery of "Finnish" culture. Karelia is that region along the Russian border that was said to have been settled by the earliest Finnish tribes and had most faithfully preserved the traditional native culture and folklore.

By the 1890s it became a center for vacationing artists seeking inspiration, among them the painter Akseli Gallen-Kallela, the composer Jean Sibelius, and the architect Lars Sonck (1870–1956), all of whom helped to popularize Finnish motifs. Perhaps the most important architect to be attracted to its lessons was Eliel Saarinen (1873–1950), who by 1897 was in partnership with Herman Gesellius (1874–1916) and Armas Lindgren (1874–1929). In 1901 Saarinen and his partners began constructing an ensemble of living and studio spaces on an isolated site on Lake Vitträsk, outside of Helsinki, and this community became a center for the rebirth of the Finnish arts and crafts movement (Fig. 65). Much of the furniture, wall hangings, and textiles

65. Eliel Saarinen, Herman Gesellius, and Armas Lindgren, living hall within the complex at Hvitträsk, started 1901. From *Decorative Kunst*, vol. 5, February 1907.

were designed by Saarinen and his wife Loja, and the high reputation of Finnish designers in the twentieth century in many respects begins here.

The arts and crafts movements in Scandinavia, Germany, Austria, and England rallied themselves, at least in part, in opposition to the hegemony of French taste. The French decorative arts, in fact, continued to dominate European high fashion until the end of the century – this despite France's continual political instability and crisis-ridden economy. The Second Empire, under the rule of Napoleon III, produced modest economic gains and radically transformed Paris but blundered into war with Germany in the summer of 1870, and within weeks the country collapsed. The so-called Third Republic was created in September of that year, but it was faced immediately with the problem of Paris, or rather with the socialist-led rebellion of the Paris Commune. This uprising ended abruptly and tragically in May 1871, with as many as 30,000 Communards killed and as many as 40,000 people taken into detention by the French army. German troops did not leave France until late in 1873, and a republican government was not successfully formed until 1879 – the first of fifty governments between 1879 and 1918. In the 1880s the country returned to a semblance of normalcy, but its economy did not fully recover. By the early 1890s the size of France's economy and industrial production had slipped from second (behind Britain) to fourth (behind Germany and the United States). Nevertheless, Paris remained the literary and artistic capital of Europe during the nineteenth century; the movements of realism, impressionism, symbolism, and postimpressionism testify to its continuing artistic vibrancy.

Even the Ecole des Beaux-Arts enjoyed a period of relative calm after the debacles of the 1860s. In 1872 Julien Guadet (1834–1908) began his association with the school, where he would later serve as the professor of architectural theory (1894–1908). His grand work, the anachronistic yet influential *Eléments et théorie de l'architecture*, appeared in four volumes between 1902 and 1904.[85] The thousands of pages of text and plates actually contain little in the way of theory or innovative ideas. In his methodical way, Guadet appeals to those "grand and immutable principles of art" and simple rules for composition – a recipe for buildings without a footing in place or time.

In the applied or decorative arts, France's strategy was to rely on international exhibitions as a means to compare and enhance its national products and promote them abroad. The country was shocked by the success of the London Exhibition of 1851, but it rapidly followed its example with in-creasingly expansive expositions in 1855, 1867, 1878, 1889, and 1900. The most important of these was the exposition of 1889, which produced the engineering masterpieces of the Gallerie des Machines and the Eiffel Tower, both of which exerted enormous influence within Europe.

Behind these endeavors however, were well-articulated national policies that were historicist at heart. The second Empire ushered in not only grand boulevards and major building campaigns but also an aristocratic taste for the late baroque and rococo that quickly took root. Empress Eugénie's historical fondness for Madame de Pompadour and Marie Antoinette – in renovating the imperial apartments at the Tuileries, Saint-Cloud, and Malmaison – led the way. Architecturally, Charles Garnier's Paris Opera (1861–75) was a triumph of the new official taste, and the rococo style that it exemplified dominated the French decorative art industries in the exposition of 1878. The most influential supporters of this style were the Goncourt brothers.[86] Their house in Auteuil, with its nostalgic interiors, carefully documented by Edmond de Goncourt's *La Maison d'un artiste* in 1881, became a center for the new decorative style and attracted artists of both official and avant-garde persuasion. The influence of the rococo in the formation of art nouveau has long been established, and it is only fitting that France's most important art nouveau artist, Émile Gallé (1846–1904), used the baroque style throughout the 1880s as the springboard to his later vitalism.[87]

The rococo revival also underlay many of the official reforms of these years. The first calls for a decorative arts museum were voiced already in 1852, again in response to Cole's success in London. In 1856 Comte de Laborde organized the Union of Arts and Industry as a sanctioning body for its creation. Two years later a decorative arts organization was formed, the Society for the Progress of Industrial Art. In 1864, at Prosper Mérimée's urging, the emperor created the Central Union of the Fine Arts Applied to Industry. This organization was charged with planning exhibitions in the decorative arts. Following the civil war of 1870–1, Marquis Philippe de Chennevières took control of a series of reforms at the Ecole des Arts Décoratifs and created a chair in the applied arts at the Ecole des Beaux-Arts. He also took charge of the Society for a Decorative Arts Museum in 1877. In 1880 this society and the Central Union combined forces to publish the *Revue des Arts Décoratifs*, the first journal in France devoted exclusively to the decorative arts. Finally, in 1882 the two organizations merged to form the Central Union of the Decorative Arts, which would control decorative arts education and promotion over the next two decades.

Although the rococo style remained the pedagogical foundation for all of these agencies and institutions, the 1880s saw a remarkable incursion of Japanese influence. Oriental art began to be studied in the early 1860s and 1870s in both Paris and London, but in France it took on a life of its own. The first comprehensive history, *L'Art japonais*, was edited by Louis Gonse in 1883, but the driving force behind the artistic movement was Samuel Bing (1838–1905). This German entrepreneur had come to Paris in the 1850s to oversee his family's business interests in the city and had become a naturalized citizen in 1876. By this date he had been touting Japanese art, and in 1880 he undertook a one-year trip to Japan to purchase goods for his three shops in Paris. Also in the 1880s he contributed items from his own collection to the Society for a Decorative Arts Museum, organized exhibits, and wrote articles for the *Revue des art décoratifs*. Perhaps his most influential undertaking was his exquisitely designed journal *Le Japon artistique*, which began publication in 1888. Its intention, as he noted in the first issue, was to appeal to those "interested in the future of our decorative arts." More specifically,

In the new forms of art which have come to us from the uttermost parts of the East, we see something more than a Platonic feast set before our contemplative dilettanti, we find in them examples worthy to be followed in every respect, not, indeed, worthy to uproot the foundations of the old aesthetic edifice which exists, but fitted to add a fresh force to those forces which we have appropriated to ourselves in all past time, and brought to the support and aid of our national genius. How could the vitality of that genius have been maintained had it not been recruited from fresh sources from time to time?[88]

Bing's fascination with and sale of Japanese art continued even after he opened his famous Maison de l'Art Nouveau in 1895.

All of this, of course, underscores the essential difference between the arts and crafts movement in France and those elsewhere in Europe. If in England Morris and the artists of the 1880s and 1890s attempted to reinvigorate the arts by applying socialist principles derived from presumed medieval practices, the tendency in cosmopolitan France was both to turn inward and to seek to infuse the country's historical legacy with the most exotic fashions imported from abroad. As Debora Silverman has pointed out, "Rather than seek to democratize art and to recover it for the people, French art nouveau sought to aristocratize the crafts, to extend the hierarchy of the arts to include the artisan."[89] Economically, these efforts would be for the most part unsuccessful, as the continuing political instability of the country resulted in the fatal protectionist policies of the 1890s. France at the start of the twentieth century, with its faltering beaux-arts institutions and waning self-confidence, would all but cease to influence architectural theory.

3. Reform Movements in the United States

The last three decades of the nineteenth century in the United States, by contrast, are marked in every field by almost excessive optimism. These were the years of unparalleled economic and industrial expansion, recessions and booms, two world fairs, the settling of the West, and the Spanish-American War. This period saw the introduction of electricity, indoor plumbing, the telephone, the automobile, the typewriter, and the assembly line. By 1900 the country would pass its nearest rival, Britain, in industrial output and have a gross national product more than twice that of Germany or Russia. Its population at the turn of the century would swell to roughly eighty million people, almost double that of France. Around the time that an assassin's bullet ended the life of President McKinley in 1901, the United States became a full-fledged world power. Theodore Roosevelt boldly reaffirmed the Monroe Doctrine, began the approval process for the Panama Canal, and invited the first "colored" man to a private White House dinner – Booker T. Washington. Suspicious of America's new might, the German government of Kaiser Wilhelm II had plans drawn up for an invasion of the United States, via "Puerteriko" and Long Island.

Unsurprisingly, a feeling of ebullience is evident in the arts. Although many American artists – like their architectural counterparts – preferred to take their training abroad, most also expressed a desire to create an autonomous artistic culture at home. In the realm of the decorative arts, the Philadelphia Centennial Exposition of 1876 provided an important impulse to reform, for here were displayed products of the British arts and crafts movement, French realist and impressionist works, and even objects from Japan. Several of the leading American artists, such as John La Farge (1835–1910) and Louis Comfort Tiffany (1848–1933), had already been affected by such influences.[90] Both had experimented with opalescent glass before this date. La Farge, a painter by training, was at this time completing the stained-glass windows for Boston's Trinity Church. In 1879 he would be the first to patent a new glass process, which would be used in the creation of many stained-glass designs in the 1880s. One window he displayed at the 1889 exposition in Paris was even hailed by the French press as a masterpiece of design.

The case of Tiffany is even more striking. The son of Charles Tiffany (founder of the famous jewelry concern), Louis Tiffany rebelled against an easy path in business and turned his attention toward art. In 1868–9 he studied painting in Paris under Leon Bailly and then visited Spain and North Africa. Upon returning to New York, he opened a studio and exhibited three oils and six watercolors in the Philadelphia Exposition of 1876. Around this time he met Candace Wheeler, who in 1877 would establish the New York Society of Decorative Art. In 1879 they formed "Tiffany and Associated Artists," in which Louis specialized in glass design, Wheeler in embroideries, Samuel Colman in fabrics and wallpapers, and Lockwood de Forest in woodcarving and decoration. The profession of interior design in America was essentially born during these years. Charles Eastlake's *Hints on Household Taste* appeared in an American edition in 1872. Clarence Cook published his *House Beautiful* in 1877. Cook also wrote the text for *What Shall We Do with Our Walls?* (1881), instigated by Warren, Fuller & Co., which also hired Tiffany and Colman to design wall and ceiling papers. Other books to appear in this period were Harriet Prescott Spofford's *Art Decoration Applied to Furniture* (1878), Henry Hudson Holly's *Modern Dwellings in Town and Country Adapted to American Wants and Climate* (1878), Falke's *Art in the House* (1879), and Constance Cary Harrison's *Woman's Handiwork in Modern Homes* (1881). For women, the decorative arts and interior decoration became an important conduit into the field of design.

Tiffany's guild of artists parted amicably in 1881, but Tiffany soon leapt to the forefront of American designers with his interior design commissions for the White House (1882–3) and the Ponce de Leon Hotel in St. Augustine, Florida (1885–7). He still collaborated during the 1880s with a number of highly talented artists and craftsmen, among them Wheeler, La Farge, Auguste Saint-Gaudens, Stanford White, and the Herter brothers. In 1881 he received the first patents for his version of opalescent glass, and in 1885 he established the Tiffany Glass Company, which initially specialized in stained glass. At the 1889 Paris Exposition he first saw the works of Émile Gallé and also met Samuel Bing, with whom he began a fruitful association. After his invention (and patenting) of "favrile" glass in the early 1890s, he began the production of his famous lamps, vases, and jewelry (Fig. 66). By the time his products were displayed in Bing's Maison l'Art Nouveau, in 1895, he had perhaps become America's most celebrated artist. His abstract use of

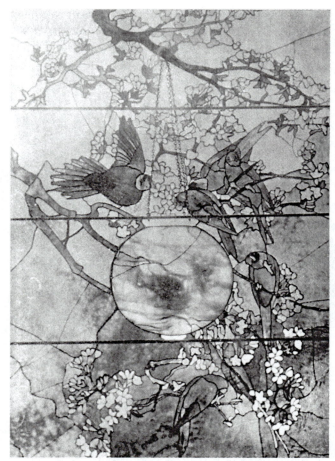

66. Louis C. Tiffany, window design. From "Exhibit Section," *Tiffany Glass & Decoration Company, Furnishers & Glass Workers* (New York, 1893).

unconventional forms and techniques is sometimes called art nouveau, but such a label only vaguely describes the originality of his designs, which in their sensitivities (parallel with trends in Europe) derive from his studies of Moorish, impressionist, and Oriental art.

Tiffany's rise to prominence in the 1880s fell in line with a burst of activity in related fields. One of his frequent architectural collaborators of this period was Stanford White (1853–1906), who also focused much of his enormous talent on interior design.[91] White initially aspired to be an artist, but he turned to architecture on the advice of La Farge, and in 1872 he joined the office of H. H. Richardson. In a little over a year he became Richardson's chief designer, replacing George McKim (1847–1909), who left the office to start his own practice. In 1879, the partnership of McKim, Meade & White was formed. Whereas the first principal had since the 1870s been drawn to American colonial and Georgian styles, White quickly established his personal flair for spatial relationships and textural shingle treatments in such works as the Newport Casino (1880); the Short Hills Casino, Short Hills, New Jersey (1880); the Isaac Bell House, Newport (1883); and the Goelet House, Newport (1883–4). Vincent Scully Jr. has defined 1883 as the year that the Queen Anne style and colonial revival gave way to the "shingle style."[92] Many shingle-style homes were illustrated in the multiple volumes of George William Sheldon's *Artistic Houses* (1883–84) and *Artistic Country–Seats* (1886–87), which also documented the residential innovations of Bruce Price, Wilson Eyre Jr., William R. Emerson, and W. Halsey Wood.[93] In essence, the legacy of Davis and Downing was now coming to fruition in the American suburban home.

Also taking formation at the start of the 1880s was the movement sometimes known as the "American Renaissance," another run with classicism prompted by McKim, Mead & White's Henry Villard House in New York (1882–3) and their Boston Public Library (1888–95) (Fig. 67).[94]

67. McKim, Mead & White, Boston Public Library, 1888–95. Corner detail. Photograph by author.

The rooms of the former were hailed by Mariana Griswold Van Rensselaer in 1885 as the finest interiors in the country, while the interiors of the Boston Public Library – behind an exterior paying homage both to Richardson and to the Bibliothèque Ste.-Geneviève – sought a spatial grandeur and a synthesis of the arts that harken back to Latrobe's work on the Capitol.[95]

On a domestic level, the classical movement is best represented by Edith Wharton and Ogden Codman's *The Decoration of Houses* (1897), which proudly underscores the great strides American interior design had made over the previous decade. Classicism, for Wharton and Codman, represents not "a style" but simply "style," and it is reflected in such attributes as attention to purpose, harmony, rhythm, logic, and proportion. Further, "beauty depends on fitness, and the practical requirements of life are the ultimate test for fitness" and "once this is clearly understood, it will be seen that the supposed conflict between originality and tradition is no conflict at all."[96] In the footnote to the last sentence, Wharton and Codman cited no less a classical authority than Durand.

More broadly, the American Renaissance movement reached its apogee in the Chicago Columbian Exposition of 1893. Indeed, few events in American architectural history have received so little analysis yet been so summarily decried. Sullivan's smug and stinging description of the event in 1924 as "a naked exhibitionism of charlatanry" is in part responsible for its dismissal, but the matter is not so simple.[97] To begin with, the "White City" – whose site plan was a joint production of John Root, Frederick Law Olmstead, and Henry Codman – was perceived in a very different light in its day. The press and the public were simply overwhelmed by its beauty and charm – and not only lay visitors but also artists, architects, and intellectuals. The New Englander Henry Adams devoted nearly a full chapter of his autobiography to its awe-inspiring success, and claimed that, while he was unsure of its ultimate meaning, it "was the first expression of American thought as a unity; one must start there."[98] Charles Eliot Norton, president of Harvard University, found the layout of buildings to be "noble, original and satisfactory, a work of fine art," and applauded in particular the "superb effect in the successful grouping in harmonious relationships of vast and magnificent structures."[99] The architectural critic Montgomery Schuler echoed this assessment when he termed the exposition "the most admired group of buildings ever erected in this country," although "the success is first of all a success of unity, a triumph of *ensemble*," and "the landscape plan is the key to the pictorial success of the Fair as a whole."[100] Finally, the critic Henry Van Brunt, who was also one of the exposition's contributing architects, stated, "Never was a combination of monumental buildings, contrived for a specific and monumental purpose, more carefully and ingeniously studied for the production of preconceived effects of order and magnificence."[101] Above all he was appreciative of the efforts of Olmstead and Root, who came up with "the brilliant idea of converting the hopeless sand-dunes and intervening marshes of this district into a series of low and broad terraces, intersected by the Basin, the canals, and the Lagoon, which form the most distinguishing and characteristic features of the Exposition."[102]

All of this is far removed from the more puritanical and socialist aspirations of the British arts and crafts reformers, and their influence in America was in fact only starting to be noticeable around this time.[103] Utopian guilds and communities, of course, had long been present in this country, with its abundant open land. One of the more successful of these was a Quaker sect known as the Shakers, who had emigrated from England in 1774 and preached communism and celibacy. A century later there were over 2,000 Shakers in the United States, grouped into fifty-eight communities occupying over 100,000 acres of land. The largest of these highly regulated communities was in New Lebanon, New York, and in 1852 it opened a furniture factory to sell simple and practical designs.

Shaker furniture and rural living may have influenced Gustav Stickley (1857–1942), whose impact on the American arts and crafts movement was enormous.[104] In 1884 he moved from Wisconsin to New York State and undertook several furniture ventures with relatives – mainly producing reproductions of established styles. In 1898 he visited Europe and met Voysey, Ashbee, and Samuel Bing, yet it was only with the first two men that he came to be philosophically allied. In 1900 he and two brothers began a company that specialized in original designs based on traditional techniques of handicraft production. In October 1901 he began the journal *The Craftsman*, devoting the first two issues to the ideas of Morris and Ruskin. Later issues, which regularly documented the innovations in American domestic practice during the first fifteen years of the twentieth century, continued to exalt the ideals of the British movement as well as the American creed of "honesty, simplicity and usefulness" that lay at the heart of Stickley's "craftsman" idea. In the 1903 catalogue for the arts and crafts exhibition held in Syracuse, Stickley briefly stated his principles as the expression of purpose, the absence of ornament, and "the strict fitting of all work to the medium in which it is executed."[105] In the more expansive essay at the conclusion of his book *Craftsman Homes* (1909), Stickley allied his furniture and bungalows designs with the sweeping social, political, and industrial attitude that views luxury or an excess of material possessions as an impediment to "individual life." The craftsman idea, by contrast, exalts the simplicity of plain and unencumbered rural living "because we firmly believe that the country is the only place to live in."[106] Here the ghost of Downing makes its presence felt.

The arts and crafts movement was influential in several cities around the turn of the century, but it was especially prominent in Chicago. The first issue of *House Beautiful* was published Chicago in December 1896, with articles by Morris, Crane, Ashbee, and Voysey; it was joined in 1897 by the American version of the British journal *Studio*, which appeared under the title *International Studio*. In 1899 the Industrial Art League was organized in Chicago and assumed for its task the creation of workshops, course instruction, libraries and museums, and publications to promote the arts and crafts. One of its founders was Oscar Lovell Triggs, a professor at the University of Chicago, who in 1901 would make a proposal for a guild and school of handicraft modeled on English examples. Triggs was also the secretary of the Chicago branch of the William Morris Society and a founding member of the Chicago Arts and Crafts Society. In his *Chapters in the History of the Arts and Crafts Movement* (1901), he saw the arts and crafts movement as entirely a British affair, which he traced through Morris's Red House back to the thought of Ruskin and Carlyle.[107] Triggs held these views even though by 1901 he was giving modest support to machine and industrial production.

Triggs may have undergone his conversion to industrialism through his contacts with Hull House, the urban center founded in 1889 by Jane Addams (1860–1935) and Ellen Gates Starr to improve the lot of immigrants. The activist Addams had visited Toynbee Hall in London in 1888, and in Chicago she sought to create a center that would combine basic social services, such as day care, English instruction, and employment assistance, with cultural amenities, including an art gallery, a library, and classes in art and music. The Chicago Arts and Crafts Society held its first meeting in Hull House in October 1897, apparently through the efforts of both Starr and Addams. Among the architects present were Frank Lloyd Wright (1867–1959), Dwight Perkins, Myron Hunt, and Robert Spencer – all of whom were sharing office space. Hull House also hosted

Wright's famous lecture of 1901, "The Art and Craft of the Machine."

Wright's conversion to and somewhat heretical withdrawal from the arts and crafts movement took place over the course of the 1890s. The inglenook and fireplace of his own shingled house in Oak Park (1889–90) – with its exterior allusions to the work of Bruce Price and Stanford White – show his early allegiance to the cause. In 1893 he walked out of Sullivan's office in a dispute over his "bootlegged" houses and soon began a period of experimentation. He passed from the classical symmetry of the Winslow House (1893–4) to such historicist intimations as the Bagley House (1894) and the Moore House (1895) to the freer spatial development and horizontal layering of the Heller House (1897) and the Husser House (1899). The last house greatly impressed Ashbee in 1900 when he visited Chicago, where he came to give ten lectures on the subject of the arts and crafts, including one at Hull House. In his journal Ashbee described the Husser House as "one of the most individual of creations that I have seen in America," and he went on to note the bald challenge that Wright already felt free to pose to him:

"My God," he said, "is Machinery; and the art of the future will be the expression of the individual artist through the thousand powers of the machine, – the machine doing all those things that the individual workman cannot do. The creative artist is the man who controls all this and understands it."[108]

This was the idea that the apostate Wright was rehearsing for his Hull House lecture of 1901, which he opened with praise for William Morris, "the great socialist," and John Ruskin, "the great moralist," for preaching "the gospel of simplicity."[109] Nevertheless, Morris in his rightful cause against vulgarity had fundamentally miscalculated the liberating potential of the machine – "the modern sphinx" – whose riddle the modern artist must solve, for in it "lies the only future of art and craft."[110] With this point made, Wright, using Sullivanesque prose, sets off on a spirited defense of the machine, leading his audience from Hugo's chapter on architecture in *The Hunchback of Notre-Dame* to the "peerless Corliss tandems whirling their hundred ton fly-wheels" in Gary, Indiana.[111] "Art in the grand old sense" is indeed dead, and Wright claims that the machine's ultimate function, when captured by the artistic spirit, is "to emancipate human expression" and, even more, to fulfill Whitman's longing for democracy.[112] For Wright, the

medieval socialism of the English arts and crafts movement is simply nostalgia; capitalism and the "nerve ganglia" of the modern city are real. The tall modern office building – "the machine pure and simple" – becomes the "hard and bony skeleton" of the new architecture, for which the artist is now to supply the enveloping fabric "with the living flesh of virile imagination."[113] To return to the past is impossible: "Artists who feel toward Modernity and the Machine now as William Morris and Ruskin were justified in feeling then, had best distinctly wait and work sociologically where great work may still be done by them. In the field of art activity they will do distinct harm. Already they have wrought much miserable mischief."[114]

With these words – no doubt startling many in his audience, including Triggs – Wright makes his break with his contemporaries. He knew full well what he was doing, or so he later pointed out with great self-righteousness. In fact, it was true, as he noted that the "Society went 'handicraft' and was soon defunct."[115] Not only had Wright broken the spell of British theory over the very large issue of politics and industry, but he created a fracture that would prove to be irreparable.

This break is also evident if we turn to the other center of the American arts and crafts movement – the West Coast. In San Francisco in the 1890s the movement could claim the circle around Bernard Maybeck (1862–1957), which included Willis Polk (1867–1924), A. C. Schweinfurth (1864–1900), the talented Ernest Coxhead (1863–1933), and John Galen Howard (1864–1931). When Maybeck arrived in San Francisco in 1890, it was already a booming city of over 300,000, and his timing could not have been better.[116] His German-American father trained him as a wood-carver, but, with very little money, he managed an entry into the Ecole des Beaux-Arts in 1882. Upon returning to New York in 1886 he joined the office of Carrière and Hastings, and it was he who supervised the construction of the extraordinary Ponce de Leon Hotel in Saint Augustine, coordinating the efforts of such designers as Tiffany. When this project was completed in 1888, Maybeck moved west in search of his future, first to Kansas City and then to San Francisco. He eventually found work in the office of A. Page Brown. In 1890 he began a translation of Semper's book on style (never completed), and in 1894 he was hired as an instructor in drawing at the University of California, Berkeley, where he trained, among others, Julia Morgan (1872–1957). Although he is generally known for such larger works as the faculty club at Berkeley (1902) and the First Church of Christ Scientist,

Berkeley (1927–9), it was housing to which his talent was most suited. Maybeck was an eclectic and combined styles in experimental ways. He began his career in the mid-1890s using the shingle style with English overtones but soon melded it with Scandinavian, Swiss, and Japanese elements. His particular strengths were his innovative spatial planning, his use of exposed structural framing, and unpainted (often redwood) timber and paneled surfaces. His interiors were often more Oriental in character than representative of the arts and crafts movement.

Southern California in the late 1890s was home to Irving Gill (1870–1936) and the Greene brothers. Gill, a native of New York, had made his way to Chicago in 1890 and actually worked for a while in the office of Adler and Sullivan under Wright's supervision.[117] In 1893 he moved to San Diego and set up practice. Beginning in 1907, he moved away from the craftsman style and gravitated toward the use of cubic, mission-inspired forms remarkably "modern" in their exploitation of smooth stucco surfaces and chaste simplicity (they lacked roof gables and any type of ornamental detailing). In 1911, in his design for the Banning House in Los Angeles, he experimented with the tilt-slab Aiken precast concrete system, and in 1914–16 he built the Dodge House in West Hollywood, one of the true masterpieces of the early twentieth century. In an essay written in 1916 for *The Craftsman*, Gill forcibly denounces eclecticism and any ornamental embellishment and insists on returning "to the source of all architectural strength – the straight line, the arch, the cube and the circle – and drink from these fountains of Art that gave life to the great men of old."[118] Incorporating native plantings both within courtyards and around the house, Gill further noted:

We should build our house simple, plain and substantial as a boulder, then leave the ornamentation of it to Nature, who will tone it with lichens, chisel it with storms, make it gracious and friendly with vines and flower shadows as she does the stone in the meadow. I believe also that houses should be built more substantially and should be made absolutely sanitary. If the cost of unimportant ornamentation were put into construction, then we would have a more lasting and a more dignified architecture.[119]

The meteoric rise of the Greene brothers at the beginning of the twentieth century is another success story.[120] Charles Henry Greene (1868–1957) and Henry Mather Greene (1870–1954) were born to parents who had moved to Saint Louis in 1869. There they were enrolled in the Manual Training High School, an experimental school run by Washington University. The force behind the school was

the professor of mathematics and applied mechanics, Calvin Milton Woodward, who was also a student of William Morris and a champion of manual training in woodworking, metalworking, and machine-tool design as a way to facilitate spatial reasoning. The two boys thrived, even if their subsequent beaux-arts training at MIT briefly dampened their interest in architecture. In 1893 the two brothers set out for Pasadena to make their mark. They first experimented with the Queen Anne style, the craftsman style, and the shingle style, but by 1902 they were already developing the West Coast version of the bungalow (low, gabled, one-and-a-half-story houses, generally with a front low pitch to the roof over a porch). Enriching their designs with Japanese and Swiss details, the two brothers (around 1907) began to produce a series of masterpieces that scarcely have an equal in American practice, among them the Blacker House (1907–9), the Ford House (1907), and the Gamble House (1908) (Fig. 68). The incomparable detailing of the last combines the craftsman idea with Oriental structural techniques, American timber uses, and the southern California landscape in a way that surely must have appeared incomprehensible to architects who had grown up with the traditional arts and crafts movement. West Coast designers were working with elements almost entirely new to American practice, and here a major center of international modernism was taking formation.

4. Camillo Sitte and Ebenezer Howard

Not unrelated to the domestic reform movements at the close of the nineteenth century were the changing attitudes regarding urban and suburban planning. The century as a whole had witnessed a radical transformation in living conditions brought about by industry, population migrations to urban centers, and the leveling of social classes. The metropolis or metropolitan center begins to make its appearance in the 1850s, and this phenomenon of high-density working and living would by century's end meet with resistance by critics often invoking earlier and simpler times. Efforts were therefore made to tame or humanize the still-expanding urban environments, even to replace them with alternative strategies and modes of living.

London and Paris were the two largest urban centers of the nineteenth century, but the French capital is a better model to examine because of its rapid transformation at the hands of Napoleon III and his city prefect, Georges-Eugène Haussmann (1809–91).[121] The latter assumed office

68. Greene and Greene, Gamble House, Pasadena, 1908. Photograph by author.

on 29 June 1853 and was immediately given a proposed plan for the city drawn by the emperor himself and on which he had penciled in a series of new streets and boulevards. A few of the proposed additions and amendments, like the rue de Rivoli and the reorganization of the area around the central market, had already been started, while others were completely new. Their purpose, in the emperor's mind, was to revamp Paris into a new imperial capital, to renovate its urban fabric and infrastructure (water, sewer), and to facilitate commerce and industry by constructing modern circulation arteries that – not incidentally – would be less vulnerable to the disruptions of mass violence.

Over the next seventeen years Haussmann succeeded on a grand scale. In 1859 he raised the cornice line of streets over 20 meters wide from 17.54 meters to 20 meters, thereby giving these streets greater visual definition. The following year he annexed many of the surrounding suburbs, immediately raising the population of Paris from 1.2 million to 1.6 million inhabitants. Most importantly, he imposed an overall and identifiable (quasi-baroque) urban structure on the city through the creation of broad, tree-lined boulevards; green spaces and public squares; fountains; and a unique cityscape of unified granite curbs, asphalt sidewalks, cobblestone streets, street lamps, protective tree grates, benches, kiosks, and newspaper stalls. The reasons given for the urban restructuring included modernity, health, efficiency, subservience of the individual buildings to the urban structure

or typology of place, and allowance for future expansion. Much of what the visitor to Paris sees today is the urban ambience of the Second Empire metropolis as reconstructed by Napoleon and Haussmann, whose changes for the most part were applauded throughout their tenure. Yet Haussmann's very success led to his dismissal in 1870. Under his design guidelines, the buildings of Paris became more regular and severe, and their individuality began to disappear. Moreover, rapid speculative development contributed to austerity and superficiality in the treatment of facades. Finally, there were as well unexpected costs to all of this activity. For example, the annexation of the suburbs, whose cost was supposed to be covered by the generation of new tax revenues, proved to be far more expensive than anticipated.

Haussman's reshaping of Paris nevertheless influenced urban strategies worldwide. It became studied in the United States around the turn of the century and was one of the inspirations for the Chicago Columbian Exposition of 1893. Soon after the exposition's close, its director of works, Daniel Burnham (1846–1912), began to apply its planning ideals to the city as a whole.[122] First came the master plan for the city of Washington, D.C., which he prepared in 1902 with the assistance of Frederick Olmstead Jr. and George McKim. Although it was essentially a reworking of L'Enfant's original plan for the city, it resurrected and strengthened the idea of a formal mall, which now extended past the Washington Monument into the unclaimed marshland beyond – to what would later become the site of the Lincoln Memorial. It further graced the banks of the Potomac River with additional parks, fields, and sites for future monuments. When President Theodore Roosevelt embraced its ideals, it survived the usually fatal political challenges and was largely implemented.

Burnham's "city beautiful" movement, as it would become known, was one of the most influential movements in American urban history. Burnham followed his plan for Washington with proposals for Cleveland (1903), San Francisco (1905), and Baguio and Manila in the Philippines (1905). The most dramatic and imposing of his proposals, however, was for his beloved Chicago. It included 142 plates (sixty-one drawings) and was published by Burnham and Edward H. Bennett in 1909. He used Grant Park, the site of the exposition, and its shoreline landscaping as the base for a radial plan whose hub was a colossal civic center a few blocks west of the river. The exceedingly tall and slender dome of the civic center and the fixed cornice lines of the surrounding buildings were lessons taken directly from Paris, as the published plan explicitly noted.[123] And even though only a few elements of the proposal were actually realized, Frank Lloyd Wright later credited Burnham for the fact that "Chicago seems to be the only great city in our States to have discovered its own waterfront."[124]

Classical aspirations were not unique to the United States. With the unification of Germany in 1871 and the economic prosperity that ensued, the "science" (*Wissenschaft*) of urban planning likewise prospered under the leadership of Reinhard Baumeister (1833–1917), whose book *Stadterweiterung* (City expansion) first appeared in 1876. Baumeister was a proponent of the modern city, and he stressed the importance of designing for efficient vehicular traffic, zoning, and public hygiene. He was opposed to the universal use of the gridiron plan because of its unsuitability to the medieval layout of so many German cities. He also differed from Haussmann in his preference for curved streets, which he felt had a redeeming aesthetic effect. Building upon Baumeister's theories was Joseph Stübben (1845–1936), who was active in the planning of Aachen, Cologne, and Posen.[125]

Still, the city most influenced by the transformation of Paris was Vienna – a city that until the late 1850s had stood virtually unchanged for seven centuries. The impulse to change was the decision made in 1857 by Emperor Franz Josef (1830–1916) to tear down the city's old ramparts (which had defended the town against Ottoman armies in 1683) and develop the exceedingly broad glacis

separating the "old town" from the rapidly expanding suburbs. The creation of the Ringstrasse in 1859 – the broad, tree-lined boulevard circumventing the city and forming a ring with the Danube – led to one of the largest urban building campaigns of the nineteenth century. Over the course of a single generation, the avenue and adjoining areas were populated with a score of new buildings: a major church, a new university, a parliament, a city hall, an opera house, a theater, and a group of large museums. Seemingly overnight this central European town transformed itself into the most splendid symbol of European modernity. Paris had been the principal model for the plan, and hundreds of speculative apartment buildings with carefully calculated cornice lines were erected to house the new middle-class partakers of modern culture.

Later additions and modifications further strengthened the idea of Vienna as a paradigm of modernity. In 1892–3 an international competition was held to produce another master plan for the still-expanding city. It was won by Otto Wagner, who in his competition report applauded the Parisian solution because "our realism, our traffic, and modern technology imperatively demand the straight line."[126] He lauded the walk from the Place de la Concorde (on a sunny spring day) up the Champs Élysées and beyond. Against the champions of the contrary "painterly" approach to urban planning, he insisted if they "would only open their eyes, they would soon be convinced that the straight, clean, practical street leading us to our destination in the shortest possible time – occasionally interrupted by monumental buildings, appropriately designed squares, beautiful and meaningful perspectives, parks, etc. – is also the most beautiful."[127] His reference to the Champs Élysées was in response to an article that appeared in the *Deutsche Bauzeitung* in 1893, in which Karl Henrici noted that he would much prefer a two-hour "alpine hike" to a stroll of similar duration down a straight avenue lined with poplars.[128]

As a result of his victory, Wagner, in 1894, was appointed architect of Vienna's new Stadtbahn (railway system), for which he would design more than forty stations, bridges, and viaducts. He reiterated his ideas about planning in his manifesto *Modern Architecture* (1896), but the most specific and expansive articulation of his views is contained in his book *Die Großstadt* (The metropolis, 1911), which he prepared for a conference held at Columbia University in 1910.[129] One of the topics under discussion at this meeting was Burnham's proposed plan for Chicago, which mirrored the ideas of Wagner.

Also similar to Wagner's notions were the urban theories of August Endell (1871–1947), whose *Die Schönheit der großen Stadt* (The beauty of the metropolis, 1908) exalts precisely the city's artificiality: the unifying spectacle of its infinitely varied aesthetic experiences against the essentially conservative tendencies of nature and "homeland."[130] Endell's aesthetics owes much to the French realists and impressionists (not to mention the *flâneur* of Baudelaire) who first glorified Haussmann's Paris.[131] He therefore shared none of the anxiety of the sociologist Georg Simmel, for whom the large city's "intensification of nervous stimulation" represented an affront to the natural rhythm of life.[132] Such a position had earlier been staked out by Ferdinand Tönnies in his *Gemeinschaft und Gesellschaft* (Community and society, 1887), which had pitted the "organic" life of the small community against the "imaginary and mechanical" life of the anonymous society.[133] Already a cleft was opening here that was essentially political, although the boundaries were not yet well drawn.

Wagner too met with resistance. His forceful remarks of 1893 against the painterly approach to town planning indicate that one battle was already being enjoined. His antagonist in this instance was Camillo Sitte (1843–1903), whose book *Der Städtebau nach seinen künstlerischen Grundsätzen* (City planning according to its artistic principles) had appeared in 1889.[134]

The son of an architect, Sitte had also received art history training under Rudolf von Eitelberger. He opened an architectural office in Vienna in 1873 but two years later changed his focus when Eitelberger offered him the directorship of a school of applied arts in Salzburg. A decade later he was chosen to head a new school of applied arts in Vienna, and his home soon became an important hub of Viennese intellectual life. Always a prolific writer, he had hardly written a word on city planning prior to his book of 1889, and it was conceived out of his concern with the broader issues of urban modernity. These included the depopulation of streetscapes, the tendency toward greater size and the commensurate lack of scale, and the psychological oppression – "yawning emptiness and oppressive ennui" – induced by the modern metropolis, where such newly diagnosed nervous disorders as "agoraphobia" were becoming evident.[135] Sitte's contention was that in the intuitively formed towns of Europe's past the shapes of streets and plazas were calculated for their visual (hence psychological) impact and that thus the architecture constituted a definitional backdrop. In modern times the situation was exactly the reverse: "Building lots are laid out as regularly shaped closed forms, and what is left over between them becomes street or plaza."[136] Sitte thus proposed "to go to school with Nature and with the old masters also in matters of town planning," and in his book he offered sundry examples of Europe's most successful old plazas and urban squares. What he meant by "painterly" (*malerisch*) was not an accidental grouping of forms with picturesque qualities but rather composed urban panoramas based on scientific laws of perspective. Buildings were not to be freely placed in their context but were to form part of the enclosing wall; plazas should always be spatially enclosed and their centers kept free. One should not copy the irregularities of old times, Sitte argued, but rather learn the lessons of scale and space and the importance of these elements for urban vitality. Endless straight streets are to be disdained because they allow no unified visual impression to emerge.

Sitte's book struck a sympathetic chord in many parts of Germany and indeed across Europe. In 1893 the Belgian Charles Buls published his *L'Esthétique des villes* (The aesthetics of cities), and as mayor of Brussels he set about transforming that city along artistic lines similar to those of Sitte. The books of Sitte and Buls were also very popular in Italy (the source of many of Sitte's examples), where the problem of accommodating the historical texture of cities to the needs of modern transportation was especially acute.[137]

Still another front at this time was being defined by strategies decidedly antiurban at heart, particularly those arising from the popularity of the suburbs. One of the earliest planned communities in America was the suburban town of Riverside, near Chicago, laid out by Frederick Olmstead and Calvert Vaux in 1869. The idea was to provide a series of housing estates surrounding a small commercial center and generous natural park system. The streets were curved and nearly all ended in green vistas. Riverside was connected to Chicago by rail and proved immediately successful as a suburb. It also greatly influenced the character of American suburban development elsewhere – from Forest Hills Gardens, Queens (1909–12), to Lake Forest, Illinois (1914–15).

One of Riverside's more interested visitors was the Englishman Ebenezer Howard (1850–1928), who in 1871 had moved from London to Nebraska with the intention of permanently settling there.[138] When his agrarian endeavor faltered he moved to Chicago to find work as a stenographer, but in 1876 he decided to return to England. During the next two decades, while working in the parliamentary bureaucracy, he put together his ideas on urban planning, drawing upon sources as remote as Edward Bellamy's *Looking*

Backward, 2000–1887, and the Russian geographer Peter Kropotkin. Howard outlined his ideas in *To-morrow: A Peaceful Path to Real Reform* (1898), whose third edition was given the more descriptive title *Garden Cities of To-morrow* (1902).[139]

Howard differed from the many utopian planners before him in his pragmatism. Working within the legal framework of the free enterprise system, he proposed to combine the human incentives of individualism ("a society in which there is fuller and freer opportunity for its members") with a quasi-socialist vision ("a condition of life in which the well-being of the community is safeguarded").[140] The garden city is proffered not as a suburb but as a satellite town: a closed entity consisting of an urban center, housing, industry, and an agricultural belt protecting it from overbuilding. The maximum size of each garden city is fixed at 30,000 inhabitants, and the land is to be municipally owned and leased to individuals. Railways ring the city and connect the individual garden cities to each other and to the larger urban centers. The cities are conceived as autonomously functioning commercial entities under the laws of free trade.

Howard put his ideas into action. In 1899 he formed the Garden City Association, and in 1903 the first garden city, Letchworth, was laid out by Raymond Unwin (1863–1940) and Barry Parker (1867–1947) on a site thirty-five miles north of London.[141] The stock company was unable to purchase the necessary land, hence the town lacked the economic self-sufficiency that was promised and did not initially achieve its intended size. It was nevertheless successful in attracting educated, middle-class residents and spawned many imitations, among them the suburban development of Hamstead Garden in north London. In 1919 Howard teamed up with Louis de Soissons to design Welwyn, the second garden city, and the garden city movement, as we will see, remained very strong throughout the 1920s.

9

EXCURSUS ON A FEW OF THE CONCEPTUAL FOUNDATIONS OF TWENTIETH-CENTURY GERMAN MODERNISM

Throughout much of the twentieth century, histories of modern architecture generally followed the lead of the practitioners of the 1920s, who tended to stress the conceptual "divide" separating the architectural thought of the late nineteenth century from that of the early-twentieth century. The basis for positing such a divide was the belief that "modern" architecture, in particular the so called functional architecture that came into vogue in the 1920s, was the inevitable terminus of Western architectural development, at least as far as its formal language. Early practitioners of modernism were nearly unanimous in stressing their "break" with the past and in rejecting the possibility of returning to historical or stylistic themes in design. The chasm separating the "then" and the "now" was deemed to be unbridgeable.

Architectural theorists in the 1970s and 1980s took a very different view of the matter. Some argued that "history" needed to be reintroduced into design to counter the "loss of meaning" or the inherent limitations of earlier functionalism. They claimed the modern vocabulary of nonhistorical forms had exhausted its artistic possibilities and in the process it had become both tedious and inhuman. The essential "postmodern" idea was to replace this presumed monovalency of form and function with a layered polyvalency of meanings, which in turn would enrich and reinvigorate form.

Historiographic models and teleological expectations also radically changed before and during these two decades. History was no longer perceived as moving in a linear, deterministic fashion toward some final end, and the aesthetic values of modernism were no longer viewed as absolute and final. Moreover, the notion of historical inevitability had

lost its historicist footing. "Narrative" rather than "history" became the operative word, at least within the confines of academic circles. But then again, postmodern theory did not in itself really define a break, or not one as serious as first surmised. The conceptual roots of postmodern thinking extended well back into the century, and many of its ideas (not to mention the reuse of its forms) were drawn from the modernist discourse of the 1920s. This simultaneous display of continuity and presumed conceptual innovation is instructive, because it sheds some light on the earlier conceptual divide that even today in many circles is widely presumed to separate the nineteenth and twentieth centuries. But is such a divide, in fact, ever plausible?

Within the confines of the history of German theory, which is generally credited with having first nurtured an industrially inspired "modern" style at the beginning of the twentieth century, the divide between modern and premodern certainly seemed real. The nonhistorical forms, first proffered under the guise of a factory aesthetic, were formally different from their historicist predecessors. And of course Adolf Loos was publicly condemned in 1909 when he attempted to erect a nearly unadorned commercial and apartment complex next to the baroque extravaganza of the Hofburg Palace. The appearance of a divide became even more vivid in the 1920s as the factory aesthetic of iron, concrete, and glass became applied to buildings of other types. Reading the new architecture simply as forms, Sigfried Giedion could – in 1928 – only trace the lineage of modernism back through the industrial buildings and the engineers of the preceding century; modern "constructors" (formerly called architects) were stripped entirely of a nineteenth-century architectural legacy. Such a historical outlook hardened even more after 1933, with the breakdown of German society and its part in the instigation of the second world war. Among architectural historians, the historiographic response to this human catastrophe was simply to cease all research on Germany history and theory. The German generation of modernists of the early twentieth century, many now residing in exile, thus became ever more regarded as a lonely island of pioneers without a continental imprint or geological history. Efforts to find some kind of token lineage in the arts and crafts aesthetic of William Morris, the rationalism of Viollet-le-Duc, or the forms of art nouveau were from the beginning utterly unconvincing.

But does history or theory – barring a major conflagration – ever operate in such a precipitous fashion with regard to its conceptual underpinnings? Posing this question in another way: How did the idea of a nonhistorical "style" (first explored by Karl Friedrich Schinkel and others near the start of the nineteenth century) arise at the end of the century from the presumed ashes of charred historicism? If we take into account the continuity of architectural thought during the preceding three hundred years (to restrict ourselves to a very discernible line of critical development), the obvious answer is that architecture never moves in such a way. New forms are always supported by ideas (among other things), and the modernism of the early twentieth century, when placed within its larger historical context, simply appears as another phase of an unfolding continuum of ideas regarding what is "modern." Semoiotic theory again supports such a contention. Rather than reading twentieth-century modernism as a final stage of formal decoding or symbolic abstraction, semioticians argue that it is more accurate to view modernism as the substitution of one semantic code for another. Any such substitution therefore has a theoretical basis.

The continuity of Germanic theory is again affirmed when we view the development of some of the key concepts of twentieth-century modernism – all of which have clear nineteenth-century roots. The idea of architectural "space" is a case in point. The first historian to explore the theme in a systematic manner was Karl Schnaase (1798–1875), who in his *Niederländische Briefe* (Netherlandish letters, 1834) treated medieval architecture as the continuous development of the (interior) spatial theme, as a creative answer to the exterior focus of classical architecture. In reflecting on the spatial play of the side aisles within the central nave of the Antwerp Cathedral, Schnaase even cited this subjective experience of space – "a pulsing organic life" –

as the most important factor in the structural evolution and detailing of medieval architecture.[1] In the 1840s the art historian Franz Kugler (1808–58), in his Berlin lectures, identified Renaissance architecture as especially known for its "spatial beauty."[2] Jakob Burchkardt (1818–97) employed the same meaning of the term in *Geschichte der Renaissance in Italien* (History of the Italian Renaissance, 1867), when he characterized Renaissance architecture as the "spatial style" (*Raumstil*) in distinction to the "organic styles" of Greece and Gothic times In his view, spatial motives can be found in Roman, Byzantine, Romanesque and Italian-Gothic architecture, but it is first fully developed as a conscious idea during the Renaissance.[3]

Another starting point for this theme is found in the theory of Gottfried Semper. The spatial motive of the wall "dressing" was central to his four-motive theory, and he defined this motive as "the oldest formal principle in architecture independent of construction and based on the concept of *space*."[4] In volume 2 of his book on style, he explored the spatial motive within the context of masonry vaulting. In his chronology, the idea of space (hollow construction) is first consciously raised to the status of an art in the fourth century B.C. It is advanced by the architects of Alexander the Great and their successors, and "perfected" by the Romans (for whom it expresses the idea of world domination). The Romans, he argued, found the "solution to the problem of how to create from the surrounding rooms themselves the supports and abutments necessary to vault even massive central halls while expending a minimum on material and in labor and surrounding spaces themselves, and with the least expense of material, obtaining the largest possible space."[5] In a lecture given in Zurich in 1869, he returned to the spatial theme, but this time he adds one important qualification. After noting that the Romans had not really advanced "the mighty art of space creation" into "a free self-sufficient idealism," he points out to his audience of architects that in this new spatial art lies "the cosmopolitan future of architecture."[6]

Semper was not alone in theorizing architecture's spatial possibilities. Within a few weeks of his lecture in Zurich, the Berlin architect Richard Lucae published an article entitled "On the Meaning and Power of Space in Architecture."[7] Lucae begins by isolating the elements of the architectural spatial experience, which are form, light, color, and scale. Form produces the aesthetic effect of space, light its character, color alters the specific mood, and scale is "the conscious perception of the spatial relation of our body to our spirit."[8] Lucae then ponders the contrasting spatial experiences of a living room, the hall of a train station, an alpine tunnel, a theater, the Cologne Cathedral, the Roman Pantheon, St. Peter's in Rome, and the Crystal Palace in Sydenham. His impressions of St. Peter's are as follows:

We stroll down the central nave like down an enormous street – involuntarily to the point at which the idea of the whole building resides. We do not stand simultaneously at the beginning and the end of the space, as in the Pantheon. The powerful barrel vaults lead our eyes there, where the half-light around us suddenly withdraws into a supernatural force of light. Surely an inhabitant of the primeval forest, someone who had not heard of Saint Peter or Christianity, would not pause before he arrives under the dome of Michelangelo. Here is a space that seals us off from the profane world of commerce. Here the source of light leads us into a region that shields our eyes from the banality of life.[9]

The Crystal Palace, by contrast, is a "piece of sculpted atmosphere" in which light fills the whole space with a "beautiful naturalness," a "magically poetic form of light."[10] What is fundamental to these differing perceptions, Lucae feels, is that each space is experienced as a psychological whole; what is inessential is the building's style, "which influences the spatial effect only to a very slight extent."[11]

In an address given later that year to the Berlin Association of Architects, Lucae connects the sensations induced by large spaces quite rightfully with the issue of iron, whose potentially large spans he interprets – presaging Giedion's point in the 1920s – as a "general symbol" for "soaring."[12] Like Semper, however, Lucae believes that the full structural development of iron lies somewhere in the future because its novel aesthetics demands a sense of lightness and slight proportions: "A succeeding generation who has grown up with iron construction, just as we have grown up with stone construction, will in many cases have the fully undisturbed sense of beauty that still eludes us today, because our cherished tradition of beauty is seemingly under assault."[13]

The art critic and theorist Conrad Fiedler (1841–95) picked up the theme of space in an essay of 1878. Fiedler had been a great admirer of Semper, and although he felt that Semper's "art-historical erudition" might have inhibited his creative potential as a designer, he was highly appreciative of his theory. In a letter to the sculptor Adolf Hildebrand in 1875, he noted that "I am once again going through his writings and I am astounded again and again by his revelations."[14] Fiedler's astonishment, in fact, led him in 1878 to write a commentary on Semper's book on style, in which he stressed not only the book's "epoch-making" attributes but also the fact that Semper "brings to historical observation and research an uncommonly profound artistic understanding."[15] The theme that Fiedler seizes on in his review is the idea of space, which he now argues is the creative solution to contemporary architecture's excessive concern with historical styles. In his opinion, neither Roman or Gothic forms have much to say to today's architect, but the "simple and formally unelaborated notion of a vaulted enclosure of space" does have something to say. Pointing to the inherent spatial possibilities of the Romanesque style, he notes that "here, by contrast, the idea of enclosing space seems to have been planned in stone from the beginning. It was a matter of expressing the idea of a continuous enclosure by means of a wall and at the same time of elevating the heavy material into a free expression of that idea."[16] Hence, the idea of space is already recognized in 1878 as a way to reduce architecture's dependence on historical content.

The Swiss architect Hans Auer (1847–1906), however, takes another track with two very important essays written in 1881 and 1883. Auer had studied with Semper in Zurich in the 1860s and thus knew his theory in all its nuances. In the first of his essays, "The Influence of Construction on the Development of Architectural Style," Auer points out that while construction should take first priority in any theory of architecture, architecture's most important task is "the creation of spaces."[17] Two years later he greatly expands upon this suggestion in an essay entitled "The Development of Space in Architecture."[18] He begins with a historical review of significant spatial creations, starting with the hypostyle hall at Karnak and concluding with the dome of St. Peter's in Rome. Within this evolutionary process of ever more efficient and more expansive spatial development, he defines the "poetry of space" as the "soul of the building," in the sense that here the human imagination is given artistic free rein. The spatial dimension of a room has a specific practical or functional value, but in works of high culture "the height [of the room] always far exceeds human need, and it is that which affects the soul of someone experiencing it as something pleasant, imposing, uplifting, and overwhelming."[19] In the present age, in which "chaos of artistic concepts" reigns, this process of spatial development becomes even more apparent, as each new train station must be larger than its predecessor. Quite simply, "We live today already in a phase in which a new style is forming under the irresistible influence of a new material that shakes its brazen fist at all traditions of the past – namely, *iron*."[20] Auer's only reservation in this regard was his belief that the large iron trusses that had been thus far employed in train stations had not yet been treated in an artistically satisfactory manner.

The early culmination to this spatial theorizing is found in a lecture given in Leipzig in 1893 by August Schmarsow (1853–1936). His starting point is again Semper's thought, but this time supplemented by the perceptual psychologies of Hermann Lotze and Wilhelm Wundt and the phenomenology of Carl Stumpf.[21] Schmarsow had just landed a professorship at Leipzig University, which he won over his rival Heinrich Wölfflin, and in contrast to Wölfflin's formalism, Schmarsow proposes a "genetic approach" to art history, one that would postulate an aesthetics "from within." If the contrary aesthetics "from without" focuses on the outward aspects of architecture, such as form or style, his approach would consider the psychological side of the artistic experience, that is, how we perceive and interpret the built world. Thus he begins by posing the question of what do such buildings as the Pantheon in Rome have in common with the troglodyte's cave or Semper's Carib hut? The answer, Schmarsow argues, is simply that all are "spatial constructs," a fact that has profound human implication: "Our sense of space and spatial imagination press toward spatial creation; they seek their satisfaction in art. We call this art architecture; in plain words, it is the *creatress of space*."[22]

In saying this, Schmarsow aligns the notion of spatial creation to a primordial human instinct – the instinct to define one's existence or presence in the world. If Auer's spatial imagination had the vertical axis as its primary field of experience, Schmarsow's spatial theory stresses the enclosure of the subject – the experience of one's orientation in space and one's directional movement through it. Moreover, recognition of the importance of space can now be seized on to reinvigorate contemporary architectural practice:

Should not architecture also today, in turning back to the time-honored inner aspect of its creations, once again find its way into the hearts of the general population by becoming the *creatress of space*? It is said that the spirit builds the body in its own image. *The history of architecture is the history of the sense-of-space [Raumgefühl]*, and thus consciously or unconsciously it is a basic constituent in the history of *worldviews*.[23]

What is interesting in Schmarsow's development of this notion – now ready-made as a concept for architectural use – is how he came to his viewpoint. Space, in his theory, is an idea that freely moves among architectural, aesthetic, psychological, and art historical parameters. Also apparent in this process is the increasing psychological nature of the notion. What began in Semper's theory as a vague intimation of a Roman sense of "world domination" becomes in Schmarsow's aesthetics an existential footing for human

self-awareness. And although recent historical studies have placed much emphasis on psychological thinking in the second half of the nineteenth century – chiefly the theories of Jean-Martin Charcot and Sigmund Freud – what is often overlooked is the large body of perceptual and physiological research, which in fact had a more direct and profound effect on architectural theory. Such research is evident elsewhere, but in Germany it includes the psychological investigations of Johann Friedrich Herbart, Robert Zimmermann, Hermann Helmholtz, Gustav Fechner, Hermann Lotze, and Wilhelm Wundt, to name but a few. What is important to note is that collectively this body of theory shifts the focus of architectural theory away from "styles" and toward something more abstract – the architectural experience itself. Historical coding is thereby eroded.

We find such a process of abstraction when we consider the complementary notion of form. The pantheistic revelations of the late nineteenth century regarding form actually have their start in the philosophy of Arthur Schopenhauer. In *The World as Will and Representation* (1819), he attempted to replace the Hegelian "spirit" with the idea of "will," and to this end he ranked the various arts as to their will. In this hierarchy, architecture was the lowest art because it employed physical matter, and gravity was attempting to collapse matter into a pile of rubble. Thus he defined architecture as the ingenious art of countering or subverting this natural will with its structural framework of walls, floors, columns, and arches. In essence, architecture is the dynamic presentation of this conflict between support and load, which conflict indeed might be articulated or highlighted by architecture's structural and ornamental vocabulary.

Schopenhauer developed this theme most extensively in the second edition of his book, which appeared in 1844, but already by that date this conception had found its way into architectural thought: first in the theory of Schinkel, and then as the central theme of Carl Bötticher's *Die Tektonik der Hellenen* (Greek tectonics, 1843–52). For Bötticher, the purpose of each architectural member's art-form (such as the shape of a column capital) is to express symbolically the mechanical functions of its structural dynamic.

A similar viewpoint is found in Semper's study on style. Columns, for Semper, do not passively resist gravity but dynamically counter it with upward energy. In classical architecture the lines of a capital are not idle decorations but symbols expressing elastic resistance and the mediation of tension. As Semper says: "Artistically enlivened, supporting elements become organisms, and frame and roof supports are expressed collectively and purely mechanically: they are the load needed to activate the life inherent in the column. At the same time, the frame and its supports are in themselves variously articulated and seem to be striving and essentially alive in their individual parts."[24]

The development of this theme next passes back to philosophical circles. Semper's friend and colleague in Zurich, Friedrich Theodor Vischer, had already interpreted architecture in this way in *Aesthetik oder Wissenschaft des Schönen* (Aesthetics or the science of the beautiful, 1846–57), in which he defined architecture as a "symbolic art" that bears the task of rhythmically animating forms by infusing "buoyant life" into inert matter. The collective symphony of these effects – architectural lines moving, rising, and falling in space – further defines for Vischer "the whole outer and inner life of nations."[25] In 1866 Vischer revisited the issue in light of Semper's lead and now gives greater emphasis to the importance of symbolism. Repudiating his earlier Hegelian position, according to which symbolism was historically limited to classical times, Vischer now insists that architectural form represents a "higher" symbolic process valid in all stages of conceptual evolution, even the most recent. The psychological impulse underlying this animation of architectural form is the human "unifying and contractive feeling" (*Ineins- und Zusammenfühlung*), that is, the pantheistic impulse to merge with the sensuous world around us.[26]

In 1873 Vischer's son Robert (1847–1933) places these ideas within the broader context of a theory by coining the word *Einfühlung*. The German word literally means "in-feeling," but its closest English equivalent is "empathy." Vischer had been fascinated with recent physiological investigations regarding the processes of human sensation or perception as well as early studies of dream interpretation. What he was seeking was a way to apply these physiological and psychological insights to the subjective experience of art. For instance, in alluding to a book on dream interpretation by Albert Scherner, Vischer notes, "Here it was shown how the body, in responding to certain stimuli in dreams, objectifies itself in spatial forms. Thus it unconsciously projects its own bodily form – and with this also the soul – into the form of the object. From this I derived the notion that I call 'empathy.'"[27]

The English word "empathy" suggests a simple projection of the emotion we may feel toward an object or person, but the German word *Einfühlung* refers to a more thoroughgoing transference of our personal ego, one in which our whole personality to some extent merges with the object.

Essentially, the network of responses that we read into an object of aesthetic contemplation, such as a building, is nothing less than the complex sum of the psychological experiences or richness of content that we at the same time project into the artistic form. The artistic process is thus always self-referential; architecture and its forms define our current and collective psychological state of mind.

The transposition of this notion of in-feeling back into architectural theory takes place in 1886 in the doctoral dissertation of Heinrich Wölfflin, "Prolegomena to a Psychology of Architecture." It opens with the simple question: "How is it possible that architectural forms are able to express an emotion or a mood?"[28] It next lays out the problem in both physiological and psychological terms based on the principle: "Physical forms possess a character only because we ourselves possess a body."[29] Saying this another way, the formal expressions that we read into architecture are nothing other than the vital feelings of our own body – the expression of will; a feeling of balance; a sense of regularity, symmetry, proportion, and rhythm. Or in Kantian terms, "Our own bodily organization is the form through which we apprehend everything physical."[30]

Wölfflin then sets off on his analysis of architecture, which he considers largely by using the now conventional paired concepts of support and load. Little is new in his remarks, except his attempt to interpret building facades as one would read human physiognomies. But he nevertheless takes a much more animate view of architecture than Schopenhauer did, with the result that he defines ornament as "an expression of excessive force-of-form."[31] In his concluding chapter, which deals with history (almost as an afterthought), he comes to the novel realization that a psychology of architecture is less applicable in individual instances but more cogent as a vivid expression of the collective psychology of a particular culture or period of time. With that, he opens a whole new field of investigation to art history, which can now examine every style as a collective and psychological sense of form.

Wölfflin was still viewing the psychology of architectural form in terms of historical styles, and it is within the context of creating a new style that the matter was more often treated in architectural circles around this time. This was, of course, the problem that Semper in 1869 had passed on to the next generation of architects, and many stepped forth with an attempted solution. The Swiss architect Rudolf Redtenbacher (1840–85) first tackles the problem in a series of articles in 1877. In one essay, "The Building Efforts of the Present," Redtenbacher analyses the current prevailing stylistic tendencies by identifying four main groups: the "fanatics" of a single style, the advocates of the Renaissance, the eclectics, and the neutrals. He is as opposed to those stressing the purity of one style as he to those who randomly select elements from every style, which leads him to the conclusion that we must become "more scientific" and "step out of the children's shoes of dilettantism."[32] What this means becomes apparent in another essay, in which he argues that "architecture begins only there where construction and the world of forms become inseparable," that is, construction must first advance to the level of an organism, like the human body, before it can be capable of genuine symbolic expression.[33]

He advances his tectonic theory in two books in the early 1880s, the second of which is entitled the *Die Architektonik der modernen Baukunst* (The architectonics of modern architecture, 1883). Here, in the first installment of his history of tectonic development, Redtenbacher takes square aim at Semper's "dressing" thesis and insists that it is more fruitful "to win architectural motives from the construction."[34] In short, Redtenbacher proposes to mine the tectonic history of the field for lessons on how to reinvigorate underdeveloped formal systems using contemporary building methods. Only an early death cut short what was becoming a Herculean project.

Redtenbacher's tectonic strategy is mirrored on the technological front by the theories of the Cologne architect Georg Heuser, who was a disciple of Semper, Darwin, and the technologist Ernst Kapp. Kapp was the author of *Grundlinien einer Philosophie der Technik* (Outline of a philosophy of technology, 1877), in which he defined the development of human tools and machines as a natural process of "organ projection," hence extensions of the human mind. Heuser, in a long series of articles beginning in 1881, analyzed the formal possibilities of "stable frames" and what he termed the "latticework style" (*Gefachstil*), and he lands on the formal solution of the I-beam for both aesthetic and engineering reasons – around the time the shape was first rolling out of American steel mills.[35] What is even more interesting is the Darwinian framework of his analyses, because he insists that changes in architectural form come about through a process of natural selection.[36] Initially, new materials and techniques are treated in the same way as older materials and technologies, but eventually new variations appear. The more variants that emerge, the more correct will be the designer's solution to the contemporary problem. If the results are unsatisfactory, a process of crossbreeding old and new methods and techniques takes place.

Thus the development of iron as a building material, Heuser argues, is instilling architecture with a new formal life.

The Viennese architect Heinrich von Ferstel, by contrast, saw the solution to the problem of creating a new style as already contained in the theory of Semper, who had "put artistic research on a completely new footing." In a formal address before the Vienna Technische Hochscule in 1880, he challenged his students to step up to the issue of a future style by returning to the study of Semper's writings: "With such a footing it will be easier for the new generation than for the preceding to fulfill the tasks that modern architecture has put forth in the higher sense of artistic design."[37]

Ferstel's Viennese colleague Josef Bayer (1827–1910) had a more specific recipe for solving the problem of a new style. He too was familiar with Semper's theory (he wrote perhaps the best interpretive account of it), although he actually taught literature at the Technische Hochschule. In an 1886 essay, "Modern Architectural Types," Bayer defines style as "a specific way of thinking and a formal manifestation of art deriving from the innermost ground and essence of the age, which can have only *one* prescribed main direction."[38] Today's *Zeitgeist* (spirit of the age), in his view, differs from that of past ages because the "personal impulses" of their styles bore the imprint of monarchical, aristocratic, or religious institutions. Today's art is essentially "social" – that is, society has become predominantly middle-class – and thus today's architecture must reflect this social imprint. The elements of a new style will therefore be found, not in the repository of historical forms, but rather in the "power of the horizontal." What he means by this is that the vertical and hierarchical buildings of the past are giving way in this democratic age to a contextual grouping of urban buildings and that these are to be judged aesthetically not individually but by "the powerfully emphasized rhythms of the masses."[39] A style grows from within, for which reason he proposes a biological metaphor: "That root seems to have long been withering; now, however, the mysterious vital forces press up and the real, true, and essential architectural form of the epoch grows powerful limbs within the traditional masks and draperies of style."[40]

In another essay of the same year, "The Style Crisis of Our Age," Bayer takes his argument one step further. The starting point is a comment Semper made in 1834: that art knows only one master – need, which today has indeed become the master of architecture. But this is not a functionalist formulation for Bayer: "It would be utterly foolish to demand that our architecture produce out of itself a new particular detail of forms – what a textbook might call style."[41] Our treasury of forms, he goes on to argue, is richer than in past ages because we have a greater command of architectural history. But the evening gowns of styles past are today unraveling at the seams: "In the end, gradually and imperceptibly, the new architectural problems are also leading to new formal ideas; and even the *changed rhythm of old forms*, ordered after a new architectural principle of living, has already won a more essential and greater victory."[42] He concludes with an intriguing statement:

I even dare to assert that the kernel-formation of a *modern style* is already here, although we will not perceive its sign if we look at our buildings from the perspective of well-known historical styles. Then only what is different becomes apparent, not what is common to them. What is new is evident in the total attitude that we bring to the design of a building – the organization of its floor plan and our age's particular compositional tasks as such.[43]

Bayer's somewhat old-fashioned Hegelian idealism and its concern with content, as his editor Robert Stiassny noted in 1919, was fundamentally at odds with the "formalism of the Herbartians," and this may also have been its only limitation.[44] Stiassny's judgment bears repeating because he was correct on one very important point. Bayer had come close to solving the problem of a new style but still could not filter out of his thinking the historical residue of styles. A solution to the problem, in fact, would come one year later and be put forth by a Herbartian theorist – Adolf Göller (1846–1902) – a professor of architecture at the Stuttgart Polytechnikum. He provided the solution, in effect, by returning to a consideration of psychological aesthetics and viewing the problem as entirely a formal one.

Göller's breakthrough came in an essay published in 1887, "What Is the Cause of Perpetual Style Change in Architecture?" Göller's bête noire was the artistic theory of Hegel and his aligning of formal beauty with the symbolic (ideal) content of the work of art. Göller insists that representational or idealized content is far less important for architecture than for the arts of painting or sculpture, because architecture, perceptually, is more generally composed of abstract geometrical forms. And if these forms – for analytical purposes – were stripped entirely of their content or historical styles, architecture could be more simply defined as "the art of pure form," whose beauty must then reside in "an inherently pleasurable, meaningless play of lines or of light and shade."[45] With this single sentence, Göller turns the essential corner of the historicist debate – in theory at least.

But Göller does more. From Wundt's psychology he borrows the notion of a cultural "memory image" (*Gedächtnisbild*), which he defines as a psychological residuum or memory of previously viewed forms. Some mental images are found pleasing, others are not, and the mental work that we do in forming the memory image, Göller argues, is the unconscious reason for the pleasure or displeasure that we feel in regarding a form. An individual's (and by extension a culture's) sense-of-form is thus dependent on past memory images. Eventually these existing images become complete or jaded, requiring no further mental work for their perception. The pleasure of the form then diminishes, and at this point artists begin to vary the form, producing a baroque phase, as it were, for each artistic style. When this phase runs its course and all forms become jaded, a new and simplified "pure form" is posited, initiating a new stylistic phase. It is the dialectical drama of these two moments – jading and the search for a new memory image – that is the psychological cause for style change in architecture.

Göller's larger study of 1888, *Die Entstehung der architektonischen Stilformen* (The origin of architectural style-forms), employs this framework, but the aim is now to glean the recurring laws of stylistic development. This is a different focus from Semper's earlier stylistic investigation, as Michael Podro has noted: "But where Semper's focus had been on the origin of architectural forms, on re-understanding them, Göller's concern is different. He is interested in the underlying motivation for transforming earlier devices and forms and in the nature of the mind's satisfaction in such transformation."[46]

Göller begins his study by disposing of Bötticher's general theory, which assigned a superior value to the Greek and Gothic styles because of their logically consistent principles. Göller argues in a relativistic way that because a culture's sense-of-form is essentially conditioned by existing memory images, notions of "good" or "bad" forms – the superiority of one period's sense-of-form over another – are aesthetically irrelevant. Göller, for instance, claims that the Roman adaptation of the Greek entablature molding to the archivolt of the arch (a decorative application of a constructional motif) was no "lie," as Bötticher had insisted, but was rather a normal part of the creative process of architectural development.[47] With myriad examples, Göller identifies fourteen ways in which forms come into being or undergo formal change, which he classifies under the general rubrics of transference, transformation, and combination. Perhaps no similarly comprehensive study of architectural form has ever been attempted, and Göller's book in many ways remains instructive.

Where Göller's book truly becomes interesting, however, is in its concluding remarks, for there the architect wrestles with the creation of a new style. His analysis seems almost schizophrenic, because his feelings continually waver back and forth. In essence, he is torn between two realizations. One is that an architectural style, according to his theory, cannot stand still – "there is no pausing!" – and that the changed sense-of-form (indicative of his age) must produce new memory images; the second is that he is unable to imagine just how these new forms will appear. For Göller the present day ultimately has only two viable options: (1) to select among the forms of an existing style or (2) to start with an existing style and carry it into a baroque phase. The reason for this paucity of options is our position in history: The field of invention today is the poorest it has ever been because we know the past too well to lose our formal bias and thus allow a new style to emerge: "our impartial feeling hinders us from singling out individual forms as the basis of a style of our own time – if such a new style would be possible!"[48]

At the same time Göller goes on to consider the progress achieved during his time. The scale of monumental works allows his generation to design beautiful floor plans, like the architects of the Roman and Renaissance eras. The reforms in domestic architecture have made the home a place of comfort and functional satisfaction. Increasing wealth and technical means, the upswing in social life – these are all benefits unknown to the past. And then there are the incredible spans and spaces that iron has afforded. Unfortunately a style of "iron and glass" is out of the question because, as Semper had argued, its forms are too insubstantial. Thus Göller is left with the extraordinary conclusion: "All simple and natural remedies for the production of art-forms have already been used."[49] Knowing this, we can only draw from the repository of the past, noting that "we create with full buckets, and in that lies just the secret of our well-being."[50] In short, Göller's psychological reduction of architecture to purely abstract forms (lines, light and shadow) had solved the architectural problem from the perspective of the 1920s (as Robert Stiassny must have seen), but his immersion in the nuances of stylistic forms did not allow him to see just how revolutionary was his entirely novel solution. But two others contemporary theorists did see it.

One of the first critics to respond to his ideas was Wölfflin, who, as mentioned, was simultaneously struggling with the same problem. In his dissertation (1886), he had focused on the individual's sense-of-form and how it relates to his reading of architecture. Only in the last few pages did he turn to the collective or cultural sense-of-form that Göller was surveying, and here Wölfflin pointed out that "the prevailing attitude and movement" of a people or a nation is reflected in every aspect of its artistic style.

This suggestion becomes the theme of his first book, *Renaissance and Baroque* (1888), in which every period is invested with a vital feeling and every style has its particular mood. In seeking to explain how the Renaissance style transformed itself into the baroque style, he now has to contend with Göller's explanation. In truth, the two men were not far apart in their psychological perspectives, even though their terminology and their construction of the problem were entirely different. Wölfflin wanted to establish the thesis that every style is a product of a particular artistic temper or sense-of-form, but at the same time he rejects the notion that this sense-of-form changes simply with cultural or individual sensibilities or through the psychological process of "jading." His objections to Göller's thesis are three in number: First, Göller separates the problem of form from its temporal or historical context; second, his formal evolution is "purely mechanical" at heart; and third, his solution does not really explain the nature of the Italian baroque.[51] Wölfflin, in a somewhat overly wrought way, regards the baroque artistic temper as something entirely new and not simply a taste that evolved through the tiring of certain Renaissance forms or proportions.

Whatever Wölfflin's rationalization of his differences with Göller in 1888, the point is really moot, because the art historian soon adopts Göller's solution to construct his formalist model of art history. But late in 1887 another review of Göller's theory appeared, one that much more astutely brings the issues into clear focus.[52] The author of this review was the architect and historian Cornelius Gurlitt. And if Wölfflin had found Göller's psychology lacking, Gurlitt saw that Göller had actually laid the basis for a future aesthetics.

Gurlitt was simply astounded with Göller's two books. He begins his review with the comment that there is a gap between theory and practice today, one that has its roots in the theoretical constructs of Schelling and Hegel, especially the belief that the beauty of an artwork necessarily resides in spiritual content. Architecturally, this translates into the principle that a building must represent a function: "Every architect knows how much trouble this demand has caused, how often he has had to create artificial functions because he does not want to do without their 'expression,' how he must often simply deny it in order to satisfy an aesthetic demand, or because a hundred technical and purely aesthetic reasons keep him from it."[53] In short, the complexity of today's architecture, the multiplicity of its purposes, defies such one-to-one representation. The architect is continually rebuked: "This cornice line expresses no purpose – it is ugly! This tower here signifies nothing – it is a reprehensible contraption! This dome does not cover the most important room of a building – it is an artistic lie!"[54]

Göller's psychology, Gurlitt goes on to argue, neatly solves this problem, essentially by overturning the Hegelian footing on which such reasoning is grounded. His "two remarkable books" have shown, first, that there is a beauty of pure form that resides solely in abstract forms, lines, and light and shadow and, second, that there are psychological laws governing a form's changing effectiveness. Moreover, Göller's notion of a "memory image" brings to a conclusion the centuries-long debate that began with the Perrault–Blondel dispute over absolute versus relative beauty.[55] Forms are not beautiful in themselves but are only judged so through our memory image (habits and conventions); the same applies to proportions and to all judgments of whether one style is superior to another. Göller in this way neatly levels the field of art history. Gurlitt, however, faults Göller on one very important point – the latter's belief that these principles of "pure form" apply only to architecture and not to the arts of painting and sculpture. Gurlitt responds in a remarkable concluding statement:

Yet what is important is not only what can be read in Göller's books; a far greater booty will be reserved for the person who logically applies the theory of the beauty of pure form to painting and sculpture – that is, for that person who shows that the world of form, now free of intellectual content, can also greatly impress our sense of beauty in these arts. He will also show by this how proper it was for German art to pass from the content-laden manner of [Peter] Cornelius to realism, or from the world of ideas to that of the sensuously felt form.[56]

Here, in 1888, is the first conceptual formulation of abstract art, written twenty years before abstract art begins to manifest itself in practice – a fitting achievement for an article that also supplies modern architecture with a novel conceptual basis.

10

MODERNISM 1889–1914

I have made the following observation and have announced it to the world: *The Evolution of culture is synonymous with the removal of ornament from objects of daily use.*

Adolf Loos (1908)

1. Otto Wagner

The break with historical forms that had been contemplated in theory for much of the nineteenth century came about largely in the exhilarating years 1889–1912. If we look at the change from the perspective of European theory, the essential tracts defining the new perspective were published between 1896 and 1901. What is as surprising as the suddenness of the transformation of modern architectural thought is the breadth of activity across two continents. The great tower and buildings of the Paris Exposition of 1889 – whose role in fostering an image of "modern life" should not be underestimated – may rightly be viewed as symbols of the new modernity, but this new phase of Western culture was also being driven from below by the widespread desire of architects – now drawing upon the existing theoretical base – to make a fresh start.

Formal innovation was widespread. In 1889 the Catalan architect Antonio Gaudí (1852–1926) was putting the finishing touches on his Palacio Güell in Barcelona. In 1890 Louis Sullivan rushed into the office of his chief draftsman, Frank Lloyd Wright, in Chicago and (with the design of the Wainwright building in hand) proudly announced that he had solved the "skyscraper" problem.[1] In 1892 Victor Horta designed the Hôtel Tassel, the building that is said to have started the fashion of art nouveau. And it was in Vienna in the early 1890s that a middle-aged and successful architect demanded that his art purge itself of its historical past. His name was Otto Wagner (1841–1918).[2]

Up to 1890, Wagner had showed considerable ambition but never any sign of revolutionary intentions. Born in Vienna – three months before Schinkel's death and three years before the birth of the American H. H. Richardson – he briefly attended the Technical University in Vienna and the Bauakademie in Berlin prior to studying at the Vienna Academy of Fine Arts. Upon graduation, Wagner settled into private practice and focused on speculative building projects. Throughout the 1870s and 1880s he was successful at making money, as indicated by the classical luxury of his first villa on Hüttelbergstrasse (1886), but he was evidently unfulfilled as an artist. Over the years he had entered a score of international competitions – for the Vienna Stock Exchange (1863), Berlin Cathedral (1867), Hamburg City Hall (1876), Berlin Reichstags Building (1882), Budapest Parliament (1882), and Amsterdam Stock Exchange (1884) – but had never captured the prize, despite his considerable design and rendering skills.

In 1889, the forty-eight-year-old architect began publishing a monograph of his designs.[3] In its preface he describes his style as "a certain free Renaissance" adapted to local circumstances and modern materials, but he goes on to speak of a "*Nutz-Stil*" (utility style) as the mode of the future. He then mentions the "breakthrough" of French realist painters and concludes with this telling remark: "That such realism in architecture can also bear quite peculiar fruit may be seen by several quite poignant examples, such as the Eiffel Tower, the Kursaal in Ostend, etc. etc. But whereas in such cases there is too much realism, the bulk of our present-day architecture shows too little."[4]

In 1894 Wagner overhauled his career. His first-place showing in the Vienna Master Plan competition was announced in February of that year; in April he was selected as the architect of the city's new rail system, the Stadtbahn. This would provide him with abundant work for the remainder of the decade, but the clincher came in July when Wagner was called to one of the two chairs of architecture at the Vienna Academy of Fine Arts. Traditionally, the two chairs were reserved for architects versed in the Gothic and Renaissance styles. Wagner quickly decided to scrap the Renaissance curriculum in favor of one pledged to defining a new style for modern times. He was the first European professor to make such a pedagogical change.

The announcement of his intentions came in a short but stunning inaugural address given in October 1894. In attendance were the students Josef Hoffmann, Leopold Bauer, and Josef Ludwig as well as the two most talented architects on Wagner's staff, Joseph Maria Olbrich and Max Fabiani. Wagner opened by defending himself as a follower "of a certain *practical trend*," but he then embarked on an assault on the use of historical styles. Architecture, he insisted, must always be a reflection of its time; it must express contemporary living conditions and methods of construction, and for the present this means that architects must embrace the pervading realism of the time: "It will not harm it, nor will any decline of art ensue as a consequence of it; rather it will breathe a new and pulsating life into forms, and in time conquer new fields that today are still devoid of art – for example, that of engineering. Only thus can we speak of a real improvement in art. I would even maintain that we must force ourselves in this way to reach a characteristic style representative of us."[5] Wagner's remarks were greeted by students with resounding applause. A few months later, in the first number of the journal *Der Architekt*, Max Fabiani turned Wagner's speech into a student manifesto by heralding "realism" as the "battle cry" of the Wagner school – a school of architecture that would attend to "the needs of modern life, our century's much expanded constructional knowledge, and the technology of wholly new materials."[6]

Wagner quickly seized this challenge as a cause. Two years later he published *Moderne Architektur: Seinen Schülern ein Führer auf diesem Kunstgebiete* (Modern architecture: A guide for his students to this field of art).[7] The original published version (1896), which would be widely read across Europe, was without pretense, but by the third edition (1902) it had become a beautifully crafted, exquisitely designed manifesto whose leading theses would be highlighted in capital letters. The preface of the first edition sets out this recurring theme:

One idea inspires this book, namely THAT THE BASIS OF TODAY'S PREDOMINANT VIEWS ON ARCHITECTURE MUST BE SHIFTED, AND

WE MUST BECOME FULLY AWARE THAT THE SOLE DEPARTURE POINT FOR OUR ARTISTIC WORK CAN ONLY BE MODERN LIFE.[8]

Wagner follows with chapters on the architect, style, composition, construction, and the practice of art, as well as a conclusion – in a pitch that is unrelenting. If the architect's happy union of idealism and realism is seen as "the crowning glory of modern man," his creations are not always seen that way by the public because of the "completely unintelligible" store of forms that he presents.[9] The chapter on style once again highlights the necessity to be modern:

ALL MODERN CREATIONS MUST CORRESPOND TO THE NEW MATERIALS AND DEMANDS OF THE PRESENT IF THEY ARE TO SUIT MODERN MAN; THEY MUST ILLUSTRATE OUR OWN BETTER, DEMOCRATIC, SELF-CONFIDENT, IDEAL NATURE AND TAKE INTO ACCOUNT MAN'S COLOSSAL TECHNICAL AND SCIENTIFIC ACHIEVEMENTS, AS WELL AS HIS THOROUGHLY PRACTICAL TENDENCY – THAT IS SURELY SELF-EVIDENT![10]

The new style must further express an emotional and intellectual change:

AN ALMOST COMPLETE DECLINE OF THE ROMANTIC, AND AN ALMOST ALL-ENCOMPASSING APPEARANCE OF REASON IN ALL OUR WORKS.[11]

This is so because

THE CLEFT BETWEEN MODERNITY AND THE RENAISSANCE IS ALREADY LARGER THAN THAT BETWEEN THE RENAISSANCE AND ANTIQUITY.[12]

The theoretical heart of Wagner's study is his chapter on construction, in which he sets out his materialist premises. He begins, as many German writers before him, by referring to Semper's four architectural motives, but he interprets these motives not as ideas or techniques but rather as form-shaping elements in their own right, leading him to the postulate that "EVERY ARCHITECTURAL FORM HAS ARISEN IN CONSTRUCTION AND HAS SUCCESSIVELY BECOME AN ART-FORM."[13] He follows with a most revealing criticism of Semper's theory: "It is Semper's undisputed merit to have referred us to this postulate, to be sure in a somewhat exotic way, in his book *Der Stil*. Like Darwin, however, he lacked the courage to complete his theories from above and below and had to make do with a symbolism of construction, instead of naming construction itself as the primitive cell of architecture."[14]

Hence Wagner rightly recognizes that Semper's motives were essentially symbolic or idealistic in nature (from above), whereas for him they should be purely constructional (from below). Wagner was also surely aware that Semper was adamant in insisting that his theory "will have nothing in common with the coarsely materialist view that holds architecture's essence to be nothing but improved construction – illustrated and illuminated statics and mechanics, as it were – or mere materiality."[15] Wagner's theoretical underpinning, which may owe something to Rudolph Redtenbacher, is thus anti-Semperian at heart.

Nevertheless, Wagner's contention is a bold one for 1896, because he is the first architect to offers suggestions on just how art forms might be taken from constructional forms. He identifies two types of building construction: the "Renaissance way of building" and "modern way of building." The former consists of "immense stone blocks" that are hoisted into place and carved on the spot in a lengthy and expensive process. In the latter method, the blocks of stone are replaced by thin exterior panels (a "planar" surface) that can be attached to a backing (to the masonry wall that Vienna's building code demanded) with bronze bolts, which he also calls rosettes. This modern way of building is superior not only in terms of time and money but also because of the fact that "IN THIS WAY A NUMBER OF NEW ARTISTIC MOTIFS WILL EMERGE."[16]

What Wagner is in fact describing in 1896 is the solution he eventually offers in his Postal Savings Bank (designed in 1903), but this building should also be placed within the context of Wagner's overall development. A starting point might be his apartment building of 1889 on Universitätsstrasse, whose formal organization bears a striking resemblance to Sullivan's skyscraper solution for the Wainwright building – except for the fact that it is bearing-wall construction are laden with baroque motifs. In its day, this was referred to as Wagner's "Empire" phase, an allusion to the style of the empire of Napoleon I. The same baroque character is also found in the decorations for the apartment building he built for himself on Rennweg Strasse in the same year. In a proposal for the church in Esseg in 1892, however, Wagner toys with the decorative and extremely slender iron posts and floral capitals that Horta was at the moment popularizing with his Hôtel Tassel. Wagner's designs for the Stadtbahn stations, beginning in 1894, show another evolution, but not one entirely in keeping with his polemics in favor of realism. They are for the most part classically composed and are Spartan in their detailing, but with certain contradictions. At the Nussdorf Dam (1894), for instance, he exposes (as one would expect) the steel trusses and the mechanism that controls the water level in the canal; at the same time he guards each entrance to the bridge with a colossal, copiously maned lion, placed atop baroque pylons. His other buildings of the mid-1890s are also Empire in their composition and decorative treatment, as the younger generation surrounding him was well aware. Fabiani in fact concludes his review of Wagner's inaugural address essentially by excusing Wagner's Empire affectations – for using "a historical style as a basis" – by explaining that it was but a temporary expedient to wean architecture away from more severe rococo abuses.[17]

In any case Wagner made his break from the Empire style in 1898. It can almost be traced to a single drawing for the apartment building at 40 Wienzeile, in which a designer's hand in his office seemed to have erased the Empire decorations of the first version of the facade and replaced them with Secessionist majolica tiles of an abstract floral design. A subtler and yet more profound break in his style is found in Wagner's 1898 proposal for a Capuchin church in Vienna, which was to serve as a crypt for the recently deceased Empress Elisabeth and other members of the Habsburg dynasty. Here he intended to sheathe the building in the thin granite panels that he describes in *Moderne Architektur*. He also proposed – in addition to a plethora of bronze statuary – to offset the light-colored granite panels with the dark bronze and the copper coping of the dome. Wagner was evidently being influenced by the color sensibilities of his friend Gustav Klimt.

This granite panel system is also the solution that Wagner proposed (in many variations) in his competition designs for the Fran Josef-Stadtmuseum (City Museum), beginning in 1900. But it was in the Postal Savings Bank design of 1903 that Wagner was first given the chance to implement his paneled "modern way of building" in a significant way (Fig. 69). That the manipulated bolt heads supposedly affixing the panels to the masonry backing represent for him one of his "NEW ARTISTIC MOTIFS" is clear from the fact that he wanted to have them gilded in order to be better seen from the Ringstrasse, one block away. Decorative bolt heads also appear everywhere inside the banking hall: from the marble wainscoting and heating vents to the slender steel columns penetrating the diaphanous membrane of the luminous ceiling. Outside, the legion of trumpeting and wreath-bearing angels (as originally proposed) is reduced to a lonely two – summoning the first triumph of Wagner's vision of modernity. For Semper, the wreath signified the conceptual starting point for art.

69. Otto Wagner, Postal Office Savings Bank, Vienna, 1903–12. From *Der Architekt*, vol. 12 (1906).

2. Realism and *Sachlichkeit*

Wagner's repeated invocation of "realism" in his manifestos of the 1890s was not something new to German theory, for the term in fact supplies the conceptual framework to which this phase of German modernism is tethered. The term, of course, goes back to the movement in French painting of the 1850s and 1860s, and briefly it was a term applied to the work of Viollet-le-Duc. In French architectural circles the term also reappeared in the 1870s and 1880s in the writings of Paul Sédille (1836–1900), the architect of the celebrated Printemps department store in Paris (1881–5).[18]

In Germany in the 1880s and 1890s the term "realism" was bandied about, and there were realist movements in German literature and painting. The novels of Adalbert Stiftner and Gottfried Keller were characterized as realist in their choice of subject matter. Among the German painters who pursued parallel themes to those in France were Adolf Menzel, Wilhelm Leibl, and Max Liebermann.

Architecturally, the term "realism" is first found in the 1860s in Germany, in the writings of Semper. The term frequently occurs in the second volume of *Der Stil*, where it becomes a synonym (and not always a positive one) for material honesty, structural display, and the straightforward expression of constructional motives. Thus one of Semper's early biographers, the Saxon architect Constantine Lipsius (1832–94), could praise his theory in 1880 for placing "the main accent on the symbolic" and for the "realist sense" with which he approached certain constructional and material issues.[19] Four years later Friedrich Pecht raised the issue in a broader context in his essay "German Art Since the Appearance of the Realist Movement." Pecht saw German realism as naturally evolving from the ascendancy of science (at the expense of religion) and the unification of Germany, which presaged for him a weaning of German art away from French models. To define the new tendency, however, he returns to Semper's definition of style: "If Semper defined style superbly as 'the accord of an art object with its genesis, and with all the preconditions and circumstances of its becoming,' there can be no question that today's realist period of art has developed a greater sense of style than all of its predecessors."[20]

By the middle of the 1880s the term became almost commonplace in German artistic literature – just as it was disappearing in France. Conrad Fiedler had even employed the concept earlier, although under his preferred term of "naturalism," a word often used interchangeably with "realism" at this time.[21] Gurlitt, as we have seen, invoked the concept in 1888 at the end of his review of Göller's book, and his use of the word was similar to Fiedler's and Pecht's. And in 1889 the Berlin architect Albert Hofmann wrote a rave review of the buildings at the Paris Exposition for the *Deutsche Bauzeitung* in which he underscored both the French realist legacy and the parallel German literary and architectural movements. Hofmann – citing the literary critics Heinrich and Julius Hart – claimed that realism was "thoroughly modern," and represented the "innermost spirit of the century."[22] One year later, K. E. O. Fritsch, the editor of the *Deutsche Bauzeitung*, wrote a lengthy summary of German architectural development in the nineteenth century solely in terms of the displacement of "idealism" by "realism." Not only does Fritsch argue that realism has clearly won the day, but he anoints Semper as "the leader of this healthy, genuine realist movement."[23] In a rejoinder later that year, Georg Heuser agreed with Fritsch's analysis but preferred to trace the phenomenon of realism not to Semper's theory but rather to Bötticher's address of 1846.[24]

Thus Wagner's embrace of realism in the 1890s was an easy acceptance of a well-defined movement that had many followers by this date. And it is only fitting that the most discerning review of *Moderne Architektur* evaluates its polemics entirely within the context of the realist movement. Its author was Richard Streiter (1864–1912), one of the least known yet most important theorists of this period.

The Franconian Streiter had pursued his architectural studies at the Technical University in Munich and worked for six years in the Berlin office of Paul Wallot, the architect of the much admired Reichstag building (German parliament). Streiter prepared a lavish graphic presentation of the building before leaving Wallot in 1894 to pursue a doctorate at the University of Munich. His expanding interests were now centered on the aesthetics of "Empathy-theory" as it was developing and taught by the noted psychologist Theodor Lipps. In 1896 Streiter completed his studies with a dissertation on the theory of Karl Bötticher – whose tectonic ideas, he argued, had now been superceded by the rise of psychological aesthetics.[25]

Streiter begins his review by noting that Wagner's "extremely progressive program" has created a "sensation" within the architectural circles of Austria and Germany and that it was therefore worthy of a serious and extended response. His informed, ninety-six-page review of nearly every issue raised in German theory over the past century was just that. In writing about Wagner's chapter on style, for instance, he looks at the debate on style as far back as K. F. Schinkel and Heinrich Hübsch and concludes by considering the recent contributions of Karl Neumann and Adolf Göller.[26] And whereas he is sympathetic to Wagner's insistence on a "modern style," he is at the same time cautious in accepting Wagner's metaphorical equation of style with a formal language. A more proper basis for the new style, for Streiter, is the realist plea for "truth," but here again with certain qualifications.

It is at this point that Streiter provides a history of the realist movement and neatly places the issues on the table. In architectural theory he sees the impulse for realism originating in the eighteenth century (beginning with Jean-Louis de Cordemoy), but he is disappointed with the recent turn realism has taken in painting and literature, where it has lapsed into "a fantastic idealism, symbolism, and mysticism, into a colorful musical cult of the passions."[27] In noting this "mannerism, affectation, thoughtless 'profundity,' dilettantish arrogance," he is of course alluding to the recent stirrings of the Jugendstil movement in Germany. And whereas the general trend of art nouveau was often described by early historians as transitional between historicism and modernism, Streiter more correctly sees it for what it really was – an epiphenomenon emanating from realist currents.

This point made, Streiter names Wagner as the leader of one school of architectural realism – what Streiter terms "tectonic" realism, which overall is a positive development: "For if ever a time, more than any other, were ready to accept the first principle of artistic truth, conciseness, and *Sachlichkeit* in architecture and the applied arts – the perfect fulfillment of purpose with the simplest means – it is ours."[28] Our age, he continues, invoking psychological aesthetics, has grown accustomed to this new "structural-technical *Sachlichkeit*," and our sense of form has been influenced by it. The extraordinary increase in the means of transportation has moreover thrown out any restraining ballast; modern technology and altered living conditions have affected our "corporeal self" and led to a "specific modern way of conceiving tectonic tasks."[29]

But this does not mean that Streiter accepts Wagner's notion of tectonic realism. Streiter's rejection of this notion becomes very clear when he turns to the chapter on "Construction" and considers in detail the thesis that art forms must arise out of construction. Streiter begins by pointing out Wagner's purposeful distortion of Semper's theory and Wagner's aversion to any "symbolism of construction." Streiter claims that Wagner is unclear on the issue: "How else could he blame Semper for clinging to a 'symbolism of construction,' when it is precisely this symbolism that allows the art-form to come out of construction."[30] Constructional forms in themselves simply will not do, Streiter insists. And he also points out a fundamental inconsistency between Wagner's theory and his practice:

Nowhere does one find that Wagner conceives the relation of construction and art-form any differently than his modern architectural colleagues have become accustomed to conceiving it; in fact, it can even be asserted that a number of English, French, American, and German architects take far greater account of the principle – the architect always has to develop the art-form out of the construction – than Wagner does himself.[31]

Again, Streiter is not pleased with Wagner's juxtaposition of the "Renaissance way of building" with the "modern way of building," especially if this means applying smooth granite panels. He asks, "But should not the art-forms of ashlars be different (more rusticated) than the art-forms of a panel cladding?"[32]

Streiter is opposed to Wagner's tectonic realism because he himself has a different interpretation of architectural realism, which he defined in 1896 in this way:

Realism in architecture is the most extensive consideration of the real conditions in the creation of a building and the most perfect fulfillment of the requirements of functionality, comfort, health – in a word, *Sachlichkeit*. But this is not all. Just as poetic realism considers the relation of the characters to their milieu, so architectural realism sees the principal goal of artistic truthfulness in developing the character of a building based not only on its purpose, but also on its milieu, local building materials, the landscape, and the historic characteristics of the region.[33]

His definition of realism is thus summarized in the notion of *Sachlichkeit*. In English, *Sachlichkeit* has often been translated in an architectural sense as "objectivity," but for Streiter it means "the most perfect fulfillment" of purpose with the simplest means, that is, the simplest, most practical solution to a problem.[34] And here is the basis of his difference with Wagner's tectonic realism – not its *sachliche* attributes but the fact that a strict "tectonic" architecture (architecture interpreted simply as construction)

is inherently limited in artistic expression. A purely practical architecture does not take into account the milieu, local building materials, landscape, or history of the region. In Streiter's 1896 essay he was in fact writing about the regional Bavarian style of Gabriel von Seidl. What also should be noted is that within German theory the term *Sachlichkeit* would replace the term *Realismus* (realism) over the next few years, while carrying the very same meaning.[35]

In addressing the issue of how the new "realist" style will arise, Streiter turns to the conceptual innovations of psychological aesthetics and explains the formalism of Heinrich Wölfflin and the spatial theory of August Schmarsow. He ultimately sides with the former, if only for the reason that he sees the new style as being driven from below: "The sense of form that should introduce a uniform feeling into the future architecture will therefore have to start with the making of individual forms and decorations."[36] And to fortify his case that there is an inherent aesthetic need to advance beyond mere tectonic or constructional form, Streiter cites the surprising example of the Chicago Columbian Exposition of 1893: "The well-worn, festive, and luxurious robe of classical architecture everywhere covered the thin iron skeleton of the gigantic hall; the exposition stands as the most shining example of the inexhaustible vitality of antique architectural forms, as the most persuasive admission of the impossibility of approaching the same artistic effect with modern construction."[37]

Streiter was not alone in espousing a regional interpretation of realism in the mid-1890s. Close to his view was Alfred Lichtwark (1852–1914), the director of the Hamburg Kunsthalle.[38] In addition to transforming his museum into a major learning center for modern art, Lichtwark was active with the association Pan (the group also published a journal by this name) as well as the nationalist causes of the Dürerband (founded in 1902 as an artistic advisory group) and the Bund Heimatschutz (founded in 1904 to advance German culture) – both important forerunners of the German Werkbund. In 1896 Lichtwark prepared an essay entitled "Realistiche Architektur" (Realist architecture) for *Pan*, but he withdrew it, as the editor later noted, to allow Streiter's essay on realism to appear. The following year Lichtwark published a revised version of the essay – which now focused on Alfred Messel's Berlin department store and equated the Christmas Eve opening with the long-awaited arrival of architectural realism in Germany: "And no doubt even the layperson has had the feeling that a new architectural organism has arisen, whose serenity and strength expresses the intention to create a realist architecture, and when he has later considered it in relation to other buildings, he may for the first time become aware that architecture is not merely columns, beams, and ornament."[39] Lichtwark went on to define realism, which he felt already had a generation of development in the other arts, as the modern solution to the twin scourges of academicism (historical styles) and romanticism (art nouveau and Jugendstil).

Lichtwark pursued the same theme in a series of essays appearing over the next two years, which he published in 1899 as *Palastfenster und Flügeltür* (Palace window and double door). Central to his architectural conception is the notion of *bürgerliche* design. *Bürgerliche* is generally translated as "middle-class," although it connotes plainness, honesty, and unpretentiousness. Lichtwark insisted that convenient building interiors should be the centerpiece of design; exteriors too should have simple masses, though set off by areas of local color – for example, plain brick walls accented by brightly painted shutters, flower boxes, and window frames. Interestingly, when Lichtwark republished his essay "Realistiche Architektur" in his anthology of writings in 1899, he changed its title to "Sachliche Baukunst" (Practical building-art), following Streiter in his preference for the new term.[40]

Also on the side of Streiter and Lichtwark in the late 1890s was the architect Fritz Schumacher (1869–1947), who saw the impulse of realism as something that was regenerating architecture from below.[41] Schumacher was born in Bremen but raised in the South American country of Columbia and in New York City. He studied architecture in the early 1890s in Berlin and Munich before taking a job with Gabriel von Seidl. Through the support of Theodor Fischer, he obtained a position in the municipal office of Leipzig in 1896, and during his tenure there he established many intellectual contacts and began to write. In 1901 Gurlitt lured Schumacher to Dresden to become a professor at that city's technical university. In 1906 – supported by Fried Naumann, Karl Schmidt, and Hermann Muthesius – Schumacher organized the successful Dresden Applied Arts Exhibition, and in the following year he gave the keynote address at the founding meeting of the German Werkbund in Munich. In 1909 he became the municipal architect of Hamburg, where he, together with Fritz Höger and Hans Poelzig, practiced a northern German style that combined the local brick and indigenous forms with the modern necessities of functional planning.

While still a student in Munich, Schumacher had become enthusiastic about the realist movement, which he viewed as "a reaction to the false world of historical and so-cietal illusions."[42] His most important early essay appeared in 1898 under the title "Style and Fashion," in which he reviewed the trends of recent years. The "historical style-carousel" that had rapidly run through the Renaissance, baroque, rococo, and Empire revivals, he felt, had abruptly ended with the "wake-up call" of the 1890s. In its place came the spirit of realism, but also the new "fashion" (disguising itself as a style) of art nouveau, emanating from the ateliers of Paris and Brussels. Instead of imitating these fashions, Schumacher calls for "organic new creations":

what can unite and hopefully will serve as a common bond may be a certain commonality of taste. And perhaps it possesses nothing more than the artistic recognition that the basis for solving tasks resides in the nature of practical purpose, in the nature of the material, in the nature of the organic world of form, in the nature of qualities of the vernacular. As different as the individual cases may appear, this could then be described as the achievement of an epoch of *realist* architecture.[43]

Still another prominent realist of the 1890s was Julius Lessing, the long-time director of the Applied Arts Museum in Berlin. Lessing had long supported Semper's ideas, and in the 1890s he emerged as one of the most sanguine voices in support of Wagner's call for realism. His important essay "New Paths" (1895) actually precedes Wagner's book and may have influenced the architect. Lessing begins by summarizing the reform movement in the German applied arts over the past thirty years and then describes naturalism as a way to wean the arts away from historicism. But far more important in the forging of this new viewpoint, he insists, should be the Semperian triad of purpose, material, and technique. He then poses two related questions: "Is it conceivable that instead of a gradual withdrawal from the historical tradition, these technical factors themselves will create completely new forms? Can we consider the recently invented, purely constructional form of a modern steel girder to be a creation similar to the Greek columns, whose hallowed form has ruled all periods of art up until today"?[44] He boldly answers, "Certainly we can and we must."[45] And after reiterating Dohme's analogy of architecture with ships and modern vehicles (now the third person to do so), Lessing draws a line from the Crystal Palace to the skyscrapers of Chicago and to the Paris Exposition of 1889. Do not fear the machine, he says in conclusion:

Like it or not, our work has to be based on the soil of the practical life of our time; it has to create those forms that correspond to our needs, our technology, and our materials. If we fashion in this a form of beauty in the manner of our scientific age, it will resemble neither the pious beauty of the Gothic nor the opulence of the Renaissance but will perhaps appear like the somewhat austere beauty of the late nineteenth century – and that is all anyone can ask of us.[46]

Semper, Lipsius, Pecht, Heuser, Gurlitt, Albert Hofmann, Wagner, Streiter, Lichtwark, Schumacher, Lessing – the adherents of architectural realism and *Sachlichkeit* had become by the 1890s the predominant school within German architectural theory.

3. Endell and van de Velde

And it is only by looking at the realist movement that one can understand the ideological complexity of the Jugendstil, Secession, and art nouveau movements of the second half of the 1890s. Art nouveau in France, for instance, was prompted in part by baroque and Oriental influences, but with the success of Henry van de Velde after 1895 it would take on another face. Two intellectual forces behind the Vienna Secession of 1898 were Joseph Olbrich and Joseph Hoffmann, both of whom were working in Wagner's office. In Berlin the Jugendstil movement was centered around the journal *Pan* (founded in 1895), but this journal also published articles by the realists Streiter and Lichtwark. And the start of the Jugendstil phase in the decorative arts is generally assigned to the 1896 exhibit of textiles by Hermann Obrist (1863–1927). By this date Richard Riemerschmid (1868–1957) was already designing furniture, which he displayed at the international exhibition held at Munich's Glaspalast in 1897.[47] Also exhibiting at this event were Bernard Pankok, Bruno Paul, Otto Eckmann, Peter Behrens, and August Endell. It was the last of these men, however, who would best translate the principles of the Jugendstil design into architectural terms.[48]

Endell, in fact, underscores just how misleading the appellation *Jugendstil* can be when applied across the board to art and architecture in the 1890s. The son of a Berlin architect, he first studied at the University of Tübingen before switching to the University of Munich in 1892, where he took courses in psychology, physiology, philosophy, and art history. He next pursued a doctorate under Theodor Lipps and was a doctoral candidate alongside Richard Streiter. In 1896 Endell met Obrist and – inspired by his work – turned his attention to the decorative arts. In a review of the Munich Exhibition of 1896, "On Beauty," Endell urged artists to become more emotional (empathetic) and less intellectual in

the pursuit of art.[49] His architectural theory was presented in two papers published early in 1898.

In the first of these, "Possibility and Goal of a New Architecture," Endell opposes current tectonic and realist tendencies and defends his position by highlighting the importance of psychological empathy. "The demand to be purposeful provides only the skeleton of the building," and beyond this requirement there is a range of aesthetic feelings that need to be addressed.[50] The architect should therefore work more generally with form and color, because "a cultivated, refined sense-of-form is the basic precondition of all architectural creation; it cannot be intellectually learned."[51] Echoing the formalism of Wölfflin, Göller, and Gurlitt, he notes, "The architect must be a form-artist; only the art of pure form leads the way to a new architecture."[52] This new art of pure form, he feels, is scarcely known at present.

In another essay of 1898, Endell further sets out his ideas. The essay is built around a single illustration of four fenestrated elevations – which, as Nikolaus Pevsner noted, are "misdatable" and "astonishingly similar" to German housing designs of the 1920s (Fig. 70).[53] Endell's intention is to demonstrate how a range of different empathetic emotions can be suggested simply by altering the shapes of window openings and mullions. The openings of Figure 2 display "tension and rapid tempo," he claims, whereas the openings of Figure 3 have "little tension and a slow tempo."[54] This example points to an interesting aspect of Endell's analytical efforts, namely, his penchant for analyzing forms abstractly and not in the naturalistic manner of so many of his Jugendstil contemporaries. He was seeking to develop a psychology of form that is concerned only with shapes, colors, proportions, and spatial relationships. What was lacking throughout his career, however, was the capacity to translate his theory into practice in a compelling way.

By the turn of the century Endell's efforts were overtaken by those of the Belgian Henry van de Velde (1863–1957), another figure of complexity and one of the most successful artists of this period.[55] Belgium itself had long been an important center for the new art. The journal *L'Art Moderne* had been founded in 1881, and three years later it began to clamor for an "art nouveau."[56] In 1883 twenty avant-garde painters seeking to exhibit their works formed Les Vingt, certainly the first secession of its kind. Over the next ten years their exhibitions stood in the forefront of the European art world by displaying the work of such contemporary artists as Georges Seurat, Paul Gauguin, and Walter Crane; at the same time the organization became increasingly radical in its promotion of socialism and anarchy, ultimately leading to its dissolution in 1893.

Van de Velde, a native of Antwerp, joined Les Vingt in 1888, shortly from returning to Belgium after his second stay in Paris. As a painter he was much influenced by Vincent van Gogh as well as by Seurat, but around 1890 he became disaffected with the elitism of painting and turned toward the decorative arts. He entered an embroidery in the Les Vingt exhibition of 1892, and in the same year he became aware of the English arts and crafts movement and William Morris. In 1893 he began teaching at the Antwerp Academy, structuring his class along the lines of the English model. In various lectures and essays over the next couple of years, he decried the division between the arts as symptomatic of larger social or class divisions and thus came to see artistic reform in terms of a larger ethical and social cause.[57]

In 1895, however, van de Velde switched his attention to furniture design and architecture, when he began work on his "cottage" in Uccle, near Brussels. In this somewhat rustic house built of stone, brick, wood, and plaster, van de Velde made his first attempt at integrating architecture, nature, and the decorative arts. Even before the house was finished, Siegfried Bing and Julius Meier-Graefe visited it to examine its interiors. Bing subsequently invited van de Velde to Paris to design three rooms for his new shop, Maison de l'Art Nouveau, which opened late in 1895. Many reviews of van de Velde's work also appeared in Germany, where he designed an interior for the Dresden Exhibition of 1897. Two years later van de Velde – now heralded by Meier-Graefe as a "genius"[58] – moved to Berlin and established a successful practice that gravitated more and more toward architecture.

Van de Velde made his design theories known through a series of writings published shortly after he moved to Germany. In the first of these, *Die Renaissance im modernen Kunstgewerbe* (The renaissance in the modern applied arts, 1901), he recounts the history of the new movement, which conveniently originates in Bing's shop in Paris. The ideas of Ruskin, Morris, and Crane were fundamental to laying the groundwork for the new movement, as were the writings of Viollet-le-Duc. But even more interestingly, he locates the new movement within the trajectory of realism and naturalism, which both redirected attention to such primitive qualities as color, line, and form and desymbolized art, thereby breaking its historical connections to the past. In van de Velde's words, "Realism and naturalism mean for the artist a rediscovery of and return to life."[59]

Also essential to his theory is his notion of the "new ornament," which he defines entirely in realist terms: "I have wanted to create a form of ornament that allows the willful artistic imagination no more free rein than is permitted to the engineer for the design of a locomotive, an iron bridge, or a hall."[60] He is obviously not referring to applied ornament, but rather to a harmony and balance of lines and colors intrinsic to the objects themselves: "Our modern buildings have no other meaning than their purpose. Our train stations, our steamboats, our bridges, our iron towers have no secret meaning."[61]

In another essay published shortly thereafter, van de Velde claims that a new style needs but two principles: reason and its offspring – logic. Again he points to the works of engineers (locomotives, bridges, glass halls) and the importance of these structures as models for the new modernity. "The engineer," he writes, "stands at the beginning of the new style and the principle of logic serves as his basis."[62] Architectural beauty is defined quite simply as "the perfect accord of the means with the purpose," and van de Velde further cites the perceptual theories of Chevreul and Helmholtz as another spur to the new style.[63] This returns him to the issue of empathy and its importance for the new art: "A line is a force that, like all elementary forces, is active. When several lines are brought together they react in the same way as several elementary forces. This fact is crucial; it is the basis of the new system of ornament but it is not its only principle."[64] Van de Velde is actually arguing that lines receive their energy through the empathetic transference of the energy expended by the eye during the perceptual process. The designer's role is to bring these potentially sympathetic lines into harmony; in effect, he is a conductor of functional, active, abstract forms.

Van de Velde continues to develop these ideas down through the first decade of the new century. What becomes difficult is to square his rationalist, empathetic theory with the flamboyance of his personal style. There is, in fact, a major shift in his design approach from the smoking room of the Maison de l'Art Nouveau (1895) or the shop for the Havana Company in Berlin (1899) to the much more subdued and neutral interiors of the Folkwang-Museum, Hagen (1901). By 1904 – with his designs for the Applied Art Museum in Weimar and the theater in Weimar – he has left behind all suggestion of a historical style and placed architecture totally on an abstract footing. At the same time his penchant for curvilinear or organic lines does not accord with the logic he found so compelling in iron towers, bridges, and large exhibition halls. Many of his contemporaries indeed perceived this lack of consistency and faulted him for it. Julius Meier-Graefe, one of van de Velde's most

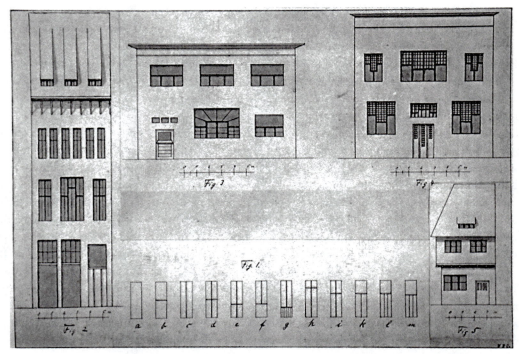

70. August Endell, illustration from "Formenschönheit und dekorative Kunst," *Dekorative Kunst*, vol. 2 (1898).

vocal supporters in the late 1890s, put his finger on van de Velde's problem in his 1901 review of the Alfred Walter Heymel apartment in Munich, designed by Alexander Schröder. He found these interiors appealing precisely because they lack the "Belgian line." That is,

Here we see that it does not require infinitely profound art or much of a 'modernism *à tout prix*' to create a suitable milieu, as the prestige of most of the leading artists of our movement would like us to believe. Without exception all of them could learn a lot from this simple solution, especially the best of the modern principles – that one cannot use too little art in order to be an artist.[65]

Van de Velde's problem was that he first achieved fame as an art nouveau designer and that after 1901, once the architectural ground again had shifted, he found it difficult to live his reputation down.

4. Olbrich, Hoffmann, and Loos

The split between van de Velde's rationalist theory and his practice is also evident in Vienna around the turn of the century. If Wagner's espousal of tectonic realism had supplied one theoretical framework for architecture's break with its

historical past, there were other variations on this theme. Indeed the cleft between theory and practice that occurs in Wagner's work around 1896 underscores the difficulty in finding the appropriate bridge between realism and art. And the fact that this was the period of the Vienna Secession – and Wagner's own Secessionist phase – further complicates the issue. Earlier biographies of Wagner tended to see the Secession as largely driving the changes in his ideas on design, but in fact the argument can more easily be made that his contacts with the Secession hindered rather than advanced his thinking.

The Vienna Secession was born of an administrative dispute overlaid with personalities, and in this respect it differs from parallel movements. Beginning in 1861, commissions in the fine arts for all state-financed projects in Vienna were approved by the Genossenschaft bildender Künstler Wiens (Vienna Artists Society). By the early 1890s divisions within the organization were already evident. State-sanctioned agencies tend to be conservative by nature and favor more established artists and styles. When Viennese artists such as Hermann Bahr and Gustav Klimt began to change their styles in line with European developments, and when younger artists already aligned with these movements demanded more rapid change, a clash over the direction of the Genossenschaft became inevitable. It took the form of an administrative coup in April 1897, when Klimt organized the Veneinigung bildender Künstler Österreichs (Austian Association of Artists). Klimt intended it to be a subgroup within the Genossenschaft, but unsympathetic reactions from the established society led to a formal break in May.

Wagner was in the middle of the controversy and leaned both ways. On the one hand, he had been awarded numerous commissions over the years through his association with the Genossenschaft, and at the time of the split he was serving on an important committee within the organization. On the other hand, his artistic sympathy for change fell in line with the new developments. Wagner did in fact join the Secession in 1899, but it was a move that he seems to have soon regretted because it only added fuel to the controversy over his design for the City Museum. Any talk of a "Secession style" for Wagner is thus difficult, even though his proposal for a new academy of fine arts in 1897 can be counted among the most baroque of all the Secessionist fantasies. In fact, the Secessionist decorations that Wagner applied to such works as his apartment buildings on the Wienziele are almost certainly the work of his younger staff. Only when Wagner succeeded in peeling away this artistic "tattooing" – as Adolf Loos would soon refer to it – did this architect move on to the more rational forms of his later years.

A similar dichotomy is also evident in the work of two of Wagner's younger colleagues, Joseph Maria Olbrich (1867–1907) and Joseph Hoffmann (1870–1956). Olbrich attended the Academy of Fine Art but studied under Wagner's predecessor, Carl Hasenauer.[66] Equally important was Olbrich's earlier decorative training at the applied arts school in Vienna headed by Camillo Sitte. Olbrich returned from his tour of the South in 1894 and joined Wagner's office, where he remained for four years, primarily assisting in the Stadtbahn buildings. He assimilated the master's style, more so than anyone else, as his early competition designs of these years demonstrate. And his great success with the Secession building itself (1898) – probably the most widely publicized building on the Continent in the 1890s – deservedly has been called Wagnerian for its combination of a relatively straightforward presentation of a gallery and the high (gilded) claims of idealism. Olbrich himself saw its slightly battered cubic forms not as representative of a new modern style but rather as a primeval and timeless temple to art in which "I only wanted to hear the sound of my own sensation, to see my warm feeling ossified in cold walls."[67]

His youthful enthusiasm and quasi-mystical exuberance at the same time left him without a rationale to ground his own sense of design. His work over the next few years was mainly limited to interior decoration (in the worse sense of this term), as he followed the leads from Uccle, Paris, Munich, and Glasgow. His several rooms at the Paris Exposition of 1900 were perhaps the most ornate of all the ones on display – naturalistic and exceedingly overbearing. When he failed to obtain the teaching position that Wagner sought for him in Vienna, he accepted the invitation of Grand Duke Ernst Ludwig in 1899 to join the artist colony at Darmstadt, where in the final years of his short life he pursued his cultic fantasies to their mystical ends. From the perspective of theory, his designs had already become irrelevant around the time the "unknown" prophet descended the steps of his Ernst Ludwig House in 1901 to receive the crystalline form, inaugurating the opening of the colony. The Darmstadt experiment, with its monkish pageantry, would prove to be short-lived, as would the Nietzschean idolatry that Olbrich shared with van de Velde. None of this disputes Olbrich's great talent and his widespread influence up to the time of his death in 1907.

Hoffmann never took matters to such an extreme, but in other respects he also became an ill-formed stepchild of the Secession.[68] He won the gold medal at the Academy of Fine Arts in 1895 and toured the South, joining Wagner's office after his return. His rooms for the Paris Exposition of 1900, in their artistic pretense and visual gaudiness, rivaled those of Olbrich, but within a few years his style abruptly simplified itself, in line with developments elsewhere. In 1903 he joined Kolomon Moser and Fritz Wärndorfer to found the Vienna Werkstätte (workshops), yet another attempt to create an arts and crafts guild like those in Britain. But it also had some notable differences in its underlying conception – first and foremost its firm commitment, at least at the beginning, to the new aesthetics of modernity (planar surfaces and clean lines).

It was also in 1903 that Hoffmann received the commission for the building that would arguably be his finest architectural achievement, the Purkersdorf Sanatorium.[69] The sanatorium itself was the idea of the famed psychiatrists Richard von Krafft-Ebing and Anton Löw, who were developing innovative treatments for "nervous disorders." Hoffmann responded with a Wagnerian design – following fast on the heels of the Postal Office Savings Bank – that in some respects excelled the achievement of his mentor. The flat roofs and cubic purity of the graduated rectangular building greatly appealed to twentieth-century historians for its "modernism," but the work possesses a creative spirit and attention to detail that almost transcends this appellation.

The leitmotif of the design is "hygiene," another issue emphasized in Wagner's *Moderne Architektur*. It was a rural treatment center for patients who were suffering from various forms of neuroses and whose remedies included sunlight, fresh air, and various hydrotherapies, including hydroelectric therapy. The groupings of windows on the main facade bear an almost eerie resemblance to one of the facade studies drawn a few years earlier by Endell, but this is almost certainly a coincidence. What Hoffmann achieves at Purkersdorf is what one critic at the time referred to as a "*sachliche* matter-of-factness": a practical, well-lit (by electricity), rational, and hygienic design, above all a design imbued with the spirit of modernity.[70] Unfortunately, it was one of the last successes in Hoffmann's lengthy career. His design for the Palais Stoclet in Brussels (1905–11) lacks the compelling architectural logic and forms of Purkersdorf, and by the second decade of the century Hoffmann had lapsed into what might be called a pilaster style: heavy, bulky, squat forms capped with large roofs.

The transformation in Hoffmann's work around 1903 may owe something to the intense café discussions he had with his Moravian compatriot and later antagonist Adolf Loos (1870–1933).[71] As an architect, Loos's importance around 1900 is tenuous at best; as a polemicist and critic, his significance is without question. Loos was born in Brno, a city in the present-day Czech Republic. He was educated at a state college in Bohemia and at the technical school in Dresden (1890–3). This is important for two reasons: first, he could not have escaped the Semperian legacy in Dresden; second, the fact that he did not attend the Vienna Academy of Fine Arts precluded him from higher state appointments in the bureaucracy of the Habsburg Empire. He was thus destined to remain an "outsider" in Vienna. Meanwhile, came three years in the United States, where Loos visited an uncle in Philadelphia and worked odd jobs in New York City, Saint Louis, and Chicago, the site of the Columbian Exposition of 1893. Though he later exploited the United States and the Whitmanesque notion of "democracy" to his polemical advantage, it is difficult to assess the architectural impact of his stay abroad. Yet when he returned to live in Vienna in 1896, he did so with a critical edge far sharper than that of his colleagues.

His life in Vienna was not initially easy. He first gravitated toward the circle of the Secessionists, and in 1898 he even published two articles in their journal *Ver Sacrum*. In one of these, "Potemkin City," he sarcastically equated the historicist architecture of the Ringstrasse with the canvas-and-pasteboard villages supposedly erected by Grigori Potemkin in the Crimea to dupe the visiting Empress Catherine. Already evident in this essay is the sardonic, sometimes caustic wit that would endear Loos around this time to fellow Moravian critic Karl Kraus, who in April 1899 would start his satirical journal *Die Fackel*. Loos's falling out with the Secession, and especially with Hoffmann (supposedly over the latter's refusal to allow Loos to exhibit at the Secession building), occurred sometime before this date. Toward the end of 1898, Loos published the first of several critical reviews of Hoffmann's work, in which he announced his "strongest opposition to that direction," noting, "For me tradition is everything, for me the free rule of the imagination is secondary."[72] In another essay of 1898, entitled "The Old and New Direction in Architecture," Loos reveals more of himself by claiming that the future architect must be – in this order – a classicist, a modern man, and a gentleman.[73]

In the spring and summer of 1898, Loos was engaged by Vienna's main newspaper, the *Neue Freie Presse*, to write reviews of the Vienna Jubilee Exhibition. His articles were sharp, controversial, and above all funny, as he took the occasion to vent his scorn for the Secession, art nouveau, and Austrian culture in general. The newspaper reviews cover a range of topics: from men's fashions to furniture, vehicles, and underclothes. Philosophical tangents are the norm. In his article on indoor plumbing, he launches a diatribe on the bathing habits of Austrians (or lack thereof) and urges the state to raise the standards of cleanliness: "For only that nation that approaches the English in water usage can keep pace with them economically; only that nation that exceeds the English in water usage is chosen to overtake them in world dominance."[74] His article on footwear leads him to this observation: that "Nations with a more highly developed culture walk more quickly than those that are still backward." In an article on building materials, he notes that the English export their wallpaper to Austria: "Unfortunately they cannot send over entire houses as well."[75] And in his review of women's fashions, the opening images of lustful desires, tormented men and women, and cracking whips – and, yes, the Marquis de Sade – actually serve as a prelude to a plea for a woman's right to wear pants and to have equal economic opportunity.[76]

Another literary masterpiece of these early years is his tirade "The Poor Little Rich Man" (1900), in which he expands his attack on the Secession to include the art nouveau of van de Velde.[77] It is the story of a man who has everything – that is, everything until a friend alerts him to his lack of attention to "art." He then hires an architect to redesign the interiors of his home, and the architect co-ordinates all items – walls, rugs, furniture, and clothing – down to the placement of the matchbox on the coffee table. When his wife and children present him with birthday gifts, he is temporarily elated, but then the architect appears and is appalled to find the client wearing slippers designed for the bedroom in the living area. Needless to say, the architect will not allow him to keep his gifts – art has now made his life unhappy yet "complete."

The apogee of Loos's satirical pontificating was surely the founding of his own newspaper in 1903 (only two is-sues appeared), sardonically entitled *Das Andere: Ein Blatt zur Einführung abendländischer Kulture in Österreich* (The other: A paper for the introduction of Western culture into Austria) (Fig. 71).[78] It seems the bad table manners of a countryman had convinced him of the necessity to launch an organ that had a regular column on etiquette. He promised in future issues to address such pressing con-cerns as how feasts should be celebrated, the proper protocol for social calls, and the correct wording of invitations. This confluence of the architect and critic is reminiscent of the fact that in the original (French) version of Samuel Beckett's *Waiting for Godot*, Estragon silences Vladimir in their esca-lating exchanges of grievous insults by summoning the word *architecte*. In Beckett's English translation of this play, the word is rendered as "critic."

Loos was able to write so much in his early years because his practice was small. One of his first commissions was an interior for the Goldman & Salatsch clothing store (1898), which is notable for its absence of Secessionist character and for the simple use of cut glass, fine woods, and brass fittings. Another early success was his interior scheme for the Café Museum (1899), appropriately located near the Secession building. The exterior was reduced to bare white stucco, and the interior to white walls with mahogany wainscoting, brass strips (electrical conduits), suspended lighting fixtures, mirrors, and Thornet chairs. Its lack of decoration quickly earned it the appellation "Café Nihilismus," and it became a favorite haunt of writers and artists.

Loos's many apartment interiors of the first decade of the new century vary in quality and are for the most part unre-markable. Perhaps the most intriguing is the design for the Villa Karma (1904–06), which he built for the psychiatrist Theodor Beer on the shoreline of Lake Geneva. The stark, white-stucco simplicity of the exterior, replete with a classi-cal porch at the entrance supported on four Doric columns, ran afoul of local building officials but somehow managed to be built. The vividly polychrome interiors – composed of a palette of variegated marbles, gold mosaics, and exquisitely detailed wood paneling – stand in open conflict with the image of Loos as an anti-ornamentalist. The overall design is pregnant with private fantasies and a sense of mystery. Loos did not finish the building, but this may have been due in part to a "sexual offence" on the part of Beer that caused him to flee the country suddenly.

If the Villa Karma is the most visually alluring of his early works, the so-called Looshaus in Vienna (1909–10) is cer-tainly the most famous, as few architects have been dignified by a building popularly renamed after themselves. Part of the controversy surrounding this building is due to its loca-tion on an important urban plaza outside a baroque gateway of the Hofburg Palace. Part is also due to the subterfuge with which the building was pushed past the code officials and city council.[79] The owners of the building (the clothing firm Goldman & Salatsch) invited Loos to participate in a closed competition in the summer of 1909, but Loos de-clined. He was nevertheless given the commission but had to collaborate with the architect Ernst Epstein (who in fact signed the documents). Loos worked up the plan but Epstein apparently prepared the first historicist facade drawings of March 1910, on the basis of which the building permit was issued. Three months later Loos modified the design so that it displayed horizontal, meanderlike bands throughout the four stories of flats above. All went well until the scaffolds and canvas cover came down in September, revealing the plain white stucco finish of the upper stories. The municipal council held a meeting later that month, and dozens of angry citizens stepped forth to condemn the outrage. People also flocked to the site to inspect the building (still without its marble paneling below). Loos asked for time and was given until June of the following year to come up with a new facade design. Loos and Epstein, however, waited until May 1910 to announce a competition for the new design. This design never materialized, but in July Loos offered to add flower boxes to the walls. The council refused the offer, but Loos went ahead and placed five of them on the building with-out permission, just before suffering a nervous breakdown. The matter continued to simmer, and at a meeting of the council in December over two thousand interested citizens attended to hear the proceedings. Three months later the council decided to accept the fait accompli, pending addi-tional flower boxes. Loos had by now become an interna-tional celebrity – to the near financial ruin of his clients.

In a late essay in defense of his design, Loos said that while some might still debate the building's merits, no one could call it provincial; in his preference for a "traditional way

DAS ANDERE

EIN BLATT ZUR EINFUEHRUNG ABENDLAENDISCHER KULTUR IN OESTERREICH: GESCHRIEBEN VON ADOLF LOOS   I. JAHR

TAILORS AND OUTFITTERS
GOLDMAN & SALATSCH

K. U. K. HOF-
LIEFERANTEN
K. BAYER. HOF-
LIEFERANTEN

KAMMER-
LIEFERANTEN
Sr. k. u. k. Hoheit des
Herrn Erzherzog Josef
etc. etc.

WIEN, I. GRABEN 20.

HALM & GOLDMANN
ANTIQUARIATS-BUCHHANDLUNG
für Wissenschaft, Kunst und Literatur
WIEN, I. BABENBERGERSTRASSE 5

Großes Lager von wertvollen Werken aus allen
Wissenschaften.

Einrichtung von belletristischen und Volksbiblio-
theken.

Ankauf von ganzen Bibliotheken und einzeln n
Werken aus allen Zweigen des Wissens.

Übernahme von Bücher- und Autographen-
auktionen unter kulantesten Bedingungen.

COXIN das neue Mittel zur Entwicklung
photographischer Platten, Rollfilms
ohne DUNKELKAMMER
bei Tages- oder künstlichem Licht ist in allen
einschlägigen Geschäften zu haben.

COXIN ist kein gefärbter Entwickler. — COXIN
erfordert keinerlei neue Apparate und kann immer
benutzt werden.

COXIN-EXPORTGESELLSCHAFT
Wien, VII/2, Breitegasse 3.

71. Adolf Loos, title page from first issue of *Das Andere: Ein Blatt zur Einfuehrung abendlaendischer Kultur in Oesterreich* (1903).

of building," he had sought to design "a building that can only stand in a metropolis."[80] The city of Vienna, however, received a complex and finely detailed building. The first two levels, used by Goldman & Salatsch, are sheathed in Cipolin marble, which Loos obtained on a trip to Euboea (Greece). These two levels are sharply differentiated from the four apartment levels above as well as from the copper-roofed, skylit attic. The most prominent feature of the main facade – the four columns with a strong entasis – actually have no structural value; to demonstrate this fact (in almost fiendish fashion) Loos slightly shifts them off the rhythm of the window openings above so that the two outer columns

fall into the window openings. This formal atonality also allows him wider bay windows above.

There is always subtlety in the architectural logic of Loos. As an essayist he is certainly best known for his polemic "Ornament and Crime," which was written in 1908 and first read in Vienna in January 1910.[81] The impulse for the work seems to have been an exhibition of the decorative arts held in Vienna in 1908, for which Hoffmann designed the temporary exhibition spaces. Beneath the sour humor of the piece is a serious argument, though oversimplified in places. Loos is not equating ornament with crime; he allows the cobbler the joy of creating traditional scallops on his shoes. But he does reject the use of ornament on objects of everyday use and denies it to those who attend a symphony by Beethoven. The lack of ornament for these individuals is "a sign of intellectual power." That is, in the current stage of cultural evolution, the time and money formerly exhausted on stylized decorations ("Where will Olbrich's work be ten years from now?") are redirected to higher quality objects and the general prosperity of the state.[82] Ornament is thus equated with economic stagnation: "Woe betide the nation that remains behind in its cultural development. The English become richer and we become poorer."[83]

But this does not mean that architecture lacks an aesthetic dimension. Already in an essay of 1898 devoted (of all things) to Semper's principle of "dressing," Loos very subtlety redefines Semper's thesis. If the (inherently ornamental) manufacture of the dressing actually precedes the structural framework devised to support it, he argues, the distinction between dressing and support allows us to distinguish between "*some* architects" and "*the* architect." The former simply erect walls and then look around for an appropriate dressing; the latter views things quite differently: "The artist, *the architect*, first senses the effect he wishes to produce and then envisions the space he wishes to create. The effect he wishes to bring to bear on the beholder – be it fear or horror in a prison, reverence in a church, respect for the power of the state in a government bureau, piety in a tomb, a sense of homeyness in a dwelling, gaiety in a tavern – this effect is evoked by the material and the form."[84]

In a lecture given in Berlin in the fall of 1910, in the midst of the controversy over the Looshaus, Loos returns to this idea – the primacy of emotional "effect" over tectonic design – by affirming the architect's purpose as that of awakening sentiments: "It is therefore the task of the architect to define exactly the sentiment. The room must evoke a warm feeling, the house must be pleasant to live in. The judicial building must appear as a threatening gesture to secret vice. The bank must say: here your money is secured and well protected by honest people."[85] The passage evolves from his distinction between the making of a house and the making of art. The latter is a private affair, autonomous, distracting to the viewer, and revolutionary – in a word, provocative. The former is social, purposeful, comfortable to the user, and conservative – or more simply, evocative. Thus the walls of one's house have to appeal to one's innermost feelings and sense of comfort: "Man loves everything that serves his comfort. He hates everything that wants to shake him from his safe and secure position and trouble him. And thus he loves his house and hates art."[86]

Accepting Loos at his word we can see that Semper's principle of dressing serves not only as the (nineteenth-century) theoretical underpinning of his emotive conception of architecture but also as a convenient theoretical base for his anti-ornamental crusade. If Loos regarded Hoffmann's and Olbrich's empathetic "tattooing" as a form of maudlin sentimentality (akin to the scrawl on a bathroom stall), it was because such "erotic" outbursts were no longer suited to modern sensibilities. In their place, he would substitute a more refined (and no less sentimental) form of ornamentation – the primacy of the dressing materials themselves. Citing just those used in his interior designs during these years, these include variegated and costly materials ranging from brass and copper, gold mosaics, floor tiles, painted glass, decorative plaster, wallpaper, expensive wood paneling, and above all an array of highly chromatic marble dressings, all exquisitely detailed to maximize their effects. Hoffmann and Olbrich sought to impose high art from above on the crafts; Loos limited his craftsmanship to the dressing. Loos, the son of a stone mason, knew how to cut his marble dressings (with the veining patterns at the joints carefully considered) thinner than other architects of his time knew how to cut them. They could have been paper thin for his purposes, for they were preeminently ornamental dressings – smooth and planar, yet with costly and durable patterns.

Of course, all of these colorful sartorial effects relate only to the interior of a house, where the urban inhabitant is free to remove the social mask and be himself. The exterior, as Loos noted in this essay, must be as inconspicuous as the well-tailored black frock coat – preferably cashmere, classically styled, and with black, not brass, buttons.

5. Berlage and Wright

By 1900 this new image of modernity was beginning to take shape in every European country. In Holland, modernism during this period is more or less synonymous with Hendrik Petrus Berlage (1856–1934).[87] Although he was fifteen years younger than his friend and colleague in Vienna, Berlage shares many affinities with Wagner, not least of which was a similar architectural education and an almost parallel path of theoretical development.

Berlage was born in Amsterdam, but after some preliminary training in art he chose to pursue architectural studies in Zurich, beginning in 1875. The decision was important because even though Semper had departed the city for Vienna in 1871, the Semper program was still intact and was being taught by his students Julius Stadler and Georg Lasius. Berlage returned to Holland in 1881 and formed a partnership with Theodor Sanders, but the first years of his practice were uneventful. Like Wagner, he practiced a "certain free Renaissance" style with overtones of the Dutch Renaissance. In 1884 his picturesque Renaissance design placed in the top five in the competition for the Amsterdam Exchange, but after a second round (in 1885), the competition became mired in controversy and ended without a result. Berlage's style in the second half of the 1880s drew upon a variety of sources, as did his thinking. The Semperian grounding of his early years was complemented by the influence of Viollet-le-Duc, which emanated from the Gothic circle of P. J. H. Cuypers (1827–1921). Realism became prominent in Holland around 1890, as did the urban theory of Sitte. Through the circle of J. L. M. Lauweriks (1864–1932) and K. F. C. De Bazel (1866–1923), Berlage became acquainted with Oriental philosophies and theosophy. In addition, Berlage studied the proportional geometrical theories of Jan Hessel de Groot and was deeply influenced by Morris's socialism.

By the early 1890s Berlage had melded these influences and begun to develop a personal style that gravitated toward simplification. In an article entitled "Architecture and Impressionism" (1894), he calls for "a simpler architectural concept" that places emphasis on the distribution of masses rather than silhouettes and on simplified lines, moderate detailing, and material and labor economy, in keeping with the societal forces pushing toward social equality.[88] In 1895, with the blessing of local officials, he began to prepare in private his design for the Amsterdam Exchange, which, after the city council gave its secret approval in 1896, would become his first masterpiece. This work – his first attempt to pull away from historicism – in fact precedes Wagner's efforts in Vienna. The forces that had an impact on its creation, however, became apparent only in a series of lectures Berlage gave after its completion.

Berlage by nature was drawn to intellectual matters, and like Semper he had a great distrust for abstract or speculative theory. In an early writing, "Architecture's Place in Modern Aesthetics" (1886), he summarized the ideas of no less than fifteen aestheticians (from Immanuel Kant to Hermann Lotze), only to conclude that "the question of architecture's place within the system of the arts has not been sufficiently answered by the observations of aestheticians."[89] Yet he never surrendered his ambition to understand the course of philosophical and social development. The key texts in

the formation of his mature theory are two lectures he gave in Germany at the start of 1904, published in 1905 under the title *Gedanken über Stil in der Baukunst* (Thoughts on style in architecture).

The socialism that drives his early theory remains very much in evidence. He assigns the "ugliness" of nineteenth-century architecture to the loss of the "ideal," a decline in artistic standards brought on by capitalism and the rise of "personal interests" over social ones. Sham architecture is the result. At one point, he even blames the phenomena of historicism (and in particular the Gothic and Renaissance movements) on the sudden increase of capital brought about by industrialization.[90] But the nineteenth century, he notes, also gave us the two apostles of truth: Viollet-le-Duc and Semper. If the former defined the doctrine of structural truth, Semper was one of those great spirits who "as Heine says, 'nod to each other over the centuries.'"[91] He laid down the metaphysical principle that nature creates her myriad forms with the simplest means and with a consistent underlying logic. From this principle, Berlage derives the ideas of repose, unity, and order (geometry), which he argues will be the attributes of the new style.

Two other passages in Berlage's discussion illuminate his practice. In the first, he refers to Semper's discussion of the "seam" (*die Naht*) and its etymological relation to the German word for "necessity" (*die Not*) and his transformation of the axiom of "making a virtue out of necessity" into "making a virtue out of the seam." Berlage then makes the observation (similar to Wagner's exploitation of the "constructional motif"): "You artists should exploit, therefore, the various constructional difficulties as decorative motifs."[92] One can readily see Berlage's own decorative treatment of the seam in the main hall of the Amsterdam Exchange, where the capital imposts and bases of the granite columns flatten into the plane of the lower segmented arch (a seamless seam), where the alternating piers gently corbel out to receive the steel trusses supported on a simple pin joint, and where the upper plane of the wall again bevels out to define its termination with the ceiling (Fig. 72). Semper's figurative mask becomes for Berlage a literal mask, in which the wall patterns, materials, and structural components represent, as it were, their own constructional and nonconstructional roles as surface decorations.

In the second passage, attached as an addendum, Berlage defines architecture as "the art of spatial enclosure."[93] He is the first architect to make such a statement since Hans Auer, and it is likely – given his interest in aesthetics – that he was familiar with Schmarsow's writings. Berlage also knew

Semper well, and it is the latter whom he cites with regard to the dressing (textile) thesis, from which he draws a lesson similar to that regarding the seam: "Following the basic principle, the wall decorations should stay on the plane, that is to say, sunk into the wall, and sculptural elements should ultimately form ornamental wall components."[94]

Berlage presents his theory more fully in four lectures given in Zurich in 1908, published as *Die Grundlagen und Entwicklung der Architektur* (Foundations and development of architecture). Much of the text has to do with his geometrical theory of proportions and with his denunciation of historicism, but toward the end of the work he returns to Semper, who he considers in conjunction with Hermann Muthesius. From these two sources Berlage derives three principles for the new art: (1) Geometry should be the basis of architectural design, (2) motifs from earlier styles should be avoided, and (3) forms should be developed in "the most simple, *sachlich* way."[95] He is aware of the general meaning of the term *Sachlichkeit*, but he endows it with further nuance. *Sachlichkeit*, for Berlage, means "a renewed awareness that architecture is the art of spatial enclosure," it means care in the placement of "pictorial decorations," it means a "naked wall in all its smooth and simple beauty," it means the elimination of all decorative and material excesses, and it means a "natural simplicity and clarity."[96] And it has as well a social dimension:

The *sachliche*, rational, and therefore clear construction can become the basis of the new art, but only when this principle has penetrated deeply enough and been applied widely enough will we stand at the door of a new art. And at the same moment the new, universal spirit – the social equality of all men – will be revealed, a spirit whose ideas are located not in the beyond but here on earth, confronting all of us.[97]

Berlage's theoretical formulation becomes all the more interesting because he, like Wagner before him, reached his conceptualization of modernism prior to his arrival at a fully *sachliche* practice – which properly begins with his design for the Holland House in London (1914–16) and the St. Hubertus Hunting Lodge (1914–20). Halfway in between the Zurich lectures and these two designs, in 1911, he made a trip to the United States, where he was moved by the work of Frank Lloyd Wright. Only afterwards do words like "three-dimensional" and "plastic" enter his vocabulary.[98]

It was in part through Berlage's impressions that Wright's architecture came to have such a powerful effect on Dutch architecture, and Wright in his prewar practice was in turn influenced by developments abroad. But from the perspective of design innovations, no European paralleled Wright's achievements in the first decade of the twentieth century.[99] Wright of course arrived at the solution for his "Prairie House" around 1900, and with it an almost mature understanding of his goals and design philosophy. In his second address of that year to the Architectural League of Chicago – given eight months before his famous Hull House lecture – he vigorously objected to the "archaeological dry bones" of his day and pleaded for a regeneration of architecture, which, incidentally, "does not lie in the hands of classicists or fashion mongers of the East or the West."[100] There is already a confidence and high moralism to his tone, and one cannot help but read in his messianic idealism the healthy spirit of Emerson, Whitman, and Sullivan. "The architect," he warns the students in his audience, "primarily should have something of his own to say or keep silent. There are more legitimate fields of action for him than the field of architecture."[101] As for his mission, its scope is vast: "Elevated railway systems and freight stations, manufactories, grain elevators and office buildings, the housing of highly organized industries, monumental in power and significance, stripped and trained to the bone for action. The housing of a people – nervous, intellectual, receptive, and progressive."[102] Again: "Life is preparing the stuff to satisfy the coming demand, and the architect will know the capacities of modern methods, processes, and machines and become their master. He will sense the significance to his Art of the new materials that are his, of which steel is but one."[103]

Another of these new materials was concrete, the aesthetic properties of which Wright first seems to have become interested in as early as 1894, with his design for a "Monolith Bank," where concrete walls were relieved only by the formed decorative panels sandwiching the piers of the clerestory windows. He did not publish this project until 1901, the same year that he explored concrete's plastic potential in his sculptural display for the Universal Portland Cement Company at the Pan-American Exposition. He introduced precast concrete parts into the Larkin Building, designed in 1902, but his first important essay with the new material is Unity Temple in Oak Park, the design for which was started in 1905. It would be hard to overstate both the importance of this building for his career and the technical difficulties of its execution. The reason for these difficulties was not that reinforced concrete was such a new material but that it had never before been treated (exposed) in such a way. The creation of a monochrome surface over broad wall areas without discolorations, cracks, and pour lines

72. Hendrik Berlage, Amsterdam Exchange, 1897–1903. Pin-joint detail. Photo by author.

and with a pleasing visual texture had never before been attempted.[104] His ingenious solution (on a tiny budget) led him to propose his "Fireproof House for $5,000" (1907) and his spectacular design for a twenty-two story skyscraper in San Francisco (1912). In his understanding of the material's possibilities, Wright was many years in advance of his contemporaries.

Wright is better known in the first years of the new century for his residential designs. The horizontal layering of forms and the pinwheel plans of his prairie style first occur in his designs for the Heller House (1897) and the Husser House (1899), but the prairie style itself bursts forth in 1900 with his designs for the Bradley House and the Hickox House. His progress from this point forward was simply astounding, as in quick succession he designed the Willits House, Oak Park (1902–3); the Dana House, Springfield (1903–4); the Cheney House, Oak Park (1903–4); the Martin House,

Buffalo (1904); the Coonley House, Riverside (1907–12); and the Robie House, Chicago (1908–11). The first definitive statement of his thinking was the 1908 essay he wrote for the *Architectural Record*, which this journal published along with eighty-seven illustrations of his work.

"In the Cause of Architecture" is, however, more suggestive in its content than informative in its details. It begins with his Emersonian respect for "Nature" and "a sense of the organic," which is loosely characterized as "a knowledge of the relations of form and function."[105] In a later essay with the same title, he defines organic architecture as "an architecture that *develops* from within outward in harmony with the conditions of its being, as distinguished from one that is *applied* from without."[106] This definition is crucial to his broader philosophical outlook, although here he only intimates his beliefs. In describing the "New School of the Middle West," he chooses rather to enumerate six principles for the prairie house. The first principle – the principle of "Simplicity and Repose" – finds a parallel in Berlage's lectures of a few years earlier, but Wright elaborates upon it with design preferences, such as employing as few rooms as possible, making the openings integral with the structure, limiting detailing, and incorporating wall pictures into the wall itself. In discussing the principle that "a building should appear to grow easily from the site," he speaks in favor of gently sloping roofs, low proportions, quiet skylines, low terraces, and sequestered private gardens formed by outreaching walls, all important innovations of his in landscape theory. Other principles – that one should employ natural colors and display the nature of the materials, for example – are integral to his thinking, but he cuts short his discussion of these and other ideas to dwell on such topics as his problems with contractors. Only toward the end of the essay does he get to the issue at hand:

As for the future – the work shall grow more truly simple; more expressive with fewer lines, fewer forms; more articulate with less labor, more plastic; more fluent, although more coherent; more organic. It shall grow not only to fit more perfectly the methods and processes that are called upon to produce it, but shall further find whatever is lovely or of good repute in method or process, and idealize it with the cleanest, most virile stroke I can imagine.[107]

These words are not so much prophetic as they are suggestive of the confidence likely to be felt by a forty-one-year-old architect at what would normally be the early zenith of his creative powers. Wright's personal life, however, was at a point of crisis. In 1908 he was visited in his Oak Park studio by Kuno Francke, a professor at Harvard, who pointed out that although his work was little appreciated in the United States, the German public was ready for it; therefore, Wright should consider moving his office abroad.[108] Shortly thereafter Wright received a letter from the Berlin publisher Wasmuth offering to publish a monograph of his work. This invitation dovetailed nicely with his failing marriage and his affair with Mamah Cheney (one of his former clients), and in June 1909 Wright quit Chicago and joined Cheney on a romantic interlude in Berlin and Fiesole, where Wright prepared the drawings for the book. The monograph, at least, would prove to be a stunning success and catapult Wright to international fame, while the adultery, which was widely publicized in American newspapers, would gain for Wright unwelcome notoriety at home. The monograph becomes even more important for the essay Wright wrote for the occasion of its publication.

Perhaps the most interesting thing about this essay – which again echoes the spirit of Emerson and Sullivan – is the intensity with which he now views his redemptive mission of cleansing American architecture from the scourge of historicism. He speaks to the American ideal of democracy, to America's opportunities and individuality, and even to its self-perceived cultural inferiority, especially prevalent in the Northeast, where "our get-rich-quick citizens attempt to buy tradition ready-made and are dragged forward, facing backwards, in attitudes most absurd to those they would emulate, characteristic examples of conspicuous waste."[109] In contrast, there is the "West and Middle West, where breadth of view, independent thought, and a tendency to take common sense into the realm of art, as in life, are more characteristic."[110] It is with this pioneering garb that Wright costumes his work – organic work in which "ornamentation is conceived in the very ground plan, and is of the very constitution of the structure." With a sartorial metaphor reminiscent of Loos, Wright points out, "Where the warp and woof of the fabric do not yield sufficient incident or variety, it is seldom patched on. Tenderness has often to be sacrificed to integrity."[111] One's home in the Midwest should be designed to wear well, and this concern mandates pleasing colors, soft textures, living materials, and the horizontal line: "To Europeans these buildings on paper seem uninhabitable; but they derive height and air by quite other means and respect an ancient tradition, the only one here worthy of respect – the prairie."[112]

Wright was certainly correct in this last observation, as his floor plans, with their displaced axialities and linear extensions into a lush landscape, must have seemed exotic to European architects working with much greater spatial constraints. And while marveling at Wright's arrival at pure planar abstraction in his plans and forms, many of these same architects may also have not recognized the importance of geometry and structure for Wright. The key text here is a small book he published in 1912, entitled *The Japanese Print: An Interpretation*. In many ways it is the most illuminating of all of his writings. In speaking of the "structure" inherent in all Japanese art, he goes on to define this concept for design in general as "pure form, an organization into a very definite manner of parts or elements into a larger unity – a vital whole."[113] Geometry underlies structure in architecture; geometry is what he calls the "grammar" of form. But geometry is only the starting point for something more profound:

But there is a psychic correlation between the geometry of form and our associated ideas, which constitutes its symbolic value. There resides always a certain "spell-power" in any geometric form which seems more or less a mystery and is, as we say, the soul of the thing. It would carry us far from our subject if we should endeavor to render an accurate, convincing account of the reason why certain geometric forms have come to symbolize for us and potently to suggest certain human ideas, moods, and sentiments – as for instance: the circle, infinity; the triangle, structural unity; the spire, aspiration; the spiral, organic progress; the square, integrity. It is nevertheless a fact that more or less clearly in the subtle differentiations of these elemental geometric forms, we do sense a certain psychic quality which we may call the "spell-power" of the form, and with which the artist freely plays, as much at home with it as the musician at his keyboard with his notes.[114]

This is also what makes Wright's prewar architecture so innovative and compelling – its spell-power. Whether it is the geometrical ensemble of the Avery Coonley House plan (1906–9) or the surreal spatial composition and Mayan forms of the Midway Gardens (1914), Wright's architecture is almost always exotic, perhaps too exotic for the design deities he may have offended. Upon returning to the United States after his sojourn in Fiesole, Wright bypassed Chicago and his wife (who was refusing a divorce) and built his fellowship of Taliesin outside of Madison, Wisconsin. Here he settled Mamah and her two children, together with his office staff. One day while he was in Chicago supervising the construction of Midway Gardens, the male household cook – demented with paranoia – sealed up the house from the outside and set it on fire. He then took an axe and chopped to death those who tried to escape the flames. Altogether seven were brutally murdered, among them Mamah and her two children. Wright was devastated, and the living areas of Taliesin were reduced to ashes. It was a catastrophe from which he would barely recover.

6. Garnier, Perret, Jeanneret, and Sant'Elia

Wright's experiments with the use of reinforced concrete around the turn of the century have a parallel in France in the work of Tony Garnier (1869–1948) and Auguste Perret (1874–1954). The two architects were trained in Paris at the Ecole des Beaux-Arts under Julien Guadet, yet their work bears little resemblance to the compositional methods and classical formalism that continued to dominate the academic teachings at the turn of the century.

Garnier was a native of Lyons, the city in which he also established his architectural practice.[115] He began his architectural studies in 1889 and made no fewer than six attempts to win the *grand prix* before finally succeeding in 1899. It was while he was in Rome that he began to work out the elements of the *Cité Industrielle* (industrial city). Various drawings were exhibited in Paris in 1904, and Garnier continued to prepare designs until the project's publication in 1917. The project is utopian and within the French positivist tradition of Charles Fourier and Saint-Simon. One of its premises is that "a certain progress of social order" will eventually dictate communistic or public ownership of all land and state distribution of food, water, and medical supplies.[116] Other of its political and sociological ideas may have been influenced by the writings of Pierre-Joseph Proudhon and Frédéric Le Play and Howard's recently published ideas on the garden city. The projected size of Garnier's *Cité* (35,000 people) is the same as Howard's model, and its residential quarter, with the emphasis on pedestrian scale and greenery, is also sympathetic with Howard's vision. But Garnier's acceptance, even exaltation, of industrialization, and his willingness to grow the city as conditions warrant, project a different mindset, particularly in the attention he gives to hygiene (sun, air, vegetation) and zoning. The *Cité*, in fact, is sharply divided into residential and public areas, the latter containing administrative buildings, cultural institutions (museums, libraries), and sports facilities. The industrial section is far removed from the town, as is the hydroelectric station. Even the cemetery and hospital are placed on an adjoining hillside and separated from the urban center by green space. The drawings tend to fix one's attention on the ease of pedestrian access, while the use of (mostly empty) Parisian avenues and the traditional layouts of residential blocks at best allude to the recent introduction of motorized vehicular traffic.

Another feature that distinguishes Garnier's design is his use of reinforced concrete for all walls, floors, and ceilings. There had been extensive development of this material in France going back to François Cointereaux's experiments of the 1790s, and Garnier had the more recent example of François Hennebique's innovative concrete systems of the 1880s and 1890s. Garnier's designs in their detailing, however, always display the hand of a talented architect, and it is the consummate abstractness of his logical solutions, especially those on paper, that are innovative for this period.

After 1904 Garnier returned to Lyons, and with the election of the socialist mayor Edouard Herriot in 1908 he found a sympathetic friend who was intent on employing his talent in the cause of a socialist city. Before the war Garnier designed the concrete and steel structures for the new slaughterhouses (1909–13), the hospital Grange-Blanch (1911–27), and the Lyons Stadium (1913–18). All are without historical vestiges and are notable for their structural clarity, but none has the persuasiveness of his utopian city.

One of Garnier's classmates at the Ecole des Beaux-Arts, Auguste Perret, is better known for his work in reinforced concrete, especially for his Paris apartment building on the rue Franklin (1903–4) across the river from the Eiffel Tower.[117] He entered the Ecole in 1891 and quickly advanced to the first class but left in 1897 without a diploma to join his father's contracting firm (a diploma would have precluded his acting as a contractor). Auguste and his brother Gustave also soon formed a design partnership. The apartment house on the rue Franklin is almost contemporary with Wright's Unity Temple. The infill site was shallow, leading the brothers to devise a U-shaped plan in which the circulation is moved to the rear and all of the rooms face onto the street. For the structure the Perret brothers turned to a patented Hennebique post-and-slab system with concrete infill panels (Hennebique himself advised on the design). Six floors on each side cantilever out from the structural lines, and a series of tiles – the infill panels with a sunflower pattern – sheathe the concrete, in contrast to the exposed surfaces of Unity Temple. Roof gardens adorn the top.

Although modest in both width and height, it is an important early example of high-rise construction. Perret followed it with his concrete parking garage on the rue Ponthieu (1905) and later with the Théâtre des Champs Elysées (1911–13). Van de Velde had first designed the latter building in

1911, but the actual commission eventually passed to Perret, in what became a highly contentious matter between the two men. The final design is notable for its structural gymnastics; as a structural tour de force, however, it was exceeded in the prewar years by Max Berg's concrete Centennial Hall in Breslau.

Perret's place in early twentieth century architecture is partly defined by his relationship with Le Corbusier. Bom Charles-Edouard Jeanneret (1887–1965), he was raised in the Swiss watch-making town of La Chaux-de-Fonds, not far from the French border, and his architectural education was both spotty and extended.[118] In 1905, he attended the Ecole d'Art in his hometown as a protégé of the headmaster Charles L'Eplattenier, who guided him into architecture. He first trained in the decorative arts, however – with a curriculum that joined the principles of Owen Jones with the tendencies of art nouveau. With the help of René Chapellaz, Jeanneret designed his first house in 1906, which in a picturesque way combined medieval and Swiss chalet forms. The years 1907–11 were mostly given over to traveling: to Italy, Austria, France, and Germany. In Paris, beginning in the summer of 1909, he worked part-time for Perret in his office on rue Franklin. Little should be made of this brief apprenticeship (ending in November), because Perret was not working on any significant concrete projects, and Jeanneret in any case lacked the mathematical skills to take account of the engineering aspects of concrete design. His stay in Paris nonetheless had the benefit of exposing him to the metropolis and its cultural life.

Jeanneret spent most of 1910 back in La Chaux-de-Fonds, where he started a book on city planning, which he never finished. During these years he was smitten with the planning principles of Sitte, and in fact it was Jeanneret's desire to gather more material for this book (as well as a grant for another proposed book on German applied arts) that led him to Germany in the spring of 1910 – first to Munich, where he sought work (unsuccessfully) with Theodor Fischer. A German Werkbund Congress in Berlin attracted him to that city, where Jeanneret met Peter Behrens and visited the recently completed AEG Building. Six months later, after some effort, the young Swiss architect was accepted into Behrens's office, where he worked for five months. Here he received what was perhaps his only serious training in architecture and also surrendered his early medievalism in favor of Behrens's classicism. But this was not a happy period for the moody youth, as his letters and written statements make apparent. From Berlin Jeanneret next undertook a *voyage d'orient*, visiting the Balkans, Turkey, Greece, and Italy. Back

in La Chaux-le-Fonds in 1911, he settled down and wrote his first published book, *Étude sur le movement d'art decorative en Allemagne* (Study of the decorative-arts movement in Germany, 1912).[119]

The book is remarkably naïve, considering the experiences of the past few years. It is simplistic in its logic, arrogant in its assertions, and nationalistic in its cloying tone. It was commissioned by the Ecole d'Art, the decorative-arts school in La Chaux-le-Fonds, where Jeanneret would soon begin to teach. It opens with "General Considerations" and with Jeanneret's condemnation of the decorative arts of the nineteenth century – save for the "Empire style" of Napoleon, which he considered a momentary triumph of simple, bourgeois taste. The decorative arts, in Jeanneret's view, cease to exist by the second half of the century, "despite [Eugène] Grasset, despite Ruskin, despite Morris."[120] Meanwhile, Germany had been unified in 1871, and even though in artistic matters it had "copied France for centuries," it was now seeking to become the "champion of modernism."[121] France has little to fear, in Jeanneret's view, because Germany achieves its success simply because of its economic and organizational skills and by "the systematic absorption (purchase) of works of Parisian painters and sculptors (Courbet, Manet, Cézanne, Van Gogh, Matisse, Maillol, etc.)."[122] Therefore its recent success is little more than an "accidental fact" caused by the shortcomings of the German personality. By contrast, "in France there is a normal and progressive evolution of the thought and spirit of the people."[123]

Following this claim, Jeanneret begins the factual part of his study, where he surveys the German Werkbund, Karl Osthaus's new museum in Hagen, the efforts of the AEG, the city planning movements, and German artistic education. His descriptions are terse and provide little insight or information. In his "Final Considerations," in which he harps once again on the artistic inferiority of the German race, he acknowledges Germany's "organizational genius" but only with a certain disdain: "If Paris is the home of art, in Germany resides the center of production."[124] Two sentences from a letter written to L'Eplattenier earlier in the year, in which he rehearsed his ideas for his concluding chapter, perhaps better convey his condescending attitude toward the country: "France subjugates [subjugue] Germany. And Germany submits [s'incline]."[125] The First World War, during which similar feelings would be vented on both sides, of course lay in the near future.

In Italy, the prewar situation was more complex and somewhat happier than in France. Ruled or dominated by foreign powers for several centuries, the country was unified as a nation in 1870, but it was a unity more on paper than in practice because few Italians actually spoke the Tuscan dialect adopted by the government. The northeast maintained strong cultural ties with Habsburg Austria; the northwest looked to France. The new capital at Rome continued to be a center of classical learning, but its southern classicism was offset by a medievalism in the north. Italy's two most important architectural theorists of the nineteenth century, Pietro Selvatico (1803–80) and Camillo Boito (1836–1914), both fell in with the Gothic currents of the north.

The unification of the country, the *Risorgimento*, also brought for many Italians a desire to define a national artistic character and achieve artistic independence. In this regard Boito's introductory chapter to his 1880 book, entitled "On the Future Style of Italian Architecture," stands as a landmark in Italian theory. Boito, who was a professor of architectural history at the Brera Academy in Milan, opposed the historicism of the day and pleaded for a new national style to be founded on rational principles. Yet while accepting modern building techniques and engineering, he was at the same time opposed to severing all ties with the past. He proposed a medieval Lombard style as a rational starting point for the present, although without its archaeological garb.[126]

Opposing this view were some of the disputants in the controversies raised by the Italian Exposition of Architecture, held in Turin in 1890.[127] The foil was Raimondo D'Aronco's classically inspired exhibition hall, garnished in brilliant polychrome tones. Many raved at his audacious simplification of classical forms, while others, such as the critic Alfred Melani, lamented that "ours is an architecture suffocated by art, with inspiration stifled under the inordinate weight of stylistic erudition and under the invalid authority of a doctrinaire scholasticism."[128] Melani had early on – in his *Manuale architettura italiana* (1887) – renounced the use of historical styles, and by the fourth edition of the book (1904) he was even able to draw upon the achievements of Wagner and Hoffmann to buffer his case.[129]

This still largely academic conflict resurrected itself around the turn of the century with Italy's involvement in the Paris Exposition of 1900 and, more importantly, with Turin's International Exposition of the Modern Decorative Arts of 1902. The Paris Exhibition affected Italian designers in a negative way, as it suggested that they were lagging behind in developing the art nouveau flamboyance that was just achieving its apogee in France. At the Turin Exposition, with the brilliant Secession-inspired buildings of D'Arco once again stealing the show, the confrontation

took the form of a capitulation to the artistic invasion from the North, including works by Olbrich, Behrens, Tiffany, Mackintosh, and Horta. The alluring forms of Olbrich, in particular, were deemed by D'Aroco to be nothing less than divine (and therefore worthy to be plagiarized), and their appeal pushed the earlier question of a national style to the side, at least temporarily. The event nevertheless proved to be a stunning success.

The outgrowth of the exhibition was the birth of the so-called liberty style (also known by other names), which emerged in Italy around the time that art nouveau was collapsing elsewhere. As in other countries, the new architectural movement had the cathartic effect of weaning the younger architects away from the classical past, and in the works of the better architects of the first decade of the new century – Alfredo Melani, Guiseppe Torres, and especially Annibale Rigotti – there is evidence of a new appreciation for simpler compositional forms with traces of regional characteristics. Hence the stage was set for the more radical currents of futurism.

The leader of this avant-garde futurist group, with ties to cubist circles in Paris, was the poet Filippo Tommaso Marinetti, whose apocalyptical manifesto of spiritual alienation and technological modernity first appeared in 1909.[130] He achieved his spiritual liberation – figuratively in his account – by crashing his speeding automobile into a ditch, from which experience he could now exalt such things as "love of danger," "the beauty of speed," nationalism, the glorification of war ("the world's only hygiene"), "scorn for women," and the destruction of "museums, libraries, academies of every kind."[131] The next year Umberto Boccioni transposed the futurist agenda into painting, which now was to eschew all forms of imitation and any concept of "harmony" or "good taste."[132]

The first futurist manifesto for architecture did not appear until May 1914. It was signed by Antonio Sant'Elia (1888–1916), although his authorship has often been disputed.[133] Born in Como, Sant'Elia moved to Milan in his teens, where in 1909–11 he attended the Brea Academy. Here he passed through design studios still dominated by the influence of the Wagner school. Sant'Elia left the academy in 1911, prior to graduating, in order to pursue several design competitions, but this does not explain his sudden fascination two years later with the abstract volumetric forms of silos, power stations, and factories. These *Dinamismi* became the starting point for his visual extravaganza *La Città Nuova* (the new city), which occupied him for much of 1914. He first exhibited eleven drawings of an industrial city at a Lombard architectural exhibition in February, and around the same time he joined the Nuove Tendenze, a group of architects who followed the futurists but without the extreme rhetoric. At their exhibition in May, Sant'Elia exhibited sixteen stupendous drawings of his new urban conception – six devoted to high-rise structures, three to power plants. Mario Chiattone, who shared studio space with Sant'Elia, also produced three drawings of urban skyscrapers, and these foreshadowed future developments even more accurately. But Sant'Elia's drawings (in pen, wash, and colored pencil) were formally richer and more dynamic, with their use of the diagonal and their exaltation of pedestrian bridges, ziggurat forms, elevators, and the nervous movement of cars, planes, and trains (Fig. 73).

In the exhibition catalogue of 1914 Sant'Elia published a manifesto that became known as the *Messsaggio* (Message). It calls for architecture to throw out everything of its past and to begin anew. The world of the twentieth century demands a reformulated modern city, one devoid of the old notions of monumentality and decoration. It opposes "fashionable architecture of every country and of every kind," historical preservation, static lines, and costly materials inconsonant with modern culture.[134] In its place should be a new architecture, "the architecture of cold calculation, of fearless audacity, and of simplicity; the architecture of reinforced concrete, of iron, glass, cardboard, textiles, and all those surrogates of wood, stone, and brick that allow us to obtain the maximum elasticity and lightness."[135] In what are generally regarded as additions to the text made by Marinetti a few months later, the *Messaggio* condemns all "pseudo avant-garde architecture of Austria, Hungary, Germany, and America" and insists that the hallmarks of futurist architecture will be "obsolescence and transience."[136]

Sant'Elia and the more general movement of futurism seem in retrospect to be somewhat isolated outcroppings in the prewar years. With the advent of the war, neither the polemics nor the drawings had much immediate impact within European architectural circles, and for many years they were seen as detached from the main lines of twentieth-century theory. The British historian Reyner Banham resurrected the reputation of Sant'Elia around 1960 by promoting him as one of the pivotal figures of avant-garde theory: "with attitudes of mind, rather than formal or technical methods."[137] Although this view represented an important advance over earlier appraisals of Sant'Elia, surely it is somewhat overstated. Sant'Elia's contribution to twentieth-century modernism is largely a poetic one: exquisite and inspired drawings of a new world, but a world very much confined to paper. His last manifesto appeared in August 1914, a few days after the start of the war. Embracing the "love and danger" and nationalist ethic of militarism that Marinetti espoused, Sant'Elia became a soldier and was killed at the front in October 1916.

7. Muthesius and Behrens

The polemical battle that Loos and others were waging against the Secession and Jugendstil in the early years of the century was preceded and in the end overtaken by the criticisms of Hermann Muthesius (1861–1927).[138] The name of this Thuringian architect is generally associated with his important publications on English architecture, but to focus just on these is to overlook his far more significant contributions to twentieth-century modernism. Muthesius rightfully can be called the first major theorist of the twentieth century, and no one shaped the course of German modernism in a more concrete way than he did.

Muthesius also personified the new middle-class aspirations of the Wilhelmine era (1871–1918). He studied art history and philosophy at the University of Berlin before beginning his architectural studies at the Technische Hochschule in Berlin in 1883. He joined the Prussian government as an entry-level government architect and worked briefly in the office of Paul Wallot (narrowly missing Streiter there) before taking a position with the architectural firm Ende & Bockmann, for which he administered state-sponsored projects in Japan. After four years in the Far East, he returned to Germany in 1891 and two years later rejoined the Ministry of Public Works; it was this ministry, together with the Ministry of Commerce and Trade, that sent him to London in 1896 as an attaché to the German Embassy. His mission was to study English decorative arts and architecture, a task similar to that of Robert Dohme twelve years earlier. Muthesius adopted entirely Dohme's aesthetic outlook, and his first book on England, *Die englische Baukunst der Gegenwart* (Contemporary English architecture, 1900), therefore shared Dohme's liking for the tradition of Shaw and Webb, now updated with works of Lethaby, Voysey, Mackintosh, and others.[139] But it is important to note that this appreciation was formed within the context of Prussian state policies, and Muthesius never advocated adopting English tendencies in Germany. He could not do so because he was influenced intellectually by a host of other forces as well.

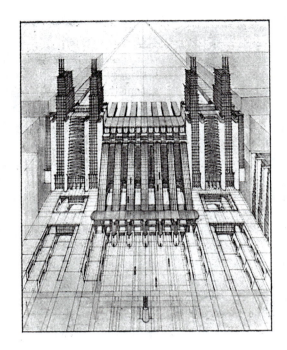
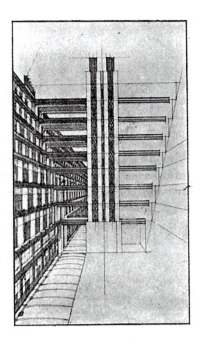

73. Antonio Sant'Elia, The Futurist Manifesto, from *Direzione del movimento Futurista Milano* (Milan, 1914).

Already in the early 1890s Muthesius had been drawn to the writings of social conservatives within the artistic reform movements in Germany, among them Ferdinand Averarius, Julius Langbehn, and Alfred Lichtwark. Many of these individuals dedicated themselves to the preservation of German culture in the face of the great social change wrought by industrialization, and art became an important refuge and source of salvation in their theories. For instance, Julius Langbehn's book *Rembrandt als Erzieher* (Rembrandt as educator, 1890) was perhaps the most widely read book of the decade.[140] In it he condemned the materialist and technological excesses of the late nineteenth century and sought to counter it with the notion of "Germanness," a cultural image exalting the simple and moral nature of the German spirit. Langbehn influenced Streiter and Schumacher and strongly colored the thought of Lichtwark. Langbehn influenced liberal politicians as well, such as Friedrich Naumann, which suggests a greater complexity than has generally been afforded to these social and political movements.

Another individual influencing Muthesius around 1900 was Julius Meier-Graefe, one of the founders of *Pan* and someone in fact who had fought with Lichtwark over the direction of the journal. Meier-Graefe became the editor of the journal *Dekorative Kunst* in 1897, but he resigned this position in 1899 to open his shop in Paris, La Maison Moderne – designed by van de Velde. Yet Meier-Graefe, as indicated by the 1901 article discussed earlier, was already distancing himself from the Belgian at this time. This is important, for it was in the pages of *Dekorative Kunst* – in 1901 – that Muthesius published his first attack on van de Velde and spoke of the "new art."

Next to Wagner's book, Muthesius's essay "New Ornament and New Art" was the second most important document of this period. It is lucid and forthright in its argument because it is a synthesis of ideas well rehearsed by earlier reformers. Muthesius begins by praising Meier-Graefe's article of a few months earlier precisely because the author was turning away from the "ludicrous" direction of the Jugendstil and the Secession. All artistic reformations, he notes, "initially begin with superficialities," a point that he interestingly illustrates by referring to William Morris's love of medieval ornaments and ways of production.[141] On the Continent, the reason for this penchant toward "frolicking" decoration is that so many of the young artists are trained in painting. Thus they seek to infuse their creations with "emotion," in one case by ridiculously constructing the back of a chair out of twenty-six pieces of wood. In one further swipe at van de Velde, Muthesius points out that these same artists, in providing a theory for their programs, put "fulfillment of purpose" at the top of the list. This goal could not be more inconsistent with their results, and these tendencies have simply led to fashion rather than the creation of something of substance.

Against the vagaries of the "new art," Muthesius proposes the touchstones of "common sense" and the fact that contemporary life strives for practicality. Following Streiter, Muthesius subsumes common sense and practicality under the rubric of *Sachlichkeit:* "'Style-making' in architecture has long blocked *sachliche* progress – no less in the applied arts. If we would simply get rid of style-making and architecture-making, we would be surprised at the *sachliche* progress. Therefore a cleansing of so-called artistic intentions is to be preferred to an introduction of new ones."[142] He therefore pleads for an "abstention from any kind of superfluous ornament or linear show," for we live

in an age of middle-class ideals and we need a middle-class art. Presaging Loos, he cites Dohme's 1888 comment to the effect that "the person of greater sensitivity no longer decorates."[143] The modern individual prefers neither "non-representational lines" nor "naturalistic roses" on his wallpaper but is likely to appreciate "the elegantly built sailing vessel shooting across the water's surface, the electric lamp, and the bicycle – these seem to capture the spirit of our time more closely than any new furniture and wallpaper of the Jugendstil or Secession style."[144] Echoing the polemics of Wagner and Lichtwark, Muthesius lauds the concern for hygiene, daylight, air, and physical comfort in domestic design: "We need bright and clean rooms without clutter or dust catchers, with smooth and simple furniture that is easy to clean and move, a room that is airy and openly arranged."[145] In short, this remarkable essay of only a few pages serves as a canonic synopsis of two decades of German realist (now *sachliche*) theory.

Muthesius wasted little time in advancing his polemic. The following year he published *Stil-Architektur und Baukunst* (Style-architecture and building art), based on two lectures given in 1901.[146] *Architektur* is a term of Greek and Latin origin that came into the German language in the eighteenth century as an appellation referring to high or monumental design; in most German writings up until the nineteenth century, the German word *Baukunst* (building art) was used. Muthesius's title is meant to contrast the high art of "styles" (imposed, foreign, eclectic) with the more authentically German "building art," in which buildings are formed in an unpretentious, realist, or *sachliche* manner.

The first part of the study is a brisk historical review filled with generalizations and overt simplifications of the past that would become incorporated into other early histories of modernism. The two authentic styles for Muthesius are the Greek and the Gothic; the Renaissance failed as a style principally because it was "cultured" and a "pale image of a superior original art," again bad because "an art for the ruling class replaced the Gothic art of the people."[147] Some improvements were made by the burghers of the early eighteenth century, but these gains were reversed at midcentury by the "second" revolution – the rise of Greek neoclassicism. The chaos born of neoclassicism led in the nineteenth century to the idealism of the various classical styles (used successfully by only a few architects, such as Schinkel) and the romanticism that gave rise to the Gothic revival movement (good, honest design). Classicists such as Semper are rudely dismissed for their "cosmopolitan architecture" and their failure to recognize a "Nordic art."[148] Gothicists such as Viollet-le-Duc and Morris are lauded, respectively, for their "constructional sensibility" and "workmanship, reasonableness, and sincerity."[149] There are no gray areas in Muthesius's account. Handicraft traditions, aided by the machine, declined and collapsed into the "nothingness" of the late century; the nineteenth century – in a refrain that would be endlessly repeated in the coming decades – could only be dubbed the "inartistic century."[150]

This hyperbolic analysis is followed by Muthesius's program for the twentieth century, in which several important ideas are put forth. If all "high" architectural production fails completely – from the use of various styles to "pasting modern plant ornaments and sapling motifs onto the old organism" – it is because architecture is on the threshold of a new period.[151] The new economic and transportation needs, new materials and principles of construction, and new expectations of comfort have all contributed to an entirely new context for present and future artistic production. The leading forces in this regard are meeting halls, railway terminals, steamships, bicycles, and the like: "Here we notice a rigorous, one might say scientific objectivity [Sachlichkeit], an abstention from all superficial forms of decoration, a design strictly following the purpose that the work should serve."[152] But Muthesius in this acknowledgment is not promoting the use of purely engineered forms for architectural practice. There is within his theory, as has been noted, a slippage between the purely "sachliche" designs of industry (what Streiter earlier called tectonic Sachlichkeit) and the more middle-class, matter-of-fact, but emotionally satisfying building art of everyday life.[153] Muthesius's view of sachliche design, as it should now be clear, is nearly identical with Streiter's 1896 definition of realism. Muthesius's understanding of Sachlichkeit is infused with the rural sentiments with which he had been inspired since the early 1890s.

Thus the pragmatic sensibility underlying these machines, vehicles, and bridges, as it were, runs parallel with the more commonplace sachliche reforms of everyday life:

While Mother Architecture found herself on a wrong path, life never rested but went on to create forms for the innovations it had produced, the simple forms of pure practicality [Sachlichkeit]. It created our machines, vehicles, implements, iron bridges, and glass halls. It led the way soberly in that it proceeded practically – one would like to say purely scientifically. It not only embodied the spirit of the time but also fitted itself to the aesthetic-tectonic views that were reformed under the same influence."[154]

And these last – the "aesthetic-tectonic views" of modern building practice – emanate not only from industry but also from the arts and crafts and other reform movements of the nineteenth century. The one crucial difference between this position and earlier ones is that Muthesius, almost alone in Germany in 1901, openly embraces the machine. In fact, it is his philosophical acceptance of the machine that grounds his pivotal architectural demand for "undecorated practical form [Sachform]."[155]

It is also this acceptance that will bring him into conflict with some members of the German Werkbund, which, beginning in 1907, becomes the primary vehicle for the dissemination of such views in Germany.[156] Of almost equal importance, however, are Muthesius's reforms undertaken for the Ministry of Commerce and Trade between 1903–7 as well as his leadership of the Verband des deutschen Kunstgewerbes (Association of the German Applied Arts). In the first role, Muthesius returned to Germany in 1903 and was given the task of reforming the trade schools and arts and crafts schools in Germany in light of his English experiences and philosophical outlook. He reorganized school curriculums, created instructional workshops, and helped to arrange exhibits, all with the intention of advancing national exports and enhancing the domestic quality of life. It was his success at these efforts – done in the name of the "modern" principle of Sachlichkeit – that laid the foundation for the Werkbund.

Muthesius was not alone in this regard. Upon his return to Germany in 1903, he was joined by Peter Behrens (1868–1940), who a few months earlier had been appointed director of the Dusseldorf Arts and Crafts School.[157] Behrens had been a recent convert to the cause of industrial modernity. He was trained as a painter in the late 1880s, worked as an artist in Munich in the 1890s, and in 1899 he heeded the Apollonian call and moved to the artist colony at Darmstadt; it was there in 1900 that he built himself a house and thus initiated his career as an architect. By 1902, however, Behrens had rejected the colony's mystical view of art and had arrived essentially at the same position as Muthesius.[158] Among the many artists and architects also aligning themselves with the efforts of Muthesius were Richard Riemerschmid (1868–1957), Karl Schmidt, and Hans Poelzig (1869–1936). The first great success of their collaborative efforts was the Third German Arts and Crafts Exhibition, held in Dresden in 1906. Its chief organizer was Fritz Schumacher, and the reforms instituted at the various schools, especially those of Bruno Paul's school in Berlin and Behrens's school in Dusseldorf, were highlighted. It was a worthy rehearsal for the founding of the Werkbund one year later.

The Werkbund was intended to be a coalition of artists and industrialists not dissimilar to Cole's alliance of the mid-nineteenth century. Very different, however, were the conflicting premises and aims brought together at its inception. Almost three hundred artists and others were invited to the first meeting in Munich in 1907. Around a hundred showed up to hear Schumacher's keynote address of 5 October – cogently entitled "The Reconquest of a Harmonious Culture" – in which he lamented the decline of preindustrial ideals while at the same time insisting upon the essential realism of modern life.[159] The time was ripe for such an organization, and over the next three years its membership would swell beyond seven hundred. A number of intellectuals from outside the arts and industry, such as the sociologist Werner Sombart and the politician Friedrich Naumann, actively participated in its deliberations. The list of architects taking part includes almost every major figure from the prewar period: Riemerschmid, Behrens, Paul, Olbrich, Hoffmann, van de Velde, Theodor Fischer, Paul Bonatz, Hans Poelzig, Heinrich Tessenow, Bruno Taut, and Walter Gropius. Never before had such a coalition of architects, craftsmen, teachers, museum directors, and theorists been assembled in this way. The Werkbund's purpose was to facilitate reforms in the industrial arts both to enhance national wealth (through exports) and to raise the living standard at home. There was as well a significant architectural agenda wrapped in the banner of practicality (*Sachlichkeit*).

Although the Werkbund pretended to impose no overall design ideology on its membership, there were indeed very serious efforts to control directions behind the scene, as Muthesius, who was elected to the governing board in 1908, continued to play a key role in the organization down through 1914. In an important address given at a trade school in 1907, Muthesius offended a union of traditional craftsmen when he insisted that they accept the modern principles of the "new movement" in the name of social progress and patriotism.[160] In response to the stir created by his comments, the Ministry of Trade insisted that Muthesius not attend the first Werkbund conference in October. But he was not out of action for long. In his address at the second Werkbund meeting in 1908, he reiterated his position, claiming that if Germany was to succeed in the international marketplace, it had to have products of superior design, and there had to be a larger national strategy of cooperation combined with a local acceptance of design principles.

Again, this was similar to Cole's agenda in the 1850s, except that the nationalist intentions of the "new movement" were more candidly admitted. And there was another crucial difference: England in the nineteenth century had a colonial empire and colonial wealth, while Germany in 1908 did not. Hence for Germany the economic stakes of design superiority were higher.

In the midst of these concerns came the garden city of Hellerau, to which the Werkbund would briefly relocate.[161] Germany had possessed a Garden-City Society since 1902, but in 1906–7 this society more or less merged with the Werkbund. The industrialist Karl Schmidt proposed erecting a garden city outside of Dresden in 1906, a factory community for the workers of the German Werkstätten. It was to be more than a community: in fact, a bold social experiment in healthy and communal living. To this end Schmidt put together committees of future Werkbund members to review the project, including Riemerschmid, Muthesius, Theodor Fischer, Schumacher, Friedrich Naumann, and Wolf Dohrn – the last the secretary of the Werkbund. Riemerschmid prepared the overall layout of winding streets and terraced houses, which in his models featured standardized doors, windows, and fixtures. He also designed the factory and the superb commercial center – all in a southern German rural vernacular. Muthesius contributed several villas and groups of row houses with gardens (Fig. 74). His English-inspired vocabulary included plastered gables with red-tile roofs, painted windows and shutters, and white picket fences. Heinrich Tessenow (1876–1950) departed from these models with his steeply gabled and severe housing blocks, pristine in their formal autonomy and simplified detailing. Hellerau could lay claim to some of the best architecture produced in Germany prior to the war, and it quickly became a Mecca for artists and intellectuals from around the world.

Controversy erupted in 1911, however, when Tessenow designed the Hellerau Institute of Rhythmic Movement and Dance – the community's health, gymnastic, and spiritual center. Tessenow's design featured as its centerpiece a tall, severely gabled temple form in antis, whose full-height square columns were reduced to abstraction and whose only relief consisted of (yin/yang) oculi in the two gables. Dohrn supported the classical design, whereas Schmidt, Riemerschmid, Muthesius, and Fischer vehemently opposed it. When a review commission backed it, the last three men resigned from the oversight committee in protest. Dohrn, in turn, was soon ousted by Muthesius as the Werkbund secretary.

74. Hermann Muthesius, row houses in Hellerau, 1910. Photograph by author.

This controversy underscores the fact that Muthesius's program of *Sachlichkeit* had yet to find its formal vocabulary. Muthesius himself returned to architectural practice in 1904 and built a number of large suburban houses around Berlin, where he combined the methods of English planning with vernacular gabled forms. As an architect, Muthesius had not advanced beyond the regional realist sentiments advocated by Lichtwark in the 1890s. By 1910, however, there had appeared two trends in Germany opposed to this rural romanticism. One was a nascent neoclassical movement more often referred to as the Beidermeier revival. Its leader was the Berlin architect Paul Mebes (1872–1938). In a lavishly illustrative study of 1908 he forcefully argued that the classically inspired, yet simple, plain burgher-architecture of the early nineteenth century offered a starting point for today's practice.[162] A countermovement, as we might expect, formed around the tectonic interpretation of *Sachlichkeit* – the factory aesthetic. Its articulate champion was the Austrian theorist Joseph August Lux (1871–1947), whose *Ingenieur-Ästhetik* (Engineer aesthetic, 1910) essentially revived a nineteenth-century debate by insisting that architects should be less like artists and more like engineers. Not only were contemporary works of engineering beautiful in their honesty and economy, but the public will soon come to see them as such: "Modern technical structures only need to become old in order to be perceived as beautiful.[163]

It is only within the context of the last two movements that we can understand the work of Peter Behrens. It was he, of course, who had orchestrated the theatrical opening of the Darmstadt colony in 1901 by proclaiming the crystal as "the sign."[164] It was Behrens who joined Muthesius within the Ministry of Commerce in 1903 with an equally strong desire for reform – a mutual allegiance that remained intact when Behrens became the director of the Dusseldorf School of Arts and Crafts in 1903–7. Architecturally, however, Behrens still needed a few years to develop. Forsaking his earlier Jugendstil manner, he toyed with an abstract conception of architecture in his exhibition pavilions at Oldenburg (1905), although with a geometrical purity that certainly owes much to the theories of the Dutch architect J. L. M. Lauweriks. At the Dresden Exhibition of 1906, Behrens designed a pavilion for a linoleum company – this time in a Florentine classical style of the early Renaissance. The same style is apparent in his design of 1906 for the crematorium at Hagen, which he carried out for the museum director Karl Osthaus. Behrens's style changed, however, in 1907, when he became the artistic advisor to the Allgemeine Elektricitäts-Gesellschaft (AEG). Behrens now not only gained access to the social circles of the German industrial elite but became the first architect to implement the design objectives of the Werkbund.

At this point he emerges as the most prominent architect in Germany, a remarkable feat considering he had been in practice less than a decade. Behrens subsequently directed all of the AEG's design activities, whether related to buildings, graphics, or electrical products. The last category included lamps, fans, heaters, kettles, and clocks – all to be made affordable through mass production. In a memorandum issued in 1907, Behrens prohibited the "copying of handcraftsmanship, historical styles, or other materials" and encouraged the accentuation of the machine process of production. "The aim," as one historian has noted of the memorandum, "was the artistic affirmation of technical production, which could be achieved by developing design methods that would correspond to and would appear aesthetically analogous to machine forms."[165] This would prove to be a remarkably forward-thinking strategy, whether applied to the design of a tea kettle or an electric light fixture.

As the staff architect, Behrens had succeeded Alfred Messel, who had designed the AEG administration building in 1905–6. Behrens put together a remarkable staff of young designers between 1907 and 1910, including Mies van der Rohe and Walter Gropius, and he deeply influenced their development. Mies's prewar houses in Berlin are virtually indistinguishable from contemporary designs by Behrens. Gropius, who first developed his interest in standardized housing in Behrens's office, spent much of his time in 1909–10 writing to industrialists and offering his services as an architect and artistic advisor. He received his first commission, for the Fagus shoe factory, through these efforts.

The signature work for Behrens is of course the AEG turbine factory in Berlin (1908–9), the so-called Temple to Industry (Fig. 75). Over the past century it has achieved the status of an icon for the modern movement – for pretty much the wrong reasons. It is, nevertheless, a complex work. Behrens was only the artistic advisor overseeing the labors of the engineer Karl Bernhard, and various features of the building, such as the steel structure and use of glass walls, were prescribed by the AEG design board. There was also some tension between the two designers. Bernhard preferred a greater use of glass and wanted it carried to the corners, and he decried the architect's use of battered concrete pylons (nonbearing and banded with strips of steel to affect rustication) and the concrete gable (supported by a concealed steel truss) "on the grounds of artistic truth."[166] For his part, Behrens forcefully opposed "the tendency of our modern aesthetics that seeks to devise all artistic forms from function and technology."[167] With regard to this issue, he was actually a "conservative" within the logic of early modernist paradigms, and he even noted – in contrast to Lux – that purely technical constructions were often "ugly"

and that it was the architect's role to conceal the ugliness with a suitable cladding. Behrens attempted to raise the factory building to the level of high art with his insistence on monumental forms.

An article published in English in the *Scientific American Supplement* in 1913 sheds further light on his intentions. He reverts to what is now the very old argument within German theory that iron and glass have a dematerializing effect on form and that architecture, by contrast, should rather be "the formation of space."[168] Thus, on the advice of August Schmarsow, he rationalizes the two corner concrete pylons as "only intended to connect and to close."[169] Their horizontal banding stands in contrast to the verticality of the steel construction, and it is through such devices that a "compactness and a feeling of aesthetical stability" is produced for "the eye used to sensuous impressions."[170] The influence of empathy theory was thus still strong. At the end of the article he stresses the suprapersonal role of the artist over and above the professional work of engineers: "All great things that have been produced in the world have been the results not of conscientious professional work, but the outcome of the energy of great and strong personalities."[171] Therefore, in a Nietzschean plea he insists on respecting these great and strong personalities, that is, "the character of modern style should be realized and carried out and that such architects and engineers as possess the required creative power and sure stylistic feeling, should get recognition."[172]

Behrens's most interesting theoretical argument, however, occurs in his lecture "Art and Technology" (1910). It opens with Houston Stewart Chamberlain's distinction between civilization (material progress) and culture (spiritual and artistic progress) and with the insistence that engineering works "created merely through the accomplishment of utilitarian and material intentions" speak to material progress but they cannot provide a base for culture.[173] With that, he falsely ascribes "utilitarian and material intentions" to Semper: "Or, as the Viennese scholar Riegl has put it, 'Semper's mechanistic view of the nature of the work of art should be replaced by a teleological view in which the work of art is seen as the result of a specific and intentional artistic volition [*Kunstwollen*] that prevails in the battle against functional purpose, raw materials, and technology.'"[174]

Although on the surface this statement appears to be no more than a miscasting of Semper's theory, similar to what Wagner had argued a little more than a decade earlier, it represents in fact the real palace coup. Early twentieth-century modernism, in all of its deterministic zeal, is born at this precise moment, endowed with a new (but nevertheless old)

75. Peter Behrens, turbine factory, Berlin, 1908–9. From Joseph August Lux, *Ingenieur Aesthetik* (Munich, 1910).

sense of finality. Semper's artistic idealism, in effect, is slain by Alois Riegl's notion of "artistic volition" (*Kunstwollen*).

This interpretation requires an explanation. The historian Riegl, a textile curator at the Museum for Art and Industry in Vienna, was throughout his career a devoted Semperian who had often used Semper's idealism to buffer his notion of artistic volition, which Riegl initially construed (in 1893) as a plea for individual artistic freedom over and above material factors determining art. In *Spätrömische Kunstindustrie* (Late-Roman art industry, 1901), however, Riegl reversed himself and accused Semper of being a materialist, because, in effect, Riegl now raised his own notion of artistic volition from a personal artistic drive to a suprapersonal or teleological *Zeitgeist* (spirit of the time) that determines artistic output for any particular age or culture.[175] Great artists step forward, but they can only express the particular spirit of their age – a view that, in essence, allows once-defeated Hegelianism (Hegel's historical model) back into architectural theory. By embracing Riegl's thesis, Behrens, fortunate to be born under a happy alignment of the stars, can now define his efforts as the search for a "mature culture," that is, as a great artist destined to reveal the temporal spirit of the new industrial age. The early Modern Movement is thus

here being outfitted in the philosophical mantle of teleological destiny, a tendency that will only become stronger and more pronounced in the 1920s. Behrens thus closes his address of 1910 with ominous words: "German art and technology will work toward one goal: toward the power of the German nation, which reveals itself in a rich material life ennobled by intellectually refined design."[176] Art is now given a scarcely concealed political mandate.

All of this brings us to the 1914 Werkbund exhibition in Cologne, when the teleological agenda of Muthesius and Behrens became fully transparent. It should first be noted that the Werkbund was now beset with a number of personal feuds and alliances. With the ouster of Dohrn, Muthesius had effectively taken control of the organization, and the Werkbund offices were moved from Hellerau back to Berlin. Muthesius, as a secretly installed "second chairman" for the event, also wrested control of the Cologne exhibition from the legal Werkbund planning council chaired by Karl Osthaus.[177] This wealthy museum director and early patron of Van de Velde and Behrens had long pursued a path independent of Muthesius. More recently he had drawn close to Gropius, for whom he had helped secure a job in Behrens's office. In 1911 he hired Gropius to assemble a photographic collection of anonymous factories, silos, and the like for his Hagen museum. Now realizing that his authority on the planning committee was being supplanted by Muthesius's invisible position within the Werkbund, Osthaus, together with Gropius, began planning what amounted to a secession from the Werkbund.

Muthesius had also alienated others with his heavy-handed administration of the (mostly governmental) monies for the exhibition. He repeatedly blocked van de Velde's design for the theater, which as a result was ready only after the opening of the exhibition. He vetoed an important commission for August Endell and relegated him to second-class status within the new pecking order. He so infuriated Poelzig that the latter withdrew as the architect of the model factory, the commission for which then went to Gropius. Muthesius also clashed with Gropius on several occasions over the factory design. Muthesius even offended his former ally Behrens at the start of the process by rejecting his site plan for the exhibition.

The forces of revolt were thus well in place before the Werkbund exhibition officially opened in May 1914. The main meeting was scheduled for 3 July, at which Muthesius was to give the keynote address. One week prior to the meeting, Muthesius distributed ten "theses," which he hoped the delegates would approve by voice vote. In response, he received from a coalition gathering around van de Velde ten countertheses in the form of opposition to his every point.[178] Muthesius tried to stave off the revolt by toning down the remarks in his address, but it was too late. Those present that night and the next day engaged in a furious debate as Gropius in the wings tried (unsuccessfully) to orchestrate a walkout from the organization. The ostensible issue in dispute was the single word *Typisierung*, the meaning of which, both then and now, has been the subject of much discussion.[179] The first thesis of Muthesius reads: "Architecture, and with it the entire creative activity of the Werkbund, strives toward the development of types [*Typisierung*]. Only in this way can architecture attain again the general significance that it had in times of harmonious culture."[180]

Earlier historians of this confrontation defined *Typisierung* as "standardization" and thus cast the dispute as a simple one between those favoring the imposition of design

standards and the proponents of artistic freedom – which it certainly was not. Van de Velde promoted this reading in his first counterthesis by insisting that the artist, as an idealist and free spontaneous creator, would always resist the imposition of a "canon." He then immediately renounced this freedom in his second counterthesis, in which he sought artistic refuge behind the stronger teleological (Hegelian) currents of the spirit of the time.

More recently historians have interpreted the dispute in other ways. The dictionary defines *Typisierung* as both stylization and as rationalization, and it seems Muthesius understood the term in both senses, that is, as the aesthetic treatment of an article that is rational and recognizable through its stylization – not at all dissimilar to the stylized lines of tea kettles that Behrens produced at the AEG. To this extent, Muthesius was merely repeating what he had stated for more than a decade, and his views could not have come as much of a shock to his audience. But Muthesius also intended this word in another sense that many did find unacceptable, although it too was not new. In his sixth thesis, he speaks of the international success of German exports as a "matter of life and death for Germany." In the following thesis, he insists that national publicity or propaganda efforts be started to ensure their commercial success. And in the ninth and tenth theses he neatly connects these efforts with the growth of large corporate enterprises. It seems that between 1912 and 1914 Muthesius had effectively aligned the efforts of the Werkbund entirely with the efforts of the Commerce Ministry, and for this "inartistic" offense he would be tumbled. He was not the only individual to lose face in the conflict. Behrens, who had stood on the sidelines during the dispute, would not recover his earlier standing. Van de Velde (who as a Belgian was soon to be placed under house arrest) was marginalized. If anyone could claim victory in the dispute, Gropius and Bruno Taut could, but of course their victory at first turned out to be a hollow one. Shortly before the contentious Werkbund congress took place, the Austrian Archduke Franz Ferdinand and his wife Sophie, on a visit to Sarajevo, were shot and killed by two rounds of an assassin's pistol. During the month of July the armies of Europe were mobilizing for what would become the first military exercise of the new era of "mature culture," better known as World War I.

11

EUROPEAN MODERNISM 1917–1933

Society is filled with a violent desire for something which it may obtain or not.
Everything lies in that: everything depends on the effort made and the attention
paid to these alarming symptoms. Architecture or Revolution. Revolution can be
avoided.

Le Corbusier (1923)

1. Spenglerism versus Taylorism

The "war to end all wars" involved nearly every country in Europe, as well as the United States, Canada, Turkey, Japan, Australia, Indochina, India, and several colonial countries in Africa. It put into uniform over fifty million troops and greatly advanced the lethal possibilities of modern warfare with such military innovations as long-range artillery, poison gas, tanks, airplanes, battleships, submarines, and machine guns. Altogether ten million soldiers died on the battlefield, and over twenty million were maimed. Turkey alone lost one-fourth of its adult male population. In Poland over four million people were killed or made homeless. In the end, sadly, it was agreed by everyone that the entire event scarcely had to happen. It came about almost accidentally through a mixture of diplomatic blundering, national arrogance, and anachronistic treaty obligations.

For two of the principal contestants – France and Germany – the war was little more than a resumption of the hostilities of 1870–1. Military alliances came first. In 1879 Germany had formed a pact with Austria-Hungary and Russia, which Italy joined in 1882. When in 1890 the new German emperor, Wilhelm II, decided not to renew the treaty with Russia, France took the occasion to sign an alliance with that country. In 1902 Britain joined the Franco-Russian alliance in a less formal way, and the principal contestants were now set. To Habsburg Austria goes the infamy of initiating the conflict. After the assassination of its archduke in Sarajevo by Serbian nationalists in June 1914, Austria decided within a month to declare war on Serbia. Russia, bound by treaty to protect Serbia, mobilized its forces. In response, Germany, France, and Britain mobilized their armies. With little or no diplomatic effort directed toward resolving what had become essentially a problem of distrust, Wilhelm II declared war on France on 31 August 1914. Four days later Britain declared war on Germany, on the very day that Germany invaded Belgium. The German strategy was simple. With supreme confidence, it intended to hold off the Russians in the East while it quickly routed France and then dealt with Britain.

The quick victory never came. German armies rapidly moved across the northern parts of France, but the invasion stalled within a month. Pressed by the Russians along the eastern front, Germany relocated some of its western forces there. Meanwhile Britain began to put its troops into France, thereby assuring a stalemate that would last for most of the next four years. The strategic draw, however, was not benign, as waves of men were sacrificed with each engagement. The Germans launched the first chlorine-gas attack in April 1915 (a more deadly mustard gas would soon follow), shortly before Italy entered the war against Austria (it later declared war against Germany). In a single battle at Verdun, in February 1916, France lost 500,000 soldiers, Germany 400,000. The United States, which had been neutral at the start, was slowly drawn into the conflict. The sinking of the cruise liner *Lusitania* in May 1915 tilted public sentiment toward the side of the allies, and the government supplied France and Britain with munitions more aggressively. In response Germany announced unrestricted submarine warfare, and the sinking of two American vessels in March 1917 led the United States to declare war on Germany a few weeks later. The mobilization and transportation of more than a million troops to Europe, however, would take nearly a year to accomplish.

In the meantime, a particularly destructive drama was unfolding in the East. German armies had moved far into Russia, and the enormous Russian casualties, combined with massive starvation in the cities, had made Czar Nicholas II a very unpopular ruler. In March 1917 he abdicated, and a provisional government under Alexander Kerensky was formed. In Zurich the Bolshevik revolutionary Vladimir Ilich Ulyanov watched the situation very closely. Better known to history as Lenin, he secretly negotiated with the German government for a train to take him and his comrades back to Russia. Germany supplied the train – on the presumption that Lenin would foment a revolution that would draw Russia out of the conflict. He arrived in St. Petersburg in mid-April, where comrade Leon Trotsky soon joined him. Their first attempt at revolution in July failed, and Lenin was forced to seek safety in Finland. But Kerensky's government, under attack from the extreme left and the extreme right, eventually collapsed on its own. Lenin began his successful revolution in October 1917 and quickly sued for peace with Germany. He came into power with the hope of setting up a new socialist society based on Marxist principles. The lengths he would go to achieve this end were revealed on the night of 16 July 1918, when he approved the murder of the hapless Czar Nicholas together with his entire family.

The revolution that Germany had made possible in Russia soon backfired back home. By the summer of 1918 the American forces were beginning to make a difference on the battlefields in France, and the German armies were in retreat. After four years of war, Germany was simply overextended and unable to maintain industrial and food production. Famine and rioting had become commonplace in the major cities, and German communists (now drawing open support from Lenin) were organizing against the government. With the subsequent mutiny of the German navy, war was no longer an option. At the end of September the supreme army commander asked Woodrow Wilson to arrange an armistice, and when the details were finalized in early November 1918, one of the conditions was the abdication of Wilhelm II and the loss of his son's claim to the throne. The first revolutionary government of November was eventually replaced by the so-called Weimar Republic (negotiators met in Weimar because of rioting in Berlin), but only after Karl Liebknecht and Rosa Luxemburg, leaders of the Spartacus League, failed in their effort to impose a "Free Socialist Republic" on Germany. These two revolutionaries were murdered on 15 January 1919 in police hands, and elections a few days later installed a moderate socialist government led by the "People's Commissar" Friedrich Ebert.

But Ebert's government had no chance of success, as the conditions worked out for the Versailles Treaty (signed in May 1919) deprived Germany of the material and economic resources it needed to survive. Germany lost so many of its territories that it now had less than half of the coal production it required. France insisted on huge indemnities of over $30 billion. Inflation became such a severe problem in the first part of the 1920s in Germany that its currency collapsed, and only the American infusion of money through the Dawes Plan averted a complete economic disaster. Victorious France and Britain were scarcely better off. France in particular had been destroyed militarily, politically, and economically, and its condition would scarcely stabilize before the Great Depression of 1929. The Depression, of course, led to another catastrophic political collapse and eventually to renewed warfare.

The war and its aftermath make European artistic developments in the 1920s a special case. When architectural historians talk about the revolution of "modern architecture" between the two world wars, they are generally referring – at least as far as built works – to the years 1924–30, when construction in most countries briefly came alive. And because a shortage of housing was the most acute problem facing postwar Europe, nearly all building efforts focused on alleviating this shortage. Moreover, housing shortages carry with them a specific set of demands – that the maximum number of units (better concentrated in high densities) be built with the minimum cost and time of construction. These criteria in themselves push architectural theory far beyond its traditional bounds with regard to such issues as ornament and style. Quite simply, the brutal reality of the war had profoundly changed the parameters of architectural practice.

Still, there was another broad architectural revolution during these years – in the realm of theory – and in many respects this revolution was born of the forced idleness of so many architects. But here again we should approach the issue with some caution. The architectural modernism of the 1920s has in recent years become conflated with parallel avant-garde movements in painting and literature, resulting in the blurring of crucial ideological distinctions.[1] On the one hand, it is possible to argue that European architectural theory of the 1920s is less an innovation and more a consolidation of ideas put forth prior to the war, in fact before 1900. On the other hand, the phenomenon of avant-gardism – with its political dimension – was indeed novel, to say the least. Only in a few historical instances, such as after the French Revolution, has architectural thinking assumed such an overtly political coloration, and rarely has theory been so radicalized in its presentation. So-called avant-garde theory was voiced in the midst of the massive political and economic devastation of the postwar years.

Certainly the most significant political event affecting European thinking in the first half of the 1920s was the Russian Revolution of 1917. However one may interpret the course of communism over the twentieth century, no one can deny the airy hopes that it released across a war-ravaged Europe. Intellectuals and artists, especially in the early postwar years, were convinced that the spread of communism to all of Europe was inevitable. There was a wide-ranging consensus that Europe was entering a new period of human social development – a teleological destiny that would move humanity beyond the possibility of future wars.

This hope, however, was also infused with an equal measure of pessimism, as we see in the success of Oswald's Spengler's *Decline of the West* (1918) – the most widely read book in Europe in its time. The parallels and contrasts between the ideas of Lenin (1870–1924) and Spengler (1880–1936) are myriad. Both men dealt with the "problem of civilization" and believed that Western culture was at the end of its natural historical cycle, both believed in the historical inevitability of this change, both argued that industrialization and economic interests had essentially created this spiritual crisis, and both eschewed the former "eternal truths" of Western humanism. But whereas the materialist Lenin envisioned singing comrades-in-arms marching into their promised land, the metaphysician Spengler saw everywhere only pending doom. For the latter, the Faustian soul of Western modernity had been born not in 1917 but in the tenth century, concomitant with spiritual rediscovery and Romanesque architecture. After the false Apollonian regression of the Renaissance, it had taken on its autumnal colors in the seventeenth and eighteenth centuries during baroque and rococo times. The nineteenth century witnessed the West's ailing winter, as the declining culture of the Faustian spirit (now devoid of all creativity) surrendered itself to the inchoateness of "civilization," with its positivist delusions. What was left for the twentieth century, Spengler concluded, was to acknowledge but one truth: "Money is overthrown and abolished only by blood."[2] In the end, the three "high priests" of the machine – the entrepreneur, the engineer, and the factory worker – might be spared, but only through the religious cleansing of imperialism, more warfare, and "Caesarism."

Although the Marxism of Lenin and the conservatism of Spengler are sometimes interpreted as symbols of the larger conflict between communist and capitalist worldviews, such a juxtaposition seems to blur the fine line between ideology and theory – so essential for interpreting architectural thought. Spengler concluded his book with two chapters on "Money" and the "Machine," not because he saw his own beliefs essentially at odds with socialism (which he preferred to Weimar Republicanism), but because he saw Germany as morally betrayed by the excessive optimism bred of technology and industrialization. When viewed in this light, his philosophical outlook finds its proper theoretical antithesis not in Marxism but rather in the ideas of the American engineer Frederick Winslow Taylor (1856–1915).

Spenglerism and Taylorism indeed form the ideological field on which European theory plays itself out in the 1920s. Taylor, like Spengler, was not an academic. In the 1880s and 1890s he was a manager employed by two American steel companies, and in the name of efficiency he became interested in quantifying productivity. This interest would lead him in 1911 to write *The Principles of Scientific Management* – perhaps the second most widely read book of the postwar years. "The principal object of management," he noted in his opening sentence, "should be to secure the maximum prosperity for the employer, coupled with the maximum prosperity for each employee."[3] Taylor's approach was to break down each particular phase of the production process; analyze and time each movement with a stopwatch; eliminate all false, slow, or useless movements; and, where necessary, train the worker in new and more efficient movements. To make this analysis even more "scientific," he often employed Frank Gilbreth to record a worker's movements with a camera, aided by the use of small lights attached to limbs. The result of applying such techniques is sometimes portrayed as the worst kind of mindless drudgery, but Taylor's dual aim was to increase productivity and provide the workers with shorter working hours, higher wages, and regular working breaks. For instance, in one study of masons, Gilbreth discovered that with the use of an adjustable scaffold for the bricks he could eliminate all bending and lifting. By tempering the mortar, the mason could bed the brick to its proper depth without tapping. These improvements increased the rate of brick laying from 120 bricks per man-hour to 350. In another study related to ball-bearing inspection, Taylor was able to triple efficiency, raise workers' wages 80–100 percent, reduce working hours from $10\frac{1}{2}$ to $8\frac{1}{2}$ a day, and provide two consecutive days of paid vacation each month.

Nowhere were these methods applied with greater success than in the American automotive industry. Henry Ford (1863–1947) was a relatively late pioneer in a field that had developed in the late nineteenth century through the efforts of such inventors as Gottlieb Daimler, Karl Benz, and Ranson Eli Olds. Ford's first two ventures in automobile production failed around the turn of the century, but by 1903 he had formed the Ford Motor Company, and two years later he was producing 10,000 automobiles a year with a price tag of $400 a vehicle. These were small cars offered at well below the average price of other automobiles, but Ford remained intent on improving quality while reducing cost. In 1908 he introduced the Model T (originally priced at $950), which was by far the strongest, most durable, and most advanced car of its time. In 1909 he hired Albert Kahn (1869–1942) to build a new assembly plant in Highland Park, where, inspired by Taylor's ideas, Ford created a sophisticated assembly line with conveyor belts, moving platforms, and overhead rails to minimize worker movements. It took several years to perfect the production cycle, but by 1914 (as Europe was hurtling into war) Ford had improved the system to the point where he had decreased assembly time by 50 percent, doubled the wages of the workers, and reduced their daily working hours from nine to eight. When he decided to add a third daily production shift in that year, the result was a previously unimaginable event: men rioting outside of his plant in their eagerness to be hired. By 1923 the cost of a Model T had been lowered to $260, and even before this date Ford's employees became the first workers in the world able to afford this former luxury item. He thus proved Taylor's contention that "the cheapening of any article in common use almost immediately results in a largely increased demand for that article," thereby defeating unemployment.[4] European intellectuals were well aware of his ideas. The German sociologist Jakob Walcher aptly summed up the situation in 1925 with the title of his book: *Ford oder Marx. Die praktische Lösung der sozialen Frage* (Ford or Marx? The practical solution of the social problem).

2. Soviet Rationalism and Constructivism

Ford was not the only leader during this period drawing upon the principles of "scientific management." As early as 1918 Lenin announced his intention to incorporate Taylor's ideas into the Soviet system of industrialization, but of course the obstacles he faced were more severe. Marxist theory has construed communism as the final stage of a sociopolitical evolution that included feudalism and capitalist economic development. The October Revolution of 1917 had occurred in a society that was still largely feudal and that lagged far behind the West in industrial development. Yet issues of production made up only a small proportion of the problems confronting Lenin. The Germans in the Brest-Litovsk peace accords of 1918 had dealt the Russians a harsh blow by seizing a third of their land and population and 90 percent of their coal production. When the Bolsheviks came to power, they immediately nationalized all private lands and the banking system and gradually nationalized all industries. Although some of these measures were rolled back briefly under Lenin's New Economic Policy of 1921, the damage to the struggling economy had been done: civil warfare, widespread chaos, and mass famine ensued. Lenin himself was seriously wounded in an assassination attempt in August 1918, and he responded by initiating the "Red Terror" campaign, which in 1918–21 executed over 12,000 political opponents. During the war of the "Reds" and the "Whites," Trotsky rebuilt the Soviet army, increasing its size from 100,000 to 5 million. Lenin, however, suffered his first stroke in 1922 and died early in 1924. In a bitter struggle with Trotsky, Josef Stalin emerged as Lenin's successor. He would eventually lead the revolution down his own particular path of human brutality.

Within this unstable economic and political context, it seems almost heroic that Soviet artists and architects during these same years would briefly seize the lead in Europe.[5] Painters to some extent led the way. Kasimir Malevich (1878–1935) began experimenting with pure abstraction in 1913 and two years later exhibited his celebrated *Black Square*. By 1919 he had defined "suprematism" as a dematerialized and nonobjective form of art exploring "new frameworks of pure colour," a scaleless and measureless world independent "of any aesthetic considerations of beauty, experience or mood."[6] Malevich introduced suprematism to the art school at Vitebsk in 1919, and in the following year he organized UNOVIS (Union of the New Art) among whose members was El Lissitzky (1890–1947). Lissitzky was at the time developing his three-dimensional abstract Prouns (acronym for "Project for the Affirmation of the New").

Also advocating abstract art were the brothers Naum Gabo (1890–1977) and Anton Pevsner (1886–1962), who taught at the Free Art Studios in Moscow. In "The Realist Manifesto" (1920), originally issued as a poster, they opposed color as a pictorial element and favored it as material body, opposed the line as a descriptive value and favored it as a direction of static forces and rhythm, opposed any notion of pictorial and plastic space and favored simple depth, and opposed sculptural mass: "We affirm *in these arts a new element of kinetic rhythms as the basic forms of our perception of real time.*"[7]

Another front within Soviet art was being defined by constructivism, founded by Vladimir Tatlin (1885–1953), a painter and sculptor whose "counter-reliefs" were first shown in 1913–14. Tatlin proposed his Monument to the Third International in 1919–20: a dynamic steel-and-glass tower consisting of two intertwining helixes that would have reached a height of 1,300 feet (400 meters). Close to Tatlin in his emphasis on constructional values was Alexander Rodchenko (1891–1956). In two programs issued in 1921–2 (the second with his wife, Varvara Stepanova), Rodchenko referred to constructivism as the "art of the future," and the art whose "scientific communism" was based on the three disciplines of tectonics, facture, and construction.[8] These terms were defined by Rodchenko – and by Aleksei Gan in his book *Konstruktivizm* (1922) – in highly political and rather abstruse ways. Tectonics for him relates to the socialist exploitation of the most recent materials and industrial techniques in the creation of utilitarian art; facture relates to the choice and manipulation (processing) of materials; construction is the "organizational function of constructivism," or the most efficient fabrication of the product possible.

The two vehicles for the dissemination and refinement of constructivist ideas were VKhUTMAS (State Higher Artistic and Technical Studios) and INKHUK (Institute of Artistic Culture). Both were founded in Moscow in 1920. The first was a new school of art and architecture that attracted many of the leading theorists of the new art. In architecture, the first- and second-year course of Nikolai Ladovsky (1881–1941) became renowned across Europe for its new rationalist syntax of machine forms and formal abstraction, based at least in part on his "empathy" research. INKHUK not only funded artistic research but also prepared exhibitions for travel abroad and had regular contacts with such sister institutions as the Bauhaus. Coordinating and infusing these efforts were state agencies: first, the propaganda direction of Prolekult (Proletarian Cultural and Educational Organizations); second, the economic mandate for machine-made and mass-produced products; and, third, the Taylorism of the Central Institute for Labor. Artists contributed in various ways. In the early 1920s, for instance, Tatlin and Rodchenko were involved in designing workers' clothing and machine-made furniture for the masses. Thus architecture and art in the Soviet Union were accepted from the start as extensions of the larger economic and political body.

76. Vesnin Brothers, Palace of Labor competition project, 1923. From Walter Gropius, *Internationale Architektur* (Berlin, 1925).

The architectural consolidation of these currents resulted in 1923 in the founding of ASNOVA (Association of New Architects) and in a brilliant architectural flowering – on paper at least. ASNOVA, whose members called themselves rationalists, had as its mission the liberation of architecture from the "atrophied forms" of the stylistic past, and although centered at VKhUTMAS, it reached across the artistic spectrum to embrace the work of Lissitzky, Malevich, and Konstantin Melnikov (1890–1974). The first indication of what constituted the idea of constructivist architecture is found in the work of the Vesnin brothers: Leonid (1880–1937), Victor (1882–1950), and especially Alexander (1883–1959). The three combined in 1923 to produce the remarkable competition design for the Palace of Labor in Moscow (Fig. 76), and in the following year Alexander and Victor designed their famous project for the Leningrad Pravda building. The Palace of Labor combined a central office tower with oval assembly hall but also sported an array of radio masts and cables as well as docking ports for aircraft; the Pravda building had a glass tower with a separate glazed elevator and incorporated the amenities of a loudspeaker, searchlight, clock, and pipe railing. Actual construction, however, was scarcely possible in the first half of the 1920s, and thus the first palpable expression of the new Soviet architecture is perhaps Melinkov's wooden pavilion at the Exposition of the Decorative Arts in Paris in 1925, which featured an open tower and diagonal circulation elements cut into the rectangular plan. Inside, designed by Rodchenko, was a workers' club with chess tables.

The absence of building activity forced many to turn to theory, led by Moisei Ginzburg (1892–1946). Before the war he had studied at the Ecole des Beaux-Arts in Paris and in Toulouse before attending the Academy of Fine Arts in Milan – at the height of futurist activities. He spent the war years at the Riga Polytechnical Institute and graduated with a degree in engineering in 1917. After spending four years in the Crimea, he came to Moscow in 1921 and began teaching history and theory at VKHUTMAS. There he befriended the Vesnin brothers and joined with them in 1925 in founding the first constructivist group of architects, the OSA (Society of Modern Architects). By this date Ginzburg had already published two books. In the first, *Ritm v arkhitekture* (Rhythm in architecture, 1923), he spoke of the constructivist preference for dynamic forms in rhythmic motion and the phenomenological relation to human experience. In his second book, *Stil' I epokha* (Style and epoch, 1924), he produced a pathbreaking study that moved Soviet theory to the forefront of European thought.[9]

Ginzburg was not only an architect but an intellectual. With his education in France and Italy and his knowledge of German and American developments, he brought a European perspective to Soviet theory. There are discernible traces of Wölfflin's historiography, Spengler's despair, and Taylor's scientific efficiency in his thinking; others have noted the ideas of Paul Frankl, Wilhelm Wörringer, and Le Corbusier.[10] His study is original, however, in its quick synthesis of relatively old ideas into a new model. He defines styles in a Wölfflinian fashion as "certain kinds of natural phenomena that impose definite traits on all manifestations of human activity, large and small, quite irrespective of whether or not their contemporaries have aspired to or even have been at all aware of them."[11] All styles for him move through three stages of development: youth (constructive), maturity (organic), and old age (decorative). And he basically draws upon the Saint-Simonian notion that a new stylistic synthesis will emerge from the two principal styles

from the past (Graeco-Italic and Gothic). Additionally, he accepts the Spenglerian idea that European practice has been in decline for the past two centuries, and even these two centuries are isolated from the present by the "grandiose cataclysm" of World War I and the Russian Revolution. Hence, there is the optimism that "the language of modernity," residing in *the true essence of the present day, its rhythm, its everyday labor and concerns, and its lofty ideal*," will produce a new evolutionary phase of practice.[12]

What is also of interest in his analysis is how he isolates the factors of the new style. His historical survey concludes with a "picture of complete decline" as far as European practice is concerned (including a rejection of Behrens's monumentalizing of the factory aesthetic at the AEG) and an appreciation of American industrial might: "An American tempo of life is emerging, utterly different from that of Europe – businesslike, dynamic, sober, mechanized, devoid of any romanticism – and this intimidates and repels a placid Europe."[13] What he is alluding to are the models of industrial development (factories and grain silos), which he initially defines through the "*purposive clarity* of the spatial solution" and "*dynamics and its penetrating force.*"[14] As the first task of the modern world is the construction of workers' housing and industrial factories, the latter should provide the formal paradigm for the new architecture.

More precisely, the metaphor that Ginzburg uses is the machine, which he views as the undecorated vehicle of "utmost organization" and as a motor for mobility. If unadorned organization leads to "precision in formulating a creative idea," mobility can be illustrated by a locomotive or in the Vesnin brothers' design for the Palace of Labor of 1923, which Ginzburg very instructively reduces to a series of vertical and diagonal arrows representing visual forces. This empathic force field is for him a sweeping conceptualization of theoretical importance; not only is the machine's "tension and intensity, as well as its keenly expressed direction" now the chosen emblem of the new style, but the machine also engenders a specific architectural preference for "a form that is asymmetrical or that, at best, has no more than a single axis of symmetry, which is subordinated to the main axis of movement and does not coincide with it."[15] From this perspective, constructivism is the first "constructive" stage of the new style.

Ginzburg's study might be instructively compared with El Lissitzky's *Russland* (Russia, 1930), a book that first appeared in Vienna.[16] Lissitzky was, if anything, more buoyant in interpreting the significance of this "new page in human history." He had spent much of the 1920s in Germany and

Switzerland as an artist and cultural ambassador, where he had a major influence on the course of events. At the conclusion of his book, he summarizes the new architecture using three principles: (1) Architecture is not "a mere emotional, individualistic, and romantic affair"; (2) a *sachliche* approach to design should be employed; and, most importantly, (3) architecture should be "goal directed" and scientific.[17] Russian architecture, Lissitzky admits, has for centuries lagged behind that of the West, but at the same time he is critical of European developments of the 1920s (its aesthetic tendencies) and adamant in presenting architecture as a socialist or revolutionary art. The two most pressing concerns for Soviet architecture are housing (to be solved by building large complexes with communal kitchens and kindergartens) and workers' clubs, whose purpose is cultural reeducation. It is not hard to read – behind his utopianism – the severity of the economic problems still limiting the realization of so many designs. By 1930 Lissitzky was also meeting opposition from both professional and political circles within Russia.

The competition for Palace of the Soviets (1931–3) – the swan song for this phase of Soviet practice – is a case in point. Already in 1929 a professional group (under the acronym VOPRA [All-Union Organization of Proletarian Architects]) had formed to oppose both the machine aesthetic and the Western-inspired roots of the OSA. The announcement of the competition in June 1931 coincided with a speech by a Communist Party secretary who lamented the lack of aesthetic considerations in contemporary architectural practice.[18] To further complicate the judging, in April 1932 Stalin issued his decree "Concerning the Reorganization of Literary-Artistic Societies," which laid the basis for establishing what would be known as "socialist realism" (a version of neoclassicism) as the official state style. Thus the outcome of the competition was close to being decided before the actual event unfolded. Over 160 entries from around the world were submitted to the committee at the end of 1931. The best known was the project of Le Corbusier. It was rejected in the early stages of the judging because it "cultivates the aesthetic of a complicated machine."[19] The most brilliant design was by the Vesnin brothers, and it lasted until the later rounds. The winning scheme, by Boris Iofan, Vladimir Shchuko, and Vladimir Gelfreik, featured a neoclassical tower 315 meters high, capped by a colossal statue of Lenin. Construction on the project began in 1937, only to be halted by the war.

By the late 1930s the avant-garde chapter of Soviet architecture had long since ended, and nearly all of the formerly "modern" architects had been forced from practice or sent to labor camps. Thus this momentary flowering of Soviet architecture collapsed overnight into the black historical hole of Stalinism.

3. De Stijl and Dutch Modernism

As Holland was one of the few neutral countries during World War I, its architecture displays a continuity not seen elsewhere in Europe. It was also one of the few European countries where avant-garde thinking had a direct and noticeable effect on architectural practice, and earlier than elsewhere on the Continent. Its building activity, combined with its surprisingly varied lines of competing ideologies, also made it the most vibrant European country architecturally in the first half of the 1920s.

The continuity of Dutch developments is seen in the work of Berlage, who continued to get commissions almost unabated throughout the war years. In 1914–16 he erected the Holland House in London, at the same time that he was designing a sumptuous hunting lodge for the Kröller-Müller family in Hoenderloo (1914–20). In 1919 he began design work on the museum at The Hague, and throughout this period he was making urban proposals for Amsterdam South, the first plans for which he had produced in the early 1900s. Behind these proposals was a new program for building 3,500 housing units put forth in 1915 by the new mayor of Amsterdam. Over the next two years, Berlage reworked his earlier schemes and produced a plan of unified roads and blocks of housing, distinct in logic but not unrelated in character to the concentric system of canals to the north.

Amsterdam South became the venue for the housing estates of Pieter Kramer (1881–1961) and Michel de Klerk (1884–1923), the leaders of the so-called Amsterdam school. These two architects got their start in the office of Eduard Cuypers, and both were active in the Dutch Communist Party. Both too were sympathetic with the editorial direction of Theo van der Wijdeveld (b. 1886) at the Dutch journal *Wendingen*, which during the war years championed European expressionist and Dutch vernacular movements. De Klerk's two designs for the housing and community estate Eigen Haard (1913–16) and his and Kramer's combined work on the Dageraad estate (1920–2) represent a vivid alternative to earlier barracks-style housing owing to their attention to detail and mastery of scale, the formal variety of the designs, and the inventive use of masonry textures.

Two other architects of great talent working within the Amsterdam school were J. M. van der Mey and J. F. Staal.

Not unrelated to the work of the Amsterdam school, and strongly influenced by Frank Lloyd Wright, were the efforts of the very talented Willem Dudok (1884–1974). In 1918 he became the municipal architect of Hilversum, and it was here that he created (among several other impressive buildings) the asymmetrical grouping of volumes for the Town Hall (1924–30). Dudok himself may have denied Wright's influence, but two of the latter's strategies – the extension of spatial volumes outward and the horizontal layering of elements with a vertical anchor – have here been mastered by Dudok in a way that cannot be disputed.

Yet Dutch modernism in the late teens and early 1920s is almost synonymous with the influential *De Stijl* journal and movement of the same name. Its two founders were the painters Pieter Mondrian (1872–1944) and Theo van Doesburg (1883–1931).[20] That the movement arose in Holland had much to do with the turmoil created by the war. Mondrian, who had started his career as a painter in Holland before 1900, moved to Paris in 1911 and became strongly attracted to cubist developments. He was on a visit home in 1914 when the war broke out, and thus he remained in Holland. For a few years he had been experimenting with abstraction and was pursuing a path that would lead him to his black-line compositions of the late teens. Van Doesburg, who was eleven years younger, developed his ideas only slightly later. He was called into Dutch military service in 1914 to guard the Belgium frontier, and it was during this period that he first read Wassily Kandinsky's *Concerning the Spiritual in Art* (1910), which emphasized the empathetic values of color and the appropriateness of abstraction as a spiritual means to rid art of its contaminating materialism.[21]

Also influencing Mondrian were his conversations with Mathieu Schoenmaekers (1875–1944). This influential Dutch Theophist-Christophist published his theories in two books that appeared in 1915 and 1916: *Het nieuwe wereldbeeld* (The new image of the world) and *Beginselen der beeldende wiskunde* (The principles of plastic mathematics). Schoenmaekers referred to his beliefs as a "positive mysticism"; they have been called Neoplatonic and redemptive, although they are not far removed from the Renaissance belief in an overriding cosmic unity or harmonic proportions operating within the universe. Schoenmakers also rejected the "appearance" of nature (the world) and preferred to view its forms as arcane symbolic truths that must be penetrated so that their inner mathematical order can be intuitively revealed to the mind.[22] The real world, as opposed to the apparent world, is rational, plastic, and mathematical, or more simply an abstraction fashioned by or susceptible to reason. Behind this esotericism lurks, once again, a Spenglerian dread about worldly events; the war, even in Holland, had shattered all belief in the values of the old social order. The idea of progress came to be viewed with disillusion, and the escape to utopianism owes much to the political and moral plight of Europe.

Similar sentiments are found in the first *De Stijl* manifesto of 1918, which opens with this thesis: "There is an old and a new consciousness of time. The old is connected with the individual. The new is connected with the universal. The struggle of the individual against the universal is revealing itself in the world war as well as in the art of the present day."[23] This "new consciousness of time," which emphasizes the present and rejects the traditions of the past, defines itself essentially through abstraction or through the negation of the emotional and the personal. Against the individuality of the past (which has only led to war), there must now arise a new conception of the collective. The collective must acknowledge the commonality of humanity and manifest its style through the objectivity of abstraction.

In painting, the elements of this abstract art are planes (often square or rectangular), lines, and color. In van Doesburg's textbook of 1925, he reduces the expressive means of the painter simply to color: positive (the primaries red, blue, yellow) and negative (black, white, and gray).[24] The crucial point here is the belief that an evolution has taken place from natural forms to "plastic" elements. For architecture, there is a similar evolution of means. In one manifesto of 1923, van Doesburg notes that architecture now consists only of the laws of space and color.[25] Two years later he limits architectural expression to "surfaces, masses (positive), and space (negative). The architect expresses his aesthetic experience through relationships of surfaces and masses to interior spaces and to space."[26]

The translation of these principles into practice is of course a more elusive task, and van Doesburg took some years to develop an understanding how to achieve this. At De Stijl's inception in 1917, there were in fact three architects associated with the movement: Robert van't Hoff (1887–1979), Jan Wils (1891–1972), and J. J. P. Oud (1890–1963). The first two men were attracted to the cubic austerity and constructional lessons of Wright, but this grounding in materiality eventually made their efforts incompatible with the planar abstraction van Doesburg was seeking. The case of Oud is different because he had discussed with van Doesburg the possibility of forming the journal *De Stijl* as early as 1915, and he was a close friend of Mondrian as well. This is important because at least one De Stijl painter – Bart van der Leck – specifically opposed allowing architects into De Stijl because of their tendency to meddle with color.[27]

Van der Leck's fears were actually borne out by the subsequent collaboration and breakup of Oud and van Doesburg. Oud had received his architectural training at the Technical University in Delft and worked briefly for Theodor Fischer in Munich. In 1914 he moved to Leiden, where he collaborated with Dudok on one project. The next year he came under the influence of Berlage – both formally and politically – and it was the latter who, in 1917, passed to Oud the commission for a community center in Leiden. The twin-gabled symmetrical building designed by Oud was constructed of brick and had red-tiled roofs in the manner of Berlage but featured a color scheme by van Doesburg. The scheme called for painted window frames and a series of colored-brick panels on the exterior and colored-tile floor patterns and painted doors and fames in the interior. The modulated Dutch-brick detailing on the exterior creates an odd juxtaposition with the incorporated "art." Around this time, however, Oud began experimenting on paper and in practice with more abstract compositions. His renovation of and addition to a seaside villa at Katwijk aan Zee (1917) rightfully might be called the first architectural success achieved using the De Stijl vocabulary.

The split between Oud and van Doesburg came during their collaboration on the "Spangen" housing blocks in Rotterdam, which Oud designed early in 1918. Van Doesburg prepared two color schemes for the project in 1920 and 1921 – that is, after Mondrian weighed in on the architecture by suggesting that a building should be conceived as a multiplicity of planes in which color is integral and everywhere present. The problem is that Oud's designs for Spangen were still gabled and somewhat traditional in form, and van Doesburg sought to overlay the designs with strong interior and exterior color schemes. When Oud balked at the preeminence of color over form, van Doesburg responded with his famous "either this – or nothing" letter. Oud opted for the latter.[28]

The split was advantageous to Oud, as in 1918 he received an important appointment, as the municipal architect for Rotterdam. As a socialist tending ever more toward European rationalism, Oud in his new role as city architect began turning to simple, straightforward, and economical solutions to housing problems and retreating from what he regarded as the pretension and cost of De Stijl gamesmanship. It is interesting that in his article of June 1921, written

a few months prior to his breakup with van Doesburg, he scarcely mentions color (except for the admonition not to paint brick). He opens this important essay with a nod to the "new, spiritual living-complexes" that are forming and the role of futurism and cubism in altering aesthetic perspectives, but he just as quickly leaves them behind for what is almost a replay of the polemics of Muthesius and Loos of twenty years earlier. The issues are by now much clearer. Architects, because of architecture's grounding in usefulness and the reality of machine production, should look to autos, ships, yachts, electrical and sanitary articles, and men's clothing as departure points for the "new art." Further, they should realize that its new "expressive means par excellence" resides not in ornament but in detailing.[29] For steel construction, this means a minimum of material and hence a focus on the created "empty space"; for reinforced concrete, it means a coherence of the supporting and supported parts and (preempting Giedion) "an almost hovering appearance."[30] Above all there should be a higher form of *Sachlichkeit*, one seen in sophisticated materials, shining finishes and colors, and the glitter of steel:

Thus there is the tendency of architectonic development toward a building-art that in its essence is tied to the material more so than in the past, but in its appearance will go far beyond the material; it will be a building-art free of all impressionistic and atmospheric design, one whose purity of proportions will be seen in the fullness of light, in a brightness of color and an organic clarity of form that, through the absence of anything secondary, will far exceed classical purity.[31]

The split with Oud was also helpful to van Doesburg, because it allowed him to rethink his earlier position, which he did during his two stays in Berlin and Weimar in 1921–2. He first visited Berlin in December 1920 and met Bruno Taut, Adolf Behne, and Walter Gropius, the last of whom invited him to visit the Bauhaus in Weimar. Van Doesburg accepted the invitation early in 1921, and after finishing scheduled lectures elsewhere, he returned in April to set up shop near the school and publish his journal from Weimar. De Stijl's membership at this stage consisted essentially of van Doesburg and Mondrian, the last of whom had moved back to Paris in 1919. Van Doesburg's quest was thus that of a missionary: to proselytize his ideas and solicit new converts to the cause. On both counts he was successful, so much so that his unauthorized, off-campus studio and lectures nearly caused the Bauhaus to go into open revolt against the teachings of Gropius. More importantly, he met El Lissitzky and now joined his ideas with the spatial lessons of suprematism.

The next year van Doesburg met the young Dutch architect Cornelis van Eesteren and another alliance ensued, just as van Doesburg was preparing a De Stijl exhibition for Léonce Rosenberg's gallery in Paris. The hypothetical design of a villa for Rosenberg became the basis for three projects shown in 1923, and among the items displayed were the well-known axonometric drawings of three-dimensional planes suspended in space. The idea behind those drawings owes everything to Malevich and Lissitzky, but van Doesburg's and Mondrian's contribution was to apply color to the full planar surfaces. This idea also inspired another recent convert to the movement, Garrit Rietveld (1888–1964), to design his Schröder House in Utrecht in 1924 (Fig. 77). It was located at the end of a row of three-story brick townhouses and could not have been more anticontextual. The grouped horizontal and vertical planes were painted white and in four shades of gray; window frames, supports, and railings were originally white, gray, black, blue, red, and yellow. It had a startling appearance as an object of art, although it was actually constructed of brick and wood. Notwithstanding the abundance of praise that has been lavished on its design, it is a work that in its conceptual and constructional naïveté underscores vividly the limited possibilities of a De Stijl architecture within existing technology.

This lack of constructional honesty was also becoming apparent to other Dutch architects by 1925, as a distinct change of direction occurs around this time. Oud was establishing himself as the leading Dutch designer with several Rotterdam housing projects. The traditionally conceived brick housing blocks that he used at Spangen gave way in 1922 to the low, village-like architecture of the Oud-Mathenesse estate and even more dramatically to concrete-and-glass elements of the estate at Hook of Holland (1924–7). The two linear stretches of two-story units at Hook featured a continuous second-level balcony and a pavilion-like termination at the four ends: elegant cylinders in which the supporting columns are visible behind the large expanses of curved glass for the ground-level shops. A few years later, Henry Russell Hitchcock and Philip Johnson would regard this feature as the icon for the international style. Oud followed in short order with two other masterpieces: the Café de Unie in Rotterdam (1924) and his Kiefhoek housing estate (1925–9).

Oud was soon joined by talented competitors. In 1925 the young Mart Stam returned to Holland after working for several years in Germany and Switzerland; he joined the office of Johannes Andreas Brinkman (1902–49) and

Leendert Cornelis van der Vlugt (1902–49). The gifted van der Vlugt had already displayed his design skill with his highly respected concrete-and-glass arts and crafts school at Groningen in 1922. The firm of Brinkman and van der Vlugt soon produced several other notable buildings, chief of which was the Van Nelle Tobacco Factory Office Building, Leiden (1925–7), and the Van Nelle Factory, Rotterdam (1926–30). Of all of the built works in Europe in the 1920s, these buildings, with their flat roofs, glass walls, geometric forms, and streets "in the sky," best captured what the constructivists had put down on paper earlier in the decade. Another Dutch architect of considerable talent who emerged during these years was Johannes Duiker (1890–1935). His sanatorium at Hilversum (1926–8), designed with Bernard Bijvoet, was a much admired and much emulated example of international modernism. Arguably, it is one of the most important buildings of the decade.

4. Expressionism and the Bauhaus

With its devastating defeat in the war, Germany was scarcely in a position to dominate European theory in the immediate postwar years. Architectural production had largely ceased in Germany by 1917, and in the following year starvation and housing had become the principal problems of every city. Further, the terms of the Treaty of Versailles prevented the country from immediately rebounding. Inflation rapidly eroded the value of the currency, and attempts at revolution from political extremists on both ends of the spectrum were rampant between 1918 and 23. The industrial optimism of 1914 that had seeded the war (warmly embraced by intellectuals) had been transformed into spiritual malaise and political pessimism. The paranoiac specters of Marx, Nietzsche, and Spengler thus haunted intellectual discourse. A return to the crafts, a withdrawal into "visionary" utopianism, and a dreamy expressionist concern with fanciful images were outlets for architects now forced into prolonged idleness and bare subsistence.

Indicative of the first tendency, without the utopianism, were the efforts of Fritz Schumacher and Heinrich Tessenow. Schumacher left Dresden in 1909 to become the chief architect for the city of Hamburg, where he was to exert enormous influence on the city through his designs and his regional planning endeavors. In two books of 1917, *Die Kleinwohnung* (The small dwelling) and *Das Wesen des neuzeitlichen Backsteinbaues* (The nature of contemporary brick building), he argues for the mass production of urban

77. Garrit Rietveld, Schröder House, Utrecht, 1924–5. From Walter Gropius, *Internationale Architektur* (Berlin, 1925).

housing and for giving special attention to materials, local building traditions, and detailing.[32]

Tessenow, in the postwar years, brings the handicraft interests and modern classicism of his prewar period into sharper focus. Already in *Der Wohnhausbau* (House building, 1909), he had called for the standardization of the small house through the use of elementary forms. With *Hausbau und Dergleichen* (House building and such things, 1916) and *Handwerk und Kleinstadt* (Handicraft and small town, 1918), he defined his theoretical outlook even more succinctly.[33] In the former, for instance, he reduced his elementary design (and concern for the *bürgerliche*) to the principles of *Sachlichkeit* (now "truth in industrial work"), order, regularity, and purity. In 1919 Tessenow returned to Hellerau and produced his best domestic work, partially owing to his obsession with detail.

That German architecture of the postwar years is more generally considered under the rubric of "expressionism" brings with it problems.[34] For one thing the term has been widely applied to a number of philosophical, artistic, and literary movements from Sören Kierkegaard to Edvard Munch. In painting, it has been assigned to the Brücke (Bridge), founded in 1905 by Ludwig Kircher, and to the Blaue Reiter (Blue Rider), founded in 1911 by Wassily Kandinsky and Franz Marc. In architecture, the term is widely employed to refer to a number of different formal conceptions, from the fantasy sketches of Han Poelzig, Bruno Taut, and Hermann Finsterlin to the buildings of Rudolf Steiner, Erich Mendelsohn, and Fritz Höger. The problem is that there is simply no single theoretical thread that connects these various approaches.

The architectural ideas of Rudolf Steiner (1861–1925) reveal the more esoteric side of expressionist thinking without the prevailing despondency. An Austrian by birth, Steiner had been a scholar of Goethe when he moved to Berlin in 1897 and first made contact with literary and artistic circles. By 1902 Steiner had become the leader of the German Theosophical Society, but a decade later he had come to reject its Eastern orientation in favor of his own, more "scientific" individualism. To further his ideas, he founded the Anthroposophical Society, whose goal was to advance human mental or spiritual powers through a series of progressive exercises. Around 1907 Steiner became interested in designing a building for the practice of his religious beliefs, and four years later he designed his first "Goetheanum," which he planned to build in Munich. When city officials turned down his request, he moved the project to Dornach, in the Jura foothills of Basel. Construction began in 1913 on the huge double-domed timber structure set atop a concrete base. More than just a religious place of meditation, it formed part of a spiritual community somewhat modeled on Hellerau.

Although Steiner's design for the first Goetheanum (destroyed by fire in 1922) bears some resemblance to van de Velde's theater for the Werkbund exhibition, his rationale for the design was entirely different, and his intentions were essentially symbolic.[35] In lectures given in the summer of 1914, he demonstrates his familiarity with the ideas of Alois Riegl, Semper, Bötticher, and Adolf Hildebrand – all of whom he rejects for their materialism. He knows as well the ideas on empathy of Wilhelm Wörringer, explained in Wörringer's important and highly influential *Abstraktion und Einfühlung* (Abstraction and empathy, 1908). This leads him to an emphasis on haptic forms underlain with a mathematical and symbolic cosmology. As one of the highest manifestations of the "spiritual science," architecture's task is to create a "whole living organism" in which the soul becomes spiritually shaped by the imprint of sensuous surfaces. The analogy he uses is the baking mold, in which the dough (now space) takes its negative shape: "In our building, however, nothing is mere wall. The forms grow out of the wall. That is the essential thing. And when we pass around inside our building we shall find one plastic form, a continuous relief sculpture on the capitals, plinths, architraves."[36] Thus the soul finds "union with the Spirit" by filling out spatially to the continuous organic forms and partaking of their movement, color, and symbolic imprints.

More representative of the expressionist movement in Germany is the work of Hans Poelzig (1869–1936).[37] He studied architecture at the Technical University in Berlin and in 1900 moved to Breslau to teach at the School of Art and Applied Arts. In 1903 he became the school's director, which puts him on a parallel path with his near contemporary Behrens at Dusseldorf. Even though he was active in the Werkbund, he never accepted the agenda of Muthesius and Behrens. In his speech at the Dresden Exhibit of Applied Art of 1906, he stressed both architecture's tie with tradition and the importance of "tectonic constructional form" imbued with the quality of *Sachlichkeit*.[38] And this craft-based emphasis on sound construction with vernacular overtones became the hallmark of his prewar successes, including Werdermühle Factory on the Oder Island in Breslau (1906) and his Upper Silesia Tower for the Posen Exhibition (1911). His pergola and exhibition building for the Breslau Exhibition of 1913, by contrast, are historical and oddly clash with Max Berg's brilliant concrete exercise, Centennial Hall.

The war years were for the most part lost to Poelzig, but his career rebounded forcefully in 1919, during which year he was elected president of the German Werkbund and designed the Berlin Playhouse. He used his address to the Werkbund conference in Stuttgart – the first since 1914 – to reject the policies of Muthesius and to condemn the linkage of art to mass production and trade policies. He insisted that the Werkbund return to its earlier idealism based in craftsmanship, which he defined as "something absolutely spiritual, a basic attitude of the mind, not technical perfection in some sector or another."[39] It is also an "ethical concept" in its commitment to creating forms with "strong expression." Poelzig thus sought to pull the Werkbund back to the "emotional" and "artistic" side of production: free use of color, original forms, forms with enthusiasm, and a recultivation of a national culture.

Poelzig at the same time set a direction for practice with his design for the Berlin Playhouse. The German theater director Max Reinhardt had purchased a dilapidated market hall in 1919 and hired Poelzig to transform the structure into a theater for 5,000 people. Poelzig responded by constructing a large dome over the projecting stage and arena seating and suspended from it a series of stalactite forms in which he concealed colored lighting. The visually complex cavelike intensity of the forms, justified on both acoustical and lighting grounds, astounded war-weary visitors. A series of foyers (the first brilliant green) with fanlike supports and light columns progressively intensified the emotional drama experienced by the spectators as they moved from the port red theater exterior into the unreal and cathartic world of the stage. The following year he proposed a series of grander schemes for a festival theater complex in Salzburg, but these intense, almost demented proposals were not to be realized. Among Poelzig's designs of the 1920s were also several movie sets.

Poelzig, however, remained an anomaly and – the Werkbund notwithstanding – somewhat aloof from the changing architectural situation. The inspirational force behind the short-lived burst of expressionist activity around 1919 was not Poelzig but rather Bruno Taut (1880–1938).[40] The latter was a tireless promoter and organizer, and by 1919 he was coordinating in Berlin the efforts of a circle of intellectuals that included Walter Gropius (1883–1969) and Adolf Behne (1885–1948). This was the group that was gaining control of German theory, and would direct it for most of the 1920s.

Taut in retrospect appears an unlikely leader. After studying architecture in Berlin and working for Theodor Fischer, he studied urban planning under Theodor Goecke at Berlin's Technical University. Taut opened an office with Franz Hoffmann in 1909 but still largely concentrated his efforts on the organizational front. His design for the Glass Pavilion at the Stuttgart Werkbund Exhibition of 1914 is a case in point. It was not one of the official Werkbund pavilions but a project that Taut himself implemented, first by designing it, then by seeking contributions from glass companies for its erection. His principal client, in fact, was the German Luxfer Prism Company, a subdivision of the famous Chicago firm of glassmakers.[41]

78. Title page of the Arbeitsrat für Kunst manifesto (Berlin, 1919).

The idea for it was gained from the friendship that Taut had formed with the writer and poet Paul Scheerbart (1863–1915). In his *Glasarchitektur* (Glass architecture, 1914), which he dedicated to Taut, Scheerbart touted glass as a metaphor for social change and was ebullient over its architectural possibilities, especially as a medium of light and a stimulator of heightened sensory awareness.[42] Taut, in turn, dedicated his pavilion to Scheerbart, and inside his "cascade room" (with waterfall) he experimented with combinations of silvered glass, colored glass, mosaics, and colored lighting.

At the 1914 Cologne Exhibition, Taut sided with Gropius in opposing the proposals of Muthesius. Also present at the exhibition was Adolf Behne. He had studied both architecture and art history – the last under Heinrich Wölfflin and Georg Simmel – and in 1912 he completed his doctorate on Tuscan architecture. Like Taut, Behne enjoyed Berlin's bohemian life, and he quickly made his mark as an architectural critic and social activist, writing his first polemic on behalf of expressionist architecture in 1915.[43] The friendship of Behne, Taut, and Gropius survived the war, even though Gropius was drafted into service and served at the front. Moreover, their politics became increasingly radicalized as the military disaster unfolded. By war's end, they were committed socialists and active members of the Independent Social Democratic Party (USDP).

Thus they supported the German revolution that took place in November 1918, which provisionally led to the socialist government of Friedrich Ebert. The more radical German communists, the Spartacists, demanded a Soviet-style revolutionary council and the abolition of private property, while Ebert sought a more moderate socialism within the bounds of capitalism. After the revolutionary efforts of Karl Liebknecht and Rosa Luxemburg failed to impose a Marxist government, elections in January resulted in a constitutional body of socialist parties. On 6 February 1919 the so-called Weimar Republic was formally declared.[44]

It was in the midst of this political upheaval (and indeed in the most dire economic circumstances) that two revolutionary associations of artists – the Novembergruppe (November Group) and Arbeitsrat für Kunst (Working Council for Art) – were formed. The former, whose manifesto first appeared in December 1918, was the broader of the two, in terms of both its membership and its ideology (uniting both dadaists and expressionists). As an "alliance of radical artists," it somewhat oddly insisted on a thorough reform of museums (eliminating objects of only "scholarly value"), an overhaul of art schools and curricula, and full control of all matters pertaining to architecture, including the "suppression of artistically worthless architectural monuments."[45]

The Arbeitsrat für Kunst, founded by Taut, Gropius, Behne, and Heinrich Tessenow, was initially more radical in its aims (Fig. 78). It modeled itself on the workers' and soldiers' revolutionary councils and sought to become an official artistic soviet for the revolutionary government. Taut's six-point architectural program, issued on Christmas day 1918, demanded architectural innovations "which demonstrate the cosmic character of architecture, its religious foundations, so-called Utopias" – essentially by relocating people to large housing estates in the country and granting the architect absolute autonomy in all matters of design.[46] But the failure of the Sparticist uprising, leading to the death of Karl Liebknecht and Rosa Luxemburg, quickly changed the political tone of things. Taut resigned his chairmanship of the architectural council, and he was succeeded in March by Gropius, who now covertly plotted a somewhat more moderate, if still revolutionary course. Behne worked alongside Gropius to expand the council's membership and to merge it with the Novembergruppe. Other radicals on the council under Gropius included Max Taut, Otto Bartning, Ludwig Hilberseimer, and Hans and Wassili Luckhardt. Gropius softened the public political agenda essentially by shifting the tactics of the council from those of a political action committee to a more private "conspiratorial brotherhood" – still insisting on an "alliance of the arts under the wing of a great architecture."[47] At the same time Gropius sought to preserve Bruno Taut's expressionist and utopian agenda as a kind of spiritual cleansing, to be achieved by a return to the arts and crafts.

One of the first acts of the Arbeistrat für Kunst was the Exhibition of Unknown Architects held in April 1919. Its theme was utopia, and Gropius, Bruno Taut, and Behne wrote a three-part program articulating the aims of the organization. In Gropius's section, he called for a proletarian return to crafts, the destruction of the academies, and "the creative conception of the cathedral of the future, which will once again be all in *one* shape, architecture and sculpture and painting."[48] Taut bemoaned the ill effects of an "all-devouring society, parasites in the fabric of a society that knows no architecture, wants no architecture and therefore needs no architects!"[49] The less stricken Behne pointed out that the sketches on display were for sale but then nobly insisted that they were not to be purchased by the "snob" who was only in search of "a sensation, an effect."[50] The exhibition, predictably, was a failure; meanwhile, at the nearby Paul Cassirer Gallery, the ink drawings of Erich Mendelsohn were concurrently on display.

At this point revolutionary polemics took one of the oddest turns in all of political history. Shortly after the exhibition, Taut initiated the artists of Gropius's "conspiratorial brotherhood" into his similarly secretive "Crystal Chain": fourteen artists and architects under pseudonyms inspiring one other with chain letters and sketches. Taut encouraged them in the first letter of 24 November 1919 to "consciously be 'imaginary architects'!" and therefore restrict themselves entirely to the world of fantasy.[51] In the same year Taut published *Die Stadtkrone* (City crown) and *Alpine Architektur* –

the first continuing his fascination with the crystal, the second dealing with the creation of mystical shrines and crystalline caves in the Alps. He followed in 1920 with *Die Auflösung der Städte* (The dissolution of cities), which presented childlike sketches of the relocation of people to the countryside; he also began editing the magazine *Frühlicht* (1920–1). Only Taut's appointment as the municipal architect of Magdeburg in 1921 ended his period of pathos.

In more ways than one, the years 1921–3 came to be pivotal for modern German theory. These were the years in which the compelling ideas of Russian constructivism and the Dutch De Stijl began to become known in Germany. It was during these years as well that the Bauhaus first gained notice as a workshop for modern design. Its near cultic reputation in later years, however, did not come easy.

World War I, among other things, created a crisis for German artistic education. Before the war, academies of art and the applied arts had functioned admirably – largely under the control of Muthesius. Afterwards, there was the question of reconstituting their curricula in light of the changed political attitudes and ruinous economic conditions. The prewar arts and crafts school at Weimar had been the creation of Henry van de Velde, who had been invited there in 1902 by the grand duke of Saxe-Weimar as an artistic advisor. Out of this invitation came the decision to build a new school of the applied arts (1904–6), for which van de Velde designed the building and of which he became the first director. Van de Velde also designed the adjacent building for the art school (1904–11), which operated independently. His tenure at the School of Applied Arts, however, ended with the German invasion of Belgium in August 1914, which resulted in his arrest as a Belgian national. Only in 1917, in fact, was the thoroughly humiliated artist allowed to take refuge in Switzerland.

Late in 1914 Gropius, who a few months earlier had supported van de Velde at the Werkbund convention, wrote him to express his sympathy. Van de Velde responded with a letter in which he noted that the grand duke was threatening to close the School of Applied Arts, but that van de Velde had nevertheless recommended Gropius, August Endell, or Hermann Obrist as his successor.[52] The school did indeed cease to exist on 1 October 1915; it served as a military hospital for the remainder of the war. The next day, interestingly enough, Gropius received a letter from Fritz Mackensen, the director of the Weimar Art School, who queried him on the possibility of forming an architecture department within the school.[53] Gropius responded from the war front that the architecture school should be independent and all else secondary to it.[54] Negotiations must have continued through the early winter, because in January 1916 Gropius sent to the state ministry in Weimar his recommendations for the reform of artistic education, especially relating to the crafts.[55] These recommendations were similar to those proposed in Berlin by Wilhelm von Bode, who was the general director of the Berlin museums and was in charge of reforms at the national level.

The war, of course, took its turn for the worse, and it was not until the end of 1918 that Gropius picked up the thread of earlier contacts. He first wrote to Baron von Fritsch in the Berlin ministry and noted that he had been selected for the Weimar directorship earlier and wanted to know if an appointment would still be forthcoming [56] Negotiations must have resumed shortly thereafter, because in April 1919 the details of his appointment had been worked out. He would become director of the Art School (not the defunct School of Applied Arts) and reform it into a school for craft-based instruction, presumably leading to instruction in architecture. Through a bureaucratic backdoor, Gropius got the name of the new school changed to the Staatliches Bauhaus based on the idea that the term *Bauhaus* (literally, construction house) invokes the metaphor of a medieval guild. The first Bauhaus program, written in April, during the same days as the revolutionary brochure for the "Exhibition of Unknown Architects," stressed the same medieval theme, that is, that architects, painters, and sculptors must first return to the crafts for purification, as it were: "Together let us desire, conceive, and create the new structure of the future, which will embrace architecture and sculpture and painting in one unity and which will one day rise toward the heaven from the hands of a million workers like the crystal symbol of a new faith."[57] Gropius further defined the new school as a workshop with no teachers or pupils but rather with masters, journeymen, and apprentices. And although architecture was listed as the first area of instruction, all training was based in the crafts: woodcarving, blacksmithing, cabinetmaking, etching, printing, weaving, drawing, anatomy, and color theory. Thus a fine arts academy was converted into a Morris-inspired crafts school with the ostensible aim of teaching architecture.

To add further to the pedagogical confusion, Gropius's first faculty appointments came from the fine arts: the Blue Rider painter and printmaker Lyonel Feininger (print shop), the sculptor Gehard Marcks (pottery), and the painter Johannes Itten. Moreover, the last artist, who would teach the famed *Vorkurs* (preliminary course) on design, brought with him to Weimar several students steeped in the cultic rituals of the Mazdaznan religion that Itten professed, which required shaved heads, regular meditation, fasts, and a diet of garlic.

The rest of the staff gradually took shape. Among the masters hired in 1920 were Oskar Schlemmer (sculpture and stage), Georg Muchs (weaving), and Paul Klee (stained glass). In 1921 Wassily Kandinsky arrived to take over the wall-painting studio, and in 1923 László Moholy-Nagy was hired to run the metal workshop. It is said that Alma Mahler, the estranged wife of Gropius, had been the one to advise her husband that the success of the school required the hiring of celebrities.[58]

Thus it should not be surprising that in its first years the school struggled for its very survival against attacks on many fronts. The students were alarmed when they learned that their expectation of becoming "artists," which had brought them to the art school in the first place, was at odds with the director's insistence on a return to the crafts. The first student demonstration took place in July 1919 over the faculty jury's awarding of student prizes and its negative evaluation of the work done during the previous year. A more serious walkout of students took place at the start of 1921.[59] The faculty inherited by Gropius similarly felt resentment toward the new director, as their rationale as fine art instructors was unceremoniously dismissed. At the beginning of January 1920, they produced "A Public Declaration of the Artists of Weimar," signed by forty artists, professors, and friends of art, in which they took exception to the "onesided and intolerant rule in the Bauhaus of the extremist Expressionism" and demanded "the restoration on its old premises of the Art Academy in which every art trend can develop freely."[60] This faculty revolt did not simmer down. In 1921 the same professors officially staged a "secession" from the Bauhaus and took over one wing of the building for the reconstitution of the art school.

Still, the opposition from within the school almost paled in comparison with the opposition from without. In this regard, it must be said that Gropius made several tactical errors. He had changed the name of the school to the Bauhaus at one governmental level but bypassed the relevant regulating office, which had opposed the change of name. The first appointment he made – of the "Cubist" Feininger – offended the national minister, von Bode, to whom Gropius had just given private assurances that he would create a craft school.[61] Local residents of Weimar also soon demonstrated en masse against the new director. Their reasons for opposing the Bauhaus were legion: the dismantling of the prestigious academy faculty; the "Expressionist" narrowness of the new curriculum; the "contempt" shown by the new faculty toward the local population; the "Spartacist" political orientation of most students; their abusive behavior toward one nationalist student; and their poor dress, vulgar language, and rowdy behavior. There was also the very real fear of local tradesmen that the Bauhaus workshops would compete with them and reduce their profits. Although it is convenient to dismiss the opposition as politically motivated (leftists in support of Gropius and rightists against), it is surely a mistake to do so. Each side had legitimate arguments, and in any case Gropius himself was eager to flaunt his political colors with his concurrent directorship of the Arbeitsrat für Kunst. Further, Germany had just lost a war and was undergoing a revolution, and its people were cold, hungry, and bitterly divided along political lines.[62]

In 1921, the pedagogical situation began to evolve, partly as a result of several converging forces, chief of which were an awareness of Dutch developments and an appreciation for the new Soviet art. In regard to the influence of Dutch architecture, Behne helped to prepare the way. He traveled to Holland in 1920 and met most of the leading architects. This trip led to his book *Holländische Baukunst in der Gegenwart* (Present-day Dutch architecture, 1922). The De Stijl artist van Doesburg made his first trip to Berlin in December 1920, where he met Gropius at the home of Bruno Taut. He visited Weimar some weeks later, and he returned to the town in April 1921 – much to Gropius's chagrin – to live for the next nine months. He strongly opposed Gropius's crafts-based agenda, and his advocacy of the machine and spatial abstraction caused sharp divisions within both the faculty and the student body. When Gropius refused to let him teach, van Doesburg set up his own unofficial studio, lectured, and had numerous contacts with students.[63]

The influence of constructivism on the Bauhaus is owed to the efforts of El Lissitzky, who arrived in Berlin late in 1921.[64] With Illya Ehrenburg, he started the journal *Vea/Objet/Gegenstand*, the first two issues of which appeared in April 1922, the third and final issue in May.[65] It was a far-ranging cultural journal, mostly in Russian, yet covering all of the arts. The first (double) issue published articles by van Doesburg and Le Corbusier. Early in 1923 Lissitzky had an exhibition in Hanover, where Kurt Schwitters first promoted his Prouns. Lissitzky shortly thereafter became involved editorially with the Berlin journal *G*, which he coedited with Hans Richter and Werner Gräff.[66] The dadaist Richter, who was a friend of van Doesburg and Moholy-Nagy, was the intellectual force behind this journal, while

Gräff was a Bauhaus student during the two previous years. And it was this broader circle of artists who were simultaneously awakening Mies van der Rohe from his Spenglerian slumber. Mies designed his first (acute angled) skyscraper for the Friedrichstrasse competition in 1921 and in the same year developed his rounded, glass version, which appeared in Taut's *Frühlicht* in May 1922. For the first issue of *G* he presented his concrete office building.

There were other forces driving theoretical debate during these years, the most prominent of which was a movement known as *Amerikanismus* (Americanism), which swept through Germany in the early 1920s. It had of course been present prior to the war, but *Amerikanismus* now became a catchphrase (for both proponents and opponents) for everything related to modernity in film, music, dance, industry, and the modern city. Gropius himself had been much attracted to the economic and rational image of America in 1910 when he published his "Program for the Founding of a General Housing-Construction Company Following Artistically Uniform Principles."[67] If the war and Spengler had temporarily halted his interest in technology and mass production, it had fully revived by the early 1920s.

The strongest exponent of Taylorism and American production methods after the war was Gropius's close friend Martin Wagner (1885–1957), later the municipal architect of Berlin. In 1918 Wagner published *Neue Bauwirtschaft* (Modern construction business), which advocated American building methods and business models. In his journal *Soziale Bauwirtschaft* (Social construction business), articles repeatedly pointed to the principles of Taylor as a way to revive the dire German economy. One of the forty-one articles Behne published in 1921, "Mittelalterliches und modernes Bauen" (Medieval and modern building), appeared in Wagner's journal.[68] By 1923 the issue of American mass production literally exploded in Germany with the German translation of Henry Ford's autobiography, which quickly became a best-seller. The idea of American workers not only working at good wages but driving their automobiles to their single-family homes could not have seemed more exotic to impoverished Europeans.

The sudden interest in skyscrapers in Germany was another manifestation of this fascination. When Mies published his glass skyscraper of 1922, he justified its glass aesthetically on the basis that "the impression of the high-reaching steel skeletons is overpowering."[69] And the principal architectural event of this year was the Chicago Tribune Competition, in which no fewer than thirty-seven German architects participated.

Thus the years 1921–3 saw Gropius's growing disaffection with the crafts-based constitution of the Bauhaus and his return to his earlier position regarding technology and mass production – now with new aesthetic justifications. It is evident both in his architectural practice and in the growing divisiveness within the Bauhaus faculty.

In the first regard, the year 1921 defines the turning point. The topping-out ceremony for the Sommerfeld residence took place in December 1920, and the hand-crafted, mostly wood-paneled interiors were finished (in the Bauhaus workshops) a few months later. The Bauhaus student Fred Forbat (1897–1972) oversaw the construction of this log–cabin house set on a limestone base, which symbolized perfectly the Bauhaus's ideal of returning to the crafts. Gropius also had his hand in the design of a nearby office building and lumberyard for Sommerfeld, which many saw as "Chinese" or "Indian" in appearance and as reflecting – according to Forbat – Gropius's strong contemporary interest in Eastern culture.[70]

In 1921, however, Gropius and Meyer designed three other projects that reflect a sense of uncertainty. The Otte House in Berlin-Zehlendorf (1921–2), with its axiality and frontal symmetry (not to mention its odd window proportions), is an unsuccessful hybrid of elements gleaned from Frank Lloyd Wright and the Sommerfeld House. The design for the Kallenbach House (1921–2) is no less awkward, with its clumsy use of the diagonal and the De Stijl color scheme of its site plan. The renovation of the theater in Jena, for which Gropius received the commission in November 1921, defines a partial break, for the outside has plain stucco walls and flat roofs. Inside he put Oskar Schlemmer in charge of the color scheme and the painting of a large fresco. When this scheme was severely criticized by van Doesburg the following spring, Gropius had the whole interior repainted with a De Stijl color scheme. Mies van der Rohe, recalling his 1923 visit to the refinished theater, stated that he was still "rather disappointed" with its decorative superficiality.[71]

Gropius, as has often been noted, was not an especially talented architect, but he did persist in moving forward. In the spring of 1922 – enthused by *Amerikanismus* and Le Corbusier's writings – he developed a renewed interest in mass-produced housing and asked Forbat to prepare a site plan and a standardized housing scheme for a Bauhaus settlement in nearby Am Horn. Forbat advanced the block-like scheme as far as obtaining building permits in July, until code officials objected to the flat roofs. The project then languished until other students reworked the scheme in 1923 for the first Bauhaus exhibition. An experimental

house, designed by the painter Georg Muche (assisted by the student Marcel Breuer), was also erected as an exhibit, but it was widely criticized for its unworkable floor plan. Gropius had in the meantime prepared his Chicago Tribune design and was now firmly committed to technology and industry.

Parallel with this architectural transformation were the battles that Gropius waged with his own faculty over the same issue. Itten seems to have initiated the conflict at a faculty meeting toward the end of 1921 by opposing any school requirements for solving practical tasks. Gropius responded at a faculty meeting in December with the admonition that real problems should be taken into account and that the economic viability of the school depended on outside commissions.[72] The following February Gropius issued an eight-page circular in which he reiterated his views.[73] He pointed to the experiments in Russia, praised the engineer for his "clear and organic forms," and called for a unity of art and industry. Over this issue Gropius and Itten became engaged in what was widely recognized as a personal power struggle for control of the school, and interestingly most of the painters on the faculty were opposed to Gropius. Gropius's close friend Feininger adamantly opposed any contact with industry, as did Muche and Schlemmer.[74]

The showdown came in the summer of 1923 in connection with the first Bauhaus exhibition. It was also a critical juncture for the existence of the school. In 1920 the Bauhaus had been given a three-year budget, and it was now time for the students to demonstrate the strides they had made in their crafts-based education. Outside opposition toward the school had only intensified over the years, and it is to the credit of Gropius that he stood steadfast against both internal and external political pressure. He set a new direction for the school in August with his keynote address kicking off "Bauhaus Week," entitled "Art and Technology: A New Unity." His vision, however, was rudely contested by a manifesto written by Schlemmer for the exhibition catalogue. The artist – using some of Gropius's own words from four years before – glorified the Bauhaus as a lonely and idealistic "cathedral of socialism" against "the materialism and the mechanization of art and life." He also proclaimed much more – the death of God, the unholy "speed and supertension of commercialization," the force of capitalism negatively delivering "the work of man against man."[75] Gropius, who had not seen the text before its publication, worked feverishly on the eve of the exhibition opening to remove the overtly political manifesto from the catalogues, but it was too late; a few advance copies had been sent to the press.

The exhibition itself was a huge event, located in several sites around Weimar and lasting six weeks. Oud came from Holland to lecture. A new score by Igor Stravinsky was first performed. Many architects from Berlin and elsewhere came to view the International Exhibition of Architecture that Gropius had simultaneously arranged and that supplied the material for his first book. This was really the first attempt on the part of Gropius to define the new movement according to his own architectural ideas. And while some of the competing currents of modernism were represented (as manifest in works by Mies van der Rohe, Erich Mendelsohn, and Hans Poelzig), other approaches were pointedly omitted (those of Hugo Häring and Hans Scharoun). Mies, as has often been noted, was privately quite critical of Gropius's efforts as well as his narrow selection of work to be shown.[76]

Reviews of the exhibitions were generally favorable, but with qualifications. Walter Passarge noted that the Bauhaus project was not yet "finished and complete," but he praised the "earnestness and determination" with which the task of integrating art and technology was being pursued. He also noted the "homogeneity, relevance, and clarity" of the international architectural work exhibited and saw it as closer to the spirit of the time than "all 'Utopian' and 'Expressionistic' architecture" – a critique certainly of the earlier positions of Gropius and Taut.[77] Another discerning critique of the event was written by Adolf Behne. He rightly pointed out that the new theme of technology was not at all evident in the "small-mindedness of handicrafts" that dominated the show.[78] He also noted that Gropius was personally at a crossroads: forced to choose between his changing designs of the past few years and the theme of *Sachlichkeit* that he would ultimately have to embrace.

Itten, having now lost the showdown with Gropius, left the school immediately after the event, but local antagonism toward the school did not cease. A Communist insurrection in Thuringia in October brought in the national army and swung political sentiment to the right. Gropius, at one point, had his house searched by agents of the army.[79] The fate of the school was decided by the Thuringian elections of early 1924, in which the ruling left-wing coalition of socialists was defeated by a right-wing coalition of parties. Gropius struggled to save the school throughout the year, but in December the Thuringian Diet voted to close the "cathedral of socialism" and dismiss the faculty.

In retrospect, this decision worked out well for the school. In the winter of 1925 Gropius negotiated with Fritz Hesse, the socialist mayor of Dessau, to relocate the school there and erect new facilities – Gropius's first major commission

and one of the more advanced examples of the new style. At Dessau, in interim quarters, Gropius began operating the Bauhaus printing press, which became an invaluable propaganda vehicle for the school. What is generally referred to today as Bauhaus design – the industrial household products, the graphics of Moholy-Nagy, the Breuer chrome chairs – mostly originated at Dessau, although certainly some excellent designs came out of Weimar. In 1927 the curriculum expanded to include an architecture school, shortly before Gropius resigned his post early in 1928.

The mid-1920s became a defining moment in German modernism in another sense: The first two histories of the "modern movement" were published during these years. Adolf Behne actually wrote *Der moderne Zweckbau* (The modern functional building) in 1923 but was unable to find a publisher, in part owing to the competing and inhibiting efforts of his erstwhile friend Gropius. It finally appeared in 1926, one year after Gropius published his first book, *Internationale Architektur*, which was compiled from the exhibition documents of 1923. Both articulate interpretations of the changes in European architecture since the war.

Der moderne Zweckbau is by far the more theoretical of the two.[80] Behne builds his book around the dual notions of *Zweck* (function, purpose) and *Sachlichkeit*. He never defines the last term, which in the era of Streiter and Muthesius signified the simple and practical solution to a problem. The notion as resurrected by Behne seems to have had this meaning and a bit more. In his forward to Max Taut's *Bauten und Pläne* (Buildings and plans, 1927), Behne wrote a short essay on the notion, which he defined over several pages. It is not a small concept, he notes, and it does not mean dryness, plainness, or spare schematization: "*Sachlichkeit* means responsible thinking, it means a work that satisfies all purposes with and out of the imagination. For imagination belongs to it: to grasp the purpose where it uncovers its revolutionary meaning."[81] There is also a social dimension for Behne; a design is *sachlich* when it attends to a social concern, when it satisfies a "healthy function in human society."[82] In *Der moderne Zweckbau*, the term *Sachlichkeit* is depicted as a progressive unfolding of three conceptual stages of formal development, as revealed by three chapter headings. "No Longer a Facade but a House" is the first stage – represented by Wagner, Berlage, Messel, and Wright – when the concept of a historical facade in design gives way to a shaping of the floor plan according to functional necessity. "No Longer a House but Shaped Space" represents the second stage, when the house or the box itself gives way to a stricter *Sachlichkeit*. Behrens's work at the AGE and the ideas of Henry Ford initiate this phase, which is also represented in American grain silos and in the designs of such architects as Henry van de Velde and Erich Mendelsohn. In the third chapter, "No Longer Shaped Space but Designed Reality," Behne sees *Sachlichkeit*'s highest mediation in the merging in Germany of (Eastern) constructivist demands with the (Western) rationalist sensibilities of Dutch and French architects. Interestingly, for Behne, as opposed to Gropius, it is the organic functionalism of Hugo Häring and Hans Scharoun that best exemplifies this amalgamation in Germany. Further, Behne's large selection of illustrations is extremely wide ranging. Modernism for him is broad based and also open ended in its allowance for future development.

Gropius's *Internationale Architektur* contains only a short foreword, but it is a powerfully worded manifesto of what he deems to be the new and deterministic spirit of functionalism. Against the sentimental, aesthetic, and decorative conceptions of the past, there has slowly arisen a new "universal will-to-form" rooted in the totality of society and life, a profound spiritual change that in architecture seeks "to design the buildings of our surroundings from an inner law without lies and ornamentation, to represent functionally their meaning and purpose through the tension of their architectural masses and to reject everything superfluous that masks their absolute form."[83] This overwhelming *Zeitgeist* further "recognizes a **unified** world image of our time, it presumes the longing to free spiritual values from their individual limitation and to raise them to **objective validity**."[84] Architects and people obviously cannot stand in the way of the new international movement; its appearance is predestined. Hence the earlier determinism of Peter Behrens is erected as the ideological premise of the modern movement.

The selection of illustrations here is narrower than in the book by Behne. The genealogy of this new international architecture starts with Behrens and Wright and (most importantly) with the prewar factories of Gropius (Meyer is not credited in the captions). Gropius, in fact, is far and away the architect most often illustrated, and therefore we must presume him to be the architect most smitten by this indomitable world spirit. There is, nevertheless, an informed selection of works from Russia, France, Czechoslovakia, Holland, and Germany. Projects for tall buildings are of special interest; in fact, the illustrations close with an aerial photograph of the lower part of Manhattan. Overall, in this overlaid conception of a *Zeitgeist* we find the creation of the first historical myth of European modernism. Spengler is refuted by being transformed.

5. Le Corbusier and Giedion

Charles-Édouard Jeanneret watched the travesty of World War I from his home in La Chaux-de-Fonds.[85] Upon leaving Germany in the summer of 1911, he had made his *voyage d'orient* to Turkey and Greece, which he reached by way of the Balkans and returned from by way of Italy. Shortly after arriving back in Switzerland he began teaching decorative and interior design at the Ecole d'Art. He had two residential commissions prior to the war. The first, the Villa Jeanneret-Perret (1912), was built for his parents on a steep hillside above La Chaux-de-Fonds. Jeanneret responded with a nearly symmetrical neoclassical solution that is reminiscent of the style of Behrens. The young architect's ambition also got the better of him, as the size and costly details of the rather large villa were far beyond his parents' means. Thus the house, which his parents were eventually forced to sell at a significant loss, had the effect of exhausting their life's savings. The second project, the Villa Favre-Jacot (1912–13), was fortunately built for a wealthier client, and its Mediterranean classicism, together with its colored columns and piers, shows something of a break from Germanic influence. A third prewar project (done in 1914) – his so-called *Cité Jardin* – was a plan for a residential neighborhood that featured winding streets. In its general character, it is reminiscent of the garden city at Hellerau, which he visited for a second time in June 1914. Jeanneret was to be the architect for the houses in the development, but the war intervened.

The war had the effect of virtually shutting down Jeanneret's architectural career. He lost his teaching position in May 1914 over a flap with the school commission that was in part political (opposition from socialists), in part pedagogical. He visited the Werkbund conference in Cologne in June, and in December he entered a competition for a masonry bridge over the Rhone River near Geneva. This arched design is significant only because it helped to renew his friendship with Max Du Bois, an engineer and childhood friend who was now working in Paris. For Jeanneret it was an entirely one-way relationship, as the architect had no training in mathematics or structural engineering. He continually exploited the good graces of Du Bois to obtain structural advice and the most detailed design services free of charge. Around 1915 Jeanneret became involved with his "Dom-ino" housing system, which is perhaps the most misunderstood and overrated project of his career.

The intention was to design a concrete slab and pier system that could be used in mass-produced housing.[86] The idea of a slab supported on recessed columns in itself was certainly not new, but the self-imposed restrictions that Jeanneret insisted upon greatly complicated the solution to a simple problem. He wanted a flat slab (flat on both sides) supported on square piers without the customary swelling or outward angling at the top of the column to facilitate the transfer of shear forces. Moreover, he wanted it to be produced at the site without temporary wooden forms and with unskilled labor. Given these criteria, the solution – which seems to have cost Du Bois and another engineer hundreds of hours of work, although Jeanneret applied for the patent in his name only – can simply be described as naive. It consisted of a series of hollow tiles resting on the top flanges of temporary I beams with concrete poured around the tiles and strengthened with reinforcing bars. For the pour, the I beams rested on another set of temporary I beams secured to the columns. It was by no means an economical solution, and it certainly could not have been carried out by unskilled labor or have been supported on uncured or freshly poured piers. Further, it made little sense as an idea in that the flat slab disallowed cavities for wiring and ducts and (once poured) could only have been penetrated (for pipes, chimneys, and vents) by drilling. The sketches of houses that Jeanneret made to display his system scarcely redeem the design; it is minimal housing of the most primitive kind, and it is little wonder that the system was never used by Jeanneret or anyone else.

The only project that Jeanneret built during the war – if we disallow his pirated scheme for the cinema La Scala – demonstrates his growing interest in concrete. The Villa Schwob (1916–18) was designed as a concrete structure, but it was engineered by a Zurich firm with a conventional joist and slab system. The symmetrical design of the house – with its empty billboard facade on the north and awkward detailing on both sides at the attic level – has been extensively analyzed for Jeanneret's first use of a geometrical proportional system. The project, however, was better known in its day for its huge cost overruns, which eventually resulted in a lawsuit. Jeanneret sued Raphael Schwob for his failure to pay the architect's fee. The latter countersued the architect for allowing an original budget of 115,000 francs to climb to over 300,000 and for his lack of architectural oversight (malpractice). These suits took place in 1918, just as Jeanneret found himself enmeshed in another complicated series of lawsuits emanating from the technical problems surrounding leakage at the cinema La Scala (1916). Here, at least, he was not sued for secretly taking over the commission and pirating the design of another architect. It was,

nevertheless, an unfortunate finale to his habitation in his hometown.

In January 1917 Jeanneret moved to Paris to put these experiences behind him. He was approaching the age of thirty and had been in practice for a little over a decade. At best he was a mediocre architect, and he had failed to establish any hint of an original style. France was still very much at war. In fact the German shelling of Paris by long-range artillery began in March, but Jeanneret was all but oblivious to it. Du Bois had kindly prepared his triumphant arrival into the metropolis by arranging an office, a secretary, and a job as manager of a plant producing building materials. For the next five years Jeanneret built no buildings, except for a water tower and a double-house for a proposed housing estate in Normandy. His work, however, brought him face to face with the issue of building materials, and his reading now encompassed Taylorism, which for him would become his ideological creed for all things related to architecture.[87] He wrote a book-length manuscript entitled "France ou Allemagne," which played to France's wartime nationalism by touting its superiority to Germany in art and architecture. He also developed his interest in painting. This interest mushroomed in the winter of 1917–18 when Perret introduced Jeanneret to the painter Amédée Ozenfant (1886–1966) – his new mentor and, for a while, his new best friend.

If the engineer Du Bois had rescued Jeanneret from provincial life, it was Ozenfant who taught him how to become an artist. Ozenfant introduced Jeanneret into the artistic circles of Paris and, most importantly, provided him with a set of "architectonic" principles – to use a term employed by Alfred H. Barr more than a half-century ago – that were fully translatable into architecture.[88] In 1920 Ozenfant even helped him create a new name to go along with his new persona: Le Corbusier.[89]

Ozenfant's campaign of Purism had begun in 1915 when he founded the journal L'Elan, which grew out his cubist period and featured articles on Picasso, Matisse, and Apollinaire. The first reference to Purism was published there in December 1916 under the title "Notes sur le cubisme." In these notes Ozenfant referred to cubism as "a movement of purism" but described it as lately suffering from its repetitive motifs and undue focus on the fourth dimension.[90] Jeanneret met the painter early in 1917, during the period in which Ozenfant was contemplating a larger manifesto. The friendship was swiftly cemented, and in fact Jeanneret moved his easel into Ozenfant's studio, where he was daily tutored on both the theory and practicalities of working with oils. In September 1917 the two collaborated on *Après le cubisme*, the manifesto to accompany the first exhibition of Purist paintings, scheduled for the end of the year. In its intellectual tenor, Purism was idealistic and conservative rather than "avant-garde" – it called for order, clarity, logic, and a common ground on which to meet the modern world of technology. It was also a dry run for better things, because in 1920 the two men teamed up with the poet Paul Dermée to launch the journal *L'Esprit Nouveau*, Jeanneret's springboard to fame.[91]

The principles of Purism were pivotal to Le Corbusier's theoretical development. Purism is often construed as part of a larger *rappel à l'ordre* (call to order) especially evident in French art. If it grew out of the cubist movement, it was at the same time a critique of cubism's individualist and fragmentary images. Purism stressed "plastic" form of a more intellectual nature, that is to say, "a work of art should induce a sensation of a mathematical order, and the means of inducing this mathematical order should be sought among universal means."[92] Therefore it emphasized precision of contour, cleanness of line, volumetric representation, flattening in the overlaying of planes, overall ordering of objects and contours, and Cartesian rationalization. Its colors tended toward the cool grays and cool browns and the deeper tones of red and green, and on this issue the Purists stood in vivid opposition to De Stijl and the constructivists. Above all, its painterly themes were "objets-types" – bottles, glasses, pipes, guitars – or typical forms that had been created for their usefulness but at the same time had achieved cultural status. Ozenfant and Jeanneret spoke of a "mechanical selection" of objects as parallel to Darwinian "natural selection" and of a world in which these objects of use have become purified by a process of economy, human scale, and mathematical harmony.[93] These types, when portrayed on the canvas, moreover, were carefully arranged with regulating lines to form asymmetric compositions, but at the same time were carefully ordered. The emphasis on plastic form, simple volumes, clean lines, smooth surfaces, flattened planes, and ruling geometry was directly translatable into architecture.

L'Esprit Nouveau was conceived more broadly as a cultural entity dedicated to modernity. According to the opening issue, "There is a new spirit: it is a spirit of construction and of synthesis guided by a clear conception." Therefore the journal would be "truly dedicated to the living aesthetic."[94] Dermée saw it primarily as an aesthetic journal, but with his ouster (for his dadaist leanings) after three issues, the subtitle was subsequently changed by Ozenfant and Jeanneret to "Revue internationale illustrée de l'activité contemporaine" (International illustrated review of

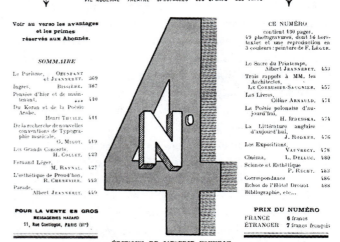

79. Cover of the fourth issue of *L'Esprit Nouveau* (Paris, 1920).

contemporary events) (Fig. 79). It now purported to cover all fine arts and literature, also the pure and applied sciences, experimental aesthetics, engineering aesthetics, urbanism, philosophy, sociology, economics, the moral and political sciences, modern life, theater, exhibitions, sports, and special events. The name apparently derived from a lecture by Apollonaire, but for Ozenfant and Jeanneret it expressed a commitment to the industrial future and to a brave new world to be governed by an intellectual elite. Its twenty-eight issues spanned almost six years – its survival in part was due to Jeanneret's success at selling advertisements to industrialists and manufacturers.[95] It brought together voices as distinct as Victor Basch, Adolf Loos (his "Ornament and Crime" essay), Fillipo Tommaso Marinetti, and Theo van Doesburg.

L'Esprit Nouveau was the forum in which Le Corbusier published the series of articles (coauthored with Ozenfant under the pseudonym Le Corbusier-Saugnier) that he later reassembled in four books, the first of which was *Vers une architecture* (Toward an architecture, 1923).[96] It is surely the best known architectural manifesto of the twentieth century, although it represents a decidedly odd combination of past and future tendencies within Le Corbusier's intellectual development. It is also an easy book to read and notable for its juxtaposition of modern and classical images.

In one of the earlier analyses of its content, the British historian Reyner Banham reduced this juxtaposition to twin categories, the "Academic" and the "Mechanistic."[97] In the first of these he placed the "Three Reminders to Architects" (mass, surface, plan) as well as the chapter on "Regulating Lines," both of which derive from Le Corbusier's purist aesthetics and revolve around his definition of architecture as "the masterly, correct and magnificent play of masses brought together in light."[98] North American grain elevators as well as the works of Perret and Garnier are suggested as sources for such a conception, while the rationale for proportional regulation is provided by such classical works as the Capitol in Rome and the Petit Trianon at Versailles. Historical justification also underlies the subsection on "Architecture," which pays homage to Michelangelo – "the man of the last thousand years" – and to the plastic forms of the Parthenon.[99] The last images are particularly effective in conveying Le Corbusier's underlying ethic. A fragment of a metope, for instance, is succinctly captioned "Austere profiles. Doric morality," while a section of a Doric capital excites a similar sentiment: "The fraction of the inch comes into play. The curve of the echinus is as rational as that of a large shell. The annulets are 50 feet from the ground, but they tell more than all the baskets of acanthus on a Corinthian capital. The Doric state of mind and Corinthian state of mind are two things. A moral fact creates a gulf between them."[100]

The two "Mechanistic" sections of *Vers une architecture* sandwich the "Academic" sections and focus on another crucial aspect of Le Corbusier's theory: his love of the machine. The originality of the machine as an architectural metaphor at the same time has been vastly overconsidered – as it had been a regular feature of German theory for more than thirty years. Nevertheless, with his impassioned acceptance of industrial models and his belief in technology, he stands – outside of the constructivists – virtually alone in Europe in the years 1921–2. Again, "Americanism" and especially the theories of Taylor underlay his faith; it was strongly supported as well by the French tradition of technocratic positivism extending back to Saint Simon.[101] For better or for worse, Le Corbusier was one of the first to view the architect as a form – maker charged with the mission

of changing the world architecturally and therefore socially. Once again it is a formulation – in opposition to the pessimism of Spengler – that could only have been envisioned in these desperate years.

This meliorist theme is already announced in an early chapter, "The Engineer's Aesthetic and Architecture." The prevailing social crisis for Le Corbusier is a crisis of the spirit, or rather a crisis of architectural uncertainty and untruth:

A man who practices religion and does not believe in it is a poor wretch; he is to be pitied. We are to be pitied for living in unworthy houses, since they ruin our health and our *morale*. It is our lot to have become sedentary creatures; our houses gnaw at us in our sluggishness, like a consumption. We shall soon need far too many sanatoriums. We are to be pitied. Our houses disgust us; we fly from them and frequent restaurants and night clubs; or we gather together in our houses gloomily and secretly like wretched animals; we are becoming demoralized.[102]

Against this architectural fraud stands the ethical honesty of engineers, who by contrast "are healthy and virile, active and useful, balanced and happy in their work," while "our architects are disillusioned and unemployed, boastful and peevish."[103] It is an old and often repeated argument, but with the first images of an ocean liner (also the cover image) we also see that the argument has fundamentally shifted. Muthesius, for instance, evoked the metaphor of the ship only to shy away from a strict interpretation of *Sachlichkeit*, that is, to counter an overly mechanistic interpretation of the concept. Le Corbusier embraced the machine metaphor precisely for its moral urgency. Under the caption for a deck of the liner *Empress of France*, he writes, "An architecture pure, neat, clear, clean and healthy. Contrast with this our carpets, cushions, canopies, wall-papers, carved with gild furniture, faded or 'arty' colours: the dismalness of our Western Bazaar."[104] The startling conclusion is thus entirely logical and self-evident: "A house is a machine for living in."[105]

The compelling images of airplanes and automobiles reveal another innovative feature of the book. Le Corbusier is perhaps the first architect to understand the power of the image in the same way that publicists and advertisers were beginning to understand it as a tool for commerce. He is one of the first to conceive an architectural manifesto less as a reasoned intellectual argument and more as a visual catalogue specifically designed to seduce the architect. A few years later Sigfried Giedion, in his 1928 hagiography of Le Corbusier, would describe his own book as written for the "hurried reader" who, if pressed for time, need only glance at the images and captions. He learned this from Le Corbusier.[106]

Vers une architecture is also polemical in another sense. The heart of the book is found in the last two chapters, "Mass Production Houses" and "Architecture or Revolution," and it is here that we meet the principal focus of his efforts during the 1920s – housing. It had in fact been his chief concern since his arrival in Paris in 1917, as his various proposals for housing estates make clear. For example, in 1917, for Saint-Nicholas-d'Aliermont he proposed workers' housing (one housing unit was built) in a regional style characterized by brick construction and exposed timber beams – similar the work of Tessenow. At Troyes, in 1919, his solution closely followed the example of Tony Garnier. This period ended with his Ville Contemporaine (Contemporary City), which he devised in 1922 for a showing at the Salon d'Automne.[107] Taylorization and efficiency of movement is the running theme of this ideal city for three million people, which is bisected at the center by two vehicular axes and has no fewer than seven levels of transportation, including an airport on the uppermost level. The transportation core is surrounded by twenty-four 60-story skyscrapers, cruciform in plan, intended to serve business and administrative functions. Surrounding this ring are medium-rise housing units for the social elite: administrators, scientists, intellectuals, and artists. The workers are pushed to the perimeter, beyond them is a green belt, and beyond that is the industrial area.

In "Mass Production Houses," Le Corbusier presents such a city as a private-enterprise venture, constructed – as he emphasizes – for profit; the coalition is "one between architects and men of taste, and the universal love of the home."[108] This alliance of the perspicacious was a constant refrain of Le Corbusier during the first half of the decade. The Citrohan House (1920–2) is named for the automobile manufacturer André Citroën, and the 1925 Voisin plan of Paris was named for Gabriel Voisin. Social attitudes and social expectations have changed, he insisted, and politicians and captains of industry had better take heed. The options are simple: "Architecture or Revolution."[109]

When Le Corbusier wrote this last chapter for *Vers une architecture* in 1923, he was just completing his first two houses in France, the studio for Ozenfant in Paris and a small villa in Vaucresson. He had worked assiduously over the previous five years with no architectural results, but now the economic situation here, as in Germany, was beginning to improve. Between 1923 and 1927 he would emerge as one of Europe's leading architects and in a striking way. The

80. Le Corbusier, Ozenfant studio, Paris, 1920–3. From Walter Gropius, *Internationale Architektur* (Berlin, 1925).

minimalism of the Ozenfant studio, with its ship's ladders and squared frames of industrial sash, signals the new direction (Fig. 80). On the exterior, Le Corbusier was approaching what Frank Lloyd Wright would later facetiously call "cardboard" architecture, that is, simple surfaces stripped of any moldings, cornices, sills, or three-dimensional texture. The drive toward machinelike abstraction is nearly complete; detailing almost completely disappears.

In 1923 Le Corbusier would also receive from his friend the art collector Raoul La Roche the commission for his house in Auteuil, where the use of horizontal windows and interior spatial complexity underwent considerable refinement. Before this large house was completed, he had in hand the housing project in Pessac, near Bordeaux, and the Pavilion L'Esprit Nouveau for the exposition of 1925. Both were important steps in his career. The housing project, a daring experiment carried out for the sugar manufacturer Henri Frugès, was originally intended to be a low-income complex of 135 units. The design was standardized on a five-meter module, the walls were built of insulating cinder block, concrete beams were poured on site, and the most intriguing innovation was the use of the Ingersoll Rand's cement gun. The poor quality of the construction was somewhat mitigated by the application of Purist colors to the walls: sky blue, light green, and burnt sienna. The formal abstraction of the six building types must have seemed unworldly in 1926 – especially as the units remained unoccupied for three years. A series of financial, legal, code, and administrative difficulties (this time due only in part to Le Corbusier's managerial incompetence) allowed the finished project to sit and deteriorate until the city finally turned on the water in 1929.

The Pavilion L'Esprit Nouveau, constructed for the 1925 Exposition Internationale des Arts Decoratifs et Industriels Modernes, was conceived as a two-story demonstration unit of the "immeuble-villa" of 1922. It was a plug-in unit for high-rise buildings with a partial two-story living area and a two-story terrace. Although each was fitted with a minimal kitchen, the units were also to be supported by a central system of services that included day care, halls, and clubs run by a staff of stewards and stewardesses. The similarity of this model with later communist models is only superficial. Le Corbusier envisioned his projects not for the proletariat but for "men of taste."

In 1924–5 Le Corbusier published three other books based on the *L'Esprit Nouveau* articles. Only on *Le peinture moderne* (Modern painting) did he allow Ozenfant's name to appear as the coauthor, even though Ozenfant had collaborated on nearly all the material.[110] *Urbanisme* is the largest of these books, and it provides a good summary of Le Corbusier's ideas in the mid-1920s.[111] It speaks of the urban problems of Paris: air pollution, slums, congestion, and rampant illnesses such as tuberculosis. It presents a number of historical examples of urban plans and uses them to demonstrate the virtues of order and geometry and the superiority of the straight road, *Le Chemin des Hommes* (the path of men), over the curved street, *Le Chemin des Ânes* (the path of donkeys). He claims that the essence of the modern city, in a way recalling Otto Wagner, is time and transportation, specifically the speed of travel made possible by airplanes, trains, and automobiles. Pedestrians who

want to take a stroll are now directed to the vast urban park areas, for which his "Contemporary City" again serves as the model. Also on display in published form for the first time (it was exhibited at the exposition of 1925) is Le Corbusier's Plan Voisin, his application of the principles of the contemporary city to the right bank of Paris. Here he (infamously) calls for the removal of virtually all of the existing urban fabric of the city north of the Ile de la Cité and south of Montmartre, save a few isolated monuments.

L'art decorative (The decorative art) is similar in layout and polemical in tone. Again it proffers a number of alluring images – from filing cabinets (preeminent "type furniture") to straw hats and pipes (used by Le Corbusier himself), even lines of Hermes bags and images of dreadnought artillery. It also has its oracular overtones:

Great art lives by humble means.
Glitter is going under.
The hour of proportion has arrived.
A spirit of architecture is asserting itself.
What has occurred? A machine age has been born.[112]

Its leading theme, for which he cites the precedent of Loos, is the end of ornamentation. In his own words (aimed at the official name of the exposition of 1925), "Modern decorative art is not decorated."[113]

Beginning in 1926 Le Corbusier became active in the Redressement Français (Recovery of France), a political movement led by Ernest Mercier, which sought a drastic technocratic overhaul of the economy of the Third Republic along the philosophical lines of Ford and Taylor.[114] This overtly Saint-Simonian movement assembled a number of working committees and had its own propaganda journal. Le Corbusier joined the urban study committee and wrote two articles in 1928: the first proposing the implementation of the principles of his Plan Voisin, the second drawing attention to his work at Pessac and to the new housing exhibition at Stuttgart. The political victory of the Union Nationale party in 1928 resulted in some housing legislation being drawn up, but the economic crash of 1929 just as quickly ended any hope of implementation. For many Europeans the crash also ended the lure of "Americanism" in general.

Le Corbusier was, however, expanding his cultural horizons. In 1929 he made his first trip to Latin America, where he gave a series of lectures in Argentina and Brazil. In 1930 he published a book containing the substance of these lectures, *Précisions sur un état present de l'architecture et de l'urbanisme* (Precisions on the present state of architecture and city planning).[115] The lectures are freewheeling, animated, respectful, and in awe of the topography of sea, mountains, and rivers. The trip was important in that it helped him to reconsider some of the Cartesian absolutes of his earlier urbanistic schemes, such as the severe rectilinearity of his Plan Voisin and its inapplicability to hilly terrain. The grids and towers proposed for Paris, for instance, give way in Montevideo to a proposal for roadways extending out from the perch of the hill, with "seascrapers" descending below. For São Paulo he similarly proposed a cross axis of elevated roadways spanning hillsides forty-five kilometers apart, again with offices below. Le Corbusier returned to South America again in 1936, and these trips became the basis for the enormous influence he would later exert there.

Le Corbusier also made three trips to Moscow in 1928–30, partly in an official capacity to comment on a plan for the reconstruction of Moscow. Here he once again demanded the virtual leveling of the old city and its replacement with a Cartesian grid of towers, but this time he placed the business or administrative center (in diagrammatic form) at the top of the scheme, while below were cultural amenities along with residential areas clustered into compact quadrants to each side.[116] The elite residential centers of his earlier schemes now give way to a single "classless" residential area: ribbons of meandering housing units allowing 150 square feet per occupant. Again, it was intended as a universal solution capable of expansion or compression to any size, but it is also a radical and severe solution that the architect is seeking to impose on the world, one demanding state regulation of every facet of human life. That this plan was published in the same year that Frank Lloyd Wright presented his "Broadacre City" points to the common utopian thinking fostered by the Great Depression.

In the second half of the 1920s Le Corbusier designed his famous villas. In 1926 he published "Les 5 points d'une architecture nouvelle" (Five points of a new architecture), which affirmed his architectural type-features: *pilotis* (columns), free plan, free facade, horizontal sliding windows, and roof garden.[117] The most important was the Villa Stein-de-Monzie at Vaucresson (1926). Gabrielle de Monzie was the co-owner, together with the Americans Sarah and Michael Stein. The commission could be considered a "breakthrough" project because of the free plan, nautical motifs, rear terrace, and qualitative standards of construction. Le Corbusier himself was so enamored with it that he teamed up with Pierre Chenal to have a movie made of the house, starring himself, of course. In the movie, he – with cigarette in mouth all the while – drives up to the house in his automobile and makes his way through the house to the upper roof terrace.[118] Also included were scenes from his Villa Savoye, a commission he received in 1928. Now the *pilotis* are fully brought into play and are teamed with the staircases and ramps; it is a masterful creation, if only for its minimalist, purist language.

Le Corbusier was much less successful with his larger projects. In 1928 he won the competition for the Central Union of Consumers' Cooperatives, Moscow, which when completed in 1936 was the last of the "modern" buildings to be built in that city. The building is indeed modern in appearance, although his plan to circulate heated and cooled air through a double-glazed facade was never implemented; inside he used a series of ramps for circulation. Also intended for Russia was his competition entry for the Palace of the Soviets, which he prepared in the fall of 1931. Le Corbusier and his cousin Pierre Jeanneret were among the nine foreign firms invited to participate. His elaborate design, with the concrete shell of the main parliamentary hall suspended from a parabolic arch, failed to place, even though the now skilled publicist sent a film to Moscow to impress the judges.

His best-known competition design, however, was for the Palace of Nations, a forerunner to the United Nations. The competition for the building in Geneva was announced in the summer of 1926 and attracted 367 entries. Le Corbusier greatly enlarged his Paris staff and put much effort into the design, which featured a secretariat along the lake and an asymmetrical grouping of offices behind it. After much jury wrangling he was voted one of nine first-place winners – fueling a controversy, to the delight of the European press. The "classical" schemes preferred by politicians were eventually combined to win the day, but not before Le Corbusier sent a circular letter to world luminaries (among them Henry Ford and James Joyce) and sued the League of Nations.

What Le Corbusier lost by missing out on this prestigious commission, he gained tenfold from the international controversy surrounding the badly handled affair. He also took the occasion to publish one of his best-written and most philosophical books, *Une Maison – Un Palais* (A house – A palace), which appeared in November 1928.[119] The second half of the book is a comprehensive explanation and justification of his design for the League of Nations buildings, and it contains a number of interesting mementos from the competition. One painful chapter, "The Voice of the Academy," contains the classical solutions, the official correspondence, and the judges' minutes, while a chapter entitled "Some Voices beyond the Grave" provides citations from Rondelet, Viollet-le-Duc, and others. The first half of the book is an inspired commentary on human life and dwelling, the meaning of progress, and the nature of the modern spirit. It fittingly closes with an abundance of images of his two buildings at the Stuttgart exhibition and the Villa Stein-de-Monzie. Oddly, it is one of the few books that has not been translated into English, but it reveals him to be a master of argument and polemic. By this date he had become the ablest propagandist for the modern movement in Europe.

And Le Corbusier would soon in fact have his coronation. It came at the hands of a young and energetic observer of the new movement – Sigfried Giedion (1888–1968).[120] This Swiss national (born in Prague) first studied engineering in Vienna, but in 1915 he began university studies in Zurich and Munich, where he took a doctorate in art history under Heinrich Wölfflin. Instead of pursuing a career in teaching, however, he became attracted to literary circles and in 1923 he traveled to the Bauhaus exhibition at Weimar to write a review. Here he met Gropius and became a quick convert to the cause, although he was still pursuing a career as a dramatist. In September 1925, on the advice of Moholy-Nagy, Giedion wrote to Le Corbusier and asked for a meeting on a planned visit to Paris.[121] He was contemplating a number of essays on "the modern movement" and he wanted to survey the situation in France. The meeting must have impressed the young critic, because he now turned his attention to Le Corbusier and eventually altered his theme to focus entirely on French architecture, ignoring German developments completely. In 1928 he published *Bauen in Frankreich, Bauen in Eisen, Bauen in Eisenbeton* (Building in France, building in iron, building in ferro-concrete), one of the first books to explore the intellectual foundations of modernism as a whole.[122]

As a book it owes everything to Le Corbusier. From the original layout sheets, it is clear that the visual message was crucial to Giedion's deliberations. He began by pasting images on blank sheets and underscoring them with captions. The actual text was simply labeled "text" and was obviously secondary to the images. These sheets were then passed on to Moholy-Nagy, who refined the typography and layout and designed the cover. The text itself is punctuated with words having extra space between the letters, uppercase words, and words in italics; the smallest print is relegated to footnotes. Arrows serve as indices for the reader. The book's content is thus layered, depending on the willingness of the reader to move beyond the powerful images. Moreover, its tone, as well as such devices as "voices" from the past and the repetitive use of key words, clearly derives from Le Corbusier.

The book opens by identifying a new task for the historian: not to dwell on the past but "to extract from the vast complexity of the past those elements that will be the point of departure for the future."[123] In short, the past is only significant defining the path of development that should be embraced by the present. And what is happening at present – once again – is being propelled by supraindividual force of the modern (Hegelian) *Zeitgeist:*

We are being driven into an indivisible life process. We see life more and more as a moving yet indivisible w h o l e. The boundaries of individual fields blur. Where does science end, where does art begin, what is applied technology, what belongs to pure knowledge? Fields permeate and fertilize each other as they overlap. It is hardly of interest to us today where the conceptual boundary between art and science is drawn. We value these fields not hierarchically but as equally justified emanations of the highest impulse: LIFE! To grasp life as a totality, to allow no divisions, is among the most important concerns of the age.[124]

With such a spirited prelude, Giedion begins his genealogy of the present, which actually goes back the Saint-Simonian concept of "industry" and the theme of iron. Architecture as a living art ceased to exist around 1830, as the *Zeitgeist* seemingly chose to vacate the halls of the Ecole des Beaux-Arts and to haunt instead the structural labs of the Ecole Polytechnique. Henri Labrouste was the last nineteenth-century architect of consequence, and his intellectual successors were the great engineers of the exhibition halls, market halls, railway stations, and department stores. The indomitable spirit first expresses its full force at the Paris Exposition of 1889 in the creation of the Eiffel Tower and Gallerie des Machines. This point is vividly illustrated with Giedion's own brilliant photographs of carefully selected parts of the Eiffel Tower and the Pont Transbordeur at Marseilles (by Ferdinand-Joseph Arnondin), in which partial images are always shot from above and below to emphasize the diagonal webwork of supports.

Le Corbusier makes his appearance in part two of the book, in the shorter section on ferro-concrete. If this section is briefer it is because the historical legacy is shorter. It begins with Perret, then discusses Garnier, and ends with the great "constructor" himself (architects, Giedion argues, have ceased to exist). Giedion's photographs of the Pessac housing complex are of historical importance, and the book closes with his own apology for the League of Nations competition. The outcome was still in dispute when the book went to press, but Giedion correctly appraised the situation. For those unhurried readers willing to glance down at the footnote, he cites Frantz Jourdain, the eighty-year-old architect of the Samaritaine, as noting, "C'est une second affaire Dreyfus."[125] Le Corbusier thus became the first architect of the modern movement to experience both his sacrificial martyrdom and his glorious apotheosis.

6. The Breadth of the Early Modern Movement

Traditional accounts of the modern movement in Europe focused primarily on the achievements of its three or four leading personalities. More recently, it has come to be seen less as a movement and as much more broadly based in its practice. In fact, its multiple tendencies have less formal homogeneity than was once thought, and several have been overlooked or forgotten. A good example is the situation in France in the 1920s, where Le Corbusier was by no means alone in his embrace of modernism and was not even the most successful architect on the scene. His mentor and friend Perret – now with classicist tendencies – had remained very active throughout this decade, as was his contemporary Henri Sauvage (1873–1932). The latter built the famous La Maison à Gradins in 1912, the first terraced apartment building in the city. He topped this effort in 1922 with his terraced complex on the rue des Amiraux, which he executed in reinforced concrete.

The most prominent modern architect in Paris in the 1920s was Robert Mallet-Stevens (1886–1945). Like Corbusier, he was influenced by the Vienna Secession, cubism, and Dutch practice. Mallet-Stevens was a gifted designer with many ties to the avant-garde, and in 1923 he designed the modern set for Marcel L'Herbier's film *L'Inhumaine*. In the same year he designed a cubist villa on the Riviera for Vicomte de Noailles, which he quickly topped with his modernist villa for Paul Poiret (half-built but never completed). In 1927 Mallet-Stevens was responsible for a group of exquisitely detailed modern apartment buildings on the rue Mallet-Stevens, which Giedion could already reprove one year later for their "remnants of the old ostentation."[126] Mallet-Stevens's modernist vocabulary – his "rich" style – was now being rejected, it seems, because architecture was being judged on the basis of its relevance to the lower classes. This was the case even though the two rooms that Mallet-Stevens designed for the Salon d'Automne in 1913 and his portfolio of urban buildings, *Un cité modern* (1918), were both important stimuli to the development of Le Corbusier.[127]

Le Corbusier's architecture as well was rebuked by the militant communist André Lurçat (1894–1970), who also repeatedly rejected his appeal to industrialists.[128] Lurçat's studio house for his brother Jean (1924–5) and his grouping of eight houses for the Cité Seurat (1924–5) were better detailed than Le Corbusier's first villas and initially were better known. Giedion detects "a certain austerity, coolness" in them, but in 1929 Henry-Russell Hitchcock considered Luçat a better architect than Le Corbusier.[129] Hitchcock points out that the blocklike houses at the Cité Seurat mark a "distinct advance" on the work of Le Corbusier, while his two villas at Versailles (1925–6) depict a "solid reality, a plausibility" as opposed to the "ethereal and fantastic quality of Le Corbusier's visions." Therefore in his domestic designs Lurçat has achieved a "real superiority."[130] Hitchcock also condemns Le Corbusier's "Messianism" and "dogmatism" and by contrast welcomes Lurçat's "very healthy direct influence on many young architects."[131] In 1934, however, Lurçat moved to the Soviet Union and dutifully converted to Stalin's neoclassicism. His lone theoretical text, written after his eventual return to France, is an odd reaffirmation of the classical tradition of Guadet.[132]

Another architect obscured by the shadow of Le Corbusier was Eileen Gray (1879–1976).[133] Born in Ireland, initially trained at the Slade School of Fine Arts in London, Gray moved to France shortly after 1900, where she lived for most of her life. She began her artistic career in the decorative arts, creating such items as lacquer, screens, furniture, and carpets. By the early 1920s she had shifted her focus to interior design and then to architecture. In 1926 she started a house for herself and a friend along the Mediterranean coast (known as E-1027), which in a startling way enacted Le Corbusier's "Five Points." It was subsequently made famous by two events: Le Corbusier's despoiling of its walls with his uncommissioned murals (while staying there on holidays) and later by his death by drowning in the waters below.

Neighboring Belgium was home to Victor Bourgeois (1897–1962). His 300 housing units for La Cité Moderne in Berchem-lez-Bruxelles (1922–5), which were much influenced by Garnier, catapulted him to European prominence. He also traveled in avant-garde circles (as a friend of René Magritte and Fernand Léger) and was active in social causes. In 1927 he participated in the Weissenhof Exhibition, and in the following year he became a founding member of the Congrès Internationaux d'Architecture Moderne (CIAM).

Modernism in Italy in the 1920s was affected by politics. The country had fought on the winning side in World War I but had suffered dearly in the conflict, with 600,000 soldiers killed and another quarter of a million maimed. Politically the country began to collapse even before the end of the war, but the situation grew more desperate with the inflation of the postwar years. By 1920 the country was besieged by political anarchy, strikes, armed communist uprisings, the revolutionary tribunals of the first "Red Guards," and fierce opposition from various nationalist parties. The turmoil ended with the coup d'état of October 1922, when Benito Mussolini, the leader of Italy's Fascist Party, entered Rome and declared himself king. His usurpation of power was initially quite popular. His first cabinet was composed of members of the major parties, and the elections of 1924 testify to the success of the Fascists in their early efforts to eliminate political corruption and stabilize the economy.

The war had killed off futurism in Italy, and the most significant architectural movement in the first half of the decade was the Novecento. In its underpinnings it was related to the *rappel à l'ordre* in France, except that here the artistic source was the "metaphysical school" of Carlo Carrà and Carlo de Chirico; it combined avant-garde subject matter with a neoclassical concern for order, balance, chiaroscuro, and chromatic colors.[134] In architecture – and especially through the efforts of Giovanni Muzio (b. 1893) and Gio Ponti (1891–1979) – these principles were translated into a decorative surface treatment, but one reduced or abstracted to simulate in a subtle way the rhythms and simplified contours of the neoclassical vocabulary.[135] Muzio's exhibition building at Diano Marina (1921) is overtly Palladian and scenographic in character, while his highly controversial Ca'Brutta in Milan (1920–2) was nearly demolished because of its whimsical use of aediculae and its layering of a three-story travertine base with upper floors of dark and light stucco. By contrast, his tennis club in Milan (1922–3) is almost "postmodern" in its cheerful use of classical motifs and symmetrical, round projecting bays. Gio Ponti, together with Emilio Lancia, built the more baroque house on Via Randaccio, Milan (1924–6), and followed that with the much admired Casa Borletti (1927–8), Milan – both of which are superbly detailed and crowned with elegant obelisks. In 1928 Ponti became the editor of the newly created journal *Domus*, which became the principal organ of the Novecento.

By this date the abstracted neoclassicism of the Novecento (in contrast to the academic classicism still strong in Italy) was already facing a challenge by the Italian rationalist movement, which formed in 1926.[136] The impetus was the Milanese Group 7, led by Giuseppe Terragni (1904–43). The Group 7 issued the first of four manifestoes in December 1926,[137] and in their "strict adherence to logic, rationality," we see Gropius and Le Corbusier mediated by a Latin appreciation for tradition.[138] The northern socialist language regarding workers' housing and urbanism is evident, as are the formal motifs of cantilevered balconies, corner windows, structural expression, machine architecture, and the strict expression of function. But *razionalismo* (which seems to have been the Italian translation of *Sachlichkeit*) also encompasses a high respect for Mediterranean culture, together with a Corbusian compulsion toward elitist intervention – all within the context of a Fascist (centrally directed) political order.[139] Through the efforts of Adalberto Libera (1903–63), also of Group 7, the broader Italian Movement for Rationalist Architecture (MIAR) was founded in Rome in 1928, in conjunction with the first Exposition of Rational Architecture. Giuseppe Pagano (1896–1945), who in 1928 joined with Edoardo Persico (1900–36) in editing the magazine *Casabella*, provided an early demonstration of rationalist architecture with his work at the Turin Exhibition of 1928. A better-known icon for the new movement, however, was Terragni's Novocomum apartment building in Como (1927–9; Fig. 81).[140] With its concrete structure, rounded and squared corners, projecting balconies with pipe rails, and bands of windows, it was a modernist tour-de-force, decked out in brilliant tones of beige, orange, gray-green, and blue.

Terragni's efforts in northern Italy were soon rivaled in the south, as Mussolini strove to transform Rome into a world capital. Several post offices of the early 1930s are notable for their modernism, especially those of Mario Ridolfi (b. 1904) on the Piazza Bologna (1933) and of Libera in the Quartiere Aventino. Libera, in particular, was enormously talented, and he designed the elementary school in Trento (1931–3), the Italian Pavilion at the Chicago World's Fair (1933), and the apartments on the Ostia Lido (1933).

Two early books on Italian modernism are interesting for their different approaches. *Architettura d'oggi* (Architecture today, 1930), by Marcello Piacentini (1881–1960), is a wide-ranging and intelligent summary of European and American trends, but it favors the more classically inspired works of architects such as Peter Behrens, Mies van der Rohe, Joseph Hoffmann, and Dominikus Böhm.[141] For Italian work, Piacentini attaches the greatest importance to the ambiance of Italy: its regional character and classical heritage. In contrast, *Gli elementi dell'architettura funzionale* (The elements of a functional architecture, 1932), by Alberto Sartoris (b. 1901), is essentially polemical and stands as a testament to the influence of Le Corbusier.[142] The

81. Giuseppe Terragni, Novocomum apartment building, Como, 1927–9. Photograph by author.

latter, in fact, wrote the preface to the first edition and was apparently instrumental in Sartoris's changing "rational" to "functional" in the title – the first use of *funzionale*. Sartoris was also one of the first historians of the modern movement to stress the connection of architecture with painting and sculpture.

Italy, of course, differed from other European countries in that its political rule was neither socialist nor Marxist but Fascist, and nearly all of the rationalist architects at some point supported Fascism.[143] Terragni joined the party in 1928, and he built its regional headquarters in Como in the mid-1930s. Pagano, who would later die in a wartime concentration camp, embraced Fascism in the early 1930s. At the second MIAR exhibition in Rome in 1931, the rationalist movement issued a manifesto encouraging Mussolini to accept rationalism as the national style while at the same time insisting that rationalist architecture should "respond to the character of masculinity, force, and pride in the Revolution."[144] Although Mussolini and his cultural committees did not embrace rationalism, they also did not reject modernism either – in contrast to the political dictatorships of Germany and the Soviet Union. In short, the aims of the popular government and the modern architectural movement dovetailed in certain respects and were mutually supportive throughout the 1920s and early 1930s. This alliance, however, faltered after Mus-

solini declared his "Third Rome" (new Roman empire) in 1936 and began to forge his political alliance with Adolf Hitler.

The situation in Spain mirrored events in Italy in a few respects although it was less stable politically. Spain had remained neutral in World War I but did not escape economic and political unrest. The right-wing coup d'etat of Don Miguel Primo de Rivera in 1923 resulted in a dictatorship that lasted throughout the decade, but the country's transition to a republic in the 1930s was beset with instability and bitter factional and regional divisions. These led to a multitude of changing governments and eventually to the mutiny of General Francisco Franco and to the Spanish Civil War (1936–9). Spain's break with the classical past began only after 1927 with the Madrid journal *Arquitectura*. The first important modern architect was José Luis Sert (b. 1902), who had studied architecture in Barcelona and worked in the Paris office of Le Corbusier. Upon returning to Spain in 1930, Sert organized GATCPAC, which rapidly advanced the new architecture in Catalonia. Sert also built some striking modern buildings, among them the Galobart House (1932) and the Casa Bloc (1932–36), both in Barcelona. His early style is entirely indebted to Le Corbusier, and this is true for Spain's other prominent modernist from these years, J. Manuel Aizpurúa (1904–36).

The modern movement established itself in Switzerland by somewhat different means. The country had an accomplished early "modern" master in the person of Karl Moser (1860–1936), whose career in the first years of the century resembled those of Wagner and Berlage, for he too broke with the classical past and was a revered teacher, at the Swiss Federal Institute of Technology (ETH) in Zurich. The country also had a long tradition of innovative engineering, which is well represented in the first part of the century in the work of Robert Maillet (1872–1940). His first experiments with flat concrete slabs (integral with column supports) were undertaken in the first decade of the century, and many of his most daring bridges – canonized by Giedion in *Space, Time and Architecture* – date from the late 1920s and 1930s. The indigenous material of concrete was also joined at an early stage with the Swiss tradition in domestic architecture. The architect and historian Peter Meyer, in his book *Moderne schweizer Wohnhäuser* (Modern Swiss housing, 1928), records a number of modern houses built or designed by this date, among them works by Hans Hofmann, Max Ernst Haefeli, Paul Artaria and Hans Schmidt, Rudolf Steiger-Crawford, and Rudolf Preiswerk.[145]

Giedion's book on France appeared in 1928, and he followed it in 1929 with *Befreites Wohnen* (Liberated living), a small but another very important contribution to modern theory (Fig. 82). Giedion's theme here is the dwelling, and he demands liberation from the house's "value of eternity" as well as liberation from steep rents, thick walls, the house as monument, the house that enslaves the occupant by its upkeep, and the house that devours the time and energy of the housewife.[146] The demand for liberation from the value of eternity emanates, as he notes, from Sant'Elia's call for a new house for each generation, while the lowering of rents will result from the use of industrial techniques of production. Thick walls will be eliminated by non-bearing-wall construction: "Today we need a house whose structure finds accord with our bodily feeling, as it has been liberated by sports, gymnastics, and our corresponding way of life – **light, transparent, flexible.**"[147] The cover image is that of a liberated modern couple sitting out on their sunny open terrace. Many of the eighty-six illustrations depict the work of Le Corbusier, but there are also a number of other surprising images. Among these are buildings by Artaria & Schmidt, Mart Stam, Marcel Breuer, Bijoet & Duiker, and Richard J. Neutra (from Los Angeles) – making it a brief, up-to-date survey of international modern architecture. The book closes with such memorable photographs as an aerial view of vernacular housing in Morocco, a female tennis player in shorts, and sunbathers in a Zurich park. Like Richard Neutra in California, Giedion was selling modern architecture not as an aesthetic fashion but as an entire lifestyle. From 1928 onward, he was also director of CIAM and ran it from his home in the Zurich-Doldertal.

If Giedion introduced Switzerland to the French modernism of Le Corbusier, another and more militant strain of modernism was also being drawn from De Stijl and constructivist circles. The vehicle was the journal *ABC:Beiträge zum Bauen* (Contributions to building), which was founded in 1924 in Zurich under the editorial direction of Hans Schmidt (1893–1972) and the Dutchman Mart Stam (1899–1986).[148] Schmidt met Stam while working in Rotterdam in the early 1920s, before Stam had moved to Berlin and befriended El Lissitzky. Without work, Stam ended up moving to Switzerland in 1923 to join the office of Moser and Arnold Itten. There he finalized the details of the new venture with Schmidt and encouraged the involvement of Lissitzky, who was moving to Ticino early in 1924 to undergo treatment for tuberculosis. The Russian Marxist was most doubtful of revolutionary possibilities in Switzerland; in a letter to Oud he called it "one of the most reactionary countries in central Europe."[149]

Nevertheless, ten issues of *ABC* appeared in 1924–8 and articulated what was essentially a constructivist ideology of strict functionalism. Stam opened the first issue with an article on "Collective Design," and the numbers were often illustrated with examples of student work at VKhUTMAS. Idealized modern construction and the "Dictatorship of the Machine" were keynotes of the polemics. Stam's very accomplished projects – especially his design for the Geneva-Cornavin train station – were first displayed in the journal, as were projects of Mies van der Rohe and Hans Wettwer (1894–1952). One issue of 1926 is notable because it was put together by Hannes Meyer (1889–1954), another Swiss modernist to emerge at this time.[150]

Initially a classicist, Meyer had undergone a professional crisis in 1924. After becoming familiar with the principles of De Stijl and the work of Bourgeois, he converted to Marxism, and in 1926 he teamed up with Wettwer to design the Petersschule in Basel, a school project noteworthy for its far-extended terrace cantilevered off of steel cables. The next year Meyer and Wettwer placed third in the competition for the League of Nations, with a design that many architects saw as more advanced than the project of Le Corbusier. This sudden notoriety led to Meyer's invitation in 1927 (extended by Gropius) to head the new department of architecture at the Dessau Bauhaus. The importance of this invitation was

82. Sigfried Giedion, cover of *Befreites Wohnen* (Zurich, 1929).

compounded a few months later (in February 1928) when Gropius resigned. Meyer, with only a slender portfolio of built works, now found himself the director of the most famous design school in the world.

His appointment would prove a disaster, and Gropius soon regretted his recommendation.[151] Indeed, Meyer was in a difficult position from the beginning. Several key faculty members – Muche, Breuer, Moholy-Nagy – had left with Gropius in 1928, and the new director lost no time in alienating Klee and Kandinsky with his antiaesthetic, functionalist polemics, which were first voiced in his essay "building,"

published in the new journal *bauhaus*. In the essay, Meyer insisted that the whole process of architecture could be reduced to the "functional diagram and the economic program," and architecture was therefore "pure construction," or in essence "unartistic."[152] Meyer also allowed the school again to be politicized as a leftist institution, which naturally met with a fierce reaction from the growing Nationalist Socialist party in Germany. In response to widespread dissension both inside and outside of the school, the mayor of Dessau was forced to dismiss the Swiss director in the summer of 1930, an act that Meyer resisted with bitterness.

Although his actions and words often said otherwise, Meyer in an open letter to a newspaper vehemently protested the charge of being a Marxist. Yet by the end of the year he had led a "brigade" (consisting of seven graduates of the Red Bauhaus brigade) to Russia, "where a truly proletarian art is developing."[153]

In Austria, the legacy of Otto Wagner, who lived until 1918, was only somewhat effaced by the war, the death of Franz Josef, and the dissolution of the Habsburg Empire. The countries of Czechoslovakia, Poland, Yugoslavia, and Hungary were created out of the political dissolution, and Austria itself became a semifunctioning republic of loosely aligned political entities. Elections in 1919 resulted in a coalition government of Social Democrats and Christian Socialists, with Vienna and the industrial parts of the country aligning themselves with the first party and rural areas with the second. When the Christian Socialists gained control of the national assembly in the following year, "Red Vienna" became effectively a semiautonomous socialist state within a state. For some, it was viewed as a "third way," between orthodox Marxism on the left and other parties on the right, but it was decidedly "revolutionary" in aspiration. As housing was the most pressing need following the war, the city commenced on a political process of land and property expropriation through taxation – together with rent control – that both enraged dispossessed owners and resulted in a number of city-financed housing projects.

The results of this experiment in socialist planning have been variously interpreted and reinterpreted.[154] One housing solution was offered by Adolf Loos, who in 1921–4 was the chief architect of the municipal housing authority. He favored a low-density, single-family *Siedlung* (housing estate) concept, with vegetable gardens to combat food shortages. In his official capacity he designed four prototypical estates of row houses, the most significant of which was Am Heuberg. Here he employed his *Haus mit einer Mauer* (house with one wall) system. In this system, foundations were laid only for the two lateral walls, and the front and back walls were suspended from a timber beam that spanned the full width of the unit.

By 1923 the land-intensive garden-estate concept fell into disfavor, and city officials gave their approval instead to the *Hof* (courtyard) solution: large housing blocks of minimal, labor-intensive apartments and communal facilities (laundries, kindergartens, clinics, libraries, cinemas) built around open courtyards. The most publicized of these "proletarian" complexes was the Karl Marx-Hof (1926–30), built by Karl Ehn. It consisted of 1,400 units stretched over several city blocks (over one kilometer in overall length). With its long enclosed courtyards, realist sculptural motifs, red hues, and parade of masts highlighting the monumental central square, this "red fortress" epitomized for many the city's radical politics. Not surprisingly, it became an actual battleground when the political situation turned ugly in 1934.

Even larger (nearly 1,600 units) was the Sandleiten Seidlung (1924–8), laid out by Wagner's students Emil Hoppe and Otto Schönthal and two other firms. Altogether 64,000 units were constructed during this period. Loos's single *Hof* – the Otto Haas-Hof (1924) – is perhaps the most tedious building in his portfolio and presents him as a lesser architect than his younger contemporary Josef Frank (1885–1967), who also much preferred the low-rise *Siedlung*. Other notable architects contributing to the housing campaign were Joseph Hoffmann, Margarete Lihotzky, and Peter Behrens, the last of whom had assumed Wagner's old chair in 1921.

After Loos resigned his position with the city in 1924, he made his way to Paris to join the avant-garde circle of Tristan Tzara, where he remained until 1927. His writings during this time are minimal and of little consequence. His two best buildings of the decade – the Moller House, Vienna (1928), and the Müller House, Prague (1930) – both came near the end of his career, when his creative powers or his interest in architecture were beginning to wane. One Austrian modernist who achieved little of the recognition due him was Lois Welzenbacher (1889–1955), whose atelier was in Innsbruck.[155] In the mid-1920s his personal style began to mature, as shown by a series of remarkable reinforced-concrete buildings that he designed, culminating in the Turmhotel Seeber, Innsbruck (1930–1). With its gentle curve and cantilevered balconies (with pipe rails), it may owe something to Alvar Aalto's near contemporary sanatorium in Paimio.

The fragmentation of the former Habsburgs Empire led to a number of architectural developments within the newly established entities. The Slovene architect Jože Plečnik (1872–1957), a famed student of Otto Wagner, moved from Prague to his native Ljubljana in 1921, where he continued to pursue a classically inspired, intensely mystical modernism, as seen in his work on Prague Castle, the Church of the Sacred Heart, Prague (1928–31), and the Insurance Building, Ljubljana (1928–30).[156]

In Hungary the short-lived Communist government collapsed in 1919, which sent into political exile the one modernist with ties to the Wagner tradition, József Vágó (b. 1877), who had participated in the 1912 Werkbund debate in support of Muthesius.[157] By the mid-1920s the modernist tradition had been renewed through the designs of Farkas Molnár (1897–1945) and József Fischer (1901–95). Molnár had trained at the Bauhaus in Weimar and had even worked in the office of Gropius. He was, however, much more moved by the theories of van Doesburg, and his first designs, such as his colorful 6 × 6 houses (six meters), are constructivist- or De Stijl–inspired. This influence would eventually give way to that of Le Corbusier, who also influenced the vocabulary of Fischer.

Also from Hungary came the painter László Moholy-Nagy (1895–1946).[158] He moved to Berlin in 1919 and gravitated toward "Elementist Art," which he (together with Raoul Hausmann, Hans Arp, and Ivan Puni) defined in the pages of *De Stijl* in 1921 as "something pure, liberated from usefulness and beauty, something elemental which can arise in each person."[159] In Berlin he and van Doesburg also joined forces with the circle of Lissitzky. Moholy-Nagy, in fact, was hired by Gropius in 1923 because of his reputation as a constructivist; he was chosen to replace Itten and became a significant artistic force at the school over the next five years. His most important book of the 1920s was *Von Material zu Architektur* (From material to architecture, 1929), which graphically presents the principles of his abstract design course.[160] In the fourth section of the book, entitled "Space (architecture)," Moholy-Nagy is the second of his generation (Rudolf Schindler was the first) to proclaim: "The root of architecture lies in the mastery of the problem of space."[161] In drawing upon the relevance of the airplane (its views from above), he concludes with this statement:

The task is not completed with a single structure. The next stage will be space creation in all directions, space creation in a continuum. Boundaries become fluid, space is conceived as flowing – a countless succession of relationships.[162]

This becomes, of course, one of the leading themes of Giedion's *Space, Time and Architecture* (1941).

The modern movement rapidly insinuated itself in the countries of northern Europe as well. The Polish architect Szymon Syrkus (1893–1964), who had contacts with De Stijl circles, became one of the first practitioners of the new style in Poland and by the end of the decade had built a successful practice with his wife Helena. Czechoslovakia was also receptive to modernism. As a former part of the Habsburg Empire rich in mineral deposits, the new country quickly became a wealthy industrial center after the war. Prague's geographic proximity to both Dresden and Berlin created a Germanic cultural axis; in addition, the Bohemian, Moravian, and Slovakian people had a long tradition of intellectualism and preeminence in the arts. One important early figure of Czech modernism was Jan Kotěra (1871–1923), a student of Wagner during the second half of the 1890s.[163] He was impressed with the work of Frank Lloyd Wright and by 1906 had arrived at a clean spatial conception of architecture. Prague was home to the so-called Czech cubists, who included Pavel Janák (1882–1956), Josef Goár (1880–1945), Vlastislav Hofman (1884–1964), and Josef Chochol (1880–1956). In this brief and very complex movement, formal aspects of the baroque joined the influence of French cubism and the perceptual psychology of "empathy theory."[164] It was an experiment both formally sophisticated and unique in Europe.

The 1920s brought with it the influence of constructivism, which caused the architectural situation in Czechoslovakia to come alive. A spate of avant-garde journals – a reconstituted *Stravba, Disk, Pásmo, ReD,* and *MSA* – led the way. All embraced the new spirit; nearly all were either founded or intellectually dominated by Karel Teige (1900–51), the poet, art historian, and spokesman for the radical Devstil group.[165] Initially he was most impressed by Le Corbusier, whom he met in Paris in 1922, and he subsequently republished several articles from *L'Esprit Nouveau.* Teige also forged contacts with Behne, van Doesburg, Oud, Stam, Hannes Meyer, and eventually Giedion. In theoretical outlook, he was closer to Stam and Meyer, but polemically he played the same role in Czechoslovakia as Giedion did in Switzerland. His broad campaign to publicize European developments led to a rapid consolidation of the new architecture after 1925 and helped make known the work of a number of young and talented designers, among them Oldřich Tyl (1883–1939), Jamomír Krejcar (1895–1959), Bohuslav Fuchs (1895–1972), Jasoslav Frager (1898–1967), Evžen Linhardt (1898–1949), Josef Hanlek (1899–1961), and Karel Honzík (1900–66), to name but a few. This activity culminated in 1928 in Brno with the International Exhibition of Contemporary Culture and the Czech Werkbund housing development (*Novy dum*). If the latter was little more than a replay of Stuttgart's Weissenhof settlement of the previous year (especially in its easy imitation of Le Corbusier's style), the former allowed the prodigious talent of Fuchs, one of the most underrated European architects of the 1920s,[166] to be put on international display.

Teige's most comprehensive exposition of his ideas came in his *Modern Architecture in Czechoslovakia* (1930), largely written in 1927–8. Here he sees the 1920s as the decade of constructivism, which he interprets broadly. Its genesis lies in the Soviet Union, in Dutch practice, and in the work of (the Moravian) Loos and Le Corbusier. At its core, modernism is for Teige preeminently a socialist movement: "New architecture must begin anew on a new societal basis. This is not just a matter of inventing free forms and subjective compositions, this is not a matter of fashion: a right angle, antidecorativism, flat roof – all those are attractive, desirable, almost given features. They are not sufficient, however, nor are they decisive as inventions."[167] Constructivism, as he defines it, is "not an artistic or architectural 'ism' but rather a guideline of universal creativity, a methodology for human work in all disciplines, a means to functionalist, dialectical, materialist – in a word, socialist – thinking."[168] The new architecture must also be antiformalist, antiaesthetic, and anticapitalist and represent "*maximum functionality*."[169] The task of the modern architect "is not improvement, but renewal: a revolution," that is, a revolution predicated on class struggle and a Marxist worldview.[170]

These sentiments apparently became so strong over the course of writing the book that by the end he wrote a postscript to apologize to the reader for including the chapter on Loos, who apparently could no longer pass political muster. One year earlier, Teige even more famously took Le Corbusier to task for his politically *retardataire* desire to produce "monuments" rather than socialist "instruments."[171] The specific object of Teige's attack was Le Corbusier's project for the "Mundaneum" – a world museum proposed by the architect to be erected close to the League of Nations. Le Corbusier was apparently so stung by the attack that – four years later – he published a rare defense of his work.[172] This debate, in fact, underscores a sharp split already evident within the modern movement by 1930. Of all the early historians of modernism, Teige was the most politically uncompromising, and it is sad that his personal demise, as with so many others, can be attributed to the coming of his long-desired communist revolution, which indeed swept through his country in 1948. He then became the object of a slander campaign and died, without work, in 1951.

Finland was another creation of 1918, granted independence after almost six centuries of domination by Sweden and Russia. The national romantic movement of the turn of the century, encouraged by the work of Lars Sonck, Eliel Saarinen, and Armos Lindgren, continued well into the 1920s, even though Saarinen immigrated to the United States in 1923. It was in competition with a neoclassical movement whose roots were in Germany and with the influence of the Bauhaus, which begins to appear around the middle of the decade. Finland's two most important modernists of the 1920s were Erik Bryggman (1891–1955) and Alvar Aalto (1898–1976).[173] In competition designs of 1927, Bryggman moved past his earlier neoclassical leanings and became the first to experiment with the modernist vocabulary. These designs influenced the younger Aalto, who had been in practice with his wife Aino Marsio since 1924. The Aaltos' first office was in Jyväskylä, where they executed their neoclassical workers' club in 1924–5. They then moved to Turku after winning the competition for the Southwestern Agricultural Cooperative building in 1927 – a building that reflects their new interest in modernism. The transformation was complete with their design for the Turun Sanomat Newspaper Building in Turku (1928–30) and the extraordinary tuberculosis sanatorium at Paimio (1928–33). The last design was also influenced by the Aaltos' visit to Hilversum, where they saw the recently completed sanatorium of Johannes Duiker. The third leg of their early success was the Viipuri Library (1933–6), the competition for which they won in 1928.

Swedish architecture in the early 1920s was dominated by the efforts of Erik Gunnar Asplund (1885–1940).[174] His initial designs for the Woodlawn Cemetery date from 1916 and combine both classical and vernacular elements. His Ledouxian Stockholm Public Library (1920–8), with its geometrical lyricism and exquisite interior detailing, made him the most famous architect in Sweden. This was an honor that he would soon solidify with his well-publicized conversion to international modernism around 1930, though the ground had been prepared by Sven Markelius (1889–1972) and Uno Åhrén (1897–1977), editor of the architectural journal *Byggmästaren*.[175] The prompt for Asplund's conversion was the Stockholm design and handicraft exhibition of 1930. Not only did Asplund supervise the planning but he gave form to the exhibition through his much admired pavilion and restaurant, erected almost entirely of steel girders, glass, and cables. With Gunnar Sundbarg, Åhrén directed the housing section of the exhibition, which again drew inspiration from the recent event in Stuttgart.

The success of the exhibition led Asplund, Åhrén, Markelius, Wolter Gahn, Gregor Paulsson, and Eskil Sundahl to publish their socialist manifesto of 1931, *acceptera* (acceptance), which, while surveying modern developments elsewhere, encouraged the acceptance of Fordism, industrialization, and collective social responsibility for mass housing.[176] The very same recommendations were made two years later in Arne Sørensen's *Funktionalisme og samfund*

(Functionalism and society), which in fact used many of the same images as well.[177] In an even more forceful way, the book puts forward international modernism as the socialist and egalitarian solution to the problems of housing and town planning, helping to lay the ideological basis for the Scandinavian welfare state after the war.

The leading architect in the 1920s in Denmark was Kay Fisker (1893–1965), a student of Martin Nyrop. Fisker practiced a purist geometric style of brick and wood construction and also edited the journal *Architekten*, which in the years 1919–27 monitored international developments.[178] His student Arne Jacobsen (1902–71) was the first Dane to embrace fully the new forms, which he (with Flemming Lassen) introduced in a striking way with his competition-winning circular design for the "House of the Future," displayed in 1929 at a Copenhagen exhibition.[179] Around the same time Jacobsen completed a house for himself with a roof terrace, composed as a variation on a cube.

If many architects in the smaller countries of central and northern Europe looked to Germany as ideological for architectural ideas, it is because this country remained the most varied in its cultivation of the new architecture in the years 1922–28. And whereas the Bauhaus under the directorship of Gropius may have been (from abroad) one of the most closely followed institutions during these years, it is easy to overestimate its importance within the larger German context. If we look at the architectural situation in Germany at the start of 1926, for instance, we see that two of the most active German architects, Erich Mendelsohn (1887–1953) and Ernst May (1886–1970), were far removed from the Dessau circle.

Mendelsohn was arguably also the most talented, if not the most thoughtful, architect in Germany.[180] He had graduated from Munich Technical University in 1914, where he trained under Theodor Fisher and had artistic contacts with the Blue Rider group. During the war he served on the Eastern front and prepared the famous sketches that were first displayed in Paul Cassirer's Berlin Gallery in 1919. His first building was the Einstein Tower (1918–22), which he intended to be made of concrete but which was in the end constructed of brick with a stucco finish. Because of this building and his early sketches, he has generally been considered an expressionist, although he differed from expressionists in two important ways. First, he embraced modernism and technology and in fact was thoroughly intrigued by it. Second, while others fantasized utopian and visionary schemes, Mendelsohn built and learned to build well. His hat factory in Luckenwalde (1921–3) is a masterpiece of functional design, with its clean lines and concrete skeletal framework. His renovation of and addition to the Mossehaus publishing house, Berlin (1922–3), is a remarkably forward-looking transformation of an urban corner. He also designed a number of well-publicized commercial buildings, and late in 1925 he won his first commission for the Schocken Department Store. These and related works by Hans Scharoun (1893–1972), Hugo Häring (1882–1958), Hans Luckhardt (1890–1954), and Wassily Luckhardt (1889–1972) make up a body of innovative architectural design that rightfully dominated the journals of the 1920s, though they have since received much less attention.

Mendelsohn was also important on the theoretical front. He was easily the most traveled German architect of the 1920s. He visited the Netherlands in 1921 and 1923 and established close contacts there, not only with the Amsterdam school but with Oud in Rotterdam. In a lecture given in the former city and indicative of his outlook during this period, he encouraged young architects to "form the functions of its [the earth's] reality with the dynamics of your blood," that is, to "raise its functions to dynamic transcendency" with clear, bold, spatial construction.[181] Mendelsohn also visited Palestine in 1923, and in the following year he made an extended tour of the United States, which culminated with his pilgrimage to Taliesin. Mendelsohn's illustrated *Amerika: Bilderbuch eines Architekten* (America: Picture book of an architect, 1926) was the fruit of this endeavor.

In 1925–6 Mendelsohn made three trips to the USSR in conjunction with a factory commission there. For him this trip brought to the fore the American/Soviet dilemma facing Europe, and it resulted in his book *Russland-Europa-Amerika: Ein architektonischer Querschnitt* (Russia-Europe-America: An architectural cross-section, 1929). Although built around lightly captioned contrasting images, it is an intelligent and highly critical assessment of the contemporary situation. Mendelsohn interprets the theme of Russia and America as a dilemma for a "between" Europe. He sees America as "not only a wild, exploitatious and mechanical nation, but a nation becoming profound."[182] This new "master of the world," with its unlimited wealth and industrial shrewdness, nevertheless romantically longs for culture; it builds tall buildings but "has not yet recognized their daring conception or the spirit of expressing them."[183] Russia, on the other hand, is the stepchild of Asia and the Orient, a mystical and fantastic culture that now has become a laboratory "in its sacrifice toward the beginning of a new order."[184] Nevertheless, its success remains in doubt because of its technological backwardness, its poverty, and its undue emphasis on industry as a means of salvation. Mendelsohn goes on to characterize a chemical factory by Nikolai Ladowsky as "a symbol of a future architecture" and a Pittsburgh skyscraper by Charles Klauder as "a symbol of her [America's] longing for depth, for spiritual recollection."[185] At the same time he labels one suprematist sculpture "an intellectual play, a cubistic toy, a color game," while devaluing a design for a Moscow cinema by Ivan Leonidov as an appeal to "constructed graphics, instead of to realistic construction."[186]

Mendelsohn's analysis becomes all the more interesting when in his final section he turns to Europe. If the object of the earlier dialectic is a presumed mediation between these two technological and political alternatives, the path is blocked in Europe, on the one hand, because "her spiritual tension is too lax, her climate too temperate, and United Europe too far away," and, on the other hand, because of Europe's tendency toward rationality and theoretical gamesmanship.[187] One of the objects of his scorn is Le Corbusier. In commenting on a matter-of-fact American advertisement for steel joists, for instance, he concludes with this remark: "There is no fuss about its containing any of 'the five basic points of a fundamentally new esthetics.'"[188] A few pages later he juxtaposes an image of Oud's Hook of Holland – which "combines economical figuring with both sensitivity and technical appearance" – with Le Corbusier's taller housing scheme for Weissenhof.[189] The latter is far less successful because its cost stands "in major contrast to its useful living area," while "its [domestic] management extends over four floors."[190] This pointed remark not only brings into question the "rational" basis of this well-known icon, but it also underscores what Mendelsohn perceives to be Le Corbusier's basic aesthetic formalism. In short, it is a precocious declaration of war against what would become the aestheticism of the international style.

Unfortunately, it was a war that the Jewish Mendelsohn was destined to lose in Europe. His private practice started to collapse in 1931 with the Great Depression. Even before the legalization of anti-Semiticism in Germany, he chose the course of exile. In March 1933 he traveled briefly to Holland, next moved to England and then Palestine, and finally migrated to the United States in 1941.

Mendelsohn's critique of what was already a consolidating modernism was matched on another front by the theorizing of Ernst May, the most visible German architect involved with the housing problem of postwar Germany.[191] May too had been a student of Fischer, but he was also influenced by the garden city ideas of Raymond Unwin, with whom he worked during his university studies in London. In 1918 May assumed his first post, as a technical director for the Silesian building department in Breslau, and by the early 1920s he was constructing multifamily housing complexes using traditional building materials and forms in a manner influenced by the prewar scheme at Hellerau. His ideas continued to evolve over the next few years as he experimented with color, methods of prefabrication and rapid assembly, and even concrete panels and flat roofs. It was in Breslau that he – together with Grete Schütte-Lihotsky – began to design standardized kitchens and baths.[192] Important sources for the idea of using standardization were two books by American proponents of Taylorism in domestic design: *Principles of Domestic Engineering* (1915) by Mary Pattison (1869–1951) and *Household Engineering* (1919) by Christine Frederick (translated into German in 1920).[193]

May subsequently refined his earlier concepts to arrive at a modified garden city solution, and in 1925, the year he became the director of planning for Frankfurt, he began designing and building standardized, low-cost housing estates on the outskirts of the city. The "Frankfurt kitchen" designed for these estates by Margarete Lihotzky was engineered to provide maximum efficiency with a minimum of space through such features as built-in ironing boards and storage, but May extended the concept of efficiency to the house overall, first by standardizing such elements as doors, windows, furniture, lighting fixtures, and hardware, and second by expediting the construction process. The goal was to construct the maximum number of affordable housing units in the shortest possible time. The most innovative constructional feature of these projects, all done in collaboration with other architects and financed by the city, was a precast concrete wall system that was hoisted into place with cranes (it was first used at the Praunheim Siedlungen in 1926). These experiments were widely disseminated in May's journal *Das neue Frankfurt* (The new Frankfurt), which he started in 1926. The economic downturn at the close of the decade ended these efforts, and in October 1930 May led yet another German "brigade" of sixteen architects to work in the Soviet Union in support of Stalin's first five-year plan.[194] After this venture failed, May tried to return to Germany in 1934, but he was denied reentry. He spent the next eleven years in Kenya, Uganda, and South Africa.

May's housing efforts were by no means unique in Germany; in fact, his ideas on low-cost housing were closely watched by Gropius, Bruno Taut, and Martin Wagner, all of whom were devising similar approaches. Gropius's first experiments with mass-produced housing – following upon his earlier interest – took place in the summer of 1926 outside of Dessau, near the village of Törten. Here, his faith in Taylor never stronger, he brought together an assembly line of workers and a crane to build thirty-one units with precast concrete floor and roof slabs laid on walls of cinder block manufactured on the site.[195] The construction process was carefully analyzed to find out how to make each worker maximally efficient, but Gropius's first designs left much to be desired. The very small units had only an outhouse and no bathroom (the bathtub was placed in the kitchen), and it was from the outhouse that the inhabitants were supposed to acquire the manure for their rear gardens. Poor structural analysis also led to fracturing in many front walls. In subsequent phases, Gropius corrected some of these problems, but his professional reputation had been damaged. In 1928 he resigned his directorship of the Bauhaus to devote more time to practice, and in the same year he traveled for the first time to the United States to visit Wright, Rudolf Schindler, Richard Neutra, the Taylor Society, and the automobile factories surrounding Detroit.

Martin Wagner (1885–1957) and Bruno Taut were both active in Berlin, where in 1927 they collaborated on the famous horseshoe development at Britz.[196] Wagner was a communist, an organizer of the Berlin circle Der Ring, and in the first half of the decade he had put much effort into organizing guilds and cooperatives to finance low-cost housing based on Taylor's principles. This expertise led to his appointment in 1926 as head of Berlin's planning department. There he would form a close working relationship with Taut, who in 1921–4 had worked as a municipal architect for the town of Magdeburg. Upon returning to his native Berlin, Taut continued to focus his attention on housing, which led to his surprising small book *Die neue Wohnung: Die Frau als Schöpferin* (The new dwelling: The woman as designer).[197] Drawing upon the work of the American Christine Frederick, Taut called for the elimination of dust-collecting objects and the liberation of the housewife from her tedious tasks; he also proposed ideal house layouts reminiscent of Taylor's studies of factories. For the next few years Taut did his best work as an architect – both with Wagner on the very large scheme at Britz and with Hugo Häring and Otto Salvisberg at Berlin-Zehlendorf. These complexes were by far the best public housing produced in Germany in the 1920s and were notable as well for their efficient construction methods. Wagner publicized the results in his journal *Das neue Berlin*, which he coedited with Adolf Behne in 1929.[198]

7. Weissenhof and CIAM

The most famous of the new German housing settlements was the experimental Weissenhof Siedlung, a housing exhibition built in 1927 on a hillside above Stuttgart. Here German modernism begins a process of distillation in which competing approaches to design are filtered out and a new purified modernism emerges from the doctrinaire efforts of a self-annointed few. Stuttgart also signals the rise to prominence of another German architect who had been slowly making his way into the limelight – Ludwig Mies van der Rohe (1886–1969).[199]

Mies had been active prior to the war as a draftsman in Behrens's office and as the architect of a few Schinkelesque villas on the outskirts of Berlin. He served the last part of the war in Bulgaria but saw no action, and when he returned to Berlin in 1919, he was intellectually and artistically at a crossroads. On the one hand, he seems to have wanted to settle back into a cozy private practice designing large classical villas for wealthy suburbanites. On the other hand, in the early 1920s he was drawn into the avant-garde circle of Richter, Lissitzky, van Doesburg, and the journal *G* – a group and a periodical Mies's involvement with which has never been satisfactorily explained. Mies, who philosophically during this time was still much attracted to Spengler, may have participated in the circle more out of friendship for the dadaist Richter than out of any commitment to a particular artistic creed or ideology. Also, after 1921 Mies was sharing an office with Hugo Häring, who was active in avant-garde circles and had just married the actress Emilia Unda. The idea for *G*, with the subtitle *Material für elementare Gestaltung* (Material for elementary design), was put forth by van Doesburg on his visit to Berlin in 1920; the title was suggested by Lissitzky (*G* short for *Gestaltung*); and the first issue, published in July 1923, was edited by Richter, Lissitzky, and Werner Gräff, the last a former Bauhaus student who had chosen van Doesburg over Gropius. Richter and Mies edited the second and third issues (published in late 1923 and early 1924), and at this time the journal was assembled in Mies's Berlin office. The architect is also said to have contributed financially to the publication of at least one issue.[200]

It was in this journal that Mies published two of his early designs: the "concrete office building" and the "concrete house" of 1923. These had followed his two skyscraper schemes and should be evaluated within their context. The first skyscraper scheme – for a glass tower on Friedrichstrasse – was drawn up late in 1921 for a competition organized by a local business society. The competition was little more than an unofficial attempt to rejuvenate downtown business development along the American model, taking no account of the postwar economic reality. Mies's sketch (one of 145 entries) did not follow the competition guidelines and paid no attention to the very basic structural issues and heating and cooling problems associated with a glass-wall structure of this size. The curvilinear follow-up tower of 1922, which appeared in Taut's journal *Fruhlicht*, was no less fanciful, and its "organic" perimeter seems to owe everything to the fact that Mies was sharing office space with Häring during this period.[201] Mies's concrete office building was an exercise in employing a cantilevered slab, which the Swiss Maillart had perfected prior to the war. And the concrete country house – if one examines it next to the contemporary concrete schemes by Arthur Korn (business quarter in Haifa, 1923) and Hugo Häring (modern version of the Rio de Janeiro club, 1922–3) – appears as neither original nor especially compelling. Only with his brick country house of 1924, with its De Stijl floor plan, do we find the first signs of "avant-garde" influence.

The contrast of Mies's work with that of Häring deserves a few comments.[202] The latter, a student of Paul Wallot and Fritz Schumacher, had come to Berlin in 1921 to promote the acting career of his wife, and he was a man of considerable substance. Gut Garkau (1922–6), a farm complex north of Lübeck for which he received the commission, suggests the nature of his "organic" approach to practice. Not only did he use curvilinear forms and expressive materials but he paid great attention to the scientific and functional management of farming. His ideas were given clear theoretical form in his essay of 1925, "Wege zur Form" (Paths to form). Against the "geometric" architectural cultures of the past, with their imposition of form over function, Häring sees present-day society as demanding a new design attitude more attuned to nature and human needs:

We must seek out things and let them unfold their own forms. It is wrong to give a form to them, to determine their form from without, to force upon them arbitrary laws, to dictate to them. We are wrong when we make them display historical demonstrations; we are likewise wrong when we make them objects of our individual whims. And we are to a similar extent wrong when we reduce things to geometric or crystalline basic figures, because we thereby once again subjugate them (Corbusier).[203]

Häring seeks not an objective or rational functionalism but an expressive one. It was, incidentally, this organic

position that had led to Gropius's much criticized decision in 1923 to disallow the work of Häring at the Bauhaus exhibition – because, as Gropius explained in a letter to Mies, he wanted to focus solely on the "cubic-dynamic determined by construction."[204] This decision may be viewed as the birth of the split within German modernism that would become so evident by the end of the decade.

Returning to Mies – his terse aphoristic statements at this time do little to clarify his evolving direction. The leading theme of his two manifestoes in *G* (responding to Gropius's decision to exclude Häring from the Bauhaus exhibition) is the condemnation of aesthetic "formalism," that is, paying attention to form as opposed to "elementary design."[205] But this in the end is a difficult position to square with Mies's own formalism, which is evident in all of his "avant-garde" work. Another frequent Miesian theme of these years – that "Building art is the spatially apprehended will of the epoch" – owes as much to Riegl and Spengler as it does to van Doesburg.[206] And Mies's often cited remark of his essay of 1924 – "one cannot walk forward while looking backward, and one cannot be the instrument of the will of the epoch if one lives in the past" – is fully inconsistent with a design Mies completed a few months later for the Mosler House (1924–6). It could easily be mistaken for a Georgian manor in Virginia.[207] A classical architect by inclination, an avant-gardist in his spare time, Mies before 1925 was clearly searching for his way.

There is another side to Mies during these same years that should be stressed: his organizational and self-promotional focus. If Mies first saw his avant-garde contacts as a way to acquire the blessing of artistic legitimacy, his self-promotional efforts attest to a driving ambition. It is interesting that Mies did not join the Novembergruppe in 1919 but rather waited until 1922, after the group had jettisoned its politics and merged with the Arbeitsrat für Kunst. Mies served as its architectural director in 1923–5 and was in charge of planning several exhibitions. He also actively exhibited his few "visionary" drawings at the Bauhaus exhibition of 1923, at the Paris exhibition of 1923, and again in Berlin, Jena, Gera, Mannheim, Düsseldorf, Wiesbaden, Poland, Italy, and Russia.[208]

In the summer of 1923 Mies joined the Bund Deutscher Architekten (BDA) and quickly became a regional director, but this did not preclude him the following April from teaming up with Häring to form a renegade group within the BDA called the Der Ring (the ring), which demanded "freedom for all artistically creative architects of whatever direction."[209] Initially it was a diverse group of mainly Berlin architects, among them Häring (its secretary), Poelzig, Behrens, Mendelsohn, Hilberseimer, Bruno and Max Taut, Otto Bartning, and Gropius. This was the group that in 1926 was successful in lobbying for the appointment of Martin Wagner to the Berlin planning post. Also around the start of 1923, Mies joined the Society of Friends of the New Russia. This step seems to have been taken not out of political sympathy but because of Mies's courtship of a potential client, Eduard Fuchs, a high-ranking member of the German Communist Party.[210] Mies never received the commission of the coveted villa, but he was engaged by Fuchs in 1926 to design the highly controversial monument to Karl Liebknecht and Rosa Luxemburg: brick forms emblazoned with a stainless-steel star and hammer and sickle. If this commission seems surprising, it is because up to this point Mies had never revealed any interest in politics. Thus we must presume – despite his later willingness to curry the favor of the National Socialists – that during these years he was vacillating politically as well. Finally, in the spring of 1924, Mies joined the German Werkbund, the organization that he had avoided for so many years. His decision to join would prove to be the pivotal one for his career, because the Werkbund became his power base and the reason for his involvement with the Weissenhof exhibition.

Of all the exhibitions of the 1920s, Weissenhof stands out as the most significant within Germany.[211] The exhibition was conceived early in 1925 by Gustaf Stotz, the regional director of the Württemberg branch of the Werkbund. One year earlier Stotz had put on an exhibition in Stuttgart entitled "Die Form ohne Ornament" (Form without ornament), and in 1925 he proposed a much grander affair devoted to the new architecture. Mies's name, as a possible artistic director, would have arisen by virtue of his experience with exhibitions for the Novembergruppe, and after discussions within the Werkbund Stotz asked Mies in June 1925 to manage the architectural side of the event. The idea of a housing exhibition, which would require substantial funds, then had to be sold to the Württemberg chapter of the Werkbund and to city officials. This proved to be a delicate task that would take more than a year of negotiations to complete. It also involved a number of misleading statements by the organizers on what they really wanted to achieve. When the city council eventually approved funding for the event in July 1926 – now scheduled for the following year – it was with the understanding that it would be an estate-type housing development and involve several architects from Württemberg. What they eventually received from Stotz, Mies, and Häring

(who worked as an organizer along side Mies) was something very different.

Contention arose over the size of the project and even more over the selection of participating architects. Mies presented the first site plan to the city in October 1925, but the project was soon substantially reduced in size. The city officials wanted low-cost model dwellings in keeping with their plan to populate the hillside with small single-family houses. They were open to the possibility of multifamily units, especially if these could offer lessons on standardized (economical) construction. Mies favored larger or more luxurious architectural units, although he was not opposed to a few demonstration models built to exemplify low-cost schemes.

The selection of architects, which better reveals Mies's true intention, was a complicated process involving Mies, Häring, Stotz, and Württemberg officials. Stotz's original list, put forward in September 1925, consisted of twenty-five names and included five architects from Stuttgart. It also included six architects from outside Germany: Oud, Le Corbusier, van Doesburg, Stam, Frank, and Loos. Mies vetoed Loos and the Stuttgart architect Paul Bonatz and added van de Velde – and the negotiating process was underway. The final list was arrived at only in the following November. The German architects who made the cut were Mies, Schneck, Gropius, Hilberseimer, Bruno and Max Taut, Poelzig, Döcker, Scharoun, Behrens, and Adolf Rading. Schneck and Döcker were now the only two representatives from Stuttgart. Hilberseimer, who was primarily an urban planner, was included undoubtedly because of his friendship with Mies. Poelzig, Scharoun, Bruno Taut, and Behrens were added late, after Tessenow and Mendelsohn had declined invitations. Mendelsohn was by now opposed to Mies's leadership of Der Ring, and this internecine squabble, which resounded within European architectural circles, eventually claimed the presence of Häring, whom Mies unceremoniously dumped at the last minute after they clashed over control of the designs. Notably absent among the German architects was May, who had never made it onto any list, although he was the most experienced and best-known designer of housing estates.

The foreign architects on the list were Le Corbusier, Oud, Frank, Stam, and Bourgeois. Frank was the lone Austrian, although Loos's name had continued to reappear on and disappear from the list. Missing was Hannes Meyer, whom Mies personally rejected, as well as any architect from Czechoslovakia. Le Corbusier was given the two most prominent sites (facing the city) and by far the largest budget. This was the beginning of a personal relationship between Le Corbusier and Mies, formed at least in part in opposition to Gropius. Mies retained for himself the largest of the projects, the three-story apartment building at the crown of the site. Gropius, in the end, was relegated to two small units (one a prefab model), somewhat in the shadows of Le Corbusier's taller buildings.

From the point of view of design, Weissenhof was anything but the architectural success it is often presented as having been. Delays in the approval process and the lateness of several architects pushed the opening back by one week from its scheduled date of 17 July 1927, and many units were not finished until the end of August. The construction was shoddy, the detailing was poor, and cost overruns were rampant. Few buildings complemented each other, either compositionally or aesthetically. Further, many of the interiors lacked furnishings. In all it was a motley performance by sixteen architects, some of whom produced houses with touches of inspiration (Scharoun), others of whom showed little or no imagination (Bruno and Max Taut, Gropius, Hilberseimer, Bourgeois). The most positive thing about Mies's project was that for the first time he used steel-frame construction, although it was not indicated in the design.

But the lack of architectural success does not mean that the exhibition was not a success in a more important way – as a generator of publicity for the new movement. In fact, publicity was perhaps the one most attended-to aspect of the event, and Mies early on employed Werner Gräff to prepare two official publications (*Bau und Wohnung* and *Inneräume*) and to lead a carefully orchestrated campaign that – as Richard Pommer and Christian Otto have reported – engaged sixty press agencies and forty correspondents on the continents of Europe and North and South America.[212] Never before had an exhibition been so geared to press coverage. In effect, Weissenhof turned its version of modernism into a recognizable "modern movement." Mies van der Rohe, for one, would never return to designing classical villas. His next three commissions were for the sumptuous Herrmann Lange House, Krefeld (1927–8), the Barcelona Pavilion (1928–9), and the Tugendhat House, Brno (1928–30).

Another measure of the exhibition's success was the burst of publications that christened this view of modernism. Leading the way were Walter Curt Behrendt's *Der Sieg des neuen Baustils* (The victory of the new building style) and Ludwig Hilbereimer's *Internationale neue Baukunst* (International new architecture), both of whose appearances were planned with the exhibition's opening in mind and

formed part of the larger propaganda campaign. Behrendt (1884–1945), who had a doctorate in architecture, underwent various changes of position in the 1920s, especially after taking over the editorship of the Werkbund journal *Die Form* in 1925. His book, whose cover shows a photograph of Weissenhof (Fig. 83), opens by citing "the mighty drama of a sweeping transformation" that is now taking place, "the birth of the *form of our time*."[213] This transformation involves coming to terms "with the new realities of our time" (tools, machines, methods of construction, materials, spiritual changes) and mastering them *"creatively through design."* The resulting style – characterized by functionality, engineering, use of color, light, and space – Behrendt calls the *"technical style."*[214]

Hilberseimer's *Internationale neue Baukunst*, the first in a series of books on architecture oriented toward the public and put out by the Stuttgart publisher Julius Hoffmann, also opens with the image of Weissenhof.[215] It is, with the exception of a one-page summary of principles, a pictorial study obviously intended to emphasize the international nature of the new movement, for it includes images and projects from the United States, Holland, Italy, Russia, Switzerland, and France as well as Germany. The principles, which are subordinate only to the "creative will of the architect," give prominence not to aesthetic elements but rather to the functional character – materials and construction – and balance of all the elements: "It is not a faddish matter of forms, as many have assumed, but an elementary expression of a new architectural sensitivity."[216] In the same year (1927), Hilberseimer published *Grossstadtarchitektur* (Metropolitan architecture), a book conceived partly in response to Le Corbusier's urban theories.[217] Against both the horizontality of Le Corbusier's extension and the chaos of the vertical American cities, Hilberseimer proposes the vertical development of the city in a strict homogeneous manner. The result is a sterile, positively surreal vision of a cellular future city in which the first five stories of near continuous buildings are given over to offices and shops, while the upper fifteen stories of narrower rectilinear blocks contain the housing for residents. The darkened, faceless figures in the drawings commute to their offices below on foot by means of intermediate pedestrian ramps. Hilberseimer followed this effort in 1928 with a book co-written with Julius Vischer, *Beton als Gestalter* (Concrete as form-giver), notable for being the first European book to draw attention to the work of Richard Schindler.[218]

Also appearing in 1927 was Gustav Platz's *Die Baukunst der neuesten Zeit* (The most recent architecture), which is

83. Image of the Weissenhof housing exhibition on the cover of Walter Curt Behrendt's *Der Sieg des neuen Baustils* (Stuttgart, 1927).

a truly impressive and broadly based historical summary of the movement that praises its functional planning and social content.[219] Platz takes the roots of the modern movement back to Joseph Paxton and the Great London Exhibition. Along the way he underscores the achievements of Wagner, Berlage, Louis Sullivan, and others but also cites the contributions of such architects as Heinrich Tessenow, Theodor Fischer, Paul Bonatz, and Ludwig Hoffmann. Platz attempts to analyze the new architecture in terms of its tectonics, dynamics, rhythm, proportion, economy, surface effects, color, and ornament.

In the years 1928–30 there appeared a veritable flood of books dedicated to chronicling the new architecture in its various aspects, led by Henry-Russell Hitchcock's *Modern Architecture*, a new edition of Walter Müller-Wulckow's *Deutsche Baukunst der Gegenwart* (Present-day German architecture), Arthur Korn's *Glas im Bau und als Gebrauchsgegenstand* (Glass in building and the household), and Bruno Taut's *Modern Architecture* (published in English and German).[220] Teige's book on Czechoslovakian architecture came out in 1930, as did the three-part series *Neues Bauen in der Welt* (New building in the world), edited by Joseph Gantner in Vienna. It consisted of Roger Ginsburger's *Frankreich*, Richard Neutra's *Amerika*, and El Lissitzky's *Russland*.[221]

Müller-Welckow's book, still employing the old German script, is of interest only for the way it attempts to combine the work of Mendelsohn, May, and Gropius and the work of such traditionally minded designers as Bonatz, Richard Döcker, and Paul Mebes. Korn's book on the modern use of glass begins as something of a paean to Mies and Gropius, but it is also an invaluable visual encyclopedia of glass usage in the 1920s. The Marxist Korn would leave Germany in the early 1930s for the Soviet Union, but, failing to make a go of it as an architect there, he ended up in England in 1937.

Taut would also have a brief fling at living in the USSR, in 1932. His book *Modern Architecture* (1929) is the most interesting of this group – if only for the oddity of its intentions. During a stay in England Taut wrote an international history of modern architecture specifically for a British audience, and indeed he succeeded in assembling a credible visual chronicle of European developments. His problem is to integrate England and the United States (of which he knew exceedingly little) into his socialist mindset – a problem that becomes especially acute in his concluding chapter on England, where he manages to join scarcely concealed condescension toward his British readers with strong anti-Americanism.

Many of these historical surveys of modern practice, however, would soon meet resistance by a circle of activists who would effectively take control of the modern movement. Häring's expulsion from the Werkbund circle of Mies in 1926 was but a prelude to the discussions that were held before and during the exhibition of the following summer. Sometime in June 1927, Mies first indicated to Giedion that the "Movement must now be cleaned up" through a "secret cleansing" that would be carried out by an inner-circle elite and by press articles and exhibitions.[222] Giedion, who was meeting with all of the major figures at this time, seems to have interpreted this as a call to arms, and at the end of July he wrote to Oud to assure him that he was one of the "Seven Lamps of Architecture" accepted into the inner circle and to inform him that one of the lamps (probably Häring or Mendelsohn) was no longer burning.[223] Later that year, in another letter to Oud, Giedion identified the seven lamps as Mies, Gropius, Oud, Stam, Le Corbusier, Schmidt, and the Dutchman Cornelis van Eesteren (1887–1988) – the last of whom was admitted into the circle because of his interest in city planning. This group subsequently met in Stuttgart in October and considered collaborating on a journal. Giedion, in fact, probed Oud about the possibility of their assuming control of the new Dutch journal *i10*, but Oud and the publisher would ultimately decline this offer.

The plan to collaborate seems to have gone nowhere, but it was revisited along another front in the first months of 1928 with the creation of the Congrès Internationaux d'Architecture Moderne (CIAM).[224] Again Weissenhof was the venue for the initial discussions, and Giedion was instrumental in the founding of this organization, although he was at this time working extensively with Le Corbusier in trying to overturn the League of Nations competition verdict as well as in putting the finishing touches on his book about France. In a conversation with the Swiss Werkbund secretary Friedrich Gubler, Hélène de Mandrot, a Swiss, had suggested a concerted propaganda campaign on behalf of modernism and offered her castle at La Sarraz, Switzerland, as a meeting place. Gubler spoke with Gropius while in Stuttgart and later with Le Corbusier in Paris. The latter, fearing the dominance of German and Swiss-German architects in such an organization, was at first hesitant, but he assented when he was told he could draw up the working program for the first conference. Two dozen or so architects and officials (by invitation only) assembled in La Sarraz in late June 1928 to lay the groundwork for the new organization; they were mostly from France, Switzerland, and Germany.

The two goals of the first congress, according to Giedion, were to formulate a contemporary program of architecture and to create a vehicle for its implementation.[225] Le Corbusier proposed a four-part working program focused on modern techniques, standardization, the general economic system, and urbanism. Karl Moser was elected (honorary) president, while Giedion assumed the organizational duties as secretary of CIAM. Neither Gropius nor Mies attended the first meeting. Apparently the leading voices were those of Le Corbusier, May, Stam, Schmidt, Meyer, and Lurçat.[226] With the exception of Le Corbusier, all were communists who would later emigrate to the Soviet Union; most too had an overriding interest in urban design.

The so-called La Sarraz Declaration was drafted from the conference's discussions and only generally affirmed the aims of the architects attending the congress: "They have joined together with the intention of seeking to harmonize the elements that confront them in the modern world and of setting architecture back on its true program, which is of an economic and sociological order, dedicated solely to the service of the human being."[227] Sociology on an urban level implied the division of the city based on the three primary functions of dwelling, working, and recreation. The sociological order demanded that "subdivision, sales, and speculation, must be superseded by an economy that will regroup real-estate holdings" – effectively a plea to eliminate the private ownership of land.[228] No specific design strategy was put forward, but there was an emphasis throughout on the new industrial world and the need to accommodate architecture to the new conditions.

The second CIAM conference, held in Frankfurt in October 1929, was hosted by May and focused exclusively on the issue of housing. It produced the (later) highly controversial *Existenzminimum* standards (suggesting acceptible minimal housing square footage).[229] Here at CIAM's first planned conference (ominously coinciding with the crash of the stock market in New York) 130 architects and guests from eighteen countries gathered to study the work of May's municipal office, which was discussed, visited, and shown in exhibits. The political radicals were still in control of the agenda. Le Corbusier was on a South American tour and thus did not attend. Gropius, however, played a prominent role and sparked a controversy with his lecture (read by Giedion) "The Sociological Foundations of the Minimum Dwelling."[230] Following the sociological research of Franz Müller-Lyer, he divided human evolution into four cultural stages: kinship and tribal law, family law, individual law, and the future era of communal law. The third stage (aligned with the individual (ancestral) dwelling) coincides with the Enlightenment and is presently coming to an end with the emancipation of women. Gropius provided statistics to demonstrate the inverse proportionality of (1) industrialization and the birth rate, (2) the divorce rate and the illegitimate birth rate, and (3) the number of employed women and the number of individual households. These facts led Gropius toward the communal society and to the solution of the minimal dwelling, that is, to the idea of a contracted urban apartment with a maximum of light, sun, and ventilation. Pursuing this logic to its end, Gropius, employing charts, sought to demonstrate that the taller the buildings (arrayed in parallel and spaced to eliminate shadows), the more units can be fitted on less land. In a conclusion of great importance, he notes that "the large apartment building satisfies more nearly the sociological requirements of present-day industrial populations with their symptomatic liberation of the individual and early separation of the children from the family."[231] Gropius had just such a model in mind: one variation of his recent competition-winning scheme for the Berlin-Spandau-Haselhorst housing estate (1928–9). Here he proposed twelve-story high-rises, but the jury rejected this variation in favor of his alternative two-story and five-story units.

Gropius's approach to housing was different from that reflected in May's minimal-dwelling row houses, with their private gardens and other amenities and their direct relationship with adjoining green spaces. The split that had so

long been evolving now became inevitable. And although May was successful in deleting all references to Gropius's preference for the high-rise from the official CIAM conference publication, this issue of high- versus low-rise was about to be settled in a different way.[232]

The third CIAM conference, which took place in Brussels in November 1930, would have been the natural venue for carrying on this debate, but the voluntary departure of the various brigades for the Soviet Union essentially removed May and several of the other hard-liners from CIAM. With their departure, power now devolved back to Le Corbusier, his faithful lieutenant Giedion, and Gropius. This camp was strengthened by the election of van Eesteren as the new president. Le Corbusier set the tone and the agenda by presenting sixteen boards of his "Ville Radieuse" (Radiant City) featuring his high-rise solutions. And Gropius forcefully sided with him in his paper "Low-, Mid-, or High-Rise Building?" in which he again provides statistics (from commuter studies in Los Angeles) to prove the superiority of high-rise construction.[233] In an olive branch to Martin Wagner, Gropius accepts that the minimal dwelling cannot be applied to the single-family house and to large families, but he nevertheless argues that "well-organized, modern high-rise apartment blocks cannot be considered a necessary evil; they are a biologically motivated type of dwelling, a genuine by-product of our age."[234] This position was supported by the Austrian émigré Richard Neutra, visiting from Los Angeles, who pointed out that the high-rises in the United States were directed at the luxury market.

The fourth and final prewar CIAM conference took place in the summer of 1933, in the midst of deteriorating political and economic conditions; it codified CIAM's emphasis on Le Corbusier's "Functional City." It had been scheduled to be held in Moscow in 1932, but Soviet authorities had become ambivalent about the conference and the modern movement in general. The situation in Germany was also rapidly changing. Hitler had assumed power in March, and the architectural annex of the Bauhaus in Berlin had been closed in April. Leftists were beginning to fear losing their government jobs, and CIAM organizers responded by renting a cruise ship to transport the architects from Marseilles to Athens. Here 100 delegates convened, examined the plans of thirty-three cities, and composed the Athens Charter, all the while being filmed by Moholy-Nagy's camera. Le Corbusier assumed control of CIAM by default, as the three most prominent German members – Gropius, Mies, and Marcel Breuer – could not attend because of the worsening situation at home.

The heart of the Athens Charter (published only in 1943) were 95 propositions organized under the four functional categories of habitation, leisure, work, and traffic.[235] It is certainly one of the more remarkable documents of the modern movement, if only for its brazen intention to remake human society in its entirety. It is also a codification of Le Corbusier's urban ideas of the 1920s and 1930s, hardly surprising given that the French architect himself wrote the Athens Charter during the early 1940s on behalf of a now suspended CIAM. The functional categories of habitation, leisure, work, and traffic are treated not so much as conceptual categories but as the basis for actual physical divisions of the city. The various propositions regarding housing, for instance, call for the demolition of slums and the physical separation of residential areas from traffic and working areas and their integration with green areas. The hated antithesis of Le Corbusier's version of the garden city is the suburb, which in its American manifestation "constitutes one of the greatest evils of the century."[236] Against it, Le Corbusier mandates his solution: "High buildings, set far apart from one another, must free the ground for broad verdant areas."[237] These green areas are to be the venue for leisure-time activities. Work areas and traffic arteries are to be rigidly separated.

Le Corbusier's manifesto, of course, raised a score of legal, land-use, and economic issues that were not addressed. Its summary propositions, however, did not skirt around the problem. In fact, according to the concluding proposition, "Private interest will be subordinated to the collective interest," entailing the elimination of private ownership of land.[238] Just how the relevant government "authority" should seize land for pubic development we shall see when we consider his writings of the early 1940s. What is of interest in the Athens Charter is the power it now bestows upon the architect, to whom all of the seized lands are to be turned over. This is a key point for CIAM: "Architecture is responsible for the well-being and the beauty of the city. It is architecture that takes charge of its creation or improvement, and it is architecture that must choose and allocate the different elements whose apt proportions will constitute a harmonious and lasting work. Architecture is the key to everything."[239] That the Athens Charter dovetails perfectly with Le Corbusier's image of himself as someone destined to direct such a tectonic shift in human thought need not be overly emphasized. What should also be noted is that by 1933 the European modern movement – shortly to be scattered in different directions by a political cataclysm – is now reduced to the ideological mission of one individual. Left standing is the lone prophet Le Corbusier.

12

AMERICAN MODERNISM 1917–1934

We are contemplating a new architecture of a civilization.

Hugh Ferriss (1922)

1. The American Skyscraper

Of the two images of the American landscape most often published in European architectural journals in the 1920s – the grain silo and the skyscraper – it was the latter that was more intriguing to European observers. More so than the automobile and the ocean liner, more so than the airplane and the assembly line, the skyscraper served as a quintessential metaphor for American modernity, even if European building codes and zoning laws would not permit its construction at home. It was an icon of industrial prowess, of technological innovation and advanced assembly methods, of the new, more dynamic, more prosperous world. After a "Gothic" design won the Chicago Tribune competition of 1922, however, it was also seen by many Europeans as a sign of American architectural confusion and cultural backwardness.

This view was not restricted to Europeans, for American practice had its share of homegrown critics during these years. Henry-Russell Hitchcock, in his *Modern Architecture* (1929), saw the skyscraper as America's singular calling but also its greatest architectural failing: "The skyscraper therefore awaits the first American New Pioneer who will be able to take the engineering as a basis and create directly from it a form of architecture."[1] The bold drawings of Frank Lloyd Wright had failed Hitchcock; the art deco designs of the 1920s had failed him; the visionary explorations of Hugh Ferriss had failed him. Hitchcock believed that only Richard Neutra – in his hypothetical skyscraper design for "Rush City Reformed" (1927) – had come near to the solution.[2] The Europhile Hitchcock did not like the stepped forms imposed by the New York City zoning ordinance. He would

come to like even less the soaring and scalloped form of William van Alen's Chrysler Building, under construction in 1929.

Hitchcock's became the standard historical view of the skyscraper down through the 1950s and 1960s, but it was a view seriously flawed in its premises. For one thing, it presumed a lone formal solution to the skyscraper that was entirely structural and rectilinear. For another, it presumed the superiority of the paper designs of Le Corbusier, Gropius, and Mies van der Rohe, and as a historian who was not an architect, he underestimated the complexity of the technical and constructional task. He was unaware of the pragmatic issues with which American architects were grappling and of the problems that were in fact being ingeniously solved. His vision of the skyscraper was entirely a paper vision.

The skyscraper's genesis in New York in the 1860s and in Chicago in the 1880s has been well documented. Chicago is usually given precedence because there a consistent type of tall commercial building developed over a period of twenty years: the U-shaped or L-shaped block with offices generally restricted to two or three fronts.[3] The great Chicago fire of 1871 set in motion the necessary market forces for its creation: need for commercial space, speculative land values, code and zoning changes, and new tax laws. Among the necessary technological innovations were the electric passenger elevator; fireproofing; advances in plumbing, heating, lighting, and ventilation; and the telephone. The loamy soil of Chicago demanded a theoretical approach to footing analysis, which was largely carried out by German engineers who had emigrated to the Midwest, such as Friedrich Baumann and Denkmar Adler.[4] The essential material innovation was the introduction of Bessemer steel in the mid-1880s, which allowed the tall metal frame. Even something as seemingly insignificant as a revolving door (invented in 1888) was a crucial technological innovation in a building above a certain height. The overall form of the commercial building was dictated almost entirely by the economics of the leasable floor area, the material and labor costs, and the duration of construction. As the architectural critic Montgomery Schuyler noted of Chicago architecture in 1895, "the primary and co-ordinating qualification" for their architects is that of an administrator.[5]

The evolution of the steel frame was inhibited by the structural factor of wind loads. If we look at its development in the 1880s – from the Montauk Building (1881-2) of Burnham and Root to the Home Insurance Building (1884-5) of William Le Baron Jenney to the Tacoma Building (1888-9) and Marquette Building (1893-5) of Holabird and Roche – the principal structural issue was lateral wind force. The more the skeleton frame becomes a true frame, which in turn allows the outer walls to be non-load-bearing and therefore lighter, the more the building is vulnerable to the effects of wind. The Montauk Building had bearing walls on the exterior and an iron frame within. In the Home Insurance Building, which opened onto two streets, iron columns were moved to the exterior walls facing the street (and encased in concrete and brick), but the rear and north walls of the structure were bearing for reasons of stability. In the L-shaped Tacoma Building, the streets facades were considerably lightened and hung with cladding and glass, but the side walls and two interior walls were still bearing. Only in the second Marquette Building did the architects remove the bearing walls and achieve a true steel frame, because the U-shaped floor plan itself provided additional stability.[6]

These structural and technical considerations of course did not preclude a concern for aesthetics, an issue that increasingly comes to the fore in the 1890s. The deliberate John Wellborn Root (1850-91), who was much influenced by H. H. Richardson, often employed a Romanesque vocabulary for his tall buildings, as seen in the Rookery, Chicago (1885-8).[7] For his Monadnock Building, Chicago (1888-92), which in an earlier version had Egyptian ornamentation, he sculpted the building into a rectangular monolithic form and stripped it of all decoration or modulation except for a flaring at the top and bottom and the undulation of continuous bay windows. It was one of the last bearing-wall buildings, achieving the maximum possible height of sixteen stories.

It was Louis Sullivan who "solved" the conceptual problem of the early skyscraper with the Wainwright Building, Saint Louis (1890-1), and the Guaranty Building, Buffalo (1893-96). In the nine-story Wainwright Building, he devised a tripartite division: a two-story commercial base, intermediate floors of offices with structural piers, and an attic story for mechanical equipment. The taller and more animated Guaranty Building was one of the masterpieces of nineteenth-century American architecture. His essay "The Tall Office Building Artistically Considered," written at the completion of this building, summarizes his intentions. His epithet "form ever follows function" rationalizes the formal treatment of the various parts, with the most important part being those "indefinite number of stories of offices piled tier upon tier, one tier just like another tier, one office just like all the other offices – an office being similar to a cell in a honeycomb, merely a compartment, nothing more."[8] The tall building's chief aesthetic characteristic is to be "lofty," thrilling, and expressive of its nature: "It must be tall, every inch of it tall. The force and power of altitude must be in it, the glory and pride of exaltation must be in it. It must be every inch a proud and soaring thing, rising in sheer exultation that from bottom to top it as a unit without a single dissenting line – that it is the new, the unexpected, the eloquent peroration of the most bald, most sinister, most forbidding conditions."[9]

The critic Montgomery Schulyer celebrated Sullivan's achievement: "I know of no steel framed building in which the metallic construction is more palpably felt through the envelope of baked clay."[10] Claude Bragdon in 1918 viewed it as a milestone still not sufficiently appreciated. Here, he felt, democracy had at last found its rule in those rows and rows of utilitarian windows, regularly spaced and of equal size, suggesting "the equality and monotony of obscure laborious lives," while the impressed vertical piers stand for their "hopes and aspiration, and the unobtrusive, delicate ornament which covers the whole with a garment of fresh beauty is like the very texture of their dreams. The building is able to speak thus powerfully to the imagination because its creator is a poet and prophet of democracy."[11] Here was a uniquely American perspective that could scarcely have been voiced in Europe at this time.

Sullivan was not alone in his Chicago success. In 1895 Frank Lloyd Wright sketched out a checkerboard glass skyscraper of ten stories for the Luxfer Prism Company, and a few years later he completed the Larkin Building, Buffalo (1902-6). Charles B. Atwood's Reliance Building (1894) and Holabird and Roche's Williams Building (1897-98) and

Republic Building (1902–04) were other distinctive tall buildings constructed in Chicago in roughly the same period.

The situation in New York City around the turn of the century was quite different. First, Manhattan is an island with bedrock just a few feet below the surface, which greatly eases the structural problem. Second, the Northeast still tended to look to Europe for its artistic values. Not only were many architects from this region trained at the Ecole des Beaux-Arts in Paris, but the major architecture schools in the Northeast were almost entirely Beaux-Arts in their orientation. For these reasons, as well as the presence of older and greater concentrations of wealth, the architectural climate was considerably more conservative. The traditional styles, as some critics noted, were purchased from abroad and thus remained in fashion longer here than in Europe or in other parts of North America.

As result of these factors, although the skyscraper developed in New York earlier than in Chicago, in the former city it remained clothed in historical forms down through World War I.[12] The elevator made its first appearance in the Equitable Life Assurance Building (1868–70), where it hoisted people up to the seventh floor, which was tucked under a Mansard roof. Richard Morris Hunt's nine-story Tribune Building (1873–75), also sporting a Mansard roof but with a Florentine tower, rose to an elevation of 260 feet more than a decade before a Chicago building would achieve this height. The first tall building to leap past Trinity Church's steeple was the Pulitzer Building (1889–90), designed by George B. Post, which at 309 feet far surpassed anything in Chicago. One of the most unusual and widely acclaimed buildings of the late nineteenth century was Bruce Price's American Surety Building (1894–96), a near contemporary of the Guaranty Building. Though it stands twenty stories high, the severe rustic piers composing the intermediate stories are capped off at the top with colossal statuary and a series of Italian loggia motifs. If it falls short of Sullivan's building in functional assurance, it certainly is not lacking in animation and verve; it speaks as well to the optimism of the 1890s.

Skyscraper construction in New York just before World War I jumped dramatically in scale but retained its historicist inclinations. Notable in the last regard were the Flatiron Building (1903) of Daniel Burnham and the Times Tower (1904) of Cryus L. W. Eidlitz, but these were soon to be dwarfed by the 600-foot, forty-seven-story Singer Loft Building (1906–8) of Ernest Flagg. Here the narrow tower rises from a slightly earlier French mansard building; its central vertical band of factory glazing is framed at the sides with a stone molding and brick corner piers, punched with single windows. At the top, the tower actually mushrooms out to accommodate another mansard roof, which is capped with a lantern reminiscent of a mausoleum. This academic effort was soon to be outdone, however, by the Gothic Woolworth Tower (1911–13) of Cass Gilbert – the 792-foot building that eclipsed the Eiffel Tower as the tallest structure in the world. In fact, this "Cathedral to Commerce" housed 14,000 workers, nearly 3,000 telephones, and the fastest elevators in the world. Contemporary writers raved about the building's success.

All of this was to change with World War I and the decade of "the Twenties." The United States emerged from the conflict the wealthiest and most powerful nation in the West. The period that followed was the era of Prohibition, speakeasies, female suffrage, sexual upheaval, mass immigration, concentrated wealth, F. Scott Fitzgerald and Sinclair Lewis, George Gershwin, the radio, and even the appearance of the television. Architecturally it was a period of boom and of attempts to erect the world's tallest building. The 1920s, of course, also ended with the greatest economic crash in American history.

The key event as far as the skyscraper is concerned was the 1916 revision of the New York City zoning law.[13] The revision was conceived in part as a response to the twin blocks of Ernest Graham's Equitable Building of 1915, which rose to thirty-two stories without setbacks and housed over a million square feet of floor space. The law prescribed urban districts and a "zoning envelope." A building could rise vertically to a prescribed height but then had to step back at an angle determined by a line drawn from the street's center. And although the law imposed no height restriction, the final tower could occupy no more than 25 percent of the lot.

With the war and a postwar recession, the law took a few years to find an interpretation. John Taylor Boyd Jr. reviewed it for the *Architectural Record* in 1920 and saw it as a measure to overcome the urban chaos of the past. He also saw it as a city-planning tool that would dramatically change the nature of the city: "In a word, one may compare this new conception of a city with the older one by saying that older ideas picture the city as a kind of fungus, in which the street and block system are the cells; while the new ideal created by the Zoning Resolution conceives it to be a mechanism of related parts, or units, in the shape of neighborhoods."[14] Various other interpretations of the law followed, many of which stressed, among other things, the likelihood that a new American style would emerge from the law.[15] In 1921 Irving K. Pond, who had been wrestling with the issue of tall-building design since the 1890s, viewed the enforced "setbacks and modified corners" as a means of making a direct appeal to sentiment; that is, horizontal and vertical elements "are introduced into the structures in such manner that each may make its own appeal to the emotions and be held in restraint by the other."[16] In the same year the architect Bertram Grosvenor Goodhue (1869–1924) proposed a 1,000-foot, eighty-story tower next to Madison Square Garden, with an enormous church as its base. The architect and delineator Hugh Ferriss prepared a number of sketches for the proposed Convocation Building, which in its attenuating and stepped-back form reflected (only at a much grander scale) the silhouette of Goodhue's Nebraska State Capitol Building, which was just then starting construction.[17]

The key breakthrough for the new law and its effect on skyscraper design came in 1922 – the result of four sketches prepared by Hugh Ferriss (1889–1962) (Fig. 84).[18] Ferriss by this date was well known as a brilliant delineator. Trained as an architect, he had arrived in New York from Saint Louis in 1913, but in 1915 he established an independent practice as a professional renderer, working chiefly with charcoal and carbon pencil. His very unique chiaroscuro style lent itself to "visionary" thinking, but the extraordinary originality of his architectural creations was unpredictable. Sometime around the start of 1922 Ferriss began working with Harvey Wiley Corbett, a protégé of Gilbert and (with Frank Helmle) the architect of the much admired Bush Terminal, New York (1916–17). Corbett, a proponent of the skyscraper, had made some diagrams to explain the new law, and Ferriss transformed them into sketches. They first appeared in an exhibition of the Architectural League of New York in February 1922 and in *The New York Times Magazine* – that is, just before the Chicago Tribune competition was announced.[19] The first two of the drawings, with diagonal lines resembling a Lyonel Feininger woodcut, convey the legal setback from a line drawn at the center of the street sculpted into volumes for light. The mass in the center is the tower unrestricted in height but occupying only twenty-five percent of the lot. In the next drawing, the three principal masses begin to assume a ziggurat form. In the fourth drawing, the stepped-back mass of a building gains final form.

Two things are of importance in these sketches. First, the very convincing three-dimensional ensemble presents an entirely new vision of a skyscraper; second, these compo-

sitions are essentially sculpted from the zoning envelope in a way highly suggestive of a design strategy. Ferriss himself understood the design implications of the law: "Architects will cease to be decorators and will become sculptors."[20] And he also noted – in the quotation cited at the beginning of this chapter – that this change in outlook carries with it the possibility of a new architecture for American civilization.[21]

Over the next few years Ferriss created a series of futuristic drawings that refined his ideas. In 1923, for a planning commission headed by Corbett, Ferriss prepared drawings that proposed second-story pedestrian bridges for the commercial centers of Manhattan.[22] In 1924 he began working with the architect Raymond Hood on futuristic proposals. One was for "A City of Needles": attenuated 1,000-foot towers widely spaced and connected by streaming freeways.[23] Ferriss developed this idea over the next two years into a crystalline city of glass towers 1,500 feet tall placed in a park setting and flooded by spotlights, with airplanes flying overhead.[24] In another rendering of 1925, Ferriss and Hood proposed habitable suspension bridges: The pylons are office towers and the double system of cables on each side are transformed into suspended office and apartment buildings located between the catenary curve of the upper cable and the roadway.[25]

During the period, the only other architect comparably imaginative in his treatment of the tall building was Frank Lloyd Wright. His astonishing project for the National Life Insurance Company in Chicago (1923–4) – far more advanced in design and technological sophistication than any contemporary building – was conceived structurally as an ingenious system consisting of a spine with four intersecting and parallel towers whose floors were cantilevered off interior pylons (Fig. 85). The "opalescent, iridescent copper-bound glass" modular skyscraper was to be sheathed with a series of "suspended, standardized sheet-copper screens" into which glass was substituted in single or multiple panels.[26] The interior walls likewise were designed as prefabricated wall-and-door systems to allow maximum flexibility, with heating, plumbing, and electric systems supplied in modular trunk lines to assure their easy removal and relocation. Wright employed the structural logic that he had used on the Imperial Hotel in Tokyo, and he argued that his system would result in a building one-third lighter and three times stronger than any comparable existing skyscraper: "But of chief value, as I see it, is the fact that the scheme as a whole would legitimately eliminate the matter of 'architecture' that now vexes all such buildings, from field construction, all such elements of architecture 'exterior'

84. Hugh Ferris, four sketches depicting New York City's new zoning ordinance. From *The Metropolis of Tomorrow* (New York, 1929).

or interior becoming a complete shop-fabrication – assembled only in the field."[27] Wright's design was a real commission for a real client, Albert Mussey Johnson, a businessman but also a "fanatic and mystic; Shylock and the humanist."[28] Had this extraordinary design been realized, it would have radically altered the course of the American tall building.

Given the intense spirit of experimentation in the first years of the decade, the now somewhat notorious competition for the Chicago Tribune Tower of 1922 must be seen as having less importance for American practice than earlier assumed. It was a well-publicized and much-watched event, particularly in Europe, where few architects had work on the boards. Further, the contested decision to award first

85. Frank Lloyd Wright, design for National Life Insurance Company, Chicago, 1924. The Frank Lloyd Wright Foundation.

place to the scheme of John Mead Howells and Raymond Hood over the second-place design of Eliel Saarinen stirred up controversy at home and abroad.

The competition was the brainchild of Robert McCormick and Joseph Patterson, the two owners of the *Chicago Tribune* – "The World's Greatest Newspaper" – and its publishing empire.[29] On 9 June 1922 they announced an international architectural competition for their new building, which was to be "the most beautiful and distinctive office building in the world." Although the competition was open, ten American firms were specially invited to enter and were each to receive $2,000 for their efforts. The first-place winner was promised $50,000, and second- and third-place

winners were to receive $20,000 and $10,000 respectively. The program was ready by the beginning of August, and American participants were to have their entries submitted by the start of November; foreign entries were given another thirty days for the mail. In the end, 263 architects submitted entries, although seventy-four projects from abroad (including that of Gropius and Meyer) arrived too late to be counted or considered. The composition of the jury says everything about the owners' expectations and the nature of the competition itself. It consisted of five members: four officers from the *Chicago Tribune* and one architect – Alfred Granger, president of the Illinois Chapter of the American Institute of Architects. In essence, then, it was a lay jury with

86. Walter Gropius and Adolf Meyer, entry for the Chicago Tribune Tower competition, 1922. From Walter Gropius, *Internationale Architektur* (Munich, 1925).

four members having little or no architectural experience. And because many of the invited firms had business or social connections with the paper's owners, the fact that two of the three winning schemes came from this group was entirely predictable.[30]

The competition and its significance have been misunderstood in several respects. For one thing, many of the schemes favored by twentieth-century historians were impractical, if not technically impossible. Sigfried Giedion, in 1941, argued on behalf of the (unconsidered) scheme of Walter Gropius and Adolf Meyer over the winning scheme of Howells & Hood, but it is difficult to understand just what Giedion meant by the building's superior "architectonic expression"[31] (Fig. 86). The projecting, uncovered balconies are completely inappropriate for the Windy City's severe winters, and in any case their thin pipe railings would

hardly have given the building's occupants a sense of security while enduring the gusts off the nearby lake. Again, the proposed floor-to-ceiling "Chicago style" windows would not have handled the wind loads, as glass-and-mullion technology in 1922 was simply not up to the task. Other projects praised by Giedion, such as those of Bruno Taut and Max Taut, were simply naive from any structural or aesthetic viewpoint.

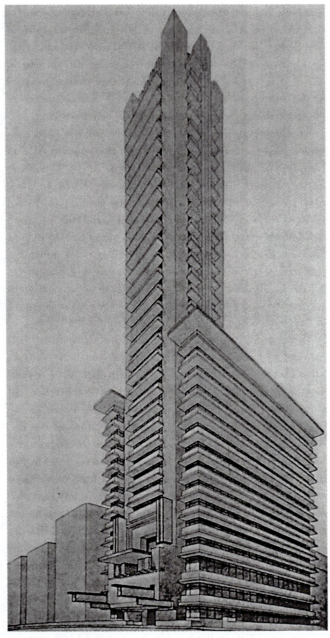

87. Bernard Bijvoet and Johannes Duiker, entry for the Chicago Tribune Tower competition, 1922. From Walter Gropius, *Internationale Architektur* (Munich, 1925).

There were several projects, however, that displayed a real understanding of the skyscraper and its technology. The entry of Bijvoet and Duiker of Holland, which was much influenced by Wright's ideas for the tall building, proposed a well-reasoned tower braced by two lower horizontal structures, with corner piers to accommodate mechanical services (Fig. 87). The project of Hans and Wassili Luckhardt, designed in association with Alfons Anker, is an ingenious sandwiching of narrow slabs, with the tallest at the center; it is both viable and eminently detailed. Perhaps the best of the American designs was that of Wright's former apprentice Walter Burley Griffin (1876–1937), who sent in his design from Australia, where he was designing the new capital city.[32] It is a setback building remarkably similar in spirit to the contemporary zoning drawings of Ferriss, yet more compacted and slenderer in its vertical articulation.

Another respect in which the competition has been misunderstood concerns the impetus that the controversy surrounding it gave to skyscraper design. In 1923 Sullivan notably fanned the controversy with an article in *Architectural Record* in which he stated that the winning project of Howells & Hood "evolved of dying ideas" and that Saarinen had indeed grasped the intricate problem of the skyscraper "in such wise as no American architect has as yet shown the required depth of thought and steadfastness of purpose to achieve."[33] But such a view does little justice to the career of Raymond Hood and even misconstrues the case with regard to Saarinen.

To begin with, the design of the Finnish architect was inspired by Gothic forms, although in a somewhat abstract way. The principal motif of the design lies in its overall step-back composition, which resembles the exercises of Ferriss, and Saarinen may even have been aware of the delineator's published efforts. Another feature of the design is the heavy use of figurative sculpture throughout the building. Sullivan found this ornamentation acceptable, but many of Saarinen's European colleagues fiercely opposed it. His relative success in the competition, in any case, induced Saarinen to immigrate to the Midwest, where he got a teaching job at the University of Michigan. The following year he began his association with the Cranbrook Academy, near Detroit, later a vital center for American modernism.

The case of Hood (1881–1934) is not all that dissimilar to that of Saarinen. John Mead Howells (1868–1959) received one of the ten invitations to enter the competition, and reportedly he met Hood one day in Grand Central Station and the two men decided to team up on the project.[34] Hood, like Howell, had studied at the Ecole des Beaux-Arts, but his New York office was unsuccessful and without work in 1922. He prepared the Gothic-inspired design on his own, no doubt influenced by Cass Gilbert's very successful Woolworth Building. But what is interesting is that Hood soon altered his design approach to the tall building in a striking way. This change was first reflected in the American Radiator Building, New York (1924), in which he turned back to the lessons of Ferriss and attenuated his tower, crowning it with a headpiece as well. Hood, in fact, became the master of the setback style, as shown by his designs for the New York Daily News Building (1928–30) and RCA Building at Rockefeller Center (1929–33), one of the finest office complexes of the century. Hood's final masterpiece was the McGraw-Hill Building (1929–31), one of the few American works to find its way into Hitchcock and Johnson's exhibition in 1932.[35]

Around 1925 another element began to work itself into the setback style – the decorative forms of art deco. Its first brilliant flowering can be seen in the apartment complex at 2 Park Avenue (1924–7), designed by Ely Jacques Kahn (1884–1972).[36] Kahn had trained at the Ecole des Beaux-Arts, and his style was certainly influenced by his visit to the exposition in Paris in 1925. But art deco is broader in its intentions, and it can be interpreted as the attempt to import to the new cubic forms of the setback style an original and dynamic (modern) animation – in keeping with the energetic pace of this period. Lewis Mumford regarded Kahn's use of art deco as that "something more" that was essential to imbue the new functional forms with artistic feeling. He thus called Kahn's apartment building on Park Avenue "the boldest and clearest note among all our recent achievements in skyscraper architecture."[37] Hitchcock, by contrast, vehemently opposed the effort to add "something more," and he grouped Kahn with those architects who "are generally very little more excellent than many of those which in their ornamentation imitate the styles of the past."[38]

Another source of art deco was the new interest in nonclassical archaeology. Kahn pursued his fascination with Persian and Oriental archaeology, and Ferriss worked with Corbett in 1923–4 on an extensive reconstruction of Solomon's Temple and its citadel.[39] Ferriss was also much intrigued by current fantasies about Babylon. In a book published in 1929, he included images of hanging gardens and the Assyrian ziggurat form as lessons to be applied to contemporary design.[40] The similarity between the setback style and the stepped pyramids of the Mayans was noticed by others as well. Wright was intrigued with pre-Columbian American motifs in Los Angeles in the late teens. The Sears

Roebuck store in Los Angeles (1926) carried Mayan ornaments, as did the more famous office building on Sutter Street, San Francisco (1929–30), the work of Timothy L. Pflueger. In 1925 the English architect Alfred C. Bossom, working in New York, called the pyramid at Tikal "the original American skyscraper" and argued for the appropriateness of its form for office buildings.[41] One result of such thinking was Francisco Mujica's extraordinary book of 1929, *The History of the Skyscraper*. Mujica, a Chilean architect and former professor at the University of Mexico, was fully informed about skyscraper developments since Jenny's Home Insurance Building, and he moved from his archaeological reconstructions of the Mayan pyramids at Tikal, Papantla, and Chichén Itzá into a "*new* line" of "Neo-American" architecture in part deriving from these stepped pyramidal forms.[42] His rich visual history concludes with his own design for a sixty-eight–story skyscraper decorated with pre-Columbian ornamentation but similar in its overall logic to the designs of Ferriss and Hood.

Ferriss's *Metropolis of Tomorrow* (1929) appeared in the same year, and this majestic work summarized his visionary ideas. It was divided into three parts: cities of today, projected trends, and an imaginary metropolis. The metropolis of the future is fed by 200-foot-wide avenues at half-mile intervals and has parklands and districts for business, art, and science. The buildings vary from large blocks that skip over avenues to isolated towers placed in a natural setting. It is a theosophical, quasi-mystical vision of the future but has a considerable basis in current realities.

A contemporary realization of one such vision, and a synthesis of the tendencies of the late 1920s, was the Chrysler Building (1928–30), designed by William van Alen (1883–1946). This 1,046-foot tower was not a corporate headquarters but a personal initiative of Walter P. Chrysler, the brilliant automotive engineer and entrepreneur.[43] Van Alen has rarely received from historians the honor he deserves. Like so many, he was a graduate of the Ecole des Beaux-Arts but he made his reputation in New York in the 1920s as a designer of fashionable store fronts, restaurants, and advertising displays. The Chrysler Building came about almost by accident, as van Alen had planned a tall building on this site for another client. When the financial backing for the project fell through, Chrysler picked up the project but insisted on owning the tallest building in the world. His ambition proved historic. When, after construction started, another building was announced to be taller by a few feet – the Bank of the Manhattan Company, designed by H. Craig Severance – Chrysler had van Alen secretly design a new

and taller topping for the structure. The celebrated arched and scalloped headdress, which (like many other details) was inspired by the metallic sleekness of automobile design, was constructed of a special chromium-nickel steel (Nirosta) that Chrysler had manufactured at the Krupp steelworks in Germany after his engineers had thoroughly tested its metallurgic properties for resistance to tarnish and deterioration. It was but one of many extraordinary feats of engineering, including the raising of the pinnacle needle from inside the scalloped dome, the design of an elevator that would exceed 1,500 feet per minute without its vibration damaging the eardrum, and (exceedingly rare for this time) the erection of the building without a serious worker accident or fatality.

The Chrysler Building has one further distinction beyond its role as an icon of American architecture: This artistic and technological wonder was not included in Hitchcock and Johnson's exhibition of 1932, although George Howe and William Lescaze's PSFS Office Tower (1931–2) in Philadelphia, in addition to the work of Raymond Hood, was shown. The Chrysler Building symbolized for many unabashed ambition, artistic audacity, and – like nearby Rockefeller Center – the technical bravado and dizzying heights to which American architecture could aspire in the closing days of the 1920s. It was also one of the last monuments of its kind, for on 29 October 1929 the American stock market collapsed at the height of its irrational exuberance. The three-and-a-half billion dollars of design work done by architectural offices in 1928 would be reduced to half a billion dollars by 1932. Nearly half of the architectural offices in the country would go bankrupt during the same period. The decade of the greatest prosperity and optimism in American history quickly gave way to the gloomiest of times.

2. Wright: The Lost Years

The inability of Frank Lloyd Wright to maintain a practice in the 1920s was another misfortune for American architecture. The Midwesterner was still attracting some of the best young architects to his studio at Taliesin, and his prodigious talent and architectural imagination were still clearly on the ascent. After the fire and homicidal tragedy of 1914, he rebuilt his homestead in Wisconsin. Three years later he prepared his final design for a new hotel in Tokyo, and in the summer of 1919 he moved there to oversee the work, which would engage him for most of the next four years. In 1923 the just completed Imperial Hotel, based on a symmetrical

Beaux-Arts plan, attained international celebrity when it escaped damage in a major earthquake that leveled most of the city and resulted in more than 100,000 deaths. Wright had engineered a structural system in which the floor slabs, independent of the exterior walls, were cantilevered off two interior supports aligned with the central corridor and resting on thin concrete pins or piles. The principle, as Wright noted in his autobiography, is that of a waiter's tray supported by the fingers of the hand in the center.[44]

Another major achievement was his design for the Hollyhock House (1918–20) in the Olive Hill section of Hollywood.[45] Aline Barnsdall was a wealthy oil heiress who had met Wright in Chicago before 1914 but had since moved to Los Angeles, where the movie industry was just establishing itself. The project was intended to be a cultural center and to include theaters for drama and cinema, a restaurant, residences for artists, and shops. Only the central mansion and a few outbuildings were contructed, but the former represents a decisive step in Wright's development. Confronted for the first time with the sunny yet temperate climate of the Southwest and a city with a Spanish mission heritage, Wright turned to pre-Columbian America, principally the Mayan culture, for architectural inspiration. The result was a regional abstraction of partially battered, adobe-scale masses (actually tile and stucco) sculpted with nonrepresentational forms and fitted to the "tan-gold" foothills and radiant climate. It was also a highly metaphoric exercise in mythological thinking and naturally was greeted with incomprehension by contemporary critics. Hitchcock in 1929, with his European taste, lashed out at the "monstrous weight of the design" and the "ornament of unparalleled inappropriateness, suggesting whittling rather than moulding," and he found it less satisfactory than the "houses of the better Néo-Spanish architects."[46]

In 1923–5 Wright built four houses in Los Angeles, the city in which he relocated his office following his return from Japan. All were constructed with "textile block," a new system of construction that reflected "a distinctly genuine expression of California life in terms of modern industry and American opportunity."[47] The four-inch concrete blocks were cast on the site in a decorative mold sixteen inches square, and they were used for the interior and exterior walls, separated by an air cavity. Vertical dowels were set into the footing sixteen inches on center, and the blocks, which had a rounded notch on their edges, were slipped between them. The narrow cavities were filled with grout, and horizontal dowels were laid across the top of each row and between the wall membranes and were similarly grouted. Wright, alluding to this invention, referred to himself as a "weaver," and the poetic allusion to the Semperian "dressing" is unmistakable, if inexplicable.[48] The Pasadena house of Alice Millard, "La Miniatura," was the first of these highly tactile creations, intended to absorb and (with openings) diffuse the brilliant sunlight. Planned in early 1923, this small masterpiece is situated in a lush natural ravine aside the road and is entered at the second level. It even has a roof terrace and garden above – three years before Le Corbusier made it one of his "five points."

In 1923, however, Wright's fortunes dipped as a result of his involvement with a speculative and failed venture in Beverly Hills, the so-called Doheny Ranch Project. The project called for the construction of twenty-five textile-block houses carved into a steep canyon hillside and was to feature terraces, hanging gardens, and natural waterfalls. Once again pre-Columbian influences were central to Wright's conception, and here also he first experimented with diagonal (or diamond) floor plans.

Adding to his difficulties were two other notable but unrealized projects, a resort at Lake Tahoe and a ranch compound for the "Shylock" Albert Johnson in Death Valley. In 1924 Wright, without work, abandoned Los Angeles and went to live in the desert to ponder the most recent downturn of his personal, legal, and financial affairs. His situation, in fact, had become unbearable, and in an odd way it was related to his Florentine interlude with Mamah Bouton Borthwick years before. While in Florence, Borthwick, who was a disciple of the Swedish feminist and socialist Ellen Key, had started translations of several of her writings. It was a project on which Wright assisted, and he even helped to defray the cost of publication.[49] Key advocated a number of marital, child-rearing, and educational reforms, and her ideas have sometimes been distilled into a "free love" philosophy that denounces legal marriage and divorce laws. Wright was in sympathy with at least the tenor of these beliefs and thus chose to live with Borthwick in a state of criminal adultery after his first wife refused him a divorce. He remained true to these ideals after the murder of Borthwick in 1914, and a few months later he entered into an affair with Maud Miriam Noel. The relationship was a rocky one, with many ups and downs over the years. Nevertheless, after his wife finally agreed to a divorce in 1922, Wright married the unstable Noel in November of the next year. It proved to be a terrible decision, as Noel, with ever worsening mental problems, left him a few months later to live in Los Angeles and pursue a movie career. Wright, after meeting Olgivanna Lazovich Hinzenberg, sued Noel for divorce at the end of 1924. When Noel found out about Wright's new lover, she chose to be vindictive in the most extreme way. The matter became public in the summer of 1925, a few months after another fire (this time from faulty wiring) had again destroyed much of Taliesin. Wright went into great debt to rebuild it and then was confronted with a series of legal actions by Noel, which included a countersuit for $100,000, a demand for the possession of Taliesin, a legal warrant for Wright's arrest on the charge of adultery (for which Wright spent two nights in a Minneapolis jail), and various other assaults on his privacy and reputation. Wright and Olgivanna, a Montenegrin national educated in Russia, were forced into hiding, and things got worse when the bank soon thereafter foreclosed on Taliesin, though the estate was retrieved by a friendly legal corporation late in 1927. The bitter divorce was granted in the same year, but only after the bankrupt Wright, hounded by the yellow press, had witnessed the destruction of his public reputation once again. Noel soon thereafter collapsed into full insanity and death.

Wright was virtually a nonpracticing architect in the years 1924–7, and the remainder of the decade brought many projects but little relief. In 1928 he was living in a desert compound in Arizona, preparing the designs for a 110-room hotel to be built by Dr. Alexander John Chandler: St. Marcos-in-the-Desert.[50] Carved into the slope of a mountain, with the lone road on site running beneath it, it was another magisterial combination of textile-block construction, respect for nature, and desert symbolism worked out on a 30/60 planning diagonal. The Great Depression, however, ended Chandler's chance of financing the project, and its collapse left the architect (who had already spent $19,000 on its design development) without a fee and even greater in debt. Wright's other major unrealized project of this period – his skyscraper design for the apartment building S. Mark's-in-the-Bouwerie Tower (1928–30) – is a brilliant variation on some of the ideas for his earlier project in Chicago. He rotated the two-story units every other floor at a 30° angle to create a tall living space. Again the floors were cantilevered from central pier-walls, creating a distinctive look and feel in three-dimensional form that only Wright could muster. And he again proposed to employ his prefabricated copper-sheet system, only now with an expanded use of glass.

Wright's lack of work led him – between 1927 and 1932 – to write. In 1926 the architect was approached by M. A. Mikkelsen, the editor of *Architectural Record*, who was both sympathetic to his status and desirous of helping him financially. Wright was initially commissioned to write five articles for the magazine in 1927, and because of their success,

Wright wrote another nine articles the following year under the title "In the Cause of Architecture."[51] In the first group of essays, the themes tend to be more introductory – the machine, steel, fabrication and imagination, the new world – and Wright in a general way addresses his concerns as an architect. In the second series, he largely dwells on the poetic nature of stone, concrete, sheet metal, and terra-cotta.

In September 1928 Wright also published a review of Le Corbusier's *Towards a New Architecture*, and with it begins a polemic that he would develop in essays and lectures over the next several years. The starting point is an unpublished article he had probably penned shortly before, in which he takes dead aim at Henry-Russell Hitchcock's forthcoming book *Modern Architecture*. Wright was upset with Hitchcock's characterization of him as a "New Traditionalist," as opposed to one of the more enlightened "New Pioneers," and even more upset with Hitchcock's Europhilic affectations: "These continental discoveries affect our provincial 'historians' with all the charm of French novelty . . . 'Toujours L'etranger!' for them."[52] In his review of Le Corbusier's book – in which he describes the architect's style as being as "stark as one of the gas-pipe railings at the end of one of his 'new' cantilevered porches" – Wright attacks the notion that architecture is simply "surface and mass," and therefore neglecting the third dimension of depth.[53]

This became an important issue for Wright, and his assault broadens over the next few years, as the architect couples his earlier critique with his unease with the "International Style" exhibition being organized by Hitchcock and Philip Johnson at the Museum of Modern Art. In a spirited piece published in *Architectural Record* in 1929, Wright defends his "organic" conception – material weight, textural ornamentation, and depth – against the gas-pipe rails, thin slabs, and naked steel features of the European modernists: "These artificially thin walls like cardboard, bent, folded, and glued together, are frankly, likewise dedicated *not to the Machine but to machinery!* Therefore they do not live."[54] Moreover, Europeans lack sympathy with nature, and their "stark boxes blister the eyes by refusing the sun-acceptance trees, rocks, and flowers love."[55]

In an unpublished essay of 1930, Wright again returns to Hitchcock, who "occasionally comes over from Paris to teach young ladies at Vassar what they should think about Architecture." As another dig, he states that it is "useless to ask why men will strike attitudes and write about things they know only haphazard."[56] Against Hitchcock's remark that Wright's time has passed in relation to his younger European colleagues, the architect lashes out with understandable passion: "And I warn Henry right here and now that, having a good start, not only do I fully intend to be the greatest architect who has yet lived but fully intend to be the greatest architect who will ever live."[57] The expression of these feelings is only slightly moderated by Wright in his Kahn lectures, delivered at Princeton University in the spring of 1930 – collectively a superb summary of his architectural beliefs. In the lecture on "The Cardboard House," he reiterates his earlier critique of Le Corbusier and his followers:

The cardboard forms thus made are glued together in box-like forms – in a childish attempt to make buildings resemble steamships, flying machines, or locomotives. By way of a new sense of the character and power of this machine age, this house strips and stoops to conquer by emulating, if not imitating, machinery. But so far, I see in most of the cardboard houses of the "modernistic" movement small evidence that their designers have mastered either the machinery or the mechanical processes that build the house. I can find no evidence of integral method in their making. Of late, they are the superficial, badly built product of this superficial, new 'surface-and-mass' aesthetic falsely claiming French painting as a parent. And the houses themselves are not the new working of a fundamental architectural principle in any sense.[58]

Wright's other great literary endeavor during these difficult years was his *Autobiography*, a highly ornate confession of his personal and philosophical outlook.[59] He began the book in 1926 and wrote most of it over the next three years in the midst of trials and tribulations. Wright finished it in 1932, as he was turning sixty-five. Understandably, it seemed to most observers that the sun had indeed set on Wright's career. No one could have imagined, not even the architect himself, that almost three decades of architectural practice and some of his best work lay ahead.

3. Schindler and Neutra

Despite Wright's many problems in the 1920s, his studio at Taliesin and elsewhere still attracted a number of young European architects. Foremost among these were the Austrians Rudolph M. Schindler (1887–1953) and Richard Neutra (1892–1970), who, unlike other disciples from abroad, remained in the United States and built successful careers. And it is perhaps inaccurate to call them disciples at all, because both brought with them rather mature architectural conceptions. In their relationships with Wright,

the latter played more the role of a spiritual mentor than of an instructor of design.

Schindler, who was five years older than Neutra, is one of the least appreciated innovators of the 1920s.[60] After engineering studies, he enrolled in the Vienna Academy of Fine Arts in 1910 and was one of the last students of Wagner, who retired in 1912. At the same time, he attended Adolf Loos's "private school," a series of informal lectures in which Loos defied academic teachings. A short manifesto handwritten by Schindler in 1913 already displays his sense of independence. It is divided into the four themes of space, construction, monumentality, and the dwelling. Schindler first argues that for modern architecture "the only idea is space and its organization."[61] He takes on as well Wagner's insistence that art-forms must arise out of construction: "The residential artist's attempt to make a symbol of construction or to give construction an artistically expressive form is dead."[62] In its place is merely "the freedom of the cantilever, the openness of the span, the space-forming surfaces of the large partition walls."[63] Lastly, he responds to Loos's claim that a home should be "comfortable" and "homey." These terms, Schindler says, have changed their meaning: "The comfort of the dwelling no longer resides in its formal development, but in the possibility of controlling within its confines light, air, and temperature."[64] Around this time Schindler became aware of Wright's work through the Wasmuth publication of 1910, and this book fueled his interest in a professional stay in the United States.

Schindler graduated from the Vienna Academy of Fine Arts in 1913 and soon answered a newspaper advertisement for a draftsman in Chicago. One year prior, Schindler had befriended Neutra, and the latter planned to join him after his graduation. The war interrupted these plans, and it also led Schindler to decide to remain in the United States after his three-year work contract was finished. His situation became more complicated after the United States entered the war against the side of Austria, and in 1918 Schindler, fearing deportation, appealed to Wright for a job. The latter accepted him in his studio at Taliesin without pay, and the next three years Schindler gained Wright's trust and eventually a salary. Among other things, he operated the Los Angeles office and supervised the construction of the Barnsdall House while Wright was working in Japan.

In 1921, in a bold move, Schindler opened an office in Los Angeles. His first project was a duplex house/studio that he and Clyde Chase designed and built for their own families in suburban West Hollywood, very near Irving Gill's Dodge House (1916). Modeling it on a campsite he had just visited in

88. Rudolf M. Schindler, vacation house, Newport Beach, California, 1922–6. From *Architectural Record*, vol. 66 (September 1929).

Yosemite Park, Schindler devised an unusual plan of three L's rotating about the center, enclosing a series of private patios and gardens. This free pinwheel plan was completely original, but it was not the house's only unusual feature. The bearing walls along one side of each wing consisted of a meandering series of four-foot tapered concrete panels without a facing on either side, opposite which he inserted a light redwood framework with glass walls open to the private interior courts. This play of the contrasting Semperian themes of masonry and tectonics fascinated Schindler in several of his early houses, and it, together with the bare simplicity of structural elements, lends this particular house almost a Japanese character.

Schindler built two houses in the mid-1920s that are landmarks of the international modern movement, although they passed virtually unnoticed at the time. The Lovell vacation house in Newport Beach (1922–6) is a glass-and-concrete structure composed of a series of open, freestanding frames on which stairs and the diagonal spatial interpenetration of stepped levels and exterior balconies rest (Fig. 88). The first sketches were done in 1922, preceding by several years Le Corbusier's refinement of his villa concept, to which Schindler's design might be compared. Schindler, however, topped this effort with the Wolfe House on Catalina Island (1928–9). The narrow site was on a steep slope overlooking the harbor, and instead of carving out the hillside, Schindler anchored a number of pin supports into the ground and essentially floated the house's three stepped

terraces, with their cantilevered canopies, above the landscape. In its formal and technical sophistication, it reveals Schindler's enormous talent. His tragedy is that he – of bohemian inclination – was never able to bring the business side of his practice to a commensurate level.

His later writings are of some interest. Dr. Philip Lovell, for whom the Newport Beach house was built, was a physician known for his "natural" health treatments and for his advocacy of exercise, massages, hydrotherapy, nude sunbathing, sexual freedom, and vegetarianism. Schindler was sympathetic to some of these prescriptions, and at Lovell's urging he published a number of articles in the *Los Angeles Times* in 1926 on the architectural requirements of a healthy house – ventilation, plumbing, heating, lighting, furniture, exercise areas, and landscape.[65] In another essay, entitled "Space Architecture" (1934), Schindler takes aim at both Wright (their friendship now over) and Le Corbusier. The former carries the distinction of being the first architect to think in terms of spatial development, but in his more recent work he has lost the way by becoming too "sculptural," as when "he tries to weave his buildings in to the character of the locality through sculptural forms."[66] This is also a fault of some futurists and cubists, who play with "highly conventionalized contrasting sculptural forms."[67] On the other hand, there are the "functionalists" of the International Style who deny form by harping on the ideal of the machine, to which their creations are much inferior. Le Corbusier's houses, Schindler notes, are "crude 'contraptions' to serve a purpose. The man who brings such machines into his living room is on the same level of primitive development as the farmer who keeps cows and pigs in his house. Mere instruments of production can never serve as a frame for life."[68] Modern architecture instead should deal with "space forms" as the "new medium to serve as a vehicle for human expression."[69]

Schindler by the late 1920s had met his chief architectural rival in southern California in the person of his friend Richard Neutra, who after some delay had arrived in the United States.[70] The war intervened before Neutra's graduation from the Technische Hochschule in Vienna, and he was sent to the Balkan front, where he soon came down with malaria and tuberculosis. He completed his architectural degree in 1918 and, still suffering from the residual effects of these maladies, moved to Switzerland in 1919 to seek a cure. There he briefly studied with Karl Moser. His desired path to America was blocked by the fact that a peace treaty between the two countries had yet to be worked out, so instead Neutra moved to Berlin, where he eventually found a job with Erich Mendelsohn. Neutra quickly became a job captain and did much design work during the two years that he was with Mendelsohn. They parted amicably in the late summer of 1923 when the peace treaty between Austria and the United States was finalized, thus allowing the recently married Neutra to obtain a visa and sail for New York in October.

He landed in that city without a job. His two objectives, after gaining work experience, were to work for Wright and eventually to team up with Schindler in California. Neutra made his way to Chicago at the start of 1924, where he moved into Hull House and took a job with the firm of Holabird and Roche. Wright was still in the West, so Neutra sought out and befriended Sullivan, who would die within a few weeks of their first meeting. It was at his funeral that he met Wright for the first time and as a result received an invitation to visit Taliesin. Wright had little work on the boards, but he took on Neutra at a small salary, and the latter was able to contribute to the National Life Insurance Company project. Wright's personal life was at this time collapsing, and in January 1925 Neutra and his wife set out for Los Angeles. Here the couple moved into Schindler's house and eventually occupied the half formerly owned by the Chases.

Neutra had landed at his destination, but without money or professional standing. His reunion with Schindler was both friendly and cool. They respected one another but had very different temperaments. Schindler was outgoing, cynical, and content with smaller residential commissions.

Neutra was serious, more optimistic, and ambitious. They collaborated with each other in a fellowship known as the Architectural Group for Industry and Commerce (AGIC), but it achieved little success, and during Neutra's first few years in Los Angeles he took jobs in other offices to survive. Nevertheless, he worked on three projects that would ultimately change the course of his career. The first was a visionary urban planning scheme known as "Rush City Reformed," which was a futuristic design for a city of skyscrapers that incorporated the elements of speed, traffic, and mass transit. The second was a book that he had worked on for some years and completed in 1927. Titled *Wie baut Amerika?* (How America builds?),[71] it is both an analytical study of American urban problems and engineering accomplishments and a prescription for improvements and innovations. The third project was a bold cantilevered design for the League of Nations competition that Neutra teamed up with Schindler to prepare. Although it did not place in the final deliberations, many European architects saw it as one of the better schemes submitted to the competition, and it was widely exhibited across Europe. Thus by the end of 1927 Neutra had emerged as one of the best-known modernists practicing in the United States – almost before he had built a single building.

His lack of designs realized would end in short order, as the commission that would establish his professional reputation also came in this year – the Lovell health house (1927–9). Schindler had just completed the Lovell vacation house at Newport Beach, but the physician, still promoting a healthy living style, turned to Neutra for his large mansion in the Hollywood hills. The reason for his not using Schindler again may have been Schindler's organizational inexperience with larger projects, but it may also have been Schindler's dalliance with the doctor's wife.[72] In any case Neutra accepted the commission with trepidation (it would rupture his friendship with Schindler) but poured every ounce of his energy into the project over the next two years. Concrete foundations were carved into two sides of a canyon wall, and upon them Neutra constructed a large steel frame. Panels of concrete and steel, together with window systems, were affixed to the sides as walls; balconies were suspended from the roof; all the amenities of a spa were carefully built into the house and its lavish grounds. With its completion in 1929, it was undoubtedly the most technologically advanced residence in the world.

In 1930 Neutra embarked on a trip around the world, beginning with Japan and China. He arrived in Europe in the summer, where he lectured widely, attended the CIAM conference in Brussels, and reestablished his connections with European modernists. Mies invited him to teach a design studio at the Bauhaus for a month, and Neutra seriously contemplated remaining in Europe. His decision to return to the United States, however, would prove to be a judicious one, for the obvious reason of his Jewish heritage. In a prolonged stay in New York on his return home, Neutra promoted his work and sought out, among others, Lewis Mumford, Buckminster Fuller, Henry-Russell Hitchcock, and Philip Johnson. Many of these would assist him in building his career in the 1930s; a distinct coalition of American modernists was now forming.

4. Mumford and Fuller

Neutra's importance for modern theory would emerge only at a later date, but by 1930 Lewis Mumford (1895–1990) and Richard Buckminster Fuller (1895–1983) had already made important contributions to the development of American modernism. Their ideas, in fact, would continue to influence architectural thought for much of the twentieth century. The expansive range of their interests in itself testifies to the vibrant but little appreciated intellectual climate in the United States during the 1920s.

Mumford, the most important American critic of the twentieth century, came to his interest in architecture by a somewhat circuitous route.[73] Born in Flushing, he grew up on the Upper West Side of Manhattan and in 1912 began night studies at City College of New York. A tubercular spot kept him out of the military for most of the war (he was a Navy radio operator in 1918), and he used this time to gain a broad humanist and scientific education, largely on his own. He never took a degree, and in his early years he remained aloof from academe, and in fact such independence was a badge of honor for many intellectuals in the 1920s.[74] Their view was that universities were failing in their mission by stifling learning and inhibiting intellectual development – first through fostering the specialization of knowledge and a scholastic detachment from the problems of the real world, second by ever narrowing the range of acceptable ideologies and avoiding critical debate or serious discourse. This was a generation of cultural critics, feminists, and social activists at odds with the notions of progress and materialism of the 1920s – a generation including Kenneth Burke, Malcolm Cowley, Van Wyck Brooks, Margaret Naumberg, Waldo Frank, Edmund Wilson, Margaret Sanger, and Walter Lippmann.

Driving their criticism were related currents within American intellectual life, among them William James's pragmatism (the necessary reciprocity of theory and practice), John Dewey's instrumentalism (the integration of theory with action), the economic criticisms of Thorstein Veblen, the feminist movement (the nineteenth amendment, on women's suffrage, passed in 1920), and the community activism of Jane Addams. In 1918, for instance, Veblen expanded his earlier attack on the leisure class with *Higher Learning in America*, in which he took aim at the bureaucracy of the university system and its symbolic pretensions of faculty production and student learning. A few years earlier Dewey, in *Democracy and Education* (1916), had defended the traditional thesis that the study of history promotes understanding of the present, but his view of history was not the usual one:

The great heroes who have advanced human destiny are not its politicians, generals, and diplomatists, but the scientific discoverers and inventors who have put into man's hands the instrumentalities of an expanding and controlled experience, and the artists and poets who have celebrated his struggles, triumphs, and defeats in such language, pictorial, plastic, or written, that their meaning is rendered universally accessible to others.[75]

Even more influential in Mumford's early development were the Scottish biologist and sociologist Patrick Geddes (1854–1932) and the garden city theorist Ebenezer Howard. The latter, as we have seen, emphasized regional planning and the marrying of rural and urban life in his planned communities. Geddes, an avid follower of Auguste Comte and Herbert Spencer, viewed society as an ecological organism in progressive development or evolution along with its environment and therefore accessible to both research and human direction.

Mumford's first book, *The Story of Utopias* (1922), was written under the sway of Geddes. The first part of the study is an intellectual history of utopian thinking from Plato to William Morris and H. G. Wells. Against this backdrop Mumford develops the notion of "eutopia" or "good place," which implies a critique not only of past idealizations of utopia but also of the notions of a national state, megalopolis, and the "proletarian myth." Mumford envisions his eutopia as the result of a regionally conceived and implemented strategy that is in line with a pervasive reform of social values but also has "plans and layouts and detailed projections, such as a town planner might utilize."[76] In this regard, he refers us to the work of James Buckingham and Ebenezer Howard, and regional strategy of this type will become a cornerstone of his later urban theory.

Mumford followed with *Sticks and Stones: A Study of American Architecture and Civilization* (1924). He had been studying and occasionally writing about American architecture since the start of the decade, and although this book does not represent his mature thinking on the subject, it is nevertheless a milestone in American architectural thought. Not only is it the first history of American architecture but it discusses this architecture specifically within the context of American (rather than European) culture.

As Mumford notes, its genesis was impelled by two written works. One was a popular essay written in 1918 by Van Wyck Brooks entitled "On Creating an Usable Past."[77] Mumford had worked alongside Brooks as a freelance critic for the magazine *Freeman* in 1920, at which time the latter was critical of Mumford's sociological perspective. Brooks's essay proposes to rescue American history from its sterile use within the university system, effectively by resurrecting writers of critical integrity and using their example to build a new tradition of American thought. The essay was a virtual manifesto for many literary critics of the 1920s, as – one by one – Ralph Waldo Emerson, Henry David Thoreau, Walt Whitman, Herman Melville, and Mark Twain received new life through literary reevaluation.[78] The fact that the past, according to Brooks, was to be "created" rather than "found" underscores the artistic side of this intervention.

The second influential study behind Mumford's book is Claude Bragdon's *Architecture and Democracy* (1918), parts of which also appeared on the pages of *Architectural Record*. Bragdon (1866–1946) had started his career in architecture in the late 1880s and began writing on the subject around the turn of the century – ultimately becoming a spirited defender of Louis Sullivan, whom he called the "prophet of democracy." His interests included theosophy, and in 1923 he would retire from practice to become a set designer for the celebrated stage actor Walter Hampden. The central theme of *Architecture and Democracy* – a theme that derives from Sullivan – is that American architects have yet to create a uniquely American architecture in line with its democratic principles. Architectural production can be divided into two orders: *Arranged* and *Organic*. Arranged architecture – the legacy of the Beaux-Arts and other eclectic traditions – is bookish, composed, and self-conscious, "a product of a pride, a knowledge, a competence, a confidence staggering to behold. It seems to say of the works of Nature, 'I'll show you a trick worth two of that.'"[79] Organic architecture, by contrast, is private, inventive, "both creative

and imaginative. It is non-Euclidian, in the sense that it is higher-dimensional – that is, it suggests extension in directions and into regions where the spirit finds itself at home, but of which the senses gives no report to the brain."[80]

What Bragdon had underscored for Mumford was the need for an uniquely American architecture to be built on creativity and tradition – a "usable past." For Mumford, in *Sticks and Stones*, this tradition became translated into the Puritanical tradition of New England, the "worldly perfection" of its rural villages, where "the essential elements in a garden-city are the common holding of land by the community, and the cooperative ownership and direction of the community itself."[81] This "garden city in every sense of the word" becomes the touchstone for Mumford against which all other American architectural developments would later fail to measure up: the "Heritage of the Renaissance," the "Classical Myth" (Jefferson), the "Diaspora of the Pioneer," Romanticism (highlighted by Richardson), and finally the "Imperial Façade" of Beaux-Arts extraction. Mumford's aversion to the "paper symmetry of axial avenues" of the city beautiful movement, echoing Bragdon's contempt for "arranged" architecture, is now ingrained as a formal (even self-contradictory) predilection of his taste. It arises because the images of Haussmann's Paris neglect "the deeper and more genuine beauties of, let us say the High Street in Oxford or Chipping Camden, or of many another European town that had achieved completion in its essentials before the nineteenth century."[82] Essentially, then, Mumford's vision of the city and its architecture is medieval, or at least preindustrial, in its scale. What is also important is that at this date he was still unfamiliar with the work of Sullivan and Wright; thus his book remains wedded to the relatively small world of the Northeast.

This perspective leads him into ambivalence in his chapter on the "Age of the Machine," where he addresses the architecture of New York City in the early 1920s – with which he has a love-hate relationship mostly tending toward hate. If the "engineer has recovered his supremacy" (with the Brooklyn Bridge), it has been at the expense of the human condition, or rather of human control – leading to the machine's rapid production, the quick turnover of goods, laissez-faire building habits, tall buildings that can only be seen in photographs, and the preeminence of the automobile, with its tendency to induce urban sprawl.[83] Mumford rejects the present that he sees unfolding, yet he is also powerless to oppose it with anything other than vague generalities: "Until our communities are ready to undertake the sort of community planning that leads to garden-cities, it will be empty eloquence to talk about the future of American architecture. Sheltered as an enjoyment for the prosperous minority, or used as a skysign for the advertisement of business, architecture will still await its full opportunity for creative achievement."[84]

Planning now becomes a main focus of his efforts. In the spring of 1923 Mumford came together with a number of sympathetic architects, planners, and specialists at the Hudson Guild Farm in Mount Olive, New Jersey, to found the Regional Planning Association of America (RPAA). The architect Clarence S. Stein (1883–1975) was nominated president, while Mumford served as the association's secretary and chief publicist. Other members included Stein's partner Henry Wright (1878–1936), the conservationist Benton MacKaye (1879–1975), and the editor Charles Harris Whitaker (1872–1938). The goals of the association were twofold. It advocated not only regional planning but also the dispersion of the populations of large cities, such as New York, to regional garden cities, along the lines of Letchworth and Welwyn in Britain.

With this agenda the RPAA competed with the Regional Plan Association (RPA), an agency funded by the Russell Sage Foundation and officially charged with preparing a regional plan for New York City and its environs. There were strong ideological differences, to be sure, but the debate between the rival organizations was scarcely a conflict, as it is sometimes characterized, between the "regressive" RPA and the "progressive" efforts of Stein and Mumford.[85] The RPA architects and planners, prominent among them Thomas Adams and Hugh Ferriss, accepted the urban realities of centralization, private enterprise, and skyscraper zoning and sought to improve cities by encouraging urban neighborhoods, planned suburbs, and rational transportation lines. The RPAA, by contrast, went against the underlying economic and political realities and militantly called for a "fourth migration" out of the city and into the region, yet without a political or economic structure in place to accomplish this end. Thus, while the RPAA may have acted as a moral conscience in its opposition to untamed speculative development (the Great Depression would soon play its part), it turned its philosophical back to the commercial and urban culture that it was presumably trying to save.

Whereas RPAA can be faulted for its idealism, it did achieve practical successes. In 1924 the association founded the City Housing Corporation with the goal of funding planned developments. Its first venture was Sunnyside Gardens in Long Island, a housing estate designed by Stein and Wright in which terrace houses and apartments were grouped around common green areas. In 1927 the corporation purchased two square miles in New Jersey and began the construction of the garden suburb Radburn, following a plan in which housing backed up to common green areas and pedestrian paths were separated from vehicular traffic.[86] Again the project was successful, and this small community quickly became a model for suburban development over the next several decades. In contrast to European housing schemes, however, these were typical suburban houses without architectural distinction; their design nevertheless reflected the long-standing desire for suburban living within the American collective psyche.

Both Sunnyside Gardens and Radburn were built with little knowledge of contemporary European settlements. Mumford, however, would soon become aware of these parallel efforts. In 1924 he met Erich Mendelsohn, who was touring the United States, and in 1925 he met both Ernst May and Walter Curt Behrendt, who had come to New York to attend an international city-planning conference sponsored by RPAA. Mumford viewed May's schemes for Frankfurt as a manifestation of his garden city ideas, but his relationship with Behrendt was even more important.[87] The latter was assuming the editorship of the Werkbund's journal Die Form, and he found in Mumford both an ideological ally and someone who could help expand the influence of the Werkbund in the United States. Behrendt at this time was initiating a campaign within German circles against the American skyscraper. Mumford discovered in him the social commitment he thought was lacking in American architects. Mumford soon thereafter wrote two articles for Die Form highly critical of the skyscraper and of American trends in general.[88] Behrendt, for his part, saw to it that Mumford's Sticks and Stones was quickly translated into German.[89]

In early 1927 Mumford traveled to Chicago specifically to view the work of Sullivan and Wright. Their efforts were now important to him because of the esteem in which Europeans held these two individuals but also because he began to see modernism as an international movement with a somewhat common ideological footing. The fact that he also saw American practice at least in part through Behrendt's European perspective, however, created inconsistencies and confusion when he began to reflect on the differences between the two cultures.

In an important 1928 essay, "The Search for 'Something More,'" Mumford returned to the theme of the skyscraper in a somewhat less critical way. He now compares the "extreme position" of Gropius and the "inexorable logic" of Le Corbusier (allowing no decoration) somewhat unfavorably with the moderate approaches of two American buildings – Ralph Walker's design for the Barclay-Vesey Building and Ely Jacques Kahn's design for 120 Park Avenue.[90] Kahn's decorative feeling was indeed just that "something more" for which Mumford was searching: "With a warm buff brick as a foundation, the Park Avenue Building works up into bands of sunny terra-cotta, broken and accentuated with red, green, bright sky-blue. The pattern is abstract; and every part, down to the lighting fixtures, has the same finish, rigor, swiftness, perfection."[91] In finding this just synthesis between "structure" and "feeling," Mumford believed it offered an alternative to European rationalists:

This building seems to me an answer both to Europeans who, despairing of synthesis, have sought to enjoy the grimness and inflexibility of modern forms by sitting hard on their organic feelings, and to those who, equally despairing of synthesis, have permitted the human, sensuous note to break out irrelevantly – either in stale archaeology, in fussy handicraft, or in unrelated bursts of modern decoration.[92]

On the domestic front, the works of Wright – "deeply regional in feeling" – again provide the right synthesis for "they are 'home' and not merely an abstract expression of the machine age."[93]

In another important essay, "Mass-Production and the Modern House" (1930), Mumford voiced similar concerns – but this time about mass-produced housing being modeled on the productive techniques of the automobile industry.[94] While recognizing the benefits in hygiene, engineering, and living comfort of prefabricated light-shell construction, he is at the same time dubious of its viability. For one thing, the cost savings would be minimal, as so much of the cost of a house derives from the cost of the land and the supporting infrastructure of roads and utilities. For another thing, the planned obsolescence and increasing cheapness of the process would lead to rapid changeover in the production cycle. In essence, mass-produced housing would become, like the automobile, a slave to the imperatives of a free-market economy.

The Brown Decades (1931), published on the eve of his first European tour and his involvement with the International Style exhibition, fittingly concludes this phase of his architectural development. It is cultural study dealing with architecture as well as literature, painting, and engineering. The title is both literal (brownstones, for instance) and metaphorical: the other side of classical (white) American cultural development between 1865 and 1895. The longest chapter, "Towards Modern Architecture," discusses the architecture of H. H. Richardson, John Root, Sullivan, and Wright. It can be seen as a further attempt to codify a "usable past."

In effect, Mumford arrives at what will become his standard interpretation of the near American past and revises many of his earlier views in light of his better knowledge. Richardson, who almost single-handedly created "the beginnings of a new architecture," achieved "the standards of a functionalist architecture" with his windows at Austin Hall at Harvard.[95] John Root, in his design for the Monadnock Building in Chicago, "finally stripped the face of the office-building, making it as austere as a steamship."[96] Sullivan solved the problem of the tall building, although Mumford has a problem with his ornamental exuberance. His was an architecture of "individuality" and "personality," while architecture as "a social art . . . must stand and fall by its collective achievement."[97] Wright's works are now given due appreciation, but interestingly only his earlier houses. Mumford is aware of his design for St. Mark's-in-the-Bouwerie, but he lacks a sense of the technical and conceptual evolution of Wright's ideas.[98] The chapter concludes with a few comments on Irving Gill and Bernhard Maybeck, but these are also architects known to Mumford only through photographs. Mumford thus seems to concede to Europeans the advantage in the 1920s. The connection between the early work of Wright and American architecture of the late 1920s is never made or even suggested.

This failure must be partly attributed to Mumford's uncertainty at this juncture in time. The doubts that he expressed in 1930 about the feasibility of mass-produced housing, for instance, were in part a response to the Dymaxion house of Buckminster Fuller, another American factor complicating Mumford's earlier European model. Fuller at this time was certainly the most advanced thinker in the world in his "structuralist" reflections about the future of architecture, and in the late 1920s and early 1930s he was also very much a part of the Greenwich Village bohemian life that had once appealed to Mumford. But the personalities of the two men were worlds apart. Fuller was born in Massachusetts, the descendent of a colonial family that included Margaret Fuller, the Transcendentalist friend of Emerson and founder of the journal *The Dial.* After twice being expelled from Harvard, he matured as an engineer in the navy during the war, before settling on Long Island in the 1920s. In the mid-1920s he helped devise a lightweight synthetic brick constructional system that was to be applied to housing, but the business venture that grew out of this, along with several other of his business ventures, failed during this

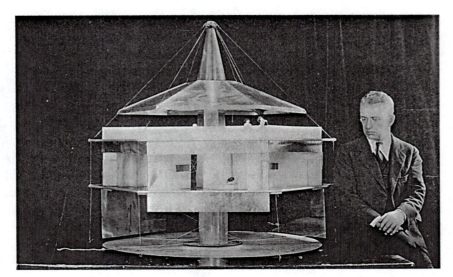

89. Buckminster Fuller, Dymaxion house, 1928. From *Shelter* (January 1932).

period. In 1927, after another business setback in Chicago, Fuller decided to remove himself from the business world and give his time entirely to his inventions – a bold and decisive step.[99]

It was at this point that he began to develop his Dymaxion house. The starting point was his effort in February 1928 to create "Lightful Houses" assembled from prefabricated parts. These structures were conceived as supported on a central mast from which rings (circular or square) were suspended for each floor. Pointing out that the cost of a cubic foot of residential architecture was three times the cost of a cubic foot of a skyscraper, Fuller argued in favor of an engineer's sense of efficiency:

We have arrived at our new artistic era of architectural expression, when our buildings will have lost their last trace of feudalistic depression; when we arise in our buildings in concentrated area of compression in opposition to gravity by means of mast or caisson reach out in space from the vertical by tension and compression, compression diminishing as we fall off from the vertical, until we finally flow downward in direct tension. Then will our exteriors, hanging from the outward flow of the top like a great fountain be full of lithsomness, light and color.[100]

In April or May of 1928, while he was still living in Chicago, his sketches for houses evolved into designs for his 4D (four-dimensional) house, the first drawings for which were actually based on a rectangular plan and a cubic house. Already he was thinking in terms of a central structural core with multiple cantilevered stories, not too dissimilar from

Wright's skyscraper designs, except that the walls and floors were now suspended from trusses above. Fuller at this time was working with the French architect Paul Nelson, a student of Le Corbusier, who left for France in the spring of 1928 to promote the 4D design in a housing competition in France. Fuller offered the patent for the 4D house to the American Institute of Architects, whose members were meeting in Saint Louis in May, but they rejected it on the grounds that the "American Institute of Architects is opposed to any kind of house designs that are manufactured like-as-peas-in-a-pod."[101]

By the end of 1928 Fuller had advanced to his Dymaxion house, which took full advantage of his background in mechanical, chemical, and structural engineering (Fig. 89). His planning module, as he explained it in 1929, was now hexagonal. The central structural spine, which contains all the electrical and air supply and waste systems, "is made of duralumin tubes, inflated to high pressure, in triangulation with piano-wire steel – similar to the battleship mast or dirigible mooring," allowing the weight of all floors to be suspended in a triangulation of cables.[102] The exterior walls consist only of "two thicknesses of translucent, transparent or opaque material such as we make from casein, with a vacuum between, providing ideal insulation against both sound and heat."[103] Casein is a phosphoprotein or natural solid derived from milk. All living or functional modules, such as for cooking, sanitation, and storage, are to be prefabricated plug-in units. Water is to be captured from rain or drawn from wells and recycled. Forced air is similarly to be recycled. The lighting sources are diffused within a ceiling grid. Fuller was even then thinking in terms of generating electricity from wind and solar panels. Although the models for this house display but a single unit, the concept is perfectly adaptable to high-rise structures. The projected price was $3,000–$5,000 less than the average cost of a house in 1929. He had taken Le Corbusier's analogy of a "machine for living" to heart, producing a prototype without parallel in either Europe or America.[104]

Fuller spent much of 1929 promoting his invention. He first exhibited the Dymaxion house at the Marshall Field Department Store in Chicago. He published his ideas in the journal *Architecture* in June and presented a lecture at the annual meeting of the Architectural League of New York in July, where he was introduced by Harvey W. Corbett and questioned afterwards by Raymond Hood and Ralph Walker, among others.[105] The Chicago publisher Charles Scribner proposed publishing a book based on his New York lecture, but the crash of the stock market squashed these plans. By the fall of 1929 Fuller had moved back to New York and was living in Greenwich Village, where he formed part of an artistic circle that included the architect and theater designer Frederick Kiesler (who had emigrated from Vienna in 1926), the Danish émigré architect Knud Lönberg-Holm, the sculptor Isamu Noguchi, and the dancer Martha Graham.

In 1932 Fuller sold his last remaining assets and purchased the magazine *T-Square*, which had formerly been funded in part by the Philadelphia architect George Howe. Fuller changed its name to *Shelter*, and over its brief run of five issues it became one of the more interesting intellectual journals ever produced in the United States. Fuller contributed a regular column on "Universal Architecture," and other contributors included Kiesler, Neutra, Lönberg-Holm, and Frank Lloyd Wright. The first issue – arranged by the guest editors George Howe, Henry-Russell Hitchcock, Alfred Barr, and Philip Johnson – was largely given over to the International Style exhibition that had just taken place. These articles, in turn, sparked a debate between the "stylists" of this camp and the "structuralists," led by Fuller, who was representing a group known as the Structural Study Association (SSA). The structuralists unequivocally rejected all stylistic or aesthetic summations of modernism. For Fuller in particular, architecture was only a part of a much broader ecological vision.[106]

The Great Depression again foreclosed any possibility of the Dymaxion house finding an industrial application. Fuller, however, was not deflated. By the start of 1933 he was already producing the prototype for the Dymaxion au-tomobile, and once more he would achieve an extraordinary breakthrough in advanced engineering.

5. The International Style Exhibition

Certainly one of the more dramatic events in American architecture was the exhibition held at the newly founded Museum of Modern Art in 1932, "Modern Architecture: International Exhibition." It produced both an exhibition catalogue and an accompanying book – *The International Style: Architecture since 1922* – both of which deeply affected the course of American architectural practice.[107] Whatever one's position on the reception of the event, it must be conceded that it ushered in several new personalities who would leave a deep imprint on twentieth-century American practice. The exhibition was the brainchild of Alfred H. Barr Jr., the first director of the new museum.[108] The event was curated by two young historians still in their twenties – Henry-Russell Hitchcock (b. 1903) and Philip Johnson (b. 1906) – who also coauthored the catalogue and book.[109]

The three men brought to the exhibition different skills and strengths. Johnson was born into a family of wealth and had been educated at Harvard University, but he had struggled in his early years for reasons of health and immaturity. In the 1920s he was a regular traveler to Europe, and in the spring of 1929 he met Barr, a young professor at Wellesley College. Barr was an enthusiast of modern European art, while Johnson, who had still not graduated from Harvard, knew next to nothing about modern art or architecture. A friendship formed, and one month later Barr was appointed director of the newly created Museum of Modern Art. Johnson, who was desperately searching for a mission in life, decided he would like to be a part of the new institution. Therefore, in the summer of 1929 he set out on another extended tour of Europe to educate himself about the nuances of the new architecture and thus he came to examine the work of Oud in Holland, the exhibition buildings in Stuttgart, and the Bauhaus at Dessau. Sometime in the winter of 1929–30, while finishing up his work at Harvard, he met Hitchcock on a trip to New York. Barr and Hitchcock had already been friends for some years from their Harvard days, and the Barr-Johnson-Hitchcock alliance was now formed.

Although Barr had very specific views on modern architecture (he had visited both the Bauhaus and VKhUTEMAS in 1927), it was Hitchcock who was the guiding intellectual force of this trio. He had graduated from Harvard in 1924 with the intention of attending the Ecole des Beaux-Arts and becoming an architect, yet he decided to return to Harvard in 1925 to take a master's degree in fine arts. He graduated in 1927 and promptly visited the Stuttgart exhibition, where his fascination with Le Corbusier had its start. After teaching at Vassar College, he moved in 1929 to Wesleyan College. Before writing *Modern Architecture*, Hitchcock wrote several essays on the subject for the Harvard journal *The Hound & Horn*, which in the years 1927–9 was edited by Lincoln Kirstein. Hitchcock's first published work, "The Decline of Architecture," is stilted and pretentious in style, juvenile in tone, and somewhat short on content. If the patient reader survives the dash of French epithets and the affected references to Spengler and Henry Adams, he will eventually come to the main point: what Hitchcock calls "the surrealist theory of contemporary architecture." This is the thesis "that all conscious aesthetic additions to technical perfection are 'embellishment' in as evil a sense as the scagliola of Mr. Loew's palaces or the American Beauty capitals of Dr. Mannings's Metropolitan."[110] In other words, present-day architecture is in decline and there is no field for its development beyond its technical dimension.

The proud student sent the issue containing his article to Mumford in New York and received polite approval from the critic, and this courtesy initiated a relationship between the two writers. In their exchanges, Mumford encouraged Hitchcock in his researches on contemporary European architecture, and the latter pleaded with Mumford, who was then writing on literary themes, to return to architectural ones.[111] Hitchcock did advance his interest in European architecture. In 1928, in another essay for *The Hound & Horn*, he refers to the work of Neutra and William Lescaze, to Le Corbusier's book of 1923, and to the appearance of "an international style."[112] Hitchcock supplied this term with the definite article "the" at the end of the following year, but Barr was the first to capitalize the term, in Hitchcock and Johnson's book of 1932.[113]

Hitchcock's book of 1929, *Modern Architecture: Romanticism and Reintegration*, was a much more sophisticated and ambitious endeavor than this earlier essays; it was brilliant in parts but also deeply flawed as a historical study. Through his own extensive travels, the author had become thoroughly familiar with recent European architectural developments, especially the work of Oud, Gropius, and Le Corbusier. His knowledge of contemporary American practice was slim at best and restricted to the Northeast. His thesis, however, is very clear: Contemporary architecture in France, Holland,

and Germany is synonymous with the creation of a new style; architecture in every other country, in particular the United States, has fallen seriously behind the times.

The historiography of the book is what is particularly interesting.[114] Hitchcock first of all defines modern architecture, in keeping with nineteenth-century histories, in a broad sense, as comprising all post-Gothic architecture (from the early Renaissance on), although his historical focus spans from 1750 to the late 1920s. All nuances within this modern period (such as the baroque, the neo-Gothic, or neoclassicism) are "phases" rather than "styles." Within the restricted time frame of 1750–1929, two notable phases are discernible: romanticism and the New Tradition. The first begins in 1750 and concludes sometime around 1875. Its highpoint is found in the work of Soufflot, Latrobe, Percier & Fontaine, Hittorff, Labrouste, Soane (Hitchcock's favorite historical architect), Pugin, Schinkel, and Charles Garnier. Whereas romanticism had some notable successes, it is (particularly after 1850) a period to be regarded "with little pleasure."[115] The same is generally true of the New Tradition, whose transitional point is best located in the work of Henry Hobson Richardson. The crucial changes, which Richardson draws from G. G. Scott, is the replacement of an "eclecticism of taste" by an "eclecticism of style."[116] In general the architects of the New Tradition are identified by their adherence to good craftsmanship and engineering, to which they generally applied increasingly abstract ornamental motifs. In Europe, Berlage, Wagner, Behrens, and Perret all fall into this group, and in the United States so do Richardson, Root, Sullivan, and Wright. The last architect, as we have seen, was infuriated by this placement in this category and by Hitchcock's dismissal of almost everything done after his Chicago period. Hitchcock at this time clearly had little regard for Wright's work, even though he had written a small monograph on Wright's career.[117] He describes the Midway Gardens, for instance, as "fantastic and decorative," while the Imperial Hotel, with its "unskillfully exotic ornament," is "vastly ineffective."[118] The Barnsdall House is "one of his least successful buildings"; only in Millard House does he succeed "in bringing into harmony his various discordant tendencies."[119]

The final section of Hitchcock's book is given over to the "New Pioneers," who collectively define a "new style" or new stylistic period succeeding the entire modern period. It is a new day, so new that this style, with its posteclectic premises, has as yet appeared only in France, Holland, and Germany. The style was presaged by three buildings at the 1914 Werkbund exhibition – van de Velde's theater, Taut's glass pavilion, and Gropius's model factory – but its true appearance begins with Le Corbusier's pavilion for the 1925 exposition. The efforts of this architect are now joined by those of Lurçat, Oud, Rietveld, Bijvoet & Duiker, Brinkman & Van der Flugt, Gropius, May, and Mies – with secondary reverberations elsewhere. For America this style still belongs "only to the future," because "its full meaning has been little understood either at home or abroad."[120] This cultural backwardness, Hitchcock interjects with quintessential academic sarcasm and disdain for his own country, "is hardly surprising, considering how slowly America is coming generally to accept even the New Tradition."[121]

The edification of American architects was, of course, the chief aim of Hitchcock's book, and in a rather didactic way he set out to inform them of the principles of the new style. Still, there is a certain ambiguity in this aspect of his presentation. Although the principles of the new style derive from the new methods of construction, the new materials, the new treatment of interior spaces, and the absence of ornament (now replaced by detailing), its essence for Hitchcock seems grounded simply in a few design clichés – roof terraces, cantilevers, asymmetries, screen walls, and corner and horizontal windows. Perhaps it would be accurate to say that Hitchcock envisions the new style entirely in terms of its visual features, and his focus on corresponding rules is even more striking in his published writings surrounding the exhibition. *Modern Architecture* is nevertheless expansive in its research and authoritative in its style. If weak in its limited formalist reasoning, it is still an invaluable document of this period.

Prior to publication, Hitchcock asked Mumford to read the manuscript, and the latter objected specifically to the division between the New Tradition and the New Pioneers as well as to Wright's low standing.[122] But there were several other aspects of Hitchcock's study to which he could have objected. Mumford was first of all a regionalist and certainly did not accept the design implications of the new international style Hitchcock was promoting. Mumford was also less attracted to the work of Le Corbusier and to his mechanical analogies.[123] And as we have seen, in his 1928 essay "The Search for 'Something More,'" he was still open to the possibility of ornament, providing it was "organic" to the design. Finally, there was Mumford's emphasis on the social purpose of architecture, which is altogether absent from Hitchcock's study. Thus he must have felt a sense of dismay at the historical course Hitchcock was tracking.

Barr in his review of Hitchcock's book was very positive, as we might expect. He opens by claiming that Hitchcock

has established himself "as very possibly the foremost living historian of his subject" and that the work itself stands in vivid contrast to other American books on modern architecture, which "have been as provincial, as ill-informed, as complacent and as reactionary as are most American architects and American schools of architecture."[124] Barr, however, does criticize Hitchcock for the timidity of his concluding chapter, his "parsimonious" use of illustrations, and for his pretentious literary style – "a little too much influenced by the German, and his spelling by the French: '-ism' is, after all, preferable in English to '-isme' and 'neo' to 'néo.'"[125]

Johnson, who met Hitchcock around the time the book appeared, was equally impressed by its content, and shortly thereafter the two men planned a joint summer tour of Europe. It was on this trip – in June 1930 – that Johnson, who had been considering writing a book on architecture himself, convinced Hitchcock that they should collaborate on a popular version of *Modern Architecture*.[126] On this trip Johnson also met Le Corbusier and Oud (whom he asked to design a house for his mother in Pinehurst, North Carolina) for the first time, but the highpoint was the time he spent in Berlin, where he met Mies van der Rohe. Johnson made two trips to Brno (one with Mies) to view the Turgendhat House, and later he would commission Mies to redo his New York apartment. By late summer or early fall, the decision was made by Barr, Hitchcock, and Johnson to combine the projected book with an exhibition. The initial proposal for the exhibition that Johnson submitted to the board of directors divided the event into three sections.[127] The first and most important would feature the work of "nine of the most prominent architects in the world," whom he listed as Hood, Wright, Norman Bel Geddes, Howe & Lescaze, the Bowman Brothers, Mies, Gropius, Le Corbusier, and Oud. The second section would focus on tall-building technology, industry, and housing. The third section would consist of an international student competition. As a didactic rationale for the event, Johnson, whose knowledge of American architecture was scant at best, claimed that "American architecture finds itself in a chaos of conflicting and very often unintelligent building. An introduction to an integrated and decidedly rational mode of building is sorely needed. The situation and direction which an exhibition of this type can give to contemporary architectural thought is incalculable."[128]

The next year was given over to preparations, which for Hitchcock and Johnson entailed another trip to Europe. Changes were also made to the organization of the exhibition. Neutra replaced Bel Geddes, who in fact was devoting the bulk of his considerable energy to stage productions and industrial design. The second section was now to focus entirely on housing, and rather than a student competition, the third section was to be a general survey of the lesser luminaries of the new style. The biggest obstacle to the main section of the event turned out to be Wright, who on several occasions threatened to pull his work out. He had been infuriated by Hitchcock's book, and he had even less respect for Johnson, whom he regarded – quite rightly – as an architectural dilettante. Johnson indeed still had much to learn. One story often told is that when preliminary discussions were held in New York on who was to be included in the show, Johnson had summarily dismissed the work of Wright on the grounds that he was dead.[129] Wright, too, had little desire to be exhibited alongside Le Corbusier and Gropius, whose work he disdained, and he certainly did not want his own vision of modernism to be superceded by an architectural style that looks "as though cut from cardboard with scissors."[130] In addition, Wright objected to the American section being represented by two European-born architects – Lescaze and Neutra – and in fact he sarcastically referred to the latter as "the eclectic 'up to date,' copying the living."[131] On one occasion his withdrawal was prevented only by Johnson's agreement to publish "Of Thee I Sing" in the issue of *Shelter* that he was guest editing. This essay was a scathing denouncement of the anti-individualist, communistic, and Spenglerian *"Geist der Kleinlichkeit"* (spirit of paltriness) emanating from Europe and threatening "to strip hide and horns from the living breathing organism that is modern architecture." Conversely, Wright concludes, "Our pioneer days are not over."[132]

On another occasion, on the eve of the opening, it was Mumford who saved the day. After Wright again announced his withdrawal, the latter telegraphed him, stating it would be a "CALAMITY PLEASE RECONSIDER YOUR REFUSAL I HAVE NO CONCERN WHATEVER ON BEHALF OF MUSEUM BUT AM INTERESTED IN YOUR OWN PLACE AND INFLUENCE STOP WE NEED YOU AND CANNOT DO WITHOUT YOU."[133] Mumford, interestingly, shared Wright's disdain for the coming event and had only reluctantly agreed to participate. In a letter to Catherine Bauer written early in 1931, in which he also alluded to Johnson's architectural shortcomings, he noted, "I am afraid it will be a typical Museum of Modern Art modern exhibition – and that's pretty, pretty bad – Barbarous in fact."[134]

Modern Architecture: International Exhibition opened on 10 February 1932 and ran until 23 March. The catalogue of the same title appeared alongside Hitchcock and

Johnson's now famous book. The exhibition concluded with the work of four individuals: Le Corbusier, Mies van der Rohe, Oud, and Wright. Models played a prominent role. Wright provided a model of his project for a house on the mesa, Denver (1932), while Le Corbusier was represented by his Savoye House (1929–30), Oud by his house in Pinehurst, and Mies by the Turgendhat House, Brno (1930). Gropius, who was relegated to the preceding room, showed a model of his Bauhaus Building, Dessau (1925–26); it appeared next to a model of the Lux Apartments, Evanston (1931), designed by the Bowman Brothers of Chicago. Other models shown were of a country tower (1932) by Raymond Hood, two projects for the Chrystie-Forsyth Housing Development by Howe & Lescaze, the project for Ring Plan School by Richard Neutra, and the Rothenberg Housing Development in Kassel by Otto Haesler. Photographs of works by architects in Belgium, Austria, Switzerland, Spain, Sweden, Finland, England, Italy, Japan, Czechoslovakia, and the USSR were also displayed.

The exhibition catalogue and Hitchcock and Johnson's book were similar, although with some differences. The catalogue, which on its cover features an image of Mies van der Rohe's Turgendhat House, Brno, Czechoslovakia (Fig. 90), is actually more impressive, as it contains a foreword by Barr, a "Historical Note" by Johnson, an essay on "The Extent of Modern Architecture" by Johnson and Hitchcock, and another on "Housing" by Mumford. Barr's foreword was a sharply worded polemic condemning the work of American architects in general. In it, he states that he regards the exhibition as an "assertion that the confusion of the past forty years, or rather of the past century, may shortly come to an end."[135] He viewed the new "International Style" (his capitals) as a product of principles emanating from the nature of modern materials, modern structure, and modern requirements in planning. He was also apologetic about including the work of Wright (who was a "source" but not a practitioner of the International Style) and Hood. The new movement for Barr was defined by Gropius, Le Corbusier, Oud, and Mies van der Rohe. Americans had no standing.

In his "Historical Note," Johnson was even more selective, restricting the "international style" (his lowercasing) to work after 1922, although rooted in neoplasticism in Holland and expressionism in Germany. For Johnson, Le Corbusier's *Vers une architecture* signaled the beginning of the new style. "The Extent of Modern Architecture" by Hitchcock and Johnson took a similar track in anointing German architects and Le Corbusier as the leaders of the new style and harshly condemning the work of American designers for their art deco affectations, "without any real understanding of what modern architecture may be."[136]

"Housing," Mumford's essay, was a substantial effort to define the new house as a "biological institution" in terms of hygiene, health, and physical fitness as well as educational and leisure-time activities (for example, listening to the phonograph or radio, watching television, or working in the garden). Mumford insisted on abundant sunlight and air, private kitchens and baths, and streets screening all through-traffic. He also demanded comprehensive planning, large-scale operations, mass production, efficient design, limited profits, low mortgages, and state subvention or public housing subsidies. The model of Otto Haesler's Rothenberg Housing Complex outside of Kassel (1930), with its repetition of barracklike row houses, must have seemed incomprehensible to many American visitors, but for Mumford this European offering – like the displayed projects of Stein and Wright, Oud, and Ernst May – represented the ideal type of housing.

Much more important than the catalogue in historical impact, however, was the book *The International Style*, which in fact was written first. It is composed of ten short chapters, the first seven of which build upon one other. For instance, the introductory chapter, entitled "The Idea of Style," touches on the failed efforts of architects in the nineteenth century to create a new style but triumphantly announces that finally a "single new style has come into existence."[137] The new style is modern and international and was created by a few pioneers. Described as "architecture as volume rather than as mass," it is characterized by regularity rather than axial symmetry and by the absence of decoration.[138]

In the second chapter, entitled "History," the authors confront the problem of Wright and his glaring omission from their book. They claim, "In his refusal of the shackles of a fixed style he has created the illusion of infinite possible styles, like the mathematicians who have invented non-Euclidean geometries. His eternally young spirit rebels against the new style as vigorously as he rebelled against the 'styles' of the nineteenth century."[139] In thus refusing to walk lockstep with his European colleagues, the individualist Wright must be relegated to the status of a pioneer of the new style. Instead, the three great leaders of the new movement are Gropius, Oud, and Le Corbusier, with Mies quickly gaining ground. Gropius, whose work was just as quickly falling out of favor with the authors, still employs some "conceptions of traditional architecture," and thus his

work is not pure as a model to be followed.[140] Oud made his mark as a designer and is still held in high favor, although his star too would soon decline. Le Corbusier (Hitchcock's preferred architect) in his design for the Ozenfant studio "crystallized" and "dramatized" the new style, while Mies (Johnson's favorite architect) in his skyscraper sketches of the early 1920s "carried technical innovation even further than Gropius, further indeed than anyone has yet gone in practice."[141] This last assertion borders on the preposterous and again underscores Hitchcock and Johnson's lack of technical training.

One other preliminary chapter, entitled "Functionalism," is of great importance because it forcefully articulates Hitchcock and Johnson's belief that the "aesthetic element" rather than architecture's functional or social (political) relevance is of primary importance for the new style. Here the authors go after the presumed functionalism of Sigfried Giedion and Hannes Meyer, who hold that design choices should be "wholly determined by technics and economics."[142] Although the authors insist that their own position is more a matter of wording than a deeply felt tenet, it is based on two factors. First is their effort to depoliticize European modernism and strip it of its socialist premises – whether they do so consciously or unconsciously is another question. But this elision of politics for the authors also carries with it a further delimiting of architecture's technical, social, and programmatic aspects. Both authors, like Barr, in fact looked at architecture from the perspective of art, or rather painting. From such a perspective, a building is primarily a two-dimensional image to be captured and analyzed in a photograph.[143]

Thus the next chapter, on "Volume," the "First Principle" of the new style, focuses not on space but on the "plane surfaces" bounding a volume.[144] The first axiom here is to keep surfaces simple, which entails such features as uncomplicated forms, flat roofs, continuous surfaces, and the movement of the window planes to the outer edge of the screening walls (eliminating shadows). The fifth chapter, on "Surfacing Material," extends these rules by mandating the use of nontextural materials such as glass, plate sheathing, and glazed tiles in lieu of the natural materials of wood, brick, and stone. The second principle, "Regularity," also reinforces this point, while the third principle, "The Avoidance of Applied Decoration," lays out another set of aesthetic parameters and requires architects to forgo decoration in favor of detailing. Independent sculpture, lettering, and color are permitted, but the rule is always restraint. Dozens of other design rules are proffered, obviously drawn from

90. Cover photograph of the exhibition catalogue *Modern Architecture: International Exhibition*, Museum of Modern Art (1932). © 1932 The Museum of Modern Art, New York. Reproduced by permission.

the authors' study of European buildings. The end result is an extraordinary intrusion by a critic and a historian into the architect's domain.

The final three chapters revert to general issues and again are strongly anti-American in their tone. The chapter "Architecture and Building" returns to the problem of functionalism, or rather to the ability of the leading European architects to combine technical and aesthetic innovations. American architects simply do not measure up to their European counterparts, and thus they "have much to learn from the leaders of the international style, even if they cannot accept sincerely the aesthetic discipline those leaders have brought into being."[145] These artistic shortcomings are made especially apparent in the final chapter, on the "Siedlung," where the Europeans are claimed to generally achieve a "neutral aesthetic level of good building."[146] At the two ends of the architectural continuum are the functionalists, who "build for some proletarian superman of the future," and the sentimental Americans, who nostalgically adhere to the "notion" of the home.[147] This notion, Hitchcock and Johnson believe, implies such features as windows "arranged for strange forms of ventilation," flower pots, "rooms catering to special methods of drying clothes indoors," and solid shutters on the second floor, "to which no burglar could climb."[148] In insisting on the superiority of the European Siedlung as the model for American housing, Hitchcock and Johnson push the architect as social engineer to a new extreme in their condescension toward the unfortunate values of the American client:

The Architect has a right to distinguish functions which are major and general from those which are minor or local. In sociological building he ought certainly to stress the universal at the expense of the particular. He may even, for economic reasons and for the sake of general architectural style, disregard entirely the peculiarities of local tradition unless these are soundly based on weather conditions. His aim is to approach an ideal standard. But houses should not be functionally so advanced that they are lived in under protest.[149]

Such a patronizing attitude, of course, can be excused for reasons of youth, but the overall tone of this particular invective in an odd way recalls that sense of American cultural inferiority that was so evident in the first half of the nineteenth century, that is, before the tradition of Richardson, Sullivan, and Wright asserted itself.[150] That this same sense of cultural inferiority could also be found within the ivory towers of most American universities of the early 1930s, where architectural training was still largely Beaux-Arts in character, is a moot point. What is interesting here is how the new Museum of Modern Art not only came to embrace a didactic mission to initiate the artistically unsophisticated into the higher reaches of art but also came to demand from them radical social change – a fundamental revolution in their living habits. In Europe similar institutional aspirations had always been centrally coordinated and aligned with more modest goals. In New York, however, the institutional mission was aesthetic but only partially so. The "art" of architecture had now become a smart commodity (style) to be imported from abroad and sold in the museum bookshop with the opening of each year's exhibition. This is not to deny the positive educational value of the exhibition of 1932 and the enrichment it brought to the American architectural debate. It came, however, at a certain price – not just for American practice but for international practice as well. It inserted the influence of a cultural institution in what before had been a professional matter – an insinuation that will be repeated in the second half of the century by institutions possessing ever larger endowments and an ever growing command of the media. The global shutdown in building activities caused by the Great Depression and World War II, however, would delay this inevitability for a few decades.

13

DEPRESSION, WAR, AND AFTERMATH
1934–1958

> I really cannot believe that you did not realize that the whole book circles around
> a single idea: to show the tragic consequences of a split personality, of a split
> culture...
>
> Sigfried Giedion, Letter to an Editor (1941)

1. Totalitarianism in Germany and Italy

The global Great Depression of 1929–33 did not in itself cause the unraveling of Europe's fragile political stability of the 1920s, but it certainly accelerated its demise. The reasons for the vast economic downturn were myriad and complex. Economic expansion in both the United States and Europe had been strong between 1924 and 1929, and financial speculation abounded. The injection of American money into Germany through the Dawes Plan, beginning in 1924, created not only an artificial economic boom (by 1926 Germany would again push past Great Britain in industrial production) but also a situation of fiscal dependency. In addition, there was the problem of war reparations, which Germany could not and, later, would not repay. The crash of the American stock market in October 1929 in itself simply signaled a period of deflation. A dramatic fall in industrial production led to a fall in the price of consumer goods, a fall in wages, and a sharp rise in unemployment. With the collapse of two German banks in 1931, the world's system of credits and currencies was thrown into disarray. Communists and socialists blamed the deteriorating situation on laissez-faire capitalism. Capitalists and financiers blamed the problem on the conservative monetary and fiscal policies endorsed by politicians. The latter, in turn, pointed to artificial trade barriers and imbalances, the antiquated gold standard, and the lack of international monetary coordination. Economic theory was obviously still in its infancy.

Behind these difficulties, however, were problems of political extremism that had never been resolved after World War I. The German Weimar Republic may have looked on paper like a genuine democracy in 1925, when Field Marshal Paul von Hindenburg was elected president, but it was a democracy that was continually being undermined by the political left and right. Communists were still expecting the spontaneous revolution they felt had been promised in 1919, while nationalists on the right were still smarting from Germany's defeat on the battlefield and the national humiliation that followed. France's foreign policy exacerbated the political divisions in Germany. Using the pretext of a delay in reparation payments, French armies marched into and occupied the Ruhr in 1922–3 and sought political control of this mineral-rich province and the Rhineland, but this act only fanned nationalist outrage. In the face of massive strikes, the French partially retreated. The situation improved somewhat in 1925 with the Locarno Agreements, which guaranteed the Franco-German border and permitted Germany to join the League of Nations. The Young Plan of 1929 set out another schedule for reparations. Now, however, the problem was the collapsing economy.

The Weimar Republic effectively fell into its final crisis in March 1930 with the new chancellorship of Heinrich Brünig, who was given extraordinary powers in the face of massive unemployment. The National Socialist Party at this time controlled only 18 percent of the vote, and the Communist Party had 13 percent. These numbers would change with the continuing economic decline, and the National Socialists would eventually displace the Social Democrats as the largest political party. After several crises, Hindenburg replaced Brünig in May 1932, and the next two chancellors, both ineffective, quickly suffered the same fate. Meanwhile, the social unrest and violence intensified, and the issue of how to respond ultimately came down to a choice between turning the government over to the military or to the National Socialist Party. Finally, in January 1933, Hindenburg offered the chancellorship to a former Austrian corporal in the German army, Adolf Hitler, who knew how to act decisively. On 27 February he set fire to the Reichstag Building and blamed it on the Communists. Their alleged guilt then became the pretext for removing them from the parliamentary body. In elections held in March, the ever more popular National Socialists took 44 percent of the vote. The Reichstag fire was also used as the justification for the Enabling Act of March 23, which gave the prime minister near dictatorial powers by curtailing the powers of the Reichstag. On April 1 Hitler announced a boycott of all Jewish shops in Germany, and a week later the government began the termination of all Jews from civil service. On April 26 Hitler created the Gestapo, and on June 14 he declared the National Socialist Party to be the only legal political party in Germany. By the following summer, with the death of Hindenburg, his power as *Führer* was supreme.

Hitler came into office in a time of political and economic crisis, and he made two promises dear to many Germans: to end unemployment and to restore the lost honor of the country. He succeeded in the first by implementing massive public works programs (the creation of the autobahn and the Volkswagen, among them), building a huge police force, and, most importantly, pursuing the rapid rearmament of Germany. His success in restoring Germany's honor almost surely exceeded his own expectations. Germany reoccupied the disputed parts of the Rhineland in 1936; it invaded and assimilated Austria and most of Czechoslovakia in 1938; it attacked Poland in 1939 (precipitating war with France and Britain); and it attacked Denmark, Norway, Belgium, Holland, and France in 1940. In 1941 it began an initially successful invasion of Russia. Only the heroism of the British people under Winston Churchill, the military intervention of the United States, and Hitler's growing megalomania saved Western Europe from complete despotism.

Within Germany and its occupied lands, Hitler employed the tools of racism, and his immortal legacy is the Holocaust. Here too he moved with gruesome dispatch. After initially eliminating Jews from most professions and even preventing them from entering Aryan shops, he pushed through a series of "citizenship" measures in September 1935, restricting the right of Jews to vote, hold office, or have sexual relations with "Germans." The systematic takeover of Jewish property began in 1937, and in the following year came the destruction of synagogues and the relocation of Jews to concentration camps. The so-called Final Solution of 1941 involved the creation of extermination camps, where 6 million European

Jews perished. The vast majority of these victims were Polish (3.3 million, or 90 percent of the Polish Jewish population) or Ukrainian (1.5 million). Jews were not the only targets of Nazi racial policies, however, and it is estimated that as many as 15 million civilians were killed. Hundreds of thousands of others were incarcerated or forcibly sterilized.

In modern history, Hitler's crimes against humanity were exceeded only by those of Joseph Stalin. By 1928 Stalin had assumed absolute control of the USSR, and his first five year plan – the plan that attracted so many German Communists and architects to the country – prescribed forced agricultural collectivization in the early 1930s and essentially put the government at war with resisting landowners and peasants (*kulaks*). It is estimated that somewhere between 5 and 15 million peasant men, women, and children were executed or forced into starvation during that decade. The so-called Great Terror of 1936–9, which was intended to eliminate political opposition, claimed another 1.2 million lives and relocated another 8 million political prisoners into a vast complex of labor camps (gulags) by the end of 1938.[1] Hitler's tyranny was open and, until the war years, visible to much of the West. The hideous madness of Stalin operated in secrecy and was later concealed, and its full extent is still being assessed.

The impact of these events on the practice of architecture was of course enormous. If the Depression severely curtailed building activity during the first years of the 1930s, the war – or preparations for war – effectively brought the practice of architecture to an end by the last years of the decade. Then followed the 1940s, which saw the wartime destruction of many cities in Europe, especially in Germany. Recovery throughout Western Europe was slow and painful and in most areas did not occur before the mid or late 1950s. Improvement was even slower in the Communist East, where the Iron Curtain and the threat of imprisonment sundered all intercourse with the West.

The architectural situation in Nazi Germany during the 1930s was complex, and it certainly goes well beyond the question of an "official" Nazi style.[2] The great symbol for the defeat of modernism in Germany traditionally has been the Bauhaus, whose fate was decided in 1933 when Mies closed the doors of the school. But the issues here are not as simple as sometimes portrayed, because personal political animosities also played a significant part in its demise. Because the majority of German architects in the 1920s and 1930s were state employees, they owed their appointments to the ruling political parties. And as most German state governments in the 1920s were Social Democratic or socialist, key appointments were restricted to those of a leftist political persuasion – such as May's appointment in Frankfurt (1925) and Martin Wagner's in Berlin (1926). Conversely, when the National Socialists formed a ruling coalition in Thuringia in 1930, they abruptly replaced the modernist Otto Bartning with the nationalist Paul Schultze-Naumburg (1869–1949). Thus architects in many cases lived or died by their political allegiance, which was often formed very early in their training. For instance, Hitler's favorite architect, Albert Speer (1905–81), relates that when he studied at the Technische Hochschule in Berlin in the late 1920s, Communist students joined the studio of Hans Poelzig, while National Socialist students gathered around Heinrich Tessenow, though neither of these teachers was especially political.[3]

Modernism, furthermore, was never a single ideological movement. Poelzig and Tessenow, for example, were both prominent modernists of their generation, yet the former's work was regarded as expressionist, the latter's often characterized as classical. Another and more vivid illustration is the controversy that erupted over the exclusion of Paul Bonatz (1877–1956) and Paul Schmitthenner (1884–1972) from the Werkbund exhibition in Stuttgart in 1927. Bonatz, in particular, had sparkling modern credentials. He worked in the office of and was a faculty assistant to Theodor Fischer, whose architectural style he also emulated. And when Fischer left Stuttgart for a position in Munich in 1908, Bonatz succeeded him in the Stuttgart chair. Two of Bonatz's early commissions – the Tübingen Library (1909–12) and the Stuttgart Railway Station (1913–28) – were widely admired as among the earliest modern buildings in Germany. In the immediate postwar years, Bonatz was a Social Democrat, but then he changed his political stance. Schmitthenner, his younger associate on the Stuttgart faculty, had studied in Karlsruhe and during the war was an architect at the national Ministry of Housing. In that capacity he designed a famous garden city *Siedlung* (*Gartenstadt Staaken*) in Berlin, much influenced by Richard Riemerschmid's plan for Hellerau. Schmitthenner joined the faculty at Stuttgart in 1918 as a housing specialist and was active in the Bund für Heimatschutz (a conservation and regionalist association) as well as in the German Werkbund. Because Bonatz and Schmitthenner were distinguished local architects, and because the Stuttgart exhibition was initially organized by the Württemberg branch of the German Werkbund and was supported by municipal funds, their participation in the event would have been logical, not to mention tactful. But as we have seen, the selection of architects for this event was largely controlled by the Berlin chapter of the Werkbund,

effectively by Mies van der Rohe. As a result, Schmitthenner never made it on the list of potential architects. Bonatz was on the first list given to Mies in September 1925, but his name was deleted.[4] The Württemberg chapter returned his name in the spring of 1926, but Mies delayed his consent. When Mies did finally relent one month later, it was too late, as Bonatz and Schmitthenner had just published an attack on the hodgepodge nature of Mies's overall plan and the absence of any architects with regionalist sensibilities. Schmitthenner, who was vice-president of the Württemberg chapter of the Werkbund, complained that his chapter had been deceived by the Berlin Werkbund office and had lost its control to a very small faction of the Werkbund.[5] What Reyner Banham recognized almost a half-century ago was in fact true – the exhibition was indeed a great victory for Berlin's Der Ring, that is, the German architects represented at Stuttgart "were mostly Berliners by professional domicile, birth or attachment."[6]

The outgrowth of such regional bitterness further fractured the modern movement in Germany – that is, beyond the split already apparent between the political functionalism of Hannes Meyer and the aesthetic formalism practiced by architects such as Mies. Some architects now saw contemporary German architecture as splitting into "evolutionary" and "revolutionary" camps.[7] A direct response to the Stuttgart exhibition was the creation of Der Block (the block) in opposition to Der Ring; originally it was a group of eight architects led by Bonatz, Schmitthenner, Schultze-Naumburg, and German Bestelmeyer.[8] Their moderate agenda of 1928 called for seeking a "unique expression for the building tasks of our time" by taking into account both the wishes of the people and the peculiarities of the natural landscape and by paying strict attention to "all the implications and possibilities of the new materials and forms," yet without dispensing with "inherited traditions and what has already been achieved."[9] In short, they picked up the theoretical thread of the realist and *Sachlichkeit* movements of the 1890s as enunciated by Richard Streiter, Fritz Schumacher, Alfred Lichtwark, and Friedrich Naumann.

But this agenda at this particular time and place further complicated the situation in architecture. For what might be described as a split between the left and right wings of the modern movement – the split between the advocates of constructional and regional forms – now becomes joined by a decidedly political reaction to modernism bordering on fanaticism. Those who were part of this reaction have captured the attention of many historians intent on discerning a "fascist" architecture, but such a stylistic-political generalization does not in any way explain the long-noted ambivalence within the Nazi Party and its architectural course. Adding to the problem is the fact that many of the regionally minded moderates of the late 1920s jumped sides as the political and economic situation deteriorated after 1930.

Schultze-Naumburg is a good example of this switching of sides, although his jump was slightly earlier. Before the war he had been primarily a designer of housing and was seen as a "progressive" architect because of his abstracted Biedermeyer style, that is, smooth surfaces and stripped-down neoclassical forms, similar to those of Tessenow, Paul Mebes, Behrens, and even Mies. Such early books of his as *Häusliche Kunstpflege* (Housing artistic concerns, 1900) were influenced by the domestic reform movement and expanded the functionalist arguments of Hirth, Dohme, Gurlitt, and Lichtwark.[10] After World War I, however, Schultze-Naumburg's career began to decline, for his traditionally based forms came increasingly under attack by the left wing of the modern movement. It was thus with some bitterness that he published his *ABC des Bauens* (ABC of building, 1926), in which, in the format of a technical handbook, he sharply criticized modern architects for their technical incompetence and unfamiliarity with the skills of the building trades – in other words, for shoddy construction.[11] He opposed, in particular, the flat roof because of its incompatibility with the German climate and German customs. In 1928, however, his critique began to take a far more sinister turn, as his polemical tract *Kunst und Rasse* (Art and race) sought to align the development of modern architecture with an alleged cultural and racial decadence.[12] It is important to note, however, that Schultze-Naumberg found little acceptance for his extremist stance, and his views in fact were not identical with those of the National Socialist Party. A few years later, an architecturally aware Hitler, who fully shared Schultze-Naumberg's racial outlook, angrily tossed his prize-winning design for a Party Forum into the trash bin, noting that "it looks like an oversized marketplace for a provincial town."[13] Another moderate regionalist, Fritz Schumacher, who joined Der Block because of his respect for Bonatz and Bestelmeyer, resigned from the group in 1933 over what he regarded as its contamination by the "fanatical" agitation of Schultze-Naumberg.[14]

There were other outlets for this extremism in the late 1920s and early 1930s. In 1923 Alfred Rosenberg, who was originally trained as an architect, became the editor of the newspaper *Völkischer Beobachter* (People's observer), the organ of the National Socialist Party. It did not, however, concern itself much with artistic matters until 1928, and only around 1930 did it reverse its earlier praise of the social modernism of Gropius, Martin Wagner, and Ernst May.[15] With its reversal, however, it too moved far to the extreme by joining its criticism of modern construction with the racial and antiurban theories of Richard Walter Darré – the source of the much-repeated phrase "blood and soil." Another strident voice in this regard was the Kampfbund für deutsche Kultur (Fighting league for German culture), which was founded in 1929 and had its own architectural wing, led by Rosenberg and Schultze-Naumburg. But this organization too would become marginalized soon after the Nazis assumed power, and the reasons have much to do with Hitler's interest in architecture.

Hitler was born in 1889 into impoverished circumstances in a small town on the Austro-German border. By 1907 he made his way to Vienna in the hope of studying art at the Academy of Fine Arts. After shifting his interest to architecture, he was stunned and humiliated by the rejection of his application to the architecture school – his acceptance, of course, would have dramatically transformed the course of the twentieth century. He subsequently refused to reapply or take work in an office; instead he devoted all of his time to self-instruction in the rudiments of architecture and its history, even as his daily existence depreciated into a vagrant's life. Only with the war did he eventually find employment (in military service), but the architectural sketches he produced in prison in 1924–5 demonstrate a good facility with the pencil. After he assumed political power in 1933, architecture remained his only true interest, and he would fret away many long nights on his architectural passion. The architect Albert Speer, who became one of Hitler's closest friends, describes his taste as "arrested in the world of his youth: the world of 1880 to 1910, which stamped its imprint on his artistic taste as on his political and ideological conceptions."[16] This taste embraced the theatrical designs of Semper and Garnier as well as the more *sachlichen* tendencies of the early century. Hitler's first and most important mentor upon his assumption to power was the Westphalian architect Paul Ludwig Troost (1878–1934), with whom he would happily and regularly pass many hours. Troost, who worked in the style of Behrens and Tessenow, designed the House of German Art in Munich, which began construction in 1933 in a severe, plain, neoclassical style, not too different from (although not as refined as) the contemporary Beaux-Arts classicism of Paul Cret. Hitler regarded architecture as the most important art, and he believed that on a state level heroic monumentality was its most essential feature. In other areas, however, he tended toward practical and functional design and in fact often employed the term *Sachlichkeit* when speaking of architecture.[17] He believed that factories built by the government should be modern, rural youth hostels should be rustic or Alpine, and houses similarly should be vernacular with pitched roofs. Thus, there was no single architectural ideology or stylistic outlook dominating Nazi practice in the 1930s. The neoclassicism of Speer, which emerged in the second half of the decade with Hitler's plan for rebuilding Berlin, was more a reflection of Hitler's megalomania and penchant for state symbolism than of his insistence on a classical style.[18]

There is again an odd relation between modernism and the politics of National Socialism. The door to an official tolerance of modernism was open because when Hitler created the Ministry of Culture in November 1933, he purposely bypassed Rosenberg (who had pleaded for its formation) and appointed Josef Goebbels to the top post. The latter was the lone cabinet minister with a doctorate, and he was a long-time foe of Rosenberg. Goebbels in his early speeches actually supported modernism over its alternatives, and he was a sincere admirer of German expressionism. His appointment of the expressionist painter Hans Weidemann to the art bureau of the Ministry of Culture was a sign of his opposition to the policies supported by Rosenberg. Goebbels's failing, however, was his habit – as Speer pointed out – of groveling before Hitler, and not confronting his political opponents head on.[19] Rosenberg, initially, was given a much less significant post within the government, but he still had control of the newspaper *Völkischer Beobachter* and the Kampfbund, and it was through these vehicles that he (until 1935) challenged the cultural views of Goebbels.

Indeed, many of the purges of modern architects from official or organizational offices were orchestrated at a local level by Rosenberg through adverse publicity campaigns. Already in the summer of 1931, the *Völkischer Beobachter* promised, once the Nazi Party gained control, to "settle accounts" with Der Ring architects for their leftist politics, and threats of this kind prevailed in the politically charged atmosphere of 1933.[20] Jewish artists and architects at all levels were attacked, and Erich Mendelsohn joined the first wave of Jewish refugees to leave the country. The offensive against modernism, however, was as much ideologically or politically driven as religious. Late in 1933 Hans Scharoun and Adolf Rading were ousted from their design studios at the Breslau Art Academy. In the same year Hans Poelzig was forced to resign his new appointment in Berlin after the Kampfbund loudly opposed him. Hermann Goering, who was at this time the new Prussian Minister of the Interior,

also dismissed Martin Wagner and Walter Curt Behrendt from the Prussian building administration.

The situation of Gropius and Mies differed only to a certain extent. For many within the Nazi party, Gropius had become synonymous with the leftist politics of the Bauhaus. And because his political affiliations were well known, he was easy to attack for his constructional shortcomings. As an architect in private practice, however, he could endure these attacks with little damage. Projects continued to come through his office up to 1934, when, owing as much to the economic situation as to anything else, they abruptly fell off. During these years Gropius entered several competitions – among them the Palace of the Soviets competition of 1931 and the Berlin Riechsbank competition of 1933 – and although he was unsuccessful, they allowed him to produce some of his best work as a designer. He also actively lobbied on behalf of modern architecture by sending letters to public officials and organizational heads.[21] He supported the cause through the first half of 1934, before the lack of work in October forced him to depart Germany for England. Originally his intention had been to remain in England for only a few years and return to Germany when the economy improved.

Mies stayed in Germany much longer, and he left the country with the greatest reluctance.[22] Even his connection with the Bauhaus did not hurt him. Gropius had suddenly appeared in his Berlin office one summer day in 1930 and appealed to him to become the new director of the Bauhaus in Dessau. Meyer had just been fired, and his militant communist views had galvanized that wing of the school into action. Gropius believed that Mies could rectify the situation. Mies accepted the challenge, and at the start of the fall semester he was greeted with a student demonstration and a list of ridiculous demands, to which he responded by calling in the police and shutting down the school for one month. His first task, then, was to depoliticize the institution and refocus its energies on art and architecture. But just as in Weimar a decade earlier, the damage within the local community had already been inflicted, and Mies was from the start fighting a losing battle. It took two more years, but on 22 August 1932 the Dessau City Council, against the wishes of the mayor, voted to shut down the institution. Mies responded a few months later by leasing a vacant warehouse in Steglitz, a suburb of Berlin, and in October he reopened the school there with most of its former faculty and students. But Berlin brought politics back into play, as now the number of National Socialists in the student body approximated the number of Communists, and political clashes again became commonplace. This was the context within which Mies arrived at the school on the morning of 11 April 1933 and found its offices being ransacked by the Gestapo.

It was also a period of great confusion within the government. The Nazis had just assumed power but had no official policies regarding architecture. The Ministry of Culture had not yet been created, and Hitler was entirely preoccupied with consolidating his grip on power. The raid, as it turns out, was not aimed at destroying the Bauhaus but was part of an investigation of Mayor Hesse of Dessau, who was now in detention on vague charges of misappropriating funds. In addition, the Communist Party had been banned, and the Gestapo was certainly interested in the Bauhaus students who were members. The next few months were thus very difficult ones for Mies, for while he was fighting to save the school, he was also a potential accomplice in the Hesse investigation. Moreover, he was in the midst of the competition for the Reichsbank – the largest governmental architectural competition in Germany in years. In fact, in early July his symmetrical scheme was named one of the six finalists.[23] In a desperate move late one evening, he actually called on Alfred Rosenberg in his ministry office. The latter had been unaware of the raid, but he nevertheless had a chilly conversation with Mies about the school and its political orientation, which Mies insisted he had now amended. This conversation did in fact help the situation, because in July the Gestapo allowed the school to reopen – conditional upon the dismissal of Wassily Kandinsky and Ludwig Hilbersheimer. It was at this point that Mies, together with the faculty, decided to close the school permanently. It was therefore a decision of the faculty and not the government that closed the Bauhaus.

Mies in a sense had won his showdown with the new government, and he would continue his efforts to make peace with it over the next five years. One the one hand, his tenure at the Bauhaus and his design of the Liebnecht-Luxemburg monument detracted from his standing; on the other hand, except for his membership in Der Ring, he had never been overtly political, and he was fairly well respected as an architect in some quarters of the Nazi government. Hitler himself, in any case, decided the Reichsbank competition by rejecting all of the winning schemes for their lack of monumentality and for having the appearance of normal office buildings.[24] The appointment of Goebbels as cultural minister late in 1933 offered some hope to modernists, and in the following year Mies was invited to participate in two government-sponsored competitions – one for the German national pavilion at the World's Fair in Brussels in 1935. Also in 1934 he prepared a mining display for the German

workers' exhibition in Berlin. When he was officially cleared in the Hesse investigation in 1935, it may have seemed his career could resume, but Mies was in fact losing favor in Germany, though not for ideological reasons but because of his minimalist style. His design for a house for Ulrich Lange in 1935 – with a flat roof – worked its way through the local zoning board only with great difficulty, and Lange decided not to build it because of the stipulation that it had to be shielded from the street.

In December 1935 Mies received an offer from Mills College in California to teach a summer course, but he had no interest in leaving Germany at this time. A letter from the Amour Institute of Technology arrived in March 1936, exploring his interest in a faculty position, and Mies, at the urging of Lily Reich, for the first time began to consider leaving his homeland. In June of that year Mies also received a visit from Alfred E. Barr. The museum director spoke of the possibility of designing the new building for the Musuem of Modern Art, and he relayed Harvard University's interest in considering him for the directorship of the Graduate School of Design. Mies preferred both of these possibilities to Chicago and – secure in his own superiority to his competitor Gropius – he broke off negotiations with the Armour Institute. Neither of these two possibilities materialized, as the Harvard position eventually went to Gropius. At the same time Mies seems to have been in the running for the commission to rebuild Berlin (Speer eventually was chosen), but the documentation is lacking to verify this. As Mies was receiving the disappointing news about Harvard, he was at work on a textile exhibition in Berlin, scheduled to open in March 1937. A few weeks before its opening, however, he was forced to resign as the architect through the personal intervention of Hermann Göring. The situation had again changed.

It was a bitter blow on top of a disappointing year, and Mies, with the greatest reluctance, decided to leave Germany with or without a job. In July 1937, using his brother's passport, he walked across the Dutch border at Aachen; a few days later, in Paris, he met Barr, who helped him gain an architectural commission in Wyoming. Mies returned to Germany to obtain the legal papers for his departure, and on 20 August he arrived in New York City. In December he concluded negotiations with the Armour Institute and moved to Chicago. When he left Germany, he was an architect who had still built relatively little, certainly nothing of great dimension or scale.

The architectural situation in the other Fascist country in Europe – Italy – was similar to that in Germany in at least one regard: There was never an official national policy regarding style. In fact, the diversity of approaches in Italy was greater than in Germany, despite the strong appeals made by the Italian rationalists to the government of Mussolini in the early 1930s. Further, as nearly all of the leading modernist architects – foremost Giuseppe Pagano and Guiseppe Terragni – remained supporters of Fascism throughout this decade, there was also no political divide among architects, that is, until the implications of the political pact between Hitler and Mussolini (anti-Semitism and war) began to be felt.

Politics aside, Italian modernism differed from other variants of European modernism in other respects. The very word "international," so warmly embraced by Hitchcock and Johnson in 1932, stood decidedly in conflict with one important aspect of Italian Fascism: its nationalism, or rather its celebration of an Italic cultural unity with historical roots extending back to the Roman Empire. This meant that Italian rationalists had to be more sensitive to cultural values and national aspirations, and consequently they had a special affinity for monumental expression as well as a genuine appreciation of regional materials and building methods and indeed the southern climate. Monumentality, sometimes bordering on pomposity, in fact dominated to such an extent that by the end of the decade the designs of the rationalists are virtually indistinguishable from the designs of more traditionally minded architects, whose classical motifs (influenced by modernism) had become increasingly more abstract.

The pace of building activity in Italy in the 1930s was also relatively high, seemingly higher than elsewhere in Europe.[25] Part of the explanation is that various building campaigns were initiated by Mussolini, who – although knowing little about architecture – nevertheless recognized its representational importance to the Fascist state. He also had the encouragement of his mistress, Margherita Sarfatti, a wealthy Venetian lady with an artistic background and a sympathy for modern developments. Mussolini was preoccupied above all else with Rome, the center of his new imperial government, which he was determined to turn into a world metropolis. The first master plan for the city, prepared in 1931 by Marcello Piacentini, focused on its classical core and called for the creation of two avenues emanating from the Piazza Venezia on either side of the monument to Vittorio Emmanuele II. One was to turn south toward Ostia; the other, the Via dell'Impero, was to run alongside the imperial forums and the Coliseum. The Via dell'Impero, once constructed, then became the intended site for a museum dedicated to the revolution, the Palazzo del Littorio, and in 1934–7 there was a major competition for the design of the building. The competition generated considerable discussion and controversy because of the building's placement next to classical monuments and the Coliseum. One scheme prepared by a group of rationalists, including Terragni, proposed a curved, seemingly hovering wall of porphyry of the scale of the Coliseum, with a platform jutting forth. Another, prepared by several architects and the firm BBPR, reduced the museum to a long horizontal slab designed in a Corbusian manner.

The problem, of course, was how to give modern expression to classical monumentality or grandeur – a problem that Piacentini was already attempting to solve with his master plan and his design for the new University of Rome (1932–5). Piacentini, with his ideological pluralism and willingness to seek a middle way between the opposite sides in contemporary disputes, is a difficult architect to characterize. The son of a famed architect, he gained prominence prior to World War I and was a shrewd and prolific critic of modern developments in the 1920s and 1930s. He opposed neoclassicism and academic eclecticism, but he also opposed modernism – both for its abstraction and for the unsuitability of some of its materials (such as glass) for the warm Roman climate. The key to his later style is his design for the post office he built in Brescia around 1930, which took the form of an abstract cubic building with a portico of tall rectangular piers horizontally banded with contrasting layers of stone. With regard to the University of Rome project, his intention was to design a unified, semi-classical complex yet without columns or arches. The completed buildings, executed by Piacentini and others, are held together by the central forum, square piers, and common travertine walls.

The largest of Piacentini's many tasks on behalf of the Fascist government was his overall management of the complex for the Esposizione Universale di Roma (EUR), initiated in 1937 and planned for completion in 1942 (it was built but never opened because of the war). The featured structure of this complex of classical proportions is the near cubic, arch-layered Palazzo della Civiltà (1938–9), designed by Ernesto La Padula, Giovanni Guerrini, and Mario Romano.

Piacentini's classical and restrained modernism, however, was only one of several approaches competing with each other in the 1930s. The Novocento style of Giovanni Muzio and Gio Ponti was still evident; the latter architect in particular moved closer to modernism with his design for the Montecatini office building in Milan (1939). Rationalists were also quite active in this decade and thereafter. Firms such as BBPR (Gian Luigi Banfi, Lodovico Belgiojoso, Enrico Peressutti, and Ernesto Rogers) and architects such as Pagano, Edoardo Persico, Adalberto Libera, and Ignazio Gardella continued to practice a refined modernism infused with Latin sensibility. BBPR's heliotherapy clinic in Legnano (1938) already portends postwar concerns for the *genius locus* with its break from "white" modernism, while Gardella's tuberculosis clinic in Alessandria (1936–6) does the same and even more so with its use of colorful brick grillwork. These were two of the more sophisticated European designs of the decade.

The most significant modern Italian architect of the 1930s was unquestionably Terragni, who among the rationalists of this time was also the most adamant supporter of Fascist politics.[26] Not only was his Novocomum apartment building (1927–9) the first distinctly modern building in Italy, but his Casa del Fascio (1932–6) – Como's regional Fascist headquarters – has been widely acclaimed as Italy's first modern masterpiece (Fig. 91). The grounds for accepting this evaluation, however, remain in dispute. Terragni's founding concept for the building (taken from a speech by Mussolini) – "a glass house into which everyone can peer," where "leaders could not imagine special or secret exits" – could be taken as the most benign concept for a town hall, yet this was the provincial headquarters of a political party that shares responsibility for plunging the world into war.[27] And notwithstanding Terragni's professed desire to make "absolutely no reference to buildings of a representational nature"[28] – variously interpreted as everything from Chiricoesque "naked masks" to syntactic self-absorption[29] – the building was in fact overtly rhetorical, with its interior mural of Mussolini, large photos of officials and solders, and didactically carved monoliths representing the principles of order, authority, and justice. On the exterior, Terragni, working with Marcello Nizzoli, planned no less than to transform one large section of blank wall into a political billboard surmounted with a colossal image of the Duce.[30] What cannot be disputed, however, is the quality of the building as it exists today, stripped of these accoutrements: the clarity of the conception and structure, the abundance and play of light, the highly successful manipulation of the four facades, and the beautiful materials detailed in a highly refined manner.

Terragni built several other buildings in the 1930s, but no project was more important to him than the Danteum (1938), which Mussolini personally approved for construction in 1938 on the Via dell'Impero opposite the ruins of the Basilica of Maxentius.[31] This museum to the poet Dante had been proposed by a private source, and the design combines an abstract spatial conception (stairs ascending from hell to purgatory to paradise) with a material reading of the three eternal resting places within this sequence. Highly symbolic in its proportions and numerology, the museum was to bring the visitor through a darkened forest of 100 marble columns at the bottom to a paradisiacal space containing thirty-three glass columns supporting a transparent framework open to the sky.

This work, as its historical interpreters have unanimously maintained, is powerful, even metaphysical. But if one cannot dispute Terragni's talent, even genius, there is also the troubling fact that he was inventing these allegories while the political situation was deteriorating. The Danteum's patron, Rino Valdameri, commissioned Terragni and Pietro Lingeri in October 1938 to prepare the design, only a few months after Hitler made his famous visit to Italy and a few weeks before the Fascist government issued its infamous "Manifesto of Racial Scientists," which allowed the systematic persecution of Italian Jews.[32] Dark days were descending, and some of the rationalist architects themselves were not averse to participating in the coming purge of fellow architects.[33] Diatribes in the press eventually escalated into events far more diabolical. Giuseppe Pagano, Gian Luigi Banfi, and Raffaello Giolli would all die in German concentration camps as a result of their resistance to the regime. Ernesto Rogers was arrested in 1943 but fortunately escaped to Switzerland.[34] Terragni himself died in 1943, after returning from the Russian front in what has been described as a state of mental and moral breakdown.[35] Politics and a bad conscience have long haunted the historical treatment of Italian modernism of the late 1930s and 1940s.

2. Prewar Theory Elsewhere in Europe

Although the rest of Europe saw little architectural activity during the decade of the 1930s, there was development along a theoretical front. In Finland during the years 1929–33, a period of the economic downturn, the Aaltos, working with the manufacturer Otto Korhonen, began to develop and manufacture bent-plywood chairs, which were exhibited in London in 1933 at the behest of the critic Morton Shand. Their interest in furniture culminated in the founding of the Artek workshop in 1936 and the creation of an important line of high-quality furniture of Scandinavian design.

The Aaltos' architectural commissions during these years were few, but they did design two pavilions for the world

91. Giuseppe Terragni, Casa del Fascio, Como, 1932–6. Photograph by author.

fairs in Paris (1937) and New York (1939) as well as their own house at Munkkiniemi (1936) and the Villa Mairea (1938–9). In the latter building in particular, the complex informality of the floor plan combined with the warmth of the detailing (now mostly with wood) helped to define a personal and hospitable style quite different from what had become the norm on the Continent.

In 1937 the Californian architect William Wurster met the Aaltos in Helsinki, and as a result the Finnish architects made their first visit to the United States in October 1938, where Alvar lectured in New York City and at Cranbrook Academy. On their second visit, in 1939, the couple toured the country for five months and exhibited their furniture and fabrics in San Francisco. The following year Alvar Aalto was scheduled to teach a full semester at M.I.T., but he returned to Finland before its conclusion because of the deteriorating political situation.

Modernism also became prominent in England in the 1930s. The interest in modernism was in part related to the stream of German Jewish art historians and architects who immigrated to England after 1933 – among the first group, Wolfgang Herrmann (1899–1995), Rudolf Wittkower (1901–71), and Nikolaus Pevsner (1902–83). Their arrival coincided with two not unrelated events: the founding of the Courtauld Institute of Art in 1932 and the arrival of the 60,000-volume art library of the late Aby Warburg (1866–

1929) from Hamburg. Within a few years, these two institutions would be assimilated into the University of London, and Britain, which up to this time had lacked a tradition in art history, would emerge as one of the leading centers for the study of art.

Pevsner's famous work *Pioneers of the Modern Movement: From William Morris to Walter Gropius* (1936) was immediately influential in Britain.[36] The book's genealogy, however, borders on idiosyncrasy. The full title wrapping around the dual portraits of Morris and Gropius indicates its starting and stopping points. Pevsner traces tripartite roots for the triumphant phenomenon of Gropius and German modernism: William Morris and the arts and crafts movement, art nouveau, and engineers of the nineteenth century. Such a lineage oddly strips German theory and practice of its Germanic legacy, and it also leads to an overemphasis on Morris and the British tradition – which tactfully served to make the new movement more popular in Britain. Because the first manifestations of the new style are the Fagus Factory and Model Factory for the Werkbund exhibition, its principles for Pevsner are those of the factory aesthetic: glass, industrial sash, steel, flat roofs, simple planes, and the absence of all ornament. Joined with them is an extraordinary psychological implication: "The warm and direct feelings of the great men of the past may have gone; but then the artist who is representative of this century of ours must needs be cold, as he stands for a century cold as steel and glass, a century the precision of which leaves less space for self-expression than did any period before."[37] And because it is a "genuine style" and not a "passing fashion," its essential distinguishing mark is "totalitarian."[38] Moreover, he concludes, "It is the creative energy of this world in which we live and work and which we want to master, a world of science and technique, of speed and danger, of hard struggles and no personal security, that is glorified in Gropius's architecture."[39] Never had modernism been extolled with such ominous overtones.

In an even more imperious insistence on English conformity to the emergent *Zeitgeist*, Pevsner followed this book with *An Enquiry into Industrial Art in England* (1937), whose emphasis is on manufacturing design.[40] The range of products surveyed is impressive, but the general tone of the book is reminiscent of Henry Cole's and Richard Redgrave's scathing critiques of almost a century earlier, only the more recent model of the Bauhaus is now squarely, if tacitly, in view.

The first of the German architects to come to England was Erich Mendelsohn, who arrived in the summer of 1933 and remained for six years, although he worked much of the time in Palestine. He formed a partnership with the Russian Serge Chermayeff (1900–96), and in early 1934 the firm won the competition for the De La Warr Pavilion in Bexhill, a modern complex that included an auditorium, restaurant, glazed spiral staircase, and seaside terrace. Chermayeff had studied in London during World War I and became a refugee following the Russian Revolution. Very active in Fabian socialist circles, he had worked as an interior designer throughout the 1920s but then expanded his interest into architecture and became a designer much in demand in the mid-1930s. In addition to collaborating with Mendelsohn, Chermayeff designed the interiors for the BBC studios (1932, with Raymond McGrath and Wells Coates) and his own house in Bentley Wood, Sussex (1938). Two years later, following bankruptcy, he left England for the United States.

When Gropius arrived in London in 1934 – encouraged to move there by Jack Pritchard – he teamed up informally and later formally with another British champion of modernism, Maxwell Fry (1899–1987). Fry had studied architecture at the University of Liverpool and worked in a traditional manner in London in the second half of the 1920s; a decade later, he was experimenting with modernism and built several important works, among them the Sun House, Hampstead (1935), and the Miramonte House, Surrey (1937). The most important of the joint ventures of Gropius and Fry was the Impington Village College in Cambridgeshire (1936), a very cordial, well-lit, single-story secondary school spread out over the site and accentuated with an auditorium.

Marcel Breuer (1902–81) came to England in 1935, where he would eventually team up with Francis Yorke (1906–62), another early British practitioner of modernism. Yorke, a specialist in reinforced concrete, was one of the founders of the Modern Architectural Research Group (MARS), the British arm of CIAM. Still another émigré with modernist interests was the Georgian Berthold Lubetkin (1901–80), who arrived in 1931. Lubetkin was also experienced in reinforced concrete and contributed to the founding of MARS. With a group of young architects, he formed the professional group TECTON, which built several impressive works, among them the Highpoint Apartment House (1933–5) and the Penguin Pool at the London Zoo (1934).

Still, it is easy to overestimate the importance of the refugees to an already awakened British architectural scene. Chermayeff, Fry, and Yorke were all talented designers who had developed their modern styles before their partnerships, and the pages of England's leading journal, *Architectural Review*, in the first half of the 1930s were filled with works by accomplished modern designers, such as Raymond McGrath, Wells Coates, Jack Pritchard, R. D. Russell, Marian Pepler, Stewart L. Thomson, Connell and Ward, George Checkley, Colin Lucas, Godfrey Samuel, and Oliver Hill. Regular contributors to this journal – such as P. Morton Shand, John Gloag, and J. M. Richards – were also very active in providing the historical context of recent events and championing the new forms. Shand, a close ally of Chermayeff, contributed to this journal a very impressive seven-part "Scenario for a Human Drama" in 1934–5, which comprehensively outlined the beginnings and evolution of modernism on the Continent.[41] In 1934 Yorke published the *The Modern House*, which devoted only fourteen pages to modern English examples. In a follow-up article in *Architectural Review* of 1936, however, he devoted nearly as many pages to chronicling recent developments and rightly dispensed with his earlier apologetic tone.[42] In an addendum to the same issue (which was focused on the use of concrete), no fewer than eleven British reinforced-concrete houses were displayed – laying the basis for the postwar fascination with this material. It is fair to say that in the second half of the 1930s there was more "modern" architecture being built in Britain than on the Continent.

This interest in modernism culminated with J. M. Richards's *An Introduction to Modern Architecture* (1940).[43]

92. Le Corbusier, model of *La Ville Radieuse*, 1936. From *The Architectural Review*, vol. 80 (October 1936).

Aimed at the layperson, Richards discusses the modern machinery, new materials, and new methods underlying this new kind of architecture. His historical survey considers Thomas Telford, William Morris, and Charles F. A. Voysey before he turns to manifestations of the new style on the Continent. British work from the 1930s is well documented, but unfortunately the book appeared during the bombing of London, and the war had now overtaken all other interests.

France during the 1930s was far less active architecturally than Britain, in part because of the country's collapsing economy. In 1930 Le Corbusier had a series of large projects on his drafting table: the Centrosoyuz Building in Moscow (1928–35) and the Pavilion Suisse (1930–32) and Cité du Refuge (1929–33) in Paris. But by 1933 he was virtually without work – a situation that would not improve for the next twelve years. Painting thus became one of his outlets. Another was his continuing involvement with the Syndicalist movement, an authoritarian, antiparliamentary group of reformed Taylorists and technocrats who argued for a constructive overhaul of the capitalist system through

large-scale planning.[44] Le Corbusier threw himself into the business of writing, editing, and attending meetings, and he made proposals for urban and agrarian reforms in dozens of articles. One architectural manifestation of this interest was his National Center for Collective Festivals (1935), a colossal oval stadium for 100,000 people in which the speaker's platform was placed on one long side. The spirit of Nuremberg, it seems, had become infectious.

Le Corbusier's Syndicalist urban ideas were brought together in his book *La Ville Radieuse* (Radiant city), which he published in 1935.[45] The concept of a Radiant City draws upon his Contemporary City of the 1920s as well as his work in Moscow (Fig. 92). Indeed, in 1930, on his third trip to Russia, he was asked to comment on a competition for a "Green City," which had been won by Nikolai Ladovsky. This was a proletarian health resort to be located outside of the city, and it followed the recent trend of many Soviet planners, who favored a decentralization of the conventional capitalist city. Le Corbusier responded in June with a fifty-nine-page "Reply to Moscow," containing twenty-one drawings defining an alternative urban model for Moscow. It rejected decentralization in favor of high-density business, administrative, and residential areas running perpendicular to a central vehicular spine and surrounded by greenbelts. He again proposed destroying most of Moscow and raising the city on *pilotis* – in the now classless society, living space would be allocated on a per-person basis. Le Corbusier redrew his Moscow plan in general terms for the CIAM conference of 1930, and in *Le Ville Radieuse* he expanded the concept with thoughts on Buenos Aires, São Paulo, Antwerp, Algeria, Geneva, and other cities. He also expressed a general concern for human biological or physical well-being: health, sunlight, solar orientation, ecology, and spiritual calm. In addition, he developed planning proposals for the *Ferme Radieuse* (Radiant farm) and *Village Radieuse* (Radiant village), which were attempts to theorize utopian plans for rural collectives and cooperatives.

Also forming part of his work during these years were the six proposals he made for the city of Algiers (*Projet Obus*) between 1931 and 1942. The most famous of the six joins the organic forms of housing blocks with a series of rectilinear towers in the financial district, mediated by a sinuous elevated viaduct (housing underneath) following the curved coastline. Again the project takes on the complexion of a private obsession born of forced idleness. Le Corbusier was not paid for his unofficial efforts, except for a seat on the Comité de Plan Régional in 1938, and because of its sweeping scale, reduced with each successive proposal, the project had no chance of becoming realized.

Another of Le Corbusier's foreign ventures of the 1930s – his trip to the United States in 1935 – is summarized in his book *Quand les Cathédrales étaient Blanches* (When cathedrals were white, 1937).[46] Echoing the "alternating hate and love of New York of so many European books of the late 1920s, Le Corbusier provided the *New York Times Magazine* with a scandalous headline when he noted that Gotham's skyscrapers were "too small," that is, "out of line" with the rationality of the Cartesian skyscraper schemes.[47] Other things annoyed, frustrated, and attracted him during his trip: suburbs, traffic congestion, and American women, the last of whom he seems to have viewed, with some trepidation, as independent-minded "Amazons."[48] The book not only has the usual air of European cultural superiority but, more evidently, exhibits a genuine incomprehension of the reality and pulse of American life. Le Corbusier and the United States would remain – by cultural attitudes, personalities, and timing – a poor fit.

3. American Practice and Academic Reforms, 1934–1941

The Great Depression of the 1930s produced more than just a slowdown in building activity in North America. It fundamentally altered the relationship between private enterprise and government and opened new facets of social and political dialogue. Many of these changes in the United States in fact were presaged by the early promise of the administration of Herbert Hoover. This geologist and engineer had made his name prior to World War I as an entrepreneur of global mining operations, and he achieved a second reputation during the war for coordinating food programs in Europe. As the secretary of commerce during the Harding and Coolidge administrations (1921–8), he employed his engineer's sense for efficiency (Taylorization) in attempting to impose standardization in production and in arguing for a planned economy. After his landslide presidential victory in 1928, however, he seemed unable initially to grasp the severity of the deflation underlying the ensuing downturn and, following the Republican loss of the House in 1930, he lacked the congressional support to implement the economic measures needed to reverse it. In terms of economic numbers, 1932 was the worst year of the Great Depression. Somewhere between twelve and fifteen million workers were unemployed, which resulted in Hoover's ouster and the election of Franklin Delano Roosevelt as president.

What Roosevelt's New Deal programs actually delivered in the six or seven years of their existence was the full engagement of Washington in drafting national economic policies. Now working with congressional support, Roosevelt rapidly implemented a series of measures in his first 100 days: major banking and agricultural reforms, creation of the Civilian Conservation Corps (CCC), abandonment of the gold standard, creation of the Tennessee Valley Authority, passage of the Home Owner's Loan Act, and creation of the National Recovery Administration (NRA), which funded both the Works Projects Administration (WPA) and various housing programs such as the Resettlement Administration. After several of these measures failed constitutional muster or proved to be ineffective, Roosevelt instituted his Second New Deal in 1935–8, which among other things led to the passage of the Social Security Act of 1935. These policies did not fully bring the Great Depression to an end (only World War II would do that), but they did succeed in increasing federal authority over areas such as banking, agriculture, corporate business, labor, and public welfare. A new social awareness was being ushered in.

Architecture was obviously much affected by the economic downturn. Building activity was reduced virtually to a standstill by 1933, and the vast majority of architects were unemployed. The young Louis I. Kahn (1901–74) is a case in point. He had completed his education at the University of Pennsylvania in 1924 under Paul Philippe Cret (1876–1945), a Beaux-Arts–trained architect who had come over from France in 1903 and established a brilliant career as a classicist. Kahn next prepared designs for the Philadelphia Sesquicentennial Exhibition of 1926 and visited Europe before returning to Cret's office. He was laid off in 1932 and joined thirty other unemployed architects in founding the Architectural Research Group in Philadelphia, which studied the housing problem, slum clearance, city planning, and the use of new construction methods. Between 1933 and 1935 he was a squad leader in charge of housing for the Philadelphia planning commission, a program funded by the WPA. In the last years of the decade he similarly worked as a consulting architect for both the Philadelphia Housing Authority and the U.S. Housing Authority. One of his two built projects of the 1930s was for a slum block clearance project in Hightstown, New Jersey, which he codesigned with Alfred Kastner. Thus for most of this decade he was largely supported by federal funds, and his focus was almost entirely on low-income housing and urban planning. The same is true for his friend and later partner Oscar Stonorov (1905–70).

The goals of Clarence Stein and Lewis Mumford's Regional Planning Association of America (RPAA) were similar to those of some of the New Deal programs, although the fit of public and private agencies was not entirely successful. The RPAA had for many years lobbied for an increase in the federal role in housing, and the need for such an increase became ever more pressing in 1934 when the RPAA's developmental arm, the City Housing Corporation, went bankrupt. Many of the RPAA members next turned their efforts to influencing national programs. Mumford orchestrated a lobbying campaign against Roosevelt officials, whom he felt were too timid in the scope of their planning.[49] Brenton MacKay advised the Tennessee Valley Authority; Frederick Ackerman, Clarence Stein, and Henry Wright were employed by the Public Works Administration; and Catherine Bauer became an advisor to the Federal Housing Authority. The RPAA's first achievement in this regard was their successful lobbying for the three Greenbelt towns built in the mid-1930s by the Resettlement Administration, headed by Rexford Tugwell. Stein, Bauer, and Wright provided advice on Greenbelt, Maryland (1935–37), a suburb halfway between Washington

REHOUSING URBAN AMERICA

BY

HENRY WRIGHT

NEW YORK: MORNINGSIDE HEIGHTS

COLUMBIA UNIVERSITY PRESS
1935

93. Henry Wright, cover of *Rehousing Urban America* (New York, 1935).

and Baltimore. Two other such towns were built in Ohio and Wisconsin (twenty-two others were planned), but Congress halted this program in 1936 after constitutional issues were raised. The built towns, moreover, were unsuccessful. They were conceived as decentralized garden suburbs, but without an employment base they became dormitory suburbs for urban commuters, essentially advancing suburban sprawl.

The members of the RPAA also failed in their efforts to curtail the building of single-family houses, which by now had become a deeply rooted value in American life. In 1933 Henry Wright, on the basis of statistical analysis, prophesied that the single-family house was "doomed to a permanent recession."[50] In his ambitious 1935 book *Rehousing Urban America* (Fig. 93), he tried to tackle head on the "Anti-American" sentiment associated with multifamily housing by invoking the colonial village and its commons: "land held by the community, around which the village was grouped; rational open spaces; exposure and protection for every house; an orderly arrangement with due regard for human amenities."[51] Nevertheless the models he proposed for emulation, based on his trip to Germany in 1932–3, were the new housing estates in Frankfurt and Berlin.

Stein was not the only one presenting European models to an American audience. Catherine Bauer (1905–64), who had emerged as another articulate critic for the cause, in 1934 published her book *Modern Housing*, which summarized her European tour, made in 1930. The book is a classic exposition of the RPAA viewpoint, written in the depths of the Depression. It opens with a quick historical survey of the nineteenth-century's failings: the "Black Congestion," "Wasteful Expansion," and "Victorian Mind and Matter" of the Industrial Age.[52] Along the way, reforms had been suggested by William Cobbett, Robert Owens, Karl Marx, Friedrich Engels, John Ruskin, William Morris, the Fabians, Ebenezer Howard, Patrick Geddes, and the "great idea" of nineteenth-century socialism.[53] But the crucial change for Bauer was brought about by the labor and social-democratic policies of the 1920s, which, although not entirely successful, nevertheless pointed the way to future developments. Bauer's "Minimum Standards in Practice" for housing are found nowhere in the United States; instead she refers the reader to Holland, Germany, Austria, and even the Soviet Union. Indeed, citing "American architects" who have worked there, she states that "there seems on the whole to be more leeway for free architectural experiment in Russia today than in any other country."[54]

Obviously Bauer would not have made this claim if she had possessed firsthand knowledge of the gruesome reality of Russia during these years, but she is tough-minded in her revolutionary insistence on "new form" rather than "reform."[55] Her ideal of housing is impossible, she candidly admits, "within the present class-property-profit economic system," and so she urges (1) the end of the speculative market, (2) the municipal purchase and expropriation of land, and (3) the subsidizing of construction by the various arms of the government.[56] The issue of the single-family house is decided by one argument: "Why should money be spent for extra outside walls, extra land which always lies useless in the shadow of one house or the other, dead windows (or windows looking directly into other people's rooms), extra feet of pipe-line and street-pavement, and extra interior heat?"[57] Her faith in the European models is no less passionate. On her European tour of 1930 she reported

on Weissenhof in a letter to Mumford: "Even if van der Rohe's roofs *do* leak in winter – even if it *does* break dishes in a Le Corbusier basement when a man drops his shoe on the top floor – I don't give a damn – nobody ought to drop shoes anyway & it's a serious reflection on the human race if members of it can't live comfortably in those swell houses."[58]

Mumford was no less vocal in the 1930s on the same issues with his two books *Technics and Civilization* (1934) and *The Culture of Cities* (1938). The former – one of the great books of the century – shines with its critique of the machine age and captures Mumford's radical idealism at its height. Here he defines himself ideologically as a "communitarian" through the notion of "basic communism" – a post-Marxian planned economy freely dispensing certain basic services such as food, shelter, and medical care.[59] It is an organic and regionalized society that is Taylorized in theory, anti-consumptive in practice, and not dissimilar to the earlier utopian scheme of Edward Bellamy. This break with capitalism is possible because Western culture, in Mumford's view, had evolved through its golden eotechnic stage (1000 A.D. to 1750), had concluded its dark paleotechnic stage (1750–1900), and had entered a neotechnic era that allows the promise, at least, of the mechanization process – that is, values assimilating the advantages of the electric lamp, gas engine, and airplane and new metals such as aluminum. It is a promise, however, that demands a dynamic social equilibrium that is at the same time regional, industrial, agricultural, and communal. Mumford demands tidiness, precision, calculation, flawlessness, objectivity, simplicity, economy, and order in his ideal society, although he does not surrender his fondness for medievalism. He captions his aerial photograph of the geometrically moated Dutch village of Naarden, for instance, with this remark: "The definite pattern of the town and its sharp contrast to the country is still immensely superior to any of the succeeding types of urban development: above all, to the amorphous dribble of Paleotechnic land-speculation."[60] Mumford in the end regarded the local balance of communitarian values to be the individual's hedge against the assaulting scourges of liberalism, commercialism, environmental destruction, population growth, war, and economic deflation.

The *Culture of Cities* is equally expansive in its ambition to chronicle the city in history and report on the "general miscarriage and defeat of civilized effort" that arises from the social disruption of modern urban life. It is a lament born more of the dread of catastrophic war than of the poverty of the Depression:

Instead of accepting the state cult of death that the fascists have erected, as the proper crown for the servility and the brutality that are the pillars of their states, we must erect a cult of life: life in action, as the farmer or the mechanic knows it: life in expression, as the artist knows it: life as the lover feels it and the parent practices it: life as it is known to men of good will who meditate in the cloister, experiment in the laboratory, or plan intelligently in the factory or the government office.[61]

Notwithstanding his vision of an alternative, the book is deeply pessimistic in its undertones. In a subchapter entitled "A Brief Outline of Hell," he offers this disturbing vision of contemporary urban culture:

The sirens sound. School-children, factory hands, housewives, office workers, one and all don their gas masks. Whirring planes overhead lay down a blanket of protective smoke. Cellars open to receive their refugees. Red Cross stations to succor the stricken and the wounded are opened at improvised shelters: underground vaults yawn to receive the gold and securities of the banks: masked men in asbestos suits attempt to gather up the fallen incendiary bombs. Presently the anti-aircraft guns sputter. Fear vomits: poison crawls through the pores. Whether the attack is arranged or real, it produces similar psychological effects. Plainly, terrors more devastating have been reintroduced into modern urban existence.[62]

The book rather neatly summarizes his urban ideas of the past fifteen years: the plea for regionalism, utopianism, satellite garden cities, environmental conservation, and above all urban planning with a sense of order. The preferred models are once again entirely European, and often his polemics lapse into the intellectual's disdain for all things American, as when he likens the neoclassical design for the Palace of the Soviets to the "swaggering skyscraper blunders of American businessmen."[63] Naiveté, too, is perhaps the only word to characterize his alternative of a "spacious, verdure-lined, composed" example of modern Russian housing under Stalin, but these are minor shortcomings of his overall argument.[64] With secular annoyance, he insists that the school rather than the church should form the community nucleus.[65] Political and social engineering is the very fiber of Mumford's being.

Not entirely unrelated to Mumford's quest for regional order is Frank Lloyd Wright's decentralized concept of Broadacre City, which he began proposing in the early 1930s.[66] The elements are first outlined in his book *The Disappearing City* (1932), but the antiurbanism is already forcefully expounded in the last of his Princeton lectures of 1930, which he opens with the question, "Is the city a natural triumph of the herd instinct over humanity, and therefore

a temporal necessity as a hangover from the infancy of the race, to be outgrown as humanity grows?"[67] His answer is that the city of today is plunging toward its death, or rather being asphyxiated by a congestion facilitated by electricity, the automobile, the telephone, and the airplane. The skyscraper with its speculative leased space is but the latest symbol of this tyranny, but oddly enough the technological advances that have facilitated its development are precisely those that will allow the overcrowded urban population – the "mobocracy" – to be dispersed into the countryside. His philosophy is one of decentralized smallness: smallness of industry, agriculture, professional pursuits, schools, commerce, and government. Television has eliminated the need to visit the cinema or the concert hall; the automobile has liberated the individual and potentially enhanced each person's freedom, that is, once he or she has been freed from urban congestion and its related ills.

In *The Disappearing City*, Wright, drawing upon the antiurban spirit of Jefferson, Emerson, Whitman, Thoreau, and others, overlays this model with more radical suggestions. The idea behind Broadacre City is that every family should be guaranteed at least one acre of land (allowing basic farming, sun, light, air, and privacy) and one automobile: "Light, strong houses and workplaces will be solidly and sympathetically built out of the nature of the ground into sunlight. Factory workers will live on acre home units within walking distance or a short ride away from the future factories. Factories beautiful, smokeless and noiseless."[68] Homes will be constructed with steel and glass, be integrated into the landscape, and be located no more than ten miles from a market. Tall buildings with festooned balcony terraces will stand free in rural parks. The monetary currency is to be replaced with a "social credit" system, and absentee ownership of property and the private ownership of inventions or public necessities are to be eliminated. In his famous model of 1935 – of a four-square-mile section (first shown at Rockefeller Center) – Wright presented an architectural vision of the concept. The key to the low-density diffusion of small, single-family houses (Fig. 94) is the automobile and inter-county arterial highways surmounted by a high-speed rail system. Locally, the gas station functions as the community center and distribution point for services. Schools, factories, and recreational facilities are organized on a countywide basis.

More interesting are the intellectual sources from which Wright drew many of his social ideas.[69] As has often been noted, there are aspects of the Jeffersonian land ethic, the Transcendental lineage of Emerson, Ruskin's communitarianism, the utopianism of Bellamy and H. G. Wells, the decentralization ethic of Ebenezer Howard, and even the "progressive" populism – the "Wisconsin Idea" – of the various La Follettes, who served as both governors and senators in that state. Other theorists also influenced Depression-era theory, some of whom Mumford took into account. Thorstein Veblen's book *Engineers and the Price System* (1921) launched a "Technocracy" movement in the early 1930s; this movement espoused guaranteed minimal incomes and the embrace of technical automation in the collective service of society. In the same vein were the anti-monopolistic ideas of C. H. Douglas, articulated in his book *Social Credit* (1921).

More important for Wright's conception of Broadacre City seems to have been the American social theorist Henry George and the economic arguments of Silvio Gesell. George's now classic study *Progress and Poverty* (1879) was written while he was living in California. His thesis is that despite the "prodigious increase in wealth-producing power" and the great promise of technology and industrialization, these boons have not relieved the "suffering and anxiety of the working classes," the majority of whom still struggle to put food on their tables.[70] Drawing upon Herbert Spencer and the tenet that wealth in all its forms is the product of labor applied to land, George's "remedy" for the situation is to make land common property, which he proposes to achieve neither by purchase nor by confiscation; rather, taxation should be shifted from the cycle of production to land values, effectively making the state the universal landlord. George's theories were enormously popular in the late nineteenth century, and on two occasions he was narrowly defeated in the mayoral race in New York City through the intervention of the corrupt Tammany machine.

Similarly, the German economist Gesell in *The Natural Economic Order* (1929; German original, 1916) proposed an anti-Marxist socialism founded on egoism – "the ideal of all true lovers of freedom." The natural economic order is an order "in which men compete on equal terms with the equipment given them by nature, an order in which, consequently, the leadership falls to the fittest, an order in which all privileges are abolished, in which the individual, obeying the impulse of egoism, goes straight for his aim undisturbed by scruples alien to economics – scruples which he will have opportunities enough of obeying outside economic life."[71] The competitive rights of the individual are enhanced by an economic policy that nationalizes land (with just compensation), mandates free trade, and gradually eliminates the monetary system through scheduled depreciation.

Wright acknowledged his debt to George and Gesell, describing their books as "two of the finest things in recorded English. Both are an exposition of Principle rather than panaceas: both dealing with Land and Money with a simplicity seeming naive to the prestidigitators of interest: our professional economists."[72]

For Wright, Broadacre City became a virtual obsession after 1935, as he continued to lobby on its behalf in exhibitions, lectures, and published writings. Mumford initially praised the back-to-the-soil, decentralized concept, even though he disapproved of Wright's use of the single-family house.[73] Wright responded to Mumford's criticism in a letter written in his usual blunt manner: "I don't know what you can mean by preferring the German tenement and slum solution as preferable to the Broadacre's minimum house and maximum of space. There can be no possible comparison between the two as to privacy, light and air, living accommodations – or what have you – at $600."[74]

Catherine Bauer was considerably less deferential in her review for *The Nation*. She attacked the scheme as romantic, utopian, politically naive, and socially inept; most especially she disliked the individualism of a man who "puts his car in the garage and is king of all he surveys."[75] Like Mumford, she countered with the solution "the Germans have been evolving," where a house is a "planned and equipped community unit; it has a garden, rents for what an average man can pay, and is situated not more than twenty minutes away from a good place to swim and a large stretch of forest or mountain permanently preserved from gas stations."[76] Meyer Schapiro assailed Wright's concept in the *Partisan Review* as feudalistic and indifferent to the class struggle and property relations.[77] The *New Masses*, a Marxist journal, applauded its anticapitalist premises but condemned Wright's "adolescent idealism."[78] Wright responded in the same journal shortly thereafter by acknowledging his plan was anticapitalist, but he also insisted that the scheme was also anticommunist and antisocialist.[79] This individualist refrain aptly summarizes his own politics, which, like Sullivan's before him, espouses the sovereignty of the individual and rural "common sense."

Out of the Broadacre concept came the Usonian house, Wright's solution to providing low-cost, single-family homes. He first spelled out the details of this "house of moderate cost" using images of the Jacobs House, Madison, in a special issue of *Architectural Forum* devoted to his resurgent career, the issue was published in 1938 and edited by Howard Myers.[80] The house, which was built at a cost of $5,500 (including the architect's fee of $450), achieved its

94. Frank Lloyd Wright, model of a car house, Broadacre City Exhibition, 1935. From *Architectural Record* (1935).

economy by eliminating all unnecessary materials in construction, using the mill to good advantage, and simplifying the heating, lighting, and sanitation system. Wright employed flat roofs; replaced the garage with a carport; minimized the basement; employed radiant heating in the floor slab; and eliminated all interior trim, built-in light fixtures, paint (by using a stain), plaster, gutters, and downspouts. The house was informally laid out on a two-by-four-foot grid with a double board-and-batten system of construction. The kitchen was efficiently planned, the dining room was eliminated, and the glazed wall faced out onto private gardens or terraces, with clerestories used elsewhere for light. Perhaps no other architect of prominence in the twentieth century devoted so much of his energy to the problem of the middle-class house.

The special issue of *Architectural Forum* on Wright's career also featured such recent projects as "Falling Water" at Bear Run and the Johnson Wax Company in Racine. In 1938 Wright built Taliesin West, near Scottsdale, and in 1943 he designed the Guggenheim Museum in New York (built 1957–64). His creative star had never shown brighter, but his foremost cause during these years remained Broadacre City. In 1943 Wright drafted a petition asking "that the Administration of our Government authorize Frank Lloyd Wright to continue the search for Democratic FORM as the basis for a true capitalistic society now known as Broadacre City."[81] It was signed by numerous intellectuals and artists, among them John Dewey, Albert Einstein, Buckminster Fuller, Norman Bel Geddes, Walter Gropius, Henry-Russell Hitchcock, Albert Kahn, Georgia O'Keefe, Eero Saarinen, Mies van der Rohe, and Thornton Wilder. In what is perhaps its equal

as a testimonial, Ayn Rand, the eloquent purveyor of her philosophy of individualism and egoism, glorified Wright as a national icon in her 1943 novel *The Fountainhead*.

Wright was also at least a minor figure of interest during these years within the ivory towers of American academe. In the 1930s and 1940s architectural programs across the country were undergoing wholesale reformation, largely from decorative Beaux-Arts instruction to training oriented toward modern design. The ideological split that is apparent during this period – between the "organic" regionalism of Wright and European modernism, which was more popular, particularly along the Atlantic seaboard – was in fact a long-standing one. Its roots extend back to two of the first schools of architecture in the United States; Massachusetts Institute of Technology and the University of Illinois at Urbana-Champaign.[82]

The program at M.I.T. was initiated by Robert Ware in the fall of 1868 with four students, but its program became better defined in 1872 with the arrival of the French-trained architect Eugène Letang, who started a Beaux-Arts program of instruction. Many of the other private institutions in the Northeast – such as Syracuse University (1873), Columbia University (1881), and the University of Pennsylvania (1874) – did not fully implement Beaux-Arts programs until around the turn of the century. When the swing came, however, it came with a vengeance, as such institutions as the Society of Beaux-Arts Architects and the American Academy were formed to standardize architectural educational programs based solely on the Beaux-Arts model.[83] This preference assumed greater importance with the creation of the Association of Collegiate Schools of Architecture, established in 1912. In one of the association's first surveys, carried out in 1915, only five of the twenty curricula reviewed did not offer a Beaux-Arts program in design.[84]

The school of architecture at the University of Illinois at Urbana-Champaign was one of the five, but its well-respected curriculum had been long established by this date, and in fact the school touted itself in 1915 as the largest in the world.[85] It had been founded in 1873 by Nathan Clifford Ricker (1843–1924), who did so by designing a program for his own graduation. To broaden his perspective, he traveled to Europe, where he was most impressed with the technically oriented curricula at German schools, particularly the Bauakademie in Berlin. Over the next several decades he implemented a program that combined a thorough grounding in the constructional sciences and materials with generous instruction in history and theory, for which he himself translated nearly all of the major texts of the last half of the nineteenth century. His program explicitly shunned Beaux-Arts composition and its decorative vocabulary; it was oriented more toward construction and practice and was more regional in its outlook.

There were a few other schools that rejected the Beaux-Arts model. The graduate program at Harvard University, which was founded in 1895 by Herbert Langford Warren (1857–1917), initially had a Germanic bias and a focus on construction.[86] The School of Architecture and the Allied Arts at the University of Oregon, founded in 1914 by Ellis F. Lawrence (1879–1946), was formed initially along Beaux-Arts lines. But after its accreditation in 1919, the school dropped this program because academic concerns "have been largely supplanted by practical problems given under much of the same conditions as exist in general architecture practice."[87] The school's curriculum included a greater emphasis on the conditions of the site as well as cross-instruction in the various arts. No other school in the 1920s – save Yale University – had such an artistic bent, although Knud Lönberg-Holm offered a de Stijl studio at the University of Michigan.[88]

The Depression quickly changed everything. Most of all it vividly underscored to educators the irrelevance of French-based academic training for designers, who now of necessity had to turn their attention to mass housing and government-funded rural programs, for example. Thus by the early to mid-1930s there were curricular reforms underway in nearly all American schools of architecture, and these were chronicled by professional journals.[89] In one report published in *Architectural Record* in 1936, the author noted reforms at the University of Cincinnati, M.I.T., the

University of Michigan, and the Cranbrook Academy of Art and stated that "there is no school that has not made modifications in curricula during the past five years. Some, in fact, have introduced a complete change in teaching method and the nature of problems."[90] Some of these reforms had occurred even earlier. The University of Cincinnati, for instance, went to a four-week work and classroom cycle of instruction in the 1920s, while Cornell University dropped its Beaux-Arts program in 1929.[91] In 1930 the University of Southern California implemented a program that de-emphasized drawing in favor of working with models and stressed both realistic problems and the development of the imagination.[92] And the University of Kansas in 1932 initiated a design program in which the instruction began with abstract, three-dimensional models and perspectives and later focused on problems of a realistic nature.[93]

The most watched reforms, at least in the Northeast, were those implemented in the mid-1930s by Joseph Hudnut (1884–1968), first at Columbia University and then a few years later at Harvard University. The reforms at the last school culminated in the appointment of Walter Gropius in 1937.[94] This Hudnut–Gropius partnership – and their subsequent public feud – speaks volumes about the way institutions and schools of higher learning in America have often been controlled by an exceedingly small circle of people whose authority has been established as much by circumstance as by accomplishment. It illustrates as well that in the 1930s, along the Atlantic seaboard at least, the conservative cultural dependency on Europe had in no way lessened.

Hudnut, the son of a wealthy Michigan banker, followed his undergraduate studies at Harvard by enrolling in the architecture program at the University of Michigan. He taught and practiced in Alabama, and in 1916 he took a master's degree at Columbia University. He next opened a small office in New York City, where he maintained an eclectic, largely classical practice that has been characterized as Georgian colonial. He was an undistinguished designer, but on the recommendation of his former teacher at Columbia – the historian Friske Kimball – he was appointed to head the architecture program at the University of Virginia in 1923. Three years later he returned to Columbia as a history professor, gave up practice, and served as a protégé to Dean William Boring, one of the founders of the Society of Beaux-Arts Architects. With Boring's retirement in 1934, Hudnut stepped in as his replacement and followed the precedent of other schools in dismantling the Beaux-Arts program.

It seems clear that Hudnut's pedagogical conversion to modernism took place sometime around 1930, but what is less apparent is the depth of his understanding of modernism. The historian Jill Pearlman has stressed the influence of Dewey's educational ideal of social engagement on Hudnut's outlook as well as the latter's brief working relationship with the German planner Werner Hegemann.[95] In an article published in 1931, "The Education of an Architect," Hudnut is very unspecific in expressing his views. He belittles the "hocus-pocus of Vignola" and stresses the "economic and intellectual currents in which the student lives" but offers little concrete advice regarding education.[96] His brief excursus deriding the doctrine of "functionalism" in an odd way rehearses the polemics of Hitchcock and Johnson of 1932 and suggests he was already close to this circle of fellow Harvard alumni.[97] Shortly after assuming the deanship at Columbia, Hudnut hired the Swedish modernist Jan Ruhtenberg to teach a design studio, and he considered the idea of approaching Gropius in England and Oud in Holland.[98] He also hired Henry Wright and Hegemann to teach studios on town planning, which demonstrates his acceptance of the RPAA and its European approach.

Whatever his understanding of European theory, Hudnut was able to make known his reforms, and his efforts soon brought him to the attention of Harvard University President James B. Conant, who in the mid-1930s also wanted a change in the university's curriculum. Conant hired Hudnut as dean in the spring of 1935, and Hudnut's first task was to combine the schools of architecture, landscape architecture, and city planning into a graduate school of design. Hudnut assumed his new post in the summer, and in a series of symbolic acts he banned history books from the library (although he himself was a historian), removed plaster casts from the atrium of Robinson Hall, and renovated the building's interior with a coat of white paint.[99] Modernism had overnight come to Cambridge, and the fortunate retirement in 1936 of the Beaux-Arts professor Jean-Jacques Haffner created a convenient faculty opening. Hudnut privately conferred only with Conant (who had little knowledge of architecture) and Alfred E. Barr in choosing his successor – the ideological christening of the new graduate school program.

The fact that Hudnut considered only Oud, Mies van der Rohe, and Gropius – three Europeans – for the chairmanship of the Department of Architecture underscores his ties with the Museum of Modern Art. The selection process quickly resolved itself. Barr, who was traveling in Europe in the spring of 1936, first approached the three men. When Hudnut followed him two months later, Oud (whom Hudnut had initially favored) said he was not interested in the position. Hudnut's next choice was Mies, but this architect's lack of patience (particularly at being considered alongside Gropius) soon eliminated him from contention.[100] Hudnut was left with Gropius, who by contrast was eager to take the job. Hudnut had effectively purchased for Harvard the package of German modernism portrayed in the MoMA exhibition of 1932, and Gropius, beginning in April 1937, now became its American icon.

It was a bold move that required an effective publicity campaign – aimed not so much at combating internal opposition as at enhancing Harvard's reputation nationwide. Hudnut stepped up to the task by publishing a series of articles in various scholarly journals, by writing the preface to Gropius's new book, and by helping to orchestrate an exhibition at MoMA in 1938 on the Bauhaus.[101]

Gropius responded by preparing a book in English, *The New Architecture and the Bauhaus* (1937), a generally self-serving history of his contributions to European modernism. It had originally been written to introduce himself to a British audience but was now copublished by Faber and Faber in London and the Museum of Modern Art in New York. In its preface, Hudnut (who was apparently unaware that the Bauhaus had no architecture program until 1927) not only praised the Bauhaus for its "invention of a new system of architectural education" but aligned this workshop system of apprenticeship in the arts with the "coming Renaissance," in which the principles "starkly given" in Europe will find "new expression" on American soil.[102] Gropius reiterated his earlier themes of standardization and rationalization and ended his book with a spirited exposition of the main goal of the Bauhaus, which was not "to propagate any 'style,' system, dogma, formula, or vogue, but simply to exert a revitalizing influence on design."[103] Again, the very idea of a " 'Bauhaus Style' would have been a confession of failure and a return to that very stagnation and devitalizing inertia which I had called it into being to combat."[104]

The exhibition at MoMA in 1938 was accompanied by a book that was edited by Herbert Bayer, Walter Gropius, and Ise Gropius and that contained a historical sketch of the Bauhaus by Alexander Dorner.[105] It was a relatively comprehensive and informed compilation of photographs and facts about an institution that was now being raised to epic proportions. The fact that the drama broke off in 1928, the year of Gropius's departure, only underscored his centrality to the institution's history. The well-orchestrated propaganda campaign proved to be enormously successful – at least in helping to cultivate Harvard University's own self-image. In his "President's Report" of 1938–9, Conant could proudly boast that Harvard had become "the leading school of modern architecture on this continent and perhaps in the entire world."[106] This was the case despite the fact that Gropius had just arrived and the program had yet to undergo any significant change.

Gropius, nevertheless, wasted little time in making his presence felt in Cambridge, in particular in his quest to reconstitute the German Bauhaus. In the fall of 1937 he brought Marcel Breuer over from England, and the next year hired the former Berlin planner Martin Wagner, who had been working in Turkey. In 1939 Gropius, in his first curricular change, reduced the number of required history courses from three to one. His biggest battle, and the one that would estrange him from Hudnut, was his campaign, beginning in 1937, to bring the painter Josef Albers to the Harvard architectural faculty to teach a Bauhaus-inspired preliminary course on design. Interestingly, it was a move firmly resisted by Hudnut, who intellectually was no match for Gropius. Hudnut, for all his easy acceptance of MoMA's image of European modernism, still saw architectural training in vague pedagogic terms as a form of personal and liberal "expression" in service to a larger social context. In an article published in 1938, he spoke of exploiting this expression through the three ideas of human space, human values, and community.[107] In another series of lectures delivered some fourteen years later, he, alluding to Ruskin, even reduced modern architecture to the three "lamps" of progress, nature, and democracy.[108] Gropius saw modern architecture in starker and more universal terms as a creation of his German generation. The fact that this puffy administrator was now stymieing his pedagogical efforts led to hard feelings. Hudnut successfully resisted the hiring of Albers until 1950, when Gropius managed to circumvent him politically and have the course introduced on a trial basis using his own graduate school budget. When Hudnut resumed control of the purse strings and cancelled the course two years later, Gropius famously resigned.

Nevertheless, it was Gropius who increasingly dominated the school during the 1940s, and it was his graduate program that would leave its imprint on American architectural education. And while the success or failure of this imprint has been much debated, Gropius was highly influential in many other ways. One example is the Charles Eliot Norton Professorship he secured for Sigfried Giedion in the academic year 1938–9. Although relatively safe in Switzerland, Giedion was eager to find a temporary base in the United States, and he used the occasion of these formal, university-wide lectures to write what was one of the most important architectural textbooks of the century – *Space, Time and Architecture: The Growth of a New Tradition* (1941) – a book that would forcefully shape architectural thought for several decades.[109]

This classic work at times assumes the character of a surging psychological novel. Much of Giedion's earlier book – *Bauen in Frankreich, Bauen in Eisen, Bauen in Eisenbeton* (1929) – is simply translated into English and incorporated into the text, but it is the addition of a larger historical framework that raises the book to quite another level. It opens with an explanation of the author's method, the same "metaphysical air" that students attending his lectures found puzzling.[110] Giedion proudly announces himself to be a "disciple of Heinrich Wölfflin," and with that he speaks of the great *Zeitgeist* that both shapes the thought of each age and reduces the images of the "ideal historian" (the disinterested chronicler who is now compelled to be a biased, active agent) to fiction.[111] Everything for Giedion moves within a larger continuum of change, universality, and destiny. The theme constantly reiterated throughout the text is the divorce between "thinking and feeling" that dominated Western consciousness from the early nineteenth century until around 1930. Founded in the preeminence of the sciences over the arts, this divorce resulted in a "split personality" of the Western mind that, implicitly at least, has culminated in the (still not fully imagined) cataclysms of the twentieth century. Freud now steals through the backdoor into architectural theory.

It is within this somber context that Giedion's tense history unfolds. He begins with the Renaissance and the new spatial conceptions of painters and architects, such as Alberti and Brunelleschi; these conclude with the arresting spatial forms of Borromini, which Giedion juxtaposes with works by Picasso and Tatlin. French and Italian gardens are briefly considered next, leading Giedion to the Industrial Revolution, where "the paths of science and the arts diverged; the connection between methods of thinking and methods of feeling was broken."[112] The divorce manifests itself in the hated eclecticism of the nineteenth century, although Giedion's thesis is somewhat ambivalent here. "If our culture," he notes, "should be destroyed by brutal forces – or even if it should continue to be terrorized by them – then the nineteenth century will have to be judged as having misused men, materials, and human thought, as one of the most wretched of periods."[113] If, on the other hand, we utilize the century's technological potential with proper feeling, "then the nineteenth century, in spite of the human disorder it created and in spite of the consequences which are still developing out of it, will grow into new and heroic dimensions."[114] In any case, this phase of human development ends around 1890, when "the smoldering hatred of eclecticism came to a head in Europe with startling suddenness."[115] The spirits igniting the next phase of development, which he calls "The Demand for Morality in Architecture," are Hendrik Berlage, Henry van de Velde, Victor Horta, Otto Wagner, Auguste Perret, Tony Garnier, and Frank Lloyd Wright. Rarely, if ever, has an architectural history been written with such emotion, and architectural design is now endowed – in a way that Pugin would have appreciated – with a supreme moral mandate.

A chapter on "American Development," no doubt written for his American audience, serves the purpose of poetic relief, as Giedion's principal concerns are with anonymous technical inventions such as hammers, locks, the balloon frame, and unadorned brick surfaces. All represent the driving force of the *Zeitgeist*, or architecture without architects, for the spirit of a country can also be read through its "anonymous ethos." This section ends with the Chicago school, Sullivan's "split personality" (his functionalism and ornamentation), and of course Wright. Although the author includes a few images of the Johnson Wax Building, they serve almost as an afterthought. Wright, in Giedion's analysis, was part of that "sacrificed generation" whose historical importance derives entirely from the influence he exerted on the European masters shortly after the turn of the century. Hence his historical mission was finished by 1909.

Giedion is now poised to embark on his most important section, "Space-Time in Art, Architecture, and Construction," in which the new era and its conceptual innovations dramatically unfold. A dizzying Hegelian synthesis of the arts and sciences was attained when artists "tried to enlarge our optical vision by introducing the new unit of space-time into the language of art. It is one of the indications of a common culture that the same problems should have arisen simultaneously and independently in both the methods of thinking and the methods of feeling."[116] Similar in breadth and historical importance to the start of the Renaissance (in science comparable to Aristotle and the Pythagoreans), the physics of Einstein and the mathematics of Hermann Minkowski now converge with the cubism of Picasso, the futurism of Umberto Boccioni, the constructivism of Malevich, and the neoplasticism of Theo van Doesburg in the new "space-time" phase of human development.[117]

Between 1925 and 1930 the two architectural titans of this new heroic phase assumed their place on the world stage: Gropius and Le Corbusier. Giedion likens the founding of the Bauhaus and its effort "to unite art and industry, art and daily life," to the creation of the Ecole Polytechnique.[118] And Gropius's design for the Dessau building is most memorably compared with Picasso's painting *L'Arlésienne*, a juxtaposition of transparencies that would haunt architectural theory for many years to come: "In this case it is the interior and the exterior of a building which are presented simultaneously. The extensive transparent areas, by dematerializing the corners, permit the hovering relations of planes and the kind of 'overlapping' which appears in contemporary painting."[119] Repaying the debt of Gropius's invitation to Harvard in full, Giedion scarcely sees a worldly rival to this profound Teutonic soul: "Gropius, like many German artists, has a strong and solid rather than a quick imagination. But, working very quietly, he arrives at new and startling conclusions. Albrecht Dürer's ponderous figures lack the grace of the Venetian school; nevertheless, Dürer's conceptions are characterized by an inherent depth."[120] All other architects, save Le Corbusier, pale in significance. Mendelsohn has no place here, Mies scarcely exists, and Wright, whose earth-bound buildings, "like the exploratory tentacles of some earth-bound animal" – well, this "may explain why Wright is somewhat repelled by what has been done in Europe since his appearance."[121]

Giedion's historical coup d'etat would take still a few years to reach its full impact. The first review of the book, by a Harvard student, was critical of Giedion's "confusing picture" and his failure to "understand or accept the real, material world."[122] With the complete demise of architectural history within architectural programs during these same years, Giedion – in one book – presents all the history that the "space-time" architect needs to know, and he does so in such a sweeping and dramatic fashion that every architectural student cannot help but feel blessed at having been born during such a momentous time. After all, the idea of space-time architecture is a conceptual breakthrough of such vast teleological proportions that it could only occur every half a millennium or so!

4. The 1940s and 1950s in the United States

The Second World War, of course, consumed the middle decades of the century. The conflict ended with the sack of Berlin in May 1945, one month after Roosevelt's death and the beginning of Harry Truman's presidency. The alliance between Britain, the United States, and the Soviet Union did not survive long thereafter. The political "spheres of influence" had already been worked out in February 1945, when Churchill, Stalin, and Roosevelt had their third meeting in Yalta, in the Crimea. Stalin agreed to join the war in the Pacific in return for territorial concessions and control of Manchuria. Poland, victimized by terrible massacres and atrocities by both the Germans and the Russians, was unofficially ceded to Soviet dominion. Stalin also promised to establish interim governments in the eastern half of Germany, Austria, Hungary, Czechoslovakia, Bulgaria, and Romania and hold free elections. He instead installed puppet communist regimes in all but Austria and erected the Iron Curtain in a tragic attempt to save his new empire. The Cold War thus commenced before the hot war concluded, and the specter of Yalta would haunt the world for decades. Stalin's attempt to seize West Berlin in June 1948 was countered by a massive airlift of supplies and by the creation of NATO the following April. Five months later the Soviets detonated their first nuclear bomb, and the Cold War suddenly became a matter of human survival.

Several unresolved "trouble spots" were part of the legacy of the war. Thousands of Jews from central and eastern Europe immigrated to Palestine, which since 1919 had been ruled by British mandate. When Britain announced its plans to surrender its charge, the United Nations in 1949 created the Republic of Israel, which survived despite dire military predictions and the hostility of neighboring Arab populations. On the other side of the world, Washington and Moscow divided up Korea along the 38th parallel. When the northern dictator Kim Il Sung, supplied with Russian arms, crossed the parallel in June 1950, it resulted in a three-year conflict, massive slaughter, and a tense truce. One of North Korea's allies was China, whose long civil war concluded late in 1949 with the Communist rule of Mao Tse-tung. Again, millions would die in the struggle. After Korea, China turned its support to insurgents in French Indochina. With the crushing French defeat at Dien Bien Phu in 1954, the country was divided in two at yet another conference in Geneva. The Communist government of North Viet Nam was to be ruled by Ho Chi Minh and the South by Ngo Dinh Diem. This solution would prove disastrous.

The postwar period in the United States was a time of high anxiety as well as guarded optimism. The fiasco of Yalta and the standoff of the Cold War had the effect of helping to foster McCarthyism (1950–3) and contributed as well to Truman's failure to win the nomination of his own party in 1952. The eight-year presidency of Dwight D. Eisenhower was characterized by moderate prosperity and limited engagement with the world, partly in response to two decades of economic depression and war. The detonation of the first hydrogen bomb in 1952 may have been the most widely watched event of the decade, but the new logic incorporated into a Princeton computer by the Hungarian mathematician John von Neumann earlier in the same year proved to be of far greater consequence. In September 1956 the United States successfully launched the first Jupiter C rocket, but the Soviets countered the following spring with their first intercontinental ballistic missile (ICBM) and then with the satellite Sputnik. The development of the ICBM and of Sputnik may have checked any growing sense of hubris on the part of Americans, but this does not mean that the national persona of the 1950s suffered the "existential" dread that was so fashionable in Europe and in remote corners of American academe. The 1950s in the United States was a decade of quiet optimism and economic growth – the era of the interstate highway system, Marilyn Monroe, the Supreme Court decision in Brown versus the Board of Education, Elvis Presley, the deep-freezer, Fidel Castro, and automobile fins. The McDonald brothers had actually set up their first fast-food restaurant in 1948.

Still another sign of the optimism across the country was the phenomenon of Levittown.[123] Planners and architects aside – William Levitt's idea in 1946 (following in the footsteps of Frederick Taylor and Henry Ford) had been to devise an efficient, economical system for home construction that would make the single-family house affordable to the average family, especially to veterans returning from the war. It was a dream that rapidly became identified with American culture, and one on which this war-weary generation of delayed family-makers subsequently constructed their peaceful hopes and aspirations. If many sociologists and planners could not understand the appeal of clear air, greenery, the backyard swing set, and a modern kitchen, these goods were part and parcel of a human urge that could not be easily thwarted. Levitt alone built over 17,000 houses, and his industry peers were more than eager to accommodate this generation of blue-collar and white-collar workers. In fact, nothing else, save perhaps the G.I. Education Bill, more widely enhanced the standard of living in the country – suburbia's many shortcomings notwithstanding.

American architectural theory during these years has been little studied and appreciated, and indeed this period is often characterized as one of little innovation or serious architectural deliberation. The documents of the day, however, tell a very different story. The critical literature relating to the practice of architecture in the postwar years in fact far exceeds – in both quantity and sophistication – anything produced in any comparable period prior to the war. Moreover, much of what began as European theory now becomes assimilated and transformed by American discussions, advanced certainly by the massive immigration of European architects and intellectuals to this country.

This last phenomenon itself has spawned its own series of misconceptions. Whereas the presence of Gropius at Harvard and Mies in Chicago did have a direct effect on American developments, even within these centers there were mediating forces in place that both resisted and altered earlier perspectives. European ideas, in turn, were influenced by the different social, technological, and political context in which they were now situated.

Another fact too little appreciated is that during these years there were a multitude of regional interpretations of modernism – a phenomenon that must be weighed against the increasing loss of cultural dominance on the part of the Northeast. One of the first books to chronicle modern architecture in the United States – James Ford and Katherine Morrow Ford's *The Modern House in America* (1940) – broke the examples down by states. This was done not for organizational reasons but because of the various regional interpretations of modernism.[124] Katherine Morrow Ford made this point clear in a follow-up article one year later, "Modern Is Regional," in which she distinguishes regional styles for New England, Pennsylvania, Florida, the Great Lakes, Arizona, the Northwest, and California.[125] Pennsylvanian modernism, for example, is affected by its tradition of barns and its abundance of stone, Northwest modernism by its timberlands, and Californian modernism by the state's "amazing variety in topography and climate."[126] In the book, incidentally, California walks away with the prize for the most modern residential buildings, even thought it was written by authors in Lincoln, Massachusetts, under the watchful eyes of Gropius and Giedion.

Such widely acknowledged regionalism calls into question the importance of the so-called International Style. The influence of the New York exhibition and its underlying institutional campaign indeed lingered, but it had an effect mainly within its own geographic area. As one of several competing forces within American practice, the Harvard–MoMA ideological axis helped to refine the new concept of modernity, but it did not in any way direct the larger process. And departure from its credo by no means signified a regression, nationalist or otherwise, as has sometimes been argued. There arose in the late 1940s a new American conception of one's work and habitat born of the Depression, the war, and distinctly American cultural values, and it was

a complex image. If a few European architects restarting their careers in a new country did not at first understand or appreciate these differences, they soon enough had to adapt to them.

Such a process of assimilation and adaptation can even be seen in the career of Gropius in New England.[127] Soon after arriving at Harvard, he began what was at first a relatively modest practice, which he initially (until 1941) formed in partnership with Marcel Breuer. One early venture was Gropius's own house in Lincoln, Massachusetts, not far from Walden Pond – a wood-framed rectangular prism with vertical redwood siding painted white and partially carved out with a terrace. A screened dining porch extended into the garden. Giedion, a few years later, deemed the work, with its "big front porch," to be a prime example of the "new regionalism" – in contrast to the sameness of the "International Style."[128] If this was overstating the case somewhat, it demonstrates Gropius's and Giedion's awareness that the climate and vegetation of New England were quite different from those of Europe.

Gropius's venture into the prefabricated housing market in the 1940s also reveals evidence of a learning curve. Gropius and Breuer had a falling out in 1941, and the latter eventually left Harvard to devote himself exclusively to his practice. Gropius next formed an association with Konrad Wachsmann (1901–80), a Jewish refugee and former student of Tessenow and Poelzig. Wachsmann had undergone some harrowing years in a French detention camp before being rescued by the combined efforts of Gropius and Albert Einstein.[129] Like Gropius, Wachsmann had long been interested in prefabricated housing, beginning with his work for a German manufacturing firm in 1926. In fact, Wachsmann met Einstein in 1929 when he designed his house in Potsdam utilizing the packaged components of this firm. Gropius's interest in industrially produced housing went back even further – to 1910. In addition to his well-known project at Törten-Dessau in the late 1920s, he also advised a German firm on the idea of a "copper house" in the early 1930s.

The venture at first appeared promising. Gropius's contribution was largely organizational. Wachsmann modified the wood-panel system he had designed in France by adapting it to a forty-inch module and revising his earlier Y-shaped connector hooks with plates built into the edges of the four-way panels. When the two men patented the system in 1942 as a "Packaged House," their timing seemed to be good, as prefabricated housing was an essential part of the American war effort and congressional money had been appropriated for its expansion. But even though Wachsmann secured funding and the General Panel Corporation was formed in anticipation of production, the venture never moved forward. The war window was missed (by Gropius and Wachsmann but not by competing firms), and then the revised version of 1944, aimed at the postwar domestic housing market, failed to go into production, even with fresh corporate support and a new plant in California. Part of the explanation for their failure was Wachsmann's ever expanding range of interests, part was the way the corporation came to be structured, and part was the packaging of the components as components rather than as "houses," which precluded FHA-approval and mortgage financing. Giedion's attribution of the corporation's bankruptcy to the "present attitude of the house purchaser" betrays his unfamiliarity with the workings and realities of the business and housing worlds.[130] There was no reason why a modular, prefabricated timber system of this type could not have been successful. Levitt's contemporary approach to fast-track housing construction – which was to provide roads, utilities, and the physical communities themselves – certainly did find broad success and emulation.

Gropius too had many friends and allies. In the 1940s he had become a U.S. citizen, testified before Congress, been a vocal advocate of planning at all levels, and served as an advisor to several corporations, including a stint with General Lucius Clay on the reconstruction of Germany. His first published work in the United States, *Rebuilding Our Communities* (1945), is a summary statement of his housing and planning ideas. Based on a lecture given in Chicago, the book speaks forcefully to what he sees as the main aspects of the housing problem: piecemeal or nonexistent government planning, excessive urban density, and urban blight. Gropius pleads for reforms in marketing, financing, and taxation and in building technologies and makes a case for his Packaged House system, "wife-saving" devices, and "hobby" rooms in houses. At a larger scale, he proposes to relocate the poor into rural neighborhood communities that offer farm-related jobs, and to rebuild cities systematically at a lower density, with more parks, and with a nucleus formed by community centers. He justifies these proposals by emphasizing their health benefits. Citing the work of two British biologists, he argues that the key to one's personal health is the broader social health, or the cultivation of the "social soil," achievable through the intervention of community centers. These new neighborhood centers, with facilities for swimming and gymnastics, cafeterias, nurseries, and play areas, thus become the linchpin in his plan for the revitalization of democratic society.[131]

In 1952 Gropius published *Architecture and Design in the Age of Science* and his better known *Scope of Total Architecture*. The first, actually a nine-page pamphlet, succinctly summarizes his argument for teamwork. Society in modern times, with its "gallup-poll mentality" and "mechanistic conception," is out of balance and harmony, with the sciences predominating over the arts and "re-search" taking precedence over the creativity of the "search." A state of balance can only be restored, he argues, by bringing the architect and designer back into the industrial process alongside the scientist, engineer, market analyst, and salesperson: "The old conception of the prima donna architect, catering to wealthy clients and acting as their gentleman trustee, finds only a limited application nowadays. Unless the architect can make himself into an indispensable part of tomorrow's production process itself, his influence will dwindle."[132]

The Scope of Total Architecture is largely a collection of essays and articles published earlier, the more recent of which concern the familiar themes of teamwork, large-scale planning, the need to build whole communities, and architectural education. The last theme, laid out in his "Blueprint of an Architect's Education," stresses the social and psychological components of design, above all "creativity" as a program that "*will lead our potential architects from observation to discovery to invention and finally to an intuitive shaping of our contemporary scene.*"[133] This statement could stand as a rejoinder to the frequent criticisms that have been made of his rational and "passionless" approach to design, deemed by some to be his educational legacy at Harvard.[134]

However justified or unjustified this last criticism may be, Gropius's influence on the American architectural profession around midcentury is indisputable. In 1945 he looked favorably upon a suggestion by John Harkness to launch a cooperative office, The Architects Collaborative (TAC), which within a few years came to epitomize the ideas of team design and planning.[135] Prominent among the firm's early ventures was the design of the Harvard University Graduate Center (1948–9).

And then there is the legacy of the Harvard graduates schooled under his tenure, students who in the 1940s included Edward L. Barnes, John Johansen, Philip Johnson, I. M. Pei, Henry N. Cobb, Paul Rudolph, and Victor Lundy. All would enjoy success by the 1960s. Johnson had been accepted into the architectural program in 1940 after some very dark years, during which time (beginning in 1934) he had resigned his position at MoMA to embrace the politics of Adolf Hitler. This turn toward Nazism evolved into political infatuations in the mid-1930s with a couple of American populists (Huey Long and the Rev. Charles E. Coughlin) and even into a short-lived attempt to start an American political party modeled on the National Socialists. By the end of the decade, however, Johnson had drifted back to the German cause and became an apologist for Hitler and his policies.[136] The German Propaganda Ministry, for instance, invited Johnson in 1939 to follow (in his Lincoln Zephyr) their panzer divisions into Poland. Johnson's political activities would come back to haunt him during the war years when they were publicly revealed, and while attending Harvard he seems to have come very close to being charged with sedition. Johnson also served as a private in the U.S. Army in 1943–4, before returning to New York City in 1945 to open an office with Landis Gores. MoMA immediately welcomed him back into the fold, despite the fact that Barr had been "dismissed" in 1943 for a combination of personal problems, administrative shortcomings, and lack of scholarly output. The former director, however, had managed to keep an office in the library of the museum and soon worked his way back into power and influence.[137] Johnson's first show was a 1947 exhibition devoted to the work of Mies van der Rohe, who was then exerting a great influence on Johnson's practice and ideas.[138]

Johnson, with his connections to MoMA and the Rockefellers, received the commission for the annex (1949–50) to the recent museum building of Philip Goodwin and Edward Durell Stone. But the project that made his professional name was the "Glass House" in New Canaan (1948–9).[139] In the article that he wrote for the *Architectural Review* in 1950, Johnson, somewhat glibly, traced its intellectual roots to Mies and the Farnsworth House, Ledoux, Schinkel, Le Corbusier, van Doesburg, Malevich, and the Acropolis and also, somewhat surrealistically, to a "burnt wooden village I saw once where nothing was left but foundations and chimneys of brick."[140] And while the suggestion of such an image (acquired in Poland?) was undoubtedly intensely personal (in one interpretation, an act of political atonement), it is far too easy to inflate the pavilion's architectural importance.[141] Much of Johnson's practice in his early years as an architect was eclectic and faddish and lacked a direction.

Architectural practice in New York in the early 1950s is better represented by the work of Gordon Bunshaft (1909–90) of the office of Skidmore, Owens & Merrill. Bunshaft had been trained at M.I.T. in the 1930s, and after traveling to Europe, he was hired into the office of Skidmore and Merrill in 1937, where he became the firm's New York designer.[142] Several of his early projects – such as the Venezuelan Pavilion for the New York World's Fair (1939) and the Hostess House, Great Lakes Naval Training Center, Illinois (1942) – display the young firm's commitment to modernity. After a lengthy period in the army, Bunshaft in 1949 was named to be one of the firm's (now Skidmore, Owens & Merrill) seven partners, who collectively guided mostly corporate projects through design and construction, with consistently high results. The Lever House (1949–52) on Park Avenue is Bunshaft's first masterpiece. It stands out against such nearby rivals as the United Nations Building (1947–50) by virtue of its overall conception and detailing: a thin slab of glazed, open offices seemingly hovering above the horizontal box forming the third-story roof terrace. The skin of green glass with stainless steel columns and aluminum mullions set an aesthetic standard that was much emulated in the 1950s.

Beyond New York and New England, a score of vital regional centers of architectural thought either sprang up or matured across the country. The Detroit area, for instance, became defined in the early 1950s by the Cranbrook Academy of Art, the rich architectural legacy of Eliel Saarinen and his son Eero (1910–61). This campus of schools and advanced workshops in the Detroit suburb of Bloomfield Hills began with the commission Eliel received in 1924 from the publisher George Booth.[143] Since the turn of the century Booth had been active in the arts and crafts movement, and in the mid-1920s he decided to channel his wealth into a campus of schools: an elementary school, higher schools for boys and girls, an academy of art, an institute of science, and the Cranbrook Museum and Library. The academy was the heart of the conception, and Booth wanted it to become a center for accomplished artists in residence, similar to the American Academy in Rome. Relatively quickly the plan took shape, and the four master studios and residences (for the teaching of architecture, painting, sculpture, and design) were completed by 1932, the year in which Eliel became president of the academy. The Depression intervened, however, and it was not until the late 1930s that the program was up and running. Prominent architects and designers attracted to the school during these years included Edmund N. Bacon, Florence Schust Knoll, Benjamin Baldwin, Charles Eames, Harry Weese, Ralph Rapson, and David Runnels. Eero Saarinen was in charge of the architecture program between 1939 and 1941.

Eliel's philosophy had also changed over the years toward industrial production and away from the arts and crafts tradition.[144] He was drawn to urban issues, as seen in the first of the two books he wrote in the 1940s, *The City: Its Growth, Its Decay, Its Future* (1943). *The City* contains a lucid discussion of the planning problems well evident in American cities at this time. Saarinen's approach is somewhat Sittesque, and his ideal in planning is to achieve what he calls an "organic order," for which he proposes the notion of "organic decentralization."[145] It is the "surgical" removal of deteriorated, misplaced, or blighted areas of the city and the dispersal of their residents into decentralized zones, allowing both the rehabilitation of the affected areas and employment for the displaced. Such a process, he argues, should take place over a half-century or more and involve the displaced residents receiving municipal-owned land in outlying areas. In the revitalized central areas, gasoline stations, signs, billboards, and other forms of exaggerated advertisement are to be banned; transportation is to be rationalized along European lines. Helsinki is one of his preferred models.

In SEARCH FOR FORM: A Fundamental Approach to Art (1948), Saarinen brings the same notion of "organic order" to art, now manifesting itself as the expressiveness and correlation of form. This is not a textbook with prescribed rules but a philosophical discussion of such ideas as good will, accord, truth, sincerity, creative vitality, and youthfulness of spirit. Artistic education is not something that can be put into a system but is simply the byproduct of good individuals, good human relations, and a good social order. Architecture begins with the room – "the most indispensable form-problem in civilized human life" – whose spiritual power is displayed in its proportions, its color, and the smallest details of its furnishings.[146] At the opposite level, architecture extends itself to the organic grouping of buildings and the higher organism of the city. Art, for Saarinen, is quintessentially the human act of politeness, civility, and accommodation.

It is from this traditionally minded yet progressive background that the work of the younger Saarinen took its own distinctive direction.[147] Eero first studied sculpture at the Grande Chaumière in Paris and returned to the United States to take his architecture degree at Yale in 1934, completing a five-year program in three years. After traveling in Europe for two years and also working in Finland, he returned to Bloomfield Hills in the summer of 1936 to teach and work for his father. It was during these years that he had his fruitful collaborations with Eames, Rapson, Weese, and others. In partnership with his father, he was also involved in a number of increasingly important commissions, including an influential elementary school and the competition-winning design for the Smithsonian Gallery of Art in Washington, D.C. (1939–41, unbuilt). This phase of

Eero's life ended with the war, during which he worked in the Office of Strategic Service (oss) in Washington D.C.

At its conclusion, Saarinen's reputation rapidly advanced. In 1948 he won the competition for the redesign of the Saint Louis riverfront with his catenary-arch monument and park. In that year he began the redesign work on the prestigious commission for the General Motors Technical Center (1945–55), which would showcase his considerable talent (Fig. 95). Situated in the Detroit suburb of Warren, the 320-acre design and research campus originally consisted of seven primary complexes of buildings (including the domed auditorium and central restaurant) grouped around a twenty-two-acre pool with water jets, a stainless steel water tower, Calder fountains, and a sculpture by Antoine Pevsner. The work is often called Meisian for its similarities to the campus of IIT, but closer inspection shows the derivation to be less than might first appear, and Saarinen himself preferred to attribute its industrial inspiration to the factory buildings of Albert Kahn. In plan, composition, and overall effect, the design is in fact much superior to the Chicago campus, but its strongest point (due in part certainly to GM's deeper pockets) is its exquisite detailing, which helps make it one of the most intelligently and flawlessly conceived architectural creations of the century. The end walls of the five research divisions are composed of colored glazed brick in brilliant tones of blue, red, yellow, orange, tangerine, gray, and black. The neutral infill of glass and solids pioneers such new technologies as the neoprene gasket and porcelain paneling; inside are flexible luminous ceiling panels with integrated mechanical systems. The sculptural interior furnishings are entirely original and his own design, worked out in collaboration with Knoll International, with which he had been involved since 1943. He followed this commission with such well-known designs as the M.I.T. Auditorium and Chapel, (1950–5), the TWA Terminal (1956–62), and Dulles International Airport (1958–62). If his view on architecture can be encapsulated, it is in the goal "To shelter and enhance man's life on earth and to fulfill his belief in the nobility of his existence."[148] His offices in Michigan and Connecticut also trained a bevy of exceptional designers, among them Gunner Birkerts, John Dinkeloo, Kevin Roche, Cesar Pelli, and Robert Venturi.

Vying with the Cranbrook in the Midwest was the city of Chicago, whose reputation in large part centered on the work of Mies van der Rohe.[149] The German refugee arrived there in 1938 to head the architecture program at the Armour Institute of Technology. In the following year he had received his first commission: the new campus for

95. Eliel and Eero Saarinen, Dynamometer Building, General Motors Technical Center, Warren, Michigan, 1945–55. From *Architectural Forum*, vol. 95 (November 1951).

this school, shortly to be renamed the Illinois Institute of Technology. The site consisted of 110 acres of land cleared for rehabilitation on the south side of Chicago. Mies, after several preliminary designs (done in collaboration with Ludwig Hilbersheimer), imposed a twenty-four-foot grid on the site and staggered the placement of nineteen rectangular buildings. The first of the new buildings, the Minerals and

Metals Research Building (1941–3), drew upon the factory aesthetic and became the proving ground for his characteristic tectonic language of I-beams and H-columns (Fig. 96). Kenneth Frampton has described Mies's approach as a transition from "building as volume" to the tectonics of the frame and the interfacing membrane, with the points of contact always articulated.[150] Such an approach had enormous

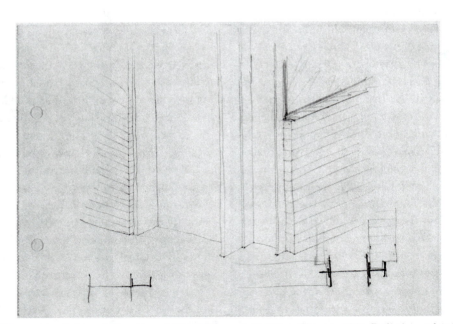

96. Mies van der Rohe, IIT Minerals and Metals Research Building, Chicago, 1941. Preliminary sketch of a building corner. Collection Centre Canadien d'Architecture/Canadian Centre for Architecture, Montréal.

appeal for architects, for it demonstrated how conventional rolled forms could be assembled in an imaginative way and speak a tectonic language of their own.

It was a lesson in detailing that Mies subsequently refined in the Farnsworth House (1945–51), the two apartment towers on Lake Shore Drive in Chicago (1949–51), and the Seagram Building in New York (1954–8). In the case of the two Chicago towers, he added projecting I-beams to the nearly continuous skin both to stiffen the mullions and to create a shadow line, almost achieving the desired "absence of architecture" that he was quoted in 1947 as seeking.[151] At the same time the Semperian "four elements" of the Farnsworth House reveal a purely aesthetic architectural conception with serious design limitations.[152] In his quest for conceptual purity, Mies denied the pavilion any cooling ducts or insect screens, making this rural retreat essentially uninhabitable in the summer and winter. In short, a rigorous logical consistency was attained at the expense of the comfort of the client and user, who in this case eventually litigated the matter. Most critics, however, were more forgiving in their assessment of this primal solution. Peter Blake, the German-British-American editor of *Architectural Forum*, lauded the Farnsworth House as "a clear and somewhat abstract expression of an architectural idea – the ultimate in skin-and-bones architecture, the ultimate in 'less is more,' the ultimate in objectivity and universality."[153] One of the few critics to take issue with Mies's approach was Mumford, who in 1943 characterized this architect's work as a descent into "the Ice Queen's palace of sterile formalism."[154]

Even Mumford, however, could not withhold praise for the Seagram Building, one of the most significant American buildings of the decade.[155] Plans for a new headquarters for Joseph E. Seagram and Sons were underway in 1954 when Samuel Bronfman's daughter, Phyllis Lambert, intervened from Paris. Her father reconsidered, and Lambert began a systematic search for an architect that included getting advice from Nikolaus Pevsner (in London), Peter Blake, and Lewis Mumford, and arranging face-to-face meetings with such architects as Marcel Breuer, Walter Gropius, Louis Kahn, George Howe, John Johansen, Minoru Yamasaki, and Eero Saarinen. The joint commission was given to Mies and Philip Johnson in October, with Lambert overseeing the process as director of planning.[156] The sixty-eight-year-old Mies moved to New York and threw himself wholeheartedly into the design work, with Johnson making his contribution by designing the restaurant, lighting, graphics, and detailing of the public spaces. The result is indisputably a masterpiece.

Mies was not the only Bauhaus refugee to leave a significant mark on Chicago. László Moholy-Nagy came to the city in 1937 – by way of Holland and England – at the invitation of the Association of the Arts and Industry. Based on the recommendation of Gropius, he had been hired to open the New Bauhaus, American School of Design.[157] The venture struggled mightily at first and in 1939 was restructured as the School of Design. It was, however, only when the program received accreditation as a college in 1944 (now renamed the Institute of Design) that it began to thrive. One of the pedagogical foundations of the program was the basic course of design that Moholy-Nagy had professed in his Bauhaus book *Von Material zu Architektur* (1929), translated into English in 1930 as *The New Vision*.[158] Moholy-Nagy defined the institute's main objective as follows:

to produce an adequate rhythm between the biological capacities of the student and the contemporary scene. The goal is no longer to recreate the classical craftsman, artist and artisan, with the aim of fitting him into the industrial age. By now technology has become as much a part of life as metabolism. The task therefore is to educate the contemporary man as an *integrator*, the new *designer* able to re-evaluate human needs warped by machine civilization.[159]

The basic course included workshop training with machines; materials; shapes, and surfaces; spatial and motion studies, using such elements as life drawing; photography, group poetry; and a smattering of psychology, philosophy, sociology, mathematics, and physics.

What was also exceptional about the institute in the first decade of its existence was the faculty – many members of which worked for little or no pay. One of the founding members was the linguist Charles Morris, who was developing a theory of semiotics that would later have a major effect on architectural theory. Another was the Hungarian artist Gyorgy Kepes (b. 1906), whose now classic book *Language of Vision* (1944) – with dual forewords by Giedion and S. I. Hayakawa – had been much influenced by Moholy-Nagy's artistic experiments as well as by Giedion. In it Kepes spoke of such things as utilizing a "**visual representation** of contemporary space-time events" and organizing them into "a contemporary **dynamic iconography**."[160] Between 1937 and 1943 he taught the course on drawing and color and the light workshop at the institute, before moving on to M.I.T.

The first head of the Department of Architecture at the institute was George Fred Keck (1895–1980).[161] This Wisconsin native had passed through the program at the University of Illinois at Champaign in the late teens and opened an office in Chicago in 1926. Within a few years he, in his designs, was drawing upon the main lines of European modernism, beginning with his design for the Miralago Ballroom and Shops, Cook County (1929). Even more exotic were two futuristic houses he designed in 1933 and 1934 with Leland Atwood for the Century of Progress exhibition. The first, the completely glazed "House of Tomorrow," was heavily influenced by Fuller's Octagon and Dymaxion houses, with its central service core, lightweight steel frame, and a garage at ground level for the owner's airplane.[162] His "Crystal House" of the following year was also remarkable as a fully glazed structure, as it was supported on the outside by a latticework of lightweight steel trusses.

In the fall of 1942 Keck was succeeded at the institute by Ralph Rapson (b. 1914).[163] The gifted Rapson had studied at the University of Michigan before his fellowship at Cranbrook in 1938. He joined Harry Weese, Charles Eames, Benjamin Baldwin, and David Runnells in that year and during his stay forged an increasingly close relationship with Eero Saarinen, with whom he worked on several prize-winning national competition entries. His first built projects date from 1939 and were entirely modern in character. He moved to Chicago in 1942 to collaborate with Robert Bruce Tague and to oversee the architecture curriculum at the institute, which he did until he too was lured to the faculty at M.I.T.

Although Moholy-Nagy died of leukemia in 1946, the institute remained a lively place even after its assimilation into the Illinois Institute of Technology in 1950. The school in its early years had operated virtually without a budget yet regularly attracted eminent visiting lecturers and critics. Other faculty members in the 1940s included Wachsmann and, for a brief period of time, Buckminster Fuller. The latter, following his work on the Dymaxion car in the early 1930s, had turned his attention to such inventions as the prefabricated Dymaxion bathroom (1936), galvanized steel emergency shelters for the British War Relief Organisation (1940), the prefabricated aluminum Wichita house (1944–6), and the Dymaxion world map, which he developed as part of the war effort to provide more accurate global information. His theories – still little understood – had also been promulgated in his *Nine Chains to the Moon: An Adventure Story of Thought*, which appeared in 1938. Beginning in 1946, with the creation of the Fuller Research Foundation in Forest Hills, New York, he turned his attention back to geometry and developed (around 1947) the first of his various geodesic structures.[164] Although much of this work was done at Black Mountain College in North Carolina (where Josef Albers had

relocated), Fuller devised and built his "Penthahexaedron" version of a dome at the Institute of Design in 1948.

Wachsmann came to the institute in 1949 while still involved with Gropius and the General Panel Corporation. The creation of the Department of Advanced Building Research (and a commission to design aircraft hangers for the United States Air Force) allowed him to continue his research on wide-span structural systems and space frames, an increasing interest of his since 1944. These systems, of course, opened up another wide field of architectural exploration.[165]

Still another prominent teacher to be connected with the institute during these years was Serge Chermayeff, who succeeded Moholy-Nagy as the institute's director in 1946.[166] After coming to the United States from England in 1940, he had done a few architectural jobs in California but had failed (because of the war) to find a teaching job at the University of Oregon or at Berkeley – despite strong support by Pietro Belluschi and William Wurster, respectively. At the end of 1941 he obtained the chairmanship of the Art Department at Brooklyn College. He also had several contacts with the Museum of Modern Art in 1943 and 1944, before being offered – through the intervention of Gropius – the directorship of the Institute of Design. There, until his departure in 1951, he introduced curricular reforms and brought architecture under the rubric of "environmental design."

In the 1940s several other regional centers of design and theory came into prominence in the American West. California – physically remote from Europe and less swayed by European developments than the East Coast – was notable for the high level of cross-fertilization that occurred there and for its melding of vernacular traditions with Asian and European influences. Wright was camped out (part of the year) in nearby Arizona, and Oregon was laying the basis for a regional modernism in the Northwest.

Certainly central to architecture in southern California was the work of Richard Neutra and Rudolf Schindler. Neutra had by now gained ascendency.[167] On the one hand, he had designed a series of well-publicized luxury houses in the 1930s and 1940s, such as the von Sternberg House, Northridge (1935), the Lewin House, Santa Monica (1938), the Kaufmann House, Palm Springs (1946), and the Tremaine House, Montecito (1948). On the other hand, he showed a strong commitment to social issues and technical innovation. Beginning with the design of his own house of 1932, which he called the "VDL Research House," he often experimented with low-cost, high-tech, prefabricated solutions. In the "all metal" Beard House, Altadena (1934), he employed radiant heating and prefabricated "self-cooling" cellular wall modules with air circulation – all for a cost of $5,000. In the case of the nearby Richter House in Pasadena (1936, built for the seismologist who devised the Richter scale), he designed it to be earthquake-proof – at a cost of $4,300. That same year he produced his "Plywood Model House" for a Los Angeles exhibition featuring inexpensive housing solutions. In the 1930s, he designed the "Diatom house" (which used building panels of diatomaceous and shell aggregate), the Steelcraft house, and low-cost homes for *Better Homes and Gardens* and *Ladies' Home Journal*. He also worked on migrant housing and in the early 1940s collaborated with David Williams and Roscoe Dewitt on Avion Village, Grand Prairie, Texas. The three architects designed a low-income community in which prefabricated units could be assembled in an hour.

Back in California, Neutra designed several wartime communities in the early 1940s, among them Hacienda Village, Pueblo del Rio, and Channel Heights in San Pedro, which provided housing for shipyard workers. One of his most concerted efforts during the war came out of his involvement with Rexford Tugwell, now the the governor of Puerto Rico, and the Committee on Design of Public Works. Taking into account the tropical climate of Puerto Rico, Neutra designed hundreds of open-air schools and health clinics, as well as five hospitals. These were incorporated into his first American book, *The Architecture of Social Concern in Regions of Mild Climate* (1948), which he wrote following a lecture tour of South America.[168]

Neutra was also very much concerned with the psychology and physiology of design, which led him in the 1940s to write *Survival through Design* (1954). The book is a single-minded exploration of the "pathology" of current design, that is, the pejorative health effects of visual and environmental pollution, sensory overload, and the little regard given human psychology in design. Drawing upon various recent experiments with the human brain, Neutra addresses the breadth of neurological responses to color, lighting, space, sound, and haptic sensations. His thesis is simple: "Acceptance of design must turn from a commercial into a physiological issue. Fitness for assimilation by our organic capacity becomes a guiding principle for judging design because such fitness aids the survival of the individual, the community, the race itself."[169] Neutra's book was in fact a harbinger of the interest in anthropology and psychology so prevalent in the 1960s.

Schindler, who had over the years grown increasingly estranged from Neutra, American functionalism, and the international style, continued his inventive and highly original practice in Los Angeles up until his death in 1953. He never succeeded in promoting himself in the way that Neutra did, and thus his output was smaller. By the end of the 1940s, however, both Neutra and Schindler were but a small part of a very lively and generally youthful architectural scene in Los Angeles.

The midwesterner Charles Eames (1907–78) was certainly representative of the younger class of talented Los Angeles architects.[170] He had attended Washington University in Saint Louis for a few years before going into practice at the start of the Great Depression. He worked for the WPA, and after a church he had designed came to the attention of Eliel Saarinen, he was offered a fellowship in 1938 to study at Cranbrook. In the following year he became an instructor in design at the intermediate school and – like Rapson – began collaborating with the younger Saarinen. The two men entered the Organic Design in Home Furnishings Competition held at the Museum of Modern Art in 1940–1 and won two first prizes for their line of chairs, storage units, sofas, and tables. Their molded plywood chairs, in particular, became the basis for the success they achieved individually in furniture design in the 1950s.

Eames moved to Los Angeles in 1941, shortly after marrying the artist Ray Kaiser, and the two shortly thereafter formed a circle with John Entenza (b. 1905) – effectively establishing a modernist bridge between Cranbrook and Los Angeles. Entenza had purchased the highly respected magazine *California Arts and Architecture* from Jere Johnson in 1939, and in an effort to expand the regional scope of the magazine, he dropped the first word in the title. It became a wide-ranging journal of the arts, encompassing music, literature, cinema, art, and above all architecture; it also regularly reviewed the work of Neutra, Ralph Soriano, William Wurster, Pietro Belluschi, and others. At the height of the war – in 1943 – Estenza and Charles Eames organized the competition Designs for Postwar Living, which echoed the widespread interest in prefabrication and industrial mass production during the war years.[171]

Out of this interest also emerged the famous Case Study Program, the goal of which Estenza announced in January 1945.[172] In the original conception, the magazine was to act as a client and select architects to prepare affordable but innovative designs that employed the latest in industrial applications; the houses would be built and opened to the public for educational purposes before being sold. The magazine thus hoped "not merely to preview, but to assist in giving some direction to the creative thinking on

97. Charles Eames and Eero Saarinen, House #8, 1945, Case Study Program. From *Arts and Architecture* (December 1945).

housing being done by good architects and good manufacturers whose joint objective is good housing."[173] The first architects commissioned were J. R. Davidson, Sumner Spaulding, Richard Neutra, Eero Saarinen, William Wilson Wurster, Charles Eames, and Ralph Rapson.

The idea quickly expanded, and over the next several years twenty-three houses were built out of thirty-four projected models. The most celebrated were #8 and #9, the two houses designed jointly by Charles Eames and Eero Saarinen. House #9 was built and occupied by Entenza himself, and house #8, built a few yards away on a canyon site in Pacific Palisades, became the home of Charles and Ray Eames (Fig. 97). Originally it was a "bridge" house – based on a 1934 sketch by Mies – placed perpendicular to the hill, but before construction Eames rotated it to be parallel with the ridgeline.[174] The double house and studio were built as light steel-frame structures with open joists and industrial sash (the frame was erected in a day and a half); all items except the furnishings and circular staircase were industrially produced and off-the-shelf. The success of the buildings seemed to assure Eames a promising architectural career, but within a few years he turned away from architecture to focus on furniture design for Hermann Miller.

The Case Study Program, with its national and even international publicity, helped shed light on a group of California modernists who came to prominence during this time. Several, such as Gregory Ain (b. 1908), Raphael Soriano (1907–88), and Harwell Hamilton Harris (1903–90), had moved through Neutra's office in the 1930s. Soriano, who had immigrated to California from Greece in 1924, perhaps remained closest to Neutra in style through the years, although by 1950 he had developed an interest in using steel in residential design. Ain, who had been featured in 1940 in the publication of James Ford and Katherine Morrow Ford, had spent several years with Neutra in the early 1930s but had a particularly bitter breakup with him in 1935 when he left to start his own practice. After the war, he worked on several housing projects with the landscape architect Garrett Eckbo and continued to pursue interest in low-cost housing.

Harris, who began his working relationship with Neutra in 1928, was the most independent of the three in his later development, and by the 1940s he had established himself as one of the leading architects in the country.[175] His association with Neutra went back to Neutra's Kings Road office and the design of the Lovell House, where he gained his first architectural exposure (he had been trained as a sculptor). Shortly after leaving Neutra, around 1933, he cultivated his interest in Wright by studying his work in California and soon produced a remarkable series of residential designs that lie somewhere between Wright, Japanese architecture (another early influence), Schindler (whose work he preferred to that of Neutra), and German modernism. His most lauded work of this period, the Weston Havens House in Berkeley (1940–1), is a masterpiece of redwood and projecting balconies, perched on a steep cliff and with a view of the bay. As a modern residential architect, Harris was arguably without peer in the United States in the 1930s.

With the advent of the war, Harris and his wife, Jean Murray Bangs, moved to New York City for an extended stay (1941–4) that would have important consequences for his theoretical development, for it was here that he became aware of the distinctly different West Coast and East Coast perceptions of modern architecture. On one front, he came into regular contact with many of the European émigrés, including Giedion, Sert, Gropius, and Breuer – all of whom he held in respect. At the same time, through the historical and literary interests of his wife, he was introduced to a growing and entertaining debate that was just unfolding, roused by forces who were resisting both the European agenda of the Museum of Modern Art and the faddishness of Bauhaus-inspired programs within academe.

A spirited discussion, for instance, was opened in the early 1940s by the irreverent British-American writer T. H. Robsjohn-Gibbings. He was a New York interior designer who had architectural interests and whom the *New York Sun* once called "the most literate designer extant."[176] In his first book, *Good-Bye, Mr. Chippendale* (1944), he poked fun at the furniture manufacturers of Grand Rapids as well as the millionaires of Palm Beach – "the last big production number of the Gilded Age" – for their stylish knockoffs and tasteless desire to turn their interiors into the "rubbish dumps of Europe."[177] In a controversial article published in *House Beautiful*, he encouraged Americans to cease worshipping the "myth" of European culture and appreciate better its own artistic and architectural legacy.[178] For architecture, this meant looking to the recent houses of California, Texas, and the Middle West, where the creative spirit of Wright and Sullivan was still very much alive.

Robsjohn-Gibbings's criticisms became far more pointed in his satirical book *Mona Lisa's Mustache* (1947), where in an aggressive yet learned tone he sets out to argue the premise "that the art we call modern art today was actually a revival of the systems used in primitive and ancient magic."[179] His thesis is not as eccentric as it might seem. Artistically, he is appreciative of the modern work of Renoir,

Monet, Degas, Cézanne, and Pissarro, but he is highly critical of the direction art takes in the twentieth century, spawned by the religious pretensions of the Pre-Raphaelites, the numinous (anti-Western) primitivism of Paul Gauguin, the antibourgeois mysticism of Apollinaire, and the political showmanship of Filippo Tommaso Marinetti. His point is simply that the artist – the self-proclaimed "Man of Genius" in Gauguin's case – has recently confused the production of art with theatrics, inspiration, esotericism, politics, literary ramblings, and other matters nonartistic, and indeed there is a troubling coincidence of these extra-artistic outpourings with the military catastrophes of the twentieth century. His current villains are the Bauhaus, Salvador Dali, and the Museum of Modern Art – the last being the place where all things "erotic" and "chic" from abroad find a seasonable showing.

Allied with Robsjohn-Gibbings in the debate of the 1940s was Elizabeth Gordon, the editor of *House Beautiful*, who throughout this decade and into the next enjoyed contrasting the "individualism" of American architects such as Wright with those self-anointed arbiters of taste who continually swoon at the latest European fashions. In the April 1953 issue of *House Beautiful*, Gordon lashed out at the "unlivability, stripped-down emptiness, lack of storage space and therefore lack of possessions" of many international style designs as well as "the frauds, the over-publicized phonies, the bullying tactics of the self-chosen elite who would dictate not only taste but a whole way of life."[180] In the next issue, her executive editor Joseph Barry, in an article entitled "Report on the American Battle between Good and Bad Modern Houses," publicized the controversy between Edith Farnsworth and Mies van der Rohe over her recently completed glass house: "poised in the middle of a small field like a fishbowl or, better, like an emptied aquarium on a steel stand." In Barry's view it was a particularly "fine example of the *bad* modern architecture to which we are opposed."[181]

Gordon sent the April issue of her magazine to all the major architectural journals in New York – "A person cannot be mad so long without finally exploding" – obviously relishing a response.[182] From Thomas H. Creighton, the editor of *Progressive Architecture*, she drew an open letter pleading for moderation. While acknowledging "many of the things you say need saying," he characterized her outburst as an appeal to "chauvinists and flag-wavers" and disagreed with her "personal definition" of comfort and beauty.[183] He of course did not address the central point of her assault – the uncritical acceptance of the "International Style" by the New

York media, which acted as power and fashion brokers. She based her argument on "The Beauty of Common Sense" and the regional nuances of climate, landscape, materials, and lifestyle.[184] The modern images of *House Beautiful* homes that Barry published over the years were an important update to the Fords' earlier book, once again exalting the regional differences between states such as Wisconsin, Arizona, California, Oregon, Oklahoma, Texas, Louisiana, and Florida.[185]

This same debate had in fact been rehearsed a few years earlier in a 1947 *New Yorker* "Sky Line" article written by Lewis Mumford on the "Bay Region Style." His argument was twofold. On the one hand "new winds," which "may hit even backward old New York," have shifted the accent of design from the machine aesthetic of the past to "living" in and of itself: a cruel blow to "those academic American modernists who imitated Le Corbusier and Mies van der Rohe and Gropius, as their fathers imitated the reigning lights of the Ecole des Beaux Arts."[186] On the other hand, this new "native and humane form of modernism" – inaugurated by the likes of John Galen Howard, Bernard Maybeck, and William Wurster – has shown the country an alternative with "a free yet unobtrusive expression of the terrain, the climate, and the way of life on the Coast."[187] Thus the Bay Region style, for Mumford, is a clear indication that American modernism is finally putting away the "quixotic purities" of its "modern" adolescence.

The column raised such an uproar in "backward old New York" that the Museum of Modern Art decided to hold a symposium on the matter in the following year, posing the question "What Is Happening to Modern Architecture?"[188] The event attracted a number of luminaries, including Gropius, Breuer, Chermayeff, Edgar Kaufmann Jr., Matthew Nowicki, Eero Saarinen, and Vincent Scully. Barr, Hitchcock, and Johnson were there to defend the International Style against Mumford's insinuations; the Englishman Gerhard Kallmann was called to the podium to argue for the side of the "New Empiricism," the ideological camp in which Barr placed the Bay Region style. Mumford was the last speaker before a lively question session.

The symposium of course solved nothing. Barr was the most defensive in insisting that the International Style was no "kind of rigid straight-jacket requiring architects to design cubistic, white stucco boxes on Lally columns, with flat roofs and glass walls."[189] He also, with a certain meanness, went on to refer to the "informal and ingratiating kind of wooden domestic architecture" as "the International Cottage Style" – likening it in fact to a "kind of

neue Gemütlichkeit."[190] Gropius emphasized his expansive notion of modernism of the 1920s. Kallmann defended the British movement of New Empiricism as "enrichment of our architectural idiom responding to "psychological requirements."[191] And Mumford saw the Bay Region style as "the healthy state that we should have in every part of the world. To me, that is a sample of internationalism, not a sample of localism and limited effort."[192]

The event nevertheless had at least a few reverberations in the Northeast. Shortly thereafter Joseph Hudnut chose to weigh in on the issue with his essay "The Post-Modern House" (1949).[193] Here he railed against the assembly-line, factory-built houses of Gropius and others and insisted on a more balanced melding of emotional values with technology.

The most important result of this debate, however, was the effect it had on Harris, who after returning to California remained close to the circle of Robsjohn-Gibbings and Gordon.[194] In the late 1940s Harris and Bangs began to reexamine the California architectural tradition of Bernard Maybeck, Greene & Greene, Willis Polk, Myron Hunt, and Irving Gill, and it is from this reassessment that Harris in the early 1950s developed his notion of a "Regionalism of Liberation," in contrast to a "Regionalism of Restriction." In the former, architects in each region develop a creative response to that region's influences as well as a critical response to what may be gleaned from the broader body of architectural thought:

A region may develop ideas. A region may accept ideas. Imagination and intelligence are necessary for both. In California in the late Twenties and Thirties modern European ideas met a still developing regionalism. In New England, on the other hand, European Modernism met a rigid and restrictive regionalism that at first resisted and then surrendered. New England accepted European Modernism whole because its own regionalism had been reduced to a collection of restrictions.[195]

A restrictive regionalism lives in the past and inhibits innovation; a free regionalism is a studied "manifestation of a region that is **especially in tune with the emerging thought of the time.** We call such a manifestation 'regional' only because it has not yet emerged **elsewhere.** It is the genius of this region to be more than ordinarily aware and more than ordinarily free. Its virtue is that its manifestation has **significance for the world outside itself.**"[196]

Gordon, Mumford, and Harris had together poked the soft underbelly of international modernism, at least as it was sanctioned at the Museum of Modern Art, but they also gave greater visibility to an already strong regional movement. In northern California, for instance, there was the work of William Wilson Wurster (1895–1972) and Joseph Esherick (b. 1914). Wurster had studied architecture at the University of California at Berkeley in the 1910s and had developed a highly refined modern sensibility in the late 1920s.[197] He espoused honest, simple, and clean expression, whether working with California native woods, corrugated steel, or oversized concrete block. In 1940 Wurster married Catherine Bauer, and between 1944 and 1950 he served as dean at M.I.T., where he was able to renew his earlier friendship with Aalto. His partnership with Theodore Bernardi and Don Emmons in 1945 initiated the second phase of his design career, noted for its refined elegance. Wurster returned to California in 1950 to take over the departmental chair of architecture at Berkeley, where in 1959 he became the first dean of the school's new College of Environmental Design.

Joseph Esherick was another architect who went west in the postwar years. A Philadelphia native, Esherick had been trained at the University of Pennsylvania in the 1930s, was close to the circle of Kahn and Howe, and, after relocating to the West Coast, put together a mostly residential practice in the Bay Area, producing designs noted for their informality and lack of attention to "aesthetics." Notwithstanding, he was a highly thoughtful architect in his approach to practice: an early advocate of placing mathematical models and computer systems in the service of design; an advocate of the social, psychological, economic, and political dimensions of design work; and an antiformalist. For Esherick, form in a Kahnian sense ("what things are and what they do") was central to his approach.[198]

Farther north, in Oregon, another state emerging as a regional center in the 1940s, there was the work of the Italian-American architect Pietro Belluschi (1899–1994), who had first come to the United States in 1923.[199] His Sutor House, Portland (1937–8), was cited by the Fords in 1940 as indicative of a developing Northwest regional style, and his remarkable Equitable Savings & Loan Association Building, Portland (1943–8), has the distinction of being the first sealed, glazed tower (aluminum and green glass) in the United States – preceding both the United Nations Building and the Lever House in New York. His work remained little known outside of the West, however, until he succeeded Wurster as dean at M.I.T. in 1951.

Florida and Texas were two other architecturally important states in the 1940s and 1950s. Elizabeth Gordon was struck in particular by the tropical lushness of southern Florida and the possibility of opening up entire walls of houses to gardens and water, and on several occasions she published the work of Alfred Browning Parker. The character of Miami also became defined in the 1950s through the colorful creations of Morris Lapidus (b. 1902).[200] Though armed with an architecture degree from Columbia obtained in the late 1920s, Lapidus for many years had a successful career in retail design in New York City before making a transition back into architecture in the early 1950s with the design for the Fontainebleu Hotel, Miami Beach (1952–4). His Americana Hotel in Bal Harbour, Florida (1955), deserves a place in architectural lore – if only because its tropical gaiety incited Sirs Nikolaus Pevsner and Basil Spence (at an American Institute of Architects convention) into a fit of rudeness toward the architect, who happened to be present to hear their condemnation of the building.[201] Lapidus is a hard architect to assess within his time. With his sweeping and curving forms, garish use of color (less obviously garish in the context of southern light), and mastery of sceneographic effects, his work is much closer to postmodern sensibilities than to the international modernism of the 1950s, yet he very successfully captured the recreational instincts of his era. Somewhat fittingly, he entitled his autobiography *An Architecture of Joy* (1979).[202]

Texas also had a strong regional tradition. In the 1920s and 1930s it followed the art deco trends of the East, but in the late 1930s and the 1940s it spawned a varied modern tradition, exemplified by the work of Karl Kamrath in Houston; David R. Williams, Howard R. Meyer, Luther Sadler, and Walter C. Sharpe in Dallas; and Chester Nagel in Austin.[203] In the 1930s Robert H. H. Hugman began work on the famed Paseo del Rio waterway in San Antonio. In 1951 Hamilton Harwell Harris was persuaded to leave California and take charge of the architectural program at the University of Texas at Austin. Through some luck, he soon put together a faculty that would become known as the "Texas Rangers."[204] The Swiss Berhard Hoesli (1923–84) was hired at the same time as Harris, and it was he whom Harris charged in 1953 with revamping the design curriculum. Joining the school as new faculty members in the 1950s were Colin Rowe (b. 1920), John Hejduk, Robert Slutzky (b. 1929), Lee Hirsche, John Shaw, Lee Hodgden, and Werner Seligmann, who collectively reorganized the studios and shifted the program away from the functionalist and social orientation of the schools in the East and toward a formalism that stressed visual devices and reassessed the origins of modernism. It was a change in curriculum that paid off handsomely, primarily because of the enthusiasm of the faculty. Hoesli, for instance, had worked for Le Corbusier and studied painting in the studio of Fernand Léger; he would later become one of Europe's leading educators of design at the Swiss Federal Institute of Technology in Zurich. Rowe, who was a classmate of James Sterling at Liverpool University, had also just studied with Rudolf Wittkower at the Warburg Institute in London. Hejduk would later become one of the "New York Five," while the painter Slutzky had been a student of Josef Albers at Yale and had a specialty in Gestalt psychology. Rowe and Slutzky's two essays on "Transparency," which in the mid-1960s would have a dramatic effect on American theory, were written in 1955–6.

Still another innovative university program that prospered in the early 1950s was that at North Carolina State University in Raleigh. The initial force behind the curricular reforms here was Dean Henry Kamphoefner, but the initiative was quickly taken up by the Polish architect Matthew Nowicki (1910–50), who around the time of his tragic death was just emerging as a highly influential voice on the American scene.[205] He had graduated from the Warsaw Polytechnic in 1936 and briefly enjoyed success in Warsaw before the Nazi invasion. As a lieutenant in the Polish army reserve, he was actually training with an antiaircraft battery on the outskirts of the city in September 1939 when hundreds of German bombers flew overhead to initiate the war – the same bombers that had evoked the enthusiasm of Philip Johnson.[206] Nowicki joined the Polish underground, and after surviving years of considerable dangers, he was rewarded in 1945 with the post of chief city planner for Warsaw. He was visiting the United States as the Polish delegate to the United Nations planning commission in 1947 when the polish Communists seized control of the government and forced him into exile.

Nowicki's proposed curriculum at North Carolina State University was different in one important respect from those of most other programs. Not only did it stress the unity of architecture with city planning and landscape design and include the core components of design, structures, and drawing, but it added a fourth grouping of courses under the heading "Humanities and History." Further, the five courses in this group, which culminated with "Human Behavior and Urban Sociology" and "Philosophy of Design," offered an intensive introduction to architectural history, which elsewhere had nearly disappeared from architecture programs by 1950.[207]

The reasoning behind this strong humanistic program was explained in two articles by Nowicki, one published in

1949 and the other posthumously in 1951. The earlier article, almost certainly influenced by the recent symposium at MoMA that Nowicki had attended, is a mild critique of Hitchcock and Johnson's international style for its voguish and overregulated formalism and its scant attention to human "psychological relations to space."[208] In the later essay, "Origins and Trends in Modern Architecture," Nowicki constructs a more sustained attack on the International Style, which he now acknowledges as having become an accepted "style" in which "form follows *Form* and not *function*."[209] He also criticizes its idealization and dematerialization of form and its "functional exactitude," whereby architecture is ultimately reduced to a machine-inspired "decoration of function."[210] Against this approach, he proposes a functionalism of "flexibility" that gives "priority to the psychological rather than to the physical function of humans."[211] If functional exactitude leads to a decoration of function, a humanistic and flexible functionalism – now picking up a thread of structural development from the nineteenth century – exalts a "decoration of structure" as well as attends to the "minute exigencies of life."[212]

Nowicki's one completed building in Raleigh, the double-parabolic tensile-structured arena for the North Carolina State Fair, designed with William Henley Deitrick, represents the structuralist side of his humanism, but it is misleading if it suggests a preoccupation with structure. It was Nowicki's other grand architectural project of 1950 – the planning and design of the new capital of Chandigarh, India (for the American firm of Mayer & Whittlesey) – that rather reveals the focus of his energies as a designer.

Nowicki in an interesting way completes a circle that returns us to his principal champion, Mumford. In the early 1950s Mumford was continuing to express his earlier reservations regarding the international style, and he embraced Nowicki, as he did Wurster earlier, as the way to advance his own humanist and regionalist critique of the contemporary situation. Mumford's modernism takes a slightly different turn in a series of lectures he gave at Columbia in 1951, which he published as *Art and Techniques* (1952). In his lecture "Symbol and Function" he echoes Nowicki's criticism of modernism in attacking its self-imposed impoverishment of expression and neglect of "biological needs, social commitments, and personal values."[213] At one point – presaging postmodern critiques – he even condemns Adolf Loos and Gropius for having "by now succeeded in eliminating from the practice of architecture almost every historic or archaic mode of symbolism."[214] Mumford once again exalts Wright's organic metaphor as an antidote, but he now seems even more impressed with the philosophy of Nowicki, who in Mumford's view was better able "to effect a fuller reconciliation of the organic and the mechanical, the regional and the universal, the abstract-rational and the personal."[215] This last comment neatly packages almost all of the issues raised in the debate in the preceding decade.

Mumford's other book from the 1950s, *From the Ground Up* (1956), is a collection of his "Sky Line" columns in the *New Yorker* from 1949 to 1955, and here one finds his views ever hardening on behalf of his liberal causes. In several articles written against the powerful Robert Moses, the commissioner of parks and coordinator of the Office of City Construction, Mumford opposed his policies of urban renewal, especially the Stuyvesant Town redevelopment project, which he portrayed not just as an "unrelieved nightmare" but as "the architecture of the Police State, embodying all the vices of regimentation one associates with state control at its unimaginative worst."[216] In another series of articles he was critical of the design of the United Nations Building in New York (1947–50). Mumford faulted its design on every level, from its small site and lack of symbolic hierarchy to its nonfunctionality. He opposed the physical dominance of the Secretariat slab over the General Assembly Building and Conference building. And as for the "cellophane" wrapping of the first glass curtain-wall high-rise tower in the city, he condemned the tower's east-west orientation, which indeed did create several mechanical problems: "Apparently, though, the Board of Design Consultants were hypnotized by Le Corbusier, and Le Corbusier has long been hypnotized by the notion that the skyscraper is a symbol of the modern art. But the fact is that both the skyscraper and Le Corbusier are outmoded."[217]

Mumford's views on planning, however, were coming under critical scrutiny at this time. The new boom in suburban development was creating a number of allied problems not addressed by conventional planning models, and among those who were reassessing the suitability of European cities as examplars for American planning was Victor Gruen (1903–80), an Austrian who had fled his homeland when the Nazis came to power in 1938. He had been trained at the Vienna Academy of Fine Arts in the early 1920s under Peter Behrens. In the late 1940s he moved to Los Angeles and formed Victor Gruen Associates, which specialized in urban and suburban planning. In response to suburban sprawl and the "miracle mile" condition of strip malls, he proposed to organize and plan these amenities into regional shopping and office centers (crystallization points) at the interface of urban and suburban areas. The shopping mall was a bold idea that he first sold to J. L. Hudson in Detroit, and it was finally realized in 1954 at Northland Center. Here continuous rows of shops, connected with arcades, were grouped around gardens and the Hudson Department Store. Two years later Gruen modified his concept in designing the first enclosed shopping mall in Southdale, Minnesota, outside of Minneapolis. Now the objective became the creation of a festive or café atmosphere with multistory interiors, sculptures, fountains, gardens, and such cultural amenities as symphony concerts and play areas for children. Gruen in his writings always stressed the desire to provide safe, vibrant, and beautiful areas for the pedestrian and venues for social, cultural, civic, and recreational activities for the public at large.[218]

In his redevelopment plan for Fort Worth, Texas (1956), he proposed turning the entire downtown area into a landscaped pedestrian zone by limiting vehicular access to a series of large parking garages along the perimeter, with a walking time of four minutes or less to the city center.[219] Through careful attention to details, he argued, the pedestrian streets could form a colorful and active scene containing exhibits, sculptures, fountains, gardens, and so on.

By contrast Edmund N. Bacon (b. 1910), who became executive director of the Philadelphia City Planning Commission in 1949, turned his attention to revitalizing the city center and its historic landmarks and integrating them with a series of parks, new housing projects, and shopping areas, with arterial transportation pushed to boundaries.

The Philadelphian who defined this city as a preeminent regional center in the 1950s, however, was Louis Kahn.[220] After struggling during the Depression years, he formed two partnerships in the early 1940s, first with George Howe (1886–1955) and next with Oscar Stonorov. Howe, together with William Lescaze, had designed the PSFS Building, and in 1950 he took over the chairmanship of the Yale architecture program.[221] Stonorov, too, was an architect of complexity. Born in Germany, he had been trained as a sculptor in Paris, studied in Zurich under Karl Moser, and worked for André Lurcat in 1925–8, before immigrating to the United States. Kahn and Stonorov collaborated on two pamphlets on city planning in the early 1940s (sponsored by the Revere Copper and Brass Corporation) and worked as consultants for the Philadelphia City Planning Commission and the Housing Authority. The first pamphlet, "Why City Planning Is *Your* Responsibility" (1942), is a guide for urban residents collectively to organize and rehabilitate their neighborhoods through such planning devices as closing off

98. Louis I. Kahn, Richards Medical Center, Philadelphia, 1957–61. Photo by author.

streets and condemning run-down buildings.[222] The second pamphlet, "You and Your Neighborhood" (1944), is another primer for effecting community change, by insisting on safe streets, local grade schools, public parks and playgrounds, and nursery and social centers.[223] Kahn's design work on the Mill Creek Housing Development, carried out in association with Kenneth Day, Louis McAllister, and Anne Tyng, also began in 1946, although the first phase of construction dates from 1952.

In 1945 Kahn began his years as a visiting critic at Yale University, which brought him into contact with circles in the Northeast, and Kahn's few residential commissions of the late 1940s – as Vincent Scully has suggested – in fact betray the influence of Marcel Breuer. But this phase of his continuing development ends with his residence at the American Academy in Rome in 1950, where he renewed his interest in the classical and preclassical past. An article by Kahn in 1944 on "Monumentality" speaks to some of his later concerns. It was a response to a manifesto issued in 1943, "Nine Points on Monumentality," by José Luis Sert, Fernand Léger, and Sigfried Giedion, in which they had defended the notion of monumentality and its compatibility with modern architecture.[224] Kahn in most respects affirms their view but also stresses that architectural monumentality should be based on "a striving for structural perfection," rather than on the nostalgic pursuit of old images of monumentality.[225] This emphasis on structure would come to characterize much of his work of the 1950s as Kahn moved away from the spatial abstractions and functional-

ist preoccupations of international modernism and instead sought an absolute and internal order for architecture.

Structural thinking is central to the Art Gallery at Yale University (1951–3), where – under the influence of Buckminster Fuller – he made the tetrahedronal concrete space frame the dominant formal element. Structure is also central to his collaboration with Anne Tyng (b. 1920) on several triangulated "city tower" projects in the mid-1950s. The coda to this particular period of his search is his famous paean "Order and Form," which appeared in the Yale journal *Perspecta* in 1955. The opening and closing lines are as follows:

Order is
Design is form-making in order
Form emerges out of a system of construction . . .

Order is intangible
It is a level of creative consciousness
forever becoming higher in level
The higher the order the more diversity in **design**

Order supports integration
From what the space wants to be the unfamiliar may be revealed to the architect.
From order he will derive creative force and power of self-criticism to give form to this unfamiliar.
Beauty will evolve[226]

The year 1955 is generally considered to be the crucial year for Kahn's evolving design philosophy, as he now begins to express this "order" through the topos of place – really a rejection of the modernist nonhierarchical and undefined notion of space. This making of an ordered place – also the reestablishing of the preeminence of distinct rooms in spatial planning – is first seen in the plan for the Adler House of 1954, but it crystallizes in the final design for the Trenton Bath House (1955–6), where even the residual court in the center is endowed with roomlike presence by the very absence of a canopy. It was a concept still evolving when he designed the Richards Medical Center, Philadelphia (1957–61) (Fig. 98). The conceptual leap that takes place between this work and his designs for the Salk Institute for Biological Studies, La Jolla (1959–65), can be attributed to a new looser "order" as well as to a return to a classical concept of monumentality. Kahn's office in Philadelphia, by this date, had become a stopping-place for students of architecture from around the world. The so-called Philadelphia school had become a reality.

5. Postwar Modernism in South America, Asia, and Europe

Opposing the northern light of Mies and Kahn in the 1950s was the southern nova of Le Corbusier. His architectural career, uneven in production from the start, had undergone even more severe fits and starts in the 1930s and reached its nadir around 1940 with the German occupation of France. Le Corbusier fled first to Vezelay, next to the village of Ozon in the foothills of the Pyrenees. From there he set his sights on obtaining a post within the Vichy government of Marshal Pétain, where many syndicalists had resituated themselves.[227] After several rejected overtures, he managed to obtain a spot on a planning commission in Vichy in January 1941, and for eighteen months (until he was dismissed) he once again set about making proposals. In the years 1941–5 he composed no fewer than seven publications, most of which reiterated his earlier views but with special wartime urgency. *Sur les 4 Routes* (The Four Routes, 1941), for instance, draws upon his earlier syndicalist regional proposals, now arranged around the themes of highways, railroads, water, and air.[228] In the chapter on highways, for instance, he proposed a series of transportation arteries for Paris and France that would connect the future Radiant City with the Radiant Farms and Radiant Villages. The pamphlet *Destin de Paris* (Fate of Paris, 1941) outlines a housing program for the new Vichy government, one that justifies Radiant City principles on the grounds that such a city would be less susceptible to fire, bombing, and gas attacks – an odd exercise

in wartime thinking for someone who chose to sit out the conflict.[229]

Le Corbusier followed this pamphlet with *La Maison des hommes* (The home of man, 1942) and *La Charte d'Athènes* (The Athens charter, 1943), both of which were started shortly after he arrived in Vichy. The text of the first was written by François de Pierrefeu and reads as a call to arms directed at the building industry as well as a plea for support for the authoritarian policies of the Vichy government. Here the two authors propose a national corporation of architects composed of master builders (*Maître d'oeuvre*) and a supreme regulator (*Ordonnateur*), who would be the czar of all postwar reconstruction.[230] The architect's illustrations (including radiant city images) and commentary occupy the bulk of the book. *La Charte d'Athènes* was intended to inform government officials of the international work on housing carried out by CIAM in 1932.[231] Le Corbusier portrayed *La Charte* as the official CIAM conference report.

Le Corbusier's one other significant wartime book, *Les trois établissements humains* (1945, The three human establishments), is very much the product of ASCORAL (Assemblée de Constructeurs pour une Rénovation Architecturale).[232] ASCORAL was a diversified group of mostly young architects that Le Corbusier organized in 1942 – into eleven sections and twenty-two committees – to undertake research for the postwar reconstruction of France. Urban issues were central to their research, but so were topics such as architectural modules, health, agrarian reforms, and factories. The "green factory," which had been recycled in Le Corbusier's sketches since 1939, became transformed by ASCORAL into a linear industrial city in which individual industrial complexes are strung out in natural settings along a major circulation artery. His tripartite "radiant" scheme for cities, agriculture, and industry is now complete, in theory at least; in effect, fifteen years of quixotic intellectual effort ended with France's liberation by British and American forces.

In 1944 Le Corbusier's old friend Raoul Dautry was appointed minister of reconstruction and urbanism in the new French government, and through him Le Cobusier soon received commissions for the reconstruction of the cities of La Rochelle-Pallice and Saint-Dié and for the prototypical Unité d'Habitation in Marseilles (1945–52). The first two projects did not move forward, but the last project was conceived to be a mass-produced, low-cost housing prototype for 1,800 people. As has often been noted, the design synthesizes ideas he had been gathering since the early 1920s: a housing block raised off the ground, two-story living areas with a second-story sleeping area extending over to the other side of the building, corridors at every third level, a midlevel shopping street with hotel, and roof terraces and recreational facilities. With its *béton brut* (rough-board concrete) finish, it signals Le Corbusier's new aloofness from the technological direction of postwar modern architecture in favor of a more primitive and sculptural expression. The Marseilles building, with its ruddy textural appearance and tended maintenance over time, seems far more successful than the other Unités in its visual confrontation with the mountains and the sun-swept Mediterranean – perhaps because it never functioned as a low-cost housing project.

Le Corbusier's other large project from the 1940s, the United Nations Building (1947–53), was far less successful. The original idea had been to create a large "world capital" situated somewhere in the United States and encompassing various meeting and administrative buildings as well as libraries, museums, housing, and commercial facilities. In 1946 Le Corbusier was nominated by the French government to an international commission charged with finding an appropriate site and developing plans for cities of two, five, ten, twenty, and forty square miles.[233] The search focused on Westchester County, New York, and Fairfield County, Connecticut, but then John D. Rockefeller Jr. stepped in late in 1946 and offered a parcel of land along the East River. The idea of a city gave way to the notion of a complex consisting of a few buildings. Shortly after viewing the site, Le Corbusier, in his usual quick fashion, one night sketched a proposal for the Secretariat Tower, Conference Center, and Assembly Hall. This sketch was later translated into a model (Project 23A), which in turn became the basis for the design.

The traditional reason given for the widely recognized failure of the project is that Le Corbusier was never given control of the design.[234] Control instead went to the American firm of Wallace K. Harrison and Max Abramovitz, who were to be advised by a team of ten experts, among them Le Corbusier, Oscar Niemeyer, and Sven Markelius. But the problems with the final design were in fact more deeply rooted than the administrative delegation of responsibilities. For the Secretariat Tower, Le Corbusier lobbied mightily for his *brise-soliel* (sun screens) and a sandwich glass-wall with filtered air (first proposed for his Centrosoyus project in 1929), but these solutions were in fact poor technological responses to a bad east-west orientation in the first place, and, more importantly, a weak overall concept – as Mumford rightly suggested. The all-important Assembly Hall

simply fails to raise itself as an effective counterpoint to the tower.

The 1950s nevertheless proved to be the most prolific decade of Le Corbusier's long career. Two of his finest buildings of this period – Notre-Dame du Haut, Ronchamp (1950–5), and the Monastery of Sainte-Marie de La Tourette, Eveux-sur-l'Arbesle (1953–9) – were built on French soil, and interspersed with his labors on these was his work at Chandigarh and Ahmedabad in India. These efforts collectively demonstrate the turn he had taken in his approach to design – presaged in one regard by his paintings and sculptures in the 1940s, in which he left behind his Purist or machine-age idioms in favor of more organic themes and primary colors.[235] The shift was also partly induced by his wartime interest in symbolism itself, which – as has been shown – "became a comprehensive system dominating his architecture" after 1947, one filled with alchemical allusions.[236] Ronchamp and La Tourette also transcend the normal bounds of architecture with their profusion of spiritual and symbolic content. They are above all sculptural and figurative creations, unyielding except on the primal level of archetypical form and esoteric meaning. James Sterling, in his highly favorable review of the church and "Europe's greatest architect" in 1955, called it "the crisis of rationalism."[237] Le Corbusier's esoteric withdrawal from the modern world concludes at Chandigarh, where the architect casts a litany of primordial symbols (sun, moon, clouds, lightening) into the city's monuments and then tries to convince Jawaharlal Nehru to build the signs of his private philosophical language: the modular, the harmonic spiral, the solar cycle, the play of the two solistices, and above all the symbolic "open hand."[238] If indeed one considers the extent to which his architecture of the 1950s follows directly upon his painterly and sculptural interests, one cannot regard these latter interests as secondary; rather, Le Corbusier might be better seen as foremost a painter and sculptor who occasionally, and with quite differing levels of success, applied his talent to architectural practice. It is largely for his painterly and tactile sensibility, at least, that he became an artistic figurehead of the 1950s and 1960s.

Still, his earlier rationalism did not dissolve away entirely. His foremost preoccupations during and shortly after the war included mathematics and the development of the modular. In 1946 he published the article "L'Architecture et l'esprit mathématique" (Architecture and the mathematical spirit), and four years later he published *Le Modular*, which proposed a universal system of progressive measurement for architecture based on the golden section.[239] This effort had been prompted by the Vichy's government's attempt (through the Association Française pour une Normalisation du Bâtiment) to devise a metric module for postwar reconstruction. Le Corbusier rejected the arithmetic approach and the abstraction of the metric system, and he worked on devising a proportional system more sympathetic to the measurements of the human body. Drawing upon two mathematical books regarding the golden section by Elisa Maillard and Matila Ghyka, and with help from ASCORAL, he eventually arrived at a double Fibonnaci progression of numbers based on the average human height of 183 cm (6′-0″) and room height of 226 cm (7′-5″).[240] The result has become outdated but is nevertheless intriguing – even if one does not accept the underlying Ouvardian premise of a grander cosmic connection.

What cannot be disputed is Le Corbusier's fame and influence throughout the architectural world in the 1940s and 1950s, that is, everywhere except the United States. His influence in South America was particularly strong, in large part owing to his visits to Argentina, Uruguay, and Brazil in 1929 and his return trip to Brazil in 1936.[241]

In the last country the ground had been prepared by the Russian-born, Italian-educated Gregori Warchavchik (1896–1975), who moved to Brazil in 1923. Another São Paulo designer of modern persuasion was Rino Levi (1901–56), who had also trained in Italy in the 1920s. His practice gained international prominence in the 1940s.[242] Yet it was Le Corbusier's trip to Rio de Janeiro in 1936 that had the decisive impact on the future of the country's architecture. The purpose of the trip was to advise a team of architects, led by Lúcio Costa (b. 1902), on the design of the new Ministry of Education and Health. Costa had been born in France but educated in Brazil. It was his curricular reforms at the National School of Fine Arts in 1930 (replacing a Beaux-Arts curriculum with European modernism) that attracted Warchavchik to the school. Costa was soon forced out of his position, but the design of the Ministry of Education and Health (1937–43) is entirely Corbusian in its planning and style: the first tall building in fact combining *pilotis, brise-soleil*, a roof garden, a concrete frame, and glass panels. Other members on this design team included Jorge Moreira (b. 1904), Affonso Eduardo Reidy (1909–64), and Oscar Niemeyer (b. 1907), all of whom would enjoy distinguished careers. Moreira and Reidy remained firmly within the Corbusian style, while Niemeyer, who made his reputation with a series of sculptural designs for the Belo Horizonte suburb of Pampulha, would emerge alongside Costa as Brazil's best-known architect.[243] Niemeyer's fame, however,

resides with his appointment in 1955 as the chief architect for the new capital, Brasília, which was laid out by Costa. If Costa's urban plan owes much to Chandigarh and the urbanistic theory of Le Corbusier, Niemeyer's designs at times dare to cross Corbusian sculptural forms with Miesian severity.

Another South American country on which Le Corbusier had a substantial impact was Argentina, through architects such as Antonio Bonet (b. 1913), Jorge Ferrari Hardoy (1914–76), and Juan Kurchan. Hardoy and Kurchan, who later formed a partnership, worked in Le Corbusier's studio in Paris in the late 1930s and continued in his style. Bonnet, a Spaniard who worked for both José Luis Sert and Le Corbusier, formed the AUSTRAL group in Argentina in 1939 – the same year in which he completed his much admired Studio Apartments in Buenos Aires. Bonnet, however, eventually transformed his modernism into a regional style, both in Argentina and later back in his native Spain.

One of Chile's leading modernists, Emilio Duhart (b. 1917), spent a year working in Le Corbusier's office, although he took a graduate degree at Harvard University under Walter Gropius in the 1940s. The Uruguayan architect Juilio Vilamajó (1894–1948) practiced a more independent and regional modern style, exemplified by the Engineering Building at the University of the Republic, Montevideo (1935–38), and even more by the houses and hostels of the Villa Serrana (1943–7) in Minas.

The work of the Venezuelan modernist Carlos Raúl Villanueva (1900–75) owes something to Le Corbusier, although he too is best known for his highly refined regional modernism.[244] The son of a Venezuelan diplomat, he was born in London and trained in France, and his work from the 1930s is strikingly modern in its plastic expression, especially his designs for many buildings of the Central University of Venezuela in Caracas, beginning in 1944.

Relative independence from Corbusian motifs is also evident in the highly colorful architectural production of Mexico.[245] The start of the modern movement here is generally attributed to José Villagran Garcia (b. 1901), both because of the teaching reforms he introduced at the Universidad Nacional de Mexico in 1923 and because of his design of the Hygiene Institute in Poptla in 1925. His lead was taken up by one of his first students, Juan O'Gorman (b. 1905), who by 1930 was already practicing a Corbusian modernism with the familiar motifs of large glass openings and pipe rails. After a hiatus in the 1940s, O'Gorman returned to practice in the 1950s with a regional style that was notable for its brilliant murals and mosaics with pre-Columbian motifs. The breathtaking polychromy of the National Library,

University City, Mexico City (1952–3), is his conception. Another architect who often combined modern forms with murals was Mario Pani (b. 1911). In the design of his National School for Teachers (1945–7), he collaborated with Mexico's most famous painter, José Clemente Orozco (1883–1949). Polychromy, however, is only one of several currents found within the richness of Mexican architecture, which encompasses the more vernacular forms of Max Cetto (1903–80) as well as the structural brilliance of Félix Candela (b. 1910).

Above all, Mexican architecture in the 1950s is known for the intensely introspective work of Luis Barragán (1901–87).[246] This engineer (by training) made several trips to Europe in his youth and went through a distinct Corbusian phase in the 1930s. He later discarded this style, in part through the influence of the French landscape theorist Ferdinand Bac, in part through his visual confrontation with the Alhambra, and in part through his increasing fascination with Mexico's ranch and courtyard tradition. Theory almost ceases with the work of Barragán, at least in the traditional literary sense; his architectural world is one of intense colors and quiet emotional effects, accessible only to intuition and sensory contemplation. At El Pedregal (1945–50) he attempted to transform 865 acres of lava desert into an Edenic housing estate with no visible houses, only fountains and open courtyards defined by abstract and natural walls. They serve as an architecture metaphor for serene self-meditation: the primal intersection of sky, earth, water, and human limitation.

Le Corbusier's influence on Japan was as strong as his influence in South America. It was first brought to the country through the efforts of two gifted students, Kunio Maekawa (b. 1905) and Junzo Sakakura (1904–68), who worked in his Paris atelier in 1928–30 and 1931–6, respectively.

Japan, however, already had a Western architectural legacy.[247] German architects had been active in the country at the turn of the century, and the Czech-American architect Antonin Raymond (1888–1976), who had followed Wright to Tokyo in 1919 to work on the Imperial Hotel, opened his own office there in the 1920s. In 1923 Raymond designed a reinforced-concrete house that was one of the first "cubist" houses anywhere in the world.[248] This modernism was soon complemented by the work of Japanese architects who had been trained in the West. Several Japanese students – Kikuji Ishimoto, Iwao Yamawaki, Bunzo Yamaguchi, and Chikatada Kurata – spent periods at the Bauhaus. And the young architect Mamoru Yamada, like his countryman Maekawa, even attended the second CIAM conference of 1929

in Frankfurt; his design for the Electrical Testing Office in Tokyo was the sole Japanese representative at the International Style exhibition of 1932. The result was that by the early 1930s there were several offices in Japan mediating Western modes with traditional styles and approaches.

The devastation brought on by the war demanded massive rebuilding as well as radical cultural change. Sakakura and Maekawa now stepped forth to take the lead, along with Raymond, who returned to Japan from the United States. The trio were soon joined by a fourth architect of international stature, Kenzo Tange (b. 1913), who was a protégé of Maekawa.[249] The differences in the work of these four men reflect the difficulties in melding the prototypes of two cultures, and in fact one could argue that the mediation never really comes about. Raymond's Reader's Digest Office, Tokyo (1950–2), resting on *pilotis*, is now Miesian in character, although its lighter, timberlike scale and proportions are Japanese. Sakakura's Museum of Modern Art, Kamakura (1951), shows the influence of Le Corbusier. Mawakama's apartment building at Haruma, Tokyo (1957–8), owes much to the Unité at Marseilles. Only Tange's work gradually moves away from the Corbusian style. His first major work, the competition-winning design for the Atomic Memorial Museum, Hiroshima (1949–55), is close to Le Corbusier, with its heavier supports and *briese-soleils*, but as his work advances in the 1950s – in the design of the Kagawa Prefectural Office (1955–8), for instance – his translation of traditional Japanese timber techniques into concrete defines a uniquely Asian modernism with distinct Corbusian undertones. Still, the influence of Ronchamp is seen in Tange's ponderous town hall at Kurashiki (1958–60) and the Totsuka Country Clubhouse (1960–1). Only in the 1960s, in fact, do Japanese architects break out of the Corbusier mold.

The work of the Egyptian architect and planner Hassan Fathy (1899–1989), by contrast, consciously rejects the architectural forms and methods of the West. Beginning with his design for the (failed) rural village of New Gourna (1945–48), near Luxor, and continuing with such projects as Mit-el-Nasara (1954), Fathy creates an Egyptian architecture for the poor: an indigenous cultural regionalism that frankly draws upon preindustrial materials and construction methods.

Theory and practice in Europe in the postwar years varies considerably from country to country. Spain is a special case, owing to its civil war of the 1930s, the cultural policies of the Franco regime, and the poverty and technological backwardness of the country.[250] In the early 1950s, Spanish architecture was characterized by an interesting dialectic between a revived international modernism, which had been essentially outlawed in the late 1930s, and the strong pull of vernacular traditions. The latter even seem to have taken precedence. The architect José Luis Fernández del Amo was involved in the reconstruction of several villages in the 1950s – especially Vegaviana in Cáceres (1954–8) – and his designs employed regional materials in a poetic manner. Whereas the work of Alejandro de la Sota (b. 1913) is more individualist and imbued with surrealist undertones, it is nevertheless rooted in tradition. In his design for the village of Esquivel, in the province of Seville (1948–55), he employs the traditional Andalusian motifs of grilles and tiles but with the wry humor characteristic of his compositions.

A similar dialogue between modernism and tradition is found in the work of the two leading Spanish architects of the 1950s: Josep Maria Sostres (b. 1915) and José Antonio Coderch (1913–84). These Catalonians were instrumental in founding *Grupo R* in 1952, which was committed to re-aligning Spanish architecture with developments elsewhere. Sostres, who had earlier founded *Amigos de Gaudí*, was a theorist, teacher, and architect whose his early career is defined by the Augustí house, Sitges (1955–8). Coderch perhaps went further in interpreting Catalonian architecture in a contemporary way, beginning with his Ugalde house, Caldes d'Estrach (1951–2), and his much admired apartment building Casa de la Marina, Barcelona (1951–4).

Similar ideas of a vernacular tradition were also evident during the 1950s in Italy – a country that now assumes (with Britain) the leading position in European theory. The rapid ascent of Italian theory is propelled, above all, by the compelling figure of Bruno Zevi (b. 1918).[251] Born in Rome, he began his architectural studies in 1936 but soon became active in anti-Fascist causes. His anti-Fascism and his Jewish ancestry made his life untenable in Italy, and he left the country in 1939 to continue his studies at the Architectural Association in London and at Harvard, where he graduated in 1941. By 1943 he was back in London participating in the Allies' war effort. During the nighttime hours – and the flood of V-2 rockets – he wrote his first book, *Verso un'architettura organica* (Towards an organic architecture, 1945)[252] (Fig. 99). In the same year he founded the Association for Organic Architecture (APAO) and the journal *Metron*, dedicated to improving society.

Towards an Organic Architecture is a complex study by a young historian. It was written partly in response to Sigfried Giedion's *Space, Time and Architecture*, whose rationalist principles it opposes. It is also a sharply yet subtly worded critique of the limits of European rationalism of the 1920s.

One of the key chapters of the historical survey concerns the stalling of the modern movement in the 1930s, which Zevi traces to three reasons: (1) people wearied of the "rational-utilitarian" polemics, which at the same time were delimiting architecture's full expressive potential; (2) there was logical inconsistency between Le Corbusier's rational language and the creative magic of his "objets à reaction poetique"; and (3) functionalist or rationalist theory itself had become impersonal, abstract, and overly dogmatic in application.[253] For Zevi modern architecture survived in the late 1930s and 1940s only in Scandinavia and the United States, whose architects today "are leading the way both in theory and in practice."[254] The reason for this is that they have moved away from the rationalist limitations or clichés of the earlier generation and are practicing an "organic" architecture: "Architecture is organic when the spatial arrangement of a room, house and city is planned for human happiness, material, psychological and spiritual. The organic is based therefore on a social idea and not on a figurative idea. We can only call architecture organic when it aims at being human before it is humanist."[255]

Aalto points the way in Scandinavia, and one of the examples of his organic approach is the anthropomorphic shaping of his plywood furniture, in contrast to the steel and chrome industrial aesthetic of the earlier rationalists. For Zevi the term *organic* implies both accommodation of the material and psychological needs of people and a higher democratic ideal. Wright epitomizes this direction in the United States, and unlike Giedion, who regards him only as a "forerunner" of European developments, Zevi places the American architect after his European counterparts to emphasize his contemporary relevancy. Zevi is also alone among European historians in recognizing the many regional centers of American practice. In fact he argues for the superiority of West Coast practice over that of the East Coast, because the last has remained culturally dependent on Europe. Thus the work of Gregory Ain, Ralph Soriano, Hamilton Harwell Harris, and William Wurster are included in his account, as is the work of Erik Gunnar Asplund and Sven Markelius.

Over the next few years, Zevi came to define the idea of organic architecture increasingly with the notion of space, the theme that he pursues in his next book, *Sapere vedere l'architettura* (Learning to see architecture, 1948; translated into English as *Architecture as Space*).[256] At first glance it seems to be little more than a reiteration of Schmarsow's argument of a half-century earlier (to which Zevi does not refer) – namely, that "The history of architecture is primarily

BRUNO ZEVI

VERSO UN'ARCHITETTURA ORGANICA

EINAUDI

99. Bruno Zevi, title page of *Verso un'architettura organica* (Turin, 1945).

the history of spatial conceptions."[257] But its framework is also expanded, as Zevi is intent on establishing for architecture "a clarity of method" and "a cultural order" in which the manifestoes and polemics of the avant-garde (sculptural and pictorial values) give way to a single standard for evaluating architecture as space.[258] Once again he considers architecture's development historically, tracing spatial conceptions from the Greeks to the baroque era to modern times. He reduces modern spatial conceptions to two competitors: (1) the rationally interpreted, free or open plan of the functionalists (contained within a regular overall geometry), and (2) the organic spatial conception of Wright. Only now Zevi seizes Wright's spatial complexity as yet another justification for his organic conception:

For Wright the open plan is not a dialectic carried on within an architectural volume, but the final result of a conquest expressed in spatial terms, starting from a central nucleus and projecting voids in all directions. It follows that the resulting drama of volumetrics has an audacity and richness undreamed

of by the Functionalists, and its very insistence on decorative elements indicates, quite apart from their sometimes doubtful taste, a desire for freedom from the bare, self-flagellating severity of early European rationalism.[259]

Zevi's appreciation of Wright, however, is not founded simply on his rich spatial volumetrics. Wright's spatial approach is better because it more conscientiously – in the traditional sense of humanism – takes into account the users' needs and psychology. At this point, in fact, Zevi's critique of modern architecture expands threefold in an unexpected way. He takes into consideration formalist appraisals of architectural space, operating from such painterly concepts as unity, symmetry, balance, and contrast, although these now have but limited or secondary applicability to architecture today. He also considers appraisals of architectural space that focus on content, specifically its social content, and these appraisals remain of great importance. But under the heading of physiopsychological interpretations he now draws upon the body of "empathy" theory, and here is where his reasoning becomes original. Citing Fiedler, Wölfflin, and Geoffrey Scott, Zevi argues that in perceiving spaces "we 'vibrate' in affinity with them, since they arouse reactions both in our bodies and in our minds," and therefore "architecture transcribes states of feeling into structural forms, humanizing and animating them."[260] In this phenomenal realm of spatial experience in fact lies the gist of Zevi's organic conception, and indeed it is a conception that is far from suggesting – as some critics in his day assumed – a return to Wrightian forms. It is an antirationalist conception that allows natural materials and functional complexities back into modern architecture. In fact, the images of Wright's buildings woven throughout the book are of his highly tactile creations at Bear Run and for the Johnson Wax Company.

Zevi further refines his historiographic conception of spatial development with his *Storia dell'architettura moderna* (History of modern architecture, 1950).[261] By this date he had already won the chair of history at the University of Venice, and he had helped to form the National Institute of Town Planning, which would play an active role in the postwar reconstruction of the country. But Italian theory in the early 1950s was already a divided field rife with competing ideas and diverging forces. Against Zevi stood the art historian Giulio Carlo Argan, whose book *Walter Gropius e la Bauhaus* (Walter Gropius and the Bauhaus, 1951) interpreted the avant-garde in the 1920s as a social and political force of great significance.[262] On the one hand, Argan argues, the Bauhaus building at Dessau, with its technological rationalism and lack of concern with beauty, was the logical development of Conrad Fiedler's theory of visibility applied to the modern world. On the other hand, the building and its architect were fundamentally ideological, that is to say, dialectical expressions of democratic forces working their way through their own contradictions. From Argan's Marxist perspective – a view that would resonate in the late 1960s – it is entirely correct and important for architecture to be political.

Opposed to these two viewpoints was a newfound appreciation for regionalist or traditional expressions – an appreciation strengthened by Zevi's respect for regional movements in Scandinavia and the United States. A number of talented designers drew upon the manual aspects of local traditions, among them Carlo Scarpa, Ludovico Quaroni, Mario Ridolfi, Mario Fiorentine, Ignazio Gardella, Franco Albini, Vittorio Gregotti, Giorgio Raineri, and Giovanni Michellucci. In Ridolfi's housing complex at Cerignola (1950–1), later heralded as a "neorealist" work, he inserts plain concrete block and decorative grillwork into a concrete frame to evoke a regional spirit, and in his controversial apartment complex on the Viale Etiopia, Rome (1950–4), he adds enameled majolica and decorative elements to the windows in an allusion to the Italian tradition of hanging ceremonial textiles at festivals. Michelucci, who before the war had designed the Florence Railway Station, drew upon his Tuscan heritage for his Exchange in Pistoria (1950) and his church in Collina (1954). This joining of traditional vocabularies, representational reminiscences, and modern methods is also a keynote of the work of Gardella and Albini, as seen in their respective designs for the House on the Zattere, Venice (1954–8), and the renovation of the Museum of the Treasury of San Lorenzo, Genoa (1952–6).

Thus the stage for serious debate was already set by December 1953, when Ernesto Nathan Rogers assumed the editorship of *Casabella* and, in a controversial act, removed the word *Costruzioni* (construction) from the title page and superimposed the word *Continuità* (continuity) over the journal's title. Invoking the prewar spirit of Giuseppe Pagano and Edoardo Persico, he noted in his opening editorial that continuity means "historical awareness, awareness of a deep-running tradition," and "the eternal struggle of the creative spirit against every manifestation of formalism, past and present."[263] Continuity further implies neither "the cosmopolitan drug of the most recent academic manner" nor "demagogic folklorism" but rather an ethical aesthetic "to test the problems of quantity in the crucible of quality and at the same time strive that quality may be progressively become quantity, to bring art and craft back to their original synthesis: teché."[264] A few years later he defines the problem of tradition and continuity in more lucid terms: "The great question is to strike a balance between those who are in danger of transforming the country into a museum embalming nature and monuments, and those others who – falling into the opposite error – would make a clean slate of everything, incredibly over-simplifying the very real difficulties before them, so as to further immediate action."[265] It is now apparent that Italian theory by the mid-1950s was clearly plotting its own course – as others would soon notice.

Swiss theory during the same time was very much dominated by the efforts of Giedion, who was intent on reviving CIAM after the war. He nevertheless wrote a steady stream of books that follow upon his earlier success. In 1948 he published *Mechanization Takes Command*, which he wrote in the United States. It is an attempt to broaden the scope of his work by considering the phenomenon of "humble things" (from farm implements to Yale locks to kitchen appliances) and their "inescapable influence over our way of life, our attitudes, our instincts."[266] It is not an optimistic book, but it still assumes that events are anonymously driven by the *Zeitgeist*. And although it touches only very occasionally on architecture, it has the tortured psychological orientation typical of his earlier analyses – seeking to restore that "lost equilibrium between inner and outer reality," find "a new balance between the individual and the collective," and mediate "between the psychic spheres within the individual."[267] Restoring this "nervous dynamic equilibrium," in Giedion's view, is the lone hope for human survival in the long run.[268]

Giedion also published three other books of significance in the 1950s. In a combined French and English edition entitled *A Decade of New Architecture* (1951), he surveyed the international field of architecture over the past ten years.[269] It is the first study to draw attention to the work of South America and of course thereby affirms the international scope of the movement. Three years later, in *Walter Gropius: Work and Teamwork*, Giedion writes a hagiography of his close friend.[270] Notwithstanding the book's evident magnification of Gropius's stature, it remains one of the best studies of this architect and his ideas, in addition to being illustrated with many rare photographs. Finally, Giedion's *Architecture: You and Me* (1958) is an invaluable anthology of his shorter writings published between 1936 and 1956.[271] His essay "New Regionalism" (1954) is a classic study that demonstrates how he shifted his perspective in response to the relatively recent critiques of Mumford and Zevi. The idea of a "style" or an "international style" is inadequate, he now argues, because such a conception encourages formalism and can displace local climatic and cultural conditions. Further there exists an increasing cultural respect for non-Western civilizations, recently brought to light, he notes, by the Japanese translation of *Space, Time and Architecture*. The differing modernisms of Neutra, Niemeyer, and Sert are, in his view, indicative of this new regard for regional nuances. Giedion concludes his essay in an unexpected way. He raises the issue of nonrectilinear or circular houses with which Frank Lloyd Wright has occasionally experimented and which Giedion compares to the ancient oval houses of Crete. Although in principle Giedion is opposed to mechanically construed rounded houses (such as the mast house of Fuller) for reasons of urban design and composition, he is nevertheless somewhat attracted to the break with "the tyranny of the right angle" and to the "search for greater interior flexibility" – if only for the anthropological purpose of probing the human spirit when it makes the transition "from the life of a nomadic herdsman to that of a settled agriculturalist."[272] He concludes, "What we need more today than anything else is *imagination*."[273]

A further indication of Giedion's changing perspective is found in some comments he attached (in 1956) to an earlier essay on "Spatial Imagination." Inspired by such recent buildings as Saarinen's Kresge Auditorium and Jørn Utzon's Sydney Opera House, Giedion seizes on the shell vault as a "liberating" event for modern architecture. Above all he applauds Utzon's "sails billowing with dramatic expectancy. They prepare one for what will take place within. They seek to divorce the audience from the routine of their daily lives. At one blow, the banal stage tower is also destroyed."[274] It is clear that Giedion's earlier technocratic rationalism has now abated; it has been moderated by an architectural conception more sculptural and decidedly more baroque. As his philosophical outlook evolved into his three-volume series, *The Eternal Present* (1957–64), it became more introspective and psychologically focused on symbolic issues.[275]

With Germany's near total wartime destruction – and with the majority of its principal prewar architects scattered across the globe – its importance as a theoretical center remained minimal for several years. One attempt at recovery was the reconstitution of the Bauhaus in Ulm – the Hochschule für Gestaltung (HfG) – which combined architectural education and training in industrial design and visual communication.[276] The school's first director, the former Bauhaus student Max Bill (b. 1908), designed an austere, factorylike complex built on a hillside above the city in 1950–5, and even Gropius himself was lured back to Germany to open the school officially with a lecture. HfG, however, was in administrative and political disarray even before the new complex opened. The Swiss Bill turned out to be a combative and ineffective rector, and his high-sounding Bauhaus ambition – "to help in turning life into a work of art" – must have sounded anachronistic even to many in the mid-1950s.[277] He was forced out in 1957 and replaced by a triumvirate of faculty ultimately headed by the Argentine Tomas Maldonado. In the Bauhaus tradition of Hannes Meyer, the earlier program was then overturned in favor of a curriculum stressing "scientific operationalism" and scientific design, a form of technological rationalism. In another parallel with the Bauhaus, the school was politicized and exhibited a growing disdain for and alienation from the political forces that were sustaining its existence. Unwilling to compromise in the tumultuous year of 1968, the striking students ultimately found the school legislated out of existence.

None of this should disparage the theoretical significance of the HfG and its curriculum in the late 1950s and early 1960s, when the school became an intellectual center for ideas and discussion, with teachers and lecturers that included Max Bense, Konrad Wachsmann, Buckminster Fuller, Konrad Lorenz, Charles and Ray Eames, Joseph Rykwert, and Christian Norberg-Schulz. Maldonado also introduced a course on semiotics that, as we shall see, would have significant reverberations in the 1960s.[278] The intellectual legacy of HfG was enormous.

In terms of architectural practice, however, no part of Europe was superior to Scandinavia. Theory in the North also takes a slightly different twist in the postwar years, as we find a persistent demand for designs that are freer and less formal, that take into account the nuances of human comfort, use natural materials, are better integrated into the environment, and that fit local traditions. J. M. Richards, in writing for *Architectural Review* in 1947, dubbed this approach a "New Empiricism."[279] In a striking lead photograph emblematic of the new style, a svelte blond-haired woman – a model of fitness and health – stands nude on the backyard lawn next to a pond, turned toward a house that resembles a North American ranch-style home (Fig. 100). The low unpretentious house in its glorious birch-forested setting was designed by Sven Markelius. Richards sees "this latest style" as an effort "both to humanize the theory [of functionalism] on its aesthetic side and to get back to the earlier rationalism on the technical side," although many functionalists have come "to wonder whether the principles of objectivity in contemporary architecture they fought so hard to establish are being quietly and skillfully jettisoned by their own team-mates."[280] And even if this same tendency can be viewed as a logical continuation of the national romantic movement from the earlier decades of the century, the influence of the ranch houses of the western United States, so regularly featured in the same journal, is obviously making its presence felt in Europe.[281] In a 1948 article published in *Architectural Review*, J. M. Richards even interprets the newly coined "Bay Region" style of California as yet another manifestation of empirical regionalism – although two years later he saw the need to differentiate the two with the labels "Regional Organic" and "Empirical Organic."[282] These last two appellations also trace a line from Zevi to an emerging British theory, which will soon lead back again to Rogers.

A number of the prewar generation of Scandinavian modernists – such as Sven Markelius, Sven Backström (1903–92), Steen Eiler Rasmussen, Kay Fisker, Arne Jacobsen, Erik Bryggman, and Alvar Alto – in fact used the forced idleness of the war years, with the shortages of metals and other materials, as a chance to reevaluate both the home and the rationalism of the 1930s. In 1943, in another *Architectural Review* article, Sven Backström outlined the pertinent issues in an insightful way.[283] With Asplund's pavilions at the Stockholm Exhibition of 1930, functionalism came to Scandinavia. But as more buildings of modern design came to be built, the shortcomings of functionalism became apparent: "The big windows, for example, were all too effective as heat-conductors, and people found it difficult to accustom themselves to the heat or cold behind them. They also felt the lack of many of the aesthetic values and the little contributions to cosiness that we human beings are so dependent upon, and that our architectural and domestic tradition had nevertheless developed."[284] As a result, the architects of his generation presently began to reevaluate modernism based on growing humanist concerns:

And it was discovered that man is a highly complicated phenomenon that is not be satisfied or understood with the help of any new epoch-making formulae. And one result of this growing insight was a reaction against the all too schematic architecture of the 1930's. To-day we have reached the point where all the elusive psychological factors have again begun to engage our attention. Man and his habits, reactions and needs are the focus of interest as never before. One tries to understand them, and to adapt the building in such a way that it really serves. And there is the desire to enrich it and beautify it in a living way, so that it may be a source of joy.[285]

Similar issues were being raised in Scandinavian practice. In 1937 Alvar Aalto signaled his move away from the rationalist style with his informal design for the Villa Mairea, which was built with plank boarding, local stone, and tile and delicately placed in a natural setting. The war, whose effects were particularly harsh in Finland, interrupted his efforts, and it was not until he won the competition for the village center of Säynätsalo (1949–52) that (with the help of his second wife, Elissa Mäkiniemi) he was able to turn these tendencies into an undisputed masterpiece. His work in the 1950s is varied, but in such efforts as the church at Vuoksenniska (1956–9) he gave these tendencies free rein.[286] This last building is not far removed in spirit from the competition-winning design of Reima Pietilä and Raili Paatelainen for the Kaleva church, Tampere (1959–66), which draws upon the same Nordic roots.

Of the many new Scandinavian satellite towns of the 1950s (in part influenced by Mumford's theories), Helsinki's garden suburb of Tapiola (begun 1951), with its informal layout and idyllic natural setting within a forest of birches and pines, is certainly the most successful and attractive. Under the direction of Markelius, the Stockholm city-planning department in 1944–54 built several new towns outside of Stockholm, the best known of which is Vällingby (1952–6), designed by Backström and Leif Reinius. It has a somewhat conventional, if informal, city center restricted to pedestrians and serviced by a supply route underneath. Housing and green areas surround the center.

Danish architects were also generally focused on housing following the war, with the exception of Jørn Utzon (b. 1918), who won the international competition for the Sydney Opera in 1957.[287] Utzon's apprenticeship exemplifies both the regional continuity and the international breadth of Scandinavian modernism in this decade. He began his studies at the Royal Academy of Art in the late 1930s under Kay Fisker and Steen Eiler Rasmusson and worked for both Asplund and Aalto before traveling to Morocco in 1948 and to the United States in the following year, where he spent time with Wright at Taliesin. On the one hand, his personal style draws upon the principles of organic or biological form, as popularly illustrated in such books as Darcy Thompson's *On Growth and Form* and as revisited elsewhere during these years, particularly in the United States. On the other hand, he combines his sense of organic form with vernacular material and building traditions and with non-Western formal interests.

Rasmusson's ideas are well documented in his *Experiencing Architecture* (1959), which could also serve as a

100. Sven Markelius, house, Kevinge, Sweden. Image from *The Architectural Review* (June 1947).

primer for the aesthetic underpinnings of New Empiricism. The book treats architecture as a corporeal (visual, auditory, and tactile) and psychological art, accessible through one's sense of form and space and enhanced through such factors as light, color, texture, rhythm, and material effects.[288] Rasmusson's earlier book, *Town and Buildings* (1951), is a primer on Scandinavian planning objectives, which feature nongridded layouts, respect for nature, rootedness to place or local traditions, and the centering of neighborhood entities on housing and domestic activities.[289] Welfare-state policies and the small, homogeneous populations of the Nordic countries during these years made these objectives conceivable and at times even achievable.

If Italy and Scandinavia were the two European countries that excelled at architectural practice in the 1950s, Britain was the country in which architectural theory was pursued with special vitality. In an interesting way, architectural discourse in Britain played off the New Empiricism of the Scandinavian North against the more traditional artistic dependency on France while at the same time entertaining

a newfound interest in Palladio, American pop culture, and Britain's own picturesque tradition.

The high level of building activity following the war was the result of the bombing of London, which created both the need for reconstruction and the bureaucratic machinery to implement it. The advocacy group MARS, now led by Maxwell Fry and Berthold Lubetkin, and the Royal Academy each presented a plan for rebuilding London in 1942–3, but the radial plan adopted by the London City Council in 1944 was prepared by Leslie Patrick Abercrombie and John Henry Forshaw. Following the legacy of Howard, it called for depopulating the city center, creating a green belt around the existing suburbs, and planning an outer ring of eight new satellite towns. The creation of a socialist state, a revived London County Council (LCC), and the New Towns Act of 1946 meant that there was a legal apparatus to tackle the severe housing problem. Over the next decade London was rebuilt and ten new towns were started.[290] The leftist politics and relatively young age of the majority of architects working for the LCC assured a "modernist" victory, although in fact a victory with far more notable failures than successes.

The planning models for these towns are better considered in the following chapter, but the choice of the particular architectural vocabulary is pertinent here. Many of the older members of MARS, like their counterparts at CIAM, favored Corbusian planning and building models, and they were soon joined within the housing division of the LCC by a number of Corbusian neophytes, among them John Killick, Alan Colquhoun, William Howell, Colin St. John Wilson, and Peter Carter – all Architectural Association graduates.[291]

Also contributing to the Frenchman's popularity during this period were Colin Rowe's essays on Le Corbusier. In 1947, while a doctoral student of Rudolf Wittkower at the Warburg Institute, Rowe published "The Mathematics of the Ideal Villa," which plotted the mathematical and proportional similarities of Palladio's Villa Malcontenta and Le Corbusier's Villa Stein-de Monzie at Garches.[292] It thereby underscored the timeless properties of "le style Corbu." Three years later Rowe published in *Architectural Review* an even more provocative essay, "Mannerism and Modern Architecture," which showed that the "inverted spatial effects" of the early modernists paralleled those of the mannerist period (1520–1600).[293] The final comparison of the apses of St. Peter's with Le Corbusier's Salvation Army Building in Paris further enhanced the stature of this modern-day Bramante. Rudolf Wittkower's publication of his book on proportions, *Architectural Principles in the Age of Humanism* (1949), and the near simultaneous appearance of Le Corbusier's *The Modular* provided additional support.[294]

This tendency to idolize Le Corbusier clashed with both the Neo-Empiricist influence from Scandinavia and the stirrings of a neo-picturesque movement.[295] What is particularly interesting in this regard is that the two leaders of these movements were the historians J. M. Richards and Nikolaus Pevsner, respectively, both editors at *Architectural Review* and both with entrenched attitudes toward modernism. Pevsner's seminal study *Pioneers of the Modern Movement* (1936) had recounted the history of modernism largely within the context of the English arts and crafts movement, while Richards's *An Introduction to Modern Architecture* (1940) followed a similar track with an equally strong account of the Giedionesque *Zeitgeist* of collectivist (Soviet style) anonymity.[296] Yet with Richards there was also the suspicion that all might not be quite right with the emerging socialist utopia. In 1940, under the pseudonym "James Macquedy," he wrote a curious "Criticism" for the *Architectural Review* in which he questioned why the universal forms of the modern movement were so unpopular with

the "Man in the Street."[297] In 1942, together with John Summerson, he published *The Bombed Buildings of Britain*, which took account of Britain's historical legacy. At the CIAM meeting in Bridgwater in 1947, Richards delivered a lecture and prepared a questionnaire on "the emotional reactions of the common man to modern art."[298] In the same year he published *The Castles on the Ground* (written in Cairo, Jerusalem, Aleppo, Rhodes, and Ain Zahalta), which praised the virtues of Victorian suburbia and English bourgeois life.[299] Banham famously noted that the book "was regarded by the young as a blank betrayal of everything that Modern Architecture was supposed to stand for, and a worse act of treachery in that it had been written by the man whose 'Introduction to Modern Architecture,' had indeed served to introduce many of them to the art of architecture."[300] Thus when the now much reformed Richards wrote about Sweden's New Empiricism in 1947, this example of a regional modern style fell in line with his own populist concerns. The reconstruction efforts formed along the lines of those advocating a rationalist Corbusian style of modern design (concrete and glass) and those favoring the Swedish strategy of employing low-tech materials such as brick and wood and maintaining a sympathetic awareness of local traditions – contemporaneously and somewhat contemptuously referred to as "People's Detailing."[301]

A third front to this debate was opened by several articles by Pevsner, later summarized in a series of lectures broadcast in 1955 and published under the title *The Englishness of English Art*. Here, in commenting favorably on such new towns as Roehampton Estate and Harlow, he pointed out their informal planning legacy in English picturesque theory and claimed, "If English planners forget about the straight axes and the artificially symmetrical facades of the academy, and design functionally and Englishly, they will succeed."[302]

Underlying this debate was a serious issue that had been haunting leftist modern theory for decades. Just as the Lenin-Trotsky wing of Soviet Communism had rejected true proletariat power in favor of a ruling elite, modernists in general had always insisted on imposing avant-garde forms rather than responding to popular taste. José Ortega y Gasset echoed such sentiments in *The Revolt of the Masses* (1930) when he argued against the "mass man" and in favor of the "cultured" elite operating within the political system and sagely controlling its sundry forms of expression.[303] Clement Greenberg's much cited essay of 1939, "Avant-Garde and Kitsch," toyed with the same position, and of course Greenberg very naively saw the Marxist avant-garde as the last defense against the inevitable kitsch of populist or capitalist society.[304] Thus the question as it unfolded in socialist Britain in the early 1950s was whether elitist agencies such as CIAM or its British counterpart, MARS, would control the design process with their sometimes unpopular modern forms or whether some third middle path between the political avant-garde and populist kitsch (the Scandinavian solution) might be found. The third logical alternative – the populist idea of giving the "common" people precisely what they wanted – was naturally unthinkable.

The issue was not resolved in Britain, but its seriousness was at least understood, as witnessed by the shifting ground of the British debate. For soon a fourth front to the debate opened, one that later coalesced under the somewhat misleading banner of the "New Brutalism" – a term apparently bandied about as early as 1950 in response to the "New Empiricism" label.[305] The movement had its beginning in the polemical work of Alison (1928–93) and Peter Smithson (1923–2003) as well as in the efforts of others within the Independent Group (IG), a group loosely associated with the Institute of Contemporary Art (ICA).[306]

The Smithsons, who had attended Durham University and the Royal Academy School of Architecture, formed a partnership in 1950, one year after their marriage and their very Miesian design for the Hunstanton Secondary Modern School, Norfolk (1949–54). In 1952 they helped to form the IG, an informal group of artists and intellectuals opposed to the status quo of the London art scene. In addition to the Smithsons, early members included the historian Reyner Banham (1922–88), the sculptor Eduardo Paolozzi, Lawrence Alloway, Richard Hamilton, and the photographer Nigel Henderson. An exhibition at the ICA in 1953 entitled "Parallel of Art and Life" presented the group's ideology in the form of 169 images of nonart: machines, archaeological and biological artifacts, and primitive art and architecture. This realist leitmotif became the basis for the Smithsons' "Urban Reidentification" grids that the couple presented to the CIAM conference at Aix-en-Provence in the same year.[307] In addition to Henderson's realist (brutal) photographs of urban life, the Smithsons, presenting their Golding Lane housing scheme of 1952, proposed a free grouping of urban towers connected by residential "streets-in-the-air," evolving hierarchically into districts and cities. This design opposed the isolation of Le Corbusier's housing blocks, which disallowed growth or connection.

The non-mainstream ethos of New Brutalism became better developed in the mid-1950s along several different fronts. In one 1956 exhibition, the Smithsons prepared a full-scale mock-up of a "House of the Future," featuring glossy curves and a womblike atmosphere. In the 1956 ICA exhibition, "This is Tomorrow," Richard Hamilton produced his famous poster and collage "Just What Is It That Makes Today's Homes So Different, So Appealing?" It featured a 1950s living room with a television, an American body builder in peacock pose, an unclad woman on the sofa with oversized breasts, and a canned ham on the coffee table. By some accounts this was the beginning of pop art. Again the team of Paolozzi, Henderson, and the Smithsons collaborated on a shedlike re-creation of Henderson's backyard in Bethnal Green, "Patio & Pavilion," which featured, among the assorted junk, a rusted bicycle wheel, a rock, and tools.[308]

Inevitably the movement had to be given a name. The Smithsons provided one as early as 1953 in describing their unbuilt "House in Soho, London" (with no interior finishes): "In fact, had this been built it would have been the first exponent of the 'new brutalism' in England."[309] Four years later, in response to an anonymous panel convened by the journal *Architectural Design*, the Smithsons saw Brutalism as an attempt "to face up to a mass-produced society, and drag a rough poetry out of the confused and powerful forces which are at work."[310] The clean image of Scandinavian modernism, and any of "the romantic pasticheries of the Festival of Britain and its offspring" are rudely rejected by an *art brut*.[311]

It was the historian Banham, however, who would align his early career with promotion of the term, and he did so in 1955 in a way that would resonate more strongly with the younger generation of postwar architects now stepping into prominence. Viewing Brutalism as both an angry response to the "William Morris Revival" of the British Communists and to the new classicism made fashionable by Wittkower's book, Banham defines it in the realm of art by citing the paintings of Jean Dubuffet, Jackson Pollock, and Alberto Burri, and in the realm of architecture by citing *le beton brut* of Le Corbusier's Marseilles building, his Ronchamp, and the concrete starkness of Kahn's Yale Gallery. Transformed into ethical (not aesthetic) principles, these works together presented "1. Memorability as an Image; 2. Clear exhibition of Structure; and 3. Valuation of Materials 'as found.'"[312] Le Corbusier's Jaoul houses in Paris (1951–5) will soon fill out the founding precedents, and their rough finishes in turn will become the inspiration for the new English edition of Brutalism – the Flats at Ham Common, London (1955–8). One of the two architects, James Sterling (1926–92), had surveyed Le Corbusier's buildings while still under construction and had found their "poor" brickwork not only excusable but indicative of a new direction for the architect.[313] In effect, Brutalism now became an international phenomenon.

Yet no sooner had Banham popularly defined Brutalism than he was inventing a new direction for the movement. While working on his dissertation under Nikolaus Pevsner in the mid-1950s, he developed a fascination with American pop culture and the chrome aesthetic or styling of American automobiles – phenomena seen as examples of cultural degeneration by most British intellectuals.[314] This fascination, as we will later see, posed a far more serious threat to the status quo in British architecture than any other development of the 1950s, because it raised the question of just what social forces were really in control of design: high art (architects) or popular culture? Modern architects, of course, had always insisted on the former, but suddenly a sense of disquiet was making itself felt. And although Banham in his own unconventional way would go on to become one of the most articulate (and nearly the last) defender of the tradition of high modernism in the 1960s, the destructive genie – sometime around 1957 – was already out of the bottle. A more radical break was looming.

14

CHALLENGES TO MODERNISM IN EUROPE
1959–1967

One thing is certain: if society at large fails to come to terms with its people – what
a paradox – people will spread over the globe and be at home nowhere, for it is in
the nature of countless pseudo places made today that they are all the same.

Aldo van Eyck

1. CIAM and Team 10

Throughout the 1930s and 1940s CIAM had remained very much in the hands of Le Corbusier and Giedion. The fourth CIAM congress, held aboard the *S.S. Patris II* in 1933, produced (ten years later) the document published by Le Corbusier as the "Athens Charter," which became the definitive statement of the organization's objectives and planning policies. It was in many of its details synonymous with Le Corbusier's "Radiant City" proposals. With the collapse of modernism in Germany in the mid-1930s, Le Corbusier assumed an even more powerful role. The fifth CIAM congress was held in Paris in 1937, and Le Corbusier arranged his Pavillon des Temps Nouveaux at the Paris Exposition as a propaganda display for the organization. The theme was the functional city. The Spaniard José Luis Sert and the Dutchman Cornelis van Eesteren joined the inner circle of the organization in these years, but the German occupation of much of Europe in the 1940s dispersed once again the remnants of CIAM.

The saving grace for CIAM turned out to be England, which after the founding of MARS (Modern Architecture Research Group) in 1933 had grown increasingly active. Many German refugees, such as Gropius and Breuer, found their way to England in the mid-1930s. In 1938 a group of MARS members, among them Serge Chermayeff and Lázló Moholy-Nagy, hosted an exhibition on the "New Architecture" that played a role in England similar to that of the MoMA exhibition in New York. Nevertheless, by the time Britain became directly involved with the war, many of the refugee architects had moved to the United States.

The problem in the United States, of course, was that up to this time the country had had very little involvement with CIAM.

The two American CIAM members of the 1930s – Richard Neutra and Knud Lönberg-Holm – were both of European descent, and because of the geographical distances separating the two men from each other and from Europe, they were largely absent from CIAM meetings and inactive in setting policies. Thus one of Giedion's first tasks upon arriving in the United States in 1939 was to found a New York chapter. He organized a symposium in New York in May that attracted such people as George Howe, George Keck, and Oscar Stonorov, and at this time there were also preparations for an unofficial northeastern chapter. When Giedion later pressed for this group's formal integration into CIAM, however, people such as Howe and Stonorov backed away from active involvement. The cultural differences between American and European cities were vast, and the idea of a single American chapter representing the continent of North America was untenable. Nevertheless, Sert's book of 1942, *Can Our Cities Survive?* was written for his new American audience (although few American examples were discussed), and it proposed to distill the resolutions of the CIAM conferences of 1933 and 1937. Its model, however, mystified Lewis Mumford, who had been asked to write the foreword. He apparently could not understand how urban analysis could be reduced to the functional categories of housing, recreation, transportation, and work without taking into account the political, educational, and cultural aspects of urban life.[1] Joseph Hudnut eventually wrote the foreword, and Giedion's organizational efforts on behalf of CIAM failed on American soil.

When CIAM officially resumed its activities following the war, the base of operations therefore shifted back to England. The first postwar conference was hosted by the MARS group at Bridgwater in September 1947. Because of the disruption of the war, there was no research to present, and so the meeting focused on a few general themes. Gropius gave a talk on architectural education, and Giedion in his speech returned to the theme of monumentality and to the working relationship of architects, painters, and sculptors. J. M. Richards spoke of modern architecture and its reception by the common man. Le Corbusier made known his work with the French group ASCORAL during the war years and offered it as a vehicle of future endeavors. With the election of Sert as the president of CIAM, Le Corbusier's authority within the organization was assured. In addition, the French architect, together with Walter Gropius and Helena Syrkus of Poland, were named as vice-presidents. The revised official aim of CIAM was as follows:

To work for the creation of a physical environment that will satisfy man's emotional and material needs and stimulate his spiritual growth.

To achieve an environment of this quality, we must combine social idealism, scientific planning and the fullest use of available building techniques. In so doing we must enlarge and enrich the aesthetic language of architecture in order to provide a contemporary means whereby people's emotional needs can find expression in the design of their environment. We believe that thus a more balanced life can be produced for the individual and for the community.[2]

Yet this new emphasis on human "spiritual growth" and aesthetics required no substantial change in the four functional categories of planning, although "Recreation" was replaced by the "Cultivation of mind and body."[3] Overall the impression of the meeting seems to have been one of optimism. The young Dutch architect Aldo van Eyck (1918–99) proclaimed the end of Cartesian common sense (in favor of imagination) and asserted that the new role of CIAM "is first and foremost an affirmation of this new consciousness."[4]

At the seventh and eighth CIAM congresses, which took place in Bergamo, Italy, in 1949, and Hoddesdon, England, in 1951, this optimism began to wane. The affair at Bergamo, arranged in part by ASCORAL, was poorly organized and poorly attended. Le Corbusier chaired a session on "Applications of the Athens Charter," hoping to produce a new and broader "Charter of Habitat" to replace the earlier one. This was a proposal that would be discussed over the next several conferences without progress. Giedion again raised the issue of aesthetics, which resulted in the charge leveled

against him by the Polish architect Helena Syrkus – that the West was practicing formalism, while "In the East, where the people have reached a positive phase of development, the works of Picasso have no meaning and are forbidden."[5] The lone American representative at the conference, James Johnson Sweeny of the Museum of Modern Art, used his time, oddly, to ridicule the artistic sophistication of President Truman.[6] Giedion later published these comments under the heading "Architects and Politics: An East-West Discussion."

The most interesting result of the seventh CIAM congress was the critique of its proceedings by Bruno Zevi. In his journal *Metron*, he struck forcefully at the heart of one of CIAM's most glaring weaknesses: the dominance of the congress by the aging rationalist attitudes of Le Corbusier, Gropius, and Giedion, at the expense of excluding any other modern point of view:

The other branch of modern architecture, that which is no longer rationalistic, the movement which is called organic, or of human architecture, or of the New Empiricism, doesn't have adequate representation in the CIAM and its cultural position has been defended by architects who entered the CIAM as proponents of the rationalist school ten years ago and have since undergone an evolution. An entire generation of young architects who have contributed to the advancement of the modern movement, and all the adherents of the Wright school have been more or less excluded. Why?[7]

At this point Zevi launches what was essentially a tirade against Giedion, citing the historical shortcomings of *Space, Time and Architecture*; its exclusion of so many of the principal figures of early modernism (such as Mendelsohn); and Giedion's failure to recognize postrationalist, postwar architectural movements. CIAM, with its archaic mindset, he notes, "cannot make such a judgment without causing two great consequences: (1) first of all, it would no longer control the New Empiricism, whose road is without doubt full of difficulties and danger; (2) it would isolate itself from the current problematics of architecture, withdrawing into an ivory tower of the conquered past."[8] His conclusion also raises a seemingly new issue: the fact that CIAM was already dividing along generational lines.

The eighth conference at Hoddesdon in 1951 focused on the theme "Heart of the City," or public urban space. Another drive to encourage American participation failed, and Philip Johnson, representing MoMA, was the only native-born American to attend. Junzo Sakakura, Kunio Maekawa, and Kenzo Tange attended from Japan, but the hoped-for participation of Latin American architects failed to materialize, in part because of the high cost of travel. Once again the meeting was dominated by Le Corbusier, Sert, the Dutch architects, and the MARS group, which up to this time had been particularly successful in putting CIAM models into practice in their reconstruction efforts. A multitude of projects were presented, producing endless debate over seemingly trivial matters and little discussion of substance.

The situation was different with the ninth CIAM congress, held in Aix-en-Provence in 1953. This congress marks the beginning of the end of the organization. Many factors were now conspiring to challenge its premises. Gropius had just turned seventy and had retired from Harvard University, where Sert succeeded him. Both Giedion and Le Corbusier were in their mid-sixties and still quite active, yet both men, because of their busy schedules, expressed a desire to delegate some of their authority to the younger generation. The organization itself was celebrating its quarter-century mark, and murmurings against its aesthetic and urbanistic principles, first sounded by Zevi, were beginning to reverberate from other quarters. Equally significant, the MARS group itself had split ideologically, and those sympathetic to Scandinavian models found themselves shunned and even ousted by the younger supporters of Corbusian block-type housing solutions.

On the surface the ninth congress ran smoothly. Over 500 members from thirty-one countries attended the meetings, which centered on the theme of "Human Habitat." Six commissions reported on the issues of urbanism, visual arts, architectural education, building techniques, legislation, and social programs. The congress concluded, curiously, with a display of striptease dancers on the roof terrace of Le Corbusier's Unité in Marseilles, an event arranged by the French delegation. Never had Le Corbusier's star shown brighter to his European acolytes than at this moment, although troubling signs were also discernible.

One sign of discontent came from a group of architects working in Casablanca for the agency ATBAT-Afrique, which included Michel Écochard, Vladimir Bodiansky, Georges Candilis, and Shadrach Woods. They displayed their innovative schemes for Moroccan squatter settlements (based on the region's traditional casbahs), which placed the design emphasis on stacked courtyards as the center of family life.[9] Another group, led by Pierre-André Emery, presented an analysis of Algerian squatter settlements. In addition, Alison and Peter Smithson, together with William and Gillian Howell and John Voelcker, presented their "Urban Reidentification" scheme, which – while short on architectural

content – at least expressed the view that a "hierarchy of human associations" (house, street, district, city) should replace the functional hierarchy (housing, recreation, transportation, work) of the Athens Charter.[10]

The Smithsons also participated in the "social programs" session, chaired by Emery and Candilis, which discussed the housing needs of nonindustrial societies. Another subcommittee, on "Urbanism," led by the Dutch architect Jacob Bakema, raised similar issues and explored their social, political, economic, and geographic dimensions. The new anthropological awareness of non-European cultures, which had been almost totally absent from earlier CIAM congresses, in a subtle yet forceful way undercut not only the presumed universality of Le Corbusier's Unité solution for housing but also the functional premises of the Athens Charter. The CIAM congress in Aix-en-Provence had a symbolic ending as well. On the last day of the conference, van Eyck is said to have interrupted the applause given to an honorary speech of Gropius on teamwork, mass production, and standardization by smashing a wine bottle against a wall of the courtyard as a vituperative reply to his "dear kind industry-happy future-anti–prima-donna-teamwork design gruel."[11] The generational rift was now unbridgeable.

The insurrection that followed the conference was carried out by British and Dutch architects. At the end of 1953, the Smithsons, the Howells, and Voelcker met in London to discuss the problem of CIAM's evolution into an ineffective bureaucratic institution. In Holland, a few weeks later, a Dutch group led by Bakema, van Eyck, and Mart Stam did the same. Out of their concerns came the so-called Doorn Manifesto, written at a meeting that took place in Holland at the end of January 1954. The meeting was attended by Giedion, Sert, and van Eesteren as well as by younger architects such as Bakema, van Eyck, H. P. Daniel van Ginkel, Hans Hovens-Greve, Peter Smithson, and Voelcker. The statement, drafted by the dissidents, was based on the "valley" diagram of Patrick Geddes, which located cities at the center of the valley floor, with towns, villages, and detached buildings occupying successively higher layers of the two hillsides. The dissidents argued that the functionally divided city did not take into account "vital human associations" and thus failed to recognize cities "as communities of varying degrees of complexity."[12] If a new "Charter of Habitat" were to be developed by CIAM, they argued, it must take into account "human association" as its first principle and relegate the four daily functions to subcategories of human association. Although the possibility of a breakaway organization was discussed at this meeting, the manifesto was not intended to announce one. The goal at this point was to force CIAM to accept a new model for its deliberations and develop a new charter to replace the Athens Charter.

The manifesto first met with success. At a CIAM council meeting in Paris in June, whose order of business was to plan the next congress, to be held in Algiers in 1955, a "Committee for CIAM 10" was decreed. It consisted of Bakema, Peter Smithson, Candilis, and Rolf Gutmann; this working group was later expanded to include other future members of Team 10, such as Woods, Alison Smithson, William Howell, Voelcker, and van Eyck. The committee's task was not to write the new "charter of habitat" but to prepare statements and resolutions for drafting the charter at the conference. At another meeting in Paris (held in September 1954), the same working committee met with Le Corbusier and Giedion and produced a proposed framework for considering habitat. The report, however, was not well received by either Le Corbusier or Giedion, who deemed it too vague. The committee also argued that CIAM had grown too large to operate effectively and needed to be drastically trimmed in size. Further meetings of this committee produced little in the way of results, and the conference scheduled for Algiers was cancelled because of Algeria's war of independence against France.

When the tenth CIAM congress officially opened in Dubrovnik, Croatia, in August 1956, little had been decided – and in fact little would be. The invited members numbered only 250 and came from fifteen countries, but the split between the Team 10 group and the older members (and within Team 10 between the Dutch and English contingents) was now painfully apparent. The conference is notable for the fact that neither Gropius nor Le Corbusier attended, but the latter, in a letter read by President Sert, handed the "baton" to the younger generation, together with his wishes for a long-lived "SECOND CIAM!"[13] Dozens of papers and visual presentations produced no new charter, and at the conclusion of the conference, Sert announced that CIAM's executive committee was dissolving itself and that the various national groups would be allowed to function autonomously. Moreover, the congress voted to entrust him and Harvard University (where he had replaced Gropius) with the task of writing the new habitat charter. It was an extraordinary act of near-surrender on the part of Sert and Giedion, just short of actually dissolving the institution.

Over the next year, several strategy sessions were held to decide the fate of the organization and its reform action, with the consensus being that its size had to be reduced still further. CIAM's unofficial successor organization – Team 10 – now embarked on a more defined and independent course, as the English architects in particular opposed continuing their activities under the aegis of CIAM. Team 10's founding members were Bakema, van Eyck, the Smithsons, the Howells, Candilis, Woods, Voelcker, van Ginkel, Hovens-Greve, and Gutmann.

In Otterlo, Belgium, in September 1959, the final CIAM congress took place under the heading "CIAM: Research Group for Social and Visual Relationships." The official title of the conference – CIAM'59 – was meant to indicate that this was not simply a continuation of the earlier CIAM gatherings but a new event.[14] Forty-three carefully selected participants, including the ninety-four-year-old Henry van de Velde, attended the eight-day session in the Kröller-Müller Museum. The conference was notable for its lectures and for the many animated discussions that erupted in the final days. Louis Kahn, attending his first CIAM conference, gave an impassioned talk on his own philosophy of design as manifest in the Richards Medical Center – a talk that remains one of the best summaries of his design ideas.[15] Aldo van Eyck was equally philosophical in his lecture "Is Architecture Going to Reconcile Basic Values?" that is, where is it going "to rediscover the archaic principles of human nature" and to "stop fondling technique for its own sake – stop stumbling after progress?"[16]

The decorum shown in these lectures was in far less supply during the design presentations. The Washington architect Wendell H. Lovett was feasted upon by a number of Team 10 members, beginning with Alison Smithson, who censored him for having produced a "typical American house" that "tells us absolutely nothing new."[17] Giancarlo De Carlo endured a similar fate while presenting his brick-and-concrete housing project (featuring gables and tiled roofs) for the town of Matera in southern Italy. In his talk De Carlo pleaded for "pliant and adjustable plans which must proceed, not from abstract ideological rules, but from a detailed knowledge of historic realities which vary from country to country."[18] In short, he argued for a modernism that took into account national and historical traditions. Candilis, however, criticized De Carlo's scheme for its "rigidity," while André Wogenscky went even further and deplored its "totally Euclidian spirit, in which all the elements are fixed and of the same value."[19] The always contentious Peter Smithson likened its blocklike forms and rectilinear geometry to a "reimposition of past social contents," similar to what had taken place in the communist world.[20] Only a bruised Lovett came to De Carlo's defense by criticizing Team 10 members for "trying to find a common solution to all of the world's problems" and for insisting on "an architecture of utter conformity."[21]

Smithson's argumentative behavior emerged once again at the end of Ernesto Rogers's presentation of his firm's (BBPR) recently completed Torre Velasca in Milan. Smithson felt compelled to point out not only the design's historical allusions but its overall "irresponsibility."[22] The skyscraper, which still dominates the Milanese skyline, was controversial because the top stories, the residential floors, project out from the narrower office floors below and are supported on diagonal concrete braces. Rogers at the conference and elsewhere defended the design as a continuation of the structural explorations of Viollet-le-Duc and Perret and as a local response to the structural expressiveness of the Milan Cathedral – in effect, a response to the historical context or "atmosphere" of the city.[23] The top-heavy form of the tower, which to some called to mind the medieval towers of such cities as Florence and Siena, was, in Rogers's explanation, not the result of historical considerations, but rather the logical outcome of building in a confined urban space and accommodating the need for air and light at ground level. But at the same time he did not deny history a role in design, as he concluded his talk by noting, "The attitude of the fathers of modern architecture was anti-historical. But this was an attitude which was born of a great revolution and it was necessary that the first premise of our culture be a new attitude to history. But this is now no longer necessary."[24]

Smithson saw the medieval shape of the tower as "so explicit" and "shot through with overtones of a former plastic vocabulary, that it does not represent a model of a moral sort but of an immoral sort."[25] Jacob Bakema decried its failure to contribute to the life of the street as well as its false historical associations: "I think that form is a communication about life, and I don't recognize in this building a communication about life in our time. You are resisting contemporary life."[26]

The feud between Rogers and Smithson flared again at the end of Kenzo Tange's presentation of several of his buildings, which Rogers interpreted as supporting his position because they represented, in his view, a modernism "translated into the Japanese language."[27] Tange, however, understood Rogers's remark as implying that he practiced a form of regionalism, that is, used regional characteristics for decorative purposes, which he summarily rejected. But Smithson went further: "I am always a bit wary of what Rogers says. There is inside his statement a plea for a re-evaluation of

one's own history as an a priori. I think this is not only completely wrong but dangerous."[28]

Somewhat mercifully, the Otterlo conference ended with the quiet decision by Sert, Giedion, and others to discontinue the use of the name CIAM. A public letter published one year later and signed by Sert, Gropius, and Le Corbusier suggested that a "minority group of members" – presumably Team 10 – had undermined the intentions and effectiveness of the organization.[29]

The letter also pointed out the contributions CIAM had made to twentieth-century architecture and urban theory. Some of these contributions were unquestionably great, others were of debatable value. CIAM was an organization of many speeches, many reports, some debate, and much general discussion, but in the end, as in the case of all such entities, its agenda was tightly controlled by an inner circle. It certainly brought attention to the problems of urban design, and in fact helped to establish urban design as a serious field in its own right, but it also promoted a one-sided and, for many, flawed vision of the city. The two best-known examples of CIAM's strategies applied to urban planning – Chandigarh and Brasília – underscore the severe limitations of its conceptual framework.

The former was a new city created by Jawaharlal Nehru, the first prime minister of India, which gained its independence from Britain in 1947. Because the western part of the province of Punjab (including the capital Lahore) had been ceded to the neighboring new state of Pakistan, the Hindu part of the province needed a new capital, and so Chandigarh was created.[30] The American planner Albert Mayer was commissioned to prepare the first plan in 1949, and he hired Matthew Nowicki to head the design team to develop its architecture. Aspects of Mayer's initial plan – the location of the government palaces at the head of the scheme, the functional separation of a business center from the surrounding neighborhoods, large automobile arteries – already carry the imprint of CIAM prescriptions; only the slight curving of the streets harkened back to Sittesque ideas. Norwicki visited the site in the spring of 1950 and prepared the first sketches of what might emerge, but his death in a plane crash on his return home meant that officials had to search for a new architect to implement the Mayer plan. Maxwell Fry and Jane Drew were approached, but they were unable to devote themselves full time to the project, and they suggested that the Indians contact Le Corbusier. The latter, in turn, brought in his brother Pierre Jeanneret. As Fry later related the story, he, Drew, and the two Frenchmen arrived in the village of Chandigarh late in 1950, and before Mayer's arrival Le Corbusier sat down with a large sheet of paper and, over a period of four days, completely redrew the plan. When Mayer arrived, he was no "match for the enigmatic but determined figure of the prophet."[31] Le Corbusier, his brother, and his two British seconds now controlled the process entirely. Some earlier elements were retained yet strengthened by the straightening of the arteries and the imposition of a colossal central artery. Buildings were placed at vast distances from each other, with scarcely a suggestion of urban space or a tree to relieve the glaring sunlight. Pedestrians were consigned to buses or long bicycle rides. For all of CIAM's emphasis on planning models and research, little or no consideration was given to Indian culture and ways of living or to the demands of the climate. In the end the plan can be read as a variation of Le Corbusier's Radiant City without the Cartesian skyscrapers – it is a city somewhat naively interpreted in architectural textbooks almost entirely on the basis of the few large monuments.

The other example of a CIAM city in the 1950s, the tropical city of Brasília, was no more successful.[32] It arose out of a competition for a new capital, a city more centrally situated within the vast land area of Brazil, and its main features were rapidly built between 1957 and 1960. Its planner, Lúcio Costa, and its leading architect, Oscar Niemeyer, both had long connections with the French master, going back to the Ministry of Education and Culture in the mid-1930s. Again, the plan observes the separation of functions demanded by CIAM. In this case, two mammoth, intersecting vehicular axes transform the physical center of the city into a vast wasteland of unusable space surrounding the three levels of traffic interchanges. The symbolic civic center is pushed two kilometers to the east from this interchange and is inaccessible to pedestrians. Businesses are arrayed along the north-south axis and are functionally separated from the residential blocks. The housing groups represent some of the more unimaginative mingling of low- and high-rise blocks ever conceived. The streets are dead, the Corbusian-style housing is beyond the means of most workers, and thus the greenbelt surrounding the closed plan quickly became a symbolic barrier dividing the rich and the poor – the latter now pushed to satellite squatter settlements beyond.

Not all of the Team 10 alternatives to CIAM models offer something substantially different. In the *Team 10 Primer* (1962), the Smithsons insist that the group formed "because of mutual realization of the inadequacies of the processes of architectural thought which they had inherited from the modern movement as a whole."[33] But the precise nature of these inadequacies are nowhere spelled out except in very general terms. In the Smithsons' successive "utopian" projects of the 1950s – from their Golden Lane Deck housing design (1952) to their proposal for Sheffield University (1953) to its logical extension, the idea of a "Cluster City" (1957) – they champion the notions of identity, comprehensibility, density, structure, pattern, growth, and mobility. In the end, however, their visual proposals feature the familiar Corbusian blocks, only now with pedestrian "streets" lifted high into the air. These streets seemingly constitute the gist of their "ecological approach to the problem of habitat."[34] Ebenezer Howard's Garden City, bound to the ground and the landscape, remains the hated antithesis.

Others involved with Team 10, however, did represent something of a break. Giancarlo de Carlo, who was later drafted into the organization, was one of Italy's most talented and thoughtful architects. His housing project for southern Italy, as we have seen, was severely criticized at Otterlo in 1959 by the Smithsons for its local cultural expression, and indeed it falls in line with larger Italian regionalist developments. De Carlo showed his respect for locale in his design for the college and student dormitories at Urbino (1962–5) and in his master plan for Urbino (1966).[35] In the first case, the large housing block has been shattered, and its smaller cells are more sensitively and comfortably integrated into the beautiful sloping landscape – a design that even pays Wrightian homage to the crown of the hillside. In the second case, the historic core of the town has been fully honored and protected.

The work of Bakema and van Eyck in Holland share a concern for local anthropology and the urban environment. The Rotterdam architect and planner Bakema (1914–81), in his partnership with J. H. van den Broek, had been one of the most active architects in Holland in the postwar decades. Rotterdam had been destroyed by German bombers in 1940, and van den Broek and Bakema's creation of the Linjbaan (1948–53) defined a new city center. Mumford was one of the keenest admirers of his efforts. Since 1947 Bakema had attended all of the CIAM meetings and displayed several of his urban projects in Rotterdam and elsewhere, but one can also sense from his comments his growing discomfort with the urban premises of the organization. He was a committed socialist but at the same time a partisan of personal freedom and artistic integration; he was much attracted to Johan Huizinga's *Homo Ludens* (1938) and was convinced of the necessity of human play.[36] His break with Giedion came in 1957, and his later partnership with the Smithsons, although perplexing, must be interpreted as an attempt to strike out on a new path.

Then there is the enigmatic figure of van Eyck, who alone among the Team 10 members shifted architectural theory onto fresh ground.[37] His connections with members of CIAM were also of long standing. While attending the ETH in Zurich in 1938–42, van Eyck had met and befriended Carola Giedion-Welcker (Sigfried Giedion's wife) and through her was introduced into Zurich's avant-garde circles during the war years, which deeply affected his artistic outlook. He worked for the Amsterdam Public Works Department after the war, but his very strong anthropological inclination was cultivated during two trips he and his wife, Hannie von Roojen, made in 1951 and 1952 to the remote Saharan desert and mountain regions of southern Algeria. On a return trip in 1959 he made his way further south into the region of Timbuktu (in Mali), where he explored the little known culture of the Dogon along the steppes of the Niger River, whose villages and houses are noted for their cosmological complexity and plastic forms. Also drawing upon the structuralism of Claude Lévi-Strauss, which emphasized the universal and unchanging patterns of human thought, van Eyck in the 1950s brought together these disparate influences in subtle, geometrically based designs for playgrounds (over sixty) and schools and most famously in his masterful orphanage in Amsterdam (1955–60). This last work is a carefully arranged, open-ended, yet supremely geometric solution to the problem of housing 125 children. The individual classrooms and the play and living areas are broken down into spatially autonomous (shallow domed, inspired by a *kava* bowl from the Fiji Islands) and small-scale units and speak to his insistence on "place" and "occasion" over and above the failed abstractions of "space" and "time." Here, as well, his intention was profoundly therapeutic: "What has happened to them has twisted them in many ways and they need untwisting."[38]

Van Eyck's highly poetic writings, particularly those he published in the Dutch journal *Forum* in 1959–63, are rich in intimations and clearly express his unique concerns. Even in his first address to the CIAM congress in Bridgewater in 1947, he was forceful in his denunciation of rationalist and mechanistic thinking. As he noted at one point, "The more tangible functions – those implied by the word 'functionalism' – are only relevant in so far as they help to adjust man's environment more accurately to his elementary requirements."[39] Van Eyck ultimately rejected the term *rationalism* altogether, and elementary human requirements for him became entirely psychological and emotional. In theory and practice, van Eyck sought to address the very primal and universal human urge to obtain a just

recognition of one's individuality, identity, and presence in the world.

The small temporary sculpture pavilion van Eyck built at Arnheim in 1965–6, with its bare concrete-block walls, might serve as a visual metaphor for his notion of "labryinthian clarity" – the absolute clarity of the defining square and circle and the linear order within which the exceptional, the special case, necessarily appears as a place of pause and contemplation. "Space and time must be 'opened,'" he noted several years earlier, "interiorized so that they can be entered; persuaded to gather man into their meaning – include him."[40] From such a vantage point, the doctrines of rationalism, modernism, and functionalism fail architecture because they are abstractions that do not concern themselves with everyday experience. Van Eyck's view of architecture is essentially phenomenological in its grounding and very different, for instance, from the Smithsons' plea for a clarity of organization. With his Bachelardian focus on interior horizons or depths of human consciousness, van Eyck rather curiously aligns himself with Giedion's ethnological interests in the late 1950s and 1960s, thereby returning to one of his intellectual wellsprings.[41] At the same time, his attempt to salvage, indeed enrich, architectural meaning through his regard for human experience rather starkly confronts some of the technocratic assumptions of mainstream modernism's formal vocabulary. He may have felt a personal affinity for the French painter and architect, but he stands much closer to Louis Kahn as one of the few architects at this time willing to reexamine the tenets of modernism. Team 10 is seemingly extraneous to his pursuits.

2. The Italian "Retreat" from the Modern Movement

The collapse of CIAM and the rise of Team 10 was but one manifestation of a growing discontent with the idea of unified modernism in the late 1950s. Under Ernesto Nathan Rogers's directorship, *Casabella-Continuità*, which by the mid-1950s had become the most important theoretical journal on the Continent, provided another forum for serious debate. It was a wide-ranging journal that covered the work of major architects such as Le Corbusier, Mies van der Rohe, and Frank Lloyd Wright as well as the recent work of Italian architects, in particular, younger architects. A section at the back of the journal surveyed what other major journals around the world were publishing, which made it a compendium of sorts. Another feature was the lead editorial, which often touched on theoretical concerns. For one issue published in 1955, for instance, the art historian Giulio Carlo Argan wrote an editorial that politely chided Rogers for his laudatory coverage of Le Corbusier's Ronchamp.[42] Rogers responded directly, and in the following issue De Carlo, in another lead editorial, challenged Rogers again, claiming that his interest in such largely irrelevant works "is blocking the development of a freer and less dogmatic architecture."[43] Le Corbusier is an important master, Argan went on to say, "but we have come to a parting of the ways," and in the end he will perhaps be viewed in the same way we view Gaudi, as "a great creator of works rich in high poetic content, but outside the circle of our immediate interests and so far removed from our problems as to appear exotic."[44] In the same issue, the journal's editor, Vittorio Gregotti, praised recent works of Mario Ridolfi "based on the experience of rediscovery inherent in the spontaneous Italian tradition."[45]

The last comment of course relates to the theme of "continuity" and a respect for the Italian tradition that Rogers brought to the journal. In an earlier issue of 1955, Rogers had noted, "To pretend to build in a preconceived 'modern style' is as absurd as to demand respect for the taboo of past styles."[46] Rogers's idea of modernism thus took account of the environmental, cultural, and historical context in which a building has to be situated so it can be modified in light of historical consciousness, that is, recognized as part of the same historical development. In his words, "To be modern means simply to sense contemporary history within the order of all of history and thus to feel the responsibility of one's own acts not from within the closed barricade of an egoistic manifestation, but as a collaboration that, through one's contribution, augments and enriches the perennial contemporaneity of the possible formal combinations of universal relationship."[47] Behind this statement stands the charge that the "first masters" of the modern movement overused technology as an expressive symbol in its own right, to the exclusion of contextual influences in design. Overemphasis on the abstraction of a preconceived "modern" model, in his view, resulted in a static formalism.

In 1957 these concerns came to a head in a single issue of the journal. Rogers opens with the editorial "Continuità o crisi?" (Continuity or crisis?), which summarizes his earlier arguments for respecting tradition while not falling into the trap of historicism.[48] More interesting is what follows. Aldo Rossi writes about a contemporary art nouveau studio. Two housing complexes of Mario Ridolfi are considered, including his complex on the Viale Etiopia, which is discussed for its integration of historicist allusions and craftwork into the

concrete structure. Most interesting is a building – the *Bottega d'Erasmo* (The Erasmus Shop) – designed by the young Turinese architects Roberto Gabetti (b. 1925) and Aimaro d'Isola (b. 1928) (Fig. 101). Bringing together offices, shops, and apartments in one building, the expressive and richly detailed work exploits the use of brick and wrought iron with references to Berlage and Perret at the start of the century, an era in Italy known as the "Liberty" period.

The issue evoked little immediate discussion, but the next year another young architect, Paolo Portoghesi, published a related article entitled "Dal Neorealismo al Neoliberty" (From Neorealism to Neoliberty), which surveyed in a critical way the main lines of Italian architecture since the war.[49] His contention was that in Italy there had been two distinct phases of postwar development – first a phase of Neorealism (a term he borrows from the cinematic style of Vittorio De Sica) born of the homelessness produced by the war and represented by the populist motifs displayed in Ridolfi's housing complex on Viale Etiopia, among other works. In the second phase, the so-called Neoliberty phase, Italian architects in the mid-1950s began to explore the very first period of Italian modernism, the period between Art Nouveau and the rationalism of the late 1920s, specifically to augment the modernist vocabulary and to resituate Italian modernism within Italy's historical tradition. Regional expressiveness and material richness are the desired qualities of this phase, although the Neoliberty style more often than not lapses into a picturesqueness that is both arbitrary and conventional.

Rogers indeed was consciously posing a challenge to the vision of modernism espoused by CIAM, and that there would be a response to his views was certainly predictable – but not the particular response that occurred in the spring of 1959, on the eve of the Otterlo conference. It came not from one of the CIAM or Team 10 members (who would confront him en masse at the conference) but rather from the English historian Reyner Banham, who had become a critic for the London journal *Architectural Review*. Brashly entitled "Neoliberty: The Italian Retreat from Modern Architecture," the article struck at the heart of the reformation that Rogers was precipitating.

It was hardly a spontaneous attack. Since the early 1950s Banham had been working under Nikolaus Pevsner on a doctorate in art history, and his dissertation centered on Italian futurism. He was thus a regular visitor to Italy and had written several reviews of contemporary Italian practice over the course of the 1950s – mostly negative. In a 1952 review of the Palazzo Grande at Leghorn by Luigi Vagnetti, Banham

101. Roberto Gabetti and Aimaro d'Isola, Bottega d'Erasmo, Turin, 1953–6. From "Bottega d'Erasmo," *Casabella*, no. 215 (April-May 1957).

expressed his "disquiet and misgiving" that a "new eclecticism within the modern movement" had arisen, prompted by this building's "Quattrocento and Mannerist treatments for the stone cladding," by the Gothic rhythm of the gables, and by the symmetry of the plan and its relationship to the cathedral opposite.[50] In a 1953 review of Luigi Moretti's Casa del Girasole – the Roman apartment house that would later figure prominently in Robert Venturi's mannerist critique – Banham expresses both hatred and love for its "decorative bravado, a flourish of sumptuous effect" (born of the Italian sunlight), its "strong relationship to palazzi of the baroque past."[51]

His 1959 article, however, is decidedly more militant in its examination of the "baffling turn" recently taken by Milanese and Torinese architects. Banham sets out to examine the Neoliberty trend within the context of Italian theory in the first half of the century, which in his eyes is already

suspect, first because of its relatively late development in the 1930s (despite futurist proddings) and second because of its uneasy connection with Fascism. What Banham also finds odd is the choice of the Liberty period for historical reevaluation, which again underplays the importance of Italian futurism within Italian theory. In his view futurism was almost the only ideology of the first half of the century to embrace fully the machine aesthetic of industry and technology. Citing an article by Aldo Rossi alluding to the middle-class situation at the turn of the century, Banham argues that one can never return to the preindustrial past for inspiration, because as Marinetti "with his fanatical automobilism" already recognized in 1909, "Art Nouveau died of a cultural revolution that seems absolutely irreversible: the domestic revolution that began with electric cookers, vacuum cleaners, the telephone, the gramophone, and all those other mechanized aids to gracious living that are still invading the home, and have permanently altered the nature of domestic life and the meaning of domestic architecture."[52] Moreover, this unbridgeable chasm between the modernism after 1909 and the premodern past is further marked out by the manifesto of futurism, the European discovery of Wright, Adolf Loos, the Werkbund, and cubism – all of which have worked a radical change in aesthetic perspectives. Banham closes with a stunning verbal assault:

To want to put on those old clothes again is to be, in Marinetti's words describing Ruskin, like a man who has attained full physical maturity, yet wants to sleep in his cot again, to be suckled again by his decrepit nurse, in order to regain the nonchalance of his childhood. Even by the purely local standards of Milan and Turin, then, Neoliberty is infantile regression.[53]

Rogers countered Banham in June with an inspired retort, "The Evolution of Architecture: An Answer to the Caretaker of Frigidaires." After providing the Italian reader with a Proustian image of the odors of stuffed fish he associates with *Architectural Review* (that is, the pub in the basement of its offices at Queen Anne's Gate), Rogers rebukes Banham for his "superficial and hasty" remarks and "rigid incomprehension of many fundamental events" and makes the following claim in his own defense:

The modern Movement is not dead at all for us: our modernity consists in actually carrying on the tradition of the Masters (of course Wright's tradition as well). But our being sensitive to the beauty (and not only to the documentary values) of a number of manifestations which hitherto had not been sufficiently appreciated, is certainly to our credit. And it is also to our credit to have given a historical framework and a present-day meaning to a number of values which had been neglected in the thick of other battles.[54]

Echoing his earlier emphasis on historical continuity, he assents that the strength of the work of Ridolfi, Gardella, Michelucci, Albini, and others is really "that they understood the Modern movement as a 'continuous revolution,' that is to say, as a continuous development of the principle of adhering to the changing content of life."[55] The chasm that Banham sees between the preindustrial and industrial worlds simply does not exist for Rogers. Indeed, for Banham – this dispenser of "absolution and condemnation" – the "formal determinism according to an abstract line of development seems to take the place of the concept of history."[56]

The matter did not stop here, as Rogers, and his design for the Torre Velasca, was again ambushed by Banham's close friends – the Smithsons – at Otterlo. Rogers mounted

another defense of his Milan building in the October issue of *Casabella-Continuità* by using a metaphor of the city as a "museum," that is, as a collection of expressive historical artifacts, in the words of Marco Frascari, "for associating and generating critical images."[57] In the same issue an article by John Woodbridge on the Bay Region style offered another instructive dimension to the debate.[58] *Architectural Review* responded in kind by translating the futurist manifesto in their August-September issue and by publishing follow-up articles in December and January.[59] But this particular debate had run its course. The generational rift that had broken the back of CIAM had here expanded into a cultural divide. Banham was tacking one course and Italy quite another; the rift between these two cultures would continue into the next decade.

3. Banham, Archigram, Metabolism, and Other Utopianisms

Banham's remarks have sometimes been interpreted as an attempt by an orthodox modernist to squash heresies within a rigid modernist outlook, but in fact his position was more complex.[60] In addition to his doctoral studies and writing, Banham had been active within the Independent Group (IG). Although he knew the Smithsons well (his identification of the cause of New Brutalism with their efforts certainly advanced their standing), he was closer in his own intellectual development to the wing of IG inhabited by Richard Hamilton, Lawrence Alloway, and John McHale. Together they shared an enthusiasm for American pop culture, jazz, advertising, Hollywood films, science fiction, Detroit cars, and, increasingly, the ideas of Buckminster Fuller. This was in fact the "beatnik" beginning of the countercultural revolution that would fully manifest itself internationally by the middle of the 1960s. Banham by this time would arrive at his own historical perspective.

The book that heralded his novel viewpoint is his now classic *Theory and Design in the First Machine Age* (1960).[61] It was based on his dissertation and combines research carried out under Pevsner with a beginning chapter and a concluding chapter on the meaning of the "Second Machine Age" – that age emerging in the late 1950s. The historical component is a study of the First Machine Age. This study begins, somewhat tenuously, with chapters on Julien Guadet and Auguste Choisy and the suggestion of a linkage between French academic theory and the logical unfolding of the modern movement. Banham next works his way through the contributions of Berlage, Wright, futurism, and cubism to the expressionists and rationalists of the 1920s. The review has some notable weaknesses as well as strengths. Among the former are Banham's almost total unfamiliarity with Germanic theory in the second half of the nineteenth century (which leads him to overemphasize the influence of Guadet and Choisy) and, understandably, his limited knowledge of Soviet theory. Its principal strength, in addition to its many novel observations, is the attention that Banham gives to futurism and later to such artists as László Moholy-Nagy. The central theme of the book is that the futurists (with their emphasis on motion and disorder) were the only theorists to understand the radical implications of the machine and its irreconcilability with traditional aesthetics. Rationalists such as Gropius and Le Corbusier paid verbal homage to the machine but, in Banham's view, still conceptualized and organized their work under the formal guidelines of past academic theory. True visionary inventions – such as Buckminster Fuller's Dymaxion house – were conceived entirely as products of technological engineering and thus paid no attention to the need for an overlay of aesthetics. Therefore architects of the 1930s and later who interpreted modern architecture simply as a product of materials and construction (the functionalists) missed the essential formative factors of the First Machine Age, which resided rather within the fundamental change of living habits and attitudes brought on by such technological appliances as the automobile.

This segue leads Banham to his remarks in the opening and concluding chapters regarding the Second Machine Age, which he now sees forming. If the products of the First Machine Age were connected with electricity and the combustion engine and their limited application to individual households, they were still largely the instruments of the capitalist elite or symbols of power. Much, however, has since changed. Razors, clippers, hair dryers, radios, telephones, tape recorders, hi-fi equipment, mixers, grinders, automatic cookers, washing machines, refrigerators, and vacuum cleaners have become commonplace in the modern household, and the "housewife alone, often disposes of more horse-power today than an industrial worker did at the beginning of the century."[62] Moreover, "highly developed mass production methods have distributed electronic devices and synthetic chemicals broadcast over a large part of society – television, the symbolic machine of the Second Machine Age, has become a means of mass-communication."[63] As for the body of theory left over from the First Machine Age, well,

it is "as economically, socially, and technologically dead as the city-states of Greece."[64] A proper theory for the Second Machine Age has yet to emerge.

In the concluding chapter Banham returns to this issue. The idea of "functionalism" is, in Banham's view, as limited today as the former idea of "rationalism," and the extent of its limitation is heralded by the radically different approach of Fuller. He quotes a lengthy excerpt from a letter that Fuller sent to John McHale in 1955. In the excerpt Fuller comments on the conceptual limitations of international modernism:

> . . . the Bauhaus and International [style] used standard plumbing fixtures and only ventured so far as to persuade manufacturers to modify the surface of the valve handles and spigots, and the colour, size, and arrangements of the tiles. The international Bauhaus never went back to the wall-surface to look at the plumbing . . . they never enquired into the overall problem of sanitary fittings themselves. . . . In short they only looked at problems of modifications of the surface of end-products, which end-products were inherently sub-functions of a technically obsolete world.[65]

Banham further notes that Le Corbusier labeled his rooms with such designations as kitchen, laundry, and music room, while Fuller in the Dymaxion house collected all of the heating, lighting, cleaning, cooking, and ventilating into a functional central core and dispensed with outmoded designations or even rigid spatial definitions. Thus the ultimate failing of the rationalists of the 1920s (or even the Italian architects of the 1950s) was their choice of symbolic architectural forms conceived out of symbolic (architectural) mental processes, whereas the Second Machine Age demands a more thoroughgoing radicalization of the conceptualization process, one that redefines architecture itself, at least architecture in the traditional sense. He concludes this chapter with a flourish:

> It may well be that what we have hitherto understood as architecture, and what we are beginning to understand of technology are incompatible disciplines. The architect who proposes to run with technology knows now that he will be in fast company, and that, in order to keep up, he may have to emulate the Futurists and discard his whole cultural load, including the professional garments by which he is recognized as an architect. If, on the other hand, he decides not to do this, he may find that a technological culture has decided to go on without him.[66]

This becomes the central issue for Banham in the early 1960s, as he moves his critical campaign forward at full throttle. Shortly after his promotion at the *Architectural*

Review to assistant executive editor, he inaugurated in the spring of 1960 a series of five articles to consider technology under the framework of "Stocktaking." One takes the form of a symposium on the concept of the architect as "Universal Man."[67] Another brings in three specialists to discuss the design process of weapons systems and the impact of computers and the human sciences (Gestalt psychology, anthropology, sociology) on architectural design.[68] The most important, however, is his lead article, which consists of parallel texts, one on tradition and one on technology. In the text on tradition he returns to his polemic against the Neoliberty style, which he now lumps together with the New Empiricism and (distantly) with regionalism and neoclassicism as a capitulation to public taste – that is, a desire not "to put up buildings that the average citizen cannot understand."[69] In the text on technology he argues that technology will increasingly impinge on architecture over the next decade, bringing with it a host of new issues such as expendability, planned obsolescence, and nonrectilinear prefabrication: "It appears always possible that at any unpredictable moment the unorganized hordes of unco-ordinated specialists could flood over the architects' preserves and, ignorant of the lore of the operation, create an Other Architecture by chance, as it were, out of apparent intelligence and the task of creating fit environments for human activities."[70]

In a prominent lecture given at the Royal Institute of British Architects in February 1961, Banham again makes his case that architecture should assimilate the human sciences into design. He argues that design trends "follow the strongest available influence that can fill the vacuum of architectural theory" – Corb, Detroit styling, science fiction – and that either "British and world architects will join the intellectual adventure of Human Science and transform architecture, or it will fail to make the imaginative leap, and turn introspective again."[71]

In another six-article series written for *Architectural Review* in 1962, Banham puts contemporary architecture "On Trial," and interestingly one can here detect a change of course. Kahn, who practices a "buttery-hatch aesthetic," is out because his concept of served and servant spaces in the Richards Medical Center achieves nothing more technologically advanced than did Le Corbusier's Pavillon Suisse thirty years earlier.[72] Mies, who Banham notes has recently fallen out of favor, should be in favor because he was a "craftsman of technology" and understood that an architect's responsibility extended down to detailing and also because he knew "how to make architecture out of what is available, not just once, as with the Charles Eames house, nor through shock

tactics, as with Bruce Goff's army-surplus architecture, but by taking thought."[73] About two prefabricated systems – the British CLASP system and Jean Prouvé's "thin, bent detail" – he is ambivalent if appreciative of the effort. The article that most clearly indicates Banham's new direction is the fifth, "The Spec-Builders: Towards a Pop Architecture," which traces the phenomenon of pop architecture back to Albert Kahn's Ford Pavilion at the New York World's Fair of 1939. Arguing that technology "is morally, socially and politically neutral," Banham now takes his lead not from the space-age, high-tech images of Fuller but rather from spec builders and their conscious pandering to the vagaries of popular tastes – "architecture as package and commodity" – within a Madison Avenue society.[74] This confession is scarcely a form of catharsis for someone who, in his introduction to these articles, argues (convincingly) that suspended ceilings "constitute one of the most sophisticated elements in the technology of architecture."[75] At the same time, his almost gleeful embrace of consumerism stands in refreshing relief to the moralism of many high-minded intellectuals of the period, who regarded it as the despised outgrowth of late capitalist systems of commodity production.

By 1965 the transformation from "science for kicks" to pop was complete, and Banham (now taking his research to the United States) has advanced in his psychedelic exuberance to the point where he can now dispense with the concept of architecture altogether. His classic essay in this regard, "A Home Is Not a House," not only encapsulates his new theme but also takes architects to task for their seemingly incorrigible fixation on concealing the ever expanding role of mechanical systems in building design: "When your house contains such a complex of piping, flues, ducts, wires, lights, inlets, outlets, ovens, sinks, refuse disposers, hi-fi reverberators, antennae, conduits, freezers, heaters – when it contains so many services that the hardware could stand up by itself without any assistance from the house, why have a house to hold it up?"[76] His thesis is actually more elementary. Human beings, he notes, have since the beginning of time been living in two ways: first by hiding under a rock or tree, later translated into the permanent abode, and second by living in the open around a fireplace, which offers freedom of migration and variability. If the former defines the architecture of the past, the latter – intimated in the conceptual combination of the Fuller dome with a mobile-home package with its own gas and electrical supply – is clearly the preferred model for the future. A contemporary example of the "unhouse" is the Glass House of Philip Johnson, which (properly forgetting "all the erudition about Ledoux and Malevich and Palladio and stuff that has been published") eliminates the bounding walls and reduces itself to a heated brick slab with a fireplace.[77] The roof is of course objectionable, and Banham would replace it and the glass walls with a polyethylene air bubble, that is, "a properly set-up standard-of-living package, breathing out warm air along the ground (instead of sucking in cold along the ground like a campfire), radiating soft light and Dionne Warwick in heartwarming stereo, with a well-aged protein turning in an infrared glow in the rotisserie, and the icemaker discretely coughing cubes into glasses on the swing-out bar – this could do something for a woodland glade or creekside rock that *Playboy* could never do for its penthouse."[78] This "power-point homesteading in a paradise garden of appliances" (à la Wright's Broadacre City) might even move to other locations by riding on its own cushion of air, "like a hovercraft or domestic vacuum cleaner."[79]

If the reader is still unclear about what Banham is describing, the artist François Dallegret in the article portrays the mechanical components conveyed by a futurist GTO transcontinental automobile together with an environmental bubble plopped over a hillside, inside of which an unclothed Banham and Dallegret, in photocopied repetition, gather around the almighty entertainment center – a pristine uterine world (without "smell, smoke, ashes and mess") presumably reduced to the vibrating pulse of sex, drugs, and rock 'n' roll. This fascination with the nonarchitectural power of "gizmos," explored in another important follow-up essay, would culminate in *The Architecture of the Well-Tempered Environment* (1969) – notable for its visual juxtaposition of Fremont Street in Las Vegas with the Atomic Energy Commission's pneumatic theater.[80]

The transformation of Banham's thought in the early 1960s was in line with the intellectual ferment of these years, which was partially due to the economic recovery from the war and the rising standard of living and partially to the rapid escalation in number of young people – the "baby boom" generation – entering higher education. Members of this generation, who had generally been too young to have endured the hardships of the war, were buoyant and impulsive and optimistic about the possibility of dramatic social change. On the other hand, the intensifying social unrest and the Cuban missile crisis, for example, had emphatically made the point that technology could have severe consequences.

Also prominent in Britain in this decade was the work of Archigram, a group of young architects centered in

Hampstead and inspired in equal measure by the futuristic theories of Fuller, the technological glee of Banham, and the cultural hedonism of the period. The circle consisted of Peter Cook, Warren Chalk, Dennis Crompton, David Greene, Ron Herron, and Michael Webb. The first issue of *Archigram*, published in 1961, urgently announced, "A new generation of architecture must arise with forms and spaces which seem to reject the precepts of 'Modern' yet in fact retain these precepts. WE HAVE CHOSEN TO BYPASS THE DECAYING BAUHAUS IMAGE WHICH IS AN INSULT TO FUNCTIONALISM."[81] If such a mission initially suggests the poetry of "orbital helmets" and "body transportation methods," it had at least a semblance of architectonic form in Michael Webb's "Sin Centre," a thesis project of 1959–62 that brings together the amenities of a department store with bowling alleys, cinema, theater, dancing, coffee bars, and pubs under the conceptual umbrella of a "drive-in galleria."[82] By the journal's third issue, published in 1963, this feigned allegiance to the principles of a non-Bauhaus modernism is superceded by a more radical reconsideration of the human habitat and its space-age possibilities, beginning with Ron Heron and Warren Chalk's "Living City," based on the notion of expendability. With the appearance of Peter Cook's "Plug-In City" in the fifth issue of *Archigram*, published in 1964 – a three-dimensional infrastructure of ducts, pipes, and space frames into which are inserted "software" living capsules – this utopian vision begins to assume manic proportions. Ron Herron's "Walking City" (1964) looks to the other side of the pending nuclear holocaust, where legged urban pods housing a few lucky survivors stalk the devastated ruins of New York City. Not unrelated in intention is the "Fun Palace" of Cedric Price, a close friend of Banham. It began as a real project in 1961: a "laboratory of fun" planned for London's East End. Its three-dimensional system of space frames; ramps; moveable walls, floors, and ceilings; and air curtains was intended to serve the leisure-time activities of music, dance, drama therapy, modeling, films, and science and of course the new phenomenon of pop culture.

Preceding Archigram by a few years were the space-frame proposals of Yona Friedman (b. 1923), a Hungarian-born, Israeli-trained architect and engineer who relocated to Paris in 1957. His criticisms of the discussions of the 1956 CIAM conference led him to form the group GEAM (Groupe d'Etudes d'Architecture Mobile), which included, among others, Paul Maymont, Frei Otto, and Eckhard Schultze-Fielitz. Toward the end of 1957, Friedman had already written the first draft of his *L'Architecture Mobile* (1959), which outlined the ideas on which he would focus his efforts over the next several decades. When he talked about "mobile architecture," he did not mean a Banhamesque auto-transported system of high-tech accessories; rather, he was referring to the purported fact that the "concepts determining life in society are in perpetual transformation" but are now slanted toward leisure and are not being satisfied by the permanence of traditional architecture.[83] He proposed a global system of one thousand new cities each containing three million inhabitants. Each city would be entirely elevated on mechanical/structural supports and take the form of a colossal, multistory space frame in which inhabitants would have the freedom to locate their light weight "dwelling cells" wherever they wanted.

Friedman had his intellectual cohorts. In 1958 the Austrian artist Hundertwasser issued his "Mould Manifesto," which, in addition to allowing the apartment dweller to reach out the window and "paint everything around pink as far as he can reach with a long brush," called for pulling down "the buildings of Mies van der Rohe, Neutra, the Bauhaus, Gropius, Johnson, Le Corbusier, and so on, since in one generation they have become outmoded and morally unendurable."[84] In the same year the *Internationale Situationiste* – a Dada-inspired group – was formed by the Dutch painter Constant (Victor E. Nieuwenhuys) and the French critic Guy Debord, both men ordained by their reading of Huizinga as "specialists in play." In the formulaic language of the day, they vowed to combat the retrogressive ideologies of capitalism and come up with a solution that jointly resolved the futuristic needs of dwelling, transportation, and recreation and the social, psychological, and artistic needs of life.[85] In the late 1940s and early 1950s, Constant was associated with Aldo van Eyck and thus came to have some influence on Team 10.[86] In 1960 he left the situationists to pursue his own vision of a "New Babylon," an elevated city originally modeled on the work of Friedman.[87]

Also attracted to futurist thinking were the Japanese metabolists.[88] Their youthful alienation was different than that of the West, however, in that it grew out of the physical and psychological devastation of the war, what one historian has called an attempt to reconcile a general sense of cultural anxiety with "the euphoria of survival."[89] The name for the group, in which each architect was to propose "future designs of our coming world," was chosen because human society was a vital process, "a continuous development from atom to nebula. The reasons why we use such a biological word, the metabolism, is that, we believe, design and technology should be a denotation of human vitality."[90] The group was inspired by two projects of Kiyonori Kikutake,

who in 1958 constructed his "Sky House" in Tokyo and early the following year produced his "Marine City" project: a series of circular, plug-in house towers (300 meters tall and able to accommodate 5,000 inhabitants) accompanied by heavy industry on floating circular platforms. The plans were displayed by Kenzo Tange at the Otterlo conference in 1959.

Tange himself, the mentor rather than an official member of the group, was now past his Corbusian form-making and had become preoccupied with urban issues – first as a visiting professor at M.I.T. in 1959, where he gave his fifth-year students the project of designing a residential community for 25,000 people in Boston Harbor. He himself developed a more ambitious proposal for Tokyo Bay in 1960: a plan for a city of ten million that was nothing less than stupendous in concept and scale. Instead of adding to the concentric historic urban core of Tokyo, he suggested expanding the city by building a multilevel communication and civic axis stretching across Tokyo Bay, providing three levels of highway on each side, and concentrating the city's businesses in the field between the two flanking arteries. Emanating off the arteries and stretching out into the bay on each side were local traffic roadways, which were to feed dozens of large housing complexes (based on traditional Japanese forms) arranged perpendicular to the roadways. Tange characterized his proposal as a way to bring the city structure and its transportation into an urban unity and "to find a new urban spatial order which will reflect the open organization and the spontaneous mobility of contemporary society."[91]

The forum for Tange's proposal was the World Design Conference of 1960, a five-day meeting in May that brought to Tokyo a number of Team 10 architects along with Louis Kahn, Minoru Yamazaki, Paul Rudolph, and Raphael Soriano from the United States. The conference was also the occasion for the publication of the manifesto *Metabolism: Proposals for a New Urbanism* (1960), which featured the work of Kikutake, Kisho Kurokawa (b. 1923), Masato Ohtaka (b. 1923), and Fumihiko Maki (b. 1928); later joining this group was Arata Isozaki (b. 1931). These were the cream of a young generation of gifted Japanese architects. Kurokawa and Isozaki worked in Tange's office, Ohtaka worked for Maekawa, and Maki had been trained at Cranbrook Academy and Harvard and was then teaching at Washington University in Saint Louis. In 1961 Kurokawa proposed the idea of a "Helix Structure," based on the chromosome structure of DNA; in his conception, the helix becomes a space frame for a three-dimensional cluster system.[92] Maki and Ohtaka countered with the idea of "Group Form" – a radical antithesis to "the image we have had in architecture for thousands of years; that is, the image of the single structure, complete in itself."[93]

This futuristic, antitraditional outpouring of ideas in Japan led within a few years to some of the most brilliant visionary designs of the 1960s, such as Isozaki's "City in the Air" (1961–2), in which housing units were suspended out linearly from cylindrical service pylons. A few buildings in the following years even drew upon such suggestions. Among them were Tange's tensile structures for the 1964 Olympic Games and the Shizuoka Press and Broadcasting Center, Tokyo (1966–7), and Kurokawa's lego-like restaurant at Otome Pass (1968) and his much illustrated Nakagin Capsule Tower (1972). The showcase for metabolist-inspired works was the Osaka Exposition in 1970, although by this date the original members of the group had all pursued their own paths.

Aside from the metabolists, little of the utopian thinking of the 1960s left much of a legacy. But beneath the layer of countercultural visioning was a core of serious theorizing by engineers and others that would create a considerable estate of ideas. Wachsmann by the 1960s had built his practice into an international venture and had taught in Germany, California, and Japan. Designers such as Frei Otto (b. 1925), whose early structural investigations drew upon projects by Saarinen and Nowicki, were creating new areas of tensile investigation. And the generalist Fuller had now risen to the status of a cult figure, both in the scientific community and among the general public. In the 1960s he capped off his illustrious career with the invention of tensegrity structures, the geodesic dome he built at Expo '67 in Montréal, and his proposal for a dome over New York City (1968). The belief that technology was capable of solving many of the world's problems remained widely held and was partially supported by the accomplishments of the time. From the promising discovery of the code for DNA to the moon landing, anything and everything seemed possible.

4. Phenomenology, Structuralism, and Semiotics

Architectural theory, as we have seen, has always operated within a larger intellectual context and has often employed interdisciplinary tools in a critical way. This was also the case in the 1950s and 1960s, when various attempts were made to provide design with a more rigorous grounding or critical apparatus. Several sciences, such as physiology, psychology, and sociology, provided readily available research that could often be directly applied to the understanding and workings of the human environment. But other more abstract disciplines also offered critical systems that in their own way had an impact on architectural thought. Phenomenology, structuralism, and semiotics were three such disciplines; each dealt with the problem of perception or the dynamics of form and meaning and thus raised questions about some of the functionalist assumptions of modernism.

Phenomenology was perhaps the first to make its way into architectural discourse. A philosophical school of thought, its concepts had first been formulated by the German mathematician and philosopher Edmund Husserl in his *Logical Investigations* (1900–1) and *Ideas Toward a Pure Phenomenology and Phenomenological Philosophy* (1913).[94] In its simplest formulation, phenomenology is the study of human consciousness – that is to say, the various ways in which things present themselves as "appearances" within our everyday experience in the world. It was largely a Continental movement set up in opposition to the empirical and logical-positivist traditions of Great Britain, but it also broke with earlier Continental thought in its rejection of metaphysics, which in the nineteenth century had dealt with the human condition largely through conceptual abstractions. Husserl's plea – *Zu den Sachen selbst* (To the things themselves) – demanded a return to the realm of phenomena or essences. According to the basic phenomenological notion of "intentionality," our psychological relationship with the world is always a "consciousness of" something, an awareness directed toward concrete people, objects, and related ideas. For philosophical purposes, however, phenomenology posits a "reduction," or a placing of these appearances in brackets, by which process one suspends one's belief in and judgment of the reality of the world in order to examine phenomena free of any naive prejudices or suppositions.

Thus phenomenology might be defined as the attempt to describe the relation of the subject (my consciousness of) with the objects of the world (appearances) as a complex experiential and interpretative process. It attempts to lay bare or explicate the "horizons" of our consciousness, the mental process by which we actually live our lives. Inner horizons are the experiences, memories, desires, or concerns with which we confront or perceive the things of the world. Outer horizons define the larger context within which things appear and gain or modify their meanings. The ultimate goal of phenomenology is to achieve a greater philosophical understanding of the human condition; it constructs no models or norms for human existence but rather concerns itself in a concrete way with the "lived world" (*Lebenswelt*) of human experience.

Phenomenological thinking manifested itself in the postwar years first through the philosophical currents of existentialism, which generally dealt with ontological issues and themes of human alienation growing out of the war. Two individuals in the 1950s, however, gave phenomenology a very specific coloration with architectural implications: Maurice Merleau-Ponty (1908–61) and Martin Heidegger (1889–1976).

Merleau-Ponty's *Phenomenology of Perception* (1945) is a landmark work because of its emphasis on the prereflective, perceptual, spatial, and temporal world of everyday experience. The central theme is that the body is not a neutral, abstract entity positioned randomly within a three-dimensional vacuum of space; it is rather an amorphous, kinesthetic, perceptual field that dwells in the present and through which we generate spatial and temporal relations – a "frontier which ordinary spatial relations do not cross" – and thereby define our lived presence in the world.[95] My body determines what is interior (myself) and exterior (the world); it determines what is in front and what is behind; its orientation and motility determine how I experience certain sensations, such as those that occur as I move through a room. Moreover, the complex perceptual variables of this experiential field vary widely among people of different ages, cultures, training, and experience, thereby placing an emphasis on the qualitative aspects of these relations. Thus a generally abstract phrase such as "interpenetration of spaces" would have very little meaning from Merleau-Ponty's point of view; it is too general and would only be intelligible after a rigorous phenomenological reflection on a specific experience or set of experiences.

Merleau-Ponty's perceptual phenomenology (or phenomenology of the body) should be distinguished from Gestalt psychological theory, such as that initiated by Max Wertheimer (1880–1943) and Wolfgang Köhler (1897–1967). Gestalt theory, which seeks to be scientific, analyzes perceptual data in terms of structures (*Gestalten*) or visual wholes composed of parts. For instance, Gestalt psychologists might conduct experiments on how one perceives the space of a room as it is affected by elements of lighting, perspectives, or auditory qualities. The line between Gestalt psychology and phenomenology becomes blurred, however, in the work of Rudolf Arnheim (b. 1904), beginning with his *Art and Visual Perception: A Psychology of the Creative Eye* (1954). His interest in visual organization with respect to works of art and architecture frequently took on a distinctly

phenomenological cast, and his books were widely studied by students of architecture.

Phenomenology was also popularized in architectural circles through the later writings of Heidegger. This German philosopher completed his doctorate in 1913 and was beginning his teaching career at Freiburg University three years later when Husserl arrived to join the faculty. He worked closely with Husserl in the following period, during which he wrote his best known study, *Being and Time*, published in 1927.[96] Although phenomenological in its impulse and overall approach, Heidegger in this book departed from Husserl's method in several respects – chief of which was his hermeneutic orientation and his concern with the ontological issue of "being." Yet Heidegger's analysis, for all of its scholarly erudition, is anything but classical in form, as he pursues a phenomenological account of *Dasein* (literally "being there") – that is, the human entity "thrown" into a world of moods and situations, always projecting itself into the future while experiencing a multitude of everyday concerns. He thus brings the analytical tools of hermeneutics, which originally were used in the reading and interpretation of biblical texts but later came to be applied to law and history, into ontology in a search for an interpretative understanding of *Dasein* in its everyday life.

During the 1930s Heidegger began to shift his focus from being to such issues as art and technology, and his 1951 lecture "Building, Dwelling, Thinking" had a strong impact on architectural thought.[97] The essay considers the hermeneutic or etymological associations of the word "building." The Old English and High German word for building, *buan*, means to dwell, to stay in one place, and it is related to the German *ich bin* (I am). Building, dwelling, and existing are thus related linguistic concepts. Similarly, the German word for space, *Raum* (related to the English "room"), originally was not synonymous with the abstraction "space" (of Latin derivation) but rather meant a clearing in a forest for living or dwelling. This fact underscores the concrete relations of "belonging to" or making one's place in the world and therefore becoming "at home"; by building our world, we at the same time construct our identities. Architecture, as this argument suggests, cannot be objectified into a set of abstract rational principles, such as utility, efficiency, economy, or functionality. It has more to do with constituting the world and giving meaning to our lives.

Whereas phenomenology sought out meanings within our everyday existence, the linguistic movement of structuralism considered meanings in more general and universal terms. The underlying model for structuralism was supplied by the linguist Ferdinand de Saussure (1857–1913), whose posthumous *Course of General Linguistics* (1916) became a "scientific" paradigm for linguistics, first by distinguishing the more invariable and self-contained rules of "language" (*langue*) from the more individual and accidental elements of "speech" (*parole*) and second by considering language more generally as a closed system of conventional signs and meanings with its own internal rules (syntax) and operations.[98] The anthropologist Claude Lévi-Strauss (b. 1908) gave the theory of structuralism a more popular and general interpretation in the 1950s through such studies as *Elementary Structures of Kinship* (1949), *Tristes Tropiques* (1955), and *Structural Anthropology* (1958). Drawing upon more recent linguistic models and his own anthropological work in decoding the mythological narratives of various tribal societies, Lévi-Strauss came to argue that there were universal and unconscious mental structures operating within or guiding human thought and displayed at every communicative level from rational knowledge to primeval storytelling.[99]

Structuralism, as a general concept at least, was transposed directly to architectural theory in the late 1950s in the work of some members of Team 10 and by a school of Japanese and Dutch architects. Kenzo Tange, for example, invoked the idea of structuralism as a conceptual model for his Tokyo Bay plan of 1960. In his linear scheme he proposed to establish the major transportation lines as "large-scale structures" around which the "short life cycle" of everyday activities would be ordered: "The important task facing us is that of creating an organic link between these two extremes and, by doing so, to create a new spatial order in our cites."[100] Tange, who was working closely with the metabolists at this time, viewed the logic of structuralism as an alternative to "aestheticism." In his important essay "Function, Structure and Symbol" (1966), he touted "structuring" as a full-fledged successor to functionalism or functional design, a way of thinking that would now draw upon the insights and models of cybernetics and information theory. Indeed, he claimed that it was "the basic theme of present-day urban design to think of the spatial organization as a network of communication and as a living body with growth and change."[101]

The term *structuralism* occurred extensively in Dutch theory after 1960, especially in relation to the anthropological interests and design sensibilities of Aldo van Eyck and Herman Hertzberger (b. 1923). Anulf Lüchinger, in *Structuralism in Architecture and Urban Planning* (1981), devoted a full-length study to structuralism, which he viewed

as the successor movement (born in Otterlo) to the functional thinking of CIAM. He defined architectural structuralism as "a complete set of relationships, in which elements change, but in such a way that these remain dependent on the whole and retain their meaning. The whole is independent of its relationship to the elements."[102] Structuralism's various design strategies, on both an individual and an urban scale of building, include numerical attempts to generate rhythms and subrhythms; the use of identifiable repetitive devices; allowance for growth, coherence, and change; and most importantly the articulation of the built volume into smaller and more understandable units within a larger spatial order. Van Eyck's Amsterdam Orphanage (1957–60) – with its design dualities of large and small, inside and outside, unity and diversity – is generally seen as the paradigm for the Dutch structuralist movement. Other early examples of structuralist architecture are van den Broek and Bakema's "Growing Dwellings" (1962), the competition projects of Joop van Stigt and Piet Blom for the "Children's Village" (1962), and Hertzberger's Centraal Beheer, Apeldoorn (1970–2). Internationally, Louis Kahn's Kimball Art Museum (1967–2) and Moshe Safdie's Habitat '67 are often characterized as structuralist for their cellular treatment of form.

Related to structuralism, with its grounding in linguistic theory, is the field of semiotics or semiology, which by the early 1960s would begin to have a decisive impact on architectural thinking.[103] Semiotics concerns everything that can be taken as a "sign," which in turn can be defined as everything that, on the basis of an established convention, can be taken as "substituting for" something else. In linguistic theory, semiotics was conceived as an analytic or neutral tool for analyzing the meaning and syntax of words and propositions. But if one views buildings as complex carriers of meanings (from implied structural functions to overt symbolic associations), its application to architectural theory is readily apparent. Various models for semiotics have been devised, and in fact they divide along two lines. The structuralist dualities present in de Saussure's linguistic theory – signifier/significant, language/speaking, synchronic/diachronic – define one line of semiological thinking that finds its first codification in Roland Barthes *Éléments de sémiologie* (1964). A second line developed out of the work of the American Charles Sanders Pierce and his successor Charles W. Morris, whose *Foundations of the Theory of Signs* appeared in 1938 – while Morris was teaching at the Institute of Design in Chicago.[104]

Morris's model should take precedence because it was more widely embraced by architects. It first distinguishes three semiotic realms: pragmatics, syntactics, and semantics. The first deals with the relationship of signs to the interpreters who read them, and thus it generally addresses the psychological or sociological parameters contributing to the meaning of signs. Syntactics treats the formal relationship of signs to one another without regard to meaning; that is to say, it considers the syntactical or grammatical rules for their use. Semantics, which has had widespread application in architecture, concerns itself with the relationship of a sign to the object to which it applies, and thus in an architectural sense it concerns the meanings of particular forms or motifs. Within the realm of semantics lies another threefold division, the classification of signs into indexes, icons, and symbols. An index is a sign that bears a physical connection with its object, whether a footprint in the snow or the arrow indicating a one-way street. An icon is a sign that is similar to its object, such as a concession stand in the shape of the object it is selling. Symbols, in a precise sense, are signs that have an arbitrary or conventional relationship with their objects. The classical Greek use of Doric columns on temples dedicated to male deities (columns later used on bank buildings) is an example of a symbol of strength, and in fact architecture can be symbolic on a multitude of levels.

The emphasis on "meaning" that appears in architectural theory in the late 1950s was in many respects a response to what was seen as the impoverishment of design brought on by the one-sided focus on functional concerns. The semiotics course that Charles Morris taught at the Chicago Institute of Design in 1937–45 treated semiotics as a tool to teach design on a more conceptually rigorous or "scientific" basis and to mediate between the outlook of the artist and that of the scientist.[105] Semiotics, in its pedagogical application, was not unrelated to the use of Gestalt psychology by both Moholy-Nagy and Kepes.

It was the pedagogical usefulness of semiotics that no doubt led Tomás Maldonado to incorporate it into the curriculum at the Technical Hochschule at Ulm (HfG) in the late 1950s. Maldonado not only taught a seminar on the subject but published his ideas in two articles, one published in 1959, the other in 1962.[106] To explain why he introduced semiotics into the curriculum, he stated, "The 'meaning,' put into brackets by the specialists in telecommunication, and the information theorists, is converted into a factor which must be studied to its most subtle implications. In this semantic and pragmatic interest participate linguists, psychologists, social psychologists and

sociologists; and also, of course the representatives of modern semiotics."[107]

Maldonado's emphasis on semiotics deeply impressed Christian Norberg-Schulz (1926–2000), whose book *Intentions in Architecture* first appeared in 1963. Norberg-Schulz, who had studied under Giedion in Zurich and at Harvard and IIT, also participated in CIAM activities in the 1950s. *Intentions in Architecture*, however, is more eclectic or universal in its attempt to prepare the ground for a "satisfactory theory of architecture."[108] In addition to semiotics, the author draws upon Gestalt psychology, the educational theory of Jean Piaget, communication models, and structuralism in his quest to define the totality of the architectural experience. But the book's breadth and degree of abstraction is also a shortcoming, as semiotics becomes merely one of the quadrants of Norberg-Schulz's "structural analysis," which also comprises building tasks, forms (elements, relations, formal structures), and structural techniques. Moreover, he does not yet recognize semiotics as a powerful critical tool for interpretation but rather sees it as a methodology for design or as a conceptual medium for architectural education.[109] Norberg-Schulz, too, soon realized this limitation, because within a few years he turned away from analytical "intentions" as a grounding for his theory and toward a stricter phenomenological approach that drew more directly on Heideggerian notions of place and meaning.[110]

Intentions in Architecture should be viewed in light of the contemporary interest in enriching what many perceived as an overly abstract functionalist architecture. Another visitor to Ulm in 1957–8, Joseph Rykwert (b. 1926), first broached this theme in a highly influential essay of 1960, "Meaning in Architecture."[111] This native of Poland, who had taken his architectural studies in London during the war, had first been attracted to the thought of Giedion and Wittkower. He spent much of the 1950s living in Italy and thus participated in the lively debates there.[112] By 1960 Rykwert, writing for the journals *Domus* and *Zodiac*, took his critique in another direction with his attacks on rationalist architecture. If the "new regionalism," in his view, was only Soviet "Social Realism" stood on its head – they appealed to opposite ends of the economic spectrum – it was also time for architects to "acknowledge the emotional power of their work; this recognition depends on the methodical investigation of a content, even of a referential content in architecture."[113] For instance, Rykwert pointed out that a house is more than a means of meeting functional needs, rather "what a man requires of his house is the conviction that he is, in some sense, at the centre of the universe; that his home mediates between him and all the confusing and threatening world outside; that in some definite place the world is summed up for him in a place which is his, all his shelter and his castle."[114] Hence, those castellations that appear on British houses or the ranch motifs of American suburban houses have an important psychological or emotional underpinning. "Through a semantic study of environment," he concluded, "we can discover the means of discoursing in our buildings. Only that way will we be able to appeal to the common man again."[115]

Semiotic studies became popular in Italy as well. An important seminal piece was Sergio Bettini's "Semantic Criticism; and the Historical Continuity of European Architecture" (1958), in which the author drew upon the work of Ernst Cassirer, Erwin Panofsky, and de Saussure to argue that even modern artistic works with nonrepresentational values retain a legible linguistic structure.[116] Bettini was also one of the first theorists to speak of architectural content in terms of "signs." The mid-1960s saw a number of more encompassing studies: Giovanni Klaus Koenig's *Analisi del linguaggio architettonico* (Analysis of the language of architecture; 1964), Renato De Fusco's *Architettura come mass medium: Note per una semiologia architettonica* (Architecture as mass medium: Notes on an architectonic semiology, 1967), Maria Luisa Scalvini's "Simbolo e significato nello spazio architettonico" (Symbol and meaning in architectonic space, 1968), and Umberto Eco's *La Struttura assente: Introduzione alla ricerca semiologica* (The absent structure: Introduction to semiological research, 1968).[117] Chapters from the last work were published in English in 1973 under the title "Function and Sign: The Semiotics of Architecture."[118] Eco viewed architecture as operating within a complex series of codes – technical, syntactic, and semantic – which in turn unfold only within a more general matrix of external or anthropological codes. Hence the meaning of things can never be permanently fixed, and in fact architects have very little control over how users ultimately interpret their creations.

Interest in semiotics mushroomed in Britain in the mid-1960s. Prompted in part through the efforts of the Italians, Rykwert (who was teaching at University College), and Norberg-Schulz (who taught at Cambridge University in 1966), through the structuralism of Lèvi-Strauss, the popularity of Cassirer, and the writings of Ernst Gombrich. A strong proponent of semiotics was the Canadian George Baird (b. 1939), who in the mid-1960s was completing his doctorate in London. He broached the topic in 1966 in an article that appeared in *Arena*, "Paradox in Regents Park: A

Question of Interpretation," which emphasized the active nature of perception within the interpretative process.[119] As a follow-up, he, together with the American Charles Jencks (b. 1939), collaborated on a special issue of the *Architectural Association Journal* entitled "Meaning in Architecture." Norris K. Smith, Alan Colquhoun (whose important essay combined typology, linguistics, and structuralist ideas), Rykwert, Luigi Moretti, and George Baird contributed essays, building upon Baird's leitmotif that "those structures of meaning which so engage our consciousness are highly articulate, capable of rational discussion and analysis."[120] This issue provided the core essays for Jencks and Baird's book *Meaning in Architecture* (1969), which added contributions by Norberg-Schulz, Geoffrey Broadbent, Reyner Banham, Kenneth Frampton, Martin Pawley, Aldo van Eyck, Françoise Choay, Nathan Silver, and Gillo Dorfles.[121] It was the general tenor of this book, together with the work of Eco, that laid the basis for the burst of semiotic activity in the early 1970s.

5. Ungers, Sterling, Scarpa, and Rossi

Both the dissolution of CIAM at Otterlo and the feud between Rogers and his British critics would leave their mark on European theory in the 1960s, a decade that begins with relative calm along the theoretical front yet would end in the political and social convulsions of 1968. The initial quietude was only amplified by Le Corbusier's death in 1965, which left Europe without the acclaimed master who had so forcefully shaped its architectural thought. On the Continent, many of the architects who would establish new directions in the early 1970s – Ricardo Bofill (b. 1939), Rafael Moneo, Mario Botta (b. 1943), Hans Hollein (b. 1934), and Christian de Portzamparc, to mention but a few – were either still in school or just beginning to practice. In France the eminent constructor Jean Prouvé (1901–84) was still busy as both an architect and engineer. In Germany the architects Gottfried Böhm (b. 1920) and Karljosef Schattner (b. 1924) were quietly pursuing the possibility of a refined postmodern baroque through a renewed interest in tradition and a return to medieval craftsmanship.[122]

The one discordant chord to sound in Germany in the early 1960s was the work of Oswald Mathias Ungers (b. 1926).[123] This native of Kaisersesch was drafted into the German military toward the conclusion of World War II and ended it as a prisoner of war. He completed his architectural studies in Karlsruhe in 1950 and opened a small office in war-ravaged Cologne. He attended the CIAM conferences during the decade and eventually drew close to the Team 10 circle of architects, even though, as an admirer of Schinkel, he sided with Rogers in his dispute with Peter Smithson. His own house (1959), an abstract composition of brick cubic forms cantilevered off a concrete framework, was later cited by Banham as one of those "hard cases" for brick Brutalism, yet it is nevertheless distinguished in its erudition and by its allusions to the work of Erich Mendelsohn and Hugo Häring.[124] In the next year Ungers, together with Reinhard Gieselmann, issued a short manifesto, "Towards a New Architecture." While not especially profound or indicative of his later direction, it at least put on record his opposition to the "technological, functional methods" and "materialistic social order" of the day, which lead in his view to the uniformity and monotony of current practice.[125]

Ungers's outlook began to change around 1963, the year he began teaching at the Technical University in Berlin. His career as an instructor in fact resulted in a thirteen-year near-hiatus from practice (he also taught at Cornell and Harvard), which allowed him to focus on his evolving rationalist ideas and derive his later notions of morphology, transformation, assemblage, and fragmentation. Several unbuilt projects he designed in these years, such as the redevelopment plan for Grünzug Süd, Cologne (1962), the student housing at Twente Polytechnic, in Enschede, Holland (1964), the classically inspired German Embassy to the Vatican (1965), and the Museums for Prussian Cultural Heritage, Berlin (1965), are startlingly different from his earlier work in their typological/spatial complexity, strong and weak geometries, and recourse to primary forms. All these designs represent a very conscious departure from the spatial sameness characteristic of functionalism and are central to the developing tide of the European rationalist movement – without the political wrapping. With his departure for Cornell University in 1968, he incorporated the theme of contextualism into his already highly conceptualized design methodology.

Methodological considerations also play an important role in the teachings of Bernard Hoesli, who arrived back in Switzerland in the late 1950s from the University of Texas. He formed a partnership with Werner Aebli but more importantly became a professor at the Swiss Federal Institute of Technology (ETH) in 1959 and was charged with creating a first-year design course based on his Texas experience. Over several decades, in fact, he devised a highly methodological process that stressed design not as a formulation of building types but as an increasingly complex series of

regulated working steps alternating with specific spatial and conceptual exercises.[126] Hoesli revolutionized architectural education in Switzerland and largely defined an "ETH Style."

The situation in Britain – Banham and Archigram aside – was certainly more fragmented during these same years. Debate took place at a very high level within the pages of the various architectural journals, but this sophistication of ideas was less apparent in practice. Again, it was a period of transition. In 1964 Norman Foster, Wendy Cheeseman, Richard Rogers, and Su Brumwell set up the "Team 4" in London. The Smithsons, as well as the polemics of Banham, no doubt had a strong impact on the early architectural outlook of the firm, but so did the studies pursued by Foster and Rogers at Yale University (where the two men met), the work of Saarinen and Skidmore, Owings, and Merrill (in whose office Rogers worked), and the ideas of Buckminster Fuller (whom Forster had befriended). The Reliance Controls Factory at Swindon, their one collaboration of distinction prior to the firm's break-up in 1967, displays the influence of SOM and vividly stands apart from developments on the Continent. The great renown of the two successor firms – Foster Associates and Piano and Rogers – gradually unfolds in the 1970s.

Another prominent British architect of this time was James Stirling (1926–92). He came out of the orbit of brutalism, and his flats at Ham Common, Middlesex (1955–8, designed in partnership with James Gowan), reflect his early penchant (bordering on idolatry) for borrowing motifs from Le Corbusier. In a 1957 critical essay, "Regionalism in Modern Architecture" Sterling voices a certain ambivalence about the "new traditionalism." On the one hand, he views it as an opportunity to reevaluate the work of Voysey and Mackintosh; on the other hand, he sees it as opposed to the new world and its custom of "inventing techniques and developing the appropriate expression of the modern attitude."[127] By the early 1960s, however, his ambivalence had entirely given way to a commitment to internationalism and the machine aesthetic – a commitment certainly reinforced by his friendship with Banham.

In between lies the Engineering Building at Leicester University (1959–63), which in its pristine constructional condition was hailed by Banham as a "fantastic invention, the more so because it proceeds rigorously from structural and circulatory considerations without frills or artwork" – that is, in part because of its crude detailing, its glare, and its audible hydraulic problems (Fig. 102).[128] Sterling, who in 1963 began practicing alone, increased the use of glass in the History Faculty Building, Cambridge University (1964–8),

102. James Sterling, Engineering Building, Leicester University, 1959–63. From *The Architectural Review*, vol. 135 (April 1964).

and Florey Residential Hall, Queen's College, Oxford (1966–71), both of which were likewise plagued with constructional, mechanical, lighting, and condensation problems. Only with the Olivetti Training School, Haslemere (1969–72), did Sterling begin to move away from large glass surfaces. In part because of his friendship with Leon Krier and later Hans Hollein, Sterling's approach to design changed again in the early 1970s – underscoring the transitional nature of this period.

In addition to the writings of Banham and Norberg-Schulz, one book that had an impact in British theory in the 1960s was *The Changing Ideals of Modern Architecture 1750–1950*, published in 1965 by Peter Collins (1920–81).[129] He had studied architecture at Leeds College of Art both before and after the war, worked in Switzerland and France (on the reconstruction of Le Havre under Auguste

Perret), and in 1956 moved to Montréal to teach at McGill University. His first book, *Concrete, the Vision of a New Architecture* (1959), was a historical study of this material and its development under Perret. *The Changing Ideals of Modern Architecture* is more broadly conceived as a survey – much in the spirit of R. G. Collingwood's *The Idea of History* (1946) – of the intellectual development of modern architecture. And as it begins not in the nineteenth century but with the Enlightenment, it forms in its structure and ideology a critique of the earlier genealogical investigations of Pevsner and Giedion. The book is superbly researched and has early chapters on neoclassicism, picturesque theory, and the various revivals of the eighteenth and nineteenth centuries. What is even more striking and original is Collins's sympathetic treatment of nineteenth-century eclecticism, which he defines – in the spirit of Denis Diderot, Victor Cousin, and Thomas Hope – as a learned and "composite system of thought made of views selected...from various other systems" and therefore an inevitable outgrowth of the new historical awareness.[130] Eclecticism, in its true sense, is to be distinguished from both idealist reimpositions of styles and a weak-minded "indifferentism," which allows any and all influences to mix. In mid-nineteenth century Europe, Collins points out, eclecticism gave rise to one of the most sophisticated debates in architectural history – here is where the concepts of modernism were worked out.

The key concept to Collins's understanding of contemporary architecture is the notion of "rationalism," which he traces back to César Daly's definition of the term in 1864 as the reconciliation of architecture with modern science and industry.[131] Once this merger had been forged, Daly believed, architecture would pass beyond its rationalist phase and seek a further conciliation with "sentiment," thereby elevating itself artistically. The first phase of the rationalist reconciliation, Collins argues, was achieved around the turn of the century in the work of Perret, but here also is where the argument takes an unexpected turn. Although a "genuine Classicism" of the modern "style" was achieved in the 1930s and 1940s across Europe and North America, not all went well. Architecture came to see itself as an art in alliance with sculpture and painting (and therefore pretending to operate with similar space-time concepts), yet in doing so it undercut its rationalist basis as a constructional art. In effect, Collins is opposed to such individualist "form-givers" as Le Corbusier and to their conception of architecture as the sculptural manipulation of form. Painting for Le Corbusier, Collins argues, was simply a means of rejecting all vestiges of revivalism, yet attempts to apply the lessons of painting and sculpture to architecture today "may well prove more of a hindrance to architectural creativity than an aid."[132] Instead, Collins calls for a judicious form of eclecticism, invoking such examples as Perret and the Torre Velasca of BBPR. Architects, he concludes, have a right once again to be "banal" (in the sense of "common to all") and can therefore harmonize buildings with the urban landscape. They once again have the freedom to suggest historical motifs, "*provided that they do not betray the contemporary principles of stylistic unity*," namely, the fulfillment of the program and "the honest expression of the structural means employed."[133] Collins values above all else the "humane human environment"; that is to say, he thoroughly rejects both the brutalist aesthetic and the technological euphoria of Banham.

Italy too remained lively in its theory and practice in the 1960s. Its debates – debates that by the end of the decade would again strike at the heart of modern theory – were in part an outgrowth of Otterlo and the "Italian Retreat," in part a result of the growing politicalization of architectural theory. The intense ideological coloration that would push theory well past the point of crisis was nevertheless backed up by the work of several exceptional designers.

The vitality of architectural theory in Italy to some degree was the result of the multiplicity of competing currents and an openness to experimentation. Many of the leading architects in the 1950s – BBPR, Albini, Gardella, Ridolfi, Michelucci, Garbetti and Isola, and Giancarlo De Carlo – remained active and pursued their contextual concerns into the 1960s in varying ways. De Carlo emerged as perhaps the most talented of this group, while Rogers retained editorial control of *Casabella-Continuità* until he was forced out in 1965. He continued to advance his earlier themes under the rubric "the utopia of reality," by which he meant the mediation of invention by the contextual influences of Italian culture and the quest to build a better society.[134]

In the second half of the 1950s there appeared the bright star of Carlo Scarpa (1906–78), whose artistic roots had preceded and infused the Italian Movement for Rational Architecture (MIAR) in the late 1920s.[135] His late rise, as with Kahn, testifies to the long period of gestation and endurance (survival) needed to produce a truly great architect. After early private practice in Venice in the late 1920s, he began his collaboration with the Venini glass factory of Murano, which drew him into the orbit of the crafts. He passed the war years quietly, specializing in the creation of exhibition spaces. No project, however, explains his leap forward in the late 1950s with a quick succession of notable projects: the Canova Plaster Cast Gallery, Possagno (1955–7), the Museo di Castelvecchio, Verona (1956–73), the Olivetti Showroom, Venice (1957–8), and above all the Palazzo Querini Stampalia (1961–3).

Scarpa, of course, is frequently coupled with Kahn because of his nearly simultaneous rejection of modern functionalism and its underlying machine aesthetics. Scarpa's approach to design involves a painstaking search for original form carried out entirely on the drafting table in myriad drawings. As a result, Scarpa's works defy pedestrian description or theoretical labeling; they are often viscerally accessible in their sensuous materiality (color, opaqueness, and texture), idealized irrationality, and extreme artisanship of detail. They are also rooted in the historical atmosphere of the Veneto and thus imbued with very specific mnemonic qualities of narration and animation, respected by but nearly reticent to outsiders. If his forms cannot be replicated elsewhere, they also show, as he noted, "that modern architecture cannot do without a knowledge of the architectural values that have always existed."[136] In a word, they are ornamental, but, as Francesco Dal Co has noted, only in the sense of the Greek word *kosmos*, which has the double meaning of "order" and "ornament" and implies that ornament is in essence decorative ordering or attention to form.[137] By virtue of his poetic and mythological interests, Scarpa's order also carries with it a certain accidental quality of discomfort or unease, a spiritual ennui seemingly out of character with this period. All of his work, in fact, seems removed to an ideal architectural time. It is little wonder that within professional circles he remained invisible for so long; his Byzantine talent was that unique.

Also rooted in a strong historical tradition were the buildings and writings of Paolo Portoghesi (b. 1931), who in his early years combined the pursuits of architect, critic, and historian.[138] Two of his early historical studies were centered on Guarino Guarini and Francesco Borromini,[139] and it is from this baroque spirit and sense of space that he and Vittorio Gigliotti, who was trained as a structural engineer, devised the open forms and flared surfaces of their Casa Baldi, Rome (1959–62). In another respect, this tufa domicile epitomized the antifunctionalist tendencies of the time, with its use of local stone and artisan building techniques. Later works of this decade are characterized by the use of geometric fields rendered dynamic by their overlay of disturbing "force" centers. The Casa Andreis, Scandriglia (1965–7), was planned on five overlapping circular grids, but in the case of the colorfully tiled Casa Papanice, Rome (1966–70), the field logic is also reflected three-dimensionally in the modulated ceilings. This entirely unique methodological approach to design achieves an early culmination in the library and cultural center at Avezzano (1968–83) and the Church of the Holy Family, Salerno (1969–74).

The work of Vittorio Gregotti (b. 1927) has unique aspects as well. He was the chief editor of *Casabella-Continuità* under Rogers in the late 1950s, and his articles on the work of Ridolfi and others contributed to the Neoliberty debate. Around 1960, however, Gregotti's outlook began to change, and over the course of this decade he developed his interest in phenomenology and structuralism and the larger issues of regional planning. His popular book *Il territorio dell'architettura* (The territory of architecture, 1966) is a collection of essays on the themes of progress, history, and typology and – most important for his later interests – on the reading of the regional landscape as an archeological structure or environmental culture.[140]

If there was a mainstream to be found in Italy in the early 1960s, it was that defined in academic circles by a reassertion of the principles of rational modernism. The *Storia dell'architettura moderna* (History of modern architecture, 1960) of Leonardo Benevolo (b. 1923) professes the aim of reaffirming the continuity or unity of the present with the historical modern movement, which of course also presumes the correctness of its founding principles and models.[141] Benevolo's vision of modernism is at heart a rational social vision of practice applied to objective social needs; in its necessary moderation it must posit a balance between the polarities of art and technology. On the larger theme of urbanism, Benevolo in 1957 participated in the Società di Architettura e Urbanistica (SAU), a coalition of planners seeking to call attention to the larger social problems. Similar associations were widespread in Italy. In 1959 Bruno Zevi countered Benevolo by establishing the National Institute of Architecture (INARCH), a coalition of architects, engineers, and industrialists invoking the spirit of the Werkbund and in service to national political decisions. At the University of Venice, Zevi founded the prestigious Institute for Architectural History, which would within a few years emerge as an important center for Italian theory.

Urbanism was a major focus of Italian theory throughout the 1960s, as seen in the efforts of Giuseppe Samonà (1898–1983) and Carlo Aymonino (b. 1926). Samonà, who had started practicing in the 1920s, was a shrewd critic of contemporary developments and a medieval historian of some stature, and between 1945 and 1974 he directed the University Institute for Architecture in Venice and turned it into one of the leading schools of Italy. His book *L'urbanistica e l'avvenire della città negli stati europei* (Urban planning and the future of the European city, 1959) defended the large city against the proponents of regional decentralization and viewed the city by looking at textural characteristics that extended over centuries.[142] It thereby prepared the ground for the multitude of studies on the urban structure published in the 1960s.

Aymonino, who had been aligned with the neorealist movement of the 1950s, published a series of books in the mid-1960s, including *La città territorio* (The urban territory, 1964), *La formazione del concetto di tipologia edilizia* (The formation of the concept of building typology, 1965), and *Origine e sviluppo della città moderna* (Origin and development of the modern city, 1965). Like Samonà, he was Marxist in his outlook and favored the use of strong geometrical elements. His interest in building typology, first exhibited in his lectures of 1963, derived from his morphological interests and would later fall in line with the Italian rationalist movement. His major project of the 1960s was the Monte Amiata Housing Complex (1967–73) on the outskirts of Milan, on which Aldo Rossi also collaborated.

The ideological circle of Samonà and Aymonino found an echo in the efforts of Manfredo Tafuri (1935–94) and Aldo Rossi (1931–97). For Tafuri, these years defined a period of varied intellectual gestation. He received his diploma from the University of Rome in 1960, and between 1961 and 1966 he served as an assistant professor in architectural design to Saul Greco, Alalberto Liberna, and Ludovico Quaroni. Tafuri never entered practice; instead, he pursued an interest in a variety of topics, including the Renaissance, Borromini, William Morris, city planning, and contemporary practice. His first published writing was on Rome's via Nazionale, one essay in a large volume on Rome published in 1961 and edited by Quaroni.[143] Early books include a long monograph on his mentor Quaroni (1964), a much smaller study of modern architecture in Japan (1964), and a book on mannerism (1966).[144] Tafuri's broader intellectual interests were also developing during these increasingly tumultuous years. His curiosity extended to Ernesto Rogers, Giulio Carlo Argan, Alberto Asor Rosa, Theodore Adorno, Georges Lukács, Walter Benjamin, Karl Mannheim, semiotics, psychoanalysis, and the cinema. His thinking would coalesce around 1968 with his professorship in Venice and the first of his critical books, *Theorie e storia dell'architettura* (1968, Theories and history of architecture), which will be considered later.

Rossi was simultaneously evolving his critical position, in part under the tutelage of Rogers and Samonà (at the Polytechnical School in Milan) and later under the tutelage of Gardella and Quaroni.[145] He began writing for *Casabella-Continuità* in 1955 as an assistant to Rogers (though still a student in Milan), and thus he had a front-row seat for the Neoliberty debate. In 1961 he began serving with Francesco Tentori as one of the two editors of the journal, and he wrote articles on the British new towns, Rome, Milan, Venice, the garden city, Vienna, and Berlin. His theoretical outlook began to mature around 1963, the year he started teaching. His architectural practice lagged behind his critical reputation at this point. His two built projects in the first half of the 1960s were his villa at Ronchi (1960, with L. Ferrari) and his Monument to the Partisans in the town square of Segrate (1965). The Loosian style and *Raumplan* of the former (bordering on plagiarism) are significant only in that the work represents the first of the "modern" revivals to appear in the 1960s. In the latter work, as he explained in a letter of 1963, he had arrived at his "rigid world with few objects" – a world precluding modern architecture's "redemptive" powers – which would become the hallmark of his later style.[146]

In 1966 Rossi promulgated his urban theory in *L'architettura della città* (The architecture of the city).[147] The book has often been compared to Robert Venturi's *Complexity and Contradiction in Architecture* (1966) because of its hostility toward functionalist thinking, but its intentions and methodology are entirely different. Rossi's book, which is quintessentially Italian in its urban perspective, is more phenomenological in outlook, though equally infused with the rigidity of Ferdinand de Saussure's linguistics and Claude Lévi-Strauss's structuralism. Rossi draws heavily on studies done by European (mostly French) geographers, with the one notable exception: his mention of Kevin Lynch's *The Image of the City* (1960).[148] At the heart of his study is his "Critique of Naive Functionalism," in which he attacks the view that architectural forms should be defined or shaped by their application to specific functions. Naive functionalism has not only misled modernism but "is regressive because it impedes us from studying forms and knowing the world of architecture according to its true laws."[149] Forms should rather arise from their own historical and urban typology.

His study's pivotal concept is the notion of "urban artifact" (*fatto urbano*), which implies, as Peter Eisenman notes, "not just a physical thing in the city, but all of its history, geography, structure, and connection with the general life of the city."[150] The leading example is the Palazzo della Ragione, the basilica-like structure in the heart of Padua, which has served a multitude of functions over the centuries and still acts as a vital urban center and focus. Rossi sees the city as a spatial structure largely defined by its monuments, routes, and geographical features, as something possessing the collective historical consciousness always active and evolving through its residents, yet with a longevity or permanence transcending time. Thus the possibility of mapping a city through a process of urban typology becomes important to Rossi, who uses a notion of "type" dating back to Antoine Chrysostome Quatremère de Quincy.[151] It is presented quite abstractly as a means for classifying buildings and urban structures; it is not something to be copied (a model) but rather the underlying idea that might serve as a rule for the model.

By contrast, Rossi distinguishes the notion of *locus* ("a relationship between a certain specific location and the buildings that are in it") from the less concrete idea of "context."[152] This distinction, for Rossi, carries important design implications: "It is hardly surprising that this concept of context is espoused and applied by those who pretend to preserve the historical cities by retaining their ancient facades or reconstructing them in such a way as to maintain their silhouettes and colors and other such things; but what do we find after these operations when they are actually realized? An empty, often repugnant stage."[153] In making this statement, Rossi may have had a specific project in Frankfurt in mind, but at the same time the tenor of the passage can be seen as problematic for someone whose work was purposefully sceneographic in its mute Platonic exploitation of form.

For all of Rossi's (now subsumed) political fervor, *The Architecture of the City* is distinctly conservative in its apparent reduction of form to monumentality and in the author's search for an architecture that is timeless and primeval in its phenomenological essence. His ideal monuments are serious and quiet in their antifunctional rhetoric, but at the same time the examples that he presents – for instance, the amphitheaters at Nimes and Arles – are rich in overlays of transposed meanings acquired over centuries. They do not in fact define a pure architecture of silent historicity.

Working alongside Rossi in his quest for philosophical reduction was his good friend Giorgio Grassi (b. 1935), whose book *La costruzione logica della architettura* (The logical construction of architecture) appeared in 1967.[154] Grassi completed his studies in Milan in 1960, worked as an editorial assistant at *Cassabella-Continuità*, and also taught as an assistant under Rossi. Grassi's book was the first to speak openly of the possibility of a new rationalist architecture, but it is more important historically for the typology of architectural elements (walls, doors, windows, columns, roofs, plans) that it proposes for easy assembly into compositions – following in part the typological efforts of the German Alexander Klein.[155] Just as Rossi's classicized modern revival had earlier celebrated Loos, Grassi is attracted to the housing schemes of Mies, Gropius, Tessenow, Oud, and Ludwig Hilberseimer. Marxist underpinnings, for Grassi, also prescribe the use of ascetic, nonexpressive, abstract forms. The joint competition project of Grassi and Rossi for the Monza San Rocco in 1966 illustrates perfectly their theoretical consensus at this time. Drawing upon such uninspiring models as the Karl Marx Hof in Vienna, it builds a virtual chessboard of two-story and four-story housing units around small enclosed courtyards, acoustically troubling at the very least.

Architecture aside, Rossi and Grassi in the late 1960s opened an entirely new avenue for architectural theory, one that would become enormously popular in Europe after its official baptism as a new "rational architectural" at the fifteenth Triennale of Milan in 1973. Rossi, in the exhibition catalogue, returned to the formulation of Adolf Behne: his distinction between a "functionalist," who tries to make each function "unique and momentary" in its solution, and the "rationalist," who "gives thought to the enduring qualities of buildings, which perhaps see many generations with changing requirements and therefore cannot live without leeway."[156] In the same catalogue, Massimo Scolari set out additional parameters for this new "global refounding of architecture," whose genesis he traces back to the faculty at Milan in the years 1967–8. In distancing it from the efforts of political radicals and from the professional status quo – which represents "the commodification of culture and establishes its objectives in the area of personal profit within a traditional bourgeois society" – Scolari, somewhat amazingly, characterizes rational architecture as a mute desire "to give free rein to architecture without political, sociological or technological subordination or tutelage."[157] In a widely read review of the Triennale of a few months later, a skeptical Joseph Rykwert denounced the "neo-rationalist" revival not only for its overt tendentiousness and ideological inconsistency but also for its many displays of bad architecture: "So that's it, then. Architecture may stay alive as long as she stays dumb. Dumb and beautiful maybe, but dumb."[158]

15

==

CHALLENGES TO MODERNISM
IN AMERICA

Architects can no longer afford to be intimidated by the puritanically moral language
of orthodox Modern architecture.

Robert Venturi (1966)

1. Mumford, Jacobs, and the Failure of the
American City

Volumes have been written about the social and physical
deterioration of the American city in the 1950s and 1960s
as well as the contrary boom of the American suburb. And
while a multitude of reasons have been adduced for the urban conflagrations of the late 1960s – racism, war, poverty,
drugs, unemployment – it is difficult to fault the fiscal commitment of the federal government itself. New Deal programs such as the Federal Housing Administration (1936),
the United States Housing Authority (1937), and the Federal
National Mortgage Association (1938) not only survived the
war but were expanded into major housing and rehabilitation programs during the Truman and Eisenhower administrations. The housing act of 1949, the cornerstone of all
postwar legislation, promised a "decent home and a suitable
living environment for every American family" and created
the Urban Redevelopment Agency, which (armed with the
new constitutional powers of eminent domain) authorized
federal funds for the condemnation, purchase, and clearance of slums. Eisenhower signed into law an even more
comprehensive housing act in 1954, which expanded such
federal programs as FHA Mortgage Insurance and allowed
the idea of urban rehabilitation to be translated into a full-
fledged urban renewal program. The Interstate Highway Act
of 1957 created a new national system of freeways, which
would soon be extended into the cities. Federal programs
were further expanded during the Kennedy and Johnson
administrations, with such legislation as the Housing Act of
1961, the Area Redevelopment Act of 1961, the Housing Act
of 1964, the Urban Mass Transportation Act of 1964, the

Model Cities Program of 1966, and the Housing and Urban
Development Act of 1968. Johnson's "War on Poverty" program, announced in the spring of 1964, was the centerpiece
of his Great Society agenda, which also included the Civil
Rights Act (1964), the Economic Opportunity Act (1964), the
Voting Rights Act (1965), the Higher Education Act (1965),
the Educational Opportunity Act (1968), the Child Health
Improvement and Protection Act (1968), and the Medicaid
Act (1968). In 1965 the various arms of the housing and
redevelopment programs were collected under the administrative umbrella of the Department of Housing and Urban
Development (HUD). By every contemporary account, it was
the heyday of liberal planning, theory, and spending. Testi-
fying before Congress in 1966, Sargent Shriver confidently
predicted that urban poverty would be eliminated within a
decade.[1]

But something obviously went very wrong. Whereas there
were successes in some downtown areas – notably San
Francisco's Ghirardelli Square, Minneapolis's Nicolett Mall,
the Boston Government Center, and Pittsburgh's Golden
Triangle – major failures of urban renewal were far more
commonplace. By the early 1960s the bulldozing of aging
urban neighborhoods and their systematic replacement with
high-rise and low-rise projects had created such well-known
abominations as Pruit-Igoe in Saint Louis, the Columbus
Houses in Newark, the Van Dyke and Baruch Towers in
New York, and the Rosen Houses in Philadelphia. The architectural and social cure turned out to be far worse than
the problem.

Of course, many other factors within the changing fabric
of American society were inhibiting the chances of success
within the field of housing. At a national level there had

been a fundamental shift in federal policies over the course of the postwar years. Much of the public housing legislation enacted in the prewar years was fiscally neutral, or nearly so, and was written specifically to advance the upward mobility of the working poor. Public subsidized housing in the early 1950s screened tenants, mandated a rent sufficient to meet operating expenses, and enforced standards of social behavior and cleanliness with the power of eviction. One decade later nearly all of these social restraints had given way to more liberalized federal programs that brought about massive dislocation of the poor and had far more permissive standards or social expectations. In fact the working poor in the 1960s were often excluded from subsidized housing in favor of those without jobs and on welfare, that is, those who, because of their lack of educational tools, did not have a realistic possibility of upward mobility.[2] Many of the poor in need of better shelter refused to move to the new projects precisely because of the social stigma attached to living there.

Working hand and glove with these policies were the changing demographics of the cities themselves. The migration of poor blacks into the cities and of white workers into the surrounding suburbs had been a trend in the United States since the 1920s. But in the 1950s the trend underwent a very significant change. The poor, especially from impoverished rural areas in the South, were attracted to the larger cities in ever greater numbers, in part because of the promise of assistance from federal programs, while workers and their employers – now trying to escape the concomitant problems of crime, substance abuse, decreasing property values, and growing blight – intensified their flight to the suburbs. The larger cities virtually overnight became havens for the uneducated and unemployed and simultaneously lost the tax base needed to address the escalating social problems.

What also had been been lacking in the first years of urban renewal was a comprehensive discussion of the architectural nature of public housing. The American aloofness toward CIAM and its debates regarding the city may be cited as one reason for this professional lethargy, but the lack of serious debate before 1960 is even striking within the academic system. Such European paradigms as the Radiant City high-rises were blithely accepted as solutions with little or no discussion of their relevance to the cultural and economic conditions in the United States. The German-inspired urban program that Gropius introduced at Harvard – his plea for community centers – is a case in point, although his efforts were by no means the most lamentable within the newly "modernized" American schools of architecture. More often

than not, a profound ignorance of the most basic facts and strategies reigned. One fairly comprehensive study produced for the American Institute of Architects in 1965, for instance, not only wrongly characterized the quite different planning approaches of Constantine Doxiadis, Charles Abrams, and Buckminster Fuller as thinking that "could be categorized along the lines of MacKaye, Le Corbusier, and the other regionalists" but went on to offer a fairly comprehensive range of urban strategies – without a thought as to their sociological implications or relevance to American cities.[3]

With such odd critical detachment on the part of the architectural profession, it is not surprising then that the vast majority of policy and urban-design decisions of the 1950s and 1960s were made not by planners or architects but by politicians or politically entrenched bureaucrats. One of the more famous of these power brokers was Robert Moses, New York City's long-standing commissioner of parks and coordinator of the Office of City Construction. He also happened to be a fan of the Corbusean high-rise set out on a grassy lawn.[4] Moses had been entrenched in power since 1924, and by World War II he had largely defined the physical character of the New York metropolitan area through his construction of parkways, bridges, beaches, and parks. Between 1945 and 1958 he was responsible for more than a thousand public housing structures housing more than a half million people, that is, more than most American cities. Among the enormous ventures under his control were Stuyvesant Town, Peter Cooper Village, and Bronx Co-op City.

Moses, at least, had the distinction in his later years of fomenting discussion. His chief nemesis during his later reign was Lewis Mumford, whose opposition to Moses dates back to the late 1940s – to his crusade against the plan for Stuyvesant Town, which Mumford faulted for its high density, lack of social amenities, and Cartesian high-rise towers.[5] In the mid-1950s Mumford took up his pen against the commissioner's penchant for new highways, both within and around New York City.[6] Mumford in the late 1950s also fought Moses's attempt to extend Fifth Avenue under Washington Square Park and connect it with projected new routes. The automobile was the archvillain for Mumford, even though he (like the highwayman Moses) never learned to drive.

Mumford's concern with urban issues in the late 1950s culminated in his decision to write *The City in History* (1961), which in some respects is a revision and expansion of *The Culture of Cities* (1938). It is one of Mumford's lengthiest and most widely applauded books and is still regarded by many to be his crowning achievement in this field. It is as well an interesting book in its quasi-archaeological quest to tie the level of human culture to the management of cities, which of course lies at the heart of his contemporary critique. After leading the reader through an account of the rise of paleolithic and neolithic culture and the development of the *polis* in Mesopotamia, Egypt, Minos, Greece, Rome, the Middle Ages (still the highpoint of urban achievement), the Renaissance, and the nineteenth century (its coketowns remaining the low point), Mumford arrives at the almost equally problematic period of the twentieth century, characterized by urban sprawl, suburbia (the anticity), automobile traffic, and worse. The principal failing of suburbia, in his viewpoint, is its social isolation:

The town housewife, who half a century ago knew her butcher, her grocer, her dairyman, her various other local tradesmen, as individual persons, with histories and biographies that impinged on her own, in a daily interchange, now has the benefit of a single weekly expedition to an impersonal supermarket, where only by accident is she likely to encounter a neighbor. If she is well-to-do, she is surrounded with electric or electronic devices that take the place of flesh and blood companions: her real companions, her friends, her mentors, her lovers, her fillers-up of unlived life, are shadows on the television screen, or even less embodied voices. She may answer them, but she cannot make herself heard: as it has worked out, this is a one-way system. The greater the area of expansion, the greater the dependence upon a distant supply center and remote control.[7]

Mumford is now quite inflexible in reiterating his earlier views. Disorder in the modern city is the rule, and its tonic is planning. Inhibiting such a sane response are a multitude of intangibles: the population boom, the city's symbolic representation of sovereign power, "giantism" for its own sake, and the technological lure of an arrogant anthropocentrism seeking ecological control. What he prescribes, however, is not a physical plan for reversing the process but only a vague plea for a more fundamental change of attitude, "in which significant improvements will come only through fresh dedication to the cosmic and ecological processes that enfold all the autonomous activities, the symbiotic associations that have long been neglected or suppressed."[8] In other essays of this period, Mumford turns back to the garden city of Howard and to the lessons of such examples as Radburn and Raymond Unwin's Hamstead Gardens, that is, to an urban-suburban cell limited in size to somewhere between 30,000 and 300,000 people.[9] His city-planning views, therefore, had essentially remained unchanged over the past thirty-five years.

Yet such a perspective had little concrete assistance to offer the rapidly deteriorating American city of the early 1960s, and it is only in the face of this genuine crisis that a serious debate begins to emerge. The starting point, interestingly, is not Mumford's writings but *The Death and Life of Great American Cities* by Jane Jacobs (b. 1916). Jacobs, like Mumford, had no formal training in architecture or urban design, yet her book would nevertheless reformulate many of the terms of the debate.

The object of Jacobs's ridicule is that twentieth-century planning ideology she terms the "Radiant garden city Beautiful" movement: the conventional wisdom of current models based on the images of Le Corbusier's towers, Howard's decentralized garden city (with its scorn of automobiles), and Daniel Burnham's monumental civic cores (around which usually assemble "an incongruous rim of ratty tattoo parlors and second-hand clothing stores").[10] The essential insight underlying her critique is that drinking a soda on an urban stoop with a neighbor is a vastly different social exercise than having that same soda on the neutral turf of a community center or in another anonymous setting. Thus her attention is centered not on urban architecture, which has generally been the sole focus of architects, but rather on the social fabric that generates a successful urban street and neighborhood – successful in the sense that community values are self-regulated and the crime is absent. She views most of the housing and rehabilitation programs of the twentieth century as working to destroy the city and its imperative social fabric. The antiurban and pessimistic demand of garden city enthusiasts (read Mumford) for decentralization, in her view, lies at the heart of this destruction, and she takes square aim at its underlying thesis:

To reinforce and dramatize the necessity for the old order of things, the Decentrists hammered away at the bad old city. They were incurious about successes in great cities. They were interested only in failures. All was failure. A book like Mumford's *The Culture of Cities* was largely a morbid and biased catalog of ills. A great city was Megalopolis, Tyrannopolis, Nekropolis, a monstrosity, a tyranny, a living death. It must go. New York's midtown was "solidified chaos" (Mumford). The shape and appearance of cities was nothing but "a chaotic accident...the summation of the haphazard, antagonistic whims of many self-centered, ill-advised individuals" (Stein). The centers of cities amounted to "a foreground of noise, dirt, beggars, souvenirs and shrill competitive advertising" (Bauer). How could anything so bad be worth the attempt to understand it?[11]

Pointing to such vibrant urban neighborhoods as Boston's North End (which planners saw as consisting of slums), Jacobs counters with an analysis of social factors that make a city work. Her twin pillars – active sidewalks (fostering social contact at all levels while retaining privacy) and functional diversity – can be achieved by (1) mixing residential and small commercial functions (the butcher to whom Mumford's housewife no longer spoke), (2) using short city blocks for pedestrians (inviting multiple routes and contacts), (3) mingling buildings of different ages (leading to visual variety and neighborhood maintenance), and (4) concentrating people (far more than allowed by modern planners). Better neighborhoods, Jacobs argues, cannot be planned by architects or planners, at least not in the traditional way. Nor can better neighborhoods be decreed by the bulldozer and large-scale "urban renewal" projects. The money for renewal (and less of it) is best spent at the local level in the form of small neighborhood loans for the maintenance and enhancement of older structures.

Many other "myths" of conventional planning also come under Jacob's scrutiny. Mumford's belief that automobiles in themselves are detrimental to the life of the city is disputed by her, at least up to a certain point. More interesting is her argument that neighborhood parks are often not the amenities that planners presume them to be. The idea that they are somehow the healthy "lungs of the city" is refuted by simple scientific facts; moreover, the removal of children by their mothers from play activities on the city's sidewalks to the "safety" of a defined playground, Jacobs argues, is matriachical and inhibits rather than promotes the learning of important social skills: "The opportunity (in modern life it has become a privilege) of playing and growing up in a daily world composed of both men and women is possible and usual for children who play on lively, diversified city sidewalks."[12] Saying this another way, the simple ability to "fool around" in unsupervised games is once again different socially from being coerced into "recognized games" on the playground. Children, she argues, much prefer the former, and in the end what urban designers and critics fear most is lack of control or the presence of chaos. But it is precisely chaos, she insists, that defines the urban experience and allows the urban neighborhood to thrive.

Mumford was quick to respond to Jacobs in a lengthy and highly critical "Sky Line" article in the *New Yorker*.[13] Although he could not have agreed more with her condemnation of the high-rise as an urban renewal "solution," he firmly opposed her effort to push "out of existence every desirable innovation in urban planning during the last

century," not least of which was Howard's model for neighborhoods of roughly 30,000 people, or the size of Jacobs's beloved Greenwich Village.[14] Acknowledging the livability of this precinct, he yet points out the blight of similarly dense neighborhoods in Brooklyn, Queens, and Harlem. Her ideal, he continues, is mainly conceived for the prevention of crime, but recent increases in crime rates are rather due to the "increasing pathology of the whole mode of life in the great metropolis, a pathology that is directly proportionate to its overgrowth, its purposeless materialism, its congestion, and its insensate disorder – the very conditions she vehemently upholds as marks of urban vitality."[15] He continues: "Her simple formula does not suggest that her eyes have ever been hurt by ugliness, sordor, confusion, or her ears offended by the roar of trucks smashing through a once quiet residential neighborhood, or her nose assaulted by the chronic odors of ill-ventilated, unsunned housing at the slum standards of congestion that alone meet her ideal standards for residential density."[16]

At this point Mumford's critique of Jacobs's book turns decidedly pessimistic: "Today, military power, scientific power, technical power, financial power, and, in fact, 'cataclysmic' power in every manifestation operate most successfully, on their own terms, by wiping out diversity and doing away with every mode of organic growth, ecological partnership, and autonomous activity."[17] The urban problems, he concludes, cannot be solved by "a few tricks of planning." Even more ominously he states, "If our urban civilization is to escape progressive dissolution, we shall have to rebuild it from the ground up."[18] Five years later, in testimony before the Ribicoff congressional committee on federal expenditures, Mumford again joins Jacobs in condemning the current urban renewal high-rises but then condemns her naiveté in linking "the rapes, the robberies, the destructive delinquencies, the ever-threatening violence" with simple planning decisions. The reasons for these urban pathologies lie much deeper, he insists: "There is no planning cure for this machine-centered existence which produces only psychotic stresses, meaningless 'happenings,' and murderous fantasies of revenge."[19]

The quarrel between Mumford and Jacobs in the early 1960s gave form to a materializing debate, which soon exploded into a broad critique of the American city and federal urban renewal programs that had been put into place by a cadre of architects, planners, ecologists, and sociologists. As would be expected, architects and planners naturally emphasized the physical elements of the city and the bringing of order to the urban environment. The landscape architect

Lawrence Halprin (b. 1916), for instance, stressed the need for urban vitality in his first book, *Cities* (1963). He did so by providing a visual documentation of design possibilities for everything from granite setts to bollards.[20] Peter Blake, since 1950 the editor of *Architectural Forum*, was a regular critic of the deterioration of the city, and in 1964 he published his famous book *God's Own Junkyard* – a book written not in anger but in "fury" (Fig. 103). A self-professed Jeffersonian, Blake sees the insensitive defacement of the skyscape, carscape, roadscape, landscape, and townscape (as the book's subtitle discloses) as the "planned deterioration of America's landscape" induced by unbounded commercialism and greed. Speaking of the American city, he says, "We walk or drive through them each day; this is where we work, shop, and are also born, exist, and die. What manner of people is being reared in these infernal wastelands?"[21]

Another solution for urban blight was presented in Victor Gruen's book of the same year, *The Heart of Our Cities: The Urban Crisis: Diagnosis and Cure*.[22] Gruen, of course, had earlier helped to create the suburb with his concept of shopping and office malls. Now he offers a solution based on urban compactness, vibrant public amenities, and small-grain patterning. He also devises a (biologically inspired) cellular approach to urban planning that isolates core areas of high density that are arranged around a central core and separated by geographic features while connected by roadways. The end result, as he himself belatedly came to see, is startlingly similar to Howard's garden city and the new satellite towns of Scandinavia.

Another theorist to focus attention on the city's physical characteristics, only in a more theoretical and psychological way, was Kevin Lynch (b. 1918). After spending his early adult years in Chicago, where he shared an apartment with Ralph Rapson, Lynch moved to Cambridge in the mid-1940s to study at M.I.T. There he eventually joined Gyorgy Kepes at the school's Center of Urban and Regional Studies, one of the first institutes of its kind. In his initial work, Lynch focused on the problem of urban form and its physical patterning. He analyzed urban textures for their building typologies, quantity, densities, grain, focal organizations, and spatial distributions. In one paper, "The Pattern of Urban Growth" (1960), he addressed the broader issue of urban planning typologies – from gridded-street patterns to galaxy layouts – and proposed what he termed a "multi-centered net" of cores dispersed within an interrelated matrix.[23]

In his first book, *The Image of the City* (1960), which would play an important role in Rossi's urban theory, he takes his research in a slightly different direction. Through the use of readings, interviews with urban inhabitants, and field surveys of three American cities (Boston, Jersey City, Los Angeles), Lynch adduces the psychological notion of "imageability" as crucial for urban design, that is, "that quality in a physical object which gives it a high probability of evoking a strong image in any given observer."[24] Imageability he further likens to the ideas of "*legibility*" and "*visibility* in a heightened sense, where objects are not only able to be seen, but are presented sharply and intensely to the senses."[25] What Lynch is in fact drawing attention to is the inhabitants' phenomenological experience of the city and the importance, for planning, orientation, and the inhabitants' need to have an overall conceptual understanding of the main features of the city in order to form a relationship with them. Hence, the components of this environmental image are presented by a combination of five structural and conceptual features: paths, edges, districts, nodes, and landmarks. Although this study offers few specific pointers for the urban designer – aside from the claim that the city should be a "well-knit *place*" and should encourage "the deposit of a memory trace"[26] – it represents a departure from the research of the 1950s, which was concerned mostly with the issue of density and only occasionally with aesthetics. The clear definition of a city's paths, nodes, and landmarks, Lynch argues, is essential for the inhabitants' self-esteem and self-understanding; therefore, architects and planners should be exceedingly cautious before removing or altering them or adding new ones.

Lynch's investigations fell in line with research that materialized in the 1960s under the rubric of "ecology." The concept (as used in biology) had been bandied about since the 1920s, but as it evolved over the decades, it became transformed into a full-fledged science comprising the workings of the environment, geography, and social phenomena. The field was popularized in the early 1960s by such books as George A. Theodorson's *Studies in Human Ecology* (1961), Rachel Carson's *Silent Spring* (1962), and Leonard J. Duhl's *The Urban Condition: People and Policy in the Metropolis* (1963). Carson's book helped to define what would eventually become an environmental movement, while Duhl's book looked at the "crisis of urbanization" from the perspective of the urban terrain, racial relations, and mental health.[27]

Also dealing with a broad overview of issues were Roger Barker's *Ecological Psychology* (1968) and Ian McHarg's *Design with Nature* (1969). McHarg (b. 1920), who became the chairman of the Department of Landscape Architecture and Regional Planning at the University of Pennsylvania, came

103. Peter Blake, two contrasting images from *God's Own Junkyard* (New York, 1964).

to his regional concerns through his initial interest in the city and the problem of physical health.[28]

Paralleling studies of the physical urban environment and ecology were numerous sociological investigations done in the early 1960s, such as those of Herbert J. Gans and Robert Gutman. The former, who received his doctorate in sociology from the University of Chicago, began his career with his well-known study of Levittown in the late 1950s, but *The Urban Villagers*, published in 1962, was a more representative work.[29] It describes the plight of Boston's West End, a largely Italian-immigrant community shortly

to be eradicated by a form of "urban renewal," the construction of luxury housing.[30] The book, in fact, provides a well-documented context for Jacobs's ideas regarding the make-up, social dynamics, and generational continuity of a neighborhood, while at the same time it underscores the lack of understanding of these issues by policymakers. Gutman, a professor of sociology at Rutgers University in the mid-1960s, became involved with the architecture school at Princeton University, where he developed his expertise on the relationship between the physical environment and social ills and patterns of behavior.[31] His role in training architects in itself reflected the dramatic increase in the popularity of sociology during these same years within architectural circles.

One outgrowth of this interest in the social sciences is the increasing body of criticism of urban renewal programs and planning models of the 1960s. Early critiques are often defensive and somewhat tentative. For instance, Elizabeth Wood, a consultant to the New York Citizens' Housing and Planning Council, argued in 1961 that the principal problem with high-rise solutions lay not with the building type itself but rather with their failure to deal with the communicational or social needs of people. Her position was that high-rises should include outdoor amenities such as places for loitering, car washing, conversation, recreation, and accidental social contact.[32]

The executive director of New York's Housing and Planning Council, Roger Starr, took a somewhat similar tack in his book *The Urban Choices: The City and Its Critics* (1967). He argued – against the easy assumptions of Jacobs in particular – that the problems of the city are essentially structural and traceable to a changing social-economic-political system. As for the question of high-rises (or the remedy of returning to a traditional street and its urban life), he remains blithely noncommittal: "The street is dying because butcher, baker, greengrocer, fish dealer, delicatessen store proprietor, and stationer have been amalgamated into the chain store and the supermarket and the discount house, whose store window is the television set or radio."[33]

But such moral smugness would soon be overtaken by events. The crisis beginning to unfold in ghettos across America had very little to do with recreation rooms or the proliferation of television sets, although it was arguably television that was educating the poor as to the tragedy of the cities, their failing schools and disappearing employment bases. On a policy level, the pending crisis was first intimated by Martin Anderson's controversial 1964 study, *The Federal Bulldozer: A Critical Analysis of Urban Renewal 1949–62* (Fig. 104).[34] Written while Anderson was still a student at M.I.T., his book is a condemnation of existing urban renewal programs and a strongly worded plea for their suspension, based on data largely collected from federal agencies. Anderson points out that the federal and state programs had failed in their most basic mission of supplying housing to the poor; for instance, in the 1950s over 126,000 housings units in urban centers had been destroyed while only 28,000 new units had been built. Moreover, the rent for most of these new projects was often far higher than the rent for the properties they replaced. The problem was only growing worse,

as over 1.6 million people were living in areas targeted for urban renewal. In addition to the social uprootedness caused by present programs, urban renewal, Anderson insists, had also failed to achieve two other essential goals. First, businesses had been severely hurt by the programs. In fact, 40 percent of the businesses displaced simply folded, which in turn intensified the problem of urban unemployment. Second, the overall effect of urban renewal on the tax base was to reduce it rather than cause the expected fourfold increase. His conclusion was that such programs should be replaced by private enterprise initiatives, which – in the same period studied – had been far more successful in upgrading housing and rebuilding the cities.

Appearing on the eve of the Great Society programs, Anderson's book was greeted with a barrage of criticism from vested bureaucratic and liberal academic interests. Robert P. Groberg, the assistant director of the National Association of Housing and Redevelopment Officials, faulted the book for various reasons, above all for its statistical analysis and its failure to see the "historical perspective and the limits of federal aid for slum clearance and redevelopment."[35] Herbert Gans actually concurred with the central point of Anderson's book, but he too criticized the statistics of this "ultraconservative economist and often free-swinging polemicist."[36] Gans insisted that urban policies had failed because they had been constructed as "a method for eliminating the slums in order to 'renew' the city, rather than as a program for properly re-housing slum dwellers."[37] Another prominent protagonist in the debate, James Q. Wilson, acknowledged that there were problems in the existing urban programs but felt they could be eliminated, in part by creating neighborhood associations and thus ending political alienation.[38]

One of the more interesting defenses of urban renewal policies came from Charles Abrams (1902–70), the longstanding chairman of the City Planning Department at Columbia University and one of the founders of the New York Housing Authority.[39] In opposing Anderson, he argued not for the abolition of federal programs but rather for their vast amplification – and the creation of a federal Urban Space Agency (URSA), obviously akin in spirit to NASA.[40] Abrams was critical of the overreliance of federal programs on slum clearance, their speculative motive, and the fact that they placed little emphasis on solving the underlying social ills, but at the same time he felt that they directed much needed attention toward land use planning, issues of urban aesthetics, and the need for civic and cultural improvements, among other things. He was appreciative of the fact that prominent architects had recently been

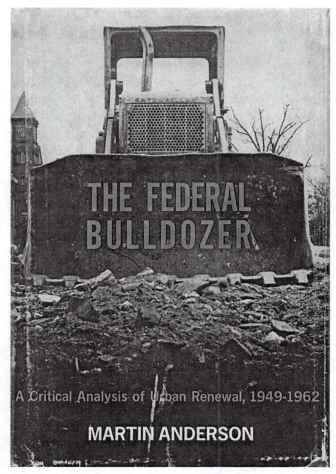

104. Cover of Martin Anderson's *The Federal Bulldozer* (Cambridge, Massachusetts, 1964).

brought into the picture and were now designing model projects – architects such as I. M. Pei, Mies van der Rohe, Paul Rudolph, William W. Wurster, and Minoru Yamasaki.[41] Hence, the answer for Abrams ultimately lay with architects' ability to solve social problems through masterful and aesthetically pleasing design.

By the mid-1960s, however, this view was being challenged. A consensus was forming that the large-scale removal of slums and their replacement with anonymous highrises had become an unmitigated urban nightmare in need of major rethinking. Pressing for a reevaluation was Paul Davidoff (1951–85), one of the founders of the advocacy planning movement. Davidoff's contention was that urban renewal programs were mainly benefiting the pockets of developers, who were siphoning off federal funds at the expense of the dislocated poor. Planning decisions were also inherently skewed in that planning commissions were generally controlled by narrow political representation and not by the citizens affected. Davidoff's early writings – beginning with "A Choice Theory of Planning" (1962, with Thomas Reiner) – together with his various legal challenges to federal funding, exclusionary zoning, and access to suburban housing, helped to sharpen the highly contentious political atmosphere of the late 1960s.[42] Various architectural groups also took up the cause of advocacy – the Architects' Renewal Committee in Harlem, Urban Planning Aid in Boston, and PARS (Planners and Architects for Neighborhood Regeneration) in San Francisco – although usually with only marginal success.

Events in any case overtook all discussion. The riot in Watts in the summer of 1965 was followed the next year by racial violence and extensive fires in no fewer than seventy cities – from Oakland to Pompano Beach to Providence. In 1967 the country witnessed urban rioting that decimated whole areas of Boston, Newark, and Detroit, leaving dozens of people killed, thousands injured, and large areas burned out. All of this unrest led to the violent atmosphere of 1968, one of the worst years in American history. Whether the psychological collapse of the collective American spirit is to be attributed to the enduring legacy of slavery and racial discrimination, the concomitant Vietnam War buildup, the failure of the free enterprise system, or the philosophical shortcomings of classic liberalism itself, the fact remains that urban renewal polices, their architectural consequences, and their theoretical foundation had over the past two decades proved entirely inadequate to the formidable task at hand. The issue of whether architects or planners could indeed solve or assuage the more pervasive social problems was at the same time brought front and center. In other words, the meliorist social premises of modernism had been placed in question.

2. From a Pattern Language to the I-Ching

The response to these ever more pressing problems can be followed in the narrower field of architecture proper, as programs in environmental design and social studies began to be integrated into architecture curricula. An early work in this vein was Serge Chermayeff and Christopher Alexander's *Community and Privacy* (1963).[43] Chermayeff, as we have seen, had been the director of Chicago's Institute of Design and in 1952 had moved to Harvard University as one of the first appointments of José Luis Sert. His research in the 1950s had centered on the sociology of housing from the functional perspective of the user, and he began to use this research to develop what he termed the "science of environmental design."[44] Underlying it was the premise that architectural design could be improved by availing itself of analytical modeling and integrating the research generated by the social sciences. *Community and Privacy* is in part an environmental tract that attributes the deterioration of the natural environment and the urban habitat to the scourges of suburbia, the automobile, and intensifying psychological stress. The aim is to develop design prototypes for community housing as alternatives to the single-family suburban house, following in the footsteps of Gropius and the European planners. Part two of the study, largely written by Alexander, is a computer-aided analysis of the variables of zoning residential functions and is largely concerned with protection against noise transmission. This refinement of the functionalist or rationalist approach to design is a principal merit of the study.

Christopher Alexander's involvement with this project was not ancillary. The Austrian-born, British-naturalized theoretician had studied mathematics, physics, and architecture at Cambridge University, before arriving at Harvard University in 1958 to begin his doctoral studies under Chermayeff. He completed his dissertation late in 1962, and the published version, *Notes on a Synthesis of Form* (1964), startled the architectural community with its mathematical premises and opened the door to a field scarcely imagined – use of an analytical method of research and computer operations capable of being translated into architectural form.

The premise underlying Alexander's work is that design has become too complex, too detailed in specialized information and variables, and too urgent, with the result that designers have reached the point of being overtaxed. Seizing an analogy from D'Arcy Thompson's *Growth of Form*, which defined form as "a diagram of forces," Alexander argues that good design is the "fitness" of form with regard to a specific context, and he conceives of fitness as a relationship of "frictionless coexistence."[45] In theory, this thesis is functionalism at its purest, but what makes Alexander's approach unique is his proposal for mapping functional variables on a computer through the mathematic tools of set theory after a sufficient number of "constructive diagrams" have been manufactured.[46] What is also new in his approach is the strong emphasis he places on psychological and anthropological variables in design; the bibliography of his dissertation, for instance, contains twice as many references to books in psychology, problem solving, and anthropology than in architecture.[47] In an appendix, Alexander even imposes his mathematical rigor on the design ele-

ments for an Indian village, and from it he devises a series of stem- or tree-like diagrams that organize the relationships of variables.

Alexander presented the tree-like mapping of the Indian village at a Team 10 meeting at Royaumont in 1962, after which he got into a debate with Aldo van Eyck over their individual uses of the tree analogy.[48] Alexander responded to the discussion a few years later with an article in *Architectural Forum* entitled "A City Is Not a Tree." It represents an advance on his earlier model, for he now realizes that a tree diagram (a successive and isolating branching of limbs, branches, twigs, and leaves) disallows the possibility of "overlap, ambiguity, and multiplicity of aspect," which are features of the experience of reality.[49] Actual human experience is akin to a semilattice, where the different branches of a matrix are able to communicate or intersect with one another. Supporting this view is Alexander's very shrewd insight that a university campus – for example, Cambridge University – need not exist as an isolated "campus" with logically distinct teaching, residential, and recreational areas but might function extremely well within an ambiguous town setting in which individual colleges are interspersed with and sometimes indistinguishable from the surrounding coffeeshops, pubs, and stores, with student lodging above: "In Cambridge, a natural city where university and city have grown together gradually, the physical units overlap because they are the physical residues of city systems and university systems which overlap."[50] In the same essay, Alexander points out that the new cities of Columbia and Greenbelt, Maryland, the greater London plan of 1944, Chandigarh, and Brasília were all laid out according to a tree or functional diagram, and this is another reason for their evident artificiality and failure. Urban design, he concludes, is an exceedingly complex fabric of variables, "the structure of living things; of great paintings and symphonies."[51]

Alexander's concern with design methodology was representative of a discernible movement of the 1960s that was strong in America but perhaps even stronger in Britain. In 1970 the British architect C. Christopher Jones summarized thirty-five "new methods" applicable to architectural design – almost all devised in the 1960s.[52] Many emanated from related fields in engineering, but many others, such as Jones's own "Collaborative Strategy for Adaptable Architecture" (CASA), were designed specifically to apply to architecture. His claim is that increasing the amount of time in design analysis not only ensures that a larger number of design variables are considered but also decreases the time needed to reach a synthetic solution. Perhaps the most influential architectural theorist in this regard was Geoffrey Broadbent. With Colin Ward – and based on a conference on design methodologies held in Birmingham in 1965 – he edited *Design Methods in Architecture* (1969) for the Architectural Association in London.[53] By this date Broadbent's developing interest in semiotics had made him very critical of Alexander's earlier work and led him to propose a design methodology of "deep structures" modeled on Noam Chomsky's syntactic studies.[54]

Alexander, too, was not content to accept his own earlier work, and in the second half of the 1960s, he not only developed his argument for the semilattice model but replaced the idea of a "diagram" with the more flexible notion of a "pattern," which he later defined as that which "describes a problem which occurs over and over again in our environment, and then describes the core of the solution to that problem, in such a way that you can use this solution a million times over, without ever doing it the same way twice."[55] His first presentation of this idea came in *A Pattern Language Which Generates Multi-Service Centers* (1968).[56] Here the problem, derived from his long-standing anthropological interests, is to define the parameters for the design of a multipurpose community center in a low-income neighborhood based for the most part on sociological and psychological research. There were evident strengths, but also inherent limitations, in such an approach. On the one hand, there are patterns for selecting the site, for the diagrammatic functioning of the center, and for many design details, such as the placement of windows, the shape of rooms, and height of the receptionist's seat. On the other hand, the idea of a pattern language is in itself culturally formulated and requires (architectural) judgments subject to conventions and ultimately reflecting the biases of the pattern makers. The proposed niches off the street for people to "stop, linger and become familiar with the building's service" both betray the behaviorist approach very evident at this time and suggest a shielding device subject to vandalism and one that, in high-crime areas, people might very well cross the street to avoid.[57] Alexander in his later work with pattern languages sought to provide more generalized anthropological formulas, but at this point he had ceased to believe in the possibility of a comprehensive design methodology.[58]

Alexander's social focus and his desire to make architectural design more "scientific" in its bearings were complemented along various other fronts in the 1960s. In a paper presented to the Architectural Association in London in 1963, Stanford Anderson spoke out against the "technological determinism" and antirevivalism of Banham by invoking the distinction between tradition (a necessary ground upon which to operate) and traditionalism ("tombstone polishing").[59] Anderson also employed the philosophical constructions of Karl Popper to argue that scientific inquiry was little more than the maintenance by scientists of "an active critical, or argumentative attitude toward their guesses" (theories) and that such a strategy could be adapted to architecture: "The radical step would be to formulate problems and hypotheses within our own architectural problem situation, and then to criticize and test them as rigorously as our current information and methods permit."[60] Anderson further pointed to the areas of sociology, psychology, and biology as having specific application to architecture; tradition in architecture (our existing formal solutions) plays a role similar to the body of scientific knowledge in that our known assumptions are continually tested and augmented in an orderly fashion.

Anderson's paper was re-presented two years later, along with several other papers, at the teacher seminar held at Cranbrook Academy in 1964, which brought such foreign visitors as Bruno Zevi, Reyner Banham, and Peter Collins together with Chermayeff and Sibyl Moholy-Nagy. The theme of the conference was the teaching of the history, theory, and criticism of architecture. Although the papers presented very different viewpoints, it is interesting to see how far the pendulum had swung toward a scientific grounding for theory and criticism. In responding to the rigorous methodological approach of Richard Llewellyn-Davies, even the humanist Peter Collins went so far as to define theory "as the principles which relate the form of a building to the sociological, technological, economic and aesthetic conditions presiding over its inception" – that is, to something akin to algebraic functionalism.[61]

This outlook, of course, was also being driven by the behavioral research undertaken inside the social science departments of American universities in the 1960s, much of which was focused on the architectural environment. Perhaps foremost among these researchers was the anthropologist Edward T. Hall, who in *The Silent Language* (1959) surveyed the unconscious cultural patterns underlying human behavior and dealt with such issues as cultural temporality, territoriality, and subliminal modes of communication. In *The Hidden Dimension* (1966), Hall analyzed the spatial experiences of buildings through their visual, auditory, olfactory, thermal, and tactile parameters, again emphasizing the cultural basis of these experiences. Hall also on occasion participated in architectural debates. He was, for example, an outspoken opponent of high-rise housing for low-income people – "less distressing to look at than slums but more disturbing to live in than much of what it replaced" – largely on the grounds that the scale and functioning of the buildings were alien to the largely uneducated people moving into the cities from rural areas.[62] The destruction of Boston's West End was also a fiasco, in Hall's view, because "slum clearance and urban renewal failed to take into account the fact that the working-class neighborhoods were quite different from those of the middle class."[63] On the positive side, he praised Bertrand Goldberg's Marina City and Chloethiel Smith's work in Washington, D.C., as important landmarks in the revitalization of urban centers.

Hall's studies on human spatiality and territoriality were among numerous books that were not architectural in the strict sense but had an impact on architectural thinking, beginning with – to name but a few – Robert Ardrey's *African Genesis* (1961) and *The Territorial Imperative* (1966), Thomas Kuhn's *Structure of Scientific Revolutions* (1962), Erving Goffman's *Behavior in Public Places* (1963), and Robert Sommer's *Personal Space: The Behavioral Basis of Design* (1969). Sommer was a psychologist at the University of California, Davis, and he directed his research toward architecture in particular. His results, however, are better summarized in the later book *Tight Spaces: Hard Architecture and How to Humanize It* (1974), where he takes direct aim at the federally funded "hard" spaces created over the past two decades – renewal projects such as Pruitt-Igeo in Saint Louis.[64]

Another influential book that had its beginning in the social problems and "social science" atmosphere of the 1960s was Oscar Newman's *Defensible Space: Crime Prevention through Urban Design* (1972). Newman, who had attended and written the history of the CIAM conference at Otterlo in 1959, defined "defensible space" as "a surrogate term for the range of mechanisms – real and symbolic barriers, strongly defined areas of influence, and improved opportunities for surveillance – that combine to bring an environment under the control of its residents."[65] The term also suggests that "certain kinds of space and spatial layout favor the clandestine activities of criminals."[66] Newman, who was the director of the Institute of Planning and Housing at New York University, builds a forceful case that high-rise, double-loaded corridor apartment buildings, which invariably create "the most difficult crime problems" in urban situations, should be banned from all multifamily housing projects."[67] The inadequacies of CIAM's policies and of its architectural research and assumptions, at least for low-income housing, had over the course of a single decade become painfully evident.

By the mid-1960s this spate of social and behavioral studies began to be augmented, if not eclipsed, by a group of popular books that addressed the human condition in more philosophical, political, and countercultural terms – and here is where architectural thinking becomes severely affected by the concomitant social upheaval. The problems now facing the country were multifaceted: the Vietnam War and military draft, the Civil Rights and Black Power movements, feminism and the New Left, runaway pollution and the environmental movement, and a disenchanted younger generation and its embrace of hallucinogenic drugs. The one idea uniting ideological credos as diverse as Stokely Carmichael's *Black Power* (1967), Paul Ehrlich's *The Population Bomb* (1968), and Timothy Leary's "Turn on, Tune in, Drop out" was that a historic cultural revolution was not only inevitable but already well underway. In his famous book *The Medium Is the Message* (1967), the Edmonton thinker Marshall McLuhan (1911–80) regarded its content not in political terms but as something intrinsic to the new media of the electronic era:

Electric circuitry has overthrown the regime of "time" and "space" and pours upon us instantly and continuously the concerns of all other men. It has reconstituted dialogue on a global scale. Its message is Total Change, ending psychic, social, economic, and political parochialism. The old civic, state, and national groupings have become unworkable. Nothing can be further from the spirit of the new technology than "a place for everything and everything in its place." You can't *go* home again.[68]

Invoking Pierre Teilhard de Chardin's analogy of electricity and the central nervous system, McLuhan – the "Oracle of the Electronic Age" – tossed in just the right number of quotations from Bob Dylan, John Cage, and James Joyce to prove to youthful readers that the "groundrule of that universe, upon which so much of our Western world is built, has dissolved."[69]

It was an alluring thesis that enchanted millions of youths across the globe, especially as it demanded nothing of its converts other than a rejection of the present status quo (in every form) and the simple intoxicating desire to feel good. Tens of thousands of students of course did drop out, and within the architectural profession prophets appeared. The charismatic Paolo Soleri (b. 1919), who had arrived in the United States in 1947 to train under Wright, was by the mid-1960s drawing hundreds of architecture students from across the country to his Arizona desert compound to help build the new city of Arcosanti. Also influenced by the ideas of Teilhard de Chardin, Soleri in his book *Arcology: The City in the Image of Man* (1969) professed a complex philosophy of mental and physical symbiosis with nature and envisioned self-contained and self-balancing urban ecosystems in harmony with the characteristics of the landscape.[70]

This combination of ecological awakening, political activism, and messianic fervor is also seen in the work of the landscape architect Lawrence Halprin, in whom the forces of Jewish mysticism, Gestalt psychology, Carl Jung, the Eastern religions, and Timothy Leary seamlessly coalesce. Halprin was one of the most active landscape designers of the 1960s, and he was certainly one of the most talented, as shown by his plaza designs for Lovejoy Plaza, Portland (1962), Ghiradelli Square, San Francisco (1962), and Nicollet Mall, Minneapolis (1966) and his overall site plan for Sea Ranch, Mendocino County (1962–9). Through the evolving principles of his design process (with input from his wife, a choreographer) and his increasing involvement with various Haight-Ashbury "happenings" in the second half of the 1960s, Halprin devised his "RSVP Cycles" (Resources, Scores, Valuaction, Performance) as a creative strategy to oppose traditional (passive) planning and therefore as something generally geared toward community involvement and collective action. His "scoring" (the "S" of RSVP) is meant to provide a nonjudgmental and nonhierarchical system for evaluating creativity in everything from the Sydney Opera house to the hexagrams of the *I-Ching*. And although the "scores" (landscape studies) for his own designs are not so far removed from conventional landscape design (best seen in his work for Sea Ranch), his political and ecological commitments were revolutionary. Also evident in his radicalism is the somewhat pervasive sense of dread among the young, abetted by a spate of apocalyptic "scientific" studies on energy, population growth, and other prophecies of impending doom. Citing the disintegrating family and political system, the questioning of morality and the venality of war, the polluting of the atmosphere, land, and water, Halprin passionately argues that "we face social catastrophe, psychological catastrophe, personal catastrophe, national catastrophe, family catastrophe, community catastrophe. It is not enough to say this one or that one is at fault. We need creative mechanisms for change, based on aggregates of self-interest leading to community. We need a score."[71] If LSD and the parables of the *I-Ching* could be employed as weapons in righting this tottering condition of imbalance, so much the better for this generation enduring a collective psychological breakdown.

3. Louis I. Kahn

This sense of doom was less evident within the upper echelons of the architectural profession, which in fact enjoyed unparalleled prosperity during these same years. For instance, this was true of the architects of the war-time class at Harvard – Edward Larrabee Barnes, John Johansen, Philip Johnson, Paul Rudolf, Ulrich Franzen, Henry N. Cobb, and I. M. Pei – many of whom had been involved in the 1940s with the socially conscious student journal *TASK*. All had by the 1960s settled into conventional practices that regularly produced postcard images for the journals.

Barnes (1915–2004) remained the most restrained of the group and had an austere and consistent style: always proficient but with little complexity or drama.[72] Nevertheless, with his signature use of the sloped roof, he produced some genuinely inspired works, beginning with the Haystack Mountain School of Crafts, Deer Isle, Maine (1958–61), and including in fact many of his educational buildings of the 1960s. At the other end of the spectrum were many less than inspiring works, such as his U.S. Consulate in Tabriz, Iran (1958–66), and the Neiman Marcus Shopping Center, Fort Worth (1963).

Philip Johnson, of course, was still being Philip Johnson: the outspoken, irreverent aesthete-turned-eclectic, who in 1959 announced in a lecture at Yale University that he was "bored" with the International Style and its aesthetic legacy.[73] Although curiously impressed with the intellectual foment around him, he now chose to take refuge in traditionalism – a strategy he shared with Edward Durell Stone and Minoru Yamasaki – and among the many expressions of Johnson's marble monumentality during this decade are the Amon Carter Museum of Western Art, Fort Worth (1962), the Museum for Pre-Columbian Art, Washington, D.C. (1963), the Kline Science Center, New Haven (1965), and the New York State Theater, New York (1965).[74]

Monumentality, although of a different sort, is also found in the work of Ulrich Franzen (b. 1921) and John Johansen (b. 1916), both of whose buildings were often successful with design-award juries. Franzen passed from his Miesian forms of the 1950s to a Kahnian style, as seen in the thirteen-story towers of the Agronomy Building at Cornell University (1968).[75] Franzen's Alley Theater, Houston (1965–8), and Johansen's Mummers Theater, Oklahoma City (1965–70), both show the belated influence of Archigram, although the former, in its unapologetic formalism, still strives to be a whole. Johansen's theatre is radically fragmentary and deeper in its underlying conception. The architect claims that he made his escape from his earlier neoclassicism and "establishment modern" through conversations with McLuhan and his reading of Fuller and Peter Cook.[76] His design for the Mummers is only seemingly whimsical in its arbitrary composition and agrarian machine aesthetic. It is actually organized in accord with the "techno-esthetics" of electronic circuitry, with a chassis (structural framework), components (halls), subcomponents (mechanical elements), and harnesses (mechanical, vehicular, and pedestrian pathways).[77]

The Cantonese Pei (b. 1917) taught at the Harvard Graduate School of Design after completing his degree there in 1946, but he was lured away in 1948 by the real estate developer William Zeckendorf, for whom he worked as an architect until 1960.[78] In his early practice, he was noticeably influenced by his mentors Gropius and Breuer, but he eventually assembled a talented office staff of his own, and indeed the 1960s became the "Pei decade." The first of his major commissions, the National Center for Atmospheric Research (1961–7), was where he honed his talent for sculptural composition and refinement of material – in this case concrete made with sand ground from a nearby quarry. It led to a long line of major commissions, including the JFK Library, Boston (1964–79), the John Hancock Tower (1966–76), and the East Wing of the National Gallery (1968–78).

After Saarinen's death in 1961, the high standards of his office were maintained by Gunnar Birkerts (b. 1925), Caesar Pelli (b. 1926), Kevin Roche (b. 1922), and John Dinkeloo (1918–81). Birkerts was a formalist of the first order and was perhaps best known in the 1960s for the catenary curves of the Federal Reserve Bank of Minneapolis, which he completed in 1968.[79] The Irishman Roche, who teamed up with Dinkeloo after Saarinen's death, had contacts with both Maxwell Fry and Mies van der Rohe before joining Saarinen's office in 1950, and he claims to have been much affected by the social and political turmoil of the 1960s.[80] Yet his firm's architectural work displays little of this urgency; it tends toward what Robert A. M. Stern enthusiastically praised in 1969 as "a passion for strong and simple imagery."[81] This passion is apparent in the purposefully overscaled forms of the Ford Foundation Building, New York (1963–8), and the Knights of Columbus Building, New Haven (1965–9). It is also apparent in the scaleless neoclassical geometry of the three reflecting-glass towers of the College Life Insurance Company complex in Indianapolis (1967–71).

The American architect with perhaps the largest international following in the 1960s was Paul Rudolph (1918–

97), who was also the most talented of the Harvard wartime graduates.[82] His background was also different. A native of Kentucky and the son of a Methodist minister, he attended Alabama Polytechnic Institute before being accepted into the Harvard program in 1941. After the interruption of naval service, he graduated in 1947 and moved back to the South to start a practice in Sarasota, Florida. The designs of his early buildings are derivative of the modernism of the 1950s but very cognizant of the Floridian climate and landscape. His Walker guest house on Sanibel Island (1957) is a masterpiece in light framing and open planning in a beach setting (Fig. 105). One of his first architectural statements – written on the eve of assuming the chairmanship of the Yale School of Architecture in 1958 – is in fact entitled "Regionalism in Architecture." It is a forcefully worded attack on the international style and Miesien objectivity in design as well as a plea for regionalism as "one way toward that richness in architecture which other movements have enjoyed and which is so lacking today."[83] He speaks at length about designing in the South and mentions sunlight, scale, color, and texture as recurring features of southern design that should be exploited to bind the new with the past.

Such an emphasis, however, is altogether missing from his curriculum at Yale and his later architectural practice. His alumni day address in 1958 is notable for his insistence that "theory must again overtake action," but his chairmanship at Yale (until 1965) is characterized – as Stern has noted – by the dominance of personalities over ideas and by a free-moving, formalist atmosphere that was essentially eclectic in its lack of direction.[84] In these same years, Rudolph's personal style changes, inspired now by the European influences of Le Corbusier and New Brutalism. His Yale Art and Architecture Building (1958–63), very unpopular with students, is highly plastic (with its exposed and striated concrete) and deserves the appellation "heroic and original" that would soon generally apply to his approach to architecture.[85] Rudolph's enormous architectural output in the second half of the 1960s would also follow the megastructural and metabolic tendencies of this decade, including such projects as Strafford Harbor, Virginia (1966), the Graphic Arts Center, New York (1967), and the Lower Manhattan Expressway Project (1967–72). His built works during these same years are always compositionally masterful, and Rudolph possessed an abundance of talent, but there is also, as with many other architects, a disconnect between his designs and the events of the world at large.

The one strong force in American practice in the 1960s is, of course, the work of Louis Kahn, whose escape from

105. Paul Rudolph, Walker guest house on Sanibel Island, Florida, 1957. From *Architectural Record*, vol. 121 (February 1957).

the status quo of the day seems almost to have been revealed by mystical decree. Kahn finally came into his own in the late 1950s with the Richards Medical Research Center, Philadelphia (1957–61), and the Salk Institute for Biological Studies, La Jolla (1959–65). In between the design work for the Philadelphia laboratories and La Jolla buildings falls the Otterlo address, a legitimate starting point for assessing his outlook in the midst of this transformation. It begins by posing the question "What is feeling?" and Kahn answers by joining feeling with thought and realization as representative of that introspective period preceding design, when the architect first wrestles with the issue of "what a building wants to be."[86] Such a romantic impulse in the 1920s would have been labeled expressionism, in contrast to rationalism, but for Kahn feeling has little to do with expression. It is rather connected with the search for that mysterious sense of order, for that Platonic form or idea that precedes any functional design considerations. As Kahn himself notes, "There are new problems, tremendous new problems today, which have not been touched by the architect because he is thinking about exterior forms. He is thinking of all kinds of extraneous things before he arrives at a kind of realization of what a space really wants to be."[87] In fact, his chief criticism of the CIAM conference is that it dealt with the circumstantial aspects of architectural problems rather than with the essence of each problem itself. If an auditorium "wants to be an instrument," as he suggests, then its ideal (nonmaterial) form is tonality or timbre.[88] He concludes his talk, interestingly, by extending his appreciation to Aldo van Eyck for simply talking about the meaning of a door: "I think it is a

wonderful thing to review the aspects of architecture from that sense."[89]

The Salk Institute also brings something else to the table, which is history – or rather the usurpation and adaptation of those timeless abstractions (forms) of history. In the design of the La Jolla complex on the Pacific Ocean, Kahn's classical training fully erupts in almost startling fashion. One theme of the design was prompted, he claimed, by the problem of glare he faced in designing the American Consulate at Luanda, Portuguese Angola (1959–61), for which, out of consideration for the intense atmosphere, he came up with the idea "of wrapping ruins around buildings."[90] But perhaps equally pertinent to the design deliberations, as Vincent Scully long ago suggested, were the geometric layouts (in ruins) of Hadrian's villa and Giovanni Battista Piranesi's Roman reconstruction of the buildings on the Campus Martius; indeed engravings of Piranesi's reconstruction were spliced together and hung on the wall in front of Kahn's Philadelphia desk.[91] Thus, the primitive double-wrapping of the reading rooms and dining rooms of the proposed conference center at La Jolla represents a quiet secession from the modern movement, what Manfredo Tafuri would later characterize as a veritable "guilt complex" toward architectural history.[92] Other critics opposed it in even more vehement terms. Writing for the British journal *Architectural Design*, Robin Middleton in 1967 described the historicist reminiscences of Kahn, Rudolph, and Johnson as "a number of adaptations of the most limited and limiting kind," comparable to "composing with fragmentary rubbish. It would seem that they are no longer prepared to accept engagement in the architectural struggle. They have turned it down."[93]

Kahn's continuing search for order and geometric clarity in the 1960s takes additional twists and turns, as exemplified by the structural design for the Kimball Art Museum, Fort Worth (1967–72), the rotation of three squares in the composition of his dormitories at Bryn Mawr College (1960–5), and the library at Phillips Exeter Academy (1965–72), where the future ruins of the circle and square form the principal atrial motif and the grand piano becomes the room's silent timbre (Fig. 106). And here also, in this spiritual atrium ornamented with railings, is where Kahn's favorite themes of analysis – order, form, design – fall short in their descriptive hermeneutics, as do the scholarly soundings (however worthy and valuable) of his intellectual influences: Egyptology, Taoism, Jungian psychology, Jewish mysticism, and a Goethean worldview.[94] Rather, Kahn's architecture in the end is overtly primal in its underlying instinct. It starkly confronts our unconscious complacency with its pure geometry, austere materiality, thermal extremes (the contrast between warm wood and cold concrete), and tactile and auditory qualities and above all its preoccupation with light, to which Kahn regularly referred in near religious terms. In this sensible way, his desire to view architecture as an exercise of the spirit was ultimately transcendental in its philosophical intentions, no less so than Ruskin's rapture with the elongated statuary at Chartres.

4. Colin Rowe, Peter Eisenman, and CASE

Against the mysticism of Kahn and the pragmatism of professional practice, there appeared an alternative line of theoretical development in the 1960s emanating from the ideas and writings of Colin Rowe (b. 1920) and Peter Eisenman (b. 1932). The two men – a professor and a graduate student – met at Cambridge University in 1960, but the source of their mutual concerns lay earlier in time.

Rowe, as we have seen, was one of the "Texas Rangers" at the University of Texas in the mid-1950s. He had been in his fourth year of training in the architectural program at Liverpool University in 1942 when he was drafted into military service. An injury in parachute school subsequently prevented him from working over a drafting table, and in the late 1940s he turned his interest to architectural history and studied under Rudolf Wittkower at the Warburg Institute. Rowe moved to Yale University in 1950 to study under Henry-Russell Hitchcock, who would also decisively influence him. After traveling around Canada, the United States, and Mexico, he settled into the program at Austin and later took a job as a visiting critic at Yale before returning to England to teach at Cambridge University in 1958. He taught there until 1963, when he accepted a professorship at Cornell University.

Rowe's early theory was encapsulated in two – still unpublished – essays, co-authored with Robert Slutzsky, on "Transparency."[95] The architectural notion of transparency has its roots in Giedion's book *Space, Time and Architecture* and in the efforts of MoMA in the 1940s to interpret twentieth-century architecture and painting as parallel conceptual pathways. Such a connection was also implicit in the exhibition of 1932 and was repeatedly reinforced by Alfred E. Barr and others in such exhibitions as "Cubism and Abstract Art" (1936).[96] Giedion accepted the thesis as a proverb in *Space, Time and Architecture*, where he famously illustrated it with complementary full-page images of Picasso's *L'Arlésienne* (1911–12) and the glass corner-detail of the Dessau Bauhaus. In the legend for the latter image, he noted the "hovering relations of planes and the kind of 'overlapping' that appears in contemporary painting."[97]

The influence of painting on architecture was also the subject of Henry-Russell Hitchcock's book *Painting toward Architecture* (1948), which grew out of an exhibition at MoMA of abstract paintings from the Miller Company collection. Rowe, of course, would know this book well. In his introductory essay, Hitchcock recited what by now had become an axiom at MoMA – namely, that the architecture of the 1920s was formally and conceptually inseparable from the abstract art of cubism, purism, Dutch abstract art, and the work done at the Bauhaus (Wright had earlier been influenced by Japanese art). And if this "tangency" of painting and architecture was less pronounced at the time of writing, when paintings were "less profoundly novel than those of a quarter of a century ago," painting nevertheless remained important because it made available to architects "the results of a kind of plastic research that can hardly be undertaken at full architectural scale."[98]

Rowe and Slutzsky in their first essay on "Transparency" adopted this premise, and their starting point is Giedion's juxtaposition of the images from Picasso and the Bauhaus. Their theme has by now been enriched by the writings of Lázló Moholy-Nagy and Gyorgy Kepes, and it is from the latter that they adopt the definition of visual "transparency" (as seen, for instance, in the work of Cézanne, Braque, Picasso, Delaunay, and Gris) as "a simultaneous perception

106. Louis I. Kahn, atrium of the Phillips Exeter Academy library, 1965–72. Photograph by author.

of different spatial locations" that leads visually to a situation of contradiction or ambiguity.[99] Still keeping to painting, transparency can be literal ("a translucent object in a deep, naturalistic space") or phenomenal ("articulated presentation of frontally displaced objects in a shallow, abstracted space"), which the authors feel is ultimately richer in its possibilities.[100] But here the two authors turn to Giedion's example with unmistakable Oedipal overtones. The image of the Bauhaus that Giedion displayed (a building designed by Gropius) does not illustrate phenomenal transparency at all but only the simpler type of literal transparency found

in the planar use of transparent glass. It is therefore a poor example to put beside the phenomenal transparency found in the paintings of Picasso.

With this decided, Rowe and Slutzsky seek examples of phenomenal transparency in architecture, and they immediately land on the garden facade of Le Corbusier's villa at Garches, which had also been the subject of Rowe's essay of 1947. Although this facade has continuous glass in horizontal bands, it is not here that phenomenal transparency is to be found. The key to the facade's phenomenal transparency consists of the two lateral walls of the roof terrace that stop short of the rear wall, together with the recessed ground story, which stops on the same invisible plane (actually along the columnar line). This creates the suggestion that the wall plane of the upper stories actually floats in front of "a narrow slot of space traveling parallel to it," and this implied spatial stratification of vertical planes is further enhanced by the recessed slot of the terrace, the third-floor balcony within the terrace, the projecting stair terrace, and the elements on the roof terrace, which together compose a layerlike series of similar stratifications.[101] In short, the garden facade at Garches has "succeeded in alienating architecture from its necessary three-dimensional existence" and flattened its depth on the retina to a shallow succession of hypothetical vertical planes.[102]

This is entirely a "painterly" interpretation of architectural form, and the theme is repeated in a second essay on transparency in 1956, in which Rowe and Slutzky analyze two-dimensional phenomenal transparency in such examples as Le Corbusier's skyscraper, Giacomo da Vignola's Villa Farnese, and Michelangelo's proposal for San Lorenzo in Florence.[103] The second essay concludes with an extended discussion of Gestalt psychology and its "phenomenal identity" and "double representation," thereby revealing another important basis for these theoretical hypotheses.

The two essays on transparency, although not published until later, handed architectural theory three very important things: 1) a rigorous concern with visible form that was at the same time a critique of the functionalist preoccupations of the 1950s; 2) a notion of formal ambiguity not unrelated to that later proffered by Robert Venturi in his literary exposition of the theme (although far removed from his populist bent); and 3) a view of architectural design as a purely formal and intellectual process no longer specifically concerned with those nagging social issues that would come to the fore in the 1960s. Rowe and Slutzky were essentially projecting an architectural theory of formal autonomy, that is, a kind of aesthetic formalism operating within its own inner sanctum of visual laws.

It was at this point that Peter Eisenman met Rowe. The former had completed his architectural studies at Cornell in the first half of the 1950s and had enrolled in a graduate program at Columbia in 1959. The following year he accepted a fellowship to Cambridge University to study Gothic architecture. There, under the prompting of Leslie Martin and Rowe, he shifted his interest to theory, a decision that was reinforced by two European tours that Rowe and Eisenman undertook in the summers of 1961 and 1962. Eisenman's unpublished doctoral dissertation, "The Formal Basis of Modern Architecture," was accepted by Trinity College in August 1963.[104]

The dissertation appeared ten months after Christopher Alexander had completed his dissertation, "The Synthesis of Form," and the themes of the two works are similar. Whereas Alexander saw form in quasi-mathematical terms as a synthesis of social and functional parameters, Eisenman viewed architectural form as a conceptual issue in and of itself – that is, as a logical problem stripped of functional, iconographic, perceptual (Gestalt), metaphysical, and aesthetic dimensions. His search, as he begins his exercise, is for a "language" of form, one that is universally valid, and whose "contention will be that formal considerations are basic to all architecture regardless of style, and that these considerations derive from the formal essence of any architectural situation. It will provide a means of communication evolved from this absolute basis; a language that will communicate the nature of the formal essence of any architecture."[105] Another premise is that this "ordering of form" must be considered "a necessary precondition for any valid or rational architecture."[106] Eisenman, in his quest for a truly rational architecture, further claims that he is hoping to devise a "terminology" for architectural form that "might serve as a basis for communication" between a teacher and a student, an architect and a client, or a critic and the public. He also refers to his hypothetical model as "an organization of architectural form within the design process."[107] This blurring of the line between purely formal analysis and design methodology, however, has its dangers.

And his development of this model will further compound the difficulties. After initially defining architecture as "in essence the giving of form (itself an element) to intent, function, structure and technics,"[108] Eisenman goes on to distinguish between generic form (Platonic, universal, transcendent) and specific form (the building) and chooses to give his attention only to the first. The properties of generic form are simply volume, mass, surface, and movement, the elements that alone must constitute his formal analysis because he has already eliminated all perceptual, phenomenological, and aesthetic concerns. Therefore, an architectural concept such as "space" – taking note of Bruno Zevi – must be subsumed within the category of volume. Still, the weakness of the system becomes fully manifest in the fourth chapter, where he passes from abstract discussion to formal analyses of eight buildings: two each by Le Corbusier, Frank Lloyd Wright, Alvar Aalto, and Giuseppe Terragni. It now becomes clear that his universal "formal system" is little more than an elaborate series of diagrams, consisting of axes and arrows.

When imposed upon the plan of the Pavillon Suisse in Paris or the Martin House in Buffalo, they yield nothing from the trapezoidal common areas of the former and an incomprehensible discussion of counterpoised and stuttered axes from the latter – an overly mute analytical language accessible to neither students nor clients nor the public. If his formal system is slightly more successful when applied to the facades of Terragni's Casa del Fascio, it is because here, in lieu of diagrams, he applies Rowe's notion of phenomenal transparency to surface planes and reduces the result to abstract line drawings.

In his final chapter, Eisenman concludes with a general discussion of theory that has little basis in the preceding discussion but is nevertheless revealing of the author's later development. His fetish for a "total rational order" and a "total ordered environment" is made clear by his reference to notions of the "organic" in design, "which by their very nature obscure the clarity of any order, and indeed create the impression that there has been no planning at all."[109] The general thrust of his argument is opposed to those (long-deceased) closed theories propounded by Alberti, Durand, and Guadet, for example, and supportive of a definition of theory that allows for an open-ended methodology centered solely on the rational and the logical. Why and how such a theory can be found, as the author suggests, by the humanist and empathetic theorist Geoffrey Scott is never made clear. Nevertheless, the path of Eisenman's future development is evident; his is a theory of architecture struggling to purge from its domain all social and semantic concerns. Rowe's idea of formal autonomy has spawned an even purer intellectual offspring.

Eisenman returned to the United States in 1963 and joined the faculty of Princeton University in the same year, where he became a colleague of Michael Graves (b. 1934). The two collaborated on several projects, including the New Jersey Corridor Project and (with Princeton students) a Manhattan waterfront project. The last was included in an exhibition held at the Museum of Modern Art early in 1967, together with urban projects from Cornell, Columbia, and M.I.T..[110] The exhibition, organized by Arthur Drexler, was an effort to tackle the problematic "urban renewal" issue head on. At this time Eisenman was also cementing his connections with the museum; in 1966 he was denied tenure at Princeton and thus needed a financial base.

Another project in which Eisenman was heavily involved was the founding of the Conference of Architects for the Study of the Environment (CASE), which grew out of a seminar organized by Eisenman, Graves, and Emilio Ambasz in

the spring of 1964. In retrospect, CASE, despite its brief duration, was an organization of some importance. For one thing it brought together a number of young faculty from the Ivy League power centers of architectural education. Eisenman and Graves represented Princeton, Henry Millon and Stanford Anderson came down from M.I.T., and Colin Rowe had just taken a position at Cornell. Richard Meier, a cousin of Peter Eisenman, directed the New York chapter. Vincent Scully and Robert Venturi also attended the first conference but left before its conclusion. Others to participate in CASE events during the next several years included Jacquelin Robertson, Anthony Vidler, Anthony Eardley, Kenneth Frampton, Roselind Krauss, John Hejduk, Charles Gwathmey, Arthur Drexler, Mario Grandelsonas, and Oscan Newman.

The ideology of CASE is hard to pin down. At one meeting in 1968 Meier asked each member to bring a copy of the *Team 10 Primer* (he would distribute the Athens Charter), which suggests an urban focus and even the desire to emulate the efforts of Team 10.[111] In a letter a few weeks later, Meier announced that the purpose of CASE was "to formulate a proposition for a National Planning Policy," that is, to act as a political action group to influence the decision-making process.[112] A draft of a statement on behalf of a proposed CASE journal, to be edited by Anderson and Vidler, claimed that CASE was intended to be a "critical forum for selected architectural ideas" and "to translate current humanist, social, psychological and scientific thought into architectural relevancy to man's global situation."[113] The same draft, in keeping with the spiritual despondency of the time, also noted the "rising brutality and despair," the "increasing violence," and the "deteriorating quality of human life" brought on by "runaway population" and pollution. In what appears to be a later draft with input from the editorial board, Eisenman inserts text expressing the desire "to review the theoretical basis of the early modern movement in an effort to determine clearly those principles which still appear to possess validity."[114] This too presages his later direction.

In January 1968, CASE split into two regional branches: CASE/Princeton-New York and CASE/Boston. Eisenman, had by this date grown discontented with this "ugly child" who was "ill-formed and without direction," but he nevertheless participated in its events up to its last meeting in the early 1970s.[115] It is not hard to find the reason for Eisenman's dwindling interest. A few years prior, CASE, in his view, had been superseded by a new brainchild that was indeed destined to make a substantial impact on American architectural theory. This was the Institute for Architecture and Urban Studies (IAUS).

5. Complexity and Contradiction in Architecture

Also coming to the forefront of American architectural theory in the second half of the 1960s were two self-professed disciples of Kahn who would make formidable contributions to the escalating criticism of modern architecture. At first glance, the polemical and built work of Charles Moore (1925–93) and Robert Venturi (b. 1925) appear congenial and similar in their impulses – almost complementary in their pop art insistence on challenging the accepted maxims of the profession – but in fact Moore and Venturi differed significantly in their outlook. Their one common denominator was that both used history as a tool to critique the professional status quo.

The midwesterner Moore cannot be separated from his adopted home of California.[116] Born in Benton Harbor, Michigan, he entered the architecture program at the University of Michigan in 1942 and graduated five years later. He next cast his lot with the dream of California and moved to San Francisco, seeking employment first in the office of Wurster, Bernardi and Emmons but (after being turned down) ending up in the office of Mario Corbett and later Joseph Allen Stein. Nineteen forty-seven was the year that both Mumford and MoMA became interested in the merits of the Bay Region style, and this particular influence remained idiomatic in much of Moore's later work. First, however, came a traveling scholarship and a visit to Europe, teaching at the University of Utah, a period in military service, and the decision in 1954 to enter the master's and doctoral program at Princeton University.

Moore's years at Princeton were important to his development in many ways. His dissertation, "Water in Architecture," was scarcely historical or theoretical yet nevertheless announced one of his main interests. He worked in design studios and was already hostile to such "establishment" architects and critics as Edward Durrell Stone, Gordon Bunshaft, Paul Rudolph, and Sigfried Giedion.[117] He met and befriended a number of colleagues, among them Venturi, Hugh Hardy, Donlyn Lyndon, and William Turnbull. Under the tutelage of the Italian Enrico Peressutti (of BBPR), he developed an appreciation for historical context and the debate that was then underway in Italy. And most importantly, in his last two years at Princeton he led a studio whose designs were regularly critiqued by Louis Kahn. In

1959 Moore moved back to California, where he joined the faculty at Berkeley under William Wilson Wurster's deanship. Moore remained there until 1965, when – bypassed for a full professorship – he accepted the chairmanship at the Yale School of Art and Architecture. By this date he was arriving as one of the first "star" architects of the electronic age.

Moore differs from almost every American architect of his generation in the breadth of his travel experience and in his knowledge of history. His various writings of the 1960s, however, reveal his design philosophy in a somewhat roundabout way. In several reviews written for *Architectural Record* and *Architectural Forum* in the middle years of the decade, he is a relatively mild-mannered critic, although in his article "Discrimination in Housing Design" he rather forcefully goes after the architect's use of "bubble diagrams" and some of the spatial/housing assumptions drawn from them.[118] In another article he expresses his deep appreciation for the second Bay Region style of Joseph Esherick, in particular, for the "extraordinary architectural wonders" brought forth in his retail transformation of the Cannery, adjacent to Fisherman's Wharf in San Francisco.[119] In a piece written for the Yale journal *Perspecta*, originally entitled "Plug It In, Rameses, and See If It Lights Up, Because We Aren't Going to Keep It Unless It Works," Moore articulates one of the recurring themes of his writings – architecture as the creation of "place."[120] In a McLuhanesque manner, he argues that replicating such accepted formulas for "places" as the Piazza San Marco makes little sense because the modern world has become dislocated and unhierarchical in its content. Equally to be rejected is the architecture of exclusion, fostered by such architects as Frank Lloyd Wright and Mies van der Rohe in their adherence to the geometrical grid. "Robert Venturi's search for ambiguity" and the "homely matter-of-factness" of his "gold-anodized television antenna" points in the direction of inclusion, but interestingly this is not the form of inclusion that Moore himself chooses.[121] He prefers the eclectic coziness of the grotto-like Madonna Inn, near San Luis Obispo – even though the electric eye that sets in motion the waterfall in the smaller grotto of the men's urinal is somewhat disquieting. On second thought, "It is not at all disquieting, but rather exhilarating, to note that here there is everything instead of nothing."[122]

A slightly more serious side of Moore is revealed in his book *Body, Memory, and Architecture* (1977, with Kent C. Bloomer), which is based on a freshman course Moore and Bloomer put together at Yale in the mid-1960s.[123]

Although the book is meant to be an introductory guide to a few basic concepts of architectural design, the content is rather meaty, for the authors draw upon sources as diverse as Gaston Bachelard, Mircea Eliade, Edward T. Hall, Adolf Hildebrand, Lawrence Halprin, Theodor Lipps, Geoffrey Scott, Kevin Lynch, and the Gestalt psychologist Max Wertheimer. What is also striking here is the great importance that Moore places on paths, places, urban patterns, orientation, identifying elements, and comic allusions, such as the mock monumental entrance to the laundry of Kresge College at the University of California, Santa Cruz. At the very least, he promotes an architecture rife with human and communicative values.

His work of the 1960s – almost always designed jointly with Lyndon, Turnbull, and Richard Whitaker – vividly defines the initially quiet revolution taking place with respect to mainstream architecture at home and abroad. His one-room bachelor's house in Orinda (1960–2), certainly his own creation, announces its originality with sliding barn doors and twin interior aediculae (derived from reading John Summerson): baldachins each supported on four Tuscan columns with painted capitals salvaged from a nineteenth-century building. One defines a living space, the other a ritualized sunken bath. There is no sympathy in this space for a Breuer chair; its showpieces are a grand piano and an eighteenth-century boudoir armchair. Comfort, in other words, is chosen over modern cliché.

The firm of MLTW (Moore, Lyndon, Turnbull, and Whitaker) achieved national renown with the Sea Ranch condominiums of 1964–5. Ten miles of rugged northern California coastline (totaling 5,000 acres) were developed in an ecologically sensitive way following the parameters laid down by Halprin's office. Joseph Esherick designed the first set of cluster houses, and MLTW simultaneously designed the condos in a post-and-beam redwood style (shed roofs, no overhangs, board siding) that – thanks to timely and extensive promotion by the firm – quickly established it as *the* West-Coast regional style of the 1960s. Again Moore preferred to define a single room under one roof, within and around which he constructed interior "houses" (loft areas) and saddlebag additions.

The firm's two other works of this decade – Kresge College (1965–74) and the Santa Barbara Faculty Club (1966–8) – underscore Moore's strengths and weaknesses as a designer. At the same time they proclaim a decisive break with modernism – shattering, as Heinrich Klotz noted, "the doctrines of a moralizing architectural theory."[124] Both in fact aim to be a mockery of "serious" architecture. In the former,

Kahn's double walls (layering) are transformed into "cardboard" architecture at its theatrical finest, although not without the expected leaky windows and high-maintenance upkeep. The Santa Barbara Faculty Club, with its irreverent moose heads, neon banners, and tacky chandeliers, seems to be an attempt to monumentalize the trivial. Moore and Turnbull were, as one biographer stated, "*trying* to shake students up, to change their lives," but at the same time he admitted that "the trivial can sometimes end up self-defeating and hollow."[125] The use of similar mock devices in Moore's low-income Church Street housing complex in New Haven (1966–8) demonstrates this point: they scarcely enhance the barrackslike project, which became yet another urban renewal disaster.

This project also raises the question whether Moore, as a phenomenon and laid-back child of the 1960s, was allowing his regard for architecture as a revolutionary force within a society to spin out of control. His appointment in 1965 by Kingman Brewster as the new chair of the Department of Architecture at Yale (over Robert Venturi and Romaldo Giurgola) in itself seems a little odd in retrospect, as he had just been turned down for tenure at Berkeley. In fact Berkeley had been shut down in 1964 by the violence of the "Free Speech" movement, to which Moore was at least sympathetic. At Yale, Moore replaced an increasingly unpopular Rudolph, and for all of his presumed anti-elitism, he was still sufficiently smug in his condescension toward the "pampered aristocratic Marxist Yalies" of the late 1960s, who "were far more to the right than I was."[126] But such radical chic also contains no small amount of cynicism, however much it may have bemused or angered Brewster and other defenders of the liberal establishment.[127] The turmoil came to a head in June 1969, when students (it must be presumed) set fire to the Art and Architecture Building. This act of arson suggests that Moore's nonauthoritarian style of running the school and dealing with disenchanted students had come home to roost.

Much has been made of his curricular changes – the introduction of Eastern studies, the instilling of environmental consciousness, the decrease in emphasis on drafting and classroom work and the increase in time spent on field trips, and the inauguration of thematic design studios – but here again the evidence can be interpreted in different ways.[128] If some may view them as fully in step with the "seismic shift in our cultural and political landscape," others may treat them as a purposeful demeaning of academic standards, a slippery slope down which many schools would slide in the 1970s.[129] In any case, Moore's tenure at Yale, it should be said, took a toll on his career. While it cannot be denied that this architect came to New Haven with considerable talent, it is also true that, during his stay, he largely frittered it away by his general lack of focus, not to mention the academic duties that consumed his time and energy. In short, Moore, for all of his amiableness and good intentions, personifies the free-swinging and easy atmosphere of disenchantment of the late 1960s.

Robert Venturi worked from a very different persona and intellectual background.[130] He enrolled at Princeton in 1944, where he completed his undergraduate studies in three years. In 1950 he obtained his master's degree at the same school (Louis Kahn and George Howe were on the jury) with a thesis on the precocious theme of "Context in Architectural Composition."[131] His first jobs were with Oscar Stonorov, Louis Kahn (part-time), and Eero Saarinen. With Kahn's backing, Venturi won the Rome Prize in 1954, which allowed him two years of study in the Italian capital and the opportunity to develop his interest in the mannerist and baroque periods. Upon returning to Philadelphia, he rejoined Kahn's office and began teaching at the University of Pennsylvania, initially as an assistant to Kahn. In 1957, he entered private practice, first alone and then in association with Mather Lippincott and Paul Cope. In 1960 he joined forces with William H. Short and in 1964 with John Rauch.

Venturi's early designs, most of which remained unbuilt, have sometimes been overlooked, but within the context of the late 1950s they are both instructive and original in their thinking. Kahn, as might be expected, certainly had a strong influence on his outlook, but even more important were the mannerist tendencies that Venturi gleaned not only from Rome but from the domestic work of Wilson Eyre and from Vincent Scully's *Shingle Style* (1955). With his design for a hypothetical beach house in New Jersey (1959), his renovation of Grand's Restaurant (1961–62), and his building for the North Penn Visiting Nurse Association, Ambler (1961–3), Venturi proved himself to be one of the few architects on the East Coast (Romaldo Giurgola was another) who was both taking an interest in American cultural traditions and exploring them with innovative élan.

The gestation of *Complexity and Contradiction in Architecture* (1966) is earlier than the publication date suggests. In 1962, after the controversial Guild House was designed, Venturi received a grant from the Graham Foundation to transform his lectures from a course on architectural theory that he was teaching at Penn with the assistance of Denise Scott Brown (b. 1931). A preliminary manuscript was sub-

mitted in March 1963, and a text was copyrighted in 1964. A portion of this text – almost forty pages – appeared in the Yale journal *Perspecta* in the following year, under the book's eventual title (Fig. 107).[132] The final, substantially edited version was published by the Museum of Modern Art in the following year. Venturi wrote the book alone, but he acknowledged being assisted critically along the way by Scott Brown, Vincent Scully, and Robert Stern (a student of Venturi at Yale). Other sources are evident as well. The conceptual dualities of van Eyck, who taught at Penn in 1960, are everywhere present, as are the ideas of Henry Millon and August Heckscher, whose book *The Public Happiness* (1962) addressed the baroque complexity of modern life. Also informing the work are Gestalt psychology and the writings of Josef Albers, Georgy Kepes, T. S. Eliot, Cleanth Brooks, and William Empson, especially the latter's *Seven Types of Ambiguity* (1955). Finally, Venturi pays homage to an important essay by John Summerson, written in 1941, in which the historian faulted architects for talking around architecture rather than about architecture; this too must be read as a rebuttal to the technological euphoria of Banham and to the computer-aided programming of Alexander.[133]

The book is thus conceptually grounded in the 1950s and early 1960s. Venturi's master's thesis had focused on the issue of context, and his first published writing, which appeared in 1953, was a short excerpt on the Campidoglio, the Roman senatorial complex recast into a mannerist vocabulary by Michelangelo.[134] Michelangelo's rhetorical exaggerations seem to be one of the architectural influences on the book, but these also include examples of baroque sensibility as disparate as the architectural works of Nicholas Hawksmoor, John Soane, Frank Furness, Edwin Lutyens, Le Corbusier, Armando Brazini (a neobaroque architect whom Venturi met in Rome), Alvar Aalto (whose Finnish buildings Venturi visited in 1965), and of course Louis Kahn. From such a range of sources, Venturi composes "A Gentle Manifesto" on behalf of a modern theory: straightforwardly yet with unexpected richness of ideas.

The leading theme is supremely simple: "I like complexity and contradiction in architecture."[135] The author endorses these two elements first because of the "richness and ambiguity of modern experience" within the rapidly changing world, and second because the overemphasis that orthodox modern architecture placed on simplicity and function has now run its historical course, leading us into "an attitude common in the Mannerist periods."[136] Thus the adage of Mies – less is more – is turned on its head: "Blatant simplification means bland architecture. Less is a bore."[137]

57a,b

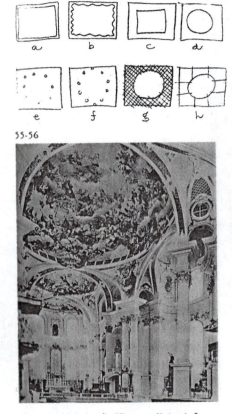

55-56

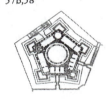

57b,58

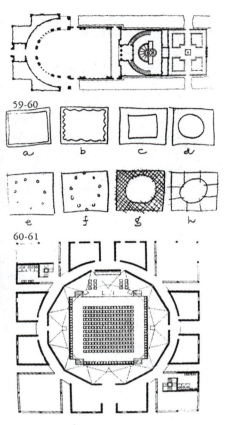

59-60

60-61

common with it (55f). The open lining inflects to touch its frame when it nears it. The sinuous inflections of nearing layers at Neresheim in Southern Germany (56) (inner circle and outer oval) is even more pronounced in plan and section. These intraspatial relationships are at once more complex and more ambiguous than St Stephen Walbrook's.

Detached linings leave spaces in between. But the architectural recognition of the in-between varies. The residual spaces are closed at Edfu and they almost dominate in volume the space they enclose. In Charles I's palace at Granada (57), the Villa Farnese at Caparola (58), or the Villa

Giulia (59), the dominant-shaped courtyards make the primary space; the rooms within the contrasting perimeter become residual (60h). As in the preliminary scheme of Kahn's Unitarian Church in Rochester (61), the residual spaces are closed. The linings of columns and piers in SS. Sergius and Bacchus, St. Stephen Walbrook, Vierzenheiligen, and Neresheim define residual spaces that are open; they open into the dominant spaces, yet they are separate from them in varying degrees. The distinctions implied between dominant and residual spaces in the main hall of

107. Page from Robert Venturi's article "Complexity and Contradiction in Architecture," *Perspecta 9/10: The Yale Architectural Journal* (1965).

So far, Venturi is indeed a "quiet" revolutionary. His study unfolds over eight chapters and eighty-five pages in a rather conventional way – reminiscent of Boffrand – by transforming elements of literary ambiguity and complexity into architectural theory and illustrating the points with a bevy of examples drawn for virtually every period of architecture. The parallel with Epson's book on ambiguity is striking. For instance, Venturi's "Both-and" echoes Empson's third type of ambiguity, in which "two apparently unconnected meanings are given simultaneously." Venturi's "Double-Functioning Elements" approach Empson's second type of ambiguity, in which "two or more alternative meanings are fully resolved into one." And Venturi's "Contradiction Juxtaposed"

recalls Empson's seventh type of ambiguity, the "full contradiction, marking a division in the author's mind." Most interesting is Venturi's concluding chapter, "The Obligation toward the Difficult Whole," which seems to mirror Empson's fourth type of ambiguity, in which "the alternative meanings combine to make clear a complicated state of mind in the author."[138] These literary guidelines or lamps can only apply to architecture as rules for the manipulation of conventions or forms, leading Venturi to expound a formalist theory.

Slightly over halfway into the book, however, the reader becomes aware of a subtheme developing within the analysis. This subtheme first appears in Venturi's discussion of the kind of ambiguity brought about when a conventional element undergoes changes and acquires additional meanings. For him this evolution of a conventional motif produces a "rhetorical element," which "discourages clarity of meaning"; with its ambiguous message, its "rhetoric offends orthodox Modern architecture's cult of the minimum."[139] Examples of reprogrammed conventional elements are to be found in "Michelangelo's architecture and what might be called Pop architecture" as well as in designs of C.-N. Ledoux, Paul Rudolph, and John Vanbrugh.[140] The designation "Pop architecture," which appeared earlier in the 1960s in the writings of Banham, is a term Venturi discussed in a 1965 article entitled "A Justification for a Pop Architecture." There he defined pop architecture as something that "embraces the commonplace, or rather the just obsolete commonplace, as the actual elements of building."[141]

The theme, however, becomes radicalized in *Complexity and Contradiction*, where Venturi addresses it under the appellation "Pop Art." In discussing the use of honky-tonk elements – the need for architecture to survive the cigarette machine – he gives another reason for their use: "The main justification for honky-tonk elements in architectural order is their very existence. They are what we have. Architects can bemoan or try to ignore them or even try to abolish them, but they will not go away."[142] And here also is where his argument becomes more engaging. One reason architects should resign themselves to accepting these elements – and this point defines an immense generational chasm – is that they can no longer pretend to live in some futurist world in which technology will somehow sweep the residue of populist culture away. Thus by the mid-1960s the optimism of early modernism or even Banham's optimism is, in Venturi's view, forever a thing of the past: "Technical innovations require investments in time and skills and money beyond the architect's reach, at least in our kind of society."[143] Another and even more startling rationale is given a few pages later: "The architect who would accept his role as combiner of significant old clichés – valid banalities – in new contexts as his condition within a society that directs its best efforts, its big money, and its elegant technologies elsewhere, can ironically express in this indirect way a true concern for society's inverted scale of values."[144] What he means by "inverted scale of values" is clearer in his earlier article on pop architecture, where he more candidly asserts that the "Federal government and the big industry it supports have largely directed expensive computer research towards the enterprises of war or, as is said, national security, over the forces

for the enhancement of life."[145] His ultimate reasoning in *Complexity and Contradiction*, in short, is that the clichés and honky-tonk elements (on which, incidentally, the architect spends a client's money) should serve as a kind of social protest against the policies of the government! Using honky-tonk elements is one of the few ways (privileged, Ivy League–trained) architects can show their disenchantment with, if not disdain for, the false society in which they live.

It is on this issue that Venturi's ideas merge with those of Denise Scott Brown, the other ideological force now affecting his outlook.[146] Scott Brown, neé Lakofski, was born in Zambia and first trained as an architect at the University of Witwatersrand in Johannesburg; in 1952 she moved to London to study at the Architecture Association. This was the era of the British welfare state, the new towns, the acclaim for Mies van der Rohe, and, most importantly, the theoretical escapades of the Smithsons and the ICA. In 1955 Denise married Robert Scott Brown, and three years later the two applied to the graduate school of the University of Pennsylvania, hoping to study with Kahn. Having not had time to prepare portfolios for the architecture school, they were only accepted into the new Department of Land and City Planning, which was set up by Dean G. Holmes Perkins and was dominated by the Philadelphia planner Edmund Bacon, on the one hand, and by David Crane, Herbert Gans, William Wheaton, and Paul Davidoff, all of whom had a sociological bent, on the other. Denise Scott Brown's ideological sympathies lay with this circle, and she brought an activist perspective, together with the social realism she knew from England, to her teaching at Penn.[147] She started as an instructor in 1960 (Robert was tragically killed in an automobile accident in 1959), and it was then that she met Venturi, who was also on the faculty. Scott Brown and Venturi collaborated on the theory course between 1962 and 1964, occasionally in practice, as with the fountain competition for Benjamin Franklin Parkway in 1965. In the same year Scott Brown's essay "The Meaningful City" announced her interest in mass communication and the dynamics of popular culture.[148] That year also saw the two architects leave Philadelphia. Venturi returned to the American Academy in Rome to complete his manuscript, then moved on to a visiting professorship at Yale University (offered by Moore). Scott Brown took a visiting position at Berkeley (where she taught a course on urbanism with Melvin Webber) before accepting a position at UCLA.

Their mutual interest in popular culture surfaces again in the final pages of *Complexity and Contradiction*, as Venturi in effect moves beyond his literary or aesthetic justification for ambiguity in favor of an all-out populist position. The call to order espoused by Peter Blake in comparing the University of Virginia to Main Street becomes the foil against which Venturi poses his famous question: Besides the irrelevancy of the comparison, "is not Main Street almost all right?"[149] In answering he reasons, "The seemingly chaotic juxtapositions of honky-tonk elements express an intriguing kind of vitality and validity," and architects should by now have learned lessons from pop art and awakened "from prim dreams of pure order."[150] Hence his conclusion: "And it is perhaps from the everyday landscape, vulgar and disdained, that we can draw the complex and contradictory order that is valid and vital for our architecture as an urbanistic whole."[151]

Venturi's book, published by the Museum of Modern Art, would prove to be a milestone for American practice, although its impact would take a few years to become fully realized. The architecture and design director at MoMA, Arthur Drexler, described the book in his foreword as a "remarkable study" opposed to "what many would consider Establishment," and Vincent Scully in his otherwise melancholic introduction more famously called it "the most important writing on the making of architecture since Le Corbusier's *Vers une Architecture*, of 1923."[152] Scully's general point was that Venturi's thought is humanistic and his roots are twofold: On the one hand, he "is an Italian architect of the great tradition – whose contact with that tradition came from art history at Princeton and a fellowship at the American Academy in Rome"; on the other hand, "he is one of the few architects whose thought parallels that of the Pop painters – and probably the first architect to perceive the usefulness and meaning of their forms."[153]

Europeans generally took a very different view of the book. Colin Rowe – in a double review covering *Complexity and Contradiction* and Reyner Banham's *The New Brutalism* (1966) – saw intellectual similarities between the two books, including their presumption that the earlier view of modern architecture as an active agent for social change had indeed run its course: "Modern architecture now exists in abundance; but the hoped for Utopia has scarcely ensued. Nor is it clear that mankind is so very much

further ahead on the road to its redemption; and hence, there has followed a certain deflation of optimism."[154] Alan Colquhoun, approaching Venturi from his socialist perspective, was not so happy with the book's "lack of complete theoretical framework" and selective reading of the past: "At this point one becomes aware of an attempt to annex to the world of 'art' the most degenerate aspects of American vernacular, and to see the categories of Pop art being brought in to shore up procedures of precarious historical validity."[155] The Marxist Manfredo Tafuri as well could not stomach Venturi's populist bent. While acknowledging his "many perceptive observations," Tafuri is nevertheless adamant in rejecting, "on one side, the failed historicisation of architectural ambiguity, that becomes, therefore, an *a priori* category with only generic meanings; on the other, the conclusions of his research that, through historiographical flattening and confusion between analyses and planning methods, manages to justify personal figurative choices."[156]

Not all Europeans, however, were so unimpressed. Joseph Rykwert, writing in the summer of 1967, found the book "ironic, charming and really rather self-deprecatory," if a little too "all right." And although he rejected Venturi's "nonchalant eclecticism and the atrophied system that lies behind it," he also admitted, "I am on Venturi's side. The functionalists too have misled us – buildings are polyvalent: polyvalence of volume and surface in terms of denotation and therefore of connotation, is what we must learn to talk about."[157] Christian Norberg-Schulz, who was advancing his own model beyond what he presented in *Intentions* a few years earlier, saw Venturi's book and its exploration of "levels of meaning" in an even more positive light: as a study that "ought to be carried further as soon as possible" within the art historical formalist tradition.[158] In the spirit of Summerson and self-criticism, he too blamed architects for focusing on "sociology and psychology, economy and ecology, mathematics and communication theory" at the expense of architecture: "*At last an architect who has the courage to write about architecture!*"[159] It is for this reason, among others, that Venturi's book marks a sharp divide.

EPILOGUE

We are in the presence of anachronism, nostalgia, and, probably, frivolity.
Colin Rowe (1968)

1968

Architectural theory is conventionally said to be a phenomenon born out of a tradition and therefore one that generally operates by evolution rather than by revolution. In quiet times this is generally the case. Very little, if anything, is ever new to architectural theory, and often generations of architects grapple with the very same issues, albeit within a changing historical context. But theory, too, is almost always visibly shaken by momentous intellectual, political, and economic events. The intellectual foment surrounding the Enlightenment defined one such moment within the course of Western history. World War I made its mark on theory, and the Great Depression ushered in a new era of thought. The year 1968 seems to define another such moment.

Nineteen sixty-eight was above all a year of political convulsion and violence.[1] In Europe the year opened and closed with the uplifting and disheartening events in Czechoslovakia. In early January, Antonín Novotný, the first secretary of the Communist Party, was ousted from his position by the Slovak Alexander Dubček (1927–93), who promised "socialism with a human face." With the further removal of Novotný loyalists from the cabinet in March, the "Prague Spring" became a cause of worldwide celebration. The country's censorship laws were quickly revoked, and people in the streets reveled in their newfound freedom of expression. Their enthusiasm was echoed in neighboring Poland, where students took to the street to oppose that country's communist rulers and censorship laws.

From Moscow, however, the Soviet ruler Leonid Brezhnev watched the developments with growing concern – despite Dubček's commitment to socialism and friendship with the USSR. The response came in August when Brezhnev ordered 500,000 Warsaw Pact troops to cross the Czechoslovakian border and occupy the city of Prague. The resurrected secret police rounded up and beat demonstrators. Dubček was flown to Moscow in chains and undoubtedly would have been killed had not the Czechoslovakian people bravely resisted the Soviet attempt to impose an interim government. Finally, under extreme duress, Dubček was forced to sign the draconian Moscow Protocol and was brought back to Prague, where, before a national television audience, he tearfully renounced his crimes and announced the revocation of his earlier measures. The following spring he was officially replaced by Gustáv Husák, and the Iron Curtain was back in place.

The streets of Western Europe were also flooded with demonstrators in the spring and summer of 1968, but for very different reasons. In Germany demands for university reforms and the sudden popularity of such drugs as LSD and hashish were among the factors contributing to the demonstrations taking place at most German universities and politically orchestrated by the Socialist Students League (SDS). The shooting in April of one student activist, Rudi Dutschke, led to a sharp escalation in the number of demonstrations and inspired demonstrators to carry placards with pictures of Rosa Luxemburg and Karl Liebknecht, the Spartacist revolutionaries who were killed in 1919. Somewhat ironically, the center of the student insurrection in Germany was the Free University in Berlin, which had been founded in 1948 because Berlin's famed Humboldt University was located in what became the Soviet-controlled sector of the city.

England was also politically active in the spring and summer of 1968, the two principal issues being its new immigration (racial) problems and the Vietnam War, to which there was growing opposition. Far more significant in size and intensity, however, was the unrest in France and Italy. The so-called May Movement in Paris actually began at the Nanterre campus of the University of Paris in March 1968, when students, led by Daniel Cohn-Bendit, took over the administration building. The school was subsequently closed at the start of April, was reopened after the Easter recess, but was closed again on 2 May because of renewed demonstrations. The decision to close the school a second time intensified the problem by bringing the insurgents into the city. The arrest of a few students in a courtyard of the Sorbonne on 3 May ignited the explosion. Massive demonstrations, guerilla tactics, strikes, and simple rioting engulfed Paris for the rest of the month. Barricades were erected in the Latin Quarter, and eventually the Sorbonne and Ecole des Beaux-Arts were occupied. Sympathetic "intellectuals" were regularly featured on nightly newscasts.

The reasons for the French upheaval were complex. One of its historians, Alain Touraine, has insisted that it heralded a new form of class struggle against technocracy, consumerism, and the commercialization of human and sexual relations.[2] Another reason was that the university system had scarcely kept abreast of the growing numbers or changing interests of the postwar generation and needed to be reformed. And then there were the contingents of Marxist-Leninists, Trotskyites, Maoists, and anarchists who, under the banner of anticolonialism and concern over the war, were seeking the overthrow of the sociopolitical "system" in its entirety.

Architectural students occupying the Ecole des Beaux-Arts shared many of these diverging interests. The "Motion of 15 May," issued a day after students occupied the building, called for various school reforms, such as open admissions and the end of examinations and competitions, but also paid lip service to the abstraction of the "workers' struggle" and the need to combat "the conditions of architectural production, which in fact subordinate it to the interests of public or private developers."[3]

The simultaneous demonstrations in Italy – demonstrations that replicated those that had been taking place regularly since 1964 – were equal in size and more overtly political. Once again the causes were the difficult economic conditions in Italy and the outmoded academic system, which were jointly responsible for the fact that fewer than half of the architecture school graduates found

work within the field. Teaching reforms along far more radical lines were demanded, however. For instance, "Red Guard" students at the University of Turin insisted upon the election of professors and the grading of all examinations by student committees.[4] The most persistent disruptions took place in the universities located in the major cites: Rome, Florence, Milan, Naples, Venice, Pisa, and Turin. By the end of March, twenty-six universities were under siege, and the disruptions, combined regularly with workers' strikes and revolutionary calls to action, persisted through the year and over the next several years, in fact, bringing the Italian government to a virtual standstill. A militant Marxism – despite the events occurring in Czechoslovakia – became the panacea of Italian intellectuals and students.

This trend is reflected in architectural theory nowhere better than in the ideas of Manfredo Tafuri (1935–94), who arrived in Venice in the spring of 1968 as the newly appointed professor at the Institute of Architectural History.[5] The city was already in the midst of political and social turmoil. The Piazza San Marco and other areas of the city were scenes of repeated occupation by students and clashes with police. Tafuri's arrival was also nearly simultaneous with the publication of the first of his critical studies, *Teorie e storia dell'architettura* (Theories and history of architecture), which had been written in 1966–7.[6] Eager to join the revolutionary cause, he drew close to the two editors of *Contropiano*, Alberto Asor Rosa and Massimo Cacciari. *Contropiano* was a newly formed militant journal whose focus (until its dissolution in 1971) was "the analysis of the questions to do with class struggle" and with "the analysis of the ideal and cultural superstructures of mass capitalistic society."[7] Tafuri's first article for this journal, "Per una critica dell'ideologia architettonica" (Toward a critique of architectural ideology), was written in the final months of 1968 and significantly advanced his thought.[8] In addition, at the institute Tafuri quickly assembled a cadre of radical historians and theoreticians into what became a collective working program of Marxist analyses. Among them were Mario Manieri Elia, Francesco Dal Co, Giorgio Ciucci, and Marco De Milchelis.

What took place in 1968 in Venice also has to be seen against the backdrop of the debates of the 1950s and early 1960s. Italian modernism had emerged from World War II with something of a bad conscience because of its wartime association with Fascism. The leading Italian historians of the immediate postwar years, such as Bruno Zevi and Leonardo Benevolo, in their own ways retreated from the problem: in Zevi's case through his support for an "organic" modernism founded on American and Scandinavian models, in Benevolo's case through advocating a modernism bound to social activism. The effort of Ernesto Rogers in the late 1950s to inject history and memory into modern architecture too can be viewed as an attempt to decontaminate modernism from its recent past – essentially by mediating modernism with the broader historical context of Italy. Tafuri in the late 1960s was coming to reject these attempts as well as their underlying humanist bases. His historical approach in the years around 1968 has been variously defined as one of total disenchantment, iconoclasm, destructuring, and Nietzschean-inspired nihilism, but his analyses at heart were always rigorous in their Marxist premises and were offered in service to revolutionary praxis. If one of his main historical interests was the European avant-garde of the 1920s and 1930s – dada, surrealism, the Bauhaus, constructivism – his ideological and critical framework was likewise the leftist sociological framework of this period, as found in the works of Georg Simmel, Max Weber, Karl Mannheim, Georg Lukács, and Walter Benjamin. The ideas of these thinkers were updated by the negative dialectics of Theodore Adorno and the structuralism of Roland Barthes. Architecture as building now virtually recedes from sight; critical theory in itself becomes its own operative yardstick.

Teorie e storia dell'architettura outlines a new path, although it is by no means a fully formed work. Overtly it addresses itself to the perceived "crisis" of contemporary history and theory, but not in the manner of earlier historians, who were generally keen to point the way out of the dilemmas. The book purports to be "a courageous and honest scrutiny of the very foundations of the Modern Movement; in fact, a thorough investigation of whether it is still legitimate to speak of a Modern Movement as a monolithic corpus of ideas, poetics and linguistic traditions."[9] What the book delivers is an abstruse "labyrinthine" discussion in which boundless names and references pop up, only to fall back without commentary or deliberation. On the one hand, a Foucauldian sense of conspiracy surfaces, allowing fantastic but dubious conceptual speculations imbued with urgent psychoanalytical drama.[10] On the other hand, structuralism, semiology, and typology are drafted into the service of critical theory. Further, the role that history plays as an "instrument" of architectural thinking is avowed to be ambiguous. For Tafuri, the task of the historian is no longer that of the delineator of genealogies directed toward present (design) consumption; his now more hostile purpose

is to break the hidden code between architectural metalanguage and ideology, to reveal the anxiety that lies beneath the surface.

If the book lacks coherence, it is almost moot because crucial change overtakes Tafuri's outlook took in the second half of 1968. His revised position first appears in his essay "Toward a Critique of Architectural Ideology." Its overtly political argument, drawing heavily on the nihilism of Cacciari, is far more pessimistic in its tone, though without sacrificing any of its conspiratorial air. For instance, he notes that "there exists, between the avant-gardes of capital and the intellectual avant-gardes, a kind of tacit understanding, so tacit indeed that any attempt to bring it into the light elicits a chorus of indignant protest."[11] Tafuri sees all architectural development since the Enlightenment as walking in lockstep with capitalism and thus in an insoluble state of crisis. In this period, the utopianisms of Laugier and Piranesi of the 1830s and the 1920s follow a rather precise dialectical process of accommodation and feigned redemption, as K. Michael Hays reports, "a unitary development in which the avant-gardes' visions of utopia come to be recognized as an idealization of capitalism, a transfiguration of the latter's rationality into the rationality of autonomous form – architecture's 'plan,' its ideology."[12] There is no way, Tafuri argues, to rid architecture of this bourgeois contamination, even by participating in "the economic and social conflicts exploding with ever greater frequency" and assisting capitalism in its inevitable fall:

This has forced a return to activism – to strategies of stimulus, critique, and struggle – on the part of the intellectual opposition, and even of class problems and conflicts. The harshness of the struggle over urban-planning laws (in Italy as well as the US), over the reorganization of the building industry, over urban renewal, may have given many the illusion that the fight for planning could actually constitute a moment in the class struggle.[13]

Architecture, because of its false ideology, has therefore lost its capacity to offer any vision for a postcapitalist world. It has reached the beginning of its natural end. As Tafuri later summarizes the matter in his *Progetto e Utopia* (1973, translated into English as *Architecture and Utopia*): "There is no more 'salvation' to be found within it; neither by wandering restlessly through 'labyrinths' of images so polyvalent that they remain mute, nor by shutting oneself up in the sullen silence of geometries content with their own perfection."[14] Tafuri's apocalyptic vision has been rightly criticized on several levels – from its nihilistic abstractions and psychoanalytical pretensions to its internal logical limitations.[15] As a politicization of architecture theory, it of course rises and falls on its own political premises. But the critique also in a very shrewd way explodes many of the naive beliefs of historians up to this time. It highlights not only attempts to subjugate the past and future with prescribed narratives in service to the present but also the very impossibility of a one-to-one relationship between form and meaning – an idea that "deconstruction" would soon entertain in full. It also succinctly captures the "crisis" of theory in 1968: this time a genuine architectural crisis of colossal magnitude.

The concomitant convulsions of theory in the United States in 1968 emanate from very different causes and emotional grounds. For one thing, the problems troubling American society were long simmering and if anything far more severe than those abroad, driven as they were by an unpopular war, vestiges of racism, and a nearly spontaneous breakdown of social values. For another thing, the cultural diversity and pragmatic eclecticism of American intellectual thought tended to reject overly rigid philosophical systems (such as Marxism) or any single explanation for the vast cultural and social breakdown.

In any case, in the 1960s events, rather than ideology, were causing the unrest. The assassination of John F. Kennedy in 1963 created the first crack in the Cold War facade of social optimism. Lyndon B. Johnson further ruptured it with his disastrous decision late in 1964 to escalate the Vietnam conflict into a war. He not only sent hundreds of thousands of American ground troops into battle but initiated a relentless and ineffective bombing campaign against the communist North that ensured a widening of the hostilities. As the American ground forces could only be supplied by a much-expanded military draft, the draft itself provided a rallying point for social opposition among the young – opposition that grew proportionally with the increasing number of battlefield casualties. The proliferation of peace marches and antidraft demonstrations in 1966 and 1967, foremost the march on the Pentagon itself in October 1967, set the stage for the cataclysms of 1968.

The other factor driving American social unrest – the Civil Rights movement – began in earnest in the spring of 1963 with the marches of Martin Luther King in Alabama, where he was opposed by Governor George Wallace and "Bull" Connor. In 1964 came the landmark civil rights legislation and the summer project of voter registration in Mississippi. The disturbances in Selma and Watts followed the next year, and in 1966 rioting broke out in several American cities,

although these events were not always driven by racial issues. By the mid-1960s the Civil Rights movement had split in two, with King retaining control of the nonviolent wing. On his flank now appeared a militant wing consisting of separatists, Black Nationalists, and self-described Marxists who openly advocated violence and insurrection.

Paralleling these events were various other developments. Feminism became a discernible and active political movement with the appearance of Betty Friedan's *The Feminine Mystique* in 1963 and the founding of the National Organization of Women in 1966. William H. Masters and Virginia E. Johnson published *Human Sexual Response* in the same year, and their research stood in the vanguard of a sexual (marriage and divorce) revolution, assisted in large part by the introduction of an effective birth control pill. To San Francisco's Haight-Ashbury district in the mid-1960s came the hippies, the Grateful Dead, and the Jefferson Airplane, and its emerging drug culture – popularized in musical lyrics – would rapidly spread across the nation and in fact the world. On the opposite end of the counter cultural spectrum were the radical politics of the New Left and such groups as the Students for a Democratic Society (SDS), which would reach their peak of influence around 1968. Fidel Castro, Ernesto Che Guevara, Ho Chi Minh, Mao Tse-tung, Herbert Marcuse, V. I. Lenin, and Karl Marx were the ideological saints of the increasingly alienated political counter culture. Like many of the student movements in Europe, the New Left and other radical groups in North America saw American culture as suffering from greed and consumerism and manipulated by special interests, corporations, and the military-industrial complex.

All of these disparate forces came to a head in 1968, the year that opened ominously with the capture of the USS *Pueblo*, a surveillance ship, off the coast of North Korea. The Tet offensive followed at the end of January, and during this period an estimated 60,000 Viet Cong forces crossed into the south and attacked nearly every urban center, including Saigon (where the U.S. Embassy came under assault). The "My Lai Massacre" – in which a platoon of soldiers under Lt. William L. Calley Jr. slaughtered an estimated 450–500 civilians – took place in March, although the full details would not be known for some time. The growing number of American casualties provoked the antiwar candidacy of Eugene McCarthy, who mounted a direct challenge to a seated Democratic president. McCarthy's show of strength in the New Hampshire and Wisconsin primaries forced President Johnson, on 31 March, to withdraw his bid for a second term in office.

On 4 April, Martin Luther King was assassinated in Memphis, which prompted rioting in 110 cities and the call-up of 75,000 National Guardsmen. In all, the violent disturbances left thirty-nine more people dead. Meanwhile, Robert Kennedy, who had early deferred to McCarthy in mounting a challenge, changed his mind and jumped into the presidential race. By early June he had taken over the lead in the race for his party's nomination, before he was gunned down in Los Angeles. The summer saw only modest urban turmoil, that is, in comparison with the previous three years. This relative calm, however, broke in August when Democrats converged on Chicago to hold their national convention. There the political delegates were met by a well-coordinated contingent of antiwar activists, Black Power leaders, hippies, and the newly formed Yippies (Youth International Party) – the last of whom promised to lace the city's water supply with LSD and nominate a pig for president. All of the self-annointed celebrities of the political left flocked to the event and the media limelight: Tom Hayden, Abbie Hoffman, Norman Mailer, and Allen Ginsberg, among many others. The eventual nomination of Hubert Humphrey over McCarthy was in the end completely overshadowed by the "police riot" of the same evening that started when battle-weary police officers, not without considerable provocation, decided to clear out Grant Park and the surrounding area. It was an act of blue-collar retribution against the white-collar–bred protestors, indicative of another stratification within American society. The Democratic candidate Humphrey was defeated in November by the Republican Richard M. Nixon, but the scars that had divided the country along political, racial, economic, and generational lines were now too deeply etched for any chance of reconciliation. It is not an exaggeration to say that the year had been one of civil warfare, and contempt for the system felt by many protestors would never fully abate, nor would the wounds experienced by both sides fully heal.

The unrest was no less evident within the universities, where, by one count, in the first six and a half months of the year over 100 campuses had suffered a total of 221 major demonstrations involving 39,000 students and faculty.[16] Buildings were being damaged and defaced, offices occupied and vandalized, presidents, deans, and professors accosted. Perhaps the most publicized of these disruptions was the rioting that took place at Columbia University in April, memorialized in an open letter by SDS president Mark Rudd (quoting LeRoi Jones) to university president Grayson Kirk: "Up against the wall, motherfucker, this is a stick-up."[17] The ostensible reasons for the "stick-up" were plans for a new gymnasium and Columbia's minor involvement with the federal Institute of Defense Analysis. That these were pretexts was freely admitted by Rudd himself.[18] Among his stated motivations for the sit-ins were Vietnam, changes in the draft regulations, the death of King, and the popularity of McCarthy on campus, which Rudd (an admirer of the Cuban revolution) feared would lead to political co-optation back into the American electoral system. In any case, he did not act alone. On 23 April, after he and others trashed the fence surrounding the planned gymnasium site, Rudd led his group of demonstrators to Hamilton Hall, where the acting dean of Columbia College, Harry Coleman, was taken as hostage. When later in the evening the black militants among the demonstrators demanded that the white SDS students depart this building, Rudd took his group to Low Library, where he occupied and vandalized the presidential office. Additional contingents of students successively "liberated" (occupied) various other buildings on campus, including Avery Hall, which housed the School of Architecture. Although Kirk quickly put the plans for the gymnasium on hold, the event had already transcended itself. Prominent radicals from across the country rushed to the scene to announce their support for the protest. The occupation ended on 30 April when an exasperated Kirk asked the police to clear the buildings and arrest the trespassers. Many students left without incident, but others barricaded the entrances and sabotaged stairways, forcing a violent showdown. Over 700 students and sympathetic outsiders were arrested. The school, physically and psychologically displaying the scars of warfare, was mercifully shut down for the remainder of the academic year, only to reignite in the fall.

The American Civil War of 1968 would obviously leave its imprint on architectural theory – if only psychologically. And its intensity can indeed be measured. The "gentle" retreats from modernism intimated by Venturi and Moore a few years earlier now seemed tame in relation to the current upheaval, and the divide already evident within American theory – between American and European-inspired outlooks – would become even more prominent. In the first regard, the "complexity and contradiction" advocated by Venturi transformed itself into full-blooded Las Vegas style "populism." Indeed Denise Scott Brown should take precedence over Venturi in this matter. She and Venturi were married on the front porch of her Santa Monica home in July 1967, one year after they had taken their first trip together to Las Vegas, and the West Coast years, as has been noted, had also been fertile in furthering her intellectual development.[19] In 1965 she taught a course at Berkeley with the sociologist Melvin Webber, whose essay "The Urban Place and the Nonplace Urban Realm" had challenged the European sociological assumptions that then formed the basis of urban theory. Against the model of the city as a central active hub from which all commercial and cultural activities dissipate outward, Webber offered a futuristic "communications systems" model in which electronic and other media access to information increasingly diminishes the importance of "place" and the need for human contact. Thus place-based notions such as neighborhood, suburb, city, region, or nation gradually lose their relevance in an area like the San Francisco Bay Region, where residents may "not participate in the metropolitan realm at all, their linkages being primarily with Washington or New York or Hong Kong or with their local-residence realms."[20] This model, of course, preceded and presaged the access to communications and information offered by tools such as the Internet and the cell phone.

Scott Brown approached this theme from a slightly different perspective. In her 1965 essay published in the *A.I.A. Journal*, she analyzed the city as a "message system" using the categories of "Perception and Meaning," "Messages," "Movement and Meaning," and "A Modern Image," and she posed the question of just how "messages" are given and received in the urban environment. Her tripartite answer – through "heraldry" (written and graphic signs), "physiognomy" (the sizes and shapes of buildings and spaces), and "location pattern" (the pattern of buildings and spaces) – echoes, as she herself notes, her former teacher David Crane's formulation in the "The City Symbolic" (1960). But just as importantly it provides a model for analyzing the contemporary noncore city, which developed following the introduction of the automobile.[21] Another key stimulus to her deliberations came in 1967 when she and Venturi were hired to teach a joint design studio at Yale, one that would entail both research and field investigation (and conversely little design). The first of these special studios centered on the theme of redesigning Herald Square, a New York City subway station, but the second, offered in the fall of 1968, carried the title "Learning from Las Vegas, or Form Analysis as Design Research." The third studio, taught the following year, drew upon the research of another Penn faculty member – Herbert J. Gans's work on Levittown.

The findings of the Las Vegas studio of 1968, which of course included a field trip to Nevada, had been anticipated much earlier by Scott Brown and Venturi. The article that later formed the basis for Part 1 of *Learning from Las Vegas* (1972) – "A Significance for A&P Parking Lots or Learning

108. Robert Venturi and Denise Scott Brown, image of Las Vegas, from "A Significance for A&P Parking Lots or Learning from Las Vegas," *Architectural Forum* (March 1968).

from Las Vegas" – was first published in *Architectural Forum* in March 1968 (Fig. 108). Appearing in the midst of global unrest, it was an important essay that in its own odd way announced their secession from all earlier forms of modernism: "Architects," the two authors noted, "are out of the habit of looking nonjudgmentally at the environment because orthodox Modern architecture is progressive, if not revolutionary, utopian and puristic; it is dissatisfied with *existing* conditions. Modern architecture has been anything but permissive: architects have preferred to change the existing environment rather than enhance what is there."[22] The cozy Italian piazza that American architects discovered in the 1940s here becomes the foil for their new vision of the city: "Two decades later architects are perhaps ready for similar lessons about large open space, big scale, and high speed."[23] The new "big scale" of course is dictated by the automobile, the big space by parking, and the heraldic sign becomes the crucial communicative element, "the building at back, a modest necessity."[24] Las Vegas is, for Venturi and Scott Brown, not the city of fountains that Audrey Hepburn learned to love but in an eerie way the city of the future.

The theme of Part 2 of *Learning from Las Vegas* also appeared in 1968, in a short article "On Ducks and Decoration." Loos's equation of decoration with "sin" has now increased tenfold: "Our thesis is that most architects' buildings today are ducks: buildings where an expressive aim has distorted the whole beyond the limits of economy and convenience; and that this, although an unadmitted one, is a kind of decoration and a wrong and costly one at that."[25] Scott Brown and Venturi now prefer the decorated shed, for "it permits us to get on with the task of making conventional buildings conventionally and to deal with their symbolic needs with a lighter, defter touch."[26] But this preference carries with it other interesting architectural implications: "We believe a new interest in the architecture of communication involving symbols and mixed media will lead us to reevaluate the eclectic and picturesque styles of the last century, to reappraise our own commercial architecture – Pop architecture, if you wish – and finally to face the question of decoration."[27]

It was a point of view, obviously, that many Europeans would never be willing to adopt. Vincent Scully's *American Architecture and Urbanism* and Robert A. M. Stern's *New Directions in American Architecture* created a mini-firestorm in Britain when the two books alluded to such ideas: the former because of what Martin Pawley termed "the irrelevance of the creative efforts catalogued in his [Scully's] book" and the latter because of the postscript, in which (a young) Stern opined that the future was being signified by the student unrest at Columbia and Yale and by Venturi and Scott Brown's studies of Las Vegas: "The Attitude, this anxiety over real problems, is as near to the new direc-

tion as anything in this book."[28] Pawley, after noting the "rent campuses, brawling streets and retributive trials" in the United States, goes on to denounce the relevance of Venturi's strip and then concludes that "if he represents the real *avant-garde* in America, it will be the first time in history that the bearers of that proud title have sought refuge in the Emperor's Palace instead of joining the revolution."[29] Venturi and Scott Brown responded with a tart rejoinder: "But we feel our pathetic, imperfect, expedient, limited, immediate, activist approach is more useful (or at least less harmful) for the near future than is your reviewer's arrogant, authoritarian, sensational, simplistic, indulgent, condescending, apocalyptic, heroic, meaningless, easy, disastrous utopianism."[30]

A more serious and no less livid response to Scott Brown was touched off a few months later when *Casabella* published her article "Learning from Pop," together with a rejoinder by Kenneth Frampton and a reply by the author.[31] In "Learning from Pop," Scott Brown not only reiterated her earlier arguments regarding Las Vegas but peppered them with comments on the failure of American urban renewal policies, which she traced back to "the 'rationalist,' Cartesian formal orders of latter day Modern architecture."[32] Also taking a shot at futuristic British theorists of the 1960s, she noted, "The forms of the pop landscape are relevant to us now as were the forms of antique Rome to the Beaux-Arts, Cubism and machine architecture to the early Moderns, and the industrial midlands and the Dogon to Team 10, which is to say extremely relevant, and more so than the latest bathysphere, launch pad, or systems hospital (or even, 'pace' Banham, the Santa Monica pier)."[33]

Frampton, who had arrived in the United States a few years earlier from England, responded in his article with a lengthy attack on Scott Brown and Venturi, which he introduced by juxtaposing images of the Vesnin brothers' design for the Pravda building (1923) and an aerial view of the Las Vegas strip. Frampton's argument is elaborately constructed. Leading with a quotation by Hermann Broch on the subtheme of "kitsch," he starts the text proper by claiming, "The recent writings of Denise Scott Brown and Robert Venturi extend the syncretic capacity of the English picturesque tradition beyond its tractable limits."[34] His point is that the pop art polemics of these two designers are but a latter-day manifestation of the English picturesque/humanist/townscape movement of the late 1940s and early 1950s, mediated along the way by the analyses of Richard Hamilton, Kevin Lynch, Herbert Gans, Melvin Webber, and, most importantly, Madison Avenue. There is as well a strong note of moral condemnation directed at the apostasy of Venturi and Scott Brown. On the one hand, "Design oriented expertise in Western European and American universities stands largely transfixed before the technical prowess and success of Western Neo-Capitalism"; on the other hand, the "socio-political critical faculty" has been seduced by "the so-called democratization of consumption and by the inevitability of that, which I have elsewhere characterized as the 'instant utopia' of Los Angeles."[35] Frampton next invokes the Marxist Herbert Marcuse on the ideological poverty of defining "the standard of living solely in terms of automobiles, television sets and airplanes."[36] But aside from applauding the structuralist planning schemes of Candilis and Woods of the early 1960s, Frampton does not rush to the defense of CIAM determinism. Instead, he closes with a threatening question: "Or is it that the present triumph of kitsch is testament in itself, without the illuminations of Pop Art, that our urban society is organized towards self defeating ends, on a sociopolitical basis that is totally invalid?"[37]

Scott Brown's response to Frampton is equally revealing of the political dimensions of the theoretical divide. On the cultural front she makes the trenchant observation: "The majority of the population may not like what Levitt offers, although there is no proof of this, but they support even less the architects' alternatives. The critique of Madison Avenue is old now and a bore."[38] Politically, the reference to Marcuse provokes a more strident defense. Not only is the "broad-gauge, European-based dismissal of the entire American society over easy and not useful," but it is also fundamentally disingenuous, for "there is something distasteful about sitting in a plush American university with enough financing to do one's thing full-time instead of part-time, as most European based architectural scholars must, and taking superior armchair-revolutionary pot shots at the capitalists that support you there."[39]

In any case, by 1971, Frampton had indeed chosen sides, and it was not with Marcuse but with the circle of individuals who had come together at the Institute for Architecture and Urban Studies (IAUS) in New York City. Here also is where European theory now mounts its counterattack.

The institute had been founded in early 1967, and historically it was related to CASE in that it grew out of Eisenman's dissatisfaction with the lack of direction of that organization. Apparently sometime in 1966 Eisenman approached Arthur Drexler, who was the director of the Department of Architecture and Design at the Museum of Modern Art, and proposed the creation of an institute that would become a center for studying urban problems. Drexler supported the idea, a few wealthy donors were found to provide startup funds, and in October 1967, at the first meeting of the trustees for the new institute, Eisenman was elected president and Drexler chairman of the board.[40] The board is notable for the absence of Colin Rowe, who up to this point had been working closely with Eisenman. If the institute's financial and ideological ties to the Museum of Modern Art recalls 1932, it should. MoMA would again work closely with the new institute to shape its theoretical position.

The objectives of the IAUS were multifaceted. One purpose was "to propose and develop new methods and new solutions for problems of the urban environment," but it was also intended to be an education center developing "new methods for education and research in physical design and planning."[41] In addition it was "to develop a body of theory concerned with architecture and physical planning," drawing on the social sciences, and "to provide a new learning and work experience for students."[42] Thus it was to function as a design studio, with Eisenman and others securing city, state, and federal monies for projects; it was also to have a faculty who would lead the projects and conduct seminars. A library, exhibitions, and a journal were also anticipated. Eisenman performed his role in 1968 by securing municipal and federal funding for projects in New York and Baltimore. The original faculty consisted of Eisenman, Rowe, Drexler, and Robert Gutman.[43] Also in 1968 Gutman, Emilio Ambasz, and Robert Slutzky were awarded Graham Foundation fellowships (John Entenza, a former Californian, was the director of the Graham Foundation as well as a board member at the IAUS).[44]

Obtaining students was another problem, and Eisenman's plan was to form relationships with university urban-study centers whereby their students would be given a stipend to work temporarily in New York City. The first collaboration formed was with the Urban Design Group at Cornell University, headed by Colin Rowe and Alexander Caragonne, both of whom also came down to the city one day a week to teach. The presence of Slutzky, Rowe, and Caragonne at the IAUS effectively reconstituted the Texas Rangers in the Northeast, but this coalition would soon shatter. In keeping with the spirit of 1968, students working at the IAUS in the fall began expressing their disapproval of Eisenman, the institute, and the disorganized nature of the projects. Eisenman, as Louis Martin has noted, interpreted the revolt as a power play by Rowe to take control of the institute, and somewhat infamously he changed the locks on the doors to force Rowe and his students out.[45] In March of the following year, Rowe and Caragonne resigned from the IAUS, after efforts at mediation failed.

In 1969 and 1970 the ideological direction of the institute was also changing. Kenneth Frampton and Stanford Anderson were brought into the institute during these years. Audiotapes from a gathering that took place in 1969 – attended by Eisenman, Frampton, Anderson, Rykwert, Michael Graves, Richard Meier, and others – demonstrate that the IAUS (at this moment indistinguishable from CASE) functioned in part as a private club in which members critiqued the architectural work of fellow members.[46] These efforts soon culminated – on both a practical and theoretical front – in two not unrelated ventures: the book *Five Architects* (1972) and the journal *Oppositions* (1973).

Although these ventures are outside of our time frame, they should be considered because they descend directly from earlier efforts. *Five Architects* grew out of a CASE meeting held at the Museum of Modern Art in May 1969, and it essentially launched a full-fledged Le Corbusier revival.[47] The five architects – Eisenman, Graves, Charles Gwathmey, John Hejduk, and Richard Meier – were at the early stages of their careers. The book contained three projects (two hypothetical, one unbuilt) of Hejduk, formerly a Texas Ranger, all of which had been exhibited at the Cooper Union in 1968. Gwathmey, who since 1970 had been in partnership with Robert Siegel, published his own cedar-sided house and studio on Long Island (1966) and two similar residences in Bridgehampton (1970). Graves displayed his Hanselmann House, Fort Wayne (1967), and an addition to the Benacerraf House in Princeton (1969). Richard Meier, who since 1965 had enjoyed an increasingly successful practice, displayed his already well-publicized Smith House (1965) in Darien, Connecticut, and the Saltzman House, East Hampton (1967). Eisenman opened the catalogue with "House I," Princeton (1967), and "House II," Hardwick, Vermont (1969).

The distinct Corbusian flavor of most of these designs (save Eisenman's) is consciously understated in the accompanying texts of both architects and critics. Meier, whose work of the early 1960s displayed overtones of Marcel Breuer and Mies, characterized the design of the Smith House as "a spatially layered linear system," thereby evoking at least a faint homage to Rowe and Slutzky's notion of transparency and the Villa Stein at Garches.[48] His use of expansive glass surfaces and Corbusian motifs – conceptual rather than functional – would of course intensify in the

early 1970s, at least with his residential designs. William La Riche, who introduced Graves's work, makes frequent mention of Le Corbusier, but he also compares Graves's designs to the cubism of Juan Gris, to the dislocation of a David Hockney painting, and to the representational values of Mircea Eliade.[49] Kenneth Frampton, in his introductory essay, "Frontality vs. Rotation," analyzes the work of the five architects entirely from a formal perspective. He too acknowledges the "syntactical references to Le Corbusier" but insists that "none of them manipulate space in a way that at all resembles the work of Le Corbusier."[50] A few years later, while acknowledging the presence of a "rehabilitated Purism" in the work of the five, Frampton again argues that their "openness to the Spartan hedonism of Le Corbusier's aesthetic was restricted from the outset, and, in some instances, had hardly ever existed. Their supposed involvement in post-Corbusean space was but a convenient way of characterizing critically their common concern for the generation of highly abstract but lyrical formal systems."[51] One can quibble with this point, although it is now moot.

Only Rowe in his introductory essay – one of the most important theoretical statements of the twentieth century – meets the underlying issues head on, by pronouncing the death of (politically) revolutionary modernism. Brashly, he does so in a way that is not entirely complimentary to the five architects:

For we are here in the presence of what, in terms of the orthodox theory of modern architecture is heresy. We are in the presence of anachronism, nostalgia, and, probably, frivolity. If modern architecture looked like this c. 1930 then it should not look like this today; and, if the real political issue of the present is not the provision of the rich with cake but of the starving with bread, then not only formally but also programmatically these buildings are irrelevant. Evidently they propound no obvious revolution; and, just as they may be envisaged as dubiously European to some American tastes, so they will seem the painful evidence of American retardation to certain European and, particularly, English judgments.[52]

Rowe, in fact, does not go on to supply the designs with any justification but merely allows their publication within the difficult "context of choices." In two paragraphs added to his introduction in 1974, he makes his point even more eloquently:

However, perhaps the great merit of what follows lies in the fact that its authors are not enormously self-deluded as to the immediate possibility of any very violent or sudden architectural or social mutation. They place themselves in the role,

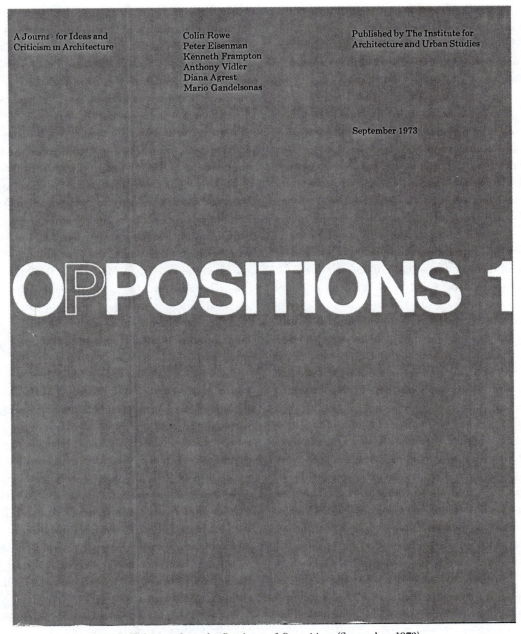

A Journal for Ideas and
Criticism in Architecture

Colin Rowe
Peter Eisenman
Kenneth Frampton
Anthony Vidler
Diana Agrest
Mario Gandelsonas

Published by The Institute for
Architecture and Urban Studies

September 1973

OP POSITIONS 1

109. Title page from the first issue of *Oppositions* (September, 1973).

the secondary role of Scamozzi to Palladio. Their posture may be polemical but it is not heroic. Apparently they are neither Marcusian nor Maoist; and, lacking any transcendental sociological or political faith, their objective – at bottom – is to alleviate the present by the interjection of a quasi-Utopian vein of poetry.[53]

Arthur Drexler expresses the same sentiment more succinctly in his preface to *Five Architects*, when he notes that their work was "*only* architecture, not the salvation of man and the redemption of the earth."[54] In orthodox modernist terms of the 1920s, this intention of course constitutes a true surrender.

If there was one theoretical position to be salvaged here, it was that of Eisenman, who had turned to Terragni for inspiration. Since 1967 he had been evolving the idea of "cardboard architecture," whose premises first appeared in two *Casabella* articles published in 1970 and 1971.[55] In the first (which reiterated much of his dissertation on Terragni),

Eisenman credits the Como architect with instituting a major shift over and above the work of Le Corbusier, "from the semantic domain to the syntactic domain: and from the traditionally-held notions of the relation of the structure, in its technological sense, to form."[56] In the second of these articles, "Notes on Conceptual Architecture: Towards a Definition," Eisenman squares this shift with Noam Chomsky's linguistic model – the distinction between "a perceptual or surface structure" (semantics) and "a conceptual or deep structure" (syntactics).[57] The idea behind "cardboard architecture" is to strip architecture entirely of its semantic connotations and to view it as a closed notational system: "Cardboard is used to signify the result of the particular way of generating and transforming a series of primitive integer relationships into a more complex set of specific relationships which become the actual building. In this sense 'cardboard' is used to denote the particular deployment of columns, walls, and beams as they define space in a series of thin planar, vertical layers."[58] Although he treats cardboard architecture as a "virtual or implied layering" of form, Houses I and II, as seen in *Five Architects*, are very much an actual layering of planar and columnar forms. Rowe and Slutzky's notion of transparency has here been interpreted in an extreme way.

Oppositions: A Journal for Ideas and Criticism in Architecture represents another culmination of CASE/IAUS activities (Fig. 109). After two years of labor, the first issue appeared in September 1973 under the editorship of Eisenman, Frampton, and Mario Gandelsonas.[59] The idea of a journal, as we have seen, originated in 1965 with the CASE group, although its realization took a very different form. The short editorial statement speaks only of the need for "critical assessment and re-assessment" and claims that the aim of the journal is to "address itself to the evolution of new models for a theory of architecture."[60] The first issues contain essays by the three editors, the most important of which (for suggesting a future direction) is the joint article by Gandelsonas and Diana Agrest entitled "Semiotics and Architecture: Ideological Consumption or Theoretical Work." An essay of Rowe, written in the mid-1950s was also published, as was an article by Anthony Vidler, who would soon join the editorial staff issue. Beginning with the third issue, Julia Bloomfield would become the managing editor.

The international cast of early contributors to *Oppositions* – Rowe, Frampton, Vidler, Agrest, Gandelsonas – is one of the distinguishing marks of the journal in its early days, as is the distinctly ideological (political) slant of many of its analyses. This last tendency was strengthened in the early 1970s through the association of the IAUS with Tafuri and Rossi – an association that resulted (somewhat oddly) in the work of the New York Five being included in the 1973 Milan exhibition on "Rational Architecture." Eisenman may have wanted *Oppositions* to enhance critical discussion within the United States, but the journal with its European orientation simply mirrored the long-standing predilection of the Ivy League architectural schools, to import their faculty and intellectual fashions from abroad. Its thematic fixation, aside from the work of the New York Five, was entirely on European theory and European architects – Le Corbusier, Soviet constructivism, and Italian rationalism, in particular. Once again, the Europhilic parallel with the efforts of the Museum of Modern Art in 1932 is striking, only less so because architecture by the end of the 1960s had become an international field in every way. On a historical and theoretical front, the journal did make many valuable contributions; it always functioned at a very high level in its presentation of history and theory.

Looking back on the year 1968, if there was one idea that bound together the IAUS, the work of the New York Five, the populism of Venturi and Moore, and Italian rationalism, it was the idea of revival or revisitation: the revival of the now iconic forms of the 1920s, of baroque mannerisms and popular vernaculars, of an idealized, even Laugier-inspired neoclassicism. This judgment is by no means intended to be a pejorative one, for revivals have always been an integral part of modern theory and practice. Perrault's design for the east facade of the Louvre, for instance, was as much an effort to initiate a pseudosystyle revival as it was an attempt to articulate a French declaration of independence from the Italian Renaissance. Such is the circular nature of theory and practice.

But revivals also occur at certain junctures, and this is what makes the phenomenon of 1968 (give or take a few years) so striking in retrospect. The pent-up postwar energy that progressively exploded in the realm of architectural theory during the 1950s and early 1960s, giving voice to a host of competing (and confident) ideologies and directions, visibly dissipates by the middle to late 1960s. Options, in fact, seem to disappear almost with each passing day, and a very real sense of cynicism sets in. The ongoing social and political upheaval beyond the walls of the design studios no doubt played a very important part in forcing a fundamental reevaluation of architecture's social and cultural assumptions, but architecture too operates with a finite storehouse of ideas and ideologies that also with a certain regularity exhaust themselves. If one wants to characterize 1968, one could well argue that above all else it was a year of exhaustion – emotional, psychological, intellectual.

Whether one looks at the year as the beginning of the end of modern theory or simply as a period of retrenchment and critical reassessment, it cannot be disputed that architectural theory would never again be the same. A new (or old) direction had to be found.

NOTES

Preface

1. David Leatherbarrow, *The Roots of Architectural Invention: Site, Enclosure, Materials* (New York: Cambridge University Press, 1993), 218–20.
2. Aristotle *Metaphysics* 1003^{b}15, 1083^{b}18.
3. Cicero, *Letters to Atticus*, trans. E. O. Winstedt (London: William Heinemann, 1918), 7:6.
4. Vitruvius, *On Architecture*, trans. Frank Granger (Cambridge, Mass.: Harvard University Press, 1998), bk. 4, chap. 5, 103–7.
5. See Luigi Grassi and Mario Pepe, *Dizionario della critica d'arte* (Turin: Utet, 1978), 2:599. The article cites usages of *teoria* by Lorenzo Ghiberti, Leonardo da Vinci, Vincenzo Danti, Georgio Vasari, and Giovanni Lomazzo.
6. Georgio Vasari, *Le vite de' più eccellenti pittori scultori e architettori* (Novara, Italy: Instituto Geografico de Agostini, 1967), 2:411. The Italian passage reads: "Chi non conosce che bisogna con matura considerazione sapere, o fuggire, o apprendere, per sé solo, ciò che si cerca mettere in opera, senza avere a raccomandarsi alla mercé dell'altrui teorica, la quale separata dalla pratica il più del volte giova assai poco?"
7. Vitruvius, *I dieci libri dell'architettura, tr. et commentati da monsignor Barbaro* (Vinegia, Italy: Marcolini, 1556).
8. Jean Martin, *Architecture, ou, Art de bien bastir de Marc Vitruve Pollion* (Paris: Gazeau, 1547).
9. Blaise Pascal, *Les Provinciales, ou lettres écrit par Louis de Montalte*, ed. Charles Louandre (Paris: Charpentier, 1873), 135. "Encore que cette opinion, qu'on peut tuer pour une médisance, ne soit pas sans probabilité dans la théorie, il faut suivre le contraire dans la pratique."
10. *An Abridgment of the Architecture of Vitruvius, Containing a System of the Whole Works of that Author* (London: Unicorn, 1692). Art. 2 (pp. 23–4) reads in part: "Architecture is a Science which ought to be accompanied with a Knowledge of a great many other Arts and Sciences, by which means it forms a correct Judgment of all the Works of other Arts that appertain to it. This Science is acquired by *Theory* and *Practice*." This book is a translation of the abridged French book *Architecture generale*

de Vitruve reduite en abreg', par Mr. Perrault, which appeared in 1674 and 1681.
11. *The Theory and Practice of Architecture; or Vitruvius and Vignola Abridg'd* (London: R. Wellington, 1703).
12. For instance, the group of late grammarians called the *Neoterici* used the term *Neotericus* to refer to recent writers. See Ernst Curtius, *European Literature and the Latin Middle Ages*, trans. Willard R. Trask (New York: Pantheon Books, 1953), 251.
13. On the quarrel and its implications for modernity, see Matei Calinescu, *Five Faces of Modernity: Modernism, Avant-Garde, Decadence, Kitsch, Postmodernism* (Durham: Duke University Press, 1987), 26–35. The two classic works describing the artistic event are Ange-Hippolyte Rigault's *Histoire de la querelle des anciens et des modernes* (Paris: Hachette et cie: 1856) and Huber Gillot's *La querelle des anciens et des modernes en France* (Paris, 1914).
14. The citation is from Theodor Adorno, *Aesthetic Theory*, trans. C. Lenhardt (London: Routledge & Kegan Paul, 1984), 34. The full sentences reads: "What guarantees the authentic quality of modern works of art? It is the scars of damage and disruption inflicted by them on the smooth surface of the immutable." The sentence of course also alludes to the well-known models and terms of Max Horkheimer, Walter Benjamin, and Adorno himself.
15. Francesco Dal Co, review of *Architecture Theory Since 1968*, edited by K. Michael Hays, *Journal of the Society of Architectural Historians* 59 (June 2000): 271.

1. Prelude

1. Juan Bautista Villalpanda, *In Ezechielem, explanationes et apparatus urbis, ac templi hierosolymitani commentariis et imaginibus illustratus*, 3 vols. (Rome, 1596–1604). This large study was begun by Jerónimo Prado, who is generally credited as the book's coauthor.
2. See René Descartes, *Rules for the Direction of the Mind*, in *The Philosophical Writings of Descartes*, trans. John Cottingham,

Robert Stoothoff, and Dugald Murdoch (Cambridge: Cambridge University Press, 1988), 1:13. The *Rules* were written before 1628 in Latin (*Regulae ad Directionem Ingenii*) but not published until 1684. They were, however, soon expanded by Descartes in his *Discourse on Method* (1638), in which this particular rule appears as the first "resolution" of his method.

3. Roland Fréart de Chambray, *Parallèle de l'architecture antique avec la moderne* (Paris: Martin, 1650), 1–2; cited from the English translation of John Evelyn, *A Parallel of the Antient Architecture with the Modern* (London: Roycroft, 1664), 1–2.

4. Ibid., 3.

5. For the life and activities of Colbert, see Inès Murat, *Colbert*, trans. Robert Francis Cook and Jeannie Van Asselt (Charlottesville: University Press of Virginia, 1984).

6. Voltaire, *The Age of Louis XIV*, in *The Works of Voltaire* (New York: Dingwall-Rock, 1927), 12:5.

7. For information on the Accademia del Disegno and the Accademia de San Luca, see Nikolaus Pevsner, *Academies of Art Past and Present* (Cambridge: Cambridge University Press, 1940), 42–66.

8. For details on these academic institutions, see Frances A. Yates, *The French Academies of the Sixteenth Century* (London: Warburg Institute, University of London, 1947; reprint, Millwood, N.Y.: Krause, 1968), 290–311. See also Anthony Blunt, *Art and Architecture in France 1500–1700* (London: Penguin, 1977), 324–35, 344–5.

9. For the details of Blondel's life, see C. Vigoureux, *Nicolas-François de Blondel: Ingénieur et Architecte du Roi (1618–1686)* (Paris: A. Picard, 1938). See also Henry Lemonnier's introduction to *Procès-Verbaux de l'Académie Royale d'Architecture, 1671–1793* (Paris: Jean Schemit, 1911–29).

10. The verbal transcripts of the Academy of Architecture were published by Henry Lemonnier in ten volumes as *Procès-Verbaux de l'Académie Royale d'Architecture, 1671–1793* (see note 9). Blondel's lecture was printed at the start of his *Cours d'architecture* (1675).

11. This was the order, at least, in which Blondel discussed these theorists in the first months of the academy's existence. See Lemonnier, *Procès-Verbaux de l'Académie Royale d'Architecture*, 1:6–8.

12. The best discussion of Blondel's theory remains that of Wolfgang Herrmann, which is contained in *The Theory of Claude Perrault* (London: Zwemmer, 1973).

13. R. Ouvrard, *Architecture harmonique, or application de la doctrine des proportions de la musique à l'architecture* (Paris, 1679), 1. For details of Ouvard's theory, see Joseph Rykwert, *The First Moderns: The Architects of the Eighteenth Century* (Cambridge: M.I.T. Press, 1980), 13.

14. See especially the invaluable study of Robert W. Berger, *The Palace of the Sun: The Louvre of Louis XIV* (University Park: Pennsylvania State University Press, 1993), 13–16. Much of the chronology that follows derives from Berger's book.

15. François Le Vau's project differed from the executed project in that the coupled-column peristyle and straight entablature ran below the attic story and the roofs of the main fabric and corner pavilions. See Berger, *Palace of the Sun*, pls. 24–32.

16. See, for instance, Rykwert, *First Moderns*, 30–1.

17. According to Charles Perrault, the king's decision was indicated by his silence with regard to the question of whether the project should be carried out. See *Charles Perrault: Memoirs of My Life*, trans. Jeanne Morgan Zarucchi (Columbia: University of Missouri Press, 1989), 77–8.

18. The initial proceedings of this council are chronicled in detail by Berger, *Palace of the Sun*, 25–45.

19. See Herrmann, *Theory of Claude Perrault*, 18. Another excellent study devoted to Perrault is Antoine Picon's *Claude Perrault, 1613–1688, ou La Curiosité d'un Classique* (Paris: Picard, 1988).

20. See "Dessein d'un Obélisque," in Claude Perrault, *Voyage à Bordeaux* (Paris: Renouard, 1909), 234–41. The project was not built.

21. For details of the observatory, see Michel Petzet, "Claude Perrault als Architekt des Pariser Observatoriums," *Zeitschrift für Kunstgeschichte* (Munich: Deutscher Kunstverlag, 1967): 1–53.

22. This seems to be the consensus viewpoint, based on the research that has been devoted to this problem over the last thirty years.

23. These changes are described by Berger, *Palace of the Sun*, 35–40. Berger also argues that Perrault's changes were made under the direct influence of Roland Fréart de Chambray, who was advising the committee on the project.

24. See Berger (in collaboration with Rowland J. Mainstone), *Palace of the Sun*, 65–74.

25. In Perrault's translation, *Les dix livres d'architecture de Vitruve* (Paris: Coignard, 1673). The first two chapters are condensed into one, hence the relevant passage is listed in the second chapter.

26. Ibid., 76. "Le goust de nostre siecle, ou du moins de nostre nation, est different de deluy des Anciens & peut-estre qu'en cela il tient un peu du Gothique: car nous aimons l'air le jour & les dégagemens. Cela nous a fait inventer une sixiéme maniere de disposer ces Colonnes, qui est de les accoupler & de les joindre deux à deux, & de mettre aussi l'espace de deux entre-colonnemens en un.... Cela a esté fait à l'imitation d'Hermogene.... Cette maniere pourroit estre apellée *Pseudosystyle*" (original spelling and accentuation).

27. Perrault, *Voyage à Bordeaux*, 155. Perrault continues: "La voûte qui est en berceau, ayant des fenêtres qui ne s'élèvent pas jusque en haut comme en l'ordre gothique, mais qui sont en lunette, est portée sur de grosses colonnes qui ont leurs bases de chapiteaux approchant assez de l'ordre antique." For sketches of this trip, see Herrmann, *Theory of Claude Perrault*, p. 27 and pls. 20–2. See also Robin D. Middleton, "The Abbé de Cordemoy and the Graeco-Gothic Ideal: A Prelude to Romantic Classicism," *Journal of the Warburg and Courtauld Institutes* 25 (1962): 298.

28. Berger suggests that the desire to see the Piliers de Tutelle was the reason Perrault undertook his trip to the south (*Palace of the Sun*, 99–103).

29. See Berger, *Palace of the Sun*, 47–52.

30. Wolfgang Herrmann has chosen these words for his translation of Marc-Antoine Laugier's use of the word *âpreté* in *Essay on Architecture* (London: Hennessey & Ingalls, 1977).

31. See Lemmonier, *Procès-Verbaux de l'Académie Royale d'Architecture*, 1:87.

32. François Blondel, *Cours d'architecture* (Paris, 1698 ed.), 237.

33. Ibid., 232–6.

34. See Pierre Patte, *Mémoires sur les objets les plus importans de l'architecture* (Paris: Rozet, 1769), 269–75.

35. Blondel, *Cours d'architecture*, 2:230. "Je m'estonne, dis-je, qu'ils n'ayent pas veu la difference qu'il y a entre ces restes qui ont l'approbation universelle & ces bâtimens demi Gothiques ou les Anciens ont couplé des Colonnes ou des Pilastres."

36. Ibid., 235. "Je n'ay rien à dire sur cette amour que l'on attribue à nostre Nation pour le jour & les degagemens, puisqu'on avoüe en même temps qu'il tient encore du Gothique, & qu'il est en cela fort different du goust des Anciens."

37. Ibid. "Il est pourtant tres veritable que c'est ce même raisonnement qui a ouvert la porte de tout temps au dereglement qui se trouve dans l'Architecture & dans les autres Arts.... Les Architectes Goths n'ont rempli leurs edifices de tant d'impertinences, que parce qu'ils ont cru qu'il leur étoit permis d'ajoûter aux inventions des Grecs & des Romains."

38. Perrault, *Les dix livres d'architecture* (Paris, 1684), 79–80, n. 16. "La principale objection sur laquelle on appuye le plus, est fondée sur un prejugé & sur la fausse supposition qu'il n'est permis de se départir des usages des Anciens; que tout ce qui n'imite pas leurs manieres doit passer pour bizarre & pour capricieux, & que si cette Loy n'est inviolablement gardée, on ouvre la porte à une licence qui met le déreglement dans tous les Arts. Mais comme cette raison prouve trop, elle ne doit rien prouver: car il y a beaucoup plus d'inconvient à fermer la porte aux belle inventions, qu'à l'ouvrir à celle qui estant ridicules se doivent détruire d'elle-mesmes.... Mais le plus grand reproche que l'on croit faire à nostre Pseudosystyle est de dire qu'il tient du Gothique. J'estois demeuré d'accord du fait dans ma notte; mais supposé que le Gothique en general, & à considerer tout ce qui le compose ne fust pas le plus beau genre d'Architecture, je ne pensois pas que tout ce qui est dans le Gothique fut à rejetter. Le jour dans les Edifices & les dégagemens dont il s'agit, sont des choses en quoy les Gothiques different des Anciens: mais ce n'est pas en cela que le Gothique est à reprendre."

39. Claude Perrault, *Ordonnance of the Five Kinds of Columns after the Method of the Ancients*, trans. Indra Kagis McEwen (Santa Monica, Calif.: Getty Publications Program, 1993), 52. Originally published as *Ordonnance des cinq espèces de colonnes selon la méthode des anciens* (Paris: Jean Baptiste Coignard, 1683).

40. Fréart de Chambray, *Parallèle de l'Architecture antique avec la Moderne*.

41. See Wolfgang Herrmann, "Antoine Desgodets and the Académie Royale d'Architecture," *The Art Bulletin*, March 1958, 23–53.

42. Antoine Desgodetz, *Les Edifices antiques de Rome dessinés et mesurés très exactement* (Paris: J. B. Coignard, 1682).

43. Desgodetz's drawings were examined by the academy in the last session of 1677 (13 December) and on one occasion in 1678, but no conclusions were reached from these discussions. The book itself, which appeared in 1682, was not considered by the academy until 1694, or eight years after Blondel's death. There were also other reasons contributing to the silence about the book in 1682. Colbert, for one thing, was quickly losing favor with the king, and he would die in the following year. By this time, his successor, Michel le Tellier Louvois, had implemented austerity measures that limited academic theoretical discussion.

44. Perrault, *Ordonnance of the Five Kinds of Columns*, 54.

45. Perrault, preface to *Les dix livres*, 12 n. 3, 100 n. 1, 102 n. 2. See also Herrmann's treatment of this issue and related ones in *The Theory of Claude Perrault*, 132 ff.

46. Perrault, preface to *Ordonnance of the Five Kinds of Columns*, 50.

47. Ibid., 51.

48. Perrault's treatise, for instance, precedes by seven years John Locke's *Essay Concerning Human Understanding* (1690).

49. Perrault, *Ordonnance of the Five Kinds of Columns*, 48–9.

50. Ibid., 52.

51. Ibid., 57.

52. Charles had his poem read to the academy by his friend the Abbé de Lavau. He published it at the conclusion of the first part of his *Parallèle des anciens et des modernes en ce qui regarde les arts et les sciences: Dialogues* (1692–7; reprint, Geneva: Slatkine Reprints, 1971), 79–85. See also Rykwert's account of the quarrel in *The First Moderns*, 24–8.

53. For a detailed history of the quarrel, see Hippolyte Rigault, *Histoire de la Querelle des Anciens et des Modernes* (Paris: Hachette et cie: 1856): 146. Voltaire later insisted that many parts of the debate were personal. In his *Age of Louis XIV* (14:242 n. 1), he suggested Boileau's hostility toward the Perraults was due to a "private pique." In the article "Ancients and Moderns," of his *Philosophical Dictionary*, Voltaire characterized the dispute in this way: "Boileau seeks only to vindicate Homer against Perrault, at the same time gliding adroitly over the faults of the Greek poet, and the slumber with which Horace reproaches him. He strove to turn Perrault, the enemy of Homer, into ridicule.... But it is not at all improbable that Perrault, though often mistaken, was frequently right" (3:160–1 n. 6).

54. Among the many famous fairy tales he authored were Little Red Riding Hood, Cinderella, Sleeping Beauty, and Bluebeard.

55. Rigault, *Histoire de la Querelle des Anciens et des Modernes*, 49.

56. Charles Perrault's memo "Dessin d'un Portail pour l'Église de Sainte-Geneviève a Paris" was first published by Michel Petzet, under the title "Un Projet des Perrault pour l'Église Sainte-Geneviève à Paris," in *Bulletin Monumental* 115, pt. 2 (1957): 81–95.

57. Perrault, *Les dix livres*, pls. XXXIV, XXXV, XL, LIV.

58. Petzet, "Un Projet des Perrault pour l'Église Sainte-Geneviève à Paris," 92.

59. See Pierre Bourget and Georges Cattaui, *Jules Hardouin Mansart* (Paris: Éditions Vincent, 1960), 161–2.

60. See Blunt, *Art and Architecture in France*, 223–4.

61. See Middleton, "The Abbé de Cordemoy and the Graeco-Gothic Ideal," 290–9.

62. Philibert de L'Orme, *Premier tome de l'architecture* (Paris: Federic Morel, 1567). See bk. 4, chaps. 8–10. De L'Orme referred to Gothic vaulting as "la voute moderne."

63. André Duschesne (1584–1640) was an antiquarian. His study of 1609 was entitled *Les Antiquités et recherches des villes, châteaux et places les plus remarquables de toute la France*. One of the first structural assessments of Gothic architecture was carried out by the architect and mathematician François Derand (1591–1644); his findings were published in *L'Architecture des voûtes, ou l'art des traits et coûpes des voûtes* (1643). Both men are discussed by Middleton, "The Abbé de Cordemoy and the Graeco-Gothic Ideal," 293, 296.

64. The academy, after reading parts of Scamozzi, began reading the fifth chapter of de L'Orme on 23 November 1676 and continued

intermittently until October 1677. See Lemonnier, *Procès-Verbaux de l'Académie Royale d'Architecture*, 1:125–53.

65. Ibid., 168–248. Colbert's request was read to the academy by Perrault on 12 July 1678. The academicians visited Notre Dame de Chartres on 3 September.

66. Jean-François Félibien, *Historique de la vie et des ouvrages des plus célèbres architectes* (Paris: Trevoux, 1725).

67. Ibid., preface, 15.

68. Ibid., bk. 4, 20–1.

69. Ibid., 21.

70. Ibid., 210.

71. Middleton, "The Abbé de Cordemoy and the Graeco-Gothic Ideal."

72. Michel de Frémin, *Memoires critiques d'architecture* (Paris: Charles Saugrain, 1702), avertissement. On Frémin, see Dorothea Nyberg, "The *Mémoirs critiques d'architecture* by Michel de Frémin," *Journal of the Society of Architectural Historians* 22 (December 1963): 217–24.

73. Ibid.

74. Ibid., chap. 44.

75. Ibid., 34.

76. Ibid., 37.

77. Ibid., 30–1.

78. Ibid., 27–9.

79. The discussion of Frémin's book, as Nyberg reported (see "*Mémoires critiques d'architecture*, by Michel de Frémin," 219) seems to have taken place at the meetings held on 2 July and 9 July 1704, although Frémin is not specifically named as the author of the work under discussion. The academy proceedings indicate that the book contains useful discussion on the materials used in basements. See Lemonnier, *Procès-Verbaux de l'Académie Royale d'Architecture*, 3:196.

80. For a discussion of Cordemoy's life and theory, see Middleton, "The Abbé de Cordemoy and the Graeco-Gothic Ideal," and his article in the *Macmillian Encyclopedia of Architects* (New York: The Free Press, 1982), 1:453.

81. Jean-Louis de Cordemoy, *Nouveau Traité de toute l'architecture or l'art de Bastir; utile aux entrepreneurs et aux ouvriers*, 2nd ed. (Paris: Coignard, 1714), 52. "... puisqu'elle a seule, & cette beauté qui résulte de l'âpreté ou du serrement des Colonnes, qui plaisoit tant aux Ancients, & ce dégagement que les Modernes recherchent avec tant de soin."

82. Ibid., 109. "... ne seroit-elle pas infiniment plus belle, si au lieu de toutes ces inutiles & pesantes arcades, de ces Pilastres & ces larges Piédroits, qui occupent mal-à-propos bien de la place, & qui causent nécessairement de l'obscurité, on n'y eût mis que des Colonnes pour porter le reste de l'édifice tel qu'il est? Son Dôme, si beau d'ailleurs, ne l'auroit-il pas été davantage, s'il eût été soûtenu par une Colonnade, plûtôt que par les quatre arcades, sur lesquelles il porte à faux?"

83. Ibid., 111. "Je regarderois en effet une Eglise dans le goût du Portique de l'entrée du Louvre, ou de celuy de l'invention de l'Illustre P. de Creil à l'Abbaye de Sainte Geneviéve de Paris, comme la plus belle chose du monde."

84. For Frézier's remarks, see Middleton, "The Abbé de Cordemoy and the Graeco-Gothic Ideal," 287–90.

85. Various letters and responses were published in the *Mémoires de Trévoux*, September 1709, July 1710, August 1710, September 1711, and July 1712.

86. Cordemoy, *Nouveau Traité de toute l'architecture or l'art de bastir*, 135 ff. "Extrait d'une lettre de l'auteur au R. P. de Tournemine Jesuite, pour servir de réponse aux Remarques de M. Frezier Ingénieur Ordinaire du Roy, insérées dans le *Journal de Trevoux* du mois de Septembre 1709."

2. The Enlightenment and Neoclassical Theory

1. On this issue, see Richard A. Etlin's chapter "The System of the Home," in *Symbolic Space: French Enlightenment Architecture and its Legacy* (Chicago: University of Chicago Press, 1994), and Michel Gallet, *Stately Mansions: Eighteenth Century Paris Architecture* (New York: Praeger, 1972).

2. What prompted Diderot's text was recent surgery that cured the congenital blindness of a woman. The problem, first discussed by John Locke (*An Essay on Human Understanding*, bk. 2, chap. 9. sect. 8), was whether a person born blind, and having learned to distinguish by touch the difference between a cube and a sphere, would be able to distinguish them, without touching them, if sight were restored. Condillac considered it again in his *Essai sur l'origine des connaissances humaines* (1846), pt. 1, sect. 6.

3. See the Prospectus in *Oeuvres complètes de Diderot*, ed. J. Assézat (Paris: Garnier Frères, 1876), 8:129–64.

4. Jean Le Rond d'Alembert, *Preliminary Discourse to the Encyclopedia of Diderot*, trans. Richard N. Schwab (Indianapolis: Bobbs-Merrill, 1981).

5. See *Encyclopédie, ou Dictionnaire raisonné des Sciences, des Arts et des métiers, par une société de Gens de Lettres* (1751; reprint, New York: Readex Microprint Corporation, 1969), 616–18. See also Joseph Rykwert, *The First Moderns: The Architects of the Eighteenth Century* (Cambridge: M.I.T. Press, 1980), 417–18, 474 n. 24.

6. French censorship laws had been broadened in 1723 and prohibited everything that questioned matters of religion, public order, and sound morality. The laws were more loosely interpreted in 1750 when Chrétien Guillaume de Lamoignon de Malesherbes was appointed chief censor. Malesherbes supported the encyclopedia project and Diderot, but even he was not always successful in thwarting the opposition. With the assassination attempt on Louis XIV in 1757, the laws again became more strictly enforced.

7. J. J. Rousseau, *The First and Second Discourse*, ed. Roger D. Masters, trans. Roger D. Masters and Judith R. Masters (New York: St. Martin's Press, 1964), 38.

8. Ibid., 141.

9. Ibid., 181.

10. The trip was carefully planned in its most minute details by the Marquise de Pompadour herself, who in the course of thirty-one letters counseled her younger brother throughout. Some of these letters are published in the account of Edmond and Jules de Goncourt, *Madame de Pompadour* (Paris: Fremin-Didot, 1888), 75–82. She referred to Soufflot as "a very gifted architect" in a letter of 1749 to the Duc de Nivernais, cited by Nancy Mitford, *Madame de Pompadour* (New York: Harper & Row, 1958), 140.

The classic work on Soufflot's life and career is Jean Monval, *Soufflot, Sa vie. Son oeuvre. Son esthétique* (Paris: Alphonse Lemerre, 1918). See also *Soufflot et son temps (1780–1980)* (Paris: Caisse Nationale des Monuments Historiques et des Sites, 1980), and the chapter on him in Allan Braham, *The Architecture of the French Enlightenment* (Berkeley: University of California Press, 1989).

11. J. J. Soufflot, "Mémoire sur les proportions de l'architecture," in Michel Petzet, *Soufflots Sainte-Geneviève und der französische Kirchenbau des 18. Jahrhunderts* (Berlin: Walter de Gruyter, 1961), 132.

12. Ibid., 135.

13. J. J. Soufflot, "Mémoire sur l'architecture gothique," in Petzet, *Soufflots Sainte-Geneviève*, 136.

14. Ibid., 140. "Quand à la construction, pour peu qu'on examine celle des églises gothiques, on verra qu'elle est plus ingénieuse, plus hardie, et même plus difficile que celle des nôtres."

15. Ibid., 142. Wolfgang Herrmann, in *Laugier and Eighteenth Century French Theory* (London: Zwemmer, 1962), points out that the Latin sentence added to this passage – *Omne tulit punctum qui miscuit utile dulci* (He has gained every vote who blends the useful with the agreeable) – derives from Horace (p. 82).

16. For a discussion of this paper, see Herrmann, *Laugier and Eighteenth Century French Theory*, 81, app. VIII, 5.

17. For comments on Frézier's paper "Dissertation historique et critique sur les orders d'architecture," see Robin Middleton, "The Abbé de Cordemoy and the Graeco-Gothic Ideal: A Prelude to Romantic Classicism," *Journal of the Warburg and Courtault Institutes* 25 (1962): 290.

18. See Herrmann, *Laugier and Eighteenth Century French Theory*, 81, app. VIII, 5.

19. Soufflot, "Mémoire pour servir de solution à cette question: savoir si dans l'art de l'architecture le goût est préférable à la science des règles ou la sciences des règles au goût," in *Nouvelles archives statisques, historiques et littéraires de départment du Rhône* (Lyons: Barret, 1832), 1:113.

20. Ibid., 114, 116.

21. Soufflot was presented to the Academy of Architecture in November 1749, shortly after his selection to accompany the future marquis. Marigny was able to advance his promotion to the first class in 1755.

22. The drawings were published by Dumont in 1764, under the title *Suite de plans, coupes, profils . . . de Pesto . . . mesurés et dessinés par J. G. Soufflot, architecte du roy en 1750.*

23. For details of the design and construction of the church, see Petzet, *Soufflots Sainte-Geneviève.*

24. Maximilien de Brébion, "Mémoire à Monsieur Le Comte de la Billarderie d'Angiviller Directeur et Ordonnateur Général des Bâtimens" (1780), published in Petzet, *Soufflots Sainte-Geneviève*, 147. "Le principal objet de M. Soufflot en bâtissant son église, a été de réunir sous une des plus belles formes la légèreté de la construction des édifices gothiques avec la pureté et la magnificence de l'architecture grecque."

25. See Anton Picon, *French Architects and Engineers*, trans. Martin Thom (New York: Cambridge University Press, 1992), 142–4.

26. Patte's letter, "Mémoire sur la construction du dôme projeté pour couronner l'église de Sainte-Geneviève," stirred a controversy when it was published in 1770. Both Soufflot and Perronet published replies in *Mercure* (April 1770), and Gauthy responded with his "Mémoire sur l'application des principes de la méchanique à la construction des voûtes et des dômes" in 1771. For the details of this dispute, see Picon, *French Architects and Engineers*, 168–80.

27. See Braham, *Architecture of the French Enlightenment*, 56, 77.

28. Rykwert, *First Moderns*, 453. Both Rykwert and Braham provide extensive and masterful analyses of this church.

29. The classic work on Laugier is Herrmann, *Laugier and Eighteenth Century French Theory*.

30. Laugier had schooling in Lyons in the 1730s, although the precise dates are unknown. Rykwert points out that the Jesuits in the first half of the century maintained a strong intellectual presence within the Lyons Academy, and thus Soufflot's views would have been known to many within the Jesuit community. Laugier may even have heard reports of Soufflot's lecture on Gothic architecture in 1741 when living in Avignon or Nîmes. See Rykwert, *First Moderns*, 444–5.

31. See Herrmann, *Laugier and Eighteenth Century French Theory*, 205. Herrmann's book contains part of the letter.

32. Friedrich Melchior Grimm, *Correspondance littéraire, philosophique et critique, adressée a un souverain d'Allemagne depuis 1753 jusqu'en 1769, par Le Baron de Grimm et par Diderot* (Paris: Longchamps, 1813), 100. "Cet ouvrage, dont on nous prépare une second édition fort augmentée, a eu un grand succès à Paris, dans le temps que son auteur se cachait soigneusement à Lyon."

33. Ibid., 103–4. "Le P. Laugier est jeune; il y a apparence que ses talens et son goût pour les arts ne resteront pas enseveli dans un cloître, et que nous le compterons bientôt dans le nombre des ex-jésuites qui ont fait honneur à la littérature."

34. M.-A. Laugier, *Observations sur l'architecture* (Paris: A La Haye, 1765).

35. Grimm, *Correspondance littéraire, philosophique et critique*, 101.

36. Marc-Antoine Laugier, *An Essay on Architecture*, trans. Wolfgang Herrmann and Anni Herrmann (Los Angeles: Hennessey & Ingalls, 1977), 8, 16, 20, 24, 26, 34, 37, 92, 104.

37. Ibid., 17, 20, 24, 37, 61, 104–5.

38. Ibid., 17.

39. Ibid., 23, 93, 101, 104.

40. Charles-Étienne Briseux, *Traité du beau essentiel dans les arts . . . avec un traité des proportions harmoniques* (Paris: Grange Bateliére, 1752), 2–3. On the theory of Briseux, see Hanno-Walter Kruft, *A History of Architectural Theory from Vitruvius to the Present*, trans. Royald Taylor, Elsie Callander, and Anthony Wood (New York: Zwemmer & Princeton Architectural Press, 1994), 146–8.

41. Briseux, *Traité du beau*, 46, 60.

42. Ibid., 4–5. "Il n'a donc pas été possible d'en constater de fixes, mais tous les auteurs sont d'accord sur la nécessité d'en observer."

43. Denis Diderot, "Recherches philosophiques sur l'origine et la nature du beau," in *Oeuvres complètes de Diderot*, ed. J. Assézat (Paris: Garnier Frères, 1876), 10:5–42.

44. Ibid., 27.

45. Ibid., 28–30.

46. On Diderot's sources, see R. Loyalty Cru, *Diderot as a Disciple of English Thought* (New York: Columbia University Press, 1913), 408–10.

47. Briseux, with La Font de Saint-Yenne, wrote a joint review, "Examen d'un Essai sur l'Architecture, *Journal de Trévoux*, March 1754. Frézier's review, "Remarques sur quelques livres nouveaux concernant la beauté et le bon goût de l'Architecture," was published in *Mercure de France*, July 1754. For details, see Herrmann, *Laugier and Eighteenth Century French Theory*, 148–60.

48. Laugier, *Essay on Architecture*, 1.

49. Ibid., 62.

50. Ibid., 63.

51. Ibid., 2.

52. Marc-Antoine Laugier, *Essai sur l'architecture* (1755; reprint Farnborough, England: Gregg Press, 1966), 255, 260. See also Laugier, *Essay on Architecture*, 63–4.

53. Laugier, *Essai sur l'architecture*, 260.

54. Ibid., 256.

55. Ibid., 257. "Je me représente ce beau primitif comme un point de perfection, qui résulte de l'assemblage d'une foule de qualités particulieres."

56. The reading began on 20 January 1755 and only continued until 17 March, and therefore it covered only the first two chapters. See Henry Lemonnier, *Procès-Verbaux de l'Académie royale d'Architecture* (Paris: Édouard Champion, 1920), 6:230–3.

57. Ibid., 7:219–21. The relevant parts of Blondel's *Cours* were read 15 July, 22 July, and 29 July 1765.

58. Fiske Kimball, *The Creation of the Rococo* (Philadelphia: Philadelphia Museum of Art, 1943), 152 ff.

59. Jean-François Blondel, *De la Distribution des maisons de plaisance* (Paris: Jombert, 1737–8), xv. The full passage reads: "Mon intention sur tout est d'engager ceux qui veuent professer l'Art de bâtir, à puiser dans l'ancienne Architecture les premiers élemens de cet Art, & que par là on accoûtume son génie à connoître ce qui est véritablement beau, & à éviter tout ce que les caprices de la nouveauté ont introduit depuis quelques années."

60. For Caylus's view on architecture and his interest in Soufflot, see Braham, *The Architecture of the French Enlightenment*, 32. For his views on painting, see Samuel Rocheblave, *Essai sur le Comte de Caylus: L'homme, l'artiste, l'antiquaire* (Paris: Hachette, 1889), 213–30. For more on Caylus, see Robin Middleton's introduction to Le Roy's *Ruins of the Most Beautiful Buildings in Greece* (Los Angeles: Getty Publications Program, 2004).

61. Laugier, *Essay on Architecture*, 61.

62. See Middleton, "The Abbé de Cordemoy and the Graeco-Gothic Ideal."

63. Construction of this large church, which shares many similarities with Ste.-Geneviève, never proceeded beyond the foundations. Napoleon later caused the design to be abandoned and in 1806 ordered a new church to be built based on a new design by Pierre Vignon.

64. J.-F. Blondel, *Discours sur la nécessité de l'étude de l'architecture* (Paris: Jombert, 1754), 88 n. Blondel also referred his readers to Cordemoy's treatise.

65. In responding to a letter from Marigny, Soufflot (in September 1758) recommended the publication of a manuscript on architectural theory by the architect Silvy based on the fact that Laugier was assisting Silvy on it. See Herrmann, *Laugier and Eighteenth Century French Theory*, 11–12, 153, 206.

66. Ibid., 173–5. Herrmann documents these passages extensively.

67. Ibid., 175–7.

68. See Robin Middleton and David Watkin, *Neoclassical and 19th Century Architecture* (New York: Electa, 1987), 195.

69. Goethe discussed Laugier's ideas in his famous anticlassical essay "On German Architecture," written about the Strasbourg Cathedral. Goethe insisted that the wall, not the column, was the essence of German architecture, and in his romantic idealism he opposed the burdening of architecture with precepts.

70. On Laugier's influence in this circle, see Fritz Neumeyer's introduction to *Friedrich Gilly: Essays on Architecture, 1796–1799* (Santa Monica, Calif.: Getty Publications Program, 1994), 33–5.

71. For a thorough examination of this claim, see Herrmann, *Laugier and Eighteenth Century French Theory*, 160–6.

72. On the students at the French Academy in Rome in the 1740s and 1750s, see Braham, *Architecture of the French Enlightenment*, 52–61, 83–107.

73. François Blondel, *Cours d'architecture enseigné dans l'Academie Royale d'Architecture* (Paris: Lambert Roullandm, 1675), 1:4.

74. Roland Fréart de Chambray, *Parallèle de l'architecture antique avec la moderne* (Paris, 1650), 3.

75. Blondel, *De la Distribution des maisons de plaisance*, xii.

76. Laugier, *Essay on Architecture*, 8. Laugier underscores this theme in stronger terms a few pages later: "It is therefore true that architecture is only under moderate obligation to the Romans and that it owes everything that is valuable and solid to the Greeks alone" (p. 40).

77. On this confusion, see Kruft, *History of Architectural Theory*, 215–17.

78. On the relationship between Soufflot and the Gazzoli circle see S. Lang, "The Early Publications of the Temples at Paestum," *Journal of the Warburg and Courtauld Institutes* 13 (1950): 48–64.

79. Ibid.

80. Jacques-Philippe d'Orville, *Sicula, quibus Siciliae Veteris Rudera*, 2 vols. (Amsterdam, 1764).

81. J. J. Winckelmann, "Anmerkungen über die Baukunst der alten Tempel zu Girgenti in Sicilien," in *Johann Winckelmanns sämtliche Werke*, ed. Joseph Eiselein (Donauöschingen: Verlage deutscher Classiker, 1825), 2:306. "Der sogenannte Tempel der Concordia zu Girgenti ist ohne Zweifel eines der ältesten griechischen Gebäude in der Welt, und hat sich von aussen unbeschädigt erhalten."

82. For instance, the British ambassador to Constantinople from 1621 to 1628, Thomas Roe, served as an agent for the Duke of Buckingham and the Earl of Arundel. See Fani-Maria Tsigakou, *The Rediscovery of Greece: Travellers and Painters of the Romantic Era* (New Rochelle, N.Y.: Caratzas Brothers, 1981). See also Robin Middleton's incomparable discussion of the history of the growing knowledge of Greece in his introduction to *Julien-David Le Roy: The Ruins of the Most Beautiful Monuments of Greece*.

83. Jacob Spon, *Voyage d'Italie, de Dalmatie, de Grèce, et du Levant* (Lyons, 1678).

84. Fischer's study – for its feverish imagination, one of the most spectacular studies of world architecture ever produced – was entitled *Entwurff einer historischen Architekur* (1725).

85. Richard Pococke, *Description of the East ... and Some Other Countries*, 2 vols. (London, 1743–5). Richard Dalton visited Egypt, Turkey, and Greece with Lord Charlemont in 1749 and published engravings in 1751; his *Antiquities and Views of Greece and Egypt* appeared only in 1791.

86. Robert Wood and James Dawkins, *The Ruins of Palmyra, otherwise Tedmor in the Desart* (London, 1753); idem, *The Ruins of Balbec, otherwise Heliopolis in Coelosyria* (London, 1757).

87. Wood and Dawkins, *The Ruins of Palmyra*, 1.

88. Wood and Dawkins, *The Ruins of Balbec*, 6.

89. James Stuart and Nicholas Revett, preface to *The Antiquities of Athens* (London: John Haberkorn, 1762), v. n. For details of Stuart's life and career, see David Watkin, *Athenian Stuart: Pioneer of the Greek Revival* (London: George Allen & Unwin, 1982).

90. Ibid.

91. For these and other details of Stuart and Revett's journey, see Dora Wiebenson, *Sources of Greek Revival Architecture* (University Park: Pennsylvania State University Press, 1969).

92. Le Roy was thus the subject of bad reports sent from Rome back to Marigny in Paris. See Wiebenson, *Sources of Greek Revival Architecture*, 33 n. 58.

93. Published in Wiebenson, *Sources of Greek Revival Architecture*, 85–7.

94. Cochin notes this in his *Mémoires inédits de Charles-Nicolas Cochin* (Paris: Baur, 1880), 78–9.

95. Cited from Wiebenson, *Sources of Greek Revival Architecture*, 102.

96. Julien-David Le Roy, *Les ruines des plus beaux monuments de la Grece* (Paris: Guerin & Delatour, 1758), 1:vii. See also Wiebenson, *Sources of Greek Revival Architecture*, 34.

97. On the great importance of Le Lorrain, see Rykwert, *First Moderns*, 357–63; Middleton and Watkin, *Neoclassical and 19th Century Architecture*, 69–70; and Braham, *Architecture of the French Enlightenment*, 58–9. On Piranesi's connection with the French Academy, see John Wilton-Ely, *The Mind and Art of Giovanni Battista Piranesi* (London: Thames & Hudson, 1978), 21. On his life and work of Panini, see Michael Kiene, *Giovanni Paolo Pannini: Römische Veduten aus dem Louvre* (Braunschweig: Herzog Anton Ulrich-Museum, 1993).

98. "Lovers of Polite Literature" is a phase taken from Stuart and Revett's first proposal for a tour of Greece. See Wiebenson, *Sources of Greek Revival Architecture*, 77.

99. Le Roy, *Les ruines des plus beaux monuments de la Grece*, 1:ix.

100. Ibid., 1:xiii.

101. Ibid., 2:ii.

102. Julien-David Le Roy, *Histoire de la disposition et des formes différentes que les chrétiens ont données à leurs temples depuis le règne de Constantin le Grand jusqu' à nous* (Paris: Dessaint & Seillant, 1764).

103. Ibid., 59.

104. The principal biography of Winckelmann remains Carl Justi's *Winckelmann und seine Zeitgenossen*, 3 vols. (Leipzig: F. C. W. Vogel, 1923). See also David Irwin's introduction to *Winckelmann: Writings on Art* (New York: Phaidon, 1972).

105. English translation by David Irwin in *Winckelmann: Writings on Art*, 61–85. See also Johann Joachim Winckelmann, *Reflection on the Imitation of Greek Works in Painting and Sculpture*, trans. Elfriede Heyer & Roger C. Norton (La Salle, Ill.: Open Court, 1987).

106. The German phrase is "eine edle Einfalt, und eine stille Grösse." The German word "stille," like the English "still," connotes not only the notion of stillness but in this instance also an imperturbable or superhuman poise. The phrase "noble simplicity" is used increasingly from the 1740s on, particularly in French literature.

107. See Justi, *Winckelmann*, 2:403.

108. Winckelmann, *Anmerkungen über die Baukunst der Alten*, in *Johann Winckelmanns Sämtliche Werke*, 1:347. On Winckelmann's disappointment with it, see Rykwert, *First Moderns*, 352.

109. Winkelmann, *Anmerkungen über die Baukunst der Alten*, 1:391–2.

110. Ibid., 441.

111. Ibid., 443.

112. Ibid., 470–1.

113. See the introduction by Alex Potts to J. J. Winckelmann, *The History of the Art of Antiquity*, trans. H. F. Mallgrave (Los Angeles: Getty Publications Program, 2005).

114. Mariette's letter was published in the supplement to the *Gazette Littéraire de l'Europe* on 4 November 1764. For the translation of the letter, Piranesi's response, and the debate in general, see G. B. Piranesi, *Observations on the Letter of Monsieur Mariette* (Los Angeles: Getty Publications Program, 2002).

115. On details of Lodoli's life and architectural ideas, see Emil Kaufmann, "Piranesi, Algarotti and Lodoli (A Controversy in XVIII Century Venice)," *Gazette des Beaux-Arts* 46 (July–August 1955): 21–8; Edgar Kaufmann Jr., "Memmo's Lodoli," *The Art Bulletin* 46 (March 1964): 159–72; idem, "Lodoli Architetto," *In Search of Modern Architecture: A Tribute to Henry-Russell Hitchcock*, ed. Helen Searing (New York: The Architectural History Foundation), 31–7; Rykwert, *First Moderns*, 288–326; Marco Frascari, "Sortes Architetii in the Eighteenth-Century Veneto" (Ph.D. diss., University of Pennsylvania, 1981).

116. Winckelmann first disparages Maffei in the preface to the *Geschichte* and makes repeated references to his errors throughout the text in footnotes.

117. Notes from the drafts were taken by Andrea Memmo and published in his *Elementi d'architettura Lodoliana: Ossia l'arte del fabbricare con solidità scientifica e con eleganza non capricciosa* (1834; reprint Milan: Mazzotta, 1973). They have been translated by Edgar Kaufmann Jr. in "Memmo's Lodoli," *The Art Bulletin* 46 (March 1964): 159–72.

118. "Memmo's Lodoli," 164.

119. Ibid., 165.

120. Interpretations of Piranesi's thought in relation to Lodoli's theory have diverged sharply. For instance, Emil Kaufmann Jr. (note 115) viewed Piranesi's *Parere su l'architettura* as "a refutation of Lodoli's doctrine," while Joseph Rykwert regards Piranesi as "Lodoli's most brilliant and most influential disciple" (*First Moderns*, p. 26).

121. Much has been published on the artistic development of Piranesi, but the best study in English is John Wilton-Ely's *The Mind and Art of Giovanni Battista Piranesi* (London: Thames & Hudson, 1978). Wilton-Ely has also edited the two volumes, *Giovanni Battista Piranesi: The Complete Etchings* (San Francisco: Alan Wofsy Fine Arts, 1994) and *Giovanni Battista Piranesi: The Polemical Works, Rome 1757, 1761, 1765, 1769* (Farnborough, England: Gregg, 1972).

122. G. B. Piranesi, *Le antichità romane*, 4 vols. (Rome: A. Rotilj, 1756).

123. Allan Ramsay, "Dialogue on Taste," *The Investigator* (London, 1762; facsimile in Yale University Library), 37–8.

124. Giambattista Vico's defense of Italian culture first appears in his book *The New Science* (1720). For Lodoli's relationship with Vico and the latter's influence on him, see Kaufmann, "Memmo's Lodoli." In defense of Etruscan autonomy, Piranesi cites A. F. Gori and Thomas Dempster, but his principal sounce, as Rudolf Wittkower has indicated, may have been M. Guarnacci ("Piranesi's 'Parere su l'architecture,'" *Journal of the Warburg Institute* 2 [1938–9]: 149).

125. Piranesi, *Della Magnificenza ed Architettura, de' Romani* (Rome, 1761), in *Giovanni Battista Piranesi: The Polemical Works*, fols. XIX, XCIX.

126. See especially plates 783–7, in *Giovanni Battista Piranesi: The Complete Etchings*, 2:851–5.

127. Ibid., pl. 780, p. 848.

128. See Piranesi, *Observations on the Letter of Monsieur Mariette*, 98.

129. Wittkower was the first to comment on this plate and point out the significance of the left hand. See Wittkower, "Piranesi's 'Parere su l'architettura,'" 151.

130. Piranesi, *Observations on the Letter of Monsieur Mariette*, 94.

131. Ibid., 95.

132. Ibid., 101.

133. Ibid., 106.

134. Ibid., 108.

135. Ibid., 111.

136. Giovanni Battista Piranesi, "An Apologetical Essay in Defence of the Egyptian and Tuscan Architecture," in *Divers Manners of Ornamenting Chimneys*, in Wilton-Ely, *Giovanni Battista Piranesi: The Polemical Works*, 28–9.

137. Ibid., 5–6.

138. Ibid., 33.

139. For details on Gabriel's life and works, see Georges Gromort, *Ange-Jacques Gabriel* (Paris: Vincent Fréal, 1933), and Christopher Tadgell, *Ange-Jacques Gabriel* (London: Zwemmer, 1978).

140. See Fiske Kimball, *The Creation of the Rococo* (Philadelphia: Philadelphia Museum of Art, 1943), 218–19.

141. Perhaps the best discussion of Goindoin, who lacks a monograph, occurs in Braham, *Architecture of the French Enlightenment*, 137–45.

142. See Anthony Vidler's *Claude-Nicolas Ledoux: Architecture and Social Reform at the End of the Ancient Régime* (Cambridge: M.I.T. Press, 1990). See also Michel Gallet, *Claude-Nicolas Ledoux, 1736–1806* (Paris: Picard, 1980), and Emil Kaufmann, *Three Revolutionary Architects: Boullée, Ledoux, and Lequeu* (Philadelphia: American Philosophical Society, 1952). For Ledoux's engravings, see C. N. Ledoux, *L'Architecture* (Princeton: Princeton Architectural Press, 1984).

143. See Jennifer Montagu, *The Expression of the Passions; The Origin and Influence of Charles Le Brun's Conférence sur l'expression générale et particulière* (New Haven: Yale University Press, 1994).

144. See Germain Boffrand, *Book of Architecture: Containing the General Principles of the Art*, trans. David Britt, ed. Caroline van Eck (Aldershot, England: Ashgate Publishing, 2002).

145. Ibid., 8.

146. Ibid., 10–11.

147. Ibid., 11.

148. Ibid., 9.

149. Ibid.

150. Two articles of interest regarding Blondel are W. Knight Sturges, "Jacques François Blondel," *Journal of the Society of Architectural Historians* 11 (1952): 16–19, and Robin Middleton, "Jacques François Blondel and the *Cours d'architecture*," *Journal of the Society of Architectural Historians* 18 (1959): 140–8.

151. J.-F. Blondel, *Cours d'architecture ou traité de la décoration, distribution & construction des Bâtiments; contenant les leçons données en 1750 & les années suivantes* (Paris: Desaint, 1771–7), 1:373. "N'en doutons point, c'est par le secours de ces nuances imperceptibles qu'on parvient à mettre une distinction réelle dans les projets de deux bâtiments de même genre, mais qui néanmoins doivent s'annoncer différemment, en préférant dans l'un style sublime, noble, élevé; dans l'autre un caractere naif, simple, vrai."

152. Ibid., 3:lxxi. "C'est le goût qui établit, qui détermine le style propre à chaque genre de Bâtiment, & qui, guidé par le raisonnement de l'Architecte, lui fait varier ses façades à l'infini."

153. The classic work to first address this issue was Emil Kaufmann's *Architecture in the Age of Reason: Baroque and Post-Baroque in England, Italy, and France* (Cambridge: Harvard University, 1955).

154. Nicolas Le Camus de Mézières, *The Genius of Architecture; or the Analogy of that Art with our Sensations*. trans. David Britt, introduction by Robin Middleton (Santa Monica, Calif.: Getty Publications Program, 1992), 70.

155. Ibid., 71.

156. Ibid., 75.

157. Jean-Louis Viel de Saint-Maux, *Lettres sur l'architecture des anciens et celle des modernes* (1787; reprint, Geneva: Minkoff, 1974), 4:13.

158. Ibid., 19.

159. Ibid., 22.

160. Ibid., 7:47 n. 15, 58 n. 29.

161. Ibid., 59 n. 32.

162. Ibid., 23.

163. Two studies in English focused on Boullée and his work are Jean-Marie Pérouse de Montclos, *Etienne-Louis Boullée, 1728–1799: Theoretician of Revolutionary Architecture* (London: Thames & Hudson, 1974), and Helen Rosenau, *Boullée and Visionary Architecture, Including Boullée's 'Architecture, Essay on Art'* (New York: Harmony Books, 1976). See also Kaufmann, *Three Revolutionary Architects*, and Etlin, *Symbolic Space*.

164. Boullée, "Architecture, Essay on Art," in Rosenan, *Boullée and Visionary Architecture*, 87.

165. Ibid., 89.

166. Ibid.
167. Ibid., 105.
168. Vidler, *Claude-Nicolas Ledoux*, 312.
169. This is how he has been primarily characterized since Kaufmann's *Three Revolutionary Architects*.
170. C.-N. Ledoux, *L'architecture considerée sous le rapport de l'art, des moeurs et de la législation* (Paris, 1804), 3. "Le caractère des monuments, comme leur nature, sert à la propagation et à l'epuration des moeurs."
171. Ibid., 10.
172. Ibid., 13.
173. Ibid., 15–16. "L'Architecture est à la maçonnerie ce que la poésie est aux belles letters: c'est l'enthousiasme dramatique du métier; on ne peut en parler qu'avec exaltation. Si le dessein donne la forme, c'est elle qui répand le charme qui anime toutes les productions. Comme il n'y a pas d'uniformité dans la pensée, il ne peut y en avoir dans l'expression."
174. A.-C. Quatremère de Quincy, *Encyclopédie méthodique. Architecture* vol. 1 (Paris: Panckoucke, 1788). See also the articles on "Bossages," "Barrières," and "Dorique."
175. Charles-François Viel, *Décadence de l'architecture à la fin du dix-huitième siècle* (Paris, 1800), 9.

3. British Theory in the Eighteenth Century

1. Of Bacon's writings, see especially the forty-fifth essay, "On Building," in *The Essayes or Counsels, Civill and Morall* (1625). Locke's great masterpiece of empirical thought was *An Essay Concerning Human Understanding* (1690).
2. See Rudolf Wittkower, "Classical Theory and Eighteenth-Century Sensibility," in *Palladio and English Palladianism* (London: Thames & Hudson, 1974), 195.
3. David Hume, *A Treatise of Human Nature: Being an Attempt to introduce the experimental Method of Reasoning into Moral Subjects* (London: Noon, 1739–40),
4. Both the transcriptions of Inigo Jones and his copy of Palladio's treatise have been reproduced in *Inigo Jones on Palladio, being the notes by Inigo Jones in the copy of I Quattro Libri dell architettura di Andrea Palladio 1601*, 2 vols. (Newcastle-upon-Tyne: Oriel Press, 1970). On Jones, see John Summerson, *Inigo Jones* (New York: Yale University Press, 2000).
5. The design of the Banqueting House should also be considered together with Jones's often repeated warning against Mannerist tendencies introduced by Michelangelo: "And to saie trew all thes composed ornaments the wch Procced out of ye abundance of dessigners and wear brought in by Michill Angell and his followers in my oppignion do not well in sollid Architecture." See also John Summerson, *Architecture in Britain 1530–1830* (Harmondsworth, England: Penguin, 1963), 67.
6. Henry Wotton, *The Elements of Architecture Collected by Henry Wotton Knight, from the best Authors and Examples* (London: John Bill, 1724).
7. See John Harris, Stephen Orgen, and Roy Strong, *The King's Arcadia: Inigo Jones and the Stuart Court* (London: Arts Council of Great Britain, 1973), 56, 62.
8. Letter to Bishop Fell, 26 May 1681. Quoted from Eduard F. Sekler, *Wren and His Place in European Architecture* (London: Faber & Faber, 1956), 74. See also Lisa Jardine, *On a Grander Scale: The Outstanding Life of Christopher Wren* (New York: Harper Collins, 2002); Adrian Tinniswood, *His Invention so Fertile: A Life of Christopher Wren* (London: Jonathan Cape, 2001); Kerry Downes, *The Architecture of Wren* (Reading, England: Redhedge, 1988).
9. See "Letter to a Friend from Paris," in *Wren's "Tracts" on Architecture and Other Writings*, ed. Lydia M. Soo (New York: Cambridge University Press, 1998), 103–5.
10. Ibid., 104.
11. Ibid., "Tract I," 153.
12. Ibid., 154.
13. See J. A. Bennett, "Christopher Wren: The Natural Causes of Beauty," *Architectural History* 15 (1972): 17.
14. Wren, "Tract II," in *Wren's "Tracts,"* 157.
15. Ibid., "Tract I," 155.
16. John Summerson, "The Mind of Wren," in *Heavenly Mansions and other Essays on Architecture* (New York: Norton, 1963), 62.
17. See, for instance, Soo's interpretation of his work through the notion of "instrumentality" in *Wren's "Tracts,"* 197. For other interpretations of Wren, see Downes, *Architecture of Wren*.
18. See Tracts III, IV, and V in *Wren's "Tracts,"* 167–95.
19. On Hawksmoor, see Kerry Downes, *Hawksmoor* (London: Zwemmer, 1959); Vaughan Hart, *Nicholas Hawksmoor: Rebuilding Ancient Wonders* (New Haven: Yale University Press, 2002); and Peter Ackroyd, *Hawksmoor* (London: Hamish Hamilton, 1985). On Vanbrugh, see Kerry Downes, *Vanbrugh* (London: Zwemmer, 1977), and Geoffrey Beard, *The Work of John Vanbrugh* (London: B. T. Batsford, 1986).
20. Downes, *Hawksmoor*, 147–51.
21. Ibid., Letter 147, pp. 255–8.
22. If is of course important to note that Vanbrugh began his career as a playwright. See Frank McCormick, *Sir John Vanbrugh: The Playwright as Architect* (University Park: Penn State University Press, 1991).
23. On the genesis of the Palladian movement, see John Harris, *The Palladian Revival: Lord Burlington, His Villa and Garden at Chiswick* (New Haven: Yale University Press, 1994), and Rudolf Wittkower, *Palladio and English Palladianism* (London: Thames & Hudson, 1974).
24. Earl of Shaftesbury, "A Letter Concerning Design," in *Second Characters or The Language of Forms*, ed. Benjamin Rand (Bristol: Thoemmes Press, 1995; originally published in 1914), 21–2.
25. Ibid., 24.
26. On Shaftesbury, see Robert Voitle, *The Third Earl of Shaftesbury: 1671–1713* (Baton Rouge: Louisiana State University Press, 1984).
27. For Shaftesbury's notion of beauty, see especially his dialogue "The Moralists, a Philosophical Rhapsody," in *Characteristics of Men, Manners, Opinions, Times*, ed. Lawrence E. Klein (Cambridge: Cambridge University Press, 1999), and Stanley Grean, *Shaftesbury's Philosophy of Religion and Ethics: A Study of Enthusiasm* (Columbus: Ohio University Press, 1967), 246–57.
28. Nicholas Du Bois, translator's preface to *The Architecture of A. Palladio in Four Books . . . Revis'd, design'd, and publish'd by Giacomo Leoni*, 2 vols. (London: Watts, 1715–20), 3. The first installment of the work, its title-page date notwithstanding, was actually issued in 1716.

29. Rudolf Wittkower first pointed this out in "English Neoclassicism and the Vicissitudes of Palladio's *Quattro Libri*," in *Palladio and English Palladianism*, 85.

30. Colin Campbell, introduction to *Vitruvius Britannicus or the British Architect containing the Plans, Elevations, and Sections of the Regular Buildings, both Publick and Private, in Great Britain* (1715; reprint, New York: Benjamin Blom, 1967).

31. Ibid.

32. On the work and ideas of Lord Burlington, see Harris, *The Palladian Revival*, and Dana Arnold, ed., *Belov'd by Ev'ry Muse: Richard Boyle, 3ʳᵈ Earl of Burlington & 4ᵗʰ Earl of Cork* (London: Georgian Group, 1994).

33. William Kent, *The Designs of Inigo Jones, consisting of Plans and Elevations for Publick and Private Buildings*, 2 vols. (London: William Kent, 1727).

34. Robert Castell, *The Villas of the Ancients Illustrated* (London: author, 1728).

35. Riccardo Conte' di Burlington, *Fabbriche antiche disegnate' da Andrea Palladio Vicentino e' date in luce' da* (London: author, 1730).

36. Rudolf Wittkower, in "Lord Burlington and William Kent," *Archaeological Journal* 102 (1945): 151–64, was the first to credit many aspects of Kent's early designs to Burlington. But this view has been broadly contested by Michael Wilson, *William Kent: Architect, Designer, Painter, Gardener, 1685–1748* (London: Routledge & Kegan Paul, 1984). On the work of Kent, see also Margaret Jourdain, *The Work of William Kent: Artist, Painter, Designer and Landscape Gardener* (London: Country Life Limited, 1948).

37. Isaac Ware, *Designs of Inigo Jones and Others* (London, 1735?). The book has been variously dated.

38. Isaac Ware, *The Four Books of Andrea Palladio's Architecture* (London: author, 1748–55).

39. Robert Morris, *An Essay in Defence of Ancient Architecture; or a Parallel of the Ancient Buildings with the Modern: Shewing the Beauty and Harmony of the Former, and the Irregularity of the Latter* (London: Browne, 1728; reprint, Farnborough, England: Gregg International, 1971), iii, xii–xiii.

40. Ibid., xviii, 23.

41. Ibid., 14.

42. Ibid., 20–1.

43. Robert Morris, *Lectures on Architecture: Consisting of Rules Founded upon Harmonick and Arithmetical Proportions in Building, Design'd As an Agreeable Entertainment for Gentlemen: and More particularly useful to all who make Architecture, or the Polite Arts, their Study*, 2nd ed. (London: Sayer, 1759; originally published in 1734–7; reprint, Farnborough, England: Gregg International, 1971). David Leatherbarrow was the first to underscore these aspects of Morris's theory, in his "Architecture and Situation: A Study of the Architectural Writings of Robert Morris," *Journal of the Society of Architectural Historians* 44 (March 1985): 48–59.

44. Morris, *Lectures on Architecture*, 173.

45. R. Morris, *An Essay upon Harmony, As it relates chiefly to Situation and Building* (1739). Reprinted in Morris, *Lectures on Architecture*, 22; see also p. 18.

46. Isaac Ware, *A Complete Body of Architecture: Adorned with Plans and Elevations, from Original Designs* (London: Osborne & Shipton, 1756), 131–2. Palladio can be censured, for instance, where he joins or intersects columns (p. 254).

47. Wolfgang Herrmann has made a careful study of these instances. See *Laugier and Eighteenth Century French Theory* (London: Zwemmer, 1962), 173–5.

48. Ware, *Complete Body of Architecture*, 138–9.

49. Ibid., 237.

50. Ibid., 136.

51. Ibid.

52. Ibid., 149.

53. W. Chambers, *A Treatise on Civil Architecture* (London: Haberkon, 1759). On the life of Chambers and aspects of his thought and practice, see John Harris, *Sir William Chambers: Knight of the Polar Star* (London: Zwemmer, 1970); John Harris and Michael Snokin, eds., *Sir William Chambers: Architect to George III* (New Haven: Yale University Press, 1996); and Michael Snodin, ed., *Sir William Chambers* (London: Victoria & Albert Museum, 1996).

54. W. Chambers, *A Treatise on the Decorative Part of Civil Architecture*, 3rd ed. (London: Joseph Smeeton, 1791), 107.

55. Chambers, *Treatise on Civil Architecture*, 58.

56. Ibid., 18.

57. Ibid.

58. Ibid., 64. Chambers also echoed similar views with regard to the relative nature of proportion and Burkean psychology in his unpublished manuscripts, housed at the Royal Academy. See also David Watkin, *Sir John Soane: Enlightenment Thought and the Royal Academy Lectures* (New York: Cambridge University Press, 1996), 33–4.

59. Ibid.

60. Chambers, *Treatise on the Decorative Part of Civil Architecture*, 107.

61. Walter John Hipple attributes the first usage in 1685 to William Aglionby. See his remarks on the introduction of the term into English in *The Beautiful, the Sublime, and the Picturesque in Eighteenth-Century British Aesthetic Theory* (Carbondale: Southern Illinois University Press, 1957), 185.

62. Letter of John Vanbrugh to the Duchess of Marlborough, 11 June 1709, in *The Complete Works of Sir John Vanbrugh*, letters edited by Geoffrey Webb (Bloomsbury, England: Nonesuch Press, 1928), 4:29.

63. Ibid., 30.

64. Anthony Ashley Cooper, Third Earl of Shaftesbury, *Characteristics of Men, Manners, Opinions, Times*, ed. Lawrence E. Kleine (Cambridge: Cambridge University Press, 1999), 317.

65. Joseph Addison, in *The Spectator* (London: George Routledge & Sons, n.d.), no. 411, 593.

66. Ibid., no. 412, 594.

67. Ibid.

68. Ibid., no. 415, 599.

69. Ibid., no. 414, 597. For Addison's views on gardens, see no. 477, 682–3.

70. Stephen Switzer, *Ichnographia Rustica* (London, 1718), 3:5. Cited from David Watkin, *The English Vision: The Picturesque in Architecture, Landscape and Garden Design* (London: John Murray, 1982), 8.

71. On Pope's use of the term, see Hipple, *The Beautiful, the Sublime, and the Picturesque*, 185–6.

72. Conversation with Joseph Spence from 1727, in *Anecdotes*. Cited from Isabel Wakelin Urban Chase, *Horace Walpole: Gardenist* (Princeton: Princeton University Press, 1943), 108.

73. See Morris R. Brownell, introduction to *Alexander Pope's Villa: Views of Pope's Villa, Grotto and Garden: A Microcosm of English Landscape* (London: Greater London Council, 1980), 9.

74. Castell, *Villas of the Ancients Illustrated*, 116.

75. Ibid.

76. Ibid., 116–17.

77. Batty Langley, *New Principles of Gardening: Or, the Laying Out and Planting Parterres, Groves, Wildernesses, Labyrinths, Avenues, Parks, etc. After a more Grand and Rural Manner, than has been done before* (London: Pater-Noster Row, 1728), v–vi (p. v is misprinted as p. x).

78. Ibid., 198.

79. Ibid., 195.

80. Ibid., 202.

81. The letter is dated 23 December and is cited from Wilson, *William Kent*, 192. See also Jourdain, *The Work of William Kent*, 77.

82. Walpole's "History of the Modern Taste in Gardening," though written in 1771, first appeared in the last volume of *Anecdotes of Painting in England* (1780). The pages of the essay cited here are taken from the more recently published version in Chase, *Horace Walpole*, 25.

83. Ibid., 26.

84. In the second edition of Langley's book, the title was changed to the more familiar *Gothic Architecture: Improved by Rules and Proportions, in many Grand Designs*. The reprint by Gregg Press in 1967 is of the 1747 edition.

85. William Temple, "Upon the Gardens of Epicurus" (1685), in *Five Miscellaneous Essays by Sir William Temple*, ed. Samuel Holt Monk (Ann Arbor: University of Michigan Press, 1963), 30.

86. Addison, *The Spectator*, no. 414, 598.

87. Morris Brownell indicates this influence in his introduction to *Alexander Pope's Villa*, 6.

88. On Dickie Bateman, see John Harris, "Dickie Bateman und seine Bedeutung für die frühe Chinoiserie in England," in *Sir William Chambers und der Englisch-chinesische Garten in Europa*, ed. Thomas Weiss (Stuttgart: Gerd Hatje, 1995), 43–6. See also David Watkin, "The Rococo and Chinoiserie Phase," in *English Vision*, 31–44.

89. William Chambers, *Designs of Chinese Buildings, Furniture, Dresses, Machines, and Utensils* (London: author, 1757; reprint, New York: Benjamin Blom, 1968), 15.

90. William Chambers, *Plans, Elevations, Sections, and Perspective Views of the Gardens and Buildings at Kew in Surry* (London: Haberkorn, 1763). On Chambers's design for the House of Confucius, see John Harris, "Sir William Chambers and Kew Gardens," in *Sir William Chambers*, 56–7.

91. W. Chambers, *A Dissertation on Oriental Gardening* (London: Griffin, 1772).

92. See Alastair Smart's informative chapter "The *Dialogue on Taste* (1755)," in *Allan Ramsay: Painter Essayist and Man of the Enlightenment* (New Haven: Yale University Press, 1992), 139–48. The dialogue appeared in 1755 under the book title *The Investigator*; a second edition appeared in 1762.

93. Smart provides several reasons for connecting Hume with Colonel Freeman (*Allan Ramsay*, 139).

94. The fascination of Robert Adam for the Gothic style goes back to his involvement with the completion of the Gothic-inspired Inveraray Castle, Argyllshire, the responsibility for which he took over in 1749. This enthusiasm is seen as well in the trip that Robert and James made across England in the spring of 1759, which featured visits to several Gothic works. And Smart draws attention to the fact that the drawing James Adam holds in the portrait painted by Ramsay in 1754 originally (as infrared photography has revealed) depicted a Gothic tower (*Allan Ramsay*, 109). Ramsay also intended to write a book on Gothic architecture.

95. A. Ramsey, "On Taste," *The Investigator* (London: 1762; reprint, New Haven: Yale University Press, 1972), 33.

96. See, for instance, sec. 8, bk. 2, of *A Treatise of Human Nature* (1739–40).

97. David Hume, "Of the Delicacy of Taste and Passion," in *Essays Moral, Political, and Literary*, in *The Philosophical Works of David Hume* (Boston: Little, Brown, 1854), 1:1–5.

98. David Hume, "Of the Standard of Taste," in *Philosophical Works of David Hume*, 252. Hume's essay was originally published in his *Four Dissertations* (1757).

99. Ibid., 254–63.

100. Ibid., 268.

101. See Immanuel Kant, *Critique of Judgment*, "Analytic of the Beautiful," pars. 6–9.

102. Edmund Burke, *A Philosophical Inquiry into the Origin of our Ideas of the Sublime and Beautiful* (London: G. Bell & Sons, 1913), 53.

103. Longinus was the first-century A.D. author of the Greek study *Peri Hypsous* (On the sublime).

104. Addison, *The Spectator*, see especially no. 412. Hume's discussion takes place in "of Contiguity and Distance in Space and Time," in *A Treatise of Human Nature*, ed. L. A. Selby-Bigge (Oxford: Clarendon Press, 1951), 432–4.

105. Alexander Gerard, *An Essay on Taste*, 3rd ed. (Edinburgh: Bell & Creech, 1780; reprint, Gainesville, Fla.: Scholars' Facsimiles & Reprints, 1963), 11.

106. Ibid.

107. Burke, *Philosophical Inquiry*, 113, 74.

108. Ibid., 108.

109. On Chambers's and Soane's reading of Burke, see Watkin, *Sir John Soane*, 34–7.

110. Burke, *Philosophical Enquiry*, 121.

111. Henry Home (Lord Kames), *Elements of Criticism*, 7th ed. (Edinburgh: Bell & Creech, 1788), 2:465.

112. See Smart, *Allan Ramsay*, 121.

113. Cited from John Fleming, *Robert Adam and His Circle in Edinburgh and Rome* (London: John Murray, 1962), 170. Fleming's study remains the best account of Adam's early career.

114. On the Adam style, see Joseph and Anne Rykwert, *Robert and James Adam: The Men and the Style* (New York: Rizzoli, 1985); Eileen Harris, *The Genius of Robert Adam: His Interiors* (New Haven, Conn.: Yale University Press, 2001).

115. A point made by Fleming, *Robert Adam and His Circle*, 303. Fleming also discusses in some detail the unpublished essay of James Adam.

116. Robert Adam and James Adam, *The Works in Architecture of Robert and James Adam* (London: authors, 1778; reprint, London: Academy Editions, 1975), 45–6 n.
117. Ibid., 46 n.
118. Ibid., 50.
119. Ibid., 58.
120. William Gilpin (anonymous in first two editions), *An Essay on Prints: Containing Remarks on the Principles of Picturesque Beauty* (London, 1768), 1–2. See also idem, *Observations on the River Wye, and Several Parts of South Wales, etc. Relative chiefly to Picturesque beauty; made in the Summer of the Year 1770* (London: Blamire, 1782; reprint, Richmond: Richmond Publishing, 1973). Other titles of Gilpin that have been reprinted include *Observations on the Highlands of Scotland, Observations on the Mountains and Lakes of Cumberland and Westmorland, Observations on the Western Parts of England,* and *Remarks on Forest Scenery.*
121. Gilpin, *Observations on the River Wye*, 1–2.
122. Ibid., 17–18.
123. Ibid., 18.
124. Ibid.
125. See H. Repton, *Sketches and Hints on Landscape Gardening: Collected from Designs and Observations* (1795), in *The Landscape Gardening and Landscape Architecture of the Late Humphry Repton*, ed. J. C. Loudon (London: Longman, 1840; reprint, Farnborough, England: Gregg International, 1969), 108. Price's comment was in *A Letter to H. Repton, Esq. On the Application of the Practice As Well as the Principles of Landscape-Painting to Landscape-Gardening*, which was a response to a published letter that Repton had written Price. For details of the Repton-Price-Knight controversy, see Hipple, *The Beautiful, the Sublime, and the Picturesque*, 224–5, 238–46.
126. Repton, *Sketches and Hints on Landscape Gardening*, 113.
127. Ibid., 112.
128. See Hipple, *The Beautiful, the Sublime, and the Picturesque*, 233.
129. Repton, *Observations on the Theory and Practice of Landscape Gardening*, in *The Landscape Gardening and Landscape Architecture of the Late Humphry Repton*, 133.
130. See Joshua Reynolds, *Discourses on Art*, ed. Robert R. Wark (New Haven: Yale University Press, 1959), 240.
131. Uvedale Price, *Essays on the Picturesque as Compared with the Sublime and the Beautiful; and, on the Use of Studying Pictures for the Purpose of Improving Real Landscape* (London: Mawman, 1810; originally published in 1794), 1:244.
132. Ibid., 50.
133. Ibid., 88.
134. On the relation in theory between Burke and Price, see Hipple, *The Beautiful, the Sublime, and the Picturesque*, 203–8.
135. Price, *Essays on the Picturesque*, 2:212–15.
136. Reynolds, *Discourses on Art*, 244.
137. Price, *Essays on the Picturesque*, 2:269.
138. Ibid., 261.
139. On Knight and his thought, see Andrew Ballantyne, *Architecture, Landscape and Liberty: Richard Payne Knight and the Picturesque* (New York: Cambridge University Press, 1997).
140. Cited from Nikolaus Pevsner, "Richard Payne Knight," *Art Bulletin* 31 (December 1949): 312.
141. Knight's first book, *An Account of the Remains of the Worship of Priapus, Lately Existing at Isernia in the Kingdom of Naples*, was issued privately to members of the Society of Dilettanti in 1786 and in part reissued in his *The Symbolical Language of Ancient Art and Mythology* in 1818.
142. Knight chose to discuss the picturesque as a "kind of beauty" in the advertisement to the second edition of *The Landscape: A Didactic Poem in Three Books* (London: Bulmer, 1795).
143. Richard Payne Knight, *An Analytical Inquiry into the Principles of Taste*, 2nd ed. (London: Luke Hansard, 1805), 57.
144. Ibid., 85.
145. Ibid., 192–5.
146. Ibid., 162–6.
147. Ibid., 221.
148. Ibid., 220.
149. Ibid., 223.
150. See Watkin's important study *Sir John Soane*. Other recent monographs include Dorothy Stroud, *Sir John Soane, Architect* (London: Faber & Faber, 1984); Pierre de la Ruffinière Du Prey, *John Soane: The Making of an Architect* (Chicago: University of Chicago Press, 1982); and Gillian Darley, *John Soane: An Accidental Romantic* (New Haven: Yale University Press, 1999).
151. John Soan, *Designs in Architecture; Consisting of Plans, Elevations, and Sections* (London: Taylor, 1788). Soane added the "e" to his last name only when he married in 1784.
152. John Soane, *Sketches in Architecture, Containing Plans and Elevations of Cottages, Villas, and other Useful buildings with Characteristic Scenery* (London: author, 1793; reprint, Farnborough, England: Gregg International, 1971).
153. John Soane, *Plans, Elevations and Sections of Buildings* (London: Taylor, 1788; reprint, Farnborough, England: Gregg International, 1971), 5.
154. Ibid., 8.
155. Ibid., 9.
156. Ibid., pl. 44.
157. Ibid., 9.
158. An ample presentation of these sources is given in the introductory chapters of Watkin's *Sir John Soane*.
159. John Soane, Lecture V, in Watkin, *Sir John Soane*, 163.
160. Ibid., Lecture VII, 586.
161. Ibid., Lecture VII, 587.
162. Ibid., Lecture VI, 573–4.
163. Ibid., Lecture XI, 642.
164. Ibid., 338–9. This is a passage added to a later version of Lecture V.
165. Ibid., Lecture XI, 648.
166. Ibid., Lecture VIII, 598.
167. Ibid., Lecture XI, 648.
168. Ibid., Lecture V, 563.
169. Ibid.
170. Ibid., 555.
171. Ibid., Lecture VIII, 600.

4. Neoclassicism and Historicism

1. Burke warned of the dangers of revolutionary excesses in his *Reflections on the Revolution in France*, penned in November 1790.

Burke was particularly incensed when Louis XVI was forcibly removed from Versailles to Paris.

2. See G. P. Gooch, *Germany and the French Revolution* (London: Frank Cass, 1965). On Hegel's admiration for Napoleon, see especially Terry Pinkard, *Hegel: A Biography* (New York: Cambridge University Press, 2000), 22–6. See also Claus Träger, ed., *Die Französische Revolution im Spiegel der deutschen Literatur* (Frankfurt, 1975), and Charles Breunig, *The Age of Revolution and Reaction 1789–1850* (New York: W. W. Norton, 1970).

3. Pinkard, *Hegel*, 228.

4. J. G. Fichte, *Reden an die deutsche Nation* (Berlin, 1912).

5. For a discussion of these projects, see James Leith, *Space and Revolution: Projects for Monuments, Squares and Public Buildings in France, 1789–1799* (Montréal: McGill-Queen's University Press, 1991); Richard A. Etlin, *Symbolic Space: French Enlightenment Architecture and Its Legacy* (Chicago: Chicago University Press, 1994), 30–47; Barry Bergdoll, *European Architecture: 1750–1890* (Oxford: Oxford University Press, 2000), 105–17.

6. For details of Durand's life and thought, see Werner Szambien, *Jean-Nicolas-Louis Durand, 1760–1834: De l'imitation à la norme* (Paris: Picard, 1984). See Alberto Pérez-Gómez, *Architecture and the Crisis of Modern Science* (Cambridge: M.I.T. Press, 1983), 297–326.

7. J.-N.-L. Durand, *Recueil et parallèle des édifices de tout genre anciens et modernes* (Paris: Gillè Fils, 1799–1801; reprint, Nördlingen: Alfons Uhl, 1986).

8. J.-N.-L. Durand, *Précis des leçons d'architecture données à l'École Polytechnique* (Paris: author, 1802–5). Translated by David Britt under the title *Précis of the Lectures on Architecture, with Graphic Portion of the Lectures on Architecture*, introduction by Antoine Picon (Los Angeles: Getty Publications Program, 2000).

9. Jean-Baptiste Rondelet, *Traité théorique et pratique de l'art de bâtir*, 7 vols. (Paris: author, 1802–17). Rondelet in the 1770s became Soufflot's technical advisor on the church and brought it to completion between 1784 and 1812.

10. Durand, *Précis of the Lectures on Architecture*, 84.

11. Ibid.

12. Ibid.

13. Ibid., 86–7, and pl. 1.

14. On the life and ideas of Quatremère de Quincy, see Thomas F. Rowlands, "Quatremère de Quincy: The Formative Years, 1785–1795" (Ph.D. diss., Northwestern University, 1987); Sylvia Lavin, *Quatremère de Quincy and the Invention of a Modern Language of Architecture* (Cambridge, Mass.: M.I.T. Press, 1992); Samir Younés, *The True, the Fictive, and the Real: The Historical Dictionary of Architecture of Quatremère de Quincy* (London: Papadakis, 1999).

15. A. C. Quatremère de Quincy, *De l'architecture égyptienne, considérée dans son origine, ses principes et son goût, et comparée sous les mêmes rapports à l'architecture grecque* (Paris: Barrois, 1803), 241. "On peut affirmer que le seule école de la charpente pourvoit faire de l'Architecture un art raisonné."

16. Ibid., 242. "En effet, ce seroit bien peu connaître l'essence de l'Architecture, et la plus grande partie des moyens qu'elle a de nous plaire, que de lui enlever cette agréable fiction, ce masque ingénieux, qui, l'associant aux autres arts, lui permet de paroître sur leur théâtre, et lui fournit une occasion de plus de rivaliser avec eux."

17. A. C. Quatremère de Quincy, "Architecture," in *Encyclopédie méthodique. Architecture* (Paris: Panckoucke, 1788–1825), 1:109. "C'est l'art de bâtir suivant des proportions & des règles déterminées."

18. Ibid., 115. "Delà, la charme de la musique, du chant des poëtes, des illusions du théâtre. C'est également de cette fiction habituelle de l'architecture . . . dans l'imitation tout-à-fois illusoire & réelle de la charpente & de la cabane."

19. Ibid., 120. "L'imitation générale de la Nature dans ses principes d'ordre, d'harmonie relatifs aux affections de nos sens, & aux perceptions de l'entendement, lui ont donné l'âme, & en ont fait un art non plus copiste, non plus imitateur, mais rival de la Nature même."

20. Ibid., 116–17. "Un jeu puéril pour les artistes, & une enigme pour le commun des hommes."

21. Ibid., "Caractère," 478. "Ainsi, dans l'emploi métaphorique de ce mot, *caractère*, n'est autre chose que le signe par lequel la nature écrit sur chaque objet son essence ses qualités distinctives, ses propriétés relatives."

22. Ibid., 492. ". . . je dirai que le *caractère* d'architecture des differens peuples consiste dans une manière d'être, dans une conformation nécessitée par les besoins physiques & les habitudes morales, & dans laquelle se peignent les climats, les idées, les moeurs, les goûts, les plaisirs & le caractère même de chaque people."

23. Ibid., 510. "Voyez combien la nature, simple dans ses types, économe dans ses moyens, est cependant inépuisable & variée dans toutes les combinaisons qui modifient ses ouvrages."

24. Ibid., "Type," 3:544. ". . . que l'idée d'un élément qui doit lui-même servir de règle au modèle."

25. Ibid., "Style," 411. ". . . style, disons-nous, devient synonyme de *caractère*, ou de la manière propre, de la physionomie distinctive qui appartienneat à chaque ouvrage, à chaque auteur, à chaque genre, à chaque école, à chaque pays, à chaque siècle, etc."

26. Ibid., "Théorie," 485. "C'est, non celle qui donne les règles, mais celle qui remonte aux sources d'où les règles émanent. C'est, non celle qui rédige les lois, mais celle qui en scrute et en pénètre l'esprit. C'est, non celle qui puise ses principes dans les ouvrages, mais celle qui donne pour principes aux ouvrages, les lois même de notre nature, les causes des impressions que nous éprouvons, les ressorts par lesquels l'art nous touche, nous émeut et nous plaît."

27. J. J. Winckelmann, *Geschichte der Kunst des Alterthums* (Dresden: Walther, 1764), 147–8. "Da nun die weisse Farbe diejenige ist, welche die mehresten Lichtstrahlen zurückschicket, sogleich sich empfindlicher macht, so wird auch ein schöner Körper desto schöner seyn, je weisser er ist."

28. C. L. Stieglitz, *Archaeologie der Baukunst der Griechen und Römer* (Weimar: Verlage des Industrie-Comptoirs, 1801), 258–9. "Die Werke der Baukunst erhalten ihre Schönheit durch die schöne Form, die bey ihr, so wie bey den bildenden Künsten, an welche sie sich anschliesst, durch Ordnung und Ebenmass, durch Schicklichkeit und gute Verhältnisse hervorgebracht wird."

29. Vitruvius, *De Architectura*, bk. 4, chap. 2; Pausanias, *Guide to Greece* (Harmondsworth, England: Penguin, 1979), par. 28.

30. Pliny, *Natural History* (Cambridge: Harvard University Press, 1868), bk. 35, I.3 and XXXVII.118).

31. Winckelmann, *Geschichte der Kunst des Alterthums*, 264.

32. William Wilkins, *Atheniensia* (London: Longman, Hurst, Orme, & Rees, 1816), 86–8.

33. William Leake, *The Topography of Athens, with Some Remarks on its Antiquities*, 2nd ed. (London: J. Murray, 1841; originally published in 1824), 335.

34. Edward Dodwell, *A Classical and Topographical Tour Through Greece* (London, 1819), 342–3. See also 320–42, 365–7.

35. Cockerell and Hallerstein, together with John Foster and Jacob Linckh, found the site of the temple in 1811 but did not do extensive excavation. Brøndsted and Stackelberg returned in 1812 and unearthed it.

36. A. C. Quatremère de Quincy, *Le Jupiter olympien, ou l'art de la sculpture antique considéré sous un nouveau point de vue* (Paris: Chez Firmin Didot, 1815), 389–91.

37. Ibid., 36. "... une sorte de peinture sans être de la couleur, c'est d'être colorés sans avoir été peinte, c'est d'offrir enfin l'apparence et non la réalité de l'illusion."

38. C. R. Cockerell, "On the Aegina Marbles," *Journal of Science and the Arts* (London), 6, no. 12 (1819): 340.

39. Ibid., 341. For the account of his travels, see Samuel Pepys Cockerell, ed., *Travels in Southern Europe and the Levant, 1810–1817: The Journal of C. R. Cockerell* (London: Longmans, Green, 1903).

40. Leo von Klenze, *Versuch einer Wiederstellung des toskanischer Tempels nach seinen historischen und technischen Anlogien* (Munich, 1822), 9, 77.

41. O. M. Baron von Stackelberg, *Der Apollotempel zu Bassae in Arcadien und die daselbst ausgegrabenen Bildwerke* (Rome, 1826), 33. "Der Farbe, noch jetzt bey allen südlichen Völkern zur Belebung von Architekturmassen unentbehrlich, wandten die Griechen in der höchsten Meisterwerke der Baukunst aus dem Perikleischen Zeitalter, sowohl Dorischer als Ionischer Bauart, noch bezeugen: das Theseium, der Parthenon, der Tempel der Minerva Polias, die Propyläen, wo selbst aüssere Bauverzierungen mit Farben aufgetragen waren. Ausserdem lassen sich manche Beyspiele aufweisen in Denksteinen, in Vasengemälden aus Griechenland, in Wandgemälden aus Pompeji, welche die Allgemeinheit der Maler auszierung an architektonischen Werken darthum. Das milde Clima begünstigte diesen Gebrauch und Dorische Tempel erscheinen hiedurch viel reicher geschmückt, als man sich denkt."

42. William Kinnard, commentary to Stuart and Revett's *The Antiquities of Athens*, 2nd ed. (London, 1825), 2:44–5 n.

43. P. O. Brøndsted, *Reisen und Untersuchungen in Griechenland*, (Paris, 1825–30), 1:147.

44. Hittorff taught himself English and traveled to London in 1820 to view the Elgin Marbles, and several studies have been devoted to Hittorff and his role in the polychrome controversy. See Karl Hammer, *Jakob Ignaz Hittorff: Ein Pariser Baumeister 1792–1867* (Stuttgart: Deutsche Verlags-Anstalt, 1986); David van Zanten, *The Architectural Polychromy of the 1830s* (New York: Garland, 1977); Robin Middleton, "Hittorff's Polychrome Campaign," in *The Beaux-Arts and Nineteenth-Century French Architecture* (Cambridge, Mass.: M.I.T. Press, 1982); and Musée Carnavalet, *Hittorff: Un Architecte du XIXème* (Alençon, France: Alençonnaise, 1986).

45. See William Harris and Samuel Angell, *Sculptured Metopes discovered amongst the Ruins of the Temples of the Ancient City of Selinus in Sicily* (London, 1826), pls. 6–8.

46. While in Italy, Hittorff informed François Gérard, Ludwig von Schorn, and Charles Percier of his discoveries. He presented one paper to the French Academy in Rome in 1824, but he did not discuss his system. Between 1827 and 1830 he published forty-nine engravings in *L'Architecture antique de la Sicile*, of which three were colored, yet he did not show the drawings that he presented in 1830.

47. J. I. Hittorff, "De l'architecture polychrôme chez les Grecs, ou restitution complète du temple d'Empédocles, dans l'acropolis de Sélinunte," *Annales de l'institute de Correspondance Archéologique* 2 (1830): 263–84.

48. Ibid., 273. "C'était le degré de richesse dans les ornements dont la peinture était plus spécialement chargée, qui servait à donner plus ou moins de magnificence apparente aux édifices sacrés, selon l'éclat dont on voulait entourer les dieux."

49. The first appraisal of Hittorff's restoration is from Raoul-Rochette's review of *L'Architecture Antique de la Sicile* in the *Journal des Savants*, July 1829. The second appraisal is from his article "De la peinture sur mur chez les anciens," in *Journal des Savants*, June–August 1833. Raoul-Rochette, however, first changed his attitude toward Hittorff in an address given to the academy in July 1830.

50. The polychrome debate in Germany began in the years 1834–5, with the conflicting views of Gottfried Semper and Franz Kugler (see chapter 5). It was initiated in England with the decision of the British Museum to convene a panel to reexamine the Elgin Marbles for traces of paint (they had been scrubbed earlier with acid and were therefore clean of evidence); see "Report of the Committee Appointed to Examine the Elgin Marbles, in order to Ascertain Whether any Evidence Remains as the Employment of Colour in the Decoration Architecture and Sculpture," *Transactions of the Royal Institute of British Architects of London* 1, pt. 2 (1842): 101–8. On the controversy in Spain, see A. Zabaletas, "Arquitectura," *No me Olvides*, no. 11 (July 1837): 5–7; no. 12 (Aug 1837): 1–3. See also the forthcoming book on Spanish polychromy by María Ocón Fernández.

51. The cited phrase is that used by Fourier in the "Preliminary Discourse" to his *Théorie des quatre mouvements* (1808). See *The Utopian Vision of Charles Fourier*, translated and edited by Jonathan Beecher and Richard Bienvenu (London: Jonathan Cape, 1971), 101.

52. Saint-Simon first began a presentation of his ideas in the journal *L'Industrie*, published in four volumes in 1816–18. On his importance for the arts, see Donald Drew Egbert, *Social Radicalism and the Arts: Western Europe* (New York: Knopf, 1970), 117–33.

53. Olinde Rodrigues, "L'artiste, le savant et l'industriel. Dialogue," in *Oeuvres de Saint-Simon et d'Enfantin* (Aalen, Germany: Otto Zeller, 1964), 10:210. "C'est nous, artistes, qui vous servirons d'avant-garde; la puissance des arts est en effet la plus immédiate et la plus rapide. Nous avons des armes de toute espère: quand nous voulons répandre des idées neuves parmi les hommes, nous les inscrivons sur le marble ou sur la toile; nous les popularisons part la poésie et la chant; nous employons tour à tour la lyre ou le galoubet, l'ode ou la chanson, l'histoire ou le roman; la scène dramatique nous est ouverte, et c'est là surtout que nous exerçons

une influence électrique et victorieuse." Rodriques, a former student at the Ecole Polytechnique, also had architectural "visions," such as his project of 1832 to design a "New Jerusalem." See Spyros Papapetros, "The Symposium Issue: Spaces of Transformation" (online article), *Iconomania: Studies in Visual Culture* (1998).

54. Emile Barrault, *Aux artistes: Du passé et de l'avenir des beaux-arts. Doctrine de Saint-Simon* (Paris: Alexandre Mesnier, 1830), 9.

55. Ibid., 73. "Nous l'avons déjà vu; les arts ne peuvent fleurir qu'à la condition d'une époque organique, et l'inspiration n'est puissante et salutaire que lorsqu'elle est sociale et religieuse."

56. On the teachings of Huyot, see Robin Middleton, "The Rationalist Interpretations of Classicism of Léonce Reynaud and Viollet-le-Duc," *AA files 2* (Spring 1986): 29–48. See also Barry Bergdoll, *Léon Vaudoyer: Historicism in the Age of Industry* (New York: Architectural History Foundation, 1994), 41.

57. Among those awed by the drawings were Karl Friedrich Schinkel and T. L. Donaldson. See Frank Salmon, *Building on Ruins: The Rediscovery of Rome and English Architecture* (London: Ashgate, 2000), 106–7.

58. See especially David Van Zanten, *Designing Paris: The Architecture of Duban, Labrouste, Duc, and Vaudoyer* (Cambridge: M.I.T. Press, 1987).

59. See Bergdoll, *Léon Vaudoyer*, 103, 295 n. 77.

60. For a detailed discussion of Vaudoyer's ideas and envoi projects, see Bergdoll, *Léon Vaudoyer*.

61. On Duban's Protestant church, see David Van Zanten, "Duban's Temple Protestant," *In Search of Modern Architecture: A Tribute to Henry-Russell Hitchcock*, ed. Helen Searing (New York: Architectural History Foundation, 1982), 64–84.

62. Neal Levine has analyzed this project and others by Labrouste in *Architectural Reasoning in the Age of Positivism: Henri Labrouste and the Néo-Grec Idea of the Bibliothèque Sainte-Geneviève* (New York: Garland, 1975); "The Romantic Idea of Architectural Legibility: Henri Labrouste and the Neo-Grec," in Arthur Drexler (ed.), *The Architecture of the Ecole des Beaux-Arts* (New York: Museum of Modern Art, 1977), 325–416; "The Book and the Building: Hugo's Theory of Architecture and Labrouste's Bibliothèque Ste-Geneviève," in *The Beaux-Arts and Nineteenth-Century French Architecture*, ed. Robin Middleton (note 44), 139–173.

63. Levine, "The Romantic Idea of Architectural Legibility: Henri Labrouste and the Neo-Grec," in *The Architecture of the Ecole des Beaux-Arts* (note 62), 386.

64. L. Vaudoyer to A.-L.-T. Vaudoyer, 20 July 1829, 16 September 1829. See Bergdoll, *Léon Vaudoyer* (note 56), 90–91.

65. Victor Hugo, *Oeuvres complètes de Victor Hugo. Philosophie*, I, 1819–1834; cited from Levine, "The Book and the Building," *The Beaux-Arts and Nineteenth-Century French Architecture* (note 62), 140.

66. Victor Hugo, *The Hunchback of Notre-Dame* (New York: Penguin, 1965), 173.

67. Ibid., 185.

68. Ibid., 186.

69. See Middleton, "The Rationalist Interpretations of Classicism of Léonce Reynaud and Viollet-le-Duc," 36.

70. Léonce Reynaud, "Architecture," *Encyclopédie nouvelle, ou Dictionnaire philosophique, scientifique, littéraire et industriel*, ed. P. Leroux and J. Reynaud (Paris: Libraire de Charles Gosselin, 1836; reprint, Geneva: Slatkine Reprints, 1991), 1:772. "... qu'aucun des systèmes du passé ne peut être considéré comme ayant une valeur absolue ... ne peut être pour nous un modèle définitif et ne doit nous imposer formellement ses lois." See also Van Zanten, *Designing Paris*, 48–52.

71. Robin Middleton in "The Rationalist Interpretations of Classicism of Léonce Reynaud and Viollet-le-Duc" stresses the importance of Guizot's and Thierry's historical methodologies for this relativist architectural interpretation, as does Barry Bergdoll in *Léon Vaudoyer* (pp. 41, 84).

72. Thomas Hope, *Observations on the Plans and Elevations designed by James Wyatt, Architect, for Downing College, Cambridge, in a letter to Francis Annesley, esq., M. P.* (London: D. N. Shury, 1804). On the reactions of James and Lewis Wyatt to Hope's pamphlet, see John Martin Robinson, *The Wyatts: An Architectural Dynasty* (Oxford: Oxford University Press, 1979), 143–4.

73. Ibid., 31. On the architectural ideas of Hope, see David Watkin, *Thomas Hope 1769–1831 and the Neo-Classical Idea* (London: Murray, 1968).

74. Ibid., 17, 21.

75. Hope gave Soane a copy of his newly printed pamphlet, and Soane annotated this passage with the remark "true, and worthy of the most serious consideration of him who wishes to distinguish himself in the higher beauties of architecture." See David Watkin, *Sir John Soane: Enlightenment Thought and the Royal Academy Lectures* (New York: Cambridge University Press, 1996), 403–4.

76. William Wilkins, *The Antiquities of Magna Graecia* (London: Longman, 1807).

77. See Watkin, *Sir John Soane*, 544, 72–78.

78. On Cockerell, see David Watkin, *The Life and Work of C. R. Cockerell* (London: Zwemmer, 1974). See also Peter Kohane, "Architecture, Labor and the Human Body: Fergusson, Cockerell and Ruskin" (Ph.D. diss, University of Pennsylvania, 1993).

79. For an account of his travels in Greece and elsewhere, see Cockerell *Travels in Southern Europe and the Levant, 1810–1817*; for an account of his time in Rome, see Salmon, *Building on Ruins*, 98–101.

80. For details of the design of the Fitzwilliam Museum and St. George's Hall, see Salmon, *Building on Ruins*, 169–88, 210–26.

81. On the development of the antiquarian movements, see Nikolaus Pevsner's chapter "English Antiquarians," in *Some Architectural Writers of the Nineteenth Century* (Oxford: Clarendon Press, 1972), 16–22. The writings discussed by Pevsner include James Murphy, *Plans, Elevations, Sections, and Views of the Church of Batalha in the Province of Estremadura in Portugal* (1795); James Hall, "Essay on the Origin and Principles of Gothic Architecture," in *Transactions of the Royal Society of Edinburgh*, vol. 3 (1798); Michael Young, "The Origin and Theory of Gothic Architecture," in *Transactions of the Royal Hibernian Academy*, vol. 3 (1790); and James Anderson, "Thoughts on the Origin, Excellencies and Defects of the Grecian and Gothic Styles of Architecture," in *Recreations in Agriculture, Natural-History, Arts and Miscellaneous Literature*, vols. 2–4 (1800–1).

82. See J. W. Goethe, "On German Architecture," in *Goethe on Art* (London: Scolar Press, 1980), 115–23.

83. Viscount de Chateaubriand, *The Genius of Christianity or the Spirit and Beauty of the Christian Religion* (Baltimore: John Murphy, 1856), 384–7.

84. On Carter, see J. Mordaunt Crook, *John Carter and the Mind of the Gothic Revival* (London: W. S. Maney, 1995).

85. James Dallaway, *Observations on English Architecture, Military, Ecclesiastical, and Civil, Compared with Similar Buildings on the Continent: Including a Critical Itinerary of Oxford and Cambridge* (London: J. Taylor, 1806).

86. G. D. Whittington, *An Historical Survey of the Ecclesiastical Antiquities of France with a View to Illustrate the Rise and Progress of Gothic Architecture in Europe* (London: J. Taylor, 1809).

87. John Britton, *The Architectural Antiquities of Great Britain, Represented in a Series of Views, Elevations, Plans, Sections, and Details, of Ancient English Edifices: With Historical and Descriptive Accounts of Each*, 5 vols. (London: J. Taylor, 1807–26).

88. Thomas Rickman, *An Attempt to Discriminate the Styles of Gothic Architecture from the Conquest to the Reformation: Preceded by a Sketch of the Grecian and Roman Orders* (London: Longman, Hurst, Rees, Orme, & Brown, 1817).

89. Rickman's paper of 1815 carried the same title and appeared in the *Panorama of Science and Art* (Liverpool, 1815). For discussion of Rickman, see Pevsner's chapter, "Rickman and the Commissioners," in *Some Architectural Writers*.

90. A. Pugin, *Specimens of Gothic Architecture; selected from various Antient Edifices in England* (London: Taylor & Britton, 1821).

91. Ibid., v.

92. Ibid., x, xii, xiv, xvii, xx.

93. For details of Barry's life and career, see Alfred Barry, *Memoir of the Life and Works of the Late Sir Charles Barry* (1867; reprint, New York: B. Blom, 1970); Marcus Whiffen, *The Architecture of Sir Charles Barry in Manchester and Neighbourhood* (Manchester: Royal Manchester Institution, 1950); and Michael Harry Port, ed., *The Houses of Parliament* (New Haven: Yale University Press, 1976).

94. On Pugin, see Phoebe Stanton, *Pugin* (New York: Viking, 1971); Michael Trappes-Lomax, *Pugin: A Medieval Victorian* (London: Sheed & Ward, 1932); Paul Atterbury and Clive Wainwright, eds., *Pugin: A Gothic Passion* (New Haven: Yale University Press, 1994); Megan Aldrich and Paul Atterbury, eds., *A. W. N. Pugin: Master of the Gothic Revival* (New Haven: Yale University Press, 1975).

95. The first of the series is *The Chest*, which is dated 1832. All are in the Victoria and Albert Museum library. See Alexandra Wedgwood, "The Early Years," Atterbury and Wainwright, *Pugin*, 29–30.

96. A. Pugin and A. W. Pugin, *Examples of Gothic Architecture; Selected from Various Antient Edifices in England*, 3 vols. (London: Bohn, 1836–8). Also appearing in this year, under the "direction" of Pugin, is Thoman Walker's *The History and Antiquities of the Vicars' Close, Wells*. Walker had purchased the sketches of the elder Pugin, owned by the younger Pugin, and published them.

97. A. W. Pugin, *Gothic Furniture of the 15th Cent.* (London: Ackermann, 1835); idem, *Designs for Iron & Brass work in the style of the xv and xvi Centuries* (London: Ackermann, 1836); idem, *Designs for Gold & Silversmiths* (London: Ackermann, 1836);

and idem, *Details of Antient Timber Houses of the 15th & 16th Centuries* (London: Ackermann, 1836).

98. Letter of 6 November 1834. Cited from Alexandra Wedgwood, "The New Palace of Westminster," in Atterbury and Wainwright, *Pugin*, 220.

99. A. W. Pugin, *Contrasts: or, A Parallel between the Noble Edifices of the Middle Ages, and Corresponding Buildings of the Present Day; Shewing the Present Decay of Taste* (London: author, 1836; 2nd ed., London: Dolman, 1841; 2nd ed. reprint by Leicester University Press, 1973).

100. Pugin, *Contrasts* (1973 reprint ed.), 1.

101. Ibid., 3.

102. Ibid., 35.

103. Many of these are illustrated in color in Atterbury and Wainwright, *Pugin*.

104. The first issue of *The Ecclesiologist* appeared late in 1841 but was bound in 1842. On the activities of the society and its organ, see Nikolaus Pevsner, "The Cambridge Camden Society and the Ecclesiologists," in *Some Architectural Writers*, 123–38.

105. A. W. Pugin, *The True Principles of Pointed or Christian Architecture* (London: John Weale, 1841), 1.

106. See, for instance, his comment in *An Apology for the Revival of Christian Architecture in England* (London: John Weale, 1843), 15–16. n. "In my own case I can truly state, that in buildings which I erected but a short time since, I can perceive numerous defects and errors, which I should not now commit; and, but a few years ago, I perpetrated abominations."

107. Ibid., 2, 5.

108. Ibid., 3 n. 3.

109. Ibid., 17.

110. Ibid., 18.

111. Ibid., 38.

5. The Rise of German Theory

1. Immanuel Kant, *Prolegomena to Any Future Metaphysics*, trans. Paul Carus and James Ellington (Indianapolis: Hackett, 1977), 5.

2. See Ernst Cassirer, *Kant's Life and Thought*, trans. James Halden (New Haven: Yale University Press, 1981), 86–90, 275–326.

3. Ernst Cassirer, *The Philosophy of the Enlightenment*, trans. Fritz Koelln and James Pettegrove (Princeton: Princeton University Press, 1968), 233.

4. Winckelmann's death in 1768, Goethe later reported, "fell down into the midst of us like a thunderbolt from a clear sky," producing in Leipzig "universal mourning and lamentation." See his *Autobiography: Truth and Fiction Relating to My Life*, trans. John Oxenford (London: Amaranth Society, 1901), 1:273.

5. Goethe's celebrated essay "On German Architecture" (1772) is contained in *Goethe on Art*, ed. and trans. John Gage (London: Scolar Press, 1980), 103–12.

6. On Goethe's relationship with Hirt, see J. W. Goethe, *Italian Journey, 1786–1788*, trans. W. H. Auden and Elizabeth Mayer (San Francisco: North Point Press, 1982), 420–1.

7. Goethe, *Goethe on Art*, 3.

8. Erik Jönsson, Graf von Dahlberg, *Svecia Antiqua et Hodernia* (Stockholm, 1726); Laurids Lauridsen de Thurah, *Den Danske Vitruvius* (Copenhagen: Berling, 1746–9).

9. C. C. L. Hirschfeld, *Théorie de l'art des jardins*, 5 vols. (Leipzig: Weidmann & Reich, 1779–85). See especially the essay in the fourth volume entitled "Remarques diverses sur le nouveau goût en fait de jardins."

10. See David Watkin and Tilmann Mellinghoff, *German Architecture and the Classical Ideal* (Cambridge: M.I.T. Press, 1987), 46. See also Fritz-Eugen Keller, "Du Ry Family," in *Maxmillan Encyclopedia of Architects* (New York: The Free Press, 1982), 1:615.

11. See Carl Justi, *Winckelmann und seine Zeitgenossen* (Leipzig: Vogel, 1866–72), 1:308.

12. See Watkin and Mellinghoff, *German Architecture and the Classical Ideal*, 51.

13. Krubsacius's second book, *Ursprung, Wachstum und Verfall der Verzierungen in den schönsten Künsten* (Origin, growth, and decline of ornamentation in the fine arts), appeared in 1759.

14. The principal monograph on Gilly is Alste Oncken, *Friedrich Gilly: 1772–1900* (Berlin: Verein für Kunstwissenschaft, 1935; reprint, Gebr. Mann, 1981). Also of importance is the exhibition catalogue *Friedrich Gilly 1772–1800 und die Privatgesellschaft junger Architekten* (Berlin: Willmuth Arenhövel, 1984), which also contains the "Denkschrift" of Konrad Levezow. See also Fritz Neumeyer's highly informative introduction to *Friedrich Gilly: Essays on Architecture, 1796–1799*, trans. David Britt (Santa Monica, Calif.: Getty Publications Program, 1994).

15. Wilhelm Heinrich Wackenroder, *Werke und Breife*, ed. Friedrich von der Leyen (Jena: Diederick, 1910), 2. Quoted from Oncken, *Friedrich Gilly*, 29.

16. In addition to Gentz and Gilly, others in the private society were Hallerstein, Joachim Ludwig Zitelmann, Karl Ferdinand Langhans (son of Carl Gotthard), Friedrich Rabe, and Karl Friedrich Schinkel.

17. F. Gilly, "Some Thoughts on the Necessity of Endeavoring to Unify the Various Departments of Architecture in both Theory and Practice," in *Friedrich Gilly: Essays on Architecture*, 169.

18. Ibid., 172. As Neumeyer has noted, Gilly quotes Goethe but draws from three separate passages from Goethe's "Über Lehranstalten zu Gunsten der bildenden Künste," *Propyläen* 2, no. 2 (1799): 10, 13, 17.

19. F. Gilly, "A Description of the Villa of Bagatelle, near Paris," in *Friedrich Gilly: Essays on Architecture*, 147.

20. K. F. Schinkel to David Gilly, January 1805. See *Aus Schinkel's Nachlass: Reisetagebücher, Briefe und Aphorismen*, ed. Alfred Freiherrn von Wolzogen (Mittenwald, Germany: Mäander Kunstverlag, 1981; originally published in 1862–4), 1:173. The literature devoted to Schinkel is much too vast to summarize. The best introduction to his life and thought in English is Barry Bergdoll's *Karl Friedrich Schinkel: An Architecture for Prussia* (New York: Rizzoli, 1994).

21. Schinkel to David Gilly, December 1804, *Aus Schinkel's Nachlass*, 1:33.

22. Ibid., 1:164. ". . . aus diesem Styl ziehen, den man gewöhlich den saracenischen nennt, weil er durch die Vermischung morgenländer und antiker Architektur in der Zeit der Völkerwanderungen entstand."

23. See Kurt W. Forster, "'Only Things That Stir the Imagination': Schinkel as a Scenographer," in *Karl Friedrich Schinkel: The Drama of Architecture* (Chicago: Art Institute of Chicago, 1994), 18–35.

24. Gustav Friedrich Waagen, "Karl Friedrich Schinkel als Mensch und als Künstler," *Berlin Kalender* (1844): 330. Cited from Helmut Börsch-Supan, "Schinkel as Artist," in Michael Snoden, ed., *Karl Friedrich Schinkel: A Universal Man* (New Haven: Yale University Press, 1991), 1.

25. On Schinkel's work in these areas, see "Schinkel's Perspective Optical Views: Art between Painting and Theater," in *Karl Friedrich Schinkel: The Drama of Architecture*, 36–53. See also the various references to these works in the exhibition catalogue *Karl Friedrich Schinkel: Architektur, Malerei, Kunstgewerbe* (Berlin: Verwaltung der Staatlichen Schlösser und Gärten, 1981). See also August Grieseback, *Carl Friedrich Schinkel: Architekt, Städtbauer, Maler* (Frankfurt: Ullstein Kunstbuch, 1983; originally published in 1924), 40–69.

26. Schinkel's stage designs are also discussed at length in Forster, "'Only Things That Stir the Imagination.'"

27. Karl Friedrich Schinkel, *Collection of Architectural Designs* (New York: Princeton Architectural Press, 1989), 36.

28. See Paul Ottwin Rave, *Schinkels Lebenswerk, Berlin 1* (Berlin: Deutscher Kunstverlag, 1941; reprint, Berlin: Deutscher Kunstverlag 1981), 94.

29. K. F. Schinkel, quoted from Goerd Peschken, *Das architektonische Lehrbuch* (Berlin: Deutscher Kunstverlag, 1979), 149–50.

Als ich meine Studien in der Baukunst gegonnen, und einige Forschritte in den verschiedenen Zweigen gemacht hatte, fühlt ich bald eine Hauptempfindung in meiner Seele, die näher zu beleuchten und zu verstehn mir vor allen Dingen wichtig schien.

Ich bemerkte, dass in den Formen der Baukunst alles auf 3 Grundlage beruhe

1. auf die Formen der Konstruktion,

2. auf Formen welche durch herkömmliche geschichtliche Wichtigkeit erzeugt werden und,

3. auf Formen die an sich bedeutsam, ihr Vorbild aus der Natur entlehnen.

Ich bemerkte ferner einen grossen unermesslichen Schatz von Formen, der bereits in der Welt durch viele Jahrtausende der Entwicklung und bei sehr verschiedenen Völkern in Ausführung von Bauwerken entstanden war und niedergelegt ist. Aber ich sah zugleich, dass unser Gebrauch von diesem angehäuften Schatz oft sehr heterogener Gegenstände, willkührlich sey, weil jede einzelne Form einen eigenthümlichen Reiz bei sich trägt, der durch eine dunkle Ahnung eines nothwendigen Motivs, sey es geschichtlich oder constructive, noch erhöht wird und verführt davon Anwendung zu machen. Man glaubt seinem Werk durch einen solchen Gegenstand einen besonderen Reiz zu verleihen dass was mir Aber in seinem primitiven Erscheinen an alten Werken eine höchst erfreuliche Wirkung erzeugte, bei seiner neuen Anwendung an Werken unserer Tag oft durchaus widerstand. Besonders ward mir klar, dass in dieser Willkührlichkeit des Gebrauchs der Grund grosser Characterlosigkeit und Styllosigkeit zu finden sey, woran so viele neue Gebäude zu leiden schienen.

Es ward mir eine Lebensaufgabe hierin Klarheit zu gewinnen. Aber je tiefer ich den Gegenstand durchdrang je grösser sah ich die Schwerigkeiten die sich meinem Bestreben entgegenstellten. Sehr bald gerieth ich in die Fehler der rein radical Abstraction, wo ich die ganze Conception für eines bestimmtes

Werk der Baukunst aus seinem nächsten trivialen Zweck allein und aus der Konstruction entwickelte, in diesem Falle entstand etwas Trockenes, starres das der Freiheit ermangelte und zwei wesentliche Element: das Historische und das Poetische ganz ausschloss.

30. See especially Goerd Peschken, "Technologische Ästhetik in Schinkels Architektur," *Zeitschrift des deutschen Vereins für Kunstwissenschaft* 22 (1968): 45–81.

31. See K. Schinkel, *'The English Journey': Journal of a Visit to France and Britain in 1826*, ed. David Bindmann and Gottfried Riemann (New Haven: Yale University Press, 1993). For details of Beauth's career, see Angelika Wesenberg, "Art and Industry," in Snodin, *Karl Friedrich Schinkel*, 57–63.

32. Schinkel's personal relationship with Wilhelm Humboldt begins at least as far back as 1803, when Schinkel, financially in need, was assisted on his Italian tour by Humboldt, who was then the Prussian ambassador to Rome. In 1820, after Humboldt retired from government service, he commissioned Schinkel to redesign his suburban estate, Schloss Tegel.

33. Schinkel's relationship with Beuth, the *Vorbilder* articles, and various other details about the origin of the *Lehrbuch* are discussed by Scott C. Wolff, "Karl Friedrich Schinkel: The Tectonic Unconscious and New Science of Subjectivity" (Ph.D. diss., Princeton University, 1977), 279–317.

34. See Peschken, *Das architektonische Lehrbuch*. Peschken, in his study, defines five distinct *Lehrbuch* conceptions: first Italian trip (1804), the romantic (1810–15), the classicist (c. 1825), the technicist (c. 1830), and the legitimist (after 1835). Others have since disputed such a rigid division and stress the evolving nature of the material gathered. *See*, for instance, Erik Forssmann, *Karl Friedrich Schinkel: Bauwerke und Baugedanken* (Munich: Schnell & Steiner, 1981), 58 ff.

35. Schinkel's relation to German romantic theory has been discussed at length by Bergdoll, *Karl Friedrich Schinkel*, and by Wolff, "Karl Friedrich Schinkel."

36. Scott Wolff points this out in "Karl Friedrich Schinkel," 67.

37. Immanuel Kant, *Kritik der Urtheilskraft*, in *Kant's gesammelte Schriften* (Berlin, 1911), 5:236. "Schönheit ist Form der Zweckmässigkeit eines Gegenstandes, sofern sie ohne Vorstellung eines Zwecks an ihm wahrgenommen wird."

38. Cassirier, *Kant's Life and Thought*, 287.

39. Stephan Körner, *Kant* (New Haven: Yale University Press, 1955), 180–5.

40. Schelling considered architecture's "purposiveness" as the rational mirroring of nature's laws, and its purpose is only its condition, not its principle of absolute truth. In his famous characterization of architecture as "frozen music," he noted that architecture deals with arithmetic and spatial-geometric relations, and only in pursuing these relations does subjectivity achieve union with the objective or natural world: "Architecture, in order to be fine art, must portray the purposiveness within itself as an objective purposiveness, that is, as the objective identity between concept and thing, the subjective and objective." See Friedrich Wilhelm Joseph von Schelling, *The Philosophy of Art*, trans. Douglas W. Scott (Minneapolis: University of Minnesota Press, 1989), 163–80 (quotation from p. 168).

41. *August Schlegels Vorlesungen über schöne Litteratur und Kunst* (Heilbronn, 1884; reprint, Nendeln: Krause, 1968), 160–1. "...die Kunst schöner Formen an Gegenständen, welche ohne bestimmtes Vorbild in der Natur, frei nach einer eignen ursprünglichen Idee des menschlichen Geistes entworfen und ausgeführt werden... sie müssen auf einen Zweck gerichtet seyn."

42. Ibid., 165. "Denn die Architektur ahmt nicht in einzelnen Geständen die Natur nach sondern in ihrer allgemeinen Methode."

43. Ibid., 179. Cicero *De oratore* 3.180.

44. K. F. Schinkel, quoted from Peschken, *Das architektonische Lehrbuch*, 22. "Da Zweckmässigkeit das Grundprincip alles Bauens ist so bestimmt die möglichste Darstellung des Ideals der Zweckmässigkeit das ist der Character oder die Physionomie eines Bauwerks seinen Kunstwerth."

45. Alois Hirt, *Die Baukunst nach den Grundsätzen der Alten* (Berlin, 1809).

46. K. F. Schinkel, quoted from Peschken, *Das architektonische Lehrbuch*, 28. "Diese Frage zeigt die höchste Beschränktheit, die Vollendung der Baukunst im Ganzen mögte wohl in die undendliche Zeitriehe hinausfallen."

47. Ibid., 28. "Diese sogenannten finstern Jahrhunderte des Mittelalters wenn man etwa die der Völkerwanderung ausnehmen mögte sind für den tiefer blickenden nicht so finster sondern zeigen den Anfang einer durchaus neuen Entwickelung das durchaus neue Princip scheint Hirt nicht zu sehen."

48. On Hirt's overall architectural theory, see Jan Philipp Klaus, *Um 1800: Architekturtheorie und Architekturkritik in Deutschland zwischen 1790 and 1810* (Stuttgart: Axel Menges, 1977).

49. See Arthur Schopenhauer, *The World as Will and Representation*, trans. E. F. J. Payne (New York: Dover, 1969), 1:213–18 (sec. 43).

50. K. F. Schinkel, quoted from Peschken, *Das Architektonische Lehrbuch*, 45. "Die architectonischen Verhältnisse beruhen auf ganz allgemeine statischen Gesetzen, werden aber erst recht bedeutend durch die Beziehung und Analogie der persönlichen Existenz des Menschen zunächst oder ihm ähnlich gebildeter und organisirter Wesen der Natur."

51. Ibid., 58.

52. Ibid., 148. "Architectur unterschieden hier vom Bauen – dass Architectur bezeichnet die mit ästhetischem Gefühl erhobene Construction." Ibid., 59. "Ganz unabhängig vom sinnlichen Wohlgefallen erwecken hierdurch die Formen ein sittlich-geistiges Wohlgefallen, welches theils aus der Erfreulichkeit der angeregten Vorstellungen hervorgeht, theils auch aus dem Vergnügen welches die blosse Thätitkeit eines deutlichen Erkennens unfehlbar nach sich zieht."

53. On the museum's importance to Prussia's emerging cultural policies, see Steven Moyano, "Quality vs. History: Schinkel's Altes Museum and Prussian Arts Policy," *The Art Bulletin* 72 (1990): 585–608. See also Forster-Hahn and Kurt W. Forster, "Art and the Course of Empire in Nineteenth-Century Berlin," in *Art in Berlin 1815–1989* (Atlanta: High Museum of Art, 1990), 41–60.

54. On details of the mural designs, see Helmut Börsch-Supan, "Zur Entstehungsgeschichte," *Zeitschrift des deutschen Vereins für Kunst-Wissenschaft* 35 (1981): 36–46; Jörg Trempler, *Das Wandbildprogramm von Karl Friedrich Schinkel, Altes Museum*

Berlin (Berlin: Gebr. Mann, 2001). See also Wolff, "Karl Friedrich Schinkel," 185–90.

55. For their content, see Rave, *Karl Friedrich Schinkel*, 76–7. See also Bergdoll's discussion of the building and its decorative content in his *Karl Friedrich Schinkel*, 195–209.

56. Franz Kugler, *Karl Friedrich Schinkel* (Berlin: George Gropius, 1842), 21.

57. On Weinbrenner's many designs for monuments, several of which were directed to France, see Klaus Lankheit, *Friedrich Weinbrenner und der Denkmalskult um 1800* (Basel: Birkhäuser, 1979). See also Gottfried Leiber, *Friedrich Weinbrenners städtebauliches Schaffen für Karlsruhe* (Karlsruhe: G. Braun, 1996), and David B. Brownlee, ed., *Friedrich Weinbrenner, Architect of Karlsruhe* (Philadelphia: University of Pennsylvania Press, 1986).

58. Friedrich Weinbrenner, *Briefe und Aufsätze*, ed. Arthus Valdenaire (Karlsruhe: G. Braun, 1926), 11. "Die Schönheit liegt somit in der vollkommenen Uebereinstimmung der Form mit dem Zweck, und vollkommen ist die Form, wenn das Objekt in ihr vollendet erscheint, so dass wir für die gegebene Gestalt nichts dazu oder davon denken können." At this point Weinbrenner adds a footnote in which he discusses Kant's third moment of beauty.

59. Ibid., 11. "Schön ist demnach eine Gestalt, in deren Umrissen sich durchaus eine zweckmässige Vollendung zeigt." Idem, 12, "Das Kunstschöne beruht auf einer Idee, und darum muss der ächte und rechte Künstler neben dem Talent für technische Ausführung jene geniale Kraft besitzen, welche frei im Reiche der Formen waltet, und sie hervorzubringen und zu beleben weiss."

60. On Moller, see Marie Frölich and Hans-Günther Sperlich, *Georg Moller: Baumeister der Romantik* (Darmstadt: E. Roether, 1959).

61. See J. Görres, "Der Dom in Köln," *Rheinischer Merkur*, 20 November 1814, 125–7.

62. G. Moller, *Denkmäler der deutschen Baukunst*, 3 vols. (Darmstadt: Karl Wilhelm Leske, 1815–21); translated by W. H. Leeds, as *Moller's Memorials of German-Gothic Architecture* (London: J. Weale, 1836).

63. *Moller's Memorials of German-Gothic Architecture*, 6–7.

64. On the life and work of Klenze, see Windfried Nerdinger, *Leo von Klenze: Architekt zwischen Kunst und Hof, 1784–1864* (Munich: Prestel, 2000); Oswald Hederer, *Leo von Klenze: Persönlichkeit und Werk* (Munich: Georg D. W. Callwey, 1981); and Norbert Lieb and Florian Hufnagel, *Leo von Klenze: Gemälde und Zeichnungen* (Munich, 1979). On Gärtner, see Winfried Nerdinger, ed., *Friedrich von Gärtner: Ein Architektenleben, 1791–1847* (Munich: Klinkhardt & Biermann, 1992); Oswald Hederer, *Friedrich von Gärtner, 1792–1847: Leben, Werk Schüler* (Munich: Prestel, 1976); and Klaus Eggert, *Friedrich von Gärtner: Der Baumeister König Ludwigs I* (Munich: Verlag des Stadtarchivs München, 1963). See also Kathleen Curran's chapter on Gärtner and Munich in her new book *The Romanesque Revival: Religion, Politics, and Transnational Exchange* (University Park: Pennsylvania State University Press, 2003).

65. See also Winfried Nerdinger, "Weder Hadrian noch Augustus – Zur Kunstpolitik Ludwigs I," in *Romantik und Restauration: Architektur in Bayern zur Zeit Ludwigs I, 1825–1848* (Munich: Hugendubel 1987).

66. On the planning and decoration of the Glyptothek, see the various essays in Klause Vierneisel and Gottlieb Leinz, ed., *Glyptothek München 1830–1980* (Munich: Glyptothek, 1980).

67. On his theory, see Dirk Klose, *Klassizismus als idealistische Weltanschauung: Leo von Klenze als Kunstphilosoph* (Munich: Uni-Druck: 1999).

68. Ibid., 12–13.

69. L. von Klenze, *Der Tempel des olympischen Jupiter zu Agrigent* (Stuttgart, 1821); idem, "Versuch einer Widerherstellung des toskanischen Temples nach seinen historischen und technischen Analogien" (lecture given 3 March 1821), *Denkschriften der Königlichen Akademie der Wissenschaften* 3 (1824).

70. L. von Klenze, *Anweisung zur Architektur des christlichen Cultus* (Munich: In der Liter. Artist. Anstalt, 1822; reprint, Nördlingen: Uhl, 1990).

71. Ibid., 6–7. "Architektur in ethischen Sinne ist die Kunst, Naturstoffe zu Zwecken der menschlichen Gesellschaft und ihrer Bedürfnisse so zu formen und zu vereinigen."

72. These and other details of Klenze's life and work are given in the chapter on Klenze in David Watkin and Tilman Mellinghoff, *German Architecture and the Classical Ideal* (Cambridge: M.I.T. Press, 1987), 141–69. On the church itself, see Günther-Alexander Haltrich, *Leo von Klenze: Die Allerheiligenhofkirche in München* (Munich: Uni-Druck, 1983).

73. Kathleen Curran makes this point in "The German Rundbogenstil and Reflections on the American Round-Arched Style," *Journal of the Society of Architectural Historians* 47 (1988): 356.

74. Excerpts of Klenze's manuscripts cited by Hederer, *Leo von Klenze*, 14. "Wir leben nicht mehr in der Zeit des unbewussten, naturnotwendigen Schaffens, durch welches früher die Bauordnungen entstanden, sondern in einer Epoch des Denkens, des Forschens und der selbstbewussten Reflexion."

75. Ibid., 15. "Eine scharf ausgesprochene Anforderung der Gegenwart an die Baukunst ist die Verbindung praktischer Zweckmässigkeit mit möglichster Kostenersparnis."

76. See Werner Szambien, "Die Ausbildung in Paris (1812–1814)," in Nerdinger, *Friedrich von Gärtner*, 41–50.

77. Letter of Gärtner to Johann Martin von Wagner, 13 January 1828, in Eggert, *Friedrich von Gärtner*, 21–2. ". . . dass zwischen diesen strengen griechischen oder überhaupt den schulgerechten strengen architektonischen Regeln, und dem rein gemütlichen und phantastischen des Mittelalters etwas liege, dass wenn es vereint werden könnte sicher das beste für christliche nämentlich katholische Kirchen seyn müsste."

78. On the planning of the Ludwigskirche, see Frank Büttner, "Die Planungsgeschichte der Ludwigskirche in München," *Munchner Jahrbuch der bildenden Kunst* 35 (1984): 189–218.

79. For the details of Hübsch's life and work, see Arthur Valdenaire, *Heinrich Hübsch: Eine Studie zur Baukunst der Romantik* (Karlsruhe, 1826); Joachim Göricke, *Die Kirchen Bauten des Architekten Heinrich Hübsch* (Stuttgart: Koldewey-Gesellschaft, 1974); and Wulf Schirmer, *Heinrich Hübsch, 1795–1863: Die grosse badische Baumeister der Romantik* (Karlsruhe: C. F. Müller, 1983). For his theory and the context of his ideas, see the introduction to Wolfgang Herrmann, ed., *In What Style Should We Build? The German Debate on Architectural Style* (Santa Monica, Calif.: Getty Publications Program, 1992). See also Barry Bergdoll, "Archaeology vs. History: Heinrich Hübsch's Critique

of Neoclassicism and the Beginnings of Historicism in German Architectural Theory," *Oxford Art Journal* 5, no. 2 (1983): 3–12.

80. Rumohr first traveled to Rome in 1805 with Ludwig Tieck, where he met Madame de Staël, Wilhelm Schlegel, and the Humboldt brothers. Between 1817 and 1821 he split his time between Rome and Tuscany. Hübsch knew Rumohr well enough to send him a drawing from Greece. See Herrmann, *In What Style Should We Build? The German Debate on Architectural Style*, 4, 52 n. 13.

81. Friedrich von Rumohr, *Italienischen Forschungen*, ed. Julius Schlosser (Frankfurt: Frankrufter Verlags-Anstalt, 1920), 1:iv.

82. Ibid., 1:87. "... wir den Style als ein zu Gewohnheit gediehenes sich Fügen in der inneren Forderung des Stoffes erklären, in welchem der Bildner seine Gestalten wirklich bildet, der Maler sie erscheinen macht."

83. Hegel rejected Rumohr's materialist formulation in his lectures. See G. W. F. Hegel, *The Philosophy of Fine Art*, trans. F. P. B. Osmaston (London: Bell & Sons, 1920), 1:399.

84. Heinrich Hübsch, *Bau-Werke* (Karlsruhe: Marx, 1838), 2. Cited from Herrmann, *In What Style Should We Build? The German Debate on Architectural Style*, 5.

85. He announced this intention in the dedicatory statement at the beginning of *In welchem Style sollen wir bauen?* (Karlsruhe: Müller, 1828; reprint, Karlsruhe: Müller, 1984).

86. Hirt responded with his "Verteidigung der griechen Architecture gegen H. Hübsch" (Defense of Greek architecture in opposition to H. Hübsch). In the appendix to the second edition of his book (1824), Hübsch countered with his "Verteidigung der griechen Architectur gegen A. Hirt" (Defense of Greek architecture against A. Hirt). See Bergdoll, "Archaeology vs. History," 3.

87. Hübsch, *In welchem Style sollen wir bauen?*

88. Hübsch, *In What Style Should We Build?* 63–4.

89. Ibid., 95.

90. Ibid., 99.

91. Ibid.

92. Ibid.

93. Hegel, *Philosophy of Fine Art*, 3:90–1.

94. Hübsch, *In What Style Should We Build?* 99.

95. For a discussion of Hübsch's theater design, see Kurt Milde, *Neorenaissance in der deutschen Architektur des 19.Jahrhunderts* (Dresden: Verlag der Kunst Dresden, 1981), 117–19.

96. On Hübsch's exhibition in Munich and Gärtner's response, see Curran, *The Romanesque Revival*.

97. Rudolf Wiegmann, "Remarks on the Treatise In What Style Should We Build?" in Herrmann, *In What Style Should We Build? The German Debate on Architectural Style*, 103–4: originally published in *Kunst-Blatt* 10 (1829): 173–4, 181–3.

98. Ibid., 105.

99. Ibid., 106, 111.

100. Franz Kugler, "Über den Kirchenbau und seine Bedeutung für unsere Zeit," *Museum: Blätter für bildende Kunst* 2 (1834): 5. Cited from Herrmann, *In What Style Should We Build?* 6.

101. E. Metzger, "Über die Einwirkung natürlicher und strucktiver Gesetze auf Formgestaltung des Bauwerkes," *Allgemeine Bauzeitung* nos. 21–26 (1837): 196. "...nach einem Systeme geordneter Spannung gebildet find, enge verbunden sich wechselseitig vertreten und Stützen, wornach für das einzelne Gewölbefeld ein Flechtwerk erzeugt ist, welches als Ganzes auch für sich bestehen konnte."

102. C. A. Rosenthal, "In What Style Should We Build?" in Herrmann, *In What Style Should We Build?* 119.

103. Ibid., 120.

104. On the details of Reichensperger's life and ideas, see Michael J. Lewis, *The Politics of the German Gothic Revival: August Reichensperger* (New York: Architectural History Foundation, 1993).

105. Ibid., 57–86.

106. R. Wiegmann, "Gedanken über die Entwickelung eines zeitgemässen nazionalen Baustyls," *Allgemeine Bauzeitung* 4 (1841): 207.

107. Ibid., 208. "Dieser Eklektizismus hat nun eine Verwirrung in diese Kunst gebracht, deren Ende kaum abzusehen ist... unsere modernen Bauwerke mehr aus dem Geschichtspunkte der Mode, als dem der echten Kunst zu beurtheilen sich veranlasst fühlen."

108. Ibid., 214. "Der Versöhnung des Geistigen mit dem Sinnlichen, der vollkommenen Harmonie zwischen dem Aeusserlichen und Innerlichen."

109. J. H. Wolff, "Entgegnung," *Beilage zur Allgemeinen Bauzeitung* 2, no. 1 (1843): 1–5.

110. J. H. Wolff, "Remarks on the Architectural Questions Broached by Professor Stier at the Meeting of Architects at Bamberg," in Herrmann, *In What Style Should We Build?* 144; originally published as "Einige Worte über die von Herrn Professor Stier bei der Architekten-Versammlung zu Bamberg zur Sprache gebrachten architektonischen Fragen," *Beilage zur Allgemeinen Bauzeitung* 2, no. 17 (1845): 270.

111. Ibid., 145 (original, 270).

112. J. H. Wolff, *Beiträge zur Aesthetik der Baukunst oder die Grundgesetze der plastischen Form, nachgewiesen an den Haupttheilen der griechischen Architektur* (Leipzig: Carl Wilhelm Leski, 1834).

113. On Schinkel's notion of style synthesis, see Norbert Knopp, "Schinkels Idee einer Stilsynthese," in *Beiträge zur Problem des Stilpluralism* (Munich: Prestel Verlag, 1977), 245–54. See also the discussion of this building in Bergdoll, *Karl Friedrich Schinkel*, 99–101.

114. K. F. Schinkel, *Aus Schinkels Nachlass*, 3:334. "Könnte man, altgriechische Baukunst in ihrem geistigen Princip festhaltend, sie auf die Bedingungen unserer neuen Weltperiode erweitern, worin zugleich die harmonische Verschmelzung des Besten aus allen Zwischenperioden liegt, so möchte man für die Aufgabe vielleicht das Geeigneteste gefunden haben."

115. This is the view of Kathleen Curran in *The Romanesque Revival*.

116. E. Metzger, "Beitrag zur Zeitfrage: In welchem Stil man bauen soll!" in *Allgemeine Bauzeitung* 10 (1845): 176. "Dieses Wort ist für den Plastiker als Architekten, ich glaube es gerne, ein Schreckenswort!"

117. Ibid., 178. "...eine schlanke feingefühlte Linienbildung, aufstrebend geordnet." Ibid., 177. "Das Netz des spitzbogigen Bausystems in seiner gesammten Verspannung ist jenem, das sich der Natur des Eisens gemäss entwickelt, nahe verwandt."

118. Karl Bötticher, "The Principles of the Hellenic and German Ways of Building with Regard to their Application to Our Present Way of Building," in Herrmann, *In What Style Should We Build?* 158; originally published as "Das Prinzip der hellenischen und germanischen Bauweise hinsichtlich der Uebertragung in die

Bauweise unserer Tage," *Allgemeine Bauzeitung*, 11 (1846): 111–25.

119. Ibid., 151.

120. Ibid., 165.

121. Bötticher, *Die Tektonik der Hellenen* (Potsdam: Ferdinand Niegel, 1852), 1.

122. Bötticher, "Entwickelung der Formen der hellenischen Tektonik," *Allgemeine Bauzeitung* 5 (1840): 322.

123. Bötticher, *Die Tektonik der Hellenen*, Vorwort, xiv.

124. Ibid., xv.

125. Ibid., 28.

126. See August Hahn, *Der Maximilianstil in München: Program und Verwirklichung* (Munich: Moos, 1982), and Ebenhard Drüeke, *"Maximilianstil" Zum Stilbegriff der Architektur im 19. Jahrhundert* (Mittenwald, Germany: Mäander, 1981).

6. Competing Directions at Midcentury

1. On the Cambridge Camden Society, see James F. White, *The Cambridge Movement* (Cambridge: Cambridge University Press, 1962); Phoebe B. Standon, *The Gothic Revival and American Church Architecture: An Episode in Taste, 1840–56* (Baltimore: Johns Hopkins University Press, 1968).

2. *The Ecclesiologist* 2, nos. 14–15 (1842): 5. On the use of the romanesque or Rundbogen style for church building in Britain, see also Kathleen Curran, The *Romanesque Revival: Religion, Politics, and Transnational Exchange* (University Park: Pennsylvania University Press, 2003).

3. On Weale, see Nikolaus Pevsner, *Some Architectural Writers of the Nineteenth Century* (Oxford: Clarendon Press, 1972), 129–30.

4. Scott in his autobiography refers to Pugin's articles in the *Dublin Review* and also stresses the importance of the elder Pugin's *Specimens of Gothic Architecture*. See G. G. Scott, *Personal and Professional Recollections* (London: Sampson Low, 1879; reprint New York: De Capo, 1977), 110.

5. *The Ecclesiologist* 4, no. 4 (1845): 184.

6. G. G. Scott, *A Plea for the Faithful Restoration of Our Ancient Churches* (London: John Henry Parker, 1850).

7. Ibid., 2.

8. See Pevsner, *Some Architectural Writers*, 171–2.

9. G. G. Scott, *Lectures on the Rise and Development of Medieval Architecture* (London: J. Murray, 1879), 209.

10. T. Hope, *An Historical Essay on Architecture* (London: John Murray, 1835).

11. Ibid. (3rd ed., 1840), 492.

12. Peter Collins, *Changing Ideals in Modern Architecture 1750–1950* (London: Faber & Faber, 1965), 218.

13. W. H. Leeds, in *Studies and Examples of the Modern School of English Architecture* (London: Weale, 1839).

14. For an extensive discussion of these lectures, see Peter Kohane, "Architecture, Labor and the Human Body: Fergusson, Cockerell and Ruskin" (Ph.D. diss., University of Pennsylvania, 1993), 278–414. I thank Peter for sharing copies of various of the lectures with me.

15. See Frank Salmon, *Building on Ruins: The Rediscovery of Rome and English Architecture* (London: Ashgate, 2000), 144–5.

16. T. L. Donaldson, *Preliminary Discourse pronounced before the University College of London, upon the Commencement of a Series of Lectures on Architecture* (London, 1842), 28.

17. J. Fergusson, "Effect of the Want of Reality on the Works of Modern Architects," *The Builder*, 16 March 1850, 122.

18. A. W. Pugin, "How Shall We Build Our Churches?" *The Builder*, 23 March 1850, 134–5.

19. R. Kerr, "Copyism in Architecture," *The Builder*, 16 November 1850, 543.

20. James Fergusson, *An Historical Inquiry into the True Principles of Beauty in Art, Especially with Reference to Architecture* (London: Longman, 1849), xv.

21. J. Fergusson, *History of the Modern Styles in Architecture: Being a Sequel to the Handbook of Architecture* (London: Longman, 1849), 329.

22. Ibid., 490.

23. On the Architectural Association, see John Summerson, *The Architectural Association 1847–1947* (London: Pleiades Books, 1947).

24. R. Kerr, *The Newleafe Discourses on the Fine Art Architecture: An Attempt to Talk Nationally on the Subject* (London: Weale, 1846), 179.

25. E. L. Garbett, *Rudimentary Treatise on the Principles of Design in Architecture as Deducible from Nature and Exemplified in the Works of the Greek and Gothic Architects* (London: Weale, 1850), 130.

26. Ibid., 253.

27. Ibid., 263–4.

28. Ibid., 264.

29. R. Kerr, preface to J. Fergusson, *History of the Modern Styles of Architecture*, 3rd ed. (London: John Murray, 1891), vi.

30. Cited from Patrick Beaver, *The Crystal Palace: 1851–1936: A Portrait of Victorian Enterprise* (London: Hugh Evelyn, 1970), 41–2.

31. William Whewell, "On the General Bearing of the Great Exhibition," in *Lectures on the Progress of Arts and Science* (New York, 1856), 12.

32. On Cole, see Elizabeth Bonython, *King Cole: A Picture Portrait of Sir Henry Cole, ксв, 1808–1882* (London: Victoria & Albert Museum, n.d.). See also *Henry Cole, Fifty Years of Public Work: Accounted for in his Deeds, Speeches and Writings*, 2 vols. (London: George Bell & Sons, 1884).

33. Charles Dickens, *Hard Times* (New York: Gramercy Books, 1982), 337.

34. Cited from Bonython, *King Cole*, 1–2.

35. Quentin Bell, *The Schools of Design* (London: Routledge & Kegan Paul, 1963), 1.

36. *Journal of Design and Manufactures* 1 (March 1849): 3.

37. On Redgrave, see Susan P. Casteras and Ronald Parkinson, eds., *Richard Redgrave, 1804–1888* (New Haven: Yale University Press, 1988).

38. R. Redgrave, "Supplementary Report on Design," in *Report by the Juries* (London: William Clowes & Sons, 1852), 713.

39. O. Jones, "Gleanings from the Great Exhibition of 1851," *Journal of Design and Manufacturers* 5 (June 1851): 93.

40. O. Jones, *The Grammar of Ornament* (New York: Van Nostrand Reinhold Co., 1982; originally published in 1856), 5.

41. See John Martin Robinson, *The Wyatts: An Architectural Dynasty* (Oxford: Oxford University Press, 1979).

42. M. D. Wyatt, "The Exhibition under Its Commercial Aspects," *Journal of Design and Manufacturers* 5 (August 1851): 157.

43. M. D. Wyatt, *The Industrial Arts of the Nineteenth Century: A Series of Illustrations of the Choicest Specimens Produced by Every Nation at the Great Exhibition of Works of Industry, 1851* (London, 1851), 1:vii.

44. M. D. Wyatt, "Iron Work and the Principles of Its Treatment," *Journal of Design and Manufactures* 4 (September 1850): 78.

45. R. Kerr, "English Architecture Thirty Years Hence," paper read in 1884, reprinted in Pevsner, *Some Architectural Writers*, 299.

46. Cited from Bonython, *King Cole*, 10.

47. Among the host of books on Ruskin's life and ideas, see Quentin Bell, *Ruskin* (New York: George Braziller, 1978); Wolfgang Kemp, *The Desire of My Eyes: The Life and Work of John Ruskin*, trans. Jan van Heurck (New York: Noonday Press, 1990); and Tim Hilton, *John Ruskin*, 2 vols. (New Haven: Yale University Press, 1985–2000).

48. J. Ruskin, *The Seven Lamps of Architecture* (London: Smith, Elder & Co., 1849), 2.

49. Ibid., 7.

50. Ibid., 8.

51. Ibid., 28.

52. Ibid., 187.

53. Ibid., 192.

54. Ibid., 114, 173–4.

55. Ibid., 36.

56. Ibid., 36–7.

57. Ibid., 111.

58. Ibid., 195.

59. Ibid., 195–6.

60. Ibid., 160.

61. *Journal of Design and Manufacturers* 2 (October 1849): 72. Pevsner (*Some Architectural Writers of the Nineteenth Century*, p. 155) identifies the reviewer as Matthew Digby Wyatt.

62. Ibid.

63. Kemp, *Desire of My Eyes*, 162.

64. J. Ruskin, *The Stones of Venice*, 3 vols (New York: John W. Lovell, n.d.), 1:15.

65. Ibid., 15–16.

66. Ibid., 3.

67. Ibid., 49, 56.

68. Ibid., pl. XIII, opposite p. 291.

69. Ibid., 2:159–60.

70. Ibid., 162.

71. Ibid., 160 n.

72. Ibid., 3:101.

73. Ibid., 2:267.

74. Ibid., 83.

75. Ibid., 1:31.

76. Ibid., 399.

77. Ibid.

78. Ibid., 406–7.

79. J. Ruskin, *Lectures on Architecture and Painting, Delivered at Edinburgh in November, 1853* (London: Smith, Elder & Co, 1855).

80. J. Ruskin, "The Deteriorative Power of Conventional Art over Nations," in *The Two Paths: Being Lectures on Art, and its Application to Decoration and Manufacture* (London: Smith, Elder & Co., 1859), 34–5.

81. Among the vast number of volumes devoted to Viollet-le-Duc, see Jean-Paul Midant, *Au Moyen Âge avec Violle-le-Duc* (Paris: Parangon, 2001); Kevin D. Murphy, *Memory and Modernity: Viollet-le-Duc at Vézelay* (University Park: Penn State University Press, 2000); Laurent Baridon, *L'imaginaire scientifique de Viollet-le-Duc* (Paris: Harmattan, 1996); Françoise Bercé, *Viollet-le-Duc: Architect, Artist, Master of Historic Preservation* (Washington, D.C.: The Trust for Museum Exhibitions, 1987); M. F. Hearn, *The Architectural Theory of Viollet-le-Duc: Readings and Commentary* (Cambridge: M.I.T. Press, 1990). See also Robin Middleton's entry on Viollet-le-Duc in *Macmillan Encyclopedia of Architecture* (New York: Macmillan, 1982), and Martin Bressani's forthcoming book *Surface into Depth: A Tracing of Viollet-le-Duc's Constructive Imagination*.

82. See Murphy, *Memory and Modernity*, 39–40.

83. Viscount de Chateaubriand, *The Genius of Christianity or the Spirit and Beauty of the Christian Religion* (Baltimore: John Murphy, 1856), 385.

84. See Pevsner's discussion of Caumont in *Some Architectural Writers*, 36–44.

85. See Murphy, *Memory and Modernity*, 45–6.

86. See Bercé, *Viollet-le-Duc*. See also Bressani, *Surface into Depth*.

87. Viollet-le-Duc, "De la construction des édifices religieux en France depuis le commencement du christianisme jusqu'au XVIe siècle." The articles ran as five chapters in eight installments of the *Annales Archéologiques* from 1844 to 1847.

88. Ibid., vol. 2 (1845), 136. "Il y a là une science et un art inconnus jusqu'alors et perdus aujourd'hui, que nous croyons tout savoir et que nous avons tant de choses à retrouver."

89. Bressani, in *Surface into Depth*, traces the concept back to the theory of Père Enfantin and discusses the notion of "elasticity" at length.

90. Viollet-le-Duc, "De la construction des édifices religieux en France," vol. 2 (1845), 136.

91. Ibid., 329.

92. See especially Robin Middleton, "The Rationalist Interpretations of Classicism of Léonce Reynaud and Viollet-le-Duc," *AA Files* II (Spring 1986): 29–48, and Barry Bergdoll, *Léon Vaudoyer: Historicism in the Age of Industry* (Cambridge: M.I.T. Press, 1994), 122–43.

93. See Léonce Reynaud, "Architecture," in *Encyclopédie nouvelle, ou Dictionnaire philosophique, scientifique, littéraire et industriel*, ed. P. Leroux and J. Reynaud (Paris: Libraire de Charles Gosselin, 1836; reprint, Slatkine Reprints, 1991), 1:772.

94. Ibid. "Ce qui peut s'exprimer ainsi: Il y aura progrès toutes les fois que les supports et les parties supportées seront disposés de manière à ce que le rapport du plein au vide soit diminué, ou à ce qu'on puisse employer de plus petits matériaux."

95. On this issue, see especially Bergdoll, *Léon Vaudoyer*, 125–9.

96. Cited from Bergdoll, *Léon Vaudoyer*, 129. "Quoi! Le gothique serait notre art national! Et nous devrions répudier toutes les conquêtes qui ont été faites depuis!"

97. On the history of this journal, see Hélène Lipstadt, "The Building and the Book in César Daly's *Revue Générale de l'Architecture*,"

in *Architecturereproduction*, ed. Beatriz Colomina (New York: Princeton Architectural Press, 1988), 25–55, and idem, "César Daly and the *Revue générale de l'architecture*" (Ph.D. diss., Harvard University, 1981. See also Ann Lorenz Van Zanten, "Form and Society: César Daly and the *Revue Générale de l'Architecture*," *Oppositions* 8 (Spring 1977): 137–45.

98. César Daly, "De la liberté dans l'art," *Revue Générale de l'Architecture* 7 (1847): 393.

99. Ibid., 397. "Il croit au progrès, il respecte le passé, il veut la liberté."

100. Léonce Reynaud, *Traité d'architecture*, 2 vols. (Paris: Dalmont et Dunod, 1860–3; originally published in 1850–8), 1:14–15.

101. Ibid., 557.

102. Viollet-le-Duc, "Essai sur l'origine et les développements de l'art de Bâtir en France," *Revue Générale de l'Architecture* 10 (1852): 245. See also Bergdoll, *Léon Vaudoyer*, 201.

103. E. E. Viollet-le-Duc, *Dictionnaire raisonné de l'architecture française du XIᵉ au XVIᵉ siècle*, 10 vols. (Paris: Bance, 1854–68); idem, *Dictionnaire raisonné du moblier français de l'epoque carolingienne à la renaissance*, 6 vols. (Paris: Morel, 1858–75); idem, *Entretiens sur l'architecture* (1858–72); translated by Benjamin Bucknall as *Lectures on Architecture*, 2 vols. (New York: Dover, 1987). Parts of the *Dictionnaire raisonné de l'architecture française* have been translated by Kenneth D. Whitehead in *The Foundations of Architecture: Selections from the Dictionnaire Raisonné*, introduction by Barry Bergdoll (New York: George Barziller, 1990).

104. Viollet-le-Duc, *Dictionnaire raisonné de l'architecture française*, 1:xi.

105. Ibid., xix–xx. "...c'est que nous regardons cette étude comme pouvant rendre aux architects cette souplesse, cette habitude d'appliquer à toute chose un principe vrai, cette originalité native et cette indépendance qui tiennent au génie de notre pays."

106. Nearly seventy pages of this article have been translated by Whitehead in *The Foundations of Architecture*.

107. Again a lengthy excerpt of this important article has been translated by Whitehead in *The Foundations of Architecture*.

108. On Viollet-le-Duc drawings, see Bressani, *Surface into Depth*.

109. Viollet-le-Duc, *Dictionnaire raisonné de l'architecture*, 8:167.

110. Ibid., 169.

111. Ibid., 156–7.

112. Ibid., 196–7.

113. Ibid., 15.

114. E. E. Viollet-le-Duc, quoted from Whitehead, *Foundations of Architecture*, 242.

115. Ibid., 234.

116. Ibid., 233.

117. Ibid., 256, 248.

118. Ibid., 260.

119. E. E. Viollet-le-Duc, *Lectures on Architecture*, 1:81. In his analogy, Greek architecture is compared "to a man stript of his clothes," while Roman architecture "may be compared to a man clothed."

120. Ibid., 172.

121. Ibid., 176.

122. Ibid., 177.

123. Ibid.

124. Ibid., 184.

125. César Daly, "Introduction," *Revue Générale de l'Architecture* 24 (1866): 5, 8. "...l'école rationaliste, qui tend en ce moment à transformer l'*art architectural* en *architecture industrielle*."

126. César Daly, "Introduction," *Revue Générale de l'Architecture* 21 (1863): 9. "Il se tiendra prudemment sur cet isthme destiné à faciliter à notre faiblesse le passage du vieux monde qui achève de s'écrouler, vers ce monde nouveau qui émerge lentement du sein de l'inconnu."

127. Bourgeois de Lagny, "Salon de 1866," *Le Moniteur des Architectes*, 1 June 1866, 81–2. "Le réalisme architectural (ou la construction avec l'absence d'art)."

128. Ibid., 83.

129. Emile Zola, *Le ventre de Paris* (Paris: Librairie générale française, 1978).

130. Viollet-le-Duc, *Lectures on Architecture*, 2:58.

131. A. Choisy, *Histoire de l'architecture*, 2 vols. (Paris: Gauthier-Villars, 1899), 764. "...un système nouveau de proportions s'est fait jour; où les lois harmoniques ne seront autres que celles de la stabilité."

132. On Semper's life and ideas, see Wolfgang Herrmann, *Gottfried Semper: In Search of Style* (Cambridge: M.I.T. Press, 1984), and H. F. Mallgrave, *Gottfried Semper: Architect of the Nineteenth Century* (New Haven: Yale University Press, 1996).

133. G. Semper, *Preliminary Remarks on Polychrome Architecture and Sculpture in Antiquity*, translated by H. F. Mallgrave and Wolfgang Herrmann, in *Gottfried Semper: The Four Elements of Architecture and Other Writings* (New York: Cambridge University Press, 1989), 45–73; originally published as *Vorläufige Bermerkungen über bemalte Architectur und Plastik bei den Alten* (Altona, 1834).

134. Ibid., 65 (original 33–4). "Dabei darf neben der Malerei der metallene Zierrath, die Vergoldung, die Drapperie von Teppichen, Baldachinen und Vorhängen und das bewegliche Geräthe nicht ausser Augen gelassen werden. Auf alles dieses und mehr noch auf die mitwirkende Umbegung und Staffage von Volk, Priestern und Festüngen waren die Monumente beim Entstehen berechnet. Sie waren das Gerüste, bestimmt, allen diesen Kräften einen gemeinsamen Wirkungspunkt zu gewähren. Der Glanz, der die Einbildungskraft ausfüllt, denk man sich lebhaft in jene Zeiten zurück, macht die Nachahmungen aus denselben, wie man sich seither gefallen hat, sie den unsrigen aufzudringen, erbleichen und erstarren."

135. Ibid., 47 (original, viii–ix). "...nur auf dem Boden des Bedürfnisses und unter der Sonne der Freiheit."

136. For details of the theater, see Mallgrave, *Gottfried Semper*, 117–29.

137. Richard Wagner, *Mein Leben* (Munich: F. Bruckmann, 1911), 1:373.

138. Ibid., 479.

139. G. Semper, *The Four Elements of Architecture: A Contribution to the Comparative Study of Architecture*, in *Gottfried Semper: The Four Elements of Architecture and Other Writings*; originally published as *Die Vier Elemente der Baukunst: Beitrag zur vergleichenden Baukunde* (Braunschweig, 1851).

140. On the relation of Klemm and Semper, see H. F. Mallgrave, "Gustav Klemm and Gottfried Semper: The Meeting of

Ethnological and Architectural Theory," *RES 9: Journal of Anthropology and Aesthetics* 9 (Spring 1985): 68–79.

141. Semper, *The Four Elements of Architecture*, 102–3.

142. G. Semper, Ms. 97, fol. 1, Semper Archives, ETH-Zurich.

143. G. Semper, *Science, Industry, and Art: Proposals for the Development of a National Taste in Art*, in *Gottfried Semper: The Four Elements of Architecture and Other Writings*; originally published as *Wissenschaft, Industrie und Kunst: Vorschläge zur Anregung Nationalen Kunstgefühles* (Braunschweig: Friedrich Vieweg & Sohn, 1852).

144. Semper, *Science, Industry, and Art*, 143–4.

145. Ibid., 136 (original 15). "Styl ist das zu künstlerischer Bedeutung erhobene Hervortreten der Grundidee und aller inneren und äusseren Coefficienten, die bei der Verkörperung derselben in einem Kunstwerke modificirent einwirkten."

146. Henry Cole, "Journey to Vienna," Victoria and Albert Museum Library, 101.A.72.

147. G. Semper, *Über die bleiernen Schleudergeschosse der Alten und über zweckmässige Gestaltung der Wurfkörper in Allgemeinen* (Frankfurt: Verlage für Kunst und Wissenschaft, 1859).

148. Ibid. ". . . dass die Gesetz der Natur, wonach diese bei ihren Formengebungen die extremen Grenzen beobachtet und über Spannung herrschen lässt, nich bloss dunkel ahnten, sondern klar erkannten."

149. G. Semper, *Der Stil in den technischen und tektonischen Künsten oder praktische Ästhetik*, 2 vols. (Frankfurt: Verlag für Kunst und Wissenschaft, 1860–3); translated by H. F. Mallgrave and Michael Robinson as *Style in the Technical and Tectonic Arts, or Practical Aesthetics* (Los Angeles: Getty Publications Program, 2004).

150. G. Semper, *Ueber die formelle Gesetzmässigkeit des Schmuckes und dessen Bedeutung als Kunstsymbolik* (Zurich: Meyer & Zeller, 1856).

151. Ibid., 6. "Wo der Mensch schmückt, hebt er nur mit mehr oder weniger bewusstem tun eine Naturgeschlichkeit an dem Gegenstand, den er ziert, deutlicher hervor."

152. Semper, *Style in the Technical and Tectonic Arts*, 71.

153. Ibid., 72.

154. Ibid., 79.

155. Ibid., 80–1.

156. Ibid., 82.

157. Ibid., 469.

158. Ibid., 659.

159. Ibid., 660.

160. Ibid., 438–9.

161. G. Semper, *On Architectural Styles*, in *Gottfried Semper: The Four Elements and Other Writings*, 281; originally published as *Ueber Baustyle* (Zürich: Friedrich Schulthess, 1869), 28.

162. Ibid., 284 (original, 31).

163. For a discussion of the relationship between Nietzsche and Semper, see Mallgrave, *Gottfried Semper*, 346–52.

164. F. Nietzsche, *The Birth of Tragedy*, trans. Walter Kaufmann (New York: Vintage, 1967), 58.

165. For a discussion of the two memoranda, see Heinrich Magirius, *Gottfried Sempers zweites Dresdner Hoftheater: Entstehung, künstlerische Ausstattung, Ikonographie* (Vienna: Hermann Böhlaus, 1895), 141–4.

7. Historicism in the United States

1. On the life and work of Bulfinch, see Howard Kirker, *The Architecture of Charles Bulfinch* (Cambridge: Harvard University Press, 1969); Charles A. Place, *Charles Bulfinch: Architect and Citizen* (New York: Da Capo Press, 1968; originally published in 1925); and Ellen Susan Bulfinch, ed., *The Life and Letters of Charles Bulfinch, Architect, with other Family Papers* (Boston: Houghton Mifflin, 1896). Among the many book on Jefferson's interest in architecture, see Robert Vickery, *The Meaning of the Lawn: Thomas Jefferson's Design for the University of Virginia* (Weimar: VDG, 1998); George Green Shackelford, *Thomas Jefferson's Travels in Europe, 1784–1789* (Baltimore: Johns Hopkins University Press, 1995); Michael Brawne, *The University of Virginia, the Lawn: Thomas Jefferson* (London: Phaidon, 1994); Jack McLaughlin, *Jefferson and Monticello: The Biography of a Builder* (New York: Henry Holt, 1988); Howard C. Rice Jr., *Thomas Jefferson's Paris* (Princeton: Princeton University Press, 1976); Fiske Kimball, *Thomas Jefferson Architect* (New York: Da Capo, 1968; originally published in 1916); and Frederick Doveton Nichols, *Thomas Jefferson's Architectural Drawings* (Charlottesville, Va.: Thomas Jefferson Memorial Foundation, 1961).

2. T. Jefferson, *Notes on the State of Virginia* (1782–7), in *Thomas Jefferson: Writings* (New York: Library of America, 1984), 278.

3. See Nichols, *Thomas Jefferson's Architectural Drawings*, 4, pl. 12.

4. The quotation is from a letter to Madame de Tessé, 20 March 1787, in *Thomas Jefferson: Writings*, 891.

5. Ibid.

6. See Jefferson's "Travel Journals, a Tour to Some of the Gardens of England," in *Thomas Jefferson: Writings*, 623–8.

7. Jefferson to John Page, 4 May 1786, in *Thomas Jefferson: Writings*, 853.

8. Ibid., 853–4. On Jefferson's aesthetics, see Kenneth Hafertepe, "An Inquiry into Thomas Jefferson's Ideas of Beauty," *Journal of the Society of Architectural Historians* 59 (2000): 216–31.

9. Jefferson to Major L'Enfant, 10 April 1791, in *Thomas Jefferson: Writings*, 976.

10. See Jefferson's sketch of Hallet's plan in Nichols, *Thomas Jefferson's Architectural Drawings*, pl. 18. Jefferson sent Hallet's modified plan to President Washington on 26 March 1793, noting the poor lighting and the bad circulation of Thornton's plan, and he received a testy response from the president on 30 June 1793.

11. See Jefferson's letter to Littleton Waller Tazewell, 5 January 1805, in *Thomas Jefferson: Writings*, 1152; on the idea of an "academical village," see also the letter to Messrs. Hugh L. White and Others, 6 May 1810, in *Thomas Jefferson: Writings*, 1222–3. Mary N. Woods has suggested the source for this concept was Quatremère de Quincy's entry "Collége," in *Encyclopédie méthodique* (1788). See her "Thomas Jefferson and the University of Virginia: Planning the Academic Village," *Journal of the Society of Architectural Historians* 44 (October 1985): 272.

12. Jefferson's asked Latrobe for comments on his plan in a letter dated 12 June 1817. The latter responded with his quick sketch of 24 July 1817. See *The Papers of Benjamin Henry Latrobe*, ed.

Edward C. Carter II (New Haven: Yale University Press, 1984–8), 3:901–2, 914–16.

13. On the work of Latrobe, see *The Architectural Drawings of Benjamin Henry Latrobe*, Jeffrey A. Cohen and Charles E. Brownell (eds.), 2 vols. (New Haven: Yale University Press, 1994); Talbot Hamlin, *Benjamin Henry Latrobe* (New York: Oxford University Press, 1955). See also *The Journal of Latrobe: Being the Notes and Sketches of an Architect, Naturalist and Traveler in the United States from 1796 to 1820* (New York: B. Franklin, 1971; originally published in 1905).

14. Latrobe described in detail his overnight stay with Washington in *The Journal of Latrobe*, 50–64.

15. Jefferson to Latrobe, 2 November 1802, *The Papers of Benjamin Henry Latrobe*, 1:221.

16. See Latrobe to Mary Elizabeth Latrobe, 24 November 1802 and 30 November 1802, ibid., 1:232–3, 234–5.

17. Thornton's unabated personal attacks on Latrobe ultimately resulted in a libel suit. For details, see Hamlin, *Benjamin Henry Latrobe*, 284–6.

18. Latrobe to John Carroll, 16 April 1805, in *The Papers of Benjamin Henry Latrobe*, 2:52–4.

19. Latrobe refers to Gilly's *Handbuch der Land-Bau-Kunst* in referring to the Delorme roofing system. See Latrobe to Jefferson, 19 July 1805, ibid., 2:108.

20. Latrobe to Jefferson, 21 May 1807, ibid., 428.

21. Jefferson to Latrobe, 22 April 1807, ibid., 411.

22. Latrobe to Jefferson, 21 May 1807, ibid., 429.

23. Ibid.

24. Latrobe cited the French Revolutionary precedent for design in "Report on the South Wing of the Capitol," 27 April 1815, ibid., 3:655.

25. On his Baltimore work, see Robert L. Alexander, *The Architecture of Maximilian Godefroy* (Baltimore: Johns Hopkins University Press, 1974).

26. An excellent study devoted to Ramée is Paul V. Turner, *Joseph Ramée: International Architect of the Revolutionary Era* (New York: Cambridge University Press, 1996).

27. On the work of Jay, see Frederick Doveton Nichols, *The Architecture of Georgia* (Savannah: Beehive Press, 1976); on Hadfield, see Michael Richman, "George Hadfield (1763–1826): His Contribution to the Greek Revival in America," *Journal of the Society of Architectural Historians* 33 (1974): 234–5.

28. On Parris, see Edward F. Zimmer, "The Architectural Career of Alexander Parris (1780–1852)" (Ph.D. diss., Boston University, 1984); on Willard, see William Wheildon, *Memoir of Solomon Willard: Architecture and Superintendent of the Bunker Hill Monument* (Boston: Monument Association, 1865).

29. A. Benjamin, *The American Builder's Companion, or, A New System of Architecture, particularly Adapted to the Present Style of Building in the United States of America* (Boston: Etheridge & Bliss, 1806). See Jack Quinan, "The Architectural Style of Asher Benjamin" (Ph.D. diss., Brown University, 1973).

30. A. Benjamin, *The Country Builder's Assistant: Containing a Collection of New Designs of Carpentry and Architecture* (Greenfield, Mass.: T. Dickman, 1897).

31. A. Benjamin, *The American Builder's Companion* (New York: Dover, 1969), 30.

32. The classic work on the Greek revival is Talbot Hamlin's *Greek Revival Architecture in America* (New York: Dover, 1964; originally published in 1944).

33. See George Tucker's political biography, *The Life of Thomas Jefferson* (London, 1837).

34. George Tucker, "On Architecture," *Port Folio* (1814): 569.

35. On Town's bridge innovations, see Tom F. Peters, *Building the Nineteenth Century* (Cambridge: M.I.T. Press, 1996), 47–9.

36. See R. W. Liscombe, "A 'New Era in My Life': Ithiel Town Abroad," *Journal of the Society of Architectural Historians* 50 (March 1991): 5–17.

37. On the partnership, see Roger Hale Newton, *Town & Davis, Architects: Pioneers in American Revivalist Architecture, 1812–1870* (New York: Columbia University Press, 1942).

38. The standard biography of Mills is Helen Mar Pierce Gallagher, *Robert Mills: Architect of the Washington Monument, 1781–1855* (New York: AMS Press, 1966; originally published in 1935). See also the essays contained in John M. Bryan, ed., *Robert Mills* (Washington, D.C.: American Institute of Architects Press, 1989). The citation is from Mills's manuscript "The Architectural Works of Robert Mills," in Gallagher, *Robert Mills*, 168.

39. Robert Mills, "The Progress of Architecture in Virginia," in Gallagher, *Robert Mills*, 155.

40. Ibid., 156–7.

41. Ibid., 169.

42. Ibid., 170.

43. On Strickland, see Anges Addison Gilchrist, *William Strickland, Architect and Engineer: 1788–1854* (New York: Da Capo Press, 1969; originally published in 1950).

44. Cited from Fiske Kimball, *American Architecture* (Indianapolis: Bobbs-Merrill, 1928), 98, and Wayne Andrews, *Architecture, Ambition, and Americans: A Social History of American Architecture* (New York: The Free Press, 1978), 130.

45. Cited from Jeffrey A. Cohen's invaluable article "Building a Discipline: Early Institutional Settings for Architectural Education in Philadelphia, 1804–1890," *Journal of the Society of Architectural Historians* 53 (1994): 142.

46. J. Strickland, "Introductory," copied by Reuben Haines, Box 90, folder 65, Wyck Papers, Architectural Philosophical Society, Philadelphia, n.p.

47. Ibid.

48. Ibid.

49. Ibid.

50. On Haviland, see Matthew Eli Baigel, "John Haviland" (Ph.D. diss., University of Pennsylvania, 1965). See also Baigel's "John Haviland in Philadelphia, 1818–1826," *Journal of the Society of Architectural Historians* 25 (1966): 197–208.

51. John Haviland and Hugh Bridport, *The Builder's Assistant, Containing the Five Orders of Architecture: Selected from the Best Specimens of the Greek and Roman, with the Figured Dimensions of their Height, Projection, and Profile, and a Variety of Mouldings, Modillions & Foliage, on a Larger Scale, both Enriched and Plain*, 3 vols. (Philadelphia: John Bioren, 1818–21).

52. Ibid., preface, vol. 3.

53. On Walter, see Robert B. Ennis, *Thomas U. Walter, Architect, 1804–1887*, 2 vols. (Philadelphia: Athenaeum, 1982); see also

Glenn Brown, *History of the United States Capitol*, 2 vols. (New York: Da Capo Press, 1970; originally published in 1902).

54. Thomas U. Walter Papers, Athenaeum of Philadelphia, ms. p. 25.

55. Ibid., 37–8.

56. Ibid., 36.

57. Ibid., 61.

58. Ibid., 62.

59. Silliman's article (one of four) on Gothic architecture appeared in July 1830, no. 2. William H. Pierson has speculated that their high intellectual tone may have been due to the assistance of either Alexander Jackson Davis or Ithiel Town. See Pierson's *American Buildings and Their Architects: Technology and the Picturesque, the Corporate and the Early Gothic Styles* (New York: Anchor Books, 1980), 168–9, 468 n. 4.30.

60. Henry Russell Cleveland's book review appeared in *North American Review* 43 (October 1836): 356–84.

61. John Henry Hopkins, *Essay on Gothic Architecture, with Various Plans and Drawings for Churches: Designed Chiefly for the Use of the Clergy* (Burlington, Vt.: Smith & Harrington, 1836). Pierson discusses the remarks of Silliman, Cleveland, and Hopkins in some depth in his *American Buildings and Their Architects*, 168–72. See also Phoebe Stanton, The *Gothic Revival and American Church Architecture* (Baltimore: Johns Hopkins University Press, 1968).

62. On Upjohn, see E. M. Upjohn, *Richard Upjohn: Architect and Churchman* (New York: Columbia University Press, 1939).

63. See Pierson, *American Buildings and their Architects*, 49–205.

64. See Clarence Epstein, "Church Architecture in Montreal during the British-Colonial Period 1760–1860" (Ph.D. diss., University of Edinburgh, 1999), 216–17.

65. See Pierson's chapter on Renwick in *American Buildings and their Architects*, 206–69.

66. A. D. Gilman, "Architecture in the United States," *North American Review*, April 1844, 437–8, 440.

67. Ibid., 463.

68. A third impulse for the *Rundbogen* in this country were the efforts (beginning in the 1840s) of the Bavarian monarch Ludwig I and the Prussian monarch Friedrich Wilhelm IV. See Kathleen Curran's *The Romanesque Revival: Religion, Politics, and Transnational Exchange* (University Park: Pennsylvania State University Press, 2003).

69. *A Book of Plans for Churches and Parsonages Published under the Direction of the Central Committee appointed by the General Congregation Convention, October 1852* (New York: Daniel Burgess, 1854), 13.

70. See Gwen W. Steege, "The *Book of Plans* and the Early Romanesque Revival in the United States: A Study in Architectural Patronage," *Journal of the Society of Architectural Historians* 46 (September 1987): 215–27.

71. See Kathleen Curran, "The German Rundbogenstil and Reflections on the American Round-Arched Style," *Journal of the Society of Architectural Historians* 47 (December 1988): 373.

72. Henry-Russell Hitchcock, *Architecture: Nineteenth and Twentieth Centuries* (Hammondworth, England: Penguin, 1977), 138.

73. Thomas A. Tefft, "The Cultivation of True Taste," lecture given in Portsmouth, 25 October 1851, archives of the Rhode Island Historical Society, fol. 13.

74. Ibid., fol. 19.

75. These points were made by Michael J. Lewis in "The German Architect in America," a paper given in 1988 at a Brown University symposium.

76. On Hunt, see Paul R. Baker, *Richard Morris Hunt* (Cambridge: M.I.T. Press, 1986).

77. Cited from Baker, *Richard Morris Hunt*, 62.

78. Ibid., 58.

79. On Bogardus, see Margot Gayle and Carol Gayle, *Cast-Iron Architecture in America: The Significance of James Bogardus* (New York: W. W. Norton, 1998).

80. Henry Van Brunt's paper was given on 7 December 1858. See William A. Coles, *Architecture and Society: Selected Essays of Henry Van Brunt* (Cambridge: Harvard University Press, 1969), 79.

81. Ibid., 84.

82. Eidlitz's paper, entitled "Cast Iron and Architecture," was presented on 21 December 1858. Hunt's two stores were located at 474–6 Broadway (1871) and 478–82 Broadway (1874).

83. The best concise study of the aesthetic thought of these two men remains Charles R. Metzger's *Emerson and Greenough: Transcendental Pioneers of an American Esthetic* (Westport, Conn.: Greenwood Press, 1954; reprint, 1974). The one biography devoted to Greenough is Nathalia Wright's *Horatio Greenough: The First American Sculptor* (Philadelphia: University of Pennsylvania Press, 1963).

84. On the Transcendental movement in general, see F. O. Matthiessen, *American Renaissance: Art and Expression in the Age of Emerson and Whitman* (London: Oxford University Press, 1941), and Paul F. Boller Jr., *American Transcendentalism, 1830–1860: An Intellectual Inquiry* (New York: G. P. Putnam, 1974).

85. In a letter to Washington Allston, Greenough noted that "Thorwaldsen made the great change in my views – By a few words which said in expressing his opinion on my work – he learned me to think for myself in my art." See *Letters of Horatio Greenough: American Sculptor*, ed. Nathalia Wright (Madison: University of Wisconsin Press, 1972), 7.

86. Letter dated 19 April 1853, in *The Correspondence of Emerson and Carlyle, 1834–1872*, ed. Joseph Slater (New York: Aperature, 1980), 486.

87. Ralph Waldo Emerson, "English Traits," in *Ralph Waldo Emerson: Essays and Lectures* (New York: Library of America, 1983), 768.

88. Ralph Waldo Emerson, "Nature," in *Ralph Waldo Emerson*, 10.

89. Ralph Waldo Emerson, "The Transcendentalist," in *Ralph Waldo Emerson*, 106.

90. Ralph Waldo Emerson, "Self-Reliance," in *Ralph Waldo Emerson*, 277.

91. Ibid., 278.

92. Ibid.

93. Ralph Waldo Emerson, "Thoughts on Art," in *The Works of Ralph Waldo Emerson* (New York: Tudor Publishing, n.d.), 4:67.

94. Ralph Waldo Emerson, "The Conduct of Life," in *Ralph Waldo Emerson*, 1104.

95. Greenough to Richard Henry Wilde, 18–19 August 1836, in *Letters of Horatio Greenough*, 199.

96. Greenough to Washington Allston, October 1836, ibid., 90.

97. Ibid., 88, 90.

98. Ibid., 91.

99. H. Greenough, "American Architecture," in *Form and Function: Remarks on Art, Design, and Architecture*, ed. Harold A. Small (Berkeley: University of California Press, 1974), 51, 53.

100. Ibid., 56.

101. Ibid., 61.

102. Ibid., 61–2.

103. Ibid., 65.

104. Greenough to Emerson, 28 December 1851, in *Letters of Horatio Greenough*, 400–1.

105. H. Greenough, "Relative and Independent Beauty," in Small, *Form and Function*, 128.

106. H. Greenough, "Structure and Organization," in Small, *Form and Function*, 128.

107. H. D. Thoreau, 11 January 1852, "Journal III," *The Writings of Henry David Thoreau* (Boston: Houghton Mifflin Co., 1968; originally published in 1906), 9:181.

108. Ibid., 182.

109. Ibid., 182–3.

110. Ibid., 240.

111. Ibid., 183.

112. See Wright, *Horatio Greenough*, 188.

113. Greenough to Charles Sumner, 16–18 November 1839, in Wright, *Letters of Horatio Greenough*, 268.

114. Wright, as well, discusses Greenough's closeness to the "sphere of Lodoli's influence." See her *Horatio Greenough*, 187.

115. On Davis, his life and work, see the essays contained in Amelia Pect, ed., *Alexander Jackson Davis: American Architect 1803–1892* (New York: Rizzoli, 1992), and John Donoghue, *Alexander Jackson Davis: Romantic Architect, 1803–1892* (New York: Arno Press, 1977).

116. A. J. Davis, preface to *Rural Residences* (New York: Da Capo, 1980; originally published in 1837).

117. A. J. Davis, "Address," Davis Collection, Avery Library, Columbia University. Cited from Jane B. Davies, "Alexander J. Davis, Creative American Architect," in Pect, *Alexander Jackson Davis*, 14–15.

118. William H. Pierson, *American Buildings and Their Architects*, 298.

119. On Downing's life and ideas, see David Schuyler, *Apostle of Taste: Andrew Jackson Downing 1815–1852* (Baltimore: Johns Hopkins University Press, 1996), and George B. Tatum and Elisabeth Blair MacDougall, eds., *Prophet with Honor: The Career of Andrew Jackson Downing, 1815–1852* (Philadelphia: Athenaeum of Philadelphia, 1989).

120. A. J. Downing, *A Treatise on the Theory and Practice of Landscape Gardening: Adapted to North America, with a View to the Improvement of Country Residences, etc.* (New York: Wiley & Putnam, 1841; reprint, Washington, D.C.: Dumbarton Oaks, 1991), dedication.

121. Ibid., iii.

122. Ibid., 297.

123. Ibid., 298.

124. A. J. Downing, *Victorian Cottage Residences* (New York: Dover, 1981; originally published in 1842), vii, viii.

125. Ibid., ix.

126. Ibid., 14. Downing's citation is from Price's *Essays on the Picturesque*.

127. Ibid., 23.

128. Ibid., Design V, 89.

129. *North American Review* 118 (January 1843), Arthur Gilman's, 10.

130. Ibid., 10–11.

131. Ibid., 9.

132. *Hints to Young Architects, Calculated to Facilitate their Practical Operations by George Wightwick . . . with Additional Notes, and Hints to Persons about Building in the Country. By A. J. Downing* (New York: Wiley & Putnam, 1847).

133. Ibid., xv.

134. Andrew Jackson Downing, *The Architecture of Country Houses* (New York: Dover, 1969; originally published in 1840), 40, 257.

135. Ibid., xx.

136. Vincent J. Scully, *The Shingle Style and the Stick Style: Architectural Theory and Design from Downing to the Origins of Wright* (New Haven: Yale University Press, 1971), xxxix.

137. Samuel Sloane, *The Model Architect: A Series of Original Designs for Cottages, Villas, Suburban Residences*, 2 vols. (Philadelphia: E. S. Jones & Co., 1852); reprinted under the title *Sloan's Victorian Buildings: Illustrations of and Floor Plans for 56 Residences & Other Structures* (New York: Dover, 1980).

138. Calvert Vaux, *Villas and Cottages: A Series of Designs Prepared for Execution in the United States* (New York: Dover, 1970: originally published in 1857), 28.

139. Ibid.

140. On Furness's life and work, see James F. O'Gorman, *The Architecture of Frank Furness* (Philadelphia: Philadelphia Museum of Art, 1973), and Michael J. Lewis, *Frank Furness: Architecture and the Violent Mind* (New York: W. W. Norton, 2001).

141. Lewis, *Frank Furness*, 14–15.

142. Lewis Mumford, preface to *Roots of Contemporary Architecture* (New York: Dover, 1972), 7.

143. The literature on Richardson is quite extensive. Among the many excellent studies are Mariana Griswold Van Rensselaer, *Henry Hobson Richardson and His Works* (New York: Dover, 1969; originally published in 1888); Henry-Russell Hitchcock, *The Architecture of H. H. Richardson and his Times* (Cambridge: M.I.T. Press, 1961; originally published in 1936); James F. O'Gorman, *Living Architecture: A Biography of H. H. Richardson* (New York: Simon & Schuster, 1997).

144. See Jeffrey Karl Ochsner and Thomas C. Hubka, "H. H. Richardson: The Design of the William Watts Sherman House," *Journal of the Society of Architectural Historians* 51 (June 1992): 121–45.

145. The details of this collaboration are discussed by Francis R. Kowsky, "H. H. Richardson's Ames Gate Lodge and the Romantic Landscape Tradition," *Journal of the Society of Architectural Historians* 50 (June 1991): 181–8. The citation of Olmsted is from "A Few Annotations, For Private Use Only, Upon 'Architectural Fitness,' Humbly Submitted to the Consideration of His Omniscient Editorial Majesty, by His Prostrate Servant, F. L. O.," cited in this Kowsky article, p. 181.

146. Cited from O'Gorman, *Living Architecture*, 181.

147. H. Van Brunt, "Henry Hobson Richardson, Architect," in Coles, *Architecture and Society*, 171.

148. Louis H. Sullivan, *Kindergarten Chats and Other Writings* (New York: Wittenborn Art Books, 1947), 29.

149. Among the many excellent studies of Sullivan are Robert Twombly and Narciso G. Menocal, *Louis Sullivan: The Poetry of*

Architecture (New York: W. W. Norton, 2000); John Szarkowski, *The Idea of Louis Sullivan* (Boston: Bullfinch Press, 2000); David Van Zanten, *Sullivan's City: The Meaning of Ornament for Louis Sullivan* (New York: W. W. Norton, 2000); Nancy Frazier, *Louis Sullivan and the Chicago School* (New York: Knickerbocker Press, 1998); Robert Twombly, *Louis Sullivan: His Life and Work* (New York: Viking, 1986); Hugh Morrison, *Louis Sullivan: Prophet of Modern Architecture* (New York: W. W. Norton, 1935). Also of historical importance are Sullivan's *The Autobiography of an Idea* (New York: Press of the American Institute of Architects, 1924), and Frank Lloyd Wright's *Genius and the Mobocracy* (New York: Duell, Sloan & Pearce, 1949). The transcendental side of his thought has been stressed by Narciso G. Menocal, *Architecture as Nature: The Transcendentalist Idea of Louis Sullivan* (Madison: University of Wisconsin Press, 1981), and Sherman Paul, *Louis Sullivan: An Architect in American Thought* (Englewood Cliffs, N.J.: Prentice-Hall, 1962).

150. Walt Whitman, "Democratic Vistas," in *Walt Whitman: Complete Poetry and Collected Prose* (New York: Library of America, 1982), 929.

151. Sullivan to Whitman, 3 February 1887. Cited from Paul, *Louis Sullivan*, 2.

152. Louis Sullivan, "Inspiration," in *Louis Sullivan: The Public Papers*, ed. Robert Twombly (Chicago: University of Chicago Press, 1888).

153. On the important influence of Ruprich-Robert on Sullivan, see David Van Zanten, "Sullivan to 1890," in Wim de Wit, ed., *Louis Sullivan: The Function of Ornament* (New York: W. W. Norton, 1986).

154. Louis Sullivan, "Characteristic and Tendencies of American Architecture," in *Louis Sullivan: The Public Papers*, 3–7.

155. For its importance to Chicago, see Joesph M. Siry, "Chicago Auditorium Building: Opera or Anarchism," *Journal of the Society of Architectural Historians* 57 (June 1998): 128–59.

156. A goal voiced by the club's secretary, Herman V. von Holst, cited by Twombly, *Louis Sullivan*, 216.

157. The two papers were entitled "Style" (1888) and "The Artistic Use of the Imagination" (1889), in *Louis Sullivan: The Public Papers*, 45–52, 62–6.

158. Louis Sullivan, "What Are the Present Tendencies of Architectural Design in America?" *The Inland Architect and News Record* 9 (March 1887): 23–6. Cited from *Louis Sullivan: The Public Papers*, 29. The symposium is reprinted in Donald Hoffmann, ed., *The Means of Architecture: Buildings and Writings by John Wellborn Root* (New York: Horizon Press, 1967), 206–17.

159. Ibid., 29.

160. Louis Sullivan, "What Is the Just Subordination in Architectural Design, of Details to Mass?" *The Inland Architect and News Record* 9 (April 1887): 52–4. Cited from *Louis Sullivan: The Public Papers*, 34.

161. See Frederick Baumann, "Thoughts on Architecture" (address to the American Institute of Architects in Washington, D.C., 1890), *The Inland Architect and News Record* 16 (November 1890): 59–60, and idem, "Thoughts on Style" (address to the American Institute of Architects in Chicago, 1892), *The Inland Architect and News Record* 20 (November 1892): 34–7.

162. John Root, "Development of Architectural Style," which ran from December 1889 to March 1890 in *The Inland Architect and News Record*.

163. The point has been demonstrated by Roula Geraniotis, "German Architects in Nineteenth-Century Chicago" (Ph.D. diss., University of Illinois, 1985). See also her informative essay, "German Architectural Theory and Practice in Chicago, 1850–1900," *Winthur Portfolio* 21 (1986): 293–306.

164. Edgar Kaufmann, Jr., "Frank Lloyd Wright's 'Lieber Meister,'" in *9 Commentaries on Frank Lloyd Wright* (New York: Architectural History Foundation, 1989), 37–42.

165. See especially Rosemarie Haag Bletter, "Gottfired Semper," in *Macmillan Encyclopedia of Architects* (New York: The Free Press, 1982), 4:30.

166. Louis Sullivan "Ornament in Architecture" (1892), in *Louis Sullivan: The Public Papers*, 80.

167. Ibid., 81.

168. Louis Sullivan, "Emotional Architecture as Compared with Intellectual: A Study in Subjective and Objective" (1894), in *Louis Sullivan: The Public Papers*, 94.

169. Ibid., 102.

170. Louis Sullivan, "The Tall Office Building Artistically Considered" (1896), in *Louis Sullivan: The Public Papers*, 111.

171. L. Eidlitz, *The Nature and Function of Art: More Especially of Architecture* (New York: A. C. Armstrong & Son, 1881; reprint, New York: Da Capo Press, 1977). On Eidlitz's theory, see Biruta Erdmann, "Leopold Eidlitz's Architectural Theories and American Transcendentalism" (Ph.D. diss., University of Wisconsin, 1977).

172. Ibid., 223.

173. Ibid., 251.

174. Ibid., 288.

175. Louis Sullivan, *Kindergarten Chats and Other Writings* (New York: Wittenborn Art Books, 1947), 44–6.

176. Ibid., 46.

177. Ibid., 99.

178. Ibid., 140–1.

179. Ibid., 159. See Lauren S. Weingarden, "Louis H. Sullivan's Metaphysics of Architecture (1885–1901): Sources and Correspondences with Symbolic Art Theories" (Ph.D. diss., University of Chicago 1981).

180. For an informative discussion of Sullivan's library, see Paul, *Louis Sullivan*, 93–108.

181. Louis Sullivan, *Democracy, A Man-Search!* ed. Ellen Hedges (Detroit: Wayne State University Press, 1961). The original title for this manuscript was "Natural Thinking: A Study of Democracy."

182. Louis Sullivan, "What Is Architecture? A Study in the American People of Today" (1906), in *Louis Sullivan: The Public Papers*, 177.

183. Ibid., 179.

184. Ibid., 188.

185. Ibid.

186. Ibid., 196.

187. Louis Sullivan, *A System of Architectural Ornament: According with a Philosophy of Man's Powers* (New York: Eakins Press, 1967; originally published in 1924).

188. Ibid. On Sullivan's relation to the ideas of Swedenborg, see Menocal, *Architecture as Nature*, 24–31.

189. Louis Sullivan, *A System of Architectural Ornament*, pl. 4.

8. The Arts and Crafts Movements

1. Robert Kerr, preface to third edition of James Fergusson's *History of the Modern Styles of Architecture* (New York, 1891), vi.

2. Richard Redgrave, "Supplementary Report on Design," in *Reports of the Juries* (London, 1852), 708.

3. Henry Cole, lecture of 24 November 1852, in *Addresses of the Superintendents of the Department of Practical Art* (London: Chapman & Hall, 1853), 12.

4. Redgrave to Cole, 25 September 1852, Victoria and Albert Museum Library, Correspondence Box 14.

5. Owen Jones, *On the True and the False in the Decorative Arts: Lectures Delivered at Marlborough House June 1852* (London: Chapman & Hall, 1853), 4.

6. Ibid.

7. Anthony Burton discusses the authorship of these principles, together with the aesthetics of Redgrave in general, in "Richard Redgrave as Art Educator, Museum Official and Design Theorist," in *Richard Redgrave 1804–1888* (New Haven: Yale University Press, 1988), 64–5.

8. Richard Redgrave (?), *Principles of Decorative Art* (London: Chapman & Hall, 1853), 1.

9. R. Wornum, *Analysis of Ornament: The Characteristics of Styles*, 3rd ed. (London: Chapman & Hall, 1877), 1.

10. Michel Chevreul's *De la loi du contraste simultané des couleurs* (1839) had been translated in English in 1854. See also George Field, *Chromatography: Or a Treatise on Colours and Pigments* (London, 1835).

11. Owen Jones, *The Grammar of Ornament* (New York: Van Nostrand Reinhold, 1982; originally published in 1856), 66.

12. Ibid., 22.

13. Ibid., 5.

14. Ibid., 155.

15. On Dresser, see Michael Whiteway, *Christopher Dresser, 1834–1904* (London: Thames & Hudson, 2002); Widar Halén, *Christopher Dresser: A Pioneer of Modern Design* (London: Phaidon, 1993); Stuart Durant, *Christopher Dresser* (London: Academy Editions, 1993).

16. Christopher Dresser, *The Art of Decorative Design* (London: Day & Son, 1862; reprint, New York: Garland, 1977).

17. Ibid., 12.

18. Ibid., 37.

19. Christopher Dresser, *The Principles of Decorative Design* (London: Cassell Petter & Galpin, 1873; reprint, London: Academy Editions, 1973).

20. The standard biography is E. P. Thompson's *William Morris: Romantic to Revolutionary* (Stanford: Stanford University Press, 1988; originally published in 1955). Also of great importance are Philip Henderson's *William Morris: His Life, Work, and Friends* (New York: McGraw-Hill, 1967); John Mackail's *The Life of William Morris*, 2 vols. (London: Longmans, 1899); Nicholas

Salmon's *The William Morris Chronology* (Bristol: Thoemmes, 1996); and William Morris's *Collected Works*, 24 vols. (New York: Russell, 1910–15; reprint, New York: Russell & Russell, 1966).

21. Cited from John Mackail, *Life of William Morris*, 1:63.

22. Burne-Jones and Morris first met Ruskin at their own apartment shortly after Ruskin's return from Switzerland in October 1858. Ruskin, who was teaching drawing at the Working Men's College continued to visit the two every Thursday night.

23. Cited from Ray Watkinson, *William Morris as Designer* (London: Trefoil Publications, 1990), 16–17.

24. Much has been written on the arts and crafts movement in general. See Gillian Naylor, *The Arts and Crafts Movement: A Study of Its Sources, Ideals, and Influence on Design Theory* (London: Trefoil Publications, 1971), and Isabelle Anscombe and Charlotte Gere, *Arts and Crafts in Britain and America* (New York: Rizzoli, 1978).

25. See *Catalogue of A. H. Mackmurdo and the Century Guild Collection* (London: William Morris Gallery, 1967).

26. On Lethaby, see Godfrey Rubens, *William Richard Lethaby: His Life and Work, 1857–1931* (London: The Architectural Press, 1986), and Sylvia Backemeyer and Theresa Gronberg, *W. R. Lethaby, 1857–1931: Architecture, Design and Education* (London: Lund Humphries, 1984).

27. See *Architects of the Art Workers Guild, 1884–1894* (London: Riba Heinz Gallery, 1984).

28. Walter Crane, "Of the Revival of Design and Handicraft: With Notes on the Work of the Arts and Crafts Exhibition Society," in *Arts and Crafts Essays* (New York: Charles Scribner's Sons, 1893; reprint, New York: Garland, 1977), 3.

29. Ibid., 4.

30. Walter Crane, *The Claims of Decorative Art* (London: Lawrence & Bullen, 1892), 6, 12.

31. Ibid., 176.

32. Ibid., 74, 79.

33. See Alan Crawford, *C. R. Ashbee* (New Haven: Yale University Press, 1985); Peter Stansky, *William Morris, C. R. Ashbee and the Arts and Crafts* (London: Nine Elms Press, 1984); *C. R. Ashbee and the Guild of Handicraft: An Exhibition* (Cheltenham, England: Cheltenham Art Gallery, 1981).

34. On Philip Webb, see William Lethaby, *Philip Webb and His Work* (London: Oxford University Press, 1935).

35. On Shaw, see Andrew Saint, *Richard Norman Shaw* (London: Yale University Press, 1976); see also Reginald Blomfield, *Richard Norman Shaw, R. A. Architect, 1831–1912* (London: Batsford, 1940).

36. William Eden Nesfield, *Specimens of Medieval Architecture: Chiefly Selected from Examples of the 12th and 13th Centuries in France and Italy* (London: Day & Son, 1862).

37. Hermann Muthesius, *The English House* (New York: Rizzoli, 1979; originally published in 1904), 22.

38. Ibid., 38.

39. See Wendy Hitchmough, *C. F. A. Voysey* (London: Phaidon Press, 1995); Stuart Durant, *C. F. A. Voysey* (London: St. Martin's Press, 1992); Duncan Simpson, *C. F. A. Voysey: An Architect of Individuality* (London: Lund Humphries, 1979); David Gebhard, *Charles F. A. Voysey, Architect* (Los Angeles: Hennessey & Ingalls, 1975).

40. W. Lethaby, *Architecture, Mysticism and Myth* (New York: George Braziller, 1975; originally published in 1891), 7.

41. Ibid.

42. Ibid., 8.

43. Among the many books devoted to Mackintosh are Charlotte and Peter Fiell, *Charles Rennie Mackintosh (1868–1928)* (Cologne: Taschen, 1996); Alan Crawford, *Charles Rennie Mackintosh* (London: Thames & Hudson, 1995); James Steele, *Charles Rennie Mackintosh* (London: Academy Editions, 1994); Robert Macleod, *Charles Rennie Mackintosh: Architect and Artist* (New York: E. P. Dutton, 1983).

44. Godfrey Rubens discusses this in his introduction to the reprint of Lethaby's *Architecture, Mysticism and Myth* (xvi–xvii), and David Walker discusses it further in his excellent essay "Mackintosh on Architecture," in *Charles Rennie Mackintosh: The Architectural Papers*, ed. Pamela Robertson (Cambridge: M.I.T. Press, 1990), 170.

45. Charles Rennie Mackintosh, "Architecture," in *Charles Rennie Mackintosh: The Architectural Papers*, 207.

46. Mackintosh's borrowing in this instance, also noted by David Walker, is pieced together from two sentences of Sedding's essay "Design," in *Arts and Crafts Essays*, 411–12.

47. See the very helpful assembly of Morris's writings by Chris Miele, *William Morris: On Architecture* (Sheffield: Academic Press, 1996).

48. William Morris, "The Prospects of Architecture in Civilization," in *William Morris: On Architecture*, 65, 84, 67.

49. Ibid., 72–3.

50. Ibid., 94.

51. William Morris, "The Revival in Architecture," in *William Morris: On Architecture*, 131.

52. Ibid., 135–6.

53. Ibid., 137.

54. Ibid., 139.

55. William Morris, *News from Nowhere* (Cambridge: Cambridge University Press, 1995; originally published in 1890), 4, 10, 53.

56. Ibid., 26.

57. Ibid., 107.

58. For an early general survey of industrial art museums, see Charles R. Richards, *Industrial Art and the Museum* (New York: Macmillan Company, 1927).

59. Eitelberger to Semper, 25 November 1863, Semper Archiv, ETH-Hönggerberg.

60. Gottfried Semper, "Practical Art in Metal and Hard Materials: Its Technology, History and Styles," Victoria and Albert Museum Library, 86.FF.64 (quotations from p. 2). A copy of the manuscript was made for Eitelberger and is in the library at the museum in Vienna.

61. See Karen David-Sirocko, *Georg Gottlob Ungewitter und die malerische Neugotik in Hessen, Hamburg, Hannover und Leipzig* (Petersberg, Germany: Michael Imhof Verlag, 1997), and Michael J. Lewis, *The Politics of the German Gothic Revival: August Reichensperger, 1808-1895* (New York: Architectural History Foundation, 1993).

62. Georg Gottlob Ungewitter, *Entwürfe zu Stadt- und Landhäusern*, 2 vols. (Leipzig: Romberg, 1856–8).

63. See David Klemm and Hartmut Frank, eds., *Alexis de Chateauneuf, 1799–1853: Architekt in Hamburg, London und Oslo* (Hamburg: Dölling & Galitz, 2000).

64. On the work of these talented architects, see especially J. Duncan Berry, "The Legacy of Gottfried Semper: Studies in Späthistorismus" (Ph.D. diss., Brown University, 1989).

65. Hermann Lotze, *Geschichte der Aesthetik in Deutschland* (Munich: Cotta'schen Buchhandlung, 1868), 546–7.

66. Richard Lucae, "Der Mensch und sein Haus – my home is my castle," in *Deutsche Bauzeitung* 1 (1867): 62–4. The invaluable study for the German reform movement is Stefan Muthesius, *Das englische Vorbild: Eine Studie zu den deutschen Reformbewegungen in Architectur, Wohnbau und Kunstgewerbe im späteren 19. Jahrhundert* (Munich: Prestel-Verlag, 1974).

67. Friedrich Pecht, *Kunst und Kunstindustrie auf der Weltausstellung von 1867* (Leipzig: Brockhaus, 1867).

68. Julius Lessing, *Das Kunstgewerbe auf der Wiener Weltausstellung 1873* (Berlin: Ernst & Korn, 1874).

69. Rudolph von Eitelberger and Heinrich von Ferstel, *Das bürgerliche Wohnhaus und das Wiener Zinshaus* (Vienna, 1860). See Muthesius, *Das englische Vorbild*, 78.

70. Jakob von Falke, *Art in the House: Historical, Critical, and Aesthetical Studies on the Decoration and Furnishing of the Dwelling*, trans. Charles C. Perkins (Boston: L. Prang & Co., 1879).

71. Ibid., 172.

72. Ibid., 169–70.

73. The essay became the leading theme of his book *Zur Cultur und Kunst* (Vienna, 1878), 4–67.

74. Georg Hirth, *Das deutsche Zimmer der Renaissance: Anregungen zu häuslicher Kunstpflege* (Munich: G. Hirth's Verlag, 1880), 126–7.

75. Ibid., 1. "...dass unter den Bedingungen, die zur Hebung unseres wirthschaftlichen Lebens zusammenwirken müssen, die Heranbildung eines guten nationalen Geschmackes eine hervoragende, vielleicht die vornehmste Stelle einnimmt."

76. R. Dohme, *Das englische Haus: Eine Kultur- und baugeschichtliche Skizze* (Braunschweig: George Westermann, 1888), 42. "...hier vielmehr das Einsetzen *einer neuen Entwickelungsperiode der Kultur* vorzuliegen."

77. Ibid., 28. "Nicht Grösse und Monumentalität, nicht Reichtum und Luxus machen...sondern die Harmonie der einzelnen Räume, ihre geschickte Gruppierung, kurz die Erfüllung jener Summe von Erfordernissen, die sein praktischer Sinn und verfeinertes Lebensbedürfnis ihm als Voraussetzungen eines behaglichen Daseins ergeben haben."

78. Ibid., 42. "Man denke beispielshalber an unsere modernen Wagen und Schiffe, deren Schönheit wir unter Aufgabe all und jeden schmückenden Ornamentes lediglich in einer aus der möglichsten Zweckdienlichkeit der Objekte hergeleiteten Grazie der Linien, bei höchster Einfachheit der Formen, unter Abstreifung alles Überflüssigen suchen – und in hohem Masse erreicht haben."

79. C. Gurlitt, *Im Bürgerhause: Plaudereien über Kunst, Kunstgewerbe und Wohnungs-Ausstattung* (Dresden: Gilbers'sche königl. Hof-Verlagsbuchhandlung, 1988), 70. "Das Wesen des englischen Stiles besteht darin, dass er Niemand nachahmt, dass er vielmehr trotz einzelner aus allen Stilen der Welt zusammen

genommenen Motive ganz national ist. So lange wir nicht En-
gländer werden, werden wir keinen englischen Stil machen
können." On Gurlitt's life and ideas, see Jürgen Paul, *Cornelius
Gurlitt* (Hellerau: Hellerau-Verlag, 2003).

80. Ibid., 227. "Sie wandeln nicht nur die Gestalt der Dinge, sondern auch unser Auge. Derselbe Tisch, der uns heute zu zierlich
vorkam, kann uns in fünf Jahren als zu plump erscheinen. Giebt
es Gesetze für solchen Wandel? Giebt es Regeln der Schönheit,
wie dick ein Tischbein sein müsse? Sicher nicht."

81. Ibid., 229. "Der Zug unserer Nation geht nach vorwärts, wir leben
nicht mehr im Reich der Träume und der Geschichte, sondern
unser Wirken und Denken richtet sich zuerst auf die Vorgänge
um uns, in welchem wir uns zu bethätigen haben, in welchem
wir unsere Stellung behaupten müssen; und dann wenden wir
den Kopf nach vorwärts, um die Grösse unseres Volkes dauernd
wirksam zu schauen. Darum seien wir auch in der Kunst modern
und *nur* modern."

82. For the formation of various workshops in Russia, see Wendy R.
Salmond, *Arts and Crafts in Late Imperial Russia* (New York:
Cambridge University Press, 1996).

83. Johan Christian Dahl, *Denkmale einer sehr ausgebildeten
Holzbaukunst aus den frühsten Jahrhunderten in den inneren
Landschaften Norwegens* (Dresden: privately published, 1837).

84. For a superb summary of Scandinavian movements and their
ideologies, see Barbara Miller Lane, *National Romanticism and
Modern Architecture in Germany and the Scandinavian Countries* (New York: Cambridge University Press, 2000).

85. J. Guadet, *Eléments et théorie de l'architecture: Cours professé
à l'École nationale et spéciale des beaux-arts*, 4 vols. (Paris: Librairie de la Construction Moderne, 1902–4).

86. See especially Debora L. Silverman's chapter on the Goncourt
brothers in *Art Nouveau in Fin-de-Siècle France: Politics, Psychology, and Style* (Berkeley: University of California, 1989),
17–39.

87. On Gallé's theories of art, see Silverman, *Art Nouveau in Fin-
de-Siècle France*, 229–42. On the baroque and rococo influence,
see S. Tschudi Madsen, *Art Nouveau* (New York: McGraw-Hill,
1967), 65–8.

88. Samuel Beng, Programme, *Artistic Japan* (London, 1888), 3–4.

89. Silverman, *Art Nouveau in Fin-de-Siècle France*, 12.

90. On La Farge, see Helene Barbara Weinberg, *The Decorative Work
of John La Farge* (New York, 1977). On Tiffany, see Alastair Duncan, *Masterworks of Louis Comfort Tiffany* (New York: Abrams,
1989); Alastair Duncan, *Tiffany Windows* (New York: Simon &
Schuster, 1982); Robert Koch, *Louis C. Tiffany: Rebel in Glass*,
3rd ed. (New York: Crown Publishers, 1982); Henry Winter, *The
Dynasty of Louis Comfort Tiffany* (Boston: H. Winter, 1966?).

91. On Stanford White, see Suzannah Lessard, *The Architect of De-
sign: Beauty and Danger in the Stanford White Family* (New
York: Dial Press, 1996); David Lowe, *Stanford White's New York*
(New York: Doubleday, 1992); Paul R. Baker, *Stanny: The Gilded
Life of Stanford White* (New York: The Free Press, 1989); Charles
C. Baldwin, *Stanford White* (1931; reprint, New York: Da Capo,
1971).

92. Vincent J. Scully Jr., *The Shingle Style and the Stick Style: Architectural Theory and Design from Downing to the Origins of
Wright*, rev. ed. (New Haven: Yale University Press, 1971), 70.

93. See a reprint of the images in Arnold Lewis, *American Country
Houses of the Gilded Age (Sheldon's "Artistic Country-Seats")*
(New York: Dover, 1982).

94. On the "American Renaissance," see *The American Renaissance
1876–1917* (New York: Brooklyn Museum, 1979).

95. On the Boston Public Library, see William H. Jordy, *American
Buildings and Their Architects: Progressive and Academic Ideals
at the Turn of the Twentieth Century* (New York: Anchor Books,
1976), 314–75.

96. Edith Wharton and Ogden Codman Jr., *The Decoration of Houses*
(1897; reprint, W. W. Norton, 1978), 196, 10.

97. Sullivan's comment was made in the closing pages of *The Autobiography of an Idea* (New York: Dover, 1956; originally published
in 1924), 322.

98. Henry Adams, *The Education of Henry Adams* (New York: Modern Library, 1918), 343.

99. Charles Eliot Norton, cited from Charles Moore, *Daniel H. Burnham, Architect, Planner of Cities* (Boston, 1921), 1:79.

100. Montgomery Schuyler, "Last Words about the World's Fair," *Architectural Record* (January–March 1894); reprinted in Montgomery Schuyler, *American Architecture and Other Writings*,
2 vols. (Cambridge: Belknap Press, 1961), 2:557, 559, 563.

101. Henry Van Brunt, "The Columbian Exposition and American
Civilization" (1893), in *Architecture and Society: Selected Essays
of Henry Van Brunt*, ed. William A. Coles (Cambridge: Belknap
Press, 1969), 313.

102. Ibid.

103. On the arts and crafts movement in America, defined largely
as a British-inspired movement, see Anscombe and Gere, *Arts
and Crafts in Britain and America*; James Massey and Shirley
Maxwell, *Arts and Crafts Design in America: A State by State
Guide* (San Francisco: Chronicle Books, 1998); and Robert
Judson Clark, ed., *The Arts and Crafts Movement in America 1876–1916* (Princeton: Princeton University Press, 1972). A
somewhat broader perspective is given in various essays in Wendy
Kaplan, ed., *"The Art that is Life": The Arts and Crafts Movement in America, 1875–1920* (Boston: Boston Museum of Fine
Arts, 1987).

104. On Stickley, see Mark A. Hewitt, *Gustav Stickley's Craftsman
Farms: The Quest for an Arts and Crafts Utopia* (Syracuse: Syracuse University Press, 2001); Barry Sanders, *A Complex Fate:
Gustav Stickley and the Craftsman Movement* (New York: Preservation Press, 1996); Donald A. Dividoff, *Innovation and Derivation: The Contribution of L. & J. G. Stickley to the Arts and Crafts
Movement* (Parsippany, New Jersey: Craftsman Farms Foundation, 1995).

105. Gustav Stickley, cited from Anscombe and Gere, *Arts and Crafts
in Britain and America*, 31–2.

106. Gustav Stickley, *Craftsman Homes: Architecture and Furnishings
of the American Arts and Crafts Movement* (New York: Dover,
1979; originally published in 1909), 194–7.

107. Oscar Lovell Triggs, *Chapters in the History of the Arts and
Crafts Movement* (New York: Benjamin Blom, 1971; originally
published in 1901).

108. Charles Robert Ashbee, from his travel journal, cited from David
A. Hanks, *The Decorative Designs of Frank Lloyd Wright* (New
York: E. P. Dutton, 1979), 67.

109. Frank Lloyd Wright, "The Art and Craft of the Machine," *Frank Lloyd Wright: Writings and Buildings* (New York: New American Library, 1960), 56.

110. Ibid., 55.

111. Ibid., 72.

112. Ibid., 60.

113. Ibid., 60, 62.

114. Ibid., 64.

115. Frank Lloyd Wright, *An Autobiography* (New York: Horizon Press, 1977), 156.

116. On Maybeck's life and career, see Kenneth H. Cardwell, *Bernard Maybeck: Artisan, Architect, Artist* (Santa Barbara, Calif.: Peregrine Smith, 1977); Ester McCoy, *Five California Architects* (Los Angeles: Hennessey & Ingalls, 1987); Sally B. Woodbridge, *Bernard Maybeck: Visionary Architect* (New York: Abbeville Press, 1992).

117. On Gill's life and career, see Bruce Kamerling, *Irving Gill, Architect* (San Diego: San Diego Historical Society, 1993); McCoy, *Five California Architects*; and Thomas S. Hines, *Irving Gill and the Architecture of Reform: A Study in Modernist Architectural Culture* (New York: Monacelli Press, 2000).

118. Irving Gill, "The Home of the Future: The New Architecture of the West: Small Homes for a Great Country," *The Craftsman* 30 (May 1916): 142.

119. Ibid., 147.

120. On the Greene brothers, see William Current, *Greene and Greene: Architects in the Residential Style* (Dobbs Ferry, N.Y.: Morgan, 1974); Randell L. Makinson, *Greene and Greene*, 2 vols. (Santa Barbara, Calif.: Peregrine Smith, 1977–9); McCoy, *Five California Architects*; Randell L. Makinson, *The Passion and the Legacy* (Salt Lake City: Gibbs Smith, 1998); and Edward R. Bosley, *Greene & Greene* (London: Phaidon Press, 2000).

121. Recent studies on Haussmann include Georges Valence, *Haussmann le grande* (Paris: Flammarion, 2000); Michel Carmona, *Haussmann* (Paris: Fayard, 2000); Willet Weeks, *The Man Who Made Paris Paris: The Illustrated Biography of Georges-Eugène Haussmann* (London: London House, 1999); and David P. Jordan, *Transforming Paris: The Life and Labors of Baron Haussmann* (Chicago: University of Chicago Press, 1996). See also François Louer, *Paris Nineteenth Century: Architecture and Urbanism*, trans. Charles Lynn Clark (New York: Abbeville Press, 1988), 231–372, and David Van Zanten, *Building Paris: Architectural Institutions and the Transformation of the French Capital, 1830–1870* (New York: Cambridge University Press, 1994), 198–255.

122. On Burnham, see Thomas S. Hines, *Burnham of Chicago: Architect and Planner* (Chicago: University of Chicago Press, 1979), and Cynthia R. Field, "The City Planning of Daniel Hudson Burnham" (Ph.D. diss., Columbia University, 1985).

123. In his eagerness to solicit information on European cities while preparing his design, Burnham actually contacted the assistant secretary of state, Huntington Wilson, and pleaded for information on pre- and post-Haussmann Paris from the French government. See Hines, *Burnham of Chicago*, 323. See also Joan E. Draper, "Paris by the Lake: Sources of Burnham's Plan of Chicago," in *Chicago Architecture 1872–1922: Birth of a Metropolis*, ed. John Zukowsky, (Munich: Prestel, 1988), 107–19.

124. Wright's remarks (from an unidentified London lecture) are cited by Hines, *Burnham of Chicago*, 325. Wright went so far as to call Chicago "the world's most beautiful city."

125. H. J. Stübben, *Der Städtebau* (Darmstadt: Arnold Bergsträsser, 1890). See also Oliver Karnou, *Herrmann Josef Stübben* (Braunschweig: Vieweg, 1996).

126. Otto Wagner, "Generalregulierungsplan," in Otto Antonia Graf, *Otto Wagner: Das Werk des Architekten* (Vienna: Hermann Böhlaus, 1985), 1:94. "Unser Realismus, unser Verkehr, die moderne Technik, sie begehren heute gebieterisch die gerade Linie, . . ."

127. Ibid., 93. "Würden diese Vertreter des Malerischen die Augen öffen, so wären sie schon lange zu Ueberzeugung gekommen, dass die gerade, reine, praktische Strasse, zeitweilig unterbrochen von Monumentalbauten, mässig grossen Plätzen, schönen, bedeutenden Perspectiven, Parks, etc., die uns in kürzester Zeit ans Ziel führt, auch weitaus die schönste ist."

128. See Karl Henrici, "Langeweilige und kurzweilige Strassen," *Deutsche Bauzeitung* 27, no. 44 (June 1893): 271.

129. For an instructive essay on Wagner's urban theory, see August Sarnitz, "Realism versus Verniedlichung: The Design of the Great City," in *Otto Wagner: Reflection on the Raiment of Modernity*, ed. H. F. Mallgrave (Santa Monica, Calif.: Getty Center Publications Program, 1993), 85–112.

130. August Endell, *Die Schönheit der grossen Stadt* (Berlin: Archibook-Verlag, 1984; originally published in 1908).

131. The *flâneur* is a reference to Baudelaire's urban aesthete, as discussed in his essay "The Painter of Modern Life," in Charles Baudelaire, *The Painter of Modern Life and Other Essays*, trans. and ed. Johathan Mayne (London: Da Capo Press, 1964), 1–40.

132. Georg Simmel, "The Metropolis and Mental Life," in *The Sociology of Georg Simmel*, trans. and ed. Kurt H. Wolff (New York: The Free Press, 1964), 410.

133. Ferdinand Tönnies, *Community and Society* (New Brunswick, N.J.: Transaction Books, 1988). For a consideration of Tönnies, Simmel, and Endell, see the opening chapter of Francesco Dal Co, *Figures of Architecture and Thought: German Architecture Culture 1880–1920* (New York: Rizzoli, 1990).

134. The best brief account of the life and thought of Sitte is the introduction by George R. Collins and Christiane Crasemann Collins to their translation of Sitte's book, *Camillo Sitte: The Birth of Modern City Planning* (New York: Rizzoli, 1986); see also Daniel Wieczorek, *Camillo Sitte et les débuts de l'urbanisme moderne* (Brussels: P. Mardaga, 1981).

135. Camillo Sitte, *City Planning According to Artistic Principles*, in *Camillo Site: The Birth of Modern City Planning*, 183.

136. Ibid., 225.

137. For a discussion of Buls and Sitte and their influence in Italy, see Richard A. Etlin, *Modernism in Italian Architecture, 1890–1940* (Cambridge: M.I.T. Press, 1991), 106–9.

138. On Howard, see Kermit C. Parsons and David Schuyler, eds., *From Garden City to Green City: The Legacy of Ebenezer Howard* (Baltimore: Johns Hopkins University Press, 2002); Peter Geoffrey Hall and Colin Ward, *Sociable Cities: The Legacy of Ebenezer Howard* (New York: Wiley, 1998); and Robert Beevers, *The Garden City Utopia: A Critical Biography of Ebenezer Howard* (London: Macmillan, 1988); and Robert Fishman, *Urban Utopias in*

the *Twentieth Century: Ebenezer Howard, Frank Lloyd Wright, and Le Corbusier* (New York: Basic Books, 1977).

139. Ebenezer Howard, *To-morrow: A Peaceful Path to Real Reform* (London: Swan Sonnenschein, 1898); idem, *Garden Cities of To-morrow* (London: Sway Sonnenschein, 1902).

140. Howard, *Garden Cities of To-Morrow*, 116–17.

141. See *Letchworth in Pictures* (Letchworth, England: First Garden City Limited, 1950).

9. Excursus on a Few of the Conceptual Foundations of Twentieth-Century German Modernism

1. Karl Schnaase, *Niederländische Briefe* (Stuttgart, 1834), 200. I thank Henrik Karge for providing his research on this theme. See his "Das Frühwerk Karl Schnaase: Zum Verhältnis von Ästhetik und Kunstgeschichte im 19. Jahrhundert," in Antje Middeldorf Kosegarten, ed., *Johann Dominicus Fiorillo, Kunstgeschichte und die romantische Bewegung um 1800* (Göttingen: Wallstein Verlag, 1995), 402–19, and his "Karl Schnaase: Die Entfaltung der wissenschaftlichen Kunstgeschichte im 19. Jahrhundert," *Kunsthistorische Arbeitsblätter: Zeitschrift für Studium und Hochschulkontakt* 7–8 (July–August 2001): 87–100. On Schnaase's conception of art history in general, see Michael Podro, *The Critical Historians of Art* (New Haven: Yale University Press, 1982), 31–43.

2. David Van Zanten, *Designing Paris: The Architecture of Duban, Labrouste, Duc, and Vaudoyer* (Cambridge: M.I.T. Press, 1987), 197.

3. Jakob Burckhardt, *The Architecture of the Italian Renaissance*, ed. Peter Murray, trans. James Palmes (Chicago: University of Chicago Press, 1985), 32.

4. Gottfried Semper, *Style in the Technical and Tectonic Arts, or Practical Aesthetics*, trans. H. F. Mallgrave and Michael Robinson (Los Angeles: Getty Publications Program, 2004), 247.

5. Ibid., 756.

6. Gottfried Semper, "On Architectural Styles," in *Gottfried Semper: The Four Elements of Architecture and Other Writings*, trans. H. F. Mallgrave and Wolfgang Herrmann (New York: Cambridge University Press, 1989), 281.

7. Richard Lucae, "Ueber die Bedeutung und Macht des Raumes in der Baukunst," in *Zeitschrift für praktische Baukunst* 29 (1869).

8. Ibid., 208. "Ja wohl, der Massstab in der Baukunst ist nur das zu unserem Bewusstsein gekommene räumliche Verhältniss unserer äusseren Person zu unserem Geiste."

9. Ibid., 205. "Im Mittelschiffe wandeln wir, gleichsam in einer mächtigen Strasse, unwillkürlich zu dem Punkte hin, in welchem die Idee des ganzen Gebäudes liegt. Wir stehen nicht, wie im Pantheon, zugleich am anfange und am Ende des Raumes. Das mächtige Tonnengewölbe leitet unsere Blick dahin, wo die Dämmerung über uns plötzlich vor einer überirdischen Lichtgewalt zurückweicht. Sicherlich würde sogar ein Bewohner des urwaldes, der noch nichts vom heiligen Petrus und der christlichen Religion gehört hätte, nicht eher ruhen, als bis er in der Kuppel des Michel Angelo angekommen wäre. Auch hier ist ein Raum, der uns von dem profanen Verkehr der Welt abschliesst. Auch hier die Quelle des Lichtes in einer Region, die unseren Blicken die Alltäglichkeit des Lebens entzieht."

10. Ibid.

11. Ibid., 199. ". . . wird der Styl die Raumwirkung nur in einem sehr geringen Masse beeinflussen."

12. Richard Lucae, "Ueber die ästhetische Ausbildung der Eisen-Konstruktionen, besonders in ihrer Anwendung bei Räumen von bedeutender Spannweite," *Deutsche Bauzeitung* 4 (1870): 12.

13. Ibid., 9. "Ein Geschlecht nach uns, welches so aufwächst mit der Eisen-Konstruktion, wie wir mit der Stein-Konstruktion aufgewachsen sind, wird in manchen Fällen das volle ungestörte Gefühl der Schönheit haben, in denen wir heute noch unbefriedigt bleiben, weil eine uns liebgewordene Schönheits-Tradition scheinbar angegriffen wird."

14. Conrad Fiedler to Adolf Hildebrand, 10 December 1875, in Günther Jachmann, ed., *Adolf von Hildebrands Briefwechsel mit Conrad Fiedler* (Dresden: Wolfgang Jess, 1927), 54–5.

15. Conrad Fiedler, "Observations on the Nature and History of Architecture," in H. F. Mallgrave and Eleftherios Ikonomou, *Empathy, Form, and Space: Problems in German Aesthetics 1873–1893* (Santa Monica, Calif.: Getty Publications Program, 1994), 127–8.

16. Ibid., 142.

17. H. Auer, "Der Einfluss der Construction auf die Entwicklung der Baustile," *Zeitschrift des österreichischen Ingenieur- und Architekten-Vereins* 33 (1981), 8–18. See also J. Duncan Berry's remarks on Auer in "The Legacy of Gottfried Semper: Studies in Spathistorismus" (Ph.D. diss., Brown University, 1989), 229–33.

18. H. Auer, "Die Entwickelung des Raumes in der Baukunst," *Allgemeine Bauzeitung* 48 (1883).

19. Ibid., 66. ". . . aber die Höhe geht weit über die menschlichen bedürfnisse hinaus und sie ist es, welche angenehm, imponirend, erhebend und überwältigend auf die Seele des Eintretenden wirkt."

20. Ibid., 74. "Wir leben heute aber schon in einer Phase, in der ein neuer Styl sich bildet unter dem unwiderstechlichen einflusse eines Materials, das mit eherner Faust an allen traditionen der Vergangenheit rüttelt: nämlich des *Eisens*."

21. See the remarks on Schmarsow in the introduction to Mallgrave and Ikonomou, *Empathy, Form, and Space*.

22. A. Schmarsow, "The Essence of Architectural Creation," in Mallgrave and Ikonomou, *Empathy, Form, and Space*, 287.

23. Ibid., 296.

24. Semper, *Style in the Technical and Tectonic Arts*, 728.

25. Friedrich Theodor Vischer, *Aesthetik; oder, Wissenschaft des Schönen*, ed. Robert Vischer, 2nd ed. (1846–57; Munich: Meyer & Jessen, 1922–3), vol. 3, sec. 559.

26. Friedrich Theodor Vischer, "Kritik meiner Ästhetik," in *Kritische Gänge*, ed. Robert Vischer, 2nd ed. (1866; Munich: Meyer & Jessen, 1922), 4:316–22.

27. Robert Vischer, "On the Optical Sense of Form," in Mallgrave and Ikonomou, *Empathy, Form, and Space*, 92.

28. Heinrich Wölfflin, "Prolegomena to a Psychology of Form," in Mallgrave and Ikonomou, *Empathy, Form, and Space*, 149.

29. Ibid., 151.

30. Ibid., 157–8.

31. Ibid., 179.

32. Rudolf Redtenbacher, "Die Baubestrebungen der Gegenwart," *Allgemeine Bauzeitung* 42 (1877): 61–3, 77–80.

33. Rudolf Redtenbacher, "Ueber den Begriff der Baukunst," *J. A. Romberg's Zeitschrift für pratische Baukunst* 37, nos. 6–8 (1877):

228. "Ich möchte glauben, die Baukunst beginnt erst da, wo Construction und Formenwelt unzertrennlich wurden...."

34. Rudolf Redtenbacher, *Architektonik der modernen Baukunst: Eine Hülfsbuch bei der Bearbeitung architektonischer Aufgaben* (Berlin: Ernst & Korn, 1883), 1.

35. For some comments on Heuser's theory and images of his style proposals, see J. Duncan Berry, "From Historicism to Architectural Realism," in *Otto Wagner: Reflections on the Raiment of Modernity*, ed. H. F. Mallgrave (Santa Monica, Calif.: Getty Publications Program, 1993), 255–99.

36. The clearest affirmation of Heuser's Darwinism is in his essay "Darwinistisches über Kunst und Technik," *Allgemeine Bauzeitung* 55 (1890): 18–19, 25–27.

37. Heinrich von Ferstel, "Rede des neu antretenden Rectors" (9 October 1880), in *Reden gehalten bei der feierlichen Inauguration des für das Studienjahr 1880/81*, Library of the Technische Universität, 51. "Auf solchen Grundlagen wird es der neuen Generation weit leichter, als den vorangangenen werden, die Aufgaben, welche der modernen Baukunst im höheren kunstgestaltendem Sinne gestellt sind, zu vollführen."

38. Josef Bayer, "Moderne Bautypen," in *Baustudien und Baubilder: Schriften zur Kunst*, ed. Robert Stiassny (Jena: Eugen Diederichs, 1919), 280. "Der Stil ist eine bestimmte, aus dem innersten Grund und Wesen des Zeitalters stammende Denkweise und Gestaltungs-Äusserung der Kunst, die nur *eine* obligatorisch vorgezeichnete Hauptrichtung haben kann."

39. Ibid., 284.

40. Ibid., 281. "Jene Wurzel schien auf lange hinaus abgestorben; nun aber drängen die geheimen Lebenskräfte empor, und die eigentliche, wahre und wesentliche Baugestalt der Epoche wächst innerhalb der herbegrachten Stilmasken und Stildraperien mit mächtigen Gliedern heran."

41. Josef Bayer, "Stilkrisen unserer Zeit," in *Baustudien und Baubilder*, 293. "Wie töricht wäre es vollends, von unserer Baukunst zu verlangen, sie solle ein neues eigentümliches Formendetail – was man nach dem Schulbegriffe den 'Stil' zu nennen pflegt – aus sich heraus hervorbringen."

42. Ibid., 293–4. "Endlich werden doch allmählich und unvermerkt die neuen Bauprobleme auch zu neuen Formgedanken führen; und selbst der *veränderte Rhythmus der alten Formen*, nach einem neuen architektonischen Lebensgesetze geordnet, ist bereits ein wesentlicher und grosser Gewinn."

43. Ibid., 295. "Ich wage sogar die Behauptung: die Kernbildung eines *modernen Stiles* ist bereits da; aber die Merkmale desselben findet man freilich nicht heraus, wenn man die Bauwerke unserer Zeit nur äusserlich auf die wohlbekannten historischen Stildetails hin beguckt. Dan zeigt sich dem Blicke allerdings nur, was verschieden, nicht auch dasjenige, was gemeinsam ist. Das nachweisbar Neue aber gibt sich kund in der Gesamthaltung der Bau-Anlagen, in ihrer Durchgliederung aus den Grundrissen heraus, in den unserem Zeitalter eigenartigen Kompositions-Aufgaben als solchen." This is the passage regarding the "Stilhülse und Kern" that Werner Oechslin has taken as the leading theme of "The Evolutionary Way to Modern Architecture: The Paradigm of Stilhülse und Kern," in *Otto Wagner: Reflections on the Raiment of Modernity*, 363–410. See also Ocheslin's *Stilhülse und Kern: Otto Wagner, Adolf Loos und der*

evolutionäre Weg zur modernen Architektur (Zurich: gta/Ernst & Sohn, 1994).

44. Robert Stiassny, "Ein deutscher Humanist: Joseph Bayer (1827–1910)," in *Baustudien und Baubilder*, page. VII.

45. Adolf Göller, "What Is the Cause of Perpetual Style Change in Architecture?" in Mallgrave and Ikonomou, *Empathy, Form, and Space*, 195.

46. Michael Podro, *The Critical Historians of Art*, 56.

47. A. Göller, *Die Entstehung der architektonischen Stilformen: Eine Geschichte der Baukunst nach dem Werden und Wandern der Formgedanken* (Stuttgart: Konrad Wittwer, 1888), 3.

48. Ibid., 442–3. "... unser unparteiisches Gefühl ist das Hinderniss, ein Einselnes als Grundlage eines eigenen Stils unserer Zeit herauszugreifen – wenn ein solcher neuer Stil je möglich ist!"

49. Ibid., 448. "Alle einfachen und natürlichen Hülfsmittel zur Herstellung der Kunstformen sind schon verbrauch."

50. Ibid., 452. "... vielmehr schöpfen wir daraus mit vollen Eimern; darin liegt eben ds Geheimniss unseres Wohllebens."

51. Wölfflin's disscusses Göller's thesis in his chapter "The Cause of the Change of Style," in *Renaissance and Baroque*, trans. Kathrin Simon (Ithaca: Cornell University Press, 1964), 74–5.

52. C. Gurlitt, "Göller's ästhetische Lehre," *Deutsche Bauzeitung* 21 (17 December 1887): 602–4, 606–7.

53. Ibid., 603. "Jeder Architekt weiss, wie viel Mühe ihm diese Forderung schon bereitet hat, wie oft er sich künstlich Funktionen schaffen musste, weil er ihren 'Ausdruck' nicht missen wollte, wie oft er einfach darauf verzichten musste, die Forderung der Aesthetik zu erfüllen, weil ihn hundert technische und rein schönheitliche Gründe davon abhielten."

54. Ibid. "Diese Gesimslinie drück keinen Zweck aus – sie ist hässlich! Dieser Thurm hat hier nichts zu bedeuten – er ist ein verwerflicher Nothbehelf! Diese Kuppel überdeckt nicht den wichtigsten Raum des Hauses – sie ist eine künstliche Lüge!"

55. Ibid., 606.

56. Ibid., 607. "Aber nicht nur was in Göllers Büchern zu lesen ist, hat Bedeutung; ungleich reichere Beute wird dem zufallen, welcher die Lehre von der Schönheit der reinen Form auf Malerei und Bildnerei anwendet und nachweist, in wie hohem Grade die des geistigen Inhalts entbehrende Formenwelt auch in diesen Künsten auf unser Schönheitsgefühl wirkt, wie recht die deutsche Kunst that, dass sie von der inhaltreichen Art des Cornelius zum Realismus überging, von der Welt der Gedanken zu dem der sinnlich empfundenen Form."

10. Modernism 1889–1914

1. Wright recounts this scene with vividness in "Louis H. Sullivan – His Work," *Architectural Record* 56 (July 1924): 29.

2. The literature on Wagner is vast. The main monograph on his work in Germany is Otto Antonia Graf, *Otto Wagner: Das Werk des Architekten*, 2 vols. (Vienna: Hermann Böhlaus, 1985). A good introduction to his theory is *Otto Wagner: Reflections on the Raiment of Modernity*, ed. Harry Francis Mallgrave (Santa Monica, Calif.: Getty Publications Program, 1993).

3. Otto Wagner, *Einige Skizzen, Projecte und ausgeführte Bauwerke* (Vienna: Kunstverlag Anton Schroll, 1892); translated by Edward Vance Humphrey as *Sketches, Projects and Executed Buildings* (New York: Rizzoli, 1987).

4. Ibid., 18.

5. Otto Wagner, "Inaugural Address to the Academy of Fine Arts," in *Otto Wagner, Modern Architecture: A Guide for His Students to This Field of Art*, trans. Harry Francis Mallgrave (Santa Monica, Calif.: Getty Publications Program, 1988), 160.

6. Max Fabiani, "Aus der Wagner Schule," *Der Architekt* 1 (1895): 53.

7. Otto Wager, *Moderne Architektur: Seinen Schülern ein Führer auf diesem Kunstgebiete* (Vienna: Anton Schroll, 1896); translated by Harry Francis Mallgrave as *Modern Architecture: A Guide for His Students to This Field of Art* (see note 5).

8. Wagner, *Modern Architecture*, 60.

9. Ibid., 61, 65.

10. Ibid., 78.

11. Ibid., 79.

12. Ibid., 80.

13. Ibid., 92.

14. Ibid., 93.

15. Gottfried Semper, *Style in the Technical and Tectonic Arts, or Practical Aesthetics*, trans. Harry Francis Mallgrave and Michael Robinson (Los Angeles: Getty Publications Program, 2003), 106.

16. Wagner, *Modern Architecture*, 96.

17. Fabiani, "Aus der Wagner Schule," 54.

18. For a discussion of Sédille's use of the term "Realism," see J. Duncan Berry, "From Historicism to Architectural Realism," in *Otto Wagner: Reflections on the Raiment of Modernity* (Santa Monica, Calif.: Getty Publications Program, 1993), 261–9.

19. Constantin Lipsius, *Gottfried Semper in seiner Bedeutung als Architekt* (Berlin: Verlage der Deutschen Bauzeitung, 1880), 99. J. Duncan Berry was the first to discuss these instances of architectural realism in Germany, in his "the legacy of Gottfried Semper: Studies in *Späthistorismus*" (Ph.D. diss., Brown University 1989).

20. Friedrich Pecht, "Die deutsche Kunst seit dem Auftreten der realistischen Bewegung," in Franz von Reber, *Geschichte der neueren deutschen Kunst*, 2nd ed. (Leipzig, 1884), 211. "Wenn Semper der Styl unübertrefflich als 'die Uebereinstimmung einer Kunsterscheinung mit ihrer Entstehungsgeschichte, mit allen Vorbedingungen und Ümstanden ihres Werdens' definiert, so kann es gar keine Frage sein, das jetzige realistische Kunstperiode mehr stylegefühl entwickelt hat als alle ihre Vorgänger."

21. See especially Fiedler's essay "Moderner Naturalismus und künstlerische Wahrheit" (1881), *Schriften zur Kunst I* (Munich: Wilhelm Fink, 1991), 81–110.

22. Albert Hofmann, "Die kunstgeschichtliche Stellung der Bauten für die Weltausstellung von 1889 in Paris," *Deutsche Bauzeitung* 9 November 1889, 543.

23. Karl Emil Otto Fritsch, "Stil-Betrachtungen," *Deutsche Bauzeitung*, 30 August 1890, 423. "Führer in dies gesunden, echt realistischen Bewegung war Gottfried Semper."

24. Georg Heuser, "Ein Nachwort zu den 'Stilbetrachtungen,'" *Deutsche Bauzeitung*, 24 December 1890, 626.

25. Richard Streiter, *Karl Böttichers Tektonik der Hellenen als ästhetische und kunstgeschichtliche Theorie: Ein Kritik* (Hamburg: Leopold Voss, 1896).

26. The Neumann book that figures heavily into Streiter's discussion is *Der Kampf um die neue Kunst* (Berlin: Hermann Walther, 1896).

27. Richard Streiter, "Architektonische Zeitfragen: Eine Sammlung und Sichtung verschiedener Anschauungen mit besonderer Beziehung auf Professor Otto Wagners' Schrift 'Moderne Architektur'" (1898), in *Richard Streiter: Ausgewählte Schriften zur Aesthetik und Kunst-Geschichte* (Munich: Delphin, 1913), 79. "... in eine phantastische Gedankenkunst, in Symbolismus und Mystizismus, in einen farbenmusikalischen Stimmungskultus umschlug."

28. Ibid., 81. "Wenn je eine Zeit geeignet war, mehr wie eine andere der Anschauung Raum zu geben, dass in Architektur und Kunstgewerbe künstlerische Wahrhaftigkeit, Knappheit und Sachlichkeit, vollkommenste Erfüllung des Zweckes mit den einfachsten Mitteln als erste Bedingung gelten soll, so ist es die unsrige."

29. Ibid., 82.

30. Ibid., 102–3. "Wie könnte er sonst bei Semper das Festhalten an einer 'Symbolik der Konstruktion' beanstanden, da doch gerade diese Symbolik das ist, was aus dem Konstruktionsglied die Kunstform werden lässt."

31. Ibid., 105. "Nirgends ist zu entdecken, dass Wagner das Verhältnis von Konstruktion und Kunstform anders auffasst, als es sonst von der modernen Architektenschaft aufgefasst zu werden pflegt; ja es kann vielmehr behauptet werden, das eine Reihe englischer, französischer, amerikanischer und deutscher Architekten dem Satz: 'Der Architekt hat immer aus der Konstruktion die Kunstform zu entwickeln,' weit mehr Rechnung trägt, als Wagner selbst."

32. Ibid., 113. "Nun müssen aber doch wohl die Kunstformen Quaderschichtmauerwerk anders (derber) sein, als die Kunstformen für Platterverkleidung, ..."

33. Richard Streiter, "Aus München" (1896), in *Richard Streiter*, 32. "Realismus in der Architektur, das ist die weitgehendste Berücksichtigung der realen Werdenbedingungen eines Bauwerks, die möglichst vollkommene Erfüllung der Forderungen der Zweckmässigkeit, Bequemlichkeit, Gesundheitförderlichkeit, mit einhem Wort: die Sachlichkeit. Aber das ist noch nicht Alles. Wie der Realismus der Dichtung al seine seiner Hauptaufgaben es betrachtet, die Zusammenhang der Charaktere mit ihrem Milieu scharf ins Auge zu fassen, so sieht die verwandte Richtung in der Architektur ein vor allem erstrebenswertes Ziel künstlerischer Wahrhaftigkeit darin, den Charakter eines Bauwerks nicht aus seiner Zweckbestimmung allein, sondern auch aus dem Milieu, aus der Eigenart der jeweilig vorhandenen Baustoffe, auf der landschaftlich und geschichtlich bedingten Stimmung der Oertlichkeit heraus zu entwickeln."

34. See the passage cited in note 28.

35. See Harry Francis Mallgrave, "From Realism to Sachlichkeit: The Polemics of Architectural Modernity in the 1890s," in *Otto Wagner*, 281–321.

36. Richard Streiter, "Architektonische Zeitfragen," in *Richard Streiter*, 118–119. "Das Formgefühl, das in die Baukunst der Zukunft

eine einheitliche Grundstimmung hineinzubringen im Stande sein soll, wird also bei der Formgebung des Einzelnen und der Dekoration einsetzen müssen."

37. Ibid., 111. "Das altbewährte feierlich prunkvolle Gewand klassischer Architektur hüllte allenthalben das dürre Gerippe der in Eisen konstruierten machtigen Hallen ein: das glänzendste Zeugnis für die unversiegliche Lebenskraft der antiken Bauformen, das beredteste Zugeständnis der Unmöglichkeit, den modernen Konstruktionen eine nur annähernd gleich künstlerische Wirkung abzugewinnen."

38. For an overview of Lichtwark's theory, see Hans Präffcke, *Der Kunstbegriff Alfred Lichtwarks* (Hildesheim, Germany: Georg Olms, 1896).

39. Alfred Lichtwark, "Realistische Architektur," *Pan* 3 (1897): 230. "Und sicher hat auch der Laie das Gefühl gehabt, dass ein neuer Bauorganismus entstanden ist, in dem sich ruhig und fest der Wille ausspricht, eine realistische Architektur zu schaffen, und es mag ihm wenn er nachher andere Bauten betrachtet hat, zu erstenmale eine Ahnung davon aufgegangen sein, dass Architektur nicht blosse Säule, Bebälk und Ornament ist."

40. Alfred Lichtwark, "Sachliche Baukunst," *Palastfenster und Flügeltür*, in *Alfred Lichtwark: Eine Auswahl seiner Schriften*, ed. Wolf Mannhardt (Berlin: Bruno Cassirer, 1917), 257–73.

41. On Schumacher's life and ideas, see Dagmar Löbert, *Fritz Schumacher (1869 bis 1947): Reformarchitekt zwischen Tradition und Moderne* (Bremen: Donat, 1999), and Hartmut Frank, ed., *Fritz Schumacher: Reformkultur und Moderne* (Stuttgart: Hatje, 1994).

42. Fritz Schumacher, *Stufen des Lebens: Erinnerungen eines Baumeisters* (Stuttgart: Deutsche Verlags-Anstalt, 1938), 398 n. 33. Cited from J. Berry, "The Legacy of Gottfried Semper: Studies in Späthistorismus," 61.

43. Fritz Schumacher, "Stil und Mode" (1898), in *Im Kampfe um die Kunst: Beiträge zur architektonischen Zeitfragen*, 2nd ed. (Strassburg: J. H. Heitz, 1902), 28–9. ". . . und was als gemeinsames Band hindurch gehen kann und hoffentlich auch noch einmal hindurchgehen wird, das mag eine gewisse Gemeinsamkeit der Geschmacksunterlage sein, die vielleicht nicht mehr Gemeinsames besitzt, als dass die Künstler bei Bewältigung ihrer Aufgaben sichtlich zurückgehen zur Natur des praktischen Zwecks, zur Natur des Materials, zur Natur der organischen Formenwelt, zur Natur des volkstümlichen Eigenart. Das könnte man dann, wie verschieden es im Einzelnen aussehen mag, als die Erreichung einer Epoche *realistischer* Architektur bezeichnen."

44. Julius Lessing, "Neue Wege," *Kunstgewerbeblatt*, 1895, 3. "Ist es nun denkbar, das an Stelle historischer Überlieferung und allmählicher Weiterbildung diese technischen Faktoren durchaus neue Formen schaffen? Können wir die neu gefundene, rein konstruktive Form eines modernen eisernen Trägers also eine Schöpfung betrachten wie die griechische Säule, deren geheiligte Form bis heute alle Kunstperioden beherrscht?"

45. Ibid.

46. Ibid., 5. "Bequem oder nicht: unsere Arbeit hat einzusetzen auf dem Boden des praktischen Lebens unserer Zeit, hat diejenigen Formen zu schaffen, welche unseren Bedürfnissen, unserer Technik, unserem Material entsprechen. Wenn wir uns auf diesem Wege zu einer Form der Schönheit im Sinne unseres naturwissenschaftlichen Zeitalters emporarbeiten, so wird sie nicht aussehen wie die fromme Schönheit der Gotik oder die üppige der Renaissance, aber sie wird aussehen wie die vielleicht etwas herbe Schönheit aus dem Schlusse des neunzehnten Jahrhunderts, und das es was man von uns verlangen kann."

47. See Maria Makela, *The Munich Secession: Art and Artists in Turn-of-the-Century Munich* (Princeton: Princeton University Press, 1990).

48. On the thought and work of Endell, see Helge David, ed., *Vom Sehen: Texte 1896–1925 über Architektur, formkunst und "Die Schönen der grossen Stadt"* (Basel: Birkhäuser, 1995); Tilmann Buddensieg, "The Early Years of August Endell: Letters to Kurt Breysig from Munich," *Art Journal* (spring 1983): 41–49.

49. August Endell, *Um die Schönheit: Eine Paraphrase über die Münchener Kunstausstellung in 1896* (Munich: Franke, 1896).

50. August Endell, "Möglichkeit und Ziele einer neuen Architektur," *Deutsche Kunst und Dekoration* 3 (March 1898): 141.

51. Ibid., 143. "Ein ausgebildetes verfeinertes Formgefühl ist die Grundvoraussetzung alles architektonischen Schaffens, und das kann man nicht intellektuell erlernen."

52. Ibid., 144. "Der Architekt muss Formkünstler sein, nur durch die reine Formkunst führt der Weg zu einer neuen Architektur."

53. Nikolaus Pevsner, *Pioneers of Modern Design: From William Morris to Walter Gropius* (Harmondsworth, England: Penguin, 1968), 194–5.

54. August Endell, "Formenschönheit und decorative Kunst," *Dekorative Kunst* 2 (1898), 119–25.

55. On van de Velde's life and work, see Dieter Dolgner, *Henry van de Velde in Weimar, 1902–1917: Kunstführer* (Weimar: Verlage und Datenbank für Geisteswissenschaften, 1997); Steven Jacobs, *Henry van de Velde* (Louvain: Van Halewyck, 1996); Klaus-Jürgen Semback und Birgit Schulte, eds., *Henry van de Velde: Ein europäischer Kunstler in seiner Zeit* (Cologne: Wienand Verlag, 1992); and Klaus-Jürgen Sembach, *Henry van de Velde* (New York: Rizzoli, 1989).

56. See an excellent summary of this concept and its use in Belgium in Amy F. Ogata, *Art Nouveau and the Social Vision of Modern Living* (New York: Cambridge University Press, 2001), 5.

57. Among van de Velde's early writings are *Cours d'arts d'industrie et d'ornementation* (Brussels: Moreau, 1894); *Deblaiement d'art* (Brussels: Vve Monnom, 1894); *Apercus en vue d'une synthese d'art* (Brussels: Vve Monnom, 1895).

58. See Meler-Graefe's article in the special issue of *Dekorative Kunst* (vol. 3, 1898–9) that is devoted to van de Velde.

59. Henry van de Velde, *Die Renaissance im modernen Kunstgewerbe* (Berlin: Bruno & Paul Cassirer, 1901), 43. "Realismus und Naturalismus bedeuten für die Künstler ein Wiederzurückfinden zum Leben."

60. Ibid., 97. "Ich habe eine Form der Ornamentik aufstellen wollen, welche der Willkür der Künstlerphantasie nicht mehr frei die Zügel schiessen liess, ebensowenig wie dies einem Ingenieur für die äussere Form einer locomotive, einer eisernen Brücke oder einer Halle verstattet wäre."

61. Ibid., 100. "Unsere modernen Bauten haben keine andere Bedeutung als ihren Zweck. Unsere Bahnhöfe, unsere Dampfboote, unsere Brücken, unsere Türme von Eisen haben keineswegs den geheimen Sinn. . . ."

62. Henry van de Velde, "Principielle Erklärungen," in *Kunstgewerbliche Laienpredigten* (Leipzig: Hermann Seemann, 1902),

172. "Der Ingenieure stehen am Beginn des neuen Stils, und das Prinzip der Logik ist seine Basis."

63. Ibid., 175, 187.

64. Ibid., 188. "Eine Linie ist eine Kraft, die ähnlich wie alle elementaren Kräfte tätig ist; mehrere in Verbindung gebrachte, sich aber widerstrebende Linien bewirken dasselbe, wie mehrere gegeneinander wirkende elementare Kräfte. Diese Wahrheit ist entscheidend, sie is die Basis der neuen Ornamentik, aber nicht ihr einziges Prinzip."

65. J. Meier-Graefe, "Ein modernes Milieu," in *Dekorative Kunst* 4 (1901): 262–4. "Hier wurde der Nachweis geliefert, dass es nicht so unendlich tiefer Künste und auch nicht so sehr des *A tout prix*-Modernismus bedarf, um ein anständiges Milieu zu schaffen, as das Prestige des meisten führenden Künstler unserer Bewegung glauben lassen möchte. Sie all ohne Ausnahme können an dieser einfachen Lösung viel lernen, vor allem das beste der modernen Prinzipien, dass man nicht wenig genug Kunst anwenden kann, um Künstler zu sein."

66. On Olbrich, see Joseph August Lux, *Joseph M. Olbrich: Ein Monographie* (Berlin: Wasmuth, 1919); Ian Latham, *Joseph Marie Olbrich* (New York: Rizzoli, 1980); Robert Judson Clark, "Joseph Maria Olbrich and Vienna" (Ph.D. diss., Princeton University, 1973).

67. Joseph M. Olbrich, "Das Haus der Secession," *Der Architekt* 5 (1899): 5. "Nein, nur meine eigene Empfindung wollte ich in Klang hören, mein warmes Fühlen in kalten Mauern erstarrt sehen."

68. The classic work on Josef Hoffmann is Eduard F. Sekler's *Josef Hoffmann: The Architectural Work, Monograph and Catalogue of Works*, trans. John Maas (Princeton: Princeton University Press, 1985).

69. For the background and details of the Purkersdorf Sanatorium, see Leslie Topp's instructive chapter on this building in *Architecture, Truth and Society in Vienna, 1898–1912* (New York: Cambridge University Press, 2002).

70. Joseph A. Lux referred to the work in 1905 as guided by a *"sachliche Selbstverständlichkeit"* (*sachliche* matter-of-factness) in his review "Sanatorium," *Hohe Warte* 1 (1904–5): 407. For other reactions, see also Topp, *Architecture, Truth and Society in Vienna.*

71. The most comprehensive biography of Loos is that of Burkhard Rukschcio and Roland Schachel, *Adolf Loos: Leben und Werk* (Vienna: Residenz Verlag, 1982). Two works in English are Benedetto Gravagnuolo, *Adolf Loos: Theory and Works* (New York: Rizzoli, 1982), and *The Architecture of Adolf Loos* (London: Arts Council Exhibition, 1985).

72. Adolf Loos, "Ein wiener Architekt," *Dekorative Kunst*, 11 (1898); reprinted in Adolf Loos, *Die potemkinsche Stadt* (Vienna: Georg Prachner Verlag, 1983), 53. "Für mich ist die Tradition alles, das freie Walten der Phantasie kommt bei mir erst in zweiter Linie."

73. Adolf Loos, "Die Alt und die neue Richtung in der Baukunst," *Der Architekt* 4 (1898): 31–2; reprinted in Loos, *Die potemkinsche Stadt*, 62–8.

74. Adolf Loos, "Die Plumber," in *Ins leere gesprochen: 1897–1900* (Vienna, Georg Prachner, 1981; originally published in 1931), 105–6. Cited from my translation "Plumbers," in *Plumbing: Sounding Modern Architecture*, ed. Nadir Lahiji & D. S. Friedman (New York: Princeton Architectural Press, 1997), 18.

75. Adolf Loos, "Building Materials," in *Spoken into the Void: Collected Essays 1897–1900*, trans. Jane O. Newman and John H. Smith (Cambridge: M.I.T. Press, 1982), 65.

76. Ibid., 99–103.

77. Ibid., 124–7.

78. Adolf Loos, *Das Andere: Ein Blatt zur Einführung abendländischer Kultur in Österreich* (Vienna: Verlag Kunst, 1903).

79. Relatively detailed histories of the controversy surrounding its design are contained in Gravagnuolo, *Adolf Loos*, and in Rukschcio and Schachel, *Adolf Loos.*

80. Adolf Loos, "Heimatkunst" (1914), in *Adolf Loos: Trotzdem 1900–1930* (Vienna: Georg Prachner, 1982; originally published in 1931). An English translation of this essay appears in *The Architecture of Adolf Loos*, 110–3.

81. See Rukschcio and Schachel, *Adolf Loos*, 118.

82. Adolf Loos, "Ornament and Crime" (1908), in *The Architecture of Adolf Loos*, 102–3.

83. Ibid., 101.

84. Adolf Loos, "Das Prinzip der Bekleidung" (1898), in *Adolf Loos: Ins Leere Gesprochen*, 140. "Der künstler aber, der *architect*, fühlt zuerst die wirkung, die er hervorzubringen gedenkt, und sieht dann mit seinem geistigen auge die räume, die er schaffen will. Die wirkung, die er auf den beschauer ausüber will, sei es nun angst oder schrecken wie beim kerker; gottesfurcht wie bei der kirche; ehrfurcht vor der staatsgewalt wie beim regierungspalast; pietät wie beim grabmal; heimgefühl wie beim wohnhause; fröhlichkeit wie in der trinkstube; diese wirkung wird hervorgerufen durch das material und durch die form."

85. Adolf Loos, "Architektur," in *Adolf Loos: Trotzdem*, 102–3. "Die architektur erweckt stimmungen im menschen. Die aufgabe des architekten ist es daher, diese stimmung zu präzisieren. Das zimmer muss gemütlich, das haus wohnlich aussehen. Das justizgebäude muss dem heimlichen lastere wie eine drohende gebärde erscheinen. Das bankhaus muss sagen: hier ist dein geld bei ehrlichen leuten fest und gut verwahrt."

86. Ibid., 101. "Der mensch liebt alles, was seiner bequemlichkeit dient. Er hasst alles, was ihm aus seiner gewonnenen und gesicherten position reissen will und belästigt. Und so liebt er das haus und hasst die Kunst."

87. On the thought and designs of Berlage, see Pieter Singelenberg, *H. P. Berlage, Idea and Style: The Quest for Modern Architecture* (Utrecht: Haentjens, Dekker & Gumbert, 1972); Manfred Bock, *Anfänge einer neuen Architektur: Berlages Beitrag zur architektonischen Kultur der Niederlande im ausgehenden 19. Jahrhundert* (The Hague: Staatsuitgeverij, 1983); and Sergio Polano, *Hendrik Petrus Berlage: Complete Works* (New York: Rizzoli, 1988); and Manfred Bock et al., *Berlage in Amsterdam* (Amsterdam: Architectura & Natura Press, 1992).

88. Hendrik Petrus Berlage, "Architecture and Impressionism," in *Hendrik Petrus Berlage: Thoughts on Style, 1886–1909*, trans. Iain Boyd Whyte (Santa Monica, Calif.: Getty Publications Program, 1996), 105–21.

89. Hendrik Petrus Berlage, "Architecture's Place in Modern Aesthetics" (1886), in *Hendrik Petrus Berlage: Thoughts on Style*, 102.

90. Hendrik Petrus Berlage, "Thoughts on Style" (1905), in *Hendrik Petrus Berlage: Thoughts on Style*, 132.

91. Ibid., 137.

92. Ibid., 139.

93. Ibid., 152.

94. Ibid., 153.

95. Hendrik Petrus Berlage, "The Foundations and Development of Architecture" (1908), in *Hendrik Petrus Berlage: Thoughts on Style*, 245.

96. Ibid., 249–50.

97. Ibid., 250. "Die sachliche, vernünftige, und daher klare Konstruktion kann die Basis der neuen Kunst werden; und erst dann, wenn jenes Prinzip genügend durchgedrungen ist und auch allgemein verwendet wird, werden wir an der Pforte einer neuen Kunst stehen; aber auch in demselben Moment wird das neue Weltgefühl, die gesellschaftliche Gleichheit aller Menschen manifestiert sein, ein Weltgefühl, nicht mit seinem Ideal eines Jenseits, d.h. nicht in diesem Sinne religiös, sondern mit seinem Ideal von dieser Erde, also jenem entgegengesetzt."

98. See Berlage's *Amerikaansche reisherinneringen* (Rotterdam: W. L. & J. Brusse, 1913), 45. See also Iain Boyd Whyte's introduction to *Hendrik Petrus Berlage: Thoughts on Style*, 65.

99. On Wright's early years, see Grant Carpenter Manson, *Frank Lloyd Wright to 1910: The First Golden Age* (New York: Van Nostrand Reinhold, 1958), and Anthony Alofsin, *Frank Lloyd Wright: The Lost Years, 1910–1922: A Study of Influence* (Chicago: University of Chicago Press, 1993). For a recent general overview of Wright, see Neil Levine, *The Architecture of Frank Lloyd Wright* (Princeton: Princeton University Press, 1966).

100. Frank Lloyd Wright, "The Architect" (1900), in *Frank Lloyd Wright Collected Writings* (New York: Rizzoli, 1992), 1:48.

101. Ibid., 51.

102. Ibid., 50.

103. Ibid., 52.

104. On his decisions in this regard, see Joseph M. Siry, *Unity Temple: Frank Lloyd Wright and Architecture for Liberal Religion* (New York: Cambridge University Press, 1996), 143–8.

105. Wright, "In the Cause of Architecture" (1908), in *Frank Lloyd Wright Collected Writings*, 1:86.

106. Wright, "In the Cause of Architecture" (1914), *Frank Lloyd Wright Collected Writings*, 1:127 n.

107. Wright, "In the Cause of Architecture" (1908), *Frank Lloyd Wright Collected Writings*, 1:100.

108. See Wright's version of these events in Frank Lloyd Wright, *An Autobiography* (New York: Horizon Press, 1977), 185–6.

109. Wright, "Ausgefuhrte Bauten und Entwürfe von Frank Lloyd Wright" (1911), in *Frank Lloyd Wright Collected Writings*, 1:108.

110. Ibid.

111. Ibid., 112.

112. Ibid., 113.

113. Wright, "The Japanese Print: An Interpretation" (1912), in *Frank Lloyd Wright Collected Writings*, 1:117.

114. Ibid., 117–18.

115. On Garnier and his *Cité Industrielle*, see Dora Wiebenson, *Tony Garnier: The Cité industrielle* (New York: George Braziller, 1969). See also Tony Garnier, *L'oeuvre complete* (Paris: Editions du Centre Georges Pompidou, 1989); René Jullian, *Tony Garnier: Constructeur et utopiste* (Paris: P. Sers, 1989); and Krzysztof Kazimierz, *Tony Garnier et les débuts de l'urbanisme fonctionnel en France* (Paris: Centre de Recherche d'Urbanisme, 1967).

116. Garnier's preface to *Une Cité Industrielle* is translated at the end of Wiebenson, *Tony Garnier*, 107–12.

117. On Perret, see Peter Collins, *Concrete: The Vision of a New Architecture: A Study of Auguste Perret and His Precursors* (London: Faber & Faber, 1959); Ernesto N. Rogers, *Auguste Perret* (Milan: Il Balcone, 1955); Karla Britton, *Auguste Perret* (London: Phaidon, 2001); Roberto Gargiani, *Auguste Perret, 1874–1954: Teoria e opere* (Milan: Electa, 1993); and Kenneth Frampton's chapter on Perret in his *Studies in Tectonic Culture: The Poetics of Construction in Nineteenth and Twentieth Century Architecture* (Cambridge: M.I.T. Press, 1995).

118. On Le Corbusier's early years, see the invaluable study of H. Allen Brooks, *Le Corbusier's Formative Years: Charles-Edouard Jeanneret at La Chaux-de-Fonds* (Chicago: University of Chicago Press, 1997).

119. See Nancy J. Troy, *Modernism and the Decorative Arts in France: Art Nouveau to Le Corbusier* (New Haven: Yale University Press, 1991), 103–7.

120. Charles-Edouard Jeanneret, *Étude sur le movement d'art decorative en Allemagne* (New York: Da Capo Press, 1968; originally published in 1912), 11.

121. Ibid., 11–13.

122. Ibid., 13.

123. Ibid., 13. "Il y a en France evolution normale, progressive, de la pensées, de l'âme de ce people."

124. Ibid., 74. "Si Paris est le foyer de l'Art, l'Allemagne demeure le grand chantier de production."

125. Jeanneret to Charles L'Eplattenier, 16 January 1911. Cited from Brooks, *Le Corbusier's Formative Years*, 251. "France subjugue l'Allemagne. Et l'Allemagne s'incline."

126. Camillo Boito, "Sullo stile futuro dell'architettura italiana," in *Architettura del medio evo in Italia* (Milan: Ulrico Hoepli, 1880).

127. See Etlin's chapter describing this exposition in *Modernism in Italian Architecture, 1890–1940* (Cambridge: M.I.T. Press, 1991).

128. Alfred Melani, "Dottrinarismo architettonico," in *Prima Esposizione Italiani di Architettura in Tornio. Conferenze ottobernovembre 1890* (1891), 31–2. Cited from Etlin, *Modernism in Italian Architecture*, 6.

129. Alfred Melani, *Manuale architettura Italiana antica e moderna* (Milan: Ulrico Hoepli, 1904), 496.

130. Marinetti's manifesto was first published on 20 February 1909. For an English translation, see Charles Harrison and Paul Wood, ed., *Art in Theory 1900–2000: An Anthology of Changing Ideas* (Oxford: Blackwell, 2003), 146–9.

131. Ibid., 147–8.

132. Boccioni's manifest of 11 April 1910 was also signed by Carlo Carrà, Luigi Russolo, Giacomo Balla, and Gino Severini. See Harrison and Wood, *Art in Theory 1900–2000*, 150–152.

133. Sant'Elia's authorship has been debated throughout the second half of the twentieth century. For details of it and his career, see Esther da Costa Meyer's excellent study *The Work of Antonio Sant'Elia: Retreat into the Future* (New Haven: Yale University Press, 1995).

134. Cited from Costa Meyer, *Work of Antonio Sant'Elia*, 212.

135. Ibid.

136. Ulrich Conrads, *Programs and Manifestoes on Twentieth-Century Architecture* (Cambridge: M.I.T. Press, 1975), 36, 38.

137. R. Banham, *Theory and Design in the First Machine Age* (London: The Architectural Press, 1982; originally published in 1960), 99.

138. On Muthesius, his ideas, and his role in the German Werkbund, see Fedor Roth, *Hermann Muthesius und die Idee der harmonischen Kultur: Kultur als Einheit der künstlerischen Stils in allen Lebensäusserungen eines Volkes* (Berlin: Mann Verlag, 2001); Uwe Schneider, *Hermann Muthesius und die Reformdiskussion in der Gartenarchitektur des frühen 20. Jahrhunderts* (Worms, Germany: Wernersche Verlagsgesellschaft, 2000); John Vincent Maciuika, "Herrmann Muthesius and the Reform of German Architecture, Arts, and Crafts, 1890–1914" (Ph.D. diss., University of California, Berkeley, 1998); and Hans-Joachim Hubrich, *Hermann Muthesius: Die Schriften zu Architektur, Kunstgewerbe, Industrie in "Neuen Bewegung"* (Berlin: Mann, 1981).

139. Hermann Muthesius, *Die englische Baukunst der Gegenwart: Beispiele neuer englischer Profanbauten* (Leipzig: Cosmos, 1900).

140. See Julius Langbehn, *Rembrandt als Erzieher: Von einem Deutschen* (Leipzig: Hirschfeld, 1890).

141. Hermann Muthesius, "Neues Ornament und neue Kunst," *Dekorative Kunst* 4 (1901): 353, 356.

142. Ibid., 362–3. "In der Architektur has das 'Stilmachen' lange die Quellen sachlichen Fortschrittes verstopft, in der Nutzkunst nicht minder. Wollte man dieser Stil- und Architekturmacherei die Thüre weisen, so würde man Wunder an sachlichem Fortschritte erleben. Es gilt also hier vielmehr ein Reinigungswerk an sogenannten künstlerischen Gesichtspunkten vorzunehmen, als ein Hereintragen neuer."

143. Ibid., 364.

144. Ibid. "Das über die Wasserfläche schiessende, elegant gebaute Segelboot, der elektrische Beleuchtungskörper, das Zweirad scheinen dem Geist unserer Zeit näher gekommen zu sein, als der Jugend- und Secessionsstil unserer bisherigen neuen Möbel und Tapeten."

145. Ibid., 365. "Wir brauchen helle und saubere Räume ohne Staubecken und Staubfänge, glatte und einfache Möbel, die sich ebenso leicht abstäuben wie verschieben lassen, eine luftige und durchsichtige Disposition des ganzen Raumes...."

146. Hermann Muthesius, *Stilarchitektur und Baukunst: Wandlungen der Architektur im XIX. Jahrhundert und ihr heutiger Standpunkt* (Mülheim-Ruhr, Germany: Schimmelpfeng, 1902); translated by Stanford Anderson as *Style-Architecture and Building-Art: Transformations of Architecture in the Nineteenth Century and Its Present Condition* (Santa Monica, Calif.: Getty Publications Program, 1994). The two lectures are noted in the preface to the second edition of 1903, but no details are given.

147. Muthesius, *Style-Architecture and Building-Art*, 51–2.

148. Ibid., 68.

149. Ibid., 65, 67.

150. Ibid., 50.

151. Ibid., 78.

152. Ibid., 79.

153. See Anderson's introduction to Muthesius, *Style-Architecture and Building-Art*, 14–19.

154. Muthesius, *Style-Architecture and Building-Art*, 98.

155. Ibid., 92.

156. For two different perspectives of its founding and the purpose of the Werkbund, see Joan Campbell, *The German Werkbund: The Politics of Reform in the Applied Arts* (Princeton: Princeton University Press, 1978), and Frederic J. Schwartz, *The Werkbund: Design Theory and Mass Culture before the First World War* (New Haven: Yale University Press, 1996). See also Francesco Dal Co's chapter on the Werkbund in *Figures of Architecture and Thought: German Architecture Culture 1880–1920* (New York: Rizzoli, 1982). A short but no less important article on the aims of the Werkbund is Mark Jarzombek's "The *Kunstgewerbe,* the *Werkbund,* and the Aesthetics of Culture in the Wilhelmine Period," *Journal of the Society of Architectural Historians* 53 (March 1994): 7–19.

157. For an excellent discussion of Muthesius, Behrens, and these reforms, see J. Maciuika, "Hermann Muthesius and the Reform of German Architecture, Arts, and Crafts, 1890–1914," 185–245.

158. Ibid., 133–4.

159. F. Schumacher, "Die Wiedereroberung harmonischer Kultur," *Kunstwart* 21 (January 1908): 135–8.

160. Hermann Muthesius, "Die Bedeutung des Kunstgewerbes," *Dekorative Kunst* 15 (1907): 177–92.

161. For a discussion of Hellerau, see Maciuika, "Herrmann Muthesius and the Reform of German Architecture, Arts, and Crafts, 1890–1914," 333–63. See also Barbara Miller Lane, *National Romanticism and Modern Architecture in Germany and the Scandinavian Countries* (New York: Cambridge University Press, 2000), 155–61.

162. Paul Mebes, *Um 1800: Architectur und Handwerk im letzten Jahrhundert ihrer traditionellen Entwicklung* (Munich: F. Bruckmann, 1908).

163. Joseph August Lux, *Ingenieur-Ästhetik* (Vienna: Gustav Lammers, 1910), 38. "Die modernen technischen Konstruktionen brauchen nur älter zu werden, um als schön zu gelten."

164. Peter Behrens, *Ein Dokument deutscher Kunst: Die Austellung der Kunstler-Kolonie in Darmstadt, 1901, Festschrift* (Munich: F. Bruckmann, 1901), 9. On the life and work of Behrens, see Tilmann Buddenseig et al., *Industriekultur: Peter Behrens and the AEG, 1907–1914,* trans. Iain Boyd Whyte (Cambridge: M.I.T. Press, 1983), and Stanford Anderson, *Peter Behrens and a New Architecture for the Twentieth Century* (Cambridge: M.I.T. Press, 2000).

165. Buddensieg, *Industriekultur,* 42.

166. Karl Bernhard, "Die neue Halle für die Turbinenfabrik der Allgemeinen Elektrizitätsgesellschaft in Berlin," *Zeitschrift des Vereins Deutscher Ingenieure,* #39 (1911), 1682. Cited from Karin Wilhelm, "Fabrikenkunst: The Turbine Hall and What Came of It," in Buddensieg, *Industriekultur,* 143.

167. Peter Behrens, "Kunst und Technik," a lecture given at the AEG, published in *Berliner-Tageblatt,* 25 January 1909. Cited in Buddensieg, *Industriekultur,* 62.

168. Peter Behrens, "The Aesthetics of Industrial Buildings: Beauty in Perfect Adaptation to Useful Ends," *Scientific American,* suppl., 23 August 1913, 120.

169. Ibid.

170. Ibid.

171. Ibid., 121.

172. Ibid.

173. Peter Behrens, "Art and Technology," in Buddensieg, *Industriekultur,* 213.

174. Ibid.

175. On Riegl's later notion of *Kunstwollen*, see Margaret Olin, *Forms of Representation in Alois Riegl's Theory of Art* (University Park: Pennsylvania State University, 1992), 148–53. See also the discussion of Riegl in Harry Francis Mallgrave, *Gottfried Semper: Architect of the Nineteenth Century* (New York: Yale University Press, 1996), 372–81.

176. Peter Behrens, "Art and Technology," in Buddensieg, *Industriekultur*, 219.

177. See Maciuika, "Hermann Muthesius and the Reform of German Architecture, Arts, and Crafts, 1890–1914," 364–88, and Anna-Christa Fund, ed., *Karl Ernst Osthaus gegen Hermann Muthesius: Der Werkbundstreit im Spiegel der im Karl Ernst Osthaus Archiv erhaltenen Briefe* (Hagen: Karl Ernst Osthaus Museum, 1978).

178. For the ten theses and antitheses, see "Muthesius/Van de Velde: Werkbund theses and antitheses," in *Programs and Manifestoes on 20ᵗʰ-Century Architecture*, ed. Ulrich Conrads (Cambridge: M.I.T. Press, 1975), 28–31.

179. For an extended discussion of *Typisierung*, see Schwartz, *Werkbund*, 121–63.

180. Translation cited from Anderson, *Peter Behrens and a New Architecture for the Twentieth Century*, 215.

11. European Modernism 1917–1933

1. For the theory of avant-garde movement in literature and painting, see Peter Bürger, *Theory of the Avant-Garde*, trans. Michael Shaw (Minneapolis: University of Minnesota Press, 1984). For a broader perspective, see Matei Calinescu, *Five Faces of Modernity: Modernism, Avant-Garde, Decadence, Kitsch, Postmodernism* (Durham, N.C.: Duke University Press, 1987).

2. Oswald Spengler, *The Decline of the West*, trans. Charles Francis Atkinson (New York: Knopf, 1934) 2: 507.

3. Frederick Winslow Taylor, *The Principles of Scientific Management* (Minola, New York: Dover, 1998; originally published in New York, Harper & Bros. 1911), 1.

4. Ibid., 5.

5. Several excellent works on Soviet architecture have appeared in recent years. See especially the three studies by William Craft Brumfield, *A History of Russian Architecture* (New York: Cambridge University Press, 1993); *Reshaping Russian Architecture: Western Technology, Utopian Dreams* (New York: Cambridge University Press, 1990); and *The Origins of Modernism in Russian Architecture* (Berkeley: University of California Press, 1991). See also Victor Margolin, *The Struggle for Utopia: Rodchenko, Lissitzky, Moholy Nagy, 1917–1946* (Chicago: University of Chicago Press, 1997).

6. Kasimir Malevich, "Non-Objective Art and Suprematism," in *Art in Theory 1900–1990: An Anthology of Changing Ideas*, ed. Charles Harrison and Paul Wood (Oxford: Blackwell, 1999), 291.

7. Naum Gabo and Anton Pevsner, "The Realistic Manifesto," in Harrison and Wood, *Art in Theory 1900–1990*, 299.

8. Alexander Rodchenko, "Slogans," and Alexander Rodchenko and Varvara Stepanova, "Programme of the First Working Group of Constructivists," in Harrison and Wood, *Art in Theory 1900–1990*, 315–18.

9. Moisei Ginzburg, *Style and Epoch*, trans. & intro. Anatole Senkevitch, Jr. (Cambridge: M.I.T. Press, 1982). Senkevitch provides an excellent summary of Ginzburg's thought.

10. See Catherine Cooke, "'Form is a Function X': The Development of the Constructivist Architect's Design Method," in *Architectural Design: Russian Avant-Garde Art and Architecture*, Profile 47, vol. 53 5/6 (London: Architectural Design and Academy Editions, 1983), 38–42.

11. Ginzburg, *Epoch and Style*, 42.

12. Ibid., 47.

13. Ibid., 70.

14. Ibid., 72.

15. Ibid., 92.

16. El Lissitzky, *Russland: Die Rekonstruktion der Architektur in der Sowjetunion* (Vienna, 1930); translated by Eric Dluhosch as *Russia: An Architecture for World Revolution* (Cambridge: M.I.T. Press, 1984).

17. Lissitzky, *Russia*, 70–71.

18. On this speech and the history of this competition, see Antonia Cunliffe, "The Competition for the Palace of Soviets in Moscow, 1931–1933," *Architectural Association Quarterly* 11, no. 2 (1979): 36–48.

19. Ibid., 41.

20. The classic study of the De Stijl movement is H. L. C. Jaffé, *De Stijl 1917–1931: The Dutch Contribution to Modern Art* (Amsterdam: J. M. Meulenhoff, 1956). See also Mildred Friedman, ed., *De Stijl 1917–1931: Visions of Utopia* (Minneapolis: Walker Art Center, 1982), and Nancy J. Troy, *The De Stijl Environment* (Cambridge: M.I.T. Press, 1983). On van Doesburg, see Joost Baljeu, *Theo van Doesburg* (New York: Macmillan, 1974), and Allan Doig, *Theo van Doesburg: Painting into Architecture, Theory into Practice* (Cambridge: Cambridge University Press, 1987).

21. Wassily Kandinsky, *Concerning the Spiritual in Art* (New York: Wittenborn, 1947).

22. See especially Jaffé, *De Stijl 1917–1931*, 56–62.

23. De Stijl, "Manifesto I," in Harrison and Wood, *Art in Theory*, 278.

24. Theo van Doesburg, *Grundbegriffe der neuen gestaltenden Kunst* (Mainz, Germany: Florian Kupferberg, 1966; originally published in 1925 in the Neue Bauhausbucher series), 15.

25. "De Stijl: Manifesto V," in Ulrich Conrads, ed., *Programs and Manifestoes on Twentieth-Century Architecture* (Cambridge: M.I.T. Press, 1964).

26. Van Doesburg, *Grundbegriffe der neuen gestaltenden Kunst*, 15.

27. See Troy, *The De Stijl Environment*, 13–17.

28. Letter of van Doesburg to Oud, 3 November 1921, cited from Troy, *The De Stijl Environment*, 83–6.

29. J. J. P. Oud, "Over de toekomstige bouwkunst en haar architectonische mogelijkheden," *Bouwkundig Weekblad*, 11 June 1921. Cited from Oud's German version, "Über die zukünftige Baukunst und ihre architektonischen Möglichkeiten," *Holländische Architektur* (Mainz, Germany: Florian Kupferberg, 1976; originally published in 1926), 68.

30. Ibid., 782.73.

31. Ibid., 76. "So weist die Tendenz der architektonischen Entwicklung auf eine Baukunst, welche im Wesen mehr als früher an das Stoffliche gebunden, in der Erscheinung darüber mehr hinaus

sein wird; welche sich, frei von aller impressionistischen Stimmungsgestaltung, in der Fülle des Lichtes entwickelt zu einer Reinheit der Verhältnisses, einer Blankheit der Farbe und einer organischen Klarheit der Form, welche durch das Fehlen jedes Nebensächlichen die klassische Reinheit wird übertreffen können."

32. Fritz Schumacher, *Die Kleinwohnung: Studien zur Wohnungsfrage* (Leipzig: Quelle and Meyer, 1917); idem, *Das Wesen des neuzeitleichen Backsteinbaues* (Munich: Callwey, 1917).

33. Heinrich Tessenow, *Hausbau und dergleichen* (Braunschweig: Vieweg, 1986; originally published in 1916); translated by Wilfried Wang as "Housebuilding and Such Things," *9H*, no. 8, 1989. Idem, *Handwerk und Kleinstadt* (Berlin: Bruno Cassirer, 1919).

34. The term *expressionism* is nevertheless well established. The principal studies of the topic in English are Wolfgang Pehnt's *Expressionist Architecture* (London: Thames & Hudson, 1973) and Dennis Sharp's *Modern Architecture and Expressionism* (London: Longmans, 1966). For the principal writings of expressionist artists, see Rose-Carol Washton Long, ed., *German Expressionism: Documents from the End of the Wilhelmine Empire to the Rise of National Socialism* (New York: G. K. Hall, 1993).

35. See especially David Adams, "Rudolf Steiner's First Goetheanum as an Illustration of Organic Functionalism," *Journal of the Society of Architectural Historians* 51 (June 1992): 182–204.

36. Rudolf Steiner, *Ways to a New Style in Architecture: Five Lectures by Rudolf Steiner* (London: Anthroposophical Publishing Co., 1927), 21.

37. On Poelzig, see Christian Marquart, *Hans Poelzig: Architekt, Maler, Zeichern* (Tübingen: Wasmuth, 1995); Julius Posener, *Hans Poelzig: Reflections on His Life and Work*, ed. Kristin Feireiss (New York: Architectural History Foundation, 1992); *Hans Poelzig, Gesammelte Schriften und Werke*, ed. Julius Poesner (Berlin: Schriftenreihe der Akademie der Künste, 1970).

38. Hans Poelzig, "Fermentation in Architecture" (1906), in Conrads, *Programs and Manifestoes*, 14–17.

39. Hans Poelzig, "Address to the Werkbund" (1919), in *Hans Poelzig, Gesammete Schriften und Werke*, 130.

40. On Taut, see *Bruno Taut 1880–1938* (Berlin: Akademie der Künste, 1980); Rosemarie Haag Bletter, "Bruno Taut and Paul Scheerbart's Vision" (Ph.D. diss., Columbia University, 1973); Iain Boyd Whyte, ed. and trans., *The Crystal Chain Letter: Architectural Fantasies by Bruno Taut and His Circle* (Cambridge, M.I.T. Press, 1985); Ian Boyd Whyte, *Bruno Taut and the Architecture of Activism* (Cambridge: Cambridge University Press, 1982).

41. See Dietrich Neumann, "'The Century's Triumph in Lighting': The Luxfer Prism Companies and Their Contribution to Early Modern Architecture," *Journal of the Society of Architectural Historians* 54, (March 1995): 24–53.

42. See *Glass Architecture by Paul Scheerbart and Alpine Architecture by Bruno Taut*, trans. James Palmes and Shirley Palmer (New York: Praeger, 1972).

43. See Adolf Behne, "Expressionistische Architektur," *Der Sturm* 5 (January 1915): 175; excerpted from *Zur neuen Kunst* (Berlin: Der Sturm, 1915). See also Rosmarie Haag Bletter's introduction to Adolf Behne, *The Modern Functional Building* (Santa Monica, Calif.: Getty Publications Program, 1996).

44. One of the better political histories of this period is Detlev J. K. Peukert's *The Weimar Republic: The Crisis of Classical Modernity* (New York: Hill & Wang, 1993).

45. See "Novembergruppe: Draft Manifesto 1918 and 'Guidelines' 1919," in Harrison and Wood, *Art in Theory 1900–1990*, 262–3.

46. Bruno Taut, "A Programme for Architecture," in Conrads, *Programs and Manifestoes on Twentieth-Century Architecture*, 41–43.

47. Walter Gropius, address to the Arbeitsrat für Kunst, 22 March 1920. Cited from Whyte, *Crystal Chain Letters*, 2.

48. See Walter Gropius, "New Ideas on Architecture," in Conrads, *Programs and Manifestoes*, 46.

49. Bruno Taut, "New Ideas on Architecture," Conrads, *Programs and Manifestoes*, 47.

50. Adolf Behne, "New Ideas on Architecture," Conrads, *Programs and Manifestoes*, 48.

51. Bruno Taut, 24 November 1919, in Whyte, *Crystal Chain Letters*, 19.

52. Van de Velde to Gropius, 11 April 1915, in Hans M. Wingler, *The Bauhaus: Weimar, Dessau, Berlin, Chicago* (Cambridge: M.I.T. Press, 1978), 21. Much of the following account is taken from this invaluable documentary history of the Bauhaus.

53. Fritz Mackensen to Gropius, 2 October 1915, in Wingler, *The Bauhaus*, 22.

54. Gropius to Fritz Mackensen, 19 October 1915, in Wingler, *The Bauhaus*, 22.

55. "Recommendations for the Founding of an Educational Institution as an Artistic Counselling Service for Industry, the Trades, and the Crafts," 25 January 1916, in Wingler, *The Bauhaus*, 23.

56. Gropius to Baron von Fritsch, 31 January 1919, in Wingler, *The Bauhaus*, 26.

57. "Program of the Staatliche Bauhaus in Weimar," April 1919, in Wingler, *The Bauhaus*, 31.

58. Mies van der Rohe noted this in a conversation to Howard Dearstyne in 1957. See Howard Dearstyne, *Inside the Bauhaus*, ed. David Spaeth (New York: Rizzoli, 1986), 43.

59. Ibid., 51–4, 57–8.

60. Ibid., 261 n. 3.

61. Baron von Fritsch to Hofmarschallamt in Weimar, 20 April 1920, in Wingler, *The Bauhaus*, 33.

62. For an excellent discussion of the politics of Weimar and the early Bauhaus, see Barbara Miller Lane, *Architecture and Politics in Germany, 1918–1945* (Cambridge: Harvard University Press, 1985), 69–86.

63. On van Doesburg's stay in Weimar, see the exhibition catalogue *Konstruktivistische Internationale schöperische Arbeitsgemeinschaft, 1922–1927: Utopien für eine Europäische Kultur* (Ostfilden-Ruit, Germany: Gerd Hatje, 1992), especially the article of Rainer Stommer, "Der 'De Stijl'-Kurs von Theo van Doesburg in Weimar (1922)," 169–177. See also the chapter on Doesburg's stay and its effect in Dearstyne, *Inside the Bauhaus*, 62–7.

64. On the circle of Lissitzky in Berlin, see the second chapter of Margolin, *Struggle for Utopia*.

65. In 1994 the journal was reissued in a reprint version, in German with an English translation, by Lars Müller Publishers.

66. The two issues of *G* have also been reprinted by Kern Verlag (Munich, 1986), with an introduction by Marion von Hofacker.

67. Published in Wingler, *The Bauhaus*, 20–1.

68. Adolf Behne, "Mittelalterliches und modernes Bauen," *Sociale Bauwirtschaft*, 15 July 1921.

69. Mies van der Rohe, "Skyscrapers," *Frühlicht* 1, no. 4 (1922), 122. Cited from Fritz Neumeyer, *The Artless Word: Mies van der Rohe on the Building Art*, trans. Mark Jarzombek (Cambridge: M.I.T. Press, 1991), 240.

70. See Winfried Nerdinger, *Walter Gropius* (Berlin: Mann Verlag, 1985), 45.

71. Mies reflected back on the theater in 1969: "The main celebration was held in Jena. There was a theater there which Gropius had built or remodeled – built, I believe (no, remodeled). He did this with Adolf Meyer. We were rather disappointed and we said, 'That is so strange, it is all so decorative, like the Wiener Werkstätten.'" Cited from Dearstyne, *Inside the Bauhaus*, 79.

72. Walter Gropius, "The Necessity of Commissioned Work for the Bauhaus," in Wingler, *The Bauhaus*, 51.

73. "The Viability of the Bauhaus Idea," in Wingler, *The Bauhaus*, 51–52.

74. Lyonel Feiniger, letter to Julia Feininger, 5 October 1922, in Wingler, *The Bauhaus*, 56. "We have to steer toward profitable undertakings, toward mass production! That goes decidedly against our grain and is a forestalling of the process of evolution." See also his letter of 1 August 1923, p. 69, and Muche's essay "Bildende Kunst und Industrieform," *Bauhaus*, no. 1 (1926). The relevant passage is cited in Dearstyne, *Inside the Bauhaus*, 125. In several remarks in his diaries and letter, Schlemmer recounted the "duel" between Itten and Gropius. In remarking on Itten's likely departure in June 1922, Schlemmer noted, "He is the most capable of us pedagogically and he has a marked talent for leadership. I feel only too keenly the lack of this in me. Furthermore, if Gropius no longer has the strong opposition of Itten, he will be the much greater danger." Cited from Dearstyne, *Inside the Bauhaus*, 88.

75. Oskar Schlemmer, "The Staatliche Bauhaus in Weimar," in Wingler, *The Bauhaus*, 65–66.

76. In a letter to van Doesburg (23 August 1923), Mies criticized Gropius for his "constructivistic formalism." See excerpts of the letter in Richard Pommer and Christian F. Otto, *Weissenhof 1927 and the Modern Movement in Architecture* (Chicago: University of Chicago Press, 1991), 11–12.

77. Ibid., "The Bauhaus Exhibition in Weimar," 67–8.

78. Adolf Behne, "Das Bauhaus Weimar," *Die Weltbühne* 19 (1923) 291–2. Cited from Rosemarie Haag Bletter's introduction to Adolf Behne, *The Modern Functional Building*, trans. Michael Robinson (Santa Monica, Calif.: Getty Publications Program, 1996), 31.

79. See Letter of Complaint, 24 November 1923, in Wingler, *The Bauhaus*, 76.

80. Adolf Behne, *Der moderne Zweckbau* (Munich: Drei Masken Verlag, 1926); translated by Michael Robinson as *The Modern Functional Building* (see note 78).

81. Adolf Behne, "Von der Sachlichkeit," in *Eine Stunde Architektur* (Berlin: Architbook-Verlag, 1984), 40. "Sachlichkeit bedeutet verantwortetes Denken, bedeutet ein Schaffen, das alle Zwecke mit und aus der Phantasie erfüllt. Denn es gehört Phantasie dazu, den Zweck dort zu fassen, wo er seinen revolutionären Sinn enthüllt."

82. Ibid., 41.

83. Walter Gropius, *Internationale Architektur*, ed. Hans M. Wingler (Mainz, Germany: Florian Kupferberg, 1981; originally published in 1925), 7–8. "Ein neuer Wille wird spürbar, die Bauten unserer Umwelt aus innerem Gesetz zu gestalten ohne Lügen und Verspieltheiten ihren Sinn und Zweck aus ihnen selbst heraus durch die Spannung ihrer Baumassen zueinander funktionell zu verdeutlichen und alles Entbehrliche abzustossen, das ihre absolute Gestalt verschleiert."

84. Ibid., 7. "Im Gegenteil, der Wille zur Entwicklung eines **einheitlichen** Weltbildes, der unsere Zeit kennzeichnet, setzt die Sehnsucht voraus, die geistigen Werte aus ihrer individuellen Beschränkung zu befreien und sie zu **objektiver Geltung** emporzuheben."

85. On the early years of Le Corbusier, see H. Allen Brooks, *Le Corbusier's Formative Years: Charles-Edouard Jeanneret at La Chaux-de-Fonds* (Chicago: University of Chicago Press, 1996). For complete documentation of his work, see *The Le Corbusier Archive*, 32 vols. (New York: Garland, 1982–4).

86. On the Dom-ino system, see Eleanor Gregh, "The Dom-ino Idea," *Oppositions*, winter-spring 1979, 61–87.

87. See Mary McLeod, "'Architecture or Revolution': Taylorism, Technocracy, and Social Change," *Art Journal*, Summer 1983, 132–47.

88. Alfred H. Barr, Jr., *Cubism and Abstract Art* (Cambridge: Belknap Press, 1986), 164.

89. The name derives from the maternal side of his family, which was Lecorbesier. It was Ozenfant who suggested the variant spelling.

90. "Notes on Cubism," in *Art in Theory 1900–1990*, 223–5.

91. The twenty-eight issues of *L'Esprit Nouveau*, originally published in 1920–5, were reprinted by Da Capo Press (New York, 1968–9).

92. Amédée Ozenfant and Charles Édouard Jeanneret, "Purism," in *L'Esprit Nouveau*, no. 4, 1920; cited from Harrison and Wood, *Art in Theory 1900–1990*, 238.

93. Ibid., 239.

94. "L'Esprit Nouveau," *L'Esprit Nouveau: Revue internationale d'esthétique*, no. 1, preface and dedication.

95. See Stanislaus von Moos, "Standard and Elite: Le Corbusier, die Industrie und der Esprit nouveau," in *Die nützliche Künste: Gestaltende Technik und bildende Kunst seit der Industriellen Revolution*, ed. Tilmann Buddensieg and Henning Rogge (Berlin: Quadriga, 1981), 306–23; Beatriz Colomina, *Privacy and Publicity: Modern Architecture as Mass Media* (Cambridge: M.I.T. Press, 1996), 141–99.

96. Le Corbusier-Saugnier, *Vers une architecture* (Paris: Éditions G. Crès et Cie, 1923).

97. Reyner Banham, *Theory and Design in the First Machine Age* (New York: Praeger, 1978), 220–46.

98. Le Corbusier, *Towards a New Architecture*, trans. Frederick Etchells (London: The Architectural Press, 1927), 31. The wrong injection of "New" into the title has often been noted. A new translation by the Getty Research Institute is forthcoming.

99. Ibid., 156.

100. Ibid., 203, 198.

101. This is very much the point made by McLeod, "'Architecture or Revolution.'" McLeod has also noted that the reference to Taylorism in the chapter "Mass Production Houses" was deleted in the English translation of 1927.

102. Le Corbusier, *Towards a New Architecture*, 14.

103. Ibid.

104. Ibid., 100.

105. Ibid., 95.

106. This point was emphasized in Colomina, *Privacy and Publicity*, especially the chapter on "Publicity." On Giedion's "Preliminary Remark," see *Building in France, Building in Iron, Building in Ferro-Concrete*, trans. J. Duncan Berry (Santa Monica, Calif.: Getty Publications Program, 1995), 83.

107. See Stanislaus von Moos, *Le Corbusier: Elements of a Synthesis* (Cambridge: M.I.T. Press, 1988), 187–238; Robert Fishman, *Urban Utopias in the Twentieth Century* (Cambridge: M.I.T. Press, 1982).

108. Le Corbusier, *Towards a New Architecture*, 264.

109. Ibid., 265.

110. *Vers une architecture* first appeared in 1923 under the co-authorship of Le Corbusier–Saugnier, but Le Corbusier had the "Saugnier" (the penname of Ozenfant) deleted from the second edition.

111. Translated into English in 1929 as *The City of To-morrow and Its Planning* (reprint, Cambridge: M.I.T. Press, 1971).

112. Le Corbusier, *The Decorative Art of Today*, trans. James Dunnet (London: Architectural Press, 1987), 129.

113. Ibid., xxiii.

114. See Mary McLeod, "Urbanism and Utopia: Le Corbusier from Regional Syndicalism to Vichy" (Ph.D. diss. Princeton University, 1985), and idem, "'Architecture or Revolution,'" 141–3.

115. Le Corbusier, *Précisions sur un état present de l'architecture et de l'urbanisme* (Paris: Les Éditions G. Crès, 1930); translated by Edith Schreiber Aujame as *Precisions on the Present State of Architecture and City Planning* (Cambridge: M.I.T. Press, 1991).

116. The Moscow plan was later discussed in *La Ville Radieuse* (Boulogne: Editions de l'Architecture d'Aujourd'hui, 1935); translated as *The Radiant City* (London: Faber & Faber, 1957).

117. First published in Alfred Roth, *Zwei Wohnhäuser von Le Corbusier und Pierre Jeanneret* (Stuttgart, 1927; reprint, 1977).

118. Colomina, *Privacy and Publicity*, 289–91.

119. Le Corbusier, *Une maison – un palais: "A la recherche d'une unite architecturale"* (Paris: Les Éditions G. Crès, 1928).

120. For Giedion's life and work, see Sokratis Georgiadis, *Sigfried Giedion: An Intellectual Biography* (Edinburgh: Edinburgh University Press, 1994).

121. Colomina, *Privacy and Publicity*, 199.

122. The book was originally published by Klinkhardt & Biermann in Leipzig; translated by J. Duncan Berry as *Building in France, Building in Iron, Building in Ferro-Concrete* (Santa Monica, Calif.: Getty Publications Program, 1995).

123. Ibid., 85.

124. Ibid., 87.

125. Ibid., 189 n. 96. The Dreyfus Affair, which involved the false accusation of the Jewish soldier Alfred Dreyfus for espionage in the 1890s, gained international notoriety.

126. Ibid., 190. Giedion, in alluding to the Palais Stoclet a few lines later, makes the more radical point that "today no building conceived in luxury and unlimited expense can any longer have any importance in the history of architecture."

127. On the significance of the rooms at the Salon d'Automne, on which Jeanneret devoted six pages of sketches in his notebooks, see Brooks, *Le Corbusier's Formative Years*, 351–2. See also *Une*

cité moderne: Desseins de Rob Mallet-Stevens, Architecte (Paris: Mille-Feuille, 1922); translated as *A Modern City: Designs by Rob Mallet-Stevens, Architect* (London: Benn Brothers, 1922). The portfolio of designs is clearly influenced by the *Wagnerschule* and the Viennese Secession.

128. Manfredo Tafuri and Francesco Dal Co, *Modern Architecture* (New York: Abrams, 1979), 174.

129. Giedion, *Building in France*, 197.

130. Henry-Russell Hitchcock, Jr., *Modern Architecture: Romanticism and Reintegration* (New York: Hacker Art Books, 1970), 171–2.

131. Ibid., 173.

132. André Lurçat, *Formes, Composition et lois d'Harmonie. Eléments d'une science de l'ésthétique architecturale*, 5 vols. (Paris, 1953–7).

133. On the life and work of Gray, see Peter Adam, *Eileen Gray, Architect/Designer: A Biography* (New York: Abrams, 2000), and Caroline Constant, *Eileen Gray* (London: Phaidon, 2000).

134. For a summary of these principles, see Carlo Carrà, "Our Antiquity," Harrison and Wood *Art in Theory 1900–1990*, 229–34.

135. On the Novecento movement, see Richard A. Etlin's *Modernism in Italian Architecture, 1890–1940* (Cambridge: M.I.T. Press, 1991), 165–95.

136. Ibid., 225–597.

137. The four manifestoes appeared in the journal *La Rassegna Italiana* in December 1926, February 1927, March 1927, and May 1927. They have been translated by Ellen R. Shapiro in *Oppositions*, no. 6 (1976): 86–102.

138. Cited from Etlin, *Modernism in Italian Architecture*, 236.

139. Ibid., 237. Etlin cites the Agnoldomenico Pica in noting this connection between rationalism and German *Sachlichkeit*.

140. On this building and others of Terragni, see Thomas L. Schumacher, *Surface and Symbol: Giuseppe Terragni and the Architecture of Italian Rationalism* (New York: Princeton Architectural Press, 1991).

141. Marcello Piacentini, *Architettura d'oggi* (Rome: Paolo Cremonese, 1930).

142. Alberto Sartoris, *Gli elementi dell'architettura funzionale* (Milan: Ulrico Hoepli, 1941; originally published in 1932).

143. See especially Diane Yvonne Ghirardo's essay "Italian Architects and Fascist Politics: An Evaluation of the Rationalist's Role in Regime Building," *Journal of the Society of Architectural Historians* 39 (May 1980): 109–27.

144. *Manifesto per l'architettura razionale*, 30 March 1831. Cited from Ghirardo, "Italian Architects and Fascist Politics," 126.

145. Peter Meyer, *Moderne schweizer Wohnhäuser* (Zurich: Verlag Dr. H. Girsberger & Cie, 1928).

146. Sigfried Giedion, *Befreites Wohnen* (Zurich: Orell Füssli Verlag, 1929), 5.

147. Ibid., 7. "Wir brauchen heute ein Haus, das sich in seiner ganzen Struktur im Gleichklang mit einem durch Sport, Gymnastik, sinngemässe Lebensweise befreiten Körpergefühl befindet: **leicht, lichtduchlassend, beweglich.**"

148. The journal not only has been reproduced in a beautiful facsimile edition by Lars Müller Publishers (Baden 1993) but has been critically supplemented with several excellent articles discussing the journal's history and intellectual context. On Stam, see Werner Oechslin, ed., *Mart Stam: Eine Reise in de Schweiz 1923–1925* (Zurich: GTA Verlag, 1991); on Schmidt, see Hans

Schmidt, "The Swiss Modern Movement," *Architectural Association Quarterly* 4 (April–June 1972): 33–41.

149. Lissitzky to Oud, 8 September 1924. Cited from Claude Lichtenstein, "ABC and Switzerland: Industrialism as a Social and Aesthetic Utopia," in *ABC: Beiträge zum Bauen 1924–1928* (reprint, Baden: Verlage Lars Müller, 1993), 17.

150. Second series, no. 2, 1926.

151. See the letter of Gropius to Tomàs Maldonado, cited in Dearstyne, *Inside the Bauhaus*, 208–9.

152. Hannes Meyer, "building," in *bauhaus* 2, no. 4 (1928). Cited from Wingler, *The Bauhaus*, 153–4.

153. Ibid., 165. "My Expulsion from the Bauhaus: An Open Letter to Lord Mayor Hesse of Dessau," originally published in *Das Tagebuch* (Berlin), 16 August 1930. Citation from Christian Borngräber, "Foreign Architects in the USSR: Bruno Taut and the Brigades of Ernst May, Hannes Meyer, Hans Schmidt," *Architectural Association Quarterly* 11, no. 1 (1979): 52.

154. See especially Eve Blau, *The Architecture of Red Vienna 1919–1934* (Cambridge: M.I.T. Press, 1999). See also Helmut Gruber, *Red Vienna: Experiment in Working-Class Culture, 1919–1934* (New York: Oxford University Press, 1983); Manfred Tafuri, "'Das Rote Wien,' Politica e forma della residenza nella Vienna socialista 1919–1933," in *Vienna Rossa* (Milan, 1980); and Peter Haiko and Mara Reissberger, "Die Wohnhausbauten der Gemeinde Wien, 1919–1934," *Archithese*, no. 12 (1974): 49–55.

155. See August Sarnitz, *Lois Welzenbacher: Architekt 1889–1945* (Vienna: Residenz Verlag, 1989).

156. On Plečnik, see François Burkhardt, Claude Eveno, and Boris Podrecca eds., *Jože Plečnik, Architect: 1872–1957*, trans. Carol Volk, (Cambridge: M.I.T. Press, 1989); Damjan Prelovšek, *Jože Plečnik 1872–1957: Architectura Perennis*, trans. Patricia Crampton and Eileen Martin (New Haven: Yale University Press, 1997); and Peter Krečič, *Plečnik: The Complete Works* (New York: Whitney Library of Design, 1993).

157. Ákos Moravánszky, *Competing Visions: Aesthetic Invention and Social Imagination in Central European Architecture, 1867–1918* (Cambridge: M.I.T. Press, 1998), 377–8.

158. On Moholy-Nagy, see Sibyl Moholy-Nagy, *Moholy-Nagy: Experiment in Totality* (Cambridge: M.I.T. Press, 1969); Krisztina Passuth, *Moholy-Nagy* (London: Thames & Hudson, 1985); Margolin, *The Struggle for Utopia*; and Joseph Harris Caton, "The Utopian Vision of Moholy-Nagy" (Ph.D. diss., Princeton University, 1980).

159. Raoul Haussmann, Hans Arp, Iwan Puni, and Moholy-Nagy, "Aufruf zu Elementaren Kunst," *De Stijl* 4, no. 10 (1921): 156. Cited from the translation in Margolin, *The Struggle for Utopia*, 53.

160. László Moholy-Nagy, *Von Material zu Architektur* (Munich: Albert Langen, 1929); reissued by Florian Kuperberg in the New Bauhausbücher series in 1968; revised English translation, *The New Vision* (New York: Warren & Putnam, 1930).

161. László Moholy-Nagy, *The New Vision and Abstract of an Artist* (New York: Wittenborn, 1946), 60.

162. Ibid., 63.

163. See Vladimir Slapeta, ed., *Jan Kotěra 1871–1923: The Founder of Modern Czech Architecture* (Prague: Kant, 2001).

164. See Rostislav Švácha, *The Architecture of New Prague, 1895–1945*, trans. Alexandra Büchler (Cambridge: M.I.T. Press, 1995);

Akos Moravánszky, *Competing Visions*; Alexander von Vegesack, ed., *Czech Cubism: Architecture, Furniture, and Decorative Arts, 1910–1925* (New York: Princeton Architectural Press, 1992); and Irena Žantovska Murray, "The Burden of Cubism: The French Imprint on Czech Architecture, 1910–1914," in Eve Blau and Nancy Troy, eds., *Architecture and Cubism* (Montreal: Canadian Centre for Architecture, 1997), 41–57.

165. See especially Eric Dluhosch and Rostislav Švácha, eds., *Karel Teige: L'Enfant Terrible of the Czech Modernist Avant-Garde* (Cambridge: M.I.T. Press, 1999).

166. This is also the view of Henry-Russell Hitchcock (see his *Modern Architecture*, p. 198).

167. Karel Teige, *Modern Architecture in Czechoslovakia and Other Writings*, introduction by Jean-Louis Cohen, translation by Irene Žantovska Murray and David Britt (Los Angeles: Getty Publications Program, 2000), 291.

168. Ibid.

169. Ibid., 292.

170. Ibid., 297–8.

171. See George Baird, "Karel Teige's 'Mundaneum,' 1929, and Le Corbusier's 'In Defense of Architecture,' 1933," together with a translation of the two articles in *Oppositions*, no. 4 (1974): 79–108.

172. Ibid., 80.

173. See Riita Nikula, ed., *Erik Bryggman 1891–1955* (Helsinki: Museum of Finnish Architecture, 1988). Among the many studies of Aalto, see David Paul Pierson, *Alvar Aalto and the International Style* (New York: Whitney Library of Design, 1978); Malcolm Quantrill, *Alvar Aalto: A Critical Study* (New York: New Amsterdam, 1983); Peter Reed, ed., *Alvar Aalto: Between Humanism and Materialism* (New York: Museum of Modern Art, 1998); Winfried Nerdinger, ed., *Alvar Aalto: Toward a Human Modernism* (Munich: Prestel, 1999); and Göran Schildt's (three-volumes biography of Aalto, Rizzoli, 1984–94).

174. On Asplund, see Eric De Maré, *Gunnar Asplund: A Great Modernist* (London: Art & Technics, 1955), and Stuart Wrede, *The Architecture of Erik Gunnar Asplund* (Cambridge: M.I.T. Press, 1980).

175. On the work and ideas of Markelius and Åhrén, see Eva Rudberg, *Sven Markelius: Architect* (Stockholm: Arkitektur Förlag, 1989), and idem, *Uno Åhrén: En Föregångsman inom 1900-talets Arkitektur och Samhällsplanering* (Stockholm: Byggforskningsrådet, 1981).

176. Erik Gunnar Asplund et al., *accepterá* (Stockholm: Bokförlagsaktiebolaget Tiden, 1931).

177. Arne Sørensen, *Funktionalisme og samfund* (Copenhagen: Forlaget Fremad, 1933).

178. See Tobias Faber, ed., *Kay Fisker* (Copenhagen: Architektens Forlag, 1995), and Hans Erling Langkilde, *Arkitekten Kay Fisker* (Copenhagen: Architektens Forlag, 1960). See also the special issue of *Archithese* on Kay Fisker (vol. 15, July–August 1985).

179. See Carsten Thau and Kjeld Vindum, *Arne Jacobsen* (Copenhagen: Architektens Forlag, 2001).

180. On Mendelsohn's life and work, see Arnold Whittick, *Eric Mendelsohn* (New York: F. W. Dodge Corporation, 1940); Kathleen James, *Erich Mendelsohn and the Architecture of German Modernism* (New York: Cambridge University Press, 1997);

and Regina Stephan, *Erich Mendelsohn: Architect, 1887–1953* (New York: Monacelli Press, 1999).

181. Erich Mendelsohn, "The International Consensus on the New Architectural Concept, or Dynamics and Function" (1923), in *Erich Mendelsohn: Complete Works of the Architect*, trans. Antje Frisch (1930; reprint, New York: Princeton Architectural Press, 1992), 34.

182. Erich Mendelsohn, preface to *Russland-Europa-Amerika: Ein architektonischer Querschnitt* (1929; reprint, Basel: Birkhäuser Verlag, 1989).

183. Ibid., 160.

184. Ibid., preface.

185. Ibid., 120, 122.

186. Ibid., 138, 140.

187. Ibid., 170.

188. Ibid., 182.

189. Ibid., 188.

190. Ibid., 186.

191. On May, see D. W. Dreysse, *May-Siedlungen: Architekturführer der acht Siedlungen des neuen Frankfurt 1926–1930* (Frankfurt: Fricke, 1987), and especially Nicholas Bullock, "Housing in Frankfurt 1925–1931 and the New Wohnkultur," *Architectural Review* 163 (June 1978): 335–42. See also Barbara Miller Lane, "Architects in Power: Politics and Ideology in the Work of Ernst May and Albert Speer," in Robert I. Rotberg and Theodore K. Raab, eds., *Art and History: Images and their Meaning* (Cambridge: Cambridge University Press, 1988), 283–310.

192. On May's years in Silesia, see Susan R. Henderson, "Ernst May and the Campaign to Resettle the Countryside: Rural Housing in Silesia, 1919–1925, *Journal of the Society of Architectural Historians* 61 (June 2002): 188–211. On Schütte-Lihotsky, see Susan R. Henderson, "A Revolution in the Woman's Sphere: Grett Lihotsky and the Frankfurt Kitchen," in Debra Coleman, ed., *Architecture and Feminism* (New York: Princeton Architectural Press, 1996), 221–48.

193. Mary Pattison, *Principles of Domestic Engineering; or The What, Why and How of a Home; An Attempt to Evolve a Solution of the Domestic "Labor and Capital" Problem – to Standardize and Professionalize Housework – to Re-organize the Home upon "Scientific Management" Principles – and to Point Out the Importance of the Public and Personal Element therein, as well as the Practical* (New York: Trow Press, 1915); Christine Frederick, *Household Engineering: Scientific Management in the House* (Chicago: American School of Home Economics, 1919). On Frederick's influence in Germany, see Mary Nolan, *Visions of Modernity: American Business and the Modernization of Germany* (New York: Oxford University Press, 1994).

194. Borngräber, "Foreign Architects in the USSR, 50–62.

195. On the details of the construction at Törten, see Nerdinger, *Walter Gropius*, 18–20, 82–6.

196. On the work of Taut, see Winfried Nerdinger, *Bruno Taut, 1880–1938: Architekt zwischen Tradition und Avantgarde* (Stuttgart: Deutsche Verlags-Anstalt, 2001); Olaf Gisbertz, *Bruno Taut and Johannes Göderitz in Magdeburg: Architektur und Stätebau in Weimarer Republik* (Berlin: Mann, 2000); Bettina Zöller-Stock, *Bruno Taut: Die Innenraumentwürfe des Berliner Architekten* (Stuttgart: Deutsche Verlags-Anstalt, 1993); and Kurt Junghanns, *Bruno Taut, 1880–1938* (Berlin: Elefanten Press,

1983). On Martin Wagner, see the exhibition catalogue *Martin Wagner, 1885–1957: Wohnungsbau und Weltstadtplanung: Die Rationalisierung des Glücks* (Berlin: Akademie der Künste, 1985).

197. Bruno Taut, *Die neue Wohnung: Die Frau als Schöpferin* (Leipzig: Klinkhardt & Biermann, 1924).

198. Reprinted by Julius Poesener as *Das neue Berlin: Grossstadtprobleme* (Basel: Birkhäuser, 1988).

199. Initiated by Philip C. Johnson's exhibition catalogue – *Mies van der Rohe* (New York: Museum of Modern Art, 1947) – the literature on Mies has grown too voluminous to catalogue here. Two recent and somewhat complementary monographs are Franz Schulze, *Mies van der Rohe: A Critical Biography* (Chicago: University of Chicago Press, 1985), and Neumeyer, *The Artless Word*.

200. Schulze, *Mies van der Rohe*, 196.

201. Schulze also suggests this connection (ibid., 101–3).

202. On Häring's theory, see *Hugo Häring: Schriften, Entwürfe, Bauten*, ed. Heinrich Lauterbach and Jürgen Joedicke (Stuttgart: Karl Krämer Verlag, 1965), and Peter Blundell Jones, *Hugo Häring: The Organic versus the Geometric* (Stuttgart: Edition Axel Menges, 1999).

203. Hugo Häring, "Wege zur form," in *Hugo Häring: Schriften, Entwürfe, Bauten*, 14. "Wir wollen die dinge aufsuchen und sie ihre eigene gestalt entfalten lassen. Es widerspricht uns, ihnen eine form zu geben, sie von aussen her zu bestimmen, irgendwelche abgeleiteten gesetzhaftigkeiten auf sie zu übertragen, ihnen gewalt anzutun. Wir handelten falsch, als wir sie zum schauplatz historischer demonstrationen machten, wir handelten aber ebenslo falsch, als wir sie zum gegenstand unserer individuellen launen machten. Un gleicherwiese falsch handeln wir, wenn wir die dinge auf geometrische oder kristallische grundfiguren zurückführen, weil wir ihnen damit wiederum gewalt antun (corbusier)." (lower-cap nouns by Häring)

204. Cited from Jones, *Hugo Häring*, 38.

205. "Office Building", *G*, no. 1 (July 1923): 3, and "Building," *G*, no. 2 (September 1923): 1. Cited from Neumeyer, The *Artless Word*, 241–2.

206. "Office Building," 3; "Building Art and the Will of the Epoch!" *Der Querschnitt* 4, no. 1 (1924): 31. Cited from Neumeyer, *The Artless Word*, 241, 245.

207. "Building Art and the Will of the Epoch!" 31. Cited from Neumeyer, *The Artless Word*, 245.

208. Schulze, *Mies van der Rohe*, 118.

209. "Mies Papers," Library of Congress. Cited from Pommer and Otto, *Weissenhof 1927*, 14.

210. Schulze, *Mies van der Rohe*, 124–6.

211. A comprehensive and insightful account of the exhibition is given in Pommer and Otto, *Weissenhof 1927*.

212. Ibid., 132–8.

213. Walter Curt Behrendt, *The Victory of the New Building Style* (Los Angeles: Getty Publications Program, 2000), 89.

214. Ibid., 107, 110–14, 142.

215. Ludwig Hilberseimer, ed., *Internationale neue Baukunst* (Stuttgart: Julius Hoffmann, 1927). On Hilberseimer, see Richard Pommer, David Spaeth, and Kevin Harrington, *In the Shadow of Mies: Ludwig Hilberseimer, Architect, Educator, and Urban Planner* (Chicago: Art Institute of Chicago, 1988); and K. Michael

Hays, *Modernism and the Posthumanist Subject: The Architecture of Hannes Meyer and Ludwig Hilberseimer* (Cambridge: M.I.T. Press, 1992).

216. Ibid., 5.

217. Ludwig Hilberseimer, *Grossstadtarchitektur* (Stuttgart: Julius Hoffmann, 1927; reprint, 1978). On Hilberseimer's ideas on city planning, see Richard Pommer, "More a Necropolis Than a Metropolis: Ludwig Hilberseimer's Highrise City and Modern City Planning," in Pommer, Spaeth, and Harrington *In the Shadow of Mies*, 16–53.

218. Julius Vischer and Ludwig Hilberseimer, *Beton als Gestalter* (Stuttgart: Julius Hoffmann, 1928).

219. Gustav Platz, *Die Baukunst der neuesten Zeit* (Berlin: Im Propyläen-Verlag, 1927).

220. Henry-Russell Hitchcock, *Modern Architecture* (London: Payson & Clarke, 1929; reprint, New York: Hacker Art Books, 1970); Walter Müller-Wulckow, *Deutsche Baukunst der Gegenwart* (Leipzig: Langewiesche Verlag, 1929); Arthur Korn, *Glas im Bau und als Gebrauchsgegenstand* (Berlin: Ernst Pollak, 1929; reprint, Kraus, 1981); Bruno Taut, *Modern Architecture* (London: The Studio Limited, 1929).

221. Roger Ginsburger, *Frankreich: Die Entwicklung der neuen Ideen nach Konstruktion und Form* (Vienna: Anton Schroll, 1930); Richard Neutra, *Amerika: Die Stilbildung des neuen Bauens in den Vereinigten Staaten* (Vienna: Anton Schroll, 1930); El Lissitzky, *Russland: Architektur für eine Weltrevolution* (Vienna: Anton Schroll, 1930).

222. Noted in a letter from Giedion to Oud, 17 November 1927, in Pommer and Otto, *Weissenhof 1927*, 273 n. 1.

223. Giedion to Oud, 30 July 1927, in Pommer and Otto, *Weissenhof 1927*, 272–3 n. 1.

224. The essential history of this movement is by Eric Mumford, *The CIAM Discourse on Urbanism, 1928–1960* (Cambridge: M.I.T. Press, 2000).

225. Giedion to Cornelis van Eesteren, 10 July 1928, in Mumford, *The CIAM Discourse on Urbanism*, 10.

226. Ibid., 19.

227. Cited from *The Athens Charter*, trans. Anthony Eardley (New York: Grossman Publishers, 1973), 6.

228. Ibid., 7–8.

229. CIAM, *Die Wohnung für das Existenzminimum* (Frankfurt: Englert & Schlosser, 1930).

230. Walter Gropius, "Sociological Premises for the Minimum Dwelling of Urban Industrial Population," in *Scope of Total Architecture* (New York: Collier Books, 1974), 91–102.

231. Ibid., 100.

232. See Mumford, *The CIAM Discourse on Urbanism*, 39.

233. Gropius's origional title was "Flach-, Mittel- oder Hochbau?" Together with parts of another article, it was translated as "Houses, Walk-ups, or High-rise Apartment Blocks?" in *Scope of Total Architecture*, 103–15.

234. Ibid., 109.

235. Le Corbusier, *La Charte d'Athènes* (Paris: Plon, 1943); translated by Anthony Eardley as *The Athens Charter* (see note 227).

236. *The Athens Charter*, Proposition 20, p. 60.

237. Ibid., Proposition 29 (French Proposition 28–9), p. 65.

238. Ibid., Proposition 95, p. 105.

239. Ibid., Proposition 92, p. 104.

12. American Modernism 1917–1934

1. Henry-Russell Hitchcock, Jr., *Modern Architecture: Romanticism and Reintegration* (New York: Hacker Art Books, 1970; originally published in 1929), 201.

2. Ibid., 204.

3. The classic historical work on this era is Carl Condit, *The Chicago School of Architecture: A History of Commercial and Public Buildings in the Chicago Area 1875–1925* (Chicago: University of Chicago Press, 1964).

4. Friedrich Baumann wrote the first important study, *The Art of Preparing Foundations for all Kinds of Buildings, with particular Illustration of the "Method of Isolated Piers" as Followed in Chicago* (Chicago: Wing, 1892; originally published in 1873). On Adler's structural innovations, particularly with regard to the auditorium building, see Louis H. Sullivan, "Development and Construction" (1916), in *Louis Sullivan: The Public Papers*, ed. Robert Twombly (Chicago: University of Chicago Press, 1988), 211–22.

5. Montgomery Schuyler, "The Economics of Steel Frame Construction," *A Critique of the Works of Adler and Sullivan* (1895), cited from Lewis Mumford, ed., *Roots of Contemporary American Architecture* (New York: Dover, 1972; originally published in 1952), 236.

6. On the structure of the Tacoma and Marquette Buildings, see Robert Bruegmann, *The Architects and the City: Holabird & Roche of Chicago, 1880–1918* (Chicago: University of Chicago Press, 1997), 83–6, 124.

7. On Root's life and work, see Donald Hoffmann, *The Architecture of John Wellborn Root* (Chicago: University of Chicago Press, 1973). For his writings on architecture, see *The Meanings of Architecture: Buildings and Writings by John Wellborn Root*, ed. Donald Hoffmann (New York: Horizon Press, 1967).

8. Louis Sullivan, "The Tall Office Building Artistically Considered," in *Louis Sullivan: The Public Papers*, 105.

9. Ibid., 108.

10. Cited from Claude Bragdon, *Architecture and Democracy* (New York: Knopf, 1918), 17.

11. Ibid., 18–19.

12. The rise of the skyscraper in New York has been the subject of several historical studies over the years. A few of the most prominent are Col. William A. Starrett, *Skyscrapers and the Men Who Build Them* (New York: Scribner's, 1928); Ada Louise Huxtable, *The Tall Building Artistically Reconsidered: The Search for a Skyscraper Style* (New York: Pantheon Books, 1982); Paul Goldberger, *The Skyscraper* (New York: Knopf, 1982); Thomas A. P. van Leeuwen, *The Skyward Trend in Thought: The Metaphysics of the American Skyscraper* (Cambridge: M.I.T. Press, 1986); Carol Willis, *Form Follows Finance: Skyscrapers and Skylines in New York and Chicago* (New York: Princeton Architectural Press, 1995); and Sarah Bradford Landau and Carl Condit, *Rise of the New York Skyscraper 1865–1913* (New Haven: Yale University Press, 1996).

13. On the profound implications of this law, see Carol Willis's "Zoning and *Zeitgeist*: The Skyscraper City in the 1920s," *Journal of the Society of Architectural Historians* 40 (March 1986): 47–59.

14. John Taylor Boyd, Jr. "The New York Zoning Resolution and Its Influence upon Design," *Architectural Record* 48, no. 3 (September 1920): 193.

15. Early accounts of the effects of the new zoning law include Harvey Wiley Corbett, "High Buildings on Narrow Streets," *American Architect*, no. 119 (1921): 603–8, 617–19, and C. Matlock Price, "The Trend in Architectural Thought in America," *Century Magazine*, no. 102 (1921).

16. Irving K. Pond, "Zoning and the Architecture of High Buildings," *Architectural Forum* 35 (October 1921): 133.

17. One drawing is illustrated and described by Ferriss in his book *The Metropolis of Tomorrow* (New York: Ives Washburn, 1929; reprint, New York: Princeton Architectural Press, 1986), 41, 191.

18. On Ferriss and the importance of these sketches, see Carol Willis's portrait of him in "Drawing towards Metropolis," in Ferriss, *Metropolis of Tomorrow*, 148–84.

19. They appeared in the *New York Times Magazine* on 19 March 1922. The *Chicago Tribune* competition was announced in June.

20. Hugh Ferriss, "The New Architecture," *New York Times Magazine*, 19 March 1922, 8. Cited from Willis, "Drawing towards Metropolis," 155.

21. Cited from Willis, "Drawing towards Metropolis," 158.

22. Ibid., 160.

23. Ibid., 162. First published by Orrick Johns, "Architects Dream of a Pinnacle City," *New York Times Magazine*, 28 December 1924.

24. See Ferriss, *Metropolis of Tomorrow*, 87, 101.

25. Ibid., 71.

26. Frank Lloyd Wright, "In the Cause of Architecture VIII: Sheet Metal and a Modern Instance," in *The Architectural Record*, October 1928; reprinted in *Frank Lloyd Wright: Collected Writings, 1894–1930*, ed. Bruce Brooks Pfeiffer (New York: Rizzoli, 1992), 308.

27. Ibid., 309.

28. *An Autobiography: Frank Lloyd Wright* (New York: Horizon Press, 1977; originally published in 1932), 279.

29. On the history of the competition, see Katherine Solomonson, *The Chicago Tribune Tower Competition* (New York: Cambridge University Press, 2001).

30. The third-place winning scheme was that of Holabird and Roche.

31. See Sigfried Giedion, *Space, Time and Architecture: The Growth of a New Tradition* (Cambridge: Harvard University Press, 1949; originally published in 1941), 327, and idem, *Walter Gropius: Work and Teamwork* (London: The Architectural Press, 1954), 68. Giedion's argument is that Gropius's scheme is "much closer in spirit to the Chicago school than the Gothic tower which was executed."

32. On the careers of Griffin and his wife Marion Mahony, see Anne Watson, ed., *"Beyond Architecture": Marion Mahony and Walter Burley Griffin, America, Australia, India* (Sidney: Powerhouse Publishing, 1998).

33. Louis Sullivan, "The Chicago Tribune Competition," *The Architectural Record*, no. 153 (February 1923): 151–7; reprinted in *Louis Sullivan: The Public Papers*, 228–9.

34. On Hood, see Walter H. Kilham, *Raymond Hood, Architect: Form through Function in the American Skyscraper* (New York: Architectural Book Publishing Co., 1973), and Arthur Tappan North, *Raymond M. Hood* (New York: McGraw-Hill, 1931).

35. See Henry-Russell Hitchcock and Philip Johnson, *The International Style* (New York: W. W. Norton, 1966; originally published in 1932), 156–7.

36. On the early work of Kahn, see his monograph *Ely Jacques Kahn* (New York: McGraw, 1931).

37. Lewis Mumford, "American Architecture To-day: I. The Search for 'Something More,'" *Architecture* (1928): reprinted in Lewis Mumford, *Architecture as a Home for Man: Essays for Architectural Record*, ed. Jeanne M. Davern (New York: Architectural Record Books, 1975), 15.

38. Hitchcock, *Modern Architecture*, 103.

39. See Willis, "Drawing towards Metropolis," 160–2.

40. Ferriss, *Metropolis of Tomorrow*, 97, 99.

41. Cited from John Burchard and Albert Bush-Brown, *The Architecture of America: A Social and Cultural History* (Boston: Little, Brown, 1961), 351.

42. Francisco Mujica, *The History of the Skyscraper* (Paris: Archaeology and Architecture Press, 1929; reprint, New York: Da Capo Press, 1977).

43. For a biography of Chrysler and a chapter summarizing the history of this building, see Vincent Curcio, *Chrysler: The Life and Times of an Automotive Genius* (Oxford: Oxford University Press, 2000).

44. *An Autobiography; Frank Lloyd Wright*, 239.

45. For a interpretation of the symbolic complexity this design, see Neil Levine, *The Architecture of Frank Lloyd Wright* (Princeton: Princeton University Press, 1996), 124–47.

46. Hitchcock, *Modern Architecture*, 116.

47. *An Autobiography: Frank Lloyd Wright*, 265.

48. Wright may have learned of Semper's ideas when he first came to Chicago in 1887 and through his relationships with several German-speaking workers in his office over the years, such as Schindler and Neutra and his long-time engineer Paul Mueller. On the theme of Semper and the dressing, see Kenneth Frampton, "Frank Lloyd Wright and the Text-Tile Tectonic," *Studies in Tectonic Culture: The Poetics of Construction in Nineteenth and Twentieth Century Architecture* (Cambridge: M.I.T. Press, 1995), 93–120.

49. See Alice T. Friedman, "Frank Lloyd Wright and Feminism: Mamah Borthwick's Letters to Ellen Key," *Journal of the Society of Architectural Historians* 61 (June 2002): 140–51. On Key, see Barbara Miller Lane, *National Romanticism and Modern Architecture in Germany and the Scandinavian Countries* (New York: Cambridge University Press, 2000), 122–6.

50. On this project, see Levine's analysis in *The Architecture of Frank Lloyd Wright*, 191–215.

51. The articles appeared between May 1927 and December 1928. They are assembled in *Frank Lloyd Wright: Collected Writings*, vol. 1, 1894–1930, 225–316.

52. Wright, "In the Cause of Architecture: Purely Personal," in *Frank Lloyd Wright: Collected Writings*, vol. 1, 1894–1930, 256.

53. Wright, "Towards a New Architecture," *World Unity* (September 1928); reprinted in *Frank Lloyd Wright: Collected Writings*, vol. 1, 1894–1930, 317–18.

54. Wright, "Surface and Mass – Again!" *Architectural Record* (July 1929); reprinted in *Frank Lloyd Wright: Collected Writings*, vol. 1, 1894–1930, 327.

55. Ibid.

56. Wright, "Poor Little American Architecture," in *Frank Lloyd Wright: Collected Writings*, vol. 2, 1931–1932, ed. Bruce Brooks Pfeiffer (New York: Rizzoli, 1992), 16.

57. Ibid., 17.

58. The Kahn lectures were published by Princeton University in 1931 under the title *Modern Architecture*. They are reprinted in *Frank Lloyd Wright: Collected Writings*, vol. 2, 1931–1932, 58.

59. *An Autobiography. Frank Lloyd Wright*. The revised version of 1977 differs from the original version of 1932.

60. On the work of Schindler, see Ester McCoy, *Five California Architects* (Los Angeles: Hennessey & Ingalls, 1987). Several good articles are published in Lionel March and Judith Sheine, eds., *R. M. Schindler: Composition and Construction* (London: Academy Editions, 1993). For a German monograph on his work, see August Sarnitz, *R. M. Schindler: Architekt 1883–1957* (Vienna: Akademie der bildenden Künste, 1986). See also the many writings of David Gebhard concerning this architect, including *Schindler* (New York: Viking Press, 1971).

61. Rudolph M. Schindler, "Modern Architecture: A Program" (1913), in March and Sheine, *R. M. Schindler*, 10.

62. Ibid., 11.

63. Ibid.

64. Ibid., 12.

65. The articles appeared in the Sunday magazine section of the *Los Angeles Times* on 14 March, 21 March, 4 April, 11 April, 18 April, and 2 May 1926. Sarnitz provides German translations in his *R. M. Schindler*, 146–50.

66. Rudolph M. Schindler, "Space Architecture," in March and Sheine, *R. M. Schindler*, 55. (The essay first appeared in *Dune Forum* [Oceans, California], February 1934, 44–6).

67. Ibid.

68. Ibid.

69. Ibid., 56.

70. The most recent biography of Neutra is Thomas S. Hines, *Richard Neutra and the Search for Modern Architecture: A Biography and History* (New York: Oxford University Press, 1982). See also Ester McCoy, *Richard Neutra* (New York: Braziller, 1960), and Willy Boesiger, ed., *Richard Neutra: Buildings and Projects* (New York: Praeger, 1951–1966).

71. Richard Neutra, *Wie Bau Amerika?* (Stuttgart: Julius Hoffmann, 1927).

72. Hines, *Richard Neutra*, 76.

73. On Mumford's life and thought, see Donald L. Miller, *Lewis Mumford: A Life* (New York: Weidenfeld & Nicolson, 1989); Thomas P. Huges and Agatha C. Huges, eds., *Lewis Mumford: Public Intellectual* (New York: Oxford University Press, 1990); Robert Wojtowicz, *Lewis Mumford and American Modernism: Eutopian Theories for Architecture and Urban Planning* (New York: Cambridge University Press, 1996); and Lewis Mumford, *Sketches from Life: The Autobiography of Lewis Mumford: the Early Years* (New York: Dial Press, 1982).

74. See Steven Biel, *Independent Intellectuals in the United States, 1919–1945* (New York: New York University Press, 1992).

75. John Dewey, *Democracy and Education: An Introduction to the Philosophy of Education* (New York: The Free Press, 1966), 216.

76. Lewis Mumford, *The Story of Utopias* (New York: Boni & Liveright, 1922), 303.

77. Van Wyck Brooks, "On Creating a Usable Past," *Dial*, 11 April 1918, 337–41. Robert Wojtowicz is especially informative in pointing out the importance of Brooks (see *Lewis Mumford and American Modernism*, 54).

78. Mumford helped bring about this literary reevaluation with his *A Golden Day: A Study in American Experience and Culture* (1926) and *Herman Melville* (1929).

79. Bragdon, *Architecture and Democracy*, 52.

80. Ibid., 52–5.

81. Lewis Mumford, *Sticks and Stones: A Study of American Architecture and Civilization* (New York: Boni & Liveright, 1924; New York: Dover, 1955), 9–10.

82. Ibid., 60.

83. Ibid., 72.

84. Ibid., 111.

85. On the details of the debate between the RPAA and RPA, see John L. Thomas, "Lewis Mumford, Benton MacKaye, and the Regional Vision," in Huges and Huges, *Lewis Mumford*, 66–99. See also Robert Wojtowicz's chapter on it in *Lewis Mumford and American Modernism*, 113–60.

86. See Daniel Schaffer, *Garden Cities for American: The Radburn Experience* (Philadelphia: Temple University Press, 1982).

87. See M. David Samson's excellent essay "Unser Newyorker Mitarbeiter: Lewis Mumford, Walter Curt Behrendt, and the Modern Movement," *Journal of the Society of Architectural Historians* 55 (June 1996): 126–39.

88. L. Mumford, "Die Form in der amerikanische Zivilisation," *Die Form* 1 (November 1925); idem, "Amerikanische Baukunst," *Die Form* 1 (February 1925).

89. The German translation of *Sticks and Stones – Vom Blockhaus zum Wolkenkratzer* (From Log Cabin to Skyscraper) – appeared in 1926.

90. Mumford, "American Architecture To-day: I. The Search for 'Something More'"; reprinted in *Lewis Mumford: Architecture as a Home for Man*, 13.

91. Ibid., 15.

92. Ibid., 15–16.

93. Lewis Mumford, "American Architecture To-day: II. Domestic Architecture," *Architecture* (1928); reprinted in Mumford, *Architecture as a Home for Man*, 21.

94. Lewis Mumford, "Mass-Production and the Modern House," *The Architectural Record* (1930); reprinted in Mumford, *Architecture as a Home for Man*, 46–61.

95. Lewis Mumford, *The Brown Decades: A Study of the Arts in America 1865–1895* (New York: Harcourt, Brace, 1931), 114, 121.

96. Ibid., 137.

97. Ibid., 155.

98. Ibid., 168.

99. Of the many studies devoted to Fuller and his ideas, perhaps two recently published ones provide the best introduction: *Your Private Sky: R. Buckminster Fuller: Art Design Science*, ed. Joachim Krausse and Claude Lichtenstein (Zurich: Lars Müller Publishers, 1999), and *Your Private Sky: R. Buckminister Fuller: Discourse*, ed. Claude Lichtenstein and Joachim Krausse (Zurich: Lars Müller, 2001).

100. R. Buckminster Fuller, "Lightful Houses," in *Your Private Sky: R. Buckminster Fuller: Discourse*, 70.

101. Cited from Lloyd Steven Sieden, *Buckminster Fuller's Universe* (Cambridge, Mass.: Perseus, 2000), 138.

102. R. Buckminster Fuller, "The Dymaxion House," *Architecture* (June 1929); reprinted in *Your Private Sky: R. Buckminster Fuller: Art Design Science*, 135.

103. Ibid.

104. Fuller read Le Corbusier's *Towards a New Architecture* in 1927 or 1928. In a letter to his sister in 1928 he noted that he had been "stunned" by "the almost identical phraseology of his telegraphic style of notation with the notations of my own set down completely from my own intuitive searching and reasoning and unaware even to the existence of such a man as Corbusier." See the letter in *Your Private Sky: R. Buckminster Fuller: Discourse*, 80.

105. See "Dymaxion House, Meeting Architectural League, New York, Tuesday, July 9, 1929," in *Your Private Sky: R. Buckminster Fuller: Discourse*, 84–103.

106. For some details of this debate, see *Your Private Sky: R. Buckminster Fuller: Art Design Science* 158, and "R. Buckminster Fuller: Universal Architecture" (1932), in Ulrich Conrads, ed., *Programs and Manifestoes on Twentieth-Century Architecture* (Cambridge: M.I.T. Press, 1970), 128–36.

107. Alfred H. Barr, Henry-Russell Hitchcock, and Philip Johnson, *Modern Architecture: International Exhibition* (10 February–23 March 1932) (New York: Museum of Modern Art, 1932); Henry-Russell Hitchcock and Philip Johnson, *The International Style: Architecture since 1922* (New York: W. W. Norton, 1932; citations from 2nd ed., 1966). For its history, see Terence Riley, *The International Style: Exhibition 15 and the Museum of Modern Art* (New York: Rizzoli, 1992).

108. See Riley, *The International Style*, 19, 91–3. On Barr, see Sybil Gordon Kantor, *Alfred H. Barr, Jr. and the Intellectual Origins of the Museum of Modern Art* (Cambridge: M.I.T. Press, 2002).

109. On Philip Johnson, see his *Writings* (New York: Oxford University Press, 1979); Hilary Lewis and John O'Connor, eds., *Philip Johnson: The Architect in His Own Words* (New York: Rizzoli, 1994); and Franz Schulze, *Philip Johnson: Life and Work* (New York: Knopf, 1994).

110. Henry-Russell Hitchcock, "The Decline of Architecture," *The Hound and Horn* 1 (September 1927): 31.

111. On their relationship, see Wotjowicz, *Lewis Mumford and American Modernism*, 57–9.

112. Henry-Russell Hitchcock, "Four Harvard Architects," *The Hound and Horn* 2 (September 1928): 41–7.

113. See Hitchcock, *Modern Architecture*, 162, and Hitchcock and Johnson, *The International Style*, 11.

114. See Panayotis Tournikiotis, *The Historiography of Modern Architecture* (Cambridge: M.I.T. Press, 1999), 113–37.

115. Hitchcock, *Modern Architecture*, 50.

116. Ibid., 115.

117. In 1928 Hitchock prepared a monograph on Wright for the Paris journal *Cahiers d'Art*.

118. Hitchcock, *Modern Architecture*, 115.

119. Ibid., 115–16.

120. Ibid., 199.

121. Ibid.

122. Wotjowicz, *Lewis Mumford and American Modernism*, 58.

123. For Mumford's first European trip in 1932, Johnson supplied him with the addresses of Le Corbusier, Gropius, Breuer, Mies, and Oud, but Mumford did not contact them. See Wotjowicz, *Lewis Mumford and American Modernism*, 95–6.

124. Alfred H. Barr, Jr., "Modern Architecture," *The Hound and Horn* 3 (April–June 1930): 431.

125. Ibid., 434–5.

126. Riley, *The International Style*, 12. The date seems to have been 18 June 1930.

127. Ibid., Appendix 1, "Preliminary Proposal for an Architecture Exhibition at the Museum of Modern Art," 213–14.

128. Ibid.

129. For the various sources of this remark, see Levine, *The Architecture of Frank Lloyd Wright*, 217, 466–7 n. 1.

130. Wright, *Frank Lloyd Wright: Collected Writings, 1930–1932*, 51.

131. Cited from Wotjowicz, *Lewis Mumford and American Modernism*, 93.

132. Wright, "Of Thee I Sing," *Shelter*, April 1932; cited from *Frank Lloyd Wright: Collected Writings*, ed. Bruce Brooks Pfeiffer 3, 1931–1939 (New York: Rizzoli, 1993), 113–15.

133. Cited from Wotjowicz, *Lewis Mumford and American Modernism*, 93.

134. Ibid., 92.

135. Alfred H. Barr, foreword to *Modern Architecture: International Exhibition* (New York: Museum of Modern Art, 1932), 13.

136. Alfred H. Barr, "The Extent of Modern Architecture," in *Modern Architecture: International Exhibition*, 22.

137. Hitchcock and Johnson, *The International Style*, 19.

138. Ibid., 20.

139. Ibid., 27.

140. Ibid., 29.

141. Ibid., 33.

142. Ibid., 36.

143. Hitchcock, of course, made this point very explicit in his later book *Painting toward Architecture* (New York: Duell, Sloan & Pearce, 1948).

144. Hitchcock and Johnson, *The International Style*, 41.

145. Ibid., 81.

146. Ibid., 91.

147. Ibid., 93.

148. Ibid.

149. Ibid., 93–4.

150. An excellent consideration of the period in American architecture between Richardson and the Museum of Modern Art exhibition of 1932 is presented by Deborah Frances Pokinski, *The Development of the American Modern Style* (Ann Arbor, Mich.: UMI Research Press, 1984).

13. Depression, War, and Aftermath: 1934–1958

1. The estimates of those murdered or starved or worked to death in labor camps under Stalin vary considerably. For a recent historical evaluation of the Stalin years in the 1930s, see Robert Conquest, *The Great Terror: A Reassessment* (New York: Oxford University Press, 1990).

2. The classic work on German architecture of this period is Barbara Miller Lane's *Architecture and Politics in Germany 1918–1945* (Cambridge: Harvard University Press, 1968); see also Anna Teut, *Architektur im Dritten Reich* (Frankfurt, 1967).

3. Albert Speer, *Inside the Third Reich: Memoirs of Albert Speer*, trans. Richard Winston and Clara Winston (New York: Macmillan, 1970), 16–17.

4. See especially Richard Pommer and Christian F. Otto, *Weissenhof 1927 and the Modern Movement in Architecture* (Chicago: University of Chicago Press, 1991), 46.

5. Ibid., 51.

6. Reyner Banham, *Theory and Design in the First Machine Age* (New York: Praeger, 1967), 275.

7. Pommer and Otto, *Weissenhof 1927*, 143.

8. Ibid., 164–5; see also Lane, *Architects and Politics in Germany*, 140.

9. The manifesto is reprinted in Teut, *Architektur im Dritten Riech*, 29. It was originally published in *Baukunst*, 4 May 1928, p. 128.

10. Paul Schultze-Naumburg, *Häusliche Kunstpflege*, 4th ed. (Leipzig: Eugen Diederichs, 1902).

11. Paul Schultze-Naumburg, ABC *des Bauens* (Stuttgart, 1926).

12. Paul Schultze-Naumburg, *Kunst und Rasse* (Munich, 1928).

13. Speer, *Inside the Third Reich*, 76.

14. Pommer and Otto, *Weissenhof 1927*, 278 n. 51.

15. Lane, *Architecture and Politics in Germany*, 152.

16. Speer, *Inside the Third Reich*, 50.

17. On Hitler's many remarks on architecture, see N. H. Baynes, ed., *The Speeches of Adolf Hitler*, 2 vols. (London, 1942).

18. Speer, of course, made this same point with regard to Troost. See Speer, *Inside the Third Reich*, 50.

19. Ibid., 32. Speer was amazed that when Hitler objected to two watercolors by Emile Nolde and Eberhard Hanfstaengl in Goebbels's house, the minister immediately had them removed.

20. *Völkischer Beobachter*, "Eine Abrechnung mit dem System May, Gropius, Taut und Konsorten!" 12–13 July 1931. Cited from Lane, *Architecture and Politics in Germany*, 165.

21. Lane, *Architecture and Politics in Germany*, 181.

22. For a study devoted specifically to these important years for Mies, see Elaine S. Hochman, *Architects of Fortune: Mies van der Rohe and the Third Reich* (New York: Fromm International Publishing, 1990).

23. For the best images of this design and other designs of Mies from the 1930s, see Philip C. Johnson, *Mies van der Rohe* (New York: Museum of Modern Art, 1947).

24. Hochman notes this from a conversation with Speer in 1974. See Hochman, *Architects of Fortune*, 201. Speer wielded considerable power. He secured commissions for Bonatz, Bestelmeyer, and Peter Behrens and did much to protect his former teacher Tessenow.

25. The best overview of Italian architecture of this period is Richard A. Etlin, *Modernism in Italian Architecture, 1890–1940* (Cambridge: M.I.T. Press, 1991).

26. The basic monograph on Terragni's work in English is Thomas L. Schumacher, *Surface and Symbol: Giuseppe Terragni and the Architecture of Italian Rationalism* (New York: Princeton Architectural Press, 1991). On the relation of the Italian rationalists to Fascism, see Diane Yvonne Ghirardo, "Italian Architects and Fascist Politics: An Evaluation of the Rationalist's Role in Regime Building," *Journal of the Society of Architectural Historians* 39 (May 1980): 109–27.

27. Giuseppe Terragni, "The Construction of the Casa del Fascio in Como," trans. Debra Dolinski, in Schumacher, *Surface and Symbol*, 143, 147.

28. Ibid., 142.

29. See Manfredo Tafuri, "Giuseppe Terragni: Subject and 'Mask,'" *Oppositions*, Winter 1977, 11; Peter Eisenman, "Dall'Ogetto alla Relazionalità," *Casabella*, 344 (January 1970): 38–41.

30. See Diane Ghirardo, "Politics of a Masterpiece: The *Vicenda* of the Façade Decoration for the Casa del Fascio, Como," *Art Bulletin* 62 (1980).

31. For its history and interpretation, see Thomas L. Schumacher, *The Danteum* (New York: Princeton Architectural Press, 1990).

32. On the correspondence surrounding the Danteum, see Schumacher, *The Danteum*, 153–60. On the anti-Semitic legislation, see Etlin, *Modernism in Italian Architecture*, 568–97.

33. Etlin, *Modernism in Italian Architecture*, 580–2. Both Terragni and Sartoris participated in the persecution of the rationalist Pagano, whose family name was Pagano-Pogatschnig.

34. On Rogers's response to the events of these years, see Richard S. Bullene, "Architetto-Cittadino Ernesto Nathan Rogers" (Ph.D. diss., University of Pennsylvania, 1994).

35. Etlin, *Modernism in Italian Architecture*, 378.

36. Nikolaus Pevsner, *Pioneers of the Modern Movement: From William Morris to Walter Gropius* (London: Faber & Faber, 1936; various reprints, beginning in 1949, under the title *Pioneers of Modern Design*). On the historiography of the book, see David Watkin, *Morality and Architecture* (Chicago: University of Chicago Press, 1984), 71–111, and Panayotis Tournikiotis, *The Historiography of Modern Architecture* (Cambridge: M.I.T. Press, 1999), 21–9.

37. Pevsner, *Pioneers of the Modern Movement*, 205–6.

38. Ibid., 206.

39. Ibid., 207.

40. Nikolaus Pevsner, *An Enquiry into Industrial Art in England* (New York: Macmillan, 1937).

41. Shand's seven-part article "Scenario for a Human Drama" appeared in *Architectural Review* between July 1934 and March 1935.

42. Francis R. S. Yorke, "The Modern English House," *Architectural Review* 80 (December 1936): 237–42.

43. J. M. Richards, *An Introduction to Modern Architecture* (Harmondsworth, England: Penguin, 1940).

44. The most comprehensive study of this phase of his life is Mary McLeod, "Urbanism and Utopia: Le Corbusier from Regional Syndicalism to Vichy" (Ph.D. diss., Princeton University, 1985); see also Robert Fishman, "From the Radiant City to Vichy: Le Corbusier's Plans and Politics, 1928–1942," in *The Open Hand: Essays on Le Corbusier*, ed. Russell Walden (Cambridge: M.I.T. Press, 1977).

45. Le Corbusier, *La Ville Radieuse: Éléments d'une doctrine d'urbanisme pour l'équipement de la civilization machiniste* (Boulogne: Editions de l'Architecture d'Aujourd'hui, 1935); translated by Pamela Knight, Eleanor Levieux, and Derek Coltman as *The Radiant City: Elements of a Doctrine of Urbanism to Be Used as the Basis of Our Machine-Age Civilization* (London: Faber & Faber, 1967).

46. Le Corbusier, *Quand les Cathédrales étaient Blanches* (Paris: Plon, 1937); translated by Francis E. Hyslop, Jr., as *When the Cathedrals Were White* (New York: McGraw-Hill, 1947).

47. Le Corbusier, *When the Cathedrals Were White*, 114, 52.

48. Ibid., 213.

49. See Robert Wojtowicz, *Lewis Mumford and American Modernism: Eutopian Theories for Architecture and Urban Planning* (New York: Cambridge University Press, 1996), 131–3.

50. Henry Wright, "The Sad Story of American Housing," *Architecture* 67 (March 1933); reprinted in Lewis Mumford, ed., *Roots of Contemporary American Architecture* (New York: Dover, 1972; originally published in 1952), 335.

51. Henry Wright, *Rehousing Urban America* (New York: Columbia University Press, 1935), 33.

52. Catherine Bauer, *Modern Housing* (Boston: Houghton Mifflin, 1934).

53. Ibid., 92.

54. Ibid., 223.

55. Ibid., 141–9.

56. Ibid., 158.

57. Ibid., 188–9.

58. Bauer to Mumford, 29 July 1930, cited from Wojtowicz, *Lewis Mumford and American Modernism*, 88.

59. Lewis Mumford, *Technics and Civilization* (New York: Harcourt, Brace, 1934), 400–6. On the history and overall conception of the book, see Rosiland Williams, "Lewis Mumford as Historian of Technology in *Technics and Civilization*," in *Lewis Mumford: Public Intellectual*, ed. Thomas P. Huges and Agatha C. Huges (New York: Oxford University Press, 1990), 43–65.

60. Mumford, *Technics and Civilization*, opposite p. 146. On Mumford's selection of images, see Stanislaus von Moos, "The Visualized Machine Age, Or: Mumford and the European Avant-Garde," in Huges and Huges, *Lewis Mumford*, 181–232.

61. Lewis Mumford, *The Culture of Cities* (New York: Harcourt, Brace, 1938), 11.

62. Ibid., 275.

63. Ibid., 357.

64. Ibid., 372.

65. Ibid., 471–9.

66. Several excellent introductions to Broadacre City are available. See Anthony Alofsin, "Broadacre City: The Reception of a Modernist Vision, 1932–1988," *Center: A Journal for Architecture in America* 5 (1989), 8–40; George R. Collins, "Broadacre City: Wright's Utopia Reconsidered," in *Four Great Makers of Modern Architecture* (New York: Columbia University Press, 1961); John Sergeant's chapter on Boardacre City in *Frank Lloyd Wright's Usonian Houses* (New York: Whitney Library of Design, 1976); Lionel March, "An Architect in Search of Democracy: Broadacre City," in *Writings on Wright: Selected Comment on Frank Lloyd Wright*, ed. H. Allen Brooks (Cambridge: M.I.T. Press, 1981).

67. *Frank Lloyd Wright: Collected Writings, 1930–1932*, ed. Bruce Brooks Pfeiffer (New York: Rizzoli, 1992), 69.

68. Frank Lloyd Wright, *The Disappearing City* (New York: William Farquhar Payson, 1932); reprinted in *Frank Lloyd Wright: Collected Writings*, ed. Bruce Brooks Pfeiffer, vol. 3, 1931–1939 (New York: Rizzoli, 1993), 92.

69. See especially March, "An Architect in Search of Democracy: Broadacre City."

70. Henry George, *Progress and Poverty: An Inquiry into the Cause of Industrial Depressions and of Increase of Want with Increase of Wealth . . . The Remedy* (New York: Robert Schalkenbach Foundation, 1956; originally published in 1879), 3, 6.

71. Silvio Gesell, *The Natural Economic Order: A plan to secure an uninterrupted exchange of the products of labor, free from bureaucratic interference, usury and exploitation*, trans. Philip Pye (San Antonio: Free Economy Publishing, 1929), 13–14.

72. *An Autobiography: Frank Floyd Wright* (New York: Horizon Press, 1977), 602.

73. Lewis Mumford, The Skyline, *The New Yorker*, 27 April 1935, 63–5. Mumford recanted his earlier praise in 1962 in an *Architectural Record* article, "Megalopolis as Anti-City," in which he lamented that Wright's vision "proved to be what his countrymen, during the next thirty years, would turn into our dismal sub-suburban present, abetted as they have been by exuberant highway building and expansive motor car production." See Lewis Mumford, *Architecture as a Home for Man: Essays for Architectural Record*, ed. Jeanne M. Davern (New York: Architectural Record Books, 1975), 122.

74. Wright to Mumford, 27 April 1937, cited from Wojtowicz, *Lewis Mumford and American Modernism*, 135.

75. Catherine Bauer, "When Is a House Not a House?" *The Nation*, 26 January 1933, 99.

76. Ibid., 100.

77. Meyer Shapiro, "Architect's Utopia," *Partisan Review* 4 (March 1938): 42–7.

78. Stephan Alexander, "Frank Lloyd Wright's Utopia," *New Masses*, 18 June 1935, 28; cited from Alfonsin, "Broadacre City," 25.

79. Frank Lloyd Wright, "Freedom Based on Form," *New Masses*, 23 July 1935, 23–4; cited from Alfonsin, "Broadacre City," 25. See also Frank Lloyd Wright, with Baker Brownell, *Architecture and Modern Life* (New York: Harper & Bros., 1937).

80. Frank Lloyd Wright, "Jacobs House," *Architectural Forum* 68 (January 1938): 78–83; reprinted in *Frank Lloyd Wright, Collected Writings, 1931–1939*, 284–90. See also Sergeant's classic study *Frank Lloyd Wright's Usonian Houses*.

81. See Appendix F, "Broadacre City Petition, 1943," in Sergeant, *Frank Lloyd Wright's Usonian Houses*, 201.

82. See Arthur Clason Weatherhead, "The History of Collegiate Education in Architecture in the United States" (Ph.D. diss., Columbia University, 1941).

83. Ibid., 150.

84. See Gwendolyn Wright, "History for Architects," in *The History of History in American Schools of Architecture, 1865–1975*, ed. Gwendolyn Wright and Janet Parks (New York: The Temple Hoyne Buell Center for the Study of American Architecture, 1990), 23.

85. See Anthony Alofsin, "Tempering the Ecole: Nathan Ricker at the University of Illinois, Langford Warren at Harvard, and Their Followers," in *The History of History in American Schools of Architecture*, 76. See also Roula Geraniotis, "The University of Illinois and German Architectural Education," *Journal of Architectural Education*, no. 38 (Summer 1984): 15–21, and Wayne Michael Charney and John W. Stamper, "Nathan Clifford Ricker and the Beginning of Architectural Education in Illinois," *Illinois Historical Journal*, no. 79 (winter 1979): 257–66.

86. See Alfonsin, "Tempering the Ecole," 77–82.

87. Ellis F. Lawrence, "Experiment in Architectural Education," *The Spectator*, 10 April 1920, 3; cited from Michael Shellenbarger, "Ellis F. Lawrence (1879–1946): A Brief Biography," in *Harmony in Diversity: The Architecture and Teaching of Ellis F. Lawrence*, ed. Michael Shellenbarger (Eugene, Ore.: Museum of Art and the Historical Preservation Program, 1989), 17.

88. See Wright, "History for Architects," 26.

89. The journal articles include Joseph Hudnut, "The Education of the Architect," *Architectural Record* 69 (May 1931): 413; C. Matlack Price, "The Challenge to Architectural Education," *Architecture*, December 1934, 311; "Columbia Changes her Methods," *Architectural Forum*, February 1935, 166 ff.; "Education of the Architect," *Architectural Record*, September 1936, R. L. Duffus, "The Architect in a Modern World," *Architectural Record*, September 1936, 181–92; and Everett Victor Meeks, "Foreign Influences on Architectural Education in American," *The Octagon*, July 1937, 36–42. See also Arthur Clausen Weatherhead, *The History of Collegiate Education in Architecture in the United States* (New York, 1942).

90. "Education of the Architect," *Architecural Record*, September 1936, 201.

91. Weatherhead, *The History of Collegiate Education in Architecture in the United States*, 195.

92. Ibid., 196.

93. Ibid.

94. On the ideas of Hudnut and the appointment of Gropius, see Jill Pearlman, "Joseph Hudnut's Other Modernism at the 'Harvard Bauhaus,'" *Journal of the Society of Architectural Historians* 56 (December 1997): 452–77, and idem, "Joseph Hudnut and the Education of the Modern Architect" (Ph.D. diss., University of Chicago, 1993). See also Winfried Nerdinger, "From Bauhaus to Harvard: Walter Gropius and the Use of History," in *The History of History in American Schools of Architecture*, 89–98.

95. Pearlman, "Joseph Hudnut and the Education of the Modern Architect," 85–103.

96. Hudnut, "The Education of an Architect," 412.

97. Hudnut, beginning in 1935, served on the Museum of Modern Art's architecture committee, but his closeness to the circle of Hitchcock and Johnson, as Pearlman suggested, dates back at least to 1933.

98. Pearlman, "Joseph Hudnut and the Education of the Modern Architect," 129–31.

99. Pearlman, "Joseph Hudnut's Other Modernism at the 'Harvard Bauhaus,'" 459–60.

100. On Mies's insistence on being the only candidate considered, see Hockman, *Architects of Fortune and the Third Reich*, 271–5.

101. Joseph Hudnut, "Architecture Discovers the Present," *The American Scholar* 1 (1938): 106–14; idem, "Architecture in a Mechanized World," *The Octagon*, August 1938; idem, "Architecture Discovers the Present," *The American Scholar* 7 (winter 1939); idem, "Architecture and the Modern Mind," *Magazine of Art* 33 (May 1940); idem, "Education and Architecture," *Architectural Record*, October 1942, 36–8.

102. Joseph Hudnut, preface to Walter Gropius, *The New Architecture and the Bauhaus*, trans. P. Morton Shand (New York: Museum of Modern Art, 1936), 7–10.

103. Ibid., 62.

104. Ibid.

105. Herbert Bayer, Walter Gropius, and Ise Gropius, eds., *Bauhaus 1919–1928* (New York: Museum of Modern Art, 1938; reprint, for the Museum of Modern Art by Arno Press, 1972).

106. James B. Conant, "President's Report," *Official Register of Harvard University, 1938–1939*. Cited from Pearlman, "Joseph Hudnut's Other Modernism at the 'Harvard Bauhaus,'" 459.

107. Joseph Hudnut, "Architecture in a Mechanized World," *The Octagon* 10 (August 1938): 6.

108. Joseph Hudnut, *The Three Lamps of Modern Architecture* (Ann Arbor: University of Michigan Press, 1952).

109. The book is also one of the most analyzed texts in the history of architecture. On its premises, see Sokratis Georgiadis, *Sigfried Giedion: An Intellectual Biography*, trans. Colin Hall (Edinburgh: Edinburgh University Press, 1994), 97–151.

110. See the comments of H. Seymour Howard, Jr., "*Space, Time and Architecture* by Sigfried Giedion," *TASK*, no. 2 (1941): 37.

111. Sigfried Giedion, *Space, Time and Architecture: The Growth of a New Tradition* (Cambridge: Harvard University Press, 1941), 2–3, 6.

112. Ibid., 116.

113. Ibid., 98.

114. Ibid.

115. Ibid., 226

116. Ibid., 364.

117. See the extensive discussion of this idea and the reaction to it in Georgiadis, *Sigfried Giedion*, 118–29.

118. Giedion, *Space, Time and Architecture*, 397.

119. Ibid., 403, illus. 230.

120. Ibid., 406.

121. Ibid., 402.

122. Howard, "*Space, Time and Architecture* by Sigfried Giedion," 37–38.

123. For the history of Levittown and contemporary reactions, see Herbert J. Gans, *The Levittowners: Ways of Life and Politics in a New Suburban Community* (New York: Columbia University Press, 1982).

124. James Ford and Katherine Morrow Ford, *The Modern House in America* (New York: Architectural Book Publishing Co., 1940).

125. Katherine Morrow Ford, "Modern Is Regional," *House and Garden*, March 1941, 35–7.

126. Ibid., 79.

127. On these years, see in particular Sigfried Giedion, *Walter Gropius: Work and Teamwork* (New York: Reinhold, 1954), and Reginald R. Isaacs, *Walter Gropius: An Illustrated Biography of the Creator of the Bauhaus* (Boston: Bulfinch Press, 1991).

128. Giedion, *Walter Gropius*, 71. Giedion also wrote an article on "New Regionalism" published in the *Architectural Record* 115 (January 1954): 132–7.

129. On Wachsmann and his association with Gropius, see Gilbert Herbert, *Dream of the Factory-made House: Walter Gropius and Konrad Wachsmann* (Cambridge, M.I.T. Press, 1985).

130. Giedion, *Walter Gropius*, 76.

131. Walter Gropius, *Rebuilding Our Communities* (Chicago: Paul Theobald, 1945), 49–53.

132. Walter Gropius, *Architecture and Design in the Age of Science* (New York: Spiral Press, 1952).

133. Walter Gropius, *Scope of Total Architecture* (New York: Harper & Bros., 1955), 57.

134. For an analysis of his design methods at Harvard, see Klaus Herdeg, *The Decorated Diagram: Harvard Architecture and the Failure of the Bauhaus Legacy* (Cambridge: M.I.T. Press, 1983), 12–13.

135. See volume 4 of *The Walter Gropius Archive: An Illustrated Catalogue of Drawings, Prints, and Photographs in the Walter Gropius Archive at the Busch-Reisinger Museum, Harvard University*, ed. John C. Harkness (New York: Garland Publications, 1991).

136. See especially Franz Schulze, *Philip Johnson: Life and Work* (New York: Knopf, 1994), 135–46.

137. For details of this period at MoMA, see Sybil Gordon Kantor, *Alfred H. Barr, Jr. and the Intellectual Origins of the Museum of Modern Art* (Cambridge: M.I.T. Press, 2002), 354–65.

138. Appearing with the exhibition was Johnson's important book *Mies van der Rohe* (New York: Museum of Modern Art, 1947).

139. See David Whitney and Jeffrey Kipnis, eds., *Philip Johnson: The Glass House* (New York: Pantheon Books, 1993).

140. Ibid., 14. The article originally appeared in the *Architectural Review*, vol. 108, September 1950.

141. On the act of atonement, see Peter Eisenman's introduction to *Philip Johnson Writings* (Oxford: Oxford University Press, 1979); also see Whitney and Kipnis, *Philip Johnson: The Glass House*, 77–9.

142. On Bunshaft, see Carol Herselle Krinsky, *Gordon Bunshaft of Skidmore, Owings & Merrill* (New York: Architectural History Foundation, 1988).

143. For the history of the Cranbrook Academy, see Robert Judson Clark et al., *Design in America: The Cranbrook Vision 1925–1950* (New York: Abrams, 1984).

144. See his comments in Robert Judson Clark, "Cranbrook and the Search for Twentieth-Century Form," in *Design in America*, 30.

145. Eliel Saarinen, *The City: Its Growth, Its Decay, Its Future* (New York: Reinhold, 1943), 22–3.

146. Eliel Saarinen, SEARCH FOR FORM: *The Fundamental Approach to Art* (New York: Reinhold, 1948); reprint edition, *The Search for Form in Art and Architecture* (New York: Dover, 1985), 127.

147. On the life and work of Eero Saarinen, see Allan Temko, *Eero Saarinen* (New York: Braziller, 1962), and *Eero Saarinen on His Work: A Selection of Buildings Dating from 1947 to 1964 with Statements by the Architect*, ed. Aline B. Saarinen (New Haven: Yale University Press, 1962).

148. *Eero Saarinen on His Work*, 5.

149. The essential work on Mies's time in Chicago, with several important essays, is Phyllis Lambert, ed., *Mies in America* (Montréal: Canadian Centre for Architecture, 2001). For biographical material, see also Franz Schulze, *Mies van der Rohe: A Critical Biography* (Chicago: University of Chicago Press, 1985).

150. Kenneth Frampton, *Studies in Tectonic Culture: The Poetics of Construction in Nineteenth and Twentieth Century Architecture* (Cambridge: M.I.T. Press, 1995), 189–95.

151. Philip C. Johnson, *Mies van der Rohe* (New York: Museum of Modern Art, 1947), 140.

152. On the Farnsworth House, see Franz Schulze, *The Farnsworth House* (Plano, Ill.: Lohan Associates, 1997), and Werner Blaser, *Mies van der Rohe, Farnsworth House: Weekend House/Wochenendhaus* (Zurich: Birkhäuser, 1999).

153. Peter Blake, *The Master Builders* (New York: Knopf, 1960), 234.

154. Lewis Mumford, "The Life, the Teaching and the Architecture of Matthew Norwicki," *Architectural Record* 116 (September 1954): 128–35; cited from Lewis Mumford, *Architecture as a Home for Man: Essays for Architectural Record*, ed. Jeanne M. Davern (New York: Architectural Record Books, 1975), 87.

155. On the Seagram building, see Phyllis Lambert, "The Seagram Building, New York (1954–1958)," in Lambert, *Mies in America*, 391–406; Franz Schulze, ed., *The Mies van Rohe Archive: Convention Hall, Seagram Building* (New York: Garland Publications, 1993); and Erza Stoller, *The Seagram Building* (New York: Princeton Architectural Press, 1999). Mumford praised the building in his "Sky Line" article "The Lesson of the Master," *The New Yorker*, 13 September 1958, 126–9.

156. On the architectural selection process, see Phyllis Bronfman Lambert, "How a Building Gets Built," *Vassar Alumnae Magazine*, February 1959, 13–19. A few other details noted here were gained in a conversation with Phyllis Lambert, for which I express my gratitude.

157. On the details of the Chicago endeavor, see Sibyl Moholy-Nagy, *Experiment in Totality* (Cambridge: M.I.T. Press, 1969; originally published in 1950). See also Hans M. Wingler, *Bauhaus: Weimar, Dessau, Berlin, Chicago* (Cambridge: M.I.T. Press, 1978).

158. László Moholy-Nagy, *The New Vision: Fundamentals of Design, Painting, Sculpture, Architecture* (New York: W. W. Norton, 1938).

159. László Moholy-Nagy, *Vision in Motion* (Chicago: Paul Theobald, 1956; originally published in 1947), 64.

160. Gyorgy Kepes, *Language of Vision* (New York: Dover, 1995; originally published in 1944), 14.

161. See Robert Piper Boyce, "George Fred Keck, 1895–1980: Midwest Architect" (Ph.D. diss., University of Wisconsin, 1986); Robert Boyce, *Keck & Keck* (New York: Princeton Architectural Press, 1993).

162. See the pamphlet *House of Tomorrow: America's First Glass House* (Chicago: R. Graham, 1933).

163. See Jane King Hession, Rip Rapson, and Bruce N. Wright, *Ralph Rapson: Sixty Years of Modern Design* (Afton, Minn.: Afton Historical Society Press, 1999).

164. For details of this invention, see Joachim Krausse and Claude Lichtenstein, eds., *Your Private Sky: R. Buckminster Fuller: Art, Design, Science* (Zurich: Lars Müller, 1999), 276–349.

165. See Konrad Wachsmann, *The Turning Point in Building* (New York: Reinhold, 1961).

166. On Chermayeff, see Alan Powers, *Serge Chermayeff: Designer, Architect, Teacher* (London: RIBA Publications, 2001).

167. On Neutra's life and work in California, see Thomas S. Hines, *Richard Neutra and the Search for Modern Architecture: A Biography and History* (New York: Oxford University Press, 1982).

168. Richard Neutra, *The Architecture of Social Concern in Regions of Mild Climate* (São Paulo: Gerth Todtmann, 1948). The book was published in both Portuguese and English.

169. Richard Neutra, *Survival through Design* (London: Oxford University Press, 1954), 91. See also Sandy Isenstadt, "Richard Neutra and the Psychology of Architectural Consumption," in *Anxious Modernisms: Experimentation in Postwar Architectural Culture*, ed. Sarah Williams Goldhage and Réejean Legault (Montréal: Canadian Centre for Architecture, 2000), 97–117.

170. On the life and architectural work of Eames, see John Neuhart, Marilyn Neuhart, and Ray Eames, *Eames Design: The Work of*

the *Office of Charles and Ray Eames* (New York: Abrams, 1969); Ralph Caplan, John Neuhart, and Marilyn Neuhart, *Corrections: The Work of Charles and Ray Eames* (Los Angeles: Los Angeles Art Center, 1976); Donald Albecht, ed., *The Work of Charles and Ray Eames: A Legacy of Invention* (New York: Abrams, 1997); and Pat Kirkham, *Charles and Ray Eames: Designers of the Twentieth Century* (Cambridge: M.I.T. Press, 1998).

171. The results of the competition were announced in the August 1943 issue. Eero Saarinen and Oliver Lundquist won first place and a design by I. M. Pei and E. H. Duhart took second place.

172. See Ester McCoy, *Case Study Houses 1945–1962* (Santa Monica, Calif.: Hennessey & Ingalls, 1977; originally published in 1962 under the title *Modern California Houses*), and Ester McCoy, ed., *Blueprints for Modern Living: History and Legacy of the Case Study Houses* (Los Angeles: Museum of Contemporary Art, 1990).

173. "Announcement: The Case Study House Program," *Arts and Architecture*, January 1945, 39.

174. See especially James Steele, *Eames House: Charles and Ray Eames* (London: Phaidon, 1994).

175. On his work and influence, see Lisa Germany, *Harwell Hamilton Harris* (Berkeley: University of California Press, 2000).

176. Cited from the back cover of *Mona Lisa's Mustache: A Dissection of Modern Art* (1947).

177. T. H. Robsjohn-Gibbings, *Good Bye, Mr. Chippendale* (New York: Knopf, 1944), 40, 81.

178. T. H. Robsjohn-Gibbings, "Postwar DREAM WORLD or.... REALITY?" *House Beautiful*, August 1944, 48–50, 88–9.

179. T. H. Robsjohn-Gibbings, *Mona Lisa's Mustache: A Dissection of Modern Art* (New York: Knopf, 1947), 6.

180. Elizabeth Gordon, "The Threat to the Next America," *House Beautiful*, April 1953, 126–7.

181. Joseph Barry, "Report on the American Battle between Good and Bad Modern Houses," *House Beautiful*, May 1953, 173.

182. Cited from Thomas H. Creighton's open letter, *Progressive Architecture*, May 1953, 234.

183. Ibid.

184. "The Beauty of Common Sense" was the title of her introduction to Joseph Barry, *The House Beautiful Treasury of Contemporary American Homes* (New York: Hawthorn Books, 1958).

185. Ibid.

186. Lewis Mumford, Sky Line, "Status Quo," *The New Yorker*, 11 October 1947, 108–9.

187. Ibid., 110.

188. "What Is Happening to Modern Architecture?" *Museum of Modern Art Bulletin* 15 (Spring 1948).

189. Ibid., 6.

190. Ibid., 8.

191. Ibid., 16–17.

192. Ibid., 18.

193. Joseph Hudnut, "The Post-Modern House," in *Roots of Contemporary American Architecture*, ed. Lewis Mumford (New York: Dover, 1972), 306–15. The essay originally appeared in Hudnut's book *Architecture and the Spirit of Man* (Cambridge, Harvard University Press, 1949), 108–19.

194. Germany draws out their points of contact most effectively in *Harwell Hamilton Harris*, 100–5, 152–4.

195. Harwell Hamilton Harris, "Regionalism and Nationalism," joint address to the Northwest Regional Council and American Institute of Architects, Eugene, Oregon, 1954. Cited from *Harwell Hamilton Harris: A Collection of His Writings and Buildings*, student publication of the School of Design, North Carolina State University of North Carolina at Raleigh, vol. 14, no. 5 (1965): 28.

196. Ibid., 27.

197. On Wurster, see Marc Treib, ed., *An Everyday Modernism: The Houses of William Wurster* (San Francisco: San Francisco Museum of Modern Art, 1995), and R. Thomas Hille, *Inside the Large Small House: The Residential Design Legacy of William W. Wurster* (New York: Princeton Architectural Press, 1994).

198. See "Joseph Esherick: Theory and Practice," *Western Architect and Engineer*, no. 222 (December 1961): 20–37.

199. On Belluschi's career and work, see Meredith L. Clausen, *Pietro Belluschi: Modern American Architect* (Cambridge: M.I.T. Press, 1994).

200. On Lapidus, see Martina Düttmann and Friederike Schneider, eds., *Morris Lapidus: Architect of the American Dream* (Basel: Birkhäuser, 1992).

201. See the account in "Morris Lapidus, Alan Lapidus," in John W. Cook and Heinrich Klotz, *Conversations with Architects* (New York: Praeger, 1973), 154.

202. Morris Lapidus, *An Architecture of Joy* (Miami: E. A. Seemann, 1979).

203. On Texas architecture prior to World War II, see Jay C. Henry, *Architecture in Texas 1895–1945* (Austin: University of Texas, 1993).

204. See Alexander Caragonne, *The Texas Rangers: Notes from an Architectural Underground* (Cambridge: M.I.T. Press, 1995).

205. The best study of Norwicki's life and work consists of four articles by Lewis Mumford published in the *Architectural Record* between June and September 1954 under the title "The Life, the Teaching and the Architecture of Matthew Nowicki"; reprinted in Mumford, *Architecture as a Home for Man*, 67–101. See also Bruce Shafer, "The Writings and Sketches of Matthew Nowicki," *Design* 19, no. 2, 27–30.

206. See Schulze, *Philip Johnson*, 137–9.

207. Mumford, "The Life, the Teaching and the Architecture of Matthew Nowicki," in *Architecture as a Home for Man*, 78.

208. Matthew Nowicki, "Composition in Modern Architecture," *The Magazine of Art*, March 1949, 108–111; cited from the reprint in Mumford, *Roots of Contemporary American Architecture*, 408.

209. Matthew Norwicki, "Origins and Trends in Modern Architecture," *The Magazine of Art*, November 1951, 273–9; reprinted under the title "Function and Form," in Mumford, *Roots of Contemporary American Architecture*. Cited from Joan Ockman, ed., *Architecture Culture 1943–1968* (New York: Rizzoli, 1993), 150.

210. Ibid., 152–4.

211. Ibid., 154.

212. Ibid., 156.

213. Lewis Mumford, *Art and Technics* (New York: Columbia University Press, 1952), 114–15.

214. Ibid., 121.

215. Ibid., 133–4.

216. Lewis Mumford, *From the Ground Up: Observations on Contemporary Architecture, Housing, Highway Building, and Civic Design* (New York: Harcourt Brace Jovanovich, 1956), 109.

217. Ibid., 37, 43.

218. In addition to various articles published in architectural magazines, Gruen's ideas were presented in *Shopping Towns USA* (with Larry Smith) (New York: Reinhold, 1960); Victor Gruen, *The Heart of Our Cities* (New York: Simon & Schuster, 1964); and idem, *Centers for the Urban Environment: Survival of the Cities* (New York: Van Nostrand Reinhold, 1973).

219. On the details of the plan, see "Transformation of Typical Downtown (Ft. Worth)," *Architectural Forum* 104 (May 1956): 146–55.

220. On Kahn's designs and ideas, see Romaldo Giurgola and Mehta Jaimini, *Louis I. Kahn* (Boulder, Colo.: Westview Press, 1975); *Louis I. Kahn: Complete Works, 1935–1974*, ed. Heinz Ronner, Sharad Jhaveri, Alessandro Vasella (Boulder, Colo.: Westview Press, 1977); and Vincent Scully Jr., *Louis I. Kahn* (New York: George Braziller, 1962).

221. On Howe, see Helen Howe West, *George Howe, Architect, 1886–1955: Recollections of My Beloved Father* (Philadelphia: W. Nunn, 1973), and Robert A. M. Stern, *George Howe: Toward a Modern Architecture* (New Haven: Yale University Press, 1975).

222. See Oscar Stonorov and Louis I. Kahn, *Why City Planning Is Your Responsibility* (New York: Revere Copper & Brass, 1942).

223. Oscar Stonorov and Louis I. Kahn, *You and Your Neighborhood: A Primer for Neighborhood Planning* (New York: Revere Copper & Brass, 1944).

224. See José Luis Sert, Fernand Léger, and Sigfried Giedion, "Nine Points on Monumentality," in Ockman, *Architecture Culture 1943–1968*, 29–30.

225. Louis Kahn, "Monumentality," in Ockman, *Architecture Culture 1943–1968*, 48.

226. Louis Kahn, "Order and Form," *Perspecta* 3 (1955) 57.

227. On these years, see especially Robert Fishman, "Le Corbusier's Plans and Politics, 1928–1942," in Walden, *The Open Hand*, 244–83.

228. Le Corbusier, *Sur les 4 Routes* (Paris: Gallimard, 1941); translated by Dorothy Todd as *The Four Routes* (London: Dennis Dobson, 1947).

229. Le Corbusier, *Destin de Paris* (Paris: Fernand Sorlot, 1941).

230. François de Pierrefeu and Le Corbusier, *La Maison des hommes* (Paris: Plon, 1942); translated by Clive Entwistle and Gordon Holt as *The Home of Man* (London: Architectural Press, 1948).

231. Le Corbusier, *La Charte d'Athènes* (Paris: Plon, 1943); translated by Anthony Eardley as *The Athens Charter* (New York: Grossman Publishers, 1973).

232. Le Corbusier, *Le trois établissements humains* (Paris: Denoel, 1945).

233. See *Report of the Headquarters Commission to the Second Part of the First Session of the General Assembly of the United Nations* (Lake Success, N.Y.: United Nations, October 1946).

234. This was certainly the predominant view of the 1950s and 1960s. See, for instance, Peter Blake, *The Master Builders: Le Corbusier, Mies van der Rohe, Frank Lloyd Wright* (New York: Knopf, 1960), 125–32, and idem, *Le Corbusier: Architecture and Form* (Baltimore: Penguin, 1960), 126–32.

235. On the importance of painting for Le Corbusier, see Stanislaus von Moos, "Le Corbusier as Painter," *Oppositions*, nos. 19–20 (Winter–Spring 1980). See also his remarks in *Le Corbusier: Elements of a Synthesis* (Cambridge: M.I.T. Press, 1982), 281–91.

236. See Richard A. Moore's superb article "Alchemical and Mythical Themes in the Poem of the Right Angle, 1947–1965," *Oppositions*, nos. 19–20 (Winter–Spring 1980) 111–39.

237. James Sterling, "Ronchamp, Le Corbusier's Chapel and the Crisis of Rationalism," *Architectural Review* 119 (January 1955): 155–61. Sterling saw Ronchamp as a form of modern mannerism, drawing upon folk architecture for its revitalization. On the religious aspect of the design, see John Winter, "Le Corbusier and the Theological Program," in Walden, *The Open Hand*, 286–321.

238. On this sculptural work, see M. P. M. Sekler, "Le Corbusier, Ruskin, the Tree and The Open Hand," and Stanislaus von Moos, "The Politics of the Open Hand," both in Walden, *The Open Hand*, 42–95, 412–57.

239. Le Corbusier, *Le Modular: Essai sur une mesure harmonique à l'échelle humaine applicable universellement à l'architecture et à la méchanique* (Boulogne-sur-Seine: Editions de l'Architecture d'Aujourd'hui, 1950); *The Modular*, trans. Peter DeFrancia and Anna Bostock (London: Faber & Faber, 1954).

240. See Elisa Maillard, *Du nombre d'Or* (Paris, 1943); Matila Ghyka, *Esthétique des proportions dans la nature et dans les arts* (Paris, 1927); and idem, *Le Nombre d'Or* (Paris, 1931). For details on his project, see Tim Benton, "The Sacred and the Search for Myths," in *Le Corbusier: Architect of the Century* (London: Arts Council of Great Britain, 1987), 241.

241. On Brazilian modernism, see Henrique Mindlin, *Modern Architecture in Brazil* (New York: Reinhold, 1956). See also Henry-Russell Hitchcock, *Latin American Architecture since 1945* (New York: Museum of Modern Art, 1955), and Francisco Bullrich, *New Directions in Latin American Architecture* (New York: Braziller, 1969).

242. Giedion, in his international survey of modernism of 1951, *A Decade of New Architecture*, cites three buildings by Levi.

243. See Stamo Papdaki, *The Work of Oscar Niemeyer* (New York: Reinhold, 1950); idem, *Oscar Niemeyer: Works in Progress* (New York: Reinhold, 1956); and Rupert Spade, *Oscar Niemeyer* (New York: Simon & Schuster, 1969).

244. See Sibyl Moholy-Nagy, *Carlos Raul Villanueva* (London: Alec Tiranti, 1964).

245. See Max L. Cetto, *Modern Architecture in Mexico*, trans. D.Q. Stephenson (New York: Praeger, 1961), and Olive Bamford Smith, *Builders in the Sun: Five Mexican Architects* (New York: Architectural Book Publishing Co., 1967).

246. See Emilio Ambasz, *The Architecture of Luis Barragán* (New York: Museum of Modern Art, 1976).

247. On the advent of modern architecture in Japan, see David B. Stewart, *The Making of a Modern Japanese Architecture: 1868 to the Present* (Tokyo: Kodansha International, 1987).

248. See Antonin Raymond, *An Autobiography* (Rutland, Vt.: Tuttle, 1970).

249. On Tange's work, see *Kenzo Tange 1946–1969*, ed. Udo Kultermann (New York: Praeger, 1970), and Robin Boyd, *Kenzo Tange* (New York: Braziller, 1962). On Maekawa's work, see Jonathan Reynolds, *Kunio Maekawa and the Emergence of Japanese Modernist Architecture* (Berkeley: University of California Press, 2001).

250. On developments in Spain, see Gabriel Ruiz Cabero, *The Modern in Spain: Architecture after 1948* (Cambridge: M.I.T. Press, 2001).

251. On Zevi and his ideas, see Andrea Oppenheimer Dean, *Bruno Zevi on Modern Architecture* (New York: Rizzoli, 1983); on Zevi as a historian, see Panayotis Tournikiotis, *The Historiography of Modern Architecture* (Cambridge: M.I.T. Press, 1999), 51–83.

252. Bruno Zevi, *Verso un'architettura organica: Saggio sullo sviluppo del pensiero architettonico negli ultimi cinquant'anni* (Turin: Einaudi, 1945); translated as *Towards an Organic Architecture* (London: Faber & Faber, 1950).

253. Zevi, *Towards an Organic Architecture*, 47–8.

254. Ibid., 139.

255. Ibid., 76.

256. Bruno Zevi, *Sapere vedere l'architettura: Saggio sull'interpretazione spaziale dell'architettura* (Turin: Einaudi, 1948); translated by Milton Gendel as *Architecture as Space: How to Look at Architecture* (New York: Horizon Press, 1957).

257. Zevi, *Architecture as Space*, 32.

258. Ibid., 21, 17.

259. Ibid., 144.

260. Ibid., 188.

261. Bruno Zevi, *Storia dell'architettura moderna* (Turin: Einaudi, 1950). The book has not been translated into English, but its main arguments reappear in Bruno Zevi, *The Modern Language of Architecture*, trans. Ronald Strom and William A. Packer (Seattle: University of Washington Press, 1978).

262. Giulio Carlo Argan, *Walter Gropius e la Bauhaus* (Turin: Einaudi, 1951).

263. See Ernesto Nathan Rogers, "Continuità," *Casabella-Continuità*, no. 199 (December 1953): 2.

264. Ibid.

265. Ernesto Rogers, "Tradition and Modern Design," *Zodiac 1* (1957): 272.

266. Sigfried Giedion, *Mechanization Takes Command: A Contribution to Anonymous History* (New York: W. W. Norton, 1969; originally published in 1948), 4.

267. Ibid., 720–1.

268. Ibid., 722.

269. Sigfried Giedion, *A Decade of New Architecture* (Zurich: Editions Girsberger, 1951).

270. Sigfried Giedion, *Walter Gropius: Work and Teamwork* (London: Architectural Press, 1954).

271. Sigfried Giedion, *Architecture: You and Me: The Diary of a Development* (Cambridge: Harvard University Press, 1958). This anthology in content is similar to his *Architektur und Gemeinschaft: Tagbuch einer Entwicklung* (Hamburg, 1956).

272. Ibid., 150–1.

273. Ibid., 151.

274. Ibid., 193.

275. Sigfried Giedion, *The Eternal Present: A Contribution on Constancy and Change*, 2 vols. (New York: Bollingen Foundation, 1962–4), and idem, *The Eternal Present: The Beginnings of Architecture* (New York: Bollingen Foundation, 1964).

276. See Herbert Lindiger, ed., *Ulm Design: The Morality of Objects, Hochschule für Gestaltung, Ulm 1953–1968*, trans. David Britt (Cambridge: M.I.T. Press, 1991). See also Kenneth Frampton, "Apropos Ulm: Curriculum and Critical Theory," *Oppositions 3*, May 1974, 17–36.

277. For an account of the agonizing political history of the school, see René Spitz, *hfg ulm: The View Behind the Foreground: The Political Hisotry of the Ulm School of Design 1953–1968* (Stuttgart: Axel Menges, 2002).

278. I thank Louis Martin for first drawing my attention to this course. It is discussed in Chapter 13.

279. J. M. Richards, "The New Empiricism: Sweden's Latest Style," *Architectural Review* 101 (June 1947), 199–204.

280. Ibid., 199.

281. The editors of the *Architectural Review* were very much attracted to western American houses. In the December 1946 issue they juxtaposed three houses in California (by Dinwiddie & Hill, Neutra, and Harris) with three not unsimilar houses in Cophenhagen.

282. See "Bay Region Commercial" and "Bay Region Domestic" in *Architectural Design*, September 1948 (pp. 111–16) and October 1948 (pp. 164–70). Under "Regional Organic" Richards included Wright's Taliesin West, the "Bay Regional Style of Pacific America," the New England style of Marcel Breuer, as well as some Danish and British work. Under "Empirical Organic" he placed the Swedish work, along with Aalto's new dormitory at M.I.T. See "The Next Step?" *Architectural Review* 107 (March 1950): 175–6.

283. Sven Backström, "A Swede Looks at Sweden," *Architectural Review* 94 (September 1943): 80.

284. Ibid.

285. Ibid.

286. See especially Malcolm Quantril, *Alvar Aalto: A Critical Study* (New York: New Amsterdam, 1983), and Asko Salokorpi, *Modern Architecture in Finland* (London: Weidenfield & Nicholson 1970).

287. On Utzon's theoretical development, see Kenneth Frampton's insightful chapter "Jørn Utzon: Transcultural Form and the Tectonic Metaphor," in *Studies in Tectonic Culture: The Poetics of Construction in Nineteenth and Twentieth Century Architecture* (Cambridge: M.I.T. Press, 1995), 247–334.

288. Steen Eiler Rasmussen, *Experiencing Architecture* (Cambridge: M.I.T. Press, 1959).

289. Steen Eiler Rasmussen, *Towns and Buildings* (Liverpool: University Press of Liverpool, 1951).

290. See especially Lionel Esher, *A Broken Wave: The Rebuilding of England 1940–1980* (London: Allen Lane, 1981).

291. On the politics of the LCC and the acclaim of Le Corbusier, see Reyner Banham, *The New Brutalism: Ethic or Aesthetic?* (London: Architectural Press, 1966), 11–16.

292. Colin Rowe, "The Mathematics of the Ideal Villa: Palladio and Le Corbusier Compared," *Architectural Review* 101 (March 1947): 101–4.

293. Colin Rowe, "Mannerism and Modern Architecture," *Architectural Review* 107 (May 1950): 289–99.

294. Rudolf Wittkower, *Architectural Principles in the Age of Humanism* (London: Warburg Institute, 1949; reprint, Academy Editions 1973). An article on Le Corbusier's modular by Matila Ghyka also appeared in the pages of the *Architectural Review*.

295. For a discussion of the "New Empiricism" movement within the context of the British CIAM debates, see Eric Mumford, *The CIAM Discourse on Urbanism, 1928–1960* (Cambridge: M.I.T. Press, 2000), 163–8, and Kenneth Frampton, *Modern Architecture: A Critical History* (New York: Oxford University Press,

1980), 262–8. Banham recounts both new empiricism and neo-picturesque situations in *The New Brutalism*, 12–13.

296. For an analysis of these two books, see David Watkin, *Morality and Architecture* (Chicago: University of Chicago Press, 1984), 51–53, 80–97. The title of Pevsner's book was changed to *Pioneers of Modern Design* in 1949.

297. James Macquedy (J. M. Richards), "Criticism," *Architectural Review* 87 (May 1940): 183–4.

298. The lecture, "Architectural Expression," was published in *Architects' Journal*, 25 September 1947, 277–81. A summary of the questionnaire, from which this citation is taken, appears in Sigfried Giedion, *A Decade of New Architecture*, 30–4.

299. J. M. Richards, *The Castles on the Ground* (London: Architectural Press, 1947).

300. Banham, *The New Brutalism*, 13.

301. Ibid., 11.

302. Nikolaus Pevsner, *The Englishness of English Art* (Hammondsworth, England: Penguin, 1964), 188.

303. José Ortega y Gasset, *The Revolt of the Masses* (New York: W. W. Norton, 1930).

304. Clement Greenberg, "Avant-Garde and Kitsch," in *Art and Culture: Critical Essays* (Boston: Beacon Press, 1961), 3–21.

305. Banham, *The New Brutalism*, 10.

306. The Smithsons, as yet, lack a comprehensive biography. See John Maule McKean, "The Smithsons: A Profile," *Building Design*, no. 345 (1977): 22–4. On the IG and ICA, see Nigel Whiteley's excellent study *Reyner Banham: Historian of the Immediate Future* (Cambridge: M.I.T. Press, 2002), 83–139. See also Anne Massey, *The Independent Group: Modernism and Mass Culture in Britain, 1945–1959* (Manchester: Manchester University Press, 1995).

307. See Whiteley, *Reyner Banham*, 85–6, and Mumford, *The CIAM Discourse on Urbanism*, 232–6. Much of the design work presented at CIAM was published in *Urban Structuring: Studies of Alison and Peter Smithson* (London: Studio Vista, 1967).

308. See Whiteley, *Reyner Banham*, 115–17.

309. Alison Smithson and Peter Smithson, "House in Soho, London," *Architectural Design*, December 1953, 342.

310. Alison Smithson and Peter Smithson, "Thoughts in Progress: The New Brutalism," *Architectural Design*, April 1957, 113.

311. Ibid., 111. Comment of the panel.

312. Reyner Banham, "The New Brutalism," *Architectural Review* 118 (December 1955): 361.

313. James Sterling, "Garches to Jaoul: Le Corbusier as Domestic Architect in 1927 and 1953," *Architectural Review* 118 (September 1955): 145–9.

314. See Louis Martin, "The Search for a Theory in Architecture: Anglo-American Debates, 1957–1976" (Ph.D. diss., Princeton University, 2002), 414. See Whiteley, *Reyner Banham*, 90–122, and Banham's essay "Machine Aesthetic," *Architectural Review* 117 (April 1955): 225–8.

14. Challenges to Modernism in Europe 1959–1967

1. See Mumford's letter in Eric Mumford, *The CIAM Discourse on Urbanism, 1928–1960* (Cambridge: M.I.T. Press, 2000), 133–134. See also José Luis Sert, *Can Our Cities Survive? An ABC of Urban Problems, Their Analyses, Their Solutions, Based on the Proposals Formulated by the C.I.A.M.* (Cambridge: Harvard University Press, 1942; reprint, Kraus, 1979).

2. Sigfried Giedion, "Post-War Activity of CIAM," in *A Decade of New Architecture* (Zurich: Editions Girsberger, 1951), 17.

3. Ibid., 25.

4. Ibid., 37.

5. Sigfried Giedion, "Architects and Politics: An East-West Discussion," in *Architecture You and Me: The Diary of a Development* (Cambridge: Harvard University Press, 1958), 87.

6. Ibid., 88.

7. Bruno Zevi, "A Message to the International Congress of Modern Architecture," in Andrea Oppenheimer Dean, *Bruno Zevi on Modern Architecture* (New York: Rizzoli, 1983), 127.

8. Ibid., 132.

9. See Monique Eleb, "An Alternative to Functionalist Universalism: Écochard, Candilis, and ATBAT-Afrique," in *Anxious Modernisms: Experimentation in Postwar Architectural Culture*, ed. Sarah Williams Goldhage and Réejean Legault (Montréal: Canadian Centre for Architecture, 2000), 55–73.

10. See the text accompanying the presentation in Mumford, *The CIAM Discourse on Urbanism*, 234–5.

11. See Francis Strauven, *Aldo van Eyck: The Shape of Relativity* (Amsterdam: Architectura & Natura, 1998), 256.

12. See Jacob Bakema et al., "Doorn Manifesto – CIAM Meeting 29-30-31 January 1954, Doorn," in *Architecture Culture 1943–1968*, ed. Joan Ockman (New York: Rizzoli, 1993), 183. The original version and drafts are published in Alison Smithson ed., *The Emergence of Team 10 out of C.I.A.M.* (London: Architectural Association, 1982), 17–34.

13. See Mumford, *The CIAM Discourse on Urbanism*, 248.

14. For details on this conference, see Oscan Newman, ed., *CIAM '59 in Otterlo* (Stuttgart: Karl Krämer Verlag, 1961).

15. Louis Kahn, "Talk at the Conclusion of the Otterlo Conference," in Newman, *CIAM '59 in Otterlo*, 205–16.

16. Newman, *CIAM '59 in Otterlo*, 26–7.

17. Ibid., 48–53.

18. Ibid., 86. De Carlo's lecture was entitled "Talk on the Situation of Contemporary Architecture."

19. Ibid., 90.

20. Ibid., 91.

21. Ibid., 90.

22. Ibid., 95.

23. See the discussion of these points in Richard S. Bullene, "Architetto-Cittadio Ernesto Nathan Rogers" (Ph.D. diss., University of Pennsylvania, 1994), 49–52.

24. Newman, *CIAM '59 in Otterlo*, 93.

25. Ibid., 96.

26. Ibid., 97.

27. Ibid., 182.

28. Ibid.

29. Mumford, *The CIAM Discourse on Urbanism*, 264–5.

30. The best study of Chardigarh is Norma Evenson, *Chandigarh* (Berkeley: University of California Press, 1966). See also the essays in Russell Walden, ed., *The Open Hand: Essays on Le Corbusier* (Cambridge: M.I.T. Press, 1977).

31. Maxwell Fry, "Le Corbusier at Chandigarh," in Walden, *The Open Hand*, 356.

32. The classic study of the city's shortcomings is James Holston, *The Modernist City: An Anthropological Critique of Brasília* (Chicago: University of Chicago Press, 1989).

33. "The Aim of Team 10," in *Team 10 Primer*, ed. Alison Smithson (Cambridge: M.I.T. Press, 1968; originally published in 1962), 3.

34. Alison Smithson and Peter Smithson, in Smithson, *Team 10 Primer*, 86. Originally published as "CIAM 10 Projects. Team 10," in *Architectural Design*, September 1955.

35. Giancarlo de Carlo, *Urbino: The History of a City and Plans for Its Development* (Cambridge: M.I.T. Press, 1970; originally published in 1966). See also Lambreto Rossi, *Giancarlo De Carlo: Architettura* (Milan: Arnoldo Mondadori Editore, 1988).

36. Cornelis Wagenaar, "Jaap Bakema and the Fight for Freedom," in Goldhage and Legault, *Anxious Modernisms*, 261–77.

37. For details on van Eyck's life and work, see Strauven, *Aldo van Eyck*. For his work as a designer of playgrounds, see Liane Lefaivre and Alexander Tzonis, *Aldo van Eyck: Humanist Rebel* (Rotterdam: 101 Publishers, 1999).

38. Cited from Newman, *CIAM '59 in Otterlo*, 30.

39. Cited from Giedion, "Post-War Activity of CIAM," 37.

40. Cited from Smithson, *Team 10 Primer*, 41.

41. See especially Giedion's trilogy *The Eternal Present*, consisting of *The Beginnings of Art* (1962), *The Beginnings of Architecture* (1964), and *Architecture and the Phenomena of Transition* (1971). The first two volumes grew out of the A. W. Mellon Lectures in the Fine Arts (1957), and many regard them as his best books.

42. *Casabella-Continuità*, no. 209 (1956), 11–2.

43. *Casabella-Continuità*, no. 210 (1956): 3. English translation on page vi.

44. Ibid.

45. Ibid., 22. Translation by *Casabella*, vii.

46. Ernesto Nathan Rogers, "Preexisting Conditions and Issues of Contemporary Building Practice," *Casabella-Continuità*, no. 204 (February–March 1955): 3. Cited from the translation by Julia Banfi in Ockman, *Architecture Culture 1943–1968*, 201.

47. Ibid., 203.

48. *Casabella-Continuità*, no. 215, (April–May, 1957), 1–2.

49. Paolo Portoghesi, "Dal Neorealismo al Neoliberty," *Comunità*, no. 65 (December 1958): 69–79.

50. Reyner Banham, "Italian Eclectic," *Architecture Review* 112 (October 1952): 213–17.

51. Reyner Banham, "Case del Girasole," *Architecture Review* 113 (February 1953): 73–7.

52. Reyner Banham, "Neoliberty: The Italian Retreat from Modern Architecture," *Architecture Review* 125 (April 1959): 235.

53. Ibid.

54. Ernesto Nathan Rogers, "The Evolution of Architecture: Reply to the Caretaker of Frigidaires," *Casabella-Continuità*, no. 228 (June 1959): 2. English translation page v.

55. Ibid., 4; *Casabella*, vi.

56. Ibid., 3; *Casabella*, v.

57. Ernesto Rogers, "Tre problemi di ambientamento: La Torre Velasca a Milano, Un edificio per uffici e apparamenti a Torino, Casa Lurani a Milano," *Casabella-Continuità*, no. 232 (October 1959): 4–24. See Marco Frascari, "Tolerance or Play: Conventional Criticism or Critical Conventionalism in Light of the Italian Retreat from the Modern Movement," in *Midgård: Journal of Architectural Theory and Criticism* 1, no. 1 (1987): 9.

58. John Woodbridge, "Il 'Bay Region Style': La tradizione architettonica della Baia di San Francisco," *Casabella-Continuità*, no. 232 (October 1959): 39–43.

59. See "Futurist Manifesto, with an Introduction of Reyner Banham," *Architecture Review* 126, # 751 (August–September 1959): 77–80; "Neo Liberty: The Debate," *Architecture Review* 126, # 754 (December 1959): 341–4; "Clarification from Milan," *Architecture Review*, 126, # 755 (January 1960): 1–2.

60. On Banham's theoretical development, see especially Nigel Whiteley, *Reyner Banham: Historian of the Immediate Future* (Cambridge: M.I.T. Press, 2002). See also the chapter on Banham in Louis Martin, "The Search for a Theory in Architecture: Anglo-American Debates, 1957–1976" (Ph.D. diss., Princeton University, 2002), 93–133.

61. Reyner Banham, *Theory and Design in the First Machine Age* (London: The Architectural Press, 1960; citations from 2nd ed., New York: Praeger, 1967).

62. Ibid., 10.

63. Ibid.

64. Ibid., 12.

65. Ibid., 326. Nigel Whiteley (in *Reyner Banham*, 155–6) points out the source and date of this letter, published in James Meller, ed., *The Buckminster Fuller Reader* (London: Pelican, 1972), 44–68.

66. Ibid., 329–30.

67. Reyner Banham, "1960: The Future of Universal Man," *Architecture Review* 127 (April 1960): 253–60.

68. Reyner Banham, "1960: The Science Side," *Architecture Review* 127 (March 1960): 183–90.

69. Reyner Banham, "1960: Stocktaking," *Architecture Review* 127 (February 1960): 96.

70. Ibid., 100.

71. Reyner Banham, "The History of the Immediate Future," *RIBA Journal*, May 1961, 255, 27.

72. Reyner Bahnam, "On Trial: 2. Louis Kahn: The Buttery-Hatch Aesthetic," *Architecture Review* 131 (March 1962): 203–6. See an extended discussion of the six articles in Whiteley, *Reyner Banham*, 151–71.

73. Reyner Banham, "On Trial: 6. Mies van der Rohe," *Architecture Review* 132 (August 1962): 128.

74. Reyner Banham, "On Trial: 5. The Spec Builders: Towards a Pop Architecture," *Architecture Review* 132 (July 1962): 43–4.

75. Reyner Banham, "On Trial: 1. The Situation: What Architecture of Technology?" *Architecture Review* 131 (January 1962): 98.

76. Reyner Banham, "A Home Is Not a House," *Art in America*, April 1965, 70; reprinted in Charles Jencks and George Baird, eds., *Meaning in Architecture* (New York: Braziller, 1969), 109–18, and in Ockman, *Architecture Culture 1943–1968*, 370–8.

77. Ibid., 79.

78. Ibid., 75.

79. Ibid., 78, 75.

80. See Reyner Banham, "The Great Gizmo," *Industrial Design*, no. 12 (September 1965): 48–59; reprinted in *A Critic Writes: Essays by Reyner Banham*, ed. Mary Banham et al. (Berkeley: University of California Press, 1996), 109–18. See also Reyner Banham, *The Architecture of the Well-Tempered Environment* (London: Architectural Press, 1969).

81. Peter Cook, *Archigram* (London: Studio Vista, 1972), 8.

82. Ibid., 12.

83. Yona Friedman, *L'Architecture mobile: Vers une cité conçue par ses habitants* (Paris: Casterman, 1970; published privately in 1959). Cited from Ockman, *Architecture Culture 1943–1968*, 274. See also Yona Friedman, "The Ten Principles of Space Town Planning" (1962), and "GEAM: Programme for a Mobile Architecture," in *Programs and Manifestoes on Twentieth-Century Architecture*, ed. Ulrich Conrads (Cambridge: M.I.T. Press, 1984), 183–4, 167–8.

84. Hundertwasser, "Mould Manifesto against Rationalism in Architecture" (1958), in Conrads, *Programs and Manifestoes*, 157–60.

85. See Constant/Debord, "Situationist Definitions" and "Situationists: International Manifesto," in Conrads, *Programs and Manifestoes*, 161–2, 172–4.

86. See Jean-Louis Violeau, "A Critique of Architecture: The Bitter Victory of the Situationist International," in Goldhage and Legault, *Anxious Modernisms*, 239–59. Constant's ideas were also published in the Dutch architectural journal *Forum* shortly after van Eyck and Bakema joined the staff as editors. See especially *Forum*, no. 6 (1959).

87. See Constant, "New Babylon," in Conrads, *Programs and Manifestoes*, 177–8. See also idem, "The Great Game to Come," in Ockman, *Architecture Culture 1943–1968*, 314–416. The portfolio *New Babylon* was published in various editions.

88. On Japanese metabolism, see Noboru Kawazoe, ed., *Metabolism 1960: Proposals for a New Urbanism* (Tokyo: Bijutsu shuppansha, 1960), and Kisho Noriaki Kurokawa, *Metabolism in Architecture* (Boulder, Colo.: Westview Press, 1977).

89. Cherie Wendelken, "Putting Metabolism Back in Place: The Making of a Radically Decontextualized Architecture in Japan," in Goldhage and Legault, *Anxious Modernisms*, 292.

90. Kiyonori Kikutake, preface to Kawazoe, *Metabolism 1960*.

91. Kenzo Tange, "A Plan for Tokyo, 1960: Toward a Structural Reorganization," in Ockman, *Architecture Culture 1943–1968*, 330.

92. Kurokawa, *Metabolism in Architecture*, 56.

93. Fumihiko Maki and Masato Ohtaka, "Metabolism 1960," in Kawazoe, 59.

94. Edmund Husserl, *Logical Investigations*, 2 vols., trans. J. N. Findlay (London: Routledge & Kegan Paul, 1976); idem, *Ideas: General Introduction to Pure Phenomenology*, trans. W. R. Boyce Gibson (New York: Collier Books, 1962).

95. Maurice Merleau-Ponty, *Phenomenology of Perception*, trans. Colin Smith (London: Routledge & Kegan Paul, 1962), 98.

96. Martin Heidegger, *Being and Time*, trans. John Macquarrie and Edward Robinson (New York: Harper & Row, 1962).

97. Martin Heidegger, "Building, Dwelling, Thinking," in *Poetry, Language, Thought*, trans. Albert Hofstadter (New York: Harper Colophon Books, 1975), 143–162.

98. Ferdinand de Saussure, *Course in General Linguistics*, trans. Wade Baskin (New York: McGraw-Hill, 1966).

99. Nearly all of Lévi-Strauss's books have been translated into English. On his life and theories, see Edmund Leach, *Claude Lévi-Strauss* (Chicago: University of Chicago Press, 1989), and Octavio Paz, *Claude Lévi-Strauss: An Introduction* (New York: Dell, 1970).

100. Kenzo Tange, "A Plan For Tokyo, 1960: Toward a Structural Reorganization," in *Kenzo Tange 1936–1969: Architecture and Urban Design*, ed. Udo Kultermann (Zurich: Verlag für Architektur Artemis, 1970), 130.

101. Ibid., 241.

102. Arnulf Lüchinger, *Structuralism in Architecture and Urban Planning* (Stuttgart: Karl Krämer, 1981), 16. See also Wim J. van Heuvel, *Structuralism in Dutch Architecture* (Rotterdam: Uitgeverij 010 Publishers, 1992).

103. For an excellent general overview of semiotics, see George Baird's "Semiotics and Architecture," in *Encyclopedia of Aesthetics*, ed. Michael Kelly (New York: Oxford University Press, 1998), 1:271–5.

104. Morris's lengthy article was published in the *International Encyclopedia of Unified Science*, vol. 1, no. 2 (Chicago: University of Chicago Press, 1938). See also *The Collected Papers of Charles Sanders Pierce*, 8 vols., ed. C. Hartshorne and P. Weiss (Cambridge: Harvard University Press, 1974).

105. See Martin, "The Search for a Theory in Architecture: Anglo-American Debates, 1957–1976," 399–408. See also Martin's ensuing discussion of semiotics at the HfG.

106. Tomas Maldonado, "Communications and Semiotics," *Ulm 5* (July 1959): 69–78; idem, "Notes on Communication," *Uppercase 5* (1962): 5–10, one of five articles related to his seminar and its results.

107. Maldonado, "Notes on Communication," 5.

108. Christian Norberg-Schulz, *Intentions in Architecture* (Cambridge: M.I.T. Press, 1965; originally published in 1963), 7.

109. Manfredo Tafuri also faults Norberg-Schulz for basing his analysis on ahistorical criteria. See Manfredo Tafuri, *Theories and History of Architecture*, trans. by Giorgio Verrecchia (New York: Harper & Row, 1917), 172.

110. The pivotal work in this regard is his *Existence, Space and Architecture* (New York: Praeger, 1971).

111. Joseph Rykwert, "Meaning and Building," *Zodiac 6* (1960): 193–6; reprinted in Joseph Rykwert, *The Necessity of Artifice* (London: Academy Editions, 1982), 9–16.

112. In response to Banham's two articles of 1952, Michael Burton and Joseph Rykwert replied with "Italian Eclecticism," *Architecture Review* 113 (February 1953): 134.

113. Rykwert, "Meaning and Building," 193.

114. Ibid., 195.

115. Ibid., 196.

116. Sergio Bettini, "Semantic Criticism; and the Historical Continuity of European Architecture," *Zodiac 2* (1958): 191–203 (English version).

117. Giovanni Klaus Koenig, *Analisi del linguaggio architettonico* (Florence: Liberia editrice Fiorentina, 1964); Renato De Fusco, *Architettura come mass medium: Note per una semiologia architettonica* (Bari: Dedalo, 1967); Maria Luisa Scalvini, "Simbolo e significato nello spazio architettonico," *Casabella*, no. 328 (1968): 42–7; Umberto Eco, *La Struttura assente: Introduzione alla ricerca semiologica* (Milan: Bompiani, 1968).

118. First published in *VIA I: The Journal of the Graduate School of Fine Arts, University of Pennsylvania*, 1973; reprinted in Geoffrey Broadbent, Richard Bunt, and Charles Jencks, eds., *Signs, Symbols, and Architecture* (Chichester, England: Wiley, 1980).

119. George Baird, "Paradox in Regents Park: A Question of Interpretation," *Arena: Architectural Association Journal* 81 (April 1966): 272–6.

120. See "Meaning in Architecture" (special issue), *Architectural Association Journal* 83 (June 1967): 7.

121. Charles Jencks and George Baird, eds., *Meaning in Architecture* (New York: Braziller, 1969).

122. For the work of Böhm and Schattner, see the recent exhibition catalogue *New German Architecture: A Reflexive Modernism*, ed. Ullrich Schwarz (Ostfildern-Ruit, Germany: Hatje Cantz Verlag, 2002).

123. On the work of Ungers, see *O. M. Ungers, Architektur, 1951–1991* (Stuttgart: Deutsche Verlags-Anstalt, 1991), and Martin Kieren, *Oswald Mathias Ungers* (Zurich: Artemis,1994).

124. Reyner Banham, *The New Brutalism: Ethic or Aesthetic?* (London: Architectural Press, 1966), 125–6.

125. Reinhard Gieselmann and Oswald Mathias Ungers, "Towards a New Architecture" (1960), in Conrads, *Programs and Manifestoes*, 165.

126. See Jürg Jansen et al., *Teaching Architecture: Bernhard Hoesli at the Department of Architecture at the ETH Zurich* (Zurich: Institut für Geschichte und Theorie der Architektur, 1989).

127. James Sterling, "Regionalism and Modern Architecture," *Architects' Year Book 7* (1957); cited from Ockman, *Architecture Culture 1943–1968*, 248.

128. Reyner Banham, "The Style for the Job," *New Statesman*, 14 February 1964, 261; cited from Mary Banham et al., *A Critic Writes*, 97.

129. Peter Collins, *Changing Ideals in Modern Architecture 1750–1950* (London: Faber & Faber, 1965). On the thought of Peter Collins, see Panayotis Tournikiotis, *The Historiography of Modern Architecture* (Cambridge: M.I.T. Press, 199), 168–91.

130. Collins, *Changing Ideals*, 118.

131. Ibid., 198–9.

132. Ibid., 284.

133. Ibid., 298.

134. Ernesto Rogers, "Utopia della realtà," *Casabella-Continuità*, no. 259 (January 1962): 1.

135. The most important studies on Scarpa include Francesco Dal Co and Giuseppe Mazzariol, eds., *Carlo Scarpa: The Complete Works* (New York: Rizzoli, 1985); Nicolas Olsberg et al., *Carlo Scarpa Architect: Intervening with History* (Montréal: Canadian Centre for Architecture, 1999); Marco Frascari, *The Body and Architecture in the Drawings of Carlo Scarpa* (Cambridge: Harvard University Press, 1987); and Maria Antonietta Crippa, *Carlo Scarpa: Theory, Design, Projects* (Cambridge: M.I.T. Press, 1986).

136. Carlo Scarpa, "Address Delivered for the Inauguration of the Academic Year 1964–1965 at the IUAV in Venice," in Dal Co and Mazzariol, *Carlo Scarpa*, 282.

137. Francesco Dal Co, "The Architecture of Carlo Scarpa," in Dal Co and Mazzariol, *Carlo Scarpa*, 56.

138. Two monographs on Portoghesi are Giovanna Massobrio, Maria Ercadi, and Stefania Tuzi, *Paolo Portoghesi: Architetto* (Milan: Skira, 2001), and Mario Pisani, *Paolo Portoghesi: Opere e progetti* (Milan: Electa, 1992). A short but instructive introduction to his early work is the English/German exhibition catalogue prepared by François Burckhardt, *Paolo Portoghesi, Vittorio Gigliotti, Architecture 1960–1969* (Hamburg: Hochschule für bildende Künste, n.d.).

139. Paolo Portoghesi, *Guarino Guarini 1624–1683* (Milan: Electa, 1956), and idem, *Borromini nella cultura europea* (Rome: Laterza, 1964).

140. Vittorio Gregotti, *Il territorio dell'architecttura* (Milan: Feltrinelli, 1987; originally published in 1966).

141. Leonardo Benevolo, *History of Modern Architecture*, trans. H. J. Landry, 2 vols. (Cambridge: M.I.T. Press, 1971).

142. Giuseppe Samona, *L'urbanistica e l'avvenire della città negli stati europei* (Bari: Laterza, 1959).

143. Manfredo Tafuri, "La prima strada di Roma moderna: Via Nazionale," in *Roma: Città e piani* (Turin: Urbanistica, 1960).

144. Manfredo Tafuri, *Ludovico Quaroni e lo sviluppo dell'architettura moderna in Italia* (Milan: Edizioni di Comunità, 1964); idem, *L'architettura moderna in Giappone* (Rocca San Caciamo: Cappelli, 1964); *L'architettura del Manierismo nel Cinquecento europea* (1966).

145. Biographical material on Rossi's early years is still lacking. For a presentation of his architectural works in English, see Peter Arnell and Ted Bickford, eds., *Aldo Rossi: Buildings and Projects* (New York: Rizzoli, 1985).

146. The letter was to Francesco Tentori, published in his "D'où venons-nous? Qui sommes-nous? Où allons-nous?" in *Aspetti dell'arte contemporanea*, exhibition catalogue, L'Aquila, 28 July to 6 October 1963 (Rome: Edizioni dell'Ateneo, 1963), 264–5.

147. Aldo Rossi, *The Architecture of the City*, trans. Diane Ghirardo and Joan Ockman (Cambridge: M.I.T. Press, 1984).

148. Rossi was interested in Lynch's emphasis on orientation as well as his comments on residential districts. See Rossi, *The Architecture of the City*, 34, 69, 101, 112.

149. Ibid., 46.

150. Ibid., 22 (editor's note).

151. Ibid., 40. Rossi cites the definition of Quatremère de Quincy given in the *Dictionnaire historique d'architecture* (1832).

152. Ibid., 103.

153. Ibid., 123.

154. Giorgio Grassi, *La construzione logica della architettura* (Padua: Marsilio, 1967).

155. Alexander Klein, *Das Einfamilienhaus, Südtyp: Studien und Entwürfe mit grundsätzlichen Betrachtungen* (Stuttgart: J. Hoffmann, 1934).

156. Aldo Rossi, introduction to *Architettura Razionale* (Milan: Franco Angeli, 1977; originally published in 1973), 24; the passage in English is cited from Adolf Behne, *The Modern Functional Building*, trans. Michael Robinson (Los Angeles: Getty Publications Program, 1996), 137–8.

157. Massimo Scolari, "Avanguardia e nuova architettura," in *Architettura Razionale*, 168–70; cited from Massimo Scolari, "The New Architecture and the Avant-Garde," trans. Stephen Sartarelli, in *Architecture Theory since 1968*, ed. K. Michael Hays (Cambridge: M.I.T. Press, 2002), 135–6.

158. Joseph Rykwert, "15ª Triennale," *Domus*, no. 530 (January 1974): 4.

15. Challenges to Modernism in America

1. Sargent Shriver, cited from Steven Hayward, "Broken Cities: Liberalism's Urban Legacy, in *Urban Society*, 9th ed. (Guildford: McGraw-Hill, 1999), 117.

2. See Martin Mayer, *The Builders: Houses, People, Neighborhoods, Governments, Money* (New York: W. W. Norton, 1978), 188–90.

3. Paul D. Spreiregen, *Urban Design: The Architecture of Towns and Cities* (New York: McGraw-Hill, 1965), 47.

4. On the career of Moses, see Robert A. Caro, *The Power Broker: Robert Moses and the Fall of New York* (New York: Knopf, 1974).

5. Mumford's essays critiquing Stuyvesant Town include "From Utopia Parkway Turn East" (1949), "Fresh Meadows, Fresh Plans" (1949), and "Prefabricated Blight" (1948), in *From the Ground Up: Observations on Contemporary Architecture, Housing, Highway Building, and Civic Design* (New York: Harcourt Brace Jovanovich, 1956), 3–10, 11–19, 108–14.

6. For his views on highways, see his four Sky Line articles published as "The Roaring Traffic's Boom" in *The New Yorker* between March and June 1955; reprinted in *From the Ground Up*, 199–243.

7. Lewis Mumford, *The City in History: Its Origins, Its Transformations, and Its Prospects* (New York: Harcourt, Brace & World, 1961), 512.

8. Ibid., 575.

9. See especially his five-part series of articles "The Future of the City," published in *Architectural Record* in 1962–3. Reprinted in Lewis Mumford, *Architecture as a Home for Man: Essays for Architectural Record*, ed. Jeanne M. Davern (New York: Architectural Record Books, 1975), 107–44.

10. Jane Jacobs, *The Death and Life of Great American Cities* (New York: Random House, 1961), 25.

11. Ibid., 20–1.

12. Ibid., 84.

13. Lewis Mumford, "Mother Jacobs' Home Remedies," *The New Yorker*, 1 December 1962; reprinted as "Home Remedies for Urban Cancer," in *The Urban Prospect* (London: Secker & Warburg, 1968), 182–207.

14. Mumford, "Home Remedies for Urban Cancer," 188.

15. Ibid., 194–5.

16. Ibid., 197.

17. Ibid., 206.

18. Ibid., 207.

19. Lewis Mumford, "A Brief History of Urban Frustration," in *The Urban Prospect*, 215.

20. Lawrence Halprin, *Cities* (Cambridge: M.I.T. Press, 1963; reprint, 1972).

21. Peter Blake, *God's Own Junkyard: The Planned Deterioration of America's Landscape* (New York: Holt, Rinehart & Winston, 1964), 33.

22. Victor Gruen, *The Heart of Our Cities: The Urban Crisis: Diagnosis and Cure* (New York: Simon & Schuster, 1964).

23. Kevin Lynch, "The Pattern of the Metropolis," in *Neighborhood, City, and Metropolis: An Integrated Reader in Urban Sociology*, ed. Robert Gutman and David Popenoe (New York: Random House, 1970), 856–71. In the same book, see also Kevin Lynch and Lloyd Rodwin, "A Theory of Urban Form" (1958), 756–76.

24. Kevin Lynch, *The Image of the City* (Cambridge: M.I.T. Press, 1971; originally published in 1960), 9.

25. Ibid., 9–10.

26. Ibid., 119.

27. L. J. Duhl, ed., *The Urban Condition: People and Policy in the Metropolis* (New York: Basic Books, 1963).

28. After graduating from Harvard University after the war, McHarg returned to his native Scotland with a severe case of tuberculosis.

29. The earlier work was published as *The Levittowners: Ways of Life and Politics in a New Suburban Community* (New York: Pantheon, 1967).

30. Herbert J. Gans, *The Urban Villagers: Group and Class in the Life of Italian-Americans* (New York: The Free Press, 1962).

31. For an important anthology of essays on this topic, see Robert Gutman, ed., *People and Buildings* (New York: Basic Books, 1972).

32. Elizabeth Wood, *Housing Design: A Social Theory* (New York: Citizens' Housing and Planning Council, 1961).

33. Roger Starr, *The Urban Choices: The City and Its Critics* (Baltimore: Penguin, 1969; originally published in 1967), 177.

34. Martin Anderson, *The Federal Bulldozer: A Critical Analysis of Urban Renewal 1949–62* (Cambridge: M.I.T. Press, 1964). See also the summary article "The Federal Bulldozer," in *Urban Renewal: The Record and the Controversy*, ed. James Q. Wilson (Cambridge: M.I.T. Press, 1966), 491–508.

35. Robert P. Groberg, "Urban Renewal Realistically Reappraised," in Wilson, *Urban Renewal*, 509–531.

36. Herbert J. Gans, "The Failure of Urban Renewal," in *People and Plans: Essays on Urban Problems and Solutions* (New York: Basic Books, 1968), 261.

37. Ibid., 265–6.

38. James Q. Wilson, "Planning and Politics: Citizen Participation in Urban Renewal," in Wilson, *Urban Renewal*, 407–21.

39. On Abrams, see A. Scott Henderson, *Housing and the Democratic Ideal: The Life and Thought of Charles Abrams* (New York: Columbia University Press, 2000).

40. Charles Abrams, *The City Is the Frontier* (New York: Harper & Row, 1965); its chapter "Some Blessings of Urban Renewal" appears in Wilson, *Urban Renewal*, 558–82. On URSA, see also "Housing in the Year 2000," in William R. Ewald Jr., ed., *Environment and Policy: The Next Fifty Years* (Bloomington: Indiana University Press, 1968), 209–40.

41. Charles Abrams, "Some Blessings of Urban Renewal," in Wilson, *Urban Renewal*, 562.

42. Paul Davidoff, "A Choice Theory of Planning," *Journal of the American Institute of Planners* 28 (1962): 103–15. See also idem, "Advocacy and Pluralism in Planning," *Journal of the American Institute of Planners* 31 (1965): 331–7, and idem, "Democratic Planning," *Perspecta* 11 (1967): 158–9, reprinted in Joan Ockman, *Architecture Culture 1943–1968: A Documentary Anthology* (New York: Rizzoli, 1993), 442–5.

43. Serge Chermayeff and Christopher Alexander, *Community and Privacy: Toward a New Architecture of Humanism* (New York: Anchor, 1965; originally published in 1963).

44. See several of his essays and speeches in Richard Plunz, ed., *Design and the Public Good: Selected Writings 1930–1980 by Serge Chermayeff* (Cambridge: M.I.T. Press, 1982). The citation is from Chermayeff and Alexander, *Community and Privacy*, 20.

45. Christopher Alexander, *Notes on the Synthesis of Form* (Cambridge: Harvard University Press, 1964), 18–19.

46. Ibid., 84–91.

47. Christopher Alexander, "The Synthesis of Form: Some Notes on a Theory" (Ph.D. diss., Harvard University, 1962). Alexander listed in his bibliography only eight books or articles on architecture,

ten books and articles under the rubric "Psychology and Problem Solving," ten books under "Mathematics and Systems Theory," and seven under "Anthropology."

48. For the details of this extended discussion, see Francis Strauven, *Aldo van Eyck: The Shape of Reality* (Amsterdam: Architectura & Natura, 1998), 397–402, 473 n. 663. The fact that Alexander was invited to this private gathering suggests that his doctoral work was followed in various circles.

49. Christopher Alexander, "A City Is not a Tree," *Architectural Forum* 122 (May 1965): 58. Part 1 of the article appeared in the April issue of *Architectural Forum*.

50. Ibid., 59.

51. Ibid.

52. J. Christopher Jones, *Design Methods: Seeds of Human Futures* (London: Wiley, 1970). See also S. Gregory, ed., *The Design Method* (London: Butterworth, 1966).

53. Geoffrey Broadbent and Colin Ward, *Design Methods in Architecture*, Architecture Association Paper No. 4 (London: Lund Humphries, 1969).

54. On the nature of his opposition to Alexander, and the latter's response, see Louis Martin, "The Search for a Theory in Architecture: Anglo-American Debates, 1957–1976" (Ph.D. diss., Princeton University, 2002), 320–7.

55. Christopher Alexander, Sara Ishikawa, and Murray Silverstein, with Max Jacobson, Ingrid Fiksdahl-King, and Shlomo Angel, *A Pattern Language: Towns, Buildings, Construction* (New York: Oxford University Press, 1977), x.

56. Christopher Alexander, Sara Ishikawa, and Murray Silverstein, *A Pattern Language Which Generates Multi-Service Centers* (Berkeley: Center for Environmental Structure, 1968).

57. Ibid., 187.

58. See especially his trilogy of books: Christopher Alexander, *The Timeless Way of Building* (New York: Oxford University Press, 1979); Alexander, Ishikawa, and Silverstein, *A Pattern Language*; and Christopher Alexander, Murray Silverstein, Shlomo Angel, Sara Ishikawa, Denny Abrams, *The Oregon Experiment* (New York: Oxford University Press, 1975).

59. Stanford Anderson, "Architecture and Tradition That Isn't 'Trad, Dad,'" *Architectural Association Journal* 80 (May 1965): 325–30; cited from Marcus Whiffen, ed., *The History, Theory and Criticism of Architecture: Papers from the 1964 AIA-ACSA Teacher Seminar* (Cambridge: M.I.T. Press, 1965), 71.

60. Ibid., 79.

61. Peter Collins, "The Interrelated Roles of History, Theory, and Criticism in the Process of Architectural Design," in Whiffen, *The History, Theory and Criticism of Architecture*, 3–4.

62. Edward T. Hall, *The Hidden Dimension* (Garden City, N.J.: Doubleday, 1966), 159.

63. Ibid., 160.

64. Robert Sommer, *Tight Spaces: Hard Architecture and How to Humanize It* (Englewood Cliffs, N.J.: Prentice-Hall, 1974).

65. Oscar Newman, *Defensible Space: Crime Prevention through Urban Design* (New York: Macmillan, 1972), 3.

66. Ibid., 12.

67. Ibid., 176.

68. Marshall McLuhan and Quentin Fiore, *The Medium Is the Message: An Inventory of Effects* (New York: Bantam, 1967), 16.

69. Ibid., 146.

70. Paulo Soleri, *Arcology: The City in the Image of Man* (Cambridge: M.I.T. Press, 1969).

71. Lawrence Halprin, *The RSVP Cycles: Creative Processes in the Human Environment* (New York: Braziller, 1969), 197.

72. See Edward Larrabee Barnes, *Edward Larrabee Barnes: Architect* (New York: Rizzoli, 1994).

73. Philip Johnson, "Whither Away – Non-Meisian Directions, 1959," in *Writings* (New York: Oxford University Press, 1979), 226–41.

74. See *The Architecture of Philip Johnson*, foreword by Philip Johnson (Boston: Bulfinch Press, 2002).

75. Peter Blake, *The Architecture of Ulrich Franzen* (Basel: Birkhäuser, 1998).

76. See John M. Johansen, *John M. Johansen: A Life in the Continuum of Modern Architecture* (Milan: L'Arca Edizione, 1995).

77. John Johansen, "An Architecture for the Electronic Age," *The American Scholar*, no. 35 (1965), and "John Johansen," in *By Their Own Design*, ed. Abby Suckle (New York: Whitney Library of Design, 1980), 67–77.

78. See Carter Wiseman, *I. M. Pei: A Profile in American Architecture* (New York: Abrams, 1990).

79. See Gunnar Birkerts, *Buildings, Projects and Thoughts 1960–1985* (Ann Arbor: University of Michigan Press, 1985).

80. See, for instance, his various comments in his interview with John W. Cook and Heinrich Klotz, *Conversations with Architects* (New York: Praeger, 1973), 52–89.

81. Robert A. M. Stern, *New Directions in American Architecture* (New York: Braziller, 1969).

82. On Rudolph, see Sibyl Moholy-Nagy, *The Architecture of Paul Rudolph* (London: Thames & Hudson, 1970), and Tony Monk, *The Art and Architecture of Paul Rudolph* (London: Wiley-Academy, 1999).

83. Paul Rudolph, "Regionalism in Architecture," *Perspecta* 4 (1957): 13.

84. See Paul Rudolph, "Alumni Day Speech: Yale School of Architecture, February 1958," *Oppositions* 4 (October 1974): 35–62, and Robert A. M. Stern, "Yale 1950–1965," ibid., 141–3.

85. An epithet given to Rudolph's work by Robert Venturi, Denise Scott Brown, and Steven Izenour, *Learning from Las Vegas* (Cambridge: M.I.T. Press, 1977; originally published in 1972), 93.

86. Louis Kahn, "Talk at the Conclusion of the Otterlo Congress," in *CIAM '59 in Otterlo*, ed, Oscan Newman (Stuttgart: Karl Krämer Verlag, 1961), 205–6.

87. Ibid., 212

88. Ibid., 206.

89. Ibid., 214.

90. Interview in Kahn's office, February 1961, reprinted in *Louis I. Kahn: Writings, Lectures, Interviews*, ed. Alessandra Latour (New York: Rizzoli, 1991), 123.

91. Vincent Scully, Jr., *Louis I. Kahn: Makers of Contemporary Architecture* (New York: Braziller, 1962), 37.

92. Manfredo Tafuri, *Theories and History of Architecture*, trans. Giorgio Verrecchia (New York: Harper & Row, 1976), 55.

93. Robin Middleton, "Disintegration," *Architectural Design* 37 (May 1967): 204.

94. Fine intellectual analyses of Kahn and his work include David Brownlee and David De Long, *Louis Kahn: In the Realm of Architecture* (New York: Rizzoli, 1991); Romaldo Giurgola and Jaimini

Mehta, *Louis I. Kahn* (Boulder, Colo.: Westview Press, 1975); August L. Komendant, *18 Years with Architect Louis I. Kahn* (Englewood, Colo.: Alvray, 1975); Alexandra Tyng, *Beginnings: Louis I. Kahn's Philosophy of Architecture* (New York: Wiley, 1984); John Lobell, *Between Silence and Light: Spirit in the Architecture of Louis I. Kahn* (Boston: Shambhala, 2000; originally published in 1979); and Joseph A. Burton, "The Architectural Hieroglyphics of Louis I. Kahn: Architecture as *Logos*" (Ph.D. diss., University of Pennsylvania, 1983).

95. Colin Rowe and Robert Slutzsky, "Transparency: Literal and Phenomenal," *Perspecta* 8 (1963); republished as *Transparency*, with a commentary by Bernhard Hoesli and an introduction by Werner Oechslin (Basel: Birkhäuser, 1997). Part 2 of the essay was published in *Perspecta* 13–14 (1971), and reprinted in part in Ockman, *Architecture Culture 1943–1968*, 205–23. On Rowe, see also Joan Ockman, "Form without Utopia: Contextualizing Colin Rowe" (review essay), *Journal of the Society of Architectural Historians* 57 (December 1998): 448–56, and the special issue of *Architecture New York* devoted to Rowe (nos. 7–8, 1994).

96. Alfred H. Barr, *Cubism and Abstract Art: Painting, Sculpture, Constructions, Photography, Architecture, Industrial Art, Theater, Films, Posters, Topography* (New York: Museum of Modern Art, 1938; reprint, 1986).

97. Sigfried Giedion, *Space, Time and Architecture: The Growth of a New Tradition* (Cambridge: Harvard University Press, 1949), 426–7.

98. Henry-Russell Hitchcock, *Painting toward Architecture* (New York: Duell, Sloan & Pearce, 1948), 46, 54.

99. C. Rowe and Slutzsky, *Transparency*, 23.

100. Ibid., 32.

101. Ibid., 37–8.

102. Ibid., 38.

103. This second essay has been recently reprinted in the first volume of Colin Rowe, *As I Was Saying: Recollections and Miscellaneous Essays*, ed. Alexander Caragonne (Cambridge: M.I.T. Press, 1996), 73–106.

104. For an extended discussion of Eisenman and the dissertation, see Martin, "The Search for a Theory of Architecture," 517–38. I thank Louis Martin for allowing me to read his copy of this dissertation.

105. Peter D. Eisenman, "The Formal Basis of Modern Architecture" (Ph.D. diss., Cambridge University, 1963), 5.

106. Ibid., 37.

107. Ibid., 38.

108. Ibid., 12.

109. Ibid., 143.

110. The exhibition was held 23 January–13 March 1967; see Museum of Modern Art Staff, *The New City: Architecture and Urban Renewal* (New York: Museum of Modern Art, 1967).

111. Letter of 26 February (for meeting of 5 February), CASE Archives, Canadian Centre for Architecture, folder B1-2.

112. Ibid., folder B1-2, letter of 26 February 1968.

113. Ibid.

114. Ibid., folder B1-5, statement of editorial board, 9 May 1965.

115. Ibid., folder B1-2, letter to Thomas Vreeland, 9 January 1968.

116. On the details of his life and work, see Kevin P. Keim, *An Architectural Life: Memoirs and Memories of Charles W. Moore* (Boston: Bulfinch Press, 1996); Charles Moore, *You Have to Pay for the Public Life: Selected Essays of Charles W. Moore*, ed. Kevin Keim (Cambridge: M.I.T. Press, 2001); David Littlejohn, *Architect: The Life and Work of Charles W. Moore* (New York: Holt, Rinehart & Winston, 1984); Gerald Allen, *Charles Moore* (London: Granada, 1980); and *Charles Moore: Buildings and Projects 1949–1986*, ed. Eugene J. Johnson (New York: Rizzoli, 1986).

117. Littlejohn, *Architect*, 122.

118. Charles Moore, "Discrimination in Housing Design," in Charles Moore and Gerald Allen, *Dimensions: Space, Shape, and Scale in Architecture* (New York: Architectural Record Books, 1976), 131–42.

119. Charles Moore, "Two Buildings by Joseph Esherick: Dedicated to the Moving Inhabitant, Not the Maker of Form," in Moore and Allen, *Dimensions*, 71.

120. The theme was first voiced in the essay (written with Donlyn Lyndon, Patrick Quinn, and Sim Van der Ryn) "Toward Making Places," published in *Landscape*, Fall 1962, 31–41; reprinted in Moore, *You Have to Pay for Public Life*, 88–107.

121. Charles Moore, "Plug It in, Rameses, and See If It Lights Up: Because We Aren't Going to Keep It Unless It Works," *Perspecta* 11 (1967): 32–43; cited from Moore, *You Have to Pay for Public Life*, 156–7.

122. Charles Moore, "Inclusive and Exclusive," in Moore and Allen, *Dimensions*, 160.

123. Kent C. Bloomer and Charles Moore, *Body, Memory, and Architecture* (New Haven: Yale University Press, 1977).

124. Heinrich Klotz, *The History of Postmodern Architecture*, trans. Radka Donnell (Cambridge: M.I.T. Press, 1988), 189.

125. Littlejohn, *The Architect*, 229.

126. Ibid., 152.

127. Ibid. As Littlejohn reports, Moore at one point wrote a manifesto and list of demands for his rebellious students, and "Kingman Brewster knew I had written it and was not at all pleased." Moore argued that his efforts had saved the architecture program, but in fact the program in the late 1960s came very close to being eliminated.

128. See *Architecture or Revolution: Charles Moore and Yale in the Late 1960s*, exhibition catalogue Eve Blau (curator) (New Haven: Yale University School of Architecture, 2001).

129. Ibid., preface by Robert A. M. Stern and J. M. Hoppin.

130. The important studies on the work of Venturi and his wife Denise Scott Brown include David B. Brownlee, David G. De Long, and Kathryn B. Hiesinger, eds., *Out of the Ordinary: Robert Venturi, Denise Scott Brown and Associates* (Philadelphia: Philadelphia Museum of Art, 2001); Stanislaus von Moos, *Venturi, Rauch & Scott Brown: Buildings and Projects*, trans. David Antal (New York: Rizzoli, 1987); and Christopher Mead, *The Architecture of Robert Venturi* (Albuquerque: University of New Mexico Press, 1989).

131. The thesis has been published in Robert Venturi and Denise Scott Brown's *Iconography and Electronics upon a Generic Architecture: A View from the Drafting Room* (Cambridge: M.I.T. Press, 1996). For a study of Venturi's years at Princeton, see Deborah Fausch, "The Context of Meaning Is Everyday Life: Venturi and Scott Brown's Theories of Architecture and Urbanism" (Ph.D. diss., Princeton University, 1999).

132. Robert Venturi, "Complexity and Contradiction in Architecture: Selections from a Forthcoming Book," *Perspecta* 9/10 (1965): 17–56. The issue was edited by Robert Stern.

133. See John Summerson, "The Mischievous Analogy," in *Heavenly Mansions and Other Essays on Architecture* (London: Cresset Press, 1949), 195–218.

134. Robert Venturi, "The Campidoglio: A Case Study," *Architectural Review*, vol. 113, 677 (May 1953): 333–4; reprinted in *A View from the Campidoglio: Selected Essays 1953–1984* (New York: Harper & Row, 1984), 12–13.

135. Robert Venturi, *Complexity and Contradiction in Architecture* (New York: Museum of Modern Art, 1966), 22.

136. Ibid., 22, 26.

137. Ibid., 25.

138. William Empson, *Seven Types of Ambiguity* (New York: New Directions, 1947), "Contents."

139. Venturi, *Complexity and Contradiction*, 44.

140. Ibid., 44–5.

141. Robert Venturi, "A Justification for Pop Architecture," *Arts and Architecture*, April 1965, 22.

142. Venturi, *Complexity and Contradiction*, 48.

143. Ibid., 49.

144. Ibid., 52.

145. Venturi, "A Justification for Pop Architecture," 22.

146. On Denise Scott Brown, see David B. Brownlee's "Form and Content," in Brownlee, De Long, and Hiesinger, *Out of the Ordinary*, 3–89.

147. Scott Brown wrote several articles for the *Journal of the American Institute of Planners* in the first half of the 1960s: "Form, Design and the City" (November 1962), "Natal Plans" (May 1964), and "The Meaningful City" (January 1965).

148. Scott Brown, "The Meaningful City"; reprinted and expanded in *Connection* 4 (spring 1967): 6–7, 12–14, 26–7, 50–1.

149. Venturi, *Complexity and Contradiction*, 102.

150. Ibid., 102–3.

151. Ibid., 103.

152. Foreword to *Complexity and Contradiction*, 11.

153. Ibid., 14.

154. Colin Rowe, "Waiting for Utopia," *New York Times*, 1967; reprinted in Rowe, *As I Was Saying*, 2:75–8.

155. Alan Colquhoun, "Robert Venturi," *Architectural Design* 37 (August 1967): 362.

156. Manfredo Tafuri, *Theories and History of Architecture*, trans. Giorgio Verrecchia (New York: Harper & Row, 1976), 213.

157. Joseph Rykwert, "Complexity and Contradiction in Architecture," *Domus*, no. 453 (August 1967).

158. Christian Norberg-Schulz, "Less or More?" *Architectural Review* 143 (April 1968): 258. "His formal descriptions mainly follow the path indicated by art historians such as Wölfflin, Frankl, Brinckmann, Wittkower, and Sedlmayr."

159. Ibid., 257.

Epilogue

1. Of the many accounts of 1968, perhaps the best is David Caute, *The Year of the Barricades: A Journey through 1968* (New York: Harper & Row, 1988).

2. Alain Touraine, *The May Movement: Revolt and Reform*, trans. Leonard F. X. Mayhew (New York: Random House, 1971).

3. "Motion of May 15, Strike Committee, Ecole des Beaux-Arts," in *Architecture Culture 1943–1968: A Documentary Anthology*, ed. Joan Ockman (New York: Rizzoli, 1993), 457. See also Donald Drew Egbert, *The Beaux-Arts Tradition in French Architecture* (Princeton: Princeton University Press, 1980), and Martin Pawley and Bernard Tschumi, "The Beaux-Arts since '68," *Architectural Design* 61 (September 1971).

4. See Caute, *Year of the Barricades*, 76.

5. The best introduction to Tafuri and his ideas are the various essays appearing in the memorial double edition of *Casabella*, nos. 619–620, (January–February 1995). See also Jean-Louis Cohen, "La coupure entre architects et intellectuals, ou les enseignements de l'italophilie," *In Extenso* 1 (1984): 182–223.

6. Manfredo Tafuri, *Theories and History of Architecture*, trans. Giorgio Verrecchia (New York: Harper & Row, 1976).

7. Alberto Asor Rosa, "Critique of Ideology and Historical Practice," *Casabella*, nos. 619–620 (January–February 1995).

8. Manfredo Tafuri, "Per una critica dell'ideologia architettonica," *Contropiano*, no. 1 (January–April 1969); translated by Stephen Sartarelli as "Toward a Critique of Architectural Ideology," in *Architecture Theory since 1968*, ed. K. Michael Hays (Cambridge: Cambridge University Press, 2000).

9. Tafuri, *Theories and History of Architecture*, 2.

10. The following passage is indicative of Tafuri's historical manner: "We can say, therefore, that for Kahn too, history is only an *ingredient* to be manipulated. He uses it to justify choices already made or to shed semantic light, through the open allusion of the references, on values that aspire towards the symbol and the institution, but that, at the same time, try to open be open and readable without betraying the code that rejects myths, symbols and permanent institutions.... The historicism of the Kahnian school harks back to the European myth of Reason: as such it becomes a phenomenon opposed to the pragmatist American tradition, balanced, by now, between a fun-fair irrationality and a guilty cynicism" (*Theories and History of Architecture*, 56–7).

11. Tafuri "Toward a Critique of Architectural Ideology," 6. On Cacciari's ideas, see Massimo Cacciari *Architecture and Nihilism: On the Philosophy of Modern Architecture*, trans. Stephen Sartarelli (New Haven: Yale University Press, 1993).

12. Ibid., introductory remarks, 2.

13. Ibid., 31.

14. Manfredo Tafuri, *Progetto e Utopia* (Bari: Laterza, 1973); translated by Barbara Luigia La Penta as *Architecture and Utopia: Design and Capitalist Development* (Cambridge: M.I.T. Press, 1976), 181.

15. One excellent critique of its logical problems is Tomas Llorens, "Manfredo Tafuri: Neo-Avant-Garde and History," in *On the Methodology of Architecture History*, ed. Demetri Porphyrios, Architectural Design Profile (1981), 82–95. On his historiography, see Panayotis Tournikiotis, *The Historiography of Modern Architecture* (Cambridge: M.I.T. Press, 1999), 193–219.

16. William Manchester, *The Glory and the Dream: A Narrative History of America 1932–1972* (Boston: Little, Brown, 1973), 1131.

17. Cited from Caute, *Year of the Barricades*, 166.

18. Ibid., 172. In a speech given in Boston shortly after the Columbia confrontation, Rudd admitted that the connection with the

Defense Department was "nothing at Columbia" and the gymnasium issue was "bull."

19. See Deborah Fausch, "The Context of Meaning Is Everyday Life: Venturi and Scott Brown's Theories of Architecture and Urbanism" (Ph.D. diss., Princeton University, 1999), esp. 138–78.

20. Melvin Webber, "The Urban Place and the Nonplace Urban Realm," in *Explorations into Urban Structure*, ed. Melvin Webber et al. (Philadelphia: University of Pennsylvania Press, 1964), 140.

21. Denise Scott Brown, "Messages," *Connection* 4 (spring 1967): 14; reprinted from the *AIA Journal*. Crane's essay, "The City Symbolic," appeared in the *Journal of the American Institute of Planners* 26 (November 1960): 280–92.

22. Robert Venturi and Denise Scott Brown, "A Significance for A&P Parking Lots or Learning from Las Vegas," *Architectural Forum* 128 (March 1968): 37.

23. Ibid., 40.

24. Ibid., 39.

25. Denise Scott Brown & Robert Venturi, "On Ducks and Decoration," *Architecture Canada* 45 (October 1968): 48.

26. Ibid.

27. Ibid.

28. First citation, Martin Pawley, "Leading from the Rear," *AD*, January 1970, 46; second citation, Robert Stern, *New Directions in American Architecture* (London: Studio Vista, 1969), 116.

29. Pawley, "Leading from the Rear," 46.

30. Robert Venturi and Denise Scott Brown, letter in response to "Leading from the Rear," *AD*, July 1970, 370.

31. *Casabella*, nos. 359–360 (1971). This was a special issue devoted to "The City as Artefact" organized by the Institute for Architecture and Urban Studies, and it contained essays by Peter Eisenman, Joseph Rykwert, Stanford Anderson, and Tom Schumacher, among others.

32. Denise Scott Brown, "Learning from Pop," *Casabella*, nos. 359–360 (1971): 15.

33. Ibid., 17.

34. Kenneth Frampton, "America 1960–1970: Notes on Urban Images and Theory," *Casabella*, nos. 359–360 (1971): 25.

35. Ibid., 33.

36. Ibid., 36.

37. Ibid.

38. Denise Scott Brown, "Reply to Frampton," *Casabella*, nos. 359–360 (1971): 43.

39. Ibid., 44–5.

40. The pertinent documents are in the CCA Archives, Montreal, Series A, file A-1.

41. Ibid., "Policies and Procedures," 14 April 1969, PDE/A/4, 1.

42. Ibid.

43. Ibid., "Faculty 1967–1968," PDE/A/4.

44. Ibid., trustee meeting 4 November 1968, Series A, file A-1.

45. Noted by Louis Martin, "The Search for a Theory in Architecture: Anglo-American Debates, 1957–1976" (Ph.D. diss., Princeton University, 2002), 554–6.

46. Transcripts of the two audiotapes are in the IAUS central file (Lot 3 086, folder B1–4) of the CCA collection. Martin (n. 45, p. 557) says that they were transcribed for a book that Eisenman wanted to title *Cardboard Architecture*.

47. *Five Architects: Eisenman, Graves, Gwathmey, Hejduk, Meier* (no publication data, 1974?).

48. Ibid., 111.

49. Ibid., 39–41, 55.

50. Ibid., 12.

51. Kenneth Frampton, introduction to *Richard Meier, Architect: Buildings and Projects 1966–1976* (New York: Oxford University Press, 1976), 8.

52. *Five Architects*, 4.

53. Ibid., 8.

54. Ibid., 1.

55. Martin discusses this notion and its genesis extensively in "The Search for a Theory in Architecture," 552–68, 589–98.

56. Peter Eisenman, "From Object to Relationship: The Casa del Fascio by Terrgni," *Casabella* 344 (January 1970): 38.

57. Peter Eisenman, "Notes on Conceptual Architecture: Towards a Definition," *Casabella*, nos. 359–360 (1971): 51.

58. Quotation from *Five Architects*, 15.

59. On the history of the journal, see Joan Ockman, "Resurrecting the Avant-Garde: The History and Program of *Oppositions*," in *Architectureproduction*, ed. Beatriz Colomina (New York: Princeton Architectural Press, 1988), 180–99.

60. Editorial statement, *Oppositions* 1 (September 1973).

INDEX